Art & Architecture Thesaurus

THE GETTY
ART HISTORY
INFORMATION
PROGRAM

The Art and Architecture Thesaurus
is a program of
The Getty Art History Information Program

Art & Architecture Thesaurus

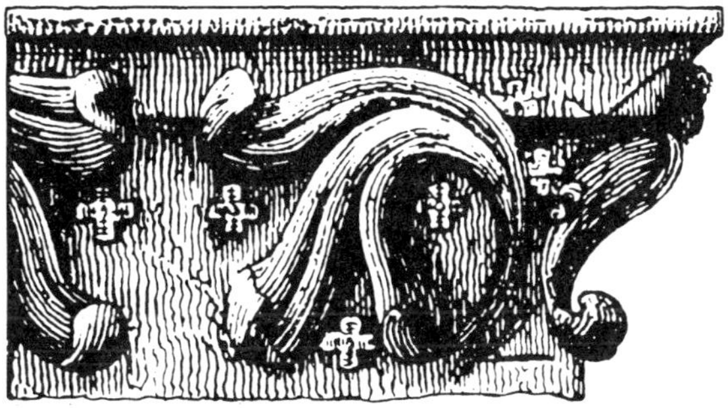

Toni Petersen
DIRECTOR

Volume 3
Part III: Alphabetical Display (continued)

Published on behalf of
The Getty Art History Information Program

OXFORD UNIVERSITY PRESS

New York · 1990 · *Oxford*

Oxford University Press

Oxford New York Toronto
Delhi Bombay Calcutta Madras Karachi
Petaling Jaya Singapore Hong Kong Tokyo
Nairobi Dar es Salaam Cape Town
Melbourne Auckland

and associated companies in
Berlin Ibadan

Published by Oxford University Press, Inc.,
200 Madison Avenue, New York, New York 10016

Library of Congress Cataloging-in-Publication Data
Art & architecture thesaurus / Toni Petersen, director.
p.
21½x28 cm.
Half t.p.: The Getty Art History Information Program.
Includes bibliographical references.
Contents: v. 1, pt. 1. Introduction. pt. 2. Hierarchical displays — v. 2. Alphabetical display, A and–Knotted — v. 3. Alphabetical display, Knotting–Zutujil.
ISBN 0-19-506403-8 (set)
1. Subject headings—Art. 2. Art—Abstracting and indexing. 3. Subject headings—Architecture. 4. Architecture—Abstracting and indexing. I. Petersen, Toni. II. Getty Art History Information Program. III. J. Paul Getty Trust. IV. Title: Art and architecture thesaurus.
Z695.1.A7A76 1990 89-26479
025.4'97—dc20 CIP

9 8 7 6 5 4 3 2 1

Printed in the United States of America
on acid-free paper

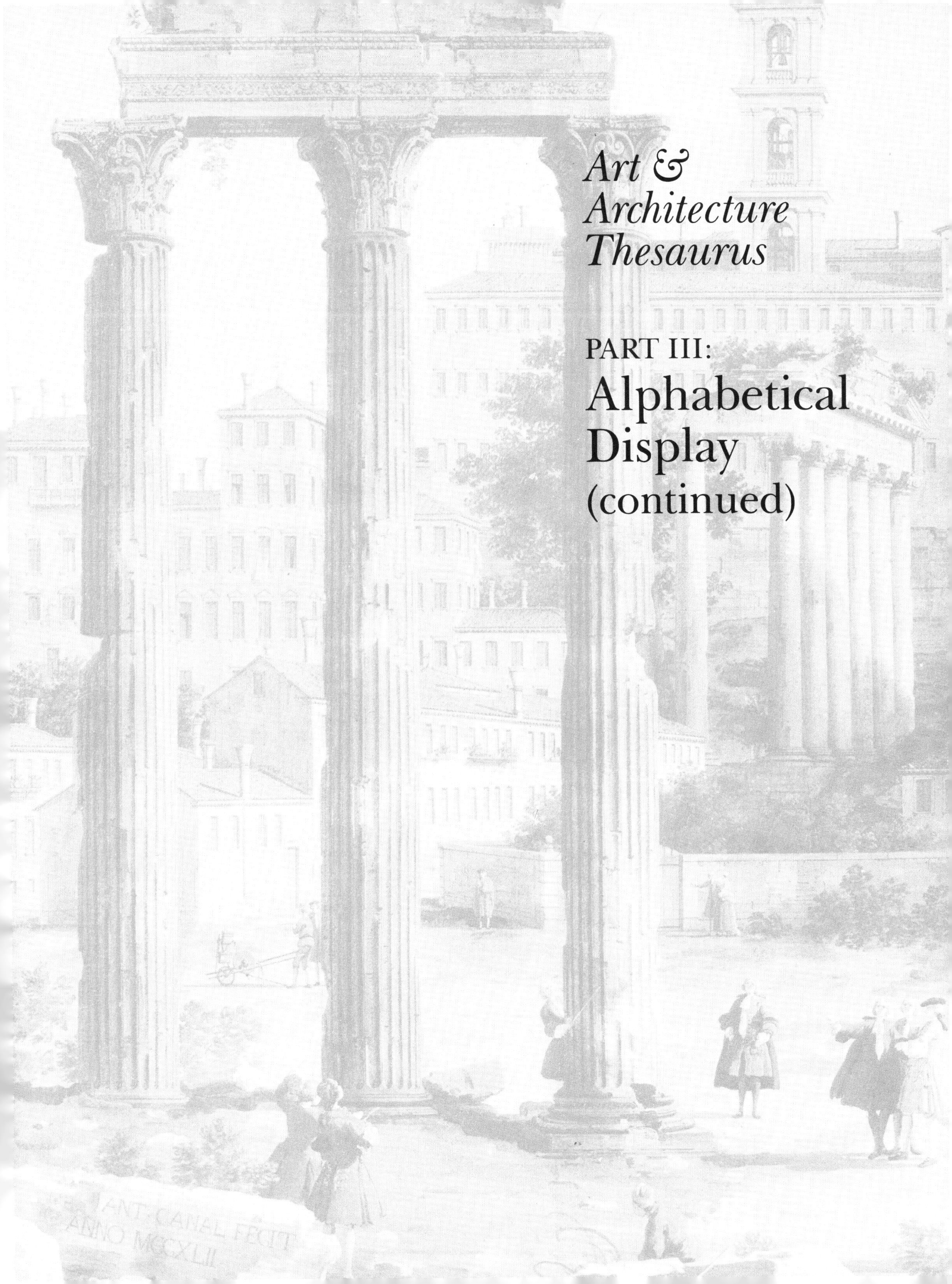

Art &
Architecture
Thesaurus

PART III: Alphabetical Display (continued)

knotting
KT.546 (L)
ALT **knotted**
CN K.KT.AFU.ALO.ELK.DUC.AFU.AXC

knotwork
DG.139
SN Use for decorative patterns that are an intricate form of interlace involving knotlike forms.
UF knot pattern, linked
linked knot pattern
pattern, linked knot
CN D.DG.AFU.ARI.ALO.BZY.AFU

knowledge
BM.586 (L,R)
CN B.BM.BUE.BCW

knowledge, sociology of
USE **sociology of knowledge**

knowledge, theory of
USE **epistemology**

knuckle hinges, olive
USE **olive knuckle hinges**

knuckle joints
TF.591
ALT **knuckle joint**
SN Hinged joints by which two rods are connected. (MEANS)
UF curb joints
curb rolls
joints, curb
joints, knuckle
rolls, curb
CN V.TF.ALO.AFU.DUC

knuckled arms
TG.812
ALT **knuckled arm**
SN The scroll ending on arms of certain kinds of Windsor chairs.
UF arms, knuckled
CN V.TG.ALO.ALO.AFU.AFU.ALO

knuckles
TF.523
ALT **knuckle**
SN Enlarged, protruding, cylindrical parts of a hinge through which the pin is inserted. (MEANS)
CN V.TF.AFU.ALO.ALO.ALO

knulled decoration
USE **gadrooning**

knulled feet
USE **scroll feet**

knulling
USE **knurling**

knurl feet
USE **scroll feet**

knurl toe feet
USE **scroll feet**

knurled feet
USE **scroll feet**

knurling
KT.142 (L)
ALT **knurled**
SN The making of knurls, small protuberances, or knobs. (W)
UF knulling
CN K.KT.AFU.ALO.DOI.BZY

Ko Kutani
FL.2027
UF Kutani, Ko
Kutani, Old
Old Kutani
CN F.FL.ALO.ARI.ALO.ALO.ALO.
ALO.ALO.CFS.ALO

Ko Seto
FL.2038
UF Old Seto
Seto, Ko
Seto, Old
CN F.FL.ALO.ARI.ALO.ALO.ALO.
ALO.ALO.DUC.ALO

koa
MT.1200 (L)
UF Acacia koa
CN M.MT.AFU.AFU.ALO.BIQ.DCU.
AFU.AFU.AFU.HCQ.AFU.AFU

Kobadian
FL.1777
UF Kobadiyan
Koban (Kobadian)
CN F.FL.ALO.ARI.AFU.ALO.BZY

Kobadiyan
USE **Kobadian**

Kobaltblau
USE **cobalt blue**

Kobaltgelb
USE **cobalt yellow**

Kobaltgrün
USE **cobalt green**

Kobaltviolet
USE **cobalt violet**

Koban (Kobadian)
USE **Kobadian**

Kobuk
FL.808
CN F.FL.ALO.ALO.ALO.AFU.ALO.
AFU.ALO.ALO.ALO.AXC

Koco
USE **Khocho**

Kodachrome (TM)
KT.369
SN A subtractive color reversal process using a film with an integral tripack of black-and-white emulsions, each layer sensitized to a separate primary color. The film contains no dyes; the color developing agents and color couplers are supplied in development, each layer being dyed and bleached separately by carefully controlled processing through three machines, with separate drying between each machine.(HAIST) For Capstaff's two-color Kodachrome process, use **two-color processes.**
CN K.KT.AFU.ALO.DUC.DIO.ALO.
DZW.AFU.ARI

Kodacolor (TM)
KT.370
SN A trademark of Eastman Kodak Company. A chromogenic process to produce subtractive-color negatives in an integral tripack. The process produces integral color masks, which give the film its characteristic orange color. First marketed in 1941, the Kodacolor process has been improved several times. All modern color negative processes are variants of the Kodacolor process.
CN K.KT.AFU.ALO.DUC.DIO.ALO.
DZW.AFU.AXC

Kodak (TM) instant color photoprints
USE **dye diffusion transfer prints**

Kodak (TM) instant prints
USE **dye diffusion transfer prints**

Kodiak
FL.786
CN F.FL.ALO.ALO.ALO.AFU.ALO.
AFU.AFU.ARI

Koeller's alloy
MT.417
UF alloy, Koeller's
CN M.MT.AFU.AFU.AFU.BZY.AFU.
AFU.AFU.ALO.BUE.ALO.BIQ

Kofun
FL.1972 (L)
UF Great Tombs period
Haniwa
Tumulus period (Kofun)
CN
F.FL.ALO.ARI.ALO.ALO.AFU.ARI.A
LO

Koguryo
FL.2111 (L)
UF Kokuryo
CN F.FL.ALO.ARI.ALO.ARI.AFU.ALO.
ALO

Koh Ker
FL.2362
CN F.FL.ALO.ARI.BCW.ALO.ARI.
ALO.BOK

Kokuryo
USE **Koguryo**

kolkhoz
RG.17
SN Use for Russian collective farms.
CN V.RG.AFU.AFU.AFU.AFU.AXC.
AFU.AFU

kolokolnya
USE **bell towers**

Kolosh
USE **Tlingit**

Kom
FL.198 (L)
UF Bikom
CN F.FL.ALO.AFU.AXC.AFU.AFU.AFU.ARI.AXC

Komo (Northeastern Zaire)
FL.511 (L)
UF Kumu
CN F.FL.ALO.AFU.AXC.ALO.ALO.BIQ.AFU.AFU.BCW

Kompong Preah
FL.2321
CN F.FL.ALO.ARI.BCW.ALO.AFU.ALO.AFU

Kong
FL.83
CN F.FL.ALO.AFU.ALO.AFU.BIQ

Kongo
FL.479 (L)
UF Bakongo
CN F.FL.ALO.AFU.AXC.ALO.ALO.AXC.AXC

Kongo Kingdom
FL.123 (L)
UF Bakongo Kingdom
Congo Kingdom
CN F.FL.ALO.AFU.ALO.ALO.AFU

Koniag
FL.1201 (L)
UF Kaniagmiut
CN F.FL.ALO.ALO.ARI.AFU.AFU.AFU.AFU.ARI

Koniagui
FL.341
UF Coniagui
CN F.FL.ALO.AFU.AXC.AFU.ARI.BIQ.BIQ

Konin
USE **Early Heian**

Konkomba
FL.385 (L)
CN F.FL.ALO.AFU.AXC.AFU.AXC.ARI.ARI.AXC

Konkrete Kunst
USE **Concrete art**

Kono
FL.327 (L)
CN F.FL.ALO.AFU.AXC.AFU.ARI.BCW.BIQ

Konso
FL.626
CN F.FL.ALO.AFU.AXC.AXC.ARI.CFS.ALO

Koran holders
USE **Koran stands**

Koran reading desks
USE **Koran stands**

Koran stands
TG.629 (L)
ALT **Koran stand**
UF holders, Koran
Koran holders
Koran reading desks
reading desks, Koran
stands, Koran
CN V.TG.AFU.AFU.BIQ.BCW.ALO.AFU.AFU

Korean
FL.2106 (L,B)
UF Corean
CN F.FL.ALO.ARI.ALO.ARI

korhogo cloth
MT.1881
UF cloth, korhogo
CN M.MT.AFU.AFU.ARI.ALO.ALO.ALO.ARI.ALO

Korin School
USE **Sotatsu-Korin School**

korina
USE **limba**

Koro
FL.215 (L)
CN F.FL.ALO.AFU.AXC.AFU.AFU.ALO.ALO.BUE

Koros
FL.2491
UF Cris-Koros
CN F.FL.ALO.AXC.AFU.BCW.BIQ

Koryak
FL.2150 (L)
CN F.FL.ALO.ARI.ARI.ALO.BCW.ALO

Koryo
FL.2108 (L)
CN F.FL.ALO.ARI.ALO.ARI.AFU.AFU

Kose School
FL.2057
CN F.FL.ALO.ARI.ALO.ALO.ALO.ARI.BZY

Kosova
USE **Gusii**

Kossi
FL.189 (L)
UF Bakosi
Nkosi
CN F.FL.ALO.AFU.AXC.AFU.AFU.AFU.ALO.AXC

Kota
FL.416 (L)
UF Bakota
Kuta
CN F.FL.ALO.AFU.AXC.ALO.AFU.AXC.AXC

Kota (Shake)
USE **Shake**

Kotah
FL.2293
CN F.FL.ALO.ARI.AXC.ALO.AFU.BZY.BCW.BCW.BUE

Kotoko
FL.369
CN F.FL.ALO.AFU.AXC.AFU.AXC.ALO.ARI

Kotokoli
USE **Tem**

Kotosh
FL.1138
CN F.FL.ALO.ALO.ALO.ARI.AXC.AFU.ALO.ALO

Kotosh Chavín
FL.1144
UF Chavín, Kotosh
CN F.FL.ALO.ALO.ALO.ARI.AXC.AFU.ARI.BCW

kotter pins
USE **cotter pins**

Koulen
USE **Kulên**

Koumbi Saleh
FL.79
UF Kumbi Saleh
CN F.FL.ALO.AFU.ALO.AFU.ALO.AFU

Koyukon
FL.1236 (L)
CN F.FL.ALO.ALO.ARI.AFU.AFU.ARI.CRG

kozo
MT.1964 (L)
SN Vegetable fiber used in papermaking.
CN M.MT.AFU.AFU.ARI.ALO.ALO.AXC.AXC.AFU.ALO

Kpe
FL.190 (L)
UF Bakwiri
CN F.FL.ALO.AFU.AXC.AFU.AFU.AFU.ALO.BCW

Kpelle
FL.328 (L)
UF Guerze
CN F.FL.ALO.AFU.AXC.AFU.ARI.BCW.BOK

Kra
USE **Wee**

Kraak porcelain
FL.1947
UF blue-and-white ware, Transitional
porcelain, Kraak
Transitional blue-and-white ware
Transitional ware
ware, Transitional
ware, Transitional blue-and-white

CN F.FL.ALO.ARI.ALO.AFU.AFU.AXC.
ARI.AXC

kraals
RD.8
ALT **kraal**
SN Designates certain Central and South African village compounds and their cattle enclosures.
CN V.RD.AFU.AFU.ALO.ALO.AFU

kraft paper
MT.1899
SN A very strong paper, usually a light brown in color, which was originally made from rope but now is produced from unbleached sulfate wood pulp. (TATEMT)
UF paper, kraft
CN M.MT.AFU.AFU.ARI.ALO.ALO.
AXC.AFU.AXC.AFU

Kran
USE **Wee**

Kremnitz white
USE **white lead**

Krems white
USE **white lead**

Kremserweiss
USE **white lead**

krepidomas
USE **crepidomas**

Krobo
FL.301 (L)
UF Kropo
CN F.FL.ALO.AFU.AXC.AFU.ARI.ALO.
AFU.AFU

Kropo
USE **Krobo**

Kru
FL.313 (L)
CN F.FL.ALO.AFU.AXC.AFU.ARI.ARI.
ALO

Kua
USE **Makua**

Kuang-hsu
USE **Guangxu**

Kuba
FL.429 (L)
UF Bakuba
CN F.FL.ALO.AFU.AXC.ALO.ALO.
AFU.AFU

Kuba Court Style
FL.432
UF Court Style, Kuba
CN F.FL.ALO.AFU.AXC.ALO.ALO.
AFU.AFU.ARI

Kuba Court Style, Revived
USE **Kuba Revived Court Style**

Kuba Folk Style
FL.434
UF Folk Style, Kuba
CN F.FL.ALO.AFU.AXC.ALO.ALO.
AFU.AFU.AXC

Kuba Kingdom
FL.124
UF Bakuba Kingdom
Bushong
Bushongo
CN F.FL.ALO.AFU.ALO.ALO.ALO

Kuba Revived Court Style
FL.433
UF Kuba Court Style, Revived
Revived Court Style, Kuba
CN F.FL.ALO.AFU.AXC.ALO.ALO.
AFU.AFU.ARI.AFU

Kubachi ware
FL.3541
UF Kubatcha ware
ware, Kubachi
ware, Kubatcha
CN F.FL.ALO.BIQ.AFU.GRC.ALO.ARI

Kubatcha ware
USE **Kubachi ware**

Kubbestols
TG.76
ALT **Kubbestol**
SN Norwegian chairs made from logs. (FAIRB)
CN V.TG.AFU.AFU.ALO.AFU.AFU.AFU.
IFM

Kuça
FL.1817
UF Ch'iu-tzu
Kucha
CN F.FL.ALO.ARI.AFU.AXC.ELK.BOK

Kucha
USE **Kuça**

Kudara
USE **Kudara Kannon**

Kudara Kannon
FL.2101
UF Kudara
CN F.FL.ALO.ARI.ALO.ALO.ALO.
BCW.ARI

Kuikuru
FL.1584 (L)
UF Cuicuru
CN F.FL.ALO.ALO.ARI.ARI.AFU.DUC

Kukhn-Kala
FL.1797
CN F.FL.ALO.ARI.AFU.AXC.CFS

Kukuruku
USE **Etsako**

Kulanapan
USE **Pomo**

Kulango
FL.362 (L)
CN F.FL.ALO.AFU.AXC.AFU.AXC.
AFU.CRG.AFU

Kulên
FL.2361
UF Koulen
Phnom Kulên
CN F.FL.ALO.ARI.BCW.ALO.ARI.
ALO.BIQ

Kulu
FL.2280
CN F.FL.ALO.ARI.AXC.ALO.AFU.BZY.
BCW.ARI.CFS

Kumbi Saleh
USE **Koumbi Saleh**

Kumeyaay
USE **Kamia**

Kumtura
USE **Kumutra**

Kumu
USE **Komo (Northeastern Zaire)**

Kumutra
FL.1818
UF Kumtura
Qumtura
Qumutra
CN F.FL.ALO.ARI.AFU.AXC.ELK.BUE

Kundu
FL.191 (L)
UF Nkundu
CN F.FL.ALO.AFU.AXC.AFU.AFU.
AFU.ALO.BIQ

Kuniyaki
FL.2024
CN F.FL.ALO.ARI.ALO.ALO.ALO.
ALO.ALO.BZY

kunstschranks
USE **schranks**

Kunstwollen
BM.323
UF aesthetic urge
will to form
CN B.BM.AFU.AXC.ELK.BIQ

kura
RK.1210
SN Use for specialized Japanese buildings devoted to storage of personal family possessions and agricultural products.
CN V.RK.AFU.ALO.ALO.GFO.AXC

Kurgan
FL.2492
UF Barrow culture
Pit-grove culture
CN F.FL.ALO.AXC.AFU.BCW.BOK

kurgans
USE **burial mounds**

Kuroba
USE **Attie**

kursaals
USE **spas**

Kurumba
FL.354 (L)
UF Fulse
CN F.FL.ALO.AFU.AXC.AFU.AXC.AFU.BCW

Kusan
USE **Coos**

Kusana
USE **Kushan**

Kushan
FL.2199 (L)
UF Kusana
CN F.FL.ALO.ARI.AXC.ALO.AFU.ARI.BCW

Kushite
FL.161 (A,L)
UF Cushite
CN F.FL.ALO.AFU.ALO.AXC.AXC.ALO

Kushite Dynasty
USE **Twenty-fifth Dynasty**

Kusinagara
FL.2169
UF Kusinara
CN F.FL.ALO.ARI.AXC.AFU.AXC.ALO.ARI

Kusinara
USE **Kusinagara**

Kusu
FL.494
UF Bakusu
CN F.FL.ALO.AFU.AXC.ALO.ALO.BCW.AXC

Kuta
USE **Kota**

Kütahya ware
FL.3522 (L)
UF Abraham of Kütahya style Iznik pottery
Iznik pottery, Abraham of Kütahya style
pottery, Abraham of Kütahya style Iznik
pottery, Kütahya
ware, Kütahya
CN F.FL.ALO.BIQ.AFU.FOG.ALO.ALO.ALO

Kutani
FL.2025 (L)
CN F.FL.ALO.ARI.ALO.ALO.ALO.ALO.ALO.CFS

Kutani, Ao
USE **Ao Kutani**

Kutani, Green
USE **Ao Kutani**

Kutani, Hachiroemon
USE **Saiko Kutani**

Kutani, Ko
USE **Ko Kutani**

Kutani, Old
USE **Ko Kutani**

Kutani, Revived
USE **Saiko Kutani**

Kutani, Saiko
USE **Saiko Kutani**

Kutchin
FL.1237 (L)
CN F.FL.ALO.ALO.ARI.AFU.AFU.ARI.CXA

Kutenai
FL.1411 (L)
UF Kitunaha
CN F.FL.ALO.ALO.ARI.AFU.BUE.BOK

Kutshu
USE **Nkutshu**

Kuva
FL.1798
UF Quba
Quva
CN F.FL.ALO.ARI.AFU.AXC.CLM

Kuyu
FL.398
CN F.FL.ALO.AFU.AXC.ALO.AFU.AFU

Kuznetsk Basin
FL.2145 (L)
CN F.FL.ALO.ARI.ARI.ALO.ALO

Kwabornament
USE **Auricular**

KWAC indexes
USE **key-word-and-context indexes**

Kwakiutl
FL.1348 (L)
CN F.FL.ALO.ALO.ARI.AFU.BIQ.DIO

Kwarasm
USE **Khorezm**

Kwele
FL.426
UF Bakwele
CN F.FL.ALO.AFU.AXC.ALO.AFU.BIQ.ALO

Kweni
USE **Guro**

Kwese
FL.466
UF Bakwese
CN F.FL.ALO.AFU.AXC.ALO.ALO.ARI.BIQ

KWIC indexes
USE **key-word-in-context indexes**

KWOC indexes
USE **key-word-out-of-context indexes**

KWOT indexes
USE **key-word-out-of-title indexes**

Kyama
USE **Ebrie**

Kyoto
FL.2029
CN F.FL.ALO.ARI.ALO.ALO.ALO.ALO.ALO.CLM

l'art brut
USE **art brut**

L'Art Informel
USE **Art Informel**

La Jolla
FL.902
CN F.FL.ALO.ALO.ALO.AFU.ALO.ARI.AFU.ARI

La Pastora
FL.981
CN F.FL.ALO.ALO.ALO.ALO.AFU.ALO.AFU.AFU.ARI.ALO

La Tène
FL.2520 (L,R)
CN F.FL.ALO.AXC.AFU.BOK.AFU.ALO

label moldings
RT.805
ALT label molding
SN Moldings or dripstones that extend horizontally across the top of openings.
UF moldings, label
CN V.RT.AFU.ALO.AFU.BOK.AFU.ALO.BZY.ALO

labeling
USE **marking**

labels
VW.759 (N)
ALT label
SN Pieces of paper or fabric or small tablets inscribed and affixed to something for identification or description.
CN V.VW.AFU.ALO.ALO.ALO

labels, book
USE **bookplates**

labels, decanter
USE **wine labels**

labels, union
USE **union labels**

labels, wine
USE **wine labels**

labor agreements, collective
USE **collective labor agreements**

labor and industrial relations
USE **industrial relations**

labor and material bonds
VW.906
ALT **labor and material bond**
UF bonds, labor and material
CN V.VW.AFU.ARI.AFU.BOK.BOK.AXC.ARI

labor camps
RG.63 (L,B)
ALT **labor camp**
UF camps, labor
CN V.RG.AFU.AFU.BOK.ALO.AFU.ALO

labor exchanges
USE **employment agencies**

labor mobility
BM.1052 (L,B)
UF mobility of labor
mobility, labor
CN B.BM.CLM.AFU.ALO.ARI.AFU

labor relations
USE **industrial relations**

labor rest homes
RK.754 (A,L)
ALT **labor rest home**
UF rest homes, labor
CN V.RK.AFU.ALO.ALO.CXA.ALO.AFU.AXC.AXC.AFU

labor unions
USE **trade unions**

labor, unskilled
USE **unskilled labor**

laboratories
RK.1159 (A,L,B)
ALT **laboratory**
SN Use for rooms, buildings, or groups of buildings equipped with apparatus for scientific experiments or other research, testing, and investigations.
CN V.RK.AFU.ALO.ALO.FIM.ALO.AFU

laboratories, aerodynamical
USE **aerodynamical laboratories**

laboratories, aeronautical
USE **aeronautical laboratories**

laboratories, agricultural
USE **agricultural laboratories**

laboratories, art restoration
USE **conservation laboratories**

laboratories, biological
USE **biological laboratories**

laboratories, chemical
USE **chemical laboratories**

laboratories, clinical
USE **medical laboratories**

laboratories, computation
USE **computer centers**

laboratories, conservation
USE **conservation laboratories**

laboratories, crime
USE **crime laboratories**

laboratories, electronics
USE **electronics laboratories**

laboratories, environmental
USE **environmental laboratories**

laboratories, language
USE **language laboratories**

laboratories, manned orbital
USE **space stations**

laboratories, medical
USE **medical laboratories**

laboratories, research
USE **research laboratories**

laboratories, space
USE **space stations**

laboratories, veterinary
USE **veterinary laboratories**

laboratory notebooks
VW.514
ALT **laboratory notebook**
UF notebooks, laboratory
CN V.VW.AFU.ALO.AFU.AFU.AFU.CLM.AFU

laboratory notes
VW.64
ALT **laboratory note**
UF notes, laboratory
CN V.VW.AFU.AFU.AFU.DZW.ALO

laborers
HG.25 (L)
ALT **laborer**
SN Workers whose duties require physical strength rather than skills or training. (RHDEL2)
UF navvies
CN H.HG.AFU.AXC.ALO.AFU.AFU

laboring class
USE **working class**

Labrador Eskimo
USE **Labrador Inuit**

Labrador Inuit
FL.1211
UF Eskimo, Labrador
Inuit, Labrador
Labrador Eskimo
CN F.FL.ALO.ALO.ARI.AFU.AFU.AFU.ALO.AFU.BCW

labyrinth gardens
USE **maze gardens**

labyrinth pattern (frets)
USE **frets**

labyrinth pattern (interlace)
USE **interlace**

labyrinths
DG.39
ALT **labyrinth**
SN Use for motifs depicting on a flat surface a path that twists around itself but never crosses itself, usually leading from an outer edge to the center. Common in Roman mosaics and inlaid in Medieval church pavements.
UF mazes (motifs)
CN D.DG.AFU.AFU.CLM

lac
MT.1503 (L)
SN A resin from the insect Coccus lacca used especially to produce shellac.
CN M.MT.AFU.AFU.ALO.BOK.CXA

lac (red pigment)
MT.1692
UF Indian lake
lake, Indian
CN M.MT.AFU.AFU.ARI.AFU.AFU.ALO.ALO.BCW.ALO.BCW

Lacandón
FL.1535 (L)
CN F.FL.ALO.ALO.ARI.ALO.BIQ.AFU.AXC

lace
MT.1870 (R)
SN Fine, openwork cloth with a ground of mesh or net on which patterns may be worked at the same time as the ground; made by looping, twisting, or knotting thread. (W)
CN M.MT.AFU.AFU.ARI.ALO.ALO.ALO.ALO.CXA

lace makers
HG.539 (L)
ALT **lace maker**
UF makers, lace
CN H.HG.AFU.AXC.BUE.ARI.CXA.CFS.ARI

lace making
KT.549 (L)
CN K.KT.AFU.ALO.ELK.DUC.AFU.BIQ

lace, bobbin
USE **bobbin lace**

lace, bone
USE **bobbin lace**

lace, hairpin
USE **hairpin lace**

lace, pillow
USE **bobbin lace**

lace, Valenciennes
USE **Valenciennes lace**

lacertine ornament
DG.140
SN Celtic and Viking interlace incorporating two- or four-legged creatures with ears, biting snout, and tail.

(LDDO)
UF lacertines
ornament, lacertine
CN D.DG.AFU.ARI.ALO.BZY.ALO

lacertines
USE **lacertine ornament**

lacewood
USE **London plane wood**

lacing courses
RT.618
ALT **lacing course**
SN Courses of brick or tile built into masonry walls for bonding and leveling purposes.
UF courses, lacing
CN V.RT.AFU.AFU.AFU.BIQ.BUE.ALO.AFU.ALO.BIQ

Laconian
FL.2630
UF Cyrenaic
CN F.FL.ALO.AXC.ALO.AFU.ALO.AXC.ALO.BCW.ALO

laconica
USE **sudatoria**

lacque carminée
USE **carmine**

lacquer
MT.2429 (L,R)
SN Glossy, quick-drying finishes that are dried by evaporation of the solvents or thinners in which a resin vehicle is dissolved. (MH12)
CN M.MT.AFU.ARI.CRG.AFU.ARI

lacquer red
USE **deep reddish orange**

lacquer, Oriental
USE **Oriental lacquer**

lacquerers
HG.482 (L)
ALT **lacquerer**
CN H.HG.AFU.AXC.BUE.ARI.BOK

lacquering
KT.668 (L)
ALT **lacquered**
CN K.KT.AFU.ALO.GRC.AFU.AXC

lacree
USE **blue lake**

lacrosse fields
RK.1482 (B)
ALT **lacrosse field**
UF fields, lacrosse
CN V.RK.ALO.ALO.BCW.AFU.BCW

lactate, butyl
USE **butyl lactate**

lacunars
USE **coffers (ceiling components)**

Ladakhi
FL.2155 (L)
CN F.FL.ALO.ARI.AXC.AFU.ARI

ladder-back chairs
USE **slat-back chairs**

ladder hooks
TF.156
ALT **ladder hook**
SN Metal projections used to secure a ladder to a ledge or to the ridge of a roof. (PUTNAM)
UF hooks, ladder
CN V.TF.AFU.AFU.AFU.AFU.CXA.BIQ

ladders
TB.478 (L,N,R)
ALT **ladder**
SN Frames, usually of wood or metal, consisting of two side pieces called stiles which are connected by crosspieces, usually round, called rungs; used as a means of climbing up or down. (DAC)
CN V.TB.AFU.ARI.ERE.ALO

ladders, aerial
USE **aerial ladders**

ladders, double-cleat
USE **double-cleat ladders**

ladders, extension
USE **extension ladders**

ladders, fish
USE **fishways**

ladders, hook
USE **hook ladders**

ladders, Jacob's
USE **rope ladders**

ladders, pompier
USE **hook ladders**

ladders, rope
USE **rope ladders**

ladders, sea
USE **rope ladders**

ladders, sectional
USE **sectional ladders**

ladders, single-cleat
USE **single-cleat ladders**

ladders, trestle
USE **trestle ladders**

lading, bills of
USE **bills of lading**

ladles, foundry
USE **melting ladles**

ladles, melting
USE **melting ladles**

ladles, pouring
USE **melting ladles**

lady chapels
RM.308
ALT **lady chapel**
SN Major chapels dedicated to the Virgin Mary, usually located in the axis of a church at its east end. (HAS)
UF chapels, lady
CN V.RM.AFU.DIO.AXC.ALO.AFU.AXC.AXC

lady's cabinet dressing tables
TG.544
ALT **lady's cabinet dressing table**
SN Lady's writing desks fitted with an adjustable looking glass above. (THORN2)
UF cabinets and writing tables, lady's
combination writing table and dressing stands
dressing tables, lady's cabinet
lady's cabinets and writing tables
tables, lady's cabinet dressing
writing table and dressing stands, combination
CN V.TG.AFU.AFU.AXC.ALO.BZY.CFS.AFU

lady's cabinets
USE **cheverets**
lady's writing tables

lady's cabinets and writing tables
USE **lady's cabinet dressing tables**

lady's chairs
TG.186
ALT **lady's chair**
SN Term generally applied to a variety of different chairs with low seats. (DOWNS)
UF chairs, lady's
chairs, pompador
pompador chairs
pompadors
CN V.TG.AFU.AFU.ALO.AFU.AFU.ALO.CRG

lady's companions
USE **lady's writing tables**

lady's cylinder writing tables
USE **lady's writing tables**

lady's desks
TG.543
ALT **lady's desk**
SN Term generally applied to a variety of small-scale desks designed for women; of a type popular in the 18th century.
UF desks, lady's
CN V.TG.AFU.AFU.AXC.ALO.BZY.CFS

lady's drawing and writing tables
USE **Carlton House tables**

lady's dressing stands
TG.637
ALT **lady's dressing stand**
UF dressing stands, lady's
stands, lady's dressing

CN V.TG.AFU.AFU.BIQ.BCW.ALO.
BCW.ALO

lady's dressing tables
TG.735
ALT **lady's dressing table**
SN Term generally applied to a variety of dressing tables which are fitted with a mirror and have drawers to hold toilet articles. For lady's dressing tables having drawers on the side which swing out and provide mirrors on a quadrant, use **Rudd's tables.** Use **toilettes** with reference to French dressing tables designed for women.
UF dressing tables, lady's
tables, lady's dressing
CN V.TG.AFU.AFU.BIQ.BOK.ALO.
CLM.AXC

lady's screen writing tables
TG.578
ALT **lady's screen writing table**
SN Writing tables with fire screens to protect the writer from the heat of the fire.
UF desks, screen
screen desks
screen tables
screen writing tables, lady's
tables, lady's screen writing
tables, screen
writing tables, lady's screen
CN V.TG.AFU.AFU.AXC.ALO.BZY.
FUA.BUE.ARI

lady's secretaries
TG.553
ALT **lady's secretary**
UF secretaries, lady's
CN V.TG.AFU.AFU.AXC.ALO.BZY.
DUC.ALO

lady's small writing desks
USE **lady's writing tables**

lady's writing fire screens
TG.15
ALT **lady's writing fire screen**
UF fire screens, lady's writing
screens, lady' writing fire
writing fire screens, lady's
CN V.TG.AFU.AFU.AFU.AFU.BIQ.ARI

lady's writing tables
TG.575
ALT **lady's writing table**
SN Small writing tables designed for women.
UF cabinets, lady's
companions, lady's
cylinder writing tables, lady's
desks, lady's small writing
lady's cabinets
lady's companions
lady's cylinder writing tables
lady's small writing desks
small writing desks, lady's
tables, lady's writing
writing desks, lady's small
writing tables, lady's
writing tables, lady's cylinder
CN V.TG.AFU.AFU.AXC.ALO.BZY.
FUA.BUE

lag bolts
TF.316
ALT **lag bolt**
SN Bolts having a wrench head, usually square or hexagonal in shape, pointed and threaded like a wood screw. (PUTNAM)
UF bolts, lag
coach screws
lag screws
screws, coach
screws, lag
CN V.TF.AFU.AFU.AFU.ALO.AFU.
ALO.AFU.BUE

lag screws
USE **lag bolts**

lagoons
RD.150 (L)
ALT **lagoon**
CN V.RD.ARI.AFU.AFU.AFU.ALO.ARI

Lagozza
FL.2493
CN F.FL.ALO.AXC.AFU.BCW.BUE

Laguna
FL.1470 (L)
CN F.FL.ALO.ALO.ARI.AFU.CFS.CRG.
AFU.AXC

Laguneta
FL.1035
CN F.FL.ALO.ALO.ALO.ALO.AFU.
ALO.ARI.AFU.ARI.BUE

laid-out elevations
VD.25
ALT **laid-out elevation**
SN Use for drawings of elevations arranged around a plan as if the walls had been laid flat.
UF elevations, laid-out
CN V.VD.AFU.AFU.BIQ.ALO.ALO.ARI

laid paper
MT.1967
SN Paper watermarked with fine lines running across the grain. (WCOL)
UF paper, laid
CN M.MT.AFU.AFU.ARI.ALO.ALO.
AXC.AXC.ALO

laity
HG.238 (L)
CN H.HG.AFU.AXC.AXC.BIQ.AFU.BIQ

Laja, Igbo
USE **Igbo Laja**

Lakabi pottery
USE **Lakabi ware**

Lakabi ware
FL.3566
UF Lakabi pottery
Laqabi pottery
Laqabi ware
pottery, Lakabi
pottery, Laqabi
ware, Lakabi
ware, Laqabi
CN F.FL.ALO.BIQ.AFU.HIK.BCW.AXC

Lake
FL.1412
CN F.FL.ALO.ALO.ARI.AFU.BUE.BUE

lake (color)
USE **dark red**
grayish reddish orange
moderate purplish red
moderate red
strong red
vivid red

lake (pigment)
USE **lake pigment**

lake asphalt
MT.977
UF asphalt, lake
CN M.MT.AFU.AFU.ALO.ALO.AFU.
AFU.ALO.ARI

lake dwellings
RK.308 (L)
ALT **lake dwelling**
UF dwellings, lake
pile-dwellings
CN V.RK.AFU.ALO.ALO.AXC.ALO
.AXC.ALO.AXC

Lake Mojave
FL.908
CN F.FL.ALO.ALO.ALO.AFU.ALO.
ARI.ALO.ARI

lake pigment
MT.1806
SN Pigments produced by dyeing clays with aniline dyes.
UF lake (pigment)
pigment, lake
CN M.MT.AFU.AFU.ARI.AFU.AFU.
ALO.ARI.AXC

Lake Sentani
FL.3634 (L)
UF Sentani
CN F.FL.ALO.BOK.ALO.BCW.AFU.
ALO.ARI

lake, blue
USE **blue lake**

lake, brown
USE **moderate red**

lake, buckthorn
USE **Persian berries lake**

lake, campeachy
USE **campeachy lake**

lake, carmine
USE **carmine**
moderate purplish red
moderate red
strong purplish red
strong red
vivid red

lake, crimson
USE **crimson lake**

lake, crimson (color)
USE **moderate red**

lake, deep
USE **dark purplish red**

lake, flavine
USE **quercitron lake**

lake, Florentine
USE **carmine**
crimson lake

lake, geranium
USE **geranium red**
vivid red

lake, grain
USE **kermes**

lake, Indian
USE **lac (red pigment)**

lake, kermes
USE **kermes**

lake, madder
USE **alizarin madder**
madder
strong purplish red
strong red

lake, mineral
USE **potter's pink**

lake, Munich
USE **carmine**

lake, Persian berries
USE **Persian berries lake**

lake, purple
USE **dark purplish red**
deep red
moderate red

lake, quercitron
USE **quercitron lake**

lake, quercitron (color)
USE **moderate orange yellow**

lake, rose
USE **dark purplish red**
grayish purplish red
moderate pink

lake, scarlet
USE **moderate red**
strong red

lake, Vienna
USE **carmine**

lake, yellow
USE **yellow lake**

lake, yellowberries
USE **Persian berries lake**

lakefronts
RK.1594
ALT **lakefront**
UF lakeshores (lakefronts)
CN V.RK.ALO.ARI.CLM.AFU.AFU

lakes
RD.131 (A,L,R)
ALT **lake**
CN V.RD.ARI.AFU.AFU.AFU.AFU.ALO.AFU

lakes, oxbow
USE **oxbow lakes**

lakeshores
RD.230 (L)
ALT **lakeshore**
CN V.RD.ARI.AFU.AXC.AFU.ALO.AXC.BUE.ARI

lakeshores (lakefronts)
USE **lakefronts**

Lakota
USE **Teton**

Lali
FL.401 (L)
UF Balali
CN F.FL.ALO.AFU.AXC.ALO.AFU.ALO.ALO

Lalitipur
USE **Patan**

lally columns
RT.94
ALT **lally column**
SN Metal pipes, sometimes filled with concrete, used to support girders or beams. (PUTNAM)
UF columns, lally
CN V.RT.AFU.AFU.AFU.AXC.BIQ.AFU.AFU.CFS

Lamaism
BM.613 (L)
SN A Western term for the religion of Tibet, not used by the Buddhists themselves. (DNCR)
CN B.BM.BZY.AFU.AFU.ALO

Lamba
USE **Namba**

Lambayeque
FL.1164
CN F.FL.ALO.ALO.ALO.ARI.AXC.AFU.BIQ.AFU

lambrequins
USE **aprons (furniture components)**

lambruscatura
USE **wainscoting**

lamella roofs
USE **lamella structures**

lamella structures
RT.21 (B)
ALT **lamella structure**
SN Use for structures based on a skewed grid of archlike forms, usually wood or metal.
UF lamella roofs
roofs, lamella
structures, lamella
CN V.RT.AFU.AFU.AFU.ALO.ALO

laminate, plastic
USE **plastic laminate**

laminated glass
USE **safety glass**

laminated plastic
USE **plastic laminate**

laminating
KT.57 (B)
ALT **laminated**
CN K.KT.AFU.ALO.BCW.BOK

Lamoka
FL.870
CN F.FL.ALO.ALO.ALO.AFU.ALO.ALO.AXC.BCW

lamp black
USE **black**

lampblack
MT.1575 (L)
SN A deep, saturated, velvety black powder often used as a pigment. (WEHLTE)
UF Lampenschwarz
noir de bougie
CN M.MT.AFU.AFU.ARI.AFU.AFU.ALO.ALO.AFU.AFU.AFU.AXC

lampblack, brown
USE **bister**

lampblack, white
USE **zinc white**

Lampenschwarz
USE **lampblack**

lampposts
RM.448 (N)
ALT **lamppost**
SN Posts usually supporting outdoor lamps or lanterns. (W)
CN V.RM.ALO.AFU.BZY

lamps, festoon
USE **festoon lighting**

Lamu
FL.152
CN F.FL.ALO.AFU.ALO.AXC.ALO.ALO

Lan Na
USE **Northern Thai**

Lan Xang
FL.2394
CN F.FL.ALO.ARI.BCW.AXC.AFU

lanais
RM.174
ALT **lanai**
SN Living spaces open in part to the outdoors.
CN V.RM.AFU.DIO.ALO.CXA.BUE.AFU

Lancashire pattern riveting hammers
USE **Warrington-pattern hammers**

Lancet
USE **Early English**

lancet arches
RT.234
ALT **lancet arch**
SN Use for pointed arches whose curves are being struck from centers farther apart than the span of the arch.
UF acute arches
arches, acute
arches, lancet
CN V.RT.AFU.AFU.AFU.BCW.AFU.AFU.AFU.CRG.AXC

lancet windows
RT.925
ALT **lancet window**
SN Slender pointed-arched windows, much used in the early 13th century. (PDARC)
UF windows, lancet
CN V.RT.AFU.ARI.AFU.AFU.BOK.AFU.AFU.CXA

lancewood
MT.1192
UF Nectrandra
yaya
CN M.MT.AFU.AFU.ALO.BIQ.DCU.AFU.AFU.AFU.FUA

land art
BM.260 (R)
SN Type of art pioneered in the late 1960s, using for materials the land itself, earth, stones, wood, and other natural objects. Use also for large-scale works that use natural forces. For other works that surround or involve the viewer, use **environmental art.**
UF art, earth
art, eco
art, ecological
art, environmental (land art)
art, land
earth art
eco art
ecological art
environmental art (land art)
CN B.BM.AFU.ARI.BCW.FOG.BIQ

land development
USE **real estate development**

land drainage
BM.418 (L,B)
UF drainage, land
drainage, soil
soil drainage
CN B.BM.AXC.AFU.AFU

land grants
VW.929 (L)
ALT **land grant**
SN Official documents from a government to an individual conveying free-simple title to public lands.
UF grants, land
land patents
patents, land
CN V.VW.AFU.ARI.AFU.BZY.AXC

land law
KD.165 (L,B)
UF law, land
CN K.KD.AFU.ALO.DOI.BCW

land ownership maps
USE **cadastral maps**

land patents
USE **land grants**

land plats
USE **plats**

land reclamation works
RK.568
ALT **land reclamation work**
UF reclamation works
works, land reclamation
works, reclamation
CN V.RK.AFU.ALO.ALO.CFS.ALO.AXC

land reform
BM.551 (L)
SN Legislative or other measures effecting a more equitable distribution of agricultural land especially by dividing large estates into small holdings. (W)
UF reform, land
CN B.BM.BOK.BUE.ALO

land registers
VW.926 (R)
ALT **land register**
UF registers, land
CN V.VW.AFU.ARI.AFU.BZY.ALO.AFU

land settlement
BM.1044 (A,L)
SN Use for the settling of permanent residents on a certain area of land.
UF settlement of land
settlement, land
CN B.BM.CLM.AFU.AFU.AFU

land subdivision
BM.1077 (A,L)
UF real estate subdivision
subdivision of land
subdivision, land
subdivision, real estate
CN B.BM.CLM.ALO.ALO.ALO.AFU

land subsidences
USE **subsidences (earth movements)**

land surveying
USE **topographical surveying**

land surveys
VW.930
ALT **land survey**
SN Use for documents, often maps, which record the measuring and marking of land.
UF surveys (land)
surveys, land
CN V.VW.AFU.ARI.AFU.BZY.BCW

land use
BM.1043 (A,L,B,R)
UF use, land
CN B.BM.CLM.AFU.AFU

land use maps
VW.194 (L)
ALT **land use map**
SN Maps showing the existing uses of a given area.
UF maps, land use
CN V.VW.AFU.AFU.AFU.FZU.AXC.AFU.ARI.AXC.BOK

land use, rural
USE **rural land use**

land use, urban
USE **urban land use**

land valuation
KG.45 (A,L,B)
UF valuation, land
CN K.KG.AFU.AFU.ARI.AFU.AFU

land, agricultural
USE **agricultural land**

land, arable
USE **arable land**

land, building
USE **building sites**

land, common
USE **common land**

land, crown
USE **crown land**

land, improved
USE **improved land**

land, public
USE **public land**

land, raw
USE **raw land**

land, serviced
USE **improved land**

land, unimproved
USE **raw land**

land, vacant
USE **raw land**

landfills
RK.1471 (A,L,B)
ALT **landfill**
CN V.RK.ALO.ALO.AXC.AFU.ALO

landfills, sanitary
USE **sanitary landfills**

landforms
RD.176 (L)
ALT **landform**
SN Geomorphic features of the earth's surface formed by natural processes which have definable composition and range of characteristics that recur wherever the features are found and that reflect similar surface and subsurface conditions. (WAYTA)
CN V.RD.ARI.AFU.AXC.AFU

landforms, aeolian
USE **aeolian landforms**

landforms, fluvial
USE **fluvial landforms**

landforms, glacial
USE **glacial landforms**

landing fields
USE **airfields**

landing newels
RT.1105
ALT **landing newel**
SN Posts at the landing point of a stair supporting the handrail. (PUTNAM)
UF newels, landing
CN V.RT.AFU.BIQ.AXC.ALO.BCW.AFU.AFU

landing stages
USE **landings (marine structures)**

landing strips
USE **airstrips**

landings
RT.1102 (B)
ALT **landing**
SN The platforms between flights of stairs, or at the termination of a flight of stairs. (PUTNAM)
UF landings, stair
paces
stair landings
CN V.RT.AFU.BIQ.AXC.ALO.AXC

landings (marine structures)
RK.1318 (B)
ALT **landing (marine sturcture)**
SN When possible use a more specific term.
UF embarcaderos
landing stages
stages, landing
CN V.RK.AFU.ALO.ALO.GLI.ARI.ARI.AXC

landings, stair
USE **landings**

landlords
HG.723 (A,L,B)
ALT **landlord**
SN Owners or holders of land or houses which are leased or rented to others. (W)
CN H.HG.AFU.BCW.DIO

landmark buildings
RK.511 (A,B)
ALT **landmark building**
UF buildings, landmark
buildings, listed
historic listed buildings
listed buildings
CN V.RK.AFU.ALO.ALO.BZY.ALO

landmarks
RK.886 (L)
ALT **landmark**
SN Use for any conspicuous monument, fixed object, or marker that helps establish the location of land boundaries or the location of a property.
CN V.RK.AFU.ALO.ALO.DOI.AFU.ALO.ARI

landscape architects
HG.86 (A,L,B)
ALT **landscape architect**
UF architects, landscape
designers, landscape
landscape designers
CN H.HG.AFU.AXC.AXC.AFU.AFU.ALO.ALO.ARI

landscape architecture
KD.16 (A,L,B,R)
UF architecture, landscape
design, landscape
landscape design
CN K.KD.AFU.AFU.AFU.AFU.ALO.AFU.AFU

landscape design
USE **landscape architecture**

landscape designers
USE **landscape architects**

landscape gardening
KT.492 (L,B)
SN The development and decorative planting of gardens and grounds. (W)
UF gardening, landscape
CN K.KT.AFU.ALO.DZW.AFU.ARI

landscape gardens
RK.1409 (A,B)
ALT **landscape garden**
SN Grounds laid out so as to produce the effect of natural scenery. (OED)
UF gardens, informal
gardens, landscape
informal gardens
CN V.RK.ALO.AFU.AFU.AFU.BCW

landscape marble
USE **forest marble**

landscape protection
KG.118 (A,L,B,R)
UF protection of landscape
protection, landscape
CN K.KG.AFU.AFU.BCW.ALO.BCW

landscape, agricultural
USE **agricultural land**

landscapes
VB.73 (L,B,R)
ALT **landscape**
CN V.VB.AFU.AXC.AXC

landscapes (environments)
RD.122 (A,L,B,R)
ALT **landscape (environment)**
SN Use broadly for portions of the earth's surface that share common repeating characteristics that can be comprehended at a glance. Landscapes are more than scenery or political units; they are systems of natural and cultural contexts. If possible use a more specific term.
CN V.RD.ARI

landscapes, cultural
USE **cultural landscapes**

landscapes, natural
USE **natural landscapes**

landscapes, suburban
USE **suburban landscapes**

landscapes, urban
USE **urban landscapes**

landscaping
KT.494 (B)
SN Arranging and modifying the effects of the natural environment for aesthetic effect. (W)
CN K.KT.AFU.ALO.DZW.ALO

landscaping plans
VD.42
ALT **landscaping plan**
UF plans, landscaping
CN V.VD.AFU.AFU.BIQ.ALO.AXC.AFU.ALO.ARI

landslide control
USE **landslide protection**

landslide protection
KG.119
UF control, landslide
landslide control
protection, landslide
CN K.KG.AFU.AFU.BCW.ALO.BIQ

landslides
KM.112 (L,B)
SN Occurrences of rapid downward movement under influence of gravity of a mass of rock, earth, or artificial fill on a slope. (W)
CN K.KM.AFU.CXA.BCW

Landuma
FL.345

CN F.FL.ALO.AFU.AXC.AFU.ARI.BIQ.BUE.ALO

lanes
RK.1535
ALT **lane**
SN Use for narrow ways generally wide enough for only a single line of moving persons or vehicles and often set between defined borders, as of hedges, fences, or buildings.
CN V.RK.ALO.ALO.BIQ.ARI.AFU.ALO.AFU.BCW

lanes (road elements)
RM.482
ALT **lane (road element)**
SN Strips of roadways adequate to accommodate a single line of vehicles. (W)
CN V.RM.ALO.ALO.ALO.ALO.BUE

lanes, acceleration
USE **acceleration lanes**

lanes, bowling
USE **bowling alleys**

lanes, bus
USE **bus lanes**

Lango
FL.684 (L)
UF Umiro
CN F.FL.ALO.AFU.AXC.AXC.BOK.CRG

Langobard
USE **Lombard**

language
BM.587 (R)
SN The words, their pronunciation, and the methods of combining them used and understood by a considerable community and established by long usage. (W)
CN B.BM.BUE.BIQ

language laboratories
RM.230 (B)
ALT **language laboratory**
SN Special rooms with sound recording and reproducing equipment for use by students studying languages. (RHDEL2)
UF laboratories, language
CN V.RM.AFU.DIO.ALO.DOI.BOK

language schools
RK.810
ALT **language school**
UF schools, language
CN V.RK.AFU.ALO.ALO.CXA.ARI.ALO.BUE

languages
KD.30
CN K.KD.AFU.AFU.ARI

Languedoc marble
MT.799
SN A compact marble of brilliant red color blotched with white. (RS)
UF French red marble
marble, French red
marble, Languedoc
red marble, French
CN M.MT.AFU.AFU.AFU.DCU.AFU.ARI.ARI.ARI.BCW.ALO

Lanna
USE **Northern Thai**

lanolin
MT.2195 (L)
SN Purified and hydrated wool grease. (MH)
UF wax, wool
wool-fat
wool wax
CN M.MT.AFU.AFU.ARI.BZY.AFU.ALO

lantern lights
RT.996 (B)
ALT **lantern light**
SN Raised skylights or small lanterns with the sides mostly glazed, erected on a roof to admit light to the space below.
UF lantern windows
lights, lantern
windows, lantern
CN V.RT.AFU.ARI.AFU.ARI.ARI.AFU

lantern slide transparencies
USE **lantern slides**

lantern slides
VJ.84 (L,N,R)
ALT **lantern slide**
SN Transparent positive images made or mounted on glass for projection, usually but not necessarily photographic, measuring 3 1/4 to 3 1/2 by 4 inches. (SAPSP)
UF hyalotypes
lantern slide transparencies
magic lantern slides
slides, lantern
slides, magic lantern
transparencies, lantern slide
CN V.VJ.AFU.AFU.BCW.ARI

lantern towers
USE **crossing towers**

lantern windows
USE **lantern lights**

lanterns of the dead
RK.478 (A,L,R)
ALT **lantern of the dead**
SN Use for slender, towerlike structures erected in cemeteries to contain a light and often an altar; common in Medieval France.
UF beacons, cemetery
cemetery beacons
graveyard lanterns
lanterns, graveyard
CN V.RK.AFU.ALO.ALO.BOK.BOK.ALO

lanterns (roof appendages)
RT.485 (B)
ALT **lantern (roof appendage)**
SN Windowed superstructures crowning a roof or dome, and serving to give light or air to the space below; in certain circumstances, such structures, whether they provide light or not.
CN V.RT.AFU.AFU.AFU.BIQ.ARI.ALO.AFU.BUE.BCW

lanterns, graveyard
USE **lanterns of the dead**

Laotian
FL.2393 (L,B)
CN F.FL.ALO.ARI.BCW.AXC

lap bottom seams
TF.658
ALT **lap bottom seam**
SN The same as lap joints, but typically used to refer to sheet metal, and sometimes plates, that are welded, soldered, or riveted at the overlapping joint. (MEANS)
UF bottom seams, lap
lap seams
seams, lap
seams, lap bottom
CN V.TF.ALO.ARI.ARI.BUE.BZY

lap joints
TF.684
ALT **lap joint**
SN In construction, joints in which two building elements are not butted up against each other, but are overlapped, part of one covering part of the other. (MEANS)
UF joints, lap
joints, overlapping
laps
overlapping joints
CN V.TF.ALO.ARI.AXC.ARI.AXC

lap seams
USE **lap bottom seams**

lapidaries
HG.484 (L)
ALT **lapidary**
SN Experts in precious stones and the art or techniques of lapidary.
CN H.HG.AFU.AXC.BUE.ARI.BUE

lapidary
KT.769 (L,R)
SN Use for processes pertaining to the art of cutting and polishing precious and semiprecious stones.
UF carving, gem
cutting, gem
gem carving
gem cutting
lapidary art
CN K.KT.AFU.ALO.HOE.ARI

lapidary art
USE **lapidary**

lapis
USE **moderate bluish green**

lapis aequipondus
USE **pietra nefritica**

lapis albanus
USE **peperino**

lapis amiantus
USE **amianto**

lapis atracius
USE **verd antique**

lapis basanites
USE **basalt**

lapis gabinus
USE **sperone**

lapis judaicus
USE **graphic granite**

lapis lazuli
MT.529 (R)
CN M.MT.AFU.AFU.AFU.CFS.AFU.ERE

lapis lazuli blue
USE **deep blue**
moderate blue

lapis lazuli (ultramarine blue)
USE **ultramarine blue**

lapis liydius
USE **pietra di paragone**

lapis ophites
USE **verde di ranocchia**

lapis porphyrite
USE **porphyry**

lapis tiburtinus
USE **travertine**

lapped drawers
USE **lipped drawers**

laps
USE **lap joints**

laps (learning modules)
USE **learning modules**

laptop computers
TB.145
ALT **laptop computer**
SN Microcomputers so compact that they can be operated while resting on the user's lap. (RHDEL2)
UF computers, laptop
CN V.TB.AFU.ARI.BCW.ARI.AFU.AFU

Laqabi pottery
USE **Lakabi ware**

Laqabi ware
USE **Lakabi ware**

larch
MT.1362 (L)
UF Larix
CN M.MT.AFU.AFU.ALO.BIQ.DCU.AFU .AFU.ALO.BZY

larch fir
USE **western larch**

larch, European
USE **European larch**

larch, Japanese
USE **Japanese larch**

larch, Montana
USE **western larch**

larch, mountain
USE **western larch**

larch, Siberian
USE **Siberian larch**

larch, western
USE **western larch**

larders
RM.200 (B)
ALT **larder**
SN Rooms where food is stored. (HAS)
CN V.RM.AFU.DIO.ALO.DCU.CFS

large
DC.120
CN D.DC.AFU.AXC.AFU

large span structures
RT.9 (A)
ALT **large span structure**
UF long span structures
structures, large span
structures, long span
CN V.RT.AFU.AFU.AFU.AFU.ALO.AFU

Large wild fauna phase
USE **Bubalus phase**

Larix
USE **larch**

Larix decidua
USE **European larch**

Larix europaea
USE **European larch**

Larix occidentalis
USE **western larch**

Larix russica
USE **Siberian larch**

Larix sibirica
USE **Siberian larch**

larkin desks
USE **desks-over-bookcases**

Las Charcas
FL.1019
CN F.FL.ALO.ALO.ALO.ALO.AFU.ALO. ARI.AFU.ALO.ARI

laser art
BM.261 (R)
UF art, laser
CN B.BM.AFU.ARI.BCW.FOG.BOK

laser beam cutting
KT.829 (L)
UF cutting, laser beam
CN K.KT.AFU.ALO.HOE.BCW.ALO.ARI .AXC

laser disks
USE **optical disks**

laser printers
TB.172 (L)
ALT **laser printer**
SN Electrophotographic printers in which a laser is used as the light source. (DOC)
UF printers, laser
CN V.TB.AFU.ARI.BCW.AXC.AXC.ALO. ARI.ALO.ALO

laser welding
KT.811 (L)
UF welding, laser
CN K.KT.AFU.ALO.HOE.BCW.ALO. AFU.ALO.BCW.ARI

latch bolts
TF.171
ALT **latch bolt**
SN Beveled spring bolts usually operated by a knob, handle, or turn. (BROWNL)
UF bolts, latch
bolts, live
live bolts
CN V.TF.AFU.AFU.AFU.AFU.DIO.AXC

latch bolts, antifriction
USE **antifriction latch bolts**

latch bolts, hinged
USE **swinging latch bolts**

latch bolts, swinging
USE **swinging latch bolts**

latches
TF.172 (N)
ALT **latch**
SN Holding devices that rely on some form of horizontal bar, such as a bolt, rod, or hook as the means of closure. Distinguished from **catches** which rely on a roller, magnet, or friction.
CN V.TF.AFU.AFU.AFU.AFU.DIO.BCW

latches, auxiliary dead
USE **auxiliary dead latches**

latches, barn-door
USE **barn-door latches**

latches, cabinet
USE **cabinet latches**

latches, cottage
USE **cottage latches**

latches, dead
USE **night latches**

latches, deadlocking
USE **auxiliary dead latches**

latches, fire-door
USE **fire-door latches**

latches, hospital
USE **hospital latches**

latches, ice box
USE **ice box latches**

latches, integral
USE **integral locks**

latches, knob
USE **knob latches**

latches, lift
USE **lift latches**

latches, mortise
USE **mortise locks**

latches, night
USE **night latches**

latches, roller
USE **roller latches**

latches, screen-door
USE **screen-door latches**

latches, secret gate
USE **secret gate latches**

latches, sliding-door
USE **sliding-door locks**

latches, spring
USE **spring latches**

latches, thumb
USE **thumb latches**

latches, two-point
USE **two-point latches**

latches, vestibule
USE **vestibule latches**

Late Antique
FL.2725 (A,R)
UF Antique, Late
Imperial, Late
Late Imperial
Late Roman
Roman, Late
CN F.FL.ALO.AXC.ALO.ALO.AFU.AXC.ARI

Late Archaic
FL.2576
UF Archaic, Late
CN F.FL.ALO.AXC.ALO.AFU.AFU.ARI.AXC.ARI

Late Assyrian
FL.2980
UF Assyrian, Late
Neo-Assyrian
CN F.FL.ALO.AXC.ARI.BCW.AFU.BUE.ARI

Late Baroque
FL.3175
UF Baroque, Late
CN F.FL.ALO.BCW.ALO.ARI.AXC.ARI

Late Benin
FL.96
UF Benin, Late
CN F.FL.ALO.AFU.ALO.AFU.BUE.AFU.ARI

Late Bronze Age
FL.29
UF Bronze Age, Late
CN F.FL.AFU.BCW.ARI.ARI

Late Byzantine
FL.3076
UF Byzantine, Late
CN F.FL.ALO.BCW.ALO.AFU.ALO.AXC

Late Chalcolithic
FL.23
UF Chalcolithic, Late
CN F.FL.AFU.BCW.ALO.ALO.ARI

Late Chiripa
FL.1146
UF Chiripa, Late
CN F.FL.ALO.ALO.ALO.ARI.AXC.AFU.ARI.BOK

Late Chou
USE **Late Zhou**

Late Classic
FL.970
UF Classic, Late
CN F.FL.ALO.ALO.ALO.ALO.AFU.AFU.AXC.ARI

Late Classical
FL.2580
UF Classical, Late
CN F.FL.ALO.AXC.ALO.AFU.AFU.ARI.BCW.ARI

Late Cocle
USE **Macaracas**

Late Corinthian
FL.2629
UF Corinthian, Late
CN F.FL.ALO.AXC.ALO.AFU.ALO.AXC.ALO.BCW.AFU.AXC

Late Cremation
FL.926
UF Cremation, Late
CN F.FL.ALO.ALO.ALO.AFU.ALO.ARI.BCW.ALO

Late Cycladic
FL.2547 (A)
UF Cycladic, Late
CN F.FL.ALO.AXC.ALO.AFU.AFU.ALO.AFU.AXC

Late Cypriote
FL.2896
UF Cypriote, Late
CN F.FL.ALO.AXC.ARI.ARI.AFU.ARI

Late Dilmun
FL.2885
UF Dilmun, Late
CN F.FL.ALO.AXC.ARI.ALO.AFU.AFU.ARI

Late Edo
FL.1985
UF Edo, Late
Late Tokugawa
Tokugawa, Late
CN F.FL.ALO.ARI.ALO.ALO.AFU.BCW.AFU.ARI

Late Etruscan
FL.2709
UF Etruscan, Late
CN F.FL.ALO.AXC.ALO.ALO.AFU.ARI.ALO

Late Formative
USE **Late Preclassic**

Late Geometric
FL.2567
UF Geometric, Late
CN F.FL.ALO.AXC.ALO.AFU.AFU.ARI.ALO.ARI

Late Gerzean
FL.2783
UF Gerzean, Late
CN F.FL.ALO.AXC.ALO.ARI.AFU.AFU.ALO.ARI.ALO

Late Gothic
FL.3096 (L,B)
UF Gothic, Late
CN F.FL.ALO.BCW.ALO.ALO.AFU.ARI.ARI

Late Heian
FL.1980 (L)
UF Fujiwara
Heian, Late
CN F.FL.ALO.ARI.ALO.ALO.AFU.AXC.ARI.ALO

Late Helladic
FL.2552
UF Helladic, Late
CN F.FL.ALO.AXC.ALO.AFU.AFU.ALO.ALO.ARI

Late Hellenistic
FL.2582
UF Hellenistic, Late
CN F.FL.ALO.AXC.ALO.AFU.AFU.ARI.BIQ.AFU

Late horizon
FL.1171
CN F.FL.ALO.ALO.ALO.ARI.AXC.AFU.BOK

Late Imperial
USE **Late Antique**

Late Intermediate period
FL.1163
UF Intermediate period, Late
CN F.FL.ALO.ALO.ALO.ARI.AXC.AFU.BIQ

Late Iron Age
FL.33
UF Iron Age, Late
CN F.FL.AFU.BCW.AXC.ARI

Late Jomon
FL.1963
UF Jomon, Late
CN F.FL.ALO.ARI.ALO.ALO.AFU.AFU.ALO.AXC

Late Malla
FL.2164
UF Malla, Late
CN F.FL.ALO.ARI.AXC.AFU.AXC.AFU.BCW.ALO

Late Medieval
FL.3097
SN Use with reference to the period c.1250 to as late as 1500 where the terms **Gothic** or **Late Gothic** are not appropriate.
UF Medieval, Late
CN F.FL.ALO.BCW.ALO.ALO.AFU.AXC

Late Minoan
FL.2559
UF Minoan, Late
CN F.FL.ALO.AXC.ALO.AFU.AFU.ALO.ARI.AXC

Late Mughal
USE **Provincial Mughal**

Late Naqada
USE **Gerzean**

Late Nara
FL.1977
UF Nara, Late
Tempyo
CN F.FL.ALO.ARI.ALO.ALO.AFU.AXC.ALO.ALO

Late Neolithic
FL.17
UF Neolithic, Late
CN F.FL.AFU.BCW.AFU.ARI.ARI

Late Orientalizing
FL.2572
UF Orientalizing, Late
CN F.FL.ALO.AXC.ALO.AFU.AFU.ARI.ARI.ARI

Late Palace period
USE **New Palace period**

Late period Californian
FL.773
UF Californian, Late period
CN F.FL.ALO.ALO.ALO.AFU.AFU.BCW.AFU.ARI

Late period (Egyptian)
FL.2826
CN F.FL.ALO.AXC.ALO.ARI.AFU.CFS

Late period Plateau
FL.780
UF Plateau, Late period
CN F.FL.ALO.ALO.ALO.AFU.AFU.BCW.ARI.AXC

Late Postclassic
FL.973
UF Decadent period
Postclassic, Late
CN F.FL.ALO.ALO.ALO.ALO.AFU.AFU.BCW.ALO

Late Preclassic
FL.965
UF Formative, Late
Late Formative
Preclassic, Late
CN F.FL.ALO.ALO.ALO.ALO.AFU.AFU.ALO.ARI

Late Renaissance
FL.3169
UF Renaissance, Late
CN F.FL.ALO.BCW.ALO.ARI.AFU.ARI

Late Republican
FL.2713
UF Republican, Late
CN F.FL.ALO.AXC.ALO.ALO.AFU.AXC.AFU.AFU

Late Roman
USE **Late Antique**

Late Tokugawa
USE **Late Edo**

Late Victorian
FL.3320
UF Victorian, Late
CN F.FL.ALO.BCW.ALO.AXC.DIO.ALO.BCW.ALO.ARI

Late Zhou
FL.2371
UF Chou, Late
Late Chou
Zhou, Late
CN F.FL.ALO.ARI.BCW.ARI.AFU.ALO

Later Andhra
FL.2198
UF Andhra, Later
CN F.FL.ALO.ARI.AXC.ALO.AFU.ARI.AXC.ALO

Later Chin
USE **Later Jin**

Later Chou
USE **Later Zhou**

later coctilis
USE **fired brick**

later coctus
USE **fired brick**

Later Han
FL.1890
UF Han, Later
CN F.FL.ALO.ARI.ALO.AFU.AFU.ALO.CLM.AXC

Later Han (Eastern Han)
USE **Eastern Han**

Later Jin
FL.1887
UF Chin, Later
Jin, Later
Later Chin
CN F.FL.ALO.ARI.ALO.AFU.AFU.ALO.CLM.AFU

Later Liang
FL.1889
UF Liang, Later
CN F.FL.ALO.ARI.ALO.AFU.AFU.ALO.CLM.ARI

Later Tang
FL.1888
UF Tang, Later
CN F.FL.ALO.ARI.ALO.AFU.AFU.ALO.CLM.ALO

Later Zhou
FL.1891
UF Chou, Later
Later Chou
Zhou, Later
CN F.FL.ALO.ARI.ALO.AFU.AFU.ALO.CLM.BCW

lateral
DC.37
CN D.DC.AFU.ALO.ARI.CRG

lateral buckling
KT.889
SN Buckling of a structural member involving lateral deflection and twist. (STEIN)
UF buckling, lateral
CN K.KT.ALO.AFU.ARI

lateral buttresses
RT.79
ALT **lateral buttress**
SN Use for buttresses standing at the corner of a building and on axis with one of the walls.
UF buttresses, lateral
CN V.RT.AFU.AFU.AFU.AXC.AXC.AXC

lateral loads
BM.1013
SN Load applied horizontally owing to wind pressure or seismic blast effects. (STEIN)
UF loads, lateral
CN B.BM.CFS.AXC.CLM.ALO.ARI.BZY

lateral sewers
RK.551
ALT **lateral sewer**
SN Sewers which discharge into branch or other sewers and have no other common sewer tributary to them. (DAC)
UF sewers, lateral
CN V.RK.AFU.ALO.ALO.CFS.ALO.AFU.ALO.ALO.AXC

laterite
MT.2064 (L)
SN A residual product of rock decay that is red in color and has a high content in the oxides of iron and hydroxide of aluminum and a low proportion of silica.(W) Used in African building construction. (OLIVER)
UF bauxite, ferroginous
ferroginous bauxite
CN M.MT.AFU.AFU.ARI.BOK.ALO.ARI

latex
MT.1002 (B)
SN A viscous, milklike fluid composed of resins or waxes in the form of tiny globules in aqueous suspension, and obtained especially from rubber trees;(MAYER) used for many rubber applications, such as adhesive. Also refers to water dispersion of synthetic rubbers and of rubberlike plastics. (MH12)
CN M.MT.AFU.AFU.ALO.AXC.BIQ

latex caulk
MT.2651
UF caulk, latex
CN M.MT.AFU.ARI.HTY.AFU.AFU

latex paint
MT.2531
SN Low sheen acrylic emulsion paint, has excellent resistance to weathering and good impact resistance.
UF latex water paint
paint, latex
paint, latex water
water paint, latex
CN M.MT.AFU.ARI.CRG.ALO.BCW.AFU.BIQ.AFU

latex water paint
USE **latex paint**

lath axes
USE **froes**

lath-back Windsor chairs
TG.108
ALT **lath-back Windsor chair**
SN Square-back Windsor chairs with narrow vertical lath instead of round spindles. (EVANS)
UF chairs, lath-back Windsor
Windsor chairs, lath-back
CN V.TG.AFU.AFU.ALO.AFU.AFU.AFU.MLC.CFS.ALO

lath hammers
USE **lathing hatchets**

lath nails
TF.441
ALT **lath nail**
UF nails, lath
CN V.TF.AFU.AFU.AFU.ALO.AFU.CFS.ALO.CRG

lath nails, metal
USE **metal lath nails**

lath rivers
USE **froes**

lath, diamond mesh
USE **diamond mesh lath**

lath, flat expanded metal
USE **diamond mesh lath**

lath, gypsum
USE **gypsum board**

lath, rib
USE **rib lath**

lath, rock
USE **gypsum board**

lathe puppets
TB.436
ALT **lathe puppet**
SN Upright supports or guides of a machine that are fastened at the bottom only. (W)
UF puppets (tools)
puppets, lathe
CN V.TB.AFU.ARI.EFQ.ALO.ALO

lathes
TB.114 (L,N)
ALT **lathe**
SN Machines in which work is rotated about a horizontal axis and shaped by a fixed cutting, boring, or drilling tool while being held in a chuck, faceplate, or mandrel or between centers in headstock and tailstock. (W)
CN V.TB.AFU.ARI.AXC.AFU.AFU

lathes, great wheel
USE **great wheel lathes**

lathes, mandrel
USE **mandrel lathes**

lathes, pole
USE **pole lathes**

lathes, spoke
USE **spoke lathes**

lathes, turret
USE **turret lathes**

lathes, wheel
USE **wheel lathes**

lathhouses
RK.69
ALT **lathhouse**
SN Structure made of laths or slats to shelter growing plants requiring shade and wind protection. (DAC)
UF houses, slat
slat houses
CN V.RK.AFU.ALO.ALO.AFU.AFU.BOK.ALO

lathing
KT.705 (L)
SN The placing of lath in forming walls, or other building elements. (DAC)
CN K.KT.AFU.ALO.GRC.CFS

lath
MT.2412 (L)
SN The surface, other than masonry, to which plaster is applied; made from various materials, including expanded metal mesh, gypsum board, or other material that will sufficiently bond the plaster. (HORNB)
UF lathing (lath)
CN M.MT.AFU.ARI.BZY.BIQ

lathing hammers
USE **lathing hatchets**

lathing hatchets
TB.893 (N)
ALT **lathing hatchet**
SN Tools having a hatchet blade and a hammer face; used for cutting and nailing wood lath.
UF hammers, lath
hammers, lathing
hatchets, lathing
lath hammers
lathing hammers
CN V.TB.AFU.BCW.CFS.ALO.AFU.DCU.ARI

lathing (lath)
USE **lath**

lathmaker's froes
USE **knife froes**

latifundia
RG.20 (L)
ALT **latifundium**
SN Large, ancient Roman agricultural estates; for modern Spanish Latin American contexts, prefer **haciendas.**
CN V.RG.AFU.AFU.AFU.ARI

Latin American
FL.1706 (L,B,R)
UF American, Latin
Hispanic
CN F.FL.ALO.ALO.AXC.ALO

Latin cross-plan
DC.81
UF plan, Latin cross
CN D.DC.AFU.ARI.ERE.AXC

Latin crosses
DG.10
SN Crosses having three short arms, at the top and sides, and a long arm at the bottom.
UF crosses, Latin
crosses, long
cruces capitatae
cruces immissae
long crosses
CN D.DG.AFU.AFU.ARI.BCW

Latin Dynasty
USE **Latin Empire**

Latin Empire
FL.3075
UF Latin Dynasty
Latin Kingdom
CN F.FL.ALO.BCW.ALO.AFU.ALO.ARI

Latin Kingdom
USE **Latin Empire**

Latinos
HG.780 (L)
ALT **Latino**
UF Americans, Hispanic
Hispanic Americans
CN H.HG.AFU.BOK.ARI.ALO

latrinas
USE **reredorters**

latrines
RK.747 (A,L,B,R)
ALT **latrine**
SN Use for detached structures in public contexts containing one or more seats and a pit serving as toilets; distinguished from **outhouses** which are similar structures in domestic contexts. For rooms that are within buildings and have such simple facilities, use **privies.**
CN V.RK.AFU.ALO.ALO.CXA.ALO.AFU.ARI.AFU

lats
RK.901
ALT **lat**
SN Freestanding Indian pillars, bearing inscriptions or surmounted by animal sculpture.
UF stambas
CN V.RK.AFU.ALO.ALO.DOI.AFU.BIQ.AFU

latten ware
USE **pewter**

lattice-back chairs
TG.158
ALT **lattice-back chair**
SN Chairs having a back formed by slender members crossing over each other in a netlike pattern.
UF chairs, lattice-back
chairs, trellis-back
trellis-back chairs
CN V.TG.AFU.AFU.ALO.AFU.AFU.AFU.NIE.ELK.AFU

lattice trusses
USE **Town lattice trusses**

lattice trusses, Town
USE **Town lattice trusses**

lattice windows
RT.926 (L)
ALT **lattice window**
SN Window casements, fixed or hinged, with mullions set diagonally. (HAS)
UF trellis windows
windows, lattice
windows, trellis
CN V.RT.AFU.ARI.AFU.AFU.BOK.AFU.AFU.DCU

lattice, Chinese
USE **Chinese fretwork**

lattices
RT.1045
ALT **lattice**
SN Networks of small light bars of wood, metal, or other material crossing at regular intervals, usually diagonally.
UF latticework
CN V.RT.AFU.AXC.ALO.AXC

lattices, garden
USE **trellises**

latticework
USE **lattices**

lauan
MT.1193
SN Wood resembling mahogany; used for furniture and cabinet woods, paneling and boatbuilding. (MH)
UF mahogany, Philippine
Philippine mahogany
shorea
tangile
CN M.MT.AFU.AFU.ALO.BIQ.DCU.AFU.AFU.AFU.FZU

Lauderdale
FL.894
CN F.FL.ALO.ALO.ALO.AFU.ALO.ALO.BOK.BUE

launch complexes
RG.220 (L)
ALT **launch complex**
UF complexes, launch
launch sites
sites, launch
CN V.RG.AFU.AFU.EFQ.AFU.ALO

launch sites
USE **launch complexes**

launch towers
RK.1310 (A)
ALT **launch tower**
UF towers, launch
CN V.RK.AFU.ALO.ALO.GLI.ARI.AFU

launching ramps
RK.1322
ALT **launching ramp**
UF boat ramps
ramps, boat
ramps, launching
CN V.RK.AFU.ALO.ALO.GLI.ARI.ARI.BCW

laundries
RK.194 (A,L,B,R)
ALT **laundry**
SN Commercial establishments where laundering is done. (W)
UF coin operated laundries
commercial laundries
houses, wash
laundries, coin operated
laundries, commercial
laundries, public
public laundries
wash houses
CN V.RK.AFU.ALO.ALO.ALO.AXC.BIQ

laundries, coin operated
USE **laundries**

laundries, commercial
USE **laundries**

laundries, public
USE **laundries**

laundry chutes
RM.213
ALT **laundry chute**
UF chutes, clothes
chutes, laundry
clothes chutes
CN V.RM.AFU.DIO.ALO.DIO.ARI.ALO

laundry rooms
RM.231 (A,B)
ALT **laundry room**
UF rooms, laundry
CN V.RM.AFU.DIO.ALO.DOI.BUE

laundry trays
RT.1482 (N)
ALT **laundry tray**
SN Deep, large sinks used for washing laundry.
UF laundry tubs
set tubs
trays, laundry
tubs, laundry
tubs, set
CN V.RT.ALO.BCW.ALO.ARI.CFS.AXC

laundry tubs
USE **laundry trays**

laurel
MT.1194 (L,R)
UF bay laurel
common laurel
laurel, bay
laurel, common
laurel, true
Laurus nobilis
true laurel
CN M.MT.AFU.AFU.ALO.BIQ.DCU.AFU.AFU.AFU.GFO

laurel magnolia
USE **magnolia graniflora**

laurel oak
MT.1242
UF oak, laurel
Quercus laurifolia
CN M.MT.AFU.AFU.ALO.BIQ.DCU.AFU.AFU.AFU.IRA.CLM

Laurel (style)
FL.871

CN F.FL.ALO.ALO.ALO.AFU.ALO.ALO.
AXC.BIQ

laurel, bay
USE **laurel**

laurel, bull
USE **magnolia graniflora**

laurel, camphor
USE **camphorwood**

laurel, common
USE **laurel**

laurel, true
USE **laurel**

Laurentian
FL.872
CN F.FL.ALO.ALO.ALO.AFU.ALO.ALO.
AXC.BOK

Lauricocha
FL.1134
CN F.FL.ALO.ALO.ALO.ARI.AXC.AFU.
AFU.ALO

Laurus nobilis
USE **laurel**

lava
MT.625 (L)
CN M.MT.AFU.AFU.AFU.DCU.AFU.AFU.
ALO.ALO.AFU

lavatories (rooms)
RM.68 (B)
ALT **lavatory (room)**
SN Use for rooms containing a sink and toilet, but neither tub nor shower.
UF half-baths
powder rooms
rooms, powder
rooms, wash
wash rooms
CN V.RM.AFU.DIO.ALO.ALO.ARI

lavatories (sinks)
RT.1486 (N,B)
ALT **lavatory (sink)**
SN Sinks used for washing the hands and face. For deep, relatively large sinks used for washing the arms and upper body, use **wash sinks.**
CN V.RT.ALO.BCW.ALO.ARI.CFS.BIQ
.ALO

lavatories, public
USE **rest rooms**

lavender
USE **light purple**
moderate purple
pale purple
very light violet
very pale violet

lavender blue
USE **brilliant purplish blue**
light purplish blue

lavender blue, deep
USE **brilliant purplish blue**

lavender blue, light
USE **light purplish blue**

lavender gray
USE **pale purplish blue**
pale violet
very pale purplish blue
very pale violet

lavender oil
MT.1988 (L)
SN A colorless to yellowish aromatic essential oil obtained from the flowers of several species of lavender;(W) used as a retardant in oil paints. (MAYER)
UF oil of lavender
oil, lavender
oleum lavandulae
CN M.MT.AFU.AFU.ARI.ARI.AFU.ARI.
AFU.ALO

lavender violet
USE **brilliant violet**

lavender violet, light
USE **light violet**

lavender violet, pale
USE **light purple**
pale purple

lavender, blue
USE **pale purplish blue**

lavender, bluish
USE **light violet**

lavender, bright
USE **light purple**
light violet
moderate purple
moderate violet

lavender, dark
USE **light purple**

lavender, dark grayish
USE **pale violet**

lavender, deep
USE **light violet**

lavender, deep dull
USE **pale purple**

lavender, deep grayish
USE **pale purple**
pale violet

lavender, dull
USE **grayish purplish pink**

lavender, grayish
USE **pale purple**

lavender, light
USE **light purple**

lavender, lilac
USE **pale violet**

lavender, pale
USE **very pale purple**

lavender, pale bluish
USE **very pale purple**
very pale violet

lavender, pastel
USE **very pale purple**

lavender, pink
USE **pale purplish pink**

lavras
RG.192
ALT **lavra**
SN Use for certain monastic complexes of the eastern Mediterranean in which hermit monks live in a loosely organized group of cells around a common central complex.
CN V.RG.AFU.AFU.DUC.AXC

law
KD.160 (A,L,B,R)
UF legal studies
studies, legal
CN K.KD.AFU.ALO.DOI

law courts
USE **courthouses**

law enforcing
KG.207 (L)
UF enforcing, law
CN K.KG.AFU.ALO.BCW.BUE

law manuscripts
USE **legal manuscripts**

law offices
RK.919 (A,L)
ALT **law office**
UF legal offices
offices, law
offices, legal
CN V.RK.AFU.ALO.ALO.DZW.ALO.
BCW

law reporters
HG.291 (L)
ALT **law reporter**
UF court reporters
reporters, court
reporters, law
CN H.HG.AFU.AXC.BCW.ALO.AFU.ARI
.ARI.ALO

law schools
RK.811 (A,L)
ALT **law school**
UF schools, law
CN V.RK.AFU.ALO.ALO.CXA.ARI.ALO.
BZY

law, civil
USE **civil law**

law, criminal
USE **criminal law**

law, environmental
USE **environmental law**

law, international
USE **international law**

law, land
USE **land law**

law, penal
USE **criminal law**

law, public
USE **public law**

law, zoning
USE **zoning law**

lawmakers
USE **legislators**

lawn tennis courts
USE **tennis courts**

lawns
RM.454 (L,R)
ALT **lawn**
CN V.RM.ALO.AFU.CFS.BCW

laws
VW.1028 (L,B,R)
ALT **law**
SN Documents stating rules of action or conduct prescribed by controlling authority and having binding legal force. (BLACKS)
CN V.VW.AFU.ARI.ALO.BCW.AFU.ARI.AFU.ARI.AFU

laws, building
USE **building codes**

laws, poor
USE **poor laws**

lawson cypress
USE **Port Orford cedar**

lawyers
HG.317 (L)
ALT **lawyer**
UF attorneys
CN H.HG.AFU.AXC.BCW.ALO.BIQ.AXC

layer, antiabrasion
USE **supercoat**

layer, nonabrasion
USE **supercoat**

layer, subbing
USE **subbing layer**

layering
KT.58
ALT **layered**
CN K.KT.AFU.ALO.BCW.BUE

laying concrete
USE **pouring concrete**

laying in
KT.246
SN Painting a canvas in a monochrome color as a first step in the development of tonal values and of the composition as a whole. (THDAT)
CN K.KT.AFU.ALO.DUC.CXA.ALO.ARI.ALO.AFU

laying, tile
USE **tile laying**

laylights
RT.997
ALT **laylight**
SN Glazed panels, usually set flush with the ceiling, serving to admit light to the room below.
CN V.RT.AFU.ARI.AFU.ARI.ARI.ALO

layout drawings
USE **site plans**

layout paper
MT.1935
UF paper, layout
CN M.MT.AFU.AFU.ARI.ALO.ALO.AXC.ARI.AXC.ALO.AFU

layouts, site
USE **site plans**

lazar houses
USE **lazarettos**

lazarettos
RK.767 (A,L,R)
ALT **lazaretto**
SN Use for hospitals treating very dangerous cantagious diseases, common during the Middle Ages; for places for the treatment of leprosy specifically, use **leprosariums.**
UF houses, lazar
lazar houses
CN V.RK.AFU.ALO.ALO.CXA.ALO.AFU.BCW.ALO.BCW.AFU

lazuline blue
USE **ultramarine blue**

Lê
FL.2432
CN F.FL.ALO.ARI.BCW.BUE.AFU.BCW

le goût grec
USE **goût grec**

le premier art roman
USE **First Romanesque**

leaching
KT.641 (L)
SN Removal of materials in solution by the passage of water through the soil. (STEIN)
CN K.KT.AFU.ALO.GFO.BCW

leaching fields
RT.1465 (L)
ALT **leaching field**
SN Systems of trenches containing coarse aggregate and distribution pipes through which septic tank effluent may seep into the surrounding soil. (DAC)
UF absorption fields
disposal fields
fields, absorption
fields, disposal
fields, leaching
leaching trenches
trenches, leaching
CN V.RT.ALO.BCW.ALO.ARI.BOK

leaching trenches
USE **leaching fields**

lead
MT.436 (A,L,B,R)
CN M.MT.AFU.AFU.AFU.BZY.AFU.AFU.ARI.BOK

lead-alkali glass
USE **lead glass**

lead alloys
MT.400 (L)
UF alloys, lead
CN M.MT.AFU.AFU.AFU.BZY.AFU.AFU.AFU.ALO.BCW

lead-antimony-tin alloys
USE **white metal**

lead-based paint
MT.2528 (L)
UF lead paint
paint, lead
paint, lead-based
CN M.MT.AFU.ARI.CRG.ALO.BCW.AFU.AXC.AFU

lead bronze
MT.382 (L)
UF bronze, lead
bronze, ordnance
ordnance bronze
CN M.MT.AFU.AFU.AFU.BZY.AFU.AFU.AFU.ALO.ARI.BCW.AXC

lead-capped nails
TF.445
ALT **lead-capped nail**
UF lead head nails
lead nails
nails, lead
nails, lead-capped
nails, lead head
nails, nonleaking roofing
nonleaking roofing nails
roofing nails, nonleaking
CN V.TF.AFU.AFU.AFU.ALO.AFU.CFS.ALO.DIO.AFU

lead (color)
USE **dark gray**

lead crystal
USE **crystal**

lead glass
MT.243
SN Glass containing a high proportion of lead oxide and having a relatively high refractive index, with poor acid resistance and low rigidity; used in many optical components, neon-sign

tubing, and light bulbs.
UF glass, lead
glass, lead-alkali
glass, lead silicate
lead-alkali glass
lead silicate glass
silicate glass, lead
CN M.MT.AFU.AFU.AFU.BIQ.AFU.AFU.AXC

lead gray
USE **dark gray**
reddish gray

lead head nails
USE **lead-capped nails**

lead monoxide, yellow
USE **litharge**

lead nails
USE **lead-capped nails**

lead oxide
USE **litharge**

lead paint
USE **lead-based paint**

lead pencils
USE **graphite pencils**

lead points
TB.256
ALT **lead point**
SN Use for instruments composed of actual lead. Distinct from **graphite pencils,** which in the 19th century were misleadingly called lead pencils.
UF points, lead
CN V.TB.AFU.ARI.CLM.AFU.ALO.CLM.ALO

lead silicate glass
USE **lead glass**

lead stannate
MT.1780
UF lead-tin yellow
stannate, lead
yellow, lead-tin
CN M.MT.AFU.AFU.ARI.AFU.AFU.ALO.ALO.BUE.ARI.BCW

lead tetroxide
USE **red lead**

lead-tin yellow
USE **lead stannate**

lead wool
MT.2652
SN A wool-like material of fine strands of lead; sometimes used as caulking in pipe joints. (DAC)
UF wool, lead
CN M.MT.AFU.ARI.HTY.AFU.ALO

lead, black
USE **graphite (black pigment)**

lead, orange
USE **red lead**

lead, red
USE **red lead**

lead, red (color)
USE **deep reddish orange**

lead, red (iron oxide red)
USE **iron oxide red**

lead, white
USE **white lead**

leaded glass
MT.248 (A)
SN Pieces of glass fixed together with strip lead; used for windows. (ACME)
UF glass, leaded
CN M.MT.AFU.AFU.AFU.BIQ.AFU.ALO.ALO

leader heads
RT.1466 (B)
ALT **leader head**
UF heads, leader
heads, rainwater
rainwater heads
CN V.RT.ALO.BCW.ALO.ARI.BUE

leaders, rainwater
USE **conductors (piping)**

leading
USE **leadwork**

leads, plastic
USE **plastic leads**

leadwork
MT.2770 (A,L)
UF leading
CN M.MT.AFU.AXC.BOK.BCW

leaf
MT.457
SN Metal beaten or rolled out to extreme thinness for use in gilding. (MAYER)
UF composition leaf
Dutch metal
leaf, composition
leaf, metal
metal leaf
metal, Dutch
CN M.MT.AFU.AFU.AFU.BZY.AFU.ALO.ARI

leaf scrolls
DG.66
ALT **leaf scroll**
SN Decorative motifs consisting of isolated or fairly discrete scrolls with foliate forms. For continuing patterns employing these, use **scrolling foliage.**
UF foliate scrolls
scrolls, foliate
scrolls, leaf
CN D.DG.AFU.AFU.DOI.ALO

leaf, composition
USE **leaf**

leaf, lily
USE **water leaf**

leaf, metal
USE **leaf**

leaf, palm
USE **palm leaf**

leaf, water
USE **water leaf**

leaflets
USE **handbills**

leafstalk
MT.1076 (L)
SN The leafstalk of palms, sometimes used in making doors in Bantu huts. (WALTON)
UF petiole
stalk, leaf
CN M.MT.AFU.AFU.ALO.BIQ.CLM.ALO

lean mortar
MT.2602
SN In masonry, a mortar that lacks cementious materials and may be weak, harsh, or difficult to spread. (PUTNAM)
UF mortar, lean
mortar, poor
poor mortar
CN M.MT.AFU.ARI.DZW.ARI.AFU.AXC.ALO

lean-to houses
USE **saltbox houses**

lean-to roofs
USE **shed roofs**

lean-tos
RK.21 (N)
ALT **lean-to**
SN Use for freestanding structures with a single-pitched roof leaning against two posts or trees. For similarly roofed minor structures built against the side of buildings use **appentices.**
CN V.RK.AFU.ALO.AFU.ALO.AXC

leaning files
USE **joint files**

learning activity packages
USE **learning modules**

learning activity packets
USE **learning modules**

learning kits
USE **learning modules**

learning modules
VW.347
ALT **learning module**
SN Packets of subject-specific teaching materials containing objectives,

directions for use, and test items. (ERIC)
UF kits, learning
laps (learning modules)
learning activity packages
learning activity packets
learning kits
learning packages
modules, learning
packages, learning
packets, learning activity
CN V.VW.AFU.AFU.ALO.CXA.BCW

learning packages
USE **learning modules**

learning resource centers
RK.702 (L)
ALT **learning resource center**
UF centers, instructional materials
centers, learning resource
centers, school media
instructional materials centers
LRCs
school media centers
CN V.RK.AFU.ALO.ALO.CRG.AXC.ALO.ALO.AFU

learning, lifelong
USE **continuing education**

leas
USE **meadows**

leased housing
USE **rental housing**

leases
VW.883 (L)
ALT **lease**
SN Contracts by which one conveys land or other property for a specified time usually for compensation or rent. (W)
CN V.VW.AFU.ARI.AFU.BOK.BOK.ALO.ALO.AFU.ALO

leather
MT.954 (L,R)
SN The skin or hides of animals. (MH)
CN M.MT.AFU.AFU.ALO.AFU.DZW.AXC

leather chairs (Boston chairs)
USE **Boston chairs**

leather chairs, Boston
USE **Boston chairs**

leather chairs, crook'd-back
USE **Boston chairs**

leather curing
USE **curing (leather)**

leather factories
USE **tanneries**

leather-upholstered chairs (Boston chairs)
USE **Boston chairs**

leather-upholstered chairs (Cromwellian chairs)
USE **Cromwellian chairs**

leather, lizard
USE **lizard leather**

leatherworkers
HG.485
ALT **leatherworker**
CN H.HG.AFU.AXC.BUE.ARI.BZY

leatherworking
KT.771
CN K.KT.AFU.ALO.HOE.AXC

leaves
MT.1038 (L,R)
ALT **leaf**
UF foliage
CN M.MT.AFU.AFU.ALO.BIQ.BIQ

leaves (hinge components)
TF.524
ALT **leaf (hinge component)**
SN Parts of hinges extending out from either side of a knuckle joint. (DITTRI)
CN V.TF.AFU.ALO.ALO.ARI

leaves (door components)
USE **door leaves**

leaves (furniture components)
TG.941
ALT **leaf (furniture component)**
CN V.TG.ALO.FCS

leaves (sheets)
VW.605
ALT **leaf (sheet)**
SN Sheets of paper or parchment, each side of which is referred to as a page. (ICA)
CN V.VW.AFU.ALO.AFU.BZY

leaves, door
USE **door leaves**

Lebanon cedar
MT.1338
UF cedar, Lebanon
Cedrus libani
CN M.MT.AFU.AFU.ALO.BIQ.DCU.AFU.AFU.ALO.ALO.BCW

lecithin
MT.1005 (L)
SN A lipoid, or fatlike substance that is found in egg yolk and other animal and vegetable matter;(MAYER) used, among other things, as an emulsifier in casein paints to regulate viscosity in printing inks. (MH12)
CN M.MT.AFU.AFU.ALO.AXC.BOK.ALO

lecterns
TG.643 (N,R)
ALT **lectern**
SN Stands with a sloping top and usually a ledge at the bottom of the slope designed to support a book or script in a convenient position for a reader standing before it. (W)
CN V.TG.AFU.AFU.BIQ.BCW.ALO.CLM

lecti
TG.390
ALT **lectus**
SN Ancient Roman couches, of a variety of forms, but generally having turned legs and often having both head and foot boards. (RICHTE)
CN V.TG.AFU.AFU.ARI.ALO.AXC

lectionaries
VW.545 (L,R)
ALT **lectionary**
SN Books containing the extracts (pericopes) from scripture appointed to be read at public worship. (ODCC)
CN V.VW.AFU.ALO.AFU.AFU.ALO.BUE.BUE

lectionaries, gospel
USE **evangeliaries**

lecture halls
RM.64 (A,L,B)
ALT **lecture hall**
SN Use for large rooms with fixed seating, designed for lectures. For large rooms designed for activities such as concerts or plays and requiring a large stage, use **auditoriums.**
UF halls, lecture
lecture theaters
theaters, lecture
CN V.RM.AFU.DIO.ALO.AFU.AXC

lecture notes
VW.65
ALT **lecture note**
UF notes, lecture
CN V.VW.AFU.AFU.AFU.DZW.ARI

lecture theaters
USE **lecture halls**

lecturers
HG.724 (L)
ALT **lecturer**
UF speakers
CN H.HG.AFU.BCW.DOI

lectures
VW.471 (L,N)
ALT **lecture**
SN Expositions of a given subject delivered before an audience or class, especially for the purposes of instruction. (AHD)
CN V.VW.AFU.AFU.ALO.FOG.AFU

ledgement tables
RT.625
ALT **ledgement table**
SN Stringcourses, usually molded; especially those carried along the lower portion of a building. (HAS)
UF ledgment tables
tables, ledgement

CN V.RT.AFU.AFU.AFU.BIQ.BUE.ALO.AFU.ALO.CFS.ARI

ledger boards
RT.700
ALT **ledger board**
SN Wood strips or boards let into the studs to add support for the ends of the joists. (DAC)
UF boards, ledger
boards, ribbon
girt strips
ribands
ribbon boards
ribbon strips
strips, girt
strips, ribbon
CN V.RT.AFU.AFU.ALO.ALO.ALO

ledgers
VW.848 (N)
ALT **ledger**
SN Volumes of final entry in accounting in which are entered debits, credits, and all other money transactions under each individual account or heading. (ICA)
CN V.VW.AFU.ARI.AFU.BIQ.CXA.AFU.BUE

ledgment tables
USE **ledgement tables**

Lee marble
MT.828
UF marble, Lee
CN M.MT.AFU.AFU.AFU.DCU.AFU.ARI.ARI.ARI.BOK.BUE

Lefkandi I
FL.2544
CN F.FL.ALO.AXC.ALO.AFU.AFU.ALO.AFU.AFU.BOK

left
DC.38
CN D.DC.AFU.ALO.ARI.CXA

leg vises
TB.768 (N)
ALT **leg vise**
SN Any of the various blacksmithing vises that have one long leg which is attached to a bench (and often supported at the foot) and a simple spring mechanism to hold the jaws open. (FARNH)
UF vises, leg
CN V.TB.AFU.BCW.BIQ.AXC.ALO.BCW.ALO

Lega
FL.512 (L)
UF Balega
Rega
Warega
CN F.FL.ALO.AFU.AXC.ALO.ALO.BIQ.AFU.AFU.BIQ

legacies
USE **bequests**

legal correspondence
VW.32 (L)
UF correspondence, legal
CN V.VW.AFU.AFU.AFU.BIQ.ALO.ALO

legal documents
VW.867 (L)
ALT **legal document**
SN Use for documents having legal relevance in general. For documents that give expression to a legal act or agreement for the purpose of creating, securing, modifying, or terminating a right, or for the purpose of furnishing evidence of a right, use **legal instruments.** (LCSH)
UF documents, legal
CN V.VW.AFU.ARI.AFU.BOK

legal files
VW.596
ALT **legal file**
SN Collections of material relating to law cases; they may include brief decisions or histories of cases. (LG)
UF files, legal
CN V.VW.AFU.ALO.AFU.BIQ.ARI.ALO.AFU

legal holidays
KM.72 (L,R)
SN Holidays established by legal authority and characterized by legal restrictions on work and transaction of official business. (W)
UF holidays, legal
CN K.KM.AFU.CFS.AFU

legal instruments
VW.876 (L)
ALT **legal instrument**
SN Use for documents that give expression to a legal act or agreement, for the purpose of creating, securing, modifying, or terminating a right, or for the purpose of furnishing evidence of a right. For documents having legal relevance in general, use **legal documents.** (LCSH)
UF instruments, legal
CN V.VW.AFU.ARI.AFU.BOK.BOK

legal manuscripts
VW.662 (R)
ALT **legal manuscript**
UF juridical manuscripts
law manuscripts
manuscripts, juridical
manuscripts, law
manuscripts, legal
CN V.VW.AFU.ALO.AFU.DZW.ARI.ALO.AFU

legal medicine
USE **forensic medicine**

legal notices
VW.316
ALT **legal notice**
SN Announcements required by law to be given for a specific purpose or case; typically required to be published in a newspaper or posted in a court house.
UF notices, legal
CN V.VW.AFU.AFU.ALO.BOK.AFU.ALO

legal offices
USE **law offices**

legal studies
USE **law**

legations
RK.336 (A,L,B)
ALT **legation**
SN Use only generally for official residences of foreign ministers. When such residences include offices for ministers appointed primarily to oversee and protect the home country's economic interests in a host country, use **consulates,** but use **embassy buildings** when the offices and residences are for ministers called ambassadors appointed to implement items of international foreign policy in a host country.
CN V.RK.AFU.ALO.ALO.AXC.ALO.BOK.BOK.AFU

legends
BM.273 (L,R)
CN B.BM.AFU.ARI.BIQ.AXC.ALO.AFU

legislating
KG.182
CN K.KG.AFU.ALO.ARI.BIQ

legislation
BM.453 (L,B)
SN The enactments of a legislator or a legislative body. (W)
UF enacting
CN B.BM.BCW.BUE

legislative acts
VW.1026
ALT **legislative act**
SN Laws or statutes passed by a legislature. (BLACKS)
UF acts, legislative
CN V.VW.AFU.ARI.ALO.BCW.AFU.ARI.AFU.ALO

legislative bills
USE **bills (legislative records)**

legislative buildings
RK.981 (A)
ALT **legislative building**
SN Use for buildings housing the legislative bodies of a government.
UF buildings, legislative
CN V.RK.AFU.ALO.ALO.ERE.AFU.BCW

legislative districts
RG.250 (L)
ALT **legislative district**
UF districts, legislative
CN V.RG.ALO.AFU.AFU.ARI.ALO

legislative records
VW.1023
ALT **legislative record**
UF records, legislative
CN V.VW.AFU.ARI.ALO.BCW.AFU.ARI

legislators
HG.676 (L)
ALT **legislator**
UF lawmakers
CN H.HG.AFU.AXC.CFS.CFS.BCW

legitimate construction
USE **linear perspective**

legs
TG.943
ALT **leg**
CN V.TG.ALO.FIM.AFU

legs, baluster
USE **baluster legs**

legs, baluster turned
USE **baluster legs**

legs, bandy
USE **cabriole legs**

legs, bowed
USE **cabriole legs**

legs, bulbous
USE **baluster legs**

legs, cabriole
USE **cabriole legs**

legs, cluster
USE **cluster legs**

legs, curule
USE **curule legs**

legs, detachable
USE **detachable legs**

legs, fly
USE **swing legs**

legs, gate
USE **gate legs**

legs, Grecian cross
USE **curule legs**

legs, hipped
USE **hipped knees**

legs, Marlboro
USE **Marlborough legs**

legs, Marlborough
USE **Marlborough legs**

legs, rectangular
USE **Marlborough legs**

legs, sabre
USE **sabre legs**

legs, scimitar
USE **sabre legs**

legs, square (Marlborough legs)
USE **Marlborough legs**

legs, straight
USE **Marlborough legs**

legs, stump
USE **stump legs**

legs, swing
USE **swing legs**

legs, therm
USE **therm legs**

legs, trumpet
USE **trumpet legs**

legs, Waterloo
USE **sabre legs**

legs, X-shaped
USE **curule legs**

lehrs
TB.101
ALT **lehr**
SN Tunnel-shaped ovens in which glass is annealed. (SPILLM)
CN V.TB.AFU.ARI.ALO.ARI.ARI

Leipzig yellow
USE **chrome yellow**

leisure
BM.332 (L,B)
SN Freedom from work or other obligatory activities.
UF free time
CN B.BM.ALO.ALO.AXC

Leithner's blue
MT.1600
SN An early variety of cobalt blue. (MAYER)
UF blue, Leithner's
CN M.MT.AFU.AFU.ARI.AFU.AFU.ALO.ALO.ALO.ARI.BCW.AFU

Lele
FL.441 (L)
UF Bashilele
CN F.FL.ALO.AFU.AXC.ALO.ALO.AFU.AFU.BCW

Lemhi
FL.1313 (L)
CN F.FL.ALO.ALO.ARI.AFU.AXC.BIQ

lemon
USE **moderate yellow**

lemon
MT.1195 (L)
UF lemonwood
CN M.MT.AFU.AFU.ALO.BIQ.DCU.AFU.AFU.AFU.GLI

lemon cadmium yellow
MT.1775
UF cadmium yellow, lemon
jaune de cadmium citron
Kadmiumgelb zitron
yellow, lemon cadmium
CN M.MT.AFU.AFU.ARI.AFU.AFU.ALO.ALO.BUE.ARI.ALO.AXC

lemon yellow
USE **barium yellow**
brilliant greenish yellow
brilliant yellow
deep greenish yellow
deep yellow
light yellow
vivid greenish yellow
vivid yellow

lemon yellow, light
USE **brilliant greenish yellow**
light greenish yellow

lemon yellow, pale
USE **light greenish yellow**

lemonwood
USE **lemon**

Lenape
USE **Delaware**

Lenca
FL.1555 (L)
CN F.FL.ALO.ALO.ARI.ALO.BOK.BIQ

lending
KG.81 (L)
SN Giving or letting out for temporary use. (W)
UF loaning
CN K.KG.AFU.AFU.AXC.AXC.CLM

Lengola
FL.513
CN F.FL.ALO.AFU.AXC.ALO.ALO.BIQ.AFU.AFU.BOK

length
BM.807
CN B.BM.CFS.ARI.AXC.BUE.BIQ

Lengua
FL.1644 (L)
CN F.FL.ALO.ALO.ARI.ARI.AXC.BZY

Lenni Lenape
USE **Delaware**

lens caps
TB.311 (N)
ALT **lens cap**
SN Caps used to protect the camera lens from dirt and abrasion. (HAND)
UF caps, lens
CN V.TB.AFU.ARI.CLM.ARI.AFU.ALO.ARI

lens hoods
TB.312
ALT **lens hood**
SN Detachable camera accessories designed to shield the lens from any extraneous light. (SWED)

UF hoods, lens
CN V.TB.AFU.ARI.CLM.ARI.AFU.ALO.AXC

lenses (photographic)
USE **photographic lenses**

lenses, anamorphic
USE **wide-angle lenses**

lenses, camera
USE **photographic lenses**

lenses, convertible
USE **convertible lenses**

lenses, fisheye
USE **fisheye lenses**

lenses, fixed-focus
USE **fixed-focus lenses**

lenses, long-focus
USE **long-focus lenses**

lenses, normal
USE **standard lenses**

lenses, photographic
USE **photographic lenses**

lenses, prime
USE **standard lenses**

lenses, separable
USE **convertible lenses**

lenses, standard
USE **standard lenses**

lenses, telephoto
USE **telephoto lenses**

lenses, varifocal
USE **zoom lenses**

lenses, wide-angle
USE **wide-angle lenses**

lenses, zoom
USE **zoom lenses**

lensless photographs
USE **photograms**

Lent
KM.84 (L,R)
CN K.KM.AFU.CFS.ARI.BOK

lenticular processes
KT.345
SN Use for photographic processes that incorporate a screen of minute lenses into the film or print. Has been used for both stereoscopic and color photography.
UF lenticular systems
CN K.KT.AFU.ALO.DUC.DIO.ALO.CXA

lenticular systems
USE **lenticular processes**

Leo symbols
DG.79
ALT **Leo symbol**
CN D.DG.AFU.AFU.ERE.BIQ

lepanto marble
MT.766
UF marble, lepanto
CN M.MT.AFU.AFU.AFU.DCU.AFU.ARI.ARI.ALO.BOK.ALO

lepers' squints
USE **lowside windows**

lepidolite
MT.530 (L)
CN M.MT.AFU.AFU.AFU.CFS.AFU.EWY

leprosariums
RK.768 (R)
ALT **leprosarium**
UF hospitals, leprosy
leprosy hospitals
CN V.RK.AFU.ALO.ALO.CXA.ALO.AFU.BCW.ALO.BCW.ALO

leprosy hospitals
USE **leprosariums**

Lesbian cymas
USE **cyma reversas**

lesbio
MT.829
UF greco giallognolo
marmor lesbium
CN M.MT.AFU.AFU.AFU.DCU.AFU.ARI.ARI.ARI.BOK.BZY

lesches
USE **clubhouses**

Lese
FL.522 (L)
UF Balesa
CN F.FL.ALO.AFU.AXC.ALO.ALO.BIQ.AFU.ALO.ARI

lesenes
USE **pilaster strips**

Lesser Vehicle
USE **Hinayana**

letter books
VW.487
ALT **letter book**
SN Books of blank or lined paper on which letters to be sent have been written; also copies of letters, originally on loose sheets, bound together, usually in chronological order. (GAHLM)
UF books, letter
CN V.VW.AFU.ALO.AFU.AFU.AFU.ALO.ALO

letter-box plates
TF.24
SN Plates, attached to the exterior side of a door, having an opening through which mail may be passed. (DAC)
UF letter plates
letter slots
mail slots
plates, letter
slots, letter
slots, mail
CN V.TF.AFU.AFU.AFU.AFU.AFU.CRG

letter chutes
USE **mail chutes**

letter plates
USE **letter-box plates**

letter slots
USE **letter-box plates**

letterers
HG.149 (B)
ALT **letterer**
CN H.HG.AFU.AXC.AXC.AFU.AFU.ALO.BCW.AFU.ALO.ARI

lettering
KT.485 (L,B,R)
ALT **lettered**
CN K.KT.AFU.ALO.DUC.EWY.ALO

lettering pens
TB.271 (N)
ALT **lettering pen**
SN Pen holders, usually made of lightweight wood, into which specially shaped nibs can be fitted. These nibs may range in size from extremely broad and flat to narrow and pointed; used in calligraphy and lettering.
UF calligraphic lettering pens
lettering pens, calligraphic
pens, calligraphic lettering
pens, lettering
CN V.TB.AFU.ARI.CLM.AFU.ALO.DOI.ARI

lettering pens, calligraphic
USE **lettering pens**

letterpress copies
VW.681
ALT **letterpress copy**
SN Documents often on tissue paper, produced by the transfer of ink through direct contact with the original, using moisture and pressure in a copy press.
UF copies, letterpress
CN V.VW.AFU.ALO.AFU.DZW.BIQ.BCW

letterpress copybooks
VW.512
ALT **letterpress copybook**
SN Books containing letterpress copies. (ICA)
UF copybooks, letterpress
CN V.VW.AFU.ALO.AFU.AFU.AFU.CFS

letterpress halftone
USE **relief halftone**

letterpress halftones
USE **relief halftones**

letters
VW.16 (L,N,R)
ALT **letter**
CN V.VW.AFU.AFU.AFU.BIQ.AFU.ARI

letters of administration
VW.1020
ALT **letter of administration**
SN Formal documents issued by probate courts that serve to appoint an administrator of an estate. (BLACKS)
UF administration, letters of
CN V.VW.AFU.ARI.ALO.BCW.AFU.ALO.ALO.AFU.AFU.AFU.ALO

letters of advice
VW.22
ALT **letter of advice**
UF advice, letters of
CN V.VW.AFU.AFU.AFU.BIQ.AFU.ARI.AXC

letters of credit
VW.832 (L)
ALT **letter of credit**
SN Use both for letters addressed by a bank to a correspondent certifying that a person named therein is entitled to draw upon his credit up to a certain sum and for letters addressed by a banker to a person to whom credit is given, authorizing that person to draw on the issuing bank. (GAHLM)
UF circular notes
commercial letters of credit
confirmed letters of credit
credit, letters of
credit, traveler's letters of
notes, circular
traveler's letters of credit
CN V.VW.AFU.ARI.AFU.BIQ.CFS.AXC

letters of intent
VW.23 (L)
ALT **letter of intent**
SN Letters customarily employed to reduce to writing a preliminary understanding of parties who intend to enter into contract. (BLACKS)
UF intent, letters of
CN V.VW.AFU.AFU.AFU.BIQ.AFU.ARI.BCW

letters of introduction
VW.24
ALT **letter of introduction**
UF introduction, letters of
CN V.VW.AFU.AFU.AFU.BIQ.AFU.ARI.BIQ

letters of marque
VW.988 (L)
ALT **letter of marque**
SN Originally, letters granted by a sovereign authorizing an individual to sieze the subjects of a foreign state, or their goods, by way of retaliation or reprisal for injuries; later, specifically, any license or extraordinary commission granted by a government to a private person to command an armed vessel at sea to take an enemy's ships and merchandise. (GAHLM)
UF marque, letters of
CN V.VW.AFU.ARI.ALO.BCW.AFU.AFU.AFU.AXC

letters of recommendation
VW.25 (L)
ALT **letter of recommendation**
UF recommendation, letters of
recommendations
CN V.VW.AFU.AFU.AFU.BIQ.AFU.ARI.BOK

letters patent
VW.989 (L)
ALT **letter patent**
SN Written communication usually signed and sealed from a government or sovereign of a nation conferring upon a designated person a grant (as a right, title, status, property, authority privilege, monopoly, franchise, immunity, or exemption) that could not otherwise be enjoyed. (GAHLM)
UF patent, letters
CN V.VW.AFU.ARI.ALO.BCW.AFU.AFU.AFU.BCW

letters testamentary
VW.1021
ALT **letter testamentary**
SN Written communications from a court, usually a probate court, or an officer informing an executor of his appointment and authority to execute the will of the testator. (GAHLM)
UF testamentary, letters
CN V.VW.AFU.ARI.ALO.BCW.AFU.ALO.ALO.AFU.AFU.AFU.ARI

letters, business
USE **business letters**

letters, circular
USE **circular letters**

letters, form
USE **form letters**

letters, love
USE **love letters**

letters, market
USE **market letters**

letters, sales
USE **sales letters**

lettres de cachet
VW.990 (L)
ALT **lettre de cachet**
SN Letters which bear an official seal, usually authorizing imprisonment without trial. (W)
CN V.VW.AFU.ARI.ALO.BCW.AFU.AFU.AFU.BIQ

Lettrism
FL.3730 (L,R)
CN F.FL.ALO.BUE.ARI.DIO

Levalloisian
FL.2453
CN F.FL.ALO.AXC.AFU.AFU.AXC

Levalloiso-Mousterian
FL.2456
CN F.FL.ALO.AXC.AFU.ALO.AFU

Levantine
FL.2909
UF The Levant
CN F.FL.ALO.AXC.ARI.AXC

Levanto-Aurignacian
FL.2913
CN F.FL.ALO.AXC.ARI.AXC.AFU.AFU.ALO

levees
RK.567 (L)
ALT **levee**
SN Use for embankments built to prevent flooding of low-lying land. For embankments built to control or retain flood waters of rivers or seas use **dikes**.
UF flood walls
walls, flood
CN V.RK.AFU.ALO.ALO.CFS.ALO.ARI.ALO

level crossings
USE **grade crossings**

leveling
KT.143 (L)
ALT **leveled**
CN K.KT.AFU.ALO.DOI.CFS

leveling planes
TB.931 (N)
ALT **leveling plane**
SN A class of planes.
UF planes, leveling
CN V.TB.AFU.BCW.CFS.ALO.AFU.DUC.ARI

levellers, cooper's
USE **sun-planes**

lever boards
USE **louver boards**

lever shears
TB.725 (N)
SN Shears constructed on the principle of the lever. (W)
UF alligator shears
crocodile shears
shears, alligator
shears, crocodile
shears, lever
CN V.TB.AFU.BCW.BIQ.ARI.ALO.BIQ.AXC

lever tumbler locks
TF.204
ALT **lever tumbler lock**

UF locks, lever tumbler
tumbler locks, lever
CN V.TF.AFU.AFU.AFU.AFU.DIO.BIQ.AFU.CFS

levers
TF.256 (N)
ALT **lever**
SN Any projecting piece by which a mechanism is operated or adjusted. (W)
CN V.TF.AFU.AFU.AFU.AFU.DOI

levers, dummy
USE **dummy knobs**

levers, rushing
USE **flagging irons**

levers, toilet tank
USE **toilet tank levers**

levigation
KT.616
ALT **levigated**
SN Process of grinding a material in a wet state, such as in preparation of paint pigments. (MAYER)
CN K.KT.AFU.ALO.FUA.CRG.AFU

lewis bolt anchors
TF.296
ALT **lewis bolt anchor**
SN Bolts shaped into wedges at the end, which are inserted into a prepared hole in a heavy unit or stone and secured in place with poured concrete or melted lead; also, eyebolts inserted into heavy stones and used in the manner of a lewis to lift and move the stones. (MEANS)
UF anchors, lewis bolt
bolt anchors, lewis
bolts, lewis
lewis bolts
CN V.TF.AFU.AFU.AFU.ALO.AFU.AFU.BUE

lewis bolts
USE **lewis bolt anchors**

lewises
TB.615 (N)
ALT **lewis**
SN Metal devices consisting of dovetail tenons; used to hoist heavy units of masonry.
CN V.TB.AFU.BCW.BCW.ALO.FIM

lexicographers
HG.196 (L)
ALT **lexicographer**
SN Persons who research information about words that make up language and write and review definitions for publication in a dictionary. (DOT)
CN H.HG.AFU.AXC.AXC.ARI.ALO.ALO.ALO

lexicons
VW.394
ALT **lexicon**
SN Dictionaries of the words of a language, especially one giving the meaning in another language. (LG)
CN V.VW.AFU.AFU.ALO.EWY.ARI.AFU.ALO

ley-lines
USE **leys**

leys
RG.206 (A,L)
ALT **ley**
SN An alignment of at least five neolithic sites in less than ten miles. (LANDSP)
UF ley-lines
straight tracks
CN V.RG.AFU.AFU.DZW.AFU.ALO

leys (meadows)
USE **meadows**

Li
FL.199
UF Bali
CN F.FL.ALO.AFU.AXC.AFU.AFU.AFU.ARI.BCW

Li (Yi)
USE **Yi**

Lia
USE **Bolia**

liability
BM.454 (A,L,B)
CN B.BM.BCW.BZY

Liang
FL.1878 (L)
CN F.FL.ALO.ARI.ALO.AFU.AFU.ALO.BUE.AFU.ALO.ARI

Liang, Later
USE **Later Liang**

Liao
FL.1892 (L)
CN F.FL.ALO.ARI.ALO.AFU.AFU.ALO.CRG

liberal arts
KD.293 (R)
SN Studies such as language, philosophy, history, literature, and abstract science, that are presumed to provide chiefly general knowledge and to develop the general intellectual capacities such as reason or judgement. (W)
UF arts, liberal
liberal studies
studies, liberal
CN K.KD.AFU.AXC.ALO

liberal arts (medieval studies)
KD.296
SN Use for the studies comprising the trivium and quadrivium in the Middle Ages, usually arithmetic, geometry, astonomy, music, grammar, rhetoric, and logic. (RHDEL2)
UF arts, liberal (medieval studies)
CN K.KD.AFU.BCW.ALO

Liberal Judaism
USE **Reform Judaism**

liberal studies
USE **liberal arts**

liberalism
BM.560 (L)
SN A political philosophy based on belief in progress, the essential goodness of man and the autonomy of the individual and standing for tolerance and freedom for the individual from arbitrary authority. (W)
UF political liberalism
CN B.BM.BOK.BZY.BIQ

liberate rolls
VW.1006 (L)
ALT **liberate roll**
SN Records of the writs authorizing delivery of money out of the treasury. (LG)
UF rolls, liberate
CN V.VW.AFU.ARI.ALO.BCW.AFU.AFU.ALO.AFU.ALO

liberty
USE **freedom**

Liberty Style
USE **Stile Liberty**

Libocendrus decurrens
USE **incense cedar**

Libra symbols
DG.80
ALT **Libra symbol**
CN D.DG.AFU.AFU.ERE.BOK

libraires, art
USE **art libraries**

librarians
HG.305 (L,B)
ALT **librarian**
SN Persons who administer libraries and perform related library services, including acquiring and processing library materials, and furnishing reference and other services to patrons.
CN H.HG.AFU.AXC.BCW.ALO.BCW.ALO

librarians, audiovisual
USE **audiovisual librarians**

librarians, circulation
USE **circulation librarians**

librarians, film
USE **audiovisual librarians**

librarians, government
USE **government librarians**

librarians, reference
USE **reference librarians**

librarians, special
USE **special librarians**

librarianship
USE **library science**

libraries
RK.691 (A,L,N,B,R)
ALT **library**
UF bibliothecae
CN V.RK.AFU.ALO.ALO.CRG.AXC

libraries (bookcases)
USE **library bookcases**

libraries (rooms)
RM.151 (A,R)
ALT **library**
CN V.RM.AFU.DIO.ALO.CFS.ARI

libraries, academic
USE **academic libraries**

libraries, architectural
USE **architectural libraries**

libraries, branch
USE **branch libraries**

libraries, Carnegie
USE **Carnegie libraries**

libraries, children's
USE **children's libraries**

libraries, corporate
USE **corporate libraries**

libraries, depository
USE **depository libraries**

libraries, medical
USE **medical libraries**

libraries, moving
USE **moving libraries**

libraries, national
USE **national libraries**

libraries, presidential
USE **presidential libraries**

libraries, private
USE **private libraries**

libraries, public
USE **public libraries**

libraries, research
USE **research libraries**

libraries, school
USE **school libraries**

libraries, special
USE **special libraries**

libraries, state
USE **state libraries**

library agencies
USE **library service agencies**

library bookcases
TG.404
ALT **library bookcase**
UF bookcases, library
cases, library
libraries (bookcases)
library cases
CN V.TG.AFU.AFU.AXC.ALO.ALO.BIQ

library bookcases, portable
USE **moving libraries**

library cards
VW.573
ALT **library card**
UF cards, library
cards, readers'
library tickets
readers' cards
readers' tickets
tickets, library
tickets, readers'
CN V.VW.AFU.ALO.AFU.ARI.BZY

library cases
USE **library bookcases**

library chairs (reading chairs)
USE **reading chairs**

library paste
MT.2353
SN A thick, white, smooth adhesive made from starch and used especially on paper and paperboard. (W)
UF paste, library
CN M.MT.AFU.ARI.ARI.AFU.ALO.ALO.ALO.ALO

library press beds
TG.346
ALT **library press bed**
UF beds, library press
bedsteads, library press
library press bedsteads
press beds, library
CN V.TG.AFU.AFU.ARI.AFU.AFU.BIQ.AFU.BIQ.AFU

library press bedsteads
USE **library press beds**

library science
KD.159 (L)
SN Study of the purpose, functions, management, operations, history, and problems of libraries, library systems and networks, and related information services. (PG)
UF librarianship
science, library
CN K.KD.AFU.ALO.DIO.AFU

library service agencies
HG.871 (L)
ALT **library service agency**
SN Commercial or professional organizations established to provide supplies, equipment, software, and services to libraries.
UF agencies, library service
library agencies
CN H.HG.ALO.DIO.ALO

library steps
TG.664 (N)
ALT **library step**
SN Ladders from which the upper shelves of a bookcase may be reached, often fitted into a chair, stool, table, or other piece of furniture. (DDA)
UF library stools
steps, library
stools, library
CN V.TG.AFU.AFU.BIQ.BIQ.ALO

library stools
USE **library steps**

library tables
TG.579 (N)
ALT **library table**
UF library writing tables
tables, library
tables, library writing
writing tables, library
CN V.TG.AFU.AFU.AXC.ALO.BZY.FUA.BZY

library tables (refectory tables)
USE **refectory tables**

library tickets
USE **library cards**

library writing tables
USE **library tables**

library writing tables, kidney
USE **kidney tables**

librettists
HG.187 (L)
ALT **librettist**
SN Persons who compose text for opera, musical plays, or extended choral works, or who adapt text to accommodate the musical requirements of composers. (DOT)
CN H.HG.AFU.AXC.AXC.ARI.AFU.AFU.BOK

librettos
VW.534 (L)
ALT **libretto**
SN Books or booklets containing the text or words of an opera or similar extended musical composition. (RHDEL1)
CN V.VW.AFU.ALO.AFU.AFU.ALO.BIQ

Libyan Dynasty
USE **Twenty-second Dynasty**
Twenty-third Dynasty

Libyco-Capsian
FL.44
CN F.FL.ALO.AFU.AFU.AFU.ALO.ARI

Licchavi
FL.2159
CN F.FL.ALO.ARI.AXC.AFU.AXC.AFU.ALO

licenses
VW.375 (L,N)
ALT **license**
SN Documents evidencing a right or permission, granted to an individual or organization in accordance with law by a competent authority, to engage in some transaction, business, or occupation, or to do some act. (GAHLM)
CN V.VW.AFU.AFU.ALO.DUC.ARI

licenses, marriage
USE **marriage licenses**

licensing
KG.148 (A)
ALT **licensed**
SN Granting lawful authority to an individual or group to do something which would be illegal or invalid without that authorization.
CN K.KG.AFU.AFU.BIQ.BOK

lich-gates
RT.894 (L,B)
ALT **lich-gate**
SN Roofed gateways at the entrances to churches or cemeteries where a coffin may be placed. (HAS)
UF lych-gates
CN V.RT.AFU.ARI.AFU.AFU.ARI.ALO.AFU.AFU.ALO

lich stones
RK.474
ALT **lich stone**
SN Large stones on which to rest a coffin momentarily at the entrance of a cementary. (RHDEL2)
UF lych stones
stones, lich
CN V.RK.AFU.ALO.ALO.BOK.BCW

lichter Ocker
USE **light ocher**

licorice, Spanish
USE **Spanish licorice**

lidos
USE **seaside resorts**

liens
BM.452 (L)
SN Charges upon real or personal property for the satisfaction of some debt or duty ordinarily arising by operation of law. (W)
CN B.BM.BCW.BOK.ALO

lierne ribs
USE **liernes**

lierne vaults
RT.552
ALT **lierne vault**
SN Vaults in which liernes are used. (DAC)
UF vaults, lierne
CN V.RT.AFU.AFU.AFU.BIQ.BOK.AFU.ARI.AFU.ALO.ALO

liernes
RT.687
ALT **lierne**
SN Use for small subordinate ribs, inserted between the main ribs of Gothic vaults.
UF lierne ribs
ribs, lierne
ribs, tertiary
tertiary ribs
CN V.RT.AFU.AFU.ALO.AFU.ARI.ARI

lieutenant governors
HG.681 (L)
ALT **lieutenant governor**
SN State officers next in rank to a governor, who take the governor's place in case of the latter's absence, disability, or death. (RHDEL2)
UF governors, lieutenant
CN H.HG.AFU.AXC.CFS.CFS.BIQ

life
BM.722 (L,R)
CN B.BM.CFS.AFU.AXC

life care communities
RD.74 (L)
ALT **life care community**
SN Use for self-contained residential communities which provide extensive services for the complete daily needs of residents, including dining, medical, recreation, entertainment and, possibly, estate care facilities. For similar facilities for retired people in which the services offered are less comprehensive, use **retirement communities.**
UF communities, life care
CN V.RD.AFU.BIQ.ARI.AFU

life drawings
VD.154 (R)
ALT **life drawing**
UF drawings, life
CN V.VD.AFU.BIQ.BCW.AFU

life-size
DC.121
CN D.DC.AFU.AXC.ALO

life, keys of
USE **ankhs**

life, quality of
USE **quality of life**

lifelong education
USE **continuing education**

lifelong learning
USE **continuing education**

lift bridges
RK.1280
ALT **lift bridge**
SN Bridges with a section or sections lifted vertically between towers by counterweights or cables.
UF bridges, lift
bridges, vertical lift
vertical lift bridges
CN V.RK.AFU.ALO.ALO.GLI.ALO.AFU.AFU.AXC.ARI

lift-ground
KT.458
SN Aquatint technique in which the image is drawn on the plate with a water-soluble solution; the plate is covered with a ground and submerged in water which dissolves the solution, lifts the ground, and exposes the image areas so the plate can be etched. (SAFF)
UF aquatint etching, lift-ground
aquatint, lift-ground
aquatint, sugar-lift
etching, lift-ground
lift-ground aquatint
lift-ground aquatint etching
lift-ground etching
sugar-lift aquatint
CN K.KT.AFU.ALO.DUC.DUC.ALO.BCW.AFU.AXC.AFU.AFU

lift-ground aquatint
USE **lift-ground**

lift-ground aquatint etching
USE **lift-ground**

lift-ground etching
USE **lift-ground**

lift latches
TF.176
ALT **lift latch**
SN Unencased surface-mounted latches consisting of a bar pivoted to a plate and engaging with a hook on the jamb, the bar being operated by a thumb piece on the outside of the door and by a lift handle on the inside. (STEIN)
UF latches, lift
CN V.TF.AFU.AFU.AFU.AFU.DIO.BCW.AFU.ARI

lift-off hinges
TF.120
ALT **lift-off hinge**
UF hinges, lift-off
CN V.TF.AFU.AFU.AFU.AFU.CLM.AFU.ELK

lift stations
USE **pumping stations**

lifters, tack
USE **tack pulls**

lifting
KT.757 (L)
ALT **lifted**
UF elevating
hoisting
raising
CN K.KT.AFU.ALO.HIK.AFU

lifting jacks
USE **jacks**

lifting (painting technique)
KT.231
SN In painting, the technique of creating a special textural effect resembling that of the dragging stroke, by layering a sheet of cloth or paper on the surface of wet paint, rubbing lightly, and lifting away. (MAYER)
CN K.KT.AFU.ALO.DUC.CXA.ALO.AFU.BZY

lifts, chair
USE **chair lifts**

lifts, chair (ski lifts)
USE **ski lifts**

lifts, chest
USE **drawer pulls**

lifts, inclined
USE **inclined lifts**

lifts, sash
USE **sash lifts**

lifts, ski
USE **ski lifts**

lifts, window
USE **sash lifts**

Ligbi
FL.363
CN F.FL.ALO.AFU.AXC.AFU.AXC.AFU.CRG.ALO

light
BM.846 (L,R)
CN B.BM.CFS.AXC.ALO.AFU.ALO.AFU

light amber
USE **dark orange yellow**
moderate orange yellow

light amethyst
USE **moderate purple**

light aqua
USE **pale blue**
pale green
very light greenish blue

light aqua blue
USE **pale blue**
very light greenish blue

light aqua green
USE **pale green**
very light bluish green

light art
BM.262 (R)
UF art, light
CN B.BM.AFU.ARI.BCW.FOG.BUE

light beige
USE **grayish yellow**
light grayish yellowish brown

light blue
DL.217
UF blue, cerulean (color)
blue, copen
blue, light
blue, light cerulean
blue, light copen
blue, pale cerulean
blue, pale Windsor
centroid color 181
cerulean
cerulean blue (color)
cerulean blue, light
cerulean blue, pale
copen blue
copen blue, light
light cerulean blue
light copen blue
pale cerulean blue
pale Windsor blue
ultramarine
Windsor blue, pale
CN D.DL.AFU.AFU.BZY.BCW

light blue green
USE **brilliant green**
light bluish green
light green

light blue violet
USE **vivid purplish blue**

light bluish gray
DL.228
UF aqua gray
baby blue
blue, baby
blue, gray
blue, white
bluish gray, light
centroid color 190
gray blue
gray, aqua
gray, light bluish
gray, pearl
pearl gray
white blue
CN D.DL.AFU.AFU.BZY.CRG.AFU

light bluish green
DL.200
UF aqua
aqua green
aqua green, bright
aqua, bright
blue green
blue green, dark
blue green, light
blue, turquoise
bluish green, light
bright aqua
bright aqua green
bright turquoise green
centroid color 163
dark blue green
dark jade green
dull green
emerald green, light
gray green
green, aqua
green, bright aqua
green, bright turquoise
green, dark jade
green, dull
green, gray
green, light blue
green, light bluish
green, light emerald
green, light jade
green, turquoise
jade green
jade green, dark
jade green, light
light blue green
light emerald green
light jade green
light turquoise
pastel turquoise green
turquoise blue
turquoise (color)
turquoise green
turquoise green, bright
turquoise green, pastel
turquoise, light
CN D.DL.AFU.AFU.BUE.DCU.ALO.BCW

light bluish violet
USE **brilliant purplish blue**
brilliant violet
strong purplish blue

light brown
DL.79
UF bistre
bistre brown
brown orange
brown, bistre
brown, light
brown, orange
brown, pale
brown, red
brown, yellow
centroid color 57
ocher (color)
orange brown
orange, brown
pale brown
raw Italian earth
raw sienna (color)
red brown
sienna, raw (color)
yellow brown
CN D.DL.AFU.AFU.AXC.ARI

light brownish gray
DL.86
UF bistre
bistre brown
black brown
black, gray
brown, bistre
brown, black
brown, gray
brown, lilac
brownish gray, light
centroid color 63
gray black
gray brown

gray lilac
gray, light brownish
gray, silver
lilac brown
lilac, gray
putty (color)
sepia (color)
silver gray
CN D.DL.AFU.AFU.AXC.BOK.AFU

light brownish olive
USE **light olive brown**

light buff
USE **pale orange yellow**
pale yellow

light cadmium
USE **vivid yellow**

light cerulean blue
USE **brilliant greenish blue**
light blue
strong greenish blue

light chartreuse
USE **brilliant yellow green**
light yellow green

light chartreuse yellow
USE **brilliant greenish yellow**
light greenish yellow
moderate greenish yellow
strong greenish yellow

light chrome green
USE **dark yellowish green**

light chrome yellow
USE **strong yellow**

light citron yellow
USE **light greenish yellow**

light construction
USE **lightweight construction**

light copen blue
USE **light blue**

light copper brown
USE **strong brown**

light cornflower blue
USE **light purplish blue**
light violet
moderate purplish blue
moderate violet

light courts
RM.47 (A)
ALT **light court**
SN Use for courts or recesses serving primarily to provide light or ventilation to windows along the walls; for very small courts used primarily for ventilation, use **air shafts.**
UF courts, light
CN V.RM.AFU.DIO.AFU.BCW.ARI.AXC

light dull bluish violet
USE **light violet**

light emerald green
USE **brilliant green**
light bluish green
light green
very light bluish green

light filters
TB.313 (L,N)
ALT **light filter**
SN Filters that absorb light of certain wavelengths or colors selectively; used for modifying the light. (W)
UF color filters
filters, color
filters, light
CN V.TB.AFU.ARI.CLM.ARI.AFU.ALO.BCW

light fuchsia purple
USE **strong reddish purple**

light garnet
USE **dark red**

light gold
USE **brilliant yellow**
moderate yellow
strong yellow

light gray
DL.302
UF aluminum (color)
blue, granite
blue, pearl
centroid color 264
drab gray, pale
granite blue
gray light
gray, light
gray, oyster
gray, pearl
gray, very light
light, gray
oyster gray
oyster white (color)
pale drab gray
pearl blue
pearl (color)
pearl gray
pearl white
very light gray
white, oyster (color)
white, pearl
CN D.DL.AFU.ALO.ALO.AFU

light gray blue
USE **grayish blue**
pale blue

light gray, medium
USE **medium gray**

light grayish blue violet
USE **light purplish blue**

light grayish brown
DL.83
UF beige
bisque
brown, dull
brown, light grayish
brown, orange
centroid color 60
dull brown
grayish brown, light
orange brown
putty (color)
CN D.DL.AFU.AFU.AXC.BIQ.AFU

light grayish olive
DL.149
UF bistre
centroid color 109
grayish olive, light
green, slate
greige
olive, light grayish
olive, pale
pale olive
slate green
CN D.DL.AFU.AFU.BIQ.AXC.AFU

light grayish purplish red
DL.59
UF bluish pink
centroid color 261
dull violet
grayish purplish red, light
lilac
mauve orchid
orchid, mauve
pink, bluish
purplish red, light grayish
red, light grayish purplish
violet, dull
CN D.DL.AFU.AFU.ALO.CFS.AFU.BIQ.AFU

light grayish red
DL.44
UF brown red
brown, red
centroid color 18
dull rose
grayish red, light
lilac
lilac rose
pale red
red brown
red, brown
red, light grayish
red, pale
rose, dull
rose, lilac
vermilion (color)
CN D.DL.AFU.AFU.ALO.BIQ.ALO

light grayish reddish brown
DL.96
UF brown, dull reddish
brown, gray
brown, light grayish reddish
brown, pale
centroid color 45
dull reddish brown
gray brown
grayish reddish brown, light
pale brown
reddish brown, dull
reddish brown, light grayish

CN D.DL.AFU.AFU.AXC.BZY.AFU.BIQ.
AFU

light grayish violet blue
USE **brilliant purplish blue**

light grayish yellowish brown
DL.105
UF beige
beige, light
bisque
bistre
bistre, brown
bistre, gray
brown bistre
brown, dull yellowish
brown, light grayish yellowish
brown, orange
brown, pale
brown, pale yellowish
brown, very pale
buff
camel
centroid color 79
dull yellowish brown
ecru
gray bistre
grayish yellowish brown, light
light beige
orange brown
pale brown
pale yellowish brown
very pale brown
yellowish brown, dull
yellowish brown, light grayish
yellowish brown, pale
CN D.DL.AFU.AFU.AXC.BZY.ALO.BIQ.
AFU

light green
DL.168
UF blue green
blue green, light
centroid color 144
dull green
emerald (color)
emerald green, light
green, dull
green, light
green, light emerald
green, light mint
green, mint
green, verdigris
light blue green
light emerald green
light mint green
mint green
mint green, light
verdigris (color)
verdigris green
CN D.DL.AFU.AFU.BUE.BCW

light green yellow
USE **light greenish yellow**

light greenish blue
DL.237
UF aqua
aqua blue
aqua green
aqua, bright
aquamarine (color)
blue turquoise
blue, aqua
blue, Bremen (color)
blue, bright
blue, light greenish
blue, light turquoise
blue, turquoise
Bremen blue (color)
bright aqua
bright aqua blue
bright blue
centroid color 172
green, aqua
green, turquoise
greenish blue, light
light turquoise
light turquoise blue
turquoise blue
turquoise (color)
turquoise green
turquoise, blue
turquoise, light
CN D.DL.AFU.AFU.BZY.DCU.AFU.BCW

light greenish gray
DL.180
UF ash, ultramarine grey
blue gray
centroid color 154
gray, light greenish
greenish gray, light
grey ultramarine ash
ultramarine ash, grey
CN D.DL.AFU.AFU.BUE.CRG.AFU

light greenish yellow
DL.139
UF barium yellow (color)
canary
centroid color 101
chartreuse
chartreuse yellow
chartreuse yellow, light
citron yellow
citron yellow, light
green yellow, light
green yellow, pale
greenish yellow, light
lemon yellow, light
lemon yellow, pale
light chartreuse yellow
light citron yellow
light green yellow
light lemon yellow
pale green yellow
pale lemon yellow
pastel yellow
sulphur (color)
sulphur yellow
yellow, barium (color)
yellow, chartreuse
yellow, citron
yellow, light chartreuse
yellow, light citron
yellow, light greenish
yellow, light lemon
yellow, pale lemon
yellow, pastel
yellow, sulfur
CN D.DL.AFU.AFU.BCW.CRG.ALO.BCW

light guideway transit
USE **personal rapid transit**

light gunmetal
USE **dark gray**

light ivory
USE **pale yellow**

light jade green
USE **light bluish green**

light lavender
USE **light purple**

light lavender blue
USE **light purplish blue**

light lavender violet
USE **light violet**

light lemon yellow
USE **brilliant greenish yellow**
light greenish yellow

light lilac
USE **light purple**
very light purple

light lime green
USE **brilliant yellowish green**
strong yellow green

light mauve
USE **light violet**
moderate pink
moderate purplish pink

light meters
TB.314 (L,N)
ALT **light meter**
SN Instruments for measuring the intensity of light in a certain place or upon a certain object, having an adjustable scale for determining the optimum relations of shutter speeds and stops at each intensity. (RHDEL2)
UF exposure meters
meters, exposure
meters, light
CN V.TB.AFU.ARI.CLM.ARI.AFU.ALO.
BIQ

light methyl blue
USE **brilliant blue**

light mint green
USE **light green**
very light green

light mustard tan
USE **light olive**

light navy
USE **dark blue**
dark purplish blue

grayish purplish blue
pale purplish blue

light navy gray
USE **medium gray**

light neutral gray
USE **medium gray**

light ocher
MT.1789
SN Natural earth pigment. (WEHLTE)
UF lichter Ocker
ocher, light
CN M.MT.AFU.AFU.ARI.AFU.AFU.ALO.ALO.BUE.ARI.CFS.ALO

light olive
DL.145
UF bistre brown
bistre, olive
bright olive green
brown, bistre
brown, yellow
centroid color 106
dull gold
dull greenish yellow
gold, dull
green, bright olive
green, lime
greenish yellow, dull
light mustard tan
lime green
mustard tan, light
olive bistre
olive green, bright
olive yellow
olive, light
tan, light mustard
yellow brown
yellow, dull greenish
yellow, olive
CN D.DL.AFU.AFU.BIQ.AFU

light olive brown
DL.108
UF beige
bistre brown
bistre, brown
bistre, deep
bistre, gray
bistre, olive
brown bistre
brown olive
brown, bistre
brown, gray
brown, light olive
brownish olive
brownish olive, light
camel
centroid color 94
dark ocher
deep bistre
dull gold
gold, dull
gold, mustard
gray bistre
gray brown
gray, silver
greige
khaki
light brownish olive
mustard
mustard gold
mustard tan
ocher, dark
olive bistre
olive, brown
olive, brownish
olive, light brownish
parchment (color)
silver gray
tan, mustard
CN D.DL.AFU.AFU.AXC.BZY.ARI.AFU

light olive drab
USE **olive gray**

light olive gray
DL.152
UF bistre, olive
black, gray
brown, gray
centroid color 112
deep olive gray
gray black
gray brown
gray green
gray, light olive
green, gray
green, slate
greige
olive bistre
olive gray, deep
olive gray, light
slate green
CN D.DL.AFU.AFU.BIQ.BCW.AFU

light olive green
USE **moderate yellow green**

light-on-dark ware
FL.2669
UF painted ware, light-on-dark
ware, light-on-dark
CN F.FL.ALO.AXC.ALO.AFU.ALO.AXC.BCW.BCW

light orange
DL.65
UF buff
centroid color 52
orange pink
orange, light
peach (color)
reddish yellow
salmon
yellow, reddish
CN D.DL.AFU.AFU.ARI.BCW

light orange yellow
DL.130
UF bright yellow
buff, orange
centroid color 70
dull yellow
Indian yellow (color)
orange buff
orange yellow, light
orange, yellowish
reddish yellow
yellow, bright
yellow, dull
yellow, Indian (color)
yellow, light orange
yellow, reddish
yellowish orange
CN D.DL.AFU.AFU.BCW.CRG.AFU.BCW

light orchid
USE **light purplish pink**
moderate purplish pink

light orchid pink
USE **pale purplish pink**

light orchid rose
USE **deep purplish pink**
moderate purplish pink

light Paris green
USE **light yellowish green**

light Payne's gray
USE **bluish gray**
pale blue

light pens
TB.155 (L,N)
ALT **light pen**
SN Hand-held pen-shaped computer devices which are light sensitive so that when they are held to a point on a video screen they allow the computer to modify data or drawings.
UF light styluses
pens, light
styluses, light
CN V.TB.AFU.ARI.BCW.AXC.AFU.BCW

light periwinkle blue
USE **light purplish blue**
light violet
very pale violet

light pink
DL.7
UF baby pink
centroid color 4
pink, baby
pink, light
rose
CN D.DL.AFU.AFU.AFU.AXC

light pinkish lilac
USE **light purplish pink**

light purple
DL.272
UF bright lavender
centroid color 222
dark lavender
lavender
lavender violet, pale
lavender, bright
lavender, dark
lavender, light

light lavender
light lilac
lilac
lilac, light
pale lavender violet
pale rose purple
purple, light
rose purple
rose purple, pale
CN D.DL.AFU.AFU.CFS.BCW

light purple drab
USE **grayish purple**

light purplish blue
DL.247
UF blue violet
blue violet, grayish
blue violet, light grayish
blue, French
blue, light cornflower
blue, light periwinkle
blue, light purplish
blue, periwinkle
blue, reddish
centroid color 199
cerulean
cornflower blue, light
French blue
gentian
grayish blue violet
grayish blue violet, light
grayish violet blue, pale
lavender blue
lavender blue, light
light cornflower blue
light grayish blue violet
light lavender blue
light periwinkle blue
pale grayish violet blue
periwinkle
periwinkle blue
periwinkle blue, light
purplish blue, light
reddish blue
ultramarine
violet blue, pale grayish
violet, blue
CN D.DL.AFU.AFU.BZY.DCU.ALO.BCW

light purplish gray
DL.284
UF blue, gray
centroid color 232
gray blue
gray lilac
gray, light purplish
gray, lilac
lilac
lilac gray
lilac, gray
purplish gray, light
CN D.DL.AFU.AFU.CFS.CRG.AFU

light purplish pink
DL.19
UF bluish pink
centroid color 249
light orchid
light pinkish lilac
lilac rose
lilac, light pinkish
orchid pink
orchid, light
pink, bluish
pink, light purplish
pink, orchid
pink, rose
pinkish lilac, light
purplish pink, light
red violet
rose
rose pink
rose, lilac
violet, red
CN D.DL.AFU.AFU.AFU.CLM.AFU.AXC

light rail transit
RD.99 (L)
SN Designates rail systems operating on private but not necessarily exclusive right of way, at street level or grade separated, generally on electric power, at medium speeds (10-30 miles per hour), and generally making frequent stops at low platforms or directly at grade-level stations.
UF LRT
rail transit, light
transit, light rail
CN V.RD.ALO.ARI.AFU.AFU.ALO.AFU

light red
USE **deep yellowish pink**
grayish reddish orange
moderate orange
moderate red
moderate reddish orange

light red brown
USE **light reddish brown**

light reddish brown
DL.92
UF brown, dull reddish
brown, light reddish
brown, pale reddish
brown, red
brown, yellow
centroid color 42
dull reddish brown
light red brown
pale red
pale reddish brown
red brown
red, pale
red, weak
reddish brown, dull
reddish brown, light
reddish brown, pale
terra cotta (color)
weak red
yellow brown
CN D.DL.AFU.AFU.AXC.BZY.AFU.ARI

light reddish purple
DL.293
UF centroid color 240
lilac, purplish
lilac, rose
orchid
purple, light reddish
purplish lilac
red violet
reddish purple, light
reddish violet
rose lilac
rose purple
violet, red
violet, reddish
CN D.DL.AFU.AFU.CFS.DCU.AFU.AXC

light rose
USE **moderate purplish pink**

light rose beige
USE **brownish pink**
grayish yellowish pink

light rose brown
USE **dark grayish red**
grayish red

light salmon
USE **light yellowish pink**

light styluses
USE **light pens**

light tan
USE **light yellowish brown**

light terre verte
USE **moderate bluish green**

light turquoise
USE **light bluish green**
light greenish blue
very light greenish blue

light turquoise blue
USE **light greenish blue**
very light greenish blue

light turquoise green
USE **very light bluish green**

light vermilion
USE **strong reddish orange**
vivid reddish orange

light violet
DL.259
UF aniline violet
blue, bright periwinkle
blue, light cornflower
blue, light periwinkle
blue, periwinkle
bluish lavender
bluish violet
bluish violet, dull
bluish violet, light dull
bright lavender
bright mauve
bright periwinkle blue
centroid color 210
cornflower blue, light
deep lavender
dull bluish violet
dull bluish violet, light

grayish violet blue
lavender violet, light
lavender, bluish
lavender, bright
lavender, deep
light cornflower blue
light dull bluish violet
light lavender violet
light mauve
light periwinkle blue
lilac
mauve, bright
mauve, light
periwinkle blue
periwinkle blue, bright
periwinkle blue, light
ultramarine
violet blue, grayish
violet, aniline
violet, bluish
violet, dull bluish
violet, light
violet, light dull bluish
CN D.DL.AFU.AFU.BZY.DCU.ARI.BCW

light violet blue
USE **strong purplish blue**

light violet gray
USE **medium gray**
purplish gray

light (weight)
USE **lightweight**

light yellow
DL.116
UF amber (color)
amber yellow
buff, orange
canary yellow
centroid color 86
cream color
ivory (color)
lemon yellow
massicot yellow
Naples yellow (color)
ocher (color)
orange buff
orpiment (color)
pastel yellow
quercitron
reddish yellow
soft yellow
Turner's yellow (color)
yellow, amber
yellow, canary
yellow, lemon
yellow, light
yellow, massicot
yellow, Naples (color)
yellow, pastel
yellow, reddish
yellow, soft
yellow, Turner's (color)
CN D.DL.AFU.AFU.BCW.BCW

light yellow green
DL.159
UF centroid color 119
chartreuse, light
chartreuse, pale
green, light yellow
light chartreuse
pale chartreuse
yellow green, light
CN D.DL.AFU.AFU.BOK.BCW

light yellowish brown
DL.101
UF amber gold
beige, yellow
bistre
bistre, gray
brown orange
brown, dull yellowish
brown, light yellowish
brown, pale
brown, very pale
buff
buff, yellow
camel
centroid color 76
dull yellowish brown
earth yellow
gold, amber
gray bistre
grayish orange
khaki
light tan
orange, brown
orange, grayish
pale brown
tan
tan, light
topaz (color)
very pale brown
yellow beige
yellow buff
yellow, earth
yellowish brown, dull
yellowish brown, light
CN D.DL.AFU.AFU.AXC.BZY.ALO.ARI

light yellowish green
DL.190
UF blue green
centroid color 135
dull green
green, blue
green, dull
green, light Paris
green, light yellowish
green, malachite (color)
green, Paris
green, pistachio
light Paris green
malachite green (color)
Paris green
Paris green, light
pistachio green
yellowish green, light
CN D.DL.AFU.AFU.BUE.DCU.AFU.BCW

light yellowish olive
USE **dark greenish yellow**

light yellowish pink
DL.28
UF baby pink
centroid color 28
flesh pink
light salmon
moderate orange pink
orange pink, moderate
pale peach
pale yellow orange
peach (color)
peach, pale
pink, baby
pink, flesh
pink, light yellowish
pink, moderate orange
rose
rose, salmon
salmon
salmon rose
salmon, light
yellow orange, pale
yellowish pink, light
CN D.DL.AFU.AFU.AFU.CLM.ALO.AXC

light, artificial
USE **artificial light**

light, gray
USE **light gray**

light, natural
USE **daylight**

light, reflected
USE **reflected light**

light, transmitted
USE **transmitted light**

lighthouses
RK.1270 (A,L,N,B,R)
ALT **lighthouse**
CN V.RK.AFU.ALO.ALO.GLI.AFU.BIQ.
ARI

lighting
RT.1352 (A,L,B,R)
UF illumination (lighting)
CN V.RT.ALO.AXC

lighting cameramen
USE **cinematographers**

lighting, accent
USE **directional lighting**

lighting, architectural
USE **architectural lighting**

lighting, artificial
USE **artificial light**

lighting, city
USE **municipal lighting**

lighting, cornice
USE **cornice lighting**

lighting, cove
USE **cove lighting**

lighting, decorative
USE **architectural lighting**

lighting, direct
USE **direct lighting**

lighting, directional
USE **directional lighting**

lighting, electric
USE **electric lighting**

lighting, emergency
USE **emergency lighting**

lighting, exterior
USE **exterior lighting**

lighting, festoon
USE **festoon lighting**

lighting, fluorescent
USE **fluorescent lighting**

lighting, general
USE **general lighting**

lighting, general diffuse
USE **general diffuse lighting**

lighting, indirect
USE **indirect lighting**

lighting, indoor
USE **interior lighting**

lighting, interior
USE **interior lighting**

lighting, local
USE **local lighting**

lighting, metropolitan
USE **municipal lighting**

lighting, municipal
USE **municipal lighting**

lighting, natural
USE **daylight**

lighting, outdoor
USE **exterior lighting**

lighting, outline
USE **architectural lighting**

lighting, stage
USE **stage lighting**

lighting, street
USE **street lighting**

lighting, supplementary
USE **supplementary lighting**

lighting, task
USE **task lighting**

lighting, valance
USE **valance lighting**

lightness
USE **brightness**

lightning
BM.748 (L,B,R)
CN B.BM.CFS.ALO.AXC.ALO.BCW

Lightning Beyazit
USE **Bayazid I**

lightning conductors
USE **lightning rods**

lightning protection
KG.120 (A,L,B)
UF protection, lightning
CN K.KG.AFU.AFU.BCW.ALO.BOK

lightning rods
RT.468 (L,B)
ALT **lightning rod**
SN Metallic cables or rods extending from the highest point on a roof to the ground that protect the building should lightning strike, by providing a direct path to the ground. (DAC)
UF conductors, lightning
lightning conductors
rods, lightning
CN V.RT.AFU.AFU.AFU.BIQ.ARI.ALO.AFU.BCW

lights
RT.969
ALT **light**
SN Openings or mediums through which daylight may pass, as a pane. (RS)
UF panes, window
window panes
windowlights
CN V.RT.AFU.ARI.AFU.AFU.BOK.ALO.ARI

lights (windows)
USE **windows**

lights, angel
USE **angel lights**

lights, batement
USE **batement lights**

lights, exit
USE **exit lights**

Lights, Feast of
USE **Hanukkah**

lights, fixed
USE **fixed windows**

lights, hopper
USE **hopper windows**

lights, lantern
USE **lantern lights**

lights, margin
USE **side lights**

lights, monitor
USE **monitors (roof appendages)**

lights, pavement
USE **pavement lights**

lights, roof
USE **skylights**

lights, side
USE **side lights**

lights, spire
USE **spire lights**

lights, stop
USE **traffic signals**

lights, sunburst
USE **fanlights**

lights, tombstone
USE **tombstone lights**

lights, traffic
USE **traffic signals**

lights, transom
USE **transom windows**

lightweight
DC.147 (B)
UF light (weight)
CN D.DC.AFU.BOK.ALO

lightweight aggregate
MT.2301
UF aggregate, lightweight
CN M.MT.AFU.ARI.ALO.ALO.ALO.AFU

lightweight concrete
MT.226 (A,L,B)
UF concrete, lightweight
CN M.MT.AFU.AFU.AFU.BCW.AFU.AXC.BCW

lightweight construction
KT.33 (L)
UF construction, lightweight
light construction
CN K.KT.AFU.ALO.BCW.ARI.AFU.BIQ

lightweight materials
MT.2807 (B)
UF materials, lightweight
CN M.MT.AFU.BCW.CXA

lightwells
RM.283 (B)
ALT **lightwell**
SN Shafts designed to admit light to the interior rooms of a building. (W)
CN V.RM.AFU.DIO.ARI.ALO.DIO.ALO

lignum vitae
MT.1196 (L)
SN The heaviest, hardest, and most dense of the commercially available woods. (MAYER)
UF guaiacum
guayacan
guayacum
CN M.MT.AFU.AFU.ALO.BIQ.DCU.AFU.AFU.AFU.GRC

liguid gas storage tanks
USE **gasoline tanks**

lilac
USE **grayish purple**
grayish purplish pink
grayish purplish red

light grayish purplish red
light grayish red
light purple
light purplish gray
light violet
moderate pink
moderate purple
moderate reddish purple
pale purple
pale reddish purple
pinkish gray
purplish gray
purplish white
very light purple
very light violet
very pale purple

lilac brown
USE **blackish red**
light brownish gray
reddish gray

lilac gray
USE **brownish pink**
grayish purple
light purplish gray

lilac lavender
USE **pale violet**

lilac purple
USE **moderate purplish red**

lilac rose
USE **deep purplish pink**
light grayish red
light purplish pink
moderate purplish red
strong reddish purple

lilac, dull
USE **grayish purplish red**
moderate violet
pale purple

lilac, gray
USE **light brownish gray**
light purplish gray
reddish gray
very pale purple

lilac, grayish
USE **blackish red**

lilac, light
USE **light purple**
very light purple

lilac, light pinkish
USE **light purplish pink**

lilac, pale
USE **pale purplish pink**
very pale purple

lilac, pastel
USE **very pale purple**

lilac, purplish
USE **light reddish purple**
moderate purplish pink

lilac, red
USE **grayish purplish red**
moderate purplish red

lilac, rose
USE **dark purplish pink**
grayish purplish red
light reddish purple
moderate purplish red

Lillooet
FL.1413 (L)
CN F.FL.ALO.ALO.ARI.AFU.BUE.BZY

lily green
MT.1644
UF green, lily
CN M.MT.AFU.AFU.ARI.AFU.AFU.ALO.ALO.AXC.ALO.AFU

lily leaf
USE **water leaf**

lily white, Jersey
USE **lithopone**

limba
MT.1197 (L)
UF afara
korina
Terminalia superba
CN M.MT.AFU.AFU.ALO.BIQ.DCU.AFU.AFU.AFU.GWW

lime
MT.327 (A,L,B,R)
SN Calcium oxide, occurring abundantly in nature. (MH)
CN M.MT.AFU.AFU.AFU.BUE

lime blue
MT.1597
UF blue, lime
CN M.MT.AFU.AFU.ARI.AFU.AFU.ALO.ALO.ALO.ARI.ARI.AFU

lime blue (artificial ultramarine blue)
USE **artificial ultramarine blue**

lime concrete
MT.203
SN A concrete made from a mixture of lime, sand, and gravel, widely used before the lime matrix was replaced by portland cement. (DAC)
UF concrete, lime
CN M.MT.AFU.AFU.AFU.BCW.AFU.AFU.BOK

lime glass
USE **soda lime glass**

lime glass, soda
USE **soda lime glass**

lime green
USE **dark greenish yellow**
grayish greenish yellow
light olive
moderate greenish yellow
strong yellow green

lime green, bright
USE **brilliant yellow green**
brilliant yellowish green
strong yellow green
vivid yellow green

lime green, light
USE **brilliant yellowish green**
strong yellow green

lime kilns
TB.100 (A,L,N,B)
ALT **lime kiln**
SN Furnace-type apparatus, usually long, tilted cylinders, that are slowly rotated; used to heat calcium carbonate above 900 degrees centigrade to produce lime. (MHDSTT)
UF kilns, lime
CN V. TB. AFU. ARI. ALO. ARI. ALO. ALO. BCW

lime mortar
MT.2600
SN A mixture of hydrated lime, sand, and water, which has a compressive strength up to 400 psi. (MH)
UF mortar, lime
CN M.MT.AFU.ARI.DZW.ARI.AFU.AXC

lime putty
MT.2656
SN Putty consisting of lime that has been slaked with water and aged, often mixed with sand or marble dust to make the several types of mortar used in the plaster support of a painting in fresco.
UF plasterer's putty
putty, lime
putty, painter's
CN M.MT.AFU.ARI.HTY.ALO.ALO

lime-sand mortar
MT.2603
UF mortar, lime-sand
CN M.MT.AFU.ARI.DZW.ARI.AFU.BCW

lime soda glass
USE **soda lime glass**

lime white
USE **chalk**

lime (wood)
USE **linden**

lime yellow
USE **brilliant greenish yellow**
brilliant yellow green
strong greenish yellow

lime, anhydrous
USE **quicklime**

lime, burnt
USE **quicklime**

lime, caustic
USE **quicklime**

lime, common
USE **common lime**

lime, common (quicklime)
USE **quicklime**

lime, fat
USE **fat lime**

lime, hydrated
USE **hydrated lime**

lime, lump
USE **quicklime**

lime, meager
USE **meager lime**

lime, poor
USE **meager lime**

lime, rich
USE **fat lime**

lime, slaked
USE **hydrated lime**

lime, small-leafed
USE **small-leafed lime**

lime, unslaked
USE **quicklime**

limestone
MT.649 (A,L,B,R)
SN General name for a great variety of calcite rocks. Includes dolomite, marble, chalk, or any mineral consisting largely of calcium carbonate. (MH)
CN M.MT.AFU.AFU.AFU.DCU.AFU.ALO.AFU.ALO.ALO

limestone, Alabama
USE **Alabama limestone**

limestone, algal
USE **algal limestone**

limestone, arenaceous
USE **siliceous limestone**

limestone, argillaceous
USE **argillaceous limestone**

limestone, Bangor
USE **Bangor limestone**

limestone, beer
USE **beer stone**

limestone, bituminous
USE **carbonaceous limestone**

limestone, bryozoa
USE **bryozoa limestone**

limestone, Caen
USE **Caen stone**

limestone, carbonaceous
USE **carbonaceous limestone**

limestone, cherty
USE **siliceous limestone**

limestone, coral
USE **coral limestone**

limestone, coraliferous
USE **coral limestone**

limestone, crinoidal
USE **crinoidal limestone**

limestone, dolomitic
USE **magnesian limestone**

limestone, ferruginous
USE **ferruginous limestone**

limestone, hydraulic
USE **hydraulic limestone**

limestone, Indiana
USE **Indiana limestone**

limestone, magnesian
USE **magnesian limestone**

limestone, Old Gothic
USE **Old Gothic limestone**

limestone, oolitic
USE **oolitic limestone**

limestone, pisolitic
USE **pisolitic limestone**

limestone, Portland
USE **Portland stone**

limestone, Queenston
USE **Queenston limestone**

limestone, rustic
USE **rustic limestone**

limestone, sandy
USE **siliceous limestone**

limestone, select
USE **select limestone**

limestone, Shelly
USE **Shelly limestone**

limestone, siliceous
USE **siliceous limestone**

limestone, standard
USE **standard limestone**

limestone, statuary
USE **statuary limestone**

limestone, tufaceous
USE **travertine**

limestone, variegated
USE **variegated limestone**

limewash
USE **whitewash**

limewashing
USE **whitewashing**

limewood
USE **linden**

limewood, American
USE **linden**

limit-load design
USE **plastic design**

limit-states design
USE **plastic design**

limit, elastic
USE **elastic limit**

limited access highways
RK.1518 (L)
ALT **limited access highway**
UF controlled access highways
highways, controlled access
highways, limited access
limited access roads
roads, limited access
CN V.RK.ALO.ALO.BIQ.ARI.AFU.AFU.ARI

limited access roads
USE **limited access highways**

limited editions
VB.124 (L)
ALT **limited edition**
SN A set number of replicas of a work of art, of which the plate, mold, or die is destroyed after the copies have been made. (MAYER)
UF editions, limited
CN V.VB.ALO.BZY.ALO.AFU

limites
RK.452 (L)
ALT **limite**
SN Designates ancient Roman fortified frontier boundaries or defense zones.
CN V.RK.AFU.ALO.ALO.BIQ.BUE

limners
HG.108
ALT **limner**
SN Once a synonym for painters; regarding British painting of the 15th and 16th centuries, refers to painters of miniature portraits; regarding Colonial America, refers to portrait painters more generally.
CN H.HG.AFU.AXC.AXC.AFU.AFU.ALO.AXC.CXA.AFU.ALO

Limoges porcelain
FL.3221 (L,R)
UF porcelain, Limoges
CN F.FL.ALO.BCW.ALO.ARI.BIQ.BIQ.ARI.ALO.AXC.ALO

limonite
MT.512 (L)
SN The common iron ore of early New England; a mineral of secondary origin formed by the water solution of other iron minerals. (MH)
UF bog iron ore
brown hematite
brown ore

hematite, brown
iron ore, bog
ore, bog iron
ore, brown
CN M.MT.AFU.AFU.AFU.CFS.AFU.CXA.ALO

linacs
USE **linear accelerators**

Lincoln rockers
TG.227
ALT **Lincoln rocker**
SN Popular term for mid-19th-century American rocking chairs with a high, upholstered back and seat and open arms with upholstered pads on the elbows.
UF chairs, Grecian rocking
chairs, Lincoln rocking
Grecian rocking chairs
Lincoln rocking chairs
rockers, Lincoln
rocking chairs, Grecian
rocking chairs, Lincoln
CN V.TG.AFU.AFU.ALO.AFU.AFU.AXC.ARI.ALO

Lincoln rocking chairs
USE **Lincoln rockers**

linden
MT.1313 (L,R)
UF American basswood
American limewood
basswood
basswood, American
lime (wood)
limewood
limewood, American
Tilia
Tilia americana
CN M.MT.AFU.AFU.ALO.BIQ.DCU..AFU.AFU.LZO.ALO

linden, common
USE **common lime**

line
BM.68 (L)
SN A narrow elongated mark drawn or projected. (W)
CN B.BM.AFU.AFU.ARI.AFU.CLM

line block prints
USE **line photoengravings**

line blocks
USE **line photoengravings**

line cuts
USE **line photoengravings**

line drawing, contour
USE **contour drawings**

line drawings
VD.129
ALT **line drawing**
UF drawings, line
CN V.VD.AFU.AXC.BIQ

line engraving
KT.453 (L,R)
SN Intaglio technique in which the image is made by scored lines of varying width in a metal plate. (SAFF)
UF engraving, line
CN K.KT.AFU.ALO.DUC.DUC.ALO.BCW.AFU.ARI.ALO

line engravings, process
USE **line photoengravings**

line graphs
VW.248
ALT **line graph**
UF graphs, line
CN V.VW.AFU.AFU.AFU.FZU.AXC.AXC.ARI

line maps
USE **outline maps**

line of beauty
USE **Hogarth's line**

line photoengravings
VJ.20
ALT **line photoengraving**
SN Photomechanical prints that involve only two tones, usually black and white, with no gradations.
UF engravings, process line
line block prints
line blocks
line cuts
line engravings, process
line photomechanical prints
photoengravings, line
photomechanical prints, line
prints, line block
process line engravings
CN V.VJ.AFU.AFU.ALO.ARI.AFU

line photomechanical prints
USE **line photoengravings**

line pins
TF.462 (N)
ALT **line pin**
SN Metal pins used in masonry work to support a horizontal string or line. The mason positions the line and then uses it as a guide in maintaining proper alignment of the work. (MEANS)
UF pins, line
CN V.TF.AFU.AFU.AFU.ALO.AFU.CXA.BCW

line printers
TB.164 (L,N)
ALT **line printer**
SN Computer output devices that produce a line of print per cycle of its operation. (DOC)
UF printers, line
CN V.TB.AFU.ARI.BCW.AXC.AXC.ALO.AFU

line-route maps
VW.155
ALT **line-route map**
SN Maps that show the actual routes and types of construction of wire circuits in an area. (DOD)
UF maps, line-route
maps, route
route maps
CN V.VW.AFU.AFU.AFU.FZU.AXC.AFU.ARI.AFU.CLM.ARI

line, Hogarth's
USE **Hogarth's line**

line, horizon
USE **horizon line**

line, phantom
USE **phantom line**

linear accelerators
RK.1157 (L,N)
ALT **linear accelerator**
SN Designates structures in which electrons, protons, or heavy ions are accelerated along a straight line by the action of alternating voltages.
UF accelerators, linear
linacs
CN V.RK.AFU.ALO.ALO.FIM.AFU.ALO

linear cities
RD.4 (A,B)
ALT **linear city**
UF cities, linear
CN V.RD.AFU.AFU.AFU.AFU

linear city
USE **linear development**

linear development
BM.1078
SN Arrangement of commercial and service facilities in a narrow belt along or over a main traffic route. (LOC)
UF city, linear
development, linear
linear city
CN B.BM.CLM.ALO.ALO.ALO.ALO

Linear Island Style
FL.2609
CN F.FL.ALO.AXC.ALO.AFU.ALO.AXC.ALO.ARI.ARI

linear pattern, continuous
USE **running ornament**

linear perspective
KT.273 (L)
SN Use for the system of perspective developed in the Italian Renaissance in which orthogonals converge toward a usually central primary vanishing point. For similar modern compositions, use **one-point perspective.**
UF artificial perspective
costruzione legittima
legitimate construction

mechanical perspective
perspectiva artificiales
perspective, artificial
perspective, legitimate
perspective, linear
perspective, Renaissance
Renaissance perspective
CN K.KT.AFU.ALO.DUC.DCU.BIQ.AXC

Linear ware
USE **Linienbandkeramik**

linearity
BM.73
ALT **linear**
SN The reliance on line for the principal effect in a drawn or painted composition, rather than on color or tone. (THDAT)
CN B.BM.AFU.AFU.ARI.AFU.CRG

linen
MT.1853 (A,L,R)
SN General name for cloth woven from the spun fibers of a type of flax plant.
CN M.MT.AFU.AFU.ARI.ALO.ALO.ALO .AFU.AXC

linen airers
USE **clotheshorses**
towel racks

linen closets
RM.197 (L)
ALT **linen closet**
UF closets, linen
CN V.RM.AFU.DIO.ALO.DCU.BOK.ARI

linen cupboards
USE **linen presses**

linen presses
TG.517 (N,B)
ALT **linen press**
SN Cupboards for the storage of linen. (DDA)
UF cupboards, linen
linen cupboards
presses, linen
CN V.TG.AFU.AFU.AXC.ALO.BUE.CXA. ALO

linen scroll
USE **linenfold**

linen, Roman
USE **Roman linen**

linenfold
DG.40
SN An ornament especially found in woodwork and furniture consisting of a panel with a motif resembling a piece of linen laid in vertical folds.
UF linen scroll
scroll, linen
CN D.DG.AFU.AFU.CRG

liner, form
USE **form lumber**

lines drawings
VD.158
ALT **lines drawing**
SN Use for drawings that show a ship's lines. Includes **sheer plans, half-breadth plans,** and **body plans,** often all drawn on one sheet.
UF drawings, lines
lines plans
lines (ships plans)
lines, ships
plans, lines
ships lines
CN V.VD.AFU.BIQ.BOK.ALO

lines plans
USE **lines drawings**

lines (ships plans)
USE **lines drawings**

lines, building
USE **building lines**

lines, electric
USE **power lines**

lines, funicular
USE **funicular lines**

lines, influence
USE **influence lines**

lines, power
USE **power lines**

lines, power transmission
USE **power lines**

lines, property
USE **property lines**

lines, ships
USE **lines drawings**

lines, sight
USE **sight lines**

lines, springing
USE **springers**

linguistic anthropology
USE **anthropological linguistics**

linguistics
KD.32 (L,B,R)
CN K.KD.AFU.AFU.AXC.AFU

linguistics, anthropological
USE **anthropological linguistics**

linguistics, applied
USE **applied linguistics**

linguistics, computational
USE **computational linguistics**

linguistics, historical
USE **historical linguistics**

linguistics, theoretical
USE **theoretical linguistics**

linguists
HG.172 (L)
ALT **linguist**
CN H.HG.AFU.AXC.AXC.ALO.AFU. ALO

Linienbandkeramik
FL.2503 (L)
UF Linear ware
ware, Linear
CN F.FL.ALO.AXC.AFU.BCW.DCU.AFU. AFU

lining
KT.645
ALT **lined**
SN Use for giving a second, inner layer such as in the conservation of oil paintings where a piece of fresh linen is applied to the back of an old canvas or in the making of a garment where an inner layer of cloth is applied.
UF relining
CN K.KT.AFU.ALO.GLI.AFU.ALO

lining petitions
USE **building permits**

linings, door
USE **doorframes**

linings, flue
USE **flue linings**

linings, window
USE **window frames**

linkage
BM.1079 (A)
ALT **linkages**
SN Denotes a planning practice that requires developers to contribute toward new urban social improvements, such as affordable housing or child care facilities, in return for concessions on new in-town developments.
CN B.BM.CLM.ALO.ALO.ALO.ARI

linked knot pattern
USE **knotwork**

links, golf
USE **golf courses**

linocut
KT.471 (L)
SN Block printing method that uses linoleum as the printing surface.
UF block-printing, linoleum
linoleum block-printing
linoleum cut
CN K.KT.AFU.ALO.DUC.DUC.ALO. BCW.ARI.ALO.AFU

linoleum
MT.2391 (A,L,B,R)
SN General name for flooring material comprised of a mixture of ground cork or wood flour, resin or other

gum, blown linseed oil, with sometimes a filler such as lithopone, on a fabric backing of burlap or canvas, rolled under pressure to give a hard, glossy surface. (MH12)
CN M.MT.AFU.ARI.BZY.AXC.AFU.AFU

linoleum block-printing
USE **linocut**

linoleum cut
USE **linocut**

linotype operators
HG.455
ALT **linotype operator**
UF operators, linotype
CN H.HG.AFU.AXC.BUE.ALO.CFS.AXC

linseed oil
MT.2011 (L)
SN Popular drying oil used as a paint medium; hardens over several weeks as components of the oil polymerize to form an insoluble matrix. (TATEMT)
UF oil, linseed
CN M.MT.AFU.AFU.ARI.ARI.AXC.AFU.BCW

linseed oil, boiled
USE **boiled oil**

linseed oil, raw
USE **raw linseed oil**

lintel courses
RT.619
ALT **lintel course**
SN In stone masonry, courses set at the level of a lintel, commonly differentiated from the wall by their greater projection, finish, or thickness which often match that of the lintel. (HAS)
UF courses, lintel
CN V.RT.AFU.AFU.AFU.BIQ.BUE.ALO.AFU.ALO.BOK

lintels
RT.354 (A,N,B,R)
ALT **lintel**
SN Horizontal structural members over an opening in a wall that carry the superimposed weight of the wall. (HAS)
CN V.RT.AFU.AFU.AFU.BCW.CFS

Linville trusses
USE **Whipple trusses**

lion and ring handles
TF.83
ALT **lion and ring handle**
UF handles, lion and ring
CN V.TF.AFU.AFU.AFU.AFU.CFS.BCW.AFU.CRG.AFU

lion's paw feet
TG.929
ALT **lion's paw foot**
SN Decorative termination to the leg of a piece of furniture (generally a chair) used from the late 17th to theearly 18th century and again in the 19th century. (DDA)
UF feet, lion's paw
CN V.TG.ALO.DZW.AFU.DCU.BIQ.ARI

Lipan Apache
FL.1452 (L)
UF Apache, Lipan
CN F.FL.ALO.ALO.ARI.AFU.CFS.AFU.AXC

liparite
USE **rhyolite**

Lipe
FL.1622
CN F.FL.ALO.ALO.ARI.ARI.ALO.ALO.BIQ

lipids
MT.1003 (L)
CN M.MT.AFU.AFU.ALO.AXC.BOK

lipped adzes
TB.817 (N)
ALT **lipped adz**
SN Adzes whose blade edges are turned upwards on each side to give a trenching cut, a square rather than round channel; also used to cut scores or notches across the grain at intervals. (SALAM)
UF adzes, dubbing
adzes, lipped
dubbing adzes
CN V.TB.AFU.BCW.CFS.ALO.AFU.AFU.BOK

lipped drawers
TG.877
ALT **lipped drawer**
UF drawers, lipped
lapped drawers
CN V.TG.ALO.DCU.AFU.AFU.ALO

Lippmann process
KT.340 (L)
SN A photographic process to produce color images in a grainless silver halide emulsion by interference.
CN K.KT.AFU.ALO.DUC.DIO.ALO.CLM.ALO

lips (lock components)
TF.568
ALT **lip (lock component)**
SN Parts of strikes that project at an angle beyond the face of the door jamb to receive the beveled latch bolt and conduct it into the strike's recess. (DITTRI)
CN V.TF.AFU.ALO.AXC.BUE

liquefied petroleum gas
MT.1011
UF bottled gas
gas, bottled
gas, liquefied petroleum
petroleum gas, liquefied
CN M.MT.AFU.AFU.ALO.BCW.ALO.ALO

liquid asphalt
MT.980
UF asphalt, liquid
CN M.MT.AFU.AFU.ALO.ALO.AFU.ALO.AFU

liquid epoxy, basic
USE **basic liquid epoxy**

Liquidambar styraciflua
USE **sweet gum**

liquids
MT.2288 (L)
ALT **liquid**
CN M.MT.AFU.ALO.JCO.ALO

liquor cases
USE **bottle cases**

Liriodendron tulipifera
USE **tulipwood**

Lisbon yellow marble
MT.844
UF marble, Lisbon yellow
yellow marble, Lisbon
CN M.MT.AFU.AFU.AFU.DCU.AFU.ARI.ARI.ARI.BUE.AFU

listed buildings
USE **landmark buildings**

listing
USE **inventorying**
registering (information handling)

lists
VW.251
ALT **list**
CN V.VW.AFU.AFU.AFU.FZU.BCW

lists (seat rails)
USE **seat rails**

lists of members
USE **membership lists**

lists of merchandise
USE **merchandise inventories**

lists of subscribers
USE **subscription lists**

lists, accession
USE **accession registers**

lists, attendance
USE **attendance lists**

lists, books
USE **bibliographies**

lists, donor
USE **donor lists**

lists, job
USE **job lists**

lists, mailing
USE **mailing lists**

lists, membership
USE **membership lists**

lists, passenger
USE **passenger lists**

lists, price
USE **price lists**

lists, publishers'
USE **publishers' catalogs**

lists, reading
USE **reading lists**

lists, shelf
USE **shelf lists**

lists, ships' passenger
USE **ships' passenger lists**

lists, subscription
USE **subscription lists**

lists, union
USE **union lists**

lists, voters'
USE **voters' lists**

lists, want
USE **want lists**

lists, warehouse
USE **merchandise inventories**

lists, wine
USE **wine lists**

litanies
VW.548 (L,R)
ALT **litany**
SN Liturgical prayers consisting of phrases recited by a leader alternating with responses by a congregation. (AHD)
CN V.VW.AFU.ALO.AFU.AFU.ALO.BUE.BZY

literary analysis
USE **literary criticism**

literary criticism
KD.56 (L,R)
UF analysis, literary
criticism of literature
criticism, literary
literary analysis
CN K.KD.AFU.AFU.BCW.ARI

literary critics
HG.198 (L)
ALT **literary critic**
UF critics, literary
CN H.HG.AFU.AXC.AXC.ARI.ALO.ARI.AFU

literary historians
HG.200 (L)
ALT **literary historian**
UF historians, literary
CN H.HG.AFU.AXC.AXC.ARI.ALO.BCW

literary history
KD.57 (L)
UF history, literary
CN K.KD.AFU.AFU.BCW.AXC

literary sketches
USE **essays**

literary theory
BM.314 (R)
UF literature, philosophy of
philosophy of literature
theory of literature
theory, literary
CN B.BM.AFU.AXC.EFQ.AXC

Literati
USE **Wen ren**

Literati Style
USE **Nanga**

literature
KD.53 (A,L,B,R)
CN K.KD.AFU.AFU.BCW

literature museums
RK.387 (L)
ALT **literature museum**
UF museums, literature
CN V.RK.AFU.ALO.ALO.BCW.AXC.ARI.AFU.AXC

literature, comparative
USE **comparative literature**

literature, philosophy of
USE **literary theory**

litharge
MT.1781
SN Lead monoxide; a heavy, yellowish powder which, when cooked with linseed oil, acts as a powerful drier. (MAYER)
UF Bleiglätte
lead monoxide, yellow
lead oxide
lithargyron
oxide, lead
plumbum ustum
yellow lead monoxide
CN M.MT.AFU.AFU.ARI.AFU.AFU.ALO.ALO.BUE.ARI.BIQ

lithargyron
USE **litharge**

litho purple
USE **dark purple**
grayish purple
moderate purple
strong purple

litho varnish
MT.2490
SN A heat-bodied linseed oil that is the vehicle in lithographic ink and usually in other printing ink. (MAYER)
UF burnt-oil varnish
oil, plate
plate oil
varnish, burnt-oil
varnish, litho
CN M.MT.AFU.ARI.CRG.AFU.BOK.ARI.ALO

lithograph stone
USE **solnhofen stone**

lithographers
HG.130 (L,R)
ALT **lithographer**
SN Persons engaged in lithography.
CN H.HG.AFU.AXC.AXC.AFU.AFU.ALO.AXC.DUC.ARI

lithographic crayons
TB.243 (N)
ALT **lithographic crayon**
SN Oily crayons with which the drawing is applied to the stone, plate, or transfer paper in lithography. (MAYER)
UF crayons, lithographic
CN V.TB.AFU.ARI.CLM.AFU.ALO.AXC.ALO

lithographic photographers
USE **photolithographers**

lithographic stone
USE **solnhofen stone**

lithography
KT.462 (L,R)
SN Planographic printmaking process in which a design is drawn on the stone or plate with a greasy substance and the surface is chemically treated to accept ink only where the design has been drawn.
CN K.KT.AFU.ALO.DUC.DUC.ALO.BCW.ALO.AFU

lithography, offset
USE **offset printing**

lithography, transfer
USE **transfer lithography**

lithol red
MT.1706
UF Harrison's red
red, Harrison's
red, lithol
CN M.MT.AFU.AFU.ARI.AFU.AFU.ALO.ALO.BCW.AXC.AXC

lithopone
MT.1733 (R)
SN Zinc sulfide coprecipitated with barium sulfate; a dense white pigment used in house paints and industrial coatings. (MAYER)
UF Becton white
Charlton white
Deckweiss
Griffith's patent zinc white
Jersey lily white
lily white, Jersey
Orr's zinc white
ponolith

white, Becton
white, Charlton
white, Griffith's patent zinc
white, Jersey lily
white, Orr's zinc
zinc white, Griffith's patent
zinc white, Orr's
CN M.MT.AFU.AFU.ARI.AFU.AFU.ALO.ALO.BOK.AFU.BIQ

lithopone, cadmium red
USE **cadmium red lithopone**

lithopone, cadmium yellow
USE **cadmium yellow lithopone**

lithozincography
USE **zincography**

litigating
KG.205 (L,B)
SN Taking legal action; carrying on a suit by judicial process. (RLG7)
UF suing
CN K.KG.AFU.ALO.BCW.BOK.BCW

litmus
MT.1524
SN Natural dyestuff used to test the acidity of chemical solutions; also used as a textile dye, wood stain, and food colorant.
CN M.MT.AFU.AFU.ARI.AFU.AFU.AFU.AFU.AFU.AXC.BCW

litmus paper
MT.1941 (N)
UF paper, litmus
CN M.MT.AFU.AFU.ARI.ALO.ALO.AXC.ARI.BIQ

lits à bateau
USE **lits en bateau**

lits à chapelle
USE **lits à la duchesse**

lits à l'ange
USE **lits d'ange**

lits à l'antique
TG.363
ALT **lit à l'antique**
SN Phrase used to describe early 19th-century French beds based on classical models. (GROER)
UF couches à l'antique
CN V.TG.AFU.AFU.ARI.AFU.AFU.CLM

lits à l'impériale
USE **lits d'ange**

lits à la duchesse
TG.327
ALT **lit à la duchesse**
SN Beds with a canopy attached to the wall behind the head or to the ceiling and not supported on posts or columns. (WATSON)
UF angel beds
beds à la duchesse
beds, angel
beds, duchesse
duchesse beds
lits à chapelle
lits à la française (lits à la duchesse)
CN V.TG.AFU.AFU.ARI.AFU.AFU.ARI.ALO

lits à la française (lits à la duchesse)
USE **lits à la duchesse**

lits à la polonaise
TG.360
ALT **lit à la polonaise**
SN Beds which stand sideways against the wall and have dome-shaped testers supported by iron rods curving up from the corners of the head boards, the rods being hidden by the bed hangings. (THORN1)
CN V.TG.AFU.AFU.ARI.AFU.AFU.BZY.ALO.AXC

lits à la romaine
TG.364
ALT **lit à la romaine**
SN French beds meant to have a separate canopy overhead; of a type made in the late 17th century. (THORN2)
CN V.TG.AFU.AFU.ARI.AFU.AFU.CRG

lits à la turque
TG.365
ALT **lit à la turque**
SN Beds with ends of equal height and an upholstered back. (PC)
CN V.TG.AFU.AFU.ARI.AFU.AFU.CXA

lits alcoves (box beds)
USE **box beds**

lits-bateaux
USE **lits en bateau**

lits brisés
USE **field beds**

lits-canapés
USE **sofa beds**

lits carrosses(box beds)
USE **box beds**

lits chapelles
USE **box beds**

lits clos
USE **box beds**

lits d'ange
TG.366
ALT **lit d'ange**
SN Beds with a flying tester suspended over the whole sleeping surface of the bed. (THORN2)
UF lits à l'ange
lits à l'impériale
CN V.TG.AFU.AFU.ARI.AFU.AFU.DCU

lits d'armée
USE **field beds**

lits d'honneur
USE **lits de parade**

lits de camp
USE **field beds**

lits de campagne
USE **field beds**

lits de chasse
USE **field beds**

lits de parade
TG.375
ALT **lit de parade**
SN 18th-century French term for magnificent state beds used in the ceremonial bedrooms of a royal residence. Not intended to be used for sleeping. (PC)
UF lits d'honneur
lits de parement
CN V.TG.AFU.AFU.ARI.AFU.AFU.ERE.AFU

lits de parement
USE **lits de parade**

lits de repos
USE **daybeds**

lits de voyage
USE **field beds**

lits en bateau
TG.372
ALT **lit en bateau**
SN Beds with two ends of equal height.
UF lits à bateau
lits-bateaux
lits en gondole
CN V.TG.AFU.AFU.ARI.AFU.AFU.EFQ.AFU

lits en forme d'armoire
USE **box beds**

lits en gondole
USE **lits en bateau**

lits fermés
USE **box beds**

lits superposés
USE **bunk beds**

liturgical architecture
USE **religious buildings**

liturgical manuscripts
VW.663 (R)
ALT **liturgical manuscript**
UF manuscripts, liturgical
CN V.VW.AFU.ALO.AFU.DZW.ARI.ALO.ALO

liturgy
BM.713 (L,R)
CN B.BM.BZY.ALO.AXC.AFU

Liu Song
FL.1877
CN F.FL.ALO.ARI.ALO.AFU.AFU.ALO.BUE.AFU.ALO.ALO

live bolts
USE **latch bolts**

live loads
BM.1016 (L)
UF loads, live
CN B.BM.CFS.AXC.CLM.ALO.ARI.CFS

live oak
MT.1243
UF oak, live
Quercus virginiana
CN M.MT.AFU.AFU.ALO.BIQ.DCU.AFU.AFU.AFU.IRA.CRG

live oak, California
USE **coast live oak**

live oak, coast
USE **coast live oak**

livery beds
TG.367
ALT **livery bed**
SN Beds for servants' use; term frequently found in 16th- and 17th-century inventories. (THORN2)
UF beds, livery
CN V.TG.AFU.AFU.ARI.AFU.AFU.DIO

livery cupboards
TG.511 (B)
ALT **livery cupboard**
SN Term which came into use in the mid-16th century in England for freestanding cupboards used for the storage of food and drink, generally in the form of a two-tier cupboard with pierced or spindle doors for ventilation. Use **aumbries** with reference to similar forms made before, after, or during the Medieval period. (DDA)
UF almoners cupboards
bread and cheese cupboards
butter cupboards
cupboards, almoners
cupboards, bread and cheese
cupboards, butter
cupboards, food
cupboards, livery
food cupboards
food lockers
lockers, food
CN V.TG.AFU.AFU.AXC.ALO.BUE.CRG

livery halls
USE **guildhalls**

livestock breeders
HG.367 (L)
ALT **livestock breeder**
UF breeders, livestock
CN H.HG.AFU.AXC.BIQ.ALO.AXC.AFU.AXC

livestock buildings
USE **animal housing**

living-halls
USE **halls**

living rooms
RM.173 (A,L)
ALT **living room**
UF rooms, living
CN V.RM.AFU.DIO.ALO.CXA.BUE

living, communal
USE **communal living**

lizard leather
MT.957
UF leather, lizard
CN M.MT.AFU.AFU.ALO.AFU.DZW.AXC.ARI

Llano
FL.744
CN F.FL.ALO.ALO.ALO.AFU.AFU.ARI.ALO.AFU

llanos
RD.245 (L)
ALT **llano**
SN Extensive grassy plains, with few trees, found in the southwest United States and Spanish America. (RHDEL2)
CN V.RD.ARI.AFU.BCW.ALO.AFU.AFU.AFU

Lo-yang
USE **Erlitou**

loadbearing walls
RT.583 (A,B)
ALT **loadbearing wall**
SN Walls that support a vertical load in addition to their own weight. (PUTNAM)
UF bearing walls
walls, bearing
walls, loadbearing
CN V.RT.AFU.AFU.AFU.BIQ.BUE.AFU.ALO.ALO

loaded brush painting
USE **impasto**

loaders
TB.44 (L,N)
ALT **loader**
SN Construction machines having a bucket, located on the front of the vehicle, which can be raised, lowered, or tilted; used to push or transport earth, crushed stone, or other construction materials. (MEANS)
CN V.TB.AFU.ARI.AFU.ARI.BCW

loaders, bucket
USE **bucket loaders**

loaders, chain bucket
USE **chain bucket loaders**

loading banks
USE **loading docks**

loading docks
RM.135 (B)
ALT **loading dock**
UF banks, loading
docks, loading
loading banks
CN V.RM.AFU.DIO.ALO.BOK.ARI

loading platforms
RT.745 (B)
ALT **loading platform**
SN Use for any raised areas, such as alongside the tracks of a railroad station, from which passengers embark or goods may be loaded.
UF platforms, loading
CN V.RT.AFU.ALO.AFU.BIQ.AFU.ARI.ALO

loads
BM.1004 (B)
SN Forces carried by a structure, or part of a structure. (DAC)
UF structural loads
CN B.BM.CFS.AXC.CLM.ALO.ARI

loads, axial
USE **axial loads**

loads, combined
USE **combined loads**

loads, concentrated
USE **concentrated loads**

loads, construction
USE **construction loads**

loads, dead
USE **dead loads**

loads, distributed
USE **distributed loads**

loads, earthquake
USE **earthquake loads**

loads, eccentric
USE **eccentric loads**

loads, impact
USE **impact loads**

loads, lateral
USE **lateral loads**

loads, live
USE **live loads**

loads, moving
USE **moving loads**

loads, short term
USE **impact loads**

loads, static
USE **dead loads**

loads, traffic
USE **traffic loads**

loads, uniform
USE **uniform loads**

loads, unsymmetrical
USE **eccentric loads**

loads, wind
USE **wind loads**

loam
MT.2065
SN Soft, easily worked soil containing sand, silt, and clay. (STEIN)
CN M.MT.AFU.AFU.ARI.BOK.ALO.AXC

loaning
USE **lending**

Lobate
USE **Auricular**

lobbies
RM.136 (A,B)
ALT **lobby**
SN Use for large halls serving as entrance spaces in public buildings or as anterooms, especially to legislative chambers. For entrance spaces in private houses, use **entrance halls.**
UF foyers
CN V.RM.AFU.DIO.ALO.BOK.AXC

lobbies, bank
USE **banking rooms**

lobby chests
TG.464
ALT **lobby chest**
UF chests, lobby
CN V.TG.AFU.AFU.AXC.ALO.AXC.DCU

lobbying
KG.38 (L)
SN Attempting to influence or sway public officials toward a desired end. (WCOL)
CN K.KG.AFU.AFU.ALO.BCW

lobbyists
HG.753 (L)
ALT **lobbyist**
CN H.HG.AFU.BCW.HZS.BIQ

lobed arches
USE **cusped arches**

lobed decoration
USE **gadrooning**

Lobedu
USE **Lovedu**

lobes
USE **foils**

Lobi
FL.355 (L)
CN F.FL.ALO.AFU.AXC.AFU.AXC.AFU.BIQ

lobing
USE **gadrooning**

loblolly pine
MT.1378 (L)
UF Oldfield pine
pine, loblolly
pine, Oldfield
pine, sap
pine, swamp
pine, yellow (loblolly pine)
Pinus taeda
sap pine
swamp pine
Virginia pine
yellow pine (loblolly pine)
CN M.MT.AFU.AFU.ALO.BIQ.DCU.AFU.AFU.ALO.CXA.BUE

local authority buildings
USE **municipal buildings**

local bibliographies
VW.260
ALT **local bibliography**
UF bibliographies, local
CN V.VW.AFU.AFU.AFU.FZU.BCW.AFU.ALO.AXC.ALO

local color
BM.112
SN Theoretically, the inherent color of an object when it is unaffected by the reflected light from another object. In practice, it is the color of an object in natural light. (MGHDIC)
UF color, local
color, surface
surface color
CN B.BM.AFU.AFU.ARI.BOK.ALO.AFU.AXC

local directories
USE **city directories**

local fire alarm systems
RT.1507
ALT **local fire alarm system**
SN Use for fire alarm systems that produce signals on the protected premises only, primarily to notify occupants.
UF alarm systems, local fire
fire alarm systems, local
systems, local fire alarm
CN V.RT.ALO.BIQ.AFU.AFU.AFU.ALO

local government
BM.544 (L,B)
UF governments, local
CN B.BM.BOK.BOK.ALO.AFU

local government buildings
USE **municipal buildings**

local government records
VW.1044
ALT **local government record**
SN Records made or received by an agency of a local government, such as a city or county, and maintained in the conduct of local government business.
UF government records, local
records, local government
CN V.VW.AFU.ARI.ALO.BCW.ALO.AFU

local history
KD.143 (L)
UF history, local
CN K.KD.AFU.ALO.CLM.AFU.ARI

local lighting
RT.1361
UF lighting, local
CN V.RT.ALO.AXC.AFU.BUE

local plans
USE **site plans**

local roads
USE **secondary roads**

local transit
RD.112 (A,L)
SN Transit systems, usually of low average speed (under 15 miles per hour) and making frequent stops, located locally within portions of cities, towns, or neighborhoods.
UF city transit
community transit
municipal transit
transit, city
transit, community
transit, local
transit, municipal
CN V.RD.ALO.ARI.AFU.ALO.ARI

Locarno Beach
FL.914
CN F.FL.ALO.ALO.ALO.AFU.ALO.ARI.ARI.ARI

location maps
VW.147
ALT **location map**
UF maps, location
CN V.VW.AFU.AFU.AFU.FZU.AXC.AFU.ARI.AFU.BOK.AFU

location of industries
USE **industrial location**

location plans
USE **site plans**

location, industrial
USE **industrial location**

location, plant
USE **industrial location**

lock plates
USE **escutcheons (hardware)**

lock rails
RT.882
ALT **lock rail**
SN The horizontal pieces of a door to which the lock is fastened. (PUTNAM)
UF rails, lock
CN V.RT.AFU.ARI.AFU.AFU.AFU.ALO.ARI.ALO.ALO.ALO

lock seams, Pittsburgh
USE **Pittsburgh lock seams**

lock sets
USE **locks**

lock stiles
RT.827

ALT lock stile
SN The vertical pieces of a door to which the lock is fastened. (PUTNAM)
UF locking stiles
shutting stiles
stiles, lock
stiles, locking
stiles, shutting
CN V.RT.AFU.ALO.ALO.AXC.ALO

lock-tenders' houses
USE **lockkeepers' houses**

lock-tenders' shacks
USE **lockkeepers' houses**

lockbands
USE **bond courses**

locker rooms
RM.69
ALT **locker room**
UF rooms, locker
CN V.RM.AFU.DIO.ALO.ALO.AXC

lockers, food
USE **livery cupboards**

locking joints
TF.670
ALT **locking joint**
UF joints, locking
CN V.TF.ALO.ARI.AXC.ALO

locking stiles
USE **lock stiles**

lockkeepers' houses
RK.334 (A,L)
ALT **lockkeeper's house**
UF houses, lockkeepers'
lock-tenders' houses
lock-tenders' shacks
CN V.RK.AFU.ALO.ALO.AXC.ALO.BOK .BIQ

locknuts
TF.453
ALT **locknut**
SN Secondary nuts used on a bolt to prevent the first nut from turning; also nuts which lock when tightened. (PUTNAM)
UF nuts, lock
CN V.TF.AFU.AFU.AFU.ALO.AFU.CLM. ARI

lockouts
KM.159 (L)
SN Situations in which employment is withheld by employers in order to gain concessions from employees. (W)
CN K.KM.AFU.EWY.AFU

locks
TF.193 (L,N,R)
ALT **lock**
SN Complete systems including all the mechanical parts and accessories of a lock, such as knobs, reinforcing plates, and protective escutcheons. (MEANS)
UF lock sets
CN V.TF.AFU.AFU.AFU.AFU.DIO.BIQ

locks, air
USE **air locks**

locks, air conditioning
USE **air conditioning locks**

locks, asylum
USE **asylum locks**

locks, auxiliary rim
USE **auxiliary rim locks**

locks, bit key
USE **bit key locks**

locks, bored
USE **bored locks**

locks, box
USE **rim locks**

locks, cabinet
USE **cabinet locks**

locks, chronometer
USE **time locks**

locks, combination
USE **combination locks**

locks, combined store-door
USE **combined store-door locks**

locks, communicating-door
USE **communicating-door locks**

locks, connecting-door
USE **communicating-door locks**

locks, conventional
USE **mortise locks**

locks, cupboard
USE **cupboard locks**

locks, cylinder
USE **cylinder locks**

locks, desk
USE **desk locks**

locks, dial
USE **combination locks**

locks, door
USE **door locks**

locks, drawer
USE **drawer locks**

locks, duplex
USE **duplex locks**

locks, French-door
USE **French-door locks**

locks, French-window
USE **French-door locks**

locks, front-door
USE **front-door locks**

locks, furniture
USE **furniture locks**

locks, guarded front
USE **guarded front locks**

locks, half-rabbeted
USE **half-rabbeted locks**

locks, hasp
USE **hasp locks**

locks, hotel
USE **hotel locks**

locks, inside-door
USE **room-door locks**

locks, instant
USE **instant locks**

locks, integral
USE **integral locks**

locks, jamb
USE **jamb locks**

locks, janus-face
USE **janus-face locks**

locks, key changing
USE **key changing locks**

locks, knob
USE **knob locks**

locks, lever tumbler
USE **lever tumbler locks**

locks, master-keyed
USE **master-keyed locks**

locks, mono
USE **preassembled locks**

locks, mortise
USE **mortise locks**

locks, office
USE **office locks**

locks, panicproof
USE **panicproof locks**

locks, patio
USE **patio locks**

locks, permutation
USE **permutation locks**

locks, preassembled
USE **preassembled locks**

locks, prison
USE **prison locks**

locks, push-pull cabinet
USE **push-pull cabinet locks**

locks, rabbeted
USE **rabbeted locks**

locks, rebated
USE **rabbeted locks**

locks, recessed front
USE **guarded front locks**

locks, reverse bevel
USE **reverse bevel locks**

locks, reversible
USE **reversible locks**

locks, rigid
USE **preassembled locks**

locks, rim
USE **rim locks**

locks, room-door
USE **room-door locks**

locks, sash
USE **window locks**

locks, ship
USE **ship locks**

locks, sliding-door
USE **sliding-door locks**

locks, store-door
USE **store-door locks**

locks, subsequent
USE **subsequent locks**

locks, subtreasury
USE **subtreasury locks**

locks, surface
USE **rim locks**

locks, three-point
USE **three-point locks**

locks, till
USE **drawer locks**

locks, time
USE **time locks**

locks, tubular
USE **tubular locks**

locks, union
USE **preassembled locks**

locks, unit
USE **preassembled locks**

locks, upright
USE **upright locks**

locks, vestibule-door
USE **vestibule-door locks**

locks, warded
USE **warded locks**

locks, window
USE **window locks**

locksaws
TB.1021 (N)
ALT **locksaw**
SN Compass saws with fine, tapered, flexible blades; used for cutting door mortises to receive locks. (KNIGHT)
UF saws, lock
CN V.TB.AFU.BCW.CFS.ALO.AFU.EWY.BUE.ALO.ALO

locksmiths
HG.515 (A,L)
ALT **locksmith**
CN H.HG.AFU.AXC.BUE.ARI.CFS.ARI.BIQ

lockups
RK.718
ALT **lockup**
SN Use for temporary holding places, as in police stations or courthouses, for persons awaiting trials or hearings; for shorter periods of confinement than jails.
CN V.RK.AFU.ALO.ALO.CXA.AFU.ARI

locomotive cranes
TB.67
ALT **locomotive crane**
SN Cranes that consist of a rotating superstructure and boom mounted on a base or car equipped for travel on railroad tracks; used to hoist and swing loads at various radii. (STEIN)
UF cranes, locomotive
CN V.TB.AFU.ARI.AFU.BCW.AXC.BIQ

locomotive sheds
USE **train sheds**

loculus
USE **arcae**

locust
MT.1198 (L)
UF Robinia
CN M.MT.AFU.AFU.ALO.BIQ.DCU.AFU.AFU.AFU.HCQ

locust bean pod
MT.1072
SN Used in binding mud in building in northern Nigeria.
UF bean pod, locust
pod, locust bean
CN M.MT.AFU.AFU.ALO.BIQ.CFS.ALO.AFU.AFU

locust, Australian
USE **Australian locust**

locust, black
USE **black locust**

locust, honey
USE **honey locust**

locust, red
USE **black locust**

lodgepole pine
MT.1379 (L)
UF pine, lodgepole
pine, pitch
Pinus contorta
pitch pine
CN M.MT.AFU.AFU.ALO.BIQ.DCU.AFU.AFU.ALO.CXA.BZY

lodges
RK.959 (A,N,B,R)
ALT **lodge**
CN V.RK.AFU.ALO.ALO.ELK.BOK

lodges (fraternal buildings)
USE **fraternal lodges**

lodges (gatehouses)
USE **gatehouses**

lodges, angling
USE **fishing lodges**

lodges, earth
USE **earth lodges**

lodges, entrance
USE **gatehouses**

lodges, fishing
USE **fishing lodges**

lodges, fraternal
USE **fraternal lodges**

lodges, hunting
USE **hunting lodges**

lodges, motor
USE **motels**

lodges, ski
USE **ski lodges**

lodges, sweat
USE **sweathouses**

lodging houses
RK.963 (A,L)
ALT **lodging house**
UF boarding houses
houses, boarding
houses, lodging
houses, rooming
rooming houses
CN V.RK.AFU.ALO.ALO.ELK.BUE

Lodi
FL.3474
CN F.FL.ALO.BIQ.AFU.EFQ

loess
RD.199 (L)
SN Wind-laid deposits of silt and dust.
CN V.RD.ARI.AFU.AXC.AFU.AFU.AXC.ALO

loft buildings
RK.1378
ALT **loft building**
SN Buildings of several floors with large areas of unobstructed space, originally rented for light industrial purposes and now frequently converted to residential occupancy. (RHDEL2)
UF buildings, loft
CN V.RK.AFU.ALO.AXC.BIQ

lofts (galleries)
USE **galleries**

lofts, choir
USE **choir lofts**

lofts, fly
USE **fly lofts**

lofts, holy
USE **rood lofts**

lofts, organ
USE **organ lofts**

lofts, rood
USE **rood lofts**

lofts, sail
USE **sail lofts**

lofts, stage
USE **fly lofts**

log
MT.1419
CN M.MT.AFU.AFU.ALO.BIQ.DCU.ALO.BIQ

log cabins
RK.316 (A,L,B,R)
ALT **log cabin**
SN Distinguished from log houses by being generally more crudely built of timbers left round and joined at the corners by overlapping saddle-shaped notches. (FGAH)
UF cabins, log
dwellings, log
log dwellings
pole shacks
shacks, pole
CN V.RK.AFU.ALO.ALO.AXC.ALO.BCW.AXC

log construction
KT.36 (B)
UF construction, log
CN K.KT.AFU.ALO.BCW.ARI.AFU.BOK

log dwellings
USE **log cabins**
log houses

log-end construction
USE **stovewood construction**

log houses
RK.317 (B)
ALT **log house**
SN Distinguished from log cabins by being generally larger and better built of carefully hewn timbers neatly notched at the corners. (FGAH)
UF continental log house
dwellings, log
houses, continental log
houses, log
log dwellings
log houses, continental
CN V.RK.AFU.ALO.ALO.AXC.ALO.BCW.BCW

log houses, continental
USE **log houses**

logarithms
BM.813 (L,B)
CN B.BM.CFS.ARI.BIQ

loggers
HG.377 (L)
ALT **logger**
SN People who cut trees for lumber. (WCOL)
UF lumberjacks
CN H.HG.AFU.AXC.BIQ.ALO.AXC.BOK.AFU

loggias
RM.247 (A,B,R)
ALT **loggia**
SN Use for covered, roomlike spaces, open to the outdoors usually through arcades or colonnades; may be contained within or adjacent to buildings.
CN V.RM.AFU.DIO.ARI.AFU.BCW

logging camps
USE **lumber camps**

logic
KD.67 (L,R)
CN K.KD.AFU.AFU.BOK.BIQ

logicians
HG.208 (L)
ALT **logician**
CN H.HG.AFU.AXC.AXC.BCW.ALO

logos
VW.706 (L,B)
ALT **logo**
SN Use for graphic images, usually derived from a company name or trademark, used in commercial contexts and often designed for ready recognition.
UF logotypes
CN V.VW.AFU.ALO.ALO.AFU.ARI

logotypes
USE **logos**

logs, ships'
USE **ships' logs**

logwood
MT.1693
UF brasil
campeachy wood
wood, campeachy
CN M.MT.AFU.AFU.ARI.AFU.AFU.ALO.ALO.BCW.ALO.BIQ

logwood blue
USE **dark bluish gray**

logwood (color)
USE **blackish purple**

Loi
FL.529
UF Baloi
CN F.FL.ALO.AFU.AXC.ALO.ALO.BIQ.ALO.AXC

Loikpo
USE **Samburu**

lokao
MT.1525
SN A green natural dyestuff of Chinese origin. (MAYER)
UF Chinese green
green, Chinese
CN M.MT.AFU.AFU.ARI.AFU.AFU.AFU.AFU.AFU.AXC.BIQ

lolling chairs
TG.77
ALT **lolling chair**
SN Period term for 19th-century American open-arm chairs with upholstered seats and backs. Seats are generally low and shallow, and the backs are high and often have serpentine cresting.
UF chairs, lolling
chairs, Martha Washington
Martha Washington chairs
CN V.TG.AFU.AFU.ALO.AFU.AFU.AFU.ILG

Loma
FL.329 (L)
UF Buzi
Toma
CN F.FL.ALO.AFU.AXC.AFU.ARI.BCW.BUE

Lomatov
FL.1801
CN F.FL.ALO.ARI.AFU.AXC.CXA.AFU

Lombard
FL.3112 (A,R)
UF Langobard
Longobard
CN F.FL.ALO.BCW.ALO.ALO.AFU.BOK.ALO.ALO.BCW

Lombard-Catalan
USE **First Romanesque**

Lombardy poplar
USE **black poplar**

Lomwe
FL.658 (L)
UF Anguru
Nguru
CN F.FL.ALO.AFU.AXC.AXC.BIQ.AFU

London plane wood
MT.1267
UF lacewood
plane wood, London
Platanus acerifolia
Platanus hispanica
Platanus hybrida
Platanus orientalis
wood, London plane
CN M.MT.AFU.AFU.ALO.BIQ.DCU.AFU.AFU.AFU.JZQ.AFU

London white
USE **white lead**

long barrows
USE **burial mounds**

long crosses
USE **Latin crosses**

long dining tables
USE **refectory tables**

Long-faced Style
USE **Buli**

long floats
USE **darbies**

long-focus lenses
TB.319
ALT **long-focus lens**
SN Any lens whose focal length is appreciably greater than the diagonal of the negative in the format in which it is used. (LANG)
UF lenses, long-focus
CN V.TB.AFU.ARI.CLM.ARI.AFU.ALO.BOK.AXC

long galleries
RM.276 (A)
ALT **long gallery**
SN Use to designate large rooms that are much longer than they are wide, such as the long galleries of Elizabethan country houses.
UF galleries (long galleries)
galleries, long
CN V.RM.AFU.DIO.ARI.ALO.CFS

long-jointer planes
USE **cooper's jointer planes**

long planes
TB.937
ALT **long plane**
SN Planes which are about 26 inches long, a shorter version of the jointer plane. (BLACKB)
UF planes, long
CN V.TB.AFU.BCW.CFS.ALO.AFU.DUC.ARI.AFU.ARI.ALO

long saws
USE **crosscut saws**

long sections
USE **longitudinal sections**

long span structures
USE **large span structures**

long tables (refectory tables)
USE **refectory tables**

long-term care facilities
USE **extended care facilities**

longhouses
RK.223 (A,R)
ALT **longhouse**
CN V.RK.AFU.ALO.ALO.AXC.AFU.BIQ

longitudinal
DC.9
CN D.DC.AFU.ALO.AFU.ARI

longitudinal-plan
USE **axial-plan**

longitudinal ridge ribs
RT.689
ALT **longitudinal ridge rib**
SN Ridge ribs running along the longitudinal axis of the space spanned by the vault.
UF ribs, longitudinal ridge
ridge ribs, longitudinal
CN V.RT.AFU.AFU.ALO.AFU.ARI.AXC.AFU

longitudinal sections
VD.71
ALT **longitudinal section**
SN Sections taken along the principal organizational axis of a structure or object.
UF axial sections
building sections
long sections
sections, axial
sections, building
sections, longitudinal
CN V.VD.AFU.AFU.BIQ.ALO.BIQ.AXC

longleaf pine
MT.1380 (L)
UF Georgia pine
hard pine
hill pine
longstraw pine
pine, Georgia
pine, hard
pine, hill
pine, longleaf
pine, longstraw
pine, rosemary
pine, southern
Pinus palustris
rosemary pine
southern pine
CN M.MT.AFU.AFU.ALO.BIQ.DCU.AFU.AFU.ALO.CXA.CFS

Longobard
USE **Lombard**

Longqing
FL.1905
UF Lung-ch'ing
CN F.FL.ALO.ARI.ALO.AFU.AFU.ALO.DIO.BUE

Longshan
FL.1846 (L)
UF Black pottery
Lung-ch'uan ware
Lungshan
pottery, Black
ware, Lung-ch'uan
CN F.FL.ALO.ARI.ALO.AFU.AFU.AFU.ARI.ARI

longstraw pine
USE **longleaf pine**

lonjas
USE **exchanges**

loo tables
TG.715
ALT **loo table**
SN Large oval or circular card tables with a central support and tilt top. (BEARD)
UF tables, loo
CN V.TG.AFU.AFU.BIQ.BOK.ALO.AXC.ALO

lookout rafters
USE **lookouts (roof components)**

lookout towers
USE **watchtowers**

lookouts (roof components)
RT.469
ALT **lookout (roof component)**
SN Short wood framing members nailed to the sides of joists or rafters to extend a roof or floor beyond an exterior wall line. (BROOKS)
UF lookout rafters
outlookers
rafters, lookout
tailpieces
CN V.RT.AFU.AFU.AFU.BIQ.ARI.ALO.AFU.BIQ

lookouts, scenic
USE **overlooks**

loom weaving
KT.555
UF weaving, loom
CN K.KT.AFU.ALO.ELK.DUC.AFU.BOK.ARI

loop-back Windsor chairs
USE **sack-back Windsor chairs**

loop handles
USE **ring handles**

loop windows
RT.1196
ALT **loop window**
SN Long, narrow, vertical windows cut in walls or parapets of Medieval structures.
UF windows, loop
CN V.RT.AFU.BUE.AFU.BIQ.AFU

loopholes
RT.1197 (B)
ALT **loophole**
SN Small openings (as in a wall or parapet) through which small arms may be discharged; similar openings to admit light and air or to permit observation. (W)
UF aleois
arrow loops
eyelets (windows)
holes, shot
loops, arrow
oillets
shot holes
slits, vision
vision slits
CN V.RT.AFU.BUE.AFU.BIQ.ALO

loops, arrow
USE **loopholes**

loose boxes
USE **box stalls**

loose fill insulation
USE **fill insulation**

loose-joint butt hinges
USE **loose-joint hinges**

loose-joint hinges
TF.99
ALT **loose-joint hinge**
SN Door hinges that can be separated by lifting. The door can thus be removed without unscrewing the hinges. (MEANS)
UF butt hinges, loose-joint
hinges, loose-joint
hinges, loose-joint butt
loose-joint butt hinges
CN V.TF.AFU.AFU.AFU.AFU.CLM.AFU.ARI.ALO

loose-leaf catalogs
VW.100 (L)
ALT **loose-leaf catalog**
SN Catalogs comprised of sheets of paper fastened together in a loose-leaf binder.
UF catalogs, loose-leaf
catalogs, sheaf
sheaf catalogs
CN V.VW.AFU.AFU.AFU.FZU.ALO.AFU.BCW

loose-pin hinges
TF.122
ALT **loose-pin hinge**
SN Hinges having a removable pin to permit the two parts of the hinge to be separated. (BROWNL)
UF hinges, loose-pin
CN V.TF.AFU.AFU.AFU.AFU.CLM.AFU.ERE

loose seats
USE **slip seats**

Lop buri
USE **Lopburî**

Lopburî
FL.2419
UF Lop buri
Lopburi School
CN F.FL.ALO.ARI.BCW.BOK.AFU.DCU

Lopburi-Khmer
FL.2409
CN F.FL.ALO.ARI.BCW.BOK.AFU.AXC.AFU

Lopburi School
USE **Lopburî**

lopers
TG.965
ALT **loper**
SN Vertical sliding pieces that when pulled out support the fall front of a desk or secretary. (W)
UF draw runners
draw slips
runners, draw
slips, draw
CN V.TG.ALO.FOG

lopping axes
TB.840
ALT **lopping ax**
SN Axes used for lopping or cutting away the branches of trees after felling. (SALAM)
UF axes, lopping
axes, shedding
axes, topping
snedding axes
topping axes
CN V.TB.AFU.BCW.CFS.ALO.AFU.AXC.BCW

Lorraine crosses
USE **crosses of Lorraine**

Los Barrancos
FL.1105
UF Barrancoid
CN F.FL.ALO.ALO.ALO.ALO.ARI.ALO

Los Chenes
USE **Chenes**

Los Ortices
FL.1067
CN F.FL.ALO.ALO.ALO.ALO.AFU.ALO.BCW.ALO.AFU

loss, heat
USE **heat loss**

lost cities
RD.38 (B)
ALT **lost city**
SN Use for settlements whose localities are no longer known or, if the general location is known, factual information about the settlement is scarce.
UF cities, lost
lost villages
villages, lost
CN V.RD.AFU.ARI.ALO

lost color ware
FL.1101
UF color ware, lost
lost-colour ware
ware, lost color
CN F.FL.ALO.ALO.ALO.ALO.ALO.ALO.ALO.AXC.ALO

lost-colour ware
USE **lost color ware**

lost pattern casting
USE **lost-wax process**

lost villages
USE **lost cities**

lost-wax process
KT.133 (L)
SN A method of casting metal in a mold, the cavity of which is formed with wax that is then heated and drained. (MAYER)
UF casting, cavityless
casting, full mold
casting, investment
casting, lost pattern
casting, vaporization
casting, wax
cavityless casting
cire perdue
full mold casting
investing (metal casting)
investment casting
lost pattern casting
mold casting, full
vaporization casting
wax casting
CN K.KT.AFU.ALO.DOI.ARI.ARI

lots
RK.1588 (B)
ALT **lot**
SN Use for parcels of land with fixed boundaries occupied or capable of being occupied by one building or use, including accessory buildings, and not divided by any public highway or alley.
UF building lots
lots, building
parcels
plots
CN V.RK.ALO.ARI.BUE

lots, building
USE **lots**

lots, meeting house
USE **greens**

lots, parking
USE **parking lots**

lots, tot
USE **tot lots**

lots, used car
USE **used car lots**

lots, vacant
USE **vacant lots**

Lotto
FL.3526
CN F.FL.ALO.BIQ.AFU.FOG.ARI.ALO

lotus
DG.59
SN Use for the decorative motif of highly conventionalized flowers or buds derived from certain Egyptian plants; common in ancient Egyptian art and, in classicizing styles, in anthemions.
CN D.DG.AFU.AFU.DIO.BUE

lotus bud capitals
USE **lotus capitals**

lotus capitals
RT.127
ALT **lotus capital**
SN Use for capitals resembling a lotus bud, common in ancient Egyptian architecture.
UF capitals, lotus
capitals, lotus bud
lotus bud capitals
CN V.RT.AFU.AFU.AFU.AXC.BIQ.ALO.ARI.AFU.CLM

Lou-tung
USE **Loudong**

Loudong
FL.1932
UF Lou-tung
CN F.FL.ALO.ARI.ALO.AFU.AFU.AXC.ALO.BOK

Louis Philippe
FL.3362
CN F.FL.ALO.BCW.ALO.AXC.DIO.BCW.ALO.BCW

Louis Quatorze
USE **Louis XIV**

Louis Quinze
USE **Louis XV**

Louis Seize
USE **Louis XVI**

Louis XIII
FL.3215 (R)
CN F.FL.ALO.BCW.ALO.ARI.BIQ.BIQ.ARI.ALO.ARI.ARI

Louis XIV
FL.3217 (R)
UF Louis Quatorze
CN F.FL.ALO.BCW.ALO.ARI.BIQ.BIQ.ARI.ALO.ARI.BCW

Louis XV
FL.3218 (R)
UF Louis Quinze
CN F.FL.ALO.BCW.ALO.ARI.BIQ.BIQ.ARI.ALO.ARI.BIQ

Louis XVI
FL.3360 (R)
UF Louis Seize
CN F.FL.ALO.BCW.ALO.AXC.DIO.BCW.ALO.ARI

Louisiade
FL.3640
CN F.FL.ALO.BOK.ALO.BCW.ALO.ARI.ALO

lounge chairs
USE **chaises longues**

loungers
USE **chaises longues**

lounges
RM.175
ALT **lounge**
CN V.RM.AFU.DIO.ALO.CXA.BZY

lounges (couches)
USE **couches**

lounges, cocktail
USE **cocktail lounges**

lounges, V.I.P.
USE **V.I.P. lounges**

louver boards
RT.1006
ALT **louver board**
SN Narrow boards placed at an angle in a louver. (DAC)
UF boards, lever
boards, louver
boards, luffer
lever boards
luffer boards
CN V.RT.AFU.ARI.ALO.ARI.ALO.AFU

louver doors
RT.857
ALT **louver door**
SN Doors containing a louver or louvers, usually with horizontal blades providing for the passage of air while the door is closed. (DAC)
UF doors, louver
doors, shutter
doors, slat
shutter doors
slat doors
CN V.RT.AFU.ARI.AFU.AFU.AFU.ALO.ARI.AFU.AFU.BOK.ARI

louver windows
RT.948
ALT **louver window**
SN Windows having a louver or louvers which fill all or part of the opening. (HAS)
UF windows, louver
CN V.RT.AFU.ARI.AFU.AFU.BOK.AFU.AFU.EWY.AXC

louvers
RT.1004 (B)
ALT **louver**
SN Assemblies of sloping, overlapping blades or slats, which may be fixed or adjustable; designed to admit air or light in varying degrees and to exclude rain or snow. Especially used in doors, windows, and the intake and discharge of mechanical ventilation systems. (DAC)
UF slats (louvers)
CN V.RT.AFU.ARI.ALO.ARI.AFU

louvers, sun
USE **brise-soleils**

Lovale
USE **Lwena**

love
BM.580 (L,R)
UF affection
CN B.BM.BUE.ARI.BZY

love letters
VW.26 (L)
ALT **love letter**
UF letters, love
CN V.VW.AFU.AFU.AFU.BIQ.AFU.ARI.BUE

love seats
TG.304 (N)
ALT **love seat**
SN 19th- and 20th-century term used for a small upholstered sofa or settee designed to seat two people. (FAIRB)
UF chairs, courting
courting chairs
seats, love
CN V.TG.AFU.AFU.ALO.ALO.BUE.AXC

Lovedu
FL.570 (L)
UF Lobedu
CN F.FL.ALO.AFU.AXC.ARI.BCW.AFU

Lovelock
FL.909
CN F.FL.ALO.ALO.ALO.AFU.ALO.ARI.ALO.AXC

low-alloy steel
USE **high-strength low-alloy steel**

low-back armchairs, Windsor
USE **low-back Windsor chairs**

low back chairs (backstools)
USE **backstools**

low-back Windsor chairs
TG.103 (N)
ALT **low-back Windsor chair**
SN Windsor armchairs with a low back that terminates at arm level and usually is comprised of a three-piece sawn arm rail that follows the outside curve of the seat. (EVANS)
UF armchairs, Windsor low-back
captain's chairs
chairs, captain's
chairs, low-back Windsor
firehouse Windsor chairs
low-back armchairs, Windsor
Windsor chairs, firehouse
Windsor chairs, low-back
Windsor low-back armchairs
CN V.TG.AFU.AFU.ALO.AFU.AFU.AFU.MLC.BOK

low-carbon steel
MT.345
SN Steel with .15% to .30% carbon. (MH)
UF machine steel
machinery steel
mild steel
steel, low-carbon
steel, machine
steel, machinery

steel, mild
CN M.MT.AFU.AFU.AFU.BZY.AFU.AFU.AFU.AFU.ALO.AFU.AFU.AFU

low cases
USE **low chests**

low cases of drawers
USE **low chests**

low chests
TG.741 (N)
ALT **low chest**
SN Popular name for a type of 18th-century American dressing table with drawers, set on high legs, and similar in form to the lower section of a high chest of drawers, which it was often made to match.
UF cases, low
chests of drawers, low
chests, half
chests, low
drawers, low chests of
half chests
low cases
low cases of drawers
low chests of drawers
lowboys
lowdaddys
CN V.TG.AFU.AFU.BIQ.BOK.ALO.CLM.BCW

low chests of drawers
USE **low chests**

low clothes presses
TG.515
ALT **low clothes press**
UF low wardrobes
presses, low clothes
wardrobes, low
CN V.TG.AFU.AFU.AXC.ALO.BUE.CXA.AFU.AFU

low cost housing
RG.70 (B)
SN Use for housing whose ultimate cost to the occupant is low, generally due to assistance from government subsidies. Distinguished from **low income housing,** which refers to the mandated low income of the occupants rather than the low cost of the units.
UF housing, low cost
housing, low rent
low rent housing
low rent public housing
public housing, low rent
CN V.RG.AFU.AFU.BOK.AXC.AFU.ALO

Low Country
USE **Netherlandish**

low-energy buildings
USE **energy efficient buildings**

low-heat cement
MT.13
UF cement, low-heat
cement, type IV
type IV cement
CN M.MT.AFU.AFU.AFU.ALO.AFU.AFU.ARI.AFU.ALO

low income housing
RG.73 (A,L)
SN Use for housing units available to occupants whose income does not exceed certain maximum income limits set by local housing authorities. Distinguished from **low cost housing,** which refers to the subsidized low rent of the units rather than the low income of the occupants.
UF housing for low income persons
housing, low income
CN V.RG.AFU.AFU.BOK.AXC.AFU.ARI

low-light photography
USE **available light photography**

low-post beds
TG.368
ALT **low-post bed**
SN Beds with two or four posts approximately four feet in height.
UF beds, low-post
beds, post
bedsteads, low-post
low-post bedsteads
post beds
CN V.TG.AFU.AFU.ARI.AFU.AFU.DOI

low-post bedsteads
USE **low-post beds**

low relief
USE **bas-relief**

low rent housing
USE **low cost housing**

low rent public housing
USE **low cost housing**

low-rise buildings
RK.9
ALT **low-rise building**
SN Use for buildings of five stories or fewer accessible by stairs only; commonly applied to apartment houses and some commercial buildings.
UF buildings, low-rise
CN V.RK.AFU.ALO.AFU.AFU.AFU.AFU

low-rise housing
RG.58 (A)
SN Use for housing of two to four stories accessible by stairs only.
UF housing, low-rise
CN V.RG.AFU.AFU.BOK.AFU.ARI

low stools
USE **joint stools**

low wardrobes
USE **low clothes presses**

low-water input gardens
USE **xeriscapes**

lowboys
USE **low chests**

lowdaddys
USE **low chests**

lower
DC.39
CN D.DC.AFU.ALO.ARI.DCU

Lower Loup
FL.920
CN F.FL.ALO.ALO.ALO.AFU.ALO.ARI.AXC.ARI

Lower Paleolithic
FL.9 (L)
UF Paleolithic, Lower
CN F.FL.AFU.BCW.AFU.AFU.AFU

Lower Perigordian
FL.2470
UF Perigordian, Lower
CN F.FL.ALO.AXC.AFU.ARI.ALO.BCW.AFU

Lower Sepik
FL.3654
UF Sepik, Lower
CN F.FL.ALO.BOK.ALO.BCW.ALO.BCW.ALO.AFU

Lowestoft, Chinese
USE **Chinese export porcelain**

Lowestoft, Oriental
USE **Chinese export porcelain**

Lowland
USE **Netherlandish**

lowside windows
RT.961 (B)
ALT **lowside window**
SN Windows, usually very small, set much below the level of the larger windows, especially in English churches. (RS)
UF lepers' squints
lychnoscopes
offertory windows
vulne windows
windows, lowside
windows, offertory
windows, vulne
CN V.RT.AFU.ARI.AFU.AFU.BOK.AFU.ARI.AXC

loxodromes
USE **portolanos**

lozenges
DG.28
ALT **lozenge**
SN Use for figures that are squares or rhombuses rotated to have their corners on the horizontal and vertical axes. Common as an isolated motif, in a diaper pattern, or in a running series.
UF diamonds (motifs)
CN D.DG.AFU.AFU.BIQ.BCW

Lozi
FL.453 (L)
UF Barotse
Barozi
Rotse
CN F.FL.ALO.AFU.AXC.ALO.ALO.ALO.ALO

LRCs
USE **learning resource centers**

LRT
USE **light rail transit**

Luang Prabang
FL.2395
CN F.FL.ALO.ARI.BCW.AXC.ALO

Luba
FL.495 (L)
UF Baluba
CN F.FL.ALO.AFU.AXC.ALO.ALO.BCW.BCW

Luba Empire
FL.126 (L)
CN F.FL.ALO.AFU.ALO.ALO.ARI.AFU

Luba-Lunda Kingdoms
FL.125
CN F.FL.ALO.AFU.ALO.ALO.ARI

Luba, Northern
USE **Buli**

lubricants
MT.2622
CN M.MT.AFU.ARI.FOG

lubricating oil
MT.1994 (L)
UF oil, lubricating
CN M.MT.AFU.AFU.ARI.ARI.ALO.ARI

Lucanian
FL.2638
CN F.FL.ALO.AXC.ALO.AFU.ALO.AXC.ALO.BIQ.BIQ

lucarnes
USE **dormers**

Luchazi
FL.454 (L)
UF Valuchazi
CN F.FL.ALO.AFU.AXC.ALO.ALO.ALO.ARI

Lucite (TM)
MT.2120 (L)
SN Methyl methacrylate made by E. I. du Pont de Nemours and Company, Inc., marketed in rolling powder and in rolls, tubes, and cast and molded sheets. (MH12)
CN M.MT.AFU.AFU.ARI.BUE.ALO.AXC.AFU.ALO.AFU.AFU

Lucknow
USE **Oudh**

lucullan marble
USE **lucullite**

lucullite
MT.776
SN Egyptian marble colored black by carbon. (W)
UF lucullan marble
marble, lucullan
CN M.MT.AFU.AFU.AFU.DCU.AFU.ARI.ARI.ARI.AFU.AXC

luffer boards
USE **louver boards**

lug chairs
USE **easy chairs**

lug sills
RT.981
ALT **lug sill**
SN Window sills in a brick or stone wall, where the sill extends beyond the width of the window opening and with the ends of the sill set in the well. Distiguished from **slip sills** which are just as long as the window is wide and fit into the walls between the jambs.
UF sills, lug
CN V.RT.AFU.ARI.AFU.AFU.BOK.ALO.BOK.ALO.ALO.AFU

lugs
USE **wings (furniture components)**

Luguru
FL.600 (L)
CN F.FL.ALO.AFU.AXC.AXC.ALO.BIQ

Luiseño
FL.1257 (L)
CN F.FL.ALO.ALO.ARI.AFU.ALO.CLM

Lule
FL.1623 (L)
CN F.FL.ALO.ALO.ARI.ARI.ALO.ALO.BOK

Lulua
FL.450 (L)
UF Bena Luluwa
CN F.FL.ALO.AFU.AXC.ALO.ALO.AFU.ALO

lumachella
MT.767
UF lumachelle marble
marble, lumachelle
CN M.MT.AFU.AFU.AFU.DCU.AFU.ARI.ARI.ALO.BOK.ARI

lumachelle marble
USE **lumachella**

lumbang oil
USE **candlenut oil**

lumbayo
MT.1205
UF Tarrietia javanica
CN M.MT.AFU.AFU.ALO.BIQ.DCU.AFU.AFU.AFU.HIK

lumber
MT.1420 (A,L)
SN Any material, such as boards, planks, or beams cut from timber to a size and form suitable for marketing. (PUTNAM)
CN M.MT.AFU.AFU.ALO.BIQ.DCU.ALO.BOK

lumber camps
RG.64 (L)
ALT **lumber camp**
UF camps, logging
camps, lumber
logging camps
CN V.RG.AFU.AFU.BOK.ALO.AFU.ARI

lumber rooms
USE **storerooms**

lumber sheds
RK.1216 (L)
ALT **lumber shed**
UF sheds, lumber
CN V.RK.AFU.ALO.ALO.GFO.BIQ.AXC

lumber, air-dried
USE **air-dried lumber**

lumber, air-seasoned
USE **air-dried lumber**

lumber, boat
USE **boat lumber**

lumber, clear
USE **clear lumber**

lumber, common dimension
USE **dimension lumber**

lumber, dimension
USE **dimension lumber**

lumber, dressed
USE **dressed lumber**

lumber, dry
USE **air-dried lumber**

lumber, factory
USE **factory lumber**

lumber, finish
USE **finish lumber**

lumber, flat-sawed
USE **plain-sawed lumber**

lumber, form
USE **form lumber**

lumber, green
USE **green lumber**

lumber, kiln-dried
USE **kiln-dried lumber**

lumber, matched
USE **matched lumber**

lumber, patterned
USE **patterned lumber**

lumber, plain-sawed
USE **plain-sawed lumber**

lumber, plank
USE **plank**

lumber, quarter-sawed
USE **quarter-sawed lumber**

lumber, rough
USE **rough lumber**

lumber, select
USE **select lumber**

lumber, shop
USE **factory lumber**

lumber, structural
USE **structural lumber**

lumber, surfaced
USE **dressed lumber**

lumber, worked
USE **worked lumber**

lumber, yard
USE **yard lumber**

lumberjacks
USE **loggers**

lumbermen
HG.376 (L)
ALT **lumberman**
SN People who engage in or oversee the cutting, processing, and marketing of lumber. (WCOL)
CN H.HG.AFU.AXC.BIQ.ALO.AXC.BOK

lumberyards
RK.163 (L,B)
ALT **lumberyard**
UF timber yards
yards, timber
CN V.RK.AFU.ALO.ALO.ALO.ARI.BIQ.AFU.CXA

Lumbu
FL.402 (L)
UF Balombo
Balumbu
CN F.FL.ALO.AFU.AXC.ALO.AFU.ALO.ARI

Lumière process
USE **Autochrome process**

luminescence
BM.857 (L,B)
CN B.BM.CFS.AXC.ALO.AFU.ALO.ALO.BCW

Luminist
FL.1751 (L,R)
ALT **Luminism**
CN F.FL.ALO.ALO.BCW.AFU.CFS.ARI

luminous ceilings
RT.731 (B)
ALT **luminous ceiling**
SN Ceiling-area lighting systems comprising a continuous surface of transmitting material with light sources mounted above it. (DAC)
UF ceilings, luminous
CN V.RT.AFU.ALO.AFU.ALO.CFS

luminous color
BM.113
SN Applies to colors which exceed in brightness the visual field and appear to emit light. (OCA)
UF color, luminous
CN B.BM.AFU.AFU.ARI.BOK.ALO.AFU.BCW

luminous paint
MT.2545
SN Any paint that glows in the dark. (MAYER)
UF paint, luminous
CN M.MT.AFU.ARI.CRG.ALO.BCW.ARI.BOK

lumiprints
USE **contact prints**

Lummi
FL.1349 (L)
CN F.FL.ALO.ALO.ARI.AFU.BIQ.DOI

lump lime
USE **quicklime**

lump sum contracts
USE **fixed-price contracts**

Luna marble
MT.830
UF lunense macchiato
marble, Luna
marmor Luniense
CN M.MT.AFU.AFU.AFU.DCU.AFU.ARI.ARI.ARI.BOK.CFS

Luna polychrome
USE **Luna ware**

Luna ware
FL.1078
UF Luna polychrome
polychrome, Luna
ware, Luna
CN F.FL.ALO.ALO.ALO.ALO.ALO.AFU.ALO.AFU.AFU

lunar bases
RK.1361 (A,L,B)
ALT **lunar base**
UF bases, lunar
bases, moon
moon bases
moon settlements
settlements, moon
CN V.RK.AFU.ALO.ARI.AXC.AXC.AFU.AFU

lunch counter stools
USE **counter stools**

lunch stools
USE **counter stools**

luncheonettes
USE **lunchrooms**

lunchrooms
RM.117 (A,L,B)
ALT **lunchroom**
SN Rooms or small restaurants specializing in light meals or snacks ready to serve or quickly prepared; includes such places where food brought from elsewhere may be eaten.
UF canteens (lunchrooms)
commissaries
luncheonettes
CN V.RM.AFU.DIO.ALO.BCW.CFS

Lunda
FL.455 (L)
UF Alunda
Tulunda
CN F.FL.ALO.AFU.AXC.ALO.ALO.ALO.AXC

Lunda Empire
FL.127 (L)
CN F.FL.ALO.AFU.ALO.ALO.ARI.ALO

Lundu
FL.192
CN F.FL.ALO.AFU.AXC.AFU.AFU.AFU.ALO.BOK

lunense macchiato
USE **Luna marble**

lunes
USE **gores**

lunette-back chairs
TG.140
ALT **lunette-back chair**
UF chairs, lunette-back
CN V.TG.AFU.AFU.ALO.AFU.AFU.AFU.NIE.CLM

lunettes
RT.927 (A,L,R)
ALT **lunette**
SN Crescent-shaped or semicircular areas on a wall or vaulted ceiling, framed by an arch or vault; includes openings or windows in such areas. (HAS)
CN V.RT.AFU.ARI.AFU.AFU.BOK.AFU.AFU.DIO

Lung-ch'ing
USE **Longqing**

Lung-ch'uan ware
USE **Longshan**

Lungshan
USE **Longshan**

Lungu
FL.545
CN F.FL.ALO.AFU.AXC.ARI.AFU.ARI

Luntu
FL.442
CN F.FL.ALO.AFU.AXC.ALO.ALO.AFU.AFU.BIQ

Luo
FL.649 (L)
CN F.FL.ALO.AFU.AXC.AXC.BCW.BUE

Lupemban
FL.58
CN F.FL.ALO.AFU.AFU.ALO.ARI.ARI

Lupembo-Tshitolian
FL.61
CN F.FL.ALO.AFU.AFU.ALO.AXC.ALO

lustre ware, Fostat
USE **Fostat ware**

lustrous
DC.136 (L)
ALT **luster**
SN Having a reflective surface less bright than glossy and giving more an impression of depth in the finish than a surface said to have a sheen.
CN D.DC.AFU.BCW.ALO

lustrous ware, black
USE **black lustrous ware**

lustrous ware, red
USE **red lustrous ware**

lute (cement)
USE **sulfur cement**

Lutheran
BM.637 (L,B)
CN B.BM.BZY.AFU.ALO.ARI.BOK

lutherns
USE **dormers**

luthiers
HG.566
ALT **luthier**
SN Makers of stringed instruments, such as violins. (W)
CN H.HG.AFU.AXC.BUE.AXC.CLM

Luvale
USE **Lwena**

luxullianite
MT.601
SN A coarse red and black stone composed of red orthoclase, gray quartz, and black tourmaline. (RS)
CN M.MT.AFU.AFU.AFU.DCU.AFU.AFU.AFU.AFU.AFU.ARI.ALO.ARI.AFU

Lwalwa
FL.443
UF Balualua
CN F.FL.ALO.AFU.AXC.ALO.ALO.AFU.AFU.BOK

Lwena
FL.456 (L)
UF Balovale
Lovale
Luvale
CN F.FL.ALO.AFU.AXC.ALO.ALO.ALO.BCW

Ly
FL.2430
CN F.FL.ALO.ARI.BCW.BUE.AFU.ARI

lycees
USE **high schools**

lyceums
RK.851 (L)
ALT **lyceum**
CN V.RK.AFU.ALO.ALO.CXA.ARI.AXC.BOK.AFU

lych-gates
USE **lich-gates**

lych stones
USE **lich stones**

lychnites marble
USE **Parian marble**

lychnoscopes
USE **lowside windows**

Lycian
FL.2863 (L)
CN F.FL.ALO.AXC.ARI.AFU.ALO.AFU

Lydenburg
FL.134
CN F.FL.ALO.AFU.ALO.ARI.ALO

Lydian
FL.2861 (L)
CN F.FL.ALO.AXC.ARI.AFU.AFU.BIQ

Lydian stone
USE **touchstone**

Lyonaise marble
MT.761
SN Coarsely mottled marble of Malletts Bay on Lake Champlain. (RS)
UF marble, Lyonaise
CN M.MT.AFU.AFU.AFU.DCU.AFU.ARI.ARI.ALO.AXC

lyre-back chairs
TG.146
ALT **lyre-back chair**
SN Use for chairs with back splats in the form of a lyre, a Regency period motif popularized by Adam, Hepplewhite, Sheraton, and Duncan Phyfe.
UF banister-back chairs, harp
chairs, harp-back
chairs, harp banister-back
chairs, lyre-back
harp-back chairs
harp banister-back chairs
CN V.TG.AFU.AFU.ALO.AFU.AFU.AFU.NIE.CXA.ALO

lyre-shaped cabinets
TG.416
ALT **lyre-shaped cabinet**
UF cabinets, lyre-shaped
CN V.TG.AFU.AFU.AXC.ALO.ARI.AFU.BCW

lyric writers
USE **lyricists**

Lyrical Abstraction
FL.3731 (R)
SN Use for certain works that continued Abstract Expressionism into the 1960s and 1970s (e.g., by Guston, Frankenthaler). For the French painting of the late 1940s sometimes called Abstraction Lyrique, use **Tachiste.**
UF Abstraction, Lyrical
CN F.FL.ALO.BUE.ARI.DOI

lyricists
HG.78
ALT **lyricist**
UF lyric writers
songwriters
writers, lyric
writers, song
CN H.HG.AFU.AXC.AXC.AFU.AFU.AFU.BIQ.BIQ.BIQ

Lysippic
FL.2687
CN F.FL.ALO.AXC.ALO.AFU.ALO.BCW.ALO.BCW

M-roofs
USE **double-gable roofs**

Ma-Hsia
USE **Ma-Xia**

Ma Karanga
USE **Karanga**

Ma-Xia
FL.1933
UF Ma-Hsia
Maxia jia
CN F.FL.ALO.ARI.ALO.AFU.AFU.AXC.ALO.BUE

Ma'adi
FL.2777
CN F.FL.ALO.AXC.ALO.ARI.AFU.AFU.AFU.AXC

Mabudu
USE **Budu**

macadam roads
USE **macadamized roads**

macadamized roads
RK.1566 (L)
ALT **macadamized road**
UF macadam roads
roads, macadamized
CN V.RK.ALO.ALO.BIQ.ARI.BCW.AFU

Macaracas
FL.1091
UF Late Cocle
CN F.FL.ALO.ALO.ALO.ALO.ALO.ALO.AFU.BIQ

Maccabees, Feast of
USE **Hanukkah**

macchie
USE **sketches**

macchine
RK.1386

ALT **macchina**
SN Structures built for festivals, ceremonies, and funerals during the 17th and 18th centuries.
CN V.RK.AFU.ALO.AXC.CFS.AFU.ALO

Macedonian Renaissance
FL.3074 (R)
UF Renaissance, Macedonian
CN F.FL.ALO.BCW.ALO.AFU.ALO.ALO.ALO

macella
RK.141
ALT **macellum**
SN Designates ancient Roman meat markets; may also be used more generally for ancient Roman food markets.
CN V.RK.AFU.ALO.ALO.ALO.ARI.AXC.AFU

Machalilla
FL.1114
CN F.FL.ALO.ALO.ALO.ARI.ALO.ALO

machicolations
RT.1193
ALT **machicolation**
SN Projecting series of corbels often surmounting the walls of later Medieval fortifications, and carrying an overhanging portion of the stone floor of the rampart; also, the openings in the floor between the corbels for the delivery of missiles on the enemy below. (RS)
CN V.RT.AFU.BUE.AFU.BCW.ALO.AXC

machine aesthetic
BM.192 (R)
SN Concept in early 20th-century art extolling the machine age and urban culture, with, visually, an emphasis on geometric shapes.
UF aesthetic, machine
CN B.BM.AFU.AFU.AXC.CLM.BIQ

machine bolts
TF.317
ALT **machine bolt**
UF bolts, machine
CN V.TF.AFU.AFU.AFU.ALO.AFU.ALO.AFU.BZY

machine-made paper
MT.1968
UF paper, machine-made
CN M.MT.AFU.AFU.ARI.ALO.ALO.AXC.AXC.ARI

machine-readable documents
USE **machine-readable records**

machine-readable records
VW.643 (L)
ALT **machine-readable record**
SN Document types in a format readable by a computer, such as on punched cards or tape or on magnetic media.
UF documents, machine-readable
electronic records
machine-readable documents
records, electronic
records, machine-readable
CN V.VW.AFU.ALO.AFU.DZW.ALO

machine screws
TF.471 (N)
ALT **machine screw**
UF screws, machine
CN V.TF.AFU.AFU.AFU.ALO.AFU.DIO.AFU.AXC

machine shops
RK.609 (L,B)
ALT **machine shop**
SN Use for places where metal and other substances are cut and shaped by machine tools.
UF shops, machine
CN V.RK.AFU.ALO.ALO.CLM.ALO.AFU.ARI

machine steel
USE **low-carbon steel**

machine tools
TB.7 (L)
ALT **machine tool**
SN Power-operated machines, such as lathes, used for general cutting and shaping of metal and other substances. (RHDEL2)
UF tools, machine
CN V.TB.AFU.AFU.ALO.ALO

machinery
TB.3 (L,R)
SN Use for the assemblage of machines or devices for doing work beyond human physical or mental limitations, or faster than the human hand.
UF machines
CN V.TB.AFU.AFU.AFU

machinery sheds
RK.1217
ALT **machinery shed**
UF sheds, machinery
CN V.RK.AFU.ALO.ALO.GFO.BIQ.BCW

machinery steel
USE **low-carbon steel**

machinery, boring
USE **boring machinery**

machinery, conveying
USE **conveyors**

machinery, crushing
USE **crushing machinery**

machinery, drilling
USE **drilling machinery**

machinery, excavating
USE **excavating equipment**

machinery, grading
USE **graders**

machinery, hoisting
USE **hoisting machinery**

machinery, hydraulic
USE **hydraulic machinery**

machinery, milling
USE **milling machinery**

machinery, pumping
USE **pumping machinery**

machinery, stage
USE **stage machinery**

machinery, theatrical
USE **stage machinery**

machinery, woodworking
USE **woodworking machinery**

machines
USE **machinery**

machines, arc welding
USE **arc welding machines**

machines, barking
USE **barkers**

machines, concrete finishing
USE **concrete finishing machines**

machines, ditching
USE **trenching machines**

machines, dividing
USE **dividing engines**

machines, drafting
USE **drafting machines**

machines, driving
USE **driving machines**

machines, fretsaw
USE **jigsaws**

machines, garden
USE **garden machines**

machines, gauffering
USE **goffering machines**

machines, goffering
USE **goffering machines**

machines, horse exercising
USE **chamber horses**

machines, planing
USE **planing machines**

machines, plastering
USE **plastering machines**

machines, sanding
USE **sanding machines**

machines, screw
USE **screw-cutting machines**

machines, screw-cutting
USE **screw-cutting machines**

machines, thread-cutting
USE **screw-cutting machines**

machines, trenching
USE **trenching machines**

machines, washing
USE **washing machines**

machines, winding
USE **winches**

machining
KT.166 (L)
ALT **machined**
SN Use for processes for changing the size or shape of a workpiece by means of machine-operated cutting tools.
CN K.KT.AFU.ALO.DOI.ERE.ALO

machinists
HG.445 (L)
ALT **machinist**
SN Persons who fabricate, assemble, or repair machinery; also craftsmen skilled in the use of machine tools. (W)
CN H.HG.AFU.AXC.BUE.ALO.BIQ

machos
TG.462
ALT **macho**
SN 15th- and 16th-century groom's chests with a single large compartment; made only in the Catalana region of Spain.
CN V.TG.AFU.AFU.AXC.ALO.AXC.CRG .ALO

Mack's cement
MT.24
SN Hard, quicksetting cement made of dehydrated gypsum to which is added a small percentage of calcined sodium sulfate and potassium sulfate; used for walls, and for floors, when mixed with sand. (MH)
UF cement, Mack's
CN M.AFU.AFU.AFU.ALO.AFU.AFU .BIQ.ALO

Mackenzie Inuit
USE **Western Arctic Inuit**

Maclura pomifera
USE **Osage orange**

Macon Plateau
FL.895
CN F.FL.ALO.ALO.ALO.AFU.ALO.ALO .BOK.BZY

macramé
KT.547 (L)
SN A technique of knotting threads; derived from the knotted fringe found on traditional Turkish towels. (THDAT)
CN K.KT.AFU.ALO.ELK.DUC.AFU.AXC. AFU

macrophotographs
VJ.115
ALT **macrophotograph**
SN Use for photographs in which the image is near life-size or larger. Distinct from the term **enlargements,** which only indicates that a photograph has been produced from a smaller photograph. For photographs taken through a microscope use **photomicrographs.**
UF photomacrographs
CN V.VJ.AFU.ARI.ALO.BOK

macrophotographs (enlargements)
USE **enlargements**

macrophotography
KT.416 (L,R)
SN Use for the techniques and the activity of producing macrophotographs.
UF photomacrography
CN K.KT.AFU.ALO.DUC.DIO.ARI.AXC. CRG

macrophotography (enlarging)
USE **enlarging**

Macú
FL.1585 (L)
UF Mahacú
Maku
Maucú
CN F.FL.ALO.ALO.ARI.ARI.AFU.DZW

Macuna
FL.1586 (L)
UF Buhagana
CN F.FL.ALO.ALO.ARI.ARI.AFU.EFQ

Macusi
FL.1587 (L)
CN F.FL.ALO.ALO.ARI.ARI.AFU.ELK

madder
MT.1526 (L)
SN Dye from the root of the madder plant, Rubia tinctorum; also used as a red pigment. It has now been largely replaced as a dyestuff by the synthetic dye alizarin.
UF alizari
crimson (natural dye)
Indian madder
lake, madder
madder lake
madder, Indian
madder, scarlet (natural dye)
munjeet
red, Turkey
root madder
scarlet madder (natural dye)
Turkey red
CN M.MT.AFU.AFU.ARI.AFU.AFU.AFU AFU.AFU.AXC.BOK

madder (color)
USE **moderate red**
moderate reddish orange
strong red
strong reddish orange

madder carmine
USE **moderate purplish red**
moderate red

madder lake
USE **alizarin madder**
madder
strong purplish red
strong red

madder lake, violet
USE **alizarin violet**

madder pink
USE **strong purplish red**

madder red
USE **moderate red**
moderate reddish orange
strong red
strong reddish orange

madder violet, dark
USE **dark grayish purple**

madder, alizarin
USE **alizarin madder**

madder, crimson
USE **vivid red**

madder, Indian
USE **madder**

madder, purple
USE **dark red**
moderate red

madder, rose
USE **strong purplish red**
vivid purplish red

madder, rose (alizarin)
USE **alizarin madder**

madder, scarlet
USE **strong yellowish pink**

madder, scarlet (natural dye)
USE **madder**

madder, synthetic
USE **alizarin madder**

madinas
USE **medinas**

Madjapahit
USE **Majapahit**

madrasas
RK.820 (A)
ALT **madrasa**
SN Use specifically for Islamic theological or law schools, especially when associated with a mosque, or generally for places of study.
CN V.RK.AFU.ALO.ALO.CXA.ARI.ALO. DOI.AFU

madre cream marble
MT.821
UF cream marble, madre
marble, madre cream

CN M.MT.AFU.AFU.AFU.DCU.AFU.ARI.
ARI.ARI.BOK.AFU.ALO

madrepore marble
MT.762
UF marble, madrepore
CN M.MT.AFU.AFU.AFU.DCU.AFU.ARI.
ARI.ALO.BCW

Madura
USE **Nayak**

magasins de nouveautés
RK.174
ALT **magasin de nouveautés**
SN Use for drapery and dry goods stores, prevalent in the early 19th century, which, contrary to standard merchandising practices of the day, kept large stocks of goods on the premises, grouping related items together in departments.
UF nouveautés, magasins de
CN V.RK.AFU.ALO.ALO.ALO.ARI.BIQ.
ALO.BCW.AFU

magazine illustration
USE **periodical illustration**

magazine illustrations
USE **periodical illustrations**

magazine racks
TG.614 (N)
ALT **magazine rack**
UF racks, magazine
CN V.TG.AFU.AFU.BIQ.AXC.ARI

magazine stands (newsstands)
USE **newsstands**

magazines
USE **periodicals**

magazines (military buildings)
RK.858 (N)
ALT **magazine (military building)**
SN Designates storage buildings for explosives and ammunition.
CN V.RK.AFU.ALO.ALO.DIO.AFU.ARI

magazines, house
USE **house organs**

magazines, powder
USE **powder magazines**

Magdalenian
FL.2468 (L)
CN F.FL.ALO.AXC.AFU.ARI.ALO.AXC

Magen Davids
USE **Stars of David**

magenta
MT.1540
UF fuchsine
CN M.MT.AFU.AFU.ARI.AFU.AFU.AFU.
AFU.ALO.ALO.AFU

magenta (color)
USE **dark purplish red**
dark reddish purple
deep purplish red
grayish purplish red
moderate purplish red
strong purple
strong purplish red
strong reddish purple
vivid purplish red
vivid violet

magenta purple, dull
USE **strong reddish purple**

magenta rose
USE **dark purplish red**
deep purplish red
moderate purplish red

magenta, deep
USE **vivid purplish red**

magic
KD.303 (L,R)
CN K.KD.AFU.BIQ.ARI

magic lantern slides
USE **lantern slides**

Magic Realist
FL.3297 (L,R)
ALT **Magic Realism**
UF Realist, Magic
CN F.FL.ALO.BCW.ALO.AXC.DCU.BIQ

magistrates
HG.682 (L)
ALT **magistrate**
SN Civil officers charged with the administration of laws. (OED)
CN H.HG.AFU.AXC.CFS.CFS.BOK

Maglemosian
FL.2481 (L)
CN F.FL.ALO.AXC.AFU.AXC.BOK

magnesia cement
MT.27 (L)
SN Magnesium oxide mixed with water, often with the addition of asbestos fibers; used to cover such things as steam pipes and furnaces. (DAC)
UF cement, magnesia
CN M.MT.AFU.AFU.AFU.ALO.AFU.AFU
.BOK

magnesian limestone
MT.684
UF dolomitic limestone
limestone, dolomitic
limestone, magnesian
CN M.MT.AFU.AFU.AFU.DCU.AFU.
ALO.AFU.ALO.ALO.AFU.ALO.AXC

magnesite
MT.531 (L,B)
SN White to bluish gray mineral used in the manufacture of bricks and as an ore of magnesium. (MH)
CN M.MT.AFU.AFU.AFU.CFS.AFU.FCS

magnesium
MT.437 (L,R)
SN A metallic element, silvery white, which is the lightest metal that is stable under ordinary conditions. (MH)
CN M.MT.AFU.AFU.AFU.BZY.AFU.AFU.
ARI.BUE

magnesium mica
USE **phlogopite**

magnetic catches
TF.48
ALT **magnetic catch**
UF catches, magnetic
CN V.TF.AFU.AFU.AFU.AFU.BCW.BUE

magnetic disks
VW.647
ALT **magnetic disk**
SN Magnetizable material in disk form, capable of storing information in the form of electromagnetic signals.
UF disks (magnetic disks)
disks, magnetic
CN V.VW.AFU.ALO.AFU.DZW.ALO.ARI

magnetic iron ore
USE **magnetite**

magnetic paint
MT.2547
UF paint, magnetic
CN M.MT.AFU.ARI.CRG.ALO.BCW.ARI
.BUE

magnetic properties
BM.946 (L)
UF properties, magnetic
CN B.BM.CFS.AXC.BZY.BIQ

magnetic push catches
TF.49
ALT **magnetic push catch**
SN Magnetic catches with an inward and outward moving strike that retract and project by means of springs on successive applications of pressure. (DITTRI)
UF catches, magnetic push
push catches, magnetic
CN V.TF.AFU.AFU.AFU.AFU.BCW.BUE.
AFU

magnetic resonance accelerators
USE **cyclotrons**

magnetic tapes
VW.649 (L)
ALT **magnetic tape**
SN Magnetizable material in tape form, capable of storing information in the form of electromagnetic signals.
UF tapes, magnetic
CN V.VW.AFU.ALO.AFU.DZW.ALO.
AXC

magnetite
MT.513 (L)
UF iron ore, magnetic
magnetic iron ore
ore, magnetic iron
CN M.MT.AFU.AFU.AFU.CFS.AFU.CXA.
ARI

magnolia
MT.1206 (L)
CN M.MT.AFU.AFU.ALO.BIQ.DCU.AFU.AFU.AFU.HOE

magnolia graniflora
MT.1207
UF bull laurel
graniflora, magnolia
laurel magnolia
laurel, bull
magnolia, laurel
CN M.MT.AFU.AFU.ALO.BIQ.DCU.AFU.AFU.AFU.HOE.AFU

magnolia, laurel
USE **magnolia graniflora**

Mah
USE **Mano**

Mahacú
USE **Macú**

Mahafaly
FL.558 (L)
CN F.FL.ALO.AFU.AXC.ARI.ARI.AXC

mahals
RK.340
ALT **mahal**
SN Use for palaces in India, especially those of the Islamic period.
CN V.RK.AFU.ALO.ALO.AXC.ALO.BOK.BOK.ALO.ARI

Mahayana
BM.614 (L)
UF Buddhism, Mahayana
Great Vehicle
Mahayana Buddhism
Vehicle, Great
CN B.BM.BZY.AFU.AFU.ARI

Mahayana Buddhism
USE **Mahayana**

Mahendravarman
FL.2326
UF Chitrasena
CN F.FL.ALO.ARI.BCW.ALO.AFU.ARI.AFU

Mahican
FL.1299 (L)
UF Mohegan
Mohican
CN F.FL.ALO.ALO.ARI.AFU.ARI.BIQ

Mahmud I
FL.3505
UF Mahmut I
CN F.FL.ALO.BIQ.AFU.FOG.AFU.FIM

Mahmud II
FL.3511
UF Mahmut II
CN F.FL.ALO.BIQ.AFU.FOG.AFU.GRC

Mahmut I
USE **Mahmud I**

Mahmut II
USE **Mahmud II**

mahoe
MT.1325
UF blue mahoe
Hibiscus elatus
mahoe, blue
majagua
Maltese wood
wood, Maltese
CN M.MT.AFU.AFU.ALO.BIQ.DCU.AFU.AFU.AFU.MQW.BCW

mahoe, blue
USE **mahoe**

mahogany
MT.1208 (L,R)
CN M.MT.AFU.AFU.ALO.BIQ.DCU.AFU.AFU.AFU.HTY

mahogany birch
USE **sweet birch**

mahogany, African
USE **African mahogany**

mahogany, Borneo
USE **Borneo mahogany**

mahogany, branch
USE **crotch mahogany**

mahogany, crotch
USE **crotch mahogany**

mahogany, Cuban
USE **South American mahogany**

mahogany, Honduras
USE **South American mahogany**

mahogany, Philippine
USE **lauan**

mahogany, South American
USE **South American mahogany**

mahogany, Spanish
USE **South American mahogany**

mahogany, West Indies
USE **West Indies mahogany**

mahogany, white
USE **white mahogany**

Mahoungoue
USE **Hongwe**

maiden towers
USE **keeps**

Maiemir
FL.2130
UF Mayemir
CN F.FL.ALO.ARI.ARI.AFU.BIQ.ALO

mail art
USE **correspondence art**

mail chutes
RM.214 (L)
ALT **mail chute**
UF chutes, letter
chutes, mail
letter chutes
CN V.RM.AFU.DIO.ALO.DIO.ARI.ARI

mail order catalogs
VW.109 (R)
ALT **mail order catalog**
UF catalogs, mail order
CN V.VW.AFU.AFU.AFU.FZU.ALO.ALO.ARI.AFU.ALO

mail slots
USE **letter-box plates**

mail, electronic
USE **electronic mail**

mailboxes
RM.498 (A,L,N,B)
ALT **mailbox**
SN Use for both public and private boxes for pickup and delivery of mail.
CN V.RM.ALO.ALO.ALO.ALO.DUC.ALO

mailing
KT.758
SN To send through a postal service. (NARA)
CN K.KT.AFU.ALO.HIK.ALO

mailing lists
VW.264 (L)
ALT **mailing list**
UF lists, mailing
CN V.VW.AFU.AFU.AFU.FZU.BCW.AFU.AXC

main (front)
USE **front**

main altars
USE **high altars**

main contractors
USE **general contractors**

main elevations
USE **front elevations**

main roads
USE **primary roads**

main sewers
RK.552
ALT **main sewer**
SN Designates public sanitary sewers into which branch sewers are connected.
UF sewers, main
sewers, trunk
trunk sewers
CN V.RK.AFU.ALO.ALO.CFS.ALO.AFU.ALO.ALO.BCW

main streets
RK.1543 (A)
ALT **main street**
SN Use only for principal thorough-

fares, usually those along which are found the primary mercantile establishments, of small to mid-size settlements.
UF streets, main
CN V.RK.ALO.ALO.BIQ.ARI.AFU.ALO.ARI.ALO

main ties
USE **tie beams**

mainframes
TB.148
ALT **mainframe**
SN Large computers, often the hub of a system serving many users. (RHDEL2)
CN V.TB.AFU.ARI.BCW.ARI.ARI

mains
RT.1471
ALT **main**
SN The principal supply pipes that feed all branches of a plumbing system. (MEANS)
CN V.RT.ALO.BCW.ALO.ARI.BZY.AXC

mains, water
USE **water mains**

maintaining
KG.110 (A,L,B)
SN Taking action which keeps people, physical objects, or property operational or sustains them in their existing state. (RLG7)
UF maintenance
CN K.KG.AFU.AFU.BCW

maintenance
USE **maintaining**

maintenance men
HG.45
ALT **maintenance man**
SN Persons who keep buildings, shops, or equipment in good repair. (W)
CN H.HG.AFU.AXC.ARI.BUE

maiolica
MT.153 (L,R)
SN Use for Italian tin-glazed earthenware produced from the Renaissance to the present. For similar but non-Italian products, especially since the mid-19th century, use **majolica.**
CN M.MT.AFU.AFU.AFU.AXC.ALO.ALO.AFU.ALO.AFU.AXC

maiolica, Castelli
USE **Castelli maiolica**

mairies
USE **hôtels de ville**

maize oil
MT.2030
UF corn oil
oil, corn
oil, maize
CN M.MT.AFU.AFU.ARI.ARI.AXC.ALO.BCW

majagua
USE **mahoe**

Majapahit
FL.2384
UF Madjapahit
CN F.FL.ALO.ARI.BCW.ARI.ALO.AXC.ALO.AFU.ALO

majolica
MT.154 (L,R)
SN Use for certain earthenware, usually lead-glazed, popular since the mid-19th century. Distinct from **maiolica,** which refers to Italian tin-glazed ware produced from the Renaissance to the present.
UF industrial majolica
majolica, industrial
CN M.MT.AFU.AFU.AFU.AXC.ALO.ALO.AFU.ALO.AFU.BCW

majolica, Castelli
USE **Castelli maiolica**

majolica, industrial
USE **majolica**

major assemblies
USE **assembly drawings**

Makah
FL.1350 (L)
UF Cape Indians
CN F.FL.ALO.ALO.ARI.AFU.BIQ.DUC

makers, color
USE **artists' colormen**

makers, furniture
USE **furniture workers**

makers, lace
USE **lace makers**

makers, nail
USE **nail makers**

makeup arrangers
HG.456
ALT **makeup arranger**
SN Persons who arrange, group, and lock galley setups of type, illustrations, and headings according to dummy makeup sheets, for printing. (DOT)
UF arrangers, makeup
hands, stone
stone hands
CN H.HG.AFU.AXC.BUE.ALO.CFS.BCW

Makiritaré
FL.1588 (L)
UF Yecuana
CN F.FL.ALO.ALO.ARI.ARI.AFU.ERE

Makonde
FL.659 (L)
CN F.FL.ALO.AFU.AXC.AXC.BIQ.ALO

Maku
USE **Macú**

Makua
FL.660 (L)
UF Kua
Wamakua
CN F.FL.ALO.AFU.AXC.AXC.BIQ.ARI

malachite
MT.532 (L)
UF copper ore, green
green copper ore
ore, green copper
CN M.MT.AFU.AFU.AFU.CFS.AFU.FIM

malachite green
MT.1642 (L)
UF green, Hungarian
green, malachite
green, mineral
green, mountain
Hungarian green
mineral green
mountain green
CN M.MT.AFU.AFU.ARI.AFU.AFU.ALO.ALO.AXC.AFU.ARI

malachite green (color)
USE **light yellowish green**

malachite green, deep
USE **moderate yellowish green**

malachite, blue
USE **azurite**

Malaga Cove
FL.903
CN F.FL.ALO.ALO.ALO.AFU.ALO.ARI.AFU.AXC

Malagan
USE **Málanggan**

Malaita
FL.3666 (L)
CN F.FL.ALO.BOK.ALO.BOK.AXC

Málanggan
FL.3661
UF Malagan
CN F.FL.ALO.BOK.ALO.BIQ.AFU.AFU

Malay Peninsular
USE **Malayan**

Malayan
FL.2398 (L)
UF Malay Peninsular
CN F.FL.ALO.ARI.BCW.BCW.AFU

Malaysian
FL.2397 (L,B)
CN F.FL.ALO.ARI.BCW.BCW

Malayu
FL.2389 (L)
UF Melayu
CN F.FL.ALO.ARI.BCW.ARI.ALO.BIQ.AFU

Malecite
FL.1300 (L)
UF Etchemin
CN F.FL.ALO.ALO.ARI.AFU.ARI.BOK

Malekula
FL.3674 (L)
CN F.FL.ALO.BOK.ALO.BUE.ARI

Mali Kingdom
FL.84 (L)
CN F.FL.ALO.AFU.ALO.AFU.BOK

Malikshah
FL.3555
CN F.FL.ALO.BIQ.AFU.HIK.ARI.ARI

Malinke
FL.376 (L)
CN F.FL.ALO.AFU.AXC.AFU.AXC.ARI.AFU.ALO

Malla
FL.2162 (L)
UF Malla of Three Kingdoms
CN F.FL.ALO.ARI.AXC.AFU.AXC.AFU.BCW

Malla of Three Kingdoms
USE **Malla**

Malla, Early
USE **Early Malla**

Malla, Late
USE **Late Malla**

malleability
BM.954
SN Property of being capable of deformation by compression without rupture.
CN B.BM.CFS.AXC.BZY.BOK.BOK

malleable materials
MT.2808
UF materials, malleable
CN M.MT.AFU.BCW.DCU

mallets
TB.468 (N)
ALT **mallet**
SN Small wood hammers used to drive another tool, such as a chisel or a gouge. (MEANS)
CN V.TB.AFU.ARI.ELK.ARI

mallets, carpenter's
USE **carpenter's mallets**

mallets, carver's
USE **carver's mallets**

mallets, caulking
USE **caulking mallets**

mallets, dead-blow
USE **dead-blow mallets**

mallets, ship-carpenter's
USE **caulking mallets**

malls (mauls)
USE **mauls**

malls (shopping centers)
USE **shopping malls**

malls (walkways)
RK.1571 (A)
ALT **mall (walkway)**
SN Use for open public areas, walks, or plazas, often lined with trees or shrubs, reserved for use by pedestrians.
UF malls, pedestrian
pedestrian malls
CN V.RK.ALO.ALO.BUE.ARI

malls, pedestrian
USE **malls (walkways)**

malls, shopping
USE **shopping malls**

malm
MT.57
UF mam (malm)
CN M.MT.AFU.AFU.AFU.AXC.AFU.AFU.BCW

malmstone
USE **calcareous sandstone**

malpractice
BM.455 (L)
CN B.BM.BCW.CFS

Maltese crosses
DG.12
ALT **Maltese cross**
SN Crosses having each arm splayed and ending in two points.
UF crosses of eight points
crosses, Maltese
CN D.DG.AFU.AFU.ARI.BIQ

Maltese wood
USE **mahoe**

maltha
MT.974
CN M.MT.AFU.AFU.ALO.ALO.AFU.AFU.ALO.AFU.AFU

malthouses
RK.72 (B)
ALT **malthouse**
SN Agricultural buildings with hop kilns for the malting of grains and with other similar equipment for brewers' work.
UF oasthouses
CN V.RK.AFU.ALO.ALO.AFU.AFU.BZY

malus
USE **applewood**

Malwa
FL.2269
CN F.FL.ALO.ARI.AXC.ALO.AFU.BZY.BCW.ALO

Mam
FL.1536 (L)
CN F.FL.ALO.ALO.ARI.ALO.BIQ.AFU.BCW

mam (malm)
USE **malm**

Mama
FL.216
CN F.FL.ALO.AFU.AXC.AFU.AFU.ALO.ALO.BZY

Mamalla
FL.2206
CN F.FL.ALO.ARI.AXC.ALO.AFU.AXC.AFU.AFU

Mambila
FL.217
CN F.FL.ALO.AFU.AXC.AFU.AFU.ALO.ALO.CFS

Mambo
FL.133
UF Chona II
CN F.FL.ALO.AFU.ALO.ARI.AFU.AFU.ARI

Mamluk
FL.3475 (A)
CN F.FL.ALO.BIQ.AFU.ELK

mamma's benches
USE **cradle benches**

Mammen Style
FL.3148 (R)
CN F.FL.ALO.BCW.ALO.ALO.AFU.BOK.ARI.BUE.ALO

mammoth plate
DC.128
SN A photographic plate size, usually 18 by 21 inches, but may vary within 15 by 18 inches to 22 by 25 inches.
CN D.DC.AFU.AXC.BIQ.ARI

mammy's benches
USE **cradle benches**

mammy's rockers
USE **cradle benches**

Mamon
FL.1011
CN F.FL.ALO.ALO.ALO.ALO.AFU.ALO.ARI.AFU.AFU.ALO

Manabi
USE **Manteño**

management
USE **managing**

management engineering
USE **industrial engineering**

management, collections
USE **collections management**

management, environmental
USE **environmental engineering**
environmental policy

management, facility
USE **facility management**

management, information

USE **information management**

management, records
USE **records management**

management, solid waste
USE **solid waste management**

management, water quality
USE **water quality management**

managers
HG.657 (L)
ALT **manager**
SN Use for persons in control of a division or phase of an institution or business. Distinct from **directors,** which denotes official heads of entire organizations.
CN H.HG.AFU.AXC.CFS.AFU.ALO

managers, hotel
USE **hotelkeepers**

managers, nursery
USE **nurserymen**

managing
KG.149 (L,B)
SN Includes organizing, carrying out, and supervising the activities of a person, group, organization, or enterprise, and controlling its human and material resources. Distinct from **administering** in that it primarily concerns the implementation rather than the formulation of policy.
UF management
CN K.KG.AFU.AFU.BIQ.BUE

Manao
FL.1589
CN F.FL.ALO.ALO.ARI.ARI.AFU.EWY

Manche
USE **Mopan**

manchettes
USE **arm pads**

Mandalay
FL.2309
CN F.FL.ALO.ARI.BCW.AFU.AFU

Mandan
FL.1387 (L)
CN F.FL.ALO.ALO.ARI.AFU.BOK.DCU

Mandara
FL.370 (L)
UF Wandala
CN F.FL.ALO.AFU.AXC.AFU.AXC.ALO.AXC

Mandi
FL.2281
CN F.FL.ALO.ARI.AXC.ALO.AFU.BZY.BCW.ARI.CLM

Manding
FL.373
UF Mandingo
CN F.FL.ALO.AFU.AXC.AFU.AXC.ARI

Mandingo
USE **Manding**

mandioca
USE **cassava**

mandrel lathes
TB.795
ALT **mandrel lathe**
UF lathes, mandrel
CN V.TB.AFU.BCW.CFS.AFU.AFU.ALO

mandrels
TB.666 (L,N)
ALT **mandrel**
SN Cylindrical tapered rods of iron or wood designed to hold a hollow part while it is being forged or turned. (SALAM)
CN V.TB.AFU.BCW.BIQ.AFU.ALO.BOK

Mangaian
FL.3690 (L)
CN F.FL.ALO.BOK.AXC.ALO.AFU

manganese
MT.438 (L,R)
SN Metallic element, Mn.
CN M.MT.AFU.AFU.AFU.BZY.AFU.AFU.ARI.BZY

manganese blue
MT.1602
UF bleu de mangane
blue, manganese
CN M.MT.AFU.AFU.ARI.AFU.AFU.ALO.ALO.ALO.ARI.BOK

manganese bronze
MT.378
SN A brass containing iron and manganese which, because of its hardness and crystalline structure, is called a bronze. (MH)
UF bronze, manganese
CN M.MT.AFU.AFU.AFU.BZY.AFU.AFU.AFU.ALO.ARI.BCW.ALO.ARI

manganese violet
MT.1712
UF Burgundy violet
mauve, permanent
mineral violet
Nürnburg violet
permanent mauve
permanent violet
violet manganèse
violet, Burgundy
violet, manganese
violet, mineral
violet, Nürnburg
violet, permanent
CN M.MT.AFU.AFU.ARI.AFU.AFU.ALO.ALO.BIQ.AFU.AFU

manganese violet (color)
USE **strong purple**

Mangarevan
FL.3693 (L)
CN F.FL.ALO.BOK.AXC.AXC.AFU

Mangbetu
FL.523 (L)
UF Ngbetu
CN F.FL.ALO.AFU.AXC.ALO.ALO.BIQ.AFU.ALO.AXC

Mangosian
FL.60
CN F.FL.ALO.AFU.AFU.ALO.AXC.AFU

mangrove
MT.1216 (L)
SN Hardwood used for timber poles in frame construction in houses in Africa;(OLIVER) also refers to the extract from the bark of the mangrove tree used in tanning leather. (MH12)
UF rhizophora
CN M.MT.AFU.AFU.ALO.BIQ.DCU.AFU.AFU.AFU.HZS

Mangue
FL.1556 (L)
UF Chorotega
CN F.FL.ALO.ALO.ARI.ALO.BOK.BOK

Manguean
USE **Chorotegan**

manhole covers
RM.488 (L,N)
ALT **manhole cover**
UF covers, manhole
CN V.RM.ALO.ALO.ALO.ALO.BZY.ALO.AFU

manholes
RM.486 (L,B)
ALT **manhole**
SN Holes, usually with a cover, through which a person may enter a sewer drain, or the like, especially one located in a city street. (RHDEL2)
CN V.RM.ALO.ALO.ALO.ALO.BZY.AFU

Manichaeism
BM.673 (L)
ALT **Manichaean**
CN B.BM.BZY.AFU.BUE

Maniera
USE **Mannerist**

Maniera greca
USE **Italo-Byzantine**

manifestoes
VW.321 (B,R)
ALT **manifesto**
SN Formal written declarations, promulgated by a sovereign or by the executive authority of a state or nation, such as to proclaim its reasons and motives for declaring a war, or other international action; also public declarations or proclamations of politi-

cal or social principles. (BLACKS)
CN V.VW.AFU.AFU.ALO.BOK.AXC

manifests
VW.935
ALT **manifest**
SN Lists or invoices of cargo or passengers, as of a ship or plane, usually containing marks or indications of contents or commodity, consignee, and other pertinent information for use at terminals or customhouses. (GAHLM)
CN V.VW.AFU.ARI.AFU.CFS.ALO

manifests, ships'
USE **ships' manifests**

manihot esculenta
USE **cassava**

manihot utilissima
USE **cassava**

Manila copal
MT.1483
SN An alcohol soluble resin tapped in the Philippines from trees of the genus Agathis. (MAYER)
UF copal, Manila
Manila resin
CN M.MT.AFU.AFU.ALO.BOK.ARI.ARI

Manila elemi
MT.1492
UF elemi, Manila
CN M.MT.AFU.AFU.ALO.BOK.BIQ.AFU

Manila hemp
MT.1829 (L)
UF abaca
fiber, Manila
hemp, Manila
CN M.MT.AFU.AFU.ARI.ALO.AFU.AFU.ALO.BIQ.AFU

Manila paper
MT.1900
SN A strong wrapping paper originally made from Manila hemp, but the name is now applied to any strong chemical wood pulp or mixed paper of a slightly buff, or Manila, color. (MH)
UF paper, Manila
CN M.MT.AFU.AFU.ARI.ALO.ALO.AXC.AFU.AXC.ALO

Manila resin
USE **Manila copal**

manioc
USE **cassava**

manipulated photographs
VJ.116 (L)
ALT **manipulated photograph**
SN Use for photographs that have been altered through interference in the optical or chemical procedures, or physically altered, as for example, sewn, marked on, or torn.
UF altered photographs
altered prints (photographs)
handworked photographs
photographs, altered
photographs, handworked
photographs, manipulated
prints, altered (photographs)
CN V.VJ.AFU.ARI.ALO.BUE

Mankot
FL.2282
CN F.FL.ALO.ARI.AXC.ALO.AFU.BZY.BCW.ARI.CRG

manlifts
RT.1322
ALT **manlift**
CN V.RT.ALO.ALO.AFU.ARI.ARI

manned orbital laboratories
USE **space stations**

Mannerist
FL.3178 (A,L,B,R)
UF Maniera
CN F.FL.ALO.BCW.ALO.ARI.BIQ.AFU

Mannerist, Artisan
USE **Artisan Mannerist**

Mano
FL.330 (L)
UF Mah
CN F.FL.ALO.AFU.AXC.AFU.ARI.BCW.BZY

manoirs
USE **manor houses**

manor houses
RK.297 (A,B)
ALT **manor house**
UF houses, manor
manoirs
manors (houses)
CN V.RK.AFU.ALO.ALO.AXC.ALO.AXC.AFU.AFU.ARI

manorial documents
USE **manorial records**

manorial records
VW.1053
ALT **manorial record**
UF documents, manorial
manorial documents
records, manorial
CN V.VW.AFU.ARI.ALO.BOK

manors
RG.21 (L)
ALT **manor**
SN Use for landed estates administered as units and consisting of the main residence (manor house), demesnes, and the land over which the lord has privileges.
CN V.RG.AFU.AFU.AFU.AXC

manors (houses)
USE **manor houses**

manpower
USE **personnel**

mansard roofs
RT.423 (A,B,R)
ALT **mansard roof**
SN Curb roofs with all four sides sloping, usually enclosing habitable spaces, and therefore having dormers.
UF double hip roofs
roofs, double hip
roofs, mansard
CN V.RT.AFU.AFU.AFU.BIQ.ARI.AFU.AFU.AFU.BOK.AFU.ALO

Mansard Style
USE **Second Empire**

manses
RK.328 (B)
ALT **manse**
CN V.RK.AFU.ALO.ALO.AXC.ALO.BOK.ARI.ALO

mansion houses
USE **mansions**

mansiones
RK.1251
ALT **mansio**
SN Use for stations, along ancient Roman and Byzantine roads (through the 7th century), spaced generally one day's travel apart and intended as stopping places for overnight stays, initially primarily reserved for imperial parties. For intermediary rest stops along these routes, use **mutationes.**
CN V.RK.AFU.ALO.ALO.GLI.AFU.ARI.AXC

mansions
RK.240 (A,R)
ALT **mansion**
SN Use for large imposing, and usually elegant and costly, dwellings.
UF homes, stately
houses, mansion
mansion houses
stately homes
CN V.RK.AFU.ALO.ALO.AXC.ALO.AFU.BUE

Manta
FL.1662 (L)
CN F.FL.ALO.ALO.ARI.ARI.BCW.CFS

mantelpieces
USE **mantels**

mantels
RT.1160 (A,L,N,R)
ALT **mantel**
SN All the work or facing around a fireplace. (DAC)
UF mantelpieces
CN V.RT.AFU.BOK.ALO.ALO.BOK

Manteño
FL.1119
UF Manabi
CN F.FL.ALO.ALO.ALO.ARI.ALO.BCW

Mantrayana
USE **Vajrayana**

manual fire alarm stations
USE **manual stations**

manual stations
RT.1514
ALT **manual station**
SN Use for manually operated fire alarms, usually boxes with a handle that is pulled.
UF boxes, fire alarm
fire alarm boxes
fire alarm stations, manual
manual fire alarm stations
stations, manual
stations, manual fire alarm
CN V.RT.ALO.BIQ.AFU.AFU.ALO.ALO

manual workers
USE **blue collar workers**

manuals
VW.348 (L,N,R)
ALT **manual**
UF handbooks
CN V.VW.AFU.AFU.ALO.CXA.BIQ

manuals, do-it-yourself
USE **do-it-yourself manuals**

manuals, employees'
USE **employees' manuals**

manuals, job
USE **project manuals**

manuals, operating
USE **operating manuals**

manuals, project
USE **project manuals**

manuals, staff
USE **employees' manuals**

manuals, style
USE **style manuals**

manuals, technical
USE **technical manuals**

manuals, training
USE **training manuals**

Manueline
FL.3158 (L,B,R)
CN F.FL.ALO.BCW.ALO.ALO.AFU.BOK.AXC.ARI.AFU

manufacturers
HG.421 (L)
ALT **manufacturer**
CN H.HG.AFU.AXC.BOK.DZW.AFU

manufacturers' catalogs
VW.113 (L)
ALT **manufacturer's catalog**
UF catalogs, manufacturers'
CN V.VW.AFU.AFU.AFU.FZU.ALO.ALO.ARI.ALO.ALO

manufacturers' directories
USE **manufacturers' registers**

manufacturers' registers
VW.409
ALT **manufacturers' register**
UF directories, manufacturers'
manufacturers' directories
registers, manufacturers'
CN V.VW.AFU.AFU.ALO.EWY.AXC.AFU.ALO.AFU

manufacturing
KG.169 (L)
SN Making goods and articles. (RLG7)
CN K.KG.AFU.ALO.AFU.BCW

manure, cattle
USE **cow manure**

manure, cow
USE **cow manure**

Manus
FL.3620 (L)
UF Admiralty Islands
CN F.FL.ALO.BOK.ALO.ALO

manuscript illumination
KT.206 (R)
UF illumination, manuscript
CN K.KT.AFU.ALO.DUC.CLM.AXC

manuscript illuminations
USE **illuminations**

manuscript maps
VW.173 (L)
ALT **manuscript map**
SN Originals of compiled maps, drawn but not printed; loosely, any map drawn by hand. (GAHLM)
UF maps, manuscript
CN V.VW.AFU.AFU.AFU.FZU.AXC.AFU.ARI.ARI.ALO

manuscripts
VW.654 (L,N,B,R)
ALT **manuscript**
SN Handwritten or typed documents, including books; also includes letter-press or carbon copies.
CN V.VW.AFU.ALO.AFU.DZW.ARI

manuscripts for publication
VW.658
ALT **manuscript for publication**
UF publication, manuscripts for
CN V.VW.AFU.ALO.AFU.DZW.ARI.AFU.ARI

manuscripts, computus
USE **computus manuscripts**

manuscripts, illuminated
USE **illuminated manuscripts**

manuscripts, juridical
USE **legal manuscripts**

manuscripts, law
USE **legal manuscripts**

manuscripts, legal
USE **legal manuscripts**

manuscripts, liturgical
USE **liturgical manuscripts**

manx tables
USE **pillar and claw tables**

Maori
FL.3697 (A,L,B)
CN F.FL.ALO.BOK.AXC.BOK.AFU

Maori, Classic
USE **Classic Maori**

map cabinets
TG.436
ALT **map cabinet**
UF cabinets, map
CN V.TG.AFU.AFU.AXC.ALO.ARI.ALO.CLM

map files
VW.599
ALT **map file**
UF files, map
CN V.VW.AFU.ALO.AFU.BIQ.ARI.ARI

map stands
TG.644
ALT **map stand**
SN Stands with a tall upright post and a sliding cross bar which can be adjusted at different heights and bears pins for suspending maps or charts. (VERNFR)
UF stands, map
CN V.TG.AFU.AFU.BIQ.BCW.ALO.CRG

Mapico Yellow
USE **Mars yellow**

maple
MT.1217 (L)
UF Acer
Aceraceae
CN M.MT.AFU.AFU.ALO.BIQ.DCU.AFU.AFU.AFU.IFM

maple, ash-leafed
USE **box elder**

maple, bigleaf
USE **bigleaf maple**

maple, bird's-eye
USE **bird's-eye maple**

maple, black
USE **black maple**

maple, broadleaved
USE **bigleaf maple**

maple, hard
USE **sugar maple**

maple, Japanese
USE **Japanese maple**

maple, Oregon
USE **bigleaf maple**

maple, red
USE **red maple**

maple, river
USE **silver maple**

maple, rock
USE **sugar maple**

maple, Russian
USE **European birch**

maple, silver
USE **silver maple**

maple, soft
USE **silver maple**

maple, sugar
USE **sugar maple**

maple, tiger
USE **tiger maple**

maple, white
USE **silver maple**

Maples Mills
FL.840
CN F.FL.ALO.ALO.ALO.AFU.ALO .ALO.ARI .AFU.BUE

mapmakers
USE **cartographers**

mapping (cartography)
USE **cartography**

Maprik
FL.3655 (L)
CN F.FL.ALO.BOK.ALO.BCW.ALO. BCW.ALO.ALO

maps
VW.138 (A,L,N,B,R)
ALT map
SN Documents depicting in graphic or photogrammetric form, normally to scale and usually on a flat medium, a selection of material or abstract features on or in relation to the surface of the earth or of a heavenly body. (ICA)
UF charts (maps)
CN V.VW.AFU.AFU.AFU.FZU.AXC.AFU. ARI

maps, aeronautical
USE **aeronautical charts**

maps, airline
USE **airline maps**

maps, base
USE **base maps**

maps, bathymetric
USE **bathymetric maps**

maps, battlefield
USE **battlefield maps**

maps, boundary
USE **cadastral maps**

maps, braille
USE **braille maps**

maps, buried cable
USE **buried cable maps**

maps, bus route
USE **bus route maps**

maps, cadastral
USE **cadastral maps**

maps, census
USE **census maps**

maps, chorochromatic
USE **chorochromatic maps**

maps, chorographic
USE **chorographic maps**

maps, choroschematic
USE **choroschematic maps**

maps, city
USE **city maps**

maps, climatic
USE **climatic maps**

maps, coastal zone
USE **coastal zone maps**

maps, computer-assisted
USE **computer-assisted maps**

maps, contour
USE **contour maps**

maps, country
USE **national maps**

maps, county
USE **county maps**

maps, demographic
USE **population maps**

maps, digital
USE **digital maps**

maps, dot
USE **dot maps**

maps, engineering
USE **engineering maps**

maps, fire insurance
USE **fire insurance maps**

maps, flood-prone-area
USE **flood-prone-area maps**

maps, flow-line
USE **flow-line maps**

maps, forestry
USE **forestry maps**

maps, geological
USE **geological maps**

maps, highway
USE **road maps**

maps, historical
USE **historical maps**

maps, hydrographic
USE **nautical charts**

maps, hydrologic
USE **hydrologic maps**

maps, hypsographic
USE **relief maps**

maps, hypsometric
USE **relief maps**

maps, index
USE **index maps**

maps, insurance
USE **fire insurance maps**

maps, isoline
USE **isoline maps**

maps, isopleth
USE **isoline maps**

maps, key
USE **index maps**

maps, land ownership
USE **cadastral maps**

maps, land use
USE **land use maps**

maps, line
USE **outline maps**

maps, line-route
USE **line-route maps**

maps, location
USE **location maps**

maps, manuscript
USE **manuscript maps**

maps, military
USE **military maps**

maps, mine
USE **mine maps**

maps, mineral
USE **mineral resource maps**

maps, mineral resource
USE **mineral resource maps**

maps, national
USE **national maps**

maps, natural-gas-pipelines
USE **natural-gas-pipelines maps**

maps, navigation
USE **navigation charts**

maps, outline
USE **outline maps**

maps, parish
USE **parish maps**

maps, photomosaic
USE **photomosaic maps**

maps, pictorial
USE **pictorial maps**

maps, planimetric
USE **planimetric maps**

maps, plat
USE **plats**

maps, population
USE **population maps**

maps, population distribution
USE **population maps**

maps, postal code
USE **postal code maps**

maps, property
USE **cadastral maps**

maps, quadrangle
USE **quadrangle maps**

maps, railroad
USE **railroad maps**

maps, railway
USE **railroad maps**

maps, raised-relief
USE **raised-relief maps**

maps, real estate
USE **cadastral maps**

maps, real property
USE **cadastral maps**

maps, regional
USE **regional maps**

maps, relative relief
USE **relief maps**

maps, relief
USE **relief maps**

maps, road
USE **road maps**

maps, route
USE **line-route maps**

maps, Sanborn
USE **fire insurance maps**

maps, seismicity
USE **seismicity maps**

maps, shaded-relief
USE **shaded-relief maps**

maps, sketch
USE **sketch maps**

maps, soil
USE **soil maps**

maps, soil survey
USE **soil maps**

maps, special-purpose
USE **thematic maps**

maps, star
USE **astronomical charts**

maps, state
USE **state maps**

maps, street
USE **street maps**

maps, strip
USE **strip maps**

maps, survey
USE **topographic surveys**

maps, tactical
USE **tactical maps**

maps, tax
USE **cadastral maps**

maps, telephone area code
USE **telephone area code maps**

maps, thematic
USE **thematic maps**

maps, time zone
USE **time zone maps**

maps, topographic
USE **topographic maps**

maps, tourist
USE **tourist maps**

maps, township
USE **township maps**

maps, transportation
USE **transportation maps**

maps, village
USE **village maps**

maps, watermain
USE **watermain maps**

maps, watershed
USE **watershed maps**

maps, weather
USE **weather maps**

maps, world
USE **world maps**

maps, zip code
USE **zip code maps**

maps, zoning
USE **zoning maps**

Mapuche
USE **Araucanian**

Mapungubwe
FL.135
CN F.FL.ALO.AFU.ALO.ARI.ARI

Maracaibo balsam
MT.1472
UF balsam, Maracaibo
CN M.MT.AFU.AFU.ALO.BOK.AFU.ARI.AFU

Maracaibo boxwood
MT.1126
UF boxwood, Maracaibo
boxwood, West Indian
Casearia praecox
Gossypiospermum praecox
West Indian boxwood
zapatero
CN M.MT.AFU.AFU.ALO.BIQ.DCU.AFU.AFU.AFU.BOK.AFU

Marajoara
FL.1128 (L)
CN F.FL.ALO.ALO.ALO.ARI.ARI.ALO.AFU

Maravi
FL.546 (L)
CN F.FL.ALO.AFU.AXC.ARI.AFU.AXC

marbelite
MT.2803
SN Artificial marble used in casting statues and small ornamental articles.
CN M.MT.AFU.BCW.CFS.ALO.ALO

marble
MT.742 (A,L,B,R)
UF marmor
CN M.MT.AFU.AFU.AFU.DCU.AFU.ARI.ARI

marble dust
MT.896
UF dust, marble
flour, marble
marble flour
CN M.MT.AFU.AFU.AFU.DCU.ALO.CXA.AFU

marble flour
USE **marble dust**

marble tables (slab tables)
USE **slab tables**

marble-topped tables
USE **slab tables**

marble, Alabama cream
USE **Alabama cream marble**

marble, Batesville
USE **Batesville marble**

marble, Belgian
USE **rance**

marble, Belgian black
USE **Belgian black marble**

marble, bird's eye
USE **coral limestone**

marble, black
USE **black marble**

marble, bougard

USE **bougard marble**

marble, breccia
USE **breccia marble**

marble, breche violette
USE **breche violette marble**

marble, brocatelle
USE **brocatelle marble**

marble, calcite
USE **calcite marble**

marble, calico
USE **Potomac breccia**

marble, campan
USE **campan marble**

marble, Carrara
USE **Carrara marble**

marble, Carystian
USE **cipollino**

marble, Cockeysville
USE **Cockeysville marble**

marble, Colorado yule statuary
USE **Colorado yule statuary marble**

marble, Connemara
USE **Connemara marble**

marble, cream blanc
USE **cream blanc marble**

marble, Egyptian breccia
USE **Egyptian breccia marble**

marble, Eleusinian
USE **Eleusinian marble**

marble, fiorto
USE **fiorto marble**

marble, fire
USE **shell marble**

marble, forest
USE **forest marble**

marble, Formosa
USE **Formosa marble**

marble, fortification
USE **fortification marble**

marble, French red
USE **griotte marble**
Languedoc marble

marble, Georgia
USE **Georgia marble**

marble, gray
USE **gray marble**

marble, green
USE **green marble**

marble, griotte
USE **griotte marble**

marble, Hymettian
USE **Hymettian marble**

marble, Iona
USE **Iona marble**

marble, Irish black
USE **Irish black marble**

marble, Istrian
USE **Istrian marble**

marble, Kilkenny
USE **Irish black marble**

marble, landscape
USE **forest marble**

marble, Languedoc
USE **Languedoc marble**

marble, Lee
USE **Lee marble**

marble, lepanto
USE **lepanto marble**

marble, Lisbon yellow
USE **Lisbon yellow marble**

marble, lucullan
USE **lucullite**

marble, lumachelle
USE **lumachella**

marble, Luna
USE **Luna marble**

marble, lychnites
USE **Parian marble**

marble, Lyonaise
USE **Lyonaise marble**

marble, madre cream
USE **madre cream marble**

marble, madrepore
USE **madrepore marble**

marble, marezzo
USE **marezzo marble**

marble, mischio
USE **mischio marble**

marble, Missouri
USE **Missouri marble**

marble, Numidian
USE **Numidian marble**

marble, onyx
USE **onyx marble**

marble, paonazzo
USE **paonazzo marble**

marble, Parian
USE **Parian marble**

marble, parmazo
USE **parmazo marble**

marble, pavonazzetto
USE **pavonazzetto**

marble, Pentelic
USE **Pentelic marble**

marble, phengites
USE **bianco e giallo antico**

marble, Phrygian
USE **pavonazzetto**

marble, pink
USE **pink marble**

marble, Porta Santa
USE **Porta Santa marble**

marble, portor
USE **portor marble**

marble, Potomac
USE **Potomac breccia**

marble, purbeck
USE **purbeck marble**

marble, red
USE **red marble**

marble, river
USE **river marble**

marble, Rockingham royal black
USE **Rockingham royal black marble**

marble, rose
USE **pink marble**

marble, rosso de levanto
USE **rosso de levanto marble**

marble, rouge antique
USE **rouge antique marble**

marble, ruin
USE **ruin marble**

marble, saccharoidal
USE **white marble**

marble, Saint Anne
USE **Saint Anne marble**

marble, Sarrancolin
USE **Sarrancolin marble**

marble, shell
USE **shell marble**

marble, Siena
USE **Siena marble**

marble, statuary
USE **statuary marble**

marble, Sussex
USE **Sussex marble**

marble, Synnadicum
USE **pavonazzetto**

marble, Tabrez
USE **Tabrez marble**

marble, Tennessee
USE **Tennessee marble**

marble, Tennessee pink
USE **Tennessee pink marble**

marble, Texas
USE **Texas marble**

marble, Thasian
USE **tasio**

marble, variegated
USE **variegated marble**

marble, veined
USE **variegated marble**

marble, Vermont white statuary
USE **Vermont white statuary marble**

marble, white
USE **white marble**

marble, white Cherokee
USE **white Cherokee marble**

marble, Winooski
USE **Winooski marble**

marble, yellow
USE **yellow marble**

marblewood
MT.1143
UF andaman marblewood
Diospyros kurzii
wood, zebra
zebra wood
CN M.MT.AFU.AFU.ALO.BIQ.DCU.AFU.AFU.AFU.CXA.AXC

marbling
KT.259 (A,L,B,R)
ALT **marbled**
SN The technique of imitating the appearance of marble, such as on wood or other surfaces; includes coloring the end papers or edges of books.
CN K.KT.AFU.ALO.DUC.CXA.ALO.BCW.ALO.ARI

marbreurs
HG.524
ALT **marbreur**
SN Persons who produce wallpaper exclusively from marblized paper, popular especially in 15th-century France. (MCCLEL)
CN H.HG.AFU.AXC.BUE.ARI.CRG.ALO

marcasite
MT.514 (L)
SN Pyrites sometimes used for gemstones, which have a yellow color with a greenish tinge; also, the mineral iron disulfide. (MH)
CN M.MT.AFU.AFU.AFU.CFS.AFU.CXA.AXC

Marcomannic
FL.3113 (L)
CN F.FL.ALO.BCW.ALO.ALO.AFU.BOK.ALO.ALO.BIQ

Mardi Gras
USE **Carnival**

marekanite
MT.629
SN Semitransparent, smoky-colored obsidian nodules of Arizona ore; used in Indian silver jewelry. (MH)
CN M.MT.AFU.AFU.AFU.DCU.AFU.AFU.ALO.ALO.ALO.AFU.AFU

marezzo marble
MT.2804 (L)
SN A cast imitation marble produced with Keene's cement. (DAC)
UF marble, marezzo
CN M.MT.AFU.BCW.CFS.ALO.ARI

margin lights
USE **side lights**

margin trowels
TB.636
ALT **margin trowel**
SN Plasterer's hand trowels on which the edges are turned up; used to finish plaster in corners. (MEANS)
UF angle trowels
trowels, angle
trowels, margin
CN V.TB.AFU.BCW.BCW.ALO.HCQ.AXC

marginal notes
USE **marginalia**

marginalia
VW.305 (L)
ALT **marginal note**
SN Notes written or printed on the margin of a page opposite the portion of text to which they refer; also, decorative work in margins, as in Medieval manuscripts.
UF adversaria
marginal notes
notes, marginal
notes, side
side notes
CN V.VW.AFU.AFU.ALO.BCW.AFU.AFU

Mari Age
FL.2975
CN F.FL.ALO.AXC.ARI.BCW.AFU.BIQ.ARI

Marianas Island
FL.3683
CN F.FL.ALO.BOK.ARI.AXC

Maricopa
FL.1458 (L)
UF Cocomaricopa
Pipatsje
CN F.FL.ALO.ALO.ARI.AFU.CFS.BCW

marigold windows
USE **rose windows**

marinas
RG.226 (A,L,B,R)
ALT **marina**
SN Secure mooring facilities primarily for recreational small craft.
UF yacht basins
CN V.RG.AFU.AFU.EFQ.ARI.ARI

marine aquariums
RK.373 (A,L,B)
ALT **marine aquarium**
UF aquariums, marine
aquariums, saltwater
oceanariums
saltwater aquariums
CN V.RK.AFU.ALO.ALO.BCW.AFU.AFU.AFU

marine archaeology
USE **underwater archaeology**

marine architects
USE **naval architects**

marine architecture
USE **naval architecture**

marine biologists
HG.329 (L)
ALT **marine biologist**
UF biologists, marine
CN H.HG.AFU.AXC.BIQ.AFU.AFU.ALO.ALO

marine charts
VW.215
ALT **marine chart**
UF admiralty charts
charts, admiralty
charts, marine
charts, sea
sea charts
CN V.VW.AFU.AFU.AFU.FZU.AXC.AFU.ARI.AXC.DIO.ALO.ALO.ALO

marine engineering
KD.229 (L)
SN Branch of engineering that deals with the construction and operation of the power plant and other mechanical equipment of seagoing craft, docks, and harbor installations. (W)
UF engineering, marine
engineering, naval
naval engineering
CN K.KD.AFU.ARI.BIQ.BUE

marine engineers
HG.639 (L)
ALT **marine engineer**
SN Engineers working in the design, construction, operation, and administration of machinery installations for seagoing vessels. (ENCYB)
UF engineers, marine
engineers, naval
naval engineers
CN H.HG.AFU.AXC.BZY.BCW.BUE

marine glue
MT.2362
SN Glue insoluble in water, made from rubber or resin solutions (or both). (MH)
UF glue, marine

CN M.MT.AFU.ARI.ARI.ARI.AFU

marine museums
USE **maritime museums**

marine painters
HG.109 (L)
ALT **marine painter**
UF painters, marine
painters, sea
sea painters
CN H.HG.AFU.AXC.AXC.AFU.AFU.ALO.AXC.CXA.AFU.ARI

marine parks
RK.1458 (A,L)
ALT **marine park**
SN Use for permanent conservation tracts located on land in contact with the sea, in submerged areas, along sea beds, or on emerged land areas near the sea coast.
UF marine reserves
marine sanctuaries
parks, marine
reserves, marine
sanctuaries, marine
CN V.RK.ALO.ALO.ARI.AFU.ALO

marine pollution
BM.435 (L)
UF pollution, marine
CN B.BM.AXC.BCW.AFU.ARI.AFU

marine reserves
USE **marine parks**

marine sanctuaries
USE **marine parks**

marine science
USE **oceanography**

marine structures
RK.1364 (L,B)
ALT **marine structure**
SN Use for structures built in relation to water in general, especially seaward of the high-water line of the major water bodies (oceans, seas, bays); use **offshore structures** for construction built on continental shelves.
UF maritime structures
structures, marine
CN V.RK.AFU.ALO.ARI.AXC.BIQ

Marine Style
FL.2670
CN F.FL.ALO.AXC.ALO.AFU.ALO.AXC.BCW.BIQ

marine subjects
USE **seascapes**

marine terminals
RG.227 (A,L)
ALT **marine terminal**
SN Use for complexes providing facilities to accommodate the movement of cargo or passengers among ships or between ships and shore.
UF ship terminals
steamship terminals
terminals, marine
terminals, ship
terminals, steamship
CN V.RG.AFU.AFU.EFQ.ARI.AXC

Mariposan
USE **Yokuts**

maritime museums
RK.398 (A,L,B)
ALT **maritime museum**
SN Use only to refer to museums dealing with the sea in general, navigation, or shipping; distinct from **naval museums,** which deal with navies, warships, or ships in general.
UF marine museums
museums, maritime
museums, nautical
nautical museums
CN V.RK.AFU.ALO.ALO.BCW.AXC.ARI.AXC.BIQ

maritime structures
USE **marine structures**

Marka
FL.377
CN F.FL.ALO.AFU.AXC.AFU.AXC.ARI.AFU.ARI

markers (drawing instruments)
TB.272
ALT **marker (drawing instrument)**
SN Pens which contain impermanent colored inks in the shaft and have a variety of pointed or blunt felt, nylon, or fiber tips. (ADAG)
UF marking pens
pens, marking
CN V.TB.AFU.ARI.CLM.AFU.ALO.DOI.AXC

markers (monuments)
RK.880
ALT **marker (monument)**
CN V.RK.AFU.ALO.ALO.DOI.AFU.ALO

market crosses
RK.883 (B)
ALT **market cross**
SN Use for structures with raised platforms and terminating in or shaped like crosses, set up in town marketplaces and used for public addresses. (RS)
UF city crosses
crosses, city
crosses, market
CN V.RK.AFU.ALO.ALO.DOI.AFU.ALO.ALO.AFU

market gardens
RK.1422
ALT **market garden**
UF gardens, market
CN V.RK.ALO.AFU.AFU.ALO.BIQ

market halls
RK.142 (B)
ALT **market hall**
UF halls, market
CN V.RK.AFU.ALO.ALO.ALO.ARI.AXC.ALO

market hamlets
USE **market towns**

market letters
VW.617
ALT **market letter**
SN Publications containing information concerning market conditions or expectations, especially those produced by firms or other financial organizations. (RHDEL2)
UF letters, market
CN V.VW.AFU.ALO.AFU.CXA.AFU.ARI.AFU

market squares
USE **marketplaces**

market towns
RD.56 (L)
ALT **market town**
UF hamlets, market
market hamlets
market villages
towns, market
villages, market
CN V.RD.AFU.AXC.BOK

market villages
USE **market towns**

market, art
USE **art market**

marketing
KG.60 (A,L)
SN Activity by which the transfer of title or possession of goods or the supplying of services from seller to buyer is effected, including advertising, shipping, storing, and selling. (RHDEL2)
CN K.KG.AFU.AFU.ARI.DCU

marketplaces
RG.39 (L,B)
ALT **marketplace**
SN Use for widened streets, neighborhood or town squares, or other mostly open public spaces where booths and stalls may be erected for public sales.
UF market squares
squares, market
CN V.RG.AFU.AFU.AXC.AFU

marketplaces, festival
USE **festival marketplaces**

markets
RK.140 (L,B,R)
ALT **market**
CN V.RK.AFU.ALO.ALO.ALO.ARI.AXC

markets (events)
KM.150 (A,L)

SN Meetings of people at a stated time and place for the purpose of trade (as in cattle, provisions, or wares) by private purchase and sale and usually not by auction. (W)
CN K.KM.AFU.ELK.ARI

markets, farmers'
USE **farmers' markets**

markets, flea
USE **flea markets**

markets, periodic
USE **periodic markets**

markets, underground
USE **underground shopping centers**

marking
KG.82
ALT **marked**
SN Use for the process of affixing an identification number, tag, or other label to an object in a collection.
UF labeling
CN K.KG.AFU.AFU.AXC.AXC.CRG

marking awls
USE **scribe awls**

marking awls, chisel-end
USE **scribe awls**

marking axes
TB.841 (N)
ALT **marking ax**
SN Axes having a head similar to a hammer; used to stamp the owner's mark onto a log.
UF axes, marking
CN V.TB.AFU.BCW.CFS.ALO.AFU.AXC.BIQ

marking brands
USE **brands**

marking pens
USE **markers (drawing instruments)**

marking, cord
USE **cord marking**

markings
USE **marks**

marks
VW.707 (B)
ALT **mark**
UF markings
CN V.VW.AFU.ALO.ALO.AFU.AXC

marks in paper
USE **watermarks**

marks of origin
VW.721 (L)
ALT **mark of origin**
SN Inscriptions, names, stamps, labels, or seals placed on articles to signify origin. (AHD)
UF origin, marks of
CN V.VW.AFU.ALO.ALO.AFU.AXC.ALO.BZY

marks, architects'
USE **architects' marks**

marks, armorers'
USE **armorers' marks**

marks, artisans'
USE **artisans' marks**

marks, artists'
USE **artists' marks**

marks, bench
USE **bench marks**

marks, bookbinding
USE **bookbinding marks**

marks, bottle makers'
USE **bottle makers' marks**

marks, cabinetmakers'
USE **cabinetmakers' marks**

marks, calligraphers'
USE **calligraphers' marks**

marks, cancellation
USE **cancellation marks**

marks, collectors'
USE **collectors' marks**

marks, country of origin
USE **country of origin marks**

marks, craftsmen's
USE **artisans' marks**

marks, date
USE **date marks**

marks, dealers'
USE **dealers' marks**

marks, deletion
USE **cancellation marks**

marks, engravers'
USE **engravers' marks**

marks, excise
USE **excise marks**

marks, factory
USE **factory marks**

marks, furniture
USE **furniture marks**

marks, gilders'
USE **gilders' marks**

marks, glass
USE **glass marks**

marks, goldsmiths'
USE **goldsmiths' marks**

marks, house
USE **house marks**

marks, masons'
USE **masons' marks**

marks, merchant
USE **trademarks**

marks, modellers'
USE **modellers' marks**

marks, ownership
USE **ownership marks**

marks, painters'
USE **painters' marks**

marks, pewter
USE **pewter marks**

marks, porcelain
USE **porcelain marks**

marks, potters'
USE **potters' marks**

marks, pottery
USE **pottery marks**

marks, printers'
USE **printers' marks**

marks, publishers'
USE **printers' marks**

marks, punch
USE **punch marks**

marks, registry
USE **registry marks**

marks, silver
USE **silver marks**

marks, silversmiths'
USE **silversmiths' marks**

marks, stone-cutters'
USE **masons' marks**

marks, swordsmiths'
USE **swordsmiths' marks**

marks, tapestry
USE **tapestry marks**

Marksville
FL.857
CN F.FL.ALO.ALO.ALO.AFU.ALO.ALO.ARI.ARI.AXC

marl
MT.58 (L)
SN Class of brick clay that comprises calcareous clays containing up to 40% calcium carbonate. (MH)
UF calcareous clay
clay, calcareous
CN M.MT.AFU.AFU.AFU.AXC.AFU.AFU.BIQ

Marlboro legs
USE **Marlborough legs**

Marlborough legs
TG.949
ALT **Marlborough leg**
SN English term for straight or tapering square legs, sometimes with a plinth

foot. Used on American furniture from the mid-18th century, often with the inside edge chamfered. (DDA)
UF legs, Marlboro
legs, Marlborough
legs, rectangular
legs, square (Marlborough legs)
legs, straight
Marlboro legs
rectangular legs
square legs (Marlborough legs)
straight legs
CN V.TG.ALO.FIM.AFU.AFU.BCW

marlstone
MT.643
SN Shale that is calcareous or dolomitic and is used with limestone in making portland cement. (MH)
CN M.MT.AFU.AFU.AFU.DCU.AFU.ALO.AFU.AFU.ARI

marmolite
MT.852
SN A thin, laminated serpentine marble, usually pale green. (MAYER)
CN M.MT.AFU.AFU.AFU.DCU.AFU.ARI.BOK.ALO

marmor
USE **marble**

marmor Africano
MT.755
UF Africano, marmor
CN M.MT.AFU.AFU.AFU.DCU.AFU.ARI.ARI.ALO.AFU.BUE

marmor batthium
USE **bigio antico**

marmor Carystium
USE **cipollino**

marmor celticum
USE **bigio e nero di francia**

marmor coraliticum
USE **palombino**

marmor corinthium
USE **giallo tigrato**

marmor Hymmetium
USE **Hymettian marble**

marmor Iassense
USE **Porta Santa marble**

marmor imezio
USE **Hymettian marble**

marmor lesbium
USE **lesbio**

marmor ligusticum
USE **serpentina comune**

marmor Luniense
USE **Luna marble**

marmor Lydium
USE **rosso brecciato**

marmor Molossium
USE **fiore di Persico**

marmor Numidicum
USE **Numidian marble**

marmor Parium
USE **Parian marble**

marmor Pentelicum
USE **Pentelic marble**

marmor phengite
USE **bianco e giallo antico**

marmor porinum
USE **porino**

marmor proconnesium
USE **bigio e nero antico**

marmor schiston
USE **brocatello**

marmor Synnadicum
USE **pavonazzetto**

marmor taenarium
USE **nero antico**

marmor thasium
USE **tasio**

marmor tyrium
USE **tirio**

marmorino
USE **scagliola**

maroger medium
MT.2507
SN A megilp or gel medium for oil painting, introduced in the United States in the 1940s by Jaques Maroger, a painter and conservator.(MAYER) It is a mixture of linseed oil, that has been saturated with lead, and mastic varnish. (AHMT)
UF medium, maroger
CN M.MT.AFU.ARI.CRG.ALO.ARI

Maronite
BM.645 (L)
UF Maronite Catholic
CN B.BM.BZY.AFU.ALO.AXC.ARI

Maronite Catholic
USE **Maronite**

maroon
USE **dark grayish red**
dark purplish red
dark red
dark reddish brown
deep reddish brown
grayish reddish brown
very dark red
very deep red

maroon purple, dark
USE **dark reddish purple**

maroon, deep
USE **dark grayish red**
dark grayish reddish brown

Marpole
FL.915
CN F.FL.ALO.ALO.ALO.AFU.ALO.ARI.ARI.AXC

marque, letters of
USE letters of marque

marquees
RT.418 (A,B)
ALT **marquee**
SN Roofs over the entrances to buildings, usually cantilevered or suspended, and of metal and glass; in the 19th and 20th centuries, common over the entrances to theaters.
UF marquises (roofs)
CN V.RT.AFU.AFU.AFU.BIQ.ARI.AFU.AFU.AFU.BCW

Marquesan
FL.3695 (L)
UF Marquesas Island
CN F.FL.ALO.BOK.AXC.BIQ

Marquesas Island
USE **Marquesan**

marquetry
KT.706 (A,L,B,R)
SN Use for the technique in which small pieces of wood or other materials are overlaid or inlaid onto another wood surface to form a decorative veneer.
CN K.KT.AFU.ALO.CRC.CLM

marquetry, boulle
USE **boulle work**

marquise chairs
USE **marquises**

marquises
TG.305
ALT **marquise**
SN A French type of small canape or large chair for two people. (DDA)
UF canapés à marquise
canapés de l'amitié
causeuses
chairs, marquise
demi-canapés
marquise chairs
CN V.TG.AFU.AFU.ALO.ALO.BUE.BCW

marquises (roofs)
USE **marquees**

marriage
BM.1130 (L,R)
CN B.BM.CRG.BUE.AXC

marriage applications
VW.956
ALT **marriage application**
UF applications, marriage

CN V.VW.AFU.ARI.AFU.DCU.ARI.ALO

marriage certificates
VW.957 (N)
ALT **marriage certificate**
SN Certificates which serve as evidence of marriage, and are executed by the persons officiating at the marriage. (BLACKS)
UF certificates, marriage
CN V.VW.AFU.ARI.AFU.DCU.ARI.ARI

marriage chests
USE **dower chests**

marriage licenses
VW.958 (L)
ALT **marriage license**
SN Licenses granted by public authority to persons who intend to marry, usually addressed to the authorized peron who is to perform the ceremony, and usually a legal prerequisite to the marriage. (BLACKS)
UF licenses, marriage
CN V.VW.AFU.ARI.AFU.DCU.ARI.AXC

marriage records
VW.954
ALT **marriage record**
SN Documents kept by a state, city, or town official which are permanent records of marriages and which include the names of the spouses, the maiden name of the wife, their addresses, and the date of marriage. (BLACKS)
UF records, marriage
CN V.VW.AFU.ARI.AFU.DCU.ARI

marriage registers
VW.959 (L)
ALT **marriage register**
UF registers, marriage
CN V.VW.AFU.ARI.AFU.DCU.ARI.BCW

marrum grass
USE **sea reed**

Mars black
MT.1577
UF black iron oxide
black, Mars
iron oxide, black
CN M.MT.AFU.AFU.ARI.AFU.AFU.ALO.ALO.AFU.ALO.AFU

Mars brown
USE **brown iron oxide**
moderate brown

Mars orange
USE **dark reddish orange**

Mars pigment
MT.1807
UF pigment, Mars
CN M.MT.AFU.AFU.ARI.AFU.AFU.ALO.ARI.BCW

Mars red
USE **dark reddish orange**
iron oxide red

Mars violet
MT.1713
UF violet, Mars
CN M.MT.AFU.AFU.ARI.AFU.AFU.ALO.ALO.BIQ.AFU.ALO

Mars violet (color)
USE **dark grayish purple**
deep reddish brown

Mars yellow
MT.1783
UF ferrite
ferrite yellow
ferrox
iron yellow
iron, yellow oxide of
jaune d'oxyde
Mapico Yellow
Oxidgelb
yellow oxide of iron
yellow, ferrite
yellow, iron
Yellow, Mapico
yellow, Mars
CN M.MT.AFU.AFU.ARI.AFU.AFU.ALO.ALO.BUE.ARI.BOK

Mars yellow (color)
USE **dark orange yellow**
deep orange yellow
moderate orange
strong orange

Marshall Island
FL.3684 (L)
CN F.FL.ALO.BOK.ARI.BCW

marshalling yards
RG.222 (L)
ALT **marshalling yard**
UF classification yards
hump yards
switching yards
yards, hump
yards, marshalling
yards, switching
CN V.RG.AFU.AFU.EFQ.ALO.AFU

marshes
RD.173 (L)
ALT **marsh**
CN V.RD.ARI.AFU.ARI.BCW

martello towers
RK.870 (A,L,B,R)
ALT **martello tower**
SN Low, circular defensive towers used, especially since the Napoleanic wars, for coastal protection; derived in name and form from the traditional Mediterranean watch towers found on Cape Martella, Corsica.
UF towers, martello
CN V.RK.AFU.ALO.ALO.DIO.ALO.AXC.ALO

martensitic stainless steel
MT.353 (L)
UF hardenable stainless steel
stainless steel, hardenable
stainless steel, martensitic
steel, hardenable stainless
steel, martensitic stainless
CN M.MT.AFU.AFU.AFU.BZY.AFU.AFU.AFU.AFU.ALO.AFU.ALO.AFU.ALO.ALO

Martha Washington chairs
USE **lolling chairs**

Martha Washington tables
USE **work tables**

martial arts schools
USE **martial arts training centers**

martial arts training centers
RK.1064 (L,B)
ALT **martial arts training center**
UF martial arts schools
schools, martial arts
training centers, martial arts
CN V.RK.AFU.ALO.ALO.EWY.AXC.BIQ.ALO.AXC.ALO

Martin's cement
MT.25
SN Cement made with potassium carbonate instead of alum. (MH)
UF cement, Martin's
CN M.MT.AFU.AFU.AFU.ALO.AFU.AFU BIQ.ARI

marts, merchandise
USE **trade marts**

marts, trade
USE **trade marts**

martyria
RK.1090 (A,L,R)
ALT **martyrium**
CN V.RK.AFU.ALO.ALO.FCS.AXC

martyrologies
VW.549 (L,R)
ALT **martyrology**
SN Lists, catalogs, histories, or accounts of religious martyrs. (AHD)
CN V.VW.AFU.ALO.AFU.AFU.ALO.BUE.CFS

Maruyama School
FL.2058 (L)
UF Maruyama-Shijo School
CN F.FL.ALO.ARI.ALO.ALO.ALO.ARI.CFS

Maruyama-Shijo School
USE **Maruyama School**

Marwar
FL.2294
CN F.FL.ALO.ARI.AXC.ALO.AFU.BZY.BCW.BCW.BZY

Marxism
BM.1090 (L,R)
SN The political, economic, and social

principles advocated by Karl Marx, Friedrich Engels, and their followers; it includes the labor theory of value, dialectical materialism, economic determination of human actions, and class struggle as a fundamental force in history. (W)
CN B.BM.CRG.ARI

Masa
FL.371 (L)
UF Banana
CN F.FL.ALO.AFU.AXC.AFU.AXC.ALO.BCW

Masai
FL.650 (L)
CN F.FL.ALO.AFU.AXC.AXC.BCW.BZY

Masco
FL.1607 (L)
CN F.FL.ALO.ALO.ARI.ARI.ALO.AFU.AXC

mashes
USE **framing hammers**

Mashhad
USE **Meshhed**

Mashhad ware
USE **Meshhed ware**

mashhads
RK.1143
ALT **mashhad**
SN Islamic shrines or shrine mosques.
CN V.RK.AFU.ALO.ALO.FCS.BOK.AXC

masjids
RK.1123 (A)
ALT **masjid**
SN Mosques, with a mihrab but no minbar, used for daily prayer by individuals or small groups, but not for Friday worship.
CN V.RK.AFU.ALO.ALO.FCS.BIQ.BIQ.ALO.ALO

masking tape
MT.2359
SN A strong brown-paper tape. (MAYER)
UF tape, masking
CN M.MT.AFU.ARI.ARI.ALO.AFU.ALO

maskmaking
KT.528
CN K.KT.AFU.ALO.ELK.CRG

masks (transparencies)
VJ.62
ALT **mask (transparency)**
SN Transparencies used in conjunction with a negative or another transparency to alter color or contrast.
UF photomasks
CN V.VJ.AFU.AFU.ARI.AXC.ARI

masks, dust
USE **dust masks**

masks, gas
USE **gas masks**

mason's axes
USE **axhammers**

masonic buildings
RK.1204 (A,B)
ALT **masonic building**
UF buildings, masonic
masonic temples
temples, masonic
CN V.RK.AFU.ALO.ALO.FZU.ALO.AFU

masonic temples
USE **masonic buildings**

Masonite (TM)
MT.1462
SN Fiberboard of the Masonite corporation made from by-product wood chips reduced to the cellulose fibers by high steam pressure. (MH)
CN M.MT.AFU.AFU.ALO.BIQ.DCU.ALO.DOI.AXC.AFU

masonry
MT.2747 (A,L,B,R)
SN Construction composed of shaped or molded units composed of stone, ceramic brick or tile, concrete, glass, adobe, or other material. (MEANS)
CN M.MT.AFU.AXC.BIQ.AFU

masonry cement
MT.14
SN A type of portland cement popular because of its workability and water retention qualities. (PUTNAM)
UF cement, masonry
CN M.MT.AFU.AFU.AFU.ALO.AFU.AFU.ARI.AFU.ARI

masonry joints, flush
USE **rough-cut joints**

masonry nails
TF.443
ALT **masonry nail**
SN Hardened-steel nails used primarily for fastening wood to masonry. (PUTNAM)
UF nails, masonry
CN V.TF.AFU.AFU.AFU.ALO.AFU.CFS.ALO.DCU

masonry plans
USE **foundation plans**

Masonry Style
USE **First Style**

masonry units
MT.2757
SN Use generally for naturally occurring or manufactured building units composed of concrete, glass, stone, or other material. (MEANS)
UF units, masonry
CN M.MT.AFU.AXC.BIQ.ALO

masonry vaults, thin
USE **timbrel vaults**

masonry walls, hollow
USE **cavity walls**

masonry, ashlar
USE **ashlar**

masonry, cyclopean
USE **cyclopean masonry**

masons
HG.597 (L,B,R)
ALT **mason**
SN Building tradesmen who build with stone or similar material, such as brick, concrete, or artificial stone. (W)
CN H.HG.AFU.AXC.BZY.AFU.DIO

masons' marks
VW.751 (A,L,B,R)
ALT **masons' mark**
UF banker-marks
marks, masons'
marks, stone-cutters'
stone-cutters' marks
CN V.VW.AFU.ALO.ALO.AFU.AXC.AXC.CLM

masons, banker
USE **banker masons**

masons, fixer
USE **fixer masons**

mass
BM.887
SN The extent of body of a solid object. (W)
CN B.BM.CFS.AXC.BCW

mass (liturgy)
KM.38 (L,R)
CN K.KM.AFU.ARI.AXC.BZY

mass books
USE **missals**

mass cards
VW.574
ALT **mass card**
SN Cards notifying the recipient that a mass is being offered for a deceased person. (WCOL)
UF cards, mass
CN V.VW.AFU.ALO.AFU.ARI.CFS

mass color
BM.114
SN Use for the surface color effect of a pigment when viewed by reflected light.
UF color, mass
mass tone
tone, mass
CN B.BM.AFU.AFU.ARI.BOK.ALO.AFU.BIQ

mass media
BM.333 (L,R)
SN Means of communication designed to reach large numbers of people and tending to set popular stan-

dards, ideas, and aims. (W)
UF media, mass
CN B.BM.ALO.ALO.BCW

mass production
BM.402
SN Methods of organizing manufacturing processes so as to attain high rates of output at decreasing unit cost. (ENCYB)
UF production, mass
CN B.BM.ARI.DUC

mass retaining walls
USE **gravity walls**

mass tone
USE **mass color**

mass transit
USE **public transit**

mass transit rail systems, urban
USE **urban rail systems**

mass transit systems
USE **public transit**

Massachusett
FL.1301 (L)
CN F.FL.ALO.ALO.ARI.AFU.ARI.BUE

massage parlors
RK.195 (L)
ALT **massage parlor**
UF body rub parlors
parlors, body rub
parlors, massage
CN V.RK.AFU.ALO.ALO.ALO.AXC.BO K

Massagetae
USE **Saka**

masses, pilaster
USE **pilaster strips**

massicot
MT.1782
UF Flemish yellow
giallolino
giallolino di Fiandra
ocher, plumbic
plumbic ocher
yellow, Flemish
CN M.MT.AFU.AFU.ARI.AFU.AFU.ALO.ALO.BUE.ARI.BIQ.AFU

massicot (color)
USE **pale yellow**

massicot yellow
USE **light yellow**
pale yellow

massies
USE **framing hammers**

Massim Area
FL.3638 (L)
CN F.FL.ALO.BOK.ALO.BCW.ALO.ARI

massing
BM.74
SN Use for the relationship between various masses or volumes of a building or structure.
CN B.BM.AFU.AFU.ARI.AFU.CXA

mast and spar axes
USE **mast axes**

mast axes
TB.842 (N)
ALT **mast ax**
SN Axes with a long blade, up to one foot, with a flared-shaped cheek and no poll; used for paring and trimming masts and spars. (SALAM)
UF axes, mast
axes, mast and spar
axes, mastmaker's
axes, spar
mast and spar axes
mastmaker's axes
spar axes
CN V.TB.AFU.BCW.CFS.ALO.AFU.AXC.BOK

mast churches
USE **stave churches**

mast drawknives
TB.907
ALT **mast drawknife**
SN Long drawknives, approximately 24 inches in length.
UF drawknives, mast
CN V.TB.AFU.BCW.CFS.ALO.AFU.DOI.ARI.BOK

mastabas
RK.490 (L,B)
ALT **mastaba**
SN Used to designate ancient Egyptian rectangular brick tombs with sloping sides and a flat top built over a burial chamber cut down into the rock below.
CN V.RK.AFU.ALO.ALO.BOK.BUE.AFU.BCW

master agreements
USE **collective labor agreements**

master copies
VW.682
ALT **master copy**
SN Copies of documents or, in some duplicating processes, the original documents, from which copies can be made. (ICA)
UF copies, master
CN V.VW.AFU.ALO.AFU.DZW.BIQ.BIQ

master drawings
VD.141
ALT **master drawing**
UF drawings, master
drawings, old master
old master drawings
CN V.VD.AFU.BCW.AFU

master files
USE **project files**

master-keyed locks
TF.205
ALT **master-keyed lock**
SN Locking systems intended for use in a series, each lock of which may be actuated by two different keys, one capable of operating every lock of the series, and the other capable of operating only one or a few of the locks. (MEANS)
UF locks, master-keyed
CN V.TF.AFU.AFU.AFU.AFU.DIO.BIQ.AFU.CLM

master keys
TF.533
ALT **master key**
SN Keys designed to open several different locks, each otherwise opened by different keys.
UF change keys
keys, change
keys, master
keys, pass
pass keys
CN V.TF.AFU.ALO.ARI.AFU.BIQ

master plans
VD.61
ALT **master plan**
UF plans, master
CN V.VD.AFU.AFU.BIQ.ALO.AXC.BIQ

master plans (reports)
USE **comprehensive plans**

master specifications
VW.797
ALT **master specification**
SN Specifications prepared as a standard for a particular type of project. (STEIN)
UF specifications, master
CN V.VW.AFU.ARI.AFU.ARI.AFU.ARI.AXC

masterpiece
BM.298 (L)
SN Use for the concept of the few outstanding works in which the artistic personality of a great artist finds its fullest expression.
UF artistic masterpiece
CN B.BM.AFU.AXC.CFS

masters
HG.767
ALT **master**
SN Use especially for artists or craftsmen qualified to teach apprentices and to carry on their trade independently; can be used broadly for persons eminently skilled in something. (RHDEL2)
CN H.HG.AFU.BIQ.BIQ

masters theses
VW.1072

ALT **masters thesis**
UF theses, masters
CN V.VW.AFU.ARI.ALO.CRG.BOK.ALO

mastic
MT.1504 (B)
SN The gum exudation of small evergreens native to the Mediterranean countries. Soluble in both alcohol and turpentine, used for artists' paints and coating lacquers.(MH) Mastic varnishes become yellow and brittle with age.
UF Bombay mastic
Chios mastic
mastic, Bombay
mastic, Chios
CN M.MT.AFU.AFU.ALO.BOK.DCU

mastic, Bombay
USE **mastic**

mastic, Chios
USE **mastic**

mastmaker's axes
USE **mast axes**

masts
RT.176 (L,B)
ALT **mast**
SN Use for vertical poles, usually stayed by guys, serving as anchorages, such as for suspension cables or to elevate antennae.
UF guyed masts
masts, guyed
CN V.RT.AFU.AFU.AFU.AXC.BZY

masts, guyed
USE **masts**

masts, radio
USE **radio towers**

mat board
MT.1915
SN A stiff cardboard with a thin facing of paper on one side, has a white or whitish base, surface may be smooth or pebbled, dull or glossy. (MAYER)
UF board, mat
CN M.MT.AFU.AFU.ARI.ALO.ALO.AXC.ALO.BIQ.AFU.AXC

mat foundations
RT.167 (B)
ALT **mat foundation**
SN Continuous foundations under the full extent of a structure. (DAC)
UF foundations, mat
CN V.RT.AFU.AFU.AFU.AXC.BUE.ARI.AFU.AFU

mat glaze
USE **matte glaze**

Mata Kuching damar
MT.1489
UF cat's eye damar
damar, cat's eye
damar, Mata Kuching
CN M.MT.AFU.AFU.ALO.BOK.AXC.AFU.AFU.AFU

Matambwe
FL.661
CN F.FL.ALO.AFU.AXC.AXC.BIQ.AXC

Matará
FL.1645
CN F.FL.ALO.ALO.ARI.ARI.AXC.CFS

Mataram
FL.2385
CN F.FL.ALO.ARI.BCW.ARI.ALO.AXC.ALO.AFU.ARI

matched boards
USE **matched lumber**

matched joints
TF.592
ALT **matched joint**
UF joints, matched
CN V.TF.ALO.AFU.DZW

matched lumber
MT.1428
SN Lumber whose edge is dressed and shaped for a tongue-and-groove joint when pieces are laid edge to edge or end to end. (STEIN)
UF boards, matched
lumber, matched
matched boards
CN M.MT.AFU.AFU.ALO.BIQ.DCU.ALO.BOK.ALO.AFU.AFU.AFU.AFU.AFU

matching planes
USE **tongue-and-groove planes**

Matebele
USE **Ndebele**

Matengo
FL.662
CN F.FL.ALO.AFU.AXC.AXC.BIQ.BCW

material culture
KD.94 (A,L,R)
SN Study of the physical objects made by a people for satisfaction of their needs, especially those articles required for sustenance and perpetuation of life. (W)
UF culture, material
CN K.KD.AFU.ALO.AFU.AXC

material, final image
USE **final image material**

material, image
USE **final image material**

material, impervious
USE **waterproof materials**

material, waterproofing
USE **waterproofing materials**

materialism
BM.360 (L,R)
SN Belief that the only or the highest values or objectives in life lie in material well-being and pleasure, and in the furthering of material progress. (W)
CN B.BM.ALO.ALO.CLM.DZW

materialism, dialectical
USE **dialectical materialism**

materials
MT.1 (L,B,R)
UF substances
CN M.MT.AFU

materials sciences
KD.245 (L)
SN Sciences concerned with the relation between the structure and properties of materials, the factors controlling the internal structure of solids, and the processes for altering the structure and properties of solids, including physical metallurgy, ceramics, polymers, and the physics and chemistry of solids. (PG)
UF sciences, materials
CN K.KD.AFU.ARI.BZY

materials, abrasion-resistant
USE **abrasion-resistant materials**

materials, absorbent
USE **absorbent materials**

materials, acid-resistant
USE **acid-resistant materials**

materials, acoustic insulating
USE **acoustical insulation**

materials, animal
USE **animal materials**

materials, architectural
USE **building materials**

materials, artists'
USE **artists' materials**

materials, audiovisual
USE **audiovisual materials**

materials, bills of
USE **quantity surveys**

materials, bituminous
USE **bituminous materials**

materials, bonding
USE **adhesives**

materials, building
USE **building materials**

materials, cartographic
USE **cartographic materials**

materials, caulking
USE **caulking compounds**

materials, cellular
USE **cellular materials**

materials, chemical-resistant
USE **chemical-resistant materials**

materials, coarse-grain
USE **coarse-grain materials**

materials, composite
USE **composite materials**

materials, conducting
USE **conductors**

materials, construction
USE **building materials**

materials, corrosive
USE **corrosive materials**

materials, fine-grain
USE **fine-grain materials**

materials, fire-resistant
USE **fire-resistant materials**

materials, flameproof
USE **fireproofing agents**

materials, flammable
USE **flammable materials**

materials, flexible
USE **flexible materials**

materials, granular
USE **granular materials**

materials, heat-resistant
USE **heat-resistant materials**

materials, honeycomb
USE **honeycomb materials**

materials, impregnated
USE **impregnated materials**

materials, inert
USE **inert materials**

materials, inflammable
USE **fire-resistant materials**

materials, instructional
USE **instructional materials**

materials, insulating
USE **insulation**

materials, jointing
USE **sealing compounds**

materials, lightweight
USE **lightweight materials**

materials, malleable
USE **malleable materials**

materials, medium-grain
USE **medium-grain materials**

materials, molding
USE **molding materials**

materials, nonbook
USE **audiovisual materials**

materials, noncombustible
USE **fire-resistant materials**

materials, nonprint
USE **audiovisual materials**
visual materials

materials, organic
USE **organic materials**

materials, packaging
USE **packaging materials**

materials, packing
USE **packaging materials**

materials, particulate
USE **granular materials**

materials, photographic
USE **photographic materials**

materials, plant
USE **plant materials**

materials, porous
USE **porous materials**

materials, pyroclastic
USE **pyroclastic materials**

materials, raw
USE **raw materials**

materials, refractory
USE **refractory materials**

materials, reinforcing
USE **reinforcing materials**

materials, sandwich
USE **composite materials**

materials, self-instructional
USE **self-instructional materials**

materials, strength of
USE **strength of materials**

materials, thermal insulating
USE **thermal insulation**

materials, visual
USE **visual materials**
visual resource collections

materials, water-resistant
USE **waterproof materials**

materials, waterproof
USE **waterproof materials**

materials, wrapping
USE **wrapping materials**

maternity hospitals
RK.770 (A,L,B)
ALT **maternity hospital**
UF hospitals, maternity
CN V.RK.AFU.ALO.ALO.CXA.ALO.AFU.BCW.ALO.BIQ

maternity wards
RM.295
ALT **maternity ward**
UF wards, maternity
CN V.RM.AFU.DIO.AXC.AFU.BCW

mates
USE **assistants**

mathas
RG.193
ALT **matha**
SN Monasteries or convents in pre-Islamic India. (PBROWN)
CN V.RG.AFU.AFU.DUC.BCW

mathematical models
BM.814 (A,L,B)
UF models, mathematical
CN B.BM.CFS.ARI.BOK

mathematical physics
KD.287 (L)
UF physics, mathematical
CN K.KD.AFU.ARI.CLM.AXC.BCW

mathematical tile
MT.167 (B)
UF geometrical tile
tile, geometrical
tile, mathematical
CN M.MT.AFU.AFU.AFU.AXC.ALO.ALO.ALO.AFU.ALO.ALO

mathematicians
HG.346 (L)
ALT **mathematician**
CN H.HG.AFU.AXC.BIQ.AFU.AFU.CLM

mathematics
KD.250 (A,L,B,R)
CN K.KD.AFU.ARI.CFS

mathematics, applied
USE **applied mathematics**

Mathura
FL.2203 (L)
CN F.FL.ALO.ARI.AXC.ALO.AFU.ARI.BIQ.ALO

Matlatzinca
FL.1501 (L)
CN F.FL.ALO.ALO.ARI.ALO.ARI.ARI

matriculating
KG.174
SN Enrolling, or admitting to membership and privileges, especially in a college or university. (RHDEL2)
CN K.KG.AFU.ALO.ALO.AFU

matt glaze
USE **matte glaze**

matt-painted ware
FL.2657
UF ware, matt-painted
CN F.FL.ALO.AXC.ALO.AFU.ALO.AXC.AXC.BIQ

matte
DC.137
SN Having a dull or lusterless surface finish.(RHDEL2) To refer to two-dimensional images lacking spatial

qualities, and to areas of color without variations, use **flat**.
UF flat (matte)
CN D.DC.AFU.BCW.ARI

matte glaze
MT.2568
SN An opaque glaze with a dull, nonreflective surface; a mat effect may be induced by adding barium or alumina (clay) to raise the maturation point of the glaze. (MAYER)
UF glaze, mat
glaze, matt
mat glaze
matt glaze
CN M.MT.AFU.ARI.CRG.ARI.ARI.AFU.ARI.ARI

matte varnish
USE **flat varnish**

Matter art
FL.3732 (R)
UF art, Matter
Matter painting
painting, Matter
CN F.FL.ALO.BUE.ARI.DUC

Matter painting
USE **Matter art**

matter, coloring
USE **colorant**

matting
KT.647 (L,B)
ALT **matted**
SN The preparation of a flat, two-dimensional art work for display by securing it inside a window mat. (REILLY)
CN K.KT.AFU.ALO.GLI.AFU.ARI

matting (roofing material)
MT.2395
CN M.MT.AFU.ARI.BZY.AXC.ALO.ALO

mattresses
TG.856 (L,N)
ALT **mattress**
CN V.TG.ALO.BIQ.CLM

mattresses, French
USE **French mattresses**

Matty Island
USE **Wuvulu Island**

Matzanel
FL.1013
CN F.FL.ALO.ALO.ALO.ALO.AFU.ALO.ARI.AFU.AFU.AXC

Maucú
USE **Macú**

Maué
FL.1590 (L)
CN F.FL.ALO.ALO.ARI.ARI.AFU.FCS

mauls
TB.470 (N)
ALT **maul**
SN Long-handled heavy wooden mallets. (MEANS)
UF batters
beaters (mauls)
malls (mauls)
CN V.TB.AFU.ARI.ELK.AXC

mauls, pin
USE **top maul hammers**

mauresques
USE **moresques**

Maurya
FL.2193 (L)
CN F.FL.ALO.ARI.AXC.ALO.AFU.ARI.ALO

mausoleums
RK.469 (A,L,N,B,R)
ALT **mausoleum**
CN V.RK.AFU.ALO.ALO.BOK.ARI.ALO.AFU

mauve
MT.1541
UF aniline purple
aniline violet
Perkin's violet
purple, aniline
violet, aniline
violet, Perkin's
CN M.MT.AFU.AFU.ARI.AFU.AFU.AFU.AFU.ALO.ALO.ALO

mauve (color)
USE **brilliant purple**
brilliant violet
moderate reddish purple
strong purple

mauve gray
USE **grayish purple**

mauve orchid
USE **light grayish purplish red**

mauve pink
USE **pale purplish pink**

mauve taupe
USE **dark grayish purple**
dark purplish gray
dark reddish gray
grayish purplish red

mauve taupe, dark
USE **dark grayish red**
dark purplish gray

mauve, bright
USE **light violet**

mauve, light
USE **light violet**
moderate pink
moderate purplish pink

mauve, orchid
USE **dark purplish pink**

mauve, pastel
USE **pale purplish pink**

mauve, permanent
USE **manganese violet**

mauve, pink
USE **pink mauve**

mauve, rose
USE **dark grayish purple**
dark purplish red
grayish purple

Mawia
FL.663
UF Wamawia
CN F.FL.ALO.AFU.AXC.AXC.BIQ.BIQ

Maxia jia
USE **Ma-Xia**

maximum-security institutions
USE **maximum-security prisons**

maximum-security prisons
RK.722
ALT **maximum-security prison**
UF high-security prisons
institutions, maximum-security
maximum-security institutions
prisons, high-security
prisons, maximum-security
prisons, super-security
super-security prisons
CN V.RK.AFU.ALO.ALO.CXA.AFU.AXC.AFU.ALO

Maya
USE **Mayan**

Mayan
FL.1531 (A,L,B)
UF Maya
CN F.FL.ALO.ALO.ARI.ALO.BIQ.AFU

Mayan blue
MT.1585
UF blue, Mayan
CN M.MT.AFU.AFU.ARI.AFU.AFU.ALO.ALO.ALO.AFU.AXC

Mayan Revival
FL.1735 (A,R)
UF Revival, Mayan
CN F.FL.ALO.ALO.BCW.AFU.BUE.AXC

maydans
RK.1445
ALT **maydan**
SN Open spaces or areas in Islamic towns used for a variety of activities, such as games, parades, and executions.
CN V.RK.ALO.AFU.ARI.AFU

Mayemir
USE **Maiemir**

Mayo
FL.1491 (L)
CN F.FL.ALO.ALO.ARI.ALO.AFU.ARI

Mayombe
USE **Yombe**

mayors
HG.683 (A,L)
ALT **mayor**
SN Chief magistrates of a city or borough. (W)
CN H.HG.AFU.AXC.CFS.CFS.BUE

Mazahua
FL.1502 (L)
CN F.FL.ALO.ALO.ARI.ALO.ARI.AXC

Mazapán
USE **Aztec I**

Mazatec
FL.1518 (L)
CN F.FL.ALO.ALO.ARI.ALO.AXC.BZY

maze gardens
RK.1405 (A,L)
ALT **maze garden**
UF gardens, labyrinth
gardens, maze
labyrinth gardens
mazes (gardens)
CN V.RK.ALO.AFU.AFU.AFU.ARI.ARI.ALO

mazes (gardens)
USE **maze gardens**

mazes (motifs)
USE **labyrinths**

mazes, hedge
USE **hedge mazes**

mazes, turf
USE **turf mazes**

mazzard
USE **sweet cherry**

Mbagani
FL.444
CN F.FL.ALO.AFU.AXC.ALO.ALO.AFU.AFU.BUE

Mbala (Kuba Folk Style)
FL.436 (L)
UF Bushongo
CN F.FL.ALO.AFU.AXC.ALO.ALO.AFU.AFU.AXC.ALO

Mbala (Western Zaire)
FL.467 (L)
UF Bambala (Western Zaire)
CN F.FL.ALO.AFU.AXC.ALO.ALO.ARI.BOK

Mbamba
FL.480
UF Ambamba
CN F.FL.ALO.AFU.AXC.ALO.ALO.AXC.AXC.AFU

Mbanza
FL.530
UF Banza
CN F.FL.ALO.AFU.AXC.ALO.ALO.BIQ.ALO.BCW

Mbata
FL.481
CN F.FL.ALO.AFU.AXC.ALO.ALO.AXC.AXC.ALO

Mbayá
FL.1646 (L)
CN F.FL.ALO.ALO.ARI.ARI.AXC.CLM

Mbeguá
FL.1694
CN F.FL.ALO.ALO.ARI.ARI.BOK.BOK

Mbembe
FL.244 (L)
CN F.FL.ALO.AFU.AXC.AFU.ALO.AFU.BIQ

Mbete
FL.417 (L)
UF Ambete
Bambete
CN F.FL.ALO.AFU.AXC.ALO.AFU.AXC.BCW

Mbokovi
USE **Mocoví**

Mbole
FL.514 (L)
UF Bambole
CN F.FL.ALO.AFU.AXC.ALO.ALO.BIQ.AFU.AFU.BUE

Mbun
FL.468
UF Babunda
Bunda
CN F.FL.ALO.AFU.AXC.ALO.ALO.ARI.BUE

Mbundu
FL.457 (L)
UF Ovimbundu
Umbundu
CN F.FL.ALO.AFU.AXC.ALO.ALO.ALO.BIQ

Mbunga
FL.588
CN F.FL.ALO.AFU.AXC.AXC.AFU.BIQ

McKean
FL.921
CN F.FL.ALO.ALO.ALO.AFU.ALO.ARI.AXC.AXC

meadow grounds
USE **meadows**

meadowlands
USE **meadows**

Meadowood
FL.873
CN F.FL.ALO.ALO.ALO.AFU.ALO.ALO.AXC.BUE

meadows
RD.246 (L)
ALT **meadow**
UF leas
leys (meadows)
meadow grounds
meadowlands
CN V.RD.ARI.AFU.BCW.ALO.AFU.AFU.ALO

meager lime
MT.331
UF lime, meager
lime, poor
poor lime
CN M.MT.AFU.AFU.AFU.BUE.ALO.ALO

mean
BM.827 (L)
UF average
CN B.BM.CFS.ARI.CRG.ALO.ARI

mean, golden
USE **golden section**

meanders
RD.159
ALT **meander**
SN Use for broad, curving, generally looplike bends in rivers or streams.
CN V.RD.ARI.AFU.AFU.ALO.ARI

meanders (patterns)
DG.141
ALT **meander (pattern)**
SN Use for running ornament consisting of continuous winding lines, either angular or curving.
CN D.DG.AFU.ARI.ALO.CFS

measured drawings
VD.100 (L,B)
ALT **measured drawing**
SN Use for drawings of an existing object, structure, or site, drawn to scale.
UF drawings, measured
drawings, survey
survey drawings
CN V.VD.AFU.ALO.BCW

measurement, color
USE **colorimetry**

measurement, photographic
USE **photogrammetry**

measuring
KT.495 (L,B,R)
ALT **measured**
CN K.KT.AFU.ALO.EFQ

meatworks
USE **slaughterhouses**

mechanical arts
KD.299 (R)
SN In Medieval times, practical areas of knowledge such as weaponry, military science, navigation, hunting, medicine, and construction arts.
UF arts, illiberal
arts, mechanical

illiberal arts
CN K.KD.AFU.BCW.ARI

mechanical drawing
USE **drafting**

mechanical drawings
VD.134 (A,L)
ALT **mechanical drawing**
SN Drawings produced with the aid of instruments such as compasses or T-squares. (DAC)
UF drawings, hard-line
drawings, mechanical
hard-line drawings
CN V.VD.AFU.AXC.BOK

mechanical drawings (building systems drawings)
VD.146
ALT **mechanical drawing (building system drawing)**
SN Use for drawings of the mechanical systems of buildings (e.g., HVAC and plumbing systems).
UF drawings, mechanical (building systems drawings)
CN V.VD.AFU.BIQ.AFU.AFU

mechanical engineering
KD.230 (L)
SN Study and application of the principles of mechanics, thermodynamics, and material properties. (PG)
UF engineering, mechanical
CN K.KD.AFU.ARI.BIQ.BZY

mechanical engineers
HG.640 (L)
ALT **mechanical engineer**
UF engineers, mechanical
CN H.HG.AFU.AXC.BZY.BCW.BZY

mechanical equipment
TB.10 (L,N)
UF equipment, mechanical
CN V.TB.AFU.ALO.ALO

mechanical furniture
TG.795
SN Refers to a great variety of furniture including barbers' chairs, wheel chairs, and space-saving office furniture; designed to solve a particular problem. (MANG)
UF furniture, mechanical
CN V.TG.AFU.ARI.BOK

mechanical pencil holders
USE **pencil holders**

mechanical pencils
TB.266 (N)
ALT **mechanical pencil**
SN Pencils whose lead is projected by a screw or other device. (W)
UF clutch pencils
pencils, clutch
pencils, mechanical
pencils, propelling
propelling pencils
CN V.TB.AFU.ARI.CLM.AFU.ALO.DIO.BCW

mechanical perspective
USE **linear perspective**

mechanical properties
BM.947
UF properties, mechanical
CN B.BM.CFS.AXC.BZY.BOK

mechanical systems
RT.1380
ALT **mechanical system**
SN In some contexts may include electrical systems and electricity-based systems, such as protection systems and communication systems.
UF systems, mechanical
CN V.RT.ALO.BCW

mechanical trowels
TB.637
ALT **mechanical trowel**
SN Machines with interchangeable metal or rubber blades; used to compact and smooth plaster. (MEANS)
UF power trowels
trowels, mechanical
trowels, power
CN V.TB.AFU.BCW.BCW.ALO.HCQ.BCW

mechanical ventilation
RT.1406
SN Use for systems supplying and exhausting fresh air by mechanical means.
UF ventilation, mechanical
CN V.RT.ALO.BCW.AFU.AFU.AXC.ALO

mechanically operated doors
RT.867 (L)
ALT **mechanically operated door**
UF automatic doors
doors, automatic
doors, mechanically operated
CN V.RT.AFU.ARI.AFU.AFU.AFU.ALO.ARI.AFU.ARI.ARI

mechanics (people)
HG.446 (L,R)
ALT **mechanic (person)**
SN Persons skilled in the construction, operation, or repair of machines or vehicles run by machines. (W)
CN H.HG.AFU.AXC.BUE.ALO.BOK

mechanics (physics)
KD.288 (L,B,R)
SN Study of forces on matter or systems, involving the identification and description of such systems by cause-and-effect associations. (PG)
CN K.KD.AFU.ARI.CLM.AXC.BIQ

mechanics, soil
USE **soil mechanics**

mechanization
BM.1141 (L,B)
CN B.BM.CXA.ALO.ARI

medal cabinets
TG.424 (N)
ALT **medal cabinet**
UF cabinets, coin
cabinets, medal
cases, medal
coin cabinets
medal cases
medalliers
CN V.TG.AFU.AFU.AXC.ALO.ARI.ALO.AXC.AFU

medal cases
USE **medal cabinets**

medalists
HG.516 (L)
ALT **medalist**
SN Designers, engravers, or makers of medals. (W)
CN H.HG.AFU.AXC.BUE.ARI.CFS.ARI.BOK

medalliers
USE **medal cabinets**

medallions (ornament areas)
DG.91 (R)
ALT **medallion (ornament area)**
SN Use for round or oval enframements, usually containing figures or ornamental motifs. Primarily found in two-dimensional media, such as textiles, stained glass, and manuscript illuminations; for circular decorated panels in architectural contexts, use **roundels.**
CN D.DG.AFU.ALO.AXC

media
MT.2623
ALT **medium**
SN Materials and techniques used in the making of a work of art (such as ink on paper, collage).
UF mediums
CN M.MT.AFU.ARI.FUA

media centers, educational
USE **audiovisual centers**

media files
USE **clippings files**

media, mass
USE **mass media**

media, visual
USE **visual materials**

Mediaeval
USE **Medieval**

medial braces
TG.980
ALT **medial brace**
SN Curved medial braces running from front to back of the seat frame. (MONTGO)

UF braces, medial
braces, sweep
medial rails
rails, medial
sweep braces
CN V.TG.ALO.GLI.ALO.ALO.AFU

medial rails
USE **medial braces**

medial strips
USE **medians**

median
BM.828
SN A value in an ordered set of quantities above and below which fall an equal number of quantities. (W)
CN B.BM.CFS.ARI.CRG.ALO.AXC

Median (Persian style)
FL.3020 (L,B)
CN F.FL.ALO.AXC.ARI.BIQ.ALO.ALO

median columns
RT.109
ALT **median column**
SN Use for the two central columns in a range, when more widely spaced than the columns to either side.
UF columns, median
CN V.RT.AFU.AFU.AFU.AXC.BIQ.AFU.ALO.BOK

median strips
USE **medians**

medians
RM.489 (L)
ALT **median**
SN Paved or planted strips of ground dividing highways into lanes according to direction of travel. (W)
UF medial strips
median strips
CN V.RM.ALO.ALO.ALO.ALO.CFS

medical centers
RK.776 (A,L,B)
ALT **medical center**
UF centers, health
centers, medical
health centers
CN V.RK.AFU.ALO.ALO.CXA.ALO.AFU.BOK

medical centers, emergency
USE **emergency medical centers**

medical clinics
USE **clinics**

medical colleges
USE **medical schools**

medical facilities
USE **health facilities**

medical illustration
KT.214 (L,R)
SN The activity of drawing or painting illustrations that are used for instruction or research in the field of medicine.
UF illustration, medical
CN K.KT.AFU.ALO.DUC.CLM.BOK.ALO

medical illustrations
VB.54 (L,R)
ALT **medical illustration**
UF illustrations, medical
CN V.VB.AFU.ALO.AXC.ALO.ARI.ALO

medical illustrators
HG.148
ALT **medical illustrator**
SN Persons engaged in medical illustration.
UF illustrators, medical
CN H.HG.AFU.AXC.AXC.AFU.AFU.ALO.BCW.AFU.ALO.ALO.ARI.AFU

medical jurisprudence
USE **forensic medicine**

medical laboratories
RK.737 (A,L,B)
ALT **medical laboratory**
UF clinical laboratories
laboratories, clinical
laboratories, medical
CN V.RK.AFU.ALO.ALO.CXA.ALO.AFU.AFU.ALO

medical libraries
RK.711 (A,L,B)
ALT **medical library**
UF libraries, medical
CN V.RK.AFU.ALO.ALO.CRG.AXC.ARI.BCW

medical museums
RK.420 (L,B)
ALT **medical museum**
UF museums, medical
CN V.RK.AFU.ALO.ALO.BCW.AXC.ARI.CFS.BCW

medical office buildings
USE **medical offices**

medical offices
RK.920 (A,L,B)
ALT **medical office**
UF doctors' offices
doctors' surgeries
medical office buildings
office buildings, medical
offices, doctors'
offices, medical
offices, physicians'
physicians' offices
surgeries, doctors'
CN V.RK.AFU.ALO.ALO.DZW.ALO.BIQ

medical photographers
HG.122
ALT **medical photographer**
SN Persons engaged in medical photography.
UF photographers, medical
CN H.HG.AFU.AXC.AXC.AFU.AFU.ALO.AXC.DOI.AXC.AFU

medical photography
KT.301 (L)
SN The activity of providing photographs to document or illustrate medical conditions or phenomena.
UF photography, medical
CN K.KT.AFU.ALO.DUC.DIO.AFU.CFS

medical records
VW.922 (L)
ALT **medical record**
UF records, medical
CN V.VW.AFU.ARI.AFU.BUE

medical schools
RK.812 (A,L,B)
ALT **medical school**
UF colleges, medical
medical colleges
schools, medical
CN V.RK.AFU.ALO.ALO.CXA.ARI.ALO.CFS

medical scientists
HG.348 (L)
ALT **medical scientist**
UF scientists, medical
CN H.HG.AFU.AXC.BIQ.AFU.AFU.CRG

medicine
KD.240 (L,R)
CN K.KD.AFU.ARI.BUE.ARI

medicine chests
TG.465 (N)
ALT **medicine chest**
SN Small chests fitted for bottles and intended to hold medical supplies; of a type made in the 18th and early 19th centuries.
UF chests, medicine
CN V.TG.AFU.AFU.AXC.ALO.AXC.DIO

medicine, forensic
USE **forensic medicine**

medicine, legal
USE **forensic medicine**

Medieval
FL.3087 (A,L,B,R)
UF Mediaeval
Medieval European
CN F.FL.ALO.BCW.ALO.ALO.AFU

Medieval European
USE **Medieval**

Medieval Indian
USE **Post-Gupta**

Medieval, Early
USE **Early Medieval**

Medieval, Late
USE **Late Medieval**

Medievalism

BM.361
SN Use for the 19th- and 20th-century interest in, or passion for, the Middle Ages.
CN B.BM.ALO.ALO.CLM.EFQ

medinas
RD.12 (A)
ALT **medina**
SN Islamic cities; may also be used for certain districts in North African cities.
UF madinas
CN V.RD.AFU.AFU.ALO.AXC.AFU

Meditation, School of
USE **Ch'an**

Mediterranean
FL.2528 (L)
CN F.FL.ALO.AXC.ALO

Mediterranean cypress
USE **classic cypress**

medium blue
USE **dark blue**
dark greenish blue
grayish purplish blue
moderate blue
moderate greenish blue

medium-carbon steel
MT.346
SN Steel having a carbon content between .3 and .6%. (DAC)
UF steel, medium-carbon
CN M.MT.AFU.AFU.AFU.BZY.AFU.AFU.AFU.AFU.ALO.AFU.AFU.ALO

medium chrome green
USE **dark green**
dark yellowish green

medium dark gray
USE **dark gray**

medium-grain materials
MT.2251
UF materials, medium-grain
CN M.MT.AFU.ALO.DOI.ALO

medium gray
DL.303
UF aluminum (color)
beige gray
black, gray
blue gray
centroid color 265
deep violet gray
gray black
gray, beige
gray, blue
gray, light navy
gray, light neutral
gray, medium
gray, medium light
gray, medium navy
gray, neutral
gray, pale neutral
gray, silver
light gray, medium
light navy gray
light neutral gray
light violet gray
medium light gray
medium navy gray
navy gray, light
navy gray, medium
neutral gray
neutral gray, light
neutral gray, pale
nickle (color)
pale neutral gray
pale violet gray
platinum (color)
silver (color)
silver gray
slate gray
violet gray, deep
violet gray, light
violet gray, pale
CN D.DL.AFU.ALO.ALO.ALO

medium light gray
USE **medium gray**

medium navy gray
USE **medium gray**

medium plate
USE **sixth plate**

medium-rise buildings
USE **mid-rise buildings**

medium-security correctional institutions
USE **medium-security prisons**

medium-security institutions
USE **medium-security prisons**

medium-security prisons
RK.723
ALT **medium-security prison**
UF correctional institutions, medium-security
institutions, medium-security
medium-security correctional institutions
medium-security institutions
prisons, medium-security
CN V.RK.AFU.ALO.ALO.CXA.AFU.AXC.AFU.ARI

medium solder
MT.423
UF solder, medium
CN M.MT.AFU.AFU.AFU.BZY.AFU.AFU.AFU.ALO.BUE.ARI.ARI

medium teal
USE **moderate greenish blue**

medium teal blue
USE **moderate greenish blue**

medium turquoise blue
USE **moderate greenish blue**

medium, maroger
USE **maroger medium**

mediums
USE **media**

mediums (photographic binders)
USE **binders**

mediums (vehicles)
USE **vehicles**

meerschaum
MT.533 (L,R)
SN Soft, white, clayey, heat-resistant mineral, a hydrous magnesium silicate, used especially for tobacco pipes. (W)
UF sepiolite
CN M.MT.AFU.AFU.AFU.CFS.AFU.FOG

meeting bars
USE **meeting rails**

meeting house benches
USE **deacon's benches**

meeting house lots
USE **greens**

meeting house seats
USE **deacon's benches**

meeting houses
RK.1115 (A,N,B,R)
ALT **meeting house**
SN Used loosely to refer to buildings of assembly for religious worship; when possible use a more specific term.
UF houses, meeting
CN V.RK.AFU.ALO.ALO.FCS.BIQ.BCW

meeting houses, Friends'
USE **Quaker meeting houses**

meeting houses, Quaker
USE **Quaker meeting houses**

meeting rails
RT.973
ALT **meeting rail**
SN In double-hung windows, the horizontal rails that meet in the middle when the window is closed. (MEANS)
UF bars, meeting
meeting bars
rails, meeting
CN V.RT.AFU.ARI.AFU.AFU.BOK.ALO.AXC

meeting rooms
USE **conference rooms**

meetings
KM.96 (L,B)
CN K.KM.AFU.CRG

meetings, town
USE **town meetings**

Mega-decoration
USE **Supermannerist**

megalithic chamber tombs
RK.485 (A,L,N,B,R)

ALT **megalithic chamber tomb**
UF chamber tombs, megalithic
dolmens
hunebedden
steinkisten
stone tables
stones, table
table stones
tables, stone
tombs, megalithic chamber
CN V.RK.AFU.ALO.ALO.BOK.BUE.AFU.ALO.ALO

megalithic monuments
RK.889 (A,L,R)
ALT **megalithic monument**
UF monuments, megalithic
CN V.RK.AFU.ALO.ALO.DOI.AFU.ARI

megaliths
MT.890 (N,B)
ALT **megalith**
CN M.MT.AFU.AFU.AFU.DCU.ALO.BUE

megalopolises
RD.19
ALT **megalopolis**
SN Great urbanized areas or clusters of urbanized areas produced by the expansion and merging of several neighboring metropolises or conurbations.
UF megapolises
CN V.RD.AFU.AFU.ALO.BIQ.ALO

megapolises
USE **megalopolises**

Megarian
FL.2622
UF Megarian ware
ware, Megarian
CN F.FL.ALO.AXC.ALO.AFU.ALO.AXC.ALO.AXC.BIQ

Megarian ware
USE **Megarian**

megarons
RK.264 (A)
ALT **megaron**
SN Designates ancient rectangular dwellings consisting of a large main space and a shallower front porch framed by projecting antae; may be used for similarly shaped central features within more complex ancient buildings.
CN V.RK.AFU.ALO.ALO.AXC.ALO.AFU.CRG.BCW

megastructures
RK.22 (A,L,R)
ALT **megastructure**
SN Use only for very large, multipurpose, adaptable structures housing all or most of the functions of a city. For less comprehensive and dominating structures, use **multiuse buildings.**
CN V.RK.AFU.ALO.AFU.ALO.BCW

megilp
MT.2508
SN Paint medium made by mixing mastic varnish with linseed oil and driers; used to give a paint body. On aging, it becomes brittle and yellow. (TATEMT)
CN M.MT.AFU.ARI.CRG.ALO.AXC

Mehmed I
FL.3486
UF Mehmed I Çelebi
Mehmet I
Muhammad I (Ottoman)
CN F.FL.ALO.BIQ.AFU.FOG.AFU.BCW

Mehmed I Çelebi
USE **Mehmed I**

Mehmed II
FL.3489
UF Mehmet II
Mehmet II Faith
Mehmet II the Conqueror
CN F.FL.ALO.BIQ.AFU.FOG.AFU.BUE

Mehmed III
FL.3495
UF Mehmet III
CN F.FL.ALO.BIQ.AFU.FOG.AFU.DCU

Mehmed IV
FL.3501
UF Mehmet IV
CN F.FL.ALO.BIQ.AFU.FOG.AFU.ELK

Mehmed V
FL.3516
UF Mehmet V Resat
CN F.FL.ALO.BIQ.AFU.FOG.AFU.HTY

Mehmed VI
FL.3517
UF Mehmet VI Vahdettin
CN F.FL.ALO.BIQ.AFU.FOG.AFU.HZS

Mehmet I
USE **Mehmed I**

Mehmet II
USE **Mehmed II**

Mehmet II Faith
USE **Mehmed II**

Mehmet II the Conqueror
USE **Mehmed II**

Mehmet III
USE **Mehmed III**

Mehmet IV
USE **Mehmed IV**

Mehmet V Resat
USE **Mehmed V**

Mehmet VI Vahdettin
USE **Mehmed VI**

Meiji
FL.1988 (A,L)
CN F.FL.ALO.ARI.ALO.ALO.AFU.BIQ.AFU

MEK
USE **methyl ethyl ketone**

melainotype
USE **tintype**

melainotypes
USE **tintypes**

melamine
MT.2163
SN A white, crystalline, slightly water-soluble solid used chiefly in organic synthesis and in the manufacture of resins, especially melamine resins. (RHDEL2)
UF formaldehyde, melamine
melamine formaldehyde
CN M.MT.AFU.AFU.ARI.BUE.ALO.AXC.ALO.ARI.AFU

melamine formaldehyde
USE **melamine**

melamine phenolic
MT.2174
UF phenolic, melamine
CN M.MT.AFU.AFU.ARI.BUE.ALO.AXC.ALO.BIQ.ARI

melancholy
BM.581 (L,R)
UF sadness
CN B.BM.BUE.ARI.CFS

Melanesian
FL.3618 (L,B)
CN F.FL.ALO.BOK.ALO

melanin
MT.1561 (L)
CN M.MT.AFU.AFU.ARI.AFU.AFU.ALO.AFU.ALO.AFU.ALO.AXC

melanorrhoea
USE **rosewood**

Melayu
USE **Malayu**

Melchite
BM.646 (L)
UF Melchite Catholic
Melkite
CN B.BM.BZY.AFU.ALO.AXC.AXC

Melchite Catholic
USE **Melchite**

Melian
FL.2688
CN F.FL.ALO.AXC.ALO.AFU.ALO.BCW.ALO.BIQ

Melkite
USE **Melchite**

mellaria

USE apiaries

melon bulb supports
TG.992
ALT **melon bulb support**
SN Modern term for a melon-shaped swelling, often carved with gadrooning, used centrally on table legs, bed posts, and press cupboard supports in the late 16th and the 17th centuries. (IDO)
UF melon supports
supports, melon bulb
CN V.TG.ALO.HIK.AFU.ALO

melon domes
USE **umbrella domes**

melon feet
TG.905
ALT **melon foot**
UF feet, melon
CN V.TG.ALO.DZW.AFU.BCW.AFU

melon supports
USE **melon bulb supports**

melting ladles
TB.693 (L)
ALT **melting ladle**
UF foundry ladles
ladles, foundry
ladles, melting
ladles, pouring
pouring ladles
CN V.TB.AFU.BCW.BIQ.ALO.ALO

melting point
BM.988 (L)
UF point, melting
CN B.BM.CFS.AXC.BZY.CFS.BIQ

Members of Congress
HG.677 (L)
ALT **Member of Congress**
UF Congress, Members of
CN H.HG.AFU.AXC.CFS.CFS.BCW.AFU

Members of Parliament
HG.679
ALT **Member of Parliament**
UF Parliament, Members of
CN H.HG.AFU.AXC.CFS.CFS.BCW.ALO

Members of the House of Representatives
HG.678 (L)
ALT **Member of the House of Representatives**
UF Congressmen
Congresspersons
Congresswomen
House of Representatives, Members of the
Representatives (Members of Congress)
CN H.HG.AFU.AXC.CFS.CFS.BCW.AFU.AFU

members, web
USE **web members**

membership lists
VW.281
ALT **membership list**
SN Lists or rolls of the collective body of members, as of a society, at a given time. (GAHLM)
UF lists of members
lists, membership
membership rolls
rolls, membership
CN V.VW.AFU.AFU.AFU.FZU.BCW.ALO.BCW

membership rolls
USE **membership lists**

membrane structures
RT.403 (B)
ALT **membrane structure**
SN Use for structures of thin, flexible surfaces that carry loads primarily through the development of tension stresses.
UF structures, membrane
CN V.RT.AFU.AFU.AFU.BIQ.ALO

Memeh
FL.3008
CN F.FL.ALO.AXC.ARI.BIQ.AFU.AFU.BZY

memel fir
USE **Scotch pine**

memorabilia
VB.102
CN V.VB.ALO.BUE.ALO

memorandums
VW.28 (L,N)
ALT **memorandum**
SN Documents recording information used for internal communication. (ICA)
UF circulars (memorandums)
memos
CN V.VW.AFU.AFU.AFU.BIQ.AFU.AXC

memorial arches
RK.894 (A,B)
ALT **memorial arch**
SN Use for usually large structures having a prominent central arch and built to commemorate events or persons; if erected to honor military victories, use **triumphal arches.**
UF arches, honorific
arches, memorial
arches, monumental
honorific arches
monumental arches
CN V.RK.AFU.ALO.ALO.DOI.AFU.AXC

memorial cards
VW.575
ALT **memorial card**
UF cards, memorial
CN V.VW.AFU.ALO.AFU.ARI.CLM

memorial columns
RK.896 (A,B)
ALT **memorial column**
UF columns, memorial
columns, monumental
monumental columns
CN V.RK.AFU.ALO.ALO.DOI.AFU.BCW

memorial volumes
USE **Festschriften**

memorials
RK.852 (A,L,N,B)
ALT **memorial**
UF commemorations
CN V.RK.AFU.ALO.ALO.DCU

memorials, war
USE **war memorials**

memos
USE **memorandums**

Memphite
FL.2802
CN F.FL.ALO.AXC.ALO.ARI.AFU.BCW.BIQ

men
HG.19 (L,R)
ALT **man**
CN H.HG.AFU.ARI.AFU

men homemakers
USE **househusbands**

menageries
RG.231 (A,L)
ALT **menagerie**
SN Places where collections of wild or unusual animals are kept or exhibited. (RHDEL2)
CN V.RG.AFU.AFU.ELK.ALO

Mende
FL.331 (L)
CN F.FL.ALO.AFU.AXC.AFU.ARI.BCW.CFS

Mendesian Dynasty
USE **Twenty-ninth Dynasty**

Mendlesham chairs
TG.109
ALT **Mendlesham chair**
SN Fancy Windsor chairs of square-back based on Sheraton's designs, and found in the region of Mendlesham, England in the early 19th century. (EVANS)
UF chairs, Dan Day
chairs, Mendlesham
chairs, Mendlesham Windsor
Dan Day chairs
Mendlesham Windsor chairs
CN V.TG.AFU.AFU.ALO.AFU.AFU.AFU.MLC.CFS.ARI

Mendlesham Windsor chairs
USE **Mendlesham chairs**

menhirs
USE **standing stones**

Menjo
USE **Bamenjo**

Mennige
USE **red lead**

Mennonite
BM.638 (L,B,R)
CN B.BM.BZY.AFU.ALO.ARI.BUE

Menominee
USE **Menomini**

Menomini
FL.1327 (L)
UF Menominee
CN F.FL.ALO.ALO.ARI.AFU.BCW.BCW

Menri School
FL.2181
CN F.FL.ALO.ARI.AXC.AFU.BOK.AFU.BCW

Menri School, New
USE **New Menri School**

mensae
USE **tables**

mensas
RT.1219 (R)
ALT **mensae**
SN In Roman Catholicism, the top of the altar, the slab. (W)
UF altar slabs
altar stones
slabs, altar
stones, altar
CN V.RT.AFU.BUE.ALO.ALO.ALO.ALO

mental health clinics
USE **psychiatric clinics**

mental health facilities
RK.778 (A,L)
ALT **mental health facility**
UF facilities, mental health
health facilities, mental
CN V.RK.AFU.ALO.ALO.CXA.ALO.AFU.BUE

mental hospitals
USE **psychiatric hospitals**

mental illness
BM.717 (L,R)
UF illness, mental
CN B.BM.CFS.AFU.AFU.AFU

mental institutions
USE **psychiatric hospitals**

mentally handicapped
HG.785 (L,B)
UF handicapped, mentally
mentally retarded
retarded, mentally
CN H.HG.AFU.BOK.AXC.ALO.AFU

mentally retarded
USE **mentally handicapped**

menuisiers
HG.562
ALT **menuisier**
SN French joiners of the 17th and 18th centuries who specialized in small objects. (DDA)
CN H.HG.AFU.AXC.BUE.AXC.BUE.ARI.AFU

menuisiers-ébéniste
USE **ébénistes**

menuisiers en ébène
USE **ébénistes**

menus
VW.266 (L,N)
ALT **menu**
SN Lists of dishes to be served or available for meals. (AHD)
UF bills of fare
CN V.VW.AFU.AFU.AFU.FZU.BCW.AFU.BCW

merawan
MT.1227
UF Hopea
CN M.MT.AFU.AFU.ALO.BIQ.DCU.AFU.AFU.AFU.ILG

mercantile buildings
RK.136 (A,L)
ALT **mercantile building**
UF buildings, mercantile
facilities, mercantile
mercantile facilities
CN V.RK.AFU.ALO.ALO.ALO.ARI

mercantile facilities
USE **mercantile buildings**

merchandise inventories
VW.367 (L)
ALT **merchandise inventory**
UF inventories, merchandise
Inventories, retail
inventories, stock
lists of merchandise
lists, warehouse
merchandise, lists of
retail inventories
stock inventories
warehouse lists
CN V.VW.AFU.AFU.ALO.DCU.ALO

merchandise marts
USE **trade marts**

merchandise, lists of
USE **merchandise inventories**

merchant marks
USE **trademarks**

merchants
HG.428 (L,R)
ALT **merchant**
SN Buyers and sellers of commodities for profit. (W)
UF traders
CN H.HG.AFU.AXC.BOK.FCS.ALO

merchants, commission
USE **commission merchants**

mercury
MT.439 (L)
UF quicksilver
CN M.MT.AFU.AFU.AFU.BZY.AFU.AFU.ARI.CFS

mercury gilding
USE **gilding**

mercury glass
USE **silvered glass**

méridiennes
TG.297 (N)
ALT **méridienne**
SN Asymmetrical seating forms with gently curved backs and having one arm higher than the other; made especially during the French Empire period. (FAIRB)
CN V.TG.AFU.AFU.ALO.ALO.BCW

Merimde
FL.2775 (L)
CN F.FL.ALO.AXC.ALO.ARI.AFU.AFU.AFU.ALO

Merina
FL.559 (L)
UF Hova
CN F.FL.ALO.AFU.AXC.ARI.ARI.BCW

merlons
RT.1192
ALT **merlon**
SN The solid portions in a battlement alternating with the embrasures.
CN V.RT.AFU.BUE.AFU.BCW.ALO.ARI.ALO.ALO

meroes
USE **pagodas**

Meroitic
FL.164 (A,L)
CN F.FL.ALO.AFU.ALO.AXC.AXC.ALO.AFU.ALO

Merovingian
FL.3108 (A,L)
CN F.FL.ALO.BCW.ALO.ALO.AFU.BOK.ALO.ALO.ARI.AFU

merry-go-rounds
RK.1005 (A,L,N,B,R)
ALT **merry-go-round**
UF carrousels
CN V.RK.AFU.ALO.ALO.EWY.AFU.AFU.ALO

Meru
FL.651 (L)
CN F.FL.ALO.AFU.AXC.AXC.BCW.CFS

Merz
FL.3393 (R)
CN F.FL.ALO.BCW.ALO.AXC.DIO.BIQ.BIQ.ARI

mesas
RD.207 (L)
ALT mesa
SN Relatively small, usually isolated, masses of land with level or nearly level tops, standing distinctly above the surrounding countryside, and having steep erosion scarps on all sides (WAYTA); smaller than plateaus, and larger than buttes.
CN V.RD.ARI.AFU.AXC.AFU.ALO.AFU.AXC

Mescalero Apache
FL.1453 (L)
UF Apache, Mescalero
CN F.FL.ALO.ALO.ARI.AFU.CFS.AFU.BCW

Meserve
FL.750
CN F.FL.ALO.ALO.ALO.AFU.AFU.ARI.ALO.ARI.AFU.AFU

mesh
MT.2256
CN M.MT.AFU.ALO.DUC

mesh lath, diamond
USE **diamond mesh lath**

Meshhed
FL.3535
UF Mashhad
CN F.FL.ALO.BIQ.AFU.GRC.AFU.ARI

Meshhed ware
FL.3542
UF Mashhad ware
ware, Mashhad
ware, Meshhed
CN F.FL.ALO.BIQ.AFU.GRC.ALO.AXC

meshrebeeyeh
RT.911 (A)
SN Projecting bay windows largely made up of carved latticework; found especially in Moorish architecture.
UF moucharaby
mushrebiyeh
CN V.RT.AFU.ARI.AFU.AFU.BOK.AFU.AFU.ALO.ALO

Meskwaki
USE **Fox**

Mesoamerican
FL.959 (L)
SN Use with reference to the Pre-Columbian period in regions from central Mexico to the western coastal area of Honduras, Nicaragua, and Costa Rica, excluding the Caribbean and those eastern regions of Central America that were subject to primarily South American cultural influences.
CN F.FL.ALO.ALO.ALO.ALO.AFU

Mesolithic
FL.13 (L)
UF Middle Stone Age
Stone Age, Middle
CN F.FL.AFU.BCW.AFU.ALO

Mesopotamian
FL.2948 (B)
CN F.FL.ALO.AXC.ARI.BCW

Mesopotamian School
FL.3437
CN F.FL.ALO.BIQ.AFU.BIQ.AFU.AFU

Mesquakie
USE **Fox**

mesquite
MT.1367 (L)
UF Algaroba
mezquite
Prosopis chilensis
CN M.MT.AFU.AFU.ALO.BIQ.DCU.AFU.AFU.ALO.CFS

mess
USE **mess halls**

mess halls
RM.113 (A,L)
ALT **mess hall**
SN May be either rooms or separate buildings.
UF commissaries
halls, mess
mess
CN V.RM.AFU.DIO.ALO.BCW.BUE.AFU

messengers
HG.47 (L)
ALT **messenger**
CN H.HG.AFU.AXC.ARI.BZY

Mestizo
USE **Provincial Highland**

Mesua ferra
USE **gangaw**

metae
RK.887
ALT **meta**
SN Designates the posts or columns placed at the turning points in Roman circuses.
CN V.RK.AFU.ALO.ALO.DOI.AFU.ALO.AXC

metal
MT.333 (A,L,B,R)
SN Any of a large group of substances that typically show a characteristic luster, are good conductors of electricity and heat, are opaque, can be fused, and are usually malleable or ductile. (W)
CN M.MT.AFU.AFU.AFU.BZY.AFU

metal alloys
USE **alloys**

metal arc welding, shielded
USE **shielded metal arc welding**

metal chasing
USE **chasing**

metal-clad cable
USE **armored cable**

metal cladding
USE **cladding**

metal-cutting
KT.825 (L)
CN K.KT.AFU.ALO.HOE.BCW.ALO.ARI

metal-cutting, electric
USE **electric metal-cutting**

metal-cutting, ultrasonic
USE **ultrasonic metal-cutting**

metal foil
USE **foil**

metal lath nails
TF.442
ALT **metal lath nail**
UF lath nails, metal
nails, metal lath
CN V.TF.AFU.AFU.AFU.ALO.AFU.CFS.ALO.CXA

metal lath, flat expanded
USE **diamond mesh lath**

metal leaf
USE **leaf**

metal molders
USE **molders**

metal plating
USE **plating**

metal points
TB.254
ALT **metal point**
SN Styluses, rods, or wires of metal, often held in a holder, used as a common tool for drawing and for writing in ancient times.
UF points, metal
CN V.TB.AFU.ARI.CLM.AFU.ALO.CLM

metal products
MT.471 (L)
UF products, metal
CN M.MT.AFU.AFU.AFU.BZY.ALO

metal-spinning
KT.850 (L)
SN Shaping sheet metal by bending or buckling it under pressure. (STEIN)
UF spinning (metal)
CN K.KT.AFU.ALO.HOE.BCW.ALO.BIQ.BCW

metal-to-wood wire hangers
TF.360
ALT **metal-to-wood wire hanger**
UF hangers, metal-to-wood wire
wire hangers, metal-to-wood
CN V.TF.AFU.AFU.AFU.ALO.AFU.BOK.ARI.ARI.AFU

metal, admiralty
USE **admiralty metal**

metal, Ashberry
USE **Ashberry metal**

metal, Babbitt
USE **Babbitt metal**

metal, bell
USE **bell metal**

metal, bidery
USE **bidri**

metal, black
USE **pewter**

metal, britannia
USE **britannia metal**

metal, Dutch
USE **leaf**

metal, Dutch white
USE **Dutch white metal**

metal, English britannia
USE **English britannia metal**

metal, expanded
USE **expanded metal**

metal, ferrous
USE **iron**

metal, Hanover white
USE **Hanover white metal**

metal, monel
USE **monel**

metal, Muntz
USE **Muntz metal**

metal, precious
USE **precious metal**

metal, queen's
USE **queen's metal**

metal, scrap
USE **scrap metal**

metal, Tutanic
USE **Tutanic metal**

metal, white
USE **white metal**

metalinguistics
KD.41 (R)
SN Branch of linguistics that deals with the relation of language to the rest of culture-determined behavior. (W)
CN K.KD.AFU.AFU.AXC.AFU.ALO.ALO

metallic brown
USE **deep brown**
deep reddish brown

metallic color
USE **metallic pigment**

metallic gray
USE **purplish gray**

metallic pigment
MT.1551
SN Particles of nonoxidized metals used as pigments to modify the optical characteristics of a paint. (GCT)
UF color, metallic
metallic color
pigment, metallic
CN M.MT.AFU.AFU.ARI.AFU.AFU.ALO.AFU.AFU.ALO

metallic red
USE **deep reddish brown**

metallic toning
KT.422
UF toning, metallic
CN K.KT.AFU.ALO.DUC.DIO.ARI.AXC.DOI.ALO

metallic ware (Anatolian pottery)
FL.2874
UF ware, metallic (Anatolian pottery)
CN F.FL.ALO.AXC.ARI.AFU.ALO.ARI.BZY

metallic ware (Levantine pottery)
FL.2940
UF ware, metallic (Levantine pottery)
CN F.FL.ALO.AXC.ARI.AXC.ALO.BIQ.BUE

metallizing
KT.710 (L)
ALT **metallized**
SN The process of coating, treating, or combining with a metal. (W)
CN K.KT.AFU.ALO.GRC.CRG

metallurgists
HG.349 (L)
ALT **metallurgist**
CN H.HG.AFU.AXC.BIQ.AFU.AFU.CXA

metallurgy
KD.247 (L,R)
SN Study of the structure of metals and alloys as related to properties that are important in their technological utilization. (PG)
CN K.KD.AFU.ARI.BZY.ALO

metals, ceramic
USE **cermets**

metals, nonferrous
USE **nonferrous metals**

metalware
MT.477
CN M.MT.AFU.AFU.AFU.BZY.ALO.BIQ

metalwork
MT.2765 (A,L,B,R)
CN M.MT.AFU.AXC.BOK

metalworkers
HG.490 (L)
ALT **metalworker**
UF smiths
CN H.HG.AFU.AXC.BUE.ARI.CFS

metalworking
KT.777 (R)
CN K.KT.AFU.ALO.HOE.BCW.AFU

metalworking, art
USE **art metalworking**

metamerism
BM.137
SN The tendency of two colored surfaces that appear alike when viewed under one kind of light to differ from each other when viewed under another. (MAYER)
CN B.BM.AFU.AFU.ARI.BOK.ALO.ALO.ARI

metamorphic rock
MT.739 (L)
UF rock, metamorphic
CN M.MT.AFU.AFU.AFU.DCU.AFU.ARI

metaphor
BM.22 (L,R)
SN A figure of speech in which a word or phrase is applied to something to which it is not literally applicable in order to suggest a resemblance. (RHDEL2)
CN B.BM.AFU.AFU.AFU.CFS.AXC

Metaphysical
FL.3405 (L,R)
UF Arte Metafisica
Pittura Metafisica
Scuola Metafisica
CN F.FL.ALO.BCW.ALO.AXC.DIO.BOK.BCW.ALO

metaphysicians
HG.209
ALT **metaphysician**
CN H.HG.AFU.AXC.AXC.BCW.ARI

metaphysics
KD.68 (L,R)
CN K.KD.AFU.AFU.BOK.BOK

Metasequoia glyptostroboides
USE **dawn redwood**

meteorological instruments
TB.539 (L,N)
ALT **meteorological instrument**
SN Artifacts originally created to be used in the observation, measurement, and recording of atmospheric phenomena. (NOM)
UF instruments, meteorological
CN V.TB.AFU.AXC.ALO.ALO

meteorological observatories
USE **meteorological stations**

meteorological stations
RK.1176 (A,L,B)
ALT **meteorological station**
UF meteorological observatories
observatories, meteorological
stations, meteorological

stations, weather
weather stations
CN V.RK.AFU.ALO.ALO.FIM.ALO.ALO.ALO.ALO

meteorologists
HG.350 (L)
ALT **meteorologist**
CN H.HG.AFU.AXC.BIQ.AFU.AFU.DCU

meteorology
KD.275 (L,B,R)
SN Science dealing with the atmosphere and all of its varied phenomena. (PG)
UF atmospheric sciences
sciences, atmospheric
CN K.KD.AFU.ARI.CLM.ARI.BOK

Metepec
FL.991
UF Teotihuacan IV
CN F.FL.ALO.ALO.ALO.ALO.AFU.ALO.AFU.AFU.CRG

meters, exposure
USE **light meters**

meters, light
USE **light meters**

meters, parking
USE **parking meters**

methanol
USE **methyl alcohol**

method, case
USE **case method**

Methodist
BM.639 (L,B)
CN B.BM.BZY.AFU.ALO.ARI.BZY

methodology
BM.1156 (A,L,R)
SN A body of methods, procedures, working concepts, rules, and postulates employed by a science, art, or discipline. (W)
UF research methods
CN B.BM.DIO.ARI

methods
USE **techniques**

methods, simulation
USE **simulation methods**

methyl acetone
MT.2698
UF acetone, methyl
CN M.MT.AFU.ARI.HZS.AFU.BOK.ARI.AFU.AFU

methyl alcohol
MT.2690 (L)
SN Nonaqueous, highly toxic alcohol distilled from grain, used as a fuel and a solvent.
UF alcohol, industrial
alcohol, methyl
alcohol, wood
Columbian spirits
industrial alcohol
methanol
spirits, Columbian
wood alcohol
CN M.MT.AFU.ARI.HZS.AFU.BOK.AFU.BIQ

methyl benzene
USE **toluene**

methyl blue
USE **vivid blue**

methyl blue, light
USE **brilliant blue**

methyl dye
MT.1543
UF dye, methyl
CN M.MT.AFU.AFU.ARI.AFU.AFU.AFU.AFU.ALO.ARI

methyl ethyl ketone
MT.2699
SN Ketone solvent used as a vinyl resin solvent. (GOTTS)
UF ketone, methyl ethyl
MEK
CN M.MT.AFU.ARI.HZS.AFU.BOK.ARI.ALO

methyl isobutyl ketone
MT.2700
UF hexone
ketone, methyl isobutyl
MIBK
CN M.MT.AFU.ARI.HZS.AFU.BOK.ARI.ARI

methyl violet
USE **vivid violet**

methylene chloride
MT.2677 (L)
UF carrene
chloride, methylene
dichloromethane
CN M.MT.AFU.ARI.HZS.AFU.BIQ.ARI.ALO

methylene oxide
USE **formaldehyde**

Metoko
FL.515 (L)
UF Banyamituku
Mituku
CN F.FL.ALO.AFU.AXC.ALO.ALO.BIQ.AFU.AFU.BZY

metonymy
BM.23 (R)
SN A figure of speech that consists in using the name of one thing for that of something else with which it is associated. (W)
CN B.BM.AFU.AFU.AFU.CFS.BCW

metopes
RT.351 (A,L,B)
ALT **metope**
SN Panels between triglyphs in the Doric frieze, often carved. (HAS)
CN V.RT.AFU.AFU.AFU.BCW.BZY.ALO.ARI.ALO.ALO

metrologists
HG.351
ALT **metrologist**
SN Specialists in weights and measures and in measuring.
CN H.HG.AFU.AXC.BIQ.AFU.AFU.DIO

metropolises
RD.13
ALT **metropolis**
SN Use for chief cities, often capital cities, of a region. (ALLABY)
CN V.RD.AFU.AFU.ALO.AXC.ALO

Metropolitan (Byzantine)
USE **Constantinopolitan**

metropolitan areas
RD.16 (L)
ALT **metropolitan area**
SN Settlement areas encompassing a central city and surrounding municipal or political jurisdictions.
UF areas, metropolitan
CN V.RD.AFU.AFU.ALO.BCW

metropolitan lighting
USE **municipal lighting**

metropolitan parks
USE **urban parks**

metropolitan railways
USE **urban rail systems**

Metropolitan Statistical Areas, Standard
USE **Standard Metropolitan Statistical Areas**

metropolitan transportation
USE **urban transportation**

metropolitans
HG.226 (L)
ALT **metropolitan**
CN H.HG.AFU.AXC.AXC.BIQ.AFU.ARI.CLM

metros
USE **subways**

meubles à hauteur d'appui
TG.417
SN Cabinets which stand at elbow height. (PC)
UF meubles d'appui
CN V.TG.AFU.AFU.AXC.ALO.ARI.AFU.BIQ

meubles à transformation
USE **multipurpose furniture**

meubles d'appui
USE **meubles à hauteur d'appui**

meubles d'entre deux
TG.418

ALT **meuble d'entre deux**
SN Cabinets intended to stand against a pier. (PC)
CN V.TG.AFU.AFU.AXC.ALO.ARI.AFU.BOK

meubles de coin
USE **corner cabinets**

meubles jardinières
USE **jardinières**

Mewan
USE **Miwok**

Mewar
FL.2295 (L)
UF Udaipur
CN F.FL.ALO.ARI.AXC.ALO.AFU.BZY.BCW.BCW.CFS

mews
RK.95 (A,B)
SN Use for urban stables with living accommodations above grouped around a courtyard or small street for use by carriage horses; may also be used by extension in modern contexts for the alleyways such stables front upon when the stables have been converted into apartments.
CN V.RK.AFU.ALO.ALO.AFU.ALO.CXA.AFU

Mexica
USE **Aztec**

Mexican
FL.715 (L,B)
CN F.FL.ALO.ALO.AFU.ARI.ARI

Mexican Americans
HG.781 (L,R)
ALT **Mexican American**
UF Americans, Mexican
Chicanos
CN H.HG.AFU.BOK.ARI.ALO.AFU

Mexican Muralist
FL.1760 (L)
UF Mexican Renaissance
Mexican school of painting
Muralist
Muralist, Mexican
Renaissance, Mexican
CN F.FL.ALO.ALO.BCW.ALO.AXC

Mexican onyx
USE **onyx marble**

Mexican Renaissance
USE **Mexican Muralist**

Mexican school of painting
USE **Mexican Muralist**

Mexican sisal
USE **henequen**

Mezcala
FL.1070
UF Guerrero
CN F.FL.ALO.ALO.ALO.ALO.AFU.ALO.BCW.AXC

mezquite
USE **mesquite**

mezzanines
RM.413 (B)
ALT **mezzanine**
SN Use for low-ceilinged stories between two stories with higher ceilings, or for balconylike stories over a part of the story below, the lower story usually, but not necessarily, being the first story.
UF entresols
CN V.RM.AFU.DUC.AXC

mezzo fresco
KT.227
SN Fresco technique common in the latter half of the 16th century where painting was done on partially dry intonaco, with lime added to the colors to enhance their adherence. (MAYER)
CN K.KT.AFU.ALO.DUC.CXA.ALO.AFU.BIQ.AFU

mezzotint
KT.454 (L,R)
SN Intaglio printing technique in which the plate is first roughened with a mezzotint rocker, then areas not to print are burnished and flattened to produce various grays and whites. (SAFF)
UF engraving, mezzotint
mezzotint engraving
CN K.KT.AFU.ALO.DUC.DUC.ALO.BCW.AFU.ARI.ARI

mezzotint engraving
USE **mezzotint**

mezzotinters
HG.132 (L)
ALT **mezzotinter**
CN H.HG.AFU.AXC.AXC.AFU.AFU.ALO.AXC.DUC.AXC

Mfinu
USE **Fumu**

Mi-son
FL.2439
CN F.FL.ALO.ARI.BCW.BUE.ALO.ALO.AFU.ALO

Mi-son A 1
FL.2440
CN F.FL.ALO.ARI.BCW.BUE.ALO.ALO.AFU.ALO.AFU

Mi-son E 1
FL.2441
CN F.FL.ALO.ARI.BCW.BUE.ALO.ALO.AFU.ALO.ALO

Mi Tsung
USE **Chen-Yen**

Miami
FL.1328 (L)
UF Twightwees
CN F.FL.ALO.ALO.ARI.AFU.BCW.BIQ

MIBK
USE **methyl isobutyl ketone**

mica
MT.534 (L)
UF glass, muscovy
muscovy glass
CN M.MT.AFU.AFU.AFU.CFS.AFU.FUA

mica diorite
MT.614
UF diorite, mica
kersantite
CN M.MT.AFU.AFU.AFU.DCU.AFU.AFU.AFU.AFU.ARI.ALO.AFU

mica-dusted ware
USE **micaceous ware**

mica (white pigment)
MT.1752
CN M.MT.AFU.AFU.ARI.AFU.AFU.ALO.ALO.BOK.ALO.CFS

mica, magnesium
USE **phlogopite**

mica, potash
USE **muscovite (mica)**

micaceous sandstone
MT.722
UF sandstone, micaceous
CN M.MT.AFU.AFU.AFU.DCU.AFU.ALO.AFU.ARI.AFU.ALO.BCW

micaceous ware
FL.2750
UF mica-dusted ware
ware, mica-dusted
ware, micaceous
CN F.FL.ALO.AXC.ALO.ALO.ALO.BUE.ALO.ARI

micarta
MT.2112
SN Commercially produced laminated products made by bonding layers of cloth or paper with a resin (as phenolic) under heat and pressure and used in the form of sheets, rod, tubes or other molded shapes. (W)
CN M.MT.AFU.AFU.ARI.BUE.ALO.ARI.ALO.ALO

Miccaotli
FL.988
UF Teotihuacan II
CN F.FL.ALO.ALO.ALO.ALO.AFU.ALO.AFU.AFU.BZY

mice
TB.156 (N)
ALT **mouse**
SN Small, button-operated computer devices that are moved around on a flat desktop or graphics tablet to

control the movement of the cursor on the monitor.
CN V.TB.AFU.ARI.BCW.AXC.AFU.BIQ

Micmac
FL.1302 (L)
CN F.FL.ALO.ALO.ARI.AFU.ARI.BZY

Micoquian
FL.2457
CN F.FL.ALO.AXC.AFU.ALO.ALO

microbiology
KD.206 (L,R)
CN K.KD.AFU.ARI.ARI.BIQ

Microcards (TM)
USE **microopaques**

microclimate
USE **climate**

microcline
MT.506
CN M.MT.AFU.AFU.AFU.CFS.AFU.CRG.AFU

microcomputers
TB.144 (L,N)
ALT **microcomputer**
SN Desk-top or portable computers, based on a microprocessor and meant for a single user. (COMBAS)
UF computers, home
computers, personal
home computers
personal computers
CN V.TB.AFU.ARI.BCW.ARI.AFU

microcopies, opaque
USE **microopaques**

microcrystalline wax
MT.2202 (L)
UF wax, microcrystalline
CN M.MT.AFU.AFU.ARI.BZY.ALO.ARI.AFU

microfiche
VW.668 (L,N,B,R)
SN Flexible, transparent sheets of film bearing a number of microimages arranged in horizontal rows and vertical columns, normally having an identifying strip legible without magnification. (ICA)
UF fiche
CN V.VW.AFU.ALO.AFU.DZW.AXC.ALO

microfiche, computer-output
USE **computer-output microfiche**

microfilm rolls
USE **microfilms**

microfilm strips
VW.672
ALT **microfilm strip**
SN Segments of microfilm that are usually inserted into microfilm jackets. (ICA)
UF strips, microfilm
CN V.VW.AFU.ALO.AFU.DZW.AXC.ARI.AFU

microfilms
VW.671 (L,N,B)
ALT **microfilm**
SN Fine-grain, high-resolution film in roll form containing, after exposure, developing, and fixing, an image, reduced in size from the original. (ICA)
UF microfilm rolls
rolls, microfilm
CN V.VW.AFU.ALO.AFU.DZW.AXC.ARI

microfilms, computer-output
USE **computer-output microfilms**

microforms
VW.664 (A,L)
ALT **microform**
SN All media used to record microimages. (ICA)
CN V.VW.AFU.ALO.AFU.DZW.AXC

microforms, computer-output
USE **computer-output microforms**

microgranite
MT.588
SN An igneous rock composed of minute crystals of quartz and alkalic feldspar. (W)
CN M.MT.AFU.AFU.AFU.DCU.AFU.AFU.AFU.AFU.AFU.ARI.AFU.AFU

micrographics
KT.216 (L)
SN Use generally for the production and use of microforms. For the process of producing microforms, use **microphotography.**
CN K.KT.AFU.ALO.DUC.CRG

micrographs
TB.258 (N)
ALT **micrograph**
SN Instruments for executing extremely minute writing and engraving; their general principle is that of the pantograph. (KNIGHT)
CN V.TB.AFU.ARI.CLM.AFU.ALO.CRG

Microlithic
FL.1838
CN F.FL.ALO.ARI.ALO.AFU.AFU.AFU.ALO.AFU

Micronesian
FL.3676 (L)
CN F.FL.ALO.BOK.ARI

microopaques
VW.673 (L)
ALT **microopaque**
SN Microimages arranged in similar manner to those on a microfiche, but on an opaque medium. (ICA)
UF Microcards (TM)
microcopies, opaque
Microprints (TM)
opaque microcopies
CN V.VW.AFU.ALO.AFU.DZW.AXC.AXC

microphotographs
VJ.119
ALT **microphotograph**
SN Photographs with images of greatly reduced size, requiring a magnification device to view, including, e.g., microfiche. Distinct from **photomicrographs,** which are photographs of minute objects, usually taken through a microscope.
CN V.VJ.AFU.ARI.ALO.BZY

microphotography
KT.417 (L)
SN Use for the techniques of producing microphotographs. For the production and use of microforms generally, use **micrographics.**
CN K.KT.AFU.ALO.DUC.DIO.ARI.AXC.CXA

Microprints (TM)
USE **microopaques**

microscope photographs
USE **photomicrographs**

microscopy
KT.15 (L,R)
SN Use generally for the use of or investigation with a microscope.
CN K.KT.AFU.ALO.AXC.ARI

Mid-Byzantine
USE **Middle Byzantine**

mid-rise buildings
RK.10
ALT **mid-rise building**
SN Use for buildings having between four or five and nine or ten stories and equipped with elevators; generally applied to commercial buidings and apartment houses.
UF buildings, medium-rise
buildings, mid-rise
medium-rise buildings
CN V.RK.AFU.ALO.AFU.AFU.AFU.ALO

mid-wall columns
RT.110
ALT **mid-wall column**
SN Use for columns supporting a wall of considerably greater thickness than itself and set more or less at the center of that thickness.
UF columns, mid-wall
CN V.RT.AFU.AFU.AFU.AXC.BIQ.AFU.ALO.BUE

middens
RK.1473 (L)
ALT **midden**
SN Use in archaeological or anthropological contexts for accumulations of household refuse, predominantly

shells and bones.
UF kitchen middens
middens, kitchen
middens, shell
mounds, shell
shell middens
shell mounds
CN V.RK.ALO.ALO.AXC.AFU.ARI

middens, kitchen
USE **middens**

middens, shell
USE **middens**

Middle Archaic
FL.2575
UF Archaic, Middle
CN F.FL.ALO.AXC.ALO.AFU.AFU.ARI.AXC.ALO

Middle Assyrian
FL.2979
UF Assyrian, Middle
CN F.FL.ALO.AXC.ARI.BCW.AFU.BUE.ALO

Middle Benin
FL.95
UF Benin, Middle
CN F.FL.ALO.AFU.ALO.AFU.BUE.AFU.ALO

Middle Bronze Age
FL.28
UF Bronze Age, Middle
CN F.FL.AFU.BCW.ARI.ALO

Middle Byzantine
FL.3072
UF Byzantine, Middle
Mid-Byzantine
Second Golden Age (Byzantine)
CN F.FL.ALO.BCW.ALO.AFU.ALO.ALO

middle cadmium yellow
MT.1776
UF cadmium yellow, middle
jaune de cadmium moyen
Kadmiumgelb mittel
yellow, middle cadmium
CN M.MT.AFU.AFU.ARI.AFU.AFU.ALO.ALO.BUE.ARI.ALO.BCW

Middle Chalcolithic
FL.22
UF Chalcolithic, Middle
CN F.FL.AFU.BCW.ALO.ALO.ALO

middle class
HG.884 (L,R)
SN Social class ranking between upper and lower classes. (W)
UF class, middle
CN H.HG.ALO.DOI.ALO.AFU

Middle Classic
FL.969
UF Classic, Middle
CN F.FL.ALO.ALO.ALO.ALO.AFU.AFU.AXC.ALO

Middle Corinthian
FL.2628
UF Corinthian, Middle
CN F.FL.ALO.AXC.ALO.AFU.ALO.AXC.ALO.BCW.AFU.ARI

Middle Cycladic
FL.2546
UF Cycladic, Middle
CN F.FL.ALO.AXC.ALO.AFU.AFU.ALO.AFU.ARI

Middle Cypriote
FL.2895
UF Cypriote, Middle
CN F.FL.ALO.AXC.ARI.ARI.AFU.ALO

Middle Dilmun
FL.2884
UF Dilmun, Middle
CN F.FL.ALO.AXC.ARI.ALO.AFU.AFU.ALO

middle distance
USE **middle ground**

Middle Edo
FL.1984
UF Edo, Middle
CN F.FL.ALO.ARI.ALO.ALO.AFU.BCW.AFU.ALO

Middle Elamite
FL.3013
UF Elamite, Middle
CN F.FL.ALO.AXC.ARI.BIQ.AFU.ALO.ARI

Middle Formative
USE **Middle Preclassic**

Middle Geometric
FL.2566
UF Geometric, Middle
CN F.FL.ALO.AXC.ALO.AFU.AFU.ARI.ALO.ALO

middle ground
BM.60
SN In pictorial arts, that part of the composition between the foreground and the background. (MAYER)
UF distance, middle
ground, middle
middle distance
CN B.BM.AFU.AFU.ARI.AFU.BCW.ALO.BCW

Middle Helladic
FL.2550
UF Helladic, Middle
CN F.FL.ALO.AXC.ALO.AFU.AFU.ALO ALO.ALO

Middle Hittite Kingdom
FL.2856
UF Hittite Kingdom, Middle
Middle Kingdom (Hittite)
CN F.FL.ALO.AXC.ARI.AFU.AFU.ARI.ALO

Middle horizon
FL.1158
CN F.FL.ALO.ALO.ALO.ARI.AXC.AFU.BCW

Middle Iron Age
FL.32
UF Iron Age, Middle
CN F.FL.AFU.BCW.AXC.ALO

Middle Jomon
FL.1962
UF Jomon, Middle
CN F.FL.ALO.ARI.ALO.ALO.AFU.AFU.ALO.ARI

Middle Kerma
FL.159
UF Kerma, Middle
CN F.FL.ALO.AFU.ALO.AXC.AXC.AFU.AFU.ALO

Middle Kingdom
FL.2803
UF Kingdom, Middle
CN F.FL.ALO.AXC.ALO.ARI.AFU.BIQ

Middle Kingdom (Hittite)
USE **Middle Hittite Kingdom**

Middle Minoan
FL.2557
UF Minoan, Middle
CN F.FL.ALO.AXC.ALO.AFU.AFU.ALO.ARI.ALO

Middle Mississippian
FL.859
UF Mississippian, Middle
CN F.FL.ALO.ALO.ALO.AFU.ALO.ALO.ARI.ARI.BCW.AFU

Middle Neolithic
FL.16
UF Neolithic, Middle
CN F.FL.AFU.BCW.AFU.ARI.ALO

middle oil
MT.2001
UF carbolic oil
oil, carbolic
oil, middle
CN M.MT.AFU.AFU.ARI.ARI.ARI.BCW.AFU

Middle Paleolithic
FL.10
UF Paleolithic, Middle
CN F.FL.AFU.BCW.AFU.AFU.ALO

Middle period Californian
FL.772
UF Californian, Middle period
CN F.FL.ALO.ALO.ALO.AFU.AFU.BCW.AFU.ALO

Middle period Plateau
FL.779
UF Plateau, Middle period
CN F.FL.ALO.ALO.ALO.AFU.AFU.BCW.ARI.ARI

Middle Preclassic

FL.964
UF Formative, Middle
Middle Formative
Preclassic, Middle
CN F.FL.ALO.ALO.ALO.ALO.AFU.AFU.ALO.ALO

middle schools
RK.838 (A,L,B)
ALT **middle school**
SN Use for schools in the United States covering grades 5 through 8 or 6 through 8 and for foreign schools covering either the last elementary school grades or combining the U.S. junior and senior high school grades.
UF schools, middle
CN V.RK.AFU.ALO.ALO.CXA.ARI.AXC.ARI

Middle Sepik
FL.3656
UF Sepik, Middle
CN F.FL.ALO.BOK.ALO.BCW.ALO.BCW.ALO.ARI

Middle Stone Age
USE **Mesolithic**

midget mounts, boudoir
USE **boudoir midget mounts**

Midland
FL.751
CN F.FL.ALO.ALO.ALO.AFU.AFU.ARI.ALO.ARI.AFU.ALO

midnight
USE **dark grayish blue**
dark grayish purple

midnight blue
USE **black**
blackish blue
blackish purple
bluish black
dark bluish gray
dark purplish blue
dark purplish gray

midways
RG.166 (A)
ALT **midway**
CN V.RG.AFU.AFU.DOI.BOK

migdols
RK.446
ALT **migdol**
SN Generally small ancient Near Eastern fortresses used from Syria to Egypt especially along borders and near oases or important road junctions. (MBRICE)
CN V.RK.AFU.ALO.ALO.BIQ.BIQ.ARI

migrant workers
HG.26 (L,R)
ALT **migrant worker**
UF workers, migrant
CN H.HG.AFU.AXC.ALO.ALO

migration
BM.1048 (R)
SN The act, process, or instance of moving from one county, region, or place to settle in another. (W)
CN B.BM.CLM.AFU.ALO

Migration (Medieval period)
USE **Migration period**

Migration period
FL.3089 (L,R)
UF Ages, Dark (Medieval)
Barbarian
Dark Ages (Medieval)
Migration (Medieval period)
CN F.FL.ALO.BCW.ALO.ALO.AFU.AFU.AFU

migration, internal
USE **internal migration**

migration, rural-urban
USE **rural-urban migration**

migration, urban-rural
USE **urban-rural migration**

mihrabs
RT.1261 (A)
ALT **mihrab**
SN Niches, chambers, or slabs in Mosques, indicating the direction of Mecca. (W)
CN V.RT.AFU.BUE.ALO.AXC.ALO

Mije
USE **Mixe**

Mijikenda
FL.601 (L)
UF Nika
Nyika
Wanika
CN F.FL.ALO.AFU.AXC.AXC.ALO.BOK

Milagro
FL.1120
CN F.FL.ALO.ALO.ALO.ARI.ALO.BIQ

mild steel
USE **low-carbon steel**

Mileke
USE **Bamileke**

mileposts
USE **milestones**

milestones
RK.888 (A,L,B,R)
ALT **milestone**
UF mileposts
miliary pillars
milliariums
pillars, miliary
CN V.RK.AFU.ALO.ALO.DOI.AFU.ALO.BCW

Milford granite
MT.598
UF granite, Milford
CN M.MT.AFU.AFU.AFU.DCU.AFU.AFU.AFU.AFU.AFU.ARI.ALO.ALO.AFU

miliary pillars
USE **milestones**

milieu de salon
USE **bornes**

military academies
RK.799 (A,L,B)
ALT **military academy**
UF academies, military
military schools
schools, military
CN V.RK.AFU.ALO.ALO.CXA.ARI.AFU BCW

military air bases
USE **air bases**

military air stations
USE **naval air bases**

military architecture
USE **military buildings**

military bases
RG.123 (L)
ALT **military base**
SN Use generally in contemporary contexts for permanent centers of operations; use **military camps** for contemporary nonpermanent posts.
UF bases (military installations)
bases, military
garrisons
military posts
CN V.RG.AFU.AFU.BZY.AFU

military bridges
RK.1289 (L)
ALT **military bridge**
UF bridges, military
CN V.RK.AFU.ALO.ALO.GLI.ALO.AFU.ALO.ALO

military buildings
RK.854 (A,L,B,R)
ALT **military building**
UF architecture, military
buildings, military
facilities, military
military architecture
military facilities
CN V.RK.AFU.ALO.ALO.DIO

military camps
RG.131 (A,L)
ALT **military camp**
SN In contemporary military contexts, use for groups of huts, tents, or other shelters set up temporarily for troops;(DODDIC) in historical contexts use for permanent or semipermanent places of encampment; use **military bases** for contemporary permanent installations.
UF camps (military)
camps, military
military encampments

military posts
CN V.RG.AFU.AFU.BZY.ALO

military cemeteries
USE **national cemeteries**
war cemeteries

military commissions
VW.992 (L)
ALT **military commission**
SN Warrants conferring authority to raise and command a body of troops; certificates conferring military or naval rank and authority on officers of certain rank. (GAHLM)
UF commissions, military
CN V.VW.AFU.ARI.ALO.BCW.AFU.AFU.AFU.BOK.AFU

military encampments
USE **military camps**

military engineering
KD.231 (L,B,R)
CN K.KD.AFU.ARI.BIQ.CFS

military engineers
HG.641 (L,B)
ALT **military engineer**
UF engineers, military
CN H.HG.AFU.AXC.BZY.BCW.CFS

military facilities
USE **military buildings**
military installations

military hospitals
RK.771 (A,L,B)
ALT **military hospital**
UF hospitals, military
CN V.RK.AFU.ALO.ALO.CXA.ALO.AFU.BCW.ALO.BOK

military housing
RG.84 (L,B)
UF army housing
housing, military
CN V.RG.AFU.AFU.BOK.BCW.ARI

military installations
RG.122 (L)
ALT **military installation**
UF installations (military complexes)
installations, military
military facilities
CN V.RG.AFU.AFU.BZY

military maps
VW.195 (L)
ALT **military map**
UF maps, military
CN V.VW.AFU.AFU.AFU.FZU.AXC.AFU.ARI.AXC.BUE

military museums
RK.399 (A,L,B)
ALT **military museum**
UF museums, military
museums, war
war museums
CN V.RK.AFU.ALO.ALO.BCW.AXC.ARI.AXC.BOK

military passes
VW.993 (L)
ALT **military pass**
SN Documents giving permission to one or more military persons to travel unimpeded, although usually with some restrictions, in a territory occupied by a military force; issued to a person or persons living in, or visiting in, the occupied area, by the commander of the military force in control thereof. (GAHLM)
UF passes, military
CN V.VW.AFU.ARI.ALO.BCW.AFU.AFU.AFU.BOK.ALO

military personnel
HG.668 (L)
UF personnel, military
CN H.HG.AFU.AXC.CFS.BOK

military perspectives
USE **cavalier oblique drawings**

military photography
KT.302 (L,R)
SN Use with regard to military applications of photography, such as for mapping or training. For photography in war for the purposes of historical documentation, use **war photography.** (LCSH)
UF photography, military
CN K.KT.AFU.ALO.DUC.DIO.AFU.CLM

military post exchanges
USE **post exchanges**

military posts
USE **military bases**
military camps

military prisons
RK.728 (L)
ALT **military prison**
SN Institutions designed to hold members of the armed forces who have been convicted of violations of the Uniform Code of Military Justice. (DOFCJ)
UF barracks, disciplinary
disciplinary barracks
prisons, military
CN V.RK.AFU.ALO.ALO.CXA.AFU.AXC.ALO.ALO

military records
VW.991
ALT **military record**
UF records, military
CN V.VW.AFU.ARI.ALO.BCW.AFU.AFU.AFU.BOK

military roads
RK.1552 (L)
ALT **military road**
UF roads, military
CN V.RK.ALO.ALO.BIQ.ARI.ALO.BCW

military schools
USE **military academies**

military towns
RD.34 (L)
ALT **military town**
SN Settlements whose primary concern is military; may also be used for settlements upon which military considerations have had a considerable formal or economic influence.
UF towns, military
CN V.RD.AFU.ALO.ALO.ALO

military training camps
RG.136 (A,L)
ALT **military training camp**
UF camps, military training
training camps, military
CN V.RG.AFU.AFU.BZY.ARI

military, the
USE **armed forces**

milk bars
RK.104 (A,B)
ALT **milk bar**
UF bars, milk
CN V.RK.AFU.ALO.ALO.ALO.AFU.AFU.AFU

milk benches
USE **water benches**

milk houses
RK.73
ALT **milk house**
UF houses, milk
CN V.RK.AFU.ALO.ALO.AFU.AFU.CFS

milking stools
TG.257 (N)
ALT **milking stool**
SN Low, usually three-legged stools with heavy circular tops set on round-bottomed bases. (CTSB)
UF stools, milking
CN V.TG.AFU.AFU.ALO.AFU.ALO.ALO.ALO

mill towns
RD.54 (A,B)
ALT **mill town**
SN Designates industrial settlements in which the primary employment is in factories for the manufacture of, for example, paper, steel, or textiles.
UF towns, mill
CN V.RD.AFU.AXC.BIQ.ALO

millboard
MT.1916 (B)
CN M.MT.AFU.AFU.ARI.ALO.ALO.AXC.ALO.BIQ.AFU.BCW

millenarianism
BM.700 (L,R)
CN B.BM.BZY.ALO.ARI.BOK

millers
HG.448 (L,R)

ALT **miller**
SN Persons who grind grain into flour. (W)
CN H.HG.AFU.AXC.BUE.ALO.BUE

milliariums
USE **milestones**

milliners
HG.538
ALT **milliner**
CN H.HG.AFU.AXC.BUE.ARI.CXA.CFS.ALO.AFU

milling (metalworking)
KT.851 (L)
ALT **milled (metalworking)**
SN In metalwork, the process of dressing a surface with various shapes of rotary cutters to produce a flat or grooved surface. (DAC)
CN K.KT.AFU.ALO.HOE.BCW.ALO.BIQ.BIQ

milling cutters
TB.709 (L)
ALT **milling cutter**
SN Rotary tool-steel cutters used in a milling machine for shaping and dressing metal surfaces. (W)
UF cutters, milling
CN V.TB.AFU.BCW.BIQ.ARI.ALO.ALO.ALO

milling equipment
USE **milling machinery**

milling machinery
TB.207 (L,N)
UF equipment, milling
machinery, milling
milling equipment
CN V.TB.AFU.ARI.BZY.AFU.AFU

millraces
RK.516
ALT **millrace**
SN Artificial channels in which water flows to and from mill wheels. (W)
CN V.RK.AFU.ALO.ALO.CFS.AFU.AFU.ALO

mills (factories)
USE **factories**

mills, bark
USE **bark mills**

mills, cotton
USE **cotton mills**

mills, flour
USE **flour mills**

mills, fulling
USE **fulling mills**

mills, gang
USE **gang sawmills**

mills, paper
USE **paper mills**

mills, planing
USE **planing mills**

mills, pulp
USE **pulp mills**

mills, rolling
USE **rolling mills**

mills, smelting
USE **smelters**

mills, smock
USE **smock mills**

mills, steel
USE **steel mills**

mills, steel rolling
USE **rolling mills**

mills, textile
USE **textile mills**

mills, tide
USE **tide mills**

mills, tube
USE **tube mills**

mills, water
USE **water mills**

mills, woolen
USE **woolen mills**

millstone grit
USE **gritstone**

millwork
MT.1449 (L)
CN M.MT.AFU.AFU.ALO.BIQ.DCU.ALO.BUE

millwrights
HG.447 (L)
ALT **millwright**
SN Persons who erect shafting, move machinery, or care for the mechanical equipment in a workshop, mill, or plant. (W)
CN H.HG.AFU.AXC.BUE.ALO.BOK.AFU

Milnesand
FL.752
CN F.FL.ALO.ALO.ALO.AFU.AFU.ARI.ALO.ARI.AFU.ARI

Milori blue
USE **Prussian blue**

mimbars
USE **minbars**

Mimbres
FL.938 (R)
CN F.FL.ALO.ALO.ALO.AFU.ALO.ARI.BIQ.BCW.ARI

Mimbres black-on-white
FL.940
UF black-on-white, Mimbres
CN F.FL.ALO.ALO.ALO.AFU.ALO.ARI.BIQ.BCW.ARI.AFU.AFU

Mimbres corrugated
FL.941
UF corrugated, Mimbres
CN F.FL.ALO.ALO.ALO.AFU.ALO.ARI.BIQ.BCW.ARI.AFU.ALO

mimeograph copies
VW.683
ALT **mimeograph copy**
SN Documents produced by a duplicating machine operating on the stencil principle; includes any documents produced by an ink bleed-through stencil. (GAHLM)
UF copies, mimeograph
CN V.VW.AFU.ALO.AFU.DZW.BIQ.BOK

mimesis
BM.7 (R)
UF imitation
CN B.BM.AFU.AFU.AFU.AXC

mimetic buildings
RK.23
ALT **mimetic building**
UF architecture parlante
architecture, programmatic
buildings, mimetic
programmatic architecture
CN V.RK.AFU.ALO.AFU.ALO.BIQ

Minai pottery
USE **Minai ware**

Minai ware
FL.3567
UF Minai pottery
pottery, Minai
ware, Minai
CN F.FL.ALO.BIQ.AFU.HIK.BCW.BCW

minarets
RK.1091 (A,L,B,R)
ALT **minaret**
SN Tall, slender towers of a mosque, from which the faithful are called to prayer. (KOSTOF)
CN V.RK.AFU.ALO.ALO.FCS.BCW

minbars
RT.1262 (A)
ALT **minbar**
SN Pulpits in mosques, having a small stand for the speaker, parapet, canopy, narrow stairs, and usually a gate at the foot of the stairs. (RS)
UF almimbars
mimbars
CN V.RT.AFU.BUE.ALO.AXC.ARI

mine buildings
RK.669 (A,L,B,R)
ALT **mine building**
UF buildings, mine
CN V.RK.AFU.ALO.ALO.CLM.ALO.ARI

mine hoists
USE **gins**

mine maps
VW.185 (L)
ALT **mine map**
UF maps, mine
CN V.VW.AFU.AFU.AFU.FZU.AXC.AFU.ARI.AXC.BCW.AFU.AFU

mine shafts
RK.678 (L)
ALT **mine shaft**
UF shafts, mine
CN V.RK.AFU.ALO.ALO.CLM.AXC.AFU

mineral baths
USE **spas**

mineral blue
USE **Antwerp blue**

mineral gray
USE **ultramarine blue**

mineral green
USE **malachite green**

mineral lake
USE **potter's pink**

mineral maps
USE **mineral resource maps**

mineral oil
MT.1984 (L)
UF oil, mineral
CN M.MT.AFU.AFU.ARI.ARI.AFU.ALO

mineral pigment
USE **inorganic pigment**

mineral pigment, artificial
USE **artificial inorganic pigment**

mineral pigment, natural
USE **natural inorganic pigment**

mineral resource maps
VW.190 (L)
ALT **mineral resource map**
UF maps, mineral
maps, mineral resource
mineral maps
resource maps, mineral
CN V.VW.AFU.AFU.AFU.FZU.AXC.AFU.ARI.AXC.BCW.BCW

mineral spirits
MT.2669
UF petroleum solvent
petroleum spirits
solvent, petroleum
spirits, petroleum
spirits, Texaco
spirits, white
spirits, mineral
Texaco spirits
varnolene
white spirits
CN M.MT.AFU.ARI.HZS.AFU.BIQ.AFU.ALO

mineral violet
USE **manganese violet**
strong purple

mineral wax
MT.2197 (L)
UF wax, mineral
CN M.MT.AFU.AFU.ARI.BZY.ALO

mineral white
USE **gypsum**

mineral yellow
USE **Turner's yellow**

mineral, orange
USE **red lead**

mineralogists
HG.342 (L)
ALT **mineralogist**
CN H.HG.AFU.AXC.BIQ.AFU.AFU.BZY.ALO

mineralogy
KD.276 (L)
CN K.KD.AFU.ARI.CLM.ARI.BUE

mineralogy museums
RK.419 (L)
ALT **mineralogy museum**
UF museums, mineralogy
CN V.RK.AFU.ALO.ALO.BCW.AXC.ARI.CFS.AXC.AFU

minerals
MT.485 (L)
CN M.MT.AFU.AFU.AFU.CFS

miners
HG.378 (L,B,R)
ALT **miner**
CN H.HG.AFU.AXC.BIQ.ALO.AXC.BUE

mines
RG.97 (A,L,N,B,R)
ALT **mine**
CN V.RG.AFU.AFU.BUE.AFU.ALO

mines, coal
USE **coal mines**

mines, copper
USE **copper mines**

mines, diamond
USE **diamond mines**

mines, gold
USE **gold mines**

mines, iron
USE **iron mines**

mines, silver
USE **silver mines**

mines, tin
USE **tin mines**

minette
USE **yellow ocher**

Ming
FL.1897 (L)
CN F.FL.ALO.ARI.ALO.AFU.AFU.ALO.DIO

Ming green
USE **strong green**

Ming-öi
USE **Kizil**

mini-parks
USE **vest-pocket parks**

Minianka
FL.356 (L)
CN F.FL.ALO.AFU.AXC.AFU.AXC.AFU.BOK

miniature
DC.122 (A,L)
CN D.DC.AFU.AXC.ARI

miniature cameras
TB.293 (L)
ALT **miniature camera**
SN General term applied to any 35mm (or smaller) camera. (LANG)
UF cameras, miniature
CN V.TB.AFU.ARI.CLM.ARI.AFU.AFU.AFU.AXC

miniature gardens
RK.1410 (A,L)
ALT **miniature garden**
UF gardens, miniature
CN V.RK.ALO.AFU.AFU.AFU.BIQ

miniature golf courses
RK.1492 (A)
ALT **miniature golf course**
UF courses, putt-putt
courses, Tom Thumb
golf courses, miniature
putt-putt courses
Tom Thumb courses
CN V.RK.ALO.ALO.BCW.BIQ.AFU

miniature theaters
RK.934 (A,L)
ALT **miniature theater**
UF theaters, miniature
CN V.RK.AFU.ALO.ALO.EFQ.ARI.BCW.AFU.ALO

miniatures (illuminations)
VB.40 (L,R)
ALT **miniature (illumination)**
SN The pictures in an illuminated manuscript, as distinct from the initials and borders. (OCA)
CN V.VB.AFU.ALO.ARI.AFU

miniaturists
HG.104 (L)
ALT **miniaturist**
SN Artists who create works in miniature, such as paintings, photographs, furniture, and other objects. For those who print or draw pictures or other decorative forms in manuscripts, use **illuminators.**
CN H.HG.AFU.AXC.AXC.AFU.AFU

.ALO.AXC.CRG

minicomputers
TB.147 (L,N)
ALT **minicomputer**
SN Mid-sized computers smaller than mainframes and usually with much more memory than microcomputers. (COMBAS)
CN V.TB.AFU.ARI.BCW.ARI.ALO

Minimal
FL.3733 (A,L,R)
ALT **Minimalism**
UF ABC
Minimalist
CN F.FL.ALO.BUE.ARI.DZW

Minimalist
USE **Minimal**

minimum-security correctional institutions
USE **minimum-security prisons**

minimum-security institutions
USE **minimum-security prisons**

minimum-security prisons
RK.724
ALT **minimum-security prison**
UF correctional institutions, minimum-security
institutions, minimum-security
minimum-security correctional institutions
minimum-security institutions
prisons, minimum-security
CN V.RK.AFU.ALO.ALO.CXA.AFU.AXC.AFU.AXC

mining
KT.617 (L,R)
CN K.KT.AFU.ALO.FUA.CXA

mining cities
USE **mining towns**

mining settlements
USE **mining towns**

mining towns
RD.55 (A)
ALT **mining town**
UF cities, mining
mining cities
mining settlements
settlements, mining
towns, mining
CN V.RD.AFU.AXC.BIQ.ARI

ministering
KG.214 (L)
SN Providing religious guidance. (RLG7)
UF ministry
CN K.KG.AFU.ALO.BIQ.ARI

ministries
RK.975 (B)
ALT **ministry**
CN V.RK.AFU.ALO.ALO.ERE.AFU.ARI.ALO

ministry
USE **ministering**

minium
USE **red lead**

minium (color)
USE **vivid reddish orange**

Minka
FL.1999
CN F.FL.ALO.ARI.ALO.ALO.ALO.AFU.BOK

Minnesota granite
MT.602
UF granite, Minnesota
CN M.MT.AFU.AFU.AFU.DCU.AFU.AFU.AFU.AFU.AFU.ARI.ALO.ARI.ALO

Minnesota stone
MT.745
UF stone, Minnesota
CN M.MT.AFU.AFU.AFU.DCU.AFU.ARI.ARI.AFU.ALO

Minnetaree
USE **Hidatsa**

Minoan
FL.2555 (A,B,R)
CN F.FL.ALO.AXC.ALO.AFU.AFU.ALO.ARI

Minoan, Early
USE **Early Minoan**

Minoan, Late
USE **Late Minoan**

Minoan, Middle
USE **Middle Minoan**

minofor
MT.412
SN Grade of butannin metal containing up to 9% zinc and up to 1% iron. (MH12)
CN M.MT.AFU.AFU.AFU.BZY.AFU.AFU.AFU.ALO.BUE.ALO.ALO.ALO

minor arts
USE **decorative arts**

minor assemblies
USE **minor assembly drawings**

minor assembly drawings
VD.113
ALT **minor assembly drawing**
UF assembly drawings, minor
component drawings
drawings, component
drawings, minor assembly
minor assemblies
CN V.VD.AFU.ALO.DCU.AFU.AFU

minor roads
USE **secondary roads**

minorities
HG.793 (L,R)
ALT **minority**
SN Use for smaller groups within a larger society that are the objects of prejudice or discrimination from the majority. For groups distinguished from the majority by their common ties of ancestry and culture, use **ethnic groups.**
CN H.HG.AFU.BOK.BUE

minsters
RK.1109 (B)
ALT **minster**
CN V.RK.AFU.ALO.ALO.FCS.BIQ.ALO.ARI.BCW

minstrel galleries
RM.36 (A)
ALT **minstrel gallery**
SN Use for galleries or balconies for players of musical instruments, whether in secular or religious buildings.
UF galleries, minstrel
galleries, music
music galleries
CN V.RM.AFU.DIO.AFU.AXC.ARI

mint
USE **dark green**

mint green
USE **light green**

mint green, light
USE **light green**
very light green

mint green, pale
USE **very light green**
very pale green

Minton
FL.3341 (R)
UF Minton porcelain and pottery
porcelain and pottery, Minton
CN F.FL.ALO.BCW.ALO.AXC.DIO.ALO.BUE.AXC.AFU

Minton porcelain and pottery
USE **Minton**

mints
RK.986 (A,L,B,R)
ALT **mint**
CN V.RK.AFU.ALO.ALO.ERE.AFU.BIQ

Minusinsk Basin
FL.2146
CN F.FL.ALO.ARI.ARI.ALO.ARI

minute books
VW.775
ALT **minute book**
SN Books in which are recorded the minutes of a collective body. (GAHLM)
UF books, minute
CN V.VW.AFU.ARI.AFU.ALO.BOK

minutes
VW.776 (L)
SN Records of what was said and done

at meetings or conferences. (ICA)
CN V.VW.AFU.ARI.AFU.ALO.BUE

Minyan ware
FL.2658
UF ware, Minyan
CN F.FL.ALO.AXC.ALO.AFU.ALO.AXC.AXC.BOK

Minyan ware, Argive
USE **Argive Minyan ware**

Minyan ware, Gray
USE **Gray Minyan ware**

Minyan ware, Yellow
USE **Yellow Minyan ware**

Mir Iskusstva
FL.3415 (R)
UF World of Art
CN F.FL.ALO.BCW.ALO.AXC.DIO.BZY.ALO.ALO

miracle plays
USE **mystery plays**

Miraflores
FL.1022
CN F.FL.ALO.ALO.ALO.ALO.AFU.ALO.ARI.AFU.ALO.BIQ

Miran
FL.1819
CN F.FL.ALO.ARI.AFU.AXC.ELK.BZY

mirror painting (reverse painting)
USE **reverse painting on glass**

mirror painting (verre églomisé)
USE **verre églomisé**

mirrored backs
TG.828
ALT **mirrored back**
UF backs, mirrored
CN V.TG.ALO.AXC.AFU.AFU

mirrored glass
USE **reflective glass**

mirroring, silver
USE **silver mirroring**

mischio marble
MT.756
UF marble, mischio
CN M.MT.AFU.AFU.AFU.DCU.AFU.ARI.ARI.ALO.AFU.BZY

mise-en-couleur
USE **pickling (metals)**

misericords
RM.322 (A,L,R)
ALT **misericord**
CN V.RM.AFU.DIO.AXC.ALO.AFU.CXA

mishima
KT.872
SN Korean technique of decorating ceramic ware in which the piece is inlaid with black and white clays and covered with a celadon glaze. (SAVAGE)
CN K.KT.AFU.ALO.HOE.BOK.AXC.AXC

Misquito
USE **Mosquito**

missals
VW.550 (L,N,R)
ALT **missal**
SN Books containing all the Roman Catholic prayers and responses necessary for celebrating the Mass throughout the year. (AHD)
UF books, mass
mass books
CN V.VW.AFU.ALO.AFU.AFU.ALO.BUE.CLM

missile bases
USE **guided missile bases**

missile ranges
USE **guided missile ranges**

missile ranges, guided
USE **guided missile ranges**

missile silos
USE **guided missile silos**

Mission
FL.1746
SN Use for the late 19th-century and early 20th-century American decorative arts style, principally with reference to furniture. Use **Mission Style** for a subtype of the Spanish Colonial Revival architecture style. (LDDO)
CN F.FL.ALO.ALO.BCW.AFU.BZY.BCW

mission churches
RK.1110 (A,B)
ALT **mission church**
SN Use only for the religious buildings of a mission.
UF churches, mission
missions (churches)
CN V.RK.AFU.ALO.ALO.FCS.BIQ.ALO.ARI.BIQ

Mission Revival
USE **Mission Style**

Mission Style
FL.1725 (A,L,R)
SN Use for a subtype of the Spanish Colonial Revival architecture style, characterized by simplicity of form and ornamentation. Use **Mission** for the late 19th-century, early 20th-century American decorative arts style, applied principally to furniture. (IAA)
UF Mission Revival
Revival, Mission
CN F.FL.ALO.ALO.BCW.AFU.ARI.AFU.AFU

mission tile
USE **Spanish tile**

missionaries
HG.227 (L,R)
ALT **missionary**
CN H.HG.AFU.AXC.AXC.BIQ.AFU.ARI.CRG

missions
RD.28 (L,R)
ALT **mission**
SN Use for self-sustaining frontier or outpost settlements created to aid in the administering of colonial wilderness enterprises, as those established by the Spanish government in America.
CN V.RD.AFU.ALO.AFU.BCW

missions (churches)
USE **mission churches**

Mississippi hackberry
MT.1170
UF Celtis mississippiensis
hackberry, Mississippi
CN M.MT.AFU.AFU.ALO.BIQ.DCU.AFU.AFU.AFU.DZW.ARI

Mississippian
FL.858 (A,L)
CN F.FL.ALO.ALO.ALO.AFU.ALO.ALO.ARI.ARI.BCW

Mississippian culture
USE **Temple Mound period**

Mississippian, Middle
USE **Middle Mississippian**

Missouri
FL.1388 (L)
CN F.FL.ALO.ALO.ARI.AFU.BOK.DIO

Missouri marble
MT.831
UF marble, Missouri
CN M.MT.AFU.AFU.AFU.DCU.AFU.ARI.ARI.ARI.BOK.CLM

Mitannian
FL.2924
CN F.FL.ALO.AXC.ARI.AXC.AFU.ARI

Mitannian pottery
USE **Atchana ware**

miter arches
RT.229
ALT **miter arch**
SN Use for arches of triangular shape, formed by two straight blocks of stone set diagonally.
UF arches, miter
arches, primitive
arches, triangular
primitive arches
triangular arches
CN V.RT.AFU.AFU.AFU.BCW.AFU.AFU.AFU.CLM

miter block planes
USE **miter planes**

miter blocks
TB.437 (N)
ALT **miter block**
SN In joinery, wood blocks arranged for sawing pieces at a 45 degree angle. (DAC)
UF blocks, miter
CN V.TB.AFU.ARI.EFQ.ALO.ARI

miter boards
TB.438
ALT **miter board**
SN Boards on which material to be planed is laid; guides or stops hold the material so that the ends of the miters can be planed at the correct angle. (DAC)
UF boards, miter
miter shoots
shoots, miter
CN V.TB.AFU.ARI.EFQ.ALO.AXC

miter-box saws
TB.991 (N)
ALT **miter-box saw**
SN Backsaws with a blade 22 to 30 inches long and 4 to 6 inches wide, designed for use with the miter box for cutting miters. (SALAM)
UF miter saws
saws, miter
saws, miter-box
CN V.TB.AFU.BCW.CFS.ALO.AFU.EWY.AFU.AXC

miter boxes
TB.439 (N)
ALT **miter box**
SN Devices for guiding hand saws at the proper angle in making a miter joint; often in the form of a narrow wood box having a bottom and two sides in which slots are cut for guiding the saw. (DAC)
UF boxes, miter
CN V.TB.AFU.ARI.EFQ.ALO.BCW

miter joints
TF.688
ALT **miter joint**
SN Joints formed by two boards with beveled edges. (NEF)
UF joints, miter
CN V.TF.ALO.ARI.AXC.ARI.BCW

miter joints, spline
USE **spline joints**

miter planes
TB.920 (N)
ALT **miter plane**
SN Planing tools used for preparing the surfaces of miter or butt joints. (MEANS)
UF miter block planes
miter shooting planes
picture-frame maker's planes
planes, miter
planes, miter block
planes, miter shooting
planes, picture-frame maker's
CN V.TB.AFU.BCW.CFS.ALO.AFU.DUC.ALO.BIQ

miter saws
USE **miter-box saws**
tenon saws

miter shooting planes
USE **miter planes**

miter shoots
USE **miter boards**

miter squares
TB.446 (N)
ALT **miter square**
SN Squares with one edge having an angle of 45 degrees; used for laying out miter joints. (MEANS)
UF squares, miter
CN V.TB.AFU.ARI.EFQ.ALO.BZY.ARI

mitering
KT.59 (L)
ALT **mitered**
SN The process of matching together in a miter joint or beveling the ends of a structural member of wood or other material for the purpose of matching together at an angle. (W)
CN K.KT.AFU.ALO.BCW.BZY

mithraea
RK.1144 (L)
ALT **mithraeum**
CN V.RK.AFU.ALO.ALO.FCS.BOK.BCW

Mithraism
BM.674 (L)
ALT **Mithraic**
CN B.BM.BZY.AFU.BZY

Mitsogo
USE **Tsogo**

mitsumata
MT.1965 (L)
SN Plant fiber used in papermaking.
CN M.MT.AFU.AFU.ARI.ALO.ALO.AXC.AXC.AFU.ARI

Mittis green
USE **emerald green**

Mittler's green
USE **viridian**

Mituku
USE **Metoko**

Miwok
FL.1258 (L)
UF Mewan
CN F.FL.ALO.ALO.ARI.AFU.ALO.CRG

Mixe
FL.1519 (L)
UF Mije
CN F.FL.ALO.ALO.ARI.ALO.AXC.CFS

mixed media
MT.2624 (R)
SN Combinations of two or more mediums in the making of a work of art. (A-Z)
CN M.MT.AFU.ARI.FUA.AFU

mixed use
BM.214
SN Use to describe projects or buildings when there is a highly site-intensive mixture of several different, major, revenue-producing functions involved.
UF use, mixed
CN B.BM.AFU.ALO.CFS.ALO

mixed-use developments
RG.237
ALT **mixed-use development**
SN Use for relatively large-scale real estate projects incorporating several revenue-producing functions, having a highly intensive use of land, and developed from a coherent plan.
UF developments, mixed-use
developments, multiuse
mixed-use projects
multiuse developments
MXDs
projects, mixed-use
CN V.RG.AFU.ALO.ALO

mixed-use projects
USE **mixed-use developments**

mixed white
USE **composite white**

mixers
TB.560 (L)
ALT **mixer**
SN Machines employed for blending the constituents of concrete, grout, mortar, or paint. (DAC)
CN V.TB.AFU.BCW.BCW.AFU.AFU

mixers, cement
USE **concrete mixers**

mixers, concrete
USE **concrete mixers**

mixers, jiffler
USE **jiffler mixers**

mixing
KT.60
ALT **mixed**
CN K.KT.AFU.ALO.BCW.CFS

mixing pressure valves
TF.283
ALT **mixing pressure valve**
UF pressure valves, mixing
valves, mixing pressure
CN V.TF.AFU.AFU.AFU.AFU.EWY.BCW

mixing rods
USE **stirring rods**

mixing tables
TG.747
ALT **mixing table**
SN Marble-topped tables with a superstructure containing drawers for decanters and having a roll top which descends to cover the marble slab when not in use. Use **slab tables** with reference to 18th-century marble-topped tables without a superstructure.
UF tables, mixing
CN V.TG.AFU.AFU.BIQ.BOK.ALO.DCU

mixing tables (slab tables)
USE **slab tables**

mixing troughs
TB.639 (N)
ALT **mixing trough**
UF troughs, mixing
CN V.TB.AFU.BCW.BCW.ARI

mixing varnish
MT.2476
SN Any varnish that may be mixed with oil paints and other coating materials, such as, damar varnish when used as an ingredient in an artist's paint vehicle. (MAYER)
UF varnish, mixing
CN M.MT.AFU.ARI.CRG.AFU.BOK.AFU.ARI

Mixtec
FL.1061 (L)
CN F.FL.ALO.ALO.ALO.ALO.AFU.ALO.AXC.ALO.AFU

Mixteca-Puebla
FL.1000
CN F.FL.ALO.ALO.ALO.ALO.AFU.ALO.AFU.ALO.ALO

mixture, additive
USE **additive mixture**

mixture, color
USE **color mixture**

mixture, optical
USE **color mixture**

mixture, subtractive
USE **subtractive mixture**

Mizui-e
FL.2079
CN F.FL.ALO.ARI.ALO.ALO.ALO.AXC.AXC

moated castles
RK.438 (B)
ALT **moated castle**
UF castles, moated
CN V.RK.AFU.ALO.ALO.BIQ.ALO.ALO

moats
RT.1207 (A,L,B,R)
ALT **moat**
CN V.RT.AFU.BUE.AFU.BZY.BOK

Moba
FL.386 (L)
CN F.FL.ALO.AFU.AXC.AFU.AXC.ARI.ARI.BCW

mobile banks
RK.131 (A,L)
ALT **mobile bank**
UF banks, mobile
CN V.RK.AFU.ALO.ALO.ALO.ALO.AFU.AXC

mobile buildings
USE **portable buildings**

mobile clinics
USE **mobile hospitals**

mobile home parks
RG.74 (A,L)
ALT **mobile home park**
SN Distinguished from **trailer camps** by being only for infrequently moved portable structures designed for year-round living.
UF mobile parks
parks, mobile home
CN V.RG.AFU.AFU.BOK.AXC.AFU.AXC

mobile homes
RK.354 (A,L,B)
ALT **mobile home**
UF homes, mobile
CN V.RK.AFU.ALO.ALO.AXC.ARI.AXC

mobile hospitals
RK.760 (A,L)
ALT **mobile hospital**
UF clinics, mobile
hospitals, mobile
mobile clinics
CN V.RK.AFU.ALO.ALO.CXA.ALO.AFU.BCW.AFU.ALO

mobile parks
USE **mobile home parks**

mobility
USE **internal migration**

mobility of labor
USE **labor mobility**

mobility, labor
USE **labor mobility**

mobility, residential
USE **residential mobility**

mobility, social
USE **social mobility**

mobility, student
USE **student mobility**

Moccasin Bluff
FL.819
CN F.FL.ALO.ALO.ALO.AFU.ALO.ALO.AFU.BIQ

Moche
USE **Mochica**

Mochica
FL.1155 (L)
UF Moche
Muchik
Proto-Chimu
CN F.FL.ALO.ALO.ALO.ARI.AXC.AFU.AXC.BCW

mock-ups
USE **models**

mockernut hickory
MT.1176
UF ballnut
Carya tomentosa
hickory, mockernut
hickory, white
hognut
white hickory
CN M.MT.AFU.AFU.ALO.BIQ.DCU.AFU.AFU.AFU.ELK.AXC

Mocobí
USE **Mocoví**

Mocoví
FL.1647 (L)
UF Mbokovi
Mocobí
CN F.FL.ALO.ALO.ARI.ARI.AXC.CRG

model apartments
RM.269 (A,L)
ALT **model apartment**
UF apartments, model
CN V.RM.AFU.DIO.ARI.ALO.BIQ.AFU.ARI

model books
USE **pattern books**

model cities
RD.83 (A,L)
ALT **model city**
SN Urban areas or communities within them whose design incorporates innovative attempts at solving specific social and physical problems; often applied to the redesign of existing settlements in the 19th and 20th centuries. For 19th-century cities built with prescribed forms to fulfill specific military or economic ideals, use **ideal cities.**
UF cities, model
CN V.RD.AFU.BUE.ARI

model houses
RK.275 (A,L,B,R)
ALT **model house**
UF demonstration houses
houses, demonstration
houses, model
houses, prototype
prototype houses
prototypes (houses)
CN V.RK.AFU.ALO.ALO.AXC.ALO.ALO.ALO

model-making
KT.529 (L,B)

CN K.KT.AFU.ALO.ELK.CXA

model villages
USE **new towns**

modeled, cursive
USE **cursive**

modelers
HG.568
ALT **modeler**
CN H.HG.AFU.AXC.BUE.AXC.CRG

modeling (forming)
KT.144 (L,R)
ALT **modeled**
SN The use of malleable material such as wax or clay to create a form which is three-dimensional. (THDAT)
CN K.KT.AFU.ALO.DOI.CLM

modeling (shading)
KT.268
ALT **modeled**
SN The suggestion of three-dimensional character using shading and highlights.
CN K.KT.AFU.ALO.DUC.DCU.BCW

modeling planes
TB.967 (N)
ALT **modeling plane**
SN Small planes, approximately 4 to 6 inches long, with the sole curved along the longitudinal axis like a compass plane. (MERCER)
UF planes, modeling
CN V.TB.AFU.BCW.CFS.ALO.AFU.DUC.BCW

modellers' marks
VW.752
ALT **modellers' mark**
UF marks, modellers'
CN V.VW.AFU.ALO.ALO.AFU.AXC.AXC.CRG

modelli
VB.56 (R)
ALT **modello**
SN Small, often quite highly finished versions of larger paintings or sculptures, made to be shown to the patron in order to indicate what is intended,(THDAT) or a highly finished drawing serving that purpose. (MEDER)
CN V.VB.AFU.ALO.BCW

models
VB.103 (A,L,N,B)
ALT **model**
SN Use for scaled representations of objects or structures, usually three-dimensional.
UF mock-ups
CN V.VB.ALO.BUE.ARI

models (people)
HG.725 (R)
ALT **model (person)**
CN H.HG.AFU.BCW.DUC

models, anatomical
USE **anatomical models**

models, architectural
USE **architectural models**

models, mathematical
USE **mathematical models**

modems
TB.157 (L)
ALT **modem**
SN Devices that enable data to be transmitted between computers, generally over telephone lines but sometimes on fiber-optic cable or radio frequencies. (COMBAS)
CN V.TB.AFU.ARI.BCW.AXC.ALO

moderate blue
DL.219
UF ash, blue ultramarine
blue ultramarine ash
blue verditer (color)
blue, bright cérulean
blue, cerulean (color)
blue, copen
blue, deep cerulean
blue, delft
blue, della robbia
blue, dull
blue, gray
blue, lapis lazuli
blue, medium
blue, moderate
blue, powder
blue, Prussian (color)
blue, royal
blue, smalt
bright cerulean blue
bright navy
centroid color 182
cerulean blue (color)
cerulean blue, bright
cerulean blue, deep
copen blue
deep cerulean blue
deep ultramarine
delft blue
della robbia blue
dull blue
gray blue
lapis lazuli blue
medium blue
navy, bright
powder blue
Prussian blue (color)
royal blue
smalt blue
ultramarine
ultramarine ash, blue
ultramarine, deep
verditer, blue (color)
CN D.DL.AFU.AFU.BZY.BIQ

moderate blue green
USE **moderate bluish green**

moderate bluish green
DL.202
UF anthracene green
aquamarine green
blue green
blue green, dark
blue green, grayish
blue green, moderate
blue, Bremen (color)
blue, cyan
blue, slate
bluish gray green, dark
bluish green, moderate
Bremen blue (color)
bright turquoise green
centroid color 164
cyan blue
dark blue green
dark bluish gray green
dark emerald green
dark jade green
deep emerald green
deep turquoise green
emerald green (color)
emerald green, dark
gray green, dark bluish
grayish blue green
green, anthracene
green, aquamarine
green, bright turquoise
green, dark emerald
green, emerald (color)
green, grayish blue
green, jade
green, moderate blue
green, moderate bluish
green, Prussian
green, teal
green, turquoise
jade green
lapis
light terre verte
moderate blue green
Prussian green
slate blue
teal
teal green
terre verte, light
turquoise (color)
turquoise green
turquoise green, bright
CN D.DL.AFU.AFU.BUE.DCU.ALO.BIQ

moderate brown
DL.80
UF brown, Cassel
brown, Mars
brown, moderate
brown, orange
brown, red
brown, sienna
brown, Van Dyke (color)
burnt umber (color)
Cassel brown
Cassel earth
centroid color 58
earth red
Mars brown

orange brown
raw umber (color)
red brown
red, earth
sienna brown
umber, burnt (color)
umber, raw (color)
Van Dyke brown (color)
CN D.DL.AFU.AFU.AXC.AXC

moderate green
DL.170
UF blue green
bright green
centroid color 145
chrome green (color)
dark viridian green
deep emerald green
emerald green (color)
emerald green, deep
gray green
green, bright
green, chrome (color)
green, dark viridian
green, deep emerald
green, emerald (color)
green, gray
green, hunter
green, jade
green, moderate
green, slate
hunter green
jade green
slate green
transparent chromium oxide
viridian (color)
viridian green, dark
CN D.DL.AFU.AFU.BUE.BIQ

moderate greenish blue
DL.239
UF azurite blue
blue green, dark
blue, azurite
blue, bright
blue, bright teal
blue, cyan
blue, deep cerulean
blue, deep peacock
blue, deep teal
blue, medium
blue, medium teal
blue, medium turquoise
blue, moderate greenish
blue, peacock
blue, teal
blue, turquoise
blue, vivid turquoise
bright blue
bright teal blue
centroid color 173
cerulean blue, deep
cyan blue
dark blue green
deep cerulean blue
deep peacock blue
deep teal blue
greenish blue, moderate
medium blue
medium teal
medium teal blue
medium turquoise blue
peacock
peacock blue
peacock blue, deep
teal
teal blue
teal blue, bright
teal blue, deep
teal blue, medium
teal, medium
turquoise blue
turquoise blue, medium
turquoise blue, vivid
turquoise (color)
vivid turquoise blue
CN D.DL.AFU.AFU.BZY.DCU.AFU.BIQ

moderate greenish yellow
DL.140
UF barium yellow (color)
bistre
centroid color 102
chartreuse
chartreuse yellow
chartreuse yellow, light
citron green
citron yellow
green, citron
green, lime
greenish yellow, moderate
light chartreuse yellow
lime green
olive yellow
pastel yellow
yellow, barium (color)
yellow, chartreuse
yellow, citron
yellow, light chartreuse
yellow, moderate greenish
yellow, pastel
CN D.DL.AFU.AFU.BCW.CRG.ALO.BIQ

moderate income housing
RG.75
UF housing, moderate income
CN V.RG.AFU.AFU.BOK.AXC.AFU.BCW

moderate olive
DL.146
UF bright olive green
brown, mustard
centroid color 107
dark greenish olive
deep olive
dull gold
gold, dull
green, bright olive
greenish olive, dark
mustard brown
mustard tan
olive green, bright
olive yellow
olive, dark greenish
olive, deep
olive, moderate
olive, yellowish
tan, mustard
yellow, olive
yellowish olive
CN D.DL.AFU.AFU.BIQ.ALO

moderate olive brown
DL.109
UF bistre
bronze (color)
brown, moderate olive
brown, red
brown, very dark grayish
brownish olive
centroid color 95
grayish brown, very dark
olive brown, moderate
olive, brownish
red brown
sepia (color)
very dark grayish brown
CN D.DL.AFU.AFU.AXC.BZY.ARI.ALO

moderate olive green
DL.208
UF bluish olive
bright olive green
centroid color 125
dark dull yellow green
deep dull yellow green
green, bright olive
green, jade
green, moderate olive
green, slate
jade green
olive green, bright
olive green, moderate
olive, bluish
peridot
slate green
yellow green, dark dull
yellow green, deep dull
CN D.DL.AFU.AFU.BUE.DCU.ARI.ARI

moderate orange
DL.66
UF brown orange
brown, pale
brown, red
brown, yellow
buff
cadmium yellow (color)
centroid color 53
copper (color)
gold ocher
golden ocher (color)
light red
Mars yellow (color)
ocher (color)
ocher, gold
ocher, golden (color)
orange brown
orange, brown
orange, moderate
orange, pastel
orange, yellow
pale brown
pastel orange
red brown
red, light

reddish yellow
yellow brown
yellow orange
yellow, cadmium (color)
yellow, Mars (color)
yellow, reddish
CN D.DL.AFU.AFU.ARI.BIQ

moderate orange pink
USE **light yellowish pink**
moderate yellowish pink

moderate orange yellow
DL.131
UF amber (color)
amber, light
antimony yellow
bistre
bright yellow
brown orange
buff
buff, dull
buff, orange
buff, yellow
cadmium yellow (color)
centroid color 71
chrome yellow, deep
deep chrome yellow
dull buff
earth, yellow
English ocher
French ocher
gold yellow
golden yellow
Indian yellow (color)
lake, quercitron (color)
light amber
ocher (color)
ocher, English
ocher, French
ocher, yellow (color)
orange buff
orange yellow, moderate
orange, brown
orpiment red
permanent yellow
quercitron lake (color)
realgar (color)
red, orpiment
reddish yellow
sandarach
yellow buff
yellow earth
yellow ocher (color)
yellow, antimony
yellow, bright
yellow, cadmium (color)
yellow, deep chrome
yellow, gold
yellow, golden
yellow, Indian (color)
yellow, moderate orange
yellow, permanent
yellow, reddish
yellowish orange
CN D.DL.AFU.AFU.BCW.CRG.AFU.BIQ

moderate pink
DL.8
UF centroid color 5
lake, rose
light mauve
lilac
mauve, light
pastel pink
pink, moderate
pink, pastel
rose
rose lake
CN D.DL.AFU.AFU.AFU.BCW

moderate portland cement
USE **modified portland cement**

moderate purple
DL.274
UF amethyst (color)
amethyst, light
bright lavender
bright violet
centroid color 223
cobalt violet (color)
lavender
lavender, bright
light amethyst
lilac
litho purple
purple, litho
purple, moderate
red violet
violet, bright
violet, cobalt (color)
violet, red
CN D.DL.AFU.AFU.CFS.BIQ

moderate purplish blue
DL.249
UF azurite blue
blue violet, grayish
blue, cornflower (color)
blue, cyanine
blue, deep royal
blue, deep sapphire
blue, gentian
blue, light cornflower
blue, moderate purplish
blue, Monastral
blue, navy
blue, reddish
blue, royal
blus, azurite
bright navy
centroid color 200
cornflower blue (color)
cornflower blue, light
cyanine blue
deep royal blue
deep sapphire blue
gentian blue
grayish blue violet
light cornflower blue
Monastral blue
navy blue
navy, bright
navy, purple
purple navy
purplish blue, moderate
reddish blue
royal blue
royal blue, deep
sapphire blue, deep
ultramarine
CN D.DL.AFU.AFU.BZY.DCU.ALO.BIQ

moderate purplish pink
DL.20
UF bluish pink
centroid color 250
dull rose
fuchsia pink
light mauve
light orchid
light orchid rose
light rose
lilac, purplish
mauve, light
orchid
orchid pink
orchid rose, light
orchid, light
pink, bluish
pink, fuchsia
pink, moderate purplish
pink, orchid
pink, rose
purplish lilac
purplish pink, moderate
red violet
rose pink
rose violet
rose, dull
rose, light
rose, light orchid
violet, red
violet, rose
CN D.DL.AFU.AFU.AFU.CLM.AFU.BCW

moderate purplish red
DL.55
UF bluish red
bluish red, dull
bright fuchsia rose
bright rose
carmine (color)
carmine lake
carmine rose
carmine, madder
carmine, rose
centroid color 258
dark rose
deep plum
deep rose
dull bluish red
fuchsia red
fuchsia rose
fuchsia rose, bright
lake (color)
lake, carmine
lilac purple
lilac rose
lilac, red
lilac, rose
madder carmine
magenta (color)
magenta rose
plum, deep

purple, lilac
purplish red, moderate
red lilac
red, bluish
red, dull bluish
red, fuchsia
red, moderate purplish
red, rose
rose
rose carmine
rose lilac
rose red
rose violet
rose, bright
rose, bright fuchsia
rose, carmine
rose, dark
rose, deep
rose, fuchsia
rose, lilac
rose, magenta
violet, rose
CN D.DL.AFU.AFU.ALO.CFS.AFU.AXC

moderate red
DL.39
UF blood red
brick red
brown lake
cadmium purple
cadmium red (color)
cadmium vermilion
carmine (color)
carmine lake
carmine rose
carmine, madder
centroid color 15
crimson lake (color)
dark rose
deep rose
dull red
geranium rose
lake (color)
lake, brown
lake, carmine
lake, crimson (color)
lake, purple
lake, scarlet
light red
madder carmine
madder (color)
madder red
madder, purple
para red (color)
permanent red
pompeian red (color)
purple lake
purple madder
purple, cadmium
quinacridone red (color)
red, blood
red, brick
red, cadmium (color)
red, dull
red, light
red, madder
red, moderate
red, para (color)
red, permanent
red, pompeian (color)
red, quinacridone (color)
red, rose
rose
rose red
rose, carmine
rose, dark
rose, deep
rose, geranium
ruby (color)
scarlet
scarlet lake
vermilion (color)
vermilion, cadmium
CN D.DL.AFU.AFU.ALO.AXC

moderate reddish brown
DL.93
UF brown, moderate reddish
brown, red
centroid color 43
dull red
earth, red
ocher, red (color)
red brown
red earth
red ocher (color)
red, dull
red, Venetian (color)
reddish brown, moderate
terra cotta (color)
Venetian red (color)
CN D.DL.AFU.AFU.AXC.BZY.AFU.AXC

moderate reddish orange
DL.72
UF brown, orange
brown, red
burnt ocher (color)
centroid color 37
copper (color)
dull vermilion
light red
madder (color)
madder red
ocher, burnt (color)
orange brown
orange red
orange vermilion (color)
orange, moderate reddish
red brown
red, light
red, madder
red, orange
red, yellowish
reddish orange, moderate
rose
vermilion (color)
vermilion, dull
vermilion, orange (color)
yellowish red
CN D.DL.AFU.AFU.ARI.BOK.AFU.AXC

moderate reddish purple
DL.294
UF centroid color 241
fuchsia purple
lilac
mauve (color)
orchid
purple, fuchsia
purple, moderate reddish
red violet
reddish purple, moderate
reddish violet
rose violet
violet, red
violet, reddish
violet, rose
CN D.DL.AFU.AFU.CFS.DCU.AFU.BCW

moderate violet
DL.261
UF anthracene violet
blackish violet
blue violet, dull
blue violet, grayish
blue, light cornflower
bluish violet
bluish violet, dark dull
bluish violet, deep dull
bright lavender
bright violet
centroid color 211
cornflower blue, light
dark dull bluish violet
deep dull bluish violet
dull blue violet
dull lilac
grayish blue violet
lavender, bright
light cornflower blue
lilac, dull
violet, anthracene
violet, blackish
violet, bluish
violet, bright
violet, dark dull bluish
violet, deep dull bluish
violet, moderate
CN D.DL.AFU.AFU.BZY.DCU.ARI.BIQ

moderate yellow
DL.117
UF amber (color)
bistre
brass (color)
brown orange
buff
buff yellow
buff, orange
canary
centroid color 87
chamois (color)
cream buff
gold (color)
gold, light
lemon
light gold
Naples yellow (color)
ocher (color)
orange buff
orange, brown
orpiment (color)
pastel yellow
reddish yellow

Turner's yellow (color)
yellow, moderate
yellow, Naples (color)
yellow, pastel
yellow, reddish
yellow, Turner's (color)
CN D.DL.AFU.AFU.BCW.BIQ

moderate yellow green
DL.160
UF bright olive green
centroid color 120
chartreuse
deep dull yellow green
gray green
green, bright olive
green, gray
green, light olive
green, moderate yellow
green, pale olive
green, pastel
green, pistachio
green, Scheele's (color)
light olive green
olive green, bright
olive green, light
olive green, pale
pale olive green
pastel green
pistachio green
Scheele's green (color)
yellow green, deep dull
yellow green, moderate
CN D.DL.AFU.AFU.BOK.BIQ

moderate yellowish brown
DL.102
UF beige, yellow
bistre
bistre brown
bronze (color)
brown, bistre
brown, dull yellowish
brown, golden
brown, moderate yellowish
brown, red
camel
centroid color 77
dull yellowish brown
golden brown
khaki
mummy (color)
raw umber (color)
red brown
tan
umber, raw (color)
yellow beige
yellowish brown, dull
yellowish brown, moderate
CN D.DL.AFU.AFU.AXC.BZY.ALO.AXC

moderate yellowish green
DL.192
UF celadon green
centroid color 136
chromium oxide
chrysocolla (color)
cobalt green (color)
deep malachite green
emerald green (color)
gray green
green, celadon
green, cobalt (color)
green, deep malachite
green, emerald (color)
green, gray
green, jade
green, moderate yellowish
green, pistachio
green, verditer
jade green
malachite green, deep
pistachio green
verdigris (color)
verditer green
yellowish green, moderate
CN D.DL.AFU.AFU.BUE.DCU.AFU.BIQ

moderate yellowish pink
DL.29
UF baby pink
bisque
bistre brown
brown orange
brown, bistre
buff
buff, orange
centroid color 29
dull orange
flesh pink
moderate orange pink
orange buff
orange pink, moderate
orange, brown
orange, dull
pastel pink
peach (color)
pink, baby
pink, flesh
pink, moderate orange
pink, moderate yellowish
pink, pastel
rose
salmon
yellowish pink, moderate
CN D.DL.AFU.AFU.AFU.CLM.ALO.
BCW

Modern Movement
FL.3280 (A,B)
SN Use with reference to the collective actions and objectives of Modernist architecture, especially, but not exclusively, of the International Style. For art, architecture, or design more generally, use **Modernist.**
CN F.FL.ALO.BCW.ALO.AXC.CRG.ARI

Modern Style (Art Nouveau)
USE **Art Nouveau**

Modern, Jazz
USE **Art Deco**

Moderne
USE **Art Deco**

Modernismo
USE **Art Nouveau**

Modernist
FL.3257 (L,B,R)
ALT **Modernism**
SN Use for certain works of art, arhcitecture, or design of the 20th century. Distinct from **Modern Movement** which is more specific to architecture.
CN F.FL.ALO.BCW.ALO.AXC.BIQ

modified portland cement
MT.15
UF cement, moderate portland
cement, modificd portland
cement, type II portland
moderate portland cement
portland cement, moderate
portland cement, modified
portland cement, type II
type II portland cement
CN M.MT.AFU.AFU.AFU.ALO.AFU.AFU
.ARI.AFU.AXC

modillions
RT.343
ALT **modillion**
SN Brackets, often in the form of a scroll with acanthus, supporting a cornice.
CN V.RT.AFU.AFU.AFU.BCW.BZY.ALO
ALO.ALO.BIQ

Modoc
FL.1414 (L)
CN F.FL.ALO.ALO.ARI.AFU.BUE.CFS

modular brick
USE **modular building brick**

modular building brick
MT.78
UF brick, modular
brick, modular building
building brick, modular
modular brick
CN M.MT.AFU.AFU.AFU.AXC.ALO
.AFU.AFU.AFU.BZY

modular construction
KT.38 (A,L)
ALT **modular**
SN Use for construction that utilizes prefabricated units and for construction based on the combination of similar subcomponents.
UF construction, modular
construction, unit
unit construction
CN K.KT.AFU.ALO.BCW.ARI.AFU.BUE

modular coordination
BM.1143 (A,L,B)
UF coordination, dimensional
coordination, modular
design, modular
dimensional coordination
modular design
rationalization (architecture)
CN B.BM.CXA.ALO.AXC.AFU

modular design
USE **modular coordination**

modules, learning
USE **learning modules**

modulus of elasticity
BM.955 (L)
UF elasticity, modulus of
Hooke's modulus
modulus, Hooke's
modulus, Young's
Young's modulus
CN B.BM.CFS.AXC.BZY.BOK.BUE

modulus, Hooke's
USE **modulus of elasticity**

modulus, section
USE **section modulus**

modulus, Young's
USE **modulus of elasticity**

Mogen Davids
USE **Stars of David**

Mogollon
FL.935 (L)
CN F.FL.ALO.ALO.ALO.AFU.ALO.ARI.BIQ.BCW

Mogollon, Chiricahua stage
USE **Chiricahua stage Mogollon**

Mogollon, Georgetown
USE **Georgetown Mogollon**

Mogollon, Pine Lawn
USE **Pine Lawn Mogollon**

Mogollon, Reserve
USE **Reserve Mogollon**

Mogollon, San Francisco
USE **San Francisco Mogollon**

Mogollon, Three Circle
USE **Three Circle Mogollon**

Mogul
USE **Mughal**

Mohammedan
USE **Islam**

Mohave
USE **Mojave**

Mohave Apache
USE **Yavapai**

Mohawk
FL.1294 (L)
CN F.FL.ALO.ALO.ARI.AFU.ARI.BCW.ALO

Mohegan
USE **Mahican**

mohel
HG.247
SN Persons who circumcise male infants in accordance with Jewish ritual. (W)
CN H.HG.AFU.AXC.AXC.BIQ.ALO.ARI

Mohenjo-daro
FL.2189 (L)
CN F.FL.ALO.ARI.AXC.ALO.AFU.AFU.ALO

Mohican
USE **Mahican**

moiré
DG.143
SN Use for patterns having a watered or rippled look. Where this produces an illusion of movement, use **moiré effect.**
CN D.DG.AFU.ARI.ALO.CLM

moiré effect
BM.151 (L,R)
UF effect, moiré
CN B.BM.AFU.AFU.ARI.BOK.BZY.ARI

moisture
BM.924 (L,B)
CN B.BM.CFS.AXC.BOK

moisture-proofing
USE **waterproofing**

Mojave
FL.1459 (L)
UF Mohave
CN F.FL.ALO.ALO.ARI.AFU.CFS.BIQ

Mojo
FL.1591 (L)
UF Moxo
CN F.FL.ALO.ALO.ARI.ARI.AFU.FIM

Mokar
USE **Ga'anda**

Moki
USE **Hopi**

Molala
FL.1415 (L)
CN F.FL.ALO.ALO.ARI.AFU.BUE.CLM

mold-blowing
USE **blow molding**

mold casting, full
USE **lost-wax process**

mold planes, bed
USE **cornice planes**

mold planes, crown
USE **cornice planes**

mold release agents
MT.2630
UF agents, mold release
CN M.MT.AFU.ARI.GLI.ALO

mold-resistant paint
USE **antifouling paint**

molded brick
MT.133 (A)
UF brick, molded
CN M.MT.AFU.AFU.AFU.AXC.ALO.AFU.AXC.ALO.ALO

molders
HG.449
ALT **molder**
UF metal molders
molders, metal
CN H.HG.AFU.AXC.BUE.ALO.BZY

molders, metal
USE **molders**

molding
ALT **molded**
CN K.KT.AFU.ALO.DOI.CRG

molding materials
MT.2625 (L)
UF materials, molding
CN M.MT.AFU.ARI.FZU

molding planes
TB.950 (N)
ALT **molding plane**
SN A class of thin-bodied planes with variously shaped soles and blades whose cutting edges form many various moldings. (BLACKB)
UF planes, molding
CN V.TB.AFU.BCW.CFS.ALO.AFU.DUC.AXC

molding planes, bead
USE **bead planes**

molding planes, centerbead
USE **centerboard planes**

molding planes, cove
USE **cove planes**

molding planes, nosing
USE **nosing planes**

molding planes, ogee
USE **ogee planes**

molding plaster
MT.2452
UF plaster, molding
CN M.MT.AFU.ARI.CRG.AFU.AXC.ALO.ALO

molding pull planes
TB.964
ALT **molding pull plane**
SN Any kind of large complex molding plane which is pulled.
UF planes, molding pull
CN V.TB.AFU.BCW.CFS.ALO.AFU.DUC.AXC.ALO.ARI

molding sand
USE **foundry sand**

molding, blow
USE **blow molding**

molding, compression
USE **compression molding**

molding, injection
USE **injection molding**

molding, reaction injection
USE **reaction injection molding**

molding, rotational
USE **rotational molding**

molding, transfer
USE **transfer molding**

moldings
RT.752 (A,L,B)
ALT **molding**
SN Long, regular channels or projections used for finishing and decorative purposes. (PUTNAM)
CN V.RT.AFU.ALO.AFU.BOK.AFU

moldings, annular
USE **roll moldings**

moldings, applied
USE **applied moldings**

moldings, balection
USE **bolection moldings**

moldings, bead
USE **bead moldings**

moldings, bead and reel
USE **bead and reel moldings**

moldings, beak
USE **beak moldings**

moldings, beakhead
USE **beakhead moldings**

moldings, bed
USE **bed moldings**

moldings, belection
USE **bolection moldings**

moldings, bellexion
USE **bolection moldings**

moldings, billet
USE **billet moldings**

moldings, bird's beak
USE **beakhead moldings**

moldings, bolection
USE **bolection moldings**

moldings, cable
USE **cable moldings**

moldings, cant
USE **cant moldings**

moldings, canted
USE **raking moldings**

moldings, cap
USE **cap moldings**

moldings, cavetto
USE **cavetto moldings**

moldings, chain
USE **chain moldings**

moldings, coin
USE **money pattern**

moldings, cove
USE **cavetto moldings**

moldings, cover
USE **cover moldings**

moldings, crown
USE **crown moldings**

moldings, dogtooth
USE **dogtooth moldings**

moldings, drop
USE **drop moldings**

moldings, egg and anchor
USE **egg and dart moldings**

moldings, egg and arrow
USE **egg and dart moldings**

moldings, egg and dart
USE **egg and dart moldings**

moldings, egg and tongue
USE **egg and dart moldings**

moldings, fillet
USE **fillet moldings**

moldings, gorge
USE **cavetto moldings**

moldings, half-round
USE **half-round moldings**

moldings, hawksbeak
USE **beak moldings**

moldings, head
USE **hood moldings**

moldings, hollow
USE **cavetto moldings**

moldings, hood
USE **hood moldings**

moldings, label
USE **label moldings**

moldings, money
USE **money pattern**

moldings, ogee
USE **cymas**

moldings, ovolo
USE **ovolo moldings**

moldings, pearl
USE **paternosters**

moldings, picture
USE **picture rails**

moldings, planted
USE **applied moldings**

moldings, quarter-round
USE **quarter-round moldings**

moldings, raised
USE **bolection moldings**

moldings, raked
USE **raking moldings**

moldings, raking
USE **raking moldings**

moldings, reel and bead
USE **bead and reel moldings**

moldings, reglet
USE **reglet moldings**

moldings, reverse ogee
USE **cyma reversas**

moldings, risen
USE **bolection moldings**

moldings, roll
USE **roll moldings**

moldings, roll-and-fillet
USE **roll-and-fillet moldings**

moldings, roll billet
USE **roll billet moldings**

moldings, rope
USE **cable moldings**

moldings, round
USE **roll moldings**

moldings, round billet
USE **roll billet moldings**

moldings, solid
USE **struck moldings**

moldings, stop
USE **stop moldings**

moldings, struck
USE **struck moldings**

moldings, talon
USE **cymas**

moldings, throat
USE **cavetto moldings**

moldings, thumb
USE **gadrooning**

moldings, undulating
USE **wave moldings**

moldings, wave
USE **wave moldings**

moldmade paper
MT.1969
UF paper, moldmade
CN M.MT.AFU.AFU.ARI.ALO.ALO.AXC.AXC.AXC

molds
TB.440
ALT **mold**
SN Hollow forms in which castings or pressings are made. (MEANS)
UF casts (molds)
CN V.TB.AFU.ARI.EFQ.ALO.BIQ

molds, bed

USE **bed moldings**

molecular biology
KD.207 (L)
UF biology, molecular
CN K.KD.AFU.ARI.ARI.BOK

moles
USE **breakwaters**

Mombasa
FL.153 (L)
CN F.FL.ALO.AFU.ALO.AXC.ALO.ARI

moment of inertia
BM.912
SN The measure of resistence of a body to angular acceleration. (CEDPS)
UF inertia, moment of
CN B.BM.CFS.AXC.BIQ.ARI.ALO

moments
BM.1021
SN The phenomena by which a force causes the body to which it is applied to rotate about a point or line. (DAC)
CN B.BM.CFS.AXC.CLM.ALO.AXC

momentum
BM.898 (L)
SN Force of motion acquired by a moving body as a result of the continuance of its motion. (W)
CN B.BM.CFS.AXC.BIQ.AFU.AXC.BCW

momie
USE **mummy**

Momoyama
FL.1986 (L)
CN F.FL.ALO.ARI.ALO.ALO.AFU.BCW.ALO

Mon
FL.2310 (L)
CN F.FL.ALO.ARI.BCW.AFU.ALO

Monagrillo
FL.1087
CN F.FL.ALO.ALO.ALO.ALO.ALO.ALO.AFU.ALO

monarchy
BM.541 (L,R)
SN Form of government having a single, usually hereditary, chief of state with life tenure who may exercise governmental powers varying from nominal to absolute. (W)
CN B.BM.BOK.BOK.AFU.ARI

monasteries
RG.194 (A,L,B,R)
ALT **monastery**
SN Places of religious retirement or seclusion from the world for persons under religious vows. (W)
CN V.RG.AFU.AFU.DUC.BIQ

monasteries, double
USE **double monasteries**

monastic churches
RK.1111 (B)
ALT **monastic church**
UF churches, monastic
CN V.RK.AFU.ALO.ALO.FCS.BIQ.ALO.ARI.BOK

monasticism
BM.692 (L,B,R)
ALT **monastic**
CN B.BM.BZY.ALO.ALO

Monastral blue
USE **dark blue**
moderate purplish blue
phthalocyanine blue

Monastral fast blue
USE **phthalocyanine blue**

Monastral green
USE **phthalocyanine green**

Mondurucu
USE **Mundurucú**

monel
MT.403 (L)
SN Natural alloy whose average composition is 67% nickel, 28% copper, and 5% other elements such as iron. (MH)
UF alloy, monel
metal, monel
monel alloy
monel metal
CN M.MT.AFU.AFU.AFU.BZY.AFU.AFU.AFU.ALO.BIQ.ALO

monel alloy
USE **monel**

monel metal
USE **monel**

monelles
USE **mullions**

money moldings
USE **money pattern**

money orders
VW.833 (L,N)
ALT **money order**
SN Orders for the payment of a specified amount of money, usually issued and payable at a bank or post office. (AHD)
UF orders, money
CN V.VW.AFU.ARI.AFU.BIQ.CFS.BCW

money pattern
DG.130
SN A running pattern of overlapping discs.
UF coin moldings
moldings, coin
moldings, money
money moldings
pattern, money
CN D.DG.AFU.ARI.ALO.BIQ.BCW

money raising
USE **fund raising**

Mongol
FL.3476 (L,R)
CN F.FL.ALO.BIQ.AFU.ERE

Mongol School
FL.3453
CN F.FL.ALO.BIQ.AFU.DIO.AFU.AFU

monials
USE **mullions**

monitor lights
USE **monitors (roof appendages)**

monitor tops
USE **monitors (roof appendages)**

monitoring
KG.101 (L)
SN Observing and collecting information about something over time or distance for some specific purpose. (RLG7)
CN K.KG.AFU.AFU.AXC.CXA

monitors
TB.158
ALT **monitor**
SN Computer components with a screen for viewing data at a computer terminal. (RHDEL2)
UF CRTs
displays (monitors)
VDTs
VDUs
CN V.TB.AFU.ARI.BCW.AXC.ARI

monitors (roof appendages)
RT.486
ALT **monitor (roof appendage)**
SN Raised central portions of roofs, along the ridge, having louvers or windows on the sides for ventilation or light.
UF lights, monitor
monitor lights
monitor tops
tops, monitor
CN V.RT.AFU.AFU.AFU.BIQ.ARI.ALO.AFU.BUE.BIQ

monk's benches (box settles)
USE **box settles**

monk's benches (chair-tables)
USE **chair-tables**

monk's chairs (chair-tables)
USE **chair-tables**

monk's chairs (sillónes frailleros)
USE **fraileros**

monk's seats
USE **chair-tables**

monkey wrenches
TB.771 (N)
ALT **monkey wrench**

SN Wrenches with one adjustable jaw which moves vertically along the shaft.
UF wrenches, monkey
CN V.TB.AFU.BCW.BIQ.AXC.ALO.BIQ.AFU.AFU

monkeys
USE **pole derricks**

monks
HG.241 (L,R)
ALT **monk**
UF friars
CN H.HG.AFU.AXC.AXC.BIQ.AFU.BUE.AFU

Mono
FL.1259 (L)
CN F.FL.ALO.ALO.ARI.AFU.ALO.CXA

mono locks
USE **preassembled locks**

Mono, Eastern
USE **Eastern Mono**

monochrome
DC.3 (R)
SN Made with a single color or hue. (WCOL)
CN D.DC.AFU.AFU.AFU

monocoque construction
KT.39 (L)
SN Type of boat, aircraft, or other construction in which the shell carries most of the stresses. (RHDEL2)
UF construction, monocoque
construction, reinforced monocoque
construction, semi-monocoque
monocoque construction, reinforced
reinforced monocoque construction
semi-monocoque construction
CN K.KT.AFU.ALO.BCW.ARI.AFU.BZY

monocoque construction, reinforced
USE **monocoque construction**

monofilament
MT.2227
CN M.MT.AFU.ALO.CRG.AFU

monograms
VW.758 (L,R)
ALT **monogram**
SN Ornamental arrangements of the initials or letters of a name, often used to indicate ownership or patronage.
UF ciphers
cyphers
initials (motif)
CN V.VW.AFU.ALO.ALO.AFU.BCW

monographic series
VW.77 (L)
UF series, monographic
CN V.VW.AFU.AFU.AFU.EWY.AFU

monographs
VW.54 (N)
ALT **monograph**
SN Written expositions of, or treatises on, a subject, usually so narrow in scope as to exclude all but a single aspect of the subject. (GAHLM)
CN V.VW.AFU.AFU.AFU.DIO

monolingual thesauri
VW.444
ALT **monolingual thesaurus**
UF thesauri, monolingual
CN V.VW.AFU.AFU.ALO.EWY.BUE.AFU

monolite yellow
USE **Hansa yellow**

monolithic churches
USE **cave churches**

monolithic columns
RT.95
ALT **monolithic column**
SN Columns shaped from a single block of stone. (DAC)
UF columns, monolithic
CN V.RT.AFU.AFU.AFU.AXC.BIQ.AFU.AFU.CLM

Monomotapa
FL.132
UF Chona I
CN F.FL.ALO.AFU.ALO.ARI.AFU.AFU.ALO

Monongahela
FL.874
CN F.FL.ALO.ALO.ALO.AFU.ALO.ALO.AXC.BZY

monopacks
USE **integral bipacks**
integral tripacks

monopodia
TG.993
ALT **monopodium**
SN Supports in form of animals' heads with one leg immediately below; used on tables and seats of the ancient world and revived in the late 18th and 19th centuries. (IDO)
UF monopods
CN V.TG.ALO.HIK.AFU.ARI

monopods
USE **monopodia**

monopolies
BM.403 (L,B)
SN Ownership or control that permits domination of the means of production or the market in a business or occupation, usually in order to control prices; it is achieved through an exclusive legal privilege, control of the source of supply, or combination or concert of action. (W)
CN B.BM.ARI.DZW

monoptera
RK.24 (R)
ALT **monopteros**
SN Circular columnar buildings that are roofed but have no cella.
CN V.RK.AFU.ALO.AFU.ALO.BOK

monorail lines
USE **monorails**

monorail railroads
USE **monorails**

monorail systems
USE **monorails**

monorails
RD.105 (A,L,B)
ALT **monorail**
UF monorail lines
monorail railroads
monorail systems
railroads, monorail
systems, monorail
CN V.RD.ALO.ARI.AFU.AFU.ALO.ALO

monotheism
BM.701 (L)
CN B.BM.BZY.ALO.ARI.BUE

monotype
KT.465 (L)
SN A printmaking process which involves painting an image onto a plate and then printing it. (BEGUIN)
CN K.KT.AFU.ALO.DUC.DUC.ALO.BCW.ALO.ALO

monsoons
KM.121 (L)
SN Periodic winds in various latitudes in the Indian Ocean and South Asia. (W)
CN K.KM.AFU.CXA.BIQ.BCW

montages (photographic)
USE **photomontages**

Montagnais
FL.1221 (L)
UF Naskapi
CN F.FL.ALO.ALO.ARI.AFU.AFU.ALO.AXC

montan wax
MT.2198
UF wax, montan
CN M.MT.AFU.AFU.ARI.BZY.ALO.AFU

Montana larch
USE **western larch**

Monte Albán
FL.1054 (L)
CN F.FL.ALO.ALO.ALO.ALO.AFU.ALO.AXC.AFU.ARI

Monte Albán I
FL.1055
CN F.FL.ALO.ALO.ALO.ALO.AFU.ALO.AXC.AFU.ARI.AFU

Monte Albán II
FL.1056

CN F.FL.ALO.ALO.ALO.ALO.ALO.AFU.ALO .AXC.AFU.ARI.ALO

Monte Albán III
FL.1057
CN F.FL.ALO.ALO.ALO.ALO.ALO.AFU.ALO .AXC.AFU.ARI.ARI

Monte Albán IV
FL.1058
CN F.FL.ALO.ALO.ALO.ALO.ALO.AFU.ALO .AXC.AFU.ARI.AXC

Monte Albán V
FL.1059
CN F.FL.ALO.ALO.ALO.ALO.ALO.AFU.ALO .AXC.AFU.ARI.BCW

monthly reports
VW.455
ALT **monthly report**
UF reports, monthly
CN V.VW.AFU.AFU.ALO.FIM.AFU.ALO .ALO

Montol
FL.231
CN F.FL.ALO.AFU.AXC.AFU.AFU.ALO. ARI.BOK

Montpellier green
USE **verdigris**

Montpellier yellow
USE **Turner's yellow**

monumental
DC.123 (L,B,R)
CN D.DC.AFU.AXC.AXC

monumental arches
USE **memorial arches**

monumental art
BM.247 (R)
UF art, monumental
CN B.BM.AFU.ARI.BCW.DZW

monumental chapels
USE **sepulchral chapels**

monumental columns
USE **memorial columns**

monumental stone
MT.906
UF stone, monumental
CN M.MT.AFU.AFU.AFU.DCU.ARI.ARI

monumentality
BM.75 (A,B)
SN Use for the impression of grandeur, nobility, permanence, and often, though not necessarily, size in a work of art or structure. (OCA)
CN B.BM.AFU.AFU.ARI.AFU.DCU

monuments
RK.877 (A,L,N,B,R)
ALT **monument**
CN V.RK.AFU.ALO.ALO.DOI

monuments, choragic
USE **choragic monuments**

monuments, henge
USE **henges**

monuments, historical
USE **historical monuments**

monuments, megalithic
USE **megalithic monuments**

monuments, national
USE **national monuments**

monuments, sepulchral
USE **sepulchral monuments**

monuments, soldiers'
USE **soldiers' monuments**

moon bases
USE **lunar bases**

moon settlements
USE **lunar bases**

moons, crescents
USE **crescents**

moonstone
MT.507 (L)
CN M.MT.AFU.AFU.AFU.CFS.AFU.CRG. ALO

moorings
RK.1323 (L)
ALT **mooring**
SN Use for semipermanent anchorages consisting of a heavy anchor, chain, mooring buoy, and penant. (CFCHAP)
UF deep-sea moorings
moorings, deep-sea
CN V.RK.AFU.ALO.ALO.GLI.ARI.ARI. BIQ

moorings, deep-sea
USE **moorings**

Moorish
FL.3604 (A,L,B)
CN F.FL.ALO.BIQ.ALO

Moorish arches
USE **horseshoe arches**

Moorish Revival
USE **Islamic Revival**

moors, peat
USE **peat bogs**

moorstone
USE **granite**

Mopan
FL.1528 (L)
UF Manche
CN F.FL.ALO.ALO.ARI.ALO.BCW.ALO

mops
TB.354 (L,N)
ALT **mop**
CN V.TB.AFU.ARI.CRG.ALO.ARI

Mopti
FL.87
CN F.FL.ALO.AFU.ALO.AFU.BOK.AFU. ALO

moraines
RD.186 (L)
ALT **moraine**
CN V.RD.ARI.AFU.AXC.AFU.AFU.ALO. AXC

moral philosophy
USE **ethics (philosophy)**

Moravian
BM.640 (L)
CN B.BM.BZY.AFU.ALO.ARI.CFS

morbidezza
BM.76
CN B.BM.AFU.AFU.ARI.AFU.DIO

mordant dye process
USE **dye toning**

mordant gilding
KT.715
SN Gilding technique in which metal leaf is laid with an oil or varnish gold size rather than with water, producing a mat finish. (MAYER)
UF gilding, mordant
CN K.KT.AFU.ALO.GRC.CRG.ALO.ARI

mordant, Dutch
USE **Dutch mordant**

mordanting
USE **dye toning**

mordants
MT.2720 (L)
SN Chemical substances that fix a dye in or on a substance by combining with the dye to form an insoluble compound. In etching, refers to corrosive substances, such as a nitric acid solution, used to corrode or bite the exposed areas of a metal plate. In gilding, refers to viscous substances used to adhere the gold leaf to a surface.
CN M.MT.AFU.ARI.IFM.ARI

moreen
MT.1855
SN In the 18th century, a stout worsted or mohair cloth; in the 19th century, often woven with a cotton warp. (NYLAN)
CN M.MT.AFU.AFU.ARI.ALO.ALO .ALO.AFU.BCW

moresques
DG.104
SN Scrolling patterns developed in 16th-century Europe as fanciful variations on Islamic arabesques. (RGRS)
UF mauresques
CN D.DG.AFU.ARI.ALO.AFU.AFU

morganite

MT.494
CN M.MT.AFU.AFU.AFU.CFS.AFU.AXC.AXC

Morgetian
FL.2702
CN F.FL.ALO.AXC.ALO.ALO.AFU.AFU.ARI

morgues
RK.465 (L,B)
ALT morgue
CN V.RK.AFU.ALO.ALO.BOK.ARI.AFU.ARI

morinda
MT.1527
SN A yellow natural dyestuff obtained from several East Indian mulberry trees and shrubs of the genus Morinda. (MAYER)
CN M.MT.AFU.AFU.ARI.AFU.AFU.AFU.AFU.AFU.AXC.BUE

mormor luculleum
USE **bigio morato**

morning rooms
RM.177
ALT **morning room**
UF rooms, morning
CN V.RM.AFU.DIO.ALO.CXA.CFS

morphemics
USE **morphology (linguistics)**

morphology (linguistics)
KD.42 (L)
UF morphemics
CN K.KD.AFU.AFU.AXC.AFU.ALO.ARI

Morris chairs
TG.78 (N)
ALT **Morris chair**
SN Armchairs with adjustable backs and loose cushions, of a type first produced by William Morris, Philip Webb, and the firm Morris, Marshall, Faulkner and Co. about 1866 in England.
UF chairs, Morris
CN V.TG.AFU.AFU.ALO.AFU.AFU.AFU.IRA

mortar
MT.2594 (A,L,B,R)
SN A pasty building material, composed of sand and lime, or cement mixed with water, which gradually hardens when exposed to air. (PUTNAM)
CN M.MT.AFU.ARI.DZW.ARI

mortar color
MT.1810
SN Pigment used to color mortar. (PUTNAM)
UF color, mortar
CN M.MT.AFU.AFU.ARI.AFU.ALO.AFU.AFU

mortar, cement
USE **cement mortar**

mortar, clay
USE **clay mortar**

mortar, clay-and-hair
USE **clay-and-hair mortar**

mortar, dry
USE **dry mortar**

mortar, fat
USE **fat mortar**

mortar, gypsum
USE **gypsum mortar**

mortar, hydraulic
USE **hydraulic mortar**

mortar, lean
USE **lean mortar**

mortar, lime
USE **lime mortar**

mortar, lime-sand
USE **lime-sand mortar**

mortar, mud
USE **mud mortar**

mortar, polymer-impregnated
USE **polymer-impregnated mortar**

mortar, poor
USE **lean mortar**

mortar, rich
USE **fat mortar**

mortarless walls
USE **dry laid walls**

mortars
TB.211 (A,L,N,R)
ALT **mortar**
SN Cup-shaped grinding vessels used in conjunction with a pestle; often made of hard stone.
CN V.TB.AFU.ARI.BZY.ALO.ALO

mortgage deeds
VW.928
ALT **mortgage deed**
SN Deeds embodying a mortgage. (GAHLM)
UF deeds, mortgage
CN V.VW.AFU.ARI.AFU.BZY.ARI.AFU

mortgages
VW.824 (L,N)
ALT **mortgage**
SN Documents expressing the conveyance of property upon condition, such as that money will be paid or a duty will be performed, which operates as a lien, so that the issuer may, under certain conditions, take possession and foreclose the property upon default.
CN V.VW.AFU.ARI.AFU.BIQ.BZY

mortgaging
KG.61
SN Conveying property to a creditor as security for the repayment of a loan. (RHDEL2)
CN K.KG.AFU.AFU.ARI.DIO

morticians
USE **undertakers**

mortise-and-tenon joints
TF.677
ALT mortise-and-tenon joint
SN Joints made when connecting two pieces of wood where a projecting tongue (tenon) of one piece is made to fit into the corresponding cutout (mortise) in the other piece. (PUTNAM)
UF joints, mortise-and-tenon
CN V.TF.ALO.ARI.AXC.ALO.BCW

mortise bolts
TF.169
ALT **mortise bolt**
UF bolts, mortise
CN V.TF.AFU.AFU.AFU.AFU.DIO.ARI.BIQ

mortise chisels
TB.858 (N)
ALT **mortise chisel**
SN Steel chisels having a heavy body with a socket shank; used for cutting mortises. (DAC)
UF chisels, heading
chisels, mortise
heading chisels
CN V.TB.AFU.BCW.CFS.ALO.AFU.BUE.ALO.AXC

mortise cylinder locks
USE **mortise locks**

mortise hinges, full
USE **full mortise hinges**

mortise latches
USE **mortise locks**

mortise locks
TF.208
ALT **mortise lock**
SN Locks designed to be cut into the edge of a door, not just applied to its surface. (BROWNL)
UF conventional locks
cylinder locks, mortise
latches, mortise
locks, conventional
locks, mortise
mortise cylinder locks
mortise latches
CN V.TF.AFU.AFU.AFU.AFU.DIO.BIQ.AFU.CRG

mortise strikes
TF.518
ALT **mortise strike**
SN Strikes mortised into the edge of a door jamb and surrounding a deeper recess in the frame. (DITTRI)

UF strikes, mortise
CN V.TF.AFU.ALO.AFU.ALO.ARI

mortising axes
TB.843 (N)
ALT **mortising ax**
SN Axes used like a chisel, in conjunction with a mallet.
UF axes, mortising
axes, post
post axes
CN V.TB.AFU.BCW.CFS.ALO.AFU.AXC.BUE

mortising knives
USE **twivels**

Morton
FL.841
CN F.FL.ALO.ALO.ALO.AFU.ALO.ALO.ARI.AFU.BZY

mortuaries
RK.466 (B)
ALT **mortuary**
SN Distinguished from **funeral homes** by having facilities only for holding, viewing, or identifying dead bodies prior to burial or cremation.
CN V.RK.AFU.ALO.ALO.BOK.ARI.AFU.AXC

mortuary chapels
USE **sepulchral chapels**

mortuary temples
RK.1136
ALT **mortuary temple**
SN Temples for ministering and offering to deified monarchs; common in ancient Egypt.
UF temples, mortuary
CN V.RK.AFU.ALO.ALO.FCS.BIQ.BZY.ALO.ARI

mosaic
KT.702
SN A method of decorating surfaces with patterns or pictures composed of small pieces of colored stone or glass, called tesserae. (A-Z)
CN K.KT.AFU.ALO.GRC.BZY.ALO

mosaicists
HG.521 (L,R)
ALT **mosaicist**
UF mosaists
CN H.HG.AFU.AXC.BUE.ARI.CLM

mosaics (photographs)
USE **photomosaic maps**

photmosaics

mosaics, aerial
USE **photomosaic maps**

mosaists
USE **mosaicists**

Mosca
USE **Chibcha**

Moshi
USE **Mossi**

Mosi
USE **Mossi**

Moslem
USE **Islam**

mosques
RK.1117 (A,L,B,R)
ALT **mosque**
CN V.RK.AFU.ALO.ALO.FCS.BIQ.BIQ

mosques, four-iwan
USE **four-iwan mosques**

mosques, hypostyle
USE **hypostyle mosques**

Mosquito
FL.1557 (L)
UF Misquito
CN F.FL.ALO.ALO.ARI.ALO.BOK.BUE

mosquito netting
TB.413 (N)
UF netting, mosquito
CN V.TB.AFU.ARI.DUC.BCW.AFU

Mossi
FL.357 (L)
UF Moshi
Mosi
CN F.FL.ALO.AFU.AXC.AFU.AXC.AFU.BUE

mossy-cup oak
USE **bur oak**

motel registers
USE **hotel registers**

motels
RK.965 (A,L,B,R)
ALT **motel**
SN Use for overnight public accommodations for motorists generally characterized by long low-rise buildings consisting of rows of attached individual sleeping quarters and having direct access between the rooms and parking spaces without an intervening lobby.
UF hotels, motor
inns, motor
lodges, motor
motor hotels
motor inns
motor lodges
CN V.RK.AFU.ALO.ALO.ELK.BZY

mother of pearl
MT.946 (L,R)
SN The hard, brilliant-colored internal layer of the pearl oystershell and of certain other marine shellfish. (MH)
UF pearl, mother of
CN M.MT.AFU.AFU.ALO.AFU.DUC.ARI

mothers
HG.14 (L,R)
ALT **mother**
CN H.HG.AFU.ALO.ALO.ALO

motifs
DG.2
ALT **motif**
SN Use for distinct or separable design elements, usually decorative, whether occurring singly as individual shapes or arrangements, or repeated or combined to form a pattern.
UF devices (motifs)
motifs, ornamental
motives
ornamental motifs
CN D.DG.AFU.AFU

motifs, bell flower
USE **husks (motifs)**

motifs, heraldic
USE **heraldic motifs**

motifs, honeysuckle
USE **anthemions**

motifs, ornamental
USE **motifs**

motifs, sunrise
USE **rising suns**

motifs, trumpet
USE **trumpet spirals**

motion
BM.893 (L,R)
SN Action or process of one body passing from one place or position to another. (W)
CN B.BM.CFS.AXC.BIQ.AFU.AXC

motion photographs
VJ.96
ALT **motion photograph**
SN Use for photographs showing successive phases of an action, usually a human figure or animal in motion; may be single exposure, composite, or a series of separate images.
UF motion study photographs
photographs, motion
photographs, motion study
CN V.VJ.AFU.ARI.AFU.ALO.AFU

motion photography
USE **chronophotography**

motion-picture cameras
TB.295 (L,N)
ALT **motion-picture camera**
SN Cameras adapted to make rapid exposure of moving objects on a strip of film. (W)
UF cameras, motion-picture
cameras, movie
cameras, moving-picture
movie cameras
moving-picture cameras
CN V.TB.AFU.ARI.CLM.ARI.AFU.AFU.

AFU.BCW

motion-picture producers
USE **filmmakers**

motion-picture reviews
USE **film reviews**

motion-picture stills
USE **film stills**

motion-picture studios
RG.138 (L,B)
ALT **motion-picture studio**
UF film studios
movie studios
moving-picture studios
studios, motion-picture
CN V.RG.AFU.AFU.CFS

motion pictures
VW.674 (A,L,R)
ALT **motion picture**
UF films
movies
moving-pictures
pictures, motion
CN V.VW.AFU.ALO.AFU.DZW.BCW

motion pictures (performing arts)
USE **film (performing arts)**

motion study photographs
USE **motion photographs**

motion study photography
USE **chronophotography**

motion, rotational
USE **rotation**

motives
USE **motifs**

motor bus systems
USE **bus transit systems**

motor bus terminals
USE **bus terminals**

motor courts
RK.966 (A,L)
ALT **motor court**
SN Public accomodations having an orderly array of individual cabins set alongside a highway and having an internal system of driveways, parking spaces, and a clearly visible and distinctly articulated office near the complex's entrance; especially popular in the United States from the late 1920s to the early 1950s.
UF auto courts
cabin camps
camps, cabin
cottage courts
courts, auto
courts, cottage
courts, motor
courts, tourist
tourist courts
CN V.RK.AFU.ALO.ALO.ELK.BZY.AFU

motor graders
USE **graders**

motor homes
RK.355 (L)
ALT **motor home**
SN Use for covered motorized vehicles equipped as traveling living quarters; for nonmotorized counterparts, use **caravans.**
UF campers
homes, motor
motorized homes
recreational vehicles
vehicles, recreational
CN V.RK.AFU.ALO.ALO.AXC.ARI.BCW

motor hotels
USE **motels**

motor inns
USE **motels**

motor lodges
USE **motels**

motor-truck terminals
USE **truck terminals**

motorized homes
USE **motor homes**

motors
TB.391 (L)
ALT **motor**
SN Rotating machines that transform electrical energy into mechanical energy. (W)
CN V.TB.AFU.ARI.DOI.AXC

motors, hydraulic
USE **hydraulic motors**

motorways
USE **throughways**

mottes
RT.1199 (R)
ALT **motte**
SN Steep mounds, a main feature of certain 11th- and 12th-century castles. (PDARC)
CN V.RT.AFU.BUE.AFU.BUE

moucharaby
USE **meshrebeeyeh**

mouchettes
RT.1029
ALT **mouchette**
SN In 14th-century Gothic tracery and derivatives, pointed, elongated openings bounded by elliptical and ogee curves. (HAS)
CN V.RT.AFU.ARI.ALO.BZY.ALO.ARI

mound breakwaters
RK.557
ALT **mound breakwater**
UF breakwaters, mound
CN V.RK.AFU.ALO.ALO.CFS.ALO.ALO .AFU.ALO

mounds
RK.1356 (A,L,N)
ALT **mound**
SN Use for piles of earth heaped up for landmarks, monuments, or as bases for other structures; for piles of earth and other debris resulting from successive superimposed occupation sites, use **tells.** For piles of earth built over grave sites, use **burial mounds.** Use **cairns** for purposely erected piles of stones.
UF artificial mounds
mounds, artificial
CN V.RK.AFU.ALO.ARI.AXC.ARI.ARI

mounds, artificial
USE **mounds**

mounds, burial
USE **burial mounds**

mounds, conical
USE **burial mounds**

mounds, effigy
USE **effigy mounds**

mounds, shell
USE **middens**

mountain architecture
USE **hillside architecture**

mountain ash
MT.1157
UF ash, mountain
Eucalyptus regnans
CN M.MT.AFU.AFU.ALO.BIQ.DCU .AFU.AFU.AFU.DIO.AXC.ALO

mountain blue
USE **Bremen blue**

mountain blue (azurite)
USE **azurite**

mountain green
USE **malachite green**

mountain hemlock
MT.1356 (L)
UF black hemlock
hemlock, black
hemlock, mountain
Tsuga mertensiana
CN M.MT.AFU.AFU.ALO.BIQ.DCU .AFU.AFU.ALO.BOK.ALO

mountain juniper
MT.1360
UF juniper, mountain
Juniperus montana
CN M.MT.AFU.AFU.ALO.BIQ.DCU .AFU.AFU.ALO.BUE.ALO

mountain larch
USE **western larch**

mountains
RD.202 (L,R)
ALT **mountain**

CN V.RD.ARI.AFU.AXC.AFU.ALO.AFU.AFU

mounting
KT.653
ALT **mounted**
SN Attaching to a support. (W)
CN K.KT.AFU.ALO.GLI.AFU.BIQ.AFU

mounting tissue
MT.2360 (N)
SN A thin sheet coated with an adhesive that becomes sticky when heated;(UPTON) used to fasten photographic prints to a mount.
UF dry-mounting tissue
tissue, dry-mounting
tissue, mounting
CN M.MT.AFU.ARI.ARI.ALO.ALO

mounting, dry
USE **dry mounting**

mounts
TF.258
ALT **mount**
CN V.TF.AFU.AFU.AFU.AFU.DUC

mounts (artists' materials)
MT.2367
ALT **mount (artist's material)**
SN Use for secondary materials on which a work, usually an image on a paper support, is mounted. For the surface on which the image resides, use **supports (artists' materials).**
UF secondary supports
supports, secondary
CN M.MT.AFU.ARI.BCW.AFU.AFU

mounts, boudoir midget
USE **boudoir midget mounts**

mourning art
USE **funerary art**

mousetail files
USE **round files**

Mousterian
FL.2458 (L)
CN F.FL.ALO.AXC.AFU.ALO.ARI

movable bookcases
USE **moving libraries**

movable bridges
RK.1277 (L)
ALT **movable bridge**
UF bridges, movable
CN V.RK.AFU.ALO.ALO.GLI.ALO.AFU.AFU.AXC

movable buildings
USE **portable buildings**

movable partitions
USE **folding partitions**

movement, women's
USE **feminism**

movement, women's liberation
USE **feminism**

movements, earth
USE **earth movements**

movie cameras
USE **motion-picture cameras**

movie houses
USE **movie theaters**

movie reviews
USE **film reviews**

movie stills
USE **film stills**

movie studios
USE **motion-picture studios**

movie theaters
RK.938 (A,L,B,R)
ALT **movie theater**
UF cinemas
film theaters
houses, movie
houses, picture
movie houses
moving-picture theaters
palaces, picture
picture houses
picture palaces
theaters, film
theaters, movie
CN V.RK.AFU.ALO.ALO.EFQ.ARI.BCW.ALO.AFU

moviemakers
USE **filmmakers**

movies
USE **motion pictures**

Movimento spaziale
USE **Spatialist**

moving
USE **transporting**

moving fillister planes
TB.918
ALT **moving fillister plane**
SN Planes with an adjustable fence which exposes the blade in proportion to the desired width of the cut;(SALAM) used to cut grooves on the side nearest the worker.
UF planes, moving fillister
CN V.TB.AFU.BCW.CFS.ALO.AFU.DUC.ALO.BCW.AFU

moving images, museums of
USE **museums of moving images**

moving libraries
TG.405
ALT **moving library**
UF bookcases, movable
bookcases, portable library
libraries, moving
library bookcases, portable
movable bookcases
portable library bookcases
CN V.TG.AFU.AFU.AXC.ALO.ALO.BIQ.AFU

moving loads
BM.1017
UF loads, moving
CN B.BM.CFS.AXC.CLM.ALO.ARI.CLM

moving-picture cameras
USE **motion-picture cameras**

moving-picture reviews
USE **film reviews**

moving-picture studios
USE **motion-picture studios**

moving-picture theaters
USE **movie theaters**

moving-pictures
USE **motion pictures**

moving ramps
RT.1298
ALT **moving ramp**
UF ramps, moving
CN V.RT.ALO.ALO.AFU.AFU.ARI

moving sidewalks
USE **moving walkways**

moving staircases
USE **escalators**

moving walks
USE **moving walkways**

moving walkways
RT.1301 (L)
ALT **moving walkway**
SN Passenger-carrying treadways on which passengers stand or walk and in which the passenger-carrying surface remains parallel to its direction of travel. (STEIN)
UF autowalks
conveyors, passenger
moving sidewalks
moving walks
passenger conveyors
sidewalks, moving
walks, moving
walkways, moving
CN V.RT.ALO.ALO.AFU.ALO.AFU

mower-knife grinders
TB.208 (N)
ALT **mower-knife grinder**
SN Small sharpening machines that utilize a horizontal, flat metal plate that is turned by means of a gearing system. The knives are held in specially designed clamps. (KNIGHT)
UF grinders, mower-knife
CN V.TB.AFU.ARI.BZY.AFU.ALO

Moxeke
FL.1142
CN F.FL.ALO.ALO.ALO.ARI.AXC.AFU.ARI.ARI

Moxo
USE **Mojo**

moynels
USE **mullions**

Mozarabic
FL.3163 (A,L,R)
CN F.FL.ALO.BCW.ALO.ALO.AFU.BOK.AXC.AXC.AXC

Mpangu
FL.482
CN F.FL.ALO.AFU.AXC.ALO.ALO.AXC.AXC.ARI

Mpemba
FL.483
CN F.FL.ALO.AFU.AXC.ALO.ALO.AXC.AXC.AXC

Mpongwe
FL.403 (L)
CN F.FL.ALO.AFU.AXC.ALO.AFU.ALO.AXC

MR chairs
TG.79
ALT **MR chair**
UF chairs, MR
CN V.TG.AFU.AFU.ALO.AFU.AFU.AFU.IWU

Mtoko
FL.136
CN F.FL.ALO.AFU.ALO.ARI.AXC

Muchik
USE **Mochica**

mucilage
MT.2354 (L)
SN Liquid adhesive made with gum arabic solution, preservative, and odorant. (MAYER)
CN M.MT.AFU.ARI.ARI.AFU.ALO.ALO.ALO.ARI

mud
MT.2066 (A,L,B)
CN M.MT.AFU.AFU.ARI.BOK.ALO.BCW

mud brick, sun-dried
USE **sun-dried brick**

mud-capping
KT.109
SN The blasting of a boulder by placing a quantity of explosives against it without confining the explosives in a drill hole. (DAC)
CN K.KT.AFU.ALO.CLM.AFU.AFU

mud cloth
MT.1882
UF cloth, mud
cloth, mud dyed
cloth, mud-resist
mud dyed cloth
mud-resist cloth
CN M.MT.AFU.AFU.ARI.ALO.ALO.ALO.ARI.ARI

mud dyed cloth
USE **mud cloth**

mud holders
USE **hawks**

mud mortar
MT.2604
UF mortar, mud
CN M.MT.AFU.ARI.DZW.ARI.AFU.BIQ

mud-plaster
MT.2447
UF plaster, mud
CN M.MT.AFU.ARI.CRG.AFU.AXC.AFU.BIQ

mud-resist cloth
USE **mud cloth**

mud rooms
RM.137 (A)
ALT **mud room**
UF rooms, mud
CN V.RM.AFU.DIO.ALO.BOK.BCW

mud spoons
TB.619 (N)
ALT **mud spoon**
SN Long-handled metal tools terminating in a small cup; used to dip stonedust from drilled holes.
UF mud spoons, quarryman's
quarryman's mud spoons
spoons, mud
spoons, quarryman's mud
CN V.TB.AFU.BCW.BCW.ALO.FUA

mud spoons, quarryman's
USE **mud spoons**

Mudéjar
FL.3164 (A,L,R)
CN F.FL.ALO.BCW.ALO.ALO.AFU.BOK.AXC.AXC.BCW

Mudejar Revival
FL.3271 (R)
UF Revival, Mudejar
CN F.FL.ALO.BCW.ALO.AXC.CLM.BOK.AFU

mudflows
KM.107 (L)
SN Occurrences of moving masses of soil made fluid by rain or melting snow, or masses of mingled volcanic particles and water that flow like lava from volcanoes. (W)
UF mudslides
CN K.KM.AFU.CXA.ALO.AXC

mudsills
USE **sill plates**

mudslides
USE **mudflows**

mudstone
MT.644
CN M.MT.AFU.AFU.AFU.DCU.AFU.ALO.AFU.AFU.AXC

muff-blown glass
USE **cylinder glass**

muff glass
USE **cylinder glass**

muffin racks
USE **muffin stands**

muffin stands
TG.645
ALT **muffin stand**
SN Small lightweight tiered stands, often folding and portable, intended to be used alongside a table for holding such light foods as muffins.
UF cake stands
muffin racks
racks, muffin
stands, cake
stands, muffin
CN V.TG.AFU.AFU.BIQ.BCW.ALO.CXA

Mughal
FL.2226 (A,L,B,R)
UF Mogul
CN F.FL.ALO.ARI.AXC.ALO.AFU.BIQ.ALO

Mughal, Late
USE **Provincial Mughal**

Mughal, Popular
USE **Popular Mughal**

Mughal, Provincial
USE **Provincial Mughal**

mugshots
USE **identification photographs**

Muhammad I
FL.3464
CN F.FL.ALO.BIQ.AFU.DUC.ALO

Muhammad I (Ottoman)
USE **Mehmed I**

Muhammad II
FL.3468
CN F.FL.ALO.BIQ.AFU.DUC.BIQ

Muhammad Mirza
FL.3584
CN F.FL.ALO.BIQ.AFU.IFM.AFU.BIQ

Muhammad Shah
FL.2235
UF Rangila
CN F.FL.ALO.ARI.AXC.ALO.AFU.BIQ.ALO.AFU.BUE

Muhammadanism
USE **Islam**

Muhammed Jafar
FL.3006
CN F.FL.ALO.AXC.ARI.BIQ.AFU.AFU.BOK

Muisca
USE **Chibcha**

mule chests
TG.466
ALT **mule chest**
SN Term used for chests having a base containing two or more drawers. (TOMLIN)
UF chests, mule
CN V.TG.AFU.AFU.AXC.ALO.AXC.DOI

muley sawmills
TB.805 (N)
ALT **muley sawmill**
SN Machines which utilize the up-and-down motion of a straight saw blade, but which depend on clamps to hold the saw blade stiff. (KNIGHT)
UF sawmills, muley
CN V.TB.AFU.BCW.CFS.AFU.BCW.ARI

mullahs
HG.228
ALT **mullah**
SN Learned teachers of the religious law and doctrines of Islam. (W)
CN H.HG.AFU.AXC.AXC.BIQ.AFU.ARI.CXA

mullions
RT.1007 (B,R)
ALT **mullion**
SN Slender, vertical, usually nonstructural bars or piers forming a division between doors, screens, or lights of windows. (W)
UF monelles
monials
moynels
moynels
munnions (mullions)
CN V.RT.AFU.ARI.ALO.AXC

multi-functional furniture
USE **multipurpose furniture**

multi-level roads
RK.1561 (B)
ALT **multi-level road**
UF roads, multi-level
CN V.RK.ALO.ALO.BIQ.ARI.ARI.ALO

multi-storey car parks
USE **parking garages**

multi-use
BM.215
SN Use with reference to the multifunctional or multipurpose nature of a built work; especially to describe those building types that are flexible enough to serve a wide variety of activities, such as gymnasiums.
UF multipurpose
CN B.BM.AFU.ALO.CFS.ARI

multifoils
DG.29
ALT **multifoil**
SN Figures composed of more than five lobes or arcs, separated by cusps.
CN D.DG.AFU.AFU.BIQ.BIQ

multifunctional epoxy
MT.2169
UF epoxy, multifunctional
CN M.MT.AFU.AFU.ARI.BUE.ALO.AXC.ALO.BCW.ALO

multigraphs
VW.684 (L)
ALT **multigraph**
SN Documents, such as letters, leaflets, or forms, produced on a small, office-type offset press used for duplicating. (GAHLM)
UF copies, multilith
multilith copies
CN V.VW.AFU.ALO.AFU.DZW.BIQ.BUE

multilingual dictionaries
USE **polyglot dictionaries**

multilingual thesauri
VW.445
ALT **multilingual thesaurus**
UF thesauri, multilingual
CN V.VW.AFU.AFU.ALO.EWY.BUE.ALO

multilith copies
USE **multigraphs**

multiple-brush painted ware
FL.2875
UF painted ware, multiple-brush
ware, multiple-brush painted
CN F.FL.ALO.AXC.ARI.AFU.ALO.ARI.CFS

multiple dwellings
RK.360
ALT **multiple dwelling**
SN Dwellings containing more than one residential unit.
UF dwellings, multiple
multiple-unit dwellings
CN V.RK.AFU.ALO.ALO.AXC.AXC

multiple exposure
KT.386
SN Use for the technique in photography of recording more than one image on a single sheet or frame of film. For the technique of printing together images from more than one negative, use **combination printing.**
CN K.KT.AFU.ALO.DUC.DIO.ARI.ARI.AXC

multiple-unit dwellings
USE **multiple dwellings**

multipurpose
USE **multi-use**

multipurpose buildings
RK.910 (A,L,B)
ALT **multipurpose building**
SN Use only for buildings designed to be flexible enough to serve different purposes at different times.
UF buildings, multipurpose
multiuse buildings
CN V.RK.AFU.ALO.ALO.DUC

multipurpose furniture
TG.797
SN Furniture designed to be used for a number of functions, e.g., writing, reading, needlework, or games, as well as larger pieces with ingeniously fitted interiors.
UF furniture, multi-functional
furniture, multipurpose
meubles à transformation
multi-functional furniture
CN V.TG.AFU.ARI.BUE

multispan bridges
RK.1282
ALT **multispan bridge**
UF bridges, multispan
CN V.RK.AFU.ALO.ALO.GLI.ALO.AFU.AFU.BCW

multistory buildings
RK.8 (A,L,B,R)
ALT **multistory building**
UF buildings, multistory
CN V.RK.AFU.ALO.AFU.AFU.AFU

multistory garages
USE **parking garages**

multiuse buildings
USE **multipurpose buildings**

multiuse developments
USE **mixed-use developments**

multiview drawings
VD.35
ALT **multiview drawing**
SN Can be used to collocate plans, sections, and elevations to distinguish them from **axonometric drawings** when that term is being used in its limited sense as an additional orthographic type.
UF drawings, multiview
CN V.VD.AFU.AFU.BIQ.ALO.ARI

multiview projection
KT.287
SN Can be used for nonaxonometric orthographic projection if **axonometric projection** is being used in its limited sense as an additional orthographic type.
UF projection, multiview
CN K.KT.AFU.ALO.DUC.DCU.BOK.ALO.ALO.AFU

Mum
USE **Bamum**

Mumienbraun
USE **mummy**

mummy
MT.1616

UF brown, Egyptian
Egyptian brown
momie
Mumienbraun
CN M.MT.AFU.AFU.ARI.AFU.AFU.ALO.ALO.ARI.ALO.AFU.AFU

mummy (color)
USE **moderate yellowish brown**

mummy brown
USE **dark yellowish brown**
grayish brown
grayish yellowish brown

Mumuye
FL.204 (L)
CN F.FL.ALO.AFU.AXC.AFU.AFU.ALO.AFU.ALO

Mun
USE **Bamum**

Mundugumor
FL.3651 (L)
CN F.FL.ALO.BOK.ALO.BCW.ALO.BCW.AFU.BCW

Mundurucú
FL.1592 (L)
UF Mondurucu
CN F.FL.ALO.ALO.ARI.ARI.AFU.FOG

Munhatta phase
FL.2920
CN F.FL.ALO.AXC.ARI.AXC.AFU.ALO.AXC

Munich lake
USE **carmine**

municipal art
USE **public art**

municipal buildings
RK.993 (A,L,B,R)
ALT **municipal building**
UF buildings, local authority
buildings, local government
buildings, municipal
local authority buildings
local government buildings
CN V.RK.AFU.ALO.ALO.ERE.ALO.AFU

municipal centers
USE **civic centers**

municipal engineers
HG.642 (L)
ALT **municipal engineer**
UF engineers, municipal
CN H.HG.AFU.AXC.BZY.BCW.CLM

municipal finance
BM.387 (A,L)
SN Used generally for city, town, borough, or village finance.
UF finance, municipal
CN B.BM.ARI.CLM.AFU

municipal government
BM.545 (L)
UF government, municipal
CN B.BM.BOK.BOK.ALO.AFU.AFU

municipal government records
VW.1046 (L)
ALT **municipal government record**
SN Records made or received by the governing body of incorporated localities.
UF government records, municipal
municipal records
records, municipal
records, municipal government
CN V.VW.AFU.ARI.ALO.BCW.ALO.AFU.ALO

municipal improvement
USE **civic improvement**

municipal lighting
RD.117 (A,L)
UF city lighting
lighting, city
lighting, metropolitan
lighting, municipal
metropolitan lighting
CN V.RD.ALO.AXC.AFU

municipal officials
USE **public officers**

municipal ordinances
USE **ordinances**

municipal plans
VW.464
ALT **municipal plan**
UF plans, municipal
CN V.VW.AFU.AFU.ALO.FIM.ARI.ALO.AFU

municipal records
USE **municipal government records**

municipal services
USE **public services**

municipal transit
USE **local transit**

municipal transportation
USE **urban transportation**

municipal universities
USE **urban universities**

municipal utilities
USE **public utilities**

municipia
RD.14
ALT **municipium**
SN Use for ancient Roman cities or towns founded with citizenship and legal rights similar to those afforded to colonies, but which were lower in status; may also be used for certain small towns during the Middle Ages.
CN V.RD.AFU.AFU.ALO.AXC.ARI

munjeet
USE **madder**

munnions (mullions)
USE **mullions**

Munshi
USE **Tiv**

muntins
RT.821 (B)
ALT **muntin**
UF bars, glazing
glazing bars
sash-bars
CN V.RT.AFU.ALO.ALO.AFU

Muntz metal
MT.389
UF metal, Muntz
CN M.MT.AFU.AFU.AFU.BZY.AFU.AFU.AFU.ALO.ARI.BIQ.ALO

muqarnas
RT.810 (A)
ALT **muqarna**
SN Use for the network of small, repeated cellular forms resembling bottomless niches and sometimes corbeled and structural, more often suspended and decorative, which form the undersurfaces of vaults and domes common in Islamic architecture.
UF honeycomb work
stalactite work
CN V.RT.AFU.ALO.AFU.BUE

Mura
FL.1593
CN F.FL.ALO.ALO.ARI.ARI.AFU.FUA

Murad
FL.3583
CN F.FL.ALO.BIQ.AFU.IFM.AFU.BCW

Murad I
FL.3484
UF Murat I
CN F.FL.ALO.BIQ.AFU.FOG.AFU.ARI

Murad II
FL.3488
UF Murat II
CN F.FL.ALO.BIQ.AFU.FOG.AFU.BOK

Murad III
FL.3494
UF Murat III
CN F.FL.ALO.BIQ.AFU.FOG.AFU.CXA

Murad IV
FL.3499
UF Murat IV
CN F.FL.ALO.BIQ.AFU.FOG.AFU.DZW

Murad V
FL.3514
UF Murat V
CN F.FL.ALO.BIQ.AFU.FOG.AFU.HIK

mural armoires
USE **hanging cupboards**

mural painters
USE **muralists**

mural photographs
USE **photomurals**

Muralist
USE **Mexican Muralist**

Muralist, Mexican
USE **Mexican Muralist**

muralists
HG.112
ALT **muralist**
UF mural painters
painters, mural
CN H.HG.AFU.AXC.AXC.AFU.AFU
.ALO.AXC.CXA.ALO.ALO

murals, photographic
USE **photomurals**

Murat I
USE **Murad I**

Murat II
USE **Murad II**

Murat III
USE **Murad III**

Murat IV
USE **Murad IV**

Murat V
USE **Murad V**

murders
KM.137 (L,R)
CN K.KM.AFU.DOI.ALO.ALO

muriatic acid
USE **hydrochloric acid**

Murngin
FL.3612 (L)
CN F.FL.ALO.BOK.AFU.AFU.ALO

Muromachi
FL.1968 (L)
UF Ashikaga
CN F FL ALO ARI ALO ALO AFU
ALO.ARI

Murphy beds
TG.350 (N)
ALT **Murphy bed**
SN Beds constructed so that they can be folded or swung into a closet; named after William L. Murphy, American inventor. (RHDEL2)
UF beds, Murphy
CN V.TG.AFU.AFU.ARI.AFU.AFU.BIQ.
ALO.AFU

musaea
RK.1338
ALT **musaeum**
SN Use for grottolike enclosures, with a water supply, thought to be the dwelling places of or dedicated to the Muses.
CN V.RK.AFU.ALO.ARI.AFU.BIQ.AFU

musallas
RK.1450
ALT **musalla**
SN Designates large, open Islamic prayer areas built to accommodate the entire population of a town; often with the mihrab as the only architectural feature.
CN V.RK.ALO.ALO.AFU

Muscovite
FL.3084
CN F.FL.ALO.BCW.ALO.AFU.ALO.
BCW.ARI.AFU

muscovite (mica)
MT.535 (L)
SN The common variety of mica; it has superior dielectric properties and is valued for radio capacitators. (MH)
UF mica, potash
potash mica
potash silicate
silicate, potash
CN M.MT.AFU.AFU.AFU.CFS.AFU.FUA.
AFU

muscovy glass
USE **mica**

museology
KD.59
UF museum studies
studies, museum
CN K.KD.AFU.AFU.BIQ

museum administration
KD.60 (R)
UF administration, museum
CN K.KD.AFU.AFU.BIQ.AFU

museum architecture
USE **museums**

museum board
MT.1919
SN Laminated type of mat board made from linen or cotton rags, or from deacidified and buffered paper pulp; often used to remount pictures backed with lower quality supports.
UF board, museum
board, rag
rag board
CN M.MT.AFU.AFU.ARI.ALO.ALO.AXC
.ALO.BIQ.AFU.BIQ

museum records
VW.1054 (L)
ALT **museum record**
UF records, museum
CN V.VW.AFU.ARI.ALO.BUE

museum registrars
USE **registrars**

museum studies
USE **museology**

museum villages
RG.139 (A,L,B)
ALT **museum village**
SN Carefully selected and situated collections of original buildings designed to illustrate not only the architecture and building forms of a given geographical area and period, but also to recreate the atmosphere and lifestyle. (NTHP85)
UF outdoor museums
village museums
villages, museum
CN V.RG.AFU.AFU.CLM

museums
RK.377 (A,L,N,B,R)
ALT **museum**
SN Use for buildings, groups of buildings, or spaces within buildings where objects of value such as works of art, antiquities, scientific specimens, or other artifacts are housed and displayed.
UF architecture, museum
museum architecture
CN V.RK.AFU.ALO.ALO.BCW.AXC

museums of moving images
RK.407
ALT **museum of moving images**
SN Use for repositories devoted to the art, history, and technology of motion pictures, television, and video. (PC)
UF moving images, museums of
CN V.RK.AFU.ALO.ALO.BCW.AXC.ARI
.BCW

museums of religious art
USE **religious museums**

museums, aeronautical
USE **aeronautical museums**

museums, agriculture
USE **agriculture museums**

museums, air and space
USE **aeronautical museums**

museums, anthropology
USE **anthropology museums**

museums, archaeological
USE **archaeological museums**

museums, architectural
USE **architectural museums**

museums, art
USE **art museums**

museums, astronautical
USE **astronautical museums**

museums, astronomical
USE **astronomical museums**

museums, automobile
USE **automobile museums**

museums, aviation
USE **aeronautical museums**

museums, botanical

USE **botanical museums**

museums, car
USE **automobile museums**

museums, children's
USE **children's museums**

museums, commercial
USE **company museums**

museums, communications
USE **communications museums**

museums, company
USE **company museums**

museums, costume
USE **costume museums**

museums, county
USE **county museums**

museums, decorative arts
USE **decorative arts museums**

museums, ethnic
USE **ethnological museums**

museums, ethnological
USE **ethnological museums**

museums, farm
USE **agriculture museums**

museums, fine arts
USE **art museums**

museums, fishery
USE **fishery museums**

museums, folk
USE **ethnological museums**

museums, folk art
USE **folk art museums**

museums, geology
USE **geology museums**

museums, historic house
USE **historic house museums**

museums, historical society
USE **historical society museums**

museums, history
USE **history museums**

museums, hunting
USE **hunting museums**

museums, industrial
USE **industrial museums**

museums, international
USE **international museums**

museums, junior
USE **children's museums**

museums, literature
USE **literature museums**

museums, maritime
USE **maritime museums**

museums, medical
USE **medical museums**

museums, military
USE **military museums**

museums, mineralogy
USE **mineralogy museums**

museums, music
USE **music museums**

museums, national
USE **national museums**

museums, natural history
USE **natural history museums**

museums, nautical
USE **maritime museums**

museums, naval
USE **naval museums**

museums, numismatic
USE **numismatic museums**

museums, open-air
USE **open-air museums**

museums, outdoor
USE **open-air museums**

museums, philatelic
USE **philatelic museums**

museums, photography
USE **photography museums**

museums, postal
USE **philatelic museums**

museums, railroad
USE **railroad museums**

museums, religious
USE **religious museums**

museums, science
USE **science museums**

museums, sports
USE **sports museums**

museums, technology
USE **technology museums**

museums, textile
USE **textile museums**

museums, theater
USE **theater museums**

museums, transportation
USE **transportation museums**

museums, war
USE **military museums**

museums, wax
USE **wax museums**

museums, zoological
USE **zoological museums**

mushrebiyeh
USE **meshrebeeyeh**

music
KD.10 (L,R)
CN K.KD.AFU.AFU.AFU.AFU.AFU.AFU.ARI

music cabinets
TG.437 (N)
ALT **music cabinet**
UF cabinets, music
CN V.TG.AFU.AFU.AXC.ALO.ARI.ALO.CRG

music cases, canterbury
USE **canterburies**

music chairs
TG.187 (N)
ALT **music chair**
UF chairs, harpsicord
chairs, music
chairs, piano
harpsicord chairs
piano chairs
CN V.TG.AFU.AFU.ALO.AFU.AFU.ALO.CXA

music conservatories
RK.814 (A,L,B)
ALT **music conservatory**
UF conservatories of music
conservatories, music
CN V.RK.AFU.ALO.ALO.CXA.ARI.ALO.CLM.AFU

music desks
USE **reading desks**

music directors (conductors)
USE **conductors (music)**

music galleries
USE **minstrel galleries**

music halls
RK.927 (A,L,B,R)
ALT **music hall**
SN Public buildings, with seating for an audience, emphasizing musical entertainment but also serving drinks.
UF halls, music
CN V.RK.AFU.ALO.ALO.EFQ.ARI.ALO.AFU

music museums
RK.408 (L)
ALT **music museum**
UF museums, music
CN V.RK.AFU.ALO.ALO.BCW.AXC.ARI.BIQ

music racks
USE **music stands**

music rooms
RM.125 (A,L,B)
ALT **music room**
UF rooms, music
CN V.RM.AFU.DIO.ALO.BIQ.AXC

music schools

RK.813 (A,L,B)
ALT **music school**
UF schools, music
CN V.RK.AFU.ALO.ALO.CXA.ARI.ALO.CLM

music scores
USE **scores**

music stands
TG.646 (N,R)
ALT **music stand**
SN Pedestals designed to hold scores or sheet music in position for reading.
UF music racks
racks, music
reading stands
stands, music
stands, reading
CN V.TG.AFU.AFU.BIQ.BCW.ALO.DCU

music stools
TG.248
ALT **music stool**
SN Stools intended for use at the piano, organ, or similar musical instrument, generally having a circular revolving or adjustable seat and sometimes a back.
UF piano stools
stools, music
stools, piano
CN V.TG.AFU.AFU.ALO.AFU.ALO.AFU.BUE

music, sheet
USE **sheet music**

musicians
HG.71 (L,R)
ALT **musician**
CN H.HG.AFU.AXC.AXC.AFU.AFU.AFU.BIQ.BIQ

musicologists
HG.167 (L)
ALT **musicologist**
CN H.HG.AFU.AXC.AXC.AFU.ALO.BCW

musicology
KD.27 (L)
CN K.KD.AFU.AFU.AFU.ALO.BIQ

Muskogee
USE **Creek**

Muslim
USE **Islam**

muslin
MT.1874
SN Plain white cotton fabric with a downy nap; sometimes used as an artist's support.
CN M.MT.AFU.AFU.ARI.ALO.ALO.ALO.ALO.DCU

Mustafa I
FL.3497
CN F.FL.ALO.BIQ.AFU.FOG.AFU.DOI

Mustafa II
FL.3503
CN F.FL.ALO.BIQ.AFU.FOG.AFU.EWY

Mustafa III
FL.3507
CN F.FL.ALO.BIQ.AFU.FOG.AFU.FUA

Mustafa IV
FL.3510
CN F.FL.ALO.BIQ.AFU.FOG.AFU.GLI

mustard
USE **dark yellow**
light olive brown

mustard brown
USE **moderate olive**

mustard gold
USE **light olive brown**

mustard oil
MT.2036 (L)
UF oil, mustard
CN M.MT.AFU.AFU.ARI.ARI.AXC.ARI.BCW

mustard tan
USE **light olive brown**
moderate olive

mustard tan, light
USE **light olive**

muster rolls
VW.994 (N)
ALT **muster roll**
SN Lists of troops actually present, made on the day of muster or review of troops in order to take account of their condition; used as the paymaster's voucher for the pay he issued. (GAHLM)
UF rolls, muster
CN V.VW.AFU.ARI.ALO.BCW.AFU.AFU.AFU.BOK.ARI

mutationes
RK.1252
ALT **mutatio**
SN Use for relay stations or rest stops set along ancient Roman and Byzantine roads (through the 7th century) and providing for the minimal needs of travelers. For stopping places for overnight stays along these ancient routes, use **mansiones.**
CN V.RK.AFU.ALO.ALO.GLI.AFU.ARI.BCW

mutes
HG.789
SN People unable to speak due to physical or psychological causes.
UF dumb
handicapped, speech
speech handicapped
CN H.HG.AFU.BOK.AXC.ALO.ALO.ARI

mutilation

BM.1102 (L)
CN B.BM.CRG.BCW.ALO.ARI.ALO

mutules
RT.344
ALT **mutule**
SN Sloping flat blocks on the soffit of the Doric cornice, usually decorated with rows of six guttae each; occur over each triglyph and each metope of the frieze. (HAS)
CN V.RT.AFU.AFU.AFU.BCW.BZY.ALO.ALO.ALO.BOK

Muzaffarid
FL.3477 (L)
CN F.FL.ALO.BIQ.AFU.EWY

Mwanza
FL.499
CN F.FL.ALO.AFU.AXC.ALO.ALO.BCW.BIQ

Mwera
FL.664 (L)
CN F.FL.ALO.AFU.AXC.AXC.BIQ.BOK

MXDs
USE **mixed-use developments**

Mycenaean
FL.2553 (A,L,B,R)
CN F.FL.ALO.AXC.ALO.AFU.AFU.ALO.ALO.ARI.AFU

mycophyta
USE **fungi**

Mylar (TM)
MT.2181
SN Clear coated polyester film.
UF film, Mylar (TM)
Mylar film (TM)
CN M.MT.AFU.AFU.ARI.BUE.ALO.AXC.ARI.AFU.AFU.AFU

Mylar film (TM)
USE **Mylar (TM)**

myrtle
MT.1368
CN M.MT.AFU.AFU.ALO.BIQ.DCU.AFU.AFU.ALO.CLM

Mysore
FL.2299
CN F.FL.ALO.ARI.AXC.ALO.AFU.BZY.BIQ.ALO

mystery plays
BM.282 (L,R)
UF miracle plays
plays, miracle
plays, mystery
CN B.BM.AFU.ARI.BIQ.BZY.AFU

mysticism
BM.514 (L,R)
CN B.BM.BIQ.AXC.CLM

mystics
HG.239 (L)

ALT **mystic**
CN H.HG.AFU.AXC.AXC.BIQ.AFU.BOK

mythology
BM.275 (L,R)
CN B.BM.AFU.ARI.BIQ.BIQ

N-butyl acetate
USE **butyl acetate**

N-power plants
USE **nuclear power plants**

N-trusses
USE **Pratt trusses**

Na-ga
USE **Nanga**

Nabatean
FL.2886 (A,R)
CN F.FL.ALO.AXC.ARI.ALO.AFU.ALO

Nabeshima
FL.2017 (L)
CN F.FL.ALO.ARI.ALO.ALO.ALO.ALO.ALO.ALO.ARI

Nabesnatana
USE **Tanana**

Nachikufan
FL.65
CN F.FL.ALO.AFU.AFU.ALO.BCW.ARI

Naco
FL.1081
CN F.FL.ALO.ALO.ALO.ALO.ALO.AFU.AXC

Nadowessioux
USE **Dakota**

Nafana
FL.358
CN F.FL.ALO.AFU.AXC.AFU.AXC.AFU.BZY

Naga School
USE **Nanga**

Nagara
FL.2248
UF Aryavarta
CN F.FL.ALO.ARI.AXC.ALO.AFU.BUE.ALO

Nagara Pathama
USE **Nakhon Pathom**

Nagare
FL.2000
CN F.FL.ALO.ARI.ALO.ALO.ALO.AFU.BUE

Nagasaki
FL.2059
CN F.FL.ALO.ARI.ALO.ALO.ALO.ARI.CLM

Nagasaki-e
FL.2080
CN F.FL.ALO.ARI.ALO.ALO.ALO.AXC.BCW

Nahane, Eastern
USE **Kaska**

Nahane, Western
USE **Tahltan**

Nahua
FL.1503 (L)
CN F.FL.ALO.ALO.ARI.ALO.ARI.BCW

nail claws
USE **tack pulls**

nail floats
USE **devil floats**

nail headers
TB.667
ALT **nail header**
UF headers, nail
CN V.TB.AFU.BCW.BIQ.AFU.ALO.BUE

nail makers
HG.517 (L)
ALT **nail maker**
UF makers, nail
CN H.HG.AFU.AXC.BUE.ARI.CFS.ARI.BUE

nail pullers
TB.420 (N)
ALT **nail puller**
SN Devices in the form of a bar with a notched end; used for gripping and drawing nails. (W)
UF pullers, nail
CN V.TB.AFU.ARI.DZW.AXC

nail punches
USE **nail sets**

nail sets
TB.976 (N)
ALT **nail set**
SN Short steel rods, usually tapered; used to drive a nail or brad below, or flush with, a wood surface. (DAC)
UF driving punches
nail punches
pin punches
punches, driving
punches, nail
punches, pin
sets, nail
CN V.TB.AFU.BCW.CFS.ALO.AFU.DZW.ARI

nail tongs
TB.759 (N)
SN Very light duty tongs. (SMITH)
UF tongs, nail
CN V.TB.AFU.BCW.BIQ.AXC.ALO.AXC.BZY

nailed joinery
MT.2786
UF joinery, nailed
CN M.MT.AFU.AXC.DOI.AFU.AFU

nailer inserts
TF.382
ALT **nailer insert**
UF inserts, nailer
CN V.TF.AFU.AFU.AFU.ALO.AFU.BZY.BCW

nailing
KT.51 (L)
ALT **nailed**
CN K.KT.AFU.ALO.BCW.BCW.ALO

nailing clips
TF.331
ALT **nailing clip**
UF clips, nailing
CN V.TF.AFU.AFU.AFU.ALO.AFU.ARI.AXC

nails
TF.386 (A,L,N)
ALT **nail**
SN Slender pieces of metal each having a point on one end which is driven into construction materials by impact. (MEANS)
CN V.TF.AFU.AFU.AFU.ALO.AFU.CFS

nails, barbed
USE **barbed nails**

nails, blunt
USE **blunt nails**

nails, box
USE **box nails**

nails, brad
USE **brads**

nails, casing
USE **casing nails**

nails, cement-coated
USE **cement-coated nails**

nails, Chinese
USE **Chinese nails**

nails, chisel
USE **chisel nails**

nails, clamp
USE **clamp nails**

nails, clasp
USE **cut nails**

nails, clout
USE **clout nails**

nails, common
USE **common nails**

nails, concrete
USE **concrete nails**

nails, cupped
USE **cupped nails**

nails, cut
USE **cut nails**

nails, cut slating
USE **cut slating nails**

nails, deck
USE **deck nails**

nails, diamond
USE **diamond nails**

nails, dog
USE **dog nails**

nails, door
USE **doornails**

nails, double-headed
USE **double-headed nails**

nails, duck bill
USE **duck bill nails**

nails, duplex
USE **double-headed nails**

nails, fencing
USE **fencing nails**

nails, finishing
USE **finishing nails**

nails, flat-head
USE **flat-head nails**

nails, flooring
USE **flooring nails**

nails, form
USE **double-headed nails**

nails, frost horseshoe
USE **frost horseshoe nails**

nails, gate
USE **gate nails**

nails, gimp
USE **gimp nails**

nails, gypsum board
USE **gypsum board nails**

nails, headless
USE **headless nails**

nails, helical
USE **helical nails**

nails, hook
USE **hook nails**

nails, hoop fastener
USE **hoop fastener nails**

nails, horseshoe
USE **horseshoe nails**

nails, hurdle
USE **hurdle nails**

nails, jobent
USE **jobent nails**

nails, lath
USE **lath nails**

nails, lead
USE **lead-capped nails**

nails, lead-capped
USE **lead-capped nails**

nails, lead head
USE **lead-capped nails**

nails, masonry
USE **masonry nails**

nails, metal lath
USE **metal lath nails**

nails, needle
USE **needle nails**

nails, nonleaking roofing
USE **lead-capped nails**

nails, plancher
USE **flooring nails**

nails, ratchet
USE **ratchet nails**

nails, ring-shank
USE **ring-shank nails**

nails, roofing
USE **roofing nails**

nails, rose
USE **rose nails**

nails, rose clench
USE **rose clench nails**

nails, rose flat
USE **rose flat nails**

nails, rose sharp
USE **rose sharp nails**

nails, scaffold
USE **double-headed nails**

nails, screw
USE **drivescrews**

nails, scupper
USE **scupper nails**

nails, shade roller pin
USE **shade roller pin nails**

nails, sheathing
USE **sheathing nails**

nails, shingle
USE **shingle nails**

nails, side
USE **side nails**

nails, siding
USE **shingle nails**

nails, staple
USE **staple nails**

nails, trunk
USE **trunk nails**

nails, umbrella
USE **umbrella nails**

nails, wallboard
USE **gypsum board nails**

nailsins
USE **gimlets**

naiskoi
RK.1145
ALT **naiskos**
CN V.RK.AFU.ALO.ALO.FCS.BOK.BIQ

naive art
BM.248 (L,R)
SN Use for works of an unaffected, individualized style produced by untrained artists.
UF art, naive
CN B.BM.AFU.ARI.BCW.EFQ

Nakhon Pathom
FL.2406
UF Nagara Pathama
Nakon Panom
CN F.FL.ALO.ARI.BCW.BOK.AFU.ARI.AFU

Nakhon Si Thammarat
FL.2411
UF Nakon Sri Thammarat
CN F.FL.ALO.ARI.BCW.BOK.AFU.BIQ

Nakipa
FL.1278
CN F.FL.ALO.ALO.ARI.AFU.ALO.FZU.AFU.AXC

Nakon Panom
USE **Nakhon Pathom**

Nakon Sri Thammarat
USE **Nakhon Si Thammarat**

Naletali
FL.140
CN F.FL.ALO.AFU.ALO.ARI.BCW.ARI

Nalu
FL.346 (L)
CN F.FL.ALO.AFU.AXC.AFU.ARI.BIQ.BUE.ARI

Namazga-depe
USE **Namazga-Tepe**

Namazga-Tepe
FL.1778
UF Namazga-depe
CN F.FL.ALO.ARI.AFU.ALO.CFS

Namba
FL.309 (L)
UF Lamba
CN F.FL.ALO.AFU.AXC.AFU.ARI.ALO.BIQ

Namban
FL.2060
CN F.FL.ALO.ARI.ALO.ALO.ALO.ARI.CRG

Nambokucho
FL.1967
UF Northern and Southern Courts
CN F.FL.ALO.ARI.ALO.ALO.AFU.ALO.ALO

name authority files
VW.590
ALT **name authority file**
UF authority files, name
files, name authority
CN V.VW.AFU.ALO.AFU.BIQ.ALO.AFU.AFU

name plates
TF.20 (N)
ALT **name plate**
UF plates, name
CN V.TF.AFU.AFU.AFU.AFU.AFU.CFS.AXC

Nanga
FL.2061
UF Bujinga
Bunjin-ga
Bunjinga
Literati Style
Na-ga
Naga School
Nanga School
Southern School (Nanga)
CN F.FL.ALO.ARI.ALO.ALO.ALO.ARI.CXA

Nanga School
USE **Nanga**

naoi
RM.337
ALT **naos**
SN The principal chamber in a Greek temple, containing the statue of the deity.
UF cellae
CN V.RM.AFU.DIO.AXC.ALO.AXC.ALO

Napatan
FL.163
CN F.FL.ALO.AFU.ALO.AXC.AXC.ALO.AFU.AFU

naphtha
MT.2670 (L)
UF benzine
naphtha, painter's
painter's naphtha
CN M.MT.AFU.ARI.HZS.AFU.BIQ.AFU.ARI

naphtha, painter's
USE **naphtha**

naphthalene violet
USE **dark reddish purple**

naphthalene violet, dark
USE **dark grayish purple**

Naples yellow
MT.1784
UF antimony yellow
brillant yellow
giallolino
giallorino
jaune brillant
jaune de Naple
Neapelgelb
yellow, antimony
yellow, brilliant
yellow, Naples
CN M.MT.AFU.AFU.ARI.AFU.AFU.ALO.ALO.BUE.ARI.BUE

Naples yellow (color)
USE **brilliant yellow**
grayish yellow
light yellow
moderate yellow
pale yellow

Naqada I
USE **Amratian**

Naqada II
USE **Gerzean**

Nara
FL.1975 (L)
CN F.FL.ALO.ARI.ALO.ALO.AFU.AXC.ALO

Nara-e
FL.2062
CN F.FL.ALO.ARI.ALO.ALO.ALO.ARI.DCU

Nara, Early
USE **Early Nara**

Nara, Late
USE **Late Nara**

narration, continuous
USE **continuous representation**

narrative
BM.9 (R)
CN B.BM.AFU.AFU.AFU.BCW

narthexes
RM.323 (L,R)
ALT **narthex**
SN Use for entrance porches in early basilican churches, and for interior vestibules across the western end of later churches.
CN V.RM.AFU.DIO.AXC.ALO.AFU.DCU

Nasca
USE **Nazca**

Naskapi
USE **Montagnais**

Nasrid
FL.3478
CN F.FL.ALO.BIQ.AFU.FCS

Nassau stoneware
USE **Westerwald stoneware**

natatione
RM.76
ALT **natatio**
CN V.RM.AFU.DIO.ALO.ALO.BOK.AXC

natatoriums
USE **swimming pools**

Natchez
FL.860 (L)
CN F.FL.ALO.ALO.ALO.AFU.ALO.ALO.ARI.ARI.BIQ

nation states
USE **nations**

national atlases
VW.133
ALT **national atlas**
UF atlases, national
CN V.VW.AFU.AFU.AFU.FZU.AXC.AFU.AFU.AFU.AXC.BCW

national bibliographies
VW.256 (L)
ALT **national bibliography**
SN Includes bibliographies that list all the books and other publications published or distributed in a particular country and bibliographies that list publications about a particular country. (LG)
UF bibliographies, national
CN V.VW.AFU.AFU.AFU.FZU.BCW.AFU.ALO.ALO

national cemeteries
RG.33 (A,L)
ALT **national cemetery**
UF cemeteries, military
cemeteries, national
military cemeteries
CN V.RG.AFU.AFU.ALO.ALO.ARI

national directories
VW.420
ALT **national directory**
UF directories, national
CN V.VW.AFU.AFU.ALO.EWY.AXC.AFU.BOK.BIQ

national domain
USE **public domain**

national forests
RD.300 (L)
ALT **national forest**
UF forests, national
CN V.RD.ARI.ALO.ALO.BIQ.ALO.AFU.AFU

national government records
VW.1048
ALT **national government record**
SN Records made or received by an agency of the government of a nation-state and maintained in the conduct of national business.
UF government records, national
records, national government
CN V.VW.AFU.ARI.ALO.BCW.ALO.ARI

national guidebooks
VW.508
ALT **national guidebook**
UF guidebooks, national
CN V.VW.AFU.ALO.AFU.AFU.AFU.BZY.ALO.ARI

national holidays
KM.73 (L,R)
SN Holidays that are observed throughout a nation. (RHDEL2)
CN K.KM.AFU.CFS.ALO

national libraries
RK.693 (A,L,B)
ALT **national library**
SN Libraries maintained out of federal government funds and serving the nation as a whole. Their broad function is to collect and preserve the books, periodicals, and newspapers published in the country. (LG)
UF libraries, national
CN V.RK.AFU.ALO.ALO.CRG.AXC.AFU .AFU

national maps
VW.231
ALT **national map**
UF country maps
maps, country
maps, national
CN V.VW.AFU.AFU.AFU.FZU.AXC.AFU. ARI.AXC.DUC.BUE

national monuments
RK.907 (L)
ALT **national monument**
UF monuments, national
CN V.RK.AFU.ALO.ALO.DOI.ALO.ARI

national museums
RK.432 (A)
ALT **national museum**
UF museums, national
CN V.RK.AFU.ALO.ALO.BCW.AXC .AXC.AXC

national organizations
HG.909
ALT **national organization**
UF organizations, national
CN H.HG.ALO.ELK.ARI

national parks
RK.1464 (A,L,B)
ALT **national park**
SN Areas of special scenic, historical, or scientific importance set aside and maintained by a national government especially for recreation or study. (W)
UF national reserves
parks, national
reserves, national
CN V.RK.ALO.ALO.ARI.ALO.AFU

national reserves
USE **national parks**

national resources
USE **natural resources**

National Socialism
BM.558 (A,L,B,R)
UF Nazism
Socialism, National
CN B.BM.BOK.BZY.AXC.AFU

national treasure
USE **cultural property**

nationalism
BM.561 (A,L,R)
SN Sense of national consciousness exalting one nation above all others and placing primary emphasis on promotion of its culture and interests as opposed to those of other nations or supranational groups. For love of one's country and devotion to its interests in general, use **patriotism.**
UF neo-nationalism
CN B.BM.BOK.BZY.BOK

nationalization
KG.183 (L,B)
ALT **nationalized**
SN Vesting control or ownership of something located or based within a country, such as natural resources or industrial enterprises, in the national government. (RHDEL2)
UF government ownership
ownership, government
CN K.KG.AFU.ALO.ARI.BOK

nations
HG.806
ALT **nation**
SN Use for usually independent political states that are distinct as to name and the characteristics or attributes of their citizens. (W)
UF countries
nation states
states (nations)
CN H.HG.ALO.ALO.BCW

Native American
FL.1194 (L)
UF American Indian
American, Native
Amerindian
Indian (American)
CN F.FL.ALO.ALO.ARI

native asphalt
USE **natural asphalt**

native clay
USE **clay**

Natufian
FL.2915
CN F.FL.ALO.AXC.ARI.AXC.AFU.AFU. AXC

natural asphalt
MT.972
SN Asphalt derived from petroleum. (STEIN)
UF asphalt, native
asphalt, natural
native asphalt
CN M.MT.AFU.AFU.ALO.ALO.AFU. AFU.ALO

natural bitumen
MT.975
UF bitumen, natural
CN M.MT.AFU.AFU.ALO.ALO.AFU. AFU.ALO.AFU.ALO

natural cement
MT.28 (L)
UF cement, hydraulic
cement, hydraulic lime
cement, natural
cement, Roman
cement, waterproof
hydraulic cement
hydraulic lime cement
Roman cement
water-lime
waterproof cement
CN M.MT.AFU.AFU.AFU.ALO.AFU.AFU BUE

natural chalk
USE **chalk**

natural dye
MT.1515
UF dye, natural
dyestuff, natural
natural dyestuff
CN M.MT.AFU.AFU.ARI.AFU.AFU.AFU. AFU.AFU

natural dyestuff
USE **natural dye**

natural fiber
MT.1814
UF fiber, natural
CN M.MT.AFU.AFU.ARI.ALO.AFU.AFU

natural gas
MT.2621 (L)
UF gas, natural
CN M.MT.AFU.ARI.FIM.ARI

natural gas pipelines
USE **gas pipelines**

natural-gas-pipelines maps
VW.204 (L)
ALT **natural-gas-pipelines map**
UF maps, natural-gas-pipelines
CN V.VW.AFU.AFU.AFU.FZU.AXC.AFU. ARI.AXC.CRG.ALO

natural history museums
RK.421 (A,L,B)
ALT **natural history museum**
UF museums, natural history
CN V.RK.AFU.ALO.ALO.BCW.AXC.ARI .CFS.BIQ

natural history photography
USE **nature photography**

natural inorganic pigment
MT.1552
UF color, earth
earth color
inorganic pigment, natural
mineral pigment, natural
natural mineral pigment

pigment, natural inorganic
pigment, natural mineral
CN M.MT.AFU.AFU.ARI.AFU.AFU.ALO.AFU.AFU.ARI

natural landscapes
RD.123
ALT **natural landscape**
SN Designates land and water areas where human effects, if present, are not ecologically significant to the area as a whole (LNDECO). Use to contrast with **cultural landscapes**, areas which are significantly altered or modified by human actions.
UF landscapes, natural
CN V.RD.ARI.AFU

natural light
USE **daylight**

natural lighting
USE **daylight**

natural mineral pigment
USE **natural inorganic pigment**

natural organic pigment
MT.1555
UF organic pigment, natural
pigment, natural organic
CN M.MT.AFU.AFU.ARI.AFU.AFU.ALO.AFU.ALO.AFU

natural red chalk
USE **red chalk**

natural resources
BM.427 (A,L)
UF national resources
resources, natural
CN B.BM.AXC.AXC

natural rubber
USE **rubber**

natural rubber, synthetic
USE **polyisoprene**

natural ventilation
RT.1407
UF passive ventilation
ventilation, natural
ventilation, passive
CN V.RT.ALO.BCW.AFU.AFU.AXC.ARI

natural vermilion
USE **vermilion**

naturalism
BM.515 (L,R)
CN B.BM.BIQ.AXC.CRG

naturalism (realism)
USE **realism (form of expression)**

Naturalistic Style
USE **Curvilinear Style**

naturalists
HG.352 (L)
ALT **naturalist**
SN Those trained or occupied in natural science, especially zoologists and botanists. (RHDEL2)
CN H.HG.AFU.AXC.BIQ.AFU.AFU.DOI

naturalization records
VW.995 (L)
ALT **naturalization record**
SN Documents which evidence the time, place, and court before which an alien is admitted to the rights and status of citizenship. (GAHLM)
UF records, naturalization
CN V.VW.AFU.ARI.ALO.BCW.AFU.AFU.AFU.BUE

naturalizing
KG.208 (L)
SN Conferring the rights and privileges of a native subject or citizen. (W)
CN K.KG.AFU.ALO.BCW.BZY

nature centers
RG.140 (A,L,B)
ALT **nature center**
UF centers, nature
CN V.RG.AFU.AFU.CRG

nature photography
KT.303 (L)
UF natural history photography
photography, natural history
photography, nature
CN K.KT.AFU.ALO.DUC.DIO.AFU.CRG

nature preserves
RK.1451 (L,B)
ALT **nature preserve**
SN Areas established for the purpose of preserving distinctive natural communities of plants and animals. (UPDC)
UF nature reserves
preserves, nature
reserves, nature
CN V.RK.ALO.ALO.ALO

nature printing
KT.475 (L)
SN A process in which an object, as a leaf or piece of lace, is pressed into a plain surface, as of soft metal, to make either a direct printing surface or a matrix. (W)
UF printing, nature
CN K.KT.AFU.ALO.DUC.DUC.ALO.BCW.ARI.ARI

nature reserves
USE **nature preserves**

nature trails
RG.185 (A,L)
ALT **nature trail**
UF trails, nature
CN V.RG.AFU.AFU.DOI.CLM.ALO

Naukratite
USE **Chian**

naumachias
KM.60
SN Ancient Roman spectacles representing naval battles. (W)
CN K.KM.AFU.BOK.AXC.ARI

nautical charts
VW.213 (L)
ALT **nautical chart**
SN Charts showing the depths of water, nature of the sea bottom, contours of the sea bottom and coastline, tides, and currents in a given sea or sea-land area. (DOD)
UF charts, hydrographic
charts, nautical
hydrographic charts
hydrographic maps
maps, hydrographic
CN V.VW.AFU.AFU.AFU.FZU.AXC.AFU.ARI.AXC.DIO.ALO.ALO

nautical museums
USE **maritime museums**

Navajo
FL.1460 (L,R)
CN F.FL.ALO.ALO.ARI.AFU.CFS.BOK

naval academies
USE **naval schools**

naval air bases
RG.125 (A,L,B)
ALT **naval air base**
UF air bases, naval
bases, naval air
military air stations
naval air stations
CN V.RG.AFU.AFU.BZY.AFU.AFU.AFU

naval air stations
USE **naval air bases**

naval architects
HG.87 (A,L)
ALT **naval architect**
UF architects, marine
architects, naval
marine architects
CN H.HG.AFU.AXC.AXC.AFU.AFU.ALO.ALO.AXC

naval architecture
KD.17 (A,L,B,R)
SN Art or science of designing and building ships and other waterborne craft. (RHDEL2)
UF architecture, marine
architecture, naval
marine architecture
CN K.KD.AFU.AFU.AFU.AFU.ALO.AFU.ALO

naval bases
RG.128 (A,L)
ALT **naval base**
SN Area naval commands normally including a seaport, which integrates shore activities that provide local logistic services to the fleet. (W)
UF bases, naval
CN V.RG.AFU.AFU.BZY.AFU.AXC

naval brass
MT.387
UF brass, naval
brass, tin
bronze, naval
naval bronze
tin brass
CN M.MT.AFU.AFU.AFU.BZY.AFU.AFU.AFU.ALO.ARI.BIQ.AFU.ALO

naval bronze
USE **naval brass**

naval engineering
USE **marine engineering**

naval engineers
USE **marine engineers**

naval museums
RK.400 (A,L,B)
ALT **naval museum**
SN Use only to refer to museums dealing with navies, warships, or ships in general; distinct from **maritime museums,** which deal with the sea in general, navigation, or shipping.
UF museums, naval
CN V.RK.AFU.ALO.ALO.BCW.AXC.ARI.AXC.BOK.AFU

naval schools
RK.800 (A,L,B)
ALT **naval school**
UF academies, naval
naval academies
schools, naval
CN V.RK.AFU.ALO.ALO.CXA.ARI.AFU.BCW.AFU

naval shipyards
RG.129 (A,L)
ALT **naval shipyard**
SN Naval bases that build, repair, dock, or convert warships, and are manned by civilian engineers and workers and administered by engineer duty officers. (W)
UF naval stations
navy yards
shipyards, naval
CN V.RG.AFU.AFU.BZY.AFU.AXC.AFU

naval stations
USE **naval shipyards**

naves
RM.277 (A,B,R)
ALT **nave**
SN Use for the main central part of an interior divided into a high center with lower side portions divided by columns or piers, usually but not always in a church. Use also for the main part of a church without aisles but with a distinct chancel.
CN V.RM.AFU.DIO.ARI.ALO.CLM

navies
HG.817 (L)
ALT **navy**
CN H.HG.ALO.AXC.ARI

navigation charts
VW.210 (L,N)
ALT **navigation chart**
UF charts, navigation
charts, pilot
maps, navigation
navigation maps
pilot charts
CN V.VW.AFU.AFU.AFU.FZU.AXC.AFU.ARI.AXC.DIO.ALO

navigation maps
USE **navigation charts**

navvies
USE **laborers**

navy
USE **blackish blue**
blackish purple
dark blue
dark grayish blue
dark grayish purple
dark purplish blue

navy blue
USE **dark purplish blue**
grayish purplish blue
moderate purplish blue

navy gray
USE **dark gray**

navy gray, deep
USE **dark gray**

navy gray, light
USE **medium gray**

navy gray, medium
USE **medium gray**

navy pitch
MT.991
UF pitch, navy
pitch, ship
ship pitch
CN M.MT.AFU.AFU.ALO.ALO.ALO.ALO.AFU.AFU

navy yards
USE **naval shipyards**

navy, bright
USE **dark blue**
deep blue
moderate blue
moderate purplish blue

navy, dark
USE **black**
blackish blue
blackish purple
bluish black
dark blue
dark bluish gray
dark grayish blue
dark purplish blue
dark purplish gray
grayish blue

navy, greenish
USE **blackish blue**
dark blue

navy, light
USE **dark blue**
dark purplish blue
grayish purplish blue
pale purplish blue

navy, purple
USE **moderate purplish blue**

navy, reddish
USE **dark violet**

Naxian
FL.2689
CN F.FL.ALO.AXC.ALO.AFU.ALO.BCW.ALO.BOK

Nayak
FL.2222 (L)
UF Madura
Nayyaks of Madura
CN F.FL.ALO.ARI.AXC.ALO.AFU.BCW.AFU

Nayarit
FL.1071 (L)
CN F.FL.ALO.ALO.ALO.ALO.AFU.ALO.BCW.BCW

Nayarit (Cora)
USE **Cora**

Nayyaks of Madura
USE **Nayak**

Nazca
FL.1156 (L)
UF Nasca
CN F.FL.ALO.ALO.ALO.ARI.AXC.AFU.AXC.BIQ

Nazism
USE **National Socialism**

NBR rubber
USE **nitrile elastomer**

Ndani
USE **Dani**

Ndebele
FL.562 (L,R)
UF Matebele
CN F.FL.ALO.AFU.AXC.ARI.AXC.AFU

Ndembu
FL.458 (L)
CN F.FL.ALO.AFU.AXC.ALO.ALO.ALO.BOK

Ndengese
FL.445
UF Dengese
CN F.FL.ALO.AFU.AXC.ALO.ALO.AFU.AFU.BZY

Ndjabi
USE **Nzebi**

Ndorobo
USE **Dorobo**

Ndumbo
FL.418 (L)
UF Andumbo
Ndumu
CN F.FL.ALO.AFU.AXC.ALO.AFU.AXC.BIQ

Ndumu
USE **Ndumbo**

Neapelgelb
USE **Naples yellow**

Near Eastern
FL.2846 (L)
CN F.FL.ALO.AXC.ARI

neat cement
MT.29
SN In masonry, a pure cement uncut by a sand mixture. (PUTNAM)
UF cement, neat
CN M.MT.AFU.AFU.AFU.ALO.AFU.AFU.BZY

Nebesna
USE **Tanana**

Nebraska
FL.922
CN F.FL.ALO.ALO.ALO.AFU.ALO.ARI.AXC.BCW

necessaries
USE **outhouses**
privies

necessary chairs
USE **commode chairs**

necessary houses
USE **outhouses**
privies

necessary stools
USE **close stools**

necessity chairs
USE **commode chairs**

necked bolts
TF.318
ALT **necked bolt**
UF bolts, necked
CN V.TF.AFU.AFU.AFU.ALO.AFU.ALO.AFU.CFS

necking
RT.139
SN The part of a column between the bottom of the capital and the top of the shaft, or the molding or moldings located here. (HAS)
UF necks
trachelia
CN V.RT.AFU.AFU.AFU.AXC.BIQ.ALO.ARI.ALO.BOK

necks
USE **necking**

necrologies
USE **death registers**

Necropolis
USE **Paracas Necropolis**

necropolises
RG.29 (A,B,R)
ALT **necropolis**
SN Use for large elaborate cemeteries of ancient cities or ancient or prehistoric burying places.
CN V.RG.AFU.AFU.ALO.AFU.ARI

Nectrandra
USE **lancewood**

needle case stakes
TB.688 (N)
ALT **needle case stake**
SN Small stakes used in sheet metal work for thin, round items such as needle cases. (RUSERW)
UF stakes, needle case
CN V.TB.AFU.BCW.BIQ.AFU.ALO.CXA.BIQ

needle files
TB.717 (N)
ALT **needle file**
SN Very small, thin files used in delicate work.
UF files, needle
CN V.TB.AFU.BCW.BIQ.ARI.ALO.ARI.ARI

needle nails
TF.426
ALT **needle nail**
UF nails, needle
CN V.TF.AFU.AFU.AFU.ALO.AFU.CFS.AFU.DIO.BOK

needle-point pens
USE **stylographs**

needle spires
RM.407
ALT **needle spire**
SN Thin spires rising from the center of a tower roof, well inside a parapet, protecting a pathway upon which scaffolding could be erected for repairs. (PDARC)
UF Hertfordshire spikes
spikes, Hertfordshire
spires, needle
CN V.RM.AFU.DOI.ALO.AFU.AXC

needlenose pliers
TB.221 (N)
SN Pliers with long, narrow, flat jaws.
UF pliers, needlenose
CN V.TB.AFU.ARI.CFS.AXC.AFU

needlepoint
KT.565
SN Process of working embroidery on a surface, such as canvas, usually with simple, even stitches across counted threads. (W)
UF point (needlepoint)
CN K.KT.AFU.ALO.ELK.DUC.ALO.BCW

needles
TB.384 (L,N)
ALT **needle**
CN V.TB.AFU.ARI.DIO.ALO

needles, spring
USE **spring needles**

needlework
KT.557 (R)
SN Includes all processes used in making ornamental patterns or designs on textiles with a needle.
CN K.KT.AFU.ALO.ELK.DUC.ALO

needs analysis
USE **needs assessment**

needs assessment
KG.7
UF analysis, needs
assessment, needs
needs analysis
CN K.KG.AFU.AFU.AFU.ALO.ALO

negative
FL.1179
CN F.FL.ALO.ALO.ALO.ARI.AXC.ALO.ALO.BCW

negative prints
VJ.39
ALT **negative print**
SN Use for photographic prints in which the tones or colors are reversed from their appearance in nature.
UF prints, negative
CN V.VJ.AFU.AFU.ARI.ARI.AFU

negative process, gelatin dry-plate
USE **gelatin dry plate process**

negative space
BM.91
SN Use for an enclosed empty space in architecture, sculpture, or painting which makes an essential contribution to the composition. (THDAT)
UF hollow volumes
negative volume
space, negative
void
volume, negative
volumes, hollow
CN B.BM.AFU.AFU.ARI.AFU.FIM.AFU

negative volume
USE **negative space**

negatives
VJ.3 (L,N)
ALT **negative**
SN Use for photographs, usually on a transparent support, in which the tones or colors are reversed from their appearance in nature. For

prints in which tones or colors are reversed, use **negative prints.** When a glass plate is painted or drawn on and a photographic print made from it, use **clichés-verre.**
UF negatives, photographic
photographic negatives
photonegatives
CN V.VJ.AFU.AFU.AFU

negatives, black-and-white
USE **black-and-white negatives**

negatives, calotype
USE **calotypes**

negatives, color
USE **color negatives**

negatives, color separation
USE **color separation negatives**

negatives, gelatin dry plate
USE **gelatin dry plate negatives**

negatives, gelatin silver
USE **gelatin silver negatives**

negatives, halftone
USE **halftone negatives**

negatives, photographic
USE **negatives**

negatives, separation
USE **color separation negatives**

negatives, silver gelatin
USE **gelatin silver negatives**

negatives, wet collodion
USE **wet collodion negatives**

negatives, wet plate
USE **wet collodion negatives**

Negativo
USE **Gallinazo**

negligence
BM.456 (L,B)
SN Failure to exercise the degree of care expected of the normally reasonable person.
CN B.BM.BCW.CLM

Negoro
FL.2011
CN F.FL.ALO.ARI.ALO.ALO.ALO.ALO.AFU.AFU

negotiable instruments
VW.826 (L)
ALT **negotiable instrument**
UF instruments, negotiable
CN V.VW.AFU.ARI.AFU.BIQ.CFS

negotiating
KG.39 (L)
SN Attempting to reach an agreement through discussion. (RLG7)
CN K.KG.AFU.AFU.ALO.BIQ

Negrillo
USE **Pygmy**

Negro
USE **African American**

Negro Movement, New
USE **Harlem Renaissance**

Negro Renaissance
USE **Harlem Renaissance**

Negroes
USE **African Americans**

neighborhood gardens
USE **community gardens**

neighborhood parks
RK.1459
ALT **neighborhood park**
UF parks, neighborhood
CN V.RK.ALO.ALO.ARI.AFU.ARI

neighborhood playgrounds
RK.1496
ALT **neighborhood playground**
UF playgrounds, neighborhood
CN V.RK.ALO.ALO.BCW.BUE.ALO

neighborhoods
RG.273 (A,L)
ALT **neighborhood**
CN V.RG.ALO.AFU.ALO.BCW.AFU

Nelson's chairs
USE **Trafalgar chairs**

Neo-Assyrian
USE **Late Assyrian**

Neo-Attic
FL.2763
CN F.FL.ALO.AXC.ALO.ALO.ALO.BZY.AFU.AXC

Neo-Babylonian
FL.2981
CN F.FL.ALO.AXC.ARI.BCW.AFU.BZY

Neo-Baroque
USE **Baroque Revival**

Neo-Brutalist
USE **Brutalist**

Neo-Byzantine
USE **Byzantine Revival**

Neo-cinquecento
USE **Stile Umberto**

Neo-Constructivist
FL.3734 (R)
ALT **Neo-Constructivism**
CN F.FL.ALO.BUE.ARI.EFQ

Neo-Dada
FL.3735 (L,R)
UF Proto-Pop
CN F.FL.ALO.BUE.ARI.ELK

Neo-Egyptian
USE **Egyptian Revival**

Neo-Expressionist
FL.3736 (R)
ALT **Neo-Expressionism**
UF Bad Painting
Expressionist, New
Neue Wilde
New Expressionist
CN F.FL.ALO.BUE.ARI.ERE

Neo-Florentine
FL.3298
CN F.FL.ALO.BCW.ALO.AXC.DCU.BOK

Neo-Geo
FL.3737 (R)
CN F.FL.ALO.BUE.ARI.EWY

Neo-Georgian
USE **Georgian Revival**

Neo-Gothic
USE **Gothic Revival**

Neo-Grec
FL.3365 (B)
CN F.FL.ALO.BCW.ALO.AXC.DIO.BCW.ARI.AFU

Neo-Greek
USE **Greek Revival**

Neo-Hittite
FL.2858
UF North Syrian
CN F.FL.ALO.AXC.ARI.AFU.AFU.ARI.AXC

Neo-Impressionist
FL.3376 (L,R)
ALT **Neo-Impressionism**
UF Divisionist
Pointillist (Neo-Impressionist)
CN F.FL.ALO.BCW.ALO.AXC.DIO.BCW.BCW.BCW

Neo-Liberty
USE **Stile Liberty**

neo-nationalism
USE **nationalism**

Neo-Norman
USE **Norman Revival**

Neo-Palladian
USE **Palladian**

Neo-Plastic
FL.3352 (R)
ALT **Neo-Plasticism**
UF Neo-Plasticist
Plastic (art movement)
CN F.FL.ALO.BCW.ALO.AXC.DIO.AXC.ARI

Neo-Plasticist
USE **Neo-Plastic**

Neo-Platonism
BM.519 (A,L,R)
UF Neoplatonism

New Platonism
Platonism, New
CN B.BM.BIQ.AXC.DIO.AFU

Neo-Rationalist
FL.3710 (A)
ALT **Neo-Rationalism**
CN F.FL.ALO.BUE.ALO.BCW

Neo-Renaissance
USE **Renaissance Revival**

Neo-Rococo
USE **Rococo Revival**

Neo-Romanesque
USE **Romanesque Revival**

Neo-Romantic
FL.3258 (R)
ALT **Neo-Romanticism**
CN F.FL.ALO.BCW.ALO.AXC.BOK

Neo-Sumerian
FL.2970
CN F.FL.ALO.AXC.ARI.BCW.AFU.BCW

Neo-Tudor
USE **Tudor Revival**

Neo-Vernacular
USE **Old English**

Neoclassical
FL.3259 (A,L,B,R)
ALT **Neoclassicism**
SN Use for architecture and art of the late 18th and the 19th centuries that follow principles of classicism. For late 18th- to early 20th-century architecture and ornament based relatively closely on ancient classical forms, use **Classical Revival.**
CN F.FL.ALO.BCW.ALO.AXC.BUE

Neoclassical Revival
USE **Classical Revival**

Neolithic
FL.14 (A,L,R)
UF New Stone Age
Stone Age, New
CN F.FL.AFU.BCW.AFU.ARI

Neolithic, Basal
USE **Basal Neolithic**

Neolithic, Early
USE **Early Neolithic**

Neolithic, Final
USE **Final Neolithic**

Neolithic, Late
USE **Late Neolithic**

Neolithic, Middle
USE **Middle Neolithic**

Neoplatonism
USE **Neo-Platonism**

neoprene
MT.2086 (L)
SN A synthetic rubber made by polymerization of chloroprene and characterized by superior resistance to oils, gasoline, sunlight, ozone, and heat, and by lower permeability to gases than rubber. (W)
UF chloroprene rubber
rubber, chloroprene
CN M.MT.AFU.AFU.ARI.BUE.AFU.AFU.BCW

neoprimitivism
USE **primitivism**

Nepalese
FL.2156 (L,B)
CN F.FL.ALO.ARI.AXC.AFU.AXC

Nepalese School
USE **Bal-bris**

nephrite
MT.526 (L)
CN M.MT.AFU.AFU.AFU.CFS.AFU.DZW.AFU

nero antico
MT.777
SN An ornamental black marble found in fragments among Roman ruins and believed to have come from Laconia. (W)
UF marmor taenarium
CN M.MT.AFU.AFU.AFU.DCU.AFU.ARI.ARI.ARI.AFU.BCW

nervures
USE **ribs**

Nespelem
FL.1416 (L)
CN F.FL.ALO.ALO.ARI.AFU.BUE.CRG

nesting tables
TG.784 (N)
SN A set of several tables, graduated in size so as to fit one over another. (ARON)
UF nests of tables
stack tables
stacking tables
tables, nest of
tables, nesting
tables, stack
CN V.TG.AFU.AFU.BIQ.BOK.AXC.AFU

Nestorian
BM.647 (L)
CN B.BM.BZY.AFU.ALO.AXC.BCW

nests of drawers
TG.878
ALT **nest of drawers**
SN Term applied to a number of small drawers framed together in the form of a box, or fitted into another piece of furniture. (DEF)
UF drawers, nests of
CN V.TG.ALO.DCU.AFU.AFU.ARI

nests of drawers, cabinet
USE **cabinets of drawers**

nests of tables
USE **nesting tables**

net structures
USE **cable net structures**

net structures, cable
USE **cable net structures**

net structures, double curvature
USE **cable net structures**

net tracery
USE **reticulated tracery**

net vaults
RT.553
ALT **net vault**
SN Use for vaults with ribs that define a network of lozenges.
UF vaults, net
CN V.RT.AFU.AFU.AFU.BIQ.BOK.AFU.ARI.AFU.ALO.ARI

Netherlandish
FL.3050
UF Low Country
Lowland
CN F.FL.ALO.BCW.AFU.CRG

nets (net structures)
USE **cable net structures**

nets, cable
USE **cable net structures**

nets, safety
USE **safety nets**

Netsilik
FL.1212
CN F.FL.ALO.ALO.ARI.AFU.AFU.AFU.ALO.AFU.BIQ

netting
KT.548 (L)
CN K.KT.AFU.ALO.ELK.DUC.AFU. BCW

netting, mosquito
USE **mosquito netting**

network pattern
USE **reticular pattern**

networks, drainage
USE **drainage systems**

networks, irrigation
USE **irrigation systems**

networks, telecommunication
USE **telecommunication systems**

networks, telephone
USE **telephone systems**

Neue Rheinische Sezession
FL.3738 (R)
CN F.FL.ALO.BUE.ARI.FCS

Neue Sachlichkeit

FL.3394 (L,R)
UF New Objectivity
Nouvelle Objectivité
CN F.FL.ALO.BCW.ALO.AXC.DIO.
BIQ.BIQ.AXC

Neue Wilde
USE **Neo-Expressionist**

Neues Bauen
FL.3281 (R)
UF Nieuwe Bouwen
Nieuwe Zakelijheid
CN F.FL.ALO.BCW.ALO.AXC.CRG.
AXC

neutral gray
USE **medium gray**

neutral gray, dark
USE **dark gray**

neutral gray, deep
USE **dark gray**

neutral gray, light
USE **medium gray**

neutral gray, pale
USE **medium gray**

neutralizers
MT.2318
CN M.MT.AFU.ARI.ALO.DIO

neutrals
DL.299
SN Colors without hue: black, white, and the grays. (RHDEL2)
CN D.DL.AFU.ALO

neutron activation analysis
KT.13 (L)
SN Using the energy and intensity of gamma rays emitted from irradiated objects to determine their trace elements in order to locate the source of raw materials used in making the artifact by matching the results to trace elements from known sources. (FOFDA)
UF activation analysis, neutron
analysis, neutron activation
analysis, radioactivation
dating, hydration ring
radioactivation analysis
ring dating, hydration
CN K.KT.AFU.ALO.AXC.AFU.AFU.AFU

Neuwieder blue
USE **blue verditer**

new blue
USE **artificial ultramarine blue**
cobalt blue

New Britain
FL.3621 (L)
UF Bihara
CN F.FL.ALO.BOK.ALO.ARI

New Brutalist
USE **Brutalist**

New Caledonian
FL.3625 (L)
CN F.FL.ALO.BOK.ALO.AXC

new communities
USE **new towns**

New England barns
USE **English barns**

New England connected barns
USE **connected barns**

New England hemlock
USE **eastern hemlock**

New England pine
USE **northern white pine**

New Expressionist
USE **Neo-Expressionist**

New Figuration
FL.3739 (R)
UF Figuration, New
Nouvelle Figuration
CN F.FL.ALO.BUE.ARI.FIM

New Georgia Island
FL.3667
CN F.FL.ALO.BOK.ALO.BOK.BCW

New Guinea
FL.3626 (L)
CN F.FL.ALO.BOK.ALO.BCW

New Guinea, Dutch
USE **Irian Jaya**

New Hebrides
USE **Vanuatu**

New Ireland
FL.3659
CN F.FL.ALO.BOK.ALO.BIQ

New Kingdom
FL.2814
UF Egyptian Empire
Kingdom, New
CN F.FL.ALO.AXC.ALO.ARI.AFU.BUE

New Menri School
FL.2182
UF Menri School, New
Sman gsar
CN F.FL.ALO.ARI.AXC.AFU.BOK.
AFU.BCW.AFU

New Negro Movement
USE **Harlem Renaissance**

New Objectivity
USE **Neue Sachlichkeit**

New Palace period
FL.2561
UF Late Palace period
Palace period, New
CN F.FL.ALO.AXC.ALO.AFU.AFU.
ALO.ARI.BIQ

New Platonism
USE **Neo-Platonism**

New Realist
FL.3740 (L,R)
ALT **New Realism**
SN Use with reference to art of the 1960s that is realist in the sense of appropriating materials from the environment or staging actions or happenings.
UF Nouveau Réaliste
Realist, New
CN F.FL.ALO.BUE.ARI.FOG

New Realist (Photorealist)
USE **Photorealist**

New Sculpture Movement
FL.3344 (L,R)
UF Sculpture Movement, New
CN F.FL.ALO.BCW.ALO.AXC.DIO.
ALO.BZY.AFU

New Stone Age
USE **Neolithic**

new towns
RD.84 (A,L,B,R)
ALT **new town**
SN New, essentially self-sufficient settlements, built in a previously undeveloped area, which provide residential, commercial, industrial, educational, recreational, and public facilities. (DAC)
UF cities, satellite (new towns)
communities, new
model villages
new communities
satellite cities (new towns)
satellite towns (new towns)
towns, new
towns, satellite (new towns)
villages, model
CN V.RD.AFU.BUE.AXC

new wave
BM.362 (R)
CN B.BM.ALO.ALO.CLM.ELK

New World Dutch barns
USE **Dutch barns**

New Year
KM.75 (L)
CN K.KM.AFU.CFS.ALO.ALO

New Year, Jewish
USE **Rosh Hashanah**

New Zealand
FL.3696 (L,B)
CN F.FL.ALO.BOK.AXC.BOK

New Zealand beech
MT.1109 (L)
UF beech, black
beech, New Zealand
black beech
Nothofagus solandri

CN M.MT.AFU.AFU.ALO.BIQ.DCU. AFU.AFU.AFU.BCW.BCW

newel caps
RT.1107
ALT **newel cap**
SN Terminal features of newels often molded, turned, or carved in a decorative shape. (HAS)
UF caps, newel
CN V.RT.AFU.BIQ.AXC.ALO.BCW. ALO.AFU

newel collars
RT.1108
ALT **newel collar**
SN Turned wood collars used to lengthen the base of a newel. (HAS)
UF collars, newel
CN V.RT.AFU.BIQ.AXC.ALO.BCW. ALO.ALO

newel drops
RT.1109
ALT **newel drop**
SN Ornamental projections at the bottom ends of newels of stairs of two or more flights.
UF drops, newel
CN V.RT.AFU.BIQ.AXC.ALO.BCW .ALO.ARI

newel posts
USE **newels**

newel stairs
RT.1073
ALT **newel stair**
SN Stairs constructed with newels at the angles to receive the ends of the strings. (RS)
UF stairs, newel
CN V.RT.AFU.BIQ.AXC.AFU.AFU.AXC

newels
RT.1104 (N,B)
ALT **newel**
SN In architecture, upright posts supporting the handrail at the top and bottom of a stairway or at the turn on a landing; also, the main posts about which circular staircases wind. (PUTNAM)
UF newel posts
posts, newel
CN V.RT.AFU.BIQ.AXC.ALO.BCW.AFU

newels, hollow
USE **hollow newel stairs**

newels, landing
USE **landing newels**

newgates
USE **prisons**

news bulletins
VW.60
ALT **news bulletin**
UF bulletins, news
CN V.VW.AFU.AFU.AFU.DUC

news photographers
USE **photojournalists**

news photographs
VJ.91
ALT **news photograph**
UF journalistic photographs
newspaper photographs
photographs, journalistic
photographs, news
photographs, press
press photographs
CN V.VJ.AFU.ALO.ALO

news photography
USE **photojournalism**

news wire photos
USE **wire photographs**

newscasters
HG.283
ALT **newscaster**
CN H.HG.AFU.AXC.BCW.ALO.AFU. ALO.AFU

newsletters
VW.616 (L,N)
ALT **newsletter**
SN In the 16th and 17th centuries, manuscript reports produced for special subscribers and issued irregularly or weekly; in the 20th century, periodic reports on the activities of a business or organization. (GAHLM)
UF bulletins
CN V.VW.AFU.ALO.AFU.CXA.AFU.ARI

newspaper clippings
USE **clippings**

newspaper columns
VW.6 (L)
ALT **newspaper column**
SN Written articles appearing regularly in a series in a newspaper. (WCOL)
UF columns, newspaper
CN V.VW.AFU.AFU.AFU.ALO.AFU

newspaper illustration
KT.207 (L,R)
UF illustration, newspaper
CN K.KT.AFU.ALO.DUC.CLM.BCW

newspaper illustrations
VB.44 (R)
ALT **newspaper illustration**
UF illustrations, newspaper
CN V.VB.AFU.ALO.AXC.AFU.ALO

newspaper indexes
VW.438 (L)
ALT **newspaper index**
UF indexes, newspaper
CN V.VW.AFU.AFU.ALO.EWY.BOK. ALO.AXC.AFU

newspaper photographs
USE **news photographs**

newspapers
VW.618 (L,N,R)
ALT **newspaper**
SN Papers that are printed and distributed daily, weekly, or at some other regular and usually short intervals and which contain news, editorials and opinions, features, advertising, and other matter considered of general interest. (GAHLM)
CN V.VW.AFU.ALO.AFU.CXA.AFU. AXC

newsprint
MT.1902 (L)
CN M.MT.AFU.AFU.ARI.ALO.ALO. AXC.AFU.AXC.ARI

newsreel photographers
USE **news photographers**

newsstands
RK.146 (A,L)
ALT **newsstand**
UF magazine stands (newsstands)
CN V.RK.AFU.ALO.ALO.ALO.ARI. BCW.ALO

newswriters
USE **journalists**

Nez Percé
FL.1417 (L)
UF Chopunnish
Nimipu
Numipu
Sahaptin
CN F.FL.ALO.ALO.ARI.AFU.BUE.CXA

Ngbaka
FL.531 (L)
UF Bwaka
Gbaya
CN F.FL.ALO.AFU.AXC.ALO.ALO. BIQ.ALO.BIQ

Ngbandi
FL.532 (L)
CN F.FL.ALO.AFU.AXC.ALO.ALO. BIQ.ALO.BOK

Ngbanya
USE **Gonja**

Ngbanyito
USE **Gonja**

Ngbetu
USE **Mangbetu**

Ngendi
FL.437
CN F.FL.ALO.AFU.AXC.ALO.ALO. AFU.AFU.AXC.ARI

Ngere
USE **Wee**

Ngindo
FL.665
CN F.FL.ALO.AFU.AXC.AXC.BIQ.BUE

Ngom

FL.419
UF Bangomo
Kalai
CN F.FL.ALO.AFU.AXC.ALO.AFU.
AXC.BOK

Ngombe
FL.533 (L)
CN F.FL.ALO.AFU.AXC.ALO.ALO.
BIQ.ALO.BUE

Ngongo
FL.438
CN F.FL.ALO.AFU.AXC.ALO.ALO.
AFU.AFU.AXC.AXC

Ngoni
FL.666 (L)
UF Angoni
CN F.FL.ALO.AFU.AXC.AXC.BIQ.BZY

Ngor School
USE **Sakya School**

Ngumba
FL.420
CN F.FL.ALO.AFU.AXC.ALO.AFU.
AXC.BUE

Nguru
USE **Lomwe**

Nguyên
FL.2433
CN F.FL.ALO.ARI.BCW.BUE.AFU.BIQ

Ngwa
FL.184
UF Bangua
Bangwa
CN F.FL.ALO.AFU.AXC.AFU.AFU.
AFU.AFU.BCW

Niani
FL.88 (L)
CN F.FL.ALO.AFU.ALO.AFU.BOK.
AFU.ARI

nibs
TB.1129
ALT **nib**
SN Pen points intended for insertion into a holder. (W)
CN V.TB.ALO.DCU

Nicaraguan
FL.706 (L,B)
CN F.FL.ALO.ALO.AFU.AFU.ALO

Nicarao
FL.1558 (L)
CN F.FL.ALO.ALO.ARI.ALO.BOK.BZY

niches
RT.656 (A,B)
ALT **niche**
SN Use generally for recesses in walls.
CN
V.RT.AFU.AFU.AFU.BIQ.BUE.ALO.
AFU.BIQ

nicked hanging wire hangers
TF.354
ALT **nicked hanging wire hanger**
UF hangers, nicked hanging wire
hanging wire hangers, nicked
wire hangers, nicked hanging
CN V.TF.AFU.AFU.AFU.ALO.AFU.
BOK.ARI.AFU.BCW

nickel
MT.440 (L,B)
SN A silvery white metal with a yellowish cast used in alloy with copper since ancient times; resistant to corrosion and to most acids except nitric. (MH)
CN M.MT.AFU.AFU.AFU.BZY.AFU.
AFU.ARI.CLM

nickel alloys
MT.401 (L)
SN Any alloy containing nickel as the base metal, or as the chief alloying element. (MH)
UF alloys, nickel
CN M.MT.AFU.AFU.AFU.BZY.AFU.
AFU.AFU.ALO.BIQ

nickel bronze
MT.379 (L)
UF bronze, nickel
CN M.MT.AFU.AFU.AFU.BZY.AFU.
AFU.AFU.ALO.ARI.BCW.ALO.AXC

nickel-copper alloys
USE **copper-nickel alloys**

nickel steel
MT.355 (L)
UF steel, nickel
CN M.MT.AFU.AFU.AFU.BZY.AFU.
AFU.AFU.AFU.ALO.AFU.ALO.ARI

nickel-titanium yellow
MT.1785
UF jaune titane de nickel
Nickeltitangelb
sun yellow
yellow, nickel-titanium
yellow, sun
CN M.MT.AFU.AFU.ARI.AFU.AFU.
ALO.ALO.BUE.ARI.BZY

nickelodeons
RK.940 (N)
ALT **nickelodeon**
UF galleries, shooting (theaters)
shooting galleries (theaters)
CN V.RK.AFU.ALO.ALO.EFQ.ARI.
BCW.ALO.AFU.ALO

Nickeltitangelb
USE **nickel-titanium yellow**

nickle (color)
USE **medium gray**

Nicoya polychrome
FL.1079
UF polychrome, Nicoya
CN F.FL.ALO.ALO.ALO.ALO.ALO.
AFU.ALO.AFU.ALO

niello
KT.704 (L,R)
SN A technique of decorating gold or silver with a black inlay. (THDAT)
CN K.KT.AFU.ALO.GRC.BZY.ARI

Niépceotype
USE **heliography**

Nieuwe Bouwen
USE **Neues Bauen**

Nieuwe Kunst
USE **Art Nouveau**

Nieuwe Zakelijheid
USE **Neues Bauen**

Nieuwe Zakelijkheid
FL.3353 (R)
CN F.FL.ALO.BCW.ALO.AXC.DIO.
AXC.AXC

Niger Delta
FL.109
CN F.FL.ALO.AFU.ALO.AFU.BUE.BUE

Nigerian
FL.92 (L)
CN F.FL.ALO.AFU.ALO.AFU.BUE

night
BM.1035 (L,R)
UF nighttime
CN B.BM.CFS.AXC.CRG.ALO

night bolts
USE **night latches**

night keys
TF.534
ALT **night key**
UF keys, night
CN V.TF.AFU.ALO.ARI.AFU.BOK

night latches
TF.177
ALT **night latch**
SN Door locks with a spring bolt that cannot be operated from the outside except by a key. (MEANS)
UF bolts, night
dead latches
latches, dead
latches, night
night bolts
CN V.TF.AFU.AFU.AFU.AFU.DIO.
BCW.AFU.AXC

night nurseries
RM.393
ALT **night nursery**
UF nurseries, night
CN V.RM.AFU.DIO.BCW.AXC.AFU

night photography
KT.396 (L)
UF photography, night
CN K.KT.AFU.ALO.DUC.DIO.ARI.ARI.
BZY.AXC

night tables

TG.749 (N,R)
ALT **night table**
SN Small tables made to stand beside a bed; includes those having a cupboard to hold a chamber pot and those with a necessary stool that pulls forward in the lower part. (OCDA)
UF bedside cabinets
bedside cupboards
bedside tables
bedstands
cabinets, bedside
chevets (night tables)
cupboards, bedside
cupboards, pot
nightstands
pot cupboards
tables d'en cas
tables de chevet
tables de nuit
tables en cas
tables, bedside
tables, night
CN V.TG.AFU.AFU.BIQ.BOK.ALO.DIO

nightclubs
RK.929 (A,L,B,R)
ALT **nightclub**
CN V.RK.AFU.ALO.ALO.EFQ.ARI.ARI

nightstands
USE **night tables**

nighttime
USE **night**

nigrosin violet
USE **dark purple**

nigrosin violet, dark
USE **dark purple**

nihilism
BM.516 (L)
SN Extreme form of skepticism that denies the objective reality of all values, beliefs, and truths. (TSIT)
CN B.BM.BIQ.AXC.CXA

Nihonga
FL.2063
UF Japanese Style
CN F.FL.ALO.ARI.ALO.ALO.ALO.ARI.DIO

Nika
USE **Mijikenda**

Nilo-Hamitic
USE **Eastern Hamitic**

Nilotes
USE **Eastern Hamitic**

Nimipu
USE **Nez Percé**

Nineteenth Dynasty
FL.2816
UF 19th Dynasty
Dynasty, Nineteenth
CN F.FL.ALO.AXC.ALO.ARI.AFU.BUE.ALO

Ninevite
FL.2995
CN F.FL.ALO.AXC.ARI.BCW.ALO.BCW.BIQ

Ninth Dynasty
FL.2799
UF 9th Dynasty
Dynasty, Ninth
CN F.FL.ALO.AXC.ALO.ARI.AFU.BCW.ARI

ninth plate
DC.129
SN A photographic plate size, about 2 by 2 1/2 inches.
CN D.DC.AFU.AXC.BIQ.AXC

Nioniosse
FL.359
CN F.FL.ALO.AFU.AXC.AFU.AXC.AFU.CFS

nippers
TB.720 (N)
SN Hand pincers with cutting jaws that meet parallel to each other rather than at an angle; used for cutting wire, thin metal rods, or the like. (DAC)
CN V.TB.AFU.BCW.BIQ.ARI.ALO.BCW

Nisa
FL.1799
CN F.FL.ALO.ARI.AFU.AXC.CRG

Nisai
FL.2030
UF Nisai-Toki
CN F.FL.ALO.ARI.ALO.ALO.ALO.ALO.ALO.CRG

Nisai-Toki
USE **Nisai**

Nishapur ware
FL.3547
UF ware, Nishapur
CN F.FL.ALO.BIQ.AFU.HCQ.AFU.AFU

Nishimura School
FL.2094
CN F.FL.ALO.ARI.ALO.ALO.ALO.AXC.BZY.CFS

Niska
FL.1351 (L)
CN F.FL.ALO.ALO.ARI.AFU.BIQ.DZW

nissen huts
USE **quonset huts**

nitrate green
USE **chrome green**

nitrate, cellulose
USE **nitrocellulose**

nitrate, silver
USE **silver nitrate**

nitric acid
MT.301 (L)
UF acid, nitric
CN M.MT.AFU.AFU.AFU.BOK.AFU.BIQ

nitrile elastomer
MT.2087 (L)
UF buna N
elastomer, nitrile
NBR rubber
nitrile rubber
rubber, NBR
rubber, nitrile
CN M.MT.AFU.AFU.ARI.BUE.AFU.AFU.BIQ

nitrile rubber
USE **nitrile elastomer**

nitrocellulose
MT.2132 (L)
UF cellulose nitrate
C N
nitrate, cellulose
CN M.MT.AFU.AFU.ARI.BUE.ALO.AXC.AFU.BCW.ARI

nitrogen dating
KT.499
SN Method used for the relative dating of bone by measuring the amount of nitrogen remaining in its collagen, which decomposes at a generally uniform rate. (FOFDA)
UF dating, nitrogen
CN K.KT.AFU.ALO.EFQ.AFU.AFU.ALO

nitroglycerin
MT.2586 (L)
UF glyceryl trinitrate
CN M.MT.AFU.ARI.DIO.ALO

nitrous oxide
MT.312 (L)
UF oxide, nitrous
CN M.MT.AFU.AFU.AFU.BOK.BCW

Nkole
FL.685
UF Ankole
Banyankole
Nyankole
CN F.FL.ALO.AFU.AXC.AXC.BOK.CXA

Nkosi
USE **Kossi**

Nkundu
USE **Kundu**

Nkutshu
FL.446
UF Bankutshu
Basongo Meno
Kutshu
Songomeno
CN F.FL.ALO.AFU.AXC.ALO.ALO.AFU.AFU.CFS

no-fines concrete
MT.227 (A,L,B)
SN A concrete mixture containing little or no fine aggregate. (DAC)
UF concrete, no-fines
CN M.MT.AFU.AFU.AFU.BCW.AFU.AXC.BCW.AFU

Noaname
USE **Chocó**

nobility
HG.889 (L,R)
SN Ruling or highly privileged social class, whose rights, property, and privileges are maintained and passed on by heredity.
CN H.HG.ALO.DOI.ALO.ARI.ALO

nodular iron
USE **ductile iron**

noir belge
USE **Belgian black marble**

noir de bougie
USE **carbon black**
lampblack

noir de vigne
USE **vine black**

noire d'ivoire
USE **ivory black**

noire d'os
USE **bone black**

noise
BM.422 (L,B)
CN B.BM.AXC.ALO.AFU

noise abatement
USE **noise control**

noise control
KG.121 (L)
UF abatement, noise
control, noise
noise abatement
noise prevention
prevention, noise
CN K.KG.AFU.AFU.BCW.ALO.BUE

noise pollution
BM.439 (A,L)
UF pollution, noise
CN B.BM.AXC.BCW.ALO.ARI

noise prevention
USE **noise control**

noise, city
USE **city noise**

noise, traffic
USE **traffic noise**

noise, transportation
USE **transportation noise**

noise, urban
USE **city noise**

noix
TG.966
SN Name given to the bosses on large stretchers linking and strengthening the legs of a table or secretaire; often very richly carved and pierced. (WATSON)
CN V.TG.ALO.FUA

Nok
FL.110
CN F.FL.ALO.AFU.ALO.AFU.BUE.BZY

nomadic furniture
USE **portable furniture**

Nomads Age, Early
USE **Early Nomads Age**

nominalism
BM.517 (L,R)
SN Theory that there are no universal essences in reality, that the mind can frame no single concept or image corresponding to any universal or general term, and that only individual concrete entities have existence. (WCOL)
CN B.BM.BIQ.AXC.DCU

non-flam film
USE **safety film**

nonabrasion layer
USE **supercoat**

nonbearing walls
RT.584
ALT **nonbearing wall**
SN Walls which support no vertical load except that of their own weight. (PUTNAM)
UF walls, nonbearing
CN V.RT.AFU.AFU.AFU.BIQ.BUE.AFU.ALO.ARI

nonbook materials
USE **audiovisual materials**

noncombustible materials
USE **fire-resistant materials**

nonconformist art
USE **dissident art**

nonconformists
USE **dissenters**

nondrying oil
MT.2031
UF oil, nondrying
CN M.MT.AFU.AFU.ARI.ARI.AXC.ARI

nonferrous alloys
MT.362 (L)
UF alloys, nonferrous
CN M.MT.AFU.AFU.AFU.BZY.AFU.AFU.AFU.ALO

nonferrous metals
MT.428 (L,B)
SN Metallic materials that do not have iron as their major ingredient. (MH12)
UF metals, nonferrous
CN M.MT.AFU.AFU.AFU.BZY.AFU.AFU.ARI

nonfiction
BM.276 (L)
SN Prose works dealing with or offering opinions or conjectures upon facts and realities. (RHDEL2)
CN B.BM.AFU.ARI.BIQ.BOK

nonfigurative art
USE **nonrepresentational art**

nonimpact printers
TB.170 (L)
ALT **nonimpact printer**
SN Printers in which the image is formed without use of mechanical impact. (DOC)
UF printers, nonimpact
CN V.TB.AFU.ARI.BCW.AXC.AXC.ALO.ARI.ALO

nonleaking roofing nails
USE **lead-capped nails**

nonmanual workers
USE **white collar workers**

Nonobjective
FL.3290 (L)
ALT **Nonobjectivism**
SN Use with reference to 20th-century art; in other contexts use **nonrepresentational art.**
CN F.FL.ALO.BCW.ALO.AXC.DCU.AFU.AFU

nonpedigreed architecture
USE **vernacular architecture**

nonprint materials
USE **audiovisual materials**
visual materials

nonreflective glass
MT.279
UF glass, nonreflective
CN M.MT.AFU.AFU.AFU.BIQ.AFU.AXC.BOK

nonrepresentational art
BM.249
SN Art which presents a visual form with no specific reference to anything outside itself.(PREBLE) With regard to 20th-century art, use **Nonobjective.**
UF art, nonfigurative
art, nonrepresentational
nonfigurative art
CN B.BM.AFU.ARI.BCW.ELK

nonrigid structures
RT.10
ALT **nonrigid structure**
SN Structures whose shape changes with

changes in the loading condition. (DS)
UF flexible structures
structures, flexible
structures, nonrigid
CN V.RT.AFU.AFU.AFU.AFU.ALO.ALO

nonshattering glass
USE **safety glass**

Nonsuch chests
TG.467
ALT Nonsuch chest
SN Chests richly decorated with marquetry patterns of arches and fantastic architecture, reminiscent of Henry VIII's (vanished) palace of Nonsuch; the appellation means unequalled. Probably made in North Germany, or by 16th-century German craftsmen who settled in London. (BEARD)
UF Baltic chests
chests, Baltic
chests, Nonsuch
CN V.TG.AFU.AFU.AXC.ALO.AXC. DUC

nonwoody plants
RD.258
ALT nonwoody plant
UF plants, nonwoody
CN V.RD.ARI.AFU.BCW.ALO.ALO.AFU

nook shafts
RT.111
ALT nook shaft
SN Use for columns set within angles formed by the features of a building, as where the jamb of a doorway meets the external face of a wall.
UF shafts, nook
CN V.RT.AFU.AFU.AFU.AXC.BIQ.
AFU.ALO.BZY

nook type hangers
TF.375
ALT nook type hanger
UF hangers, nook type
CN V.TF.AFU.AFU.AFU.ALO.AFU.
BOK.ARI.ARI.AXC.ALO.AXC

nooks
USE **alcoves**

nooks, breakfast
USE **breakfast nooks**

Nootka
FL.1352 (L)
UF Aht
Nutka
CN F.FL.ALO.ALO.ARI.AFU.BIQ.EFQ

Nor School
USE **Sakya School**

normal butyl acetate
USE **butyl acetate**

normal butyl alcohol
USE **butanol**

normal forces
USE **axial stress**

normal lenses
USE **standard lenses**

normal portland cement
USE **standard portland cement**

normal schools
USE **teachers colleges**

normal-weight concrete
MT.228
SN Concrete having a unit weight of approximately 150 pounds per cubic foot, made with aggregates of normal weight. (DAC)
UF concrete, normal-weight
CN M.MT.AFU.AFU.AFU.BCW.AFU.
AXC.BIQ

Norman
FL.3137 (A,L,B,R)
CN F.FL.ALO.BCW.ALO.ALO.AFU.
BOK.ARI.BIQ.AFU

Norman brick
MT.80
SN Brick whose nominal dimensions are 2 2/3 by 4 by 12 inches. (PCMC)
UF brick, Norman
CN M.MT.AFU.AFU.AFU.AXC.ALO.
AFU.AFU.AFU.CFS

Norman Revival
FL.3276 (A,R)
UF Neo-Norman
Revival, Norman
CN F.FL.ALO.BCW.ALO.AXC.CLM.
CLM.AFU

north
DC.47
CN D.DC.AFU.ALO.AXC.ALO

North Alaskan Eskimo
USE **Inupiaq**

North American
FL.712 (B)
UF American, North
CN F.FL.ALO.ALO.AFU.ARI

North American, Colonial
USE **American Colonial**

North Carolina pine
USE **shortleaf pine**

North River bluestone
MT.711
UF bluestone, North River
CN M.MT.AFU.AFU.AFU.DCU.AFU.
ALO.AFU.ARI.AFU.ALO.AFU.AFU.
ALO

North Syrian
USE **Neo-Hittite**

northeast
DC.48
CN D.DC.AFU.ALO.AXC.ARI

Northern and Southern Courts
USE **Nambokucho**

Northern and Southern Dynasties
FL.1868
UF Southern and Northern Dynasties
CN F.FL.ALO.ARI.ALO.AFU.AFU.
ALO.BUE.AFU

Northern Archaic
FL.809
UF Archaic, Northern
CN F.FL.ALO.ALO.ALO.AFU.ALO.
AFU.ALO.ALO.ALO.BCW

Northern Ch'i
USE **Northern Qi**

Northern Cheyenne
FL.1377
UF Cheyenne, Northern
CN F.FL.ALO.ALO.ARI.AFU.BOK.
BIQ.AFU

Northern Chou
USE **Northern Zhou**

Northern Diaguita
USE **Santa Maria (pottery style)**

Northern Dynasties
FL.1869 (L)
CN F.FL.ALO.ARI.ALO.AFU.AFU.
ALO.BUE.AFU.AFU

Northern Luba
USE **Buli**

Northern Ojibwa
USE **Saulteaux**

Northern Paiute
FL.1314
UF Paiute, Northern
Paviotso
CN F.FL.ALO.ALO.ARI.AFU.AXC.BOK

northern pine
USE **Scotch pine**

Northern Qi
FL.1873
UF Ch'i, Northern
Northern Ch'i
Qi, Northern
CN F.FL.ALO.ARI.ALO.AFU.AFU.
ALO.BUE.AFU.AFU.ALO

Northern School
FL.1934
CN F.FL.ALO.ARI.ALO.AFU.AFU.AXC.
ALO.BZY

Northern Song
FL.1894
UF Northern Sung
Song, Northern
Sung, Northern
CN F.FL.ALO.ARI.ALO.AFU.AFU.
ALO.CXA.AFU

Northern Sung
USE **Northern Song**

Northern Thai
FL.2413
UF Chiengsen
Lan Na
Lanna
Thai, Northern
CN F.FL.ALO.ARI.BCW.BOK.AFU.BUE

Northern Wei
FL.1870 (L)
UF Wei, Northern
CN F.FL.ALO.ARI.ALO.AFU.AFU.
ALO.BUE.AFU.AFU.AFU

northern white pine
MT.1381
UF New England pine
pine, New England
pine, northern white
pine, Weymouth
Pinus alba
Pinus strobus
Weymouth pine
white pine, northern
CN M.MT.AFU.AFU.ALO.BIQ.DCU
.AFU.AFU.ALO.CXA.CLM

Northern Zhou
FL.1874
UF Chou, Northern
Northern Chou
Zhou, Northern
CN F.FL.ALO.ARI.ALO.AFU.AFU.
ALO.BUE.AFU.AFU.ARI

northlight roofs
USE **sawtooth roofs**

northwest
DC.49
CN D.DC.AFU.ALO.AXC.AXC

Norton
FL.800
CN F.FL.ALO.ALO.ALO.AFU.ALO.
AFU.ALO.ALO.AFU.ARI

Norton-Hopewell
FL.820
CN F.FL.ALO.ALO.ALO.AFU.ALO.
ALO.AFU.BOK

Norway pine
MT.1382 (L)
UF pine, Norway
pine, red (Norway pine)
Pinus resinosa
red pine (Norway pine)
CN M.MT.AFU.AFU.ALO.BIQ.DCU.
AFU.AFU.ALO.CXA.CRG

Norway spruce
MT.1401 (L)
UF fir, spruce (Norway spruce)
fir, white (Norway spruce)
Picea abies
Picea glauca
spruce fir (Norway spruce)
spruce, Norway
spruce, white (Norway spruce)
white fir (Norway spruce)
white spruce (Norway spruce)
CN M.MT.AFU.AFU.ALO.BIQ.DCU.
AFU.AFU.ALO.DOI.BCW

Norwegian
FL.3060 (L,B)
CN F.FL.ALO.BCW.AFU.DUC.ARI

nose augers
TB.825 (N)
ALT **nose auger**
SN Long augers whose end terminates in a notched spoon blade with one projection sharpened to form a nose, and the other projection bent upward to clear and hold the shavings from the hole. (HUMMEL)
UF augers, downcutting
augers, nose
augers, pipe
augers, shell (nose augers)
downcutting augers
pipe augers
shell augers (nose augers)
CN V.TB.AFU.BCW.CFS.ALO.AFU.
ALO.AXC

nose bits
TB.1108 (N)
ALT **nose bit**
SN Bits with a projecting lip or notched blade which allows wood shavings to accumulate in the spoon or hollow portion of the bit. (HUMMEL)
UF bits, nose
bits, wimble
wimble bits
CN V.TB.ALO.ARI.CFS

nosing molding planes
USE **nosing planes**

nosing planes
TB.959 (N)
ALT **nosing plane**
SN Planes used to cut a semicircular convex profile on the edge of the wood, such as a stair tread or a window board. (SALAM)
UF molding planes, nosing
nosing molding planes
nosing planes, stair
nosing planes, step
planes, nosing
planes, nosing molding
planes, stair nosing
planes, step nosing
stair nosing planes
step nosing planes
CN V.TB.AFU.BCW.CFS.ALO.AFU.
DUC.AXC.AFU.BOK

nosing planes, stair
USE **nosing planes**

nosing planes, step
USE **nosing planes**

nosings
RT.1121 (B)
ALT **nosing**
SN The overhanging edges, usually half-rounds, of the tread of a step. (PDARC)
CN V.RT.AFU.BIQ.AXC.ALO.BIQ.
ALO.AFU

notarial documents
VW.1058
ALT **notarial document**
UF documents, notarial
notarial records
records, notarial
CN V.VW.AFU.ARI.ALO.BZY.AFU

notarial records
USE **notarial documents**

notaries
HG.669 (L,R)
ALT **notary**
UF notaries public
public, notaries
CN H.HG.AFU.AXC.CFS.BUE

notaries public
USE **notaries**

notations
USE **annotations**

notchboards
USE **open strings**

notching saws
USE **stairbuilder's saws**

notebooks
VW.513 (N,R)
ALT **notebook**
SN Books in which notes or memorandums are recorded, such as are used for taking notes during a class, lecture, or meeting. (GAHLM)
CN V.VW.AFU.ALO.AFU.AFU.AFU. CLM

notebooks, laboratory
USE **laboratory notebooks**

notes
VW.62 (N)
ALT **note**
SN Use for brief statements of a fact or experience, written down for review, or as an aid to memory, or to inform someone else; also includes short, informal letters. (ICA)
CN V.VW.AFU.AFU.AFU.DZW

notes, biographical
USE **biographies**

notes, circular
USE **letters of credit**

notes, field
USE **field notes**

notes, laboratory
USE **laboratory notes**

notes, lecture

USE **lecture notes**

notes, marginal
USE **marginalia**

notes, side
USE **marginalia**

Nothofagus fusca
USE **red beech**

Nothofagus solandri
USE **New Zealand beech**

notices
USE **announcements**

notices, death
USE **obituaries**

notices, legal
USE **legal notices**

notices, press
USE **press releases**

Nottingham white
USE **white lead**

Nouveau Réaliste
USE **New Realist**

nouveautés, magasins de
USE **magasins de nouveautés**

Nouvelle Figuration
USE **New Figuration**

Nouvelle Objectivité
USE **Neue Sachlichkeit**

Nsapo-Nsapo
FL.501
CN F.FL.ALO.AFU.AXC.ALO.ALO.
BCW.BOK.AFU

Ntlakyapamuk
USE **Thompson**

Ntomba
FL.534 (L)
UF Tomba
Tumba
CN F.FL.ALO.AFU.AXC.ALO.ALO.
BIQ.ALO.BZY

Nuba
FL.627 (L)
CN F.FL.ALO.AFU.AXC.AXC.ARI.CLM

Nubian
FL.155 (A,L,R)
CN F.FL.ALO.AFU.ALO.AXC.AXC

Nubian Dynasty
USE **Twenty-fifth Dynasty**

nuclear bomb shelters
RM.144 (A,L,B)
ALT **nuclear bomb shelter**
UF atomic bomb shelters
fallout shelters
radiation shelters
shelters, atomic bomb
shelters, fallout
shelters, nuclear bomb
shelters, radiation
CN V.RM.AFU.DIO.ALO.BZY.AFU.AFU

nuclear engineers
HG.643
ALT **nuclear engineer**
UF engineers, nuclear
CN H.HG.AFU.AXC.BZY.BCW.CRG

nuclear physics
KD.289 (L)
UF physics, nuclear
CN K.KD.AFU.ARI.CLM.AXC.BOK

nuclear pollution
USE **radioactive pollution**

nuclear power
BM.876 (L)
UF atomic energy
energy, atomic
power, nuclear
CN B.BM.CFS.AXC.ALO.ALO.ARI.ARI

nuclear power plants
RG.118 (A,L,N,B)
ALT **nuclear power plant**
UF atomic power plants
atomic power stations
N-power plants
plants, N-power
plants, nuclear power
power plants, atomic
power plants, nuclear
CN V.RG.AFU.AFU.BUE.ARI.AXC.ARI

nuclear reactors
TB.393 (L,B)
ALT **nuclear reactor**
SN Apparatuses in which a chain reaction of fissionable material is initiated and controlled as for generation of heat for power or for the production of plutonium from uranium. (W)
UF atomic furnaces
atomic piles
furnaces, atomic
piles (nuclear reactors)
piles, atomic
reactors, nuclear
CN V.TB.AFU.ARI.DOI.BCW

nuclear test sites
RG.215 (A)
ALT **nuclear test site**
SN Use for the locations where nuclear devices are experimentally exploded.
UF atomic test sites
sites, nuclear test
test sites, atomic
test sites, nuclear
CN V.RG.AFU.AFU.DZW.BIQ.AFU

nuclear war
BM.1122 (L,R)
UF war, nuclear
CN B.BM.CRG.BCW.CLM.ARI.ARI

nudist camps
RG.158 (L)
ALT **nudist camp**
UF camps, nudist
CN V.RG.AFU.AFU.DOI.AXC.ALO

Ñuiñe
FL.1062
CN F.FL.ALO.ALO.ALO.ALO.AFU.
ALO.AXC.ALO.ALO

Nukleet
FL.807
CN F.FL.ALO.ALO.ALO.AFU.ALO.
AFU.ALO.ALO.ALO.ARI.AFU

nulled decoration
USE **gadrooning**

nulling
USE **gadrooning**

number plates
TF.21
ALT **number plate**
UF plates, number
CN V.TF.AFU.AFU.AFU.AFU.AFU.CFS.
BCW

number symbolism
BM.15 (L,R)
SN Use for the practice of referring to intangible or religious concepts through architectural proportion or repetition of forms in works of art.
UF numbers, symbolic
numerology
symbolic numbers
symbolism of numbers
symbolism, number
CN B.BM.AFU.AFU.AFU.BZY.ALO

numbers
BM.815 (L)
CN B.BM.CFS.ARI.BUE

numbers, Fibonacci
USE **Fibonacci numbers**

numbers, symbolic
USE **number symbolism**

numerology
USE **number symbolism**

Numidian
FL.170
CN F.FL.ALO.AFU.ALO.BCW.ALO

Numidian marble
MT.812
UF giallo antico
jaune antique dore
marble, Numidian
marmor Numidicum
CN M.MT.AFU.AFU.AFU.DCU.AFU.
ARI.ARI.ARI.BIQ.BZY

Numipu
USE **Nez Percé**

numismatic museums
RK.409 (L)

ALT **numismatic museum**
UF museums, numismatic
CN V.RK.AFU.ALO.ALO.BCW.AXC.ARI.BOK

numismatics
KD.152 (L,R)
SN Study of coins, tokens, medals, paper money, and objects closely resembling them in form or purpose. (W)
CN K.KD.AFU.ALO.CLM.ALO.BCW

numismatists
HG.272 (L)
ALT **numismatist**
CN H.HG.AFU.AXC.BCW.AFU.BOK.ALO.AXC

Nuna
USE **Nunuma**

Nunatsiaqmiut
USE **Baffin Island Inuit**

nunneries
USE **convents**

nuns
HG.242 (L,R)
ALT **nun**
CN H.HG.AFU.AXC.AXC.BIQ.AFU.BUE.ALO

Nunuma
FL.360 (L)
UF Nuna
CN F.FL.ALO.AFU.AXC.AFU.AXC.AFU.CLM

Nuovo Design
FL.3711 (R)
CN F.FL.ALO.BUE.ALO.BIQ

Nupe
FL.218 (L)
CN F.FL.ALO.AFU.AXC.AFU.AFU.ALO.ALO.CLM

nuraghi
RK.869 (A,L)
ALT **nuraghe**
SN Use for ancient Sardinian large, towerlike structures, generally associated with villages, built on hilltops, and having tapering sides and corbel-vaulted interior spaces.
CN V.RK.AFU.ALO.ALO.DIO.ALO.AXC.AFU.ALO

Nürnburg violet
USE **manganese violet**

Nurpur
FL.2283
CN F.FL.ALO.ARI.AXC.ALO.AFU.BZY.BCW.ARI.CXA

nurseries (horticulture)
RK.70 (A,L,B)
ALT **nursery (horticulture)**
SN Horticultural facilities where trees, shrubs, and plants are grown for sale and transplanting elsewhere or for use as stocks for budding or grafting.
CN V.RK.AFU.ALO.ALO.AFU.AFU.BOK.ARI

nurseries (rooms)
RM.392 (A,L,B)
ALT **nursery (room)**
UF children's nurseries
nurseries, children's
CN V.RM.AFU.DIO.BCW.AXC

nurseries, children's
USE **nurseries (rooms)**

nurseries, day
USE **day care centers**

nurseries, night
USE **night nurseries**

nursery farmers
USE **nurserymen**

nursery growers
USE **nurserymen**

nursery managers
USE **nurserymen**

nursery school education
USE **early childhood education**
preschool education

nursery schools
RK.835 (A,L,B)
ALT **nursery school**
UF infant schools
schools, infant
schools, nursery
CN V.RK.AFU.ALO.ALO.CXA.ARI.AXC.AFU.ARI

nurserymen
HG.365 (L)
ALT **nurseryman**
SN Persons who own or direct plant nurseries.
UF farmers, nursery
growers, nursery
managers, nursery
nursery farmers
nursery growers
nursery managers
nurserywomen
CN H.HG.AFU.AXC.BIQ.ALO.AXC.AFU.ARI.AFU

nurserywomen
USE **nurserymen**

nurses
HG.385 (L)
ALT **nurse**
CN H.HG.AFU.AXC.BIQ.ALO.BCW.BCW

nurses' residences
RK.224 (B)
ALT **nurses' residence**
UF residences, nurses'
CN V.RK.AFU.ALO.ALO.AXC.AFU.BOK

nurses' stations
RM.296
ALT **nurses' station**
UF stations, nurses'
CN V.RM.AFU.DIO.AXC.AFU.BIQ

nursing
KD.241 (L)
CN K.KD.AFU.ARI.BUE.ARI.AFU

nursing chairs
TG.188
ALT **nursing chair**
SN Low-seated chairs, with the seats between 13 and 15 inches high, without arms.
UF chairs, nursing
CN V.TG.AFU.AFU.ALO.AFU.AFU.ALO.DCU

nursing homes
RK.750 (A,L,B,R)
ALT **nursing home**
UF homes, nursing
CN V.RK.AFU.ALO.ALO.CXA.ALO.AFU.AXC.AFU

nursing schools
RK.815 (A,L,B)
ALT **nursing school**
UF hospital-training schools
nursing, schools of
schools of nursing
schools, hospital-training
schools, nursing
CN V.RK.AFU.ALO.ALO.CXA.ARI.ALO.CRG

nursing, schools of
USE **nursing schools**

nut
MT.1041 (L)
CN M.MT.AFU.AFU.ALO.BIQ.BOK

nut inserts
TF.383
ALT **nut insert**
UF inserts, nut
CN V.TF.AFU.AFU.AFU.ALO.AFU.BZY.BIQ

Nutka
USE **Nootka**

nuts
TF.450 (L,N)
ALT **nut**
SN Short metal blocks each having a threaded hole in the center for receiving a bolt or threaded rod. (MEANS)
CN V.TF.AFU.AFU.AFU.ALO.AFU.CLM

nuts, adjusting
USE **adjusting nuts**

nuts, back
USE **back nuts**

nuts, lock
USE **locknuts**

nuts, wing
USE **wing nuts**

Nyakyusa
FL.667 (L)
CN F.FL.ALO.AFU.AXC.AXC.BIQ.CFS

Nyamwanga
FL.589
CN F.FL.ALO.AFU.AXC.AXC.AFU.BOK

Nyamwezi
FL.590 (L)
CN F.FL.ALO.AFU.AXC.AXC.AFU.BUE

Nyanja
FL.668 (L)
CN F.FL.ALO.AFU.AXC.AXC.BIQ.CLM

Nyankole
USE **Nkole**

Nyaturu
USE **Turu**

Nyika
USE **Mijikenda**

nylon
MT.2141 (L,B)
UF PA
polyamide
polyamide resin
resin, polyamide
CN M.MT.AFU.AFU.ARI.BUE.ALO.
AXC.AFU.CFS.AFU

nymphaea
RK.1337 (A,L,R)
ALT **nymphaeum**
SN Spaces or structures with fountains embellished with statues, pools, or plants and used for relaxation.
CN V.RK.AFU.ALO.ARI.AFU.BIQ

Nyoro
FL.686 (L)
UF Banyoro
CN F.FL.ALO.AFU.AXC.AXC.BOK.DCU

Nyssa aquatica
USE **tupelo**

Nyssa biflora
USE **swamp tupelo**

Nyssa ogeche
USE **ogeche tupelo**

Nyssa sylvatica
USE **black gum**

Nzebi
FL.404 (L)
UF Banjabi
Ndjabi
CN F.FL.ALO.AFU.AXC.ALO.AFU.
ALO.BCW

oak
MT.1228 (L,R)
UF Quercus
CN M.MT.AFU.AFU.ALO.BIQ.DCU.
AFU.AFU.AFU.IRA

oak, aleppo
USE **aleppo oak**

oak, Austrian
USE **Austrian oak**

oak, black
USE **black oak**

oak, British
USE **English oak**

oak, bur
USE **bur oak**

oak, California black
USE **California black oak**

oak, California live
USE **coast live oak**

oak, California white
USE **California white oak**

oak, chestnut
USE **chestnut oak**

oak, chinkapin
USE **chinquapin oak**

oak, chinquapin
USE **chinquapin oak**

oak, coast live
USE **coast live oak**

oak, durmast
USE **durmast oak**

oak, English
USE **English oak**

oak, European turkey
USE **European turkey oak**

oak, Indian
USE **teak**

oak, laurel
USE **laurel oak**

oak, live
USE **live oak**

oak, mossy-cup
USE **bur oak**

oak, Oregon
USE **western white oak**

oak, Oregon white
USE **western white oak**

oak, overcup
USE **overcup oak**

oak, pin
USE **pin oak**

oak, post
USE **post oak**

oak, red
USE **red oak**

oak, scarlet
USE **scarlet oak**

oak, schneck
USE **southern red oak**

oak, sessile
USE **sessile oak**

oak, shumard
USE **shumard oak**

oak, southern red
USE **southern red oak**

oak, swamp
USE **pin oak**

oak, swamp white
USE **swamp white oak**

oak, Texas
USE **southern red oak**

oak, valley
USE **California white oak**

oak, valonia
USE **valonia oak**

oak, western white
USE **western white oak**

oak, white
USE **white oak**

oakum
MT.2653 (L)
SN Loosely twisted hemp or jute fiber impregnated with tar or a tar derivative and used in caulking seams (as of wooden ships) and packing joints (as of pipes). (WCOL)
CN M.MT.AFU.ARI.HTY.AFU.ARI

oases
RD.291 (L)
ALT **oasis**
CN V.RD.ARI.ALO.ALO.AFU

oasthouses
USE **malthouses**

oaths
VW.477 (L,R)
ALT **oath**
SN Any forms of attestation by which persons signify that they are bound in conscience to perform an act faithfully and truthfully;(BLACKS) also affirmations of the truth of a statement given before testifying, as in a court of law.
CN V.VW.AFU.AFU.ALO.FZU.ALO

Oaxacan
FL.1050 (L)
CN F.FL.ALO.ALO.ALO.ALO.AFU.
ALO.AXC

Oba

FL.3675
UF Aoba
Omba
CN F.FL.ALO.BOK.ALO.BUE.AXC

obelisks
RK.902 (A,L,N,B,R)
ALT **obelisk**
SN Use for tall, slender, four-sided, usually monolithic stone shafts which taper upward and end in a pyramidal tip.
UF guglias
CN V.RK.AFU.ALO.ALO.DOI.AFU.BIQ.ALO

Obion
FL.848
CN F.FL.ALO.ALO.ALO.AFU.ALO.ALO.ARI.ALO.AXC

obituaries
VW.371 (L,R)
ALT **obituary**
SN Published notices of a death, usually with a brief biography of the deceased. (AHD)
UF death notices
notices, death
CN V.VW.AFU.AFU.ALO.DOI

objective art
USE **figurative art**

objects, art
USE **art objects**

objets d'art
USE **art objects**

objets de vertu
USE **art objects**

oblique arches
RT.271 (L)
ALT **oblique arch**
SN Use for arches with jambs that are not at right angles to the faces.
UF arches, oblique
arches, skew
skew arches
CN V.RT.AFU.AFU.AFU.BCW.AFU.AFU.AFU.FCS.AFU

oblique butt joints
USE **oblique joints**

oblique drawings
VD.13 (L)
ALT **oblique drawing**
SN Use for projection drawings in which parallel lines remain parallel; two spatial axes are parallel to the plane of projection (drawing surface); and the third is at an angle other than 90 degrees to the plane.
UF drawings, oblique
oblique-projection drawings
oblique projections
projections, oblique
CN V.VD.AFU.AFU.BIQ.AFU.ARI

oblique drawings, cabinet
USE **cabinet oblique drawings**

oblique drawings, cavalier
USE **cavalier oblique drawings**

oblique drawings, elevation
USE **elevation oblique drawings**

oblique drawings, facade
USE **elevation oblique drawings**

oblique drawings, general
USE **general oblique drawings**

oblique drawings, plan
USE **plan oblique drawings**

oblique joints
TF.581
ALT **oblique joint**
UF beveled butt joints
butt joints, beveled
butt joints, oblique
joints, beveled butt
joints, oblique
joints, oblique butt
oblique butt joints
CN V.TF.ALO.AFU.BOK.ALO

oblique perspectives
USE **three-point perspectives**

oblique projection
KT.284
SN Projection in which parallel projectors are oblique rather than perpendicular to the picture plane. (EW)
UF projection, oblique
CN K.KT.AFU.ALO.DUC.DCU.BOK.ALO.AFU.ARI

oblique-projection drawings
USE **oblique drawings**

oblique projections
USE **oblique drawings**

oblique sections
VD.73
ALT **oblique section**
SN Use for drawings of sections taken at angles other than 90 degrees to the axis of the structure or object.
UF sections, oblique
CN V.VD.AFU.AFU.BIQ.ALO.BIQ.BCW

oblique views
VB.27
ALT **oblique view**
UF angle views
diagonal views
views, angle
views, diagonal
views, oblique
CN V.VB.AFU.AFU.BOK.ALO.BUE

obscenity
BM.1110 (L,R)
CN B.BM.CRG.BCW.BCW

observation car elevators
RT.1308
ALT **observation car elevator**
UF elevators, observation car
CN V.RT.ALO.ALO.AFU.ARI.ALO.AFU.ALO

observation decks
RM.51
ALT **observation deck**
UF decks, observation
CN V.RM.AFU.DIO.AFU.BCW.AXC.AFU

observation towers
USE **watchtowers**

observatories
RK.1172 (L,B,R)
ALT **observatory**
CN V.RK.AFU.ALO.ALO.FIM.ALO.ALO

observatories, astronomical
USE **astronomical observatories**

observatories, meteorological
USE **meteorological stations**

obsidian
MT.628 (L)
UF glass, volcanic
volcanic glass
CN M.MT.AFU.AFU.AFU.DCU.AFU.AFU.ALO.ALO.ALO.AFU

obsidian hydration dating
KT.501 (L)
SN Method of dating by measuring, on an exposed surface of obsidian, the thickness of the hydration layer caused by the natural intake of water on that surface from the atmosphere. (HOLHZR)
UF dating, obsidian hydration
hydration ring dating
CN K.KT.AFU.ALO.EFQ.AFU.ARI

obsidian, Hawaiian
USE **tachylite**

obstacle courses
RG.175 (L)
ALT **obstacle course**
UF courses, obstacle
CN V.RG.AFU.AFU.DOI.CFS.AFU

obtuse angle arches
USE **drop arches**

obverse
DC.18
SN Use with reference to the front, top, or principal surface of a coin, medal, seal, or other two-sided object. Use **recto** to refer specifically to the principal side of a sheet of paper.
CN D.DC.AFU.ALO.ALO.BCW

occasional chairs
USE **side chairs**

occasional tables
TG.683
ALT **occasional table**

SN Small easily movable tables. (DDA)
UF faldyn tables
tables, faldyn
tables, occasional
CN V.TG.AFU.AFU.BIQ.BOK.AFU.BZY

occhio di pavone
MT.768
CN M.MT.AFU.AFU.AFU.DCU.AFU.ARI.ARI.ALO.BOK.AXC

occult sciences
KD.300 (L,R)
UF sciences, occult
CN K.KD.AFU.BIQ

occultism
BM.177 (L)
SN Includes references to or interest in hidden, mysterious, or supernatural powers, as manifested in all fields of human endeavor or creativity. Excludes occult sciences themselves.
CN B.BM.AFU.AFU.AXC.BIQ

occupancy permits
USE **certificates of occupancy**

occupancy, certificates of
USE **certificates of occupancy**

occupancy, joint
USE **joint occupancy**

occupational guidance
USE **vocational guidance**

Ocean Bay
FL.789
CN F.FL.ALO.ALO.ALO.AFU.ALO.AFU.AFU.AXC

ocean thermal energy conversion plants
RG.114 (L)
ALT **ocean thermal energy conversion plant**
SN Power plants producing electricity by utilizing temperature differentials between surface water heated by the sun and deep cold water pumped to the surface. (MHEST)
UF conversion plants, ocean thermal energy
energy conversion plants, ocean thermal
ocean thermal power plants
OTEC power plants
plants, ocean thermal energy conversion
power plants, ocean thermal
power plants, OTEC
thermal energy conversion plants, ocean
CN V.RG.AFU.AFU.BUE.ARI.ARI.AFU

ocean thermal power plants
USE **ocean thermal energy conversion plants**

oceanariums
USE **marine aquariums**

Oceanic
USE **Pacific**

oceanographers
HG.353 (L)
ALT **oceanographer**
CN H.HG.AFU.AXC.BIQ.AFU.AFU. DUC

oceanography
KD.277 (L)
UF marine science
science, marine
CN K.KD.AFU.ARI.CLM.ARI.BZY

oceans
RD.128 (L,B,R)
ALT **ocean**
SN The main water areas of the earth, lying in basins; for shallow salt water areas lying on the margins of continents, use **seas.**
CN V.RD.ARI.AFU.AFU.AFU.AFU.AFU.AFU

ocher
MT.575 (L)
SN Compact form of impure iron ore used for paint pigments and as a filler for linoleum; often containing compounds of barium or calcium. (MH12)
CN M.MT.AFU.AFU.AFU.CLM

ocher (color)
USE **brilliant orange yellow**
brilliant yellow
deep orange
light brown
light yellow
moderate orange
moderate orange yellow
moderate yellow
pale orange yellow
strong yellow
strong yellowish brown

ocher brown
USE **golden ocher**

ocher, blue
USE **blue ocher**

ocher, brown
USE **brown ocher**

ocher, burnt
USE **burnt ocher**

ocher, burnt (color)
USE **moderate reddish orange**

ocher, burnt Italian
USE **dark reddish orange**

ocher, chrome
USE **golden ocher**

ocher, dark
USE **light olive brown**

ocher, English
USE **moderate orange yellow**

ocher, French
USE **moderate orange yellow**

ocher, gold
USE **moderate orange**

ocher, golden
USE **golden ocher**

ocher, golden (color)
USE **moderate orange**

ocher, Italian
USE **yellow ocher**

ocher, light
USE **light ocher**

ocher, Oxford
USE **Oxford ocher**

ocher, plumbic
USE **massicot**

ocher, red
USE **red ocher**

ocher, red (color)
USE **moderate reddish brown**

ocher, Roman
USE **golden ocher**

ocher, spruce
USE **spruce ocher**

ocher, stone
USE **Oxford ocher**

ocher, transparent gold
USE **transparent gold ocher**

ocher, transparent gold (color)
USE **brownish orange**
strong yellowish brown

ocher, yellow
USE **yellow ocher**

ocher, yellow (color)
USE **dark orange yellow**
moderate orange yellow
strong orange yellow

Ochroma lagopus
USE **balsa wood**

Ocós
FL.1028
CN F.FL.ALO.ALO.ALO.ALO.AFU.ALO.ARI.AFU.ARI.AFU

ocote
USE **Cuban pine**

ocre brûlée
USE **burnt ocher**

ocre d'or
USE **golden ocher**

ocre jaune
USE **yellow ocher**

octagons

BM.783 (B)
ALT **octagonal**
CN B.BM.CFS.ARI.AXC.BCW.AFU.
BIQ.BCW

octastyle
DC.90
CN D.DC.AFU.ARI.ERE.BIQ.BOK

octopartite vaults
RT.528
ALT **octopartite vault**
SN Vaults divided into eight vaulting cells.
UF eight-part vaults
vaults, eight-part
vaults, octopartite
CN V.RT.AFU.AFU.AFU.BIQ. BOK.
AFU.AFU.AFU.AFU.AXC

Octopus Style
FL.2671
CN F.FL.ALO.AXC.ALO.AFU.ALO.
AXC.BCW.BOK

oculi
RT.903 (A)
ALT **oculus**
SN Use for small round or oval openings, such as windows in a wall or openings in the crown of a dome.
UF bull's-eye windows
roundels (windows)
windows, bull's-eye
CN V.RT.AFU.ARI.AFU.AFU.BCW

odea
RK.941
ALT **odeum**
SN Buildings or other roofed structures used for musical performances.
UF odeums
CN V.RK.AFU.ALO.ALO.EFQ.ARI.
BCW.ALO.ALO

odeums
USE **odea**

odorants
MT.2319
SN Any substances added to another to mask unpleasant odors, such as essential oil to paint.
CN M.MT.AFU.ARI.ALO.DOI

oeci
RM.278
ALT **oecus**
SN Use for large main rooms of ancient Greek houses and for similar rooms in ancient Roman houses, often used for dining.
CN V.RM.AFU.DIO.ARI.ALO.CRG

oeuvre
BM.299
SN The body of work of a given artist. (A-Z)
CN B.BM.AFU.AXC.CLM

oeuvre catalogues
USE **catalogues raisonnés**

offertory windows
USE **lowside windows**

office automation
BM.1139
UF automation, office
CN B.BM.CXA.ALO.AFU.AFU

office buildings
RK.911 (A,L,N,B,R)
ALT **office building**
UF buildings, office
CN V.RK.AFU.ALO.ALO.DZW

office buildings, administrative
USE **administration buildings**

office buildings, architects'
USE **architects' offices**

office buildings, government
USE **government office buildings**

office buildings, medical
USE **medical offices**

office calculators
USE **calculators**

office chairs
TG.178
ALT **office chair**
UF chairs, office
CN V.TG.AFU.AFU.ALO.AFU.AFU.
ALO.BUE.ALO

office complexes
RG.141 (A)
ALT **office complex**
UF complexes, office
CN V.RG.AFU.AFU.CXA

office files
VW.592
ALT **office file**
SN Use for records kept by public officials or other persons for their private or personal use but relating to their official duties. For private documents belonging to individuals, use **personal papers.**
UF files, office
CN V.VW.AFU.ALO.AFU.BIQ.ALO.
ALO

office locks
TF.236
ALT **office lock**
SN Locks usually having a latch bolt controlled from both sides by knobs, with the latch arranged to be set by stops so that the outside knob is inoperative and entrance is gained by key only.
UF locks, office
CN V.TF.AFU.AFU.AFU.AFU.DIO.BIQ.
ALO.ALO.BCW

office parks
RG.142 (A,B)
ALT **office park**
CN V.RG.AFU.AFU.CXA.AFU

office scretaries, Wooton cabinet
USE **Wooton cabinet office secretaries**

office secretaries, cabinet
USE **Wooton cabinet office secretaries**

office towers
RK.913
ALT **office tower**
UF towers, office
CN V.RK.AFU.ALO.ALO.DZW.AFU. AFU

office workers
USE **clerical workers**

officers' clubs
RK.873 (L)
ALT **officers' club**
UF clubs, officers'
CN V.RK.AFU.ALO.ALO.DIO.ARI.AFU

officers, cabinet
USE **cabinet officers**

officers, public
USE **public officers**

officers, security
USE **security guards**

offices
RM.232 (A,L,B)
ALT **office**
SN Use for the rooms where business, administrative, or professional activities are conducted.
CN V.RM.AFU.DIO.ALO.DOI.BZY

offices (outhouses)
USE **outhouses**

offices (privies)
USE **privies**

offices, architects'
USE **architects' offices**

offices, dental
USE **dental offices**

offices, doctors'
USE **medical offices**

offices, employment
USE **employment agencies**

offices, law
USE **law offices**

offices, legal
USE **law offices**

offices, medical
USE **medical offices**

offices, patent
USE **patent offices**

offices, physicians'
USE **medical offices**

offices, post

USE **post offices**

offices, publishing
USE **publishing offices**

offices, telegraph
USE **telegraph offices**

official architects
USE **government architects**

official documents
VW.1057
ALT **official document**
SN Records, in law, having the legally recognized and judicially enforceable quality of establishing some fact. (ICA)
UF documents, official
CN V.VW.AFU.ARI.ALO.BZY

official gazettes
USE **gazettes**

official records
USE **government records**

official reports
VW.458
ALT **official report**
UF reports, official
CN V.VW.AFU.AFU.ALO.FIM.ALO

official residences
RK.335 (A,B)
ALT **official residence**
UF residences, official
CN V.RK.AFU.ALO.ALO.AXC.ALO.BOK.BOK

officials
USE **public officers**

officials, government
USE **public officers**

officials, municipal
USE **public officers**

offset duplicating
USE **offset printing**

offset hinges
TF.123
ALT **offset hinge**
SN Hinges with one leaf offset forward or backward to account for an insetting or projecting door. (DITTRI)
UF hinges, offset
CN V.TF.AFU.AFU.AFU.AFU.CLM.AFU.EWY

offset lithography
USE **offset printing**

offset printing
KT.466 (L,R)
UF duplicating, offset
lithography, offset
offset duplicating
offset lithography
printing, offset
CN K.KT.AFU.ALO.DUC.DUC.ALO.BCW.ALO.ARI

offset pulls
TF.79
ALT **offset pull**
SN Pulls whose handles angle off to one side. Pulls offset to the right are used on right-hand doors and pulls offset to the left are used on left-hand doors. (DITTRI)
UF pulls, offset
CN V.TF.AFU.AFU.AFU.AFU.CFS.BCW.AFU.BZY

offset screwdrivers
TB.196
ALT **offset screwdriver**
SN Screwdrivers whose head is set at 90 degrees to its shaft. (MEANS)
UF screwdrivers, offset
CN V.TB.AFU.ARI.BOK.ALO.AFU

offset sections
VD.75
ALT **offset section**
SN Use for sections in which the cutting plane is jogged to expose additional important features.
UF sections, offset
CN V.VD.AFU.AFU.BIQ.ALO.BIQ.BIQ

offsets
USE **water tables**

offshore drilling platforms
RK.604
ALT **offshore drilling platform**
UF drilling platforms, offshore
petroleum production platforms
platforms, offshore drilling
platforms, petroleum production
CN V.RK.AFU.ALO.ALO.CLM.AFU.ALO

offshore drilling rigs
USE **offshore rigs**

offshore rigs
RK.602
ALT **offshore rig**
UF offshore drilling rigs
rigs, offshore
rigs, offshore drilling
CN V.RK.AFU.ALO.ALO.CLM.AFU.AFU.AFU

offshore structures
RK.1365 (L)
ALT **offshore structure**
SN Use only for structures built adjacent to the continental land masses and on the continental shelves, often located within the navigable areas of coastal waterways; use **marine structures** for construction built seaward of high-water lines of oceans, seas, or bays.
UF structures, offshore
CN V.RK.AFU.ALO.ARI.AXC.BIQ.AFU

offspring
HG.9
UF children (offspring)
CN H.HG.AFU.ALO.AFU

ogeche tupelo
MT.1160
UF Nyssa ogeche
sour tupelo
tupelo, ogeche
tupelo, sour
CN M.MT.AFU.AFU.ALO.BIQ.DCU.AFU.AFU.AFU.DIO.AXC.ARI.ALO

ogee arches
RT.235
ALT **ogee arch**
SN Pointed arches composed of reversed curves, the lower concave and the upper convex. (DAC)
UF arches, contrasted
arches, keel
arches, ogee
arches, ogival
contrasted arches
keel arches
ogival arches
CN V.RT.AFU.AFU.AFU.BCW.AFU.AFU.AFU.CRG.BCW

ogee bracket feet
TG.903
ALT **ogee bracket foot**
UF bracket feet, ogee
feet, ogee bracket
CN V.TG.ALO.DZW.AFU.AXC.ALO

ogee molding planes
USE **ogee planes**

ogee moldings
USE **cymas**

ogee moldings, reverse
USE **cyma reversas**

ogee pediments
RT.674
ALT **ogee pediment**
SN Pediments with a top in the form of two ogee curves.
UF pediments, ogee
CN V.RT.AFU.AFU.AFU.BIQ.BUE.ALO.ALO.BIQ.ALO

ogee planes
TB.965
ALT **ogee plane**
SN Planes with the profile of ogee molding. (SALAM)
UF molding planes, ogee
ogee molding planes
planes, ogee
planes, ogee molding
CN V.TB.AFU.BCW.CFS.ALO.AFU.DUC.AXC.ALO.AXC

ogee roofs
RT.419
ALT **ogee roof**
SN Roofs whose section is an ogee. (DAC)
UF roofs, ogee

CN V.RT.AFU.AFU.AFU.BIQ.ARI.AFU.
AFU.AFU.BIQ

Ogiek
USE **Dorobo**

Ogiso period
USE **Early Benin**

ogival arches
USE **ogee arches**

ogives
USE **diagonal ribs**

Ogoni
FL.245 (L)
CN F.FL.ALO.AFU.AXC.AFU.ALO.
AFU.BOK

Ohio buckeye
MT.1090
UF buckeye, Ohio
CN M.MT.AFU.AFU.ALO.BIQ.DCU.
AFU.AFU.AFU.AFU.AFU.ARI

oikos ekklesias
USE **domus ecclesiae**

oil
MT.1981 (L,B)
SN Lightly viscous, neutral combustible fatty substances, usually liquid or easily liquifiable on warming, that are insoluble in water and leave a greasy stain on paper or cloth.
CN M.MT.AFU.AFU.ARI.ARI

oil asphalt
USE **petroleum asphalt**

oil black
USE **carbon black**

oil-burning power plants
USE **oil-fired power plants**

oil color
USE **oil paint**

oil fields
RG.105 (L)
ALT **oil field**
UF fields, oil
CN V.RG.AFU.AFU.BUE.AFU.ARI

oil-fired power plants
RG.119
ALT **oil-fired power plant**
UF oil-burning power plants
plants, oil-fired power
power plants, oil-fired
CN V.RG.AFU.AFU.BUE.ARI.AXC.AXC

oil furnaces
RT.1418
ALT **oil furnace**
UF furnaces, oil
CN V.RT.ALO.BCW.AFU.ALO.AFU.
AXC.AFU.ALO

oil green
USE **chrome green**

oil-in-water emulsion
MT.2494
SN A suspension of a resinous, oily, fatty, or waxy material in a watery material. (GOTTS)
UF emulsion, oil-in-water
CN M.MT.AFU.ARI.CRG.ALO.AFU.AFU

oil-modified alkyd
MT.2160
UF alkyd, oil-modified
CN M.MT.AFU.AFU.ARI.BUE.ALO.
AXC.ALO.AFU.AFU

oil of clove
USE **clove oil**

oil of lavender
USE **lavender oil**

oil of rosemary
USE **rosemary oil**

oil of spike lavender
USE **spike oil**

oil of turpentine
USE **turpentine**

oil paint
MT.2527
SN A paint in which a drying oil is the vehicle for the pigment. (DAC)
UF color, oil
oil color
paint, oil
CN M.MT.AFU.ARI.CRG.ALO.BCW.
AFU.AXC

oil photoprints
USE **oil prints**

oil pigment prints
USE **oil prints**

oil-pigment process
USE **oil processes**

oil prints
VJ.55
ALT **oil print**
UF oil photoprints
oil pigment prints
photoprints, oil
pigment prints, oil
prints, oil
CN V.VJ.AFU.AFU.ARI.ARI.AXC.BUE.
ARI

oil processes
KT.355
SN Use for a bichromate photographic process relying on the ability of an exposed emulsion that has been soaked in cold water to resist or accept greasy inks in relation to the amount of exposure. The original print may be the end product or may be used as a master for transferring the image to another support.
UF oil-pigment process
CN K.KT.AFU.ALO.DUC.DIO.ALO.
DIO.AFU.BCW

oil refineries
USE **petroleum refineries**

oil rigs
RK.603 (L,B)
ALT **oil rig**
UF rigs, oil
CN V.RK.AFU.ALO.ALO.CLM.AFU.
AFU.ALO

oil soluble dyes
MT.1545
UF dyes, oil soluble
soluble dyes, oil
CN M.MT.AFU.AFU.ARI.AFU.AFU.
AFU.ALO.AFU

oil stain
MT.2465
UF stain, oil
CN M.MT.AFU.ARI.CRG.AFU.BIQ.AFU

oil stones
TB.739 (N)
ALT **oil stone**
SN Natural or artificial stones covered with oil; used for sharpening blades such as plane irons or chisels. (W)
UF oilstones
stones, oil
CN V.TB.AFU.BCW.BIQ.ARI.ALO.
BZY.ALO

oil storage tanks
RK.1222 (L)
ALT **oil storage tank**
UF storage tanks, oil
tanks, oil storage
CN V.RK.AFU.ALO.ALO.GFO.BOK.ALO

oil tempera
MT.2522
SN Tempera in which the vehicle is made with a water-in-oil emulsion, instead of the more usual oil-in-water emulsion. (MAYER)
UF tempera, oil
CN M.MT.AFU.ARI.CRG.ALO.BCW.
AFU.ALO.ARI.AXC

oil varnish
MT.2482
SN Varnish containing a drying oil. (PUTNAM)
UF varnish, oil
CN M.MT.AFU.ARI.CRG.AFU.BOK.
ALO.AFU

oil wells
RK.592 (L)
ALT **oil well**
UF wells, oil
CN V.RK.AFU.ALO.ALO.CFS.ALO
.BCW.CXA.AFU.ALO

oil, almond
USE **almond oil**

oil, animal
USE **animal oil**

oil, arachis
USE **peanut oil**

oil, asphalt
USE **petroleum asphalt**

oil, black
USE **black oil**

oil, blown
USE **blown oil**

oil, bodied
USE **bodied oil**

oil, boiled
USE **boiled oil**

oil, boiled linseed
USE **boiled oil**

oil, candlenut
USE **candlenut oil**

oil, carbolic
USE **middle oil**

oil, castor
USE **castor oil**

oil, China wood
USE **tung oil**

oil, clove
USE **clove oil**

oil, coal
USE **kerosene**

oil, cold-pressed
USE **cold-pressed oil**

oil, corn
USE **maize oil**

oil, cottonseed
USE **cottonseed oil**

oil, croton
USE **croton oil**

oil, curcas
USE **curcas oil**

oil, cutting
USE **cutting oil**

oil, dead
USE **creosote**

oil, drying
USE **drying oil**

oil, essential
USE **essential oil**

oil, fish
USE **fish oil**

oil, form
USE **form oil**

oil, hempseed
USE **hempseed oil**

oil, jamba
USE **jamba oil**

oil, Japanese tung
USE **Japanese tung oil**

oil, kapok
USE **kapok oil**

oil, kernel
USE **kernel oil**

oil, lavender
USE **lavender oil**

oil, linseed
USE **linseed oil**

oil, lubricating
USE **lubricating oil**

oil, lumbang
USE **candlenut oil**

oil, maize
USE **maize oil**

oil, middle
USE **middle oil**

oil, mineral
USE **mineral oil**

oil, mustard
USE **mustard oil**

oil, nondrying
USE **nondrying oil**

oil, oiticica
USE **oiticica oil**

oil, olive
USE **olive oil**

oil, paint
USE **drying oil**

oil, peanut
USE **peanut oil**

oil, perilla
USE **perilla oil**

oil, pine
USE **pine oil**

oil, pitch
USE **creosote**

oil, plate
USE **litho varnish**

oil, polymerized
USE **stand oil**

oil, poppy
USE **poppy-seed oil**

oil, poppy-seed
USE **poppy-seed oil**

oil, rape
USE **rape oil**

oil, ravison
USE **ravison oil**

oil, raw
USE **raw oil**

oil, raw linseed
USE **raw linseed oil**

oil, rice
USE **rice oil**

oil, rosemary
USE **rosemary oil**

oil, safflower
USE **safflower oil**

oil, saponified
USE **saponified oil**

oil, semidrying
USE **semidrying oil**

oil, soyabean
USE **soybean oil**

oil, soybean
USE **soybean oil**

oil, spike
USE **spike oil**

oil, stand
USE **stand oil**

oil, strong
USE **strong oil**

oil, sun-thickened
USE **sun-thickened oil**

oil, sunflower
USE **sunflower oil**

oil, thin
USE **thin oil**

oil, tobacco seed
USE **tobacco seed oil**

oil, tung
USE **tung oil**

oil, vegetable
USE **vegetable oil**

oil, walnut
USE **walnut oil**

oilcloth
MT.1883 (L)
SN Fabrics of woven cotton, jute, or hemp, heavily coated with turpentine and resin compositions. (MH)
CN M.MT.AFU.AFU.ARI.ALO.ALO.ALO.ARI.AXC

oiling out
KT.232
SN Use for the process of rubbing oil into a painting, especially popular in the 18th and 19th centuries.
CN K.KT.AFU.ALO.DUC.CXA.ALO.AFU.CFS

oilite bearing hinges
TF.124
ALT **oilite bearing hinge**
SN Hinges equipped with oil-impregnated bearings between knuckles to reduce friction. (STEIN)
UF hinges, oilite bearing
CN V.TF.AFU.AFU.AFU.AFU.CLM.AFU.FCS

oillets
USE **loopholes**

oilstones
USE **oil stones**

oiticica oil
MT.2015 (L)
SN A drying oil obtained from the kernels of the fruit of the oiticica tree that is similar to tung oil; used chiefly in varnishes, paints, and printing inks. (W)
UF oil, oiticica
CN M.MT.AFU.AFU.ARI.ARI.AXC.AFU.BIQ

Ojibwa
FL.1329 (L,R)
UF Chippewa
CN F.FL.ALO.ALO.ARI.AFU.BCW.BOK

Ojibwa, Northern
USE **Saulteaux**

Ojibwa, Plains
USE **Plains Ojibwa**

Okanagan
FL.1418 (L)
UF Okinagan
CN F.FL.ALO.ALO.ARI.AFU.BUE.DCU

Okanda
USE **Kande**

Okiek
USE **Dorobo**

Okinagan
USE **Okanagan**

Okpella
FL.254
CN F.FL.ALO.AFU.AXC.AFU.ALO.ALO.BOK

Okunev
FL.2122
CN F.FL.ALO.ARI.ARI.AFU.ALO

old age homes
RK.751 (A,L,B,R)
ALT **old age home**
UF homes for the aged
homes, old age
homes, old peoples
old peoples homes
CN V.RK.AFU.ALO.ALO.CXA.ALO.AFU.AXC.ALO

Old Assyrian
FL.2978
UF Assyrian, Old
CN F.FL.ALO.AXC.ARI.BCW.AFU.BUE.AFU

Old Assyrian Colony period
USE **Assyrian Colony period**

Old Babylonian
FL.2972
UF Babylonian, Early
Babylonian, Old
Early Babylonian
CN F.FL.ALO.AXC.ARI.BCW.AFU.BIQ

Old Bering Sea
FL.810
UF Bering Sea, Old
CN F.FL.ALO.ALO.ALO.AFU.ALO.AFU.ALO.ALO.ALO.BIQ

Old Copper Culture
FL.821
UF Copper Culture, Old
CN F.FL.ALO.ALO.ALO.AFU.ALO.ALO.AFU.BUE

Old Cordilleran
FL.734
UF Cordilleran, Old
CN F.FL.ALO.ALO.ALO.AFU.AFU.ALO.ALO.ALO

Old Elamite
FL.3011
UF Ancient Elamite
Early Elamite
Elamite, Ancient
Elamite, Early
Elamite, Old
CN F.FL.ALO.AXC.ARI.BIQ.AFU.ALO.AFU

Old English
FL.3333
UF English, Old
Neo-Vernacular
Revival, Vernacular
Vernacular Revival
CN F.FL.ALO.BCW.ALO.AXC.DIO.ALO.BOK.ALO

Old French
USE **Rococo Revival**

old fustic
USE **fustic**

Old Gothic limestone
MT.696
UF limestone, Old Gothic
CN M.MT.AFU.AFU.AFU.DCU.AFU.ALO.AFU.ALO.ALO.ARI.AFU

Old Hittite Kingdom
FL.2855
UF Hittite Kingdom, Old
Hittite Old Kingdom
Old Hittite period
CN F.FL.ALO.AXC.ARI.AFU.AFU.ARI.AFU

Old Hittite period
USE **Old Hittite Kingdom**

Old Kingdom
FL.2787
UF Kingdom, Old
CN F.FL.ALO.AXC.ALO.ARI.AFU.ARI

Old Kutani
USE **Ko Kutani**

old master drawings
USE **master drawings**

Old Order Amish
USE **Amish**

Old Oyo
FL.112
UF Katunga
Oyo Ile
Oyo, Old
CN F.FL.ALO.AFU.ALO.AFU.BUE.CFS

Old Palace period
FL.2560
UF Early Palace period
Palace period, Old
CN F.FL.ALO.AXC.ALO.AFU.AFU.ALO.ARI.BCW

old people
USE **aged**

old peoples homes
USE **old age homes**

Old Seto
USE **Ko Seto**

Old Silla
FL.2110 (L)
UF Silla, Old
CN F.FL.ALO.ARI.ALO.ARI.AFU.ALO.AFU

Old Stone Age
USE **Paleolithic**

old towns
RG.294 (A)
ALT **old town**
SN Use for older, often historic, sections of cities or towns, generally distinguished from newer parts by clear boundaries and distinctive architecture.
UF altstadts
towns, old
vieilles villes
CN V.RG.ALO.ALO.BCW

Old Village
FL.849
UF Village, Old
CN F.FL.ALO.ALO.ALO.AFU.ALO.ALO.ARI.ALO.BCW

older persons
USE **aged**

Oldfield pine
USE **loblolly pine**

Oldowen
FL.50
UF Pebble culture
CN F.FL.ALO.AFU.AFU.ALO.AFU.
AFU.ALO

olea
USE **olive**

oleoresin
USE **balsam**

oleum lavandulae
USE **lavender oil**

oleum sassafras
MT.1308
UF Sassafras officinale
sassafras, oleum
CN M.MT.AFU.AFU.ALO.BIQ.DCU.
AFU.AFU.AFU.LIG.ALO

olive
MT.1257 (L)
UF olea
CN M.MT.AFU.AFU.ALO.BIQ.DCU.
AFU.AFU.AFU.IWU

olive (color)
DL.144
CN D.DL.AFU.AFU.BIQ

olive bistre
USE **light olive**
light olive brown
light olive gray

olive black
DL.153
UF black, olive
centroid color 114
CN D.DL.AFU.AFU.BIQ.BIQ

olive brown
DL.107
UF brown, olive
CN D.DL.AFU.AFU.AXC.BZY.ARI

olive brown, dark
USE **dark olive brown**

olive brown, moderate
USE **moderate olive brown**

olive drab
USE **dark olive**
grayish olive
olive gray

olive drab, light
USE **olive gray**

olive gray
DL.151
UF black brown
black, gray
brown, black
centroid color 113
dark olive gray
dark olive gray
dark putty
deep grayish olive
drab, light olive
drab, olive
ebony (color)
gray black
gray, dark olive
gray, iron
gray, olive
grayish olive, deep
iron gray
light olive drab
olive drab
olive drab, light
olive gray, dark
olive gray, dark
olive, deep grayish
putty, dark
CN D.DL.AFU.AFU.BIQ.BCW

olive gray, dark
USE **grayish olive**
grayish olive green
olive gray
olive gray

olive gray, deep
USE **light olive gray**

olive gray, light
USE **light olive gray**

olive gray, pale
USE **yellowish gray**

olive green
DL.205
UF green, olive
CN D.DL.AFU.AFU.BUE.DCU.ARI

olive green, bright
USE **light olive**
moderate olive
moderate olive green
moderate yellow green

olive green, dark
USE **dark olive green**

olive green, dark grayish
USE **dark grayish olive green**

olive green, deep
USE **deep olive green**

olive green, grayish
USE **grayish olive green**

olive green, light
USE **moderate yellow green**

olive green, moderate
USE **moderate olive green**

olive green, pale
USE **moderate yellow green**

olive green, strong
USE **strong olive green**

olive knuckle hinges
TF.101
ALT **olive knuckle hinge**
SN Hinges designed to show only the knuckle, which is shaped like an olive, when the door is closed. (BROWNL)
UF hinges, olive knuckle
knuckle hinges, olive
CN V.TF.AFU.AFU.AFU.AFU.CLM.
AFU.ARI.ALO.AFU.AFU

olive oil
MT.2037 (L)
UF oil, olive
CN M.MT.AFU.AFU.ARI.ARI.AXC.ARI.
BIQ

olive yellow
USE **dark greenish yellow**
dark yellow
deep greenish yellow
light olive
moderate greenish yellow
moderate olive
pale yellow

olive, black
USE **dark olive**

olive, bluish
USE **dark grayish olive green**
dark olive green
deep olive green
grayish olive green
moderate olive green
strong olive green

olive, brown
USE **light olive brown**

olive, brownish
USE **light olive brown**
moderate olive brown

olive, dark
USE **dark olive**

olive, dark grayish
USE **dark grayish olive**

olive, dark greenish
USE **grayish olive**
moderate olive

olive, deep
USE **grayish olive**
moderate olive

olive, deep grayish
USE **olive gray**

olive, dull brownish
USE **dark olive brown**

olive, grayish
USE **grayish olive**

olive, light
USE **light olive**

olive, light brownish
USE **light olive brown**

olive, light grayish
USE **light grayish olive**

olive, light yellowish

USE **dark greenish yellow**

olive, moderate
USE **moderate olive**

olive, pale
USE **light grayish olive**

olive, yellowish
USE **moderate olive**

olivine
MT.538 (L)
SN Translucent mineral, usually occurring in granular form and employed as a refractory. (MH12)
UF chrysolite
chrysolith
CN M.MT.AFU.AFU.AFU.CFS.AFU.FZU

Olmec
FL.1006 (L)
CN F.FL.ALO.ALO.ALO.ALO.AFU.ALO.ALO.ALO

olympia blue
USE **cobalt blue**

olympic villages
RG.85
ALT **olympic village**
UF villages, olympic
CN V.RG.AFU.AFU.BOK.BCW.AXC

Omagua
USE **Carijona**

Omaha
FL.1389 (L)
CN F.FL.ALO.ALO.ARI.AFU.BOK.DOI

Omayyad
USE **Umayyad**

Omba
USE **Oba**

ombre tables
TG.716
ALT **ombre table**
SN Small, three-sided tables, with pits in the top to hold counters. (GLOAG)
UF tables, ombre
CN V.TG.AFU.AFU.BIQ.BOK.ALO.AXC.ARI

Ometo
FL.628
CN F.FL.ALO.AFU.AXC.AXC.ARI.CRG

on-dols
RT.1163 (A)
ALT **on-dol**
SN Use for Korean heating systems employing warm air chambers or ducts beneath the floor; similar to Roman hypocausts.
UF ontols
CN V.RT.AFU.BOK.BCW

Ona
FL.1695 (L)
UF Aona
CN F.FL.ALO.ALO.ARI.ARI.BOK.BUE

one-centered arches
RT.266
ALT **one-centered arch**
SN Arches struck from a single center, such as semicircular, segmental, or horseshoe arches. (DAC)
UF arches, one-centered
arches, single-center
single-center arches
CN V.RT.AFU.AFU.AFU.BCW.AFU.AFU.AFU.EWY.AFU

one-direction spanning slabs
USE **one-way structural systems**

one-family houses
USE **single-family dwellings**

one-hand round shaves
USE **closed scorpers**

one-man crosscut saws
TB.1024
ALT **one-man crosscut saw**
SN Three to four foot long saws generally having plain teeth; used for sawing trees into logs. (BLACKB)
UF crosscut saws, one-man
saws, one-man crosscut
CN V.TB.AFU.BCW.CFS.ALO.AFU.EWY.BUE.ARI.AFU

one-point perspective
KT.274
UF central perspective
parallel perspective (one-point perspective)
perspective, central
perspective, one-point
perspective, parallel (one-point perspective)
CN K.KT.AFU.ALO.DUC.DCU.BIQ.AXC.AFU

one-point perspectives
VD.86
ALT **one-point perspective**
UF central perspectives
elevation perspectives
frontal perspectives
parallel perspectives
perspectives, central
perspectives, elevation
perspectives, frontal
perspectives, one-point
perspectives, parallel
CN V.VD.AFU.AFU.BIQ.ARI.BCW.ALO

one-story
USE **single-story**

one-turn stairs
RT.1090
ALT **one-turn stair**
SN Stairs which turn 360 degrees as they progress from the bottom to top.
UF full-turn stairs
stairs, full-turn
stairs, one-turn
CN V.RT.AFU.BIQ.AXC.AFU.AFU.BZY.AXC

one-way beam and slab systems
RT.27
ALT **one-way beam and slab system**
SN Use for one-way structural systems in which beams occur at intervals to provide additional strength.
UF beam-and-slab floor constructions
floor constructions, beam-and-slab
systems, one-way beam and slab
CN V.RT.AFU.AFU.AFU.ALO.ARI.ALO.AFU.AFU.AFU

one-way flat plate systems
USE **one-way solid slab systems**

one-way floor and roof systems
USE **one-way structural systems**

one-way joist systems
RT.28
ALT **one-way joist system**
SN One-way structural systems in which the slab is articulated with ribs or joists, closely spaced.
UF one-way pan joist systems
one-way ribbed floors
ribbed floors, one-way
systems, one-way joist
systems, one-way pan joist
CN V.RT.AFU.AFU.AFU.ALO.ARI.ALO.AFU.AFU.ALO

one-way pan joist systems
USE **one-way joist systems**

one-way ribbed floors
USE **one-way joist systems**

one way roads
USE **one way streets**

one-way solid slab systems
RT.29
ALT **one-way solid slab system**
SN Use for structural systems in which simple, unarticulated slabs span between two supporting elements.
UF flat plate systems, one-way
one-way flat plate systems
slabs, solid
solid slabs
systems, one-way flat plate
systems, one-way solid slab
CN V.RT.AFU.AFU.AFU.ALO.ARI.ALO.AFU.AFU.ARI

one way streets
RK.1538 (L,B)
ALT **one way street**
UF one way roads
roads, one way
streets, one way
CN V.RK.ALO.ALO.BIQ.ARI.AFU.ALO.ALO.AFU

one-way structural systems
RT.26
ALT **one-way structural system**

SN Use for structural systems based on concrete slabs in which loads are transferred in one direction only.
UF floor and roof systems, one-way
one-direction spanning slabs
one-way floor and roof systems
roof systems, one-way floor and
spanning slabs, one-direction
structural systems, one-way
systems, one-way structural
CN V.RT.AFU.AFU.AFU.ALO.ARI.
ALO.AFU.AFU

Oneida
FL.1295 (L)
CN F.FL.ALO.ALO.ARI.AFU.ARI.BCW.
ARI

Oneota
FL.842 (L)
CN F.FL.ALO.ALO.ALO.AFU.ALO.
ALO.ARI.AFU.CFS

onion domes
RT.393 (A,B)
ALT **onion dome**
SN Pointed bulbous domes common in Russia and Eastern Europe, especially on churches and church towers. (PDARC)
UF bulbous domes
domes, bulbous
domes, onion
domes, Turkish
Turkish domes
CN V.RT.AFU.AFU.AFU.BIQ.AFU.AFU.
AXC

onion feet
USE **bun feet**

onion pulls
TF.80
ALT **onion pull**
SN Hand-forged pulls mounted with plates resembling a sprouting onion. (DITTRI)
UF pulls, onion
CN V.TF.AFU.AFU.AFU.AFU.CFS.BCW.
AFU.CFS

onionskin paper
MT.1908
SN Lightweight, highly finished transparent writing paper made transparent by hydration of the pulp in beaters. (MH)
UF paper, onionskin
CN M.MT.AFU.AFU.ARI.ALO.ALO.
AXC.ALO.BCW

online catalogs
VW.101 (L)
ALT **online catalog**
UF catalogs, online
online public access catalogs
OPACs
CN V.VW.AFU.AFU.AFU.FZU.ALO.
AFU.BIQ

online database search services
USE **information retrieval services**

online information retrieval services
USE **information retrieval services**

online public access catalogs
USE **online catalogs**

online publishing
USE **electronic publishing**

online reference services
HG.870
ALT **online reference service**
SN Automated reference services which provide direct answers to users' queries, or provide direct access to electronically stored databases containing the needed information. For automated information services which provide data either directly or in the form of citations to data sources, use **information retrieval services.**
UF services, online reference
CN H.HG.ALO.DIO.AFU.AXC.AFU

online retrieval
USE **online searching**

online retrieval services
USE **information retrieval services**

online search services
USE **information retrieval services**

online searching
KG.96 (L)
SN Use for the activity of querying an database, online catalog, or other collection of machine-readable documents, artifacts, or their surrogates for items having one or more attributes defined by the searcher.
UF computer searching
database searching
online retrieval
retrieval, online
searching, database
searching, online
CN K.KG.AFU.AFU.AXC.CRG.ALO.
AFU.AFU

online vendors
HG.436
ALT **online vendor**
SN Entrepreneurs who make available a number of databases through their own computer systems. (DNIT)
UF database vendors
information vendors
vendors, database
vendors, information
vendors, online
CN H.HG.AFU.AXC.BOK.FUA.AFU

Onondaga
FL.1296 (L)
CN F.FL.ALO.ALO.ARI.AFU.ARI.BCW.
AXC

ontology
KD.70 (L)
SN Branch of metaphysics concerned with the nature and relations of being. (WCOL)
CN K.KD.AFU.AFU.BOK.BOK.ALO

ontols
USE **on-dols**

onyx
MT.548
SN A variety of chalcedony silica mineral differing from agate only in the straightness of the layers; usually white and black, or white and red. (MH)
CN M.MT.AFU.AFU.AFU.CFS.AFU.
GRC.AFU.ARI.AFU.ALO

onyx marble
MT.676 (L)
UF marble, onyx
Mexican onyx
onyx, Mexican
CN M.MT.AFU.AFU.AFU.DCU.AFU.
ALO.AFU.ALO.ALO.AFU.AFU.BCW.
AFU

onyx, Mexican
USE **onyx marble**

oolite
MT.732 (L)
SN Rock consisting of small round grains that are cemented together and consist usually of calcium carbonate, but are sometimes of silica or iron oxide. (W)
CN M.MT.AFU.AFU.AFU.DCU.AFU.
ALO.ALO.ALO

oolite, Bath
USE **Bath stone**

oolite, corallian
USE **coral limestone**

oolitic limestone
MT.662
SN Limestone containing many small, rounded particles, which are concentric layers of calcium carbonate deposits. (BCMTC)
UF limestone, oolitic
roestone
CN M.MT.AFU.AFU.AFU.DCU.AFU.
ALO.AFU.ALO.ALO.AFU.AFU.ALO

Op art
FL.3741 (L,R)
UF Abstract, Perceptual
art, Op
art, Optical
Optical
Optical art
Perceptual Abstract
CN F.FL.ALO.BUE.ARI.FUA

opacity
BM.971

ALT **opaque**
SN The quality or state of a body that renders it impervious to rays of light, not transparent. (OCA)
CN B.BM.CFS.AXC.BZY.BUE.ARI

OPACs
USE **online catalogs**

opal
MT.539 (L)
CN M.MT.AFU.AFU.AFU.CFS.AFU.GFO

opal glass
MT.280 (L)
UF glass, opal
glass, opalescent
opalescent glass
opaline
CN M.MT.AFU.AFU.AFU.BIQ.AFU .AXC.BUE

opalescence
BM.970
ALT **opalescent**
CN B.BM.CFS.AXC.BZY.BUE.ALO.AFU

opalescent glass
USE **opal glass**

opaline
USE **opal glass**

opaque microcopies
USE **microopaques**

opaque watercolor
USE **gouache**

opaque white pigment
MT.1727
UF pigment, opaque white
white pigment, opaque
CN M.MT.AFU.AFU.ARI.AFU.AFU. ALO.ALO.BOK.AFU

opaquers
HG.457
ALT **opaquer**
SN Persons who apply liquid to photographic negatives to cover blemishes, especially for making printing plates. (RHDEL2)
CN H.HG.AFU.AXC.BUE.ALO.CFS.BIQ

Opata
FL.1461 (L)
CN F.FL.ALO.ALO.ARI.AFU.CFS.BUE

open-air museums
RK.380 (A,L,B)
ALT **open-air museum**
UF museums, open-air
museums, outdoor
outdoor museums
CN V.RK.AFU.ALO.ALO.BCW.AXC. ALO.AFU

open-air restaurants
USE **outdoor cafés**

open-air theaters
RK.935 (L,B)
ALT **open-air theater**
UF outdoor theaters
theaters, open-air
theaters, outdoor
CN V.RK.AFU.ALO.ALO.EFQ.ARI. BCW.AFU.ARI

open-air zoos
RG.232 (L)
ALT **open-air zoo**
UF jungle zoos
outdoor zoos
zoos, jungle
zoos, open-air
zoos, outdoor
CN V.RG.AFU.AFU.ELK.ARI

open-arm chairs
USE **elbow chairs**

open arms
TG.813
ALT **open arm**
UF arms, open
CN V.TG.ALO.ALO.AFU.AFU.ARI

open composition
BM.54
UF composition, open
CN B.BM.AFU.AFU.ARI.AFU.BCW. AFU.ALO

open cornices
USE **open eaves**

open eaves
RT.462
SN Use for eaves with visible supporting members.
UF cornices, open
eaves, open
open cornices
CN V.RT.AFU.AFU.AFU.BIQ.ARI.ALO. AFU.ALO.AFU.ARI

open-end wrenches
TB.777 (N)
ALT **open-end wrench**
SN Wrenches whose jaws have a fixed width of opening at one or both ends of the handle. (W)
UF wrenches, open-end
CN V.TB.AFU.BCW.BIQ.AXC.ALO. BIQ.BIQ

open newel stairs
RT.1078
ALT **open newel stair**
SN Spiral stairs built around an opening rather than a newel. (RS)
UF stairs, open newel
CN V.RT.AFU.BIQ.AXC.AFU.AFU. BIQ.ARI

open pit saws
TB.1026
ALT **open pit saw**
SN Thick, long, taper-bladed, two-man instruments without a frame, with an upper handle and a lower adjustable handle;(MERCER) used for cutting boards from the lengths of logs. (DISSTO)
UF pit saws, open
saws, open pit
CN V.TB.AFU.BCW.CFS.ALO.AFU. EWY.BUE.AXC

open-plan
DC.82 (A,L,B)
CN D.DC.AFU.ARI.ERE.BCW

open prisons
RK.725 (L)
ALT **open prison**
UF prisons, open
CN V.RK.AFU.ALO.ALO.CXA.AFU. AXC.AFU.BCW

open roofs
USE **open-timbered roofs**

open saws
TB.1017
ALT **open saw**
SN Saws having a handle like that of a knife, being usually long enough to be used by two hands. (SLOANE)
UF saws, open
CN V.TB.AFU.BCW.CFS.ALO.AFU. EWY.BUE

open scorpers
TB.1034 (N)
ALT **open scorper**
SN Scorpers with a round, continous blade set on a pair of handles.
UF scorpers, open
CN V.TB.AFU.BCW.CFS.ALO.AFU. FCS.ALO

open spaces
RK.1393 (A,L,B)
ALT **open space**
UF spaces, open
CN V.RK.ALO

open strings
RT.1126
ALT **open string**
SN Strings which have the upper edge notched, or otherwise worked to the shape of the steps, so that treads and risers are supported by and overlap the step-shaped edge. (RS)
UF bridgeboards
cut strings
notchboards
strings, cut
strings, open
CN V.RT.AFU.BIQ.AXC.ALO.BOK. AFU.AFU

open-timbered roofs
RT.441 (L)
ALT **open-timbered roof**
SN Roofs in which the rafters and roof sheathing are visible from below. (DAC)

UF open roofs
roofs, open
roofs, open-timbered
CN V.RT.AFU.AFU.AFU.BIQ.ARI.AFU.AFU.ALO.ARI

open web joists
RT.306
ALT open web joist
SN Steel trusses having an open web whose component parts are either hot-rolled structural shapes or cold-formed light-gauge steel shapes. (DAC)
UF bar joists
joists, bar
joists, open web
joists, trussed
trussed joists
CN V.RT.AFU.AFU.AFU.BCW.ALO.AFU.BOK.ARI

open well stairs
RT.1074
ALT open well stair
SN Stairs which rise around a rectangular well. (IGA)
UF stairs, open well
CN V.RT.AFU.BIQ.AXC.AFU.AFU.BCW

openings
RT.829 (B)
ALT opening
CN V.RT.AFU.ARI.AFU

openings (events)
KM.127 (B)
SN Formal, usually public, often invitational events by which something new is put officially into operation. (W)
CN K.KM.AFU.DCU

opera
KD.11 (L,R)
CN K.KD.AFU.AFU.AFU.AFU.AFU.AXC

opera houses
RK.928 (A,L,B,R)
ALT opera house
UF houses, opera
CN V.RK.AFU.ALO.ALO.EFQ.ARI.ALO.ALO

operating manuals
VW.355
ALT operating manual
UF manuals, operating
CN V.VW.AFU.AFU.ALO.CXA.BIQ.BCW.ALO

operating rooms
RM.297 (A,L,B)
ALT operating room
UF operating theaters
rooms, operating
theaters, operating
CN V.RM.AFU.DIO.AXC.AFU.BOK

operating (surgery)
USE **surgery**

operating theaters
USE **operating rooms**

operational drawings
USE **construction drawings**

operators, camera
USE **cameramen**

operators, engraving
USE **photoengravers**

operators, linotype
USE **linotype operators**

operators, photolith
USE **photoengravers**

ophicalcite
USE **verde di ranocchia**

ophiolite
USE **verde di ranocchia**

ophite
USE **verde di ranocchia**

ophthalmic hospitals
USE **eye hospitals**

opisthodomoi
RM.338
ALT **opisthodomos**
SN The recessed porch in the rear of a Greek temple. (DINSMR)
UF epinaoi
postica
CN V.RM.AFU.DIO.AXC.ALO.AXC.ARI

oppida
RD.10
ALT **oppidum**
SN Use for Late Iron Age and Roman period native settlements in Europe, often hillforts or otherwise lightly fortified, located as centers within the territory of local tribes.
CN V.RD.AFU.AFU.ALO.ARI.AFU

Optical
USE **Op art**

Optical art
USE **Op art**

optical correction
BM.77
SN The small variation in the form of an architectural member in order to correct an apparent bulge or sag. (THDAT)
UF correction, optical
CN B.BM.AFU.AFU.ARI.AFU.DOI

optical disks
VW.650 (L)
ALT **optical disk**
SN Data storage devices in disk form that use lasers to write and access data; can store data in analog or digital form.
UF disks, laser
disks, optical
laser disks
CN V.VW.AFU.ALO.AFU.DZW.ALO.BCW

optical glass
MT.281 (L)
SN A highly refined glass, usually a flint glass of special composition, or made from rock crystal, used for lenses and prisms. (MH)
UF glass, optical
CN M.MT.AFU.AFU.AFU.BIQ.AFU.AXC.BZY

optical illusion
BM.148 (A,L)
UF illusion, optical
CN B.BM.AFU.AFU.ARI.BOK.BZY

optical instruments
TB.540 (L,N,R)
ALT **optical instrument**
SN Artifacts originally created to be used in the observation and recording of light, including general-purpose optical equipment. (NOM)
UF instruments, optical
CN V.TB.AFU.AXC.ALO.ARI

optical mixture
USE **color mixture**

optical properties
BM.967 (L)
UF properties, optical
CN B.BM.CFS.AXC.BZY,BUE

optical science
USE **optics**

optics
KD.290 (L,R)
UF optical science
science, optical
CN K.KD.AFU.ARI.CLM.AXC.BUE

opus tessellatum
RT.817
SN Pavements with designs executed in pieces of different-colored tesserae, of larger size and more regular form than the pieces used in mosaic. (DAC)
CN V.RT.AFU.ALO.AFU.BZY.ALO.ALO

or-equal specifications
VW.798
ALT **or-equal specification**
UF specifications, or-equal
CN V.VW.AFU.ARI.AFU.ARI.AFU.ARI.BCW

oral history
KD.144 (L,R)
UF history, oral
CN K.KD.AFU.ALO.CLM.AFU.AXC

orange
DL.60 (L)
CN D.DL.AFU.AFU.ARI

orange brown

USE **brownish orange**
dark red
deep orange
grayish reddish orange
light brown
light grayish brown
light grayish yellowish brown
moderate brown
moderate orange
moderate reddish orange
strong brown
strong reddish brown

orange buff
USE **brilliant yellow**
light orange yellow
light yellow
moderate orange yellow
moderate yellow
moderate yellowish pink
strong yellow

orange-burnished ware
FL.2841
UF ware, orange-burnished
CN F.FL.ALO.AXC.ALO.ARI.ALO.AFU.AXC

orange cadmium yellow
USE **cadmium orange**

orange lead
USE **red lead**
vivid reddish orange

orange mineral
USE **red lead**

orange pigment
USE **red pigment**

orange pink
USE **brilliant orange**
light orange

orange pink, grayish
USE **grayish yellowish pink**

orange pink, moderate
USE **light yellowish pink**
moderate yellowish pink

orange red
USE **moderate reddish orange**

orange shellac
MT.2432
UF shellac, orange
CN M.MT.AFU.ARI.CRG.AFU.ARI.ALO.AFU

orange vermilion
MT.1685
SN A term sometimes applied to the more yellowish kinds of vermilion. (MAYER)
UF vermilion, orange
CN M.MT.AFU.AFU.ARI.AFU.AFU.ALO.ALO.BCW.AFU.AXC.AXC

orange vermilion (color)
USE **deep orange**
moderate reddish orange
strong reddish orange

orange yellow
DL.125
UF yellow, orange
CN D.DL.AFU.AFU.BCW.CRG.AFU

orange yellow, brilliant
USE **brilliant orange yellow**

orange yellow, dark
USE **dark orange yellow**

orange yellow, deep
USE **deep orange yellow**

orange yellow, light
USE **light orange yellow**
strong yellow

orange yellow, moderate
USE **moderate orange yellow**

orange yellow, pale
USE **pale orange yellow**

orange yellow, strong
USE **strong orange yellow**

orange yellow, vivid
USE **vivid orange yellow**

orange, antimony
USE **antimony orange**

orange, arsenic
USE **realgar**

orange, bright
USE **strong orange**
vivid orange

orange, bright reddish
USE **vivid reddish orange**

orange, bright yellowish
USE **vivid orange yellow**

orange, brilliant
USE **brilliant orange**

orange, brown
USE **brownish orange**
deep orange
grayish reddish orange
light brown
light yellowish brown
moderate orange
moderate orange yellow
moderate yellow
moderate yellowish pink
strong orange yellow

orange, brownish
USE **brownish orange**

orange, cadmium
USE **cadmium orange**

orange, cadmium (color)
USE **brilliant orange**
strong orange
vivid orange

orange, chrome
USE **chrome red**
vivid orange
vivid reddish orange

orange, dark reddish
USE **dark reddish orange**

orange, dark yellowish
USE **dark orange yellow**

orange, deep
USE **deep orange**

orange, deep reddish
USE **deep reddish orange**

orange, dull
USE **moderate yellowish pink**

orange, dull reddish
USE **grayish reddish orange**

Orange, Fine
USE **Fine Orange**

orange, grayish
USE **light yellowish brown**

orange, grayish reddish
USE **grayish reddish orange**

orange, light
USE **light orange**

orange, Mars
USE **dark reddish orange**

orange, moderate
USE **moderate orange**

orange, moderate reddish
USE **moderate reddish orange**

orange, orpiment
USE **strong orange**
vivid orange

orange, Osage
USE **Osage orange**

orange, pale yellowish
USE **pale orange yellow**

orange, pastel
USE **moderate orange**

orange, red
USE **strong reddish orange**
vivid reddish orange
vivid yellowish pink

orange, reddish
USE **reddish orange**

orange, strong
USE **strong orange**

orange, strong reddish
USE **strong reddish orange**

Orange, Thin
USE **Thin Orange**

orange, vivid

USE **vivid orange**

orange, vivid reddish
USE **vivid reddish orange**

orange, xanthine
USE **deep orange**

orange, yellow
USE **moderate orange**
strong orange

orange, yellowish
USE **brilliant orange yellow**
dark orange yellow
deep orange yellow
light orange yellow
strong orange yellow

orangeries
RK.65 (A,L,B,R)
ALT orangery
CN V.RK.AFU.ALO.ALO.AFU.AFU.BOK.AFU.ALO

Oranian
FL.45
CN F.FL.ALO.AFU.AFU.AFU.ALO.AXC

orations
VW.472 (L)
ALT oration
SN Formal addresses or speeches, especially those given on special occasions. (AHD)
CN V.VW.AFU.AFU.ALO.FOG.ALO

oratories
RM.309 (A,L,B,R)
ALT oratory
SN Use for small chapels suitable for private devotions but not used for services.
CN V.RM.AFU.DIO.AXC.ALO.AFU.AXC.BCW

orators
HG.726 (L,R)
ALT orator
CN H.HG.AFU.BCW.DZW

orbital laboratories, manned
USE **space stations**

orchards
RG.10 (L)
ALT orchard
UF groves (orchards)
CN V.RG.AFU.AFU.AFU.AFU.ARI.ARI

orchestra pits
RM.362 (B)
ALT orchestra pit
SN Pits underneath the forestage from which an orchestra plays. (W)
UF pits, orchestra
CN V.RM.AFU.DIO.AXC.AXC.ALO.ARI

orchestra shells
USE **band shells**

orchestras (audience spaces)
RM.353
ALT orchestra (audience space)
SN In modern theaters, the entire main-floor space for spectators. (RHDEL2)
CN V.RM.AFU.DIO.AXC.AXC.AFU.BCW

orchestras (stage spaces)
RM.363
ALT orchestra (stage space)
SN The semicircular spaces before the scaena in ancient theaters.
CN V.RM.AFU.DIO.AXC.AXC.ALO.AXC

orchid
USE **deep purplish pink**
grayish purplish pink
light reddish purple
moderate purplish pink
moderate reddish purple
pale purple
strong reddish purple

orchid gray
USE **grayish purple**

orchid mauve
USE **dark purplish pink**

orchid pink
USE **light purplish pink**
moderate purplish pink

orchid pink, light
USE **pale purplish pink**

orchid purple
USE **vivid reddish purple**

orchid rose
USE **deep purplish pink**

orchid rose, light
USE **deep purplish pink**
moderate purplish pink

orchid taupe
USE **dark grayish purple**
grayish purple

orchid taupe, dark
USE **dark grayish purple**
dark purplish gray

orchid, light
USE **light purplish pink**
moderate purplish pink

orchid, mauve
USE **light grayish purplish red**

orchid, pale
USE **pale purplish pink**

orchid, pink
USE **pale purplish pink**

orchid, purple
USE **strong reddish purple**

orchid, slate
USE **grayish purple**

orchil
MT.1528 (L)
UF archil
cudbear
indigo, red
red indigo
CN M.MT.AFU.AFU.ARI.AFU.AFU.AFU.AFU.AFU.AXC.BZY

order files
VW.600
ALT order file
UF files, order
CN V.VW.AFU.ALO.AFU.BIQ.ARI.AXC

order forms
VW.119 (N)
ALT order form
UF forms, order
CN V.VW.AFU.AFU.AFU.FZU.ARI.ARI

order, Composite
USE **Composite order**

order, Corinthian
USE **Corinthian order**

order, Doric
USE **Doric order**

order, Ionic
USE **Ionic order**

order, rules of
USE **rules of procedure**

order, Rustic
USE **Rustic order**

order, Solomonic
USE **spiral columns**

order, Tuscan
USE **Tuscan order**

orders, architectural
USE **architectural orders**

orders, change
USE **change orders**

orders, classical
USE **architectural orders**

orders, executive
USE **executive orders**

orders, money
USE **money orders**

orders, purchase
USE **purchase orders**

orders, variation
USE **change orders**

ordinances
VW.1030 (L)
ALT ordinance
SN Statutes or regulations, especially as enacted by local government.
UF bylaws (municipal)
city ordinances
municipal ordinances

ordinances, city
ordinances, municipal
CN V.VW.AFU.ARI.ALO.BCW.AFU.ARI.AFU.ARI.ALO

ordinances, city
USE **ordinances**

ordinances, municipal
USE **ordinances**

ordinances, zoning
USE **zoning ordinances**

ordinaries
RK.125
ALT **ordinary**
CN V.RK.AFU.ALO.ALO.ALO.AFU.BIQ.AFU

ordinary steel
USE **carbon steel**

ordinations
KM.39 (L,R)
CN K.KM.AFU.ARI.AXC.CFS

ordnance bronze
USE **lead bronze**

ordnance depots
RK.860 (B)
ALT **ordnance depot**
SN Buildings for the storage, processing, and disposition of unused ammunition, weapons, and military vehicles and equipment.
UF depots, ordnance
ordnance stores
ordnance supply depots
stores, ordnance
CN V.RK.AFU.ALO.ALO.DIO.AFU.AXC

ordnance stores
USE **ordnance depots**

ordnance supply depots
USE **ordnance depots**

Ordos
FL.2147 (L)
CN F.FL.ALO.ARI.ARI.ALO.AXC

ore
MT.540 (L)
SN A metal-bearing mineral from which a metal or metallic compound can be extracted commercially. (MH12)
CN M.MT.AFU.AFU.AFU.CFS.AFU.GLI

ore, bog iron
USE **limonite**

ore, brown
USE **limonite**

ore, carbonate
USE **siderite**

ore, green copper
USE **malachite**

ore, magnetic iron
USE **magnetite**

ore, spathic iron
USE **siderite**

Oregon cedar
USE **Port Orford cedar**

Oregon maple
USE **bigleaf maple**

Oregon oak
USE **western white oak**

Oregon pine
USE **Douglas fir**

Oregon white oak
USE **western white oak**

Oregon white pine
USE **ponderosa pine**

organ lofts
RM.37 (R)
ALT **organ loft**
SN Use for galleries or lofts in which an organ is located, often in a church.
UF lofts, organ
CN V.RM.AFU.DIO.AFU.AXC.AXC

organ screens
RT.1254 (B)
ALT **organ screen**
SN Use for ornamental screens in churches which either support an organ, or separate an organ chamber from the main space of the church.
UF screens, organ
CN V.RT.AFU.BUE.ALO.ARI.CXA.AXC

organic adhesives
MT.2340
UF adhesives, organic
CN M.MT.AFU.ARI.ARI.AFU.ALO

organic architecture
BM.226 (L,B,R)
SN A philosophy of architectural design, emerging in the early 20th century, asserting that in structure and appearance a building should be based on organic forms and should harmonize with its natural environment. (DAC)
UF architecture, organic
CN B.BM.AFU.ARI.AXC.AXC

organic black pigment
MT.1565
UF black pigment, organic
pigment, organic black
CN M.MT.AFU.AFU.ARI.AFU.AFU.ALO.ALO.AFU.AFU

organic black pigment, artificial
USE **synthetic organic black pigment**

organic black pigment, synthetic
USE **synthetic organic black pigment**

organic blue pigment
MT.1587
UF blue pigment, organic
pigment, organic blue
CN M.MT.AFU.AFU.ARI.AFU.AFU.ALO.ALO.ALO.ALO

organic blue pigment, artificial
USE **synthetic organic blue pigment**

organic blue pigment, synthetic
USE **synthetic organic blue pigment**

organic brown pigment
MT.1614
UF brown pigment, organic
pigment, organic brown
CN M.MT.AFU.AFU.ARI.AFU.AFU.ALO.ALO.ARI.ALO

organic chemistry
KD.264 (L)
UF chemistry, organic
CN K.KD.AFU.ARI.CLM.ALO.ARI

organic compounds
MT.996 (L)
UF compounds, organic
CN M.MT.AFU.AFU.ALO.AXC

organic green pigment
MT.1643
UF green pigment, organic
pigment, organic green
CN M.MT.AFU.AFU.ARI.AFU.AFU.ALO.ALO.AXC.ALO

organic green pigment, artificial
USE **synthetic organic green pigment**

organic green pigment, synthetic
USE **synthetic organic green pigment**

organic materials
MT.909 (L)
SN Substances containing carbon, including those derived from living organisms.
UF materials, organic
CN M.MT.AFU.AFU.ALO

organic pigment
MT.1554
SN Originally pigments of vegetable or animal origin, more recently pigments containing the element carbon in their composition. (MAYER)
UF pigment, organic
CN M.MT.AFU.AFU.ARI.AFU.AFU.ALO.AFU.ALO

organic pigment, artificial
USE **synthetic organic pigment**

organic pigment, natural
USE **natural organic pigment**

organic pigment, synthetic
USE **synthetic organic pigment**

organic red pigment
MT.1687
UF pigment, organic red

red pigment, organic
CN M.MT.AFU.AFU.ARI.AFU.AFU.ALO.ALO.BCW.ALO

organic red pigment, artificial
USE **synthetic organic red pigment**

organic red pigment, synthetic
USE **synthetic organic red pigment**

organic violet pigment
MT.1715
UF pigment, organic violet
violet pigment, organic
CN M.MT.AFU.AFU.ARI.AFU.AFU.ALO.ALO.BIQ.ALO

organic violet pigment, artificial
USE **synthetic organic violet pigment**

organic violet pigment, synthetic
USE **synthetic organic violet pigment**

organic yellow pigment
MT.1760
UF pigment, organic yellow
yellow pigment, organic
CN M.MT.AFU.AFU.ARI.AFU.AFU.ALO.ALO.BUE.ALO

organic yellow pigment, artificial
USE **synthetic organic yellow pigment**

organic yellow pigment, synthetic
USE **synthetic organic yellow pigment**

organization files
VW.601
ALT **organization file**
UF files, history
files, organization
history files
CN V.VW.AFU.ALO.AFU.BIQ.ARI.BCW

organizational charts
VW.240 (L)
ALT **organizational chart**
SN Diagrams of the administrative and functional structure of an organization, showing the established relationships of personnel through lines of authority and responsibility with delegated and assigned duties. (GAHLM)
UF charts, organizational
CN V.VW.AFU.AFU.AFU.FZU.AXC.ALO.BCW

organizations
HG.799 (L,B,R)
ALT **organization**
CN H.HG.ALO

organizations' buildings
USE **societies' buildings**

organizations, business
USE **business enterprises**

organizations, civic
USE **community organizations**

organizations, community
USE **community organizations**

organizations, international
USE **international organizations**

organizations, national
USE **national organizations**

organizations, professional
USE **professional associations**

organizations, standards
USE **standards organizations**

organs, house
USE **house organs**

Orhan
FL.3483
UF Orhan Bey
Orkhan
CN F.FL.ALO.BIQ.AFU.FOG.AFU.ALO

Orhan Bey
USE **Orhan**

Oribe
FL.2031 (L)
CN F.FL.ALO.ARI.ALO.ALO.ALO.ALO.ALO.CXA

oriel windows
RT.913 (L,B)
ALT **oriel window**
SN Bay windows projecting from an upper floor and not extending to the ground; usually supported by brackets or corbels.
UF windows, oriel
CN V.RT.AFU.ARI.AFU.AFU.BOK.AFU.AFU.ALO.ARI

orient yellow
USE **deep cadmium yellow**

Oriental
USE **Asian**

Oriental bazaars
USE **bazaars**

Oriental beech
MT.1110
UF beech, Oriental
Fagus orientalis
CN M.MT.AFU.AFU.ALO.BIQ.DCU.AFU.AFU.AFU.BCW.BIQ

Oriental lacquer
MT.2430
UF lacquer, Oriental
CN M.MT.AFU.ARI.CRG.AFU.ARI.AFU

Oriental Lowestoft
USE **Chinese export porcelain**

Orientalism
BM.351 (L,R)
SN Characteristics of oriental art or culture appearing in Western practice. (W)
CN B.BM.ALO.ALO.CLM.CFS.AFU

Orientalizing
FL.2569
CN F.FL.ALO.AXC.ALO.AFU.AFU.ARI.ARI

Orientalizing, Developed
USE **Developed Orientalizing**

Orientalizing, Early
USE **Early Orientalizing**

Orientalizing, Late
USE **Late Orientalizing**

orientation (architecture)
BM.79 (A,L,B)
SN Use for the positioning of a building in any determined relation to the points of the compass.
UF aspect
CN B.BM.AFU.AFU.ARI.AFU.DUC

orientation, solar
USE **solar orientation**

origami
KT.855 (L)
SN The art or process of Japanese paper folding. (W)
UF Japanese paper folding
paper-folding
paper folding, Japanese
CN K.KT.AFU.ALO.HOE.BIQ.AFU

origin, certificates of
USE **certificates of origin**

origin, marks of
USE **marks of origin**

originality
BM.40 (L,R)
CN B.BM.AFU.AFU.ALO.CFS

originals
VB.87
ALT **original**
CN V.VB.ALO.BCW

originals, camera
USE **direct positives**

Orissa
FL.2260
CN F.FL.ALO.ARI.AXC.ALO.AFU.BZY.ALO.ALO

Orkhan
USE **Orhan**

orlean
USE **annatto**

ormolu
MT.466 (R)
SN Golden or gilded bronze.
CN M.MT.AFU.AFU.AFU.BZY.AFU.ALO.AXC.ALO.ALO

ornament
VB.107 (A,L,R)
SN Decorative forms that are an integral part of a building or object but are

not essential to its structure. Regarding techniques of embellishment in general, use **decoration.**
UF ornamentation
CN V.VB.ALO.BUE.AXC

ornament drawings
VD.155
ALT **ornament drawing**
UF drawings, ornament
CN V.VD.AFU.BIQ.BIQ

ornament, drop
USE **drops**

ornament, floral
USE **floral patterns**

ornament, floriated
USE **floral patterns**

ornament, geometric
USE **geometric patterns**

ornament, lacertine
USE **lacertine ornament**

ornament, powdered
USE **powderwork**

ornament, progressive
USE **running ornament**

ornament, running
USE **running ornament**

ornament, scale
USE **scale pattern**

ornament, step
USE **step pattern**

ornament, strap
USE **strapwork**

ornament, strigil
USE **strigillation**

ornamental glass
USE **figured glass**

ornamental horticulture
KD.199 (L)
UF horticulture, ornamental
CN K.KD.AFU.ARI.ALO.AFU.ALO

ornamental motifs
USE **motifs**

ornamentation
USE **ornament**

ornaments, printers'
USE **printers' ornaments**

ornaments, type
USE **printers' ornaments**

Ornate Style
FL.2648
CN F.FL.ALO.AXC.ALO.AFU.ALO.
AXC.ARI.AXC.ARI

Ornate Style (Third Style)
USE **Third Style**

Oron
FL.246
CN F.FL.ALO.AFU.AXC.AFU.ALO.
AFU.BUE

orphan asylums
USE **orphanages**

orphanages
RK.790 (A,L,B,R)
ALT **orphanage**
UF asylums, orphan
children's homes
children's hostels
foundling hospitals
homes, children's
hospitals, foundling
hostels, children's
orphan asylums
CN V.RK.AFU.ALO.ALO.CXA.ALO
.ALO.BIQ

Orphic Cubist
USE **Orphist**

Orphist
FL.3377 (L,R)
ALT **Orphism**
UF Orphic Cubist
CN F.FL.ALO.BCW.ALO.AXC.DIO.
BCW.BCW.BIQ

orpiment
MT.1759
UF arsenic yellow
Auripigment
Chinese yellow
jaune d'arsenic
king's yellow
Rauschrot
sunflower yellow
yellow, arsenic
yellow, Chinese
yellow, king's
yellow, sunflower
CN M.MT.AFU.AFU.ARI.AFU.AFU.
ALO.ALO.BUE.AFU.AFU

orpiment (color)
USE **brilliant yellow**
light yellow
moderate yellow
strong yellow

orpiment orange
USE **strong orange**
vivid orange

orpiment red
USE **moderate orange yellow**
strong orange yellow

orpiment, red
USE **realgar**

Orr's zinc white
USE **lithopone**

orreries
USE **planetaria**

orthoclase
MT.508
CN M.MT.AFU.AFU.AFU.CFS.AFU.
CRG.ARI

Orthodox
USE **Orthodox Eastern**

Orthodox Caliphate
FL.3479
UF Caliphate, Orthodox
CN F.FL.ALO.BIQ.AFU.FIM

Orthodox Eastern
BM.629 (L)
UF Eastern Orthodox
Eastern, Orthodox
Orthodox
CN B.BM.BZY.AFU.ALO.ALO

Orthodox Judaism
BM.671 (L)
ALT **Orthodox Jewish**
CN B.BM.BZY.AFU.BOK.ALO

orthogonal drawings
USE **orthographic drawings**

orthogonal plan
USE **grid plan**

orthogonal projection
USE **orthographic projection**

orthogonal projections
USE **orthographic drawings**

orthogonals
BM.155
SN Lines in a perspective system that are perpendicular to the picture plane.
CN B.BM.AFU.AFU.ARI.BOK.CFS.ARI

orthographic drawings
VD.20
ALT **orthographic drawing**
SN Use for drawings in which the projectors are perpendicular to the plane of projection (drawing surface), i.e., a three-dimensional object is shown fully frontally at all points, with no indication of recession into depth.
UF drawings, orthogonal
drawings, orthographic
orthogonal drawings
orthogonal projections
orthographic projections
projections, orthogonal
projections, orthographic
CN V.VD.AFU.AFU.BIQ.ALO

orthographic projection
KT.286 (L)
SN Technique for representing three-dimensional objects in two dimensions using projecting lines that are perpendicular to the plane of projection. (W)
UF orthogonal projection

projection, orthographic
CN K.KT.AFU.ALO.DUC.DCU.BOK.ALO.ALO

orthographic projections
USE **orthographic drawings**

orthographs
USE **elevations**

orthophosphate, silver
USE **silver phosphate**

orthophotomaps
VW.175 (L)
ALT **orthophotomap**
SN Maps made from an assembly of perspective photographs in which tilt and relief have been removed. (DOD)
CN V.VW.AFU.AFU.AFU.FZU.AXC.AFU.ARI.ARI.ARI.AFU

orthoquartzite
USE **siliceous sandstone**

orthostats
RT.663 (A)
ALT **orthostat**
SN Large stone slabs set vertically as revetments at the lower part of walls.
CN V.RT.AFU.AFU.AFU.BIQ.BUE.ALO.AFU.CFS.AFU

orthostyles
USE **colonnades**

Osage
FL.1390 (L)
CN F.FL.ALO.ALO.ARI.AFU.BOK.DUC

Osage orange
MT.1369 (L)
SN Hard, bright orange-colored wood that yields a dye. (W)
UF bois d'arc
Maclura pomifera
orange, Osage
CN M.MT.AFU.AFU.ALO.BIQ.DCU.AFU.AFU.ALO.CRG

Osaka Print School
FL.2081
CN F.FL.ALO.ARI.ALO.ALO.ALO.AXC.BIQ

Osceola
FL.822
CN F.FL.ALO.ALO.ALO.AFU.ALO.ALO.AFU.BZY

Osman Bey
USE **Osman I**

Osman I
FL.3482
UF Osman Bey
Othman
Uthman I
CN F.FL.ALO.BIQ.AFU.FOG.AFU.AFU

Osman II
FL.3498
CN F.FL.ALO.BIQ.AFU.FOG.AFU.DUC

Osman III
FL.3506
UF Uthman III
CN F.FL.ALO.BIQ.AFU.FOG.AFU.FOG

Osmanli
USE **Ottoman**

ossuaries
RK.472 (A,N,R)
ALT **ossuary**
UF bone houses
charnel houses
houses, bone
houses, charnel
CN V.RK.AFU.ALO.ALO.BOK.ARI.ALO.ALO

Ostrogothic
FL.3110 (L,R)
CN F.FL.ALO.BCW.ALO.ALO.AFU.BOK.ALO.ALO.AXC.AFU

Ostrya
USE **hop hornbeam**

Ostrya carpinofolia
USE **European hop hornbeam**

Ostrya virginiana
USE **American hop hornbeam**

OTEC power plants
USE **ocean thermal energy conversion plants**

Othman
USE **Osman I**

Oto
FL.1391 (L)
CN F.FL.ALO.ALO.ARI.AFU.BOK.DZW

Otomi
FL.1506 (L)
CN F.FL.ALO.ALO.ARI.ALO.ARI.BIQ

Otsu-e
FL.2064
CN F.FL.ALO.ARI.ALO.ALO.ALO.ARI.DOI

Ottawa
FL.1222 (L)
CN F.FL.ALO.ALO.ARI.AFU.AFU.ALO.BCW

Ottoman
FL.3480 (A,B,R)
UF Osmanli
Ottoman Turks
Turks, Ottoman
CN F.FL.ALO.BIQ.AFU.FOG

ottoman footstools
TG.246 (N)
ALT **ottoman footstool**
UF footstools, ottoman
ottoman seats
ottomans (footstools)
seats, ottoman
CN V.TG.AFU.AFU.ALO.AFU.ALO.AFU.BIQ.ARI

ottoman seats
USE **ottoman footstools**

Ottoman Turks
USE **Ottoman**

ottomans
TG.298 (N)
ALT **ottoman**
SN Late 18th-century English name for long, low, upholstered sofas. (DDA)
UF ottomans, seat
seat ottomans
sofas, turkey
sultanes
turkey sofas
turquoises
CN V.TG.AFU.AFU.ALO.ALO.BIQ

ottomans (footstools)
USE **ottoman footstools**

ottomans, seat
USE **ottomans**

Ottonian
FL.3091 (A,L)
CN F.FL.ALO.BCW.ALO.ALO.AFU.AFU.ARI

Ouayeoue
USE **Waiwai**

oubliettes
RM.262
ALT **oubliette**
SN Shafts with openings only at the top which are often in the form of concealed pits below the floor.
CN V.RM.AFU.DIO.ARI.ALO.BCW.AFU

Oudh
FL.2261
UF Lucknow
CN F.FL.ALO.ARI.AXC.ALO.AFU.BZY.ARI

Ouobe
USE **Wee**

out-patient buildings
USE **clinics**

out-patient clinics
USE **clinics**

out-patient departments
USE **clinics**

Outagami
USE **Fox**

outboard profiles
VD.31
ALT **outboard profile**
SN Drawings that are full broadside elevations of a ship and that show more detail than in a sheer plan.
UF exterior profiles (ships)

profiles, exterior (ships)
profiles, outboard
CN V.VD.AFU.AFU.BIQ.ALO.ALO.BIQ.ALO

outbuildings
RK.1342 (L)
ALT **outbuilding**
UF ancillaries
CN V.RK.AFU.ALO.ARI.ARI

outdoor cafés
RK.120 (B)
ALT **outdoor café**
UF cafés, outdoor
open-air restaurants
restaurants, open-air
CN V.RK.AFU.ALO.ALO.ALO.AFU.AXC.BUE

outdoor furniture
TG.787
UF furniture, outdoor
CN V.TG.AFU.ALO.AFU

outdoor lighting
USE **exterior lighting**

outdoor museums
USE **museum villages**
open-air museums

outdoor recreation areas
USE **recreation areas**

outdoor theaters
USE **open-air theaters**

outdoor zoos
USE **open-air zoos**

outer baileys
RT.1169
ALT **outer bailey**
SN In complex castles, the spaces between the outer and inner walls. (IGA)
UF baileys, outer
CN V.RT.AFU.BUE.AFU.AFU.ALO

outer hearths
USE **front hearths**

outer strings
USE **face strings**

outfall sewers
RK.553
ALT **outfall sewer**
SN Sewers that receive the sewage from the collecting system and conduct it to a point of final discharge or to a disposal plant. (MEANS)
UF sewers, outfall
CN V.RK.AFU.ALO.ALO.CFS.ALO.AFU.ALO.ALO.BIQ

outhouses
RK.1343 (L,N,R)
ALT **outhouse**
SN Use for detached structures in domestic contexts containing one or more seats and a pit serving as toilets; distinguished from **latrines** which are similar structures in public contexts. For rooms that are within buildings and have such simple facilitites, use **privies.**
UF houses, necessary
necessaries
necessary houses
offices (outhouses)
CN V.RK.AFU.ALO.ARI.ARI.AFU

outlet boxes
USE **power outlets**

outlet stores
RK.176 (L)
ALT **outlet store**
UF factory outlets
outlets (stores)
outlets, factory
stores, outlet
CN V.RK.AFU.ALO.ALO.ALO.ARI.BIQ.ALO.BIQ.AFU

outlets (power outlets)
USE **power outlets**

outlets(stores)
USE **outlet stores**

outlets, factory
USE **outlet stores**

outline
BM.71
SN The visual boundary of a form, without regard to internal features; distinct from a **contour,** which may bound a form within an outline.
UF edge (outline)
profile
CN B.BM.AFU.AFU.ARI.AFU.CLM.ARI

outline drawings
VD.133
ALT **outline drawing**
SN Distinct from **contour drawings** which depict major spatial contours as well as outlines.
UF drawings, outline
CN V.VD.AFU.AXC.BIQ.ALO

outline lighting
USE **architectural lighting**

outline maps
VW.149 (L)
ALT **outline map**
SN Maps that present just sufficient geographic information to permit the correlation of additional data placed on it.
UF line maps
maps, line
maps, outline
CN V.VW.AFU.AFU.AFU.FZU.AXC.AFU.ARI.AFU.BZY

outline sketches
USE **preliminary sketches**

outline specifications
VW.799
ALT **outline specification**
UF specifications, outline
CN V.VW.AFU.ARI.AFU.ARI.AFU.ARI.BIQ

Outline Style
FL.2644
CN F.FL.ALO.AXC.ALO.AFU.ALO.AXC.ARI.ARI

outlines
VW.80 (L)
ALT **outline**
SN General descriptions covering the main points of a subject, such as summaries of written works or speeches expressed as headings and subheadings. (AHD)
CN V.VW.AFU.AFU.AFU.FCS.ALO

outlookers
USE **lookouts (roof components)**

output devices
TB.159 (L)
ALT **output device**
SN Any devices that convert the electrical signals representing information within a computer into a form that can exist or be sensed outside the computer. (DOC)
UF devices, output
CN V.TB.AFU.ARI.BCW.AXC.AXC

outremer
USE **artificial ultramarine blue**

outremer naturel
USE **ultramarine blue**

outremer violet
USE **ultramarine violet**

outshuts
RM.19
ALT **outshut**
SN Use for small parts of buildings extending beyond the general line, especially ones added at a later time.
CN V.RM.AFU.CFS

outside
USE **exterior**

outside corner trowels
TB.635
ALT **outside corner trowel**
SN Trowels which are the exact reverse of inside corner trowels in construction; used for plastering outside corners.
UF corner trowels, outside
trowels, outside corner
CN V.TB.AFU.BCW.BCW.ALO.HCQ.ARI.ALO

outsider art
USE **art brut**

outworks

RT.1200
ALT **outwork**
SN Minor defensive features established outside the principal fortification limits. (RHDEL2)
UF antemurals
CN V.RT.AFU.BUE.AFU.BZY

oval-back chairs
TG.141
ALT **oval-back chair**
UF chairs, oval-back
CN V.TG.AFU.AFU.ALO.AFU.AFU.AFU.NIE.CRG

oval-back Windsor chairs
USE **bow-back Windsor chairs**

ovals
BM.771 (L,B,R)
ALT **oval**
CN B.BM.CFS.ARI.AXC.BCW.AFU.AXC

Ovambo
USE **Ambo**

ovens
RT.1164 (L,R)
ALT **oven**
CN V.RT.AFU.BOK.BIQ

ovens (kilns)
USE **kilns**

ovens, beehive
USE **beehive ovens**

ovens, coke
USE **coke ovens**

overall patterns
USE **allover patterns**

overall views
USE **general views**

overcoat
USE **supercoat**

overcrowding
BM.1111 (L,B)
UF crowding
crowding stress
stress, crowding
CN B.BM.CRG.BCW.BIQ

overcup oak
MT.1245
UF oak, overcup
Quercus lyrata
CN M.MT.AFU.AFU.ALO.BIQ.DCU.AFU.AFU.AFU.IRA.CXA

overdoors
RT.884 (B)
ALT **overdoor**
SN Decorative members over a doorway or doorframe, such as pictures or carved panels. (W)
CN V.RT.AFU.ARI.AFU.AFU.AFU.ALO.AXC

overglazing
KT.870
ALT **overglazed**
SN Application of a second glaze to a piece of pottery. (GRCA)
CN K.KT.AFU.ALO.HOE.BOK.AXC.ARI.ARI

overhangs
RM.21
ALT **overhang**
SN Use for the projections of roofs or upper stories beyond a story immediately below.
CN V.RM.AFU.CLM

overhead door holders
TF.11
ALT **overhead door holder**
UF door holders, overhead
holders, overhead door
CN V.TF.AFU.AFU.AFU.AFU.AFU.BCW.AFU

overhead doors
RT.868
ALT **overhead door**
SN Doors of several leaves, divided horizontally, that slide up onto tracks over the space to be entered; common in the United States as garage doors.
UF doors, overhead
CN V.RT.AFU.ARI.AFU.AFU.AFU.ALO.ARI.AFU.ARI.AXC

overhead railroads
USE **elevated railroads**

overlapping joints
USE **lap joints**

overlays
VB.98
ALT **overlay**
CN V.VB.ALO.BOK.BUE

overlooks
RK.1590
ALT **overlook**
UF lookouts, scenic
scenic lookouts
CN V.RK.ALO.ARI.BZY

overmantels
RT.652 (N)
ALT **overmantel**
CN V.RT.AFU.AFU.AFU.BIQ.BUE.ALO.AFU.BCW.AXC

overpainting
KT.247
ALT **overpainted**
SN The application of a finishing coat of color to a painting after the preliminary layer or underpainting. (MAYER)
CN K.KT.AFU.ALO.DUC.CXA.ALO.ARI.ARI

overpass, pedestrian
USE **footbridges**

overpasses
RM.474 (L,B)
ALT **overpass**
CN V.RM.ALO.ALO.ALO.ALO.AXC.AFU

overprinting
KT.748
SN Process of completely printing one color over another, producing a resultant hue that is a mixture of the two. (TBL)
CN K.KT.AFU.ALO.HCQ.ALO.BIQ.ALO

overruns
RK.1506
ALT **overrun**
SN Cleared but unpaved areas at the end of runways offering extra landing roll to an airplane in an emergency. (W)
UF stopways
CN V.RK.ALO.ALO.BIQ.AFU.ARI

oversailing courses
RT.620
ALT **oversailing course**
SN Masonry courses which project beyond the general face of a wall. (HAS)
UF courses, oversailing
CN V.RT.AFU.AFU.AFU.BIQ.BUE.ALO.AFU.ALO.BUE

overstitching
KT.564
SN Using one, two, or three threads for binding a raw edge on cloth or making an ornamental edge, finish, or hem. (W)
CN K.KT.AFU.ALO.ELK.DUC.ALO.AXC.ARI

Ovimbundu
USE **Mbundu**

ovolo corners
TG.870
ALT **ovolo corner**
UF corners, ovolo
corners, sash plan
sash plan corners
CN V.TG.ALO.CRG.ARI

ovolo ends
USE **astragal ends**

ovolo moldings
RT.788
ALT **ovolo molding**
SN Convex moldings, less than a semicircle in profile; usually a quarter of a circle or a quarter-ellipse. (HAS)
UF moldings, ovolo
CN V.RT.AFU.ALO.AFU.BOK.AFU.AFU.AXC.BIQ

ovolo planes

TB.966
ALT **ovolo plane**
SN Planes used to produce ovolo or quarter-round moldings. (HUMMEL)
UF planes, ovolo
planes, quarter-round
quarter-round planes
CN V.TB.AFU.BCW.CFS.ALO.AFU.
DUC.AXC.ALO.BCW

Owasco
FL.875
CN F.FL.ALO.ALO.ALO.AFU.ALO.
ALO.AXC.CFS

owner-built houses
RK.285 (A,B)
ALT **owner-built house**
UF houses, owner-built
CN V.RK.AFU.ALO.ALO.AXCL.ACO.
ARI.ARI

owner-contractor agreements
VW.792
ALT **owner-contractor agreement**
UF agreements, owner-contractor
CN V.VW.AFU.ARI.AFU.ARI.AFU.ALO

owners
USE **proprietors**

owners, plantation
USE **plantation owners**

ownership
BM.472 (A,L,B)
UF freehold
CN B.BM.BCW.CXA.ALO.ALO.AFU

ownership marks
VW.723
ALT **ownership mark**
UF marks, ownership
CN V.VW.AFU.ALO.ALO.AFU.AXC
.ALO.CFS

ownership, government
USE **nationalization**

ownership, home
USE **home ownership**

Owo
FL.113
CN F.FL.ALO.AFU.ALO.AFU.BUE.CLM

oxbow
DC.108
SN Use to refer to furniture pieces, the fronts of which curve inward between outcurved ends and the center. (KETCH)
UF reverse serpentine
serpentine, reverse
CN D.DC.AFU.ARI.EWY.BUE

oxbow lakes
RD.132
ALT **oxbow lake**
SN Crescent-shaped lakes left in the sites of former river meanders. (ALLABY)
UF lakes, oxbow
CN V.RD.ARI.AFU.AFU.AFU.AFU.
ALO.AFU.AFU

oxbows
RD.160
ALT **oxbow**
SN River meanders with extreme curvature such that only a neck of land is left between two parts of the stream. (W)
CN V.RD.ARI.AFU.AFU.ALO.ARI.AFU

Oxford ocher
MT.1790
UF ocher, Oxford
ocher, stone
stone ocher
stone yellow
yellow, stone
CN M.MT.AFU.AFU.ARI.AFU.AFU.
ALO.ALO.BUE.ARI.CFS.ARI

oxgall
MT.1517 (L)
SN Wetting agent used in watercolors.
CN M.MT.AFU.AFU.ARI.AFU.AFU.
AFU.AFU.AFU.ALO

oxidative-reductive deterioration
KT.902
SN A deterioration of photographs, occurring when silver is attacked by any of a wide variety of oxidants that convert metallic silver atoms to highly reactive and mobile silver ions. It is the most common cause of fading of silver images. (REILLY)
UF deterioration, oxidative-reductive
CN K.KT.ALO.BCW.BOK

oxide green, transparent chromium
USE **viridian**

oxide of chromium
USE **chromium oxide green**

oxide verte de chrome opaque
USE **chromium oxide green**

oxide, antimony
USE **antimony oxide**

oxide, blue-green
USE **blue-green oxide**

oxide, lead
USE **litharge**

oxide, nitrous
USE **nitrous oxide**

oxide, Persian Gulf
USE **gulf red**

oxide, red
USE **iron oxide red**

oxide, Spanish red
USE **Spanish red oxide**

Oxidgelb
USE **Mars yellow**

Oxidrot
USE **iron oxide red**

Oxtotícpac
FL.992
CN F.FL.ALO.ALO.ALO.ALO.AFU.
ALO.AFU.AFU.CXA

oxyacetylene torches
TB.107 (N)
ALT **oxyacetylene torch**
SN Welding torches using oxygen and acetylene. (W)
UF torches, oxyacetylene
CN V.TB.AFU.ARI.ALO.ARI.BCW.AXC

oxychloric cement
MT.30
UF cement, oxychloric
cement, sorel
sorel cement
CN M.MT.AFU.AFU.AFU.ALO.AFU.
AFU.CFS

oxyhydrogen torches
TB.108 (N)
ALT **oxyhydrogen torch**
SN Welding torches using oxygen and hydrogen. (W)
UF torches, oxyhydrogen
CN V.TB.AFU.ARI.ALO.ARI.BCW.BCW

Oyo
FL.278
CN F.FL.ALO.AFU.AXC.AFU.ALO.
BCW.ALO.BIQ

Oyo Ile
USE **Old Oyo**

Oyo, Old
USE **Old Oyo**

oyster gray
USE **light gray**

oyster shell
MT.947 (L)
UF shell, oyster
CN M.MT.AFU.AFU.ALO.AFU.DUC.
AXC

oyster shell white
USE **oyster white**

oyster tables
TG.751
ALT **oyster table**
SN Specialized form of table at which one ate oysters; circular in form with a hole in the center, under which stood a basket for the empty shells. (THORN2)
UF tables, oyster
CN V.TG.AFU.AFU.BIQ.BOK.ALO.DOI

oyster white
MT.1753
UF oyster shell white
white, oyster

white, oyster shell
CN M.MT.AFU.AFU.ARI.AFU.AFU.ALO.ALO.BOK.ALO.CLM

oyster white (color)
USE **light gray**
white

ozalids
USE **diazotypes**

Ozbeg
USE **Uzbek**

ozobrome
USE **carbro process**

ozobrome process
USE **carbro process**

ozokerite
MT.2199 (L)
SN A mineral wax occurring in the vicinity of petroleum deposits. It is the crude, dark-colored wax from which ceresin is refined. (MAYER)
UF earth wax, galician
galician earth wax
wax, galician earth
CN M.MT.AFU.AFU.ARI.BZY.ALO.ALO

ozotype
USE **carbro process**

p'ai-lous
RK.501
ALT **p'ai-lou**
SN Use for Chinese ornamental gateways of one, three, or five openings, usually commemorative or triumphal.
UF pai-lous
CN V.RK.AFU.ALO.ALO.BUE.ARI

P'rapatom
USE **Pra Patom**

PA
USE **nylon**
polyamide

paces
USE **landings**

Pachacamac
FL.1162
CN F.FL.ALO.ALO.ALO.ARI.AXC.AFU.BCW.AXC

Pacheco
FL.1160
UF Coastal Tiahuanaco
Tiahuanaco, Costal
CN F.FL.ALO.ALO.ALO.ARI.AXC.AFU.BCW.ALO

pachyderm houses
USE **elephant houses**

Pacific
FL.3608 (L,R)
UF Oceanic
South Seas
CN F.FL.ALO.BOK

Pacific hemlock
USE **western hemlock**

Pacific willow
USE **western black willow**

pacifists
HG.754 (L)
ALT **pacifist**
SN Persons who believe in pacifism or are opposed to war or violence of any kind. (RHDEL2)
CN H.HG.AFU.BCW.HZS.BOK

pack ice
RD.155
SN Use for large areas of thin sheets of floating ice driven together by wind or currents to form a mass covering the entire sea surface with little or no open water.
UF ice packs
CN V.RD.ARI.AFU.AFU.AFU.ARI.ARI

package deal
USE **design-build**

package furniture
USE **knock-down furniture**

packages, learning
USE **learning modules**

packaging materials
MT.2626
UF materials, packaging
materials, packing
packing materials
CN M.MT.AFU.ARI.GFO

packers
HG.48
ALT **packer**
CN H.HG.AFU.AXC.ARI.CFS

packets, learning activity
USE **learning modules**

packing houses
USE **packing plants**

packing materials
USE **packaging materials**

packing plants
RK.635 (L)
ALT **packing plant**
UF houses, packing
packing houses
plants, packing
CN V.RK.AFU.ALO.ALO.CLM.ALO.ALO.AFU.AXC.BCW.BCW.AFU

pad feet
TG.907
ALT **pad foot**
SN Similar to club feet but resting on a disk. (TOMLIN)
UF disk feet
Dutch feet
feet, disk
feet, Dutch
feet, pad
CN V.TG.ALO.DZW.AFU.BIQ.AFU

pad saws
USE **keyhole saws**

paddles, angle
USE **angle paddles**

padlocks
TF.212 (N)
ALT **padlock**
SN Removable locks with a shackle that can be passed through a staple or link and then secured. (W)
CN V.TF.AFU.AFU.AFU.AFU.DIO.BIQ.AFU.CXA

padouk
MT.1258
CN M.MT.AFU.AFU.ALO.BIQ.DCU.AFU.AFU.AFU.JCO

pads, arm
USE **arm pads**

pads, elbow
USE **arm pads**

padstones
RT.669
ALT **padstone**
SN Stone templates used for support in walls at the end of a girder or roof truss. (RS)
CN V.RT.AFU.AFU.AFU.BIQ.BUE.ALO.ALO.ARI

Paekche
FL.2112 (L)
CN F.FL.ALO.ARI.ALO.ARI.AFU.ALO.ARI

Paestan
FL.2639
CN F.FL.ALO.AXC.ALO.AFU. ALO.AXC.ALO.BIQ.BOK

Páez
FL.1663 (L)
CN F.FL.ALO.ALO.ARI.ARI.BCW.CLM

Pagán
FL.2312
CN F.FL.ALO.ARI.BCW.AFU.ARI

paganism
BM.702 (L,R)
ALT **pagan**
UF heathenism
CN B.BM.BZY.ALO.ARI.BZY

page printers
TB.165
ALT **page printer**
SN Printers that print complete pages of output in one cycle. (DOC)
UF printers, page
teleprinters
CN V.TB.AFU.ARI.BCW.AXC.AXC.

ALO.ALO

page's chairs
USE **porter's chairs**

pageants
KM.61 (L,R)
SN Entertainments, frequently held in the open air, illustrating themes by means of spectacle rather than by consecutive narrative and dramatic characterization. (ENCYB)
CN K.KM.AFU.BOK.AXC.AXC

pagoda stone
MT.763
SN A Chinese marble. (MAYER)
UF pagodite
stone, pagoda
CN M.MT.AFU.AFU.AFU.DCU.AFU.ARI.ARI.ALO.BIQ

pagodas
RK.1124 (A,L,N,B,R)
ALT **pagoda**
UF meroes
CN V.RK.AFU.ALO.ALO.FCS.BIQ.BOK

pagodite
USE **pagoda stone**

Pahari
FL.2270 (L)
UF Punjab Hills
CN F.FL.ALO.ARI.AXC.ALO.AFU.BZY.BCW.ARI

Pahlevi
FL.3527
CN F.FL.ALO.BIQ.AFU.FUA

Pahn
USE **Sapo**

Pahouin
FL.408 (L)
UF Pangwe
CN F.FL.ALO.AFU.AXC.ALO.AFU.ARI

pai-lous
USE **p'ai-lous**

Pai miao
USE **Bai miao**

pai t'a
USE **stupas**

paillette
MT.2257
SN One of usually several small shiny objects (as spangles, sequins, beads, jewels) applied in small loosely designed clusters as a decorative trimming (as on clothing and accessories). (W)
CN M.MT.AFU.ALO.DZW

pain
BM.596 (L,R)
CN B.BM.BUE.CLM.ALO

paint
MT.2509 (A,L,N,B,R)
SN Any solution of a pigment in water, oil, or organic solvent. (MH)
CN M.MT.AFU.ARI.CRG.ALO.BCW

paint oil
USE **drying oil**

paint removers
MT.2710 (L)
UF removers, paint
CN M.MT.AFU.ARI.HZS.ALO.AFU

paint rollers
TB.519
ALT **paint roller**
SN Tubes, with a fiber surface, that are mounted on a roller and handle; used to apply paint. (MEANS)
UF rollers, paint
CN V.TB.AFU.ARI.EWY.ALO.CRG

paint shops
RK.610 (L,B)
ALT **paint shop**
UF shops, paint
CN V.RK.AFU.ALO.ALO.CLM.ALO.AFU.AXC

paint spraying
USE **spray painting**

paint thinners
USE **thinners**

paint, acrylic
USE **acrylic paint**

paint, acrylic resin
USE **acrylic paint**

paint, aluminum
USE **aluminum paint**

paint, antibacterial
USE **antifouling paint**

paint, antifouling
USE **antifouling paint**

paint, casein
USE **casein paint**

paint, chemical-resistant
USE **chemical-resistant paint**

paint, concrete
USE **concrete paint**

paint, dampproofing
USE **dampproofing paint**

paint, day-glow
USE **fluorescent paint**

paint, deck
USE **deck paint**

paint, distemper
USE **distemper paint**

paint, emulsion
USE **emulsion paint**

paint, enamel
USE **enamel paint**

paint, fire-retardant
USE **fire-retardant paint**

paint, flat
USE **flat paint**

paint, fluorescent
USE **fluorescent paint**

paint, frost-proof
USE **frost-proof paint**

paint, glue
USE **distemper paint**

paint, house
USE **house paint**

paint, latex
USE **latex paint**

paint, latex water
USE **latex paint**

paint, lead
USE **lead-based paint**

paint, lead-based
USE **lead-based paint**

paint, luminous
USE **luminous paint**

paint, magnetic
USE **magnetic paint**

paint, mold-resistant
USE **antifouling paint**

paint, oil
USE **oil paint**

paint, phosphorescent
USE **fluorescent paint**

paint, polymer
USE **polymer paint**

paint, poster
USE **poster color**

paint, rust-inhibiting
USE **rust-inhibiting paint**

paint, silicate
USE **silicate paint**

paint, vapor barrier
USE **dampproofing paint**

paintbrush feet
USE **Spanish feet**

paintbrushes
TB.505 (N)
ALT **paintbrush**
UF brushes, paint
CN V.TB.AFU.ARI.EWY.ALO.ALO.AFU

Painted Pottery
USE **Yangshao**

painted ware, Archaic

USE Archaic ware
Hassuna Archaic ware

painted ware, dark-on-light
USE **dark-on-light painted ware**

painted ware, light-on-dark
USE **light-on-dark ware**

painted ware, multiple-brush
USE **multiple-brush painted ware**

painted ware, standard
USE **Hassuna standard ware**
standard painted ware

painted ware, white
USE **white painted ware**

painter's naphtha
USE **naphtha**

painter's putty
USE **glazier's putty**

painterliness
BM.81
ALT **painterly**
CN B.BM.AFU.AFU.ARI.AFU.DZW

painters
HG.105 (L,B,R)
ALT **painter**
CN H.HG.AFU.AXC.AXC.AFU.AFU.ALO.AXC.CXA

painters' marks
VW.744 (L)
ALT **painters' mark**
UF marks, painters'
CN V.VW.AFU.ALO.ALO.AFU.AXC.AXC.AXC.AFU

painters, animal
USE **animal painters**

painters, industrial
USE **industrial painters**

painters, marine
USE **marine painters**

painters, mural
USE **muralists**

painters, sea
USE **marine painters**

painters, watercolor
USE **watercolorists**

painting
KT.218 (A,L,B,R)
CN K.KT.AFU.ALO.DUC.CXA.AFU

painting (coating)
KT.670 (B)
ALT **painted**
CN K.KT.AFU.ALO.GRC.AFU.BCW

painting books
VW.530 (L)
ALT **painting book**
UF books, painting
CN V.VW.AFU.ALO.AFU.AFU.ALO.BCW.ARI

painting techniques
KT.219 (L,R)
CN K.KT.AFU.ALO.DUC.CXA.ALO

painting, Action
USE **Action painting**

painting, American Scene
USE **American Scene**

painting, back
USE **reverse painting on glass**
verre églomisé

painting, direct
USE **alla prima**

painting, drip
USE **drip painting**

painting, dry-brush
USE **dry-brush painting**

painting, encaustic
USE **encaustic painting**

painting, finger
USE **finger painting**

painting, fresco
USE **fresco painting**

painting, Gestural
USE **Action painting**

painting, impasto
USE **impasto**

painting, loaded brush
USE **impasto**

painting, Matter
USE **Matter art**

painting, mirror (reverse painting)
USE **reverse painting on glass**

painting, mirror (verre églomisé)
USE **verre églomisé**

painting, pastose
USE **impasto**

painting, Pattern
USE **Pattern painting**

painting, roller
USE **roller painting**

painting, spray
USE **spray painting**

painting, sumi
USE **sumie**

painting, wax
USE **encaustic painting**

paintings, gouache
USE **gouaches**

paintings, pastel
USE **pastels**

Paipai
FL.1279
CN F.FL.ALO.ALO.ARI.AFU.ALO.FZU.AFU.BCW

paired windows
USE **coupled windows**

Paithan
FL.2264
CN F.FL.ALO.ARI.AXC.ALO.AFU.BZY.AXC

Paiute
FL.1462 (L)
CN F.FL.ALO.ALO.ARI.AFU.CFS.BZY

Paiute, Northern
USE **Northern Paiute**

Paiute, Southern
USE **Southern Paiute**

Pakomame
USE **Pokomam**

Pakot
USE **Pokot**

Pala
FL.2210 (L)
UF Pala-Sena (Pala)
CN F.FL.ALO.ARI.AXC.ALO.AFU.AXC.AXC

Pala-Sena (Pala)
USE **Pala**

Pala-Sena (Sena)
USE **Sena**

Pala-Tibetan
FL.2183
CN F.FL.ALO.ARI.AXC.AFU.BOK.AFU.BIQ

palace chapels
USE **royal chapels**

Palace period, New
USE **New Palace period**

Palace period, Old
USE **Old Palace period**

palace style
USE **court style**

Palace style (Mycenaean pottery)
FL.2662
CN F.FL.ALO.AXC.ALO.AFU.ALO.AXC.AXC.BUE

palaces
RK.337 (A,L,B,R)
ALT **palace**
SN Use for official residences, frequently large and impressively appointed, of sovereigns or other high dignitaries; for other large stately dwellings but not official residences, use **mansions.**
CN V.RK.AFU.ALO.ALO.AXC.ALO.

BOK.BOK.ALO

palaces, bishops'
USE **bishops' palaces**

palaces, corn
USE **corn palaces**

palaces, ducal
USE **ducal palaces**

palaces, episcopal
USE **bishops' palaces**

palaces, ice
USE **ice palaces**

palaces, imperial
USE **imperial palaces**

palaces, picture
USE **movie theaters**

palaces, royal
USE **royal palaces**

palaces, summer
USE **summer palaces**

palaeographers
USE **paleographers**

Palaeologan
FL.3077 (R)
UF Byzantine Renaissance
Palaeologue Revival
Renaissance, Byzantine
Revival, Palaeologue
Third Golden Age (Byzantine)
CN F.FL.ALO.BCW.ALO.AFU.ALO.AXC.AFU

Palaeologan, Early
USE **Early Palaeologan**

Palaeologan, High
USE **High Palaeologan**

Palaeologue Revival
USE **Palaeologan**

palaestrae
RK.1065 (A)
ALT **palaestra**
SN Ancient Greek or Roman buildings for athletic training, generally smaller than gymnasiums.
CN V.RK.AFU.ALO.ALO.EWY.AXC.BIQ.ALO.AXC.ARI

Palau
FL.3679 (L)
ALT **Palauan**
CN F.FL.ALO.BOK.ARI.ALO.AFU

palazzi
RK.303 (B)
ALT **palazzo**
SN Use for large and impressive Italian urban dwellings.
CN V.RK.AFU.ALO.ALO.AXC.ALO.AXC.AFU.ARI.ALO

palazzi pubblichi
RK.997 (A)
ALT **palazzo pubblico**
CN V.RK.AFU.ALO.ALO.ERE.ALO.AFU.AXC

pale aqua
USE **very pale blue**
very pale green

pale aqua blue
USE **very pale blue**

pale aqua green
USE **very light bluish green**
very pale green

pale blue
DL.221
UF aqua blue, light
aqua, light
aquamarine (color)
baby blue
blue, baby
blue, dull
blue, dull greenish
blue, dull reddish
blue, gray
blue, light aqua
blue, light gray
blue, pale
blue, pastel
blue, powder
centroid color 185
dull blue
dull greenish blue
dull reddish blue
gray blue
gray blue, light
gray, light Payne's
gray, pale green blue
gray, pale Payne's
gray, pearl
green blue gray, pale
greenish blue, dull
light aqua
light aqua blue
light gray blue
light Payne's gray
pale green blue gray
pale Payne's gray
pastel blue
Payne's gray, light
Payne's gray, pale
pearl gray
pewter (color)
powder blue
reddish blue, dull
ultramarine
CN D.DL.AFU.AFU.BZY.BUE

pale blue green
USE **pale green**
very pale green

pale blue violet
USE **brilliant purplish blue**

pale bluish lavender
USE **very pale purple**
very pale violet

pale bluish violet
USE **brilliant purplish blue**

pale brown
USE **light brown**
light grayish reddish brown
light grayish yellowish brown
light yellowish brown
moderate orange

pale cadmium yellow
MT.1777
UF cadmium yellow, pale
jaune de cadmium clair
Kadmiumgelb hell
yellow, pale cadmium
CN M.MT.AFU.AFU.ARI.AFU.AFU.ALO.ALO.BUE.ARI.ALO.BIQ

pale cerulean blue
USE **light blue**
very light blue

pale chartreuse
USE **light yellow green**
pale yellow green

pale cobalt arsenate
MT.1721
UF arsenate, pale cobalt
cobalt arsenate, pale
CN M.MT.AFU.AFU.ARI.AFU.AFU.ALO.ALO.BIQ.ARI.AFU.ALO

pale drab gray
USE **light gray**
white

pale emerald green
USE **very light bluish green**
very light green

pale gray green
USE **pale yellow green**

pale grayish blue
USE **very pale blue**
very pale purplish blue

pale grayish blue violet
USE **very pale purplish blue**

pale grayish violet blue
USE **light purplish blue**

pale green
DL.173
UF aqua gray
aqua green, light
aqua, light
blue green, pale
bluish gray green
bluish green, dull
celadon gray
celadon green
centroid color 149
dull bluish green
dull green
gray green, bluish
gray, aqua
gray, celadon
gray, jade

green, celadon
green, dull
green, dull bluish
green, light aqua
green, pale
green, pale blue
green, pale yellowish
green, pastel
jade gray
light aqua
light aqua green
pale blue green
pale yellowish green
pastel green
slate (color)
yellowish green, pale
CN D.DL.AFU.AFU.BUE.BUE

pale green blue gray
USE **pale blue**

pale green yellow
USE **light greenish yellow**
pale greenish yellow

pale greenish yellow
DL.142
UF centroid color 104
dull greenish yellow
green yellow, pale
greenish yellow, dull
greenish yellow, pale
pale green yellow
pastel yellow
sulphur yellow
yellow, dull greenish
yellow, pale greenish
yellow, pastel
yellow, sulphur
CN D.DL.AFU.AFU.BCW.CRG.ALO.
BUE

pale jade green
USE **very pale green**

pale lavender
USE **very pale purple**

pale lavender violet
USE **light purple**
pale purple

pale lemon yellow
USE **light greenish yellow**

pale lilac
USE **pale purplish pink**
very pale purple

pale mint green
USE **very light green**
very pale green

pale neutral gray
USE **medium gray**

pale olive
USE **light grayish olive**

pale olive gray
USE **yellowish gray**

pale olive green
USE **moderate yellow green**

pale orange yellow
DL.133
UF bisque
brown, very pale
buff
buff, dull
buff, light
buff, pale pinkish
buff, yellow
centroid color 73
dull buff
dull reddish yellow
dull yellowish orange
flesh
light buff
ocher (color)
orange yellow, pale
orange, pale yellowish
pale pinkish buff
pale yellowish orange
peach (color)
pinkish buff, pale
reddish yellow, dull
very pale brown
yellow buff
yellow, dull reddish
yellow, pale orange
yellowish orange, pale
CN D.DL.AFU.AFU.BCW.CRG.AFU.BUE

pale orchid
USE **pale purplish pink**

pale Payne's gray
USE **pale blue**

pale peach
USE **light yellowish pink**
pale yellowish pink

pale periwinkle blue
USE **very pale purple**
very pale purplish blue

pale pink
DL.10
UF centroid color 7
pink, pale
CN D.DL.AFU.AFU.AFU.BOK

pale pinkish buff
USE **pale orange yellow**

pale purple
DL.277
UF bluish violet, dull
centroid color 227
deep dull lavender
deep grayish lavender
dull bluish violet
dull lilac
dull reddish violet
dull violet
grayish lavender
grayish lavender, deep
lavender
lavender violet, pale
lavender, deep dull
lavender, deep grayish
lavender, grayish
lilac
lilac, dull
orchid
pale lavender violet
pale red purple
purple, pale
purple, pale red
red purple, pale
reddish violet, dull
rose
violet, dull
violet, dull bluish
violet, dull reddish
CN D.DL.AFU.AFU.CFS.BUE

pale purple drab
USE **grayish purplish pink**

pale purplish blue
DL.251
UF blue lavender
blue, delft
blue, dull
blue, dull reddish
blue, gray
blue, pale purplish
blue, powder
bluish violet, deep dull
centroid color 203
deep dull bluish violet
delft blue
dull blue
dull reddish blue
gray blue
gray, lavender
lavender gray
lavender, blue
light navy
navy, light
periwinkle
powder blue
purplish blue, pale
reddish blue, dull
ultramarine
violet, deep dull bluish
CN D.DL.AFU.AFU.BZY.DCU.ALO.BUE

pale purplish gray
USE **purplish gray**

pale purplish pink
DL.22
UF baby pink
bluish pink
centroid color 252
lavender, pink
light orchid pink
lilac, pale
mauve pink
mauve, pastel
orchid pink, light
orchid, pale
orchid, pink
pale lilac
pale orchid
pastel mauve

pink lavender
pink orchid
pink, baby
pink, bluish
pink, light orchid
pink, mauve
pink, pale purplish
purplish pink, pale
CN D.DL.AFU.AFU.AFU.CLM.AFU.BOK

pale red
USE **light grayish red**
light reddish brown

pale red purple
USE **pale purple**

pale reddish brown
USE **light reddish brown**

pale reddish purple
DL.297
UF centroid color 244
dull reddish violet
lilac
purple, pale reddish
reddish purple, reddish
reddish violet, dull
violet, dull reddish
CN D.DL.AFU.AFU.CFS.DCU.AFU.BOK

pale rose purple
USE **light purple**

pale turquoise green
USE **very light bluish green**

pale violet
DL.263
UF bluish violet, deep dull
centroid color 214
dark grayish lavender
deep dull bluish violet
deep grayish lavender
dull bluish violet
gray blue
gray, lavender
grayish lavender, dark
grayish lavender, deep
lavender gray
lavender, dark grayish
lavender, deep grayish
lavender, lilac
lilac lavender
violet, deep dull bluish
violet, dull bluish
violet, pale
CN D.DL.AFU.AFU.BZY.DCU.ARI.BUE

pale violet gray
USE **medium gray**
purplish gray

pale Windsor blue
USE **light blue**

pale yellow
DL.119
UF beige
bistre
buff
buff, cream
buff, light
buff, yellow
centroid color 89
cream
cream buff
dull reddish yellow
dull yellow
ecru
eggshell
ivory (color)
ivory white
ivory yellow
ivory, light
light buff
light ivory
massicot (color)
massicot yellow
Naples yellow (color)
olive yellow
parchment (color)
reddish yellow, dull
transparent yellow
white, ivory
yellow buff
yellow, dull reddish
yellow, ivory
yellow, massicot
yellow, Naples (color)
yellow, olive
yellow, pale
yellow, transparent
CN D.DL.AFU.AFU.BCW.BUE

pale yellow green
DL.161
UF centroid color 121
chartreuse, pale
dull yellowish green
gray green, pale
green, dull yellowish
green, pale gray
green, pale yellow
pale chartreuse
pale gray green
putty (color)
yellow green, pale
yellowish green, dull
CN D.DL.AFU.AFU.BOK.BOK

pale yellow orange
USE **light yellowish pink**

pale yellowish brown
USE **light grayish yellowish brown**

pale yellowish green
USE **pale green**

pale yellowish orange
USE **pale orange yellow**

pale yellowish pink
DL.31
UF alabaster (color)
brown, red
buff
buff, dull
centroid color 31
dull buff
flesh pink
gray, peach
pale peach
peach gray
peach, pale
pink, flesh
pink, pale yellowish
red brown
rose
yellowish pink, pale
CN D.DL.AFU.AFU.AFU.CLM.ALO.BOK

Palenque
FL.1632 (L)
CN F.FL.ALO.ALO.ARI.ARI.ARI.BCW

Paleo-Indian
FL.735 (L)
UF Big Game Hunting
Early American Hunter
Upper Lithic
CN F.FL.ALO.ALO.ALO.AFU.AFU.ARI

Paleo-Indian (Mesoamerican)
FL.961
CN F.FL.ALO.ALO.ALO.ALO.AFU.AFU.AFU

paleoanthropology
KD.98 (L)
SN Branch of anthropology dealing with fossil remains of the human species and its predecessors. (W)
CN K.KD.AFU.ALO.AFU.BIQ.ALO

paleogeographers
HG.262
ALT **paleogeographer**
CN H.HG.AFU.AXC.BCW.AFU.BCW.ALO

paleogeography
KD.134 (L)
SN Geography of ancient times or of a particular former geological epoch. (W)
CN K.KD.AFU.ALO.BZY.AFU

paleographers
HG.273 (L)
ALT **paleographer**
UF palaeographers
CN H.HG.AFU.AXC.BCW.AFU.BOK.ALO.BCW

paleography
KD.153 (L,R)
SN Study of ancient modes of writing, either inscribed or in manuscript form, including their identification in terms of origin or period, and the formation of individual characters. For the study and interpretation of ancient inscriptions specifically, whether of writing, pictures, or random scratchings, use **epigraphy.**
CN K.KD.AFU.ALO.CLM.ALO.BIQ

Paleolithic
FL.8 (L)

UF Eolithic period
Old Stone Age
Stone Age, Old
CN F.FL.AFU.BCW.AFU.AFU

Paleolithic, Lower
USE **Lower Paleolithic**

Paleolithic, Middle
USE **Middle Paleolithic**

Paleolithic, Upper
USE **Upper Paleolithic**

paleomagnetic dating
KT.502
SN Method of dating by measuring the direction and intensity of the magnetization of particles in clay and clay products and comparing the results to known records at fluctuations in the earth's magnetic field. (HOLHZR)
UF archaeomagnetic dating
dating, archaeomagnetic
dating, paleomagnetic
CN K.KT.AFU.ALO.EFQ.AFU.AXC

paleontologists
HG.343 (L)
ALT **paleontologist**
CN H.HG.AFU.AXC.BIQ.AFU.AFU.
BZY.ARI

paleontology
KD.278 (L,R)
SN Science dealing with the life of past geological periods, based on the study of fossil remains of plants and animals. (W)
CN K.KD.AFU.ARI.CLM.ARI.CFS

Palestinian
FL.2927 (L)
CN F.FL.ALO.AXC.ARI.AXC.ALO.ALO

palette
BM.138
SN Includes the range of color which an artist uses, the typical color range of a school or group, or the range of colors possible when mixing a prescribed group of colorants.
CN B.BM.AFU.AFU.ARI.BOK.ALO.
ALO.AXC

Pali Buddhism
USE **Theravada**

palimpsests
VW.659 (L)
ALT **palimpsest**
SN Writing material, usually parchment, that has been written upon more than once; the previous text may have been imperfectly erased, thus remaining partly legible. (ICA)
CN V.VW.AFU.ALO.AFU.DZW.ARI.
AFU.AXC

paling, Chinese
USE **Chinese fretwork**

Palingstijl
USE **Art Nouveau**

Palisades (Eskimo style)
FL.801
CN F.FL.ALO.ALO.ALO.AFU.ALO.
AFU.ALO.ALO.AFU.AXC

palisades (outworks)
RT.1208 (N)
ALT **palisade (outwork)**
SN Barriers composed of long stakes driven into the earth close together, sometimes connected by horizontal beams. (RS)
CN V.RT.AFU.BUE.AFU.BZY.BUE

Palissy ware
FL.3222 (R)
UF ware, Palissy
CN F.FL.ALO.BCW.ALO.ARI.BIQ.
BIQ.ARI.ALO.AXC.ARI

Palladian
FL.3182 (A,B,R)
ALT **Palladianism**
SN Includes works influenced by the architectural style of Andrea Palladio; excludes works by Palladio himself.
UF Neo-Palladian
Palladian Revival
Revival, Palladian
CN F.FL.ALO.BCW.ALO.ARI.BIQ.
AXC.AFU

Palladian Revival
USE **Palladian**

Palladian windows
RT.935 (R)
ALT **Palladian window**
SN Windows of large size, characteristic of Renaissance and later classicizing styles, divided by columns or piers resembling pilasters into three lights, the middle one of which is usually wider than the others and is sometimes arched. (HAS)
UF serliana
Venetian windows
windows, Palladian
windows, Venetian
CN V.RT.AFU.ARI.AFU.AFU.BOK.
AFU.AFU.ERE.ALO

palladiotype
USE **palladium process**

palladiotypes
USE **palladium prints**

palladium
MT.441 (L)
SN Rare metallic element, found in the ores of platinum. (MH12)
CN M.MT.AFU.AFU.AFU.BZY.AFU.
AFU.ARI.CRG

palladium photoprints
USE **palladium prints**

palladium prints
VJ.51
ALT **palladium print**
SN Use for photographic prints made by the palladium process.
UF palladiotypes
palladium photoprints
photoprints, palladium
prints, palladium
CN V.VJ.AFU.AFU.ARI.ARI.AXC.BOK

palladium process
KT.346
SN An iron process for making photographic prints in which palladium is reduced from a salt to form the image. Similar to the platinum process.
UF palladiotype
CN K.KT.AFU.ALO.DUC.DIO.ALO.
DCU

Pallava
FL.2205 (L)
CN F.FL.ALO.ARI.AXC.ALO.AFU.
AXC.AFU

palm capitals
RT.128
ALT **palm capital**
SN Use for capitals resembling the crown of a palm tree, the edge of the spreading top being scalloped to suggest the fronds, common in ancient Egyptian architecture.
UF capitals, palm
CN V.RT.AFU.AFU.AFU.AXC.BIQ.
ALO.ARI.AFU.CRG

palm fiber
MT.1834
SN Used in securing mangrove poles in the framework of African houses. (OLIVER)
UF fiber, palm
palmyra
CN M.MT.AFU.AFU.ARI.ALO.AFU
.AFU.ALO.CLM

palm frond
USE **palm leaf**

palm houses
RK.66 (B)
ALT **palm house**
SN Greenhouses for growing palms. (W)
UF houses, palm
palm stoves
stoves, palm
CN V.RK.AFU.ALO.ALO.AFU.AFU.
BOK.AFU.ARI

palm leaf
MT.1039
SN Used in roof and wall construction in South Africa. (OLIVER)

UF frond, palm
leaf, palm
palm frond
CN M.MT.AFU.AFU.ALO.BIQ.BIQ.AFU

palm stands
USE **plant stands**

palm stoves
USE **palm houses**

Palm Sunday
KM.85 (L)
CN K.KM.AFU.CFS.ARI.BUE

palmettes
DG.53 (R)
ALT **palmette**
SN Conventionalized ornaments featuring an erect leaf divided into lobes, like a fan or palm leaf.(RS) Common in classical and classicizing styles, used either individually or along with other conventionalized flower or foliage forms in an anthemion.
CN D.DG.AFU.AFU.DIO.ALO.AFU

palmyra
USE **palm fiber**

palombino
MT.832
SN A light gray Italian marble. (W)
UF marmor coraliticum
CN M.MT.AFU.AFU.AFU.DCU.AFU.
ARI.ARI.ARI.BOK.CRG

Pame
FL.1507 (L)
CN F.FL.ALO.ALO.ARI.ALO.ARI.BOK

pamment
MT.108
SN Tile or brick used for paving a malthouse floor. (W)
CN M.MT.AFU.AFU.AFU.AXC.ALO.
AFU.ALO.CFS.ALO

pampas
RD.247 (L)
ALT **pampa**
SN Extensive, generally grass-covered plains of South America. (W)
CN V.RD.ARI.AFU.BCW.ALO.AFU.
AFU.ARI

pampas grass
MT.1034
UF grass, pampas
CN M.MT.AFU.AFU.ALO.BIQ.AXC.
AXC.ARI

pamphlet files
USE **vertical files**

pamphlets
VW.606 (L,N,R)
ALT **pamphlet**
SN Includes unbound printed works, usually with a paper cover, containing short essays or treatises, usually on a current topic. (AHD)
UF booklets
brochures
CN V.VW.AFU.ALO.AFU.CFS

pan-and-roll roofing tile
MT.175
SN Single-lap roofing tile of two types used in combination: a flat, tapered undertile having flanges, and a half-rounded, tapered overtile. (HAS)
UF roofing tile, pan-and-roll
tile, pan-and-roll roofing
CN M.MT.AFU.AFU.AFU.AXC.ALO.
ALO.ALO.AFU.ALO.AXC.AFU.AFU.
ALO

pan breeze
USE **breeze**

Panamint
FL.1315
CN F.FL.ALO.ALO.ARI.AFU.AXC.BUE

panchromatic film
MT.2240
UF film, panchromatic
CN M.MT.AFU.ALO.CXA.ALO.BIQ

pandokeia
USE **inns**

Pandya
FL.2220 (L)
CN F.FL.ALO.ARI.AXC.ALO.AFU
.AXC.DCU

panel
MT.2258
SN Thin, flat piece of material, especially wood.
CN M.MT.AFU.ALO.EFQ

panel-back chairs
USE **wainscot chairs**

panel card photographs
USE **panel prints**

panel clamps
TB.1054
ALT **panel clamp**
SN Large clamps used to hold together the frame and panels of house doors, interior wall paneling, or the paneled doors of furniture pieces. (HUMMEL)
UF clamps, panel
CN V.TB.AFU.BCW.CFS.ALO.ALO.
BCW.BCW

panel doors
RT.858 (B)
ALT **panel door**
SN Doors having stiles, rails, and sometimes muntins which form one or more frames around thinner, recessed panels. (DAC)
UF doors, panel
CN V.RT.AFU.ARI.AFU.AFU.AFU.ALO.
ARI.AFU.AFU.BOK.AXC

panel heating
RT.1395 (L,B)
UF heating, panel
heating, radiant panel
radiant panel heating
CN V.RT.ALO.BCW.AFU.AFU.ARI.
ARI.AFU

panel houses
USE **brothels**

panel planes
TB.947 (N)
ALT **panel plane**
SN Planes used for cutting wood panels. (KEBABI)
UF planes, panel
CN V.TB.AFU.BCW.CFS.ALO.AFU.
DUC.ARI.BOK

panel prints
VJ.80
ALT **panel print**
SN Use for card photographs about 4 by 8 inches on mounts measuring 7 1/2 by 13 or larger. (SAPSP)
UF panel card photographs
photographs, panel card
prints, panel
CN V.VJ.AFU.AFU.BCW.AFU.BCW

panel saws
TB.1027
ALT **panel saw**
SN Small, light hand saws, from 10 to 24 inches long, having closely set fine teeth; used in cutting open grain and paneling.
UF saws, panel
CN V.TB.AFU.BCW.CFS.ALO.AFU.
EWY.BUE.BCW

panel tracery
USE **perpendicular tracery**

panelboards
RT.1345
ALT **panelboard**
SN Use for small electrical panels containing switches and fuses or circuit breakers. For larger panels, frames, or assemblies containing switches, fuses, instruments, and protective devices, use **switchboards.**
CN V.RT.ALO.ARI.ALO.CFS

paneling
MT.2259 (L,B,R)
CN M.MT.AFU.ALO.ELK

panelled-back chairs
USE **wainscot chairs**

panels
RT.822 (A,B)
ALT **panel**
SN Distinct portions, sections, or divisions of a surface, especially when sunk below or raised above the general level or enclosed by a frame or border.(RHDEL2) Common on

walls, ceilings, and doors, and also on furniture pieces.
UF tables (panels)
CN V.RT.AFU.ALO.ALO.ALO

panels (ornament areas)
DG.92
ALT **panel (ornament area)**
SN Areas within an ornamental scheme, usually rectangular and enframed.
CN D.DG.AFU.ALO.BCW

panels, drop
USE **drop panels**

panels, fielded
USE **fielded panels**

panes, quarrel
USE **quarrels**

panes, window
USE **lights**

Pangwa
FL.669 (L)
UF Wapangwa
CN F.FL.ALO.AFU.AXC.AXC.BIQ.CRG

Pangwe
USE **Pahouin**

Pani
USE **Pawnee**

panic bolts
TF.557
ALT **panic bolt**
SN Devices designed to grant instant exit by pushing a crossbar that releases a locking bolt or catch. (STEIN)
UF bolts, fire exit
bolts, panic
fire exit bolts
CN V.TF.AFU.ALO.AXC.AFU.BOK

panic bolts (locks)
USE **panicproof locks**

panic exit devices
USE **panicproof locks**

panicproof locks
TF.237
ALT **panicproof lock**
SN Locks that provide immediate exit from the inside at all times. (STEIN)
UF bolts, panic (locks)
exit devices, panic
locks, panicproof
panic bolts (locks)
panic exit devices
CN V.TF.AFU.AFU.AFU.AFU.DIO.BIQ.ALO.ALO.BIQ

Panjikent
FL.1823
UF Pendzhikent
Piandjikent
Pjandzikent
Pyanddzhikent
CN F.FL.ALO.ARI.AFU.AXC.ELK.CLM.ALO

Pannetier's green
USE **viridian**

panopticons
RK.25
ALT **panopticon**
SN Buildings, as prisons, hospitals, or libraries, so arranged that all parts of the interior are visible from a single point. (RHDEL2)
CN V.RK.AFU.ALO.AFU.ALO.BUE

panoramas
VB.5 (A,L,R)
ALT **panorama**
SN Use for pictorial representations that surround or are unfolded before the spectator, and for photographs that show a wide view produced by panoramic camera or by joining photographs together. May refer also to buildings in which such representations are exhibited.
CN V.VB.AFU.AFU.ARI

panoramic cameras
TB.298
ALT **panoramic camera**
SN Cameras with a special horizontally scanning lens which rotates about its rear nodal point. It produces an image on a curved plate or film and can cover a very wide angle of view. (LANG)
UF cameras, circuit
cameras, cirkut
cameras, panoramic
circuit cameras
cirkut cameras
CN V.TB.AFU.ARI.CLM.ARI.AFU.AFU.ALO.AFU

pansy green
MT.1645
UF green, pansy
CN M.MT.AFU.AFU.ARI.AFU.AFU.ALO.ALO.AXC.ALO.ALO

pantheism
BM.703 (L,R)
ALT **pantheistic**
CN B.BM.BZY.ALO.ARI.CFS

pantile
MT.181 (A,N,B)
CN M.MT.AFU.AFU.AFU.AXC.ALO.ALO.ALO.AFU.ALO.AXC.AFU.ALO.ALO

pantographs
TB.259 (L,N)
ALT **pantograph**
SN Devices consisting of four strips of wood or some other material which are hinged together in a square so that they overlap and can be adjusted to the scale of the work being copied, enlarged, or reduced. (MAYER)
UF plagiographs
planigraphs
CN V.TB.AFU.ARI.CLM.AFU.ALO.CXA

pantries
RM.201 (B)
ALT **pantry**
SN Rooms or closets in which food, groceries, and other provisions, or silverware, dishes, and other items are kept. (RHDEL2)
UF butteries
CN V.RM.AFU.DIO.ALO.DCU.CLM

pantries, butler's
USE **butler's pantries**

pao rosa
USE **Brazilian rosewood**

paonazzo marble
MT.813
UF marble, paonazzo
CN M.MT.AFU.AFU.AFU.DCU.AFU.ARI.ARI.ARI.BIQ.BZY.AFU

Papago
FL.1463 (L,R)
CN F.FL.ALO.ALO.ARI.AFU.CFS.CFS

papal briefs
USE **briefs (papal)**

papal bulls
USE **bulls**

papal crosses
DG.13
ALT **papal cross**
SN Crosses having three crossbars, with the longest near the middle and the two others above successively shorter. (W)
UF crosses, papal
crosses, pope's
pope's crosses
CN D.DG.AFU.AFU.ARI.BOK

papal encyclicals
VW.20 (L)
ALT **papal encyclical**
SN Letters addressed by the pope to all the bishops of the church. (RHDEL2)
UF encyclicals, papal
CN V.VW.AFU.AFU.AFU.BIQ.AFU.ARI.ALO.AFU.AFU

papeleras
TG.439
ALT **papelera**
SN Spanish Renaissance variation of vargueños, used for storing papers. They are usually smaller than vargueños and lack a writing lid; generally they have turned feet and may be bound with iron. (BURR)
CN V.TG.AFU.AFU.AXC.ALO.ARI.ALO.CXA

paper
MT.1892 (A,L,N,B,R)
CN M.MT.AFU.AFU.ARI.ALO.ALO.AXC

paper birch
MT.1120 (L)
UF Betula papyrifera
birch, canoe
birch, paper
canoe birch
CN M.MT.AFU.AFU.ALO.BIQ.DCU.AFU.AFU.AFU.BIQ.BIQ

paper board
USE **cardboard**

paper coatings
MT.2573 (L)
UF coatings, paper
CN M.MT.AFU.ARI.CRG.ARI.AXC

paper filigree
USE **paper quillwork**

paper-folding
USE **origami**

paper folding, Japanese
USE **origami**

paper holders
USE **toilet paper holders**

paper holders, toilet
USE **toilet paper holders**

paper-mache
USE **papier-mâché**

paper mills
RK.649 (L,B)
ALT **paper mill**
UF mills, paper
CN V.RK.AFU.ALO.ALO.CLM.ALO.ALO.AFU.AXC.BZY

paper prints, salted
USE **salted paper prints**

paper quillwork
MT.2775 (L,R)
UF filigree, paper
paper filigree
quilling (paper)
quillwork, paper
CN M.MT.AFU.AXC.BUE.AFU

paper tapes
VW.651 (N)
ALT **paper tape**
UF tapes, paper
CN V.VW.AFU.ALO.AFU.DZW.ALO.BIQ

paper, abrasive
USE **abrasive paper**

paper, absorbent
USE **absorbent paper**

paper, albanene tracing
USE **tracing vellum**

paper, aristo
USE **aristo paper**

paper, Aztec
USE **bark cloth**

paper, bark
USE **bark cloth**

paper, baryta
USE **baryta paper**

paper, Bible
USE **India paper**

paper, bituminised
USE **tar paper**

paper, blotting
USE **blotting paper**

paper, bond
USE **bond paper**

paper, book
USE **book paper**

paper, building
USE **building paper**

paper, butcher
USE **butcher paper**

paper, cannabis bark
USE **bark cloth**

paper, carbon
USE **carbon paper**

paper, carborundum
USE **carborundum paper**

paper, cartridge
USE **cartridge paper**

paper, charcoal
USE **charcoal paper**

paper, coated
USE **prepared paper**

paper, crepe
USE **crepe paper**

paper, cross-section
USE **graph paper**

paper, developing-out
USE **developing-out paper**

paper, development
USE **developing-out paper**

paper, drawing
USE **drawing paper**

paper, Egyptian
USE **papyrus**

paper, felt
USE **felt paper**

paper, fig bark
USE **bark cloth**

paper, filter
USE **filter paper**

paper, garnet
USE **garnet paper**

paper, gaslight
USE **gaslight paper**

paper, graph
USE **graph paper**

paper, grounded
USE **prepared paper**

paper, groundwood
USE **wood pulp paper**

paper, handmade
USE **handmade paper**

paper, India
USE **India paper**

paper, Japanese
USE **Japanese paper**

paper, kraft
USE **kraft paper**

paper, laid
USE **laid paper**

paper, layout
USE **layout paper**

paper, litmus
USE **litmus paper**

paper, machine-made
USE **machine-made paper**

paper, Manila
USE **Manila paper**

paper, moldmade
USE **moldmade paper**

paper, onionskin
USE **onionskin paper**

paper, photo-sensitized
USE **photographic paper**

paper, photographic
USE **photographic paper**

paper, plain salted
USE **salted paper**

paper, plant fiber
USE **bark cloth**

paper, prepared
USE **prepared paper**

paper, print-out
USE **printing-out paper**

paper, printing
USE **printing paper**

paper, printing-out
USE **printing-out paper**

paper, rag
USE **rag paper**

paper, RC
USE **resin-coated paper**

paper, resin-coated
USE **resin-coated paper**

paper, reversal
USE **reversal paper**

paper, rice
USE **rice paper**

paper, rosin-sized
USE **rosin-sized paper**

paper, salted
USE **salted paper**

paper, sensitized
USE **photographic paper**

paper, sheathing
USE **building paper**

paper, single-weight
USE **single-weight paper**

paper, solio
USE **solio paper**

paper, stripping
USE **stripping film**

paper, tar
USE **tar paper**

paper, tissue
USE **tissue paper**

paper, tracing
USE **tracing paper**

paper, transfer
USE **transfer paper**

paper, watercolor
USE **watercolor paper**

paper, wood pulp
USE **wood pulp paper**

paper, wove
USE **wove paper**

paper, wrapping
USE **wrapping paper**

paper, writing
USE **writing paper**

paperboard
USE **cardboard**

paperhanging
KT.583 (L)
CN K.KT.AFU.ALO.ERE.ARI

paperhanging brushes
USE **wallpaper brushes**

papermakers
HG.522 (L)
ALT **papermaker**
CN H.HG.AFU.AXC.BUE.ARI.CRG

papermaking
KT.856 (L,R)
CN K.KT.AFU.ALO.HOE.BIQ.ALO

papers, administrative
USE **administrative records**

papers, aristotype
USE **aristo paper**

papers, citizenship
USE **citizenship papers**

papers, estate
USE **estate records**

papers, faculty
USE **faculty papers**

papers, family
USE **family papers**

papers, House of Commons
USE **House of Commons papers**

papers, House of Lords
USE **House of Lords papers**

papers, parliamentary
USE **parliamentary papers**

papers, personal
USE **personal papers**

papers, presidential
USE **presidential papers**

papers, private
USE **personal papers**

papers, professional
USE **professional papers**

papers, ships'
USE **ships' papers**

papers, voting
USE **ballots**

paperwork
MT.2774 (L,R)
CN M.MT.AFU.AXC.BUE

paperworking techniques
KT.854 (R)
CN K.KT.AFU.ALO.HOE.BIQ

papier-mâché
MT.1971 (L,R)
SN Pulverized paper made into a water paste with an adhesive binder.
UF paper-mache
CN M.MT.AFU.AFU.ARI.ALO.ALO.BCW

Papua New Guinea
FL.3635 (L)
CN F.FL.ALO.BOK.ALO.BCW.ALO

Papua, Gulf of
USE **Papuan Gulf**

Papuan
USE **Papuan Gulf**

Papuan Gulf
FL.3642 (L)
UF Gulf of Papua
Papua, Gulf of
Papuan
CN F.FL.ALO.BOK.ALO.BCW.ALO.AXC

papyriform capitals
USE **papyrus capitals**

papyrus
MT.1894 (L,R)
UF Egyptian paper
paper, Egyptian
CN M.MT.AFU.AFU.ARI.ALO.ALO.AXC.AFU.AFU

papyrus capitals
RT.129
ALT **papyrus capital**
SN Use for Egyptian capitals in the form of a cluster of papyrus flowers, the top fanning out broadly.
UF capitals, papyriform
capitals, papyrus
papyriform capitals
CN V.RT.AFU.AFU.AFU.AXC.BIQ.ALO.ARI.AFU.CXA

para balsam
MT.1473
UF balsam, para
Para copaiba
CN M.MT.AFU.AFU.ALO.BOK.AFU.ARI.ALO

Para copaiba
USE **para balsam**

para red
MT.1707
SN A lake or toner of a bright, cherry-red color with a rather bluish undertone; made from paranitraniline, a coal tar derivative. (MAYER)
UF para toner
red, para
toner, para
CN M.MT.AFU.AFU.ARI.AFU.AFU.ALO.ALO.BCW.AXC.BCW

para red (color)
USE **moderate red**
strong red

para toner
USE **para red**

parabemata
USE **diaconica**
protheses

parabolas
BM.772 (L)
ALT **parabolic**
CN B.BM.CFS.ARI.AXC.BCW.AFU.BCW

Paracas
FL.1147 (L)
CN F.FL.ALO.ALO.ALO.ARI.AXC.AFU.ARI.BUE

Paracas Cavernas
FL.1148
UF Cavernas
CN F.FL.ALO.ALO.ALO.ARI.AXC.AFU.ARI.BUE.AFU

Paracas Necropolis
FL.1149
UF Necropolis
CN F.FL.ALO.ALO.ALO.ARI.AXC.AFU.ARI.BUE.ALO

parachute domes
USE **umbrella domes**

parades
KM.56 (L,R)
SN Use for large public processions of a festive nature, often including floats and marching bands, and held in honor of an anniversary, person, or event. For the action of a group of persons moving in orderly succession in a formal, ceremonial context, use **processions.**
CN K.KM.AFU.BOK.ARI

Paradise
BM.686 (L,R)
SN Place or state in which the souls of the righteous after death enjoy eternal bliss. (W)
CN B.BM.BZY.ALO.AFU.BIQ

paradise gardens
RK.1441
ALT **paradise garden**
SN Gardens often provided with shade, flowing water, pavilions, and elaborate plantings for private enjoyment; common in Islamic countries.
UF gardens, paradise
paradises (gardens)
CN V.RK.ALO.AFU.AFU.BCW.ALO.ALO

paradises (gardens)
USE **paradise gardens**

paraffin
MT.2201 (L)
UF paraffin wax
wax, paraffin
CN M.MT.AFU.AFU.ARI.BZY.ALO.ARI

paraffin wax
USE **paraffin**

paragone
BM.300 (R)
SN The disputatious comparison of the various arts, popular in Renaissance Humanist circles. (BARA)
CN B.BM.AFU.AXC.CRG

Paraguayan
FL.722 (L,B)
CN F.FL.ALO.ALO.AFU.AXC.BIQ

Paraguayan cedar
MT.1339
UF cedar, Paraguayan
Cedrela braziliensis
CN M.MT.AFU.AFU.ALO.BIQ.DCU.AFU.AFU.ALO.ALO.BIQ

paraline drawings
USE **axonometric drawings**

parallax stereographs
VJ.103
ALT **parallax stereograph**
UF stereographs, parallax
CN V.VJ.AFU.ARI.AFU.BOK.ALO

parallel
DC.40
CN D.DC.AFU.ALO.ARI.DIO

Parallel-flaked
FL.753
CN F.FL.ALO.ALO.ALO.AFU.AFU.ARI.ALO.ARI.ALO

parallel gable roofs
USE **double-gable roofs**

parallel perspective
KT.277
SN Use for images in which parallel projecting lines do not converge but remain parallel; common in Oriental painting. Use **elevation oblique projection** when referring to architectural drawings.
UF perspective, parallel
CN K.KT.AFU.ALO.DUC.DCU.BIQ.BCW

parallel perspective (one-point perspective)
USE **one-point perspective**

parallel perspectives
USE **one-point perspectives**

parallel projection
KT.280
SN Technique for representing three-dimensional objects in two dimensions using projecting lines that are parallel to each other. The term **parallel perspective** is used in reference to art and actually refers to methods similar to oblique projection.
UF projection, parallel
CN K.KT.AFU.ALO.DUC.DCU.BOK.ALO

parallel rules
TB.452 (N)
ALT **parallel rule**
SN Devices consisting of two flat rulers hinged together near both ends by two metal strips, on which the rulers swing parallel to each other; used in mechanical drawing to expedite the drawing of many parallel lines. (MAYER)
UF rules, parallel
CN V.TB.AFU.ARI.EFQ.ALO.CLM.AFU

parallelograms
BM.776
SN Quadrilateral figures having both pairs of opposite sides parallel to each other. (RHDEL2)
CN B.BM.CFS.ARI.AXC.BCW.AFU.BIQ.ALO.AFU

Paramara
FL.2214 (L)
UF Pawar
CN F.FL.ALO.ARI.AXC.ALO.AFU.AXC.BUE

parapet walls
USE **parapets**

parapets
RT.670 (B)
ALT **parapet**
SN Low walls, projecting from the edge of a platform, terrace, or roof, or surmounting the cornice of a building; also, walls forming the uppermost part of a defensive wall or rampart.
UF parapet walls
walls, parapet
CN V.RT.AFU.AFU.AFU.BIQ.BUE.ALO.ALO.AXC

parapets, crenelated
USE **battlements**

parascenia
RT.1266
ALT **parascenium**
SN In ancient theaters, projecting structures or wings flanking the stage on either side, and with the scene, or background, enclosing it on the sides. (RS)
CN V.RT.AFU.BUE.ARI.ALO

parastades
RT.671
ALT **parastas**
SN Those parts of the flanking walls of the cella of a temple that project beyond its front or rear, often terminating in antae. (RS)
CN V.RT.AFU.AFU.AFU.BIQ.BUE.ALO.ALO.BCW

paratransit
RD.97 (L)
SN Designates alternative nonrail transit systems, such as car pools, dial-a-rides, jitneys, and taxis.
UF demand responsive service
demand responsive transportation
transportation, demand responsive
CN V.RD.ALO.ARI.AFU.AFU.AFU.ALO

paravents
TG.17
ALT **paravent**
SN Large folding screens to provide protection against drafts. (WATSON)
CN V.TG.AFU.AFU.AFU.ALO.AFU

parcels
USE **lots**

parchment
MT.960 (L,R)
SN Skin of animals suitable for writing on or painting on in aqueous colors. (MAYER)
CN M.MT.AFU.AFU.ALO.AFU.DZW.BCW

parchment (color)
USE **dark grayish yellow**
grayish yellow
light olive brown
pale yellow

parcloses
RT.1255
ALT **parclose**
SN Screens or railings in a church, designed to exclude nonworshippers from a chapel or shrine.
UF percloses
CN V.RT.AFU.BUE.ALO.ARI.CXA.BCW

pardoning
KG.184
SN Absolving from the consequences of a fault or the punishment of a crime. (W)
CN K.KG.AFU.ALO.ARI.BUE

pardons
VW.996 (L,N)
ALT **pardon**
SN Official documents declaring the exemption of a convicted person from the penalties of an offense or crime by the power of the executor of laws. (AHD)
CN V.VW.AFU.ARI.ALO.BCW.AFU.AFU.AFU.BZY

Pare
FL.652 (L)
CN F.FL.ALO.AFU.AXC.AXC.BCW.CLM

parents
HG.12 (L,R)
ALT **parent**
CN H.HG.AFU.ALO.ALO

pargeting
MT.2777 (A,L,B)
UF pargework
parging
CN M.MT.AFU.AXC.BZY.AFU

pargework
USE **pargeting**

parging
USE **pargeting**

Parian
FL.2690 (L)
CN F.FL.ALO.AXC.ALO.AFU.ALO.BCW.ALO.BUE

Parian (British porcelain)
USE **Parian ware**

Parian cement
MT.26
SN Similar to Keene's cement with borax instead of alum as a setting accelerator. (MH)
UF cement, Parian
CN M.MT.AFU.AFU.AFU.ALO.AFU.AFU.BIQ.AXC

Parian marble
MT.833
UF greco duro
lychnites marble
marble, lychnites
marble, Parian
marmor Parium
pario
CN M.MT.AFU.AFU.AFU.DCU.AFU.ARI.ARI.ARI.BOK.CXA

Parian porcelain
USE **Parian ware**

Parian ware
FL.3342 (L)
UF Parian (British porcelain)
Parian porcelain
porcelain, Parian
porcelain, statuary
statuary porcelain
ware, Parian
CN F.FL.ALO.BCW.ALO.AXC.DIO.ALO.BUE.AXC.ALO

paring chisels
TB.859 (N)
ALT **paring chisel**
SN Long-handled chisels used to shape wood by hand without the use of a mallet. (MEANS)
UF chisels, joiner's
chisels, paring
joiner's chisels
CN V.TB.AFU.BCW.CFS.ALO.AFU.BUE.ALO.BCW

paring gouges
TB.887 (N)
ALT **paring gouge**
SN Long thin woodworking gouges, the cutting edge of which is beveled on the concave side. (MEANS)
UF gouges, paring
CN V.TB.AFU.BCW.CFS.ALO.AFU.CXA.BIQ

Parintintin
FL.1594 (L)
UF Cabahiba
Cawahib
CN F.FL.ALO.ALO.ARI.ARI.AFU.FZU

pario
USE **Parian marble**

Paris black
MT.1569
SN An inferior grade of ivory black. (MAYER)
UF black, Paris
CN M.MT.AFU.AFU.ARI.AFU.AFU.ALO.ALO.AFU.AFU.AFU.AFU.AFU.AFU

Paris blue
USE **Prussian blue**
strong blue

Paris green
USE **brilliant green**
brilliant yellowish green
emerald green
light yellowish green
strong yellowish green
vivid yellowish green

Paris green, light
USE **light yellowish green**

Paris yellow
USE **chrome yellow**

Pariserblau
USE **Prussian blue**

parish centers
USE **parish houses**

parish churches
RK.1112 (B)
ALT **parish church**
SN Use for churches serving the needs of religious administrative districts called parishes.
UF churches, parish
CN V.RK.AFU.ALO.ALO.FCS.BIQ.ALO.ARI.BUE

parish halls
USE **parish houses**

parish houses
RK.1198 (A,L,B)
ALT **parish house**
SN Buildings in connection with a church used for secular activities.
UF centers, parish
church halls
church houses
halls, church
halls, parish
houses, church
houses, parish
parish centers
parish halls
CN V.RK.AFU.ALO.ALO.FUA.BOK

parish inventories
VW.977
ALT **parish inventory**
UF inventories, parish
CN V.VW.AFU.ARI.ALO.ALO.ALO.ARI.AFU

parish maps
VW.227 (L)
ALT **parish map**
UF maps, parish
CN V.VW.AFU.AFU.AFU.FZU.AXC.AFU.ARI.AXC.DUC.AXC

parish registers

VW.978 (L)
ALT parish register
SN Registers established and kept by an ecclesiastical parish, recording chronologically baptisms, marriages, burials, and other information. (ICA)
UF registers, parish
CN V.VW.AFU.ARI.ALO.ALO.ALO.ARI.ALO

parish schools
USE **parochial schools**

parish seats
RD.27
ALT parish seat
SN County seats in Louisiana. (W)
UF seats, parish
CN V.RD.AFU.ALO.AFU.AXC.ALO

parishes
RG.257 (L)
ALT parish
SN Ecclesiastical units of area committed to one pastor. (W)
CN V.RG.ALO.AFU.AFU.BIQ.AXC

parishes (administrative bodies)
HG.807 (L)
ALT parish (administrative body)
CN H.HG.ALO.ALO.BIQ

park boards
USE **park commissions**

park commissions
HG.838
ALT park commission
UF boards, park
commissions, park
park boards
CN H.HG.ALO.BIQ.BIQ

park districts
RG.251 (A,L)
ALT park district
UF districts, park
CN V.RG.ALO.AFU.AFU.AXC

Parker trusses
RT.368
ALT Parker truss
SN Pratt trusses with polygonal top chords. (HISNEW)
UF trusses, Parker
CN V.RT.AFU.AFU.AFU.BCW.CLM.AFU.AFU.AFU.BUE.AFU

parkettes
USE **vest-pocket parks**

parking
BM.1151 (L)
CN B.BM.DCU.ALO.AFU

parking garages
RK.1226 (A,L,B)
ALT parking garage
UF car parks
car parks, multi-storey
garages, multistory
garages, parking
multi-storey car parks
multistory garages
CN V.RK.AFU.ALO.ALO.GFO.BUE.ALO.AFU

parking garages, roof
USE **roof parking garages**

parking lots
RK.1511 (A,L)
ALT parking lot
UF lots, parking
CN V.RK.ALO.ALO.BIQ.ALO.AFU

parking meters
RM.499 (L,N,B)
ALT parking meter
UF meters, parking
CN V.RM.ALO.ALO.ALO.ALO.DUC.ARI

parks
RK.1455 (A,L,B,R)
ALT park
SN Use for permanently dedicated, public recreation areas generally characterized by their natural, historic, or landscape features and administered by governmental agencies.
UF parks, public
public parks
CN V.RK.ALO.ALO.ARI

parks, amusement
USE **amusement parks**

parks, animal
USE **wild animal parks**

parks, children's
USE **playgrounds**

parks, city
USE **urban parks**

parks, community
USE **community parks**

parks, educational
USE **educational parks**

parks, game
USE **safari parks**

parks, industrial
USE **industrial parks**

parks, marine
USE **marine parks**

parks, metropolitan
USE **urban parks**

parks, mobile home
USE **mobile home parks**

parks, national
USE **national parks**

parks, neighborhood
USE **neighborhood parks**

parks, pocket
USE **vest-pocket parks**

parks, provincial
USE **provincial parks**

parks, public
USE **parks**

parks, regional
USE **regional parks**

parks, safari
USE **safari parks**

parks, skateboarding
USE **skateboarding parks**

parks, state
USE **state parks**

parks, theme
USE **theme parks**

parks, trailer
USE **trailer camps**

parks, urban
USE **urban parks**

parks, vest-pocket
USE **vest-pocket parks**

parks, wild animal
USE **wild animal parks**

parkways
RK.1525 (A,L,R)
ALT parkway
SN Use for limited access highways located within a park or parklike setting and intended for only passenger cars and noncommercial traffic. (W)
CN V.RK.ALO.ALO.BIQ.ARI.AFU.AFU.ARI.ARI

parlatories
RM.326
ALT parlatory
CN V.RM.AFU.DIO.AXC.ALO.AFU.DIO

parliament buildings
RK.985 (A,B)
ALT parliament building
UF buildings, parliament
CN V.RK.AFU.ALO.ALO.ERE.AFU.BCW.AXC

Parliament, Members of
USE **Members of Parliament**

parliamentary papers
VW.1038
ALT parliamentary paper
UF papers, parliamentary
CN V.VW.AFU.ARI.ALO.BCW.AFU.ARI.ALO.ALO

parlor cabinets
USE **étagères**

parlor chairs
TG.215
ALT parlor chair

UF chairs, parlor
CN V.TG.AFU.AFU.ALO.AFU.AFU.
ARI.AXC.BCW

parlor tables
TG.781
ALT **parlor table**
UF tables, parlor
CN V.TG.AFU.AFU.BIQ.BOK.ARI.
ALO.ARI

parlors
RM.178 (A,L)
ALT **parlor**
SN Use for rooms intended for conversation and the reception of guests in residences, hotels, monasteries, or churches; the late 20th-century living room is similar to the 19th- or early 20th-century parlor in that often another room is provided for daily family relaxation.
CN V.RM.AFU.DIO.ALO.CXA.CLM

parlors, beauty
USE **beauty shops**

parlors, betting
USE **betting parlors**

parlors, billiard
USE **pool halls**

parlors, bingo
USE **bingo halls**

parlors, body rub
USE **massage parlors**

parlors, funeral
USE **funeral homes**

parlors, ice cream
USE **ice cream parlors**

parlors, massage
USE **massage parlors**

parlors, pig
USE **pigsties**

parlors, pool
USE **pool halls**

parmazo marble
MT.790
SN A marble of Northern Italy having a coarse network of dark veins on a white or grayish ground. (W)
UF marble, parmazo
CN M.MT.AFU.AFU.AFU.DCU.AFU.
ARI.ARI.ARI.ALO.BUE

parochial records
VW.976
ALT **parochial record**
UF records, parochial
CN V.VW.AFU.ARI.ALO.ALO.ALO.ARI

parochial schools
RK.827 (L,B)
ALT **parochial school**
SN May be used for elementary or secondary schools operated, controlled, or supported by a religious body.
UF church schools
denominational schools
diocesan schools
parish schools
schools, church
schools, denominational
schools, diocesan
schools, parish
schools, parochial
CN V.RK.AFU.ALO.ALO.CXA.ARI.
ARI.AFU.AFU

parodoses
RM.354
ALT **parodos**
SN Passages in an ancient Greek theater between the audience and scaena affording access for spectators. (DAC)
CN V.RM.AFU.DIO.AXC.AXC.AFU.BIQ

parody
BM.8 (L,R)
SN Use for the form of analytical criticism in which one performance or work of art or literature subversively mimics another work or its style by adapting and inverting its characteristic features, in order to reveal weaknesses, pretensions, or lack of self-awareness in the original.
CN B.BM.AFU.AFU.AFU.AXC.AFU

paroling
KG.209 (L)
SN Officially allowing a conditional release from prison. (RLG7)
CN K.KG.AFU.ALO.BCW.CFS

parpend stones
USE **perpends**

parquetry
KT.709
SN Marquetry executed in a geometrical pattern, used especially for floors.
CN K.KT.AFU.ALO.GRC.CLM.ARI

parrotia
USE **Persian ironwood**

parsonages
RK.329 (A,L,B,R)
ALT **parsonage**
CN V.RK.AFU.ALO.ALO.AXC.ALO.
BOK.ARI.ARI

part elevations
USE **partial elevations**

Parthian
FL.3016 (L,B)
UF Arsacid
CN F.FL.ALO.AXC.ARI.BIQ.AFU.BCW

partial bibliographies
USE **selective bibliographies**

partial elevations
VD.26
ALT **partial elevation**
SN Use for elevations of only part of a structure. For drawings showing a structure as partly an exterior elevation and partly an interior elevation, use **sectional elevations.**
UF elevations, partial
part elevations
CN V.VD.AFU.AFU.BIQ.ALO.ALO.AXC

partial perspectives
VD.82
ALT **partial perspective**
SN Perspective drawings of portions of the exterior or interior of a structure.
UF perspectives, partial
CN V.VD.AFU.AFU.BIQ.ARI.ARI

partial plans
VD.62
ALT **partial plan**
SN Plan of one portion of a structure.
UF plans, partial
CN V.VD.AFU.AFU.BIQ.ALO.AXC.BOK

partial sections
VD.76
ALT **partial section**
SN Use for drawings of only part of a section through a building or object. For drawings of the exterior of a structure or object with a portion cut away so that the interior shows, use **cutaway drawings, broken-out sections, half sections,** or **sectional elevations.**
UF sections, partial
sections, strip
strip sections
CN V.VD.AFU.AFU.BIQ.ALO.BIQ.BOK

partial views
VB.18
ALT **partial view**
UF views, partial
CN V.VB.AFU.AFU.BOK.AFU.ALO

participation, citizen
USE **citizen participation**

participation, community
USE **citizen participation**

participatory design
KT.97 (A,B)
SN Participation by workers and residents in the design of the spaces, structures, or communities which they use or inhabit.
UF architecture, community
community architecture
design, participatory
CN K.KT.AFU.ALO.CFS.ALO.AFU

particle accelerators
RK.1155 (L)
ALT **particle accelerator**
SN Designates structures in which atom-

ic or subatomic particles are accelerated to high energies by means of electric and magnetic fields.
UF accelerators, particle
atom smashers
smashers, atom
CN V.RK.AFU.ALO.ALO.FIM.AFU

particle board
MT.1463 (L,B)
SN Board made from wood chips bonded with a synthetic resin.
UF board, flake
board, particle
flake board
CN M.MT.AFU.AFU.ALO.BIQ.DCU.ALO.DOI.BCW

particulate materials
USE **granular materials**

parties
KM.129 (L)
CN K.KM.AFU.DIO

parting compounds
MT.2627 (L)
SN Paste or liquid material used in casting to coat the interior of a mold in order to prevent the plaster cast from adhering to it. (MAYER)
UF abherents
agents, release
compounds, parting
release agents
CN M.MT.AFU.ARI.GLI

parting tools
TB.888 (N)
ALT **parting tool**
SN Narrow-bladed hand tools having a V-shaped gouge; used in woodworking for cutting grooves, in wood turning, or for cutting pieces in two. (DAC)
UF tools, parting
V-gouges
CN V.TB.AFU.BCW.CFS.ALO.AFU.CXA.BOK

partition tile
MT.170
SN Tile for use in building interior partitions, subdividing areas into rooms, or similar construction, carrying no superimposed loads. (DAC)
UF tile, partition
CN M.MT.AFU.AFU.AFU.AXC.ALO.ALO.ALO.AFU.ALO.ARI.ALO

partitions
RT.605 (A,B)
ALT **partition**
SN Interior walls separating one portion of a house from another; sometimes permanent inside walls which divide houses into various rooms. (PUTNAM) For entities other than walls that divide interior spaces, often incorporating bookshelves, cabinets, or drawers, use **room dividers.**
CN V.RT.AFU.AFU.AFU.BIQ.BUE.AFU.ARI.AXC.AFU

partitions, demountable
USE **demountable partitions**

partitions, folding
USE **folding partitions**

partitions, movable
USE **folding partitions**

partitions, relocatable
USE **demountable partitions**

partitions, toilet
USE **toilet compartments**

partner's desks
TG.545
ALT **partner's desk**
SN Use for desks constructed so that two people may work face-to-face; generally taking the form of a large writing table or desk with drawers on both sides.
UF desks, double
desks, partner's
double desks
CN V.TG.AFU.AFU.AXC.ALO.BZY.CLM

partners
HG.424
ALT **partner**
SN Persons associated as joint principals in carrying on an enterprise. (W)
CN H.HG.AFU.AXC.BOK.ERE

partnership
BM.457 (A,L,B)
CN B.BM.BCW.CRG

partnership agreements
VW.901
ALT **partnership agreement**
SN Documents embodying the terms and conditions of a partnership, as an association of two or more persons to carry on, as co-owners, a business for profit. (BLACKS)
UF agreements, partnership
CN V.VW.AFU.ARI.AFU.BOK.BOK.ALO.BCW

partnerships
HG.844 (L,B)
ALT **partnership**
SN Use for groups of two or more persons contractually associated as joint principals in business.(WCOL) For business enterprises considered in law as legal persons, use **corporations.**
CN H.HG.ALO.BOK.AFU.ALO

partridgewood
MT.1259
UF acapau
CN M.MT.AFU.AFU.ALO.BIQ.DCU.AFU.AFU.AFU.JII

parts, dimension
USE **dimension lumber**

Party of Color
USE **Rubenism**

party walls
RT.608 (A,L,B)
ALT **party wall**
SN Walls used jointly by two parties under easement agreement, erected upon a line dividing two parcels of land or between two dwelling units.
UF walls, party
CN V.RT.AFU.AFU.AFU.BIQ.BUE.AFU.ARI.BCW

parvises
RK.1591
ALT **parvis**
SN Use generally for the enclosed open spaces in front of and preceding the entry to European churches.
CN V.RK.ALO.ARI.CFS

pas-de-souris
RT.1095
SN In a castle, the steps leading from the moat to the entrance. (HAS)
CN V.RT.AFU.BIQ.AXC.AFU.ALO.AXC

Pasch
USE **Passover**

paseos
USE **promenades**

pass keys
USE **master keys**

passage graves
RK.487
ALT **passage grave**
SN Distinguished from **gallery graves** by having a clear distinction between the burial chamber and the tunnel-like entry passage leading to it.
UF graves, passage
CN V.RK.AFU.ALO.ALO.BOK.BUE.AFU.ALO.ALO.ALO

passages
RM.88
ALT **passage**
SN Use for relatively narrow interior spaces designed to provide access.
UF passageways
CN V.RM.AFU.DIO.ALO.ARI.AXC

passages (shopping arcades)
USE **shopping arcades**

passages, fish
USE **fishways**

passages, screens
USE **screens passages**

passageways
USE **passages**

passbooks
USE **bankbooks**

passenger conveyors
USE **moving walkways**

passenger elevators
RT.1314
ALT **passenger elevator**
UF elevators, passenger
CN V.RT.ALO.ALO.AFU.ARI.ALO.ALO.ALO

passenger lists
VW.282 (L)
ALT **passenger list**
SN Lists of persons who travel in a train, plane, ship, bus, or other conveyance without participating in its operation. (AHD)
UF lists, passenger
CN V.VW.AFU.AFU.AFU.FZU.BCW.ALO.BIQ

passenger lists, ships'
USE **ships' passenger lists**

passenger terminals
RK.1266
ALT **passenger terminal**
UF terminals, passenger
CN V.RK.AFU.ALO.ALO.GLI.AFU.BCW.ALO

passes, military
USE **military passes**

passion crosses
USE **Calvary crosses**

passion plays
BM.283 (L,R)
UF plays, passion
CN B.BM.AFU.ARI.BIQ.BZY.ALO

passionals
VW.551 (R)
ALT **passional**
SN Books containing descriptions of the sufferings of saints and martyrs, for reading on their festivals. (RHDEL2)
CN V.VW.AFU.ALO.AFU.AFU.ALO.BUE.CRG

passive solar heating
RT.1398 (L)
UF heating systems, passive solar
heating, passive solar
passive solar heating systems
solar heating, passive
systems, passive solar heating
CN V.RT.ALO.BCW.AFU.AFU.ARI.AXC.ALO

passive solar heating systems
USE **passive solar heating**

passive ventilation
USE **natural ventilation**

Passover
KM.86 (L,R)
UF Pasch
Pesach
CN K.KM.AFU.CFS.ARI.BZY

passport photographs
VJ.90
ALT **passport photograph**
UF passport photoprints
photographs, passport
photoprints, passport
CN V.VJ.AFU.ALO.AFU.AFU

passport photoprints
USE **passport photographs**

passports
VW.943 (L,N,R)
ALT **passport**
SN Official documents issued by a government that certify the identity and citizenship of individuals and grant them permission to travel abroad; includes permits issued by foreign countries allowing goods to be transported or persons to travel within that country. (AHD)
CN V.VW.AFU.ARI.AFU.CRG.ALO

paste
MT.2261 (L,R)
SN Use for any soft, plastic substance, such as an adhesive substance with a starch base. (MAYER)
CN M.MT.AFU.ALO.ERE

paste (glass)
MT.240
SN A brilliant glass of high lead content used for the manufacture of artificial gems; also an imitation gem made of this material. (W)
UF diamonds, paste
paste diamonds
strass
CN M.MT.AFU.AFU.AFU.BIQ.AFU.AFU.ALO.AFU

paste blue
USE **Prussian blue**

paste diamonds
USE **paste (glass)**

paste, library
USE **library paste**

pasteboard
MT.1909 (L)
SN Class of thick paper usually in the form of heavy sheets used chiefly for making boxes and other containers. (MH12)
CN M.MT.AFU.AFU.ARI.ALO.ALO.AXC.ALO.BIQ

pastel blue
USE **grayish blue**
pale blue
very pale blue

pastel crayons
USE **pastels (crayons)**

pastel drawings
USE **pastels**

pastel gray
USE **grayish yellow**

pastel green
USE **grayish yellow green**
moderate yellow green
pale green
very pale green

pastel lavender
USE **very pale purple**

pastel lilac
USE **very pale purple**

pastel mauve
USE **pale purplish pink**

pastel orange
USE **moderate orange**

pastel paintings
USE **pastels**

pastel pink
USE **moderate pink**
moderate yellowish pink

pastel turquoise green
USE **light bluish green**
very light bluish green

pastel yellow
USE **light greenish yellow**
light yellow
moderate greenish yellow
moderate yellow
pale greenish yellow
strong yellow

pastelists
HG.115
ALT **pastelist**
CN H.HG.AFU.AXC.AXC.AFU.AFU.ALO.AXC.DCU

pastels
VD.160 (R)
ALT **pastel**
UF drawings, pastel
paintings, pastel
pastel drawings
pastel paintings
CN V.VD.ALO

pastels (crayons)
TB.244
ALT **pastel (crayon)**
SN Colored crayons that consist of pigment mixed with just enough of an aqueous binder to hold it together; used in drawing. (MAYER)
UF crayons, pastel
pastel crayons
CN V.TB.AFU.ARI.CLM.AFU.ALO.AXC.ARI

pasticcios

USE **pastiches**

pastiches
VB.125 (L,R)
ALT **pastiche**
SN Use for artistic works that closely imitate the style of previous works, and especially those that piece together fragments from various sources.
UF pasticcios
CN V.VB.ALO.BZY.ARI

pastillage
USE **slip trailing**

pasting
KT.24
ALT **pasted**
SN Causing to adhere by or as if by means of a soft plastic mixture or composition. (W)
CN K.KT.AFU.ALO.BCW.AFU.ALO

Pasto
FL.1664 (L)
CN F.FL.ALO.ALO.ARI.ARI.BCW.CRG

pastors
HG.229 (L)
ALT **pastor**
CN H.HG.AFU.AXC.AXC.BIQ.AFU.ARI.DCU

pastose painting
USE **impasto**

pastry tables
TG.752
ALT **pastry table**
SN Marble top tables used exclusively for confectionery work. (PC)
UF tables, pastry
CN V.TG.AFU.AFU.BIQ.BOK.ALO. DUC

pastures
RD.288 (L)
ALT **pasture**
CN V.RD.ARI.ALO.AFU.AFU.BCW

Patagón
FL.1608 (L)
CN F.FL.ALO.ALO.ARI.ARI.ALO.AFU.BCW

Patan
FL.2170
UF Lalitipur
CN F.FL.ALO.ARI.AXC.AFU.AXC.ALO.AXC

Patashó
FL.1680
CN F.FL.ALO.ALO.ARI.ARI.BIQ.BUE

Patayan
FL.951
UF Hakataya
CN F.FL.ALO.ALO.ALO.AFU.ALO.ARI.BIQ.BIQ

patent furniture
TG.796
SN Use for a variety of innovative furniture forms covered wholly or in part by a registered patent. (INNO)
UF furniture, patent
CN V.TG.AFU.ARI.BOK.AFU

patent hammers
TB.606 (N)
ALT **patent hammer**
SN Two-faced hammers, each of whose faces are composed of a number of parallel thin chisels; used for dressing stone. (DAC)
UF hammers, patent
CN V.TB.AFU.BCW.BCW.ALO.EFQ.BCW

patent offices
RK.976 (A,L)
ALT **patent office**
SN Government offices for examining claims to patents and for granting patents. (W)
UF offices, patent
CN V.RK.AFU.ALO.ALO.ERE.AFU.ARI.ARI

patent yellow
USE **Turner's yellow**

patent, letters
USE **letters patent**

patents
VW.997 (L,N,R)
ALT **patent**
SN Grants made by a government to an inventor, assuring him the sole right to make, use, and sell the invention for a certain period of time. (AHD)
CN V.VW.AFU.ARI.ALO.BCW.AFU.AFU.AFU.CFS

patents, design
USE **design patents**

patents, land
USE **land grants**

pateras (motifs)
DG.49
ALT **patera (motif)**
SN Round or oval disks bearing an ornamental design in bas-relief or intaglio and used in decoration of buildings or furniture. (W)
CN D.DG.AFU.AFU.DCU

paternosters
RT.767
ALT **paternoster**
UF moldings, pearl
pearl moldings
CN V.RT.AFU.ALO.AFU.BOK.AFU.AFU.ARI.BUE

pathology, building
USE **building pathology**

paths
RK.1572 (L,B)
ALT **path**
UF pathways
CN V.RK.ALO.ALO.BUE.AXC

paths, bicycle
USE **cycling paths**

paths, bridle
USE **bridle paths**

paths, cycling
USE **cycling paths**

paths, garden
USE **garden walks**

pathways
USE **paths**

patina
MT.2549 (L,R)
SN Film or incrustation on copper or bronze; due to oxidation of the copper. (MAYER)
CN M.MT.AFU.ARI.CRG.ALO.BIQ

patio houses
USE **courtyard houses**

patio locks
TF.213
ALT **patio lock**
SN Locks designed with a push button or a turn-locking outside knob. When so locked, there is no entrance by key from the outside. (BROWNL)
UF locks, patio
CN V.TF.AFU.AFU.AFU.AFU.DIO.BIQ.AFU.DCU

patios
RM.53 (A,L,B)
ALT **patio**
SN Use for paved recreation areas adjoining 20th-century houses and the paved interior courts of Spanish or Spanish-style buildings.
CN V.RM.AFU.DIO.AFU.BCW.BCW

Patlichique
FL.985
CN F.FL.ALO.ALO.ALO.ALO.AFU.ALO.AFU.AFU.BIQ

patriarchal crosses
DG.14
ALT **patriarchal cross**
SN Crosses having two crossbars of which the lower is the longer and intersects the upright above or at its center. (W)
UF crosses, patriarchal
CN D.DG.AFU.AFU.ARI.BUE

patriarchs
HG.230 (L,R)
ALT **patriarch**
CN H.HG.AFU.AXC.AXC.BIQ.AFU.ARI.DIO

patrimony, cultural
USE **cultural property**

patriotism
BM.562 (L,R)
SN Use generally to mean love of one's country and devotion to its interests. For the sense of national consciousness exalting one nation above all others and placing primary emphasis on promotion of its culture and interests as opposed to those of other nations or supranational groups, use **nationalism.** (WCOL)
CN B.BM.BOK.BZY.BUE

patronage
BM.404 (A,L,B,R)
SN The supporting of artists and buying or funding of their work. (OCA)
CN B.BM.ARI.EFQ

patrons
HG.727 (A,L)
ALT **patron**
SN Those who give of their means or use their influence to help or benefit individuals, institutions, or causes, especially those who support the work of artists and writers. (W)
UF benefactors
CN H.HG.AFU.BCW.EFQ

Pattern and decoration (art movement)
USE **Pattern painting**

pattern-book drawings
USE **pattern drawings**

pattern books
VW.531 (A,B,R)
ALT **pattern book**
UF books, model
books, pattern
books, plan
copybooks (pattern books)
model books
plan books
CN V.VW.AFU.ALO.AFU.AFU.ALO.BCW.AXC

pattern-burnished ware
FL.2941
UF ware, pattern-burnished
CN F.FL.ALO.AXC.ARI.AXC.ALO.BIQ.BZY

pattern chairs
TG.189
ALT **pattern chair**
SN Chairs which served as models from which to work; frequently with arms or legs showing alternative forms and styles of decoration. (BEARD)
UF chairs, pattern
CN V.TG.AFU.AFU.ALO.AFU.AFU.ALO.DIO

pattern drawings
VD.101
ALT **pattern drawing**
SN Use for drawings, especially from the late Middle Ages and Renaissance, that served as exemplars in the workshop, either for apprentice copying or for transfer to final works. (A-L)
UF drawings, pattern
pattern-book drawings
CN V.VD.AFU.ALO.BIQ

Pattern painting
FL.3742 (R)
SN Use for the movement of Matisse-influenced decorative painting in New York in the 1970s.
UF Decorationist
painting, Pattern
Pattern and decoration (art movement)
CN F.FL.ALO.BUE.ARI.FZU

pattern, checker
USE **checker pattern**

pattern, continuous linear
USE **running ornament**

pattern, fish scale
USE **scale pattern**

pattern, key
USE **key pattern**

pattern, labyrinth (frets)
USE **frets**

pattern, labyrinth (interlace)
USE **interlace**

pattern, linked knot
USE **knotwork**

pattern, money
USE **money pattern**

pattern, network
USE **reticular pattern**

pattern, reticular
USE **reticular pattern**

pattern, scale
USE **scale pattern**

pattern, step
USE **step pattern**

pattern, stepped
USE **step pattern**

pattern, strigil
USE **strigillation**

pattern, striped
USE **stripes**

pattern, trumpet
USE **trumpet spirals**

pattern, wave
USE **wave pattern**

pattern, zigzag
USE **zigzags**

patterned glass
USE **figured glass**

patterned lumber
MT.1427
UF lumber, patterned
CN M.MT.AFU.AFU.ALO.BIQ.DCU.ALO.BOK.ALO.AFU.AFU.AFU.AFU

patternmakers
HG.569 (L)
ALT **patternmaker**
CN H.HG.AFU.AXC.BUE.AXC.CXA

patterns (design elements)
DG.93 (L,R)
ALT **pattern (design element)**
SN Use for ornamental designs, usually on a flat surface or in relief and composed of repeated motifs.
CN D.DG.AFU.ARI

patterns (guides)
TB.441 (L,N)
ALT **pattern (guide)**
SN Forms or models, made from a variety of materials, cut to the size or profile of the finished article and used as a guide during its construction.
CN V.TB.AFU.ARI.EFQ.ALO.BOK

patterns, allover
USE **allover patterns**

patterns, band (running ornament)
USE **running ornament**

patterns, counterchange
USE **counterchange**

patterns, diaper
USE **diaper patterns**

patterns, floral
USE **floral patterns**

patterns, flower
USE **floral patterns**

patterns, foliate
USE **foliation**

patterns, geometric
USE **geometric patterns**

patterns, overall
USE **allover patterns**

patterns, powdered
USE **powderwork**

patterns, running
USE **running ornament**

patterns, scroll
USE **scrollwork**

Patwin
FL.1260 (L)
CN F.FL.ALO.ALO.ARI.AFU.ALO.DCU

paumelle hinges
TF.100

ALT **paumelle hinge**
SN Door hinges each having a single joint, usually of modern design. (MEANS)
UF hinges, paumelle
CN V.TF.AFU.AFU.AFU.AFU.CLM.AFU.ARI.ALO.AFU

pavement lights
RT.998
ALT **pavement light**
SN Heavy glass set into a pavement to convey light to a space below. (DAC)
UF lights, pavement
CN V.RT.AFU.ARI.AFU.ARI.ARI.ARI

pavements
RT.811 (A,L,B,R)
ALT **pavement**
SN Durable coverings laid down to form the surface of a road or other outdoor area; by extension, hard floor coverings in large interiors, such as public halls or churches. (RS)
CN V.RT.AFU.ALO.AFU.BZY

pavements (sidewalks)
USE **sidewalks**

pavements, flexible
USE **flexible pavements**

pavements, rigid
USE **rigid pavements**

paver
USE **paving brick**

pavers
USE **concrete pavers**

pavers, concrete
USE **concrete pavers**

pavilion roofs
USE **pyramidal roofs**

pavilions
RK.1339 (A,L,B,R)
ALT **pavilion**
SN Light, sometimes ornamental, structures in a garden, park, or place of recreation that are used for entertainment or shelter. (W)
CN V.RK.AFU.ALO.ARI.AFU.BOK

pavilions (building divisions)
RM.22 (A,N)
ALT **pavilion (building division)**
SN Use both for the parts of buildings that project outward from the rest, especially common as corner, central, or terminal features in French architecture, and for the detached or semidetached units into which a building (as a hospital) is sometimes divided.
UF avant-corps
facade pavilions
pavilions, facade
CN V.RM.AFU.CRG

pavilions, bathing
USE **bathhouses**

pavilions, elephant
USE **elephant houses**

pavilions, facade
USE **pavilions (building divisions)**

pavilions, sports
USE **sports buildings**

pavillons (canopies)
USE **canopies (bed components)**

paving
KT.584 (A,L)
ALT **paved**
SN Laying or covering with stone, brick, asphalt, concrete, or other material, making a firm, level, or convenient surface for travel. (W)
CN K.KT.AFU.ALO.ERE.AXC

paving asphalt
MT.983
SN A dark brown to black sticky residue, predominantly derived from the refining of crude oil; used as the binder in asphaltic concrete. (DAC)
UF asphalt, paving
CN M.MT.AFU.AFU.ALO.ALO.AFU.ARI.AFU

paving brick
MT.106
SN A vitrified brick, especially suitable for use in pavements where resistance to abrasion is important. (DAC)
UF brick, paving
brick, paviour
paver
pavior
paviour brick
CN M.MT.AFU.AFU.AFU.AXC.ALO.AFU.ALO.CFS

paving sand
MT.2071
UF sand, paving
CN M.MT.AFU.AFU.ARI.BOK.ALO.BOK.AFU.ALO

paving stone
MT.907
SN A block or chunk of stone that is shaped or selected by shape for a paved surface. (DAC)
UF stone, paving
CN M.MT.AFU.AFU.AFU.DCU.ARI.AXC

paving tile
MT.2280
SN A glazed decorated tile used for floors, sidewalks, courtyards, and sometimes for walls. (W)
UF tile, paving
CN M.MT.AFU.ALO.IFM.ARI

pavior
USE **paving brick**

Paviotso
USE **Northern Paiute**

paviour brick
USE **paving brick**

Pavlovian
FL.2462
CN F.FL.ALO.AXC.AFU.ARI.AFU.ALO

pavonazzetto
MT.814
UF marble, pavonazzetto
marble, Phrygian
marble, Synnadicum
marmor Synnadicum
pavonazzetto marble
pavonazzo
Phrygian marble
Synnadicum marble
CN M.MT.AFU.AFU.AFU.DCU.AFU.ARI.ARI.ARI.BIQ.CFS

pavonazzetto marble
USE **pavonazzetto**

pavonazzo
USE **pavonazzetto**

paw feet
TG.926
ALT **paw foot**
SN Feet carved to represent an animal's paw; used on chairs, sofas, and case pieces, especially in the 19th century. (FAIRB)
UF feet, paw
CN V.TG.ALO.DZW.AFU.DCU.BIQ

Pawar
USE **Paramara**

pawnbroker's shops
USE **pawnshops**

Pawnee
FL.1392 (L)
CN F.FL.ALO.ALO.ARI.AFU.BOK.EFQ

pawnshops
RK.178 (L,B)
ALT **pawnshop**
UF pawnbroker's shops
shops, pawnbroker's
CN V.RK.AFU.ALO.ALO.ALO.ARI.BIQ.ALO.BUE

pay
USE **wages**

pay records
USE **payroll records**

Paya
FL.1559 (L)
CN F.FL.ALO.ALO.ARI.ALO.BOK.CFS

Payaguá
FL.1648 (L)
CN F.FL.ALO.ALO.ARI.ARI.AXC.CXA

paybooks
VW.850
ALT paybook
SN Individual pay records of members of the armed forces. (W)
CN V.VW.AFU.ARI.AFU.BIQ.CXA.AFU.BZY.AFU

payment bonds
VW.907
ALT payment bond
UF bonds, payment
CN V.VW.AFU.ARI.AFU.BOK.BOK.AXC.AXC

Payne's gray
USE **dark grayish blue**
grayish blue

Payne's gray, dark
USE **dark bluish gray**
dark grayish blue

Payne's gray, deep
USE **grayish blue**

Payne's gray, light
USE **bluish gray**
pale blue

Payne's gray, pale
USE **pale blue**

payroll records
VW.849
ALT payroll record
SN The records relating to the authorization, computation, distribution, and payment of wages and salaries. (GAHLM)
UF pay records
records, pay
records, payroll
CN V.VW.AFU.ARI.AFU.BIQ.CXA.AFU.BZY

payrolls
VW.851 (L)
ALT payroll
SN Lists, sometimes recorded in book form, of those entitled to receive compensation at a given time and of the amounts due to each. (GAHLM)
CN V.VW.AFU.ARI.AFU.BIQ.CXA.AFU.BZY.ALO

Pazyryk
FL.2131
CN F.FL.ALO.ARI.ARI.AFU.BIQ.ARI

PC
USE **polycarbonate**

PE
USE **polyethylene**

pe de pincels
USE **Spanish feet**

pea gravel
MT.889
UF gravel, pea
CN M.MT.AFU.AFU.AFU.DCU.ALO.BOK.AFU

peace, justices of the
USE **justices of the peace**

peach
MT.1292 (L)
CN M.MT.AFU.AFU.ALO.BIQ.DCU.AFU.AFU.AFU.KLE.AXC

peach (color)
USE **light orange**
light yellowish pink
moderate yellowish pink
pale orange yellow
strong yellowish pink

peach black
MT.1572
SN A variety of charcoal black made from peach pits, no longer in general use. (MAYER)
UF black, kernel
black, peach
kernel black
CN M.MT.AFU.AFU.ARI.AFU.AFU.ALO.ALO.AFU.AFU.AFU.ALO.ALO

peach bloom
MT.2560
UF bloom, peach
peachblow
CN M.MT.AFU.ARI.CRG.ARI.ARI.AFU.AFU.AFU.ALO

peach gray
USE **pale yellowish pink**

peach, bright
USE **strong yellowish pink**

peach, pale
USE **light yellowish pink**
pale yellowish pink

peachblow
USE **peach bloom**

peacock
USE **moderate greenish blue**

peacock blue
USE **dark greenish blue**
moderate greenish blue
strong greenish blue

peacock blue, bright
USE **brilliant greenish blue**
strong greenish blue

peacock blue, brilliant
USE **strong greenish blue**

peacock blue, dark
USE **dark greenish blue**

peacock blue, deep
USE **dark greenish blue**
moderate greenish blue

peacock blue, vivid
USE **strong greenish blue**

peak arches
USE **pointed arches**

peaks
RD.237 (L)
ALT peak
CN V.RD.ARI.AFU.AXC.ALO.BCW

peanut oil
MT.2038 (L)
UF arachis oil
oil, arachis
oil, peanut
CN M.MT.AFU.AFU.ARI.ARI.AXC.ARI.BOK

pear
MT.1260 (L)
UF pyrus
CN M.MT.AFU.AFU.ALO.BIQ.DCU.AFU.AFU.AFU.JOC

pear drop handles
TF.75
ALT pear drop handle
UF drop handles, pear
handles, pear drop
CN V.TF.AFU.AFU.AFU.AFU.CFS.BCW.AFU.BCW.AFU

pear-shaped
DC.116
CN D.DC.AFU.ARI.FCS.AXC

pear, common
USE **common pear**

pearl
MT.941 (L,R)
CN M.MT.AFU.AFU.ALO.AFU.DIO

pearl (color)
USE **light gray**

pearl blue
USE **light gray**

pearl gray
USE **light bluish gray**
light gray
pale blue
very pale blue

pearl moldings
USE **paternosters**

pearl white
USE **bismuth white**
light gray

pearl, mother of
USE **mother of pearl**

pearling
USE **beading (edging pattern)**

peasant art
USE **folk art**

peasantry
HG.886 (L,R)
SN Class of persons that till the soil, either as small landholders or as

hired laborers. (W)
UF peasants
CN H.HG.ALO.DOI.ALO.ALO

peasants
USE **peasantry**

peat
MT.2067 (L,B,R)
SN An earthy mass formed by the rapid accumulation of quick growing mosses and plants, used as a fuel. (MH)
CN M.MT.AFU.AFU.ARI.BOK.ALO. BIQ

peat bogs
RD.171 (L)
ALT **peat bog**
UF bogs, peat
moors, peat
peat moors
CN V.RD.ARI.AFU.ARI.ARI.AFU

peat gardens
RK.1412 (L)
ALT **peat garden**
SN Denotes generally hilly gardens buttressed by or built up of cut blocks of peat with terraces for plantings. (DLA)
UF gardens, peat
peat-wall gardens
CN V.RK.ALO.AFU.AFU.AFU.BOK

peat moors
USE **peat bogs**

peat-wall gardens
USE **peat gardens**

peavies
TB.1069 (N)
ALT **peavy**
SN Tools which combine the jam pike and the cant hook; used by lumbermen to pry and roll logs.
UF peevies
pevies
CN V.TB.AFU.BCW.CFS.ALO.ALO.BZY.ALO

pebble
MT.891 (L)
CN M.MT.AFU.AFU.AFU.DCU.ALO.BZY

Pebble culture
USE **Oldowen**

pebble dash
MT.2458
UF dash, pebble
dash, rock
rock dash
CN M.MT.AFU.ARI.CRG.AFU.AXC.ARI.AXC

pecan
MT.1177 (L)
UF Carya illinoensis
Carya illoinesis
hickory, pecan
pecan hickory
CN M.MT.AFU.AFU.ALO.BIQ.DCU.AFU.AFU.AFU.ELK.BCW

pecan hickory
USE **pecan**

pedal valves, foot
USE **foot pedal valves**

peddlers
HG.432 (L,R)
ALT **peddler**
UF hucksters
CN H.HG.AFU.AXC.BOK.FCS.ARI

pedestal base tables
USE **pedestal tables**

pedestal chairs
TG.81
ALT **pedestal chair**
SN Chairs constructed of a molded shell mounted on a single support on a flared base. (HAYWAR)
UF chairs, pedestal
CN V.TG.AFU.AFU.ALO.AFU.AFU.AFU.JII

pedestal desks
TG.546
ALT **pedestal desk**
SN Desks having a flat top and two boxlike supports either containing cupboards or drawers.
UF desks, pedestal
CN V.TG.AFU.AFU.AXC.ALO.BZY.CRG

pedestal end sideboards
TG.594
ALT **pedestal end sideboard**
SN Sideboards having a center drawer and a large boxlike support on either end; often these supports are partioned into divisions, or they may have drawers or shelves.
UF pedestal sideboards
sideboards, pedestal
sideboards, pedestal end
CN V.TG.AFU.AFU.AXC.ALO.CRG.BUE

pedestal sideboards
USE **pedestal end sideboards**

pedestal tables
TG.696
ALT **pedestal table**
SN Tables with a single columnar support. (FAIRB)
UF pedestal base tables
pillar pedestal tables
tables, pedestal
tables, pedestal base
tables, pillar pedestal
CN V.TG.AFU.AFU.BIQ.BOK.AFU.DUC.ALO

pedestals
RT.178 (N,B,R)
ALT **pedestal**
SN Use for solid, fixed supports found under such architectural elements as columns or balustrades, or built in to hold sculpture; usually classically divided by tripartation into base, dado, and cap.
CN V.RT.AFU.AFU.AFU.AXC.CFS.AFU

pedestals (furniture)
TG.609 (N,R)
ALT **pedestal (furniture)**
SN Use for freestanding supports, usually for decorative objects, sometimes incorporating cabinets or shelves; often classically divided by tripartition into base, dado, and cap.
CN V.TG.AFU.AFU.BIQ.ARI

pedestals with drawers
USE **cabinets of drawers**

pedestrian bridges
USE **footbridges**

pedestrian malls
USE **malls (walkways)**

pedestrian overpasses
USE **footbridges**

pedestrian roads
USE **pedestrian streets**

pedestrian streets
RK.1539 (A)
ALT **pedestrian street**
UF foot streets
pedestrian roads
roads, pedestrian
streets, foot
streets, pedestrian
streets, walking
walking streets
CN V.RK.ALO.ALO.BIQ.ARI.AFU.ALO.ALO.ALO

pedestrian walkways
USE **footbridges**

pedestrian ways
USE **walkways**

pedestrians
HG.728 (L)
ALT **pedestrian**
CN H.HG.AFU.BCW.ELK

Pedi
FL.571 (L)
CN F.FL.ALO.AFU.AXC.ARI.BCW.ALO

pediatric hospitals
USE **children's hospitals**

pedigrees
VW.334 (L,N,R)
ALT **pedigree**
SN Charts or lists showing lineage, especially those showing the ancestors of purebred animals. (AHD)
CN V.VW.AFU.AFU.ALO.CRG.ARI.AFU.ALO

pedimented dormers
RT.480
ALT **pedimented dormer**
SN Gabled dormers in which the gable is treated as a pediment.
UF dormers, pedimented
CN V.RT.AFU.AFU.AFU.BIQ.ARI.ALO. AFU.BUE.AXC.AXC.AFU

pediments
RT.672 (A,L,N,B,R)
ALT **pediment**
SN Triangular gable walls above the horizontal cornice of a classically treated building; also, triangular or roughly triangular elements, sometimes curved, or broken at the center, surmounting porticoes or openings. Common also on furniture, including as bonnet tops.
CN V.RT.AFU.AFU.AFU.BIQ.BUE. ALO.ALO.BIQ

pediments, broken
USE **broken pediments**

pediments, ogee
USE **ogee pediments**

pediments, segmental
USE **segmental pediments**

peel towers
USE **bastel houses**

peeling
KT.921
ALT **peeled**
CN K.KT.ALO.BZY.AXC

peeling chisels
USE **barking chisels**

peeling irons
USE **barking irons**

peels
USE **bastel houses**

peen hammers
TB.459
ALT **peen hammer**
SN Hammers of various designs which are roughly toothed to facilitate the cutting of stone or the breaking of brick, and sometimes having two opposite cutting edges; used especially by metal workers and stone masons. (PUTNAM)
UF hammers, peen
CN V.TB.AFU.ARI.ELK.AFU.ALO

peening
KT.153 (L)
ALT **peened**
SN The working of a metal by means of hammer blows. (DAC)
CN K.KT.AFU.ALO.DOI.CXA

peephole cards
USE **aperture cards**

peepholes
RT.953
ALT **peephole**
SN Holes or crevices (as in a furnace, oven, or door) through which one may look. (W)
UF holes, Judas
Judas holes
Judas windows
windows, Judas
CN V.RT.AFU.ARI.AFU.AFU.BOK. AFU.ALO.AFU

peevies
USE **peavies**

peg awls
TB.787 (N)
ALT **peg awl**
SN Small awls used in caning chairs.
UF awls, peg
CN V.TB.AFU.BCW.BUE.ARI

peg cutters
TB.872 (N)
ALT **peg cutter**
SN Hardened steel plates containing holes of various diameters; used to cut dowels by driving pegs through the holes to remove excess wood. (DAC)
UF cutters, dowel
cutters, peg
dowel cutters
dowel plates
plates, dowel
CN V.TB.AFU.BCW.CFS.ALO.AFU. BZY.ALO

pegmatite
MT.589 (L)
CN M.MT.AFU.AFU.AFU.DCU.AFU. AFU.AFU.AFU.AFU.ARI.AFU.ALO

pegs
TF.455 (N)
ALT **peg**
SN Small, cylindrical and pointed pieces of wood used to fasten wood members together. (MEANS)
CN V.TF.AFU.AFU.AFU.ALO.AFU.CRG

Pegu
FL.2315
CN F.FL.ALO.ARI.BCW.AFU.BCW.AFU

Peigan
USE **Piegan**

Peleset
USE **Philistine**

pelites
USE **argillaceous rock**

pellet
MT.2254
CN M.MT.AFU.ALO.DOI.ARI.AFU

pellicle, collodion
USE **collodion pellicle**

Pelos phase
FL.2538
CN F.FL.ALO.AXC.ALO.AFU.AFU. ALO.AFU.AFU.AFU

pelota courts
USE **canchas**

peltogyne
USE **purpleheart**

Pemba
FL.610
CN F.FL.ALO.AFU.AXC.AXC.ALO. BUE.ALO

Pembroke tables
TG.675 (N)
ALT **Pembroke table**
SN Dropleaf tables with a drawer or drawers below the top on either end. Introduced during the Chippendale period and intended to serve many purposes.
UF tables, Pembroke
CN V.TG.AFU.AFU.BIQ.BOK.AFU. AXC.BCW

Pembroke tables, harlequin
USE **harlequin tables**

Pembroke tables, pillar and claw
USE **pillar and claw Pembroke tables**

pen plotters
TB.162
ALT **pen plotter**
UF plotters, pen
CN V.TB.AFU.ARI.BCW.AXC.AXC. AFU.ALO

penal colonies
RG.49 (L)
ALT **penal colony**
UF colonies, penal
CN V.RG.AFU.AFU.BCW.ALO

penal institutions
USE **correctional institutions**

penal law
USE **criminal law**

pencil cedar
USE **red cedar**

pencil holders
TB.251 (N)
ALT **pencil holder**
SN Cylinders into which a medium such as a rod of graphite or silver is inserted and held by various means. (ADAG)
UF holders, mechanical pencil
holders, pencil
mechanical pencil holders
pencil holders, mechanical
CN V.TB.AFU.ARI.CLM.AFU.ALO. BZY.AFU

pencil holders, mechanical
USE **pencil holders**

pencil-post beds
TG.355
ALT **pencil-post bed**
SN Beds with hexagonal or octagonal posts, usually thought to have been made prior to the American Revolution. (MONTGO)
UF beds, pencil-post
CN V.TG.AFU.AFU.ARI.AFU.AFU.BZY.AFU

pencil sharpeners
TB.260 (N)
ALT **pencil sharpener**
UF sharpeners, pencil
CN V.TB.AFU.ARI.CLM.AFU.ALO.DCU

pencils
TB.261 (L,N)
ALT **pencil**
CN V.TB.AFU.ARI.CLM.AFU.ALO.DIO

pencils, charcoal
USE **charcoal pencils**

pencils, clutch
USE **mechanical pencils**

pencils, colored
USE **colored pencils**

pencils, graphite
USE **graphite pencils**

pencils, grease
USE **grease pencils**

pencils, lead
USE **graphite pencils**

pencils, mechanical
USE **mechanical pencils**

pencils, propelling
USE **mechanical pencils**

Pend d'Oreille
USE **Kalispel**

pendant posts
RT.515
ALT **pendant post**
SN In decorative, open-timber roof trusses, short posts set against the wall, bearing at bottom on a stone corbel or capital and supporting, generally with the aid of a curved brace, the wall end of the tie beam or hammer beam of the truss. (RS)
UF hammer posts
pendent posts
posts, hammer
posts, pendant
posts, pendent
CN V.RT.AFU.AFU.AFU.BIQ.ARI.ALO.ALO.ARI.ALO

pendants (architectural ornaments)
RT.1060
ALT **pendant (architectural ornament)**
SN Any fixed hanging architectural ornaments.
CN V.RT.AFU.BCW.BZY

Pende
FL.469 (L)
UF Bapende
CN F.FL.ALO.AFU.AXC.ALO.ALO.ARI.BZY

pendent posts
USE **pendant posts**

pendentive domes
RT.394
ALT **pendentive dome**
SN Use for domes with inner surfaces continuous with the surfaces of their pendentives.
UF domes, pendentive
handkerchief vaults
sail vaults
vaults, handkerchief
vaults, sail
CN V.RT.AFU.AFU.AFU.BIQ.AFU.AFU.BCW

pendentives
RT.182 (A,B)
ALT **pendentive**
SN Curved wall surfaces which form a transition between a dome (or its drum) and the supporting masonry. (HAS)
CN V.RT.AFU.AFU.AFU.AXC.CLM

pendulum saws
TB.1001
ALT **pendulum saw**
SN Curved saws supported on a frame on a fulcrum, which can swing back and forth, cutting as it does.
UF saws, pendulum
saws, swing
swing saws
CN V.TB.AFU.BCW.CFS.ALO.AFU.EWY.AXC.ARI

Pendzhikent
USE **Panjikent**

penetrants
MT.2320
SN Fluid added to coating material to increase penetration into a surface. (MAYER)
CN M.MT.AFU.ARI.ALO.DUC

Peninsula Yuman
FL.1284
UF Yuman, Peninsula
CN F.FL.ALO.ALO.ARI.AFU.ALO.FZU.ARI

Peninsular
FL.2412
CN F.FL.ALO.ARI.BCW.BOK.AFU.BOK

peninsulas
RD.223 (L)
ALT **peninsula**
CN V.RD.ARI.AFU.AXC.AFU.ALO.AXC.AXC

penitentiaries
USE **prisons**

penitentiaries, federal
USE **federal prisons**

penitentiaries, state
USE **state prisons**

penitentiary houses
USE **prisons**

penjing
RK.1411 (A)
SN Designates miniature Chinese plants and landscapes formed from them, often including stones, water, and miniature figures and buildings; also, the art of creating such gardens.
CN V.RK.ALO.AFU.AFU.AFU.BIQ.AFU

penknives
TB.128 (L)
ALT **penknife**
SN Small pocket knives, usually with only one blade. (W)
UF knives, pen
CN V.TB.AFU.ARI.AXC.ALO.BUE.AFU.ARI

penmanship books
USE **copybooks**

penmen
USE **calligraphers**

Pennacook
FL.1303 (L)
CN F.FL.ALO.ALO.ARI.AFU.ARI.CFS

Pennsylvania bank barns
RK.55
ALT **Pennsylvania bank barn**
SN Use for barns built into hillsides and generally characterized by stone end walls and a ramp up to a second floor containing crops and machinery which overhangs, on the barnyard side, a first floor kept for livestock.
UF bank barns, German
bank barns, Pennsylvania
barns, German bank
barns, Pennsylvania bank
barns, Pennsylvania German
barns, Pennsylvania standard
German bank barns
Pennsylvania barns
Pennsylvania German barns
Pennsylvania standard barns
CN V.RK.AFU.ALO.ALO.AFU.AFU.AFU.ARI.AFU.AFU

Pennsylvania barns
USE **Pennsylvania bank barns**

Pennsylvania Dutch
FL.1704 (L,R)
UF Dutch, Pennsylvania
German, Pennsylvania

Pennsylvania German
CN F.FL.ALO.ALO.AXC.AFU.AFU.AFU

Pennsylvania German
USE **Pennsylvania Dutch**

Pennsylvania German barns
USE **Pennsylvania bank barns**

Pennsylvania standard barns
USE **Pennsylvania bank barns**

penny arcades
RK.1034 (B)
ALT **penny arcade**
UF arcades, penny
CN V.RK.AFU.ALO.ALO.EWY.AXC.ARI.AFU.AFU

Penobscot
FL.1304 (L)
CN F.FL.ALO.ALO.ARI.AFU.ARI.CLM

pens
TB.267 (L,N,B,R)
ALT **pen**
CN V.TB.AFU.ARI.CLM.AFU.ALO.DOI

pens, ball-point
USE **ball-point pens**

pens, calligraphic lettering
USE **lettering pens**

pens, dotted line
USE **dotting wheels**

pens, felt
USE **felt-tip pens**

pens, felt-tip
USE **felt-tip pens**

pens, fountain
USE **fountain pens**

pens, lettering
USE **lettering pens**

pens, light
USE **light pens**

pens, marking
USE **markers (drawing instruments)**

pens, needle-point
USE **stylographs**

pens, quill
USE **quill pens**

pens, reed
USE **reed pens**

pens, ruling
USE **ruling pens**

pens, technical
USE **technical pens**

pensées, premières
USE **preliminary sketches**

pensions
BM.374 (A,L,B)
UF retirement pensions
CN B.BM.ARI.AXC.ALO

pensions (hotels)
RK.954 (B)
ALT **pension (hotel)**
CN V.RK.AFU.ALO.ALO.ELK.BCW.ALO

penstocks
RM.462 (L,N)
ALT **penstock**
SN Pipes conducting water from a head gate to a water wheel; also conduits for conveying water to a power plant. (RHDEL2)
CN V.RM.ALO.ALO.AFU.ALO

pent roofs (shed roofs)
USE **shed roofs**

pent roofs (skirt roofs)
USE **skirt roofs**

pentachlorophenol
MT.2640 (L)
CN M.MT.AFU.ARI.HCQ.AFU.ARI

pentagons
BM.781 (L)
ALT **pentagonal**
CN B.BM.CFS.ARI.AXC.BCW.AFU.BIQ.ARI

pentane
MT.1013
SN Any of three isometric parafin hydrocarbons found in petroleum and natural gas. (W)
CN M.MT.AFU.AFU.ALO.BCW.ALO.ALO.ALO

Pentelic marble
MT.834
UF greco fino
marble, Pentelic
marmor Pentelicum
Pentelico
Pentelikos lithos
CN M.MT.AFU.AFU.AFU.DCU.AFU.ARI.ARI.ARI.BOK.DCU

Pentelico
USE **Pentelic marble**

Pentelikos lithos
USE **Pentelic marble**

penthouse roofs (shed roofs)
USE **shed roofs**

penthouse roofs (skirt roofs)
USE **skirt roofs**

penthouses
RM.23 (A,B)
ALT **penthouse**
SN Use for structures enclosing useful space that constitute the top level of multistory buildings and have walls set back significantly from the walls of the story below; includes quite small structures, surrounded by large areas of flat roof, such as shelters for elevator machinery.
CN V.RM.AFU.CXA

pentices
USE **appentices**

pentimenti
BM.61 (R)
ALT **pentimento**
SN Refers to evidence of a painter's change of mind, apparent when areas of a picture which have been overpainted become visible. (RHLPS)
CN B.BM.AFU.AFU.ARI.AFU.BCW.ALO.BIQ

pents
USE **appentices**

people
HG.1
UF human beings
humans
persons
CN H.HG.AFU

people-movers
RT.1302
ALT **people-mover**
UF automated guideway transit
transit, automated guideway
CN V.RT.ALO.ALO.AFU.ALO.ALO

peopled scrolls
USE **inhabited scrolls**

peoplemovers, automated
USE **personal rapid transit**

peperino
MT.635
UF lapis albanus
CN M.MT.AFU.AFU.AFU.DCU.AFU.AFU.ALO.ALO.ALO.AXC.AFU

perception
BM.588 (L,R)
UF apprehension
CN B.BM.BUE.BOK

perception, figure-ground
USE **figure-ground perception**

perception, sound
USE **space perception**

perception, tactile
USE **touch**

Perceptual Abstract
USE **Op art**

percloses
USE **parcloses**

percolation, soil
USE **soil percolation**

percussive drills
USE **jackhammers**

Pere
FL.516
CN F.FL.ALO.AFU.AXC.ALO.ALO.BIQ.AFU.AFU.CFS

perennials
RD.270 (L)
ALT **perennial**
CN V.RD.ARI.AFU.BCW.ALO.ALO.ALO.AFU.BIQ

perforated brick
MT.89 (B)
UF brick, perforated
CN M.MT.AFU.AFU.AFU.AXC.ALO.AFU.AFU.ALO.ARI

perforated walls
USE **pierced walls**

perforating wheels
TB.358 (N)
ALT **perforating wheel**
SN Finely spiked or serrated wheels mounted at the end of a handle, used to perforate paper along the lines of a drawing in order to transfer it to another surface by pouncing. (MAYER)
UF pounce wheels
tracing wheels (pouncing)
wheels, perforating
wheels, pounce
wheels, tracing (pouncing)
CN V.TB.AFU.ARI.CXA.ALO

performance art
BM.263 (A,L,R)
SN Use for the genre of art works that unfold over time and that fall, by intention, between theater and object-oriented art.
UF art, performance
CN B.BM.AFU.ARI.BCW.FOG.BZY

performance artists
HG.116
ALT **performance artist**
SN Persons who formulate works of performance art. For persons in the traditional performing arts, use **performing artists.**
UF artists, performance
CN H.HG.AFU.AXC.AXC.AFU.AFU.ALO.AXC.DIO

performance bonds
VW.908 (B)
ALT **performance bond**
SN Bonds of the contractor in which a surety guarantees to the owner that the work will be performed in accordance with the contract documents. (GCIT)
UF bonds, performance
CN V.VW.AFU.ARI.AFU.BOK.BOK.AXC.BCW

performance specifications
VW.800 (B)
ALT **performance specification**
SN Specifications written according to recognized standards within the building industry, such as ASTM, and containing a complete description of the project including materials, products, designs, functions, and the performance to be expected. (STEIN)
UF specifications, performance
CN V.VW.AFU.ARI.AFU.ARI.AFU.ARI.BOK

performances
KM.57
CN K.KM.AFU.BOK.AXC

performances, first
USE **premieres**

performers
USE **performing artists**

performing artists
HG.65 (L,R)
ALT **performing artist**
SN Persons in the traditional performing arts, such as music, theater, and dance. For persons who make performance art, use **performance artists.**
UF artists, performing
entertainers
performers
showmen
CN H.HG.AFU.AXC.AXC.AFU.AFU.AFU.BIQ

performing arts
KD.5 (L,R)
UF arts, performing
CN K.KD.AFU.AFU.AFU.AFU.AFU

performing arts centers
RK.930 (A,L,B)
ALT **performing arts center**
UF arts centers, performing
centers for the performing arts
centers, performing arts
performing arts, centers for the
CN V.RK.AFU.ALO.ALO.EFQ.ARI.AXC

performing arts, centers for the
USE **performing arts centers**

perfume
MT.2631 (L,R)
CN M.MT.AFU.ARI.GRC

Pergamene
FL.2691
UF Pergamene School
CN F.FL.ALO.AXC.ALO.AFU.ALO.BCW.ALO.BZY

Pergamene pottery
USE **Pergamene ware**

Pergamene School
USE **Pergamene**

Pergamene ware
FL.2751
UF Pergamene pottery
pottery, Pergamene
ware, Pergamene
CN F.FL.ALO.AXC.ALO.ALO.ALO.BUE.ALO.AXC

pergolas
RK.1330 (A,L,N,B,R)
ALT **pergola**
SN Garden structures with open wood-framed roofs, often latticed, supported by regularly spaced posts or columns; often covered by climbing plants such as vines or roses, shading a walk or passageway. (DAC)
CN V.RK.AFU.ALO.ARI.AFU.AFU.AFU

periaktoi
RT.1267
ALT **periaktos**
SN In Greek theaters, the revolving triangular prisms on either side of the stage used for scenery changes. (KOSTOF)
CN V.RT.AFU.BUE.ARI.ARI

periboloi
RM.444
ALT **peribolos**
SN Enclosing walls or colonnades surrounding a temenos or sacred enclosure, and hence sometimes applied to the enclosure itself. (FLETCH)
CN V.RM.ALO.AFU.BOK.AFU.AFU

Pericú
FL.1283
CN F.FL.ALO.ALO.ARI.AFU.ALO.FZU.ALO.ARI

peridot
USE **grayish olive green**
grayish yellow green
moderate olive green

peridromes
USE **pteromata**

Perigordian
FL.2469 (L)
CN F.FL.ALO.AXC.AFU.ARI.ALO.BCW

Perigordian, Lower
USE **Lower Perigordian**

Perigordian, Upper
USE **Upper Perigordian**

perilla oil
MT.2016 (L)
SN A drying oil for use in house and industrial paints; not used for artists' colors. (MAYER)
UF oil, perilla
CN M.MT.AFU.ARI.ARI.AXC.AFU.BOK

period
BM.301
SN Use to mean a distinct historical or

cultural portion or division of time. (OED)
UF era
CN B.BM.AFU.AXC.CXA

period rooms
RM.98 (A,R)
ALT **period room**
SN Use for rooms in museums in which furnishings are displayed within a historically accurate architectural setting.
UF rooms, period
CN V.RM.AFU.DIO.ALO.AXC.ALO

periodic markets
KM.153
SN Markets at which buyers and sellers converge according to a regular schedule; merchants set up temporary stands or tables, usually occupying the same location in the market space and offering the same goods for sale on each occasion. (PMAALA)
UF markets, periodic
CN K.KM.AFU.ELK.ARI.ARI

periodical illustration
KT.208 (L,R)
UF illustration, magazine
illustration, periodical
magazine illustration
CN K.KT.AFU.ALO.DUC.CLM.BIQ

periodical illustrations
VB.45 (L,R)
ALT **periodical illustration**
UF illustrations, magazine
illustrations, periodical
magazine illustrations
CN V.VB.AFU.ALO.AXC.AFU.ARI

periodical indexes
VW.437 (L)
ALT **periodical index**
UF indexes, periodical
CN V.VW.AFU.AFU.ALO.EWY.BOK. ALO.AXC

periodicals
VW.619 (A,L,N,B,R)
ALT **periodical**
SN Publications issued at regular intervals of more than one day. (AHD)
UF journals (periodicals)
magazines
CN V.VW.AFU.ALO.AFU.CXA.AFU. BCW

periodicals, illustrated
USE **illustrated periodicals**

peripherals
TB.149 (N)
ALT **peripheral**
SN Any devices that are connected to a computer. (DOC)
UF computer peripherals
hardware (peripherals)
peripherals, computer
CN V.TB.AFU.ARI.BCW.AXC

peripherals, computer
USE **peripherals**

periphery walls
USE **exterior walls**

peripteral
DC.91
SN Describes buildings surrounded by a single row of columns.
CN D.DC.AFU.ARI.ERE.BIQ.BUE

peristaliths
USE **cromlechs**

peristeles
USE **standing stones**

peristyle houses
RK.258 (A)
ALT **peristyle house**
UF houses, peristyle
CN V.RK.AFU.ALO.ALO.AXC.ALO. AFU.CRG.AFU.ALO

peristyles
RT.58 (A)
ALT **peristyle**
SN Includes colonnades surrounding a building, such as a Greek temple, and Roman courtyards surrounded by a colonnade.
CN V.RT.AFU.AFU.AFU.ARI.AXC.AFU

peristyles (Roman courtyards)
USE **peristylia**

peristylia
RM.48
ALT **peristylium**
SN Use for the court toward the back of a Roman house, commonly with a small garden surrounded by a colonnade.
UF peristyles (Roman courtyards)
CN V.RM.AFU.DIO.AFU.BCW.ARI. BCW

periwinkle
USE **grayish purplish blue**
light purplish blue
pale purplish blue

periwinkle blue
USE **light purplish blue**
light violet

periwinkle blue, bright
USE **light violet**

periwinkle blue, light
USE **light purplish blue**
light violet
very pale violet

periwinkle blue, pale
USE **very pale purple**
very pale purplish blue

Perkin's violet
USE **mauve**

perlite
MT.630 (L)
SN A type of obsidian found in Oregon and California; contains about 75% silica. (MH)
UF calite
CN M.MT.AFU.AFU.AFU.DCU.AFU. AFU.ALO.ALO.ALO.AFU.ALO

Perm
FL.1800 (L)
CN F.FL.ALO.ARI.AFU.AXC.CXA

permalba
USE **composite white**

permanent blue
USE **artificial ultramarine blue**
strong purplish blue

permanent green
MT.1655
UF green, permanent
CN M.MT.AFU.AFU.ARI.AFU.AFU. ALO.ALO.AXC.ARI.BOK

permanent mauve
USE **manganese violet**

permanent red
USE **moderate red**
strong red

permanent violet
USE **manganese violet**
strong purple

permanent white
USE **blanc fixe**

permanent yellow
USE **barium yellow**
moderate orange yellow

Permanentweiss
USE **blanc fixe**

permeability
BM.978 (L,B)
ALT **permeable**
SN Property of porous material which is measured by the rate by volume at which a fluid passes through a cross section of the material. (W)
CN B.BM.CFS.AXC.BZY.BZY.ALO

permeability agents
MT.2321
SN An additive used to make hardened concrete more water-resistant. (PUTNAM)
UF agents, permeability
CN M.MT.AFU.ARI.ALO.DZW

permeability, soil
USE **soil permeability**

permits
VW.377 (N)
ALT **permit**
SN Documents which grant a person the right to do something not forbidden

by law but not allowable without such authority. (BLACKS)
CN V.VW.AFU.AFU.ALO.DUC.AXC

permits, building
USE **building permits**

permits, demolition
USE **demolition permits**

permits, occupancy
USE **certificates of occupancy**

permutation locks
TF.238
ALT **permutation lock**
SN Locks having changeable tumblers actuated by either a key or dial. (STEIN)
UF locks, permutation
CN V.TF.AFU.AFU.AFU.AFU.DIO.BIQ.ALO.ALO.BOK

permuted indexes
USE **rotated indexes**

perpendicular
DC.10
CN D.DC.AFU.ALO.AFU.AXC

Perpendicular Gothic
USE **Perpendicular Style**

Perpendicular Style
FL.3128 (L,R)
UF Gothic, Perpendicular
Perpendicular Gothic
Pointed, Third
Rectilinear Style
Third Pointed
CN F.FL.ALO.BCW.ALO.ALO.AFU.BOK.ARI.ALO.AXC.ARI

perpendicular tracery
RT.1019
SN Tracery that characterized the Perpendicular Style having repeated perpendicular mullions often rising to the curve of the arch, the mullions crossed at intervals by horizontal transoms producing repeated vertical rectangles. (HAS)
UF panel tracery
rectilinear tracery
tracery, panel
tracery, perpendicular
tracery, rectilinear
CN V.RT.AFU.ARI.ALO.BZY.AFU.AFU.ALO

perpends
MT.2759 (B)
ALT **perpend**
SN Bondstones which extend completely through the entire thickness of a masonry wall and are exposed on both wall faces. (HAS)
UF parpend stones
stones, parpend
stones, through
through stones
CN M.MT.AFU.AXC.BIQ.ALO.AFU.AFU

perpetual calendars
VW.89 (L)
ALT **perpetual calendar**
SN Charts or mechanical devices that indicate the day of the week corresponding to any given date over a period of many years. (AHD)
UF calendars, perpetual
CN V.VW.AFU.AFU.AFU.FZU.AFU.ALO

perroquets
TG.271
ALT **perroquet**
SN Pliants having a back with finials, which were often hooked forward and made to resemble parakeets. Came into fashion in France in the early 17th century; principally used at dining tables.
UF chaises à la dauphine
CN V.TG.AFU.AFU.ALO.AFU.ALO.AXC.AFU.BCW.AFU

Persian
FL.2997 (A,L,R)
CN F.FL.ALO.AXC.ARI.BIQ

Persian berries lake
MT.1766
UF buckthorn lake
lake, buckthorn
lake, Persian berries
lake, yellowberries
yellowberries lake
CN M.MT.AFU.AFU.ARI.AFU.AFU.ALO.ALO.BUE.ALO.BCW

Persian berry
USE **buckthorn berry**

Persian Gulf oxide
USE **gulf red**

Persian ironwood
MT.1190
UF ironwood, Persian
parrotia
CN M.MT.AFU.AFU.ALO.BIQ.DCU.AFU.AFU.AFU.FIM.ARI

Persian period
USE **Twenty-seventh Dynasty**

Persian red
USE **chrome red**

Persian walnut, common
USE **English walnut**

persiennes
RT.1012
ALT **persienne**
SN Exterior window shutters having horizontal slats or louvers fixed at an angle so as to admit light but exclude sun and rain. (W)
CN V.RT.AFU.ARI.ALO.BIQ.ARI

persimmon
MT.1264 (L)
UF black persimmon
persimmon, black
CN M.MT.AFU.AFU.ALO.BIQ.DCU.AFU.AFU.AFU.JTW

persimmon, black
USE **persimmon**

persimmon, common
USE **common persimmon**

personal computers
USE **microcomputers**

personal correspondence
VW.33 (R)
UF correspondence, personal
correspondence, private
private correspondence
CN V.VW.AFU.AFU.AFU.BIQ.ALO.ARI

personal papers
VW.1059
ALT **personal paper**
SN Use for the private documents belonging to an individual. For records kept by public officials or other persons for their private or personal use but relating to their official duties, use **office files.**
UF papers, personal
papers, private
private papers
CN V.VW.AFU.ARI.ALO.CFS

personal property
BM.467 (L)
SN Estate or property other than real property consisting of things temporary or movable. (W)
UF personalty
property, personal
CN B.BM.BCW.CXA.AFU.BCW

personal rail transit
USE **personal rapid transit**

personal rapid transit
RD.106 (L)
SN Use for transit systems comprised of small, automated, self-propelled vehicles, usually with rubber wheels running on concrete rails, within their own separate guideways.
UF AGT
automated guideway transit
automated guideway works
automated peoplemovers
light guideway transit
peoplemovers, automated
personal rail transit
PRT
rapid transit, personal
transit, automated guideway
transit, light guideway
transit, personal rail
transit, personal rapid
CN V.RD.ALO.ARI.AFU.AFU.ALO.ARI

personal space

BM.591 (A,L)
UF space, personal
CN B.BM.BUE.BUE

personalities, television
USE **television personalities**

personalty
USE **personal property**

personification
BM.10 (R)
CN B.BM.AFU.AFU.AFU.BIQ

personnel
HG.22
UF manpower
CN H.HG.AFU.AXC.AFU

personnel buildings
USE **employees' buildings**

personnel evaluations
VW.780 (L)
ALT **personnel evaluation**
UF evaluations, personnel
CN V.VW.AFU.ARI.AFU.ALO.BZY.ARI

personnel files
USE **personnel records**

personnel records
VW.777 (L)
ALT **personnel record**
SN Records maintained by an organization for each of its employees giving personal details and information relating to their service. (ICA)
UF files, personnel
personnel files
records, personnel
CN V.VW.AFU.ARI.AFU.ALO.BZY

personnel, military
USE **military personnel**

personnel, sales
USE **sales personnel**

persons
USE **people**

perspectiva artificiales
USE **linear perspective**

perspectival sections
USE **sectional perspectives**

perspective
KT.269 (A,L,B,R)
SN Use for any graphic method concerned with conveying an impression of depth or for representation by means of geometric projection using one or more vanishing points.
CN K.KT.AFU.ALO.DUC.DCU.BIQ

perspective drawings
VD.79 (A)
ALT **perspective drawing**
UF drawings, perspective
perspective views
skenographiae
views, perspective
CN V.VD.AFU.AFU.BIQ.ARI

perspective elevations
USE **exterior perspectives**

perspective projection
USE **central projection**

perspective views
USE **perspective drawings**

perspective, aerial
USE **aerial perspective**

perspective, artificial
USE **linear perspective**

perspective, atmospheric
USE **aerial perspective**

perspective, axial
USE **axial perspective**

perspective, central
USE **one-point perspective**

perspective, false
USE **false perspective**

perspective, frog
USE **sotto in su**

perspective, herringbone
USE **axial perspective**

perspective, inverted
USE **inverted perspective**

perspective, legitimate
USE **linear perspective**

perspective, linear
USE **linear perspective**

perspective, one-point
USE **one-point perspective**

perspective, parallel
USE **parallel perspective**

perspective, parallel (one-point perspective)
USE **one-point perspective**

perspective, Renaissance
USE **linear perspective**

perspective, reverse
USE **inverted perspective**

perspective, three-point
USE **three-point perspective**

perspective, two-point
USE **two-point perspective**

perspectives, aerial
USE **bird's-eye perspectives**

perspectives, angular
USE **two-point perspectives**

perspectives, bird's-eye
USE **bird's-eye perspectives**

perspectives, cavalier
USE **cavalier oblique drawings**

perspectives, central
USE **one-point perspectives**

perspectives, elevation
USE **one-point perspectives**

perspectives, exterior
USE **exterior perspectives**

perspectives, frog
USE **worm's-eye perspectives**

perspectives, frontal
USE **one-point perspectives**

perspectives, interior
USE **interior perspectives**

perspectives, military
USE **cavalier oblique drawings**

perspectives, oblique
USE **three-point perspectives**

perspectives, one-point
USE **one-point perspectives**

perspectives, parallel
USE **one-point perspectives**

perspectives, partial
USE **partial perspectives**

perspectives, sectional
USE **sectional perspectives**

perspectives, three-point
USE **three-point perspectives**

perspectives, two-point
USE **two-point perspectives**

perspectives, worm's-eye
USE **worm's-eye perspectives**

perspectographs
TB.279 (N)
ALT **perspectograph**
SN Tools used in perspective drawing to fix in the picture the positions of some of the outlines of objects to be represented. (W)
CN V.TB.AFU.ARI.CLM.AFU.ALO.DUC

perspex
MT.2121
SN Commercially produced, British acrylic plastic consisting essentially of polymerized methyl methacrylate. (W)
CN M.MT.AFU.AFU.ARI.BUE.ALO.
AXC.AFU.ALO.AFU.ALO

Peru balsam
MT.1475
UF balsam of Peru
balsam, Peru
CN M.MT.AFU.AFU.ALO.BOK.AFU.
BCW

perukiers

USE **wigmakers**

Peruvian
FL.723 (L,B)
CN F.FL.ALO.ALO.AFU.AXC.BOK

PES-ts
USE **thermoset polyester**

Pesach
USE **Passover**

pesthouses
RK.769 (A,L,R)
ALT **pesthouse**
SN Shelters or hospitals for those infected with a pestilential or contagious disease. (W)
CN V.RK.AFU.ALO.ALO.CXA.ALO.AFU.BCW.ALO.BCW.ARI

pesticides
USE **insecticides**

pestles
TB.212 (L,N,R)
ALT **pestle**
SN Elongated pieces of hard material, usually stone, for grinding pigments or other materials in a mortar. (GETTEN)
CN V.TB.AFU.ARI.BZY.ALO.ARI

pet cemeteries
RG.34 (A,L)
ALT **pet cemetery**
UF animal cemeteries
cemeteries, animal
cemeteries, pet
CN V.RG.AFU.AFU.ALO.ALO.AXC

pet shops
RK.164
ALT **pet shop**
UF pet stores
shops, pet
stores, pet
CN V.RK.AFU.ALO.ALO.ALO.ARI.BIQ.AFU.DCU

pet stores
USE **pet shops**

petal diaper pattern
USE **scale pattern**

petiole
USE **leafstalk**

petites tables (tables ambulantes)
USE **tables ambulantes**

petites commodes
TG.491
ALT **petite commode**
SN Small tables containing several tiers of drawers and generally set on tall legs. (WATSON)
UF commodes, petites
CN V.TG.AFU.AFU.AXC.ALO.BCW.BZY.BOK

petitions
VW.383 (L,N)
ALT **petition**
SN Includes any written requests and lists of signatures submitted to an authority to appeal for the performance of specific action.
CN V.VW.AFU.AFU.ALO.DZW

petitions for bankruptcy
VW.869
ALT **petition for bankruptcy**
SN Papers filed in a court of bankruptcy by a debtor seeking the benefits of the bankruptcy act, or by creditors alleging the commission of an act of bankruptcy by their debtor and seeking an adjudication of bankruptcy against the debtor. (BLACKS)
UF bankruptcy, petitions for
CN V.VW.AFU.ARI.AFU.BOK.AFU.AFU

petitions, lining
USE **building permits**

petkin
USE **Chinese silk**

petrochemicals
MT.1015 (L)
UF chemicals, petroleum
petroleum chemicals
CN M.MT.AFU.AFU.ALO.BCW.ALO.ARI

petrol
USE **gasoline**

petrol filling stations
USE **service stations**

petrol stations
USE **service stations**

petrol tanks
USE **gasoline tanks**

petroleum
MT.1008 (L,B)
CN M.MT.AFU.AFU.ALO.BCW.AFU

petroleum asphalt
MT.971
UF asphalt oil
asphalt, oil
asphalt, petroleum
oil asphalt
oil, asphalt
petroleum pitch
pitch, petroleum
CN M.MT.AFU.AFU.ALO.ALO.AFU.AFU.AFU.AFU

petroleum chemicals
USE **petrochemicals**

petroleum gas, liquefied
USE **liquefied petroleum gas**

petroleum jelly
MT.1016 (L)
UF jelly, petroleum
Vaseline (TM)
CN M.MT.AFU.AFU.ALO.BCW.ALO.AXC

petroleum pitch
USE **petroleum asphalt**

petroleum production platforms
USE **offshore drilling platforms**

petroleum products
MT.1009 (L)
UF products, petroleum
CN M.MT.AFU.AFU.ALO.BCW.ALO

petroleum refineries
RK.654 (A,L,B)
ALT **petroleum refinery**
UF oil refineries
refineries, oil
refineries, petroleum
CN V.RK.AFU.ALO.ALO.CLM.ALO.ALO.AFU.AXC.CXA.AFU

petroleum solvent
USE **mineral spirits**

petroleum spirits
USE **mineral spirits**

petrology
KD.269 (L)
SN Science that deals with the origin, history, occurrence, structure, chemical composition, and classification of rocks. (W)
CN K.KD.AFU.ARI.CLM.ARI.ARI.AFU

petuntze
MT.591
SN A partially decomposed feldspathic granite found in China and used with clay to make oriental porcelain. (MAYER)
UF China stone
stone, China
CN M.MT.AFU.AFU.AFU.DCU.AFU.AFU.AFU.AFU.AFU.ARI.AFU.ARI

Peul
USE **Fulani**

pevies
USE **peavies**

pew chairs
RT.1239
ALT **pew chair**
SN Seats hinged against the end of a pew to afford accommodation when needed in the aisle. (W)
UF chairs, pew
CN V.RT.AFU.BUE.ALO.ARI.BZY.ALO.AFU

pews
RT.1236 (L,N,B,R)
ALT **pew**
SN Benchlike seats, often fixed in place, having backs and being accessible by aisles, for the use of a church congregation. (RHDEL2)

CN V.RT.AFU.BUE.ALO.ARI.BZY.AFU

pews, box
USE **box pews**

pewter
MT.408 (L,R)
UF black metal
latten ware
metal, black
ware, latten
CN M.MT.AFU.AFU.AFU.BZY.AFU.
AFU.AFU.ALO.BUE.ALO

pewter (color)
USE **bluish gray**
dark gray
grayish blue
pale blue

pewter marks
VW.733 (L,R)
ALT **pewter mark**
UF marks, pewter
CN V.VW.AFU.ALO.ALO.AFU.AXC.
ARI.BOK

pewter, English
USE **English pewter**

pewter, Roman
USE **Roman pewter**

pewterers
HG.499 (L,R)
ALT **pewterer**
CN H.HG.AFU.AXC.BUE.ARI.CFS.
AFU.BIQ

pewtersmithing
KT.784 (L)
CN K.KT.AFU.ALO.HOE.BCW.AFU.BIQ

PH
USE **phenolic**

phalansteries
RG.90 (R)
ALT **phalanstery**
SN The dwellings or buildings of Fourierist communities. (W)
CN V.RG.AFU.AFU.BOK.BIQ.AFU.AFU

Phantastischer Realismus
USE **Fantastic Realist**

phantom line
BM.72
SN In technical drawing, a broken line indicating alternative position of delineated parts or the relative position of an absent part. (DAC)
UF line, phantom
CN B.BM.AFU.AFU.ARI.AFU.CLM.AXC

pharaohs
HG.699 (L,R)
ALT **pharaoh**
CN H.HG.AFU.AXC.CFS.CRG.BZY

pharmacies
USE **drugstores**

pharmacology
KD.242 (L)
SN Science of the nature and properties of drugs, particularly their actions or effects. (ERIC)
CN K.KD.AFU.ARI.BUE.AXC

pharmacy
KD.243 (L)
SN Study and practice of preparing, preserving, compounding, and dispensing drugs. (WCOL)
CN K.KD.AFU.ARI.BUE.BCW

phasotrons
USE **cyclotrons**

phengites marble
USE **bianco e giallo antico**

phenol
USE **carbolic acid**

phenol-formaldehyde resin
USE **phenolic**

phenolic
MT.2171 (L)
UF PH
phenol-formaldehyde resin
phenolic resin
resin, phenol-formaldehyde
resin, phenolic
CN M.MT.AFU.AFU.ARI.BUE.ALO.
AXC.ALO.BIQ

phenolic resin
USE **phenolic**

phenolic, melamine
USE **melamine phenolic**

phenomenologists
HG.210
ALT **phenomenologist**
CN H.HG.AFU.AXC.AXC.BCW.AXC

phenomenology
KD.71 (L,R)
CN K.KD.AFU.AFU.BOK.BUE

phenyl blue
USE **vivid purplish blue**

phenylene-based resin
MT.2139
UF resin, phenylene-based
CN M.MT.AFU.AFU.ARI.BUE.ALO.
AXC.AFU.BZY

Phi Mai
FL.2363
CN F.FL.ALO.ARI.BCW.ALO.ARI.
ALO.BUE

Phidian
FL.2692
CN F.FL.ALO.AXC.ALO.AFU.ALO.
BCW.ALO.CFS

philanthropists
HG.729 (L)
ALT **philanthropist**
CN H.HG.AFU.BCW.ERE

philatelic museums
RK.410 (L)
ALT **philatelic museum**
UF museums, philatelic
museums, postal
postal museums
CN V.RK.AFU.ALO.ALO.BCW.AXC.
ARI.BUE

philatelists
HG.274 (L)
ALT **philatelist**
CN H.HG.AFU.AXC.BCW.AFU.BOK.
ALO.BIQ

philately
KD.154 (L)
SN Study of postage stamps, revenue stamps, stamped envelopes, postmarks, post cards, covers, and similar materials relating to postal or fiscal history; also the collection of such materials. (RHDEL2)
CN K.KD.AFU.ALO.CLM.ALO.BOK

Philia stage
FL.2893
CN F.FL.ALO.AXC.ARI.ARI.AFU.AFU.
AFU

Philippine
FL.2400 (A,L,B)
CN F.FL.ALO.ARI.BCW.BIQ

Philippine mahogany
USE **lauan**

Philistine
FL.2928 (L)
UF Peleset
CN F.FL.ALO.AXC.ARI.AXC.ALO.ARI

Phillips head screwdrivers
TB.197 (N)
ALT **Phillips head screwdriver**
SN Screwdrivers used to drive or remove screws having an X-shaped indention in the head.
UF screwdrivers, Phillips head
CN V.TB.AFU.ARI.BOK.ALO.ALO

Phillips head screws
TF.482
ALT **Phillips head screw**
SN Screws each having a recessed head and an X-shaped driving indentation. (MEANS)
UF screws, Phillips head
CN V.TF.AFU.AFU.AFU.ALO.AFU.
DIO.AFU.CFS.ALO

philologists
HG.176 (L)
ALT **philologist**
CN H.HG.AFU.AXC.AXC.ALO.ALO.
ALO

philology
KD.51 (L,R)

CN K.KD.AFU.AFU.AXC.ALO.ALO

philosophers
HG.206 (L,R)
ALT **philosopher**
CN H.HG.AFU.AXC.AXC.BCW

philosophical anthropology
KD.95 (L,R)
UF anthropology, philosophical
CN K.KD.AFU.ALO.AFU.BCW

philosophy
KD.61 (L,R)
SN Critical examination of the grounds for fundamental beliefs and analysis of the basic concepts, doctrines, or practices that express such beliefs. (ERIC)
CN K.KD.AFU.AFU.BOK

philosophy of architecture
USE **architectural theory**

philosophy of art
USE **aesthetics**

philosophy of literature
USE **literary theory**

philosophy of religion
KD.77 (L)
UF religion, philosophy of
CN K.KD.AFU.AFU.BUE.AFU.ARI

philosophy of value
USE **axiology**

philosophy, moral
USE **ethics (philosophy)**

philosophy, process
USE **process philosophy**

phlogopite
MT.536
SN A magnesium mica that decomposes in sulfuric acid. (MH12)
UF magnesium mica
mica, magnesium
CN M.MT.AFU.AFU.AFU.CFS.AFU.FUA.ALO

Phnom Bakhen
USE **Bakheng**

Phnom Da
FL.2319
CN F.FL.ALO.ARI.BCW.ALO.AFU.AFU.AFU

Phnom Kulên
USE **Kulên**

Phoebe porosa
USE **imbuia**

Phoenician
FL.2929 (A,L,R)
CN F.FL.ALO.AXC.ARI.AXC.ALO.AXC

phone books
USE **telephone directories**

phone booths
USE **telephone booths**

phone tables
USE **telephone tables**

phonetics
KD.43 (L)
CN K.KD.AFU.AFU.AXC.AFU.ALO.AXC

phonocylinders
USE **phonograph cylinders**

phonodiscs
USE **phonograph records**

phonograph cylinders
VW.634 (L,N)
ALT **phonograph cylinder**
UF cylinders, phonograph
phonocylinders
CN V.VW.AFU.ALO.AFU.DZW.AFU.AFU.ALO

phonograph recordings
USE **phonograph records**

phonograph records
VW.635 (L,N,R)
ALT **phonograph record**
SN Cylinders or discs of rubber, paper, wax, metal, plastic, or other substance so prepared that sound is reproduced when played on a phonograph. (GAHLM)
UF gramophone records
phonodiscs
phonograph recordings
phonorecords
recordings, phonograph
records, gramaphone
records, phonograph
CN V.VW.AFU.ALO.AFU.DZW.AFU.AFU.ARI

phonology
KD.44 (L)
SN Study of the ways in which speech sounds form systems and patterns in language. (ERIC)
CN K.KD.AFU.AFU.AXC.AFU.ALO. BCW

phonorecords
USE **phonograph records**

phonotapes
USE **audio tapes**

phosphate, deep cobalt
USE **deep cobalt phosphate**

phosphate, silver
USE **silver phosphate**

phosphor bronze
MT.383
SN Any bronze deoxidized by the addition of phosphorus in the final state. (MH)
UF bronze, phosphor
bronze, steel
steel bronze
CN M.MT.AFU.AFU.AFU.BZY.AFU.AFU.AFU.ALO.ARI.BCW.BCW

phosphorescence
BM.973 (L)
ALT **phosphorescent**
CN B.BM.CFS.AXC.BZY.BUE.AXC

phosphorescent paint
USE **fluorescent paint**

photo composites
USE **composite photographs**

Photo-Secession
FL.1752 (R)
CN F.FL.ALO.ALO.BCW.AFU.CFS.AXC

photo-sensitized paper
USE **photographic paper**

photoaquatint
KT.432 (L)
SN A variant of photogravure in which the plate is dusted with rosin to create an irregular grain pattern with enhanced ink-holding capabilities.
UF aquatint (photography)
aquatint photogravure
aquatint process
photogravure, aquatint
CN K.KT.AFU.ALO.DUC.DOI.ARI.ARI.AFU

photochemical processes
USE **photomechanical processes**

photochemigraphy
USE **photomechanical processes**

photochromy
USE **heliochromy**

photochronography
USE **chronophotography**

photocopies
VW.685
ALT **photocopy**
SN Negative or positive copies of documents produced on or by means of sensitized material by the action of light or other radiant energy with or without intermediate negative. (ICA)
CN V.VW.AFU.ALO.AFU.DZW.BIQ. BZY

photocopying
KT.180 (L,B,R)
ALT **photocopied**
SN Reproducing a document, print, or the like photographically. (RHDEL2)
UF photoduplication
photographic reproduction
CN K.KT.AFU.ALO.DUC.BOK.AFU

photoduplication
USE **photocopying**

photoelectric detectors
RT.1517
ALT **photoelectric detector**
SN Smoke detectors that work by detect-

ing the obscuration of light by smoke.
UF detectors, photoelectric
CN V.RT.ALO.BIQ.AFU.AFU.ALO.ARI.ALO

photoengravers
HG.127
ALT **photoengraver**
SN Persons who engage in the various steps of photoengraving.
UF engraving operators
operators, engraving
operators, photolith
photolith operators
CN H.HG.AFU.AXC.AXC.AFU.AFU.ALO.AXC.DUC.AFU.AFU

photoengraving
KT.437 (L)
SN Usually refers to the production of relief printing surfaces with the aid of photography.(LANG) Can also refer to any photomechanical process to prepare chemically etched printing plates.
UF photoetching
CN K.KT.AFU.ALO.DUC.DOI.BCW. AFU

photoengravings
VJ.19
ALT **photoengraving**
SN A term used in the mid-19th century for photomechanical prints, most often those created by various relief processes, and also sometimes for those created by intaglio processes. Use a more specific term when possible.
CN V.VJ.AFU.AFU.ALO.ARI

photoengravings, line
USE **line photoengravings**

photoetching
USE **photoengraving**
photogravure

photogalvanographs
VJ.22
ALT **photogalvanograph**
SN Prints made by the process of photogalvanography.
CN V.VJ.AFU.AFU.ALO.AXC

photogalvanography
KT.430 (L)
SN Photomechanical process in which an intaglio plate is produced by the deposition of metal ions by electrical action.
CN K.KT.AFU.ALO.DUC.DOI.ARI.ALO

photogenic drawing
KT.363
SN Use for Talbot's process in which paper negatives were produced by printing out a silver image. Distinguished from **calotype**, in which the image is developed. In the mid-19th century, sometimes used as a synonym of photography.
UF drawing, photogenic
CN K.KT.AFU.ALO.DUC.DIO.ALO.DUC.ALO

photogenic drawings
VJ.14
ALT **photogenic drawing**
SN Use for Talbot's photographs produced by his photogenic drawing process, a printing-out process, some as photograms and others with a camera. Distinguished from **calotypes** which were produced by Talbot's patented developing-out process called **calotype.** In the mid-19th century, sometimes used as a synonym of photographs. For most prints made from these negatives, use **salted paper prints.**
UF drawings, photogenic
CN V.VJ.AFU.AFU.AFU.BCW.ARI

photogrammetry
KT.508 (A,L,B,R)
SN Making measurements by the means of photography. (W)
UF measurement, photographic
photographic measurement
stereophotogrammetry
CN K.KT.AFU.ALO.EFQ.ALO

photogrammetry, aerial
USE **aerial photogrammetry**

photograms
VJ.121 (L,R)
ALT **photogram**
SN Photographs produced without a camera, usually by placing an object directly on sensitized paper and exposing it to light. Includes Talbot's first photographs, which he called photogenic drawings. In the early 20th century the term was sometimes used to mean all photographs.
UF cameraless photographs
lensless photographs
photographs, cameraless
photographs, lensless
physiotypes
Rayographs
Schadographs
shadow pictures
shadowgraphs (photograms)
CN V.VJ.AFU.ARI.ALO.CFS

photograph albums
VW.488 (L,N)
ALT **photograph album**
SN Albums made up of mounted photographs, with or without identifying information. (GAHLM)
UF albums, photograph
CN V.VW.AFU.ALO.AFU.AFU.AFU.ALO.ARI

photographers
HG.117 (A,L,R)
ALT **photographer**
CN H.HG.AFU.AXC.AXC.AFU.AFU.ALO.AXC.DOI

photographers, architectural
USE **architectural photographers**

photographers, lithographic
USE **photolithographers**

photographers, medical
USE **medical photographers**

photographers, news
USE **photojournalists**

photographers, scientific
USE **scientific photographers**

photographers, still
USE **still photographers**

photographers, war
USE **war photographers**

photographers, wet plate
USE **photolithographers**

photographic apparatus
USE **photographic equipment**

photographic darkrooms
USE **darkrooms**

photographic equipment
TB.286 (L,N)
UF apparatus, photographic
equipment, photographic
photographic apparatus
CN V.TB.AFU.ARI.CLM.ARI

photographic film
MT.2230 (L)
UF film (photographic)
film, photographic
CN M.MT.AFU.ALO.CXA.ALO

photographic lenses
TB.315 (L,N)
ALT **photographic lens**
SN Solid shaped pieces of transparent material which gather and select light rays reflected from a subject so that they enter the camera and form an image of that subject on the film. (SWED)
UF camera lenses
lenses (photographic)
lenses, camera
lenses, photographic
CN V.TB.AFU.ARI.CLM.ARI.AFU.ALO.BOK

photographic materials
MT.2632 (L)
SN Use for the class of materials and material products used in the processing of photographs, including the constituent parts of the photograph itself.
UF materials, photographic
CN M.MT.AFU.ARI.GWW

photographic measurement
USE **photogrammetry**

photographic murals
USE **photomurals**

photographic negatives
USE **negatives**

photographic paper
MT.1942 (L,N,R)
UF paper, photo-sensitized
paper, photographic
paper, sensitized
photo-sensitized paper
sensitized paper
CN M.MT.AFU.AFU.ARI.ALO.ALO.AXC.ARI.BOK

photographic plates
MT.2634 (L)
ALT **photographic plate**
SN Sheets of glass, metal, porcelain, or other material coated with a light-sensitive photographic emulsion. (W)
UF plates, photographic
CN M.MT.AFU.ARI.GWW.ALO

photographic postcards
USE **picture postcards**

photographic prints
VJ.38 (N)
ALT **photographic print**
SN Use for opaque photographs, usually positive (i.e., reproducing appearances without tonal reversal, otherwise use **negative prints**), usually on paper, and generally, but not always, printed from a negative.
UF photoprints
prints (photographs)
prints, photographic
CN V.VJ.AFU.AFU.ARI.ARI

photographic processes
KT.311 (L)
SN Use for procedures by which light-sensitive materials are made to produce an image. For procedures related to how a photograph is taken or composed, or is manipulated during or after processing, use **photographic techniques.** For printing processes involving light-sensitivity at one stage, but creating a final print that was never itself light-sensitive, use **photomechanical processes.**
UF photographic processing
silver salt processes
CN K.KT.AFU.ALO.DUC.DIO.ALO

photographic processing
USE **photographic processes**

photographic reproduction
USE **photocopying**

photographic sensitometry
KT.511 (L)
UF sensitometry, photographic
CN K.KT.AFU.ALO.EFQ.ARI.AFU

photographic surveying
KT.119 (L,B)
UF surveying, photographic
CN K.KT.AFU.ALO.CXA.ARI.ALO

photographic surveying, aerial
USE **aerial photogrammetry**

photographic techniques
KT.377 (R)
SN Use with regard to specialized procedures related to how a photograph is taken or composed, or is manipulated during or after processing. Use **photographic processes** for the procedures by which light-sensitive materials are made to produce an image.
CN K.KT.AFU.ALO.DUC.DIO.ARI

photographs
VJ.1 (L,N)
ALT **photograph**
SN Use for still images produced from radiation-sensitive materials (sensitive to light, electron beams, or nuclear radiation), with the exception of reproductive prints of documents and technical drawings. May be positive or negative, opaque or transparent. Includes secondary images produced from a radiation-sensitive image, such as types of photomechanical prints and wire photographs.
UF photos
CN V.VJ.AFU

photographs, aerial
USE **aerial photographs**

photographs, altered
USE **manipulated photographs**

photographs, astronomical
USE **astrophotographs**

photographs, black-and-white
USE **black-and-white photographs**

photographs, boudoir card
USE **boudoir prints**

photographs, cabinet
USE **cabinet photographs**

photographs, cameraless
USE **photograms**

photographs, card
USE **card photographs**

photographs, carte-de-visite
USE **cartes-de-visite**

photographs, cased
USE **cased photographs**

photographs, celestial
USE **astrophotographs**

photographs, color
USE **color photographs**

photographs, composite
USE **composite photographs**

photographs, direct image
USE **direct positives**

photographs, enlarged
USE **enlargements**

photographs, gem
USE **gem photographs**

photographs, ghost
USE **spirit photographs**

photographs, handworked
USE **manipulated photographs**

photographs, identification
USE **identification photographs**

photographs, instant camera
USE **instant camera photographs**

photographs, instantaneous
USE **instantaneous photographs**

photographs, journalistic
USE **news photographs**

photographs, lensless
USE **photograms**

photographs, manipulated
USE **manipulated photographs**

photographs, microscope
USE **photomicrographs**

photographs, motion
USE **motion photographs**

photographs, motion study
USE **motion photographs**

photographs, mural
USE **photomurals**

photographs, news
USE **news photographs**

photographs, panel card
USE **panel prints**

photographs, passport
USE **passport photographs**

photographs, pigment
USE **pigment prints**

photographs, Polaroid (TM) instant color
USE **dye diffusion transfer prints**

photographs, press
USE **news photographs**

photographs, promenade card
USE **promenade prints**

photographs, psychic
USE **psychic photographs**

photographs, spirit
USE **spirit photographs**

photographs, stereoscopic
USE **stereoscopic photographs**

photographs, unique image
USE **direct positives**

photographs, wire
USE **wire photographs**

photographs, x-ray
USE **radiographs**

photography
KT.291 (A,L,B,R)
SN The art or process of making photographs.
CN K.KT.AFU.ALO.DUC.DIO.AFU

photography museums
RK.388 (A)
ALT **photography museum**
UF museums, photography
CN V.RK.AFU.ALO.ALO.BCW.AXC.ARI.AFU.BCW

photography, advertising
USE **advertising photography**

photography, aerial
USE **aerial photography**

photography, air
USE **aerial photography**

photography, ambient light
USE **available light photography**

photography, architectural
USE **architectural photography**

photography, astronomical
USE **astronomical photography**

photography, available light
USE **available light photography**

photography, balloon
USE **aerial photography**

photography, black-and-white
USE **black-and-white photography**

photography, celestial
USE **astronomical photography**

photography, close range
USE **close-up photography**

photography, close-up
USE **close-up photography**

photography, color
USE **color photography**

photography, commercial
USE **advertising photography**

photography, corona discharge
USE **Kirlian photography**

photography, documentary
USE **documentary photography**

photography, ethnographic
USE **ethnographic photography**

photography, existing light
USE **available light photography**

photography, fashion
USE **fashion photography**

photography, high-speed
USE **high-speed photography**

photography, indoor
USE **indoor photography**

photography, industrial
USE **industrial photography**

photography, infrared
USE **infrared photography**

photography, instant
USE **diffusion transfer process**

photography, journalistic
USE **photojournalism**

photography, Kirlian
USE **Kirlian photography**

photography, low-light
USE **available light photography**

photography, medical
USE **medical photography**

photography, military
USE **military photography**

photography, motion
USE **chronophotography**

photography, motion study
USE **chronophotography**

photography, natural history
USE **nature photography**

photography, nature
USE **nature photography**

photography, news
USE **photojournalism**

photography, night
USE **night photography**

photography, press
USE **photojournalism**

photography, product
USE **advertising photography**

photography, professional portrait
USE **commercial portraiture**

photography, psychic
USE **psychic photography**

photography, schlieren
USE **schlieren photography**

photography, science
USE **scientific photography**

photography, scientific
USE **scientific photography**

photography, sequential
USE **chronophotography**

photography, serial
USE **chronophotography**

photography, space
USE **space photography**

photography, spirit
USE **spirit photography**

photography, stereoscopic
USE **stereoscopic photography**

photography, stroboscopic
USE **stroboscopic photography**

photography, submarine
USE **underwater photography**

photography, three-color
USE **three-color processes**

photography, time-lapse
USE **time-lapse photography**

photography, travel
USE **travel photography**

photography, ultraviolet
USE **ultraviolet photography**

photography, underwater
USE **underwater photography**

photography, war
USE **war photography**

photography, wedding
USE **wedding photography**

photogravure
KT.431 (L,R)
SN An intaglio photomechanical process in which the metal printing plate is prepared using a bichromate process, leaving a gelatin resist of varying thickness. The plate is etched to form cells of varying depth able to hold different amounts of ink. If done with an aquatint grain, use **photoaquatint.**
UF gravure
gravure printing
heliogravure
photoetching
printing, gravure
Talbot-Klic process
CN K.KT.AFU.ALO.DUC.DOI.ARI.ARI

photogravure prints
USE **photogravures**

photogravure, aquatint
USE **photoaquatint**

photogravures
VJ.23
ALT **photogravure**
SN Photomechanical prints produced by

the process called photogravure.
UF gravure prints (photomechanical)
gravures (photomechanical)
photogravure prints
prints, gravure (photomechanical)
prints, photogravure
CN V.VJ.AFU.AFU.ALO.BCW

photojournalism
KT.304 (L,R)
UF journalistic photography
news photography
photography, journalistic
photography, news
photography, press
photoreportage
press photography
CN K.KT.AFU.ALO.DUC.DIO.AFU.CXA

photojournalists
HG.120 (L)
ALT **photojournalist**
UF news photographers
photographers, news
CN H.HG.AFU.AXC.AXC.AFU.AFU.ALO.AXC.DOI.ARI

photolith operators
USE **photoengravers**

photolithographers
HG.131
ALT **photolithographer**
UF lithographic photographers
photographers, lithographic
photographers, wet plate
wet plate photographers
CN H.HG.AFU.AXC.AXC.AFU.AFU.ALO.AXC.DUC.ARI.AFU

photolithographs
VJ.24
ALT **photolithograph**
SN Photomechanical prints produced by photolithography.
CN V.VJ.AFU.AFU.ALO.BIQ

photolithography
KT.434 (L,R)
SN A planographic photomechanical process that uses the same principle as lithography, the repulsion of oil and water, but uses a photographic process to transfer the image to the plate.
CN K.KT.AFU.ALO.DUC.DOI.AXC.AFU

photomacrographs
USE **macrophotographs**

photomacrography
USE **macrophotography**

photomaps
VW.174
ALT **photomap**
SN Maps made by superimposing cartographic data on an aerial photograph.
CN V.VW.AFU.AFU.AFU.FZU.AXC.AFU.ARI.ARI.ARI

photomasks
USE **masks (transparencies)**

photomechanical prints
VJ.16
ALT **photomechanical print**
SN Prints produced by photomechanical processes.
UF photomechanical reproductions
photomechanicals
prints, photomechanical
prints, process
process prints
reproductions, photomechanical
CN V.VJ.AFU.AFU.ALO

photomechanical prints, halftone
USE **relief halftones**

photomechanical prints, line
USE **line photoengravings**

photomechanical processes
KT.423 (L,R)
SN Processes that involve a photographic process (that is, employing light-sensitivity) to transfer an image, and then a separate process to produce a print that was never itself light-sensitive.
UF photochemical processes
photochemigraphy
processes, photomechanical
CN K.KT.AFU.ALO.DUC.DOI

photomechanical reproductions
USE **photomechanical prints**

photomechanicals
USE **photomechanical prints**

photomicrographs
VJ.98
ALT **photomicrograph**
SN Use for photographs of minute objects, usually taken through a microscope. Distinct from **microphotographs,** which are images reduced to minute size.
UF microscope photographs
photographs, microscope
CN V.VJ.AFU.ARI.AFU.AXC

photomicrography
KT.387 (L)
SN Use for techniques to photograph subjects that can be viewed only with the aid of a microscope. Use **microphotography** for techniques to produce photographs that can be viewed only with the aid of a microscope or other magnifier.
CN K.KT.AFU.ALO.DUC.DIO.ARI.ARI.BCW

photomontages
VJ.118 (L,R)
ALT **photomontage**
SN Use for combinations of photographic images, or photographic with other images, such as architectural drawings, usually arranged into a somewhat unified image. For photographs produced by printing two or more negatives as one unified image, use **composite photographs.** When pieces of photographs or other relatively flat materials are pasted together into less unified images, use **collages.**
UF montages (photographic)
CN V.VJ.AFU.ARI.ALO.BUE.ALO

photomosaic maps
VW.176
ALT **photomosaic map**
SN Maps comprised of assemblies of overlapping aerial photographs whose edges have been torn or cut and matched to form a continuous photographic representation of the earth's surface. (DOD)
UF aerial mosaics
maps, photomosaic
mosaics (photographs)
mosaics, aerial
CN V.VW.AFU.AFU.AFU.FZU.AXC.AFU.ARI.ARI.ARI.ALO

photomosaics
VJ.122
ALT **photomosaic**
SN An assemblage of photographic prints pieced together to form a continuous panorama or aerial photograph. (SAPSP)
UF mosaics (photographs)
CN V.VJ.AFU.ARI.ALO.CLM

photomurals
VJ.123 (A,B)
ALT **photomural**
SN Use for large photographic prints used as wall decorations.
UF mural photographs
murals, photographic
photographic murals
photographs, mural
CN V.VJ.AFU.ARI.ALO.CRG

photonegatives
USE **negatives**

photoprints
USE **photographic prints**

photoprints, albumen
USE **albumen prints**

photoprints, black-and-white
USE **black-and-white prints (photographs)**

photoprints, boudoir card
USE **boudoir prints**

photoprints, bromoil
USE **bromoil prints**

photoprints, cabinet card
USE **cabinet photographs**

photoprints, calotype
USE **salted paper prints**

photoprints, carbon
USE **carbon prints**

photoprints, collodion
USE **collodion prints**

photoprints, color
USE **color prints (photographs)**

photoprints, composite
USE **composite photographs**

photoprints, contact
USE **contact prints**

photoprints, dye diffusion transfer
USE **dye diffusion transfer prints**

photoprints, dye transfer
USE **dye transfer prints**

photoprints, gelatin silver
USE **gelatin silver prints**

photoprints, glass
USE **clichés-verre**

photoprints, gum bichromate
USE **gum bichromate prints**

photoprints, imperial card
USE **imperial prints**

photoprints, oil
USE **oil prints**

photoprints, palladium
USE **palladium prints**

photoprints, passport
USE **passport photographs**

photoprints, platinum
USE **platinum prints**

photoprints, promenade card
USE **promenade prints**

photoprints, salted paper
USE **salted paper prints**

photoprints, Van Dyke
USE **brownprints**

photoprints, Van Dyke brown
USE **brownprints**

Photorealist
FL.3743 (L,R)
ALT **Photorealism**
UF Cool Realist
Hyper-realist
New Realist (Photorealist)
Radical Realist
Realist, Cool
Realist, New (Photorealist)
Realist, Radical
Realist, Sharp-focus
Sharp-focus Realist
Superrealist
CN F.FL.ALO.BUE.ARI.GFO

photoreportage
USE **photojournalism**

photos
USE **photographs**

photosensitive glass
MT.282 (L)
UF glass, photosensitive
CN M.MT.AFU.AFU.AFU.BIQ.AFU .AXC.CFS

Photostats (TM)
USE **stats**

phototransparencies
USE **transparencies**

phototype
USE **collotype**

phrenology
KD.185 (L,R)
SN Study of the conformation of the skull as indicative of mental faculties and personal character. (W)
CN K.KD.AFU.ALO.EFQ.ALO.AFU

Phrygian
FL.2860 (A,L)
CN F.FL.ALO.AXC.ARI.AFU.AFU.BCW

Phrygian marble
USE **pavonazzetto**

phthalocyaninblau
USE **phthalocyanine blue**

phthalocyanine blue
MT.1608
UF bleu héliogène
blue, intense
blue, Monastral
blue, Monastral fast
blue, phthalocyanine
blue, Thalo
fast blue, Monastral
Heliogenblau
intense blue
Monastral blue
Monastral fast blue
phthalocyaninblau
Thalo blue
CN M.MT.AFU.AFU.ARI.AFU.AFU. ALO.ALO.ALO.AXC.ARI

phthalocyanine green
MT.1661 (L)
UF chloro-copper phthalocyanine
green, intense
green, Monastral
green, phthalocyanine
intense green
Monastral green
phthalocyanine, chloro-copper
CN M.MT.AFU.AFU.ARI.AFU.AFU .ALO.ALO.AXC.AXC.AFU

phthalocyanine, chloro-copper
USE **phthalocyanine green**

Phylakopi I phase
FL.2545
CN F.FL.ALO.AXC.ALO.AFU.AFU. ALO.AFU.ALO

phyllite
MT.846 (L)
CN M.MT.AFU.AFU.AFU.DCU. AFU. ARI.AXC

phys-ed buildings
USE **physical education buildings**

physical anthropologists
HG.253
ALT **physical anthropologist**
UF anthropologists, physical
CN H.HG.AFU.AXC.BCW.AFU.AFU. ALO

physical anthropology
KD.96 (L)
SN Comparative study of human physical evolution, variation, and classification, especially through measurement and observation of living people as well as human remains. (W)
UF anthropology, physical
somatology
CN K.KD.AFU.ALO.AFU.BIQ

physical education buildings
RK.1062 (A,L,B)
ALT **physical education building**
UF buildings, physical education
centers, physical training
education buildings, physical
phys-ed buildings
physical training centers
CN V.RK.AFU.ALO.ALO.EWY.AXC .BIQ.ALO.AXC

physical geography
KD.135 (L)
SN Branch of geography that deals with the exterior physical features and changes of the earth in land, sea, and air. (W)
UF geography, physical
physiography
CN K.KD.AFU.ALO.BZY.ALO

physical sciences
KD.258 (R)
UF sciences, physical
CN K.KD.AFU.ARI.CLM

physical therapists
HG.386 (L)
ALT **physical therapist**
UF physiotherapists
therapists, physical
CN H.HG.AFU.AXC.BIQ.ALO.BCW.BIQ

physical training centers
USE **physical education buildings**

physically handicapped
HG.786 (L,B)
UF handicapped, physically

CN H.HG.AFU.BOK.AXC.ALO.ALO

physically handicapped, housing for
USE **housing for the handicapped**

physicians
HG.387 (L,B,R)
ALT **physician**
UF doctors
CN H.HG.AFU.AXC.BIQ.ALO.BCW.BOK

physicians' offices
USE **medical offices**

physicists
HG.354 (L)
ALT **physicist**
CN H.HG.AFU.AXC.BIQ.AFU.AFU.DZW

physics
KD.280 (L,R)
CN K.KD.AFU.ARI.CLM.AXC

physics, applied
USE **applied physics**

physics, engineering
USE **engineering physics**

physics, high energy
USE **high energy physics**

physics, mathematical
USE **mathematical physics**

physics, nuclear
USE **nuclear physics**

physiognomy
KD.186 (L,R)
SN Study of the interpretation of facial features with respect to qualities of mind or character, shown by peculiarities of configuration or cast or characteristic expression. (W)
CN K.KD.AFU.ALO.EFQ.ALO.ALO

physiography
USE **physical geography**

physiologists
HG.331 (L)
ALT **physiologist**
CN H.HG.AFU.AXC.BIQ.AFU.AFU.ALO.ARI

physiology
KD.208 (L,B,R)
SN Biological science concerned with the mechanisms of animal function, from the level of the cell to that of the whole organism. (PG)
CN K.KD.AFU.ARI.ARI.BUE

physiotherapists
USE **physical therapists**

physiotypes
USE **photograms**

PI-tp
USE **thermoplastic polyimide**

PI-ts
USE **thermoset polyimide**

Piandjikent
USE **Panjikent**

Pianga
FL.439
CN F.FL.ALO.AFU.AXC.ALO.ALO.AFU.AFU.AXC.BCW

piani nobili
RM.414
ALT **piano nobile**
SN Use to designate second or sometimes third stories given greater apparent height or prominence on the exterior and a higher ceiling within, and containing the principal rooms of a building.
UF beaux étages
étages, beaux
CN V.RM.AFU.DUC.BCW

piano beds
TG.344
ALT **piano bed**
SN Deception beds which look like an upright piano but unfold to form a bed.
UF bedroom pianos, convertible
beds, piano
beds, piano folding
convertible bedroom pianos
folding beds, piano
piano folding beds
pianos, convertible bedroom
CN V.TG.AFU.AFU.ARI.AFU.AFU.BIQ.AFU.BCW

piano benches
TG.290 (N)
ALT **piano bench**
UF benches, piano
CN V.TG.AFU.AFU.ALO.ALO.AFU.ALO.ARI

piano chairs
USE **music chairs**

piano folding beds
USE **piano beds**

piano hinges
USE **continuous hinges**

piano maker's edge planes
USE **edge planes**

piano roll cabinets
USE **pianola roll cabinets**

piano stools
USE **music stools**

piano wire
MT.484
SN High grade, uniform steel, employed for the manufacture of special springs. (MH)
UF wire, piano
CN M.MT.AFU.AFU.AFU.BZY.ALO.BZY.ARI

Pianobor
FL.1802
CN F.FL.ALO.ARI.AFU.AXC.CXA.ALO

pianola cabinets
USE **pianola roll cabinets**

pianola roll cabinets
TG.438
ALT **pianola roll cabinet**
SN Cabinets with narrow shelves for holding piano rolls.
UF cabinets, piano roll
cabinets, pianola
cabinets, pianola roll
piano roll cabinets
pianola cabinets
roll cabinets, pianola
CN V.TG.AFU.AFU.AXC.ALO.ARI.ALO.CRG.AFU

pianos, convertible bedroom
USE **piano beds**

piazzas
RK.1446 (A,B,R)
ALT **piazza**
SN In Italian cities and towns, open public spaces usually surrounded by buildings.
CN V.RK.ALO.AFU.ARI.ALO

piazzas (porches)
USE **porches**

Picea
USE **spruce**

Picea abies
USE **Norway spruce**

Picea alba
USE **white spruce**

Picea excelsa
USE **common spruce**

Picea glauca
USE **Norway spruce**

Picea mariana
USE **bog spruce**

Picea morinda
USE **West Himalayan spruce**

Picea nigra
USE **black spruce**

Picea pangens
USE **blue spruce**

Picea rubens
USE **red spruce**

Picea rubra
USE **red spruce**

Picea sitchensis
USE **sitka spruce**

Picea smithiana
USE **West Himalayan spruce**

pickaroons
TB.1070 (N)
ALT **pickaroon**
SN Poles with a sharply pointed end and a hook, used by lumbermen in river driving and by tracklayers in aligning railroad ties. (W)
UF hookaroons
CN V.TB.AFU.BCW.CFS.ALO.ALO.BZY.ARI

picket fences
RM.438
ALT **picket fence**
SN Fences formed of a series of vertical posts, stakes, or rods, sometimes sharpened at the upper end, which are joined together by horizontal rails. (DAC)
UF fences, picket
CN V.RM.ALO.AFU.BCW.AXC

picking
KT.619
ALT **picked**
CN K.KT.AFU.ALO.FUA.DCU

picking knives
TB.785 (N)
ALT **picking knife**
SN Small knives with a wide blade; used for trimming a finished basket.
UF knives, picking
CN V.TB.AFU.BCW.BUE.ALO.AFU

pickling (metalworking)
KT.841 (L)
ALT **pickled**
SN Cleaning oxide or flux from silver or other metals by the use of extremely dilute sulphuric acid. (THDAT)
UF mise-en-couleur
CN K.KT.AFU.ALO.HOE.BCW.ALO.BCW.ARI

pickling (woodworking)
KT.884
ALT **pickled**
SN Giving wood a whitish finish by scraping off paint while leaving the remains of the gesso base still embedded in the grain. (THDAT)
CN K.KT.AFU.ALO.HOE.BUE.ALO.ALO

picks
TB.421 (N)
ALT **pick**
SN Hand tools consisting of a steel head pointed at one or both ends and mounted on a wood handle; used for loosening and breaking up compacted soil. (MEANS)
CN V.TB.AFU.ARI.DZW.BCW

picks, flinting
USE **flinting picks**

pickup tongs
TB.760 (N)
SN Tongs of all kinds that are used for picking up work as opposed to holding the work while it is forged or manipulated.
UF anvil tongs
tongs, anvil
tongs, pickup
CN V.TB.AFU.BCW.BIQ.AXC.ALO.AXC.CFS

picnic areas
RK.1493 (A,L,B)
ALT **picnic area**
UF areas, picnic
grounds, picnic
picnic grounds
CN V.RK.ALO.ALO.BCW.BOK

picnic benches
TG.291 (N)
ALT **picnic bench**
UF benches, picnic
CN V.TG.AFU.AFU.ALO.ALO.AFU.ALO.AXC

picnic grounds
USE **picnic areas**

picnic tables
TG.753 (N)
ALT **picnic table**
UF tables, picnic
CN V.TG.AFU.AFU.BIQ.BOK.ALO.DZW

pictograms
USE **pictographs**

pictographs
VB.57 (L)
ALT **pictograph**
SN Use for highly simplified images that represent an object or action, such as hieroglyphs. Use also for certain prehistoric pictures and linear designs whose meanings are uncertain.
UF pictograms
picture-writing
CN V.VB.AFU.ALO.BIQ

pictorial dictionaries
USE **picture dictionaries**

pictorial drawings
VD.6
ALT **pictorial drawing**
SN Use with regard to architectural drawings for the broad group that includes axonometric and perspective drawings, i.e., those using the forms of projection that give an impression of depth.
UF drawings, pictorial
drawings, single-view
pictorial views
single-view drawings
views, pictorial
CN V.VD.AFU.AFU.AXC

pictorial maps
VW.151 (L)
ALT **pictorial map**
UF maps, pictorial
CN V.VW.AFU.AFU.AFU.FZU.AXC.AFU.ARI.AFU.CFS

Pictorial (photography style)
USE **Pictorialist**

pictorial space
BM.92
UF space, pictorial
CN B.BM.AFU.AFU.ARI.AFU.FIM.ALO

pictorial views
USE **pictorial drawings**

Pictorialist
FL.3299
ALT **Pictorialism**
SN Use with reference to the 19th-century movement in photography.
UF Pictorial (photography style)
CN F.FL.ALO.BCW.ALO.AXC.DCU.BUE

picture books
VW.515 (L)
ALT **picture book**
UF books, picture
CN V.VW.AFU.ALO.AFU.AFU.AFU.CRG

picture dictionaries
VW.395 (L)
ALT **picture dictionary**
UF dictionaries, pictorial
dictionaries, picture
pictorial dictionaries
CN V.VW.AFU.AFU.ALO.EWY.ARI.AFU.ARI

picture-frame maker's planes
USE **miter planes**

picture-framing clamps
USE **corner clamps**

picture galleries
USE **art museums**

picture houses
USE **movie theaters**

picture moldings
USE **picture rails**

picture palaces
USE **movie theaters**

picture plane
BM.156
UF plane, picture
CN B.BM.AFU.AFU.ARI.BOK.CFS.AXC

picture postcards
VW.578 (L)
ALT **picture postcard**
UF photographic postcards
postcards, photographic
postcards, picture
CN V.VW.AFU.ALO.AFU.ARI.CXA.AFU

picture putty
MT.2657

SN Cement used by conservators for stopping or filling holes in paintings. (MAYER)
UF putty, picture
CN M.MT.AFU.ARI.HTY.ALO.ARI

picture rails
RT.653
ALT **picture rail**
SN Horizontal strips affixed to walls at or near the ceiling for supporting picture hooks.
UF moldings, picture
picture moldings
rails, picture
CN V.RT.AFU.AFU.AFU.BIQ.BUE.ALO.AFU.BCW.BCW

picture varnish
MT.2477
SN Varnish used as a final coating over a thoroughly dried oil painting to protect and preserve it and to create a uniform gloss. (MAYER)
UF varnish, picture
CN M.MT.AFU.ARI.CRG.AFU.BOK.AFU.AXC

picture windows
RT.928
ALT **picture window**
SN Outsize windows (as in a living room) placed to frame or as if to frame a desirable exterior view and often placed between two narrower windows. (W)
UF windows, picture
CN V.RT.AFU.ARI.AFU.AFU.BOK.AFU.AFU.DOI

picture-writing
USE **pictographs**

pictures, motion
USE **motion pictures**

Picturesque, the
BM.492 (A,L,R)
SN Aesthetic concept or expression, arising in Europe first in painting of the 18th century and later in architecture of the 19th century, characterized by rough, curious, or irregular forms; it applies particularly to rustic landscapes and crumbling buildings having neither the awe-inspiring grandeur of the Sublime nor the order and regularity of beauty. (RHLPS)
UF the Picturesque
CN B.BM.BIQ.AFU.BCW

Picunche
FL.1624
CN F.FL.ALO.ALO.ARI.ARI.ALO.ALO.BUE

Picuris
FL.1471
CN F.FL.ALO.ALO.ARI.AFU.CFS.CRG.AFU.BCW

pie graphs
USE **circular graphs**

pieces, apron
USE **apron pieces**

pieces, apron (furniture components)
USE **aprons (furniture components)**

pieces, carriage
USE **carriage pieces**

pieces, case
USE **case furniture**

pieces, chimney
USE **chimney breasts**

pieces, cocking
USE **sprockets**

pieces, crest
USE **crest rails**

pieces, dragging
USE **dragon beams**

pieces, dragon
USE **dragon beams**

pieces, pitching
USE **apron pieces**

pieces, plancier
USE **soffits**

pieces, sprocket
USE **sprockets**

pieces, strutting
USE **straining beams**

pieces, tie
USE **tie beams**

piecrust tables
TG.704
ALT **piecrust table**
SN Tripod, often tilt-top, circular tables whose top has a scalloped, molded rim resembling the edges of a pie.
UF tables, piecrust
CN V.TG.AFU.AFU.BIQ.BOK.AFU.DZW.ALO

pieds d'oignon
USE **bun feet**

pieds de biche
USE **hoof feet**

Piegan
FL.1375 (L)
UF Peigan
CN F.FL.ALO.ALO.ARI.AFU.BOK.BCW.ALO

pier arches
RT.281
ALT **pier arch**
SN Use for arches carried on piers, particularly the arches which divide nave from aisles in basilican churches.
UF arches, pier
CN V.RT.AFU.AFU.AFU.BCW.AFU.AFU.ARI.AXC

pier-console tables
USE **pier tables**

pier foundations
RT.151 (B)
ALT **pier foundation**
SN Foundations consisting of concrete, brick, or stone piers which deliver the load to a support stratum; the piers are usually more substantial than piles and are not clustered. Now commonly produced by excavating within a caisson.
UF caisson foundations
foundations, caisson
foundations, pier
CN V.RT.AFU.AFU.AFU.AXC.BUE.AFU.AFU

pier tables
TG.775 (N)
ALT **pier table**
SN Side tables designed to stand between two windows; often surmounted by a looking glass.
UF consoles en acajou
pier-console tables
tables, pier
tables, pier-console
CN V.TG.AFU.AFU.BIQ.BOK.ARI.AFU.ALO.AFU

pier tables (slab tables)
USE **slab tables**

pier tables, enclosed
USE **enclosed pier tables**

pierced hearts
DG.36
ALT **pierced heart**
UF hearts, pierced
CN D.DG.AFU.AFU.BUE.ALO

pierced walls
RT.579 (A)
ALT **pierced wall**
UF perforated walls
screen walls
walls, perforated
walls, pierced
walls, screen
CN V.RT.AFU.AFU.AFU.BIQ.BUE.AFU.AFU.BUE

piers
RT.184 (A,L,N,B,R)
ALT **pier**
SN Use for square or rectangular upright, masonry, supporting elements, and for similar elements of wood when classically treated; use also for massive upright supporting elements of any shape in Medieval

architecture. For cylindrical uprights, except when Medieval as described above, and for all uprights in steel and concrete frames, use **columns**; for square wooden uprights when not classically treated, use **posts.**
UF pillars
CN V.RT.AFU.AFU.AFU.AXC.CRG.AFU

piers (foundation components)
RT.154 (A,N,B)
ALT **pier (foundation component)**
SN Use for isolated masonry foundation components delivering loads to a bearing stratum; distinct from **piles,** which are smaller and may be clustered.
UF pillars (foundation components)
CN V.RT.AFU.AFU.AFU.AXC.BUE.AFU.ALO.ALO

piers (marine landings)
RK.1319 (A,L,N,B,R)
ALT **pier (marine landing)**
SN Use for structures extending from the shoreline out over water to serve as landing places or recreational or entertainment places, rather than to afford coastal protection. For structures built along or parallel to the shoreline serving as landing, loading or unloading places for vessels, use **wharves** or **quays.**
CN V.RK.AFU.ALO.ALO.GLI.ARI.ARI.AXC.AFU

piers, bundle
USE **bundle piers**

piers, buttress
USE **buttress piers**

piers, compound
USE **compound piers**

piers, gate
USE **hanging posts**

piers, wall
USE **wall piers**

pies de puente
TG.624
ALT **pie de puente**
SN Spanish Renaissance trestle stands used to support vargueños; pulls on each side of the stand support the fall front of the cabinet. (HAYWAR)
CN V.TG.AFU.AFU.BIQ.BCW.AFU.BCW.AFU

Pietersburg
FL.57
CN F.FL.ALO.AFU.AFU.ALO.ARI.ALO

pietism
BM.704 (L,R)
CN B.BM.BZY.ALO.ARI.CLM

pietra di paragone
MT.608
UF lapis liydius
CN M.MT.AFU.AFU.AFU.DCU.AFU.AFU.AFU.AFU.ALO.AFU.AFU

pietra dure
KT.703 (R)
SN Inlaid work in which pieces of hard, polished stone are set into marble or another hard surface. (MAYER)
CN K.KT.AFU.ALO.GRC.BZY.ALO.AFU

pietra nefritica
MT.853
UF lapis aequipondus
CN M.MT.AFU.AFU.AFU.DCU.AFU.ARI.BOK.ARI

pig houses
RK.87 (B)
ALT **pig house**
SN Use for buildings constructed to house pigs.
UF hoghouses
houses, pig
piggeries
CN V.RK.AFU.ALO.ALO.AFU.ALO.BUE

pig parlors
USE **pigsties**

pigeon houses
USE **dovecotes**

pigeonholes
TG.967
ALT **pigeonhole**
SN Open-fronted storage units in the well of a desk. (KETCH)
CN V.TG.ALO.FZU

piggeries
USE **pig houses**
pigsties

pigment
MT.1547 (L,R)
SN Use for any relatively insoluble organic, inorganic, or synthetic organic substance that imparts a color to another substance. Includes any coloring substance that disperses in a liquid to form a paint.
CN M.MT.AFU.AFU.ARI.AFU.AFU.ALO

pigment photographs
USE **pigment prints**

pigment prints
VJ.52
ALT **pigment print**
SN Use as a broad term for photographic prints made by any of the pigment processes.
UF photographs, pigment
pigment photographs
prints, pigment
CN V.VJ.AFU.AFU.ARI.ARI.AXC.BUE

pigment prints, oil
USE **oil prints**

pigment processes
KT.347
SN Photographic processes in which images are formed using pigments rather than silver or other metal. Common pigments included lampblack, watercolor pigments, oil paints, and oil-based inks. The pigments themselves are not light-sensitive; the photochemical action of another transparent agent makes a support bind, attract, or receive pigment.
CN K.KT.AFU.ALO.DUC.DIO.ALO.DIO

pigment, animal
USE **animal pigment**

pigment, artificial inorganic
USE **artificial inorganic pigment**

pigment, artificial inorganic black
USE **artificial inorganic black pigment**

pigment, artificial inorganic blue
USE **artificial inorganic blue pigment**

pigment, artificial inorganic brown
USE **artificial inorganic brown pigment**

pigment, artificial inorganic green
USE **artificial inorganic green pigment**

pigment, artificial inorganic red
USE **artificial inorganic red pigment**

pigment, artificial inorganic violet
USE **artificial inorganic violet pigment**

pigment, artificial inorganic yellow
USE **artificial inorganic yellow pigment**

pigment, artificial mineral
USE **artificial inorganic pigment**

pigment, artificial organic
USE **synthetic organic pigment**

pigment, artificial organic black
USE **synthetic organic black pigment**

pigment, artificial organic blue
USE **synthetic organic blue pigment**

pigment, artificial organic green
USE **synthetic organic green pigment**

pigment, artificial organic red
USE **synthetic organic red pigment**

pigment, artificial organic violet
USE **synthetic organic violet pigment**

pigment, artificial organic yellow
USE **synthetic organic yellow pigment**

pigment, black
USE **black pigment**

pigment, blue
USE **blue pigment**

pigment, brown
USE **brown pigment**

pigment, composite
USE **composite pigment**

pigment, composite green
USE **composite green pigment**

pigment, drop
USE **drop pigment**

pigment, extender white
USE **transparent white pigment**

pigment, green
USE **green pigment**

pigment, inert
USE **inert pigment**

pigment, inert white
USE **transparent white pigment**

pigment, inorganic
USE **inorganic pigment**

pigment, inorganic blue
USE **inorganic blue pigment**

pigment, inorganic brown
USE **inorganic brown pigment**

pigment, inorganic green
USE **inorganic green pigment**

pigment, inorganic red
USE **inorganic red pigment**

pigment, inorganic violet
USE **inorganic violet pigment**

pigment, inorganic yellow
USE **inorganic yellow pigment**

pigment, lake
USE **lake pigment**

pigment, Mars
USE **Mars pigment**

pigment, metallic
USE **metallic pigment**

pigment, mineral
USE **inorganic pigment**

pigment, natural inorganic
USE **natural inorganic pigment**

pigment, natural mineral
USE **natural inorganic pigment**

pigment, natural organic
USE **natural organic pigment**

pigment, opaque white
USE **opaque white pigment**

pigment, orange
USE **red pigment**

pigment, organic
USE **organic pigment**

pigment, organic black
USE **organic black pigment**

pigment, organic blue
USE **organic blue pigment**

pigment, organic brown
USE **organic brown pigment**

pigment, organic green
USE **organic green pigment**

pigment, organic red
USE **organic red pigment**

pigment, organic violet
USE **organic violet pigment**

pigment, organic yellow
USE **organic yellow pigment**

pigment, plant
USE **plant pigment**

pigment, powdered
USE **dry color**

pigment, red
USE **red pigment**

pigment, synthetic inorganic black
USE **artificial inorganic black pigment**

pigment, synthetic inorganic blue
USE **artificial inorganic blue pigment**

pigment, synthetic inorganic brown
USE **artificial inorganic brown pigment**

pigment, synthetic inorganic green
USE **artificial inorganic green pigment**

pigment, synthetic inorganic red
USE **artificial inorganic red pigment**

pigment, synthetic inorganic violet
USE **artificial inorganic violet pigment**

pigment, synthetic inorganic yellow
USE **artificial inorganic yellow pigment**

pigment, synthetic organic
USE **synthetic organic pigment**

pigment, synthetic organic black
USE **synthetic organic black pigment**

pigment, synthetic organic blue
USE **synthetic organic blue pigment**

pigment, synthetic organic green
USE **synthetic organic green pigment**

pigment, synthetic organic red
USE **synthetic organic red pigment**

pigment, synthetic organic violet
USE **synthetic organic violet pigment**

pigment, synthetic organic yellow
USE **synthetic organic yellow pigment**

pigment, transparent white
USE **transparent white pigment**

pigment, vegetable
USE **plant pigment**

pigment, white
USE **white pigment**

pigment, yellow
USE **yellow pigment**

pigments, violet
USE **violet pigments**

pignut hickory
MT.1178
UF Carya amara
Carya glabra
hickory, pignut
CN M.MT.AFU.AFU.ALO.BIQ.DCU.
AFU.AFU.AFU.ELK.BIQ

pigpens
USE **pigsties**

pigskin
MT.958
CN M.MT.AFU.AFU.ALO.AFU.DZW.
AXC.AXC

pigsties
RK.88 (A,L)
ALT **pigsty**
SN Use for enclosures for pigs that include a covered pen and yard.
UF parlors, pig
pig parlors
piggeries
pigpens
CN V.RK.AFU.ALO.ALO.AFU.ALO.BZY

Pijao
FL.1665
CN F.FL.ALO.ALO.ARI.ARI.BCW.CXA

pikes, jam
USE **jam pikes**

Pilagá
FL.1649 (L)
CN F.FL.ALO.ALO.ARI.ARI.AXC.DCU

pilaster brick
MT.109
SN A brick for constructing pilasters or slightly projecting piers, the end of which is so notched or rebated that it bonds more readily with the backing, thus increasing the stiffening of the wall. (RS)
UF brick, pilaster
CN M.MT.AFU.AFU.AFU.AXC.ALO.
AFU.ALO.CLM

pilaster masses
USE **pilaster strips**

pilaster strips
RT.659
ALT **pilaster strip**
SN Engaged piers, sometimes of only slight projection, without the capital and base of a pilaster.
UF lesenes
masses, pilaster
pilaster masses
strips, pilaster
CN V.RT.AFU.AFU.AFU.BIQ.BUE.
ALO.AFU.BOK.AFU

pilasters
RT.658 (A,N,B,R)
ALT **pilaster**
SN Shallow piers or rectangular columns projecting only slightly from a wall and, in classical architecture, conforming with one of the orders.(PDARC) Common also on furniture.
CN V.RT.AFU.AFU.AFU.BIQ.BUE.ALO.AFU.BOK

pilastrades
RT.660
ALT **pilastrade**
SN Lines of pilasters. (HAS)
CN V.RT.AFU.AFU.AFU.BIQ.BUE.ALO.AFU.BUE

pile bridges
RK.1299 (L)
ALT **pile bridge**
SN Bridges supported by pile bents. (W)
UF bridges, pile
CN V.RK.AFU.ALO.ALO.GLI.ALO.AFU.ARI.BCW

pile drivers
TB.20 (L,N)
ALT **pile driver**
SN Machines composed of a framework for holding and guiding the pile, a hammer, and a mobile plant to provide power; used for driving piles, usually by repeated blows from a free-falling or driven hammer. (MEANS)
UF drivers, pile
CN V.TB.AFU.ARI.AFU.AFU.ARI

pile driving
KT.585 (L)
SN Forcing a pile into a definite position in the ground without previous excavation, accomplished by the use of either drop hammers or steam hammers. (STEIN)
UF driving, pile
piling
CN K.KT.AFU.ALO.ERE.BCW

pile-dwellings
USE **lake dwellings**

pile foundations
RT.156
ALT **pile foundation**
SN Substructures supported on piles. (MHDSTT)
UF foundations, pile
CN V.RT.AFU.AFU.AFU.AXC.BUE.ALO.AFU

piles
RT.158 (A,L,B)
ALT **pile**
SN Use for timber, steel, or precast concrete columns serving as subsurface supports for vertical loads; distinct from **piers (foundation components)** which are larger and are never clustered.
UF pilings
CN V.RT.AFU.AFU.AFU.AXC.BUE.ALO.ALO.AFU

piles (nuclear reactors)
USE **nuclear reactors**

piles, atomic
USE **nuclear reactors**

piles, caisson
USE **caisson piles**

piles, cased
USE **cased piles**

piles, cast-in-place
USE **cast-in-place piles**

piles, driven
USE **driven piles**

piles, jacked
USE **jacked piles**

piles, precast
USE **precast piles**

Pilgrim
FL.1705
CN F.FL.ALO.ALO.AXC.AFU.AFU.ALO

pilgrimage centers
RG.213 (A)
ALT **pilgrimage center**
UF centers, pilgrimage
cities, pilgrimage
pilgrimage cities
pilgrimage sites
pilgrimage towns
sites, pilgrimage
towns, pilgrimage
CN V.RG.AFU.AFU.DZW.BCW

pilgrimage churches
RK.1102 (A)
ALT **pilgrimage church**
SN Use especially for churches built or remodeled in the 11th century, and designed for crowds of pilgrims along the main routes to the shrine at Campostela, Spain; may also be used for any large church built to receive large numbers of pilgrims.
UF churches, pilgrimage
CN V.RK.AFU.ALO.ALO.FCS.BIQ.ALO.ALO.ALO

pilgrimage cities
USE **pilgrimage centers**

pilgrimage guidebooks
VW.502 (L)
ALT **pilgrimage guidebook**
UF guidebooks, pilgrimage
CN V.VW.AFU.ALO.AFU.AFU.AFU.BZY.AFU.AFU

pilgrimage sites
USE **pilgrimage centers**

pilgrimage towns
USE **pilgrimage centers**

pilgrimages
KM.93 (L,R)
SN Journeys, usually long, undertaken as acts of homage or devotion, often to a shrine, birthplace, or sacred site.
CN K.KM.AFU.CLM.ALO

piling
USE **pile driving**

piling plans
VD.51
ALT **piling plan**
UF plans, piling
CN V.VD.AFU.AFU.BIQ.ALO.AXC.ALO.AXC

pilings
USE **piles**

pill box planes
USE **splint planes**

pillar and claw dining tables
TG.727
ALT **pillar and claw dining table**
UF dining tables, pillar and claw
tables, pillar and claw dining
CN V.TG.AFU.AFU.BIQ.BOK.ALO.BZY.ARI

pillar and claw Pembroke tables
TG.677
ALT **pillar and claw Pembroke table**
UF Pembroke tables, pillar and claw
tables, pillar and claw Pembroke
CN V.TG.AFU.AFU.BIQ.BOK.AFU.AXC.BCW.ALO

pillar and claw tables
TG.697
ALT **pillar and claw table**
SN Term applied to tables with legs jutting from a pillar, regardless of their form. (KIRK)
UF claw tables
Isle of Man tables
manx tables
tables, pillar and claw
CN V.TG.AFU.AFU.BIQ.BOK.AFU.DUC.ARI

pillar pedestal tables
USE **pedestal tables**

pillar-stones
USE **cornerstones**

pillars
USE **columns**
piers
posts

pillars (foundation components)
USE **piers (foundation components)**

pillars, bed
USE **bedposts**

pillars, bundle
USE **bundle piers**

pillars, compound
USE **compound piers**

pillars, miliary
USE **milestones**

pillow back Windsor chairs
USE **high-back Windsor chairs**

pillow capitals
USE **cushion capitals**

pillow lace
USE **bobbin lace**

pilot charts
USE **navigation charts**

pilot plants
RK.618 (L)
ALT **pilot plant**
SN Designates experimental facilities, usually small, to scaled-down versions of a planned plant, built to test manufacturing processes and generally gain experience prior to operating the final facility.
UF experimental plants
plants, experimental
plants, pilot
CN V.RK.AFU.ALO.ALO.CLM.ALO.ALO.AFU.ALO

pilotis
RT.194
ALT **piloti**
SN Use for ground-level columns or piers, either external or externally visible, which create a feeling of openness beneath an elevated building mass, as in the architecture of Le Corbusier and his followers.
CN V.RT.AFU.AFU.AFU.AXC.CXA

Pima
FL.1464 (L)
CN F.FL.ALO.ALO.ARI.AFU.CFS.CLM

pin bits
USE **spoon bits**

pin mauls
USE **top maul hammers**

pin nails, shade roller
USE **shade roller pin nails**

pin oak
MT.1246 (L)
UF oak, pin
oak, swamp
Quercus palustris
swamp oak
CN M.MT.AFU.AFU.ALO.BIQ.DCU.AFU.AFU.AFU.IRA.DCU

pin punches
USE **nail sets**

pin punches (backing-out punches)
USE **backing-out punches**

Pinatype
KT.426
CN K.KT.AFU.ALO.DUC.DOI.AFU.ALO

pincer tongs
TB.761 (N)
SN Iron tongs used for a variety of purposes, but usually used to hold heavy, round metal objects while they are being forged.
UF tongs, pincer
CN V.TB.AFU.BCW.BIQ.AXC.ALO.AXC.CLM

pincers
TB.218 (N)
SN Joined tools with a pair of jaws and handles; used to grip objects. (MEANS)
CN V.TB.AFU.ARI.CFS.ARI

pincers, carpenter's
USE **farrier's pincers**

pincers, farrier's
USE **farrier's pincers**

pinch bars
TB.418 (N)
ALT **pinch bar**
SN Steel bars with a chisel point at one end; used as a lever for lifting or moving heavy objects. (MEANS)
UF bars, pinch
bars, ripping
bars, wrecking
ripping bars
wrecking bars
CN V.TB.AFU.ARI.DZW.ALO.ALO

pine
MT.1370 (L)
UF Pinus
CN M.MT.AFU.AFU.ALO.BIQ.DCU.AFU.AFU.ALO.CXA

Pine Lawn Mogollon
FL.942
UF Mogollon, Pine Lawn
CN F.FL.ALO.ALO.ALO.AFU.ALO.ARI.BIQ.BCW.AXC

pine oil
MT.2704 (L)
UF oil, pine
CN M.MT.AFU.ARI.HZS.AFU.BZY.ALO

pine pitch
USE **pine tar**

pine tar
MT.990
UF pine pitch
pitch, pine
tar, pine
CN M.MT.AFU.AFU.ALO.ALO.ALO.ALO.AFU

pine, Alaskan
USE **western hemlock**

pine, Austrian
USE **Austrian pine**

pine, Austrian black
USE **Austrian pine**

pine, Baltic
USE **Scotch pine**

pine, black
USE **Austrian pine**

pine, Corsican
USE **Corsican pine**

pine, Cuban
USE **Cuban pine**

pine, Danzig
USE **Scotch pine**

pine, Douglas
USE **Douglas fir**

pine, Georgia
USE **longleaf pine**
southern yellow pine

pine, ginger
USE **Port Orford cedar**

pine, hard
USE **longleaf pine**
southern yellow pine

pine, hill
USE **longleaf pine**
southern yellow pine

pine, jack
USE **jack pine**

pine, Japanese stone
USE **Japanese stone pine**

pine, Japanese white
USE **Japanese white pine**

pine, Jeffrey
USE **Jeffrey pine**

pine, Jersey
USE **scrub pine**

pine, loblolly
USE **loblolly pine**

pine, lodgepole
USE **lodgepole pine**

pine, longleaf
USE **longleaf pine**

pine, longstraw
USE **longleaf pine**

pine, New England
USE **northern white pine**

pine, North Carolina
USE **shortleaf pine**

pine, northern
USE **Scotch pine**

pine, northern white

USE **northern white pine**

pine, Norway
USE **Norway pine**

pine, Oldfield
USE **loblolly pine**

pine, Oregon
USE **Douglas fir**

pine, Oregon white
USE **ponderosa pine**

pine, pitch
USE **Cuban pine**
lodgepole pine
ponderosa pine
shortleaf pine

pine, pond
USE **pond pine**

pine, ponderosa
USE **ponderosa pine**

pine, Puget Sound
USE **Douglas fir**

pine, red
USE **ponderosa pine**

pine, red (Norway pine)
USE **Norway pine**

pine, rosemary
USE **longleaf pine**
shortleaf pine

pine, sap
USE **loblolly pine**

pine, Scotch
USE **Scotch pine**

pine, Scots
USE **Scotch pine**

pine, scrub
USE **scrub pine**

pine, shortleaf
USE **shortleaf pine**

pine, slash
USE **Cuban pine**

pine, southern
USE **longleaf pine**

pine, southern yellow
USE **southern yellow pine**

pine, spruce
USE **Cuban pine**
black spruce
blue spruce
eastern hemlock
pond pine
red spruce
scrub pine
shortleaf pine
white spruce

pine, sugar
USE **sugar pine**

pine, swamp
USE **Cuban pine**
loblolly pine

pine, western yellow
USE **ponderosa pine**

pine, Weymouth
USE **northern white pine**

pine, white
USE **common spruce**

pine, yellow (loblolly pine)
USE **loblolly pine**

pine, yellow (ponderosa pine)
USE **ponderosa pine**

pine, yellow (Scotch pine)
USE **Scotch pine**

pine, yellow (scrub pine)
USE **scrub pine**

pine, yellow (shortleaf pine)
USE **shortleaf pine**

pinhole cameras
TB.299
ALT **pinhole camera**
SN Cameras whose aperture is not a lens but a tiny hole in an opaque material such as aluminum foil. (SWED)
UF cameras, pinhole
CN V.TB.AFU.ARI.CLM.ARI.AFU.AFU.ALO.ALO

pinion cutters
TB.710
ALT **pinion cutter**
SN Tools used to cut small toothed wheels, called pinions, by placing the tool over a metal rod and tapping it downwards.
UF cutters, pinion
CN V.TB.AFU.BCW.BIQ.ARI.ALO.ALO.ARI

pink
DL.3
CN D.DL.AFU.AFU.AFU

pink granite
MT.597
UF granite, pink
CN M.MT.AFU.AFU.AFU.DCU.AFU.AFU.AFU.AFU.AFU.ARI.ALO.ALO

pink lavender
USE **pale purplish pink**

pink marble
MT.795
UF marble, pink
marble, rose
rose marble
CN M.MT.AFU.AFU.AFU.DCU.AFU.ARI.ARI.ARI.AXC

pink marble, Tennessee
USE **Tennessee pink marble**

pink mauve
MT.1542
UF mauve, pink
CN M.MT.AFU.AFU.ARI.AFU.AFU.AFU.AFU.ALO.ALO.ALO.AFU

pink orchid
USE **pale purplish pink**

pink, alizarine
USE **deep pink**
strong pink

pink, baby
USE **light pink**
light yellowish pink
moderate yellowish pink
pale purplish pink

pink, bluish
USE **brilliant purplish pink**
dark purplish pink
deep purplish pink
grayish purplish pink
light grayish purplish red
light purplish pink
moderate purplish pink
pale purplish pink
strong purplish pink

pink, brilliant purplish
USE **brilliant purplish pink**

pink, brown
USE **Dutch pink**

pink, brownish
USE **brownish pink**

pink, cerise
USE **strong purplish red**

pink, dark
USE **dark pink**

pink, dark purplish
USE **dark purplish pink**

pink, dark yellowish
USE **dark yellowish pink**

pink, deep
USE **deep pink**

pink, deep purplish
USE **deep purplish pink**

pink, deep rose
USE **strong purplish pink**

pink, deep yellowish
USE **deep yellowish pink**

pink, Dutch
USE **Dutch pink**

pink, English
USE **Dutch pink**

pink, flesh
USE **light yellowish pink**

moderate yellowish pink
pale yellowish pink

pink, fuchsia
USE **deep purplish pink**
moderate purplish pink

pink, grayish
USE **grayish pink**

pink, grayish orange
USE **grayish yellowish pink**

pink, grayish purplish
USE **grayish purplish pink**

pink, grayish yellowish
USE **grayish yellowish pink**

pink, Italian
USE **Dutch pink**

pink, light
USE **light pink**

pink, light orchid
USE **pale purplish pink**

pink, light purplish
USE **light purplish pink**

pink, light yellowish
USE **light yellowish pink**

pink, madder
USE **strong purplish red**

pink, mauve
USE **pale purplish pink**

pink, moderate
USE **moderate pink**

pink, moderate orange
USE **light yellowish pink**
moderate yellowish pink

pink, moderate purplish
USE **moderate purplish pink**

pink, moderate yellowish
USE **moderate yellowish pink**

pink, orange
USE **brilliant orange**

pink, orchid
USE **light purplish pink**
moderate purplish pink

pink, pale
USE **pale pink**

pink, pale purplish
USE **pale purplish pink**

pink, pale yellowish
USE **pale yellowish pink**

pink, pastel
USE **moderate pink**
moderate yellowish pink

pink, potter's
USE **potter's pink**

pink, purplish
USE **purplish pink**

pink, rhodamine
USE **strong purplish pink**

pink, rose
USE **light purplish pink**
moderate purplish pink
vivid purplish red

pink, silver
USE **grayish pink**

pink, strong
USE **strong pink**

pink, strong purplish
USE **strong purplish pink**

pink, strong yellowish
USE **strong yellowish pink**

pink, vivid
USE **vivid pink**

pink, vivid yellowish
USE **vivid yellowish pink**

pink, yellowish
USE **yellowish pink**

pinkish buff, pale
USE **pale orange yellow**

pinkish gray
DL.13
UF centroid color 10
gray, pinkish
lilac
CN D.DL.AFU.AFU.AFU.CFS

pinkish lilac, light
USE **light purplish pink**

pinkish white
DL.12
UF centroid color 9
reddish white
white, pinkish
white, reddish
CN D.DL.AFU.AFU.AFU.BZY

pinnacles
RT.1061 (B)
ALT **pinnacle**
SN Subordinate vertical structures, generally more or less tapering, rising above the neighboring parts of a building. (RS)
UF guglias (pinnacles)
CN V.RT.AFU.BCW.CFS

pinned joints
TF.593
ALT **pinned joint**
UF joints, pinned
CN V.TF.ALO.AFU.EFQ

pinning
KT.52
ALT **pinned**
CN K.KT.AFU.ALO.BCW.BCW.ARI

pins (hardware)
TF.456 (N)
ALT **pin (hardware)**
SN Use for cylindrical pieces of wood, metal, or other material used to fasten structural members together.
CN V.TF.AFU.AFU.AFU.ALO.AFU.CXA

pins (hinge components)
TF.525
ALT **pin (hinge component)**
SN The long rods that pass through a hinge's knuckles to keep the two halves of the hinge joined together. (DITTRI)
UF hinge pins
CN V.TF.AFU.ALO.ALO.AXC

pins, barbed dowel
USE **barbed dowel pins**

pins, cotter
USE **cotter pins**

pins, dowel
USE **dowel pins**

pins, drift
USE **driftpins**

pins, escutcheon
USE **escutcheon pins**

pins, kotter
USE **cotter pins**

pins, line
USE **line pins**

pins, push
USE **push pins**

pins, sash
USE **sash pins**

pins, veneer
USE **veneer pins**

Pinto Basin
FL.910
UF Pinto-Gypssum
CN F.FL.ALO.ALO.ALO.AFU.ALO.ARI.ALO.BCW

Pinto-Gypssum
USE **Pinto Basin**

Pinus
USE **pine**

Pinus alba
USE **northern white pine**

Pinus banksiana
USE **jack pine**

Pinus caribaea
USE **Cuban pine**

Pinus contorta
USE **lodgepole pine**

Pinus echinata
USE **shortleaf pine**

Pinus jeffreyi
USE **Jeffrey pine**

Pinus lambertiana
USE **sugar pine**

Pinus mitis
USE **shortleaf pine**

Pinus palustris
USE **longleaf pine**

Pinus ponderosa
USE **ponderosa pine**

Pinus pumila
USE **Japanese stone pine**

Pinus resinosa
USE **Norway pine**

Pinus serotina
USE **pond pine**

Pinus strobus
USE **northern white pine**

Pinus sylvestris
USE **Scotch pine**

Pinus taeda
USE **loblolly pine**

Pinus virginiana
USE **scrub pine**

pioneers
HG.730 (L,R)
ALT **pioneer**
SN Persons who first enter or settle a region, thus opening it for occupation and development by others. (RHDEL2)
CN H.HG.AFU.BCW.EWY

pioury
USE **Indian yellow**

Pipatsje
USE **Maricopa**

pipe
MT.2262 (L)
SN A continuous, tubular conduit, generally leakproof, for the transport of liquids and gases. (DAC)
CN M.MT.AFU.ALO.EWY

pipe augers
USE **nose augers**

pipe chases
USE **chases**

pipe clay
USE **kaolinite**

pipe cutters
TB.711 (N)
ALT **pipe cutter**
SN Hand tools consisting of a frame with a cutting wheel and drive wheels; used for cutting pipe and tubing by forcing the cutting wheel into the pipe material and rotating the tool around the pipe. (MEANS)
UF cutters, pipe
CN V.TB.AFU.BCW.BIQ.ARI.ALO.ALO.AXC

pipe fitters
HG.602
ALT **pipe fitter**
UF fitters, pipe
CN H.HG.AFU.AXC.BZY.AFU.DOI

pipe-fitting
KT.580 (L)
CN K.KT.AFU.ALO.ERE.ALO.ARI

pipe hangers, adjustable
USE **adjustable pipe hangers**

pipe keys
TF.537
ALT **pipe key**
UF barred keys
barrel keys
keys, barred
keys, barrel
keys, pipe
CN V.TF.AFU.ALO.ARI.AFU.BZY.AFU

pipe wrenches
TB.778 (N)
ALT **pipe wrench**
SN Heavy hand tools with adjustable serrated jaws for gripping, screwing, or unscrewing metal pipe. (MEANS)
UF wrenches, pipe
CN V.TB.AFU.BCW.BIQ.AXC.ALO.BIQ.BOK

pipe wrenches, chain
USE **chain tongs**

pipelayers
HG.603
ALT **pipelayer**
CN H.HG.AFU.AXC.BZY.AFU.DUC

pipelaying
KT.582
CN K.KT.AFU.ALO.ERE.ALO.AXC

pipelines, gas
USE **gas pipelines**

pipelines, natural gas
USE **gas pipelines**

pipes, flue
USE **flues**

pipes, service
USE **service pipes**

pipestone
USE **catlinite**

piping drainage, waste and vent
USE **DWV piping**

piping (plumbing systems)
RT.1467 (N,B)
CN V.RT.ALO.BCW.ALO.ARI.BZY

piping, drainage
USE **drainage piping**

piping, DWV
USE **DWV piping**

Piqua
USE **Shawnee**

Pir Ahmad
FL.3471
CN F.FL.ALO.BIQ.AFU.DUC.BZY

Pirgos ware
USE **Pyrgos ware**

Piro
FL.1609 (L)
UF Chontaquiro
Chuntaquiro
Simirinche
CN F.FL.ALO.ALO.ARI.ARI.ALO.AFU.BIQ

Pisces symbols
DG.81
ALT **Pisces symbol**
CN D.DG.AFU.AFU.ERE.BUE

piscinae
RT.1240
ALT **piscina**
SN Basins with a drain, generally set near the sacristy and used for certain ablutions.
CN V.RT.AFU.BUE.ALO.ARI.CFS

pisé
MT.2057 (A,L,R)
SN A building material consisting of stiff earth or clay forced in between forms. (W)
CN M.MT.AFU.AFU.ARI.BOK.AFU.AXC

pisé de terre
USE **rammed earth**

pishtaqs
RK.502
ALT **pishtaq**
SN In Islamic architecture, monumental gateways or portals, especially ones with a rectangular screen wall rising above the roofline of the building beyond, usually mosques, madrasas, or caravansarais.
CN V.RK.AFU.ALO.ALO.BUE.AXC

pisolite
USE **pisolitic limestone**

pisolitic limestone
MT.673
UF limestone, pisolitic
pisolite
CN M.MT.AFU.AFU.AFU.DCU.AFU.ALO.AFU.ALO.ALO.AFU.AFU.ARI

pissoirs
USE **comfort stations**

pistachio green

USE **light yellowish green**
moderate yellow green
moderate yellowish green

pit dwellings
RK.310 (L)
ALT **pit dwelling**
SN Use for houses, common during the prehistoric periods of many cultures, whose floors are dug out deeply below the adjacent ground level; use **sunken huts** for multipurpose buildings of the first millennium AD, found in England and throughout northern Europe.
UF dwellings, pit
houses, pit
pit houses
CN V.RK.AFU.ALO.ALO.AXC.ALO .AXC.ALO.BCW

pit graves
USE **shaft graves**

Pit-grove culture
USE **Kurgan**

pit houses
USE **pit dwellings**

Pit River Indians
USE **Atsugewi**

pit saws
TB.1012 (N)
ALT **pit saw**
SN Large two-man saws used to saw boards from the lengths of logs which are placed over big pits. The saws are operated by one man standing on the log and the other standing in the pit.
UF board saws
plank saws
saws, board
saws, pit
saws, plank
CN V.TB.AFU.BCW.CFS.ALO.AFU. EWY.BCW.BIQ

pit saws, frame
USE **frame pit saws**

pit saws, open
USE **open pit saws**

pit tombs
USE **shaft graves**

pitch
MT.1505 (L)
SN Use for the black or dark viscous residue from the distillation of organic materials, especially tars, and for synthetic mixtures resembling pitch.
CN M.MT.AFU.AFU.ALO.BOK.DIO

pitch oil
USE **creosote**

pitch pine
USE **Cuban pine**
lodgepole pine
ponderosa pine
shortleaf pine

pitch, Burgundy
USE **Burgundy pitch**

pitch, Greek
USE **rosin**

pitch, navy
USE **navy pitch**

pitch, petroleum
USE **petroleum asphalt**

pitch, pine
USE **pine tar**

pitch, ship
USE **navy pitch**

pitched-brick vaults
RT.549
ALT **pitched-brick vault**
SN Use for vaults in which the rows of bricks are laid at a slight inclination, leaning against the previously laid row, thus obviating the need for formwork.
UF barrel vaults, uncentered
bovedas (pitched-brick vaults)
canted vaults
Catalan vaults
uncentered barrel vaults
vaults, canted
vaults, Catalan
vaults, pitched-brick
vaults, uncentered barrel
CN V.RT.AFU.AFU.AFU.BIQ.BOK. AFU.ARI.AFU.AFU

pitched roofs
RT.420 (B)
ALT **pitched roof**
UF roofs, pitched
CN V.RT.AFU.AFU.AFU.BIQ.ARI. AFU.AFU.AFU.BOK

pitcher houses
USE **wine cellars**

pitchers (masonry tools)
USE **pitching chisels**

pitches, cricket
USE **cricket fields**

pitches, football
USE **soccer fields**

pitches, soccer
USE **soccer fields**

pitching chisels
TB.580 (N)
ALT **pitching chisel**
SN Chisels with a wide thick edge, used by masons for rough-dressing stone. (MEANS)
UF chisels, pitching
pitchers (masonry tools)
pitching tools
tools, pitching
CN V.TB.AFU.BCW.BCW.ALO.BZY. AXC

pitching pieces
USE **apron pieces**

pitching tools
USE **pitching chisels**

pits
RK.1358 (A,L)
ALT **pit**
CN V.RK.AFU.ALO.ARI.AXC.ARI.AXC

pits (theater spaces)
RM.355
ALT **pit (theater space)**
SN Use for the ground floors of theaters, especially those at the rear; most appropriate in an English and historical rather than a modern American context.
CN V.RM.AFU.DIO.AXC.AXC.AFU.BOK

pits, gravel
USE **gravel pits**

pits, orchestra
USE **orchestra pits**

pits, seepage
USE **seepage pits**

pits, sump
USE **sumps**

pitting
KT.924
ALT **pitted**
SN Use for the appearance of small cavities or depressions in a surface caused by weathering, erosion, or other processes over time.
CN K.KT.ALO.BZY.BCW

Pittsburgh lock seams
TF.659
ALT **Pittsburgh lock seam**
UF lock seams, Pittsburgh
seams, Pittsburgh lock
CN V.TF.ALO.ARI.ARI.BUE.CFS

Pittura Colta
FL.3744 (R)
SN Use for the historicizing, classicizing movement in Italian painting of the 1980s.
CN F.FL.ALO.BUE.ARI.GLI

Pittura Metafisica
USE **Metaphysical**

piuri
USE **Indian yellow**

pivot bits
USE **tenon-cutting bits**

pivot-reinforced hinges

TF.125
ALT **pivot-reinforced hinge**
UF hinges, pivot-reinforced
CN V.TF.AFU.AFU.AFU.AFU.CLM.AFU.FIM

pivoted doors
RT.869
ALT **pivoted door**
SN Doors hung on pivots, either center pivots or offset, as distinguished from one hung on hinges or having a sliding mechanism. (DAC)
UF doors, pivoted
CN V.RT.AFU.ARI.AFU.AFU.AFU.ALO.ARI.AFU.ARI.BCW

pivoting windows
RT.950
ALT **pivoting window**
SN Windows whose sash rotates about fixed vertical or horizontal pivots, located at or toward the center. (DAC)
UF windows, pivoting
CN V.RT.AFU.ARI.AFU.AFU.BOK.AFU.AFU.EWY.BCW

Pjandzikent
USE **Panjikent**

place brick
MT.122
UF brick, place
brick, salmon
salmon brick
CN M.MT.AFU.AFU.AFU.AXC.ALO.AFU.AXC.AFU.AFU.ALO.ALO

places, endangered
USE **endangered places**

places, holy
USE **shrines**

places, imperiled
USE **endangered places**

placets
TG.249
ALT **placet**
CN V.TG.AFU.AFU.ALO.AFU.ALO.AFU.BZY

placing, concrete
USE **pouring concrete**

plafonds
USE **ceilings**

plagiarism
BM.1099 (L)
CN B.BM.CRG.BCW.ALO.ALO.AFU

plagioclase
MT.509 (L)
UF feldspar, plagioclase
plagioclase feldspar
CN M.MT.AFU.AFU.AFU.CFS.AFU.CRG.AXC

plagioclase feldspar
USE **plagioclase**

plagiographs
USE **pantographs**

plain carbon steel
USE **carbon steel**

plain cut joints
USE **rough-cut joints**

plain dovetail seams
TF.660
ALT **plain dovetail seam**
UF dovetail seams
seams, plain dovetail
CN V.TF.ALO.ARI.ARI.BUE.CLM

plain salted paper
USE **salted paper**

plain salted paper processes
USE **salted paper processes**

plain-sawed lumber
MT.1431
SN Wood cut at a tangent to the annual growth rings. (HORNB)
UF flat-sawed lumber
lumber, flat-sawed
lumber, plain-sawed
CN M.MT.AFU.AFU.ALO.BIQ.DCU.ALO.BOK.ALO.ALO.AFU

plain, Alma
USE **Alma plain**

plains
RD.217 (L)
ALT **plain**
SN Extensive areas of land having few inequalities of surface, being usually fairly flat and at low elevation. (W)
CN V.RD.ARI.AFU.AXC.AFU.ALO.ARI.ALO

Plains Cree
FL.1394
UF Cree, Plains
CN F.FL.ALO.ALO.ARI.AFU.BOK.ERE

Plains Ojibwa
FL.1395
UF Ojibwa, Plains
CN F.FL.ALO.ALO.ARI.AFU.BOK.EWY

Plains Village
FL.775
CN F.FL.ALO.ALO.ALO.AFU.AFU.BCW.ALO.AFU

plains, flood
USE **flood plains**

Plainview
FL.749
CN F.FL.ALO.ALO.ALO.AFU.AFU.ARI.ALO.ARI.AFU

plaiting
USE **braiding**

plan books
USE **pattern books**

plan diagrams
USE **plans**

plan drawings
USE **plans**

plan (formal concept)
BM.82
CN B.BM.AFU.AFU.ARI.AFU.EFQ

plan oblique drawings
VD.18
ALT **plan oblique drawing**
SN Use for drawings in oblique projection in which the horizontal plane is parallel to the plane of projection (drawing surface), and the plan is rotated to any convenient angle so that verticals may be drawn.
UF drawings, plan oblique
oblique drawings, plan
CN V.VD.AFU.AFU.BIQ.AFU.ARI.ALO

plan views
VB.29
ALT **plan view**
SN Use for depictions or photographs showing structures or sites seen from directly above. For scaled orthographic drawings specifically, use **plans.**
UF ichnographic views
views, ichnographic
views, plan
CN V.VB.AFU.AFU.BOK.ALO.BZY

plan, chessboard
USE **grid plan**

plan, Greek cross
USE **Greek cross-plan**

plan, grid
USE **grid plan**

plan, Latin cross
USE **Latin cross-plan**

plan, orthogonal
USE **grid plan**

planar trusses
RT.358
ALT **planar truss**
SN Use for trusses with all members in one plane.
UF trusses, planar
CN V.RT.AFU.AFU.AFU.BCW.CLM.AFU.AFU.AFU

plancher nails
USE **flooring nails**

planching
USE **flooring**

plancier pieces
USE **soffits**

planciers
USE **soffits**

plane figures
BM.767
SN Two-dimensional geometrical configurations.
UF figures, plane
CN B.BM.CFS.ARI.AXC.BCW.AFU

plane wood
MT.1266 (L)
UF platanus
wood, plane
CN M.MT.AFU.AFU.ALO.BIQ.DCU.AFU.AFU.AFU.JZQ

plane wood, London
USE **London plane wood**

plane, American
USE **sycamore**

plane, picture
USE **picture plane**

planers (woodworkers)
HG.545
ALT **planer (woodworker)**
CN H.HG.AFU.AXC.BUE.ARI.DIO.ALO

planes
TB.910 (L,N)
ALT **plane**
SN Tools used for leveling and smoothing the surface of wood by paring shavings from it. (BLACKB)
CN V.TB.AFU.BCW.CFS.ALO.AFU.DUC

planes (mathematics)
BM.799
CN B.BM.CFS.ARI.AXC.BIQ

planes, angle
USE **angle planes**

planes, astragal
USE **bead planes**

planes, badger
USE **badger planes**

planes, banding
USE **banding planes**

planes, banister
USE **capping planes**
handrail planes

planes, bead
USE **bead planes**

planes, bead molding
USE **bead planes**

planes, bed mold
USE **cornice planes**

planes, bench
USE **bench planes**

planes, block
USE **block planes**

planes, boxing
USE **rabbet planes**

planes, bullnose
USE **bullnose planes**

planes, bullnose rabbet
USE **bullnose planes**

planes, capping
USE **capping planes**

planes, capping (handrail planes)
USE **handrail planes**

planes, carcase grooving
USE **dado planes**

planes, centerbead molding
USE **centerboard planes**

planes, centerboard
USE **centerboard planes**

planes, check
USE **rabbet planes**

planes, chip
USE **splint planes**

planes, chisel
USE **edge planes**

planes, chiv
USE **howell planes**

planes, cleaning-out
USE **cooper's stoup planes**

planes, coffin
USE **smoothing planes**

planes, combination
USE **combination planes**

planes, compass
USE **compass planes**

planes, compass smoothing
USE **compass planes**

planes, convex
USE **guttering planes**

planes, cooper's jointer
USE **cooper's jointer planes**

planes, cooper's stoup
USE **cooper's stoup planes**

planes, cornice
USE **cornice planes**

planes, cornish
USE **cornice planes**

planes, cove
USE **cove planes**

planes, cove molding
USE **cove planes**

planes, cow
USE **roughing planes**

planes, crown
USE **cornice planes**

planes, crown mold
USE **cornice planes**

planes, dado
USE **dado planes**

planes, dado grooving
USE **dado planes**

planes, edge
USE **edge planes**

planes, finger
USE **finger planes**

planes, floor
USE **floor planes**

planes, fore
USE **jack planes**

planes, fork stail
USE **forkstaffs**

planes, grooving
USE **grooving planes**

planes, gutter
USE **guttering planes**

planes, guttering
USE **guttering planes**

planes, handrail
USE **handrail planes**

planes, heel
USE **compass planes**

planes, hollow
USE **hollow planes**

planes, housing
USE **dado planes**

planes, howell
USE **howell planes**

planes, hunter
USE **roughing planes**

planes, inclined
USE **ramps**

planes, inside
USE **cooper's stoup planes**

planes, jack
USE **jack planes**

planes, jointer
USE **jointer planes**

planes, leveling
USE **leveling planes**

planes, long
USE **long planes**

planes, long-jointer
USE **cooper's jointer planes**

planes, matching
USE **tongue-and-groove planes**

planes, miter
USE **miter planes**

planes, miter block
USE **miter planes**

planes, miter shooting
USE **miter planes**

planes, modeling
USE **modeling planes**

planes, molding
USE **molding planes**

planes, molding pull
USE **molding pull planes**

planes, moving fillister
USE **moving fillister planes**

planes, nosing
USE **nosing planes**

planes, nosing molding
USE **nosing planes**

planes, ogee
USE **ogee planes**

planes, ogee molding
USE **ogee planes**

planes, ovolo
USE **ovolo planes**

planes, panel
USE **panel planes**

planes, piano maker's edge
USE **edge planes**

planes, picture-frame maker's
USE **miter planes**

planes, pill box
USE **splint planes**

planes, plough
USE **plow planes**

planes, plow
USE **plow planes**

planes, pull
USE **short-jointer planes**

planes, quarter-round
USE **ovolo planes**

planes, rabbet
USE **rabbet planes**

planes, rabbet (badger planes)
USE **badger planes**

planes, rebate
USE **rabbet planes**

planes, roughing
USE **roughing planes**

planes, round
USE **round planes**

planes, round-both-ways
USE **cooper's stoup planes**

planes, round (guttering planes)
USE **guttering planes**

planes, rounder
USE **rounder planes**

planes, rounding (forkstaffs)
USE **forkstaffs**

planes, sash
USE **sash planes**

planes, sash fillister
USE **sash fillister planes**

planes, scabbard
USE **splint planes**

planes, scaleboard
USE **splint planes**

planes, scooper
USE **scooper planes**

planes, scoopmaker
USE **scooper planes**

planes, scraper
USE **cabinet scrapers**

planes, scrub
USE **roughing planes**

planes, scud
USE **roughing planes**

planes, scurfing
USE **roughing planes**

planes, short-jointer
USE **short-jointer planes**

planes, shoulder
USE **shoulder planes**

planes, skew
USE **skew planes**

planes, slit deal
USE **tongue-and-groove planes**

planes, slitting
USE **splint planes**

planes, smoothing
USE **smoothing planes**

planes, spelk
USE **splint planes**

planes, splint
USE **splint planes**

planes, spout
USE **guttering planes**

planes, stair
USE **capping planes**

planes, stair nosing
USE **nosing planes**

planes, stairbuilder's
USE **capping planes**
handrail planes

planes, step nosing
USE **nosing planes**

planes, straight block
USE **strike blocks**

planes, sun
USE **sun-planes**

planes, table
USE **table round planes**

planes, table round
USE **table round planes**

planes, thumb
USE **thumb planes**

planes, tongue
USE **tongue planes**

planes, tongue-and-groove
USE **tongue-and-groove planes**

planes, toothing
USE **toothing planes**

planes, trenching
USE **dado planes**

planes, trueing
USE **trying planes**

planes, trying
USE **trying planes**

planes, witchet
USE **rounder planes**

planetaria
RK.433 (A,L,B)
ALT **planetarium**
UF orreries
CN V.RK.AFU.ALO.ALO.BCW.BCW

planigraphs
USE **pantographs**

planimetric maps
VW.152
ALT **planimetric map**
SN Maps representing the horizontal position of land features and not relief. (DOD)
UF maps, planimetric
CN V.VW.AFU.AFU.AFU.FZU.AXC.AFU.ARI.AFU.CLM

planing
KT.620
ALT **planed**
SN A process for smoothing the surface of wood by shaving off small fragments. (DAC)
CN K.KT.AFU.ALO.FUA.DIO

planing machines
TB.430 (L)
ALT **planing machine**
SN Fixed or portable machines used for planing wood or steel. (MEANS)
UF machines, planing

CN V.TB.AFU.ARI.EFQ.AFU.AXC

planing mills
RK.650 (L)
ALT **planing mill**
SN Establishments primarily engaged in producing surfaced lumber, by cutting, smoothing, and matching wood.
UF mills, planing
CN V.RK.AFU.ALO.ALO.CLM.ALO.ALO.AFU.AXC.CFS

planishing
KT.154
ALT **planished**
SN The removal of irregularities from sheet metal by means of a smooth-faced hammer. (THDAT)
CN K.KT.AFU.ALO.DOI.DCU

planishing hammers
TB.663 (N)
ALT **planishing hammer**
SN Smooth-faced hammers used to planish metal surfaces.
UF hammers, planishing
CN V.TB.AFU.BCW.BIQ.AFU.ALO.BIQ.ARI

planishing stakes
TB.689 (N)
ALT **planishing stake**
SN Slightly curved, square-headed stakes, used for smoothing hammer marks out of sheet metal work. (RUSERW)
UF stakes, planishing
CN V.TB.AFU.BCW.BIQ.AFU.ALO.CXA.BOK

plank
MT.1444
SN A long, wide, square-sawn thick piece of lumber. (DAC)
UF lumber, plank
plank lumber
CN M.MT.AFU.AFU.ALO.BIQ.DCU.ALO.BOK.ARI.BCW.AFU

plank-and-beam construction
USE **post-and-beam structures**

plank chairs
USE **board chairs**

plank lumber
USE **plank**

plank saws
USE **pit saws**

planking
USE **decking**

planks (decking)
USE **decking**

planned residential developments
USE **planned unit developments**

planned unit developments
RG.78 (L)
ALT **planned unit development**
SN Use for complexes designed as unified sites that include a mix of building types and uses, common open space, and controlled density increases, rather than lot-by-lot schemes.
UF developments, planned unit
planned residential developments
PUDs
residential developments, planned
unit developments, planned
CN V.RG.AFU.AFU.BOK.AXC.ARI

planners
HG.645
ALT **planner**
CN H.HG.AFU.AXC.BZY.BIQ

planners, city
USE **city planners**

planners, town
USE **city planners**

planners, urban
USE **city planners**

planning
KD.168 (L,B)
CN K.KD.AFU.ALO.DUC

planning commissions
HG.839
ALT **planning commission**
SN Public agencies at the community level empowered to prepare comprehensive plans for future development and to evaluate proposed changes in land use for conformance with such plans. (LOFZ)
UF commissions, planning
CN H.HG.ALO.BIQ.BOK

planning districts
RG.252
ALT **planning district**
UF districts, planning
CN V.RG.ALO.AFU.AFU.BCW

planning, campus
USE **campus planning**

planning, city
USE **city planning**

planning, civic
USE **city planning**

planning, country
USE **rural planning**

planning, highway
USE **highway planning**

planning, regional
USE **regional planning**

planning, rural
USE **rural planning**

planning, space
USE **space planning**

planning, town
USE **city planning**

planning, town and country
USE **regional planning**

planning, transportation
USE **transportation planning**

planning, urban
USE **city planning**

Plano
FL.748
CN F.FL.ALO.ALO.ALO.AFU.AFU.ARI.ALO.ARI

planographic printing
KT.461
UF planographic processes
planography
printing, planographic
CN K.KT.AFU.ALO.DUC.DUC.ALO.BCW.ALO

planographic processes
USE **planographic printing**

planography
USE **planographic printing**

plans
VD.36 (A,L)
ALT **plan**
SN Use for orthographic drawings in the horizontal plane. Can also be used for a set of drawings for a project. For general reference to depictions or photographs showing structures or sites seen from directly above, use **plan views.**
UF diagrams, plan
drawings, plan
plan diagrams
plan drawings
CN V.VD.AFU.AFU.BIQ.ALO.AXC

plans (reports)
VW.460 (L,B)
ALT **plan (report)**
CN V.VW.AFU.AFU.ALO.FIM.ARI

plans, block
USE **block plans**

plans, body
USE **body plans**

plans, cadastral
USE **cadastral maps**

plans, city
USE **city plans**

plans, comprehensive
USE **comprehensive plans**

plans, construction
USE **construction drawings**

plans, deck
USE **deck plans**

plans, docking
USE **docking plans**

plans, electrical
USE **electrical plans**

plans, floor
USE **floor plans**

plans, foundation
USE **foundation plans**

plans, framing
USE **framing plans**

plans, general
USE **comprehensive plans**

plans, grading
USE **grading plans**

plans, ground
USE **ground plans**

plans, half
USE **half plans**

plans, half-breadth
USE **half-breadth plans**

plans, heating
USE **heating plans**

plans, HVAC
USE **HVAC plans**

plans, ichnographic
USE **ichnographic plans**

plans, key
USE **key plans**

plans, landscaping
USE **landscaping plans**

plans, lines
USE **lines drawings**

plans, local
USE **site plans**

plans, location
USE **site plans**

plans, masonry
USE **foundation plans**

plans, master
USE **master plans**

plans, master (reports)
USE **comprehensive plans**

plans, municipal
USE **municipal plans**

plans, partial
USE **partial plans**

plans, piling
USE **piling plans**

plans, planting
USE **planting plans**

plans, plot
USE **site plans**

plans, plumbing
USE **plumbing plans**

plans, profile
USE **profiles**

plans, property
USE **cadastral maps**

plans, reflected ceiling
USE **reflected ceiling plans**

plans, regional
USE **regional plans**

plans, regional (drawings)
USE **site plans**

plans, rigging
USE **rigging plans**

plans, sail
USE **sail plans**

plans, section
USE **sections**

plans, sheer
USE **sheer plans**

plans, ships
USE **ships plans**

plans, site
USE **site plans**

plans, street
USE **street maps**

plans, survey
USE **topographic surveys**

plans, town
USE **city plans**

plans, typical floor
USE **typical floor plans**

plans, utility
USE **utility plans**

plans, vicinity
USE **site plans**

plant communities
RD.243 (L)
ALT **plant community**
SN Naturally growing collections of plants which, for the purpose of the study of vegetation, can be usefully treated as single entities. (TANSAM)
UF communities, plant
CN V.RD.ARI.AFU.BCW.ALO.AFU

plant engineering
KD.232 (L)
UF engineering, plant
CN K.KD.AFU.ARI.BIQ.CLM

plant fiber
MT.1822 (L)
UF fiber, plant
CN M.MT.AFU.AFU.ARI.ALO.AFU.
AFU.ALO

plant fiber paper
USE **bark cloth**

plant fortifications
RK.453
ALT **plant fortification**
SN Concentric circular vegetation barriers used as defensive walls or fortifications in precolonial Africa.
UF fortifications, plant
fortifications, vegetation
plant ramparts
ramparts, plant
vegetation fortifications
CN V.RK.AFU.ALO.ALO.BIQ.BZY

plant location
USE **industrial location**

plant materials
MT.1017
UF materials, plant
CN M.MT.AFU.AFU.ALO.BIQ

plant pigment
MT.1557 (L)
UF pigment, plant
pigment, vegetable
vegetable pigment
CN M.MT.AFU.AFU.ARI.AFU.AFU.
ALO.AFU.ALO.AFU.ALO

plant publications
USE **house organs**

plant ramparts
USE **plant fortifications**

plant stands
TG.647 (N)
ALT **plant stand**
UF bouquet stands
flower stands
flower tables
palm stands
planters
stands, bouquet
stands, flower
stands, palm
stands, plant
tables, flower
CN V.TG.AFU.AFU.BIQ.BCW.ALO.DIO

Plant Style
FL.2672
CN F.FL.ALO.AXC.ALO.AFU.ALO.
AXC.BCW.BUE

plant, capital
USE **infrastructure**

plantation beds
USE **tester beds**

plantation houses
RK.298 (A)
ALT **plantation house**
UF big houses
great houses
houses, big

houses, great
houses, plantation
CN V.RK.AFU.ALO.ALO.AXC.ALO.AXC.AFU.AFU.AXC

plantation owners
HG.369 (L)
ALT **plantation owner**
UF owners, plantation
CN H.HG.AFU.AXC.BIQ.ALO.AXC.AFU.BCW

plantations
RG.22 (L,R)
ALT **plantation**
SN Large estates in a tropical or subtropical region that are generally cultivated by unskilled or semiskilled labor under central direction. (W)
CN V.RG.AFU.AFU.AFU.BCW

planted moldings
USE **applied moldings**

planters
USE **ferneries**
plant stands

planting
KT.493 (L,B)
CN K.KT.AFU.ALO.DZW.AFU.AXC

planting diagrams
USE **planting plans**

planting plans
VD.43
ALT **planting plan**
UF diagrams, planting
plans, planting
planting diagrams
CN V.VD.AFU.AFU.BIQ.ALO.AXC.AFU.ALO.ARI.AFU

planting, roadside
USE **roadside improvement**

plants
RD.257 (A,L,B,R)
ALT **plant**
CN V.RD.ARI.AFU.BCW.ALO.ALO

plants (factories)
USE **factories**

plants, assembly
USE **assembly plants**

plants, beverage processing
USE **beverage processing plants**

plants, bottling
USE **bottling plants**

plants, bulb
USE **bulbs**

plants, cement
USE **cement plants**

plants, coal-fired power
USE **coal-fired power plants**

plants, crushing
USE **crushing plants**

plants, dairy
USE **dairy plants**

plants, desalination
USE **desalination plants**

plants, experimental
USE **pilot plants**

plants, filtration
USE **filtration plants**

plants, food processing
USE **food processing plants**

plants, gas-turbine power
USE **gas-turbine power plants**

plants, geothermal power
USE **geothermal power plants**

plants, herbaceous
USE **herbaceous plants**

plants, hydroelectric power
USE **hydroelectric power plants**

plants, industrial
USE **factories**

plants, N-power
USE **nuclear power plants**

plants, nonwoody
USE **nonwoody plants**

plants, nuclear power
USE **nuclear power plants**

plants, ocean thermal energy conversion
USE **ocean thermal energy conversion plants**

plants, oil-fired power
USE **oil-fired power plants**

plants, packing
USE **packing plants**

plants, pilot
USE **pilot plants**

plants, power
USE **power plants**

plants, printing
USE **printing plants**

plants, pumped storage power
USE **pumped storage power plants**

plants, recycling
USE **resource recovery facilities**

plants, sewage treatment
USE **sewage treatment plants**

plants, smelting
USE **smelters**

plants, solar power
USE **solar power plants**

plants, steam-electric
USE **steam power plants**

plants, steam power
USE **steam power plants**

plants, tidal power
USE **tidal power plants**

plants, water treatment
USE **water treatment plants**

plants, wind power
USE **wind power plants**

plants, woody
USE **woody plants**

plaque rails
USE **plate rails**

Plaquemine
FL.861 (L)
CN F.FL.ALO.ALO.ALO.AFU.ALO.ALO.ARI.ARI.BOK

plaques
VW.608 (A,L,N,R)
ALT **plaque**
SN Use for thin flat tablets (of metal or clay, for example) of any shape, decorated or inscribed and used as decorative ornaments or commemoratives set into the surface of walls or furniture.
CN V.VW.AFU.ALO.AFU.CLM

plaster
MT.2434 (A,L,R)
CN M.MT.AFU.ARI.CRG.AFU.AXC

plaster board, gypsum
USE **gypsum board**

plaster knives
TB.613
ALT **plaster knife**
SN Knives, the blade of which is usually curved on one side and straight on the other, used to apply and smooth plaster.
UF knives, plaster
CN V.TB.AFU.BCW.BCW.ALO.FCS.ALO

plaster of Paris
MT.2442 (L,B)
SN Calcified gypsum, free of additives, used as a rapid setting plaster especially for ornamental casting. (DAC)
UF hemihydrate plaster
Paris, plaster of
plaster, hemihydrate
CN M.MT.AFU.ARI.CRG.AFU.AXC.AFU.AXC.ARI

plaster of Paris, slaked
USE **slaked plaster of Paris**

plaster, acoustical
USE **acoustical plaster**

plaster, anhydrous gypsum
USE **anhydrous gypsum plaster**

plaster, casting
USE **casting plaster**

plaster, class B gypsum
USE **retarded hemihydrate plaster**

plaster, class C gypsum
USE **anhydrous gypsum plaster**

plaster, class D gypsum
USE **Keene's cement**

plaster, fibrous
USE **fibrous plaster**

plaster, flooring
USE **gypsum cement**

plaster, gauging
USE **gauging plaster**

plaster, gypsum
USE **gypsum plaster**

plaster, hard-finish
USE **gypsum cement**

plaster, hemihydrate
USE **Plaster of Paris**

plaster, Keene's
USE **Keene's cement**

plaster, molding
USE **molding plaster**

plaster, mud
USE **mud-plaster**

plaster, retarded hemihydrate
USE **retarded hemihydrate plaster**

plaster, slag
USE **slag plaster**

plaster, tiling
USE **gypsum cement**

plasterboard
USE **gypsum board**

plasterer's putty
USE **lime putty**

plasterer's trowels
USE **trowels**

plasterers
HG.604 (L,B)
ALT **plasterer**
CN H.HG.AFU.AXC.BZY.AFU.DZW

plastering
KT.719 (L,B)
ALT **plastered**
CN K.KT.AFU.ALO.GRC.CXA

plastering machines
TB.562 (L)
ALT **plastering machine**
SN Motor-powered, portable pumps which feed plaster into a hose and onto the surface to be plastered without the use of hawks or trowels. (PUTNAM)
UF machines, plastering
CN V.TB.AFU.BCW.BCW.AFU.ALO

plasterwork
MT.2776 (A,L,B,R)
CN M.MT.AFU.AXC.BZY

plastic alloys
MT.2101
UF alloys, plastic
CN M.MT.AFU.AFU.ARI.BUE.ALO.AFU.AFU

plastic analysis
USE **plastic design**

Plastic (art movement)
USE **Neo-Plastic**

plastic design
BM.1022
SN Design of a beam that is proportioned to carry at ultimate capacity the design load multiplied by the safety factor. (MHDSTT)
UF analysis, plastic
analysis, ultimate-strength
collapse design
design, collapse
design, limit-load
design, limit-states
design, plastic
design, ultimate-load
limit-load design
limit-states design
plastic analysis
ultimate-load design
ultimate-strength analysis
CN B.BM.CFS.AXC.CLM.ALO.BCW

plastic foam
MT.2104 (L)
UF cellular plastic
expanded plastic
foam, plastic
foamed plastic
plastic, cellular
plastic, expanded
plastic, foamed
CN M.MT.AFU.AFU.ARI.BUE.ALO.ALO.ALO

plastic hinges
BM.1023
SN Regions of a member where yielding occurs as loads are increased; the regions of highest moment that develop when all fibers are fully yielded at a cross section.
UF hinges, plastic
CN B.BM.CFS.AXC.CLM.ALO.BCW.AFU

plastic-impregnated wood
USE **impregnated wood**

plastic laminate
MT.2110 (A,L)
UF laminate, plastic
laminated plastic
plastic, laminated
CN M.MT.AFU.AFU.ARI.BUE.ALO.ARI.ALO

plastic leads
TB.280
ALT **plastic lead**
SN Technical drawing leads for use on drafting film.
UF leads, plastic
CN V.TB.AFU.ARI.CLM.AFU.ALO.DZW

Plastic Style
FL.2525
CN F.FL.ALO.AXC.AFU.BOK.ALO.ALO.ALO

plastic wood
MT.2611
UF wood, plastic
CN M.MT.AFU.ARI.DZW.AXC

plastic, ABS
USE **acrylonitrile-butadiene-styrene copolymer**

plastic, acrylic
USE **acrylic**

plastic, alkyd
USE **alkyd resin**

plastic, allyl
USE **allyl resin**

plastic, casein
USE **casein plastic**

plastic, cellular
USE **plastic foam**

plastic, cellulosic
USE **cellulosic**

plastic, expanded
USE **plastic foam**

plastic, extruded
USE **extruded plastic**

plastic, extrusion blown
USE **extrusion blown plastic**

plastic, fiber reinforced
USE **reinforced plastic**

plastic, filled
USE **filled plastic**

plastic, fluorine
USE **fluoroplastic**

plastic, fluorocarbon
USE **fluoroplastic**

plastic, foamed
USE **plastic foam**

plastic, glass reinforced
USE **glass reinforced plastic**

plastic, laminated
USE **plastic laminate**

plastic, reinforced
USE **reinforced plastic**

plastic, thermosetting
USE **thermoset**

plastic, unfilled
USE **unfilled plastic**

plasticity
BM.161
SN The three-dimensional quality of a form, its roundness, palpability, apparent solidity, or quality of relief. (A-Z)
CN B.BM.AFU.AFU.ARI.BOK.CLM

plasticizers
MT.2322 (L)
SN Liquids or solids that dissolve in or are compatible with a resin, gum, or other material and render it plastic, flexible, or easy to work. (MH)
CN M.MT.AFU.ARI.ALO.EFQ

plastics
MT.2099 (A,L,B,R)
ALT **plastic**
UF artificial resins
polymers
resins (plastics)
resins, artificial
resins, synthetic
synthetic resins
CN M.MT.AFU.AFU.ARI.BUE.ALO

plastics engineering
USE **polymer science**

Plastiras type
FL.2679
CN F.FL.ALO.AXC.ALO.AFU.ALO .BCW.AFU.ARI

plat books
VW.932 (L)
ALT **plat book**
SN Records, usually public and in book form, showing the location, size, and name of the owner of each plot of land in a stated area. (STEIN)
UF books, plat
CN V.VW.AFU.ARI.AFU.BZY.BIQ

plat maps
USE **plats**

platanus
USE **plane wood**

Platanus acerifolia
USE **London plane wood**

Platanus hispanica
USE **London plane wood**

Platanus hybrida
USE **London plane wood**

Platanus occidentalis
USE **sycamore**

Platanus orientalis
USE **London plane wood**

platbands
RT.790
ALT **platband**
SN Flat, rectangular, horizontal moldings. (DAC)
CN V.RT.AFU.ALO.AFU.BOK.AFU. AFU.AXC.BOK

plate
MT.458 (L)
CN M.MT.AFU.AFU.AFU.BZY.AFU. ALO.AXC

plate anchors
USE **sill anchors**

plate beams
USE **plate girders**

plate cupboards
USE **court cupboards**

plate girders
RT.300 (L,B)
ALT **plate girder**
SN Steel girders built up of plates and angles or other structural shapes, welded or riveted together. (DAC)
UF beams, plate
girders, plate
plate beams
CN V.RT.AFU.AFU.AFU.BCW.ALO. AFU.BIQ.ALO

plate glass
MT.249 (L)
SN Any glass that has been rolled or cast into a sheet and then ground and polished. (MH)
UF glass, plate
CN M.MT.AFU.AFU.AFU.BIQ.AFU. ALO.ARI

plate negatives, gelatin dry
USE **gelatin dry plate negatives**

plate oil
USE **litho varnish**

plate rails
RT.654
ALT **plate rail**
SN Narrow shelves or rails along the upper part of the walls of a room, grooved to hold plates or decorations. (DAC)
UF plaque rails
rails, plaque
rails, plate
CN V.RT.AFU.AFU.AFU.BIQ.BUE. ALO.AFU.BCW.BIQ

plate saddle hangers
TF.358
ALT **plate saddle hanger**
UF hangers, plate saddle
saddle hangers, plate
CN V.TF.AFU.AFU.AFU.ALO.AFU. BOK.ARI.ALO.AFU.ALO

plate structures
RT.22
ALT **plate structure**
SN Use for structures based on horizontal, rigid, planar elements, typically of monolithic materials, with depths small in relation to their other dimensions.
UF plates (structures)
structures, plate
CN V.RT.AFU.AFU.AFU.ALO.ARI

plate tracery
RT.1025
SN Tracery whose openings are or seem to be pierced through slabs of stone; used especially in Early Gothic windows.
UF tracery, plate
CN V.RT.AFU.ARI.ALO.BZY.AFU.AXC

plate warmers (furniture)
TG.610
ALT **plate warmer (furniture)**
SN Pedestals designed as cupboards lined with tin and fitted with racks and a heater. (GILBR2)
UF warmers, plate (furniture)
CN V.TG.AFU.AFU.BIQ.ARI.AFU

plate, gold
USE **gold plate**

plate, Sheffield
USE **Sheffield plate**

plate, silver
USE **silver plate**

Plateau, Early period
USE **Early period Plateau**

Plateau, Late period
USE **Late period Plateau**

Plateau, Middle period
USE **Middle period Plateau**

Plateau, Transitional period
USE **Transitional period Plateau**

plateaus
RD.206 (L)
ALT **plateau**
SN Use for tablelands or flat-topped areas of considerable extent elevated above the surrounding countryside and bounded on at least one side by a vertical face.
CN V.RD.ARI.AFU.AXC.AFU.ALO. AFU.ARI

plateias
RK.1536
ALT **plateia**
SN Wide streets or avenues in ancient Greek and Roman towns.
CN V.RK.ALO.ALO.BIQ.ARI.AFU. ALO.AFU.BIQ

Plateresque
FL.3244 (A,R)
CN F.FL.ALO.BCW.ALO.ARI.BIQ.

BIQ.BUE.ALO

Plateresque, First
USE **First Plateresque**

Plateresque, Gothic
USE **First Plateresque**

Plateresque, Renaissance
USE **Second Plateresque**

Plateresque, Second
USE **Second Plateresque**

platers
USE **electroplaters**

plates (balloon and platform frame components)
RT.701
ALT **plate (balloon and platform frame component)**
SN In frame construction, horizontal boards or timbers in a wall, on top of the studs of a wall, or on the ground to receive other timbers or joists.
CN V.RT.AFU.AFU.ALO.ALO.ARI

plates (structures)
USE **plate structures**

plates, anchor
USE **anchor plates**

plates, armor
USE **armor plates**

plates, bench
USE **bench plates**

plates, bottom
USE **sill plates**

plates, card
USE **card frames**

plates, charge
USE **credit cards**

plates, combined eschutcheon
USE **combined escutcheon plates**

plates, door
USE **doorplates**

plates, dowel
USE **peg cutters**

plates, drop key
USE **drop escutcheons**

plates, escutcheon
USE **escutcheons (hardware)**

plates, folded
USE **folded plate structures**

plates, ground
USE **sill plates**

plates, gusset
USE **gussets**

plates, hinge
USE **hinge straps**

plates, key
USE **escutcheons (hardware)**

plates, kick
USE **kickplates**

plates, letter
USE **letter-box plates**

plates, lock
USE **escutcheons (hardware)**

plates, name
USE **name plates**

plates, number
USE **number plates**

plates, photographic
USE **photographic plates**

plates, pointing
USE **pointing plates**

plates, pole
USE **pole plates**

plates, push
USE **push plates**

plates, rafter
USE **roof plates**

plates, raising
USE **wall plates**

plates, roof
USE **roof plates**

plates, screw
USE **screw plates**

plates, sill
USE **sill plates**

plates, switch
USE **switch plates**

plates, threshold
USE **threshold plates**

plates, top
USE **roof plates**

plates, wall
USE **wall plates**

plates, wall (finish hardware)
USE **wall plates (finish hardware)**

plates, wire
USE **drawplates**

platform beds
TG.369
ALT **platform bed**
SN Beds, originating in Scandinavia in the 1930s, consisting of a simple shallow box for holding a mattress situated on a slightly recessed frame. (RHDEL2)
UF beds, platform
CN V.TG.AFU.AFU.ARI.AFU.AFU.DUC

platform frames
RT.40
ALT **platform frame**
SN Wood structural frames in which the studs are only one story high, the floor joist of each story rests on the top plates of the story below or on the foundation sill for the first story, and the bearing walls and partitions rest on the subfloor of each story. (DAC)
UF frames, platform
frames, western
western frames
CN V.RT.AFU.AFU.AFU.ALO.AXC.ARI

platform rockers
TG.228 (N)
ALT **platform rocker**
SN Rocking chairs which move upon a stationary base instead of rocking on curved bends.
UF chairs, platform rocking
chairs, swing rocking
platform rocking chairs
rockers, platform
rocking chairs, platform
rocking chairs, swing
swing rocking chairs
CN V.TG.AFU.AFU.ALO.AFU.AFU.AXC.ARI.ARI

platform rocking chairs
USE **platform rockers**

platform roofs
RT.433
ALT **platform roof**
SN Use for roofs with sloping sides but a substantial flat area on top. When such a roof is hipped, it will resemble a truncated pyramid.
UF roofs, platform
CN V.RT.AFU.AFU.AFU.BIQ.ARI.AFU.AFU.AFU.BOK.BOK

platforms
RT.743 (B)
ALT **platform**
SN Flat surfaces or floors, generally raised above the adjoining floor or surface, used for a speaker or performer to stand on while addressing the audience.
CN V.RT.AFU.ALO.AFU.BIQ.AFU.ARI

platforms, loading
USE **loading platforms**

platforms, offshore drilling
USE **offshore drilling platforms**

platforms, petroleum production
USE **offshore drilling platforms**

platforms, space
USE **space stations**

plating
KT.820 (L)
ALT **plated**

UF metal plating
CN K.KT.AFU.ALO.HOE.BCW.ALO.ALO.ARI

plating, electroless
USE **electroless plating**

plating, ion
USE **ion plating**

plating, zinc
USE **electrogalvanizing**

platinotype
USE **platinum process**

platinotype, sepia
USE **sepia platinotype**

platinotypes
USE **platinum prints**

platinum
MT.442 (L,R)
CN M.MT.AFU.AFU.AFU.BZY.AFU.AFU.ARI.CXA

platinum (color)
USE **medium gray**

platinum photoprints
USE **platinum prints**

platinum prints
VJ.57
ALT **platinum print**
SN Use for photographic prints made by the platinum process.
UF photoprints, platinum
platinotypes
platinum photoprints
prints, platinum
CN V.VJ.AFU.AFU.ARI.ARI.AXC.BZY

platinum process
KT.359 (L)
SN An iron process for making photographic prints in which platinum is reduced from a salt to form the image.
UF platinotype
CN K.KT.AFU.ALO.DUC.DIO.ALO.DOI

Platonism
BM.518 (L)
CN B.BM.BIQ.AXC.DIO

Platonism, New
USE **Neo-Platonism**

plats
VW.233
ALT **plat**
SN Maps, charts, or plans that show the location, boundaries, and ownership of individual properties.
UF land plats
maps, plat
plat maps
CN V.VW.AFU.AFU.AFU.FZU.AXC.AFU.AXC

play centers
USE **playgrounds**

play schools
RK.836 (L,B)
ALT **play school**
UF schools, play
CN V.RK.AFU.ALO.ALO.CXA.ARI.AXC.AFU.AXC

playbills
VW.317 (L,N,R)
ALT **playbill**
SN Programs or posters announcing a theatrical performance.
CN V.VW.AFU.AFU.ALO.BOK.AFU.ARI

playfields
USE **athletic fields**

playgrounds
RK.1494 (A,L,B,R)
ALT **playground**
UF centers, play
children's parks
children's playgrounds
parks, children's
play centers
playgrounds, children's
playgrounds, public
public playgrounds
CN V.RK.ALO.ALO.BCW.BUE

playgrounds, action
USE **adventure playgrounds**

playgrounds, adventure
USE **adventure playgrounds**

playgrounds, children's
USE **playgrounds**

playgrounds, junk
USE **adventure playgrounds**

playgrounds, neighborhood
USE **neighborhood playgrounds**

playgrounds, public
USE **playgrounds**

playgrounds, Robinson Crusoe
USE **adventure playgrounds**

playhouses (recreation buildings)
USE **children's playhouses**

playhouses (theaters)
USE **theaters**

playhouses, children's
USE **children's playhouses**

playing cards
VW.576 (L,N,R)
ALT **playing card**
SN Cards marked with rank and suit belonging to any of several decks used in playing various games. (AHD)
UF cards, playing
CN V.VW.AFU.ALO.AFU.ARI.CRG

playing fields
USE **athletic fields**

playlots
USE **tot lots**

playrooms
RM.130 (A,L,B)
ALT **playroom**
SN Use for rooms fitted out or reserved for children to play in.
UF rooms, rumpus
rumpus rooms
CN V.RM.AFU.DIO.ALO.BIQ.BCW.ALO

plays, miracle
USE **mystery plays**

plays, mystery
USE **mystery plays**

plays, passion
USE **passion plays**

playwrights
HG.188 (L,R)
ALT **playwright**
SN Persons who write original plays, such as tragedies, comedies, or dramas, or adapt themes from fictional, historical, or narrative sources, for dramatic presentation. (DOT)
UF dramatists
CN H.HG.AFU.AXC.AXC.ARI.AFU.AFU.BUE

plazas
RK.1447 (A,L,B,R)
ALT **plaza**
SN Use either for small public squares in towns or for urban, landscaped pedestrian spaces adjacent to office buildings or parking areas.
CN V.RK.ALO.AFU.ARI.ARI

plazas, corporate
USE **shopping plazas**

plazas, shopping
USE **shopping plazas**

plazas, toll
USE **toll plazas**

plazuelas
RK.1448
ALT **plazuela**
SN In Mayan architecture, exterior spaces that resemble plazas, but are of smaller size; distinguished from Mayan courtyards on the basis of the differing relationships of bordering structures. (LOTEN)
CN V.RK.ALO.AFU.ARI.ARI.AFU

pleasances
USE **pleasure gardens**

pleasure
BM.597 (L,R)
CN B.BM.BUE.CLM.ARI

pleasure gardens

RK.1423 (B)
ALT **pleasure garden**
SN Gardens, whether public or private, intended for enjoyment and amusement.
UF gardens, pleasure
grounds, pleasure
pleasances
pleasure grounds
CN V.RK.ALO.AFU.AFU.ALO.BOK

pleasure grounds
USE **pleasure gardens**

plenum chambers
RT.1441
ALT **plenum chamber**
SN Closed chambers used to distribute or collect warmed or cooled air in a forced air heating/cooling system. (MEANS)
UF chambers, plenum
plenums
CN V.RT.ALO.BCW.AFU.ALO.ARI.BUE

plenums
USE **plenum chambers**

Plessy's green
USE **chromium oxide green**

Plexiglas (TM)
MT.2122 (A,L,B)
CN M.MT.AFU.AFU.ARI.BUE.ALO.AXC.AFU.ALO.AFU.ARI

Plia chairs
USE **Plia folding chairs**

Plia folding chairs
TG.221
ALT **Plia folding chair**
UF chairs, Plia folding
folding chairs, Plia
Plia chairs
CN V.TG.AFU.AFU.ALO.AFU.AFU.AXC.AFU.ARI

pliants
TG.270
ALT **pliant**
SN French stools with folding crossed legs; distinct from **tabourets** which have fixed upright legs.
UF faldesteuils (pliants)
faldstools (pliants)
ployants
CN V.TG.AFU.AFU.ALO.AFU.ALO.AXC.AFU.BCW

pliers
TB.220 (L,N)
SN Pincer-like hand tools with scissors action, usually with serrated jaws; used for gripping, holding, bending, and cutting. (DAC)
CN V.TB.AFU.ARI.CFS.AXC

pliers, combination
USE **combination pliers**

pliers, half-round
USE **combination pliers**

pliers, needlenose
USE **needlenose pliers**

plinth brick
MT.81
UF brick, plinth
CN M.MT.AFU.AFU.AFU.AXC.ALO.AFU.AFU.AFU.CLM

plinth courses
RT.621
ALT **plinth course**
SN Masonry courses which form a continous plinth. (HAS)
UF courses, plinth
CN V.RT.AFU.AFU.AFU.BIQ.BUE.ALO.AFU.ALO.BZY

plinth feet
USE **therm feet**

plinths
RT.71 (L)
ALT **plinth**
SN Rectangular or square bases for columns, pilasters, or door framing; also solid monumental bases, often ornamented, used to support statues or memorials; or bases of external walls or the platformlike base courses of buildings. (HAS)
CN V.RT.AFU.AFU.AFU.AXC.ARI.ALO.ARI

plique-à-jour
KT.666
SN A process of enameling similar to cloisonné, except that the narrow wires or strips of metal are soldered to each other instead of to a metal base.(QUICK) Usually applies to jewelry and metal objects but may also applies to porcelain decorated by this technique such as that produced at Limoges in the 19th century. (SAVAGE)
CN K.KT.AFU.ALO.GRC.AFU.ALO.BOK

Plona folding armchairs
TG.222
ALT **Plona folding armchair**
UF armchairs, Plona folding
folding armchairs, Plona
CN V.TG.AFU.AFU.ALO.AFU.AFU.AXC.AFU.AXC

plot plans
USE **site plans**

plot surveys
USE **topographic surveys**

plots
USE **lots**

plots (computer drawings)
VD.125
ALT **plot (computer drawing)**
SN Use for computer drawings when emphasizing that they were produced on a plotter.
CN V.VD.AFU.AXC.ALO.AFU

plots, building
USE **building sites**

plots, ground
USE **ground plans**

plotters
TB.160 (N)
ALT **plotter**
SN Output devices for translating information from computers into pictorial or graphic form on paper or a similar medium. (DOC)
CN V.TB.AFU.ARI.BCW.AXC.AXC.AFU

plotters, electrostatic
USE **electrostatic plotters**

plotters, pen
USE **pen plotters**

plotting charts
VW.218 (L)
ALT **plotting chart**
SN Charts or maps showing the movements or progress of a ship, submarine, airplane, or other craft. (GAHLM)
UF charts, plotting
CN V.VW.AFU.AFU.AFU.FZU.AXC.AFU.ARI.AXC.DIO.ARI

plough planes
USE **plow planes**

ploughshare vaults
USE **plowshare vaults**

plow hammers
TB.664 (N)
ALT **plow hammer**
SN Combination tools taking the form of an iron hammer, often including an open wrench, a screwdriver, or the like. (PC)
UF hammers, plow
CN V.TB.AFU.BCW.BIQ.AFU.ALO.BIQ.AXC

plow planes
TB.921 (N)
ALT **plow plane**
SN Carpenter's grooving planes which have an adjustable fence and are capable of being fitted with various irons for cutting grooves. (PUTNAM)
UF flit plows
planes, plough
planes, plow
plough planes
plows, flit
CN V.TB.AFU.BCW.CFS.ALO.AFU.DUC.ALO.BOK

plows, angle
USE **angle plows**

plows, flit
USE **plow planes**

plowshare vaults
RT.534
ALT **plowshare vault**
SN Vaults in which the surface between the stilted wall rib and the diagonal rib is warped like a plowshare. (HAS)
UF ploughshare vaults
vaults, ploughshare
vaults, plowshare
CN V.RT.AFU.AFU.AFU.BIQ.BOK.AFU.AFU.AFU.ALO.ALO.ALO.AFU

ployants
USE **pliants**

plug bits
USE **tenon-cutting bits**

plug center bits
USE **tenon-cutting bits**

plug cutters
TB.1109
ALT **plug cutter**
SN Bits which terminate in a semicircle; used to cut around a hole to produce a core or plug which is then used to conceal recessed screwheads in hardwood floors.
UF cutters, plug
CN V.TB.ALO.ARI.CLM

plug-driving guns
USE **stud guns**

plug taps
TB.735 (N)
ALT **plug tap**
SN Cylinder-shaped taps used for cutting internal screw threads.
UF taps, plug
CN V.TB.AFU.BCW.BIQ.ARI.ALO.BUE.BCW.AFU

plugging chisels
TB.587 (N)
ALT **plugging chisel**
SN Steel rods with a star-shaped point; used for drilling holes in masonry by striking with a hammer. (MEANS)
UF chisels, plugging
drills, plugging
drills, star
plugging drills
star drills
CN V.TB.AFU.BCW.BCW.ALO.CLM.ARI

plugging drills
USE **plugging chisels**

plugs, rawl
USE **rawl plugs**

plum
MT.1293 (L)
CN M.MT.AFU.AFU.ALO.BIQ.DCU.AFU.AFU.AFU.KLE.BCW

plum (color)
USE **dark grayish purple**
dark purple
dark violet
deep purplish red
deep reddish purple
very dark purplish red
very dark reddish purple
vivid reddish purple

plum gum
USE **cherry gum**

plum purple
USE **dark violet**
very dark purple

plum violet
USE **dark purplish red**

plum, black
USE **dark grayish purple**
dark purplish gray
purplish black

plum, blue
USE **dark violet**
grayish violet

plum, dark
USE **blackish purple**
dark purplish gray

plum, deep
USE **dark grayish purple**
moderate purplish red
very dark reddish purple

plum, red
USE **dark grayish purple**
dark purplish red
very dark purplish red

plum, rose
USE **dark purplish red**
grayish purplish red
grayish reddish purple

plumbago
USE **graphite (black pigment)**

Plumbate
FL.1044 (L)
CN F.FL.ALO.ALO.ALO.ALO.AFU.ALO.ARI.ALO.ALO.ALO

Plumbate, San Juan
USE **San Juan (pottery style)**

plumber's friends
USE **plungers**

plumber's helpers
USE **plungers**

plumbers
HG.605 (L)
ALT **plumber**
CN H.HG.AFU.AXC.BZY.AFU.EFQ

plumbic ocher
USE **massicot**

plumbing
USE **plumbing systems**

plumbing drawings
VD.148
ALT **plumbing drawing**
SN Use for drawings of plumbing systems or parts thereof. For scaled floor plans specifically, use **plumbing plans.**
UF drawings, plumbing
plumbing layouts
CN V.VD.AFU.BIQ.AFU.AFU.ALO

plumbing equipment
USE **plumbing fixtures**

plumbing fixtures
RT.1478 (L,B)
ALT **plumbing fixture**
UF equipment, plumbing
fittings, sanitary
fixtures, plumbing
plumbing equipment
sanitary fittings
CN V.RT.ALO.BCW.ALO.ARI.CFS

plumbing hardware
TF.509
UF hardware, plumbing
CN V.TF.AFU.AFU.ALO.BOK

plumbing layouts
USE **plumbing drawings**

plumbing plans
VD.57
ALT **plumbing plan**
SN Use for scaled floor plans showing plumbing layout; may include an adjacent small drawing of an elevation, or a riser diagram. For other drawings of plumbing systems, use **plumbing drawings.**
UF plans, plumbing
CN V.VD.AFU.AFU.BIQ.ALO.AXC.ALO.BIQ.ARI

plumbing systems
RT.1445 (A,L,B,R)
ALT **plumbing system**
SN The systems within a building that supply water to the occupants and carry off liquid or liquid-suspended wastes; includes pipes, traps, vents, and fixtures, but not sources or destinations outside the building such as wells or septic tanks.
UF plumbing
systems, plumbing
systems, water
water systems
CN V.RT.ALO.BCW.ALO.AFU

plumbum ustum
USE **litharge**

plunger elevators
USE **hydraulic elevators**

plungers
TB.355 (N)

ALT **plunger**
SN Tools consisting of a large rubber suction cup on a wood handle; used for clearing plumbing traps of minor obstructions. (MEANS)
UF cups, force
force cups
friends, plumber's
helpers, plumber's
plumber's friends
plumber's helpers
CN V.TB.AFU.ARI.CRG.ALO.AXC

plutonic rock
MT.623
UF intrusive rock
rock, intrusive
rock, plutonic
CN M.MT.AFU.AFU.AFU.DCU.AFU.AFU.ALO.AFU

plywood
MT.1450 (A,B)
SN Wood board consisting of a number of thin layers of rotary-cut veneers glued together so that the grain of each layer is at right angles to the grain of the adjacent layer. (TATEMT)
CN M.MT.AFU.AFU.ALO.BIQ.DCU.ALO.BZY

PMMA
USE **acrylic**

pneumatic drills
TB.191
ALT **pneumatic drill**
UF air drills
drills, air
drills, pneumatic
CN V.TB.AFU.ARI.BIQ.ALO.AFU.ALO.ARI

pneumatic furniture
USE **inflatable furniture**

pneumatic hammers
USE **jackhammers**

pneumatic structures
RT.404 (L,B,R)
ALT **pneumatic structure**
SN Use for membrane structures that attain stability by internal pressurization, usually by air.
UF balloon structures
structures, balloon
structures, pneumatic
CN V.RT.AFU.AFU.AFU.BIQ.ALO.AFU

pneumatic tools
TB.14 (A,L)
ALT **pneumatic tool**
SN Tools powered by the compression or exhaustion of air.
UF tools, pneumatic
CN V.TB.AFU.ALO.ARI.ALO.AFU

pneumatic tubes
RT.1299
ALT **pneumatic tube**
UF PTs
tubes, pneumatic
CN V.RT.ALO.ALO.AFU.AFU.AXC

Poblano
FL.1712
SN Regional style of architecture in Mexico, especially around Puebla, featuring rustic and folkloristic qualities. (KELEM)
CN F.FL.ALO.ALO.AXC.ALO.AFU.ARI.ALO

pochades
VB.10
ALT **pochade**
SN Sketches that emphasize light values and overall pictorial effect, often painted.
CN V.VB.AFU.AFU.BCW.ARI

pochoir
KT.754 (L,R)
SN A stencil process for making colored prints or adding color to a printed key illustration. (W)
CN K.KT.AFU.ALO.HCQ.ALO.BUE.ALO

pocket butt hinges
TF.102
ALT **pocket butt hinge**
UF butt hinges, pocket
hinges, pocket butt
CN V.TF.AFU.AFU.AFU.AFU.CLM.AFU.ARI.ARI

pocket calculators
TB.141 (L,N,R)
ALT **pocket calculator**
UF calculators, pocket
CN V.TB.AFU.ARI.BCW.AFU.AFU

pocket chisels
USE **sash chisels**

pocket doors
RT.873
ALT **pocket door**
SN Doors that slide into a recess in a wall.
UF doors, pocket
CN V.RT.AFU.ARI.AFU.AFU.AFU ALO.ARI.AFU.ARI.BOK.AFU

pocket knives
TB.125 (L,N)
ALT **pocket knife**
SN Knives whose blade folds into the handle to fit it for being carried in the pocket. (W)
UF knives, pocket
CN V.TB.AFU.ARI.AXC.ALO.BUE.AFU

pocket parks
USE **vest-pocket parks**

pocket style hangers
TF.368
ALT **pocket style hanger**
UF hangers, pocket style
CN V.TF.AFU.AFU.AFU.ALO.AFU.BOK.ARI.ARI.ARI.ALO

Pocomchi
USE **Pokomam**

pod augers
USE **shell augers**

pod-bits
TB.1110
ALT **pod-bit**
CN V.TB.ALO.ARI.CRG

pod, locust bean
USE **locust bean pod**

Podgornoe phase
FL.2135
CN F.FL.ALO.ARI.ARI.AFU.BIQ.BCW.ALO

podiums
RM.24 (A)
ALT **podium**
SN Use to designate continuous pedestals or bases of buildings; appropriate for such elements in Roman or Etruscan temples. For similar features found in Greek temples prefer **stylobates.**
CN V.RM.AFU.DCU

pods
MT.1071 (L)
SN A dry dehiscent seed vessel or fruit. (W)
UF seedpods
CN M.MT.AFU.AFU.ALO.BIQ.CFS.ALO.AFU

poems
VW.66 (L)
ALT **poem**
SN Written or oral compositions characterized by condensed language chosen for sound and suggestive power as well as meaning, and by the use of such literary techniques as structured meter, natural cadences, rhyme, or metaphor. (AHD)
CN V.VW.AFU.AFU.AFU.EFQ

poetics
KD.58 (L)
CN K.KD.AFU.AFU.BCW.BCW

poetry
BM.280 (L,R)
CN B.BM.AFU.ARI.BIQ.BUE

poetry, concrete
USE **concrete poetry**

poets
HG.189 (L,R)
ALT **poet**
CN H.HG.AFU.AXC.AXC.ARI.AFU.AFU.BZY

Pogoro
FL.670 (L)
UF Wapogoro
CN F.FL.ALO.AFU.AXC.AXC.BIQ.CXA

point blocks
RK.12
ALT **point block**
UF blocks, point
CN V.RK.AFU.ALO.AFU.AFU.AFU.ARI.
AFU

point (needlepoint)
USE **needlepoint**

Point Peninsula
FL.876
CN F.FL.ALO.ALO.ALO.AFU. ALO.
ALO.AXC.CLM

point, dew
USE **dew point**

point, flash
USE **flash point**

point, focal
USE **focal point**

point, freezing
USE **freezing point**

point, melting
USE **melting point**

point, station
USE **station point**

point, vanishing
USE **vanishing point**

point, yield
USE **yield strength**

pointed
DC.68
CN D.DC.AFU.ARI.CRG

pointed arches
RT.230
ALT **pointed arch**
UF arches, Gothic
arches, peak
arches, pointed
Gothic arches
peak arches
CN V.RT.AFU.AFU.AFU.BCW.AFU.
AFU.AFU.CRG

pointed arches, equilateral
USE **equilateral arches**

pointed arches, four-centered
USE **Tudor arches**

pointed arches, Italian
USE **Italian pointed arches**

pointed segmental arches
RT.236
ALT **pointed segmental arch**
SN Use for pointed arches, the curves being struck from centers well below the springing line.
UF arches, pointed segmental
arches, two-centered segmental
segmental arches, pointed
segmental arches, two-centered
two-centered segmental arches
CN V.RT.AFU.AFU.AFU.BCW.AFU.
AFU.AFU.CRG.BIQ

Pointed Style
USE **Gothic**

Pointed, First
USE **Early English**

Pointed, Second
USE **Decorated Style**

Pointed, Third
USE **Perpendicular Style**

pointillism
KT.233 (L,R)
SN Painting technique whereby tones and hues are obtained by applying small areas of unmixed pigment on the canvas so that they combine optically.(OCTA) For the specific style associated especially with Seurat, use **Neo-Impressionist.**
UF divisionism
CN K.KT.AFU.ALO.DUC.CXA.ALO.
AFU.CLM

Pointillist (Neo-Impressionist)
USE **Neo-Impressionist**

pointing
KT.124 (A,B)
SN In masonry, the final treatment of joints by the troweling of mortar or a puttylike filler into the joints. (DAC)
UF joint pointing, tuck
pointing, tuck
pointing, tuck and pat
pointing, tuck joint
repointing
tuck and pat pointing
tuck joint pointing
tuck pointing
CN K.KT.AFU.ALO.DCU.ARI

pointing (sculpture)
KT.536
ALT **pointed (sculpture)**
SN A technique of reproducing a clay or plaster model or of copying a finished work through measurements. (MAYER)
CN K.KT.AFU.ALO.ELK.DIO.ALO.ARI

pointing plates
TB.281
ALT **pointing plate**
SN Tools similar to a flat file having a coarse side and a fine side; used for pointing pencils, charcoal, crayons, and pastels. (QUICK)
UF plates, pointing
CN V.TB.AFU.ARI.CLM.AFU.ALO.EFQ

pointing trowels
TB.638 (N)
ALT **pointing trowel**
SN Diamond-shaped trowels used in pointing or repointing masonry joints. (MEANS)
UF trowels, pointing
CN V.TB.AFU.BCW.BCW.ALO.HCQ.
BIQ

pointing, tuck
USE **pointing**

pointing, tuck and pat
USE **pointing**

pointing, tuck joint
USE **pointing**

points, copper
USE **copper points**

points, growth
USE **growth centers**

points, lead
USE **lead points**

points, metal
USE **metal points**

poison control centers
RK.738 (A,L)
ALT **poison control center**
UF centers, poison control
CN V.RK.AFU.ALO.ALO.CXA.ALO.
AFU.AFU.ARI

pok-ta-poks
USE **ball courts**

Pokomam
FL.1537 (L)
UF Pakomame
Pocomchi
Pokomchi
CN F.FL.ALO.ALO.ARI.ALO.BIQ.AFU.
BIQ

Pokomchi
USE **Pokomam**

Pokot
FL.629 (L)
UF Pakot
Suk
CN F.FL.ALO.AFU.AXC.AXC.ARI.CXA

polar charts
VW.197
ALT **polar chart**
UF charts, polar
CN V.VW.AFU.AFU.AFU.FZU.AXC.
AFU.ARI.AXC.BZY

polar climate
BM.742 (L,B)
SN Climate characterized by little precipitation in all seasons and consistently cold temperatures, with brief, chilly summers. (WB)
UF arctic climate

climate, arctic
climate, polar
CN B.BM.CFS.ALO.AXC.ALO.AFU.ALO

Polaroid Land (TM) film
USE **Polaroid (TM) film**

Polaroid SX-70 (TM) process
USE **internal dye diffusion transfer process**

Polaroid (TM) film
MT.2241
SN Use for the brand name photographic film that produces instant camera photographs.
UF film, Polaroid Land (TM)
film, Polaroid (TM)
Polaroid Land (TM) film
CN M.MT.AFU.ALO.CXA.ALO.BOK

Polaroid (TM) instant color photographs
USE **dye diffusion transfer prints**

Polaroid (TM) instant photographs
USE **instant camera photographs**

polders
RD.304 (L)
ALT **polder**
SN Areas of low-lying land reclaimed from the sea and enclosed by dikes. (VHINMA)
CN V.RD.ARI.ALO.ARI.ALO

pole and stands
USE **pole screens**

pole axes (froes)
USE **froes**

pole derricks
TB.76
ALT **pole derrick**
SN Small, portable derricks guyed by ropes. (PUTNAM)
UF derricks, pole
monkeys
CN V.TB.AFU.ARI.AFU.BCW.BCW.AFU.ALO

pole fire screens
USE **pole screens**

pole lathes
TB.796
ALT **pole lathe**
SN Primitive lathes in which the cord passing around the work to rotate it is fastened at its ends to the treadle and to an elastic pole above. (W)
UF lathes, pole
CN V.TB.AFU.BCW.CFS.AFU.AFU.ARI

pole plates
RT.505
ALT **pole plate**
UF plates, pole
CN V.RT.AFU.AFU.AFU.BIQ.ARI.ALO.ALO.ALO.AFU

pole screens
TG.8 (N)
ALT **pole screen**
SN Firescreens with a tripod base and an upright shaft which supports the framed panel; distinguished from **cheval fire screens** which are supported on four legs.
UF banner screens
fire screens, pole
fire screens, tripod
pole and stands
pole fire screens
pole screens, tripod
screens, banner
screens, pole
screens, pole fire
screens, tripod fire
screens, tripod pole
stands, pole and
tripod fire screens
tripod pole screens
CN V.TG.AFU.AFU.AFU.AFU.AXC

pole screens, tripod
USE **pole screens**

pole shacks
USE **log cabins**

Pole Style
FL.700
SN Style of African sculpture, typically elongated, severe, and abstract-looking.
CN F.FL.ALO.AFU.BCW.AFU

poleis
RD.15
ALT **polis**
SN Use for ancient Greek cities or city-states.
CN V.RD.AFU.AFU.ALO.AXC.AXC

poles
MT.1451 (N)
ALT **pole**
SN Use for long, cylindrical sections of timber, the approximate diameter at breast height being one foot or less.
CN M.MT.AFU.AFU.ALO.BIQ.DCU.ALO.CFS

poles, telephone
USE **utility poles**

poles, utility
USE **utility poles**

police communication systems
RD.89 (L,B)
ALT **police communication system**
UF communication systems, police
police radio
radio, police
systems, police communication
CN V.RD.ALO.ALO.AFU

police radio
USE **police communication systems**

police stations
RK.991 (A,L,N,B,R)
ALT **police station**
UF stations, police
CN V.RK.AFU.ALO.ALO.ERE.AFU.BZY.ALO

policemen
HG.49 (L)
ALT **policeman**
CN H.HG.AFU.AXC.ARI.CLM

polices, insurance
USE **insurance policies**

policing
USE **enforcing**

policlinics
USE **clinics**

policy, environmental
USE **environmental policy**

policy, government
USE **government policy**

policy, public
USE **public policy**

Polish
FL.3053 (L,B)
CN F.FL.ALO.BCW.AFU.CXA

polish (coating)
MT.2575 (L)
CN M.MT.AFU.ARI.CRG.AXC

polished ware, red
USE **red polished ware**

polishing
KT.686 (L)
ALT **polished**
UF buffing
CN K.KT.AFU.ALO.GRC.BCW.ARI

polishing rouge
USE **rouge**

political campaigns
KM.4 (L)
UF campaigns, political
CN K.KM.AFU.AFU.ALO

political cartoons
VB.37 (L,R)
ALT **political cartoon**
UF cartoons, political
CN V.VB.AFU.ALO.AFU.ARI

political liberalism
USE **liberalism**

political science
KD.175 (L,R)
UF science, political
CN K.KD.AFU.ALO.DZW

political scientists
HG.275 (L)
ALT **political scientist**
UF scientists, political
CN H.HG.AFU.AXC.BCW.AFU.BUE

political violence
USE **terrorism**

politicians
HG.670 (L,R)
ALT **politician**
CN H.HG.AFU.AXC.CFS.BZY

politics
BM.565 (A,L,R)
CN B.BM.BOK.CFS

politics, comparative
USE **comparative government**

pollutants
MT.2809
CN M.MT.AFU.BCW.DIO

pollution
BM.428 (A,L)
UF environmental pollution
CN B.BM.AXC.BCW

pollution control
KG.122
UF control, pollution
CN K.KG.AFU.AFU.BCW.ALO.BZY

pollution, air
USE **air pollution**

pollution, atmospheric
USE **air pollution**

pollution, chemical
USE **chemical pollution**

pollution, heat
USE **thermal pollution**

pollution, indoor air
USE **indoor air pollution**

pollution, marine
USE **marine pollution**

pollution, noise
USE **noise pollution**

pollution, nuclear
USE **radioactive pollution**

pollution, radioactive
USE **radioactive pollution**

pollution, soil
USE **soil pollution**

pollution, thermal
USE **thermal pollution**

pollution, water
USE **water pollution**

polo clubs
RK.1027 (B)
ALT **polo club**
UF clubs, polo
CN V.RK.AFU.ALO.ALO.EWY.AXC.
ALO.AFU.AFU

polo fields
RK.1483
ALT **polo field**
UF fields, polo
grounds, polo
polo grounds
CN V.RK.ALO.ALO.BCW.AFU.BIQ

polo grounds
USE **polo fields**

Polonnaruwa
FL.2306
CN F.FL.ALO.ARI.AXC.ARI.ALO

polyacrylate
MT.2119
UF polyacrylic resin
polymethacrylate
resin, polyacrylic
CN M.MT.AFU.AFU.ARI.BUE.ALO.
AXC.AFU.ALO.AFU

polyacrylic resin
USE **polyacrylate**

polyamide
MT.2140 (L)
USE **nylon**
polyacrylate
UF PA
CN M.MT.AFU.AFU.ARI.BUE.ALO.
AXC.AFU.CFS

polyamide resin
USE **nylon**

polybutadiene elastomer
MT.2088
UF elastomer, polybutadiene
CN M.MT.AFU.AFU.ARI.BUE.AFU.
AFU.BOK

polybutylene
MT.2143
CN M.MT.AFU.AFU.ARI.BUE.ALO.
AXC.AFU.CLM

polycarbonate
MT.2144 (L)
SN Thermoplastic polyester used in glazing, including bullet- and explosion-resistant laminates. (DIETZ)
UF PC
CN M.MT.AFU.AFU.ARI.BUE.ALO.
AXC.AFU.CRG

polychrome
DC.4 (R)
SN Relating to, made with, or decorated in several colors. (MAYER)
CN D.DC.AFU.AFU.ALO

Polychrome horizon
FL.1125
CN F.FL.ALO.ALO.ALO.ARI.ARI.AFU.
ARI

Polychrome Style
FL.3115
SN Designates work of Migration period peoples, characterized by inlays of multicolored stones, usually in gold.
UF Gem Style
CN F.FL.ALO.BCW.ALO.ALO.AFU.
BOK.ALO.ARI

Polychrome, Conte
USE **Conte Polychrome**

polychrome, Luna
USE **Luna ware**

polychrome, Nicoya
USE **Nicoya polychrome**

polychromy
BM.139 (A,L,R)
CN B.BM.AFU.AFU.ARI.BOK.ALO.
ALO.BCW

polyclinics
USE **hospitals**

polyester
MT.2179 (L,R)
CN M.MT.AFU.AFU.ARI.BUE.ALO.
AXC.ARI.AFU

polyester fiber
MT.1839 (L)
UF fiber, polyester
CN M.MT.AFU.AFU.ARI.ALO.AFU.
ALO.AFU

polyester, thermoplastic
USE **thermoplastic polyester**

polyester, thermoset
USE **thermoset polyester**

polyether
USE **acetal**

polyetherimide
MT.2145
CN M.MT.AFU.AFU.ARI.BUE.ALO.
AXC.AFU.CXA

polyethylene
MT.2146 (L)
SN A group of polyolefin polymers derived from ethylene by polymerization by heat and pressure. (MH)
UF PE
CN M.MT.AFU.AFU.ARI.BUE.ALO.
AXC.AFU.DCU

polyethylene elastomer
MT.2089
UF elastomer, polyethylene
CN M.MT.AFU.AFU.ARI.BUE.AFU.
AFU.BUE

polyformaldehyde resin
USE **acetal**

polyformaldehydes
USE **acetal**

polyglot dictionaries
VW.400 (L)
ALT **polyglot dictionary**
UF dictionaries, multilingual
dictionaries, polyglot
multilingual dictionaries
CN V.VW.AFU.AFU.ALO.EWY.ARI.

ALO.ARI.AFU

polygons
BM.773 (L)
ALT **polygonal**
CN B.BM.CFS.ARI.AXC.BCW.AFU.BIQ

polygons, funicular
USE **funicular polygons**

polyhedra
BM.793 (L)
ALT **polyhedral**
CN B.BM.CFS.ARI.AXC.BCW.ALO.AXC

polyimide
MT.2183 (L)
SN One of the superpolymers, maintains mechanical and chemical integrity above 400 degrees F for extended periods and have high strength and modulus of elasticity and excellent resistance to solvents, oils, and corrosive environments. (MH)
CN M.MT.AFU.AFU.ARI.BUE.ALO.
AXC.ARI.ALO

polyimide, thermoplastic
USE **thermoplastic polyimide**

polyimide, thermoset
USE **thermoset polyimide**

polyisoprene
MT.2090 (L)
UF isoprene
natural rubber, synthetic
rubber, synthetic natural
synthetic natural rubber
CN M.MT.AFU.AFU.ARI.BUE.AFU.
AFU.BZY

Polykleitan
FL.2684
CN F.FL.ALO.AXC.ALO.AFU.ALO.
BCW.ALO.ALO.AFU

polymer-cement concrete
USE **polymer-impregnated cement**

polymer color
USE **polymer paint**

polymer gesso
USE **polymer primer**

polymer-impregnated cement
MT.31 (L)
SN Mixture of water, hydraulic cement, aggregate, and a monomer or polymer; polymerized in place when a monomer is used. (STEIN)
UF cement, polymer-impregnated
concrete, polymer-cement
polymer-cement concrete
CN M.MT.AFU.AFU.AFU.ALO.AFU.
AFU.CLM

polymer-impregnated concrete
MT.204 (A,L,B)
SN Concrete in which an organic polymer serves as the binder. (STEIN)
UF concrete, polymer-impregnated
concrete, resin
resin concrete
CN
M.MT.AFU.AFU.AFU.BCW.AFU.AFU
.BUE

polymer-impregnated mortar
MT.2610 (L)
UF mortar, polymer-impregnated
CN M.MT.AFU.ARI.DZW.ARI.ARI.ALO

polymer paint
MT.2532
UF color, polymer
paint, polymer
polymer color
polymer tempera
tempera, polymer
CN M.MT.AFU.ARI.CRG.ALO.BCW.
AFU.BIQ.ALO

polymer primer
MT.2725
SN A white paste composed of titanium white and other white or inert pigments in polymer vehicles. (MAYER)
UF gesso, polymer
polymer gesso
primer, polymer
CN M.MT.AFU.ARI.IFM.AXC.AFU

polymer science
KD.248
SN Field dealing with the synthesis, characterization, formulation, processing, and use of polymers or plastics. (PG)
UF engineering, plastics
plastics engineering
science, polymer
CN K.KD.AFU.ARI.BZY.ARI

polymer tempera
USE **polymer paint**

polymer, ionomer
USE **ionomer polymer**

polymer, sulfone
USE **sulfone polymer**

polymer, thermoplastic
USE **thermoplastic**

polymer, vinyl
USE **vinyl**

polymerized oil
USE **stand oil**

polymers
USE **plastics**

polymethacrylate
USE **polyacrylate**

Polynesian
FL.3687 (L,B,R)
CN F.FL.ALO.BOK.AXC

polyoxide
USE **acetal**

polypropylene
MT.2147 (L)
SN Tough, lightweight, rigid plastic made by the polymerization of high-purity propylene gas in the presence of an organometallic catalyst at relatively low pressure and temperature. (STEIN)
UF PP
propylene resin
resin, propylene
CN M.MT.AFU.AFU.ARI.BUE.ALO.
AXC.AFU.DIO

polystyrene
MT.2148
SN A clear plastic or stiff foam, a polymer of styrene, used chiefly as an insulator in regrigerators and air conditioners. (RHDEL2)
UF PS
resin, styrene
styrene resin
CN M.MT.AFU.AFU.ARI.BUE.ALO.
AXC.AFU.DOI

polysulfide elastomer
MT.2092 (L)
UF elastomer, polysulfide
thiokol
CN M.MT.AFU.AFU.ARI.BUE.AFU.
AFU.CFS

polysulfone
USE **sulfone polymer**

polytechnical schools
USE **polytechnics**

polytechnics
RK.846 (B)
ALT **polytechnic**
SN Distinguished from **universities** by traditionally training technicians in business, industry, and commerce for an immediate local area, having fewer residence facilities, and offering more part-time classes. For educational institutions emphasizing training in agriculture and specific trades use **vocational schools.**
UF colleges, technical
polytechnical schools
schools, polytechnical
technical colleges
CN V.RK.AFU.ALO.ALO.CXA.ARI.
AXC.BIQ.ALO

polytheism
BM.705 (L)
CN B.BM.BZY.ALO.ARI.CRG

polyurethane
MT.2186 (L)
UF PU-tp
resin, urethane
urethane resin

CN M.MT.AFU.AFU.ARI.BUE.ALO.
AXC.ARI.ARI

polyvinyl acetal
MT.2153
SN Any of a group of thermoplastic resins made by condensing polyvinyl alcohol with an aldehyde and used chiefly in the form of sheets and films, molded products, coatings, adhesives; especially, the resin made from acetaldehyde. (W)
UF acetal, polyvinyl
CN M.MT.AFU.AFU.ARI.BUE.ALO.
AXC.AFU.EFQ.AFU

polyvinyl acetate
MT.2154
UF acetate, polyvinyl
PVAC
CN M.MT.AFU.AFU.ARI.BUE.ALO.
AXC.AFU.EFQ.ALO

polyvinyl alcohol
MT.2155
SN A thermoplastic resin that is soluble or swells in water and that is used chiefly as emulsifiers, adhesives, and films resistant to solvents and abrasion, and in making molded and extruded products and polyvinyl acetals. (W)
UF alcohol, polyvinyl
PVAL
CN M.MT.AFU.AFU.ARI.BUE.ALO.
AXC.AFU.EFQ.ARI

polyvinyl butyral
MT.2156
SN A tough, flexible, transparent, moistureproof polyvinyl acetal resin made from polyvinyl alcohol and butyraldehyde and used chiefly as the interlayer in safety glass and other laminated products and as a coating for textiles. (W)
UF butyral, polyvinyl
PVB
CN M.MT.AFU.AFU.ARI.BUE.ALO.
AXC.AFU.EFQ.AXC

polyvinyl chloride
MT.2157 (L)
SN A colorless vinyl resin used as a component of industrial paints and as a base for silkscreen inks, but not stable enough for artists' colors. (MAYER)
UF chloride, polyvinyl
PVC
CN M.MT.AFU.AFU.ARI.BUE.ALO.
AXC.AFU.EFQ.BCW

polyvinylidene chloride
MT.2175
UF chloride, polyvinylidene
PVDC
CN M.MT.AFU.AFU.ARI.BUE.ALO.
AXC.ALO.BOK

pommels (finials)
RT.1059
ALT **pommel (finial)**
SN Rounded finials. (HAS)
UF pummels (finials)
CN V.RT.AFU.BCW.BUE.ALO

Pomo
FL.1261 (L,R)
UF Kulanapan
CN F.FL.ALO.ALO.ARI.AFU.ALO.DIO

pompador chairs
USE **lady's chairs**

pompadors
USE **lady's chairs**

Pompeian blue
USE **Egyptian blue**

Pompeian red
MT.1672
UF red, Pompeian
CN M.MT.AFU.AFU.ARI.AFU.AFU.
ALO.ALO.BCW.AFU.ALO.ALO

Pompeian red (color)
USE **grayish red**
grayish reddish orange
moderate red

Pompeian red (Pozzuoli red)
USE **Pozzuoli red**

Pompeian Style
FL.3272
CN F.FL.ALO.BCW.ALO.AXC.CLM.BUE

Pompeian Style, First
USE **First Style**

Pompeian Style, Fourth
USE **Fourth Style**

Pompeian Style, Second
USE **Second Style**

Pompeian Style, Third
USE **Third Style**

pompier ladders
USE **hook ladders**

Ponca
FL.1393 (L)
CN F.FL.ALO.ALO.ARI.AFU.BOK.ELK

pond pine
MT.1383
UF pine, pond
pine, spruce
Pinus serotina
spruce pine
CN M.MT.AFU.AFU.ALO.BIQ.DCU.
AFU.AFU.ALO.CXA.CXA

ponderosa pine
MT.1384 (L)
UF Oregon white pine
pine, Oregon white
pine, pitch
pine, ponderosa
pine, red
pine, western yellow
pine, yellow (ponderosa pine)
Pinus ponderosa
pitch pine
red pine
western yellow pine
white pine, Oregon
yellow pine (ponderosa pine)
yellow pine, western
CN M.MT.AFU.AFU.ALO.BIQ.DCU.
AFU.AFU.ALO.CXA.DCU

Pondo
FL.563 (L)
CN F.FL.ALO.AFU.AXC.ARI.AXC.ALO

ponds
RD.134 (L,B,R)
ALT **pond**
SN Relatively small bodies of water, usually surrounded on all sides by land. (STEIN)
CN V.RD.ARI.AFU.AFU.AFU.AFU.
ALO.ALO

ponolith
USE **lithopone**

pontoon bridges
RK.1300 (L)
ALT **pontoon bridge**
SN Use for bridges, generally temporary, whose decks are supported on low flat-bottomed or hollow floats.
UF bridges, pontoon
floating bridges
CN V.RK.AFU.ALO.ALO.GLI.ALO.
AFU.ARI.BIQ

pony trusses
RT.380
ALT **pony truss**
SN Trusses, such as in bridges, so low that overhead bracing cannot be used. (W)
UF trusses, pony
CN V.RT.AFU.AFU.AFU.BCW.CLM.
AFU.ALO.AFU.AFU.AFU

pool halls
RK.1042
ALT **pool hall**
SN Use for public establishments equipped with pool and/or billiard tables.
UF billiard halls
billiard parlors
halls, billiard
halls, pool
parlors, billiard
parlors, pool
pool parlors
poolrooms
CN V.RK.AFU.ALO.ALO.EWY.AXC.
ARI.BOK

pool houses
USE **bathhouses**

pool parlors
USE **pool halls**

pool tables
TG.754 (N)
ALT **pool table**
SN Tables with slate surfaces covered with cloth, having six pockets and surrounded by cushioned rails. Distinct from **billiard tables** which do not have pockets.
UF tables, pool
CN V.TG.AFU.AFU.BIQ.BOK.ALO.EFQ

poolrooms
USE **pool halls**

pools
RD.136 (N,B)
ALT **pool**
SN Use for still bodies of water smaller than ponds.
CN V.RD.ARI.AFU.AFU.AFU.AFU.ALO.ARI

pools, swimming
USE **swimming pools**

poor farms
USE **almshouses**

poor laws
VW.1029 (L,R)
ALT **poor law**
UF laws, poor
CN V.VW.AFU.ARI.ALO.BCW.AFU.ARI.AFU.ARI.AFU.AFU

poor lime
USE **meager lime**

poor mortar
USE **lean mortar**

poorhouses
USE **almshouses**

Pop
FL.3745 (A,L,R)
CN F.FL.ALO.BUE.ARI.GRC

POP (paper)
USE **printing-out paper**

pope's crosses
USE **papal crosses**

popes
HG.231 (L)
ALT **pope**
CN H.HG.AFU.AXC.AXC.BIQ.AFU.ARI.DOI

popinae
RK.121
ALT **popina**
SN Ancient Roman eating places offering predominantly hot meals, usually simple, cheap, and often unsanitary establishments.
CN V.RK.AFU.ALO.ALO.ALO.AFU.AXC.BZY

poplar
MT.1269 (L)
UF populus
CN M.MT.AFU.AFU.ALO.BIQ.DCU.AFU.AFU.AFU.KFK

poplar, American
USE **American aspen**

poplar, balsam
USE **balsam poplar**

poplar, black
USE **black poplar**

poplar, English
USE **black poplar**

poplar, European black
USE **black poplar**

poplar, gray
USE **gray poplar**

poplar, Lombardy
USE **black poplar**

poplar, Virginia
USE **tulipwood**

poplar, western balsam
USE **black cottonwood**

poplar, white
USE **white poplar**

poplar, yellow
USE **tulipwood**

Popo
USE **Gun**

Popoloca
FL.1520 (L)
CN F.FL.ALO.ALO.ARI.ALO.AXC.CLM

Popoluca
FL.1521 (L)
CN F.FL.ALO.ALO.ARI.ALO.AXC.CRG

poppy oil
USE **poppy-seed oil**

poppy-seed oil
MT.2017 (L)
UF oil, poppy
oil, poppy-seed
poppy oil
CN M.MT.AFU.AFU.ARI.ARI.AXC.AFU.BUE

popular arts
USE **popular culture**

popular culture
BM.363 (L,R)
UF arts, popular
culture, popular
popular arts
CN B.BM.ALO.ALO.CLM.ERE

Popular Mughal
FL.2237
UF Mughal, Popular
CN F.FL.ALO.ARI.AXC.ALO.AFU.BIQ.ALO.ALO.AFU

population
BM.1057 (L,B)
CN B.BM.CLM.AFU.ARI

population change
BM.1058 (B)
UF change, population
CN B.BM.CLM.AFU.AXC

population decline
BM.1059 (B)
UF decline, population
CN B.BM.CLM.AFU.AXC.AFU

population density
BM.1061 (A,L,B)
UF density of population
density, population
CN B.BM.CLM.AFU.BCW

population distribution maps
USE **population maps**

population geography
KD.136 (L)
UF geography, population
CN K.KD.AFU.ALO.BZY.ARI

population growth
BM.1060
UF growth, population
increase, population
population increase
CN B.BM.CLM.AFU.AXC.ALO

population increase
USE **population growth**

population maps
VW.198 (B)
ALT **population map**
UF demographic maps
maps, demographic
maps, population
maps, population distribution
population distribution maps
CN V.VW.AFU.AFU.AFU.FZU.AXC.AFU.ARI.AXC.CFS

population specialists
USE **demographers**

population studies
USE **demography**

populism
BM.563 (L,R)
SN Political and economic doctrines advocated by the populists, including representation of agrarian interests, free coinage of silver, and government control of monopolies. (W)
CN B.BM.BOK.BZY.BZY

populus
USE **poplar**

Populus alba

USE **white poplar**

Populus balsamifera
USE **balsam poplar**

Populus candicans
USE **balm of gilead**

Populus canescens
USE **gray poplar**

Populus deltoides
USE **eastern cottonwood**

Populus gileadensis
USE **balm of gilead**

Populus grandidentata
USE **big toothed aspen**

Populus nigra
USE **black poplar**

Populus tacamahaca
USE **balsam poplar**

Populus tremula
USE **aspen**

Populus tremuloides
USE **American aspen**

Populus trichocarpa
USE **black cottonwood**

porcelain
MT.145 (L,B,R)
CN M.MT.AFU.AFU.AFU.AXC.ALO.ALO.AFU.AFU

porcelain and pottery, Minton
USE **Minton**

porcelain color
USE **ceramic color**

porcelain enamel
MT.2428 (L)
SN Generally an opaque, vitreous surface finish fused at high temperatures and used on metals. (HORNB)
UF enamel, porcelain
enamel, vitreous
vitreous enamel
CN M.MT.AFU.ARI.CRG.AFU.ALO.ALO

porcelain marks
VW.734 (L,R)
ALT **porcelain mark**
UF marks, porcelain
CN V.VW.AFU.ALO.ALO.AFU.AXC.ARI.BUE

porcelain process
USE **ceramic process**

porcelain, armorial
USE **armorial porcelain**

porcelain, Canton
USE **Chinese export porcelain**

porcelain, China trade
USE **Chinese export porcelain**

porcelain, Chinese export
USE **Chinese export porcelain**

porcelain, Compagnie-des-Indes
USE **Compagnie des Indes ware**

porcelain, East India
USE **Compagnie des Indes ware**

porcelain, five-color
USE **Wucai**

porcelain, hard paste
USE **hard paste porcelain**

porcelain, Jesuit
USE **Jesuit ware**

porcelain, Kelsterbach
USE **Kelsterbach porcelain**

porcelain, Kraak
USE **Kraak porcelain**

porcelain, Limoges
USE **Limoges porcelain**

porcelain, Parian
USE **Parian ware**

porcelain, Regensburg
USE **Regensburg porcelain**

porcelain, soft paste
USE **soft paste porcelain**

porcelain, statuary
USE **Parian ware**

porcelain, Strasbourg
USE **Strasbourg faïence**

porcelain, Tournai
USE **Tournai porcelain**

porcelain, Vezzi
USE **Vezzi porcelain**

porches
RM.248 (A,L,N,B,R)
ALT **porch**
SN Use to designate roofed spaces, open along two or more sides and adjunct to a building, commonly serving either to shelter an entrance or used as living space.
UF piazzas (porches)
verandas
CN V.RM.AFU.DIO.ARI.AFU.BIQ

porches, carriage
USE **porte-cocheres**

porches, sleeping
USE **sleeping porches**

porino
MT.835
UF grechetto duro
marmor porinum
CN M.MT.AFU.AFU.AFU.DCU.AFU.ARI.ARI.ARI.BOK.DIO

pornography
BM.218 (L,R)
ALT **pornographic**
SN Depiction or description of sexual activity in an exploitative, abusive, or violent context. For depiction or description of sexual love, use **erotica.**
CN B.BM.AFU.ARI.ALO

poros
MT.674
SN A coarse limestone found in the Peloponnesus and extensively used as a building material by the ancient Greeks. (W)
CN M.MT.AFU.AFU.AFU.DCU.AFU.ALO.AFU.ALO.ALO.AFU.AFU.AXC

porosity
BM.980 (L)
ALT **porous**
SN The ratio of the volume of the interstices of a material to the volume of its mass. (MH)
CN B.BM.CFS.AXC.BZY.BZY.ARI

porous concrete
MT.229 (A,L)
UF concrete, porous
CN M.MT.AFU.AFU.AFU.BCW.AFU.AXC.BOK

porous materials
MT.2810 (L)
UF materials, porous
CN M.MT.AFU.BCW.DOI

porphyrite
USE **red antique porphyry**

porphyritic diorite
USE **red antique porphyry**

porphyry
MT.618 (R)
UF lapis porphyrite
CN M.MT.AFU.AFU.AFU.DCU.AFU.AFU.AFU.ALO.AFU

porphyry, quartz
USE **quartz porphyry**

porphyry, red antique
USE **red antique porphyry**

port cities
USE **ports**

Port Orford cedar
MT.1345 (L)
UF cedar, Oregon
cedar, Port Orford
cedar, white
Cupressus lawsoniana
cypress, lawson
ginger pine
lawson cypress
Oregon cedar
pine, ginger
white cedar
CN M.MT.AFU.AFU.ALO.BIQ.DCU.

AFU.AFU.ALO.AXC.ALO

port saws
USE **compass saws**

Porta Santa marble
MT.815
UF Claudian stone
marble, Porta Santa
marmor Iassense
stone, Claudian
CN M.MT.AFU.AFU.AFU.DCU.AFU.
ARI.ARI.ARI.BIQ.CLM

portable bidets
TG.236
ALT **portable bidet**
SN Bidets with legs made to screw off and tops made to lock.(CABDIC). Use **traveling bidets** for those made to rise out of a chest.
UF bidets, portable
CN V.TG.AFU.AFU.ALO.AFU.ALO.
AFU.AFU.AFU.AFU

portable buildings
RK.1379 (A,L,B)
ALT **portable building**
UF buildings, mobile
buildings, movable
buildings, portable
buildings, transportable
mobile buildings
movable buildings
transportable buildings
CN V.RK.AFU.ALO.AXC.BOK

portable circular saws
USE **electric-portable saws**

portable computers
TB.146 (L)
ALT **portable computer**
UF computers, portable
CN V.TB.AFU.ARI.BCW.ARI.AFU.ALO

portable cribs
USE **folding cribs**

portable desks
TG.547 (N)
ALT **portable desk**
SN Small desks generally having a sloping surface for writing or for propping up books for reading; sometimes fitted with an inkwell or pounce-box for sand. (THORN2)
UF desks, gentleman's portable
desks, portable
desks, portable writing
desks, table
desks, writing (portable desks)
gentleman's portable desks
portable desks, gentleman's
portable writing desks
table desks
writing desks (portable desks)
writing desks, portable
CN V.TG.AFU.AFU.AXC.ALO.BZY.CXA

portable desks, gentleman's
USE **portable desks**

portable drills, electric
USE **electric drills**

portable furniture
TG.798
UF furniture, nomadic
furniture, portable
nomadic furniture
CN V.TG.AFU.ARI.BZY

portable library bookcases
USE **moving libraries**

portable writing desks
USE **portable desks**

portal frames
USE **rigid frames**

portals
RT.904 (R)
ALT **portal**
CN V.RT.AFU.ARI.AFU.AFU.BIQ

portcrayons
TB.252
ALT **portcrayon**
SN Handles for holding chalk, crayons, or charcoal, consisting of a split metal tube, usually double-ended, in which the material is secured by a ring that slides over the split end. (MAYER)
UF chalk holders
crayon holders
holders, chalk
holders, crayon
CN V.TB.AFU.ARI.CLM.AFU.ALO.
BZY.ALO

portcullises
RT.895 (B)
ALT **portcullis**
SN Defensive gratings, of massive iron or timber, movable vertically in retaining grooves cut in the jambs of fortified gateways. (HAS)
UF sarasins
CN V.RT.AFU.ARI.AFU.AFU.ARI.ALO.
AFU.AFU.ARI

porte-cocheres
RM.250 (A,L,B)
ALT **porte-cochere**
SN Use for projecting roofs or porchlike structures that shelter vehicles and passengers at the entrances to buildings; also for short vehicular tunnels through buildings, sheltering an entrance.
UF carriage porches
porches, carriage
CN V.RM.AFU.DIO.ARI.AFU.BOK

porter's chairs
TG.190 (N)
ALT **porter's chair**
SN English type of upholstered armchair with wings and an arched top making a niche to screen the occupant from drafts; made from the mid-18th century onwards. (DDA)
UF chairs, page's
chairs, porter's
page's chairs
CN V.TG.AFU.AFU.ALO.AFU.AFU.
ALO.DOI

porters
HG.50 (L)
ALT **porter**
SN Persons employed to carry baggage for patrons at a hotel or transportation terminal. (W)
CN H.HG.AFU.AXC.ARI.CRG

portfolio stands
TG.650
ALT **portfolio stand**
SN Stands for holding large prints; generally having a front which falls down and often having a lock. (LOUDON)
UF stands, portfolio
CN V.TG.AFU.AFU.BIQ.BCW.ALO.DOI

portfolios (financial records)
VW.836 (L,N)
ALT **portfolio (financial record)**
SN In investments, all securities held by one person or institution. (BLACKS)
CN V.VW.AFU.ARI.AFU.BIQ.CLM

porticoes
RM.251 (A,L,N,B,R)
ALT **portico**
SN Use for roofed porchlike spaces, open along at least one side and usually associated with an entrance, supported by columns and often surmounted by a pediment; porticoes may project from the main building mass or be recessed in it.
CN V.RM.AFU.DIO.ARI.AFU.BUE

portland blast-furnace cement
USE **portland slag cement**

portland blast-furnace-slag cement
USE **portland slag cement**

portland cement
MT.11 (L)
SN The cementitious binder for most structural concrete; obtained by pulverizing clinker consisting essentially of hydraulic calcium silicates; contains calcium sulfate as an interground addition. (DAC)
UF cement, portland
CN M.MT.AFU.AFU.AFU.ALO.AFU.
AFU.ARI.AFU

portland cement, moderate
USE **modified portland cement**

portland cement, modified
USE **modified portland cement**

portland cement, normal

USE **standard portland cement**

portland cement, standard
USE **standard portland cement**

portland cement, type I
USE **standard portland cement**

portland cement, type II
USE **modified portland cement**

portland cement, type III
USE **high-early-strength cement**

portland cement, type V
USE **sulfate-resistant cement**

Portland limestone
USE **Portland stone**

portland-pozzolan cement
MT.16
SN Portland cement blended with pozzolana.
UF cement, portland-pozzolan
CN M.MT.AFU.AFU.AFU.ALO.AFU.AFU.ARI.AFU.BCW

Portland sandstone
MT.720
UF sandstone, Portland
CN M.MT.AFU.AFU.AFU.DCU.AFU.ALO.AFU.ARI.AFU.ALO.AXC.ALO.AFU

portland slag cement
MT.17
UF cement, portland blast-furnace
cement, portland blast-furnace-slag
cement, portland slag
portland blast-furnace cement
portland blast-furnace-slag cement
slag cement, portland
CN M.MT.AFU.AFU.AFU.ALO.AFU.AFU.ARI.AFU.BIQ

Portland stone
MT.671
UF limestone, Portland
Portland limestone
stone, Portland
CN M.MT.AFU.AFU.AFU.DCU.AFU.ALO.AFU.ALO.ALO.AFU.AFU.ALO.BUE

porto marble
USE **portor marble**

portolan charts
USE **portolanos**

portolanos
VW.126
ALT **portolano**
SN Use for Medieval marine charts, used before compasses, and for Medieval navigation manuals, illustrated with charts and showing the location of ports and other navigational information.
UF charts, portolan
charts, portulan
compass maps
loxodromes
portolan charts
portolans
portulan charts
portulans
rutters
ruttiers
CN V.VW.AFU.AFU.AFU.FZU.AXC.AFU.AFU.AFU.ALO

portolans
USE **portolanos**

portor marble
MT.816
UF marble, portor
porto marble
CN M.MT.AFU.AFU.AFU.DCU.AFU.ARI.ARI.ARI.BIQ.CRG

portrait photography, professional
USE **commercial portraiture**

portraits
VB.74 (L,R)
ALT **portrait**
CN V.VB.AFU.AXC.BCW

portraits, group
USE **group portraits**

portraiture, commercial
USE **commercial portraiture**

portraiture, studio
USE **commercial portraiture**

ports
RD.57 (A,L,B,R)
ALT **port**
SN Use for settlement areas that combine a harbor and terminal facilities at the transition between land and water transportation systems.
UF cities, port
port cities
ports, sea
sea ports
CN V.RD.AFU.AXC.BUE

ports, sally
USE **sally ports**

ports, sea
USE **ports**

Portuguese
FL.3054 (L,B)
CN F.FL.ALO.BCW.AFU.DCU

Portuguese Colonial
FL.3241
UF Colonial, Portuguese
CN F.FL.ALO.BCW.ALO.ARI.BIQ.BIQ.BOK.AFU

Portuguese feet
USE **Spanish feet**

portulan charts
USE **portolanos**

portulans
USE **portolanos**

pose
BM.162
CN B.BM.AFU.AFU.ARI.BOK.CRG

positive color transparencies
USE **color transparencies**

positive transparencies
USE **transparencies**

positives
VJ.27
ALT **positive**
SN Use for photographs other than photomechanical prints in which the tones or colors correspond to (i.e., are not reversed from) their appearance in nature.
CN V.VJ.AFU.AFU.ARI

positives, calotype
USE **salted paper prints**

positives, collodion glass
USE **ambrotypes**

positives, color separation
USE **color separation positives**

positives, direct
USE **direct positives**

positives, glass-collodion
USE **ambrotypes**

positives, separation
USE **color separation positives**

positivism
BM.520 (L,R)
CN B.BM.BIQ.AXC.DOI

Possible art
USE **Conceptual**

possolan
USE **pozzolana**

possum-trot plan houses
USE **dogtrot houses**

Post-Akkad
USE **Post-Akkadian**

Post-Akkadian
FL.2968
UF Post-Akkad
CN F.FL.ALO.AXC.ARI.BCW.AFU.AXC.AFU

post-and-beam construction
USE **post-and-beam structures**

post-and-beam framing
USE **post-and-beam structures**

post-and-beam structures
RT.41
ALT **post-and-beam structure**

SN Use for any structures based on upright posts or columns supporting horizontal beams or lintels; these exclude balloon frames and platform frames, in which support is by stud walls.
UF assemblies, column and beam
column and beam assemblies
construction, plank-and-beam
construction, post-and-beam
construction, post-and-lintel
framing, post-and-beam
plank-and-beam construction
post-and-beam construction
post-and-beam framing
post-and-lintel construction
structures, post-and-beam
structures, trabeated
trabeated structures
CN V.RT.AFU.AFU.AFU.ALO.AXC.AXC

post-and-lintel construction
USE **post-and-beam structures**

Post-Angkorean
FL.2367
CN F.FL.ALO.ARI.BCW.ALO.AXC

post axes
USE **mortising axes**

post beds
USE **high-post beds**
low-post beds

Post-Conceptual
FL.3746
CN F.FL.ALO.BUE.ARI.GWW

post exchanges
RK.861 (A,L)
ALT **post exchange**
UF canteens (post exchanges)
commissaries
exchanges, military post
exchanges, post
military post exchanges
PXs
CN V.RK.AFU.ALO.ALO.DIO.AFU.BCW

Post-Gupta
FL.2204
UF Indian, Medieval
Medieval Indian
CN F.FL.ALO.ARI.AXC.ALO.AFU.AXC

post-hole diggers
TB.41 (N)
ALT **post-hole digger**
SN Tools used for digging post holes, especially those operated from the power takeoff on a tractor. (W)
UF diggers, post-hole
CN V.TB.AFU.ARI.AFU.ARI.ARI.ARI

Post-Impressionist
FL.3300 (L,R)
ALT **Post-Impressionism**
CN F.FL.ALO.BCW.ALO.AXC.DCU.BZY

Post-Minimal
FL.3747
ALT **Post-Minimalism**
UF Anti-form
CN F.FL.ALO.BUE.ARI.HCQ

post oak
MT.1247
UF oak, post
Quercus stellata
CN M.MT.AFU.AFU.ALO.BIQ.DCU.AFU.AFU.AFU.IRA.DIO

Post-object art
USE **Conceptual**

post-occupancy evaluation
KG.18
SN Use for the evaluation of building performance in terms of client needs and goals, including such things as environmental design, comfort levels, and mechanical systems as they affect human occupancy.
UF building evaluation
evaluation, building
evaluation, post-occupancy
CN K.KG.AFU.AFU.AFU.BZY.AFU.ALO

post office directories
VW.410 (L)
ALT **post office directory**
UF directories, post office
CN V.VW.AFU.AFU.ALO.EWY.AXC.AFU.ARI

post offices
RK.987 (A,L,N,B,R)
ALT **post office**
UF offices, post
CN V.RK.AFU.ALO.ALO.ERE.AFU.BOK

Post-painterly Abstraction
USE **Color-field**

post roads
RK.1553 (L)
ALT **post road**
UF roads, post
CN V.RK.ALO.ALO.BIQ.ARI.ALO.BIQ

post stations
USE **posthouses**

post stressing
USE **post tensioning**

post-tensioned prestressed concrete
MT.218 (A,L)
UF concrete, post-tensioned prestressed
prestressed concrete, post-tensioned
CN M.MT.AFU.AFU.AFU.BCW.AFU.ARI.BCW.AFU

post tensioning
KT.649
SN Method of prestressing concrete in which the tendons, such as steel cables or rods, are tensioned after the concrete has hardened. (STEIN)
UF post stressing
stressing, post
tensioning, post
CN K.KT.AFU.ALO.GLI.AFU.AXC.AFU

postal art
USE **correspondence art**

postal cards
VW.579 (A,L,R)
ALT **postal card**
SN Cards sold by the post office with a stamp already printed on them, usually mailable at a lower rate than that for letters in envelopes. (RHDEL2)
UF cards, postal
CN V.VW.AFU.ALO.AFU.ARI.CXA.ALO

postal code maps
VW.200 (L)
ALT **postal code map**
UF maps, postal code
CN V.VW.AFU.AFU.AFU.FZU.AXC.AFU.ARI.AXC.CLM

postal museums
USE **philatelic museums**

postal sculpture
USE **correspondence art**

postcard albums
VW.490 (N)
ALT **postcard album**
SN Albums made up of mounted postcards, with or without identifying information.
UF albums, postcard
CN V.VW.ALO.AFU.AFU.AFU.ALO.AXC

postcards
VW.577 (L,N,B,R)
ALT **postcard**
SN Cards on which a message may be written or printed for mailing without an envelope; often include a pictorial, comic, or other scene on one side.
CN V.VW.AFU.ALO.AFU.ARI.CXA

postcards, photographic
USE **picture postcards**

postcards, picture
USE **picture postcards**

Postclassic
FL.971
CN F.FL.ALO.ALO.ALO.ALO.AFU.AFU.BCW

Postclassic, Early
USE **Early Postclassic**

Postclassic, Late
USE **Late Postclassic**

Postclassical Ife
FL.102
UF Ife, Postclassical
CN F.FL.ALO.AFU.ALO.AFU.BUE.

BCW.ALO

poster color
MT.2515
UF color, poster
colors, show-card
paint, poster
poster paint
show-card colors
CN M.MT.AFU.ARI.CRG.ALO.BCW.AFU.ALO.AFU.ALO

poster paint
USE **poster color**

poster stamps
VW.735 (L)
ALT **poster stamp**
UF stamps, poster
CN V.VW.AFU.ALO.ALO.AFU.AXC.ARI.BZY

postern gates
USE **posterns**

posterns
RT.985
ALT **postern**
SN Back doors or gates; also, private or side entrances. (W)
UF gates, postern
postern gates
CN V.RT.AFU.ARI.AFU.ALO.AFU.AFU

posthouses
RK.1253 (A,L)
ALT **posthouse**
SN Designates stations or inns along a route providing a change of horses for couriers.
UF post stations
CN V.RK.AFU.ALO.ALO.GLI.AFU.ARI.BIQ

postica
USE **opisthodomoi**

postis
USE **jambs**

postmasters
HG.684 (L)
ALT **postmaster**
SN Officials in charge of post offices. (RHDEL2)
CN H.HG.AFU.AXC.CFS.CFS.BZY

Postmodern
FL.3704 (A,L,R)
ALT **Postmodernism**
CN F.FL.ALO.BUE.AFU

posts
RT.195 (A,N,B)
ALT **post**
SN Use for square, upright supports, usually of wood, and for similar metal elements when relatively isolated. For square uprights in classical style, and for square and rectangular masonry uprights, use **piers**; for most cylindrical uprights, and for all uprights in steel and concrete frames, use **columns.**
UF pillars
CN V.RT.AFU.AFU.AFU.AXC.DCU

posts, arm
USE **arm supports**

posts, back
USE **back rails**

posts, cased
USE **cased posts**

posts, crown
USE **crown posts**

posts, customs
USE **customhouses**

posts, gable
USE **gable posts**

posts, gate
USE **hanging posts**

posts, hammer
USE **pendant posts**

posts, hanging
USE **hanging posts**

posts, hinge
USE **hanging posts**

posts, hitching
USE **hitching posts**

posts, jamb
USE **jamb posts**

posts, king
USE **king posts**

posts, newel
USE **newels**

posts, pendant
USE **pendant posts**

posts, pendent
USE **pendant posts**

posts, princess
USE **princess posts**

posts, queen
USE **queen posts**

posts, shutting
USE **shutting posts**

posts, swinging
USE **hanging posts**

posts, tethering
USE **hitching posts**

posts, trading
USE **trading posts**

pot cupboards
USE **night tables**

pot glass
MT.263
UF glass, pot
CN M.MT.AFU.AFU.AFU.BIQ.AFU.ARI.BZY

potable water
USE **drinking water**

potash mica
USE **muscovite (mica)**

potash silicate
USE **muscovite (mica)**

potash, caustic
USE **potassium hydroxide**

potassium-argon dating
KT.505 (L)
SN Method of dating potassium-rich materials or objects by measuring the amount of radioactive decay in the ratio of potassium to argon. (HOLHZR)
UF argon-potassium dating
dating, K-Ar
dating, potassium-argon
K-Ar dating
CN K.KT.AFU.ALO.EFQ.AFU.BCW.ALO

potassium hydroxide
MT.304
UF caustic potash
potash, caustic
CN M.MT.AFU.AFU.AFU.BOK.ALO.AFU

potato printing
KT.472 (L)
UF printing, potato
CN K.KT.AFU.ALO.DUC.DUC.ALO.BCW.ARI.ALO.ALO

Potawatomi
FL.1330 (L)
CN F.FL.ALO.ALO.ARI.AFU.BCW.BUE

Potiguara
FL.1681
CN F.FL.ALO.ALO.ARI.ARI.BIQ.BZY

potlaches
KM.24 (L)
SN Ceremonial feasts given by the northwest coast Native Americans as displays of wealth, to validate or advance individual social status. They are marked by the hosts' lavish destruction of personal property and ostentatious gift giving. (W)
CN K.KM.AFU.ARI.ARI.BOK

Potomac breccia
MT.735
UF breccia, Potomac
calico marble
calico rock
marble, calico
marble, Potomac
Potomac marble
rock, calico

CN M.MT.AFU.AFU.AFU.DCU.AFU.
ALO.ALO.ARI.AFU.AFU

Potomac marble
USE **Potomac breccia**

pots, chimney
USE **chimney pots**

Potsdam sandstone
MT.727
UF sandstone, Potsdam
CN M.MT.AFU.AFU.AFU.DCU.AFU.
ALO.AFU.ARI.AFU.ALO.BIQ.AXC

potstone
MT.878
SN A more or less impure steatite used especially in prehistoric times to make cooking vessels.
CN M.MT.AFU.AFU.AFU.DCU.AFU.
ARI.BZY.ALO.AFU

potter's clay
MT.64
SN Native clay selected for its fineness, plasticity, absorbency, and other qualities that suit it to various ceramic uses. (MAYER)
UF clay, potter's
earth, potter's
potter's earth
CN M.MT.AFU.AFU.AFU.AXC.AFU.
ALO.ALO

potter's earth
USE **potter's clay**

potter's fields
RG.35
ALT **potter's field**
SN Public burial places for paupers, unknown persons, and criminals. (W)
CN V.RG.AFU.AFU.ALO.ALO.BCW

potter's flint
MT.556
UF flint, potter's
CN M.MT.AFU.AFU.AFU.CFS.AFU.
GRC.AFU.AXC.ALO

potter's pink
MT.1700
UF lake, mineral
mineral lake
pink, potter's
CN M.MT.AFU.AFU.ARI.AFU.AFU.
ALO.ALO.BCW.ARI.AXC

potteries
RK.651 (B)
ALT **pottery**
SN Places where earthen pots or vessels are made. (RHDEL2)
CN V.RK.AFU.ALO.ALO.CLM.ALO.
ALO.AFU.AXC.CLM

potters
HG.570 (L,R)
ALT **potter**
CN H.HG.AFU.AXC.BUE.AXC.DCU

potters' marks
VW.753 (L)
ALT **potter's mark**
UF marks, potters'
CN V.VW.AFU.ALO.ALO.AFU.AXC.
AXC.CXA

pottery
MT.148 (L,R)
CN M.MT.AFU.AFU.AFU.AXC.ALO.
ALO.AFU.ALO

pottery marks
VW.736 (L,R)
ALT **pottery mark**
UF marks, pottery
CN V.VW.AFU.ALO.ALO.AFU.AXC.
ARI.CFS

pottery, Abraham of Kütahya style Iznik
USE **Kütahya ware**

pottery, Arretine
USE **Arretine ware**

pottery, Black
USE **Longshan**

pottery, black-topped
USE **black-topped pottery**

pottery, Bucchero
USE **Bucchero ware**

pottery, Bunzlau
USE **Bunzlau pottery**

pottery, Damascus style Iznik
USE **Damascus ware**

pottery, Haguenau
USE **Haguenau pottery**

pottery, Hanau
USE **Hanau pottery**

pottery, Iznik
USE **Iznik ware**

pottery, Kütahya
USE **Kütahya ware**

pottery, Lakabi
USE **Lakabi ware**

pottery, Laqabi
USE **Lakabi ware**

pottery, Minai
USE **Minai ware**

pottery, Mitannian
USE **Atchana ware**

pottery, Pergamene
USE **Pergamene ware**

pottery, red-gloss
USE **red-gloss pottery**

pottery, Rhodian
USE **Rhodian ware**

pottery, Rhodian style Iznik
USE **Rhodian ware**

pottery, Rusafah
USE **Rusapha ware**

pottery, Saint Clément
USE **Saint Clément pottery**

pottery, Samarra
USE **Samarra ware**

pottery, Sarreguemines
USE **Sarreguemines pottery**

pottery, Seto
USE **Seto ware**

pottery, Sialk
USE **Sialk pottery**

pottery, Strasbourg
USE **Strasbourg faïence**

pottery, Sultanabad
USE **Sultanabad ware**

pottery, Takatori
USE **Takatori ware**

pottery, Wadi Rabah
USE **Wadi Rabah pottery**

pottery, Westerwald
USE **Westerwald stoneware**

pottery, white cross-lined
USE **white cross-lined pottery**

pottery, white-lined
USE **white-lined pottery**

pottery, white-on-red
USE **white-on-red pottery**

pouch tables
USE **work tables**

poudreuses
USE **coiffeuses**
toilettes

pouffes
TG.299
ALT **pouffe**
SN Backless upholstered seats, usually round, and large enough for several people.
UF banquettes (pouffes)
CN V.TG.AFU.AFU.ALO.ALO.BOK

poulticing (masonry)
KT.73
SN Technique of cleaning or removing stains from porous masonry; the stain is drawn out of the masonry to be reabsorbed by the poultice material. (GRIMMR)
CN K.KT.AFU.ALO.BIQ.BIQ

poultry houses
RK.89 (L,B)
ALT **poultry house**
UF fowlhouses

houses, poultry
CN V.RK.AFU.ALO.ALO.AFU.ALO.CFS

pounce bags
TB.359
ALT **pounce bag**
SN Bags made of a porous material filled with a fine powder of charcoal, chalk, or pipe clay; used in pouncing.
UF bags, pounce
CN V.TB.AFU.ARI.CXA.ARI

pounce wheels
USE **perforating wheels**

pouncing
KT.743
ALT **pounced**
SN The technique of copying a design by pricking holes in the outlines and using fine chalk or graphite powder to transfer these to a surface beneath.(THDAT) Also refers to the application of fine, powderlike substances to drawings, or pastels, to keep them from smudging while work is in progress. (RHDEL2)
CN K.KT.AFU.ALO.HCQ.ALO.AXC

pounds
USE **animal shelters**

pounds, animal
USE **animal shelters**

pouring concrete
KT.586 (B)
SN Use for the act of putting concrete in position.
UF concrete laying
concrete placing
concreting
laying concrete
placing, concrete
CN K.KT.AFU.ALO.ERE.BIQ

pouring ladles
USE **melting ladles**

Poussinism
BM.193
SN Doctrine espoused by certain French painters of the 18th century emphasizing the importance of line over color. (THDAT)
CN B.BM.AFU.AFU.AXC.CLM.BOK

poverty
BM.1112 (L,R)
UF destitution
CN B.BM.CRG.BCW.BOK

Poverty Point
FL.862 (L)
CN F.FL.ALO.ALO.ALO.AFU.ALO.ALO.ARI.ARI.BUE

powder
MT.2250 (L)
CN M.MT.AFU.ALO.DOI.AFU.ALO

powder blue
USE **bluish gray**
deep blue
moderate blue
pale blue
pale purplish blue

powder coatings
MT.2463 (A)
ALT **powder coating**
SN Thermosetting plastic coatings applied to metals resulting in a hard and resistant finish. (PC)
UF coatings, powder
powders, thermosetting
thermosetting powders
CN M.MT.AFU.ARI.CRG.AFU.BCW

powder magazines
RK.859 (L)
ALT **powder magazine**
UF magazines, powder
CN V.RK.AFU.ALO.ALO.DIO.AFU.ARI.AFU

powder process
USE **dusting-on process**

powder rooms
USE **lavatories (rooms)**

powdered ornament
USE **powderwork**

powdered patterns
USE **powderwork**

powdered pigment
USE **dry color**

powdering
USE **powderwork**

powders, thermosetting
USE **powder coatings**

powderwork
DG.97
SN Patterns in which small motifs are scattered over a usually solid ground.
UF ornament, powdered
patterns, powdered
powdered ornament
powdered patterns
powdering
CN D.DG.AFU.ARI.AFU.AFU.ALO

power dams
USE **hydroelectric dams**

power hammers
TB.463 (N)
ALT **power hammer**
SN Portable electric, pneumatic, and self-contained gasoline-driven hammers using a vibratory action principle and accommodating such tools as chisels, spade, and tampers; used for removing brick, hardened putty, mortar, and other similar applications. (PUTNAM)
UF hammers, power
CN V.TB.AFU.ARI.ELK.AFU.ARI

power lines
RM.511 (L,B)
ALT **power line**
UF electric lines
electric power transmission lines
electrical supply lines
lines, electric
lines, power
lines, power transmission
power transmission lines
transmission lines
CN V.RM.ALO.ALO.ARI.ALO

power outlets
RT.1346 (L)
ALT **power outlet**
UF boxes, outlet
outlet boxes
outlets
sockets (power outlets)
sockets, wall
wall sockets
CN V.RT.ALO.ARI.ALO.CLM

power plants
RG.108 (A,L,B,R)
ALT **power plant**
SN Use for complexes of buildings and other structures with machinery for generating electricity.
UF electric power plants
electric power stations
electrical power stations
generating stations
plants, power
power plants, electric
power stations
power stations, electrical
stations, generating
stations, power
CN V.RG.AFU.AFU.BUE.ARI

power plants, atomic
USE **nuclear power plants**

power plants, coal-fired
USE **coal-fired power plants**

power plants, electric
USE **power plants**

power plants, gas-turbine
USE **gas-turbine power plants**

power plants, geothermal
USE **geothermal power plants**

power plants, hydroelectric
USE **hydroelectric power plants**

power plants, nuclear
USE **nuclear power plants**

power plants, ocean thermal
USE **ocean thermal energy conversion plants**

power plants, oil-fired
USE **oil-fired power plants**

power plants, OTEC
USE ocean thermal energy conversion plants

power plants, pumped storage
USE pumped storage power plants

power plants, solar
USE solar power plants

power plants, steam
USE steam power plants

power plants, tidal
USE tidal power plants

power plants, wind
USE wind power plants

power producing equipment
TB.385 (L,N)
UF equipment, power producing
CN V.TB.AFU.ARI.DOI

power production, electric
USE electric power production

power resources
USE energy resources

power sanders
TB.524
ALT power sander
SN Electric-powered hand tools used for smoothing and polishing. (MEANS)
UF sanders, power
CN V.TB.AFU.ARI.EWY.ALO.CXA.AXC

power shovels
TB.49 (L,N)
ALT power shovel
SN Self-propelled, power-operated machines used to excavate or load soil or debris. (MEANS)
UF shovels, power
CN V.TB.AFU.ARI.AFU.ARI.BZY.AFU

power stations
USE power plants

power stations, electrical
USE power plants

power stations, wave
USE tidal power plants

power supply
BM.879 (L)
UF electric power supply
supply, electric power
supply, power
CN B.BM.CFS.AXC.ALO.ALO.AXC

power supply, emergency
USE emergency power supply

power supply, emergency electric
USE emergency power supply

power systems, electrical
USE electrical systems

power systems, standby
USE emergency power supply

power tools
TB.13 (L)
ALT power tool
SN Tools powered by electric motors or by gasoline engines.
UF tools, power
CN V.TB.AFU.ALO.ARI.ALO

power transmission lines
USE power lines

power trowels
USE mechanical trowels

power, covering
USE covering power

power, geothermal
USE geothermal power

power, hydroelectric
USE hydroelectric power

power, nuclear
USE nuclear power

power, solar
USE solar power

power, wind
USE wind power

powerhouses
RK.673 (R)
ALT powerhouse
SN Use for buildings in which electricity or other forms of power are generated for the operation of machinery or vehicles, or supplying power to other buildings in a complex; distinguished from **power plants** which are complexes producing power on a much larger scale.
CN V.RK.AFU.ALO.ALO.CLM.ALO.AXC.ALO.AFU

powers of attorney
VW.918 (L)
ALT power of attorney
SN Legal instruments authorizing one to act as the attorney or agent of the grantor, either generally for the management of a specified enterprise or, specifically, for the accomplishment of a particular transaction. (GAHLM)
UF attorney, powers of
CN V.VW.AFU.ARI.AFU.BOK.BOK.CLM

Powhatan
FL.1437 (L)
CN F.FL.ALO.ALO.ARI.AFU.BZY.BUE

poys, tea
USE tea tables

pozzolan cement
MT.32 (L)
SN Cement made with lime mortar and pozzolana or other material containing active silica. (HORNB)
UF cement, pozzolan
cement, pozzuolana
cement, Roman
pozzuolana cement
Roman cement
CN M.MT.AFU.AFU.AFU.ALO.AFU.AFU.CRG

pozzolana
MT.2324 (L)
SN Siliceous or siliceous and aluminous material that in itself possesses little or no cementitious value but that in finely divided form and in the presence of moisture will chemically react with calcium hydroxide at ordinary temperatures to form compounds possessing cementitious properties. (STEIN)
UF possolan
puzzolan
CN M.MT.AFU.ARI.ALO.ELK

pozzuolana cement
USE pozzolan cement

Pozzuoli blue
USE Egyptian blue

Pozzuoli red
MT.1673
UF Pompeian red(Pozzuoli red)
red, Pompeian(Pozzuoli red)
red, Pozzuoli
CN M.MT.AFU.AFU.ARI.AFU.AFU.ALO.ALO.BCW.AFU.ALO.ARI

PP
USE polypropylene

PPNA
USE Pre-pottery Neolithic A

PPNB
USE Pre-pottery Neolithic B

Pra Patom
FL.2407
UF Brah Pahdona
P'rapatom
CN F.FL.ALO.ARI.BCW.BOK.AFU.ARI.ALO

prachedis
RK.1151
ALT prachedi
SN Siamese stupas tapering from a round base to an attenuated finial.
CN V.RK.AFU.ALO.ALO.FCS.BUE.ARI

praecinctiones
RM.356
ALT praecinctio
SN Use for the walkways, concentric with the rows of seats, between the upper and lower seating tiers in a Roman theater.
CN V.RM.AFU.DIO.AXC.AXC.AFU.BUE

praetoriums

RK.346
ALT **praetorium**
SN In the ancient Roman Empire, the official residences of provincial governors. (HAS)
CN V.RK.AFU.ALO.ALO.AXC.ALO.BOK.BOK.ARI

pragmatics
KD.45 (L)
SN Study of the aspects of meaning in language that are related to the use of language in a natural context. (ERIC)
UF analysis, discourse
discourse
discourse analysis
discourse grammar
grammar, discourse
CN K.KD.AFU.AFU.AXC.AFU.ALO.BIQ

pragmatism
BM.521 (L)
CN B.BM.BIQ.AXC.DUC

Prah Khan
USE **Preah Khan**

Prah Viehear
USE **Preah Vihear**

prairie crabapple
MT.1263
UF crabapple, prairie
Pyrus ioensis
CN M.MT.AFU.AFU.ALO.BIQ.DCU.AFU.AFU.AFU.JOC.ARI

Prairie School
FL.1736 (A,L,R)
CN F.FL.ALO.ALO.BCW.AFU.BUE.BCW

prairies
RD.248 (L,R)
ALT **prairie**
SN Use for extensive unwooded grasslands, usually flat or gently rolling; found in the central portions of North America.
CN V.RD.ARI.AFU.BCW.ALO.AFU.AFU.AXC

Prasat Andet
FL.2322
CN F.FL.ALO.ARI.BCW.ALO.AFU.ALO.ALO

Pratihara
USE **Gurjara-Partihara**

Pratt trusses
RT.367
ALT **Pratt truss**
SN Trusses having parallel chords, vertical members in compression, and diagonal members (which slant toward the center) in tension. (DAC)
UF N-trusses
trusses, Pratt
CN V.RT.AFU.AFU.AFU.BCW.CLM.AFU.AFU.AFU.BUE

Praxitelean
FL.2693
CN F.FL.ALO.AXC.ALO.AFU.ALO.BCW.ALO.CLM

prayer books
VW.552 (L,R)
ALT **prayer book**
SN Books containing prayers and other forms of worship. (AHD)
UF books, prayer
CN V.VW.AFU.ALO.AFU.AFU.ALO.BUE.CXA

prayer stools
TG.258
ALT **prayer stool**
UF stools, prayer
CN V.TG.AFU.AFU.ALO.AFU.ALO.ALO.ARI

prayer walls
USE **qibla walls**

prayers
VW.384 (L,R)
ALT **prayer**
SN Use for reverent petitions made to God or another deity. (AHD)
CN V.VW.AFU.AFU.ALO.EFQ

Pre-Angkorean
FL.2317
UF Early Khmer
CN F.FL.ALO.ARI.BCW.ALO.AFU

Pre-Chellean
FL.48
CN F.FL.ALO.AFU.AFU.ALO.AFU.AFU

Pre-Columbian
FL.726 (A,L,B,R)
UF Pre-Conquest
CN F.FL.ALO.ALO.ALO

Pre-Conquest
USE **Pre-Columbian**

Pre-Dorset
FL.793
CN F.FL.ALO.ALO.ALO.AFU.ALO.AFU.ALO.AFU.ALO

Pre-Licchavi
FL.2158
CN F.FL.ALO.ARI.AXC.AFU.AXC.AFU.AFU

Pre-Maurya
USE **Saisunaga-Nanda**

Pre-Monomotapa
FL.131
CN F.FL.ALO.AFU.ALO.ARI.AFU.AFU.AFU

Pre-pottery
FL.1958
CN F.FL.ALO.ARI.ALO.ALO.AFU.AFU.AFU

Pre-pottery Neolithic A
FL.2917
UF PPNA
CN F.FL.ALO.AXC.ARI.AXC.AFU.ALO.AFU

Pre-pottery Neolithic B
FL.2919
UF PPNB
CN F.FL.ALO.AXC.ARI.AXC.AFU.ALO.ARI

Pre-projectile Point
FL.729
CN F.FL.ALO.ALO.ALO.AFU.AFU.AFU

Pre-Raphaelite
FL.3345 (L,B,R)
ALT **Pre-Raphaelitism**
CN F.FL.ALO.BCW.ALO.AXC.DIO.ALO.BZY.ALO

Pré Rup
FL.2364
CN F.FL.ALO.ARI.BCW.ALO.ARI.ALO.BZY

preaching chairs
TG.191
ALT **preaching chair**
SN Chairs having a tall back headed by a lectern so that the chair could be used as a pulpit at open-air services or worship conducted at local houses. (COMMFR)
UF chairs, preaching
chairs, pulpit
pulpit chairs
CN V.TG.AFU.AFU.ALO.AFU.AFU.ALO.DUC

preaching crosses
RK.884
ALT **preaching cross**
SN Crosses sometimes surmounting a pulpit erected outdoors at a preaching place. (W)
UF crosses, preaching
crosses, weeping
weeping crosses
CN V.RK.AFU.ALO.ALO.DOI.AFU.ALO.ALO.ALO

Preah Khan
FL.2365
UF Prah Khan
CN F.FL.ALO.ARI.BCW.ALO.ARI.ALO.CFS

Preah Vihear
FL.2366
UF Prah Viehear
CN F.FL.ALO.ARI.BCW.ALO.ARI.ALO.CLM

preassembled locks
TF.214
ALT **preassembled lock**
SN Factory assembled locks, requiring little or no alterations on installation. (MEANS)
UF locks, mono

locks, preassembled
locks, rigid
locks, union
locks, unit
mono locks
rigid locks
union locks
unit locks
CN V.TF.AFU.AFU.AFU.AFU.DIO.BIQ.AFU.DIO

precast concrete
MT.216 (A,L,B)
SN A concrete member that is cast and cured in other than its final position. (DAC)
UF concrete, precast
CN M.MT.AFU.AFU.AFU.BCW.AFU.ARI.AXC

precast piles
RT.164
ALT **precast pile**
SN Reinforced concrete piles manufactured in a casting plant or at the site. (STEIN)
UF piles, precast
CN V.RT.AFU.AFU.AFU.AXC.BUE.ALO.ALO.AFU.AXC

Preceramic
FL.1132
CN F.FL.ALO.ALO.ALO.ARI.AXC.AFU.AFU

precincts
RG.246 (L,B)
ALT **precinct**
UF wards
CN V.RG.ALO.AFU.AFU.ALO.ARI

precincts, shopping
USE **shopping districts**

precincts, voting
USE **election districts**

precious metal
MT.469 (L)
UF metal, precious
CN M.MT.AFU.AFU.AFU.BZY.AFU.ARI.AFU

precious stones
MT.573 (L,R)
SN Use for gems considered more valuable than others, especially diamonds, sapphires, emeralds, rubies, and sometimes pearls.
UF jewels
stones, precious
CN M.MT.AFU.AFU.AFU.CFS.ALO.ARI

precipitated chalk
MT.48
SN Pure, artificial calcium carbonate frequently a by-product of drug and chemical manufacturing. Used industrially as an inert pigment, as well as in gesso grounds and pastel crayons. (MAYER)
UF chalk, precipitated
CN M.MT.AFU.AFU.AFU.ARI.ALO.ALO

precipitation
BM.749 (L)
CN B.BM.CFS.ALO.AXC.ALO.BIQ

précis
USE **abstracts**

precision drawing
USE **drafting**

Precisionist
FL.1753 (L,R)
ALT **Precisionism**
UF Cubist-Realist
Cubo-Realist
Immaculate
CN F.FL.ALO.ALO.BCW.AFU.CFS.BCW

Preclassic
FL.962
UF Archaic (Preclassic)
Formative
CN F.FL.ALO.ALO.ALO.ALO.AFU.AFU.ALO

Preclassic, Early
USE **Early Preclassic**

Preclassic, Late
USE **Late Preclassic**

Preclassic, Middle
USE **Middle Preclassic**

predellas
RT.1220 (A,L,R)
ALT **predella**
SN Ledges at the backs of Christian altars and, by extension, bases of large altarpieces decorated with images related to the main panels above.
CN V.RT.AFU.BUE.ALO.ALO.ALO.ARI

Predynastic (Egyptian)
FL.2772
CN F.FL.ALO.AXC.ALO.ARI.AFU.AFU

prefabrication
KT.40
ALT **prefabricated**
SN The making of components, usually standardized and factory-made, that are later assembled during the construction of an object or structure.
CN K.KT.AFU.ALO.BCW.ARI.AFU.CFS

prehistoric
FL.4 (A,L,R)
CN F.FL.AFU.ARI

Prei Kmeng
FL.2323
CN F.FL.ALO.ARI.BCW.ALO.AFU.ALO.ARI

preliminary design drawings
USE **preliminary drawings**

preliminary designs
USE **preliminary drawings**

preliminary drawings
VD.102
ALT **preliminary drawing**
SN Done early in a design process for art or architecture; more finished than sketches.
UF designs, preliminary
drawings, preliminary
preliminary design drawings
preliminary designs
preliminary schemes
schemes, preliminary
CN V.VD.AFU.ALO.BOK

preliminary drawings (underdrawings)
USE **underdrawings**

preliminary schemes
USE **preliminary drawings**

preliminary sketches
VB.11 (L,R)
ALT **preliminary sketch**
SN Use for aids to the initial visualization of a design, especially, but not limited to, drawings. Less finished than **preliminary drawings** or **preparatory drawings.**
UF croquis
developmental sketches
initial sketches
outline sketches
pensées, premières
premières pensées
schizzi
sketches, developmental
sketches, initial
sketches, outline
sketches, preliminary
CN V.VB.AFU.AFU.BCW.AXC

preliminary sketches (underdrawings)
USE **underdrawings**

preliminary specifications
VW.801
ALT **preliminary specification**
SN Specifications, often accompanying preliminary drawings, that briefly list the materials and finishes to be used in a building project and serve as the basis for preliminary cost estimates. (STEIN)
UF specifications, preliminary
CN V.VW.AFU.ARI.AFU.ARI.AFU.ARI.BUE

preliminary studies
USE **preparatory studies**

premier art roman
USE **First Romanesque**

premieres
KM.128 (L)
UF first performances
performances, first
CN K.KM.AFU.DCU.AFU

premières pensées
USE **preliminary sketches**

prep schools
USE **preparatory schools**

preparation
USE **preparing**

preparators
HG.204
ALT **preparator**
SN People who prepare objects for exhibition.
CN H.HG.AFU.AXC.AXC.AXC.ARI

preparators, exhibition
USE **exhibition designers**

preparatory drawings
VD.105
ALT **preparatory drawing**
SN Done in preparation for further work, most often for work in a medium other than drawing, especially for printmaking. More finished than sketches. For drawings done in preparation for architectural construction, use other terms, such as **preliminary drawings** or **design drawings.**
UF designs, presentation
designs, proposed
drawings, display
drawings, preparatory
presentation drawings, architectural
CN V.VD.AFU.ALO.BUE

preparatory schools
RK.828 (L,B)
ALT **preparatory school**
SN Use for private schools intended to prepare students for more advanced formal education.
UF finishing schools
prep schools
schools, finishing
schools, preparatory
CN V.RK.AFU.ALO.ALO.CXA.ARI.ARI.AFU.ALO

preparatory studies
VB.62 (L,R)
ALT **preparatory study**
SN More finished than **preliminary sketches** and more concentrated on one portion of a design than **preparatory drawings.** Not appropriate with regard to architecture; then prefer **studies** or **detail studies.**
UF preliminary studies
studies, preliminary
studies, preparatory
CN V.VB.AFU.ALO.BOK.AXC

prepared paper
MT.1936
SN Paper having an applied coating that makes it suitable for drawing in metalpoint.
UF coated paper
grounded paper
paper, coated
paper, grounded
paper, prepared
CN M.MT.AFU.AFU.ARI.ALO.ALO.AXC.ARI.AXC.ARI

preparing
KT.591 (L,B)
ALT **prepared**
SN The action or process of making something ready for use or service or of getting ready for some occasion, test, or duty. (WCOL)
UF preparation
CN K.KT.AFU.ALO.EWY

Presbyterian
BM.641 (L,B)
CN B.BM.BZY.AFU.ALO.ARI.CLM

presbyteries
RM.327 (B)
ALT **presbytery**
SN That part in the eastern arm of a church between the choir and the sanctuary, usually reserved for the clergy. (IGA)
CN V.RM.AFU.DIO.AXC.ALO.AFU.DOI

preschool education
KD.122 (L)
UF education, nursery school
education, preschool
nursery school education
CN K.KD.AFU.ALO.BOK.AFU.AFU.AFU

prescriptions
VW.380 (L)
ALT **prescription**
SN Directions or orders of remedy for a disease or illness.
CN V.VW.AFU.AFU.ALO.DUC.BCW

presence chambers
RM.157
ALT **presence chamber**
SN Rooms where great personages formally receive company.
UF audience halls
chambers, presence
halls, audience
presence rooms
rooms, presence
CN V.RM.AFU.DIO.ALO.CLM.AFU

presence rooms
USE **presence chambers**

presence, real
USE **transubstantiation**

presentation albums
VW.491
ALT **presentation album**
UF albums, presentation
CN V.VW.AFU.ALO.AFU.AFU.AFU.ALO.BCW

presentation designs
USE **presentation drawings**

presentation drawings
VD.106 (A,L)
ALT **presentation drawing**
SN Use for architectural drawings presented to a client to illustrate how the building will look and function.
UF architectural presentation drawings
designs, presentation
designs, proposed
display drawings
drawings, display
drawings, presentation
presentation designs
presentation drawings, architectural
proposed designs
CN V.VD.AFU.ALO.BZY

presentation drawings (gifts)
VD.107
ALT **presentation drawing (gift)**
SN Finished drawings presented by the artist to a friend or patron; usually used with regard to the Renaissance-Baroque period.
UF drawings, presentation (gifts)
CN V.VD.AFU.ALO.CFS

presentation drawings, architectural
USE **preparatory drawings**
presentation drawings

preservation
KG.130 (A,L,B,R)
SN Designates actions taken to prevent further changes or deterioration in objects, sites, or structures. When such actions are taken on buildings or other structures specifically for cultural, aesthetic, or historic reasons, use **historic preservation.** When changes return an object or structure to a state of historical correctness, use **restoration.** For actions taken to return to sound condition an already deteriorated structure, use **rehabilitating.** For the activity of keeping people and things safe from harm or deterioration generally, use **protecting.**
CN K.KG.AFU.AFU.BCW.ARI

preservation districts
USE **historic districts**

preservation, historic
USE **historic preservation**

preservationists
HG.731 (A)
ALT **preservationist**
CN H.HG.AFU.BCW.FCS

preservationists, historic
USE **historic preservationists**

preservatives
MT.2635 (B)
SN Substances added to materials or food products to preserve them

against decay, discoloration, or spoilage.
CN M.MT.AFU.ARI.HCQ

preservatives, wood
USE **wood preservatives**

preserves
RG.167 (L)
ALT **preserve**
SN Areas, usually closed to the public, set apart for the propagation of game or fish and where some hunting is permitted.
UF shooting preserves
CN V.RG.AFU.AFU.DOI.BUE

preserves, nature
USE **nature preserves**

preserves, wildlife
USE **wildlife refuges**

preserving
USE **protecting**

presidential libraries
RK.712 (A,L)
ALT **presidential library**
UF libraries, presidential
CN V.RK.AFU.ALO.ALO.CRG.AXC.ARI.BIQ

presidential papers
VW.1007 (L)
ALT **presidential paper**
UF papers, presidential
CN V.VW.AFU.ARI.ALO.BCW.AFU.AFU.ALO.ALO

presidents
HG.654 (L,R)
ALT **president**
SN Elected officials serving as both chief of state and chief political executive in a republic having a presidential government; may also designate the heads of organizations such as banks, clubs, and corporations when used as the official job title for those positions. (W)
CN H.HG.AFU.AXC.CFS.AFU.AFU.ALO

presidios
RD.35 (A)
ALT **presidio**
SN Use for military settlements established by the Spanish in America often as garrisoned forts or outposts.
CN V.RD.AFU.ALO.ALO.ARI

press-back chairs
TG.148
ALT **press-back chair**
UF chairs, press-back
CN V.TG.AFU.AFU.ALO.AFU.AFU.AFU.NIE.DCU

press beds
TG.345
ALT **press bed**
SN Folding beds built into a cabinet which outwardly resembles a press or chest. (BEARD)
UF bed-chests
beds, closet
beds, cupboard
beds, press
beds, turn-up
bedsteads, cabinet
cabinet bedsteads
closet beds
cupboard beds
turn-up beds
CN V.TG.AFU.AFU.ARI.AFU.AFU.BIQ.AFU.BIQ

press beds, library
USE **library press beds**

press clippings
USE **clippings**

press cupboards
TG.518 (N)
ALT **press cupboard**
SN Large, but fairly low, cupboards with both the upper and lower sections containing enclosed storage space; of a type made in 16th- and 17th-century England and 17th-century America. Distinct from **court cupboards** which have an enclosed storage cabinet above and an open shelf or shelves below.
UF cupboards, press
CN V.TG.AFU.AFU.AXC.ALO.BUE.CXA.ARI

press cuttings
USE **clippings**

press notices
USE **press releases**

press photographers
USE **news photographers**

press photographs
USE **news photographs**

press photography
USE **photojournalism**

press releases
VW.61 (N)
ALT **press release**
SN Official or authoritative statements giving information for publication in newspapers or periodicals. (GAHLM)
UF notices, press
press notices
releases, press
CN V.VW.AFU.AFU.AFU.DUC.AFU

pressed brick
MT.138
SN A stiff mud brick made under high pressure; it is homogeneous, and has increased density and strength. (MH)
UF brick, pressed
CN M.MT.AFU.AFU.AFU.AXC.ALO.AFU.AXC.ALO.ARI

pressed wood
USE **compressed wood**

presses
TG.513
ALT **press**
SN Term of Medieval origin generally applied to tall cupboards with doors and shelves for storing linens, clothing, and kitchen utensils. For presses with sliding shelves behind closed doors, use **clothes presses.**
CN V.TG.AFU.AFU.AXC.ALO.BUE.CXA

presses à vêtements
USE **clothes presses**

presses, book (bookcases)
USE **bookcases**

presses, china
USE **china cabinets**

presses, cloth
USE **clothes presses**

presses, clothes
USE **clothes presses**

presses, drill
USE **drill presses**

presses, linen
USE **linen presses**

presses, low clothes
USE **low clothes presses**

presses, punch
USE **punch presses**

presses, wing clothes
USE **wing clothes presses**

pressing
KT.155
ALT **pressed**
CN K.KT.AFU.ALO.DOI.DIO

pressmen
HG.458
ALT **pressman**
UF pressmen, printing
printing pressmen
CN H.HG.AFU.AXC.BUE.ALO.CFS.BOK

pressmen, printing
USE **pressmen**

pressure
BM.930 (L)
CN B.BM.CFS.AXC.BUE

pressure-treated wood
MT.1452
UF wood, pressure-treated
CN M.MT.AFU.AFU.ALO.BIQ.DCU.ALO.CLM

pressure valves, mixing
USE **mixing pressure valves**

pressure welding
KT.812 (L)
ALT **pressure welded**
UF welding, pressure
CN K.KT.AFU.ALO.HOE.BCW.ALO.AFU.ALO.BIQ

pressure, air
USE **air pressure**

pressure, atmospheric
USE **atmospheric pressure**

pressure, earth
USE **earth pressure**

pressure, vapor
USE **vapor pressure**

pressure, water
USE **water pressure**

pressurized stairwells
RM.95
ALT **pressurized stairwell**
UF stairwells, pressurized
CN V.RM.AFU.DIO.ALO.ARI.BCW.AFU

prestressed concrete
MT.217 (A,L,B)
SN Concrete in which effective internal stresses are induced artificially, usually by means of tensioned steel, prior to loading the structure. (INFOD)
UF concrete, prestressed
CN M.MT.AFU.AFU.AFU.BCW.AFU.ARI.BCW

prestressed concrete, post-tensioned
USE **post-tensioned prestressed concrete**

prestressing
KT.648 (B)
ALT **prestressed**
SN Applying a load to a structure or material, such as concrete, deforming it so that it will withstand a working load more effectively or so that it will deflect less. (DAC)
CN K.KT.AFU.ALO.GLI.AFU.AXC

pretensioning
KT.650
SN A method of prestressing reinforced concrete in which the tendons, such as steel cables or rods, are tensioned before the concrete has hardened. (DAC)
CN K.KT.AFU.ALO.GLI.AFU.AXC.ALO

pretzel-back chairs
TG.154
ALT **pretzel-back chair**
SN Late 18th-century American chairs with pierced and intertwined slats and generally associated with Philadelphia cabinetmakers.
UF chairs, pretzel-back
pretzel chairs
CN V.TG.AFU.AFU.ALO.AFU.AFU.AFU.NIE.DUC.ALO

pretzel chairs
USE **pretzel-back chairs**

Preussischblau
USE **Prussian blue**

prevention of crime
USE **crime prevention**

prevention, crime
USE **crime prevention**

prevention, fire
USE **fire prevention**

prevention, noise
USE **noise control**

previews
KM.141 (L)
CN K.KM.AFU.DUC

price books
VW.535
ALT **price book**
UF books, price
CN V.VW.AFU.ALO.AFU.AFU.ALO.BOK

price lists
VW.284
ALT **price list**
SN Statements or lists of the prevailing prices of merchandise, stock, or other items for sale. (GAHLM)
UF lists, price
prices current
CN V.VW.AFU.AFU.AFU.FZU.BCW.ALO.BOK

prices
BM.405 (L)
SN Quantities of money, goods, or services that are exchanged or demanded in barter or sale for others.
CN B.BM.ARI.ELK

prices current
USE **price lists**

prick punches
TB.675 (N)
ALT **prick punch**
SN Pointed steel punches which are struck with a hammer; used to mark metal. (DAC)
UF punches, prick
CN V.TB.AFU.BCW.BIQ.AFU.ALO.BZY.BOK

pricking
KT.745
ALT **pricked**
CN K.KT.AFU.ALO.HCQ.ALO.BCW

prie-dieu chairs
USE **prie-dieus**

prie-dieus
TG.192 (N)
ALT **prie-dieu**
UF chairs, devotional
chairs, vesper
devotional chairs
prie-dieu chairs
vesper chairs
CN V.TG.AFU.AFU.ALO.AFU.AFU.ALO.DZW

priests
HG.232 (L,R)
ALT **priest**
CN H.HG.AFU.AXC.AXC.BIQ.AFU.ARI.DUC

Primaire
USE **Early Gothic**

primary colors
BM.115
SN Use for, variously, traditional paint primaries of red, yellow, and blue; psychological primaries of red, yellow, blue, and green; and physical primaries of red, blue, and green.
UF colors, primary
CN B.BM.AFU.AFU.ARI.BOK.ALO.AFU.BOK

primary education
KD.124 (L)
SN Branch of education covering kindergarten through grade 3. (ERIC)
UF education, primary
CN K.KD.AFU.ALO.BOK.AFU.ALO.AFU

primary roads
RK.1554 (B)
ALT **primary road**
UF main roads
roads, main
roads, primary
CN V.RK.ALO.ALO.BIQ.ARI.ALO.BOK

primary schools
USE **elementary schools**

primary supports
USE **supports (artists' materials)**

primary wood
MT.1411
UF wood, primary
CN M.MT.AFU.AFU.ALO.BIQ.DCU.AFU.ALO.ARI

primavera
USE **white mahogany**

prime contractors
HG.618
ALT **prime contractor**
SN Contractors who have contracts directly with an owner. (STEIN)
UF contractors, prime
CN H.HG.AFU.AXC.BZY.ALO.ALO

prime lenses
USE **standard lenses**

primer
MT.2724

SN A white ground or other coating applied to a surface before painting to give uniform texture and absorbency. (MAYER)
UF undercoat
CN M.MT.AFU.ARI.IFM.AXC

primer, polymer
USE **polymer primer**

primers
VW.357 (L)
ALT **primer**
SN Elementary textbooks, or books that cover the basic elements of a subject. (AHD)
CN V.VW.AFU.AFU.ALO.CXA.BOK

priming
KT.244
ALT **primed**
SN The application of a first coating, such as paint, varnish, or size, to a surface that is to be painted. (W)
CN K.KT.AFU.ALO.DUC.CXA.ALO. ARI.AFU

primitive arches
USE **miter arches**

primitive architecture
BM.228 (B)
SN Used as the conventional general designation for indigenous traditional architecture of the societies of Africa, Southeast Asia, the Pacific, and the Americas that, until recently, had remained undominated or uninfluenced by European, Asian, or Pre-Columbian Middle or South American civilizations; prefer specific terms for the styles or periods of such architecture. For the deliberately unsophisticated and unschooled approach to artistic creation, use **primitivism.**
UF architecture, primitive
CN B.BM.AFU.ARI.AXC.BCW.AFU

primitive art
BM.250 (L,R)
SN Use for unsophisticated and unschooled or self-taught art of any culture or period, largely uninfluenced by previous or contemporary work. Also used as a general designation for the creative works and expression of peoples whose cultures have remained undominated or uninfluenced by European, Asian, or Pre-Columbian Middle or South American civilizations; prefer specific terms for the styles or periods of such art. For the deliberately unsophisticated and unschooled approach to artistic creation, use **primitivism.**
UF art, primitive
CN B.BM.AFU.ARI.BCW.ERE

primitivism
BM.194 (L)
ALT **primitive**
SN Use generally to mean the deliberately unsophisticated and unschooled approach to artistic creation. For the Russian art movement, active from about 1905 to 1920, which combined influences from Russian folk art with ideas borrowed from Cubism and Futurism, use **Primitivist.** Distinct from **primitive art** and **primitive architecture,** which are conventional designations for the work of peoples whose cultures have remained undominated by European, Asian, or Pre-Columbian Middle or South American civilizations.
UF neoprimitivism
CN B.BM.AFU.AFU.AXC.CLM.BUE

Primitivist
FL.3416 (R)
ALT **Primitivism**
SN Russian art movement, active from about 1905 to 1920, which combined influences from Russian folk art with ideas borrowed from Cubism and Futurism.(THDAT) For the deliberately unsophisticated and unschooled approach to artistic creation, use **primitivism.**
CN F.FL.ALO.BCW.ALO.AXC.DIO. BZY.ALO.ARI

primrose yellow
USE **zinc yellow**

Prince Albert fir
USE **western hemlock**

princes
HG.700 (L,R)
ALT **prince**
CN H.HG.AFU.AXC.CFS.CRG.CFS

princess posts
RT.513
ALT **princess post**
SN In a truss, vertical posts between the queen post and the wall to supplement the support of the queen post. (DAC)
UF posts, princess
CN V.RT.AFU.AFU.AFU.BIQ.ARI.ALO. ALO.ARI.AFU.ALO

princesses
HG.701
ALT **princess**
CN H.HG.AFU.AXC.CFS.CRG.CLM

principal rafter roofs
USE **double-framed roofs**

principal rafters
RT.502
ALT **principal rafter**
SN Diagonal members of a roof truss. (RS)
UF blades (rafters)
rafters, principal
CN V.RT.AFU.AFU.AFU.BIQ.ARI.ALO. ALO.AFU.AXC

principals
HG.298 (L)
ALT **principal**
SN Directors or heads of schools. (RHDEL2)
CN H.HG.AFU.AXC.BCW.ALO.ARI.ALO

principals, roof
USE **roof trusses**

print cabinets
TG.425
ALT **print cabinet**
UF cabinets, print
CN V.TG.AFU.AFU.AXC.ALO.ARI. ALO.AXC.ALO

print dryers
TB.335 (N)
ALT **print dryer**
SN Vented cabinets equipped with suspending rods for drying films after processing. (LANG)
UF cabinets, drying
dryers, print
drying cabinets
CN V.TB.AFU.ARI.CLM.ARI.ALO.BZY

print enlargers
USE **enlargers**

print-out paper
USE **printing-out paper**

print process, carbon
USE **carbon process**

print, wax
USE **wax resist cloth**

printed ephemera
USE **ephemera**

printed forms
USE **forms**

printer's flowers
USE **fleurons**

printers
TB.163 (L,N,R)
ALT **printer**
SN Output devices that convert coded information from the processor into a readable form on paper. (DOC)
CN V.TB.AFU.ARI.BCW.AXC.AXC.ALO

printers (people)
HG.459 (L,R)
ALT **printer (person)**
SN Use for people in the commercial printing trade. For artists who make prints, use **printmakers.**
CN H.HG.AFU.AXC.BUE.ALO.CFS.BUE

printers' marks

VW.754 (L,R)
ALT **printer's mark**
SN Marks used by printers or publishers as trademarks. (ALAG)
UF devices, typographical
marks, printers'
marks, publishers'
publishers' marks
typographical devices
CN V.VW.AFU.ALO.ALO.AFU.AXC.AXC.DCU

printers' ornaments
VW.755 (L,R)
ALT **printer's ornament**
UF ornaments, printers'
ornaments, type
type ornaments
CN V.VW.AFU.ALO.ALO.AFU.AXC.AXC.DCU.AFU

printers, contact
USE **contact printers**

printers, country
USE **job printers**

printers, daisywheel
USE **daisywheel printers**

printers, dot matrix
USE **dot matrix printers**

printers, impact
USE **impact printers**

printers, impression
USE **impression printers**

printers, ink jet
USE **ink jet printers**

printers, job
USE **job printers**

printers, laser
USE **laser printers**

printers, line
USE **line printers**

printers, nonimpact
USE **nonimpact printers**

printers, page
USE **page printers**

printers, rectification
USE **rectification printers**

printing
KT.746 (L,B,R)
ALT **printed**
SN Use for processes in which an image is transferred, usually to paper or cloth; most often transferred from a plate, block, stone, or screen, but also includes the making of photographic prints. For the production of prints in a fine arts context, prefer **printmaking.**
CN K.KT.AFU.ALO.HCQ.ALO.BIQ

printing-out paper
MT.1946
UF paper, print-out
paper, printing-out
POP (paper)
print-out paper
CN M.MT.AFU.AFU.ARI.ALO.ALO.AXC.ARI.BOK.AXC

printing paper
MT.1954
UF paper, printing
CN M.MT.AFU.AFU.ARI.ALO.ALO.AXC.ARI.BUE

printing plants
RK.619 (A,L,B)
ALT **printing plant**
UF plants, printing
CN V.RK.AFU.ALO.ALO.CLM.ALO.ALO.AFU.ARI

printing pressmen
USE **pressmen**

printing processes, iron
USE **iron processes**

printing, anastatic
USE **anastatic printing**

printing, aniline
USE **aniline process**

printing, bat
USE **bat printing**

printing, block
USE **block printing**

printing, collagraph
USE **collagraph printing**

printing, color
USE **color printing**

printing, contact
USE **contact printing**

printing, double
USE **double-printing**

printing, electrostatic
USE **electrostatic printing**

printing, flock
USE **flocking**

printing, gravure
USE **photogravure**

printing, gum
USE **gum bichromate process**

printing, imbibition
USE **dye transfer process**

printing, intaglio
USE **intaglio printing**

printing, nature
USE **nature printing**

printing, offset
USE **offset printing**

printing, planographic
USE **planographic printing**

printing, potato
USE **potato printing**

printing, projection
USE **enlarging**

printing, raised-letter
USE **thermography**

printing, relief
USE **relief printing**

printing, resist
USE **resist dyeing**

printing, second
USE **double-printing**

printing, silk screen
USE **serigraphy**

printing, surface
USE **relief printing**

printing, tile block
USE **tile block printing**

printing, transfer
USE **transfer printing**

printing, wax
USE **cerography**

printing, wood-block
USE **wood-block printing**

printing, woodcut
USE **wood-block printing**

printmakers
HG.125 (L,R)
ALT **printmaker**
SN Persons who prepare, conceive, and develop drawings and other art work and prepare printmaking media used to print fine arts graphics.(DOT) For persons in the commercial printing trade, use **printers (people).**
UF artists, graphic (printmakers)
graphic artists (printmakers)
CN H.HG.AFU.AXC.AXC.AFU.AFU.ALO.AXC.DUC

printmaking
KT.440 (L,R)
SN Use for the process of making prints as works of art. For the production of other types of printed material, use **printing.**
UF arts, graphic (printmaking)
graphic arts (printmaking)
CN K.KT.AFU.ALO.DUC.DUC.AFU

printmaking techniques
KT.441 (L)
CN K.KT.AFU.ALO.DUC.DUC.ALO

printouts

VW.609
ALT **printout**
SN The printed output of a computer. (RHDEL2)
UF computer printouts
printouts, computer
CN V.VW.AFU.ALO.AFU.CRG

printouts, computer
USE **printouts**

prints (photographs)
USE **photographic prints**

prints, albumen
USE **albumen prints**

prints, albumen silver
USE **albumen prints**

prints, altered (photographs)
USE **manipulated photographs**

prints, black-and-white (photographs)
USE **black-and-white prints (photographs)**

prints, blackline
USE **blackline prints**

prints, blue process
USE **blueprints**

prints, blueline
USE **blueline prints**

prints, boudoir
USE **boudoir prints**

prints, bromoil
USE **bromoil prints**

prints, brownline
USE **brownline prints**

prints, cabinet
USE **cabinet photographs**

prints, calotype
USE **salted paper prints**

prints, cameo
USE **cameo prints**

prints, carbon
USE **carbon prints**

prints, collodion
USE **collodion prints**

prints, collotype
USE **collotypes**

prints, color (photographs)
USE **color prints (photographs)**

prints, combination
USE **composite photographs**

prints, contact
USE **contact prints**

prints, diazo
USE **diazotypes**

prints, diffusion transfer
USE **instant camera photographs**

prints, dye diffusion transfer
USE **dye diffusion transfer prints**

prints, dye transfer
USE **dye transfer prints**

prints, etched daguerreotype
USE **etched daguerreotype prints**

prints, gelatin
USE **gelatin silver prints**

prints, gelatin silver
USE **gelatin silver prints**

prints, gravure (photomechanical)
USE **photogravures**

prints, gum
USE **gum bichromate prints**

prints, gum bichromate
USE **gum bichromate prints**

prints, imperial
USE **imperial prints**

prints, instant
USE **instant camera photographs**

prints, iron process
USE **blueprints**

prints, Kodak (TM) instant
USE **dye diffusion transfer prints**

prints, line block
USE **line photoengravings**

prints, negative
USE **negative prints**

prints, oil
USE **oil prints**

prints, palladium
USE **palladium prints**

prints, panel
USE **panel prints**

prints, photographic
USE **photographic prints**

prints, photogravure
USE **photogravures**

prints, photomechanical
USE **photomechanical prints**

prints, pigment
USE **pigment prints**

prints, platinum
USE **platinum prints**

prints, process
USE **photomechanical prints**

prints, promenade
USE **promenade prints**

prints, proof
USE **contact sheets**

prints, salt
USE **salted paper prints**

prints, salt paper
USE **salted paper prints**

prints, salted paper
USE **salted paper prints**

prints, sepia
USE **sepia prints**

prints, sepia process
USE **sepia prints**

prints, silver albumen
USE **albumen prints**

prints, silver gelatin
USE **gelatin silver prints**

prints, Van Dyke (brownprints)
USE **brownprints**

prints, Van Dyke (sepia prints)
USE **sepia prints**

prints, victoria
USE **victoria prints**

prints, vintage
USE **vintage prints**

prints, white line
USE **blueprints**

priories
RG.199 (A,L,B,R)
ALT **priory**
SN Religious houses that rank immediately below abbeys and are presided over by a prior or prioress.
CN V.RG.AFU.AFU.DUC.BIQ.BCW

prismatic glass
MT.283
SN Glass in which one surface is smooth, while the other is marked by ridges of prismatic section; illuminates very large internal spaces. (RS)
UF glass, prismatic
CN M.MT.AFU.AFU.AFU.BIQ.AFU.AXC.CLM

prison camps
RG.50 (L)
ALT **prison camp**
UF camps, prison
camps, work
work camps
CN V.RG.AFU.AFU.BCW.ARI

prison locks
TF.239
ALT **prison lock**
UF locks, prison
CN V.TF.AFU.AFU.AFU.AFU.DIO.BIQ.ALO.ALO.BUE

prisoners
HG.794 (L,R)

ALT **prisoner**
UF convicts
CN H.HG.AFU.BOK.BZY

prisons
RK.719 (A,L,B,R)
ALT **prison**
SN Use for places of confinement and correction run by state or federal authorities for those adults convicted to sentences over one year for serious crimes; developed since the late 18th century and generally characterized by cell and corridor plans with separation by offense and sex, and programs of rehabilitation provided as means toward prisoner reform. Use **jails** for places for offenders sentenced either for lesser crimes or for terms up to one year.
UF houses, penitentiary
newgates
penitentiaries
penitentiary houses
CN V.RK.AFU.ALO.ALO.CXA.AFU.AXC

prisons, debtor's
USE **debtor's prisons**

prisons, federal
USE **federal prisons**

prisons, high-security
USE **maximum-security prisons**

prisons, maximum-security
USE **maximum-security prisons**

prisons, medium-security
USE **medium-security prisons**

prisons, military
USE **military prisons**

prisons, minimum-security
USE **minimum-security prisons**

prisons, open
USE **open prisons**

prisons, state
USE **state prisons**

prisons, super-security
USE **maximum-security prisons**

privacy
BM.592 (L,B)
CN B.BM.BUE.BZY

private chapels
RM.310 (B)
ALT **private chapel**
UF chapels, domestic
chapels, private
domestic chapels
CN V.RM.AFU.DIO.AXC.ALO.AFU.AXC.BIQ

private collections
HG.850 (L,R)
ALT **private collection**
UF collections, private
CN H.HG.ALO.BUE.ARI

private correspondence
USE **personal correspondence**

private gardens
RK.1439 (B)
ALT **private garden**
UF gardens, private
CN V.RK.ALO.AFU.AFU.BCW.ALO

private instructors
USE **tutors**

private libraries
RK.694 (L,B)
ALT **private library**
UF libraries, private
CN V.RK.AFU.ALO.ALO.CRG.AXC.AFU.ALO

private papers
USE **personal papers**

private roads
RK.1555 (A,L)
ALT **private road**
UF private streets
roads, private
streets, private
CN V.RK.ALO.ALO.BIQ.ARI.ALO.BUE

private schools
RK.826 (L,B)
ALT **private school**
SN Schools that are established, conducted, and primarily supported by a nongovernmental agency. (W)
UF independent schools
schools, independent
schools, private
CN V.RK.AFU.ALO.ALO.CXA.ARI.ARI.AFU

private streets
USE **private roads**

private teachers
USE **tutors**

privies
RM.70 (L,N,R)
ALT **privy**
SN Rooms or spaces that are within buildings and have one or more seats and a pit used as toilets which lack plumbing facilities, distinguished from **outhouses** which are separate structures in domestic contexts containing similar arrangements of toilet facilities. For rooms or spaces with toilets having plumbing, use **bathrooms** or **lavatories (rooms)**.
UF houses, necessary
necessaries
necessary houses
offices (privies)
CN V.RM.AFU.DIO.ALO.ALO.BCW

prizes
USE **awards**

probability
BM.829 (L)
CN B.BM.CFS.ARI.CRG.ALO.BCW

probate inventories
USE **estate inventories**

probate records
VW.1016 (L)
ALT **probate record**
SN Records generated by probate courts, which have general powers over the probate of wills, administration of estates, and, in some states, over the appointment of guardians or the adoption of minors. (BLACKS)
UF records, probate
CN V.VW.AFU.ARI.ALO.BCW.AFU.ALO.ALO.AFU.AFU

probating
KG.210
SN Establishing the authenticity or validity of a will. (RHDEL2)
CN K.KG.AFU.ALO.BCW.CLM

problems, social
USE **social issues**

procathedrals
RK.1103
ALT **procathedral**
SN Churches used temporarily as cathedrals, as, for instance, during repairs or during creation of a new diocese.
CN V.RK.AFU.ALO.ALO.FCS.BIQ.ALO.ALO.ARI

Procedural art
USE **Process art**

procedure, rules of
USE **rules of procedure**

procedures
VW.359
ALT **procedure**
SN Records of established forms or methods for conducting the affairs of a business, legislative body, or court of law. (AHD)
CN V.VW.AFU.AFU.ALO.CXA.BUE

proceedings
VW.466
ALT **proceeding**
SN Records of meetings of a society or other organization, usually published, and frequently accompanied by abstracts or reports of papers presented. (GAHLM)
UF conference proceedings
conference reports
proceedings, conference
reports, conference
transactions
CN V.VW.AFU.AFU.ALO.FIM.AXC

proceedings, bankruptcy
USE **bankruptcy proceedings**

proceedings, conference
USE **proceedings**

Process art
FL.3748 (R)
UF art, Procedural
art, Process
Procedural art
CN F.FL.ALO.BUE.ARI.HIK

process line engravings
USE **line photoengravings**

process philosophy
KD.72 (A,L)
UF philosophy, process
CN K.KD.AFU.AFU.BOK.BZY

process prints
USE **photomechanical prints**

process white
USE **blanc fixe**

processes
KT.3 (L)
ALT **process**
SN Use for the actions or procedures followed to produce some end. When emphasis is on the manner or method by which those actions or procedures are performed, use **techniques.**
CN K.KT.AFU.AFU.AFU

processes, photomechanical
USE **photomechanical processes**

processes, screen
USE **screen processes**

processing
KT.592
ALT **processed**
CN K.KT.AFU.ALO.FCS

processing plants, beverage
USE **beverage processing plants**

processing plants, food
USE **food processing plants**

processing, data
USE **data processing**

processing, electronic data
USE **data processing**

processional ways
RK.1540 (A)
ALT **processional way**
UF ways, processional
CN V.RK.ALO.ALO.BIQ.ARI.AFU.ALO.ALO.ARI

processions
KM.25 (L,R)
SN Use for the action of a group of persons moving along in orderly succession in a formal ceremonial context. For large public processions of a festive nature, often including floats and marching bands and held in honor of an anniversary, person, or event, use **parades.**
CN K.KM.AFU.ARI.ARI.BUE

proclamations
VW.322 (L)
ALT **proclamation**
SN Documents that are publicly announced or officially declared; especially a public notice by an official of some order, intended action, or state of facts. (GAHLM)
CN V.VW.AFU.AFU.ALO.BOK.BCW

procurators
HG.685 (L)
ALT **procurator**
SN Use for imperial officers of the ancient Roman empire entrusted with the management of the financial affairs of a province as agents of the emperor.
CN H.HG.AFU.AXC.CFS.CFS.CFS

procurement
USE **procuring**

procuring
KG.62 (L)
SN Acquisition of goods or services through purchase, lease, or trade.
UF acquiring
procurement
CN K.KG.AFU.AFU.ARI.DOI

produce exchanges
USE **commodity exchanges**

produce stands
RK.147
ALT **produce stand**
UF fruit and vegetable stands
fruit stands
stands, fruit
stands, produce
stands, vegetable
vegetable stands
CN V.RK.AFU.ALO.ALO.ALO.ARI.BCW.ARI

producers
USE **filmmakers**

producers, film
USE **filmmakers**

producers, motion-picture
USE **filmmakers**

product engineers
HG.157
ALT **product engineer**
SN Engineers specializing in designing, building, and testing the prototype of a product. (W)
UF engineers, product
CN H.HG.AFU.AXC.AXC.AFU.AFU.ALO.BCW.BOK.AFU

product photography
USE **advertising photography**

product specifications
VW.802
ALT **product specification**
SN Specifications describing the brand names, trade names, or manufacturers of equipment or material to be used in a building project.
UF specifications, product
CN V.VW.AFU.ARI.AFU.ARI.AFU.ARI.BZY

production
KT.593 (L)
CN K.KT.AFU.ALO.FIM

production drawings
USE **working drawings**

production specialists, film
USE **filmmakers**

production, electric power
USE **electric power production**

production, mass
USE **mass production**

Productivist
USE **Constructivist**

products, bituminous
USE **bituminous materials**

products, clay
USE **clay products**

products, concrete
USE **concrete products**

products, food
USE **food products**

products, metal
USE **metal products**

products, petroleum
USE **petroleum products**

products, wood
USE **wood products**

professional associations
HG.826 (L,B)
ALT **professional association**
UF associations, professional
organizations, professional
professional organizations
CN H.HG.ALO.BCW.BOK

professional directories
VW.411
ALT **professional directory**
UF directories, professional
CN V.VW.AFU.AFU.ALO.EWY.AXC.AFU.AXC

professional employees
USE **professionals**

professional ethics
BM.498 (A,L)

UF ethics, professional
CN B.BM.BIQ.ALO.AFU

professional organizations
USE **professional associations**

professional papers
VW.1062
ALT **professional paper**
UF papers, professional
CN V.VW.AFU.ARI.ALO.CLM

professional portrait photography
USE **commercial portraiture**

professional standards
BM.1160
UF standards, professional
CN B.BM.DIO.AXC.AFU

professionals
HG.768 (L)
ALT **professional**
SN Persons engaged in a particular pursuit, study, or science for gain or livelihood, rather than as amateurs; also persons belonging to the learned professions or any occupation requiring a great deal of training. (W)
UF employees, professional
professional employees
CN H.HG.AFU.BIQ.BOK

professors
HG.300 (L,R)
ALT **professor**
CN H.HG.AFU.AXC.BCW.ALO.ARI.ARI.AFU

profile
USE **outline**

profile plans
USE **profiles**

profile views (figures)
USE **profiles (figures)**

profiles
VD.65
ALT **profile**
SN Use for orthographic drawings of an object or structure seen in a vertical plane. In architecture, most often sections; in shipbuilding ma
UF plans, profile
profile plans
CN V.VD.AFU.AFU.BIQ.ALO.BCW

profiles (figures)
VB.30
ALT **profile (figure)**
SN Use for side views of figures, especially when a clear outline is emphasized. For certain orthographic drawings of objects or structures, use **profiles.**
UF profile views (figures)
views, profile (figures)
CN V.VB.AFU.AFU.BOK.ALO.CFS

profiles, bricklaying
USE **bricklaying profiles**

profiles, exterior (ships)
USE **outboard profiles**

profiles, inboard
USE **inboard profiles**

profiles, interior (ships)
USE **inboard profiles**

profiles, outboard
USE **outboard profiles**

profiles, soil
USE **soil profiles**

profit and loss statements
VW.823 (L)
ALT **profit and loss statement**
SN Statements showing the income and expense accounts of a business over a stated time, the difference being the profit or loss for the period. (BLACKS)
UF statements, profit and loss
CN V.VW.AFU.ARI.AFU.BIQ.BUE.ALO

programmatic architecture
USE **mimetic buildings**

programmed textbooks
VW.521 (L)
ALT **programmed textbook**
UF textbooks, programmed
CN V.VW.AFU.ALO.AFU.AFU.AFU.DIO.AFU

programmers, computer
USE **computer programmers**

programming
KG.156
SN Planning and establishing a sequence or system of actions, events, or instructions. (W)
CN K.KG.AFU.AFU.BIQ.BZY

programming (computers)
USE **computer programming**

programs
VW.68 (L,N)
ALT **program**
SN Brief outlines or explanations of the order to be pursued, or the subjects embraced, especially printed or written lists of the acts, scenes, selections, or other features composing a dramatic, musical, or other performance, with the names of the performers. (GAHLM)
UF briefs (programs)
CN V.VW.AFU.AFU.AFU.ELK

programs, building
USE **building programs**

programs, computer
USE **software**

programs, theater
USE **theater programs**

progress charts
USE **progress schedules**

progress reports
VW.786
ALT **progress report**
UF interim reports
reports, interim
reports, progress
CN V.VW.AFU.ARI.AFU.ALO.CRG.AFU

progress schedules
VW.787 (B)
ALT **progress schedule**
UF charts, progress
progress charts
schedules, progress
CN V.VW.AFU.ARI.AFU.ALO.CRG.ALO

progressions (mathematics)
USE **series (mathematics)**

progressions, arithmetic
USE **arithmetic progressions**

progressive ornament
USE **running ornament**

project architects
HG.88
ALT **project architect**
SN Architects designated to manage their firms' services related to given projects. (GCIT)
UF architects, project
CN H.HG.AFU.AXC.AXC.AFU.AFU.ALO.ALO.BCW

project calendars
VW.788
ALT **project calendar**
UF calendars, project
CN V.VW.AFU.ARI.AFU.ALO.CRG.ARI

project files
VW.598
ALT **project file**
UF files, job
files, master
files, project
job files
master files
CN V.VW.AFU.ALO.AFU.BIQ.ARI.ALO.ALO

project manuals
VW.804
ALT **project manual**
UF job manuals
manuals, job
manuals, project
CN V.VW.AFU.ARI.AFU.ARI.ALO

projected windows
RT.940
ALT **projected window**
SN Windows having one or more rotatable sashes which swing either inward or outward. (DAC)

UF projecting windows
windows, projected
windows, projecting
CN V.RT.AFU.ARI.AFU.AFU.BOK.
AFU.AFU.EWY.ALO.ALO

projecting
DC.41
CN D.DC.AFU.ALO.ARI.DOI

projecting windows
USE **projected windows**

projection
KT.278 (L)
ALT **projected**
SN Technique for representing three-dimensional objects on a two-dimensional surface following strict conventions by which imaginary sight lines project from the observer's eye to the object, transmitting an image of the object to an intervening transparent surface (the picture plane).(EW) Applies especially to technical drawings; with relation to art, use such terms as **one-point perspective** and **parallel perspective.**
CN K.KT.AFU.ALO.DUC.DCU.BOK

projection printing
USE **enlarging**

projection welding
KT.802 (L)
UF welding, projection
CN K.KT.AFU.ALO.HOE.BCW.ALO.
AFU.ALO.ALO.AFU.AFU

projection, axonometric
USE **axonometric projection**

projection, center of
USE **center of projection**

projection, central
USE **central projection**

projection, dimetric
USE **dimetric projection**

projection, isometric
USE **isometric projection**

projection, multiview
USE **multiview projection**

projection, oblique
USE **oblique projection**

projection, orthographic
USE **orthographic projection**

projection, parallel
USE **parallel projection**

projection, perspective
USE **central projection**

projection, trimetric
USE **trimetric projection**

projections, anisometric
USE **trimetric drawings**

projections, axonometric
USE **axonometric drawings**

projections, cabinet
USE **cabinet oblique drawings**

projections, cavalier
USE **cavalier oblique drawings**

projections, dimetric
USE **dimetric drawings**

projections, isometric
USE **isometric drawings**

projections, oblique
USE **oblique drawings**

projections, orthogonal
USE **orthographic drawings**

projections, orthographic
USE **orthographic drawings**

projections, trimetric
USE **trimetric drawings**

projects
BM.41
SN Use generally for proposed undertakings or creations, including the creation of works of art or architecture, or for the actual carrying out of such proposals. When emphasis is on specific conceptual schemes for the organization or appearance of graphic works, objects, structures, or systems, use **designs.**
CN B.BM.AFU.AFU.ALO.CLM

projects, housing
USE **housing projects**

projects, mixed-use
USE **mixed-use developments**

projects, rendered
USE **renderings**

projects, student
USE **student projects**

projects, unbuilt
USE **unbuilt projects**

projects, unrealized
USE **unexecuted designs**

projets rendus
USE **renderings**

proletariat
HG.891 (L)
CN H.HG.ALO.DOI.ALO.AXC.AFU

promenade card photographs
USE **promenade prints**

promenade card photoprints
USE **promenade prints**

promenade prints
VJ.81
ALT **promenade print**
SN Card photographs on mounts measuring about 7 by 4 inches.
UF card photographs, promenade
photographs, promenade card
photoprints, promenade card
prints, promenade
promenade card photographs
promenade card photoprints
CN V.VJ.AFU.AFU.BCW.AFU.BIQ

promenades
RK.1576 (A,B,R)
ALT **promenade**
SN Places for strolling; public walks. (W)
UF esplanades
paseos
CN V.RK.ALO.ALO.BUE.BCW

promissory notes
VW.834 (L)
ALT **promissory note**
SN Unconditional written promises to pay on demand, or at a fixed or determined future time, a certain sum of money to, or to the order of, a specified person or to the bearer. (GAHLM)
UF IOUs
CN V.VW.AFU.ARI.AFU.BIQ.CFS.BIQ

promontories
RD.224 (L)
ALT **promontory**
SN Use only for high points of land, bluffs, or cliffs protruding boldly into lakes or seas.
UF headlands
CN V.RD.ARI.AFU.AXC.AFU.ALO.
AXC.BCW

promoters
MT.2420
SN Substances that in very small amounts are able to increase the activity of catalysts. (W)
CN M.MT.AFU.ARI.CFS.AFU

promotions
KM.154 (L)
CN K.KM.AFU.ELK.AXC

prompt books
VW.72
ALT **prompt book**
SN Copies of plays used by a prompter, showing action of the play, cues, movements of actors, properties, costume, and scene and light plots. (GAHLM)
UF books, prompt
CN V.VW.AFU.AFU.AFU.ERE.AFU

pronaoi
RM.339 (R)
ALT **pronaos**
SN The open vestibule in front of the naos or cella of a temple.
CN V.RM.AFU.DIO.AXC.ALO.AXC.AXC

proof prints
USE **contact sheets**

proof sheets
USE **contact sheets**

proofs
VB.126 (L)
ALT **proof**
SN Use for trial printings or casts, such as of prints, photographs, or sculptures.
CN V.VB.ALO.BZY.AXC

proofs, galley
USE **galley proofs**

propaganda
BM.219 (L,R)
SN Ideas, facts, or allegations spread deliberately to support one cause or individual or to damage another. (WCOL)
CN B.BM.AFU.ARI.ARI

propane
MT.1014 (L)
SN Liquefied petroleum gas, marketed under pressure in steel cylinders as bottled gas; used especially in cook stoves. (MH)
CN M.MT.AFU.AFU.ALO.BCW.ALO.ALO.ARI

propellants
MT.2647 (L)
CN M.MT.AFU.ARI.HIK

propelling pencils
USE **mechanical pencils**

properties, acoustical
USE **acoustical properties**

properties, chemical
USE **chemical properties**

properties, electrical
USE **electrical properties**

properties, magnetic
USE **magnetic properties**

properties, mechanical
USE **mechanical properties**

properties, optical
USE **optical properties**

properties, surface
USE **surface properties**

properties, thermal
USE **thermal properties**

property
BM.459 (A,L,B)
CN B.BM.BCW.CXA.AFU

property conveyances
USE **conveyances**

property lines
BM.484
UF lines, property
CN B.BM.BCW.DUC.BCW

property maps
USE **cadastral maps**

property plans
USE **cadastral maps**

property, cultural
USE **cultural property**

property, destruction of
USE **vandalism**

property, heritage
USE **cultural property**

property, intellectual
USE **intellectual property**

property, personal
USE **personal property**

property, real
USE **real estate**

proportion
BM.85 (L,R)
SN Relation between respective parts or between parts and the whole, in a building or any work of art, whether considered purely visually or numerically.
CN B.BM.AFU.AFU.ARI.AFU.ELK

proportional compasses
TB.240 (N)
ALT **proportional compass**
UF compasses, proportional
CN V.TB.AFU.ARI.CLM.AFU.ALO.ARI.ARI

proportions, harmonic
USE **harmony**

proposal bonds
USE **bid bonds**

proposals
VW.385 (L)
ALT **proposal**
SN Includes offers by one person or organization to another of terms and conditions with reference to some work or undertaking and plans or schemes put forward for consideration, discussion, or adoption.
CN V.VW.AFU.AFU.ALO.ELK

proposals, grant
USE **grant proposals**

proposed designs
USE **presentation drawings**

propping
USE **shoring**

proprietary fire alarm systems
RT.1508
ALT **proprietary fire alarm system**
SN Use for fire alarm systems operated from a central supervising station at the protected premises.
UF alarm systems, proprietary fire
fire alarm systems, proprietary
systems, proprietary fire alarm
CN V.RT.ALO.BIQ.AFU.AFU.AFU.ARI

proprietary specifications
VW.803
ALT **proprietary specification**
SN Specifications giving the names of products and manufacturers and permitting the contractor and the client to exercise close control over product selection. (STEIN)
UF specifications, proprietary
CN V.VW.AFU.ARI.AFU.ARI.AFU.ARI.CFS

proprietors
HG.425
ALT **proprietor**
UF owners
CN H.HG.AFU.AXC.BOK.EWY

propriety
USE **decorum**

props
USE **shores (structural elements)**

props, sawyer's
USE **sawyer's props**

propylaea
RK.503 (A,B)
ALT **propylaeum**
SN Use for monumental entrances to sacred enclosures.
UF propylons
CN V.RK.AFU.ALO.ALO.BUE.BCW

propylene resin
USE **polypropylene**

propylons
USE **propylaea**

proscaenia
RM.367
ALT **proscaenium**
SN Stages of ancient Roman theaters. (JBW-P)
UF proskenia
CN V.RM.AFU.DIO.AXC.AXC.ALO.BIQ.AFU.AFU

proscenium arches
RT.1268
ALT **proscenium arch**
SN Framing arches through which, in most modern theaters, the stage setting is revealed to the audience. (TL)
UF arches, proscenium
CN V.RT.AFU.BUE.ARI.AXC

proscenium walls
RT.1269
ALT **proscenium wall**
SN Fire walls that separate a stage or enclosed platform from the public or

spectators in an auditorium. (DAC)
UF walls, proscenium
CN V.RT.AFU.BUE.ARI.BCW

prosecutors, public
USE **public prosecutors**

proskenia
USE **proscaenia**

Prosopis chilensis
USE **mesquite**

prospect doors
TG.872
ALT **prospect door**
UF doors, prospect
CN V.TG.ALO.CXA.AFU

prospects (views)
USE **views**

prospectuses
VW.81
ALT **prospectus**
SN Formal summaries of proposed commercial, literary, or other ventures. (AHD)
CN V.VW.AFU.AFU.AFU.FCS.ARI

prosperity
BM.406 (R)
CN B.BM.ARI.ERE

prostyle
DC.92
CN D.DC.AFU.ARI.ERE.BIQ.BZY

protecting
KG.132 (L)
ALT **protected**
SN Use generally for the activity of keeping people and things safe from harm or deterioration. For actions taken to prevent further changes or deterioration in objects, sites, or structures, use **preservation**. When such actions are taken on buildings or other structures specifically for cultural, aesthetic, or historic reasons, use **historic preservation.**
UF preserving
protection
CN K.KG.AFU.AFU.BCW.AXC

protection
USE **protecting**

protection of landscape
USE **landscape protection**

protection systems, fire
USE **fire protection systems**

protection, avalanche
USE **avalanche protection**

protection, burglary
USE **burglary protection**

protection, environmental
USE **environmental protection**

protection, flood
USE **flood control**

protection, flood damage
USE **flood control**

protection, landscape
USE **landscape protection**

protection, landslide
USE **landslide protection**

protection, lightning
USE **lightning protection**

protective glass, x-ray
USE **x-ray protective glass**

Protestant Episcopal
USE **Episcopal**

Protestant Reformation
USE **Reformation**

Protestantism
BM.630 (L,B,R)
ALT **Protestant**
CN B.BM.BZY.AFU.ALO.ARI

protesting
KG.40
CN K.KG.AFU.AFU.ALO.BOK

protheses
RM.311
ALT **prothesis**
SN Use for recesses, in effect chapels, used for preparation of the eucharist by the clergy, and located on the north side of the bema in Greek churches.
UF parabemata
CN V.RM.AFU.DIO.AXC.ALO.AFU.AXC.BOK

Proto-Aeolic
USE **Aeolic**

Proto-Attic
FL.2617
CN F.FL.ALO.AXC.ALO.AFU.ALO.AXC.ALO.AXC.AFU.ALO

Proto-Baroque
FL.3179
CN F.FL.ALO.BCW.ALO.ARI.BIQ.ALO

Proto-Chimu
USE **Mochica**

Proto-Corinthian
FL.2626
CN F.FL.ALO.AXC.ALO.AFU.ALO.AXC.ALO.BCW.AFU.AFU

Proto-Elamite
FL.3012
CN F.FL.ALO.AXC.ARI.BIQ.AFU.ALO.ALO

Proto-Ghassulian
FL.2922
CN F.FL.ALO.AXC.ARI.AXC.AFU.ALO.BIQ

Proto-Ionic
USE **Aeolic**

Proto-Jomon
FL.1960
CN F.FL.ALO.ARI.ALO.ALO.AFU.AFU.ALO.AFU

Proto-Pop
USE **Neo-Dada**

Proto-Renaissance
FL.3098
CN F.FL.ALO.BCW.ALO.ALO.AFU.BCW

Proto-Sesklo
FL.2532
CN F.FL.ALO.AXC.ALO.AFU.AFU.AFU.AFU

Proto-Villanovan
FL.2703
CN F.FL.ALO.AXC.ALO.ALO.AFU.AFU.AXC

Protoclassic
FL.966
CN F.FL.ALO.ALO.ALO.ALO.AFU.AFU.ARI

Protodynastic
USE **Protoliterate**

Protogeometric
FL.2563
CN F.FL.ALO.AXC.ALO.AFU.AFU.ARI.AFU

protohistoric
FL.5
CN F.FL.AFU.AXC

Protoimperial
FL.2966
CN F.FL.ALO.AXC.ARI.BCW.AFU.ARI.AFU

Protoliterate
FL.2960
UF Protodynastic
CN F.FL.ALO.AXC.ARI.BCW.AFU.ALO

Protoliterate A-B
USE **Uruk**

Protoliterate C-D
USE **Jamdat Nasr**

protomai capitals
RT.130
ALT **protomai capital**
SN Use for capitals representing the heads and necks of animals.
UF capitals, protomai
CN V.RT.AFU.AFU.AFU.AXC.BIQ.ALO.ARI.AFU.DCU

prototype houses
USE **model houses**

prototypes

VB.108 (A,B)
ALT **prototype**
CN V.VB.ALO.BUE.BCW

prototypes (houses)
USE **model houses**

provenance
BM.302
CN B.BM.AFU.AXC.DCU

Providencia
FL.1020
CN F.FL.ALO.ALO.ALO.ALO.AFU.ALO.ARI.AFU.ALO.AXC

providing
KG.133
SN Making available or supplying commodities or services, such as water or electricity. (RLG7)
UF provision
CN K.KG.AFU.AFU.BCW.BCW

provinces
HG.808
ALT **province**
CN H.HG.ALO.ALO.BOK

provincial government
BM.546 (L)
UF government, provincial
CN B.BM.BOK.BOK.ALO.ALO

Provincial Highland
FL.1713
UF Highland, Provincial
Mestizo
CN F.FL.ALO.ALO.AXC.ALO.AFU.ARI.ARI

Provincial Mughal
FL.2238
UF Late Mughal
Mughal, Late
Mughal, Provincial
Provincial School
CN F.FL.ALO.ARI.AXC.ALO.AFU.BIQ.ALO.ALO.ALO

provincial parks
RK.1465
ALT **provincial park**
SN Public parks in Canada administered by the provincial government. (DCA)
UF parks, provincial
CN V.RK.ALO.ALO.ARI.ALO.ALO

Provincial School
USE **Provincial Mughal**

provincialism
BM.364
CN B.BM.ALO.ALO.CLM.EWY

proving grounds
RG.143 (L)
ALT **proving ground**
SN Use for complexes where testing of weapons or vehicles is conducted under close-hand scrutiny; for locations where weapons are exploded at a distance from observers, use **test sites.**
UF grounds, proving
CN V.RG.AFU.AFU.DCU

provision
USE **providing**

proxemic behavior
USE **spatial behavior**

PRT
USE **personal rapid transit**

Prunus avium
USE **sweet cherry**

Prunus cerasus
USE **sour cherry**

Prunus serotina
USE **black cherry**

Prussian amber
USE **succinite**

Prussian blue
MT.1609 (L)
UF Berlin blue
bleu de Prusse
blue, Berlin
blue, bronze
blue, Brunswick
blue, Chinese
blue, iron
blue, Milori
blue, Paris
blue, paste
blue, Prussian
blue, steel
blue, Turnbull's
bronze blue
Brunswick blue
Chinese blue
iron blue
Milori blue
Paris blue
Pariserblau
paste blue
Preussischblau
steel blue
Turnbull's blue
CN M.MT.AFU.AFU.ARI.AFU.AFU.ALO.ALO.ALO.AXC.AXC

Prussian blue (color)
USE **dark greenish blue**
deep greenish blue
moderate blue
strong blue

Prussian green
USE **Brunswick green**
deep bluish green
deep greenish blue
moderate bluish green

pry bars
USE **crowbars**

prying rods
USE **flagging irons**

prytaneia
RK.988 (L)
ALT **prytaneion**
SN Use for public halls in ancient Greek cities where the sacred hearth and official headquarters of the city administration were housed and where official guests were entertained.
CN V.RK.AFU.ALO.ALO.ERE.AFU.BUE

PS
USE **polystyrene**

psalm books
USE **psalters**

psalters
VW.553 (L,R)
ALT **psalter**
SN Books containing the Book of Psalms or a particular version of, musical setting for, or selection from it. (AHD)
UF books, psalm
psalm books
CN V.VW.AFU.ALO.AFU.AFU.ALO.BUE.DCU

psammites
USE **sandstone**

psephite
USE **rudaceous rock**

pseudo-four-centered arches
RT.237
ALT **pseudo-four-centered arch**
SN Use for arches that are triangular arches in the center but with sides curved toward the springing.
UF arches, pseudo-four-centered
CN V.RT.AFU.AFU.AFU.BCW.AFU.AFU.AFU.CRG.BOK

Pseudo-Ionic
USE **Aeolic**

pseudo-three-centered arches
RT.255
ALT **pseudo-three-centered arch**
SN Use for arches that are flat in the center, but curve toward the springing.
UF arches, pseudo-three-centered
CN V.RT.AFU.AFU.AFU.BCW.AFU.AFU.AFU.ELK.AXC.ARI

pseudodipteral
DC.93
SN Describes buildings planned as dipteral but with the inner row of columns omitted.
CN D.DC.AFU.ARI.ERE.BIQ.CFS

pseudoperipteral
DC.94
SN Describes buildings having engaged columns or pilasters along the sides and rear and freestanding columns along the front.

CN D.DC.AFU.ARI.ERE.BIQ.CLM

pseudothyra
USE **secret doors**

Psychedelic
FL.3750 (R)
CN F.FL.ALO.BUE.ARI.HOE

psychiatric art
USE **art brut**

psychiatric clinics
RK.744 (A,L)
ALT **psychiatric clinic**
UF clinics, mental health
clinics, psychiatric
mental health clinics
CN V.RK.AFU.ALO.ALO.CXA.ALO.AFU.ALO.AXC

psychiatric hospitals
RK.779 (A,L,B)
ALT **psychiatric hospital**
UF asylums, insane
hospitals, mental
hospitals, psychiatric
insane asylums
institutions, mental
mental hospitals
mental institutions
CN V.RK.AFU.ALO.ALO.CXA.ALO.AFU.BUE.AFU

psychiatric windows
RT.929
ALT **psychiatric window**
SN Windows designed for use in mental institutions, characterized by heavy intermediate sections, restricted glass sizes and ventilator heights, plus special screens and hardware. (STEIN)
UF windows, psychiatric
CN V.RT.AFU.ARI.AFU.AFU.BOK.AFU.AFU.DUC

psychiatrists
HG.389 (L)
ALT **psychiatrist**
CN H.HG.AFU.AXC.BIQ.ALO.BCW.BUE

psychiatry
KD.244 (L)
SN Branch of medicine that deals with the science and practice of treating mental, emotional, or behavioral disorders, especially as originating in endogenous causes or as resulting from faulty interpersonal relationships. (W)
CN K.KD.AFU.ARI.BUE.BIQ

psychic photographs
VJ.129 (L)
ALT **psychic photograph**
SN Photographs that purport to show personal energy fields (auras), energy or personality extensions (astral projections), pre- or postcognitive mental images, or various other supranormal visual manifestations.
UF photographs, psychic
CN V.VJ.AFU.AXC.AXC

psychic photography
KT.305 (L)
SN The techniques or the activity of making psychic photographs.
UF photography, psychic
CN K.KT.AFU.ALO.DUC.DIO.AFU.DCU

psychoanalysis
KD.182 (L,R)
CN K.KD.AFU.ALO.EFQ.AFU.ALO

psychoanalysts
HG.390 (L)
ALT **psychoanalyst**
CN H.HG.AFU.AXC.BIQ.ALO.BCW.BZY

psychohistory
KD.187 (L,R)
CN K.KD.AFU.ALO.EFQ.ALO.ARI

psycholinguistics
KD.37 (L,R)
CN K.KD.AFU.AFU.AXC.AFU.AFU.AXC

psychological anthropology
USE **ethnopsychology**

psychologism
BM.291 (L,R)
SN Doctrine or theory that emphasizes psychological conceptions outside the field of psychology. (W)
CN B.BM.AFU.AXC.AXC.ALO

psychologists
HG.276 (L)
ALT **psychologist**
CN H.HG.AFU.AXC.BCW.AFU.BZY

psychology
KD.180 (L,B,R)
CN K.KD.AFU.ALO.EFQ.AFU

psychology of religion
KD.78 (L)
UF religion, psychology of
CN K.KD.AFU.AFU.BUE.AFU.AXC

psychology, cross-cultural
USE **ethnopsychology**

psychology, social
USE **social psychology**

psychotic art
USE **art brut**

pteromata
RM.340
ALT **pteroma**
SN Passageways between the walls of the cella of a classical temple and the columns of the peristyle. (HAS)
UF peridromes
CN V.RM.AFU.DIO.AXC.ALO.AXC.BCW

Ptolemaic
FL.2833
CN F.FL.ALO.AXC.ALO.ARI.AFU.CLM

PTs
USE **pneumatic tubes**

PU-tp
USE **polyurethane**

public address systems
RT.1288 (L,B)
ALT **public address system**
UF systems, public address
CN V.RT.ALO.AFU.AFU.BCW

public administrators
HG.666
ALT **public administrator**
UF administrators, public
CN H.HG.AFU.AXC.CFS.BIQ.AFU

public aquariums
USE **aquariums**

public architects
USE **government architects**

public art
BM.251 (A,L,R)
SN Use for art whose purpose is to beautify and enrich public places. For art undertaken in conjunction with particular communities, usually to produce an effect or inspire response specifically within those communities, use **community art.**
UF art, municipal
art, public
municipal art
CN B.BM.AFU.ARI.BCW.EWY

public baths
RK.780 (A,L,B,R)
ALT **public bath**
SN Use for buildings equipped with swimming pools and other facilities for bathing and swimming, traditionally the primary hygienic facility in a city or town.
UF bathhouses (public baths)
baths
baths, public
CN V.RK.AFU.ALO.ALO.CXA.ALO.AFU.BZY

public buildings
RK.967 (A,L,N,B,R)
ALT **public building**
SN Use for buildings or groups of buildings owned and operated by a governing body and often occupied by a governmental agency. (EAA)
UF buildings, civic
buildings, government
buildings, public
civic buildings
government buildings
CN V.RK.AFU.ALO.ALO.ERE

public comfort stations
USE **comfort stations**

public contracts
USE **government contracts**

public defenders
HG.319 (L)
ALT **public defender**
SN In the United States, lawyers appointed or elected by a city or county as full-time, official defenders to represent financially disadvantaged citizens in criminal cases at public expense. (RHDEL2)
UF defenders, public
CN H.HG.AFU.AXC.BCW.ALO.BIQ.AXC.ALO

public documents
USE **government records**

public domain
BM.475 (L)
UF domain, national
domain, public
domain, state
national domain
state domain
CN B.BM.BCW.DCU

public gardens
RK.1442 (B,R)
ALT **public garden**
UF gardens, public
CN V.RK.ALO.AFU.AFU.BCW.ARI

public halls
USE **assembly halls**

public health
BM.1113 (A,L,B)
SN Protection and improvement of community health by organized community effort. (WCOL)
UF health, public
CN B.BM.CRG.BCW.BUE

public health boards
USE **health boards**

public houses
USE **pubs**

public houses, coffee
USE **coffeehouses**

public housing
RG.71 (L,B,R)
SN Low cost housing, owned, sponsored, or administered by a municipal or other governmental agency. (DAC)
UF council housing
government housing
housing, council
housing, government
housing, public
CN V.RG.AFU.AFU.BOK.AXC.AFU.ALO.AFU

public housing, low rent
USE **low cost housing**

public institutions
HG.860 (L)
ALT **public institution**
UF institutions, public
CN H.HG.ALO.CXA.ALO

public land
RD.312 (L)
UF land, public
CN V.RD.ARI.ALO.AXC.AXC

public laundries
USE **laundries**

public lavatories
USE **rest rooms**

public law
KD.166 (L)
UF law, public
CN K.KD.AFU.ALO.DOI.BIQ

public libraries
RK.695 (A,L,B)
ALT **public library**
UF libraries, public
CN V.RK.AFU.ALO.ALO.CRG.AXC.AFU.ARI

public officers
HG.671 (L,R)
ALT **public officer**
UF government officials
municipal officials
officers, public
officials
officials, government
officials, municipal
CN H.HG.AFU.AXC.CFS.CFS

public parks
USE **parks**

public playgrounds
USE **playgrounds**

public policy
KD.178 (A,L)
UF policy, public
CN K.KD.AFU.ALO.DZW.ARI

public prosecutors
HG.320 (L)
ALT **public prosecutor**
SN Public officials charged with the investigation of punishable acts on behalf of the state or an internal commission. (W)
UF prosecutors, public
CN H.HG.AFU.AXC.BCW.ALO.BIQ.AXC.ARI

public records
USE **government records**

public relations
KD.114 (A,L,B)
UF relations, public
CN K.KD.AFU.ALO.ARI.AXC

public safety buildings
RK.989
ALT **public safety building**
UF buildings, public safety
CN V.RK.AFU.ALO.ALO.ERE.AFU.BZY

public schools
RK.830 (L,B)
ALT **public school**
UF schools, public
CN V.RK.AFU.ALO.ALO.CXA.ARI.ARI.ALO

public servants
USE **government employees**

public services
HG.872 (A,L)
ALT **public service**
SN Use for on-going essential services provided by government relating to the protection and maintenance of the lives and property of community members as a whole. For the actual enterprises that provide essential commodities such as water and power to the public, use **public utilities.** For the government-sponsored provision of buildings and other facilities for public use and paid for by public funds, use **public works.** For organized assistance provided by public or private agencies to individual community members, use **social services.**
UF municipal services
services, municipal
services, public
CN H.HG.ALO.DIO.ARI

public squares
USE **squares**

public toilets
USE **comfort stations**

public transit
RD.92 (A,L)
UF mass transit
mass transit systems
transit, mass
transit, public
CN V.RD.ALO.ARI.AFU

public use, dedication to
USE **dedication to public use**

public utilities
HG.862 (L,B,R)
ALT **public utility**
SN Designates public or private enterprises under strict government regulation to provide without discrimination essential public services, such as gas, electricity, and sewers.
UF municipal utilities
utilities, municipal
utilities, public
CN H.HG.ALO.DCU

public welfare
USE **welfare services**

public works

HG.874 (L,B,R)
SN Use for the government-sponsored provision of buildings and other facilities, such as post offices, roads, playgrounds, and docks, for public use and paid for by public funds.
UF works, public
CN H.HG.ALO.DIO.AXC

public, notaries
USE **notaries**

publication, manuscripts for
USE **manuscripts for publication**

publications
VW.610 (L)
ALT **publication**
SN Documents distributed to the public by sale or other transfer of ownership, or by rental, lease, or lending. (ALAG)
CN V.VW.AFU.ALO.AFU.CXA

publications, plant
USE **house organs**

publications, serial
USE **serials**

publicizing
KG.41 (L,B)
SN Disseminating information to the public. (RLG7)
UF disseminating
CN K.KG.AFU.AFU.ALO.BUE

publishers
HG.292 (L)
ALT **publisher**
CN H.HG.AFU.AXC.BCW.ALO.AFU.AXC

publishers' catalogs
VW.114 (L)
ALT **publishers' catalog**
UF catalogs, publishers'
lists, publishers'
publishers' lists
CN V.VW.AFU.AFU.AFU.FZU.ALO.ALO.ARI.ALO.ARI

publishers' lists
USE **publishers' catalogs**

publishers' marks
USE **printers' marks**

publishing
KG.102 (L,R)
ALT **published**
CN K.KG.AFU.AFU.AXC.DCU

publishing offices
RK.200 (A,B)
ALT **publishing office**
UF offices, publishing
CN V.RK.AFU.ALO.ALO.ARI.AFU.ALO

publishing, electronic
USE **electronic publishing**

publishing, online
USE **electronic publishing**

pubs
RK.105 (A,L,B,R)
ALT **pub**
SN Use for public refreshment facilities with more emphasis on drinking, normally alcoholic beverages, than on eating or entertainment, which if provided usually occurs in separate, often back rooms, and offering no accommodations; use **saloons** for similar places but with staged entertainment provided in the main room; use **taverns** for establishments offering public accommodations as well as general refreshments, but no entertainment other than social gatherings.
UF alehouses
freehouses
houses, public
public houses
CN V.RK.AFU.ALO.ALO.ALO.AFU.AFU.ALO

Pucará
FL.1152
CN F.FL.ALO.ALO.ALO.ARI.AXC.AFU.AXC.ALO

puddingstone
MT.738
SN Conglomerate rock containing numerous rounded pebbles. (STEIN)
CN M.MT.AFU.AFU.AFU.DCU.AFU.ALO.ALO.ARI.ALO.ALO

puddling
KT.139 (L)
ALT **puddled**
SN Inducing compaction in mortar or concrete by the use of a tamping rod. (DAC)
CN K.KT.AFU.ALO.DOI.BIQ.AFU

PUDs
USE **planned unit developments**

Puebla
FL.1709
CN F.FL.ALO.ALO.AXC.ALO.AFU.ALO

Pueblo
FL.1465 (L,R)
CN F.FL.ALO.ALO.ARI.AFU.CFS.CRG

Pueblo Revival
FL.1737
UF Revival, Pueblo
Revival, Pueblo-Spanish
CN F.FL.ALO.ALO.BCW.AFU.BUE.BIQ

pueblos (housing complexes)
RG.59 (A,L,R)
ALT **pueblo (housing complex)**
SN Use for multistory, multiroom complex dwellings, often built on mesas or in cliffs, common among certain Indian cultures of the southwestern United States.
CN V.RG.AFU.AFU.BOK.AFU.AXC

pueblos (settlements)
RD.29 (L,R)
ALT **pueblo (settlement)**
SN Use for Spanish civilian colonial settlements in the southwestern United States founded primarily for farming and trading.
CN V.RD.AFU.ALO.AFU.BIQ

Puelche
FL.1696 (L)
CN F.FL.ALO.ALO.ARI.ARI.BOK.BZY

Puerto Rican
FL.711 (L)
CN F.FL.ALO.ALO.AFU.ALO.AXC

Puget Sound pine
USE **Douglas fir**

pull bars
TF.25
ALT **pull bar**
UF bars, pull
CN V.TF.AFU.AFU.AFU.AFU.AFU.CXA

pull planes
USE **short-jointer planes**

pull shovels
USE **backhoes**

pullers, clip
USE **clip tongs**

pullers, nail
USE **nail pullers**

pullers, ratchet
USE **come-alongs**

pullers, staple
USE **staple pullers**

pulley blocks
TB.375
ALT **pulley block**
SN Frames that contain one or more pulleys. (MEANS)
UF blocks (pulley blocks)
blocks, pulley
CN V.TB.AFU.ARI.DCU.AFU.ARI

pulley sheaves
USE **pulleys**

pulleys
TB.376 (L,N,B)
ALT **pulley**
SN Wheels having grooved rims for carrying a rope or other line and turning in a frame. (DAC)
UF pulley sheaves
CN V.TB.AFU.ARI.DCU.AFU.AXC

pulls
TF.68
ALT **pull**
SN Handles used for pulling open a door or drawer. (MEANS)

CN V.TF.AFU.AFU.AFU.AFU.CFS.BCW

pulls, bail
USE **bail pulls**

pulls, ball and spear
USE **ball and spear pulls**

pulls, barn-door
USE **barn-door pulls**

pulls, bean
USE **bean pulls**

pulls, bin
USE **bin pulls**

pulls, button
USE **button pulls**

pulls, chest
USE **drawer pulls**

pulls, door
USE **door pulls**

pulls, door edge
USE **door edge pulls**

pulls, drawer
USE **drawer pulls**

pulls, drop
USE **drop pulls**

pulls, flush-cup
USE **flush-cup pulls**

pulls, flush ring
USE **flush rings**

pulls, heart
USE **heart pulls**

pulls, offset
USE **offset pulls**

pulls, onion
USE **onion pulls**

pulls, recessed
USE **recessed pulls**

pulls, ring
USE **ring handles**

pulls, sash
USE **sash lifts**

pulls, sliding-door
USE **sliding-door pulls**

pulls, spade
USE **spade pulls**

pulls, tack
USE **tack pulls**

pulls, window
USE **sash lifts**

pulp
MT.1056
CN M.MT.AFU.AFU.ALO.BIQ.BUE.BCW

pulp mills
RK.652 (L)
ALT **pulp mill**
UF mills, pulp
CN V.RK.AFU.ALO.ALO.CLM.ALO.ALO.AFU.AXC.CRG

pulp, soda
USE **soda pulp**

pulpboard
MT.1922
UF board, wood-pulp
wood-pulp board
CN M.MT.AFU.AFU.ARI.ALO.ALO.AXC.ALO.BIQ.ALO

pulpit chairs
USE **preaching chairs**

pulpita
RM.368
ALT **pulpitum**
SN Stages of ancient Greek theaters.
CN V.RM.AFU.DIO.AXC.AXC.ALO.BIQ.AFU.ALO

pulpits
RT.1242 (A,L,N,B,R)
ALT **pulpit**
SN Stands for a speaker, especially the preacher of a sermon. (RS)
CN V.RT.AFU.BUE.ALO.ARI.CLM.AFU

pulpwood
MT.1453 (L)
CN M.MT.AFU.AFU.ALO.BIQ.DCU.ALO.CRG

pulverized stone
USE **stone dust**

pulvinated friezes
RT.348
ALT **pulvinated frieze**
SN Friezes with a convex face. (IGA)
UF cushioned friezes
friezes, cushioned
friezes, pulvinated
friezes, swelled
swelled friezes
CN V.RT.AFU.AFU.AFU.BCW.BZY.ALO.ARI.AFU.ALO

pumice
MT.626 (L)
SN A porous, frothlike volcanic glass which did not crystallize due to rapid cooling and frothed with the sudden release of dissolved gases. Powdered or ground pumice is used as an abrasive for fine polishing. (MH)
CN M.MT.AFU.AFU.AFU.DCU.AFU.AFU.ALO.ALO.AFU.AFU

pumice (white pigment)
MT.1754
UF glass, volcanic (white pigment)
volcanic glass (white pigment)
CN M.MT.AFU.AFU.ARI.AFU.AFU.ALO.ALO.BOK.ALO.CRG

pummels (finials)
USE **pommels (finials)**

pump augers
USE **taper augers**

pump drills
TB.185 (N)
ALT **pump drill**
SN Primitive drills in which the shaft is revolved by working up and down a bar carrying a cord attached at the center to the upper end of the shaft. (W)
UF drills, pump
CN V.TB.AFU.ARI.BIQ.ALO.AFU.AFU.BCW

pump houses
USE **pumping stations**

pump rooms
RM.118 (B)
ALT **pump room**
SN Use for rooms at a spa designed for drinking mineral waters, as at Bath, England.
UF rooms, pump
CN V.RM.AFU.DIO.ALO.BCW.CLM

pump stations
USE **pumping stations**

pumped storage power plants
RG.111 (L)
ALT **pumped storage power plant**
UF plants, pumped storage power
power plants, pumped storage
CN V.RG.AFU.AFU.BUE.ARI.ALO.AFU

pumping machinery
TB.377 (L,N)
UF machinery, pumping
CN V.TB.AFU.ARI.DCU.AFU.BCW

pumping stations
RK.575 (A,L,N,B)
ALT **pumping station**
SN Use for installations with equipment for raising water in water distribution systems to a higher elevation; may be used for similar structures in sewage systems. (ALLABY)
UF houses, pump
lift stations
pump houses
pump stations
stations, lift
stations, pumping
stations, water pumping
water pumping stations
CN V.RK.AFU.ALO.ALO.CFS.ALO.BCW.BCW

pumpkin domes
USE **umbrella domes**

pumps
TB.378 (L,N)
ALT **pump**
SN Devices or machines that compress

and transport fluids, usually by pressure, suction, or both. (DAC)
CN V.TB.AFU.ARI.DCU.AFU.BCW.AFU

pumps, concrete
USE **concrete pumps**

pumps, heat
USE **heat pumps**

pumps, solar-assisted heat
USE **solar-assisted heat pumps**

Puná
FL.1610 (L)
UF Antiplano
CN F.FL.ALO.ALO.ARI.ARI.ALO.AFU.BOK

punch blocks
TB.656
ALT **punch block**
UF blocks, punch
CN V.TB.AFU.BCW.BIQ.AFU.ALO.ARI.AXC

punch marks
VW.709
ALT **punch mark**
UF marks, punch
CN V.VW.AFU.ALO.ALO.AFU.AXC.AFU.AFU

punch presses
TB.644 (N)
ALT **punch press**
SN Presses consisting of a frame containing stationary dies; used to cut or shape metal or other materials.
UF presses, punch
CN V.TB.AFU.BCW.BIQ.AFU.AFU.ALO

Punch'ong stoneware
USE **Punch'ong ware**

Punch'ong ware
FL.2118
UF Punch'ong stoneware
stoneware, Punch'ong
ware, Punch'ong
CN F.FL.ALO.ARI.ALO.ARI.ALO.AFU.AFU

punched cards
VW.652
ALT **punched card**
SN Paper cards on which machine-readable data are recorded by the punching of holes in specified positions in accordance with a predesignated code. (ICA)
UF cards, IBM (TM)
cards, punched
IBM (TM) cards
CN V.VW.AFU.ALO.AFU.DZW.ALO.BOK

puncheons
RT.198
ALT **puncheon**
SN Use for short posts and short upright pieces of timber in framing.
CN V.RT.AFU.AFU.AFU.AXC.DCU.AFU.ALO

punches
TB.360 (N)
ALT **punch**
SN Tools used to make indentations or perforations in various materials; usually in the form of a steel rod whose end may take a variety of shapes; used for marking, blanking, and decoration.
CN V.TB.AFU.ARI.CXA.AXC

punches, aligning
USE **drift punches**

punches, backing-out
USE **backing-out punches**

punches, bob
USE **countersinks**

punches, carver's
USE **carver's punches**

punches, dapping
USE **dapping punches**

punches, drift
USE **drift punches**

punches, driving
USE **nail sets**

punches, fore
USE **fore punches**

punches, hand lever
USE **hand lever punches**

punches, handrail
USE **handrail punches**

punches, nail
USE **nail sets**

punches, pin
USE **nail sets**

punches, pin (backing-out punches)
USE **backing-out punches**

punches, prick
USE **prick punches**

punches, rivet
USE **starting punches**

punches, scalloping
USE **scalloping punches**

punches, setting
USE **rivet sets**

punches, shingle
USE **shingle punches**

punches, starting
USE **starting punches**

punches, veneer
USE **veneer punches**

punchwork
MT.2771 (R)
CN M.MT.AFU.AXC.BOK.BIQ

punic wax
MT.2192
SN Treated or processed beeswax used in ancient encaustic paintings. (MAYER)
UF wax, punic
CN M.MT.AFU.AFU.ARI.BZY.AFU.AFU.AFU.AFU.AFU

punishing
KG.157 (L)
SN Imposing a penalty. (RLG7)
UF disciplining
CN K.KG.AFU.AFU.BIQ.CFS

Punjab Hills
USE **Pahari**

punk culture
BM.365 (L,R)
UF culture, punk
CN B.BM.ALO.ALO.CLM.FCS

Punu
FL.405 (L)
UF Apono
CN F.FL.ALO.AFU.AXC.ALO.AFU.ALO.BIQ

Punuk
FL.811
CN F.FL.ALO.ALO.ALO.AFU.ALO.AFU.ALO.ALO.ALO.BOK

pupils
USE **students**

pupitres
TG.968
ALT **pupitre**
SN Hinged flaps in a desk which pop up to provide a slant top reading or writing surface. (PC)
CN V.TG.ALO.GFO

pupitres (reading desks)
USE **reading desks**

puppet theaters
RK.942 (L)
ALT **puppet theater**
UF theaters, puppet
CN V.RK.AFU.ALO.ALO.EFQ.ARI.BCW.ALO.ARI

puppets (tools)
USE **lathe puppets**

puppets, lathe
USE **lathe puppets**

Puquina
USE **Uru**

purbeck marble
MT.661
UF marble, purbeck
purbeck stone

stone, purbeck
CN M.MT.AFU.AFU.AFU.DCU.AFU.ALO.AFU.ALO.ALO.AFU.AFU.AFU.BCW.AXC

purbeck stone
USE **purbeck marble**

purchase orders
VW.863
ALT **purchase order**
SN Documents authorizing a vendor to deliver materials or equipment, or to perform services, which upon acceptance constitutes a purchase contract. (GAHLM)
UF orders, purchase
CN V.VW.AFU.ARI.AFU.BIQ.CXA.AXC.ARI

purchasers
USE **buyers**

purchasing
KG.63 (L)
UF buying
CN K.KG.AFU.AFU.ARI.DOI.AFU

Pure Land sect (China)
USE **Ching-T'u**

Pure Land sect (Japan)
USE **Jodo**
Shin

pure scarlet
USE **iodine scarlet**

puree
USE **Indian yellow**

Puri-Coroado
FL.1682 (L)
CN F.FL.ALO.ALO.ARI.ARI.BIQ.CFS

purification of air
USE **air purification**

purification, air
USE **air purification**

Purist
FL.3378 (L,R)
ALT **Purism**
CN F.FL.ALO.BCW.ALO.AXC.DIO.BCW.BCW.BOK

purlins
RT.506 (B)
ALT **purlin**
UF purlins, roof
roof purlins
CN V.RT.AFU.AFU.AFU.BIQ.ARI.ALO.ALO.ALO.ALO

purlins, roof
USE **purlins**

purple
DL.266 (L,R)
CN D.DL.AFU.AFU.CFS

purple brown
USE **grayish purple**

purple drab
USE **grayish purple**

purple drab, light
USE **grayish purple**

purple drab, pale
USE **grayish purplish pink**

purple lake
USE **dark purplish red**
deep red
moderate red

purple madder
USE **dark red**
moderate red

purple navy
USE **moderate purplish blue**

purple orchid
USE **strong reddish purple**

purple slate
MT.868
UF slate, purple
CN M.MT.AFU.AFU.AFU.DCU.AFU.ARI.BUE.AFU.ARI.AFU

purple, aniline
USE **mauve**

purple, anthracene
USE **dark grayish purple**
dark purplish red

purple, blackish
USE **blackish purple**

purple, bright fuchsia
USE **deep purplish red**
deep reddish purple
strong reddish purple

purple, brilliant
USE **brilliant purple**

purple, brown
USE **grayish purple**

purple, cadmium
USE **deep red**
moderate red

purple, dark
USE **dark purple**

purple, dark grayish
USE **dark grayish purple**

purple, dark maroon
USE **dark reddish purple**

purple, dark reddish
USE **dark reddish purple**

purple, deep
USE **deep purple**

purple, deep reddish
USE **deep reddish purple**

purple, dull dark
USE **deep reddish purple**
strong reddish purple

purple, dull magenta
USE **strong reddish purple**

purple, fuchsia
USE **dark reddish purple**
deep purplish red
moderate reddish purple
strong reddish purple
vivid purplish red

purple, grayish
USE **grayish purple**

purple, grayish red
USE **grayish purple**

purple, grayish reddish
USE **grayish reddish purple**

purple, Grecian
USE **Tyrian purple**

purple, light
USE **light purple**

purple, light fuchsia
USE **strong reddish purple**

purple, light reddish
USE **light reddish purple**

purple, lilac
USE **moderate purplish red**

purple, litho
USE **dark purple**
grayish purple
moderate purple
strong purple

purple, moderate
USE **moderate purple**

purple, moderate reddish
USE **moderate reddish purple**

purple, orchid
USE **vivid reddish purple**

purple, pale
USE **pale purple**

purple, pale red
USE **pale purple**

purple, pale reddish
USE **pale reddish purple**

purple, plum
USE **dark violet**
very dark purple

purple, red
USE **dark purplish red**
deep reddish purple

purple, reddish
USE **reddish purple**

purple, rhodamine
USE **vivid purplish red**

purple, slate
USE **grayish purple**

purple, strong
USE **strong purple**

purple, strong reddish
USE **strong reddish purple**

purple, Tyrian
USE **Tyrian purple**

purple, Tyrian (color)
USE **vivid purplish red**

purple, very dark
USE **very dark purple**

purple, very dark reddish
USE **very dark reddish purple**

purple, very deep
USE **very deep purple**

purple, very deep reddish
USE **very deep reddish purple**

purple, very light
USE **very light purple**

purple, very pale
USE **very pale purple**

purple, violet
USE **deep reddish purple**

purple, vivid
USE **vivid purple**

purple, vivid reddish
USE **vivid reddish purple**

purpleheart
MT.1294 (L)
SN A strong, durable, elastic purplish wood used especially in fancy veneers. (W)
UF amaranth
peltogyne
purplewood
CN M.MT.AFU.AFU.ALO.BIQ.DCU.AFU.AFU.AFU.KQY

purplewood
USE **purpleheart**

purplish bistre
USE **brownish pink**

purplish black
DL.286
UF black plum
black, purplish
centroid color 235
plum, black
CN D.DL.AFU.AFU.CFS.CXA

purplish black, deep
USE **dark purplish gray**

purplish blue
DL.242
UF blue, purplish
CN D.DL.AFU.AFU.BZY.DCU.ALO

purplish blue, brilliant
USE **brilliant purplish blue**

purplish blue, dark
USE **dark purplish blue**

purplish blue, deep
USE **deep purplish blue**

purplish blue, grayish
USE **grayish purplish blue**

purplish blue, light
USE **light purplish blue**

purplish blue, moderate
USE **moderate purplish blue**

purplish blue, pale
USE **pale purplish blue**

purplish blue, strong
USE **strong purplish blue**

purplish blue, very light
USE **very light purplish blue**

purplish blue, very pale
USE **very pale purplish blue**

purplish blue, vivid
USE **vivid purplish blue**

purplish gray
DL.283
UF centroid color 233
dawn, gray
deep violet gray
granite (color)
gray dawn
gray violet
gray, metallic
gray, pale purplish
gray, purplish
gray, taupe
light violet gray
lilac
metallic gray
pale purplish gray
pale violet gray
purplish gray, pale
slate (color)
taupe gray
violet gray
violet gray, deep
violet gray, light
violet gray, pale
violet, gray
CN D.DL.AFU.AFU.CFS.CRG

purplish gray, dark
USE **dark purplish gray**

purplish gray, light
USE **light purplish gray**

purplish gray, pale
USE **purplish gray**

purplish lilac
USE **light reddish purple**
moderate purplish pink

purplish pink
DL.15
UF pink, purplish
CN D.DL.AFU.AFU.AFU.CLM.AFU

purplish pink, brilliant
USE **brilliant purplish pink**

purplish pink, dark
USE **dark purplish pink**

purplish pink, deep
USE **deep purplish pink**

purplish pink, grayish
USE **grayish purplish pink**

purplish pink, light
USE **light purplish pink**

purplish pink, moderate
USE **moderate purplish pink**

purplish pink, pale
USE **pale purplish pink**

purplish pink, strong
USE **strong purplish pink**

purplish red
DL.50
UF red, purplish
CN D.DL.AFU.AFU.ALO.CFS.AFU

purplish red, dark
USE **dark purplish red**

purplish red, deep
USE **deep purplish red**

purplish red, grayish
USE **grayish purplish red**

purplish red, light grayish
USE **light grayish purplish red**

purplish red, moderate
USE **moderate purplish red**

purplish red, strong
USE **strong purplish red**

purplish red, very dark
USE **very dark purplish red**

purplish red, very deep
USE **very deep purplish red**

purplish red, vivid
USE **vivid purplish red**

purplish white
DL.282
UF centroid color 231
lilac
reddish white
white, purplish
white, reddish
CN D.DL.AFU.AFU.CFS.CLM

purpurin
MT.1529
SN Any of various colored compounds obtained from chlorophyll or related

compounds by the actions of cold alcoholic alkali and oxygen and closely related to the chlorins. (W)
CN M.MT.AFU.AFU.ARI.AFU.AFU.AFU.AFU.AFU.AXC.CFS

Puruhá
FL.1666 (L)
CN F.FL.ALO.ALO.ARI.ARI.BCW.DCU

push bars
TF.26
ALT **push bar**
SN Bars, or series of bars, usually across a door, used as a means of pushing a door open. (BROWNL)
UF bars, push
CN V.TF.AFU.AFU.AFU.AFU.AFU.DCU

push catches, magnetic
USE **magnetic push catches**

push drills
TB.186 (N)
ALT **push drill**
SN Hand drills in which a spiral ratchet rotates the bit; operated by pushing on the handle. (MEANS)
UF automatic drills
drills, automatic
drills, push
drills, reciprocating
reciprocating drills
CN V.TB.AFU.ARI.BIQ.ALO.AFU.AFU.BIQ

push keys
TF.535
ALT **push key**
UF keys, push
keys, thrust
thrust keys
CN V.TF.AFU.ALO.ARI.AFU.BUE

push pins
TF.463
ALT **push pin**
UF pins, push
CN V.TF.AFU.AFU.AFU.ALO.AFU.CXA.BIQ

push plates
TF.22
ALT **push plate**
SN Plates applied to the lock stile to protect the door against soiling and wear. (BROWNL)
UF plates, push
CN V.TF.AFU.AFU.AFU.AFU.AFU.CFS.BIQ

push-pull cabinet locks
TF.248
ALT **push-pull cabinet lock**
SN Locks used principally to lock sliding cabinet doors by means of a pin extended into locked position by pushing; they are unlocked by inserting a key and pulling. (STEIN)
UF cabinet locks, push-pull
locks, push-pull cabinet
CN V.TF.AFU.AFU.AFU.AFU.DIO.BIQ.ALO.ARI.AFU.AFU

pushers, brad
USE **brad pushers**

putt-putt courses
USE **miniature golf courses**

putty
MT.2654 (L)
SN A heavy paste composed of pigment, such as whiting mixed with linseed oil; used to fill holes and cracks in wood prior to painting, or to secure and seal panes of glass in window frames. (DAC)
CN M.MT.AFU.ARI.HTY.ALO

putty (color)
USE **grayish yellow**
grayish yellow green
light brownish gray
light grayish brown
pale yellow green
yellowish gray

putty knives
TB.614 (N)
ALT **putty knife**
SN Blades of various shapes without a cutting edge; used for applying putty. (SALAM)
UF knives, putty
knives, stopping (putty knives)
stopping knives (putty knives)
CN V.TB.AFU.BCW.BCW.ALO.FCS.ARI

putty, dark
USE **olive gray**

putty, glazier's
USE **glazier's putty**

putty, lime
USE **lime putty**

putty, painter's
USE **glazier's putty**
lime putty

putty, picture
USE **picture putty**

putty, water
USE **water putty**

Puuc
FL.1040
CN F.FL.ALO.ALO.ALO.ALO.AFU.ALO.ARI.ALO.AFU.ALO

Puyallup
FL.1353 (L)
CN F.FL.ALO.ALO.ARI.AFU.BIQ.ELK

puzzolan
USE **pozzolana**

PVAC
USE **polyvinyl acetate**

PVAL
USE **polyvinyl alcohol**

PVB
USE **polyvinyl butyral**

PVC
USE **polyvinyl chloride**

PVDC
USE **polyvinylidene chloride**

pwree
USE **Indian yellow**

PXs
USE **post exchanges**

Pyanddzhikent
USE **Panjikent**

Pygmy
FL.539 (L,R)
UF Negrillo
CN F.FL.ALO.AFU.AXC.ALO.ALO.BIQ.ARI

pylons
RK.504
ALT **pylon**
SN Generally denotes monumental gateways to Egyptian temples, consisting of a pair of towerlike structures with slanting walls flanking the entrance portal;(HAS) may also be used more loosely for any large isolated structures used to mark a boundary, as at approaches to bridges or avenues. (PEVSNR)
CN V.RK.AFU.ALO.ALO.BUE.BIQ

pyramidal hipped roofs
USE **pyramidal roofs**

pyramidal roofs
RT.431
ALT **pyramidal roof**
SN Use for roofs pyramidal in form, or with a very short ridge so as to be nearly pyramidal.
UF hipped roofs, pyramidal
pavilion roofs
pyramidal hipped roofs
roofs, pavilion
roofs, pyramidal
roofs, pyramidal hipped
CN V.RT.AFU.AFU.AFU.BIQ.ARI.AFU.AFU.AFU.BOK.BCW.AFU

pyramids
RK.491 (A,L,B,R)
ALT **pyramid**
CN V.RK.AFU.ALO.ALO.BOK.BUE.AFU.BIQ

pyramids (geometric figures)
BM.795 (L,B)
ALT **pyramidal**
CN B.BM.CFS.ARI.AXC.BCW.ALO.AXC.ALO

pyres

RK.475
ALT pyre
SN Combustible heaps for burning the dead as a funeral rite. (W)
CN V.RK.AFU.ALO.ALO.BOK.BIQ

Pyrex (TM)
MT.238
SN A low expansion type of bora-silicate glass. (MH)
CN M.MT.AFU.AFU.AFU.BIQ.AFU.AFU.AFU.AFU

Pyrgos ware
FL.2673
UF Pirgos ware
ware, Pirgos
ware, Pyrgos
CN F.FL.ALO.AXC.ALO.AFU.ALO.AXC.BCW.BZY

pyrite
MT.515 (L)
SN A mineral sometimes mined for the zinc, gold, or copper associated with it, but chiefly used for producing sulfur, sulfuric acid, and coppers. (MH)
UF fool's gold
gold, fool's
iron pyrite
pyrite, iron
CN M.MT.AFU.AFU.AFU.CFS.AFU.CXA.BCW

pyrite, iron
USE **pyrite**

pyroclastic materials
MT.2811
UF materials, pyroclastic
CN M.MT.AFU.BCW.DUC

pyroclastic rock
MT.627
UF rock, pyroclastic
CN M.MT.AFU.AFU.AFU.DCU.AFU.AFU.ALO.ALO.ALO

pyrography
KT.682 (L)
UF etching, fire
fire etching
woodburning
CN K.KT.AFU.ALO.GRC.AXC.AFU

pyroxylin
MT.2135 (L)
SN A flammable mixture of cellulose nitrates usually with less than 12.5% nitrogen. (MH12)
CN M.MT.AFU.AFU.ARI.BUE.ALO.AXC.AFU.BCW.ARI.ARI

pyrus
USE **pear**

Pyrus communis
USE **common pear**

Pyrus ioensis
USE **prairie crabapple**

Pyrus malus
USE **applewood**

Pyu
FL.2313
UF Sriksetra
CN F.FL.ALO.ARI.BCW.AFU.AXC

Qadan
FL.2785
CN F.FL.ALO.AXC.ALO.ARI.AFU.ALO.AFU

Qajar
FL.3528
UF Kajar
CN F.FL.ALO.BIQ.AFU.FZU

qanats
RK.571 (L)
ALT **qanat**
SN Use for underground irrigation systems consisting of tunnels which are inclined from a water source and connected to the surface by a series of regularly spaced vertical shafts.
UF kanats
karez
CN V.RK.AFU.ALO.ALO.CFS.ALO.BCW.AFU.AFU

Qara Yawlaq Arslan
FL.3579
UF Qara Yuluk `Uthman
CN F.FL.ALO.BIQ.AFU.IFM.AFU.AFU

Qara Yuluk `Uthman
USE **Qara Yawlaq Arslan**

Qarakhanid
FL.3529
UF Great Khans
Karakhanid
CN F.FL.ALO.BIQ.AFU.GFO

Qaraman b. Nura Sufi
USE **Karaman b. Nura Sufi**

Qaramanid
USE **Karamanid**

Qasim
FL.3472 (L)
UF Kasim
CN F.FL.ALO.BIQ.AFU.DUC.CFS

qasrs
RK.439 (L)
ALT **qasr**
SN Use for Arabic castles or fortified palaces.
UF kasrs
CN V.RK.AFU.ALO.ALO.BIQ.ALO.ARI

Qatabian
FL.2887
CN F.FL.ALO.AXC.ARI.ALO.AFU.ARI

Qazwin
USE **Kazvin School**

Qement
USE **Kemant**

Qi
USE **Southern Qi**

Qi, Northern
USE **Northern Qi**

Qi, Southern
USE **Southern Qi**

Qianlong
FL.1913 (L)
UF Ch'ien-lung
CN F.FL.ALO.ARI.ALO.AFU.AFU.ALO.DOI.AXC

qibla walls
RT.1263 (A)
ALT **qibla wall**
SN Walls of a mosque or idgah oriented toward Mecca and usually containing a minbar.
UF prayer walls
walls, prayer
walls, qibla
CN V.RT.AFU.BUE.ALO.AXC.AXC

Qïlïch Arslan I
FL.3554
CN F.FL.ALO.BIQ.AFU.HIK.ARI.ALO

Qin
FL.1866 (L)
UF Ch'in
CN F.FL.ALO.ARI.ALO.AFU.AFU.ALO.BOK

Qing
FL.1909 (A,L)
UF Ch'ing
CN F.FL.ALO.ARI.ALO.AFU.AFU.ALO.DOI

Qingbai ware
FL.1948
UF Ch'ing-pai ware
ware, Ch'ing-pai
ware, Qingbai
CN F.FL.ALO.ARI.ALO.AFU.AFU.AXC.ARI.BCW

Qingliangang
FL.1840
UF Ch'ing-lien-kang
CN F.FL.ALO.ARI.ALO.AFU.AFU.AFU.ALO.ARI

Qizil
USE **Kizil**

Qoco
USE **Khocho**

Quad
FL.737
CN F.FL.ALO.ALO.ALO.AFU.AFU.ARI.AFU.AFU

quadrangle maps
VW.157

ALT **quadrangle map**
SN Maps, as those published by the United States Geological Survey, which show tracts of a country on a series of sheets and according to a specified scale.
UF maps, quadrangle
CN V.VW.AFU.AFU.AFU.FZU.AXC.AFU.ARI.AFU.CRG

quadrangles
RK.1443 (A,B)
ALT **quadrangle**
SN Use for rectangular grassy or paved areas surrounded by buildings, generally of an academic or civic nature. Distinguished from **courtyards** which generally fall within the bounds of a single building.
UF quads
CN V.RK.ALO.AFU.ALO

quadrangles (geometric figures)
USE **quadrilaterals**

quadrant
DC.69
SN Use as an adjective to mean having the shape of a quarter-circle or an arc of 90 degrees.
CN D.DC.AFU.ARI.CXA

quadrant drawers
TG.887
ALT **quadrant drawer**
UF drawers, quadrant
CN V.TG.ALO.DCU.AFU.ARI.AFU

quadrants, Dutch-door
USE **Dutch-door quadrants**

quadrel
MT.2263
SN A small piece of glass or tile, usually square or diamond-shaped; often set diagonally. (DAC)
UF quarrel
CN M.MT.AFU.ALO.FCS

quadrichrome
USE **Fresson**

quadrifrontes
USE **tetrapylons**

quadrilaterals
BM.775 (L)
ALT **quadrilateral**
SN Plane figures having four angles and four sides. (RHDEL2)
UF quadrangles (geometric figures)
CN B.BM.CFS.ARI.AXC.BCW.AFU.BIQ.ALO

quadripartite vaults
RT.526
ALT **quadripartite vault**
SN Vaults divided into four vaulting cells.
UF four-part vaults
vaults, four-part
vaults, quadripartite
CN V.RT.AFU.AFU.AFU.BIQ.BOK.AFU.AFU.AFU.AFU.ALO

quadriportici
RM.49 (A)
ALT **quadriporticus**
SN Use for enclosed Roman courtyards with porticoes on all four sides.
CN V.RM.AFU.DIO.AFU.BCW.ARI.BIQ

quadrivium
KD.298
SN Group of studies in the Middle Ages constituting the higher division of the seven liberal arts and consisting of arithmetic, music, geometry, and astronomy. (W)
CN K.KD.AFU.BCW.ALO.ALO

quads
USE **quadrangles**

Quaint Style
USE **Art Nouveau**

Quaker
BM.648 (L,B)
CN B.BM.BZY.AFU.ALO.AXC.BIQ

Quaker meeting houses
RK.1116 (L,B)
ALT **Quaker meeting house**
UF Friends' meeting houses
houses, Friends' meeting
houses, Quaker meeting
meeting houses, Friends'
meeting houses, Quaker
CN V.RK.AFU.ALO.ALO.FCS.BIQ.BCW.AFU

quaking aspen
USE **American aspen**

quality assurance
USE **quality control**

quality control
KG.170 (L,B)
SN Selecting the quality standards required for a project, and monitoring the properties of the finished work to assure compliance with those standards.
UF assurance, quality
control, quality
quality assurance
CN K.KG.AFU.ALO.AFU.BIQ

quality management, water
USE **water quality management**

quality of life
BM.1114 (L)
UF life, quality of
CN B.BM.CRG.BCW.BZY

quality, air
USE **air quality**

quality, indoor air
USE **indoor air quality**

quantity surveyors
HG.647 (A,L,B)
ALT **quantity surveyor**
UF surveyors, quantity
CN H.HG.AFU.AXC.BZY.BOK

quantity surveys
VW.811
ALT **quantity survey**
SN Detailed listings of the quantities of all items of material and equipment projected for use in a project, and the actual quantities used in the completed work. (MEANS)
UF bills of material
bills of quantity
materials, bills of
quantity, bills of
surveys, quantity
CN V.VW.AFU.ARI.AFU.AXC.BCW

quantity, bills of
USE **quantity surveys**

quantizers
USE **digitizers**

Quapaw
FL.1438 (L)
CN F.FL.ALO.ALO.ARI.AFU.BZY.BZY

quarrel
USE **quadrel**

quarrel panes
USE **quarrels**

quarrels
RT.972
ALT **quarrel**
SN A square or lozenge-shaped piece of glass, set diagonally in a lattice window, or the opening which such a piece of glass fills.
UF panes, quarrel
quarrel panes
quarries (quarrels)
CN V.RT.AFU.ARI.AFU.AFU.BOK.ALO.ARI.ARI

quarriers
HG.614
ALT **quarrier**
UF rock men
CN H.HG.AFU.AXC.BZY.AFU.FUA.AFU

quarries
RG.106 (A,L,N,B,R)
ALT **quarry**
UF stone quarries
CN V.RG.AFU.AFU.BUE.AFU.AXC

quarries (quarrels)
USE **quarrels**

quarry tile
MT.164
SN Unglazed ceramic tile, machine-made by the extrusion process from natural clay or shales. (DAC)
UF tile, quarry

CN M.MT.AFU.AFU.AFU.AXC.ALO.
ALO.ALO.ALO.AFU.AFU.AXC

quarrying
KT.621 (L,B,R)
ALT **quarried**
CN K.KT.AFU.ALO.FUA.DOI

quarryman's mud spoons
USE **mud spoons**

quarter closer
MT.113
SN A brick which has been cut to one-fourth of its normal length but is of normal thickness and width; used to space normal sized bricks. (DAC)
UF closer, quarter
closure, quarter
quarter closure
CN M.MT.AFU.AFU.AFU.AXC.ALO.
AFU.ARI.AFU.ALO

quarter closure
USE **quarter closer**

quarter plate
DC.130
SN A photographic plate size, about 3 1/4 by 4 1/4 inches.
CN D.DC.AFU.AXC.BIQ.BCW

quarter-round moldings
RT.789
ALT **quarter-round molding**
UF moldings, quarter-round
CN V.RT.AFU.ALO.AFU.BOK.AFU.
AFU.AXC.BIQ.AFU

quarter-round planes
USE **ovolo planes**

quarter-sawed lumber
MT.1432
UF lumber, quarter-sawed
CN M.MT.AFU.AFU.ALO.BIQ.DCU.
ALO.BOK.ALO.ALO.ALO

quarter-turn stairs
RT.1086
ALT **quarter-turn stair**
SN Stairs which, as they progress from bottom to top, turn 90 degrees.
UF angle stairs
stairs, angle
stairs, quarter-turn
CN V.RT.AFU.BIQ.AXC.AFU.AFU.
BZY.AFU

quarterly reports
VW.456
ALT **quarterly report**
SN Reports produced at three month intervals.
UF reports, quarterly
CN V.VW.AFU.AFU.ALO.FIM.AFU.
ALO.ARI

quarterpace stairs
RT.1082
ALT **quarterpace stair**
SN Stairs with landings at which the stair turns 90 degrees.
UF stairs, quarterpace
CN V.RT.AFU.BIQ.AXC.AFU.AFU
.BUE.AFU

quarters (districts)
RG.295 (A)
ALT **quarter (district)**
CN V.RG.ALO.ALO.BIQ

quarters, interns'
USE **interns' residences**

quarters, slave
USE **slave quarters**

quartetto tables
TG.785
ALT **quartetto table**
SN Term used by Sheraton to describe a nest of four small tables. (HAYWAR)
UF tables, quartetto
CN V.TG.AFU.AFU.BIQ.BOK.AXC.
AFU.AFU

quartz
MT.542 (L,R)
SN The most common variety of silica. (MH)
CN M.MT.AFU.AFU.AFU.CFS.AFU.
GRC.AFU

quartz (pigment)
USE **silica (white pigment)**

quartz crystal
MT.558 (L,R)
UF crystal, quartz
crystal, rock
rock crystal
CN M.MT.AFU.AFU.AFU.CFS.AFU.
GRC.AFU.BCW

quartz diorite
MT.615 (L)
UF diorite, quartz
CN M.MT.AFU.AFU.AFU.DCU.AFU.
AFU.AFU.AFU.ARI.ALO.ALO

quartz glass
USE **fused silica glass**

quartz porphyry
MT.619
UF porphyry, quartz
CN M.MT.AFU.AFU.AFU.DCU.AFU.
AFU.AFU.ALO.AFU.AFU

quartz, fused
USE **fused silica glass**

quartz, rose
USE **rose quartz**

quartzite
MT.847 (L)
SN A variety of sandstone composed largely of granular quartz which is cemented by silica forming a homogeneous mass of very high tensile and crushing strengths; especially used as a building stone, as gravel in road construction, and as aggregate in concrete. (DAC)
CN M.MT.AFU.AFU.AFU.DCU.AFU.
ARI.BCW

quatrefoils
DG.30 (R)
ALT **quatrefoil**
SN Figures composed of four equal lobes separated by cusps. (IDO)
CN D.DG.AFU.AFU.BIQ.BOK

quays
RK.1320 (A,L,B,R)
ALT **quay**
SN Use for artificial paved banks or solid landing places built parallel to and extending the shoreline to serve in the loading and unloading of vessels. For less fixed and solid structures built in similar locations and for similar purposes, use **wharves**; use **piers (marine landings)** when such lighter structures extend out over the water.
CN V.RK.AFU.ALO.ALO.GLI.ARI.ARI.
AXC.ALO

Quba
USE **Kuva**

Québec Inuit
USE **Ungava**

quebracho
MT.1295 (L)
SN The wood of Quebracho colorato, or red quebracho, found only along the west bank of the Parana and Paraguay rivers in Argentina and Paraguay. (MH)
UF schinopsis
CN M.MT.AFU.AFU.ALO.BIQ.DCU.
AFU.AFU.AFU.KWS

Quechua
FL.1611 (L)
UF Quichua
CN F.FL.ALO.ALO.ARI.ARI.ALO.AFU.
BUE

Queen Anne
FL.3198 (A,L)
SN Use with reference to the period of Queen Anne's reign (1702-14). Distinct from **Queen Anne Style**, which refers to certain decorative arts and furniture, 1870s to the present, and to the late 19th-century architecture style popularized by Richard Norman Shaw.
CN F.FL.ALO.BCW.ALO.ARI.BIQ.
BIQ.AFU.AFU.ALO.AXC

Queen Anne Revival
USE **Queen Anne Style**

Queen Anne Style
FL.3314 (A,L,B,R)

SN Use with reference to decorative arts and furniture, 1870s to the present, that revive forms from the 18th-century Queen Anne period. Use also for the late 19th-century architecture style popularized by Richard Norman Shaw. Distinct from **Queen Anne,** which refers to early 18th-century works.
UF Queen Anne Revival
Revival, Queen Anne
CN F.FL.ALO.BCW.ALO.AXC.DIO.ALO.AXC

queen closer
MT.114
SN A brick which has been cut in half along its length; it is of normal thickness but one-half normal width; used to complete a course or to space normal sized bricks. (DAC)
UF closer, queen
closure, queen
queen closure
CN M.MT.AFU.AFU.AFU.AXC.ALO.AFU.ARI.AFU.ARI

queen closure
USE **queen closer**

queen-post roofs
RT.453
ALT **queen-post roof**
SN Roofs supported by two queen posts. (DAC)
UF roofs, queen-post
CN V.RT.AFU.AFU.AFU.BIQ.ARI.AFU.ALO.ARI.BCW

queen-post trusses
RT.370
ALT **queen-post truss**
SN Trusses having two vertical posts between the rafters and the tie beam; the upper ends of the vertical posts are connected by a straining piece. (DAC)
UF queen trusses
trusses, queen
trusses, queen-post
CN V.RT.AFU.AFU.AFU.BCW.CLM.AFU.AFU.AFU.BZY

queen posts
RT.514
ALT **queen post**
SN The vertical tie beams in a truss; especially in roof trusses.
UF posts, queen
CN V.RT.AFU.AFU.AFU.BIQ.ARI.ALO.ALO.ARI.AFU.ARI

queen-size beds
TG.384
ALT **queen-size bed**
UF beds, queen-size
CN V.TG.AFU.AFU.ARI.AFU.ALO.AXC

queen trusses
USE **queen-post trusses**

queen's metal
MT.413
SN A Brittania metal with a small amount of zinc. (MH)
UF metal, queen's
CN M.MT.AFU.AFU.AFU.BZY.AFU.AFU.AFU.ALO.BUE.ALO.ALO.ARI

queens
HG.702 (L,R)
ALT **queen**
CN H.HG.AFU.AXC.CFS.CRG.CRG

Queenston limestone
MT.681
UF limestone, Queenston
CN M.MT.AFU.AFU.AFU.DCU.AFU.ALO.AFU.ALO.ALO.AFU.ALO.AFU.ALO

Querandí
FL.1697 (L)
CN F.FL.ALO.ALO.ARI.ARI.BOK.CFS

quercitron
USE **light yellow**

quercitron lake
MT.1801
SN An obsolete yellow lake pigment made from quercitron, a natural dyestuff. (MAYER)
UF flavine lake
lake, flavine
lake, quercitron
CN M.MT.AFU.AFU.ARI.AFU.AFU.ALO.ALO.BUE.AXC.ARI.AFU

quercitron lake (color)
USE **moderate orange yellow**

Quercus
USE **oak**

Quercus agrifolia
USE **coast live oak**

Quercus alba
USE **white oak**

Quercus bicolor
USE **swamp white oak**

Quercus borealis
USE **red oak**

Quercus catesbaei
USE **European turkey oak**

Quercus cerris
USE **European turkey oak**

Quercus coccinea
USE **scarlet oak**

Quercus falcata
USE **southern red oak**

Quercus garryana
USE **western white oak**

Quercus infectoria
USE **aleppo oak**

Quercus kelloggii
USE **California black oak**

Quercus laevis
USE **European turkey oak**

Quercus laurifolia
USE **laurel oak**

Quercus lobata
USE **California white oak**

Quercus lyrata
USE **overcup oak**

Quercus macrocarpa
USE **bur oak**

Quercus montana
MT.1236
CN M.MT.AFU.AFU.ALO.BIQ.DCU.AFU.AFU.AFU.IRA.BIQ.AFU

Quercus palustris
USE **pin oak**

Quercus pedunculata
USE **English oak**

Quercus petraea
USE **durmast oak**

Quercus prinus
MT.1237 (L)
CN M.MT.AFU.AFU.ALO.BIQ.DCU.AFU.AFU.AFU.IRA.BIQ.ALO

Quercus robur
USE **English oak**

Quercus rubia
USE **red oak**

Quercus sessiliflora
USE **sessile oak**

Quercus shumardii
USE **shumard oak**

Quercus stellata
USE **post oak**

Quercus velutina
USE **black oak**

Quercus virginiana
USE **live oak**

questionnaires
VW.289 (L,B)
ALT **questionnaire**
SN Documents containing a set of questions for submission to a number of persons in order to obtain statistically useful information. (GAHLM)
UF surveys (questionnaires)
CN V.VW.AFU.AFU.AFU.FZU.BIQ

Quiche
FL.1538 (L)
CN F.FL.ALO.ALO.ARI.ALO.BIQ.AFU.BOK

Quichua

USE **Quechua**

quick-service restaurants
USE **fast food restaurants**

quicklime
MT.329
SN Unslaked lime which is made from almost pure limestone. (PUTNAM)
UF anhydrous lime
burnt lime
caustic lime
common lime (quicklime)
lime, anhydrous
lime, burnt
lime, caustic
lime, common (quicklime)
lime, lump
lime, unslaked
lump lime
unslaked lime
CN M.MT.AFU.AFU.AFU.BUE.ALO

quicksilver
USE **mercury**

quietism
BM.706 (L,R)
CN B.BM.BZY.ALO.ARI.CXA

Quileute
FL.1354 (L)
UF Quillayute
CN F.FL.ALO.ALO.ARI.AFU.BIQ.ERE

quill
MT.942
CN M.MT.AFU.AFU.ALO.AFU.DOI

quill bits
USE **spoon bits**

quill pens
TB.274 (N)
ALT **quill pen**
SN Pens made from the shafts of wing feathers or quills of various birds. (MAYER)
UF pens, quill
CN V.TB.AFU.ARI.CLM.AFU.ALO.DOI.BCW

Quillacinga
FL.1667 (L)
CN F.FL.ALO.ALO.ARI.ARI.BCW.DIO

Quillayute
USE **Quileute**

quilling (paper)
USE **paper quillwork**

quillwork, paper
USE **paper quillwork**

quilting
KT.566 (L)
ALT **quilted**
SN Stitching together two or more layers of cloth, usually working the stitches into designs. (W)
CN K.KT.AFU.ALO.ELK.DUC.ALO.BIQ

quiltmakers
HG.540 (L)
ALT **quiltmaker**
CN H.HG.AFU.AXC.BUE.ARI.CXA.CFS.AXC

Quimbaya
FL.1668 (L)
CN F.FL.ALO.ALO.ARI.ARI.BCW.DOI

quinacridone red
MT.1708
UF acra red
acridone red
red, acra
red, acridone
red, quinacridone
CN M.MT.AFU.AFU.ARI.AFU.AFU.ALO.ALO.BCW.AXC.BIQ

quinacridone red (color)
USE **deep reddish orange**
moderate red
strong red

quinacridone violet
MT.1724
UF violet, quinacridone
CN M.MT.AFU.AFU.ARI.AFU.AFU.ALO.ALO.BIQ.AXC.ALO

Quinault
FL.1355 (L)
CN F.FL.ALO.ALO.ARI.AFU.BIQ.EWY

quintfoils
USE **cinquefoils**

Quioco
USE **Chokwe**

quirk beads
RT.786
ALT **quirk bead**
SN Bead moldings separated from an adjoining surface by quirks, along one or both sides. (RS)
UF beads and quirks
beads, quirk
quirks, beads and
CN V.RT.AFU.ALO.AFU.BOK.AFU.AFU.AXC.BCW.ALO.AFU

quirks
RT.809
ALT **quirk**
SN Sharp, V-shaped channels or grooves separating one element from another, as between moldings or between the abacus and echinus of a Doric capital. (HAS)
CN V.RT.AFU.ALO.AFU.BOK.ALO.ALO

quirks, beads and
USE **quirk beads**

quitch grass
USE **cutch-grass**

Quito
FL.1718
CN F.FL.ALO.ALO.AXC.ALO.AFU.AXC.ALO

Qumtura
USE **Kumutra**

Qumutra
USE **Kumutra**

quoins
RT.676 (A,N,B,R)
ALT **quoin**
SN Stones helping to form the corner of a wall of masonry, especially when accentuated by a difference in the surface treatment of the stones forming the corner from that of the rest of the wall mass. (RS)
UF coigns
coillons
coins (wall components)
coyns
cunes
CN V.RT.AFU.AFU.AFU.BIQ.BUE.ALO.ALO.BOK

quonset huts
RK.26 (A,B)
ALT **quonset hut**
SN Use for prefabricated buildings with a semicircular cross section, generally built of corrugated metal and provided with thermal insulation.
UF huts, nissen
huts, quonset
nissen huts
CN V.RK.AFU.ALO.AFU.ALO.BZY

quotations
VW.39 (L,R)
ALT **quotation**
SN Use for excerpts of parts of a literary composition, as into another book or writing; use also for statements of market price of one or more securities. (BLACKS)
CN V.VW.AFU.AFU.AFU.CFS.AFU

quotations (visual)
BM.164 (R)
SN Use for references to past visual art in another work of visual art.
CN B.BM.AFU.AFU.ARI.BOK.CXA

Quva
USE **Kuva**

Qyzyl
USE **Kizil**

Rabai
FL.606
CN F.FL.ALO.AFU.AXC.AXC.ALO.BOK.BCW

rabbet joints
TF.594
ALT **rabbet-joint**
UF joints, rabbet
joints, rebated
rebated joints
CN V.TF.ALO.AFU.ELK

rabbet joints, double
USE **double rabbet joints**

rabbet planes
TB.922 (N)
ALT **rabbet plane**
SN Wood or metal planes which are flat across the sole, in which the cutting iron extends to the extreme edge on one or both sides;(SALAM) used to cut a rabbet along the grain at the edge of the wood. (MERCER)
UF boxing planes
check planes
geelums
planes, boxing
planes, check
planes, rabbet
planes, rebate
rebate planes
CN V.TB.AFU.BCW.CFS.ALO.AFU.DUC.ALO.BUE

rabbet planes (badger planes)
USE **badger planes**

rabbet planes, bullnose
USE **bullnose planes**

rabbet saws
TB.992 (N)
ALT **rabbet saw**
SN Saw sets in a plane-like stock with an adjustable fence and blade; used to saw rabbets in the edge of a board. (KNIGHT)
UF saws, rabbet
CN V.TB.AFU.BCW.CFS.ALO.AFU.EWY.AFU.BCW

rabbeted ledge and miter joints
TF.597
ALT **rabbeted ledge and miter joint**
UF joints, rabbeted ledge and miter
CN V.TF.ALO.AFU.ELK.ARI

rabbeted locks
TF.210
ALT **rabbeted lock**
SN Locks which are fitted into and flush with the rabbet on a rabbeted door jamb. (MEANS)
UF locks, rabbeted
locks, rebated
rebated locks
CN V.TF.AFU.AFU.AFU.AFU.DIO.BIQ.AFU.CRG.ALO

rabbets, horned
USE **horned rabbets**

rabbinical seminaries
RK.821 (L)
ALT **rabbinical seminary**
UF Jewish theological seminaries
seminaries, Jewish theological
seminaries, rabbinical
CN V.RK.AFU.ALO.ALO.CXA.ARI.ALO.DOI.ALO

rabbis
HG.234 (L,R)
ALT **rabbi**
CN H.HG.AFU.AXC.AXC.BIQ.AFU.ARI.DZW

rabbit houses
USE **rabbit hutches**

rabbit hutches
RK.92 (A,L)
ALT **rabbit hutch**
UF houses, rabbit
hutches, rabbit
rabbit houses
rabbit warrens
warrens, rabbit
CN V.RK.AFU.ALO.ALO.AFU.ALO.CLM

rabbit warrens
USE **rabbit hutches**

Rabinal
FL.1539
CN F.FL.ALO.ALO.ARI.ALO.BIQ.AFU.BUE

rabs
TB.620
ALT **rab**
SN In plastering, sticks or beaters used for mixing hair with mortar. (PUTNAM)
CN V.TB.AFU.BCW.BCW.ALO.FZU

race discrimination
BM.1107 (L)
UF discrimination, race
racism
CN B.BM.CRG.BCW.ARI.AXC

race knives
TB.129 (N)
ALT **race knife**
SN Cutting tools with a blade hooked at the tip; used for marking outlines on wood or metal. (W)
UF knives, race
CN V.TB.AFU.ARI.AXC.ALO.BUE.ALO

racecourses
USE **racetracks**

racetracks
RG.176 (A,L,B,R)
ALT **racetrack**
UF racecourses
tracks (racetracks)
CN V.RG.AFU.AFU.DOI.CFS.ALO

racetracks, automobile
USE **automobile racetracks**

racetracks, horse
USE **horse racetracks**

raceways
RT.1347
ALT **raceway**
SN Any furrows or channels constructed to loosely house electrical conductors. (MEANS)
UF electric raceways
raceways, electric
CN V.RT.ALO.ARI.ALO.CRG

raceways, electric
USE **raceways**

Rachtrakuta
USE **Rashtrakuta**

racing forms
VW.623
ALT **racing form**
SN Sheets that provide detailed information about horse races, including background data on the horses and jockeys. (RHDEL2)
UF forms, racing
CN V.VW.AFU.ALO.AFU.CXA.AFU.BIQ

racing tracks, cycle
USE **velodromes**

racism
USE **race discrimination**

rack railroads
RD.102 (L)
ALT **rack railroad**
SN Use for light rail transit in which the vehicles climb grades too steep for normal rail traction modes by means of rotating gears mounted on the train that mesh with a rack between the rails. (W)
UF cog railroads
rack railways
railroads, cog
railroads, rack
CN V.RD.ALO.ARI.AFU.AFU.ALO.AFU.ALO

rack railways
USE **rack railroads**

racks
TG.611 (L,N)
ALT **rack**
UF racks, storage
storage racks
CN V.TG.AFU.AFU.BIQ.AXC

racks (hardware)
TF.269
ALT **rack (hardware)**
CN V.TF.AFU.AFU.AFU.AFU.EFQ

racks, belt
USE **belt racks**

racks, drying
USE **clotheshorses**

racks, hall
USE **hat racks**

racks, hat
USE **hat racks**

racks, magazine
USE **magazine racks**

racks, muffin
USE **muffin stands**

racks, music
USE **music stands**

racks, shoe
USE **shoe racks**

racks, storage
USE **racks**

racks, tie
USE **tie racks**

racks, towel
USE **towel racks**

racquetball courts
RK.1016 (B)
ALT **racquetball court**
UF courts, racquetball
CN V.RK.AFU.ALO.ALO.EWY.ALO.BOK

radial
DC.11
CN D.DC.AFU.ALO.AFU.BCW

radial-arm saws
TB.1002 (N)
ALT **radial-arm saw**
SN Circular saws suspended from and moving along a cantilevered arm mounted above the saw table. (DAC)
UF saws, radial-arm
CN V.TB.AFU.BCW.CFS.ALO.AFU.EWY.AXC.AXC

radial balance
USE **radial symmetry**

radial brick
USE **compass brick**

radial plan
BM.84
UF radiocentric plan
CN B.BM.AFU.AFU.ARI.AFU.EFQ.ALO

radial steps
USE **winders (steps)**

radial symmetry
BM.97
SN Arrangement of forms in which three or more forces, which are similar in visual strength and character, are distributed around a center point.
UF balance, radial
radial balance
symmetry, radial
CN B.BM.AFU.AFU.ARI.AFU.FOG.ARI

radiant heating
RT.1394 (L,B)
UF heating, radiant
CN V.RT.ALO.BCW.AFU.AFU.ARI.ARI

radiant panel heating
USE **panel heating**

radiating brick
USE **compass brick**

radiation
BM.864 (L)
CN B.BM.CFS.AXC.ALO.AFU.ARI

radiation shelters
USE **nuclear bomb shelters**

radiation, solar
USE **solar radiation**

radiation, ultraviolet
USE **ultraviolet radiation**

Radiation, UV
USE **ultraviolet radiation**

radiator units, baseboard
USE **baseboard units**

radiators
RT.1430 (A,N)
ALT **radiator**
SN Use to designate a nest of pipes, usually of cast iron and two feet or more in height, containing circulating water or steam for heating a room.
CN V.RT.ALO.BCW.AFU.ALO.ALO.ARI

Radical Realist
USE **Photorealist**

radicalism
BM.366 (L)
UF counter culture
culture, counter
ultraism
CN B.BM.ALO.ALO.CLM.FIM

radio broadcasters
HG.284
ALT **radio broadcaster**
UF broadcasters, radio
CN H.HG.AFU.AXC.BCW.ALO.AFU.ALO.ALO

radio broadcasting
KD.111 (L,B)
UF broadcasting, radio
CN K.KD.AFU.ALO.ARI.ALO.AFU

radio masts
USE **radio towers**

radio recording studios
USE **radio studios**

radio scripts
VW.73 (L)
ALT **radio script**
UF scripts, radio
CN V.VW.AFU.AFU.AFU.ERE.ALO

radio stations
RK.203 (A,L,B,R)
ALT **radio station**
UF stations, radio
CN V.RK.AFU.ALO.ALO.ARI.AFU.ARI.AFU.AFU

radio studios
RM.224 (B)
ALT **radio studio**
UF radio recording studios
recording studios, radio
studios, radio
CN V.RM.AFU.DIO.ALO.DOI.ARI.AFU

radio tables
TG.755
ALT **radio table**
UF tables, radio
CN V.TG.AFU.AFU.BIQ.BOK.ALO.ELK

radio towers
RK.212 (B)
ALT **radio tower**
UF masts, radio
radio masts
radio transmission towers
towers, radio
towers, transmitter
transmitter towers
CN V.RK.AFU.ALO.ALO.ARI.ALO.AFU

radio transmission towers
USE **radio towers**

radio, police
USE **police communication systems**

radioactivation analysis
USE **neutron activation analysis**

radioactive dating
KT.503 (L)
SN Dating by measuring processes which involve the decay of radioactive isotopes. (FOFDA)
UF dating, radioactive
dating, radiometric
radiometric dating
CN K.KT.AFU.ALO.EFQ.AFU.BCW

radioactive pollution
BM.440 (L)
UF environmental radioactivity
nuclear pollution
pollution, nuclear
pollution, radioactive
radioactivity, environmental
CN B.BM.AXC.BCW.ALO.AXC

radioactivity, environmental
USE **radioactive pollution**

radioautography
USE **autoradiography**

radiocarbon dating
KT.506 (L,R)
SN Method of dating, based on the known half-life of carbon-14, by measuring the amount of low-level radioactivity of carbon remaining in ancient and dead material of organic origin and thus determining when a plant or animal had died. (HOL-HZR)
UF C-14 dating
carbon-14 dating
dating, C-14
dating, carbon-14
dating, radiocarbon
CN K.KT.AFU.ALO.EFQ.AFU.BIQ

radiocentric plan
USE **radial plan**

radiograms
USE **radiographs**

radiographs
VJ.99 (N)
ALT **radiograph**
SN Use for images produced on photographic film by a radiation other than light, especially x-rays or gamma rays. (W)
UF photographs, x-ray
radiograms
shadowgraphs (radiographs)
skiagrams
skiagraphs
x-ray photographs
x-rays (radiographs)
CN V.VJ.AFU.ARI.AFU.BCW

radiography
KT.388 (A,L,R)
SN The making of radiographs.
UF x-ray photography
CN K.KT.AFU.ALO.DUC.DIO.ARI.ARI.BIQ

radiometric dating
USE **radioactive dating**

radius
BM.800 (L)
CN B.BM.CFS.ARI.AXC.BOK

radius brick
USE **compass brick**

radius of gyration
BM.913
SN In mechanics, the distance from the axis to a point, such that, if the whole mass of a body were concentrated at it, the moment of inertia would remain unchanged. (DAC)
UF gyration, radius of
CN B.BM.CFS.AXC.BIQ.ARI.ALO.AFU

radius rods
USE **radius tools**

radius tools
TB.621
ALT **radius tool**
SN Plastering tools consisting of a wooden arm fixed at one end to a center about which it swivels. (DAC)
UF gig sticks
radius rods
rods, radius
sticks, gig
tools, radius
CN V.TB.AFU.BCW.BCW.ALO.GFO

raffia
MT.1835 (L)
SN Strong fiber from leafstalks of the raffia palm used for weaving, basketry, and other craft work. (MAYER)
CN M.MT.AFU.AFU.ARI.ALO.AFU.AFU.ALO.CRG

raffiawork
MT.2778 (L)
CN M.MT.AFU.AXC.CFS

raft augers
TB.826 (N)
ALT **raft auger**
SN Augers for boring holes in logs, so that they can be pinned together as rafts. (SLOANE)
UF augers, raft
CN V.TB.AFU.BCW.CFS.ALO.AFU.ALO.BCW

raft foundations
RT.168 (B)
ALT **raft foundation**
SN Use for continuous foundations under the full extent of a structure that are constructed to be watertight because of their location in muck, silt, or quicksand.
UF boat foundations
foundations, boat
foundations, raft
CN V.RT.AFU.AFU.AFU.AXC.BUE.ARI.AFU.ALO

raft shackles
TB.1072 (N)
ALT **raft shackle**
SN Lengths of chain with spikes at the ends; used to bind logs together into rafts. (SLOANE)
UF shackles, raft
CN V.TB.AFU.BCW.CFS.ALO.ALO.CLM

rafter plates
USE **roof plates**

rafters
RT.497 (B)
ALT **rafter**
SN Sloping roof members that support the roof covering and extend from the ridge or the hip of the roof to the eaves. (PUTNAM)
CN V.RT.AFU.AFU.AFU.BIQ.ARI.ALO.ALO.AFU

rafters, angle
USE **hip rafters**

rafters, barge
USE **bargeboards**

rafters, common
USE **common rafters**

rafters, cripple
USE **jack rafters**

rafters, fascia
USE **bargeboards**

rafters, fly
USE **bargeboards**

rafters, hip
USE **hip rafters**

rafters, intermediate
USE **common rafters**

rafters, jack
USE **jack rafters**

rafters, lookout
USE **lookouts (roof components)**

rafters, principal
USE **principal rafters**

rafters, show
USE **show rafters**

rafters, trussed
USE **trussed rafters**

rafters, valley
USE **valley rafters**

rag board
USE **museum board**

rag felt
MT.1896
SN A type of heavy paper composed of rags impregnated with asphalt; used in the manufacture of waterproofing membranes, and for making asphalt shingles and other types of composition roofing, such as asphalt roofing. (PUTNAM)
UF felt, rag
CN M.MT.AFU.AFU.ARI.ALO.ALO.AXC.AFU.ALO.AFU

rag paper
MT.1895
UF paper, rag
CN M.MT.AFU.AFU.ARI.ALO.ALO.AXC.AFU.ALO

rag, Barnack
USE **Barnack stone**

rag, coral
USE **coral limestone**

rage
USE **anger**

Raghogarh
FL.2284
CN F.FL.ALO.ARI.AXC.ALO.AFU.BZY.BCW.AXC

raglets
USE **dado planes**

ragstone
MT.689
UF Kentish ragstone
ragstone, Kentish
CN M.MT.AFU.AFU.AFU.DCU.AFU.ALO.AFU.ALO.ALO.ALO.AFU

ragstone, Kentish
USE **ragstone**

rail bolts
USE **handrail bolts**

rail fences

RM.439
ALT **rail fence**
SN Fences of posts and split rails. (W)
UF fences, rail
CN V.RM.ALO.AFU.BCW.BCW

rail rapid transit
USE **rapid rail transit systems**

rail rapid transit systems
USE **rapid rail transit systems**

rail service, commuter
USE **commuter railroads**

rail systems, urban
USE **urban rail systems**

rail transit
USE **rail transit systems**

rail transit systems
RD.98
ALT **rail transit system**
UF fixed-guideway transit
rail transit
systems, rail transit
transit systems, rail
transit, fixed-guideway
transit, rail
CN V.RD.ALO.ARI.AFU.AFU.ALO

rail transit systems, rapid
USE **rapid rail transit systems**

rail transit, light
USE **light rail transit**

rail, suburban
USE **commuter railroads**

railing, Chinese
USE **Chinese fretwork**

railings
RT.1038 (B,R)
ALT **railing**
SN Parapets or balustrades of a lightweight, partly open, metal or wood construction.
CN V.RT.AFU.AXC.ALO.AFU.ALO

railings, window
USE **window guards**

railroad apartments
USE **railroad flats**

railroad bridges
RK.1291 (A,L,B)
ALT **railroad bridge**
UF bridges, railroad
bridges, railway
railroad viaducts
railway bridges
viaducts, railroad
CN V.RK.AFU.ALO.ALO.GLI.ALO.AFU.ALO.ARI.AFU

railroad commuter service
USE **commuter railroads**

railroad flats
RM.268
ALT **railroad flat**
SN Apartments in a substandard building having a series of rooms arranged in a line usually with each room forming the corridor to the next. (W)
UF apartments, railroad
flats, railroad
railroad apartments
CN V.RM.AFU.DIO.ARI.ALO.BIQ.AFU.ALO.ALO

railroad maps
VW.219 (L)
ALT **railroad map**
SN Maps depicting the location of systems of railroad tracks.
UF maps, railroad
maps, railway
railway maps
CN V.VW.AFU.AFU.AFU.FZU.AXC.AFU.ARI.AXC.DIO.AXC

railroad museums
RK.406 (A,L)
ALT **railroad museum**
UF museums, railroad
railway museums
CN V.RK.AFU.ALO.ALO.BCW.AXC.ARI.AXC.BZY.ARI

railroad sidings
USE **sidings**

railroad stations
RK.1240 (A,L,B,R)
ALT **railroad station**
UF depots
depots, railway
railway depots
railway stations
stations, railroad
CN V.RK.AFU.ALO.ALO.GLI.AFU.ALO.AFU.ALO

railroad terminals
RK.1241 (A,L)
ALT **railroad terminal**
UF terminals, railroad
CN V.RK.AFU.ALO.ALO.GLI.AFU.ALO.AFU.ALO.AFU

railroad tunnels
RK.1306 (A,L,N)
ALT **railroad tunnel**
UF railway tunnels
tunnels, railroad
CN V.RK.AFU.ALO.ALO.GLI.ALO.ALO.ALO

railroad viaducts
USE **railroad bridges**

railroad yards
RG.221 (L)
ALT **railroad yard**
UF railway yards
yards, railroad
CN V.RG.AFU.AFU.EFQ.ALO

railroads
RD.115 (A,L,B,R)
ALT **railroad**
UF railways
CN V.RD.ALO.ARI.ALO

railroads, cable
USE **cable railroads**

railroads, cog
USE **rack railroads**

railroads, commuter
USE **commuter railroads**

railroads, elevated
USE **elevated railroads**

railroads, funicular
USE **funicular railroads**

railroads, monorail
USE **monorails**

railroads, overhead
USE **elevated railroads**

railroads, rack
USE **rack railroads**

railroads, underground
USE **subways**

rails
RT.824
ALT **rail**
CN V.RT.AFU.ALO.ALO.ARI

rails (handrails)
USE **handrails**

rails, altar
USE **altar rails**

rails, arm
USE **arm rails**

rails, back
USE **back rails**

rails, blanket
USE **blanket rails**

rails, bottom
USE **bottom rails**

rails, chair
USE **chair rails**

rails, communion
USE **communion rails**

rails, crest
USE **crest rails**

rails, cross
USE **slats**

rails, door
USE **door rails**

rails, guard
USE **guard rails**

rails, lock

USE **lock rails**

rails, medial
USE **medial braces**

rails, meeting
USE **meeting rails**

rails, picture
USE **picture rails**

rails, plaque
USE **plate rails**

rails, plate
USE **plate rails**

rails, safety
USE **safety rails**

rails, seat
USE **seat rails**

rails, snow
USE **snow guards**

rails, toilet safety
USE **toilet safety rails**

rails, towel
USE **towel racks**

railway bridges
USE **railroad bridges**

railway buildings
RK.1238 (A,L,B)
ALT **railway building**
UF buildings, railway
railway works
works, railway
CN V.RK.AFU.ALO.ALO.GLI.AFU.ALO.AFU

railway depots
USE **railroad stations**

railway hotels
RK.955
ALT **railway hotel**
UF hotels, railway
CN V.RK.AFU.ALO.ALO.ELK.BCW.ARI

railway maps
USE **railroad maps**

railway museums
USE **railroad museums**

railway stations
USE **railroad stations**

railway tunnels
USE **railroad tunnels**

railway turntables
USE **turntables (rail transportation structures)**

railway works
USE **railway buildings**

railway yards
USE **railroad yards**

railways
USE **railroads**

railways, cable car
USE **cable railroads**

railways, elevated
USE **elevated railroads**

railways, funicular
USE **funicular railroads**

railways, metropolitan
USE **urban rail systems**

railways, street
USE **street-railroads**

railways, underground
USE **subways**

rain
BM.751 (L,B)
CN B.BM.CFS.ALO.AXC.ALO.BIQ.ALO

rain forests
RD.251 (L)
ALT **rain forest**
UF forests, rain
tropical rain forests
CN V.RD.ARI.AFU.BCW.ALO.AFU.ALO.AFU

rain, acid
USE **acid rain**

rainbow roofs
RT.436
ALT **rainbow roof**
SN Gable roofs in the form of a Gothic arch, with a gently sloping convex surface. (RHDEL2)
UF roofs, rainbow
roofs, whaleback
whaleback roofs
CN V.RT.AFU.AFU.AFU.BIQ.ARI.AFU.AFU.AFU.BUE

rainwater heads
USE **leader heads**

rainwater leaders
USE **conductors (piping)**

raised
DC.138
SN Having a pattern or design in relief; or being elevated above a surface to which it is attached or is a part. (W)
CN D.DC.AFU.BCW.AXC

raised flooring systems
USE **access floors**

raised-letter printing
USE **thermography**

raised moldings
USE **bolection moldings**

raised-relief maps
VW.160
ALT **raised-relief map**
UF maps, raised-relief
CN V.VW.AFU.AFU.AFU.FZU.AXC.AFU.ARI.AFU.CXA.ALO

raising
USE **lifting**

raising irons
USE **jumpers**

raising plates
USE **wall plates**

Rajasimha
FL.2207
CN F.FL.ALO.ARI.AXC.ALO.AFU.AXC.AFU.ALO

Rajasthani
FL.2285 (L)
CN F.FL.ALO.ARI.AXC.ALO.AFU.BZY.BCW.BCW

Rajendravarman
FL.2337
CN F.FL.ALO.ARI.BCW.ALO.ARI.AFU.BCW

Rajput
FL.2265 (L)
CN F.FL.ALO.ARI.AXC.ALO.AFU.BZY.BCW

raked joints
TF.627
ALT **raked joint**
SN Joints in a masonry wall which have the mortar raked out to a specified depth while it is still soft. (MEANS)
UF joints, raked
CN V.TF.ALO.ARI.ALO.AFU.ARI.AXC.ARI

raked moldings
USE **raking moldings**

rakers
TB.617 (N)
ALT **raker**
SN Tools used for raking out decayed mortar from the joints of brickwork. (MEANS)
CN V.TB.AFU.BCW.BCW.ALO.FOG.AFU

raking arches
USE **rampant arches**

raking cornices
RT.336
ALT **raking cornice**
SN Cornices following the slope of a gable, pediment, or roof. (HAS)
UF cornices, raking
CN V.RT.AFU.AFU.AFU.BCW.BZY.ALO.ALO.AFU.ARI

raking moldings
RT.806
ALT **raking molding**
SN Slanted moldings, as in a pediment. (W)
UF canted moldings

moldings, canted
moldings, raked
moldings, raking
raked moldings
CN V.RT.AFU.ALO.AFU.BOK.AFU.ALO.CFS

Rakka ware
USE **Raqqa ware**

raku
MT.156 (L)
SN Type of Japanese pottery which is covered with a lead glaze and fired at a very low temperature, leaving the body soft and porous. (SAVAGE)
UF raku ware
ware, raku
CN M.MT.AFU.AFU.AFU.AXC.ALO.ALO.AFU.ALO.ALO

raku ware
USE **raku**

Ramadan
KM.87 (L)
CN K.KM.AFU.CFS.ARI.CFS

Ramesside period
FL.2817
CN F.FL.ALO.AXC.ALO.ARI.AFU.BUE.ARI

ramheads
USE **froes**

ramie
MT.1836 (L)
SN A fiber used for cordage and for various kinds of coarse fabrics. (MH)
UF China grass
fiber, ramie
grass, China
ramie fiber
rhea
CN M.MT.AFU.AFU.ARI.ALO.AFU.AFU.ALO.CXA

ramie fiber
USE **ramie**

rammed earth
MT.2058 (L,B)
SN A material usually consisting of clay, sand, or other aggregate (such as sea shells) and water, which has been compressed and dried; used in building construction. (DAC)
UF earth, rammed
earth, tamped
pisé de terre
tamped earth
CN M.MT.AFU.AFU.ARI.BOK.AFU.AXC.AFU

rammers
TB.27
ALT **rammer**
SN Power-driven tools used to compact soil or other granular material. (DAC)
CN V.TB.AFU.ARI.AFU.ALO.AFU.AFU.AFU

rampant arches
RT.239
ALT **rampant arch**
SN Arches in which the impost on one side is higher than the impost on the other. (RS)
UF arches, raking
arches, rampant
arches, rising
raking arches
rising arches
CN V.RT.AFU.AFU.AFU.BCW.AFU.AFU.AFU.CXA

rampant barrel vaults
RT.542
ALT **rampant barrel vault**
SN Barrel vaults having their two springing points at different levels. (RS)
UF barrel vaults, rampant
rampant vaults
vaults, rampant
vaults, rampant barrel
CN V.RT.AFU.AFU.AFU.BIQ.BOK.AFU.ALO.AFU.AXC

rampant vaults
USE **rampant barrel vaults**

ramparts
RT.1183 (A,B)
ALT **rampart**
SN Broad embankments or mounds of earth raised as a fortification about a place. (W)
UF bulwarks
CN V.RT.AFU.BUE.AFU.BCW.AFU.AXC

ramparts, plant
USE **plant fortifications**

ramps
RT.1065 (A,L,N,B,R)
ALT **ramp**
SN Sloping floors or walks leading from one level to another. (W)
UF inclined planes
inclines (ramps)
planes, inclined
CN V.RT.AFU.BIQ.ARI

ramps, boat
USE **launching ramps**

ramps, launching
USE **launching ramps**

ramps, moving
USE **moving ramps**

ramps, wheelchair
USE **wheelchair ramps**

rance
MT.800
SN A dull-red marble with blue and read streaks and veins. (MAYER)
UF Belgian marble
marble, Belgian
CN M.MT.AFU.AFU.AFU.DCU.AFU.ARI.ARI.ARI.BCW.ARI

ranch houses
RK.251 (A,L)
ALT **ranch house**
SN Designates asymmetrically massed, one-story houses with low-pitched roofs and rambling shapes; may also be used for the main dwelling on ranches.
UF houses, ranch
CN V.RK.AFU.ALO.ALO.AXC.ALO.AFU.CLM.BCW

ranchers
HG.370 (L)
ALT **rancher**
SN Persons who own, operate, or are employed on ranches. (W)
CN H.HG.AFU.AXC.BIQ.ALO.AXC.AFU.BIQ

ranches
RG.23 (A,L,B)
ALT **ranch**
SN Denotes establishments with extensive landholdings usually for the grazing of cattle; larger than farms.
CN V.RG.AFU.AFU.AFU.BIQ

ranches, cattle
USE **cattle ranches**

ranches, dude
USE **dude ranches**

ranches, guest
USE **dude ranches**

random joints
TF.598
ALT **random joint**
SN Joints used in furniture making when pieces of veneer are joined without special attention to whether or not the various pieces are of equal widths. (PUTNAM)
UF joints, random
CN V.TF.ALO.AFU.ERE

range (agricultural landscape)
USE **rangeland**

rangefinder cameras
TB.300 (L,N)
ALT **rangefinder camera**
SN Cameras with an attachment for measuring by optical means the distance between the camera and an object. (W)
UF cameras, rangefinder
CN V.TB.AFU.ARI.CLM.ARI.AFU.AFU.ALO.ARI

rangeland
RD.289 (L)
SN Open tracts of land, usually unfenced, suitable for grazing live-

stock.
UF range (agricultural landscape)
CN V.RD.ARI.ALO.AFU.AFU.BIQ

ranges
RG.144 (L)
ALT **range**
SN Areas equipped with targets for practice in shooting weapons (RHDEL2); when possible use a more specific term.
UF target ranges
CN V.RG.AFU.AFU.DIO

ranges, archery
USE **archery ranges**

ranges, driving
USE **driving ranges**

ranges, firing
USE **firing ranges**

ranges, guided missile
USE **guided missile ranges**

ranges, rifle
USE **rifle ranges**

ranges, shooting
USE **shooting ranges**

ranges, skeet
USE **skeet ranges**

Rangila
USE **Muhammad Shah**

rapakivi
MT.603 (L)
CN M.MT.AFU.AFU.AFU.DCU.AFU.AFU.AFU.AFU.AFU.ARI.ALO.ARI.ARI

rape oil
MT.2039 (L)
SN An oil obtained from seeds of the mustard family. (MH)
UF oil, rape
CN M.MT.AFU.AFU.ARI.ARI.AXC.ARI.BUE

rapid-curing asphalt
MT.985
SN Liquid asphalt composed of asphalt cement and a naphtha or gasoline-type diluent of high volatility. (DAC)
UF asphalt, rapid-curing
CN M.MT.AFU.AFU.ALO.ALO.AFU.AXC.AFU

rapid-hardening cement
USE **accelerated cement**

rapid rail transit
USE **rapid rail transit systems**

rapid rail transit systems
RD.107 (A,L)
ALT **rapid rail transit system**
SN Systems providing heavy rail service operating on an exclusive right of way separate from other traffic systems, usually in an urban context, and with multiunit trains using electric power and moving large numbers of passengers.
UF rail rapid transit
rail rapid transit systems
rail transit systems, rapid
rapid rail transit
rapid transit
rapid transit facilities
rapid transit railways
rapid transit systems
rapid transit, rail
RRT
systems, rapid rail transit
transit systems, rapid rail
transit, rapid
CN V.RD.ALO.ARI.AFU.AFU.ALO.AXC

rapid transit
USE **rapid rail transit systems**

rapid transit facilities
USE **rapid rail transit systems**

rapid transit railways
USE **rapid rail transit systems**

rapid transit systems
USE **rapid rail transit systems**

rapid transit systems, urban
USE **urban transit systems**

rapid transit, bus
USE **bus transit systems**

rapid transit, personal
USE **personal rapid transit**

rapid transit, rail
USE **rapid rail transit systems**

Rapidographs (TM)
USE **stylographs**

rapids
RD.165 (L)
SN Irregular, partially obstructed, fast-flowing areas in rivers or streams.
UF river rapids
CN V.RD.ARI.AFU.AFU.ALO.BIQ.ALO

Raqqa ware
FL.3440 (L)
UF Rakka ware
ware, Rakka
ware, Raqqa
CN F.FL.ALO.BIQ.AFU.BIQ.ALO.AFU

Rashtrakuta
FL.2212 (L)
UF Rachtrakuta
CN F.FL.ALO.ARI.AXC.ALO.AFU.AXC.BIQ

rasp brushes
USE **file brushes**

rasps
TB.131 (L,N)
ALT **rasp**
SN Files with projecting teeth for rough work. (MEANS)
CN V.TB.AFU.ARI.AXC.ALO.BZY

rasps, cabinet
USE **cabinet rasps**

rasps, half-round cabinet
USE **cabinet rasps**

rasps, riffler
USE **riffler rasps**

Rasulid
FL.3530
CN F.FL.ALO.BIQ.AFU.GLI

rat claw feet
TG.919
ALT **rat claw foot**
SN Claw and ball feet which have very sharp and thin claws. (W)
UF claw feet, rat
feet, rat claw
CN V.TG.ALO.DZW.AFU.DCU.AFU.AFU.AFU

rat tail files
USE **round files**

rat tail hinges
USE **rattail hinges**

Ratanakosin
USE **Bangkok**

ratchet-base candlestands
USE **ratchet candlestands**

ratchet braces
TB.848
ALT **ratchet brace**
SN Braces with a ratchet-driven chuck, permitting its use in confined spaces where complete circular sweeps of an ordinary brace would be impossible. (DAC)
UF braces, ratchet
CN V.TB.AFU.BCW.CFS.ALO.AFU.BIQ.AFU

ratchet candlestands
TG.632
ALT **ratchet candlestand**
SN Candlestands with a notched mechanism for raising or lowering a support for a candle and usually with a trestle base. (FAIRB)
UF candlestands, ratchet
candlestands, ratchet-base
ratchet-base candlestands
CN V.TG.AFU.AFU.BIQ.BCW.ALO.ALO.ALO

ratchet hoists
USE **come-alongs**

ratchet nails
TF.398
ALT **ratchet nail**
SN Annular ring nails used for nailing into metal studs to hold gypsum board in drywall construction.

(PUTNAM)
UF nails, ratchet
CN V.TF.AFU.AFU.AFU.ALO.AFU.CFS.AFU.CLM

ratchet pullers
USE **come-alongs**

ratchet screwdrivers
TB.198
ALT **ratchet screwdriver**
SN Screwdrivers that are operated by the reciprocating motion of the handle which enables the user to drive a screw easily.
UF screwdrivers, ratchet
CN V.TB.AFU.ARI.BOK.ALO.ARI

ratchet screwdrivers, spiral
USE **spiral ratchet screwdrivers**

rathäuser
RK.998 (A)
ALT **rathaus**
CN V.RK.AFU.ALO.ALO.ERE.ALO.AFU.BCW

rathskellers
RM.119
ALT **rathskeller**
CN V.RM.AFU.DIO.ALO.BCW.CRG

ratings, flame spread
USE **flame spread ratings**

ratio, golden
USE **golden section**

rationalism (architecture)
BM.195 (A)
ALT **rationalist (architecture)**
SN Use for certain approaches to architecture that rely on a rethinking of architectural problems rather than on tradition, especially the specific movements in France and England in the 18th and 19th centuries, and in Italy in the 1920s.
CN B.BM.AFU.AFU.AXC.CLM.BZY

rationalism (philosophy)
BM.522 (L,R)
SN A theory that reason is in itself a source of knowledge superior to and independent of sense perception. (W)
CN B.BM.BIQ.AXC.DZW

rationalization (architecture)
USE **modular coordination**

ratonas
TG.686
ALT **ratona**
SN Spanish and Portuguese Colonial very small, low tables generally having flat carving and heavy aprons. (HAYWAR)
CN V.TG.AFU.AFU.BIQ.BOK.AFU.CFS

rattail hinges
TF.121
ALT **rattail hinge**
UF hinges, rattail
rat tail hinges
CN V.TF.AFU.AFU.AFU.AFU.CLM.AFU.ELK.AFU

rattan
MT.1022 (A,L)
CN M.MT.AFU.AFU.ALO.BIQ.ALO.AFU

Rauschrot
USE **orpiment**
realgar

rauzas
RK.471
ALT **rauza**
SN In Islamic India, mausoleums.
CN V.RK.AFU.ALO.ALO.BOK.ARI.ALO.AFU.ALO

ravelins
RT.1209
ALT **ravelin**
SN In military architecture, an outwork formed of two faces of a salient angle and constructed beyond the main ditch and in front of the curtain wall. (PDARC)
UF demilunes
CN V.RT.AFU.BUE.AFU.BZY.BZY

ravines
RD.196 (L)
ALT **ravine**
SN Narrow, steep-sided land depressions, larger than gullies and smaller than gorges and canyons, usually created by the flow of water.
CN V.RD.ARI.AFU.AXC.AFU.AFU.ARI.BUE

ravison oil
MT.2040
UF oil, ravison
CN M.MT.AFU.AFU.ARI.ARI.AXC.ARI.BZY

raw art
USE **art brut**

raw Italian earth
USE **light brown**

raw land
RD.305
SN Use for land available for building but not currently developed and lacking any improvements or utilities.
UF land, raw
land, unimproved
land, vacant
unimproved land
vacant land
CN V.RD.ARI.ALO.ARI.ARI

raw linseed oil
MT.2014
SN Linseed oil which has been refined but has not undergone further treatment, such as boiling, blowing, or bodying. (DAC)
UF linseed oil, raw
oil, raw linseed
CN M.MT.AFU.AFU.ARI.ARI.AXC.AFU.BCW.ALO

raw materials
MT.2289 (L,B)
UF materials, raw
CN M.MT.AFU.ALO.JCO.ARI

raw oil
MT.1998
UF oil, raw
CN M.MT.AFU.AFU.ARI.ARI.ARI.ARI

raw sienna
MT.1630
UF Italian earth
Sienaerde
sienna, raw
terra di Siena
CN M.MT.AFU.AFU.ARI.AFU.AFU.ALO.ALO.ARI.ARI.AXC.ALO

raw sienna (color)
USE **brownish orange**
dark orange yellow
light brown
strong yellowish brown

raw umber
MT.1633
UF brown, Sicilian
Sicilian brown
terre d'ombre naturelle
umber, raw
Umbra natur
CN M.MT.AFU.AFU.ARI.AFU.AFU.ALO.ALO.ARI.ARI.BCW.ALO

raw umber (color)
USE **dark yellowish brown**
moderate brown
moderate yellowish brown

rawashin
RT.912
CN V.RT.AFU.ARI.AFU.AFU.BOK.AFU.AFU.ALO.ALO.AFU

rawl plugs
TF.297
ALT **rawl plug**
SN Anchors for bolts and screws used to secure structural wood parts to masonry or concrete walls. (PUTNAM)
UF anchors, rawlplug
plugs, rawl
rawlplug anchors
CN V.TF.AFU.AFU.AFU.ALO.AFU.AFU.BZY

rawlplug anchors
USE **rawl plugs**

Rayist
USE **Rayonist**

Rayographs
USE **photograms**

rayon
MT.1841 (L)
CN M.MT.AFU.AFU.ARI.ALO.AFU.ALO.ALO

Rayonist
FL.3417 (R)
ALT **Rayonism**
UF Rayist
CN F.FL.ALO.BCW.ALO.AXC.DIO.BZY.ALO.AXC

Rayonnant
FL.3141 (A,B,R)
UF Gothic, Rayonnant
Rayonnant Gothic
Secondaire
CN F.FL.ALO.BCW.ALO.ALO.AFU.BOK.ARI.BIQ.ALO.ARI

Rayonnant Gothic
USE **Rayonnant**

Rayy ware
FL.3458
UF Rhages ware
ware, Rayy
ware, Rhages
CN F.FL.ALO.BIQ.AFU.DIO.ALO.ALO

razor blades
TB.132 (N)
ALT **razor blade**
UF blades, razor
CN V.TB.AFU.ARI.AXC.ALO.CFS

RC paper
USE **resin-coated paper**

reaction injection molding
KT.149
SN Plastics process in which the fast-reacting liquid ingredients of a thermosetting plastic are separately injected into a closed mold in such a way as to achieve intimate mixing. The ensuing reaction causes the mixture to harden rapidly. (DIETZ)
UF molding, reaction injection
CN K.KT.AFU.ALO.DOI.CRG.ARI.AFU

reactor containment buildings
RK.674 (L)
ALT **reactor containment building**
UF buildings, containment
buildings, reactor containment
containment buildings
containment buildings, reactor
CN V.RK.AFU.ALO.ALO.CLM.ALO.AXC.ALO.ALO

reactors, nuclear
USE **nuclear reactors**

readers' cards
USE **library cards**

readers' tickets
USE **library cards**

reading chairs
TG.193 (B)
ALT **reading chair**
SN Comfortable chairs for reading. Sometimes used specifically to mean 18th-century English armchairs with padded, leather-covered, saddle-shaped seats and an adjustable platform to hold a book projecting from the back; designed so that the occupant may either sit on it in a normal way or straddle the seat facing the back. (DDA)
UF chairs, cockfight
chairs, library (reading chairs)
chairs, reading
cockfight chairs
cockfighting chairs
library chairs (reading chairs)
CN V.TG.AFU.AFU.ALO.AFU.AFU.ALO.EFQ

reading desks
TG.548
ALT **reading desk**
UF desks, music
desks, reading
music desks
pupitres (reading desks)
reading stands
stands, reading
CN V.TG.AFU.AFU.AXC.ALO.BZY.DCU

reading desks, Koran
USE **Koran stands**

Reading green
USE **chromium oxide green**

reading lists
VW.286
ALT **reading list**
UF lists, reading
CN V.VW.AFU.AFU.AFU.FZU.BCW.ALO.BUE

reading rooms
RM.152 (A)
ALT **reading room**
SN Rooms in a club, library, hotel, or public institution especially adapted and appropriate to reading. (RS)
UF rooms, reading
CN V.RM.AFU.DIO.ALO.CFS.AXC

reading seats
USE **daybeds**

reading stands
USE **music stands**
reading desks

ready-mixed concrete
MT.219 (L,B)
SN Concrete for delivery to a site in an unhardened state for immediate use. (DAC)
UF concrete, ready-mixed
CN M.MT.AFU.AFU.AFU.BCW.AFU.ARI.BIQ

Reagen
FL.741
CN F.FL.ALO.ALO.ALO.AFU.AFU.ARI.AFU.BCW

real estate
BM.468 (L,B)
UF property, real
real property
realty
CN B.BM.BCW.CXA.AFU.BIQ

real estate agents
HG.410 (A,L)
ALT **real estate agent**
SN Persons licensed to sell, buy, lease, or rent real estate. (STEIN)
UF agents, estate
agents, house
agents, real estate
estate agents
house agents
CN H.HG.AFU.AXC.BOK.BZY.ARI

real estate development
BM.1076 (A,L)
UF development, land
development, real estate
land development
CN B.BM.CLM.ALO.ALO.ALO

real estate maps
USE **cadastral maps**

real estate subdivision
USE **land subdivision**

real presence
USE **transubstantiation**

real property
USE **real estate**

real property maps
USE **cadastral maps**

realgar
MT.1680
UF arsenic orange
orange, arsenic
orpiment, red
Rauschrot
red orpiment
roseaker
sandarac (pigment)
CN M.MT.AFU.AFU.ARI.AFU.AFU.ALO.ALO.BCW.AFU.ARI

realgar (color)
USE **moderate orange yellow**
strong orange yellow

realia
USE **artifacts**

realism (form of expression)
BM.178 (L,R)
ALT **realist (form of expression)**
SN Generally, concern for fact and reality and rejection of the impractical and visionary.(WCOL) With reference to art and literature, use for the

approach that emphasizes the depiction of things as they appear or occur.
UF naturalism (realism)
CN B.BM.AFU.AFU.AXC.BOK

realism, social
USE **social realism**

Realist
FL.3301
ALT **Realism**
CN F.FL.ALO.BCW.ALO.AXC.DCU.CFS

Realist, Cool
USE **Photorealist**

Realist, Fantastic
USE **Fantastic Realist**

Realist, Magic
USE **Magic Realist**

Realist, New
USE **New Realist**

Realist, New (Photorealist)
USE **Photorealist**

Realist, Radical
USE **Photorealist**

Realist, Sharp-focus
USE **Photorealist**

Realist, Socialist
USE **Socialist Realist**

realty
USE **real estate**

reamer bits
TB.1111
ALT **reamer bit**
SN Bits having a sharp spiral cutting edge which may be square, half-round, half-round and hollow, or five to eight-sided and with tapered ends; used for enlarging existing holes or to remove burrs from the inside of pipes.
UF bits, reamer
reamers (reamer bits)
CN V.TB.ALO.ARI.CXA

reamers
TB.192 (L,N)
ALT **reamer**
SN Tools used to smooth the surface of a hole or finish holes which have been drilled in either wood or metal.
CN V.TB.AFU.ARI.BIQ.ALO.ALO

reamers (bits)
USE **bits**

reamers (reamer bits)
USE **reamer bits**

reamers (taper augers)
USE **taper augers**

reamers, flute
USE **flute reamers**

reamers, hooked
USE **hooked reamers**

reaming
KT.167 (L)
ALT **reamed**
SN Enlarging a round hole in a piece of metal by means of a revolving-edge tool. (STEIN)
CN K.KT.AFU.ALO.DOI.ERE.ARI

rear
DC.19
SN Situated at or relating to the back or hindmost part of something. (W)
UF back
CN D.DC.AFU.ALO.ALO.BIQ

rear arches
USE **back arches**

rear elevations
RM.9
ALT **rear elevation**
UF back elevations
elevations, back
elevations, rear
CN V.RM.AFU.BCW.ARI

rear vaults
USE **back arches**

reason
BM.593 (L,R)
CN B.BM.BUE.CFS

reattribution
USE **attribution**

rebate planes
USE **rabbet planes**

rebated joints
USE **rabbet joints**

rebated locks
USE **rabbeted locks**

Rebenschwarz
USE **vine black**

rebirth
USE **reincarnation**

rec rooms
USE **recreation rooms**

recamier sofas
USE **Grecian couches**

recamiers
USE **Grecian couches**

receipt books
USE **cookbooks**

receipts
VW.865 (L,N)
ALT **receipt**
SN Written acknowledgement of the receiving or taking of goods or money delivered or paid. (GAHLM)
CN V.VW.AFU.ARI.AFU.BIQ.CXA.AXC.AXC

receipts (recipes)
USE **recipes**

receipts, trust
USE **trust receipts**

receivers, card
USE card stands

receptacles
RT.1349 (N)
ALT **receptacle**
SN Devices installed in electrical outlet boxes for the connection of portable equipment or appliances. (MEANS)
CN V.RT.ALO.ARI.ALO.CXA

reception chairs
TG.195
ALT **reception chair**
UF chairs, reception
CN V.TG.AFU.AFU.ALO.AFU.AFU.ALO.ELK

reception rooms
RM.158 (B)
ALT **reception room**
SN Use for rooms whose purpose is the formal reception of guests, tradesmen, and other visitors.
UF rooms, reception
CN V.RM.AFU.DIO.ALO.CLM.ALO

receptions
KM.132
CN K.KM.AFU.DIO.ARI

recessed arches
USE **back arches**

recessed front locks
USE **guarded front locks**

recessed joints
TF.599
ALT **recessed joint**
UF joints, recessed
joints, reveal
joints, shadow
reveal joints
shadow joints
CN V.TF.ALO.AFU.EWY

recessed pulls
TF.81
ALT **recessed pull**
UF pulls, recessed
CN V.TF.AFU.AFU.AFU.AFU.CFS.BCW.AFU.CLM

recesses
USE **alcoves**

recesses, dining
USE **dining alcoves**

recipe books
USE **cookbooks**

recipes

VW.346 (L,N)
ALT **recipe**
SN Sets of directions with a list of ingredients for making or preparing something, especially food. (AHD)
UF receipts (recipes)
CN V.VW.AFU.AFU.ALO.CXA.AXC.AFU

reciprocating drills
USE **push drills**

recitals
KM.62
CN K.KM.AFU.BOK.AXC.BCW

reclamation
KG.135 (B)
SN Making areas of the natural landscape available for human use by changing natural conditions. (WCOL)
CN K.KG.AFU.AFU.BCW.BIQ

reclamation works
USE **land reclamation works**

recliners
USE **reclining chairs**

reclining chairs
TG.223 (N)
ALT **reclining chair**
SN Easy chairs with a back and footrest adjustable up or down to comfort the user. (RHDEL2)
UF chairs, reclining
recliners
CN V.TG.AFU.AFU.ALO.AFU.AFU.AXC.ALO

recommendation, letters of
USE **letters of recommendation**

recommendations
USE **letters of recommendation**

RECON
USE **retrospective conversion**

reconstruction
KT.46
ALT **reconstructed**
SN Use only to refer to construction of new structures built to resemble old ones based on historic, archaeological, or other similar evidence.
CN K.KT.AFU.ALO.BCW.ARI.ALO.AXC

reconstructions
VB.109 (R)
ALT **reconstruction**
SN Use for drawings or models that propose how something may have looked at a previous time. May also be full-scale new objects or structures based on historical, archaeological, or other similar evidence.
CN V.VB.ALO.BUE.BIQ

record cabinets
TG.440 (N)
ALT **record cabinet**
UF cabinets, record
CN V.TG.AFU.AFU.AXC.ALO.ARI.ALO.DCU

record drawings
VD.108
ALT **record drawing**
SN Use for architectural drawings made to serve as records or reminders of an existing structure or its details.
UF drawings, record
CN V.VD.AFU.ALO.CLM

recording
KG.104 (L,B)
SN Creating a record of data or information in some lasting form, such as writing on paper or electronic signals on magnetic tape.
CN K.KG.AFU.AFU.AXC.DIO

recording studios
RM.237 (A,B)
ALT **recording studio**
UF studios, recording
CN V.RM.AFU.DIO.ALO.DOI.CXA.AFU

recording studios, radio
USE **radio studios**

recordings, audio
USE **sound recordings**

recordings, phonograph
USE **phonograph records**

recordings, sound
USE **sound recordings**

recordings, tape
USE **audio tapes**

recordings, video
USE **video recordings**

recordings, video tape
USE **video recordings**

recordings, videodisc
USE **videodiscs**

recordings, wire
USE **wire recordings**

records
VW.387 (L,B)
ALT **record**
SN Recorded information, regardless of medium, created, received, and maintained by an agency, institution, organization, or individual in pursuance of its legal obligations or in the transaction of business. (ICA)
CN V.VW.AFU.AFU.ALO.ERE

records disposition schedules
USE **records schedules**

records management
KG.99 (A,L)
SN Area of information management concerned with achieving economy and efficiency in the creation, use, handling, control, maintenance, and disposition of records. (ALAG)
UF management, records
CN K.KG.AFU.AFU.AXC.CRG.AXC

records retention schedules
USE **records schedules**

records schedules
VW.291
ALT **records schedule**
SN Documents describing the recurring records of an organization or administrative unit, specifying those records to be preserved as having archival value, and authorizing, on a continuing basis and after the lapse of specified retention periods and the occurrence of specified actions or events, the destruction of the remaining records. (ICA)
UF comprehensive record schedules
disposition schedules
disposition schedules, records
records disposition schedules
records retention schedules
retention schedules
retention schedules, records
schedules, comprehensive record
schedules, disposition
schedules, records retention
schedules, retention
schedules, transfer
transfer schedules
CN V.VW.AFU.AFU.AFU.FZU.BOK.AFU

records surveys
VW.368
ALT **records survey**
SN Surveys involving the gathering of basic information about records regarding the quantity, physical form and type, location, physical condition, storage facilities, rate of accumulation, uses, and similar data for the purpose of planning acquisition and disposal programs, microfilming operations, new facilities, and related archival activities. (ICA)
UF surveys, records
CN V.VW.AFU.AFU.ALO.DCU.ARI

records, accession
USE **accession records**

records, administrative
USE **administrative records**

records, architectural
USE **architectural records**

records, attendance
USE **attendance records**

records, audiovisual
USE **audiovisual materials**

records, Bible
USE **Bible records**

records, birth

USE **birth records**

records, bookkeeping
USE **bookkeeping records**

records, burial
USE **burial records**

records, business
USE **business records**

records, capitular
USE **church records**

records, cartographic
USE **cartographic materials**

records, cathedral
USE **church records**

records, census
USE **census records**

records, church
USE **church records**

records, civil court
USE **civil court records**

records, communion
USE **communion records**

records, company
USE **business records**

records, congressional
USE **congressional records**

records, congressional committee
USE **congressional committee records**

records, corporation
USE **corporation records**

records, county government
USE **county government records**

records, court
USE **judicial records**

records, credit
USE **credit records**

records, criminal court
USE **criminal court records**

records, custom
USE **customs records**

records, death
USE **death records**

records, diocesan
USE **diocesan records**

records, divorce
USE **divorce records**

records, electronic
USE **machine-readable records**

records, estate
USE **estate records**

records, estate administration
USE **estate administration records**

records, executive
USE **executive records**

records, exhibition
USE **exhibition records**

records, family
USE **family papers**

records, federal government
USE **federal government records**

records, financial
USE **financial records**

records, first communion
USE **communion records**

records, government
USE **government records**

records, gramaphone
USE **phonograph records**

records, graphophone
USE **graphophone records**

records, hospital
USE **hospital records**

records, House of Representatives
USE **House of Representatives records**

records, housekeeping
USE **administrative records**

records, immigration
USE **immigration records**

records, insurance
USE **insurance records**

records, intergovernmental
USE **intergovernmental records**

records, judicial
USE **judicial records**

records, legislative
USE **legislative records**

records, local government
USE **local government records**

records, machine-readable
USE **machine-readable records**

records, manorial
USE **manorial records**

records, marriage
USE **marriage records**

records, medical
USE **medical records**

records, military
USE **military records**

records, municipal
USE **municipal government records**

records, municipal government
USE **municipal government records**

records, museum
USE **museum records**

records, national government
USE **national government records**

records, naturalization
USE **naturalization records**

records, notarial
USE **notarial documents**

records, official
USE **government records**

records, parochial
USE **parochial records**

records, pay
USE **payroll records**

records, payroll
USE **payroll records**

records, personnel
USE **personnel records**

records, phonograph
USE **phonograph records**

records, probate
USE **probate records**

records, public
USE **government records**

records, sales
USE **sales records**

records, school
USE **school records**

records, Senate
USE **Senate records**

records, shipment
USE **shipping records**

records, shipping
USE **shipping records**

records, state government
USE **state government records**

records, tax
USE **tax records**

records, territorial
USE **territorial records**

records, vestry
USE **church registers**
churchwardens' accounts

records, vital
USE **vital records**

records, vital statistics
USE **vital statistics records**

recovery facilities, resource
USE **resource recovery facilities**

recovery rooms
RM.298 (L)
ALT **recovery room**
SN Hospital rooms which are equipped

with apparatus for meeting post-operative emergencies and in which surgical patients are kept during the immediate post-operative period for care and recovery from anesthesia. (W)
UF rooms, recovery
CN V.RM.AFU.DIO.AXC.AFU.BUE

recreation
BM.334 (L,B,R)
CN B.BM.ALO.ALO.BIQ

recreation areas
RG.151 (A,L,R)
ALT **recreation area**
UF areas, recreation
facilities, recreation
outdoor recreation areas
recreation areas, outdoor
recreation areas, scenic
recreation facilities
scenic recreation areas
CN V.RG.AFU.AFU.DOI

recreation areas, outdoor
USE **recreation areas**

recreation areas, scenic
USE **recreation areas**

recreation buildings
RK.1023 (A,B,R)
ALT **recreation building**
UF buildings, recreation
facilities, recreation
recreation facilities
CN V.RK.AFU.ALO.ALO.EWY.AXC

recreation centers
RK.1043 (A,L,B)
ALT **recreation center**
UF canteens (recreation centers)
centers, recreation
CN V.RK.AFU.ALO.ALO.EWY.AXC.AXC

recreation centers, community
USE **community centers**

recreation facilities
USE **recreation areas**
recreation buildings

recreation rooms
RM.126 (L,B)
ALT **recreation room**
UF hobby rooms
rec rooms
rooms, hobby
rooms, rec
rooms, recreation
rooms, rumpus
rumpus rooms
CN V.RM.AFU.DIO.ALO.BIQ.BCW

recreational vehicles
USE **motor homes**

recruiting
KG.154 (L)
SN Seeking out and enlisting people for an enterprise, usually for a stated period of time, on either a paid or volunteer basis. (RLG7)
UF enlisting
CN K.KG.AFU.AFU.BIQ.BUE.BCW

rectangles
BM.777 (L)
ALT **rectangular**
CN B.BM.CFS.ARI.AXC.BCW.AFU.BIQ.ALO.AFU.AFU

rectangular legs
USE **Marlborough legs**

rectification printers
HG.462
ALT **rectification printer**
UF printers, rectification
CN H.HG.AFU.AXC.BUE.ALO.CFS.BUE.ARI

Rectilinear Style
USE **Perpendicular Style**

rectilinear tracery
USE **perpendicular tracery**

recto
DC.20
SN Use with reference to the principal side of a sheet of paper. Use **obverse** to refer to the front, top, or principal surface of a coin, medal, seal, or currency note bearing the main design.
CN D.DC.AFU.ALO.ALO.BOK

rectories
RK.330 (A,L,B,R)
ALT **rectory**
CN V.RK.AFU.ALO.ALO.AXC.ALO.BOK.ARI.AXC

rectors
HG.235 (L)
ALT **rector**
CN H.HG.AFU.AXC.AXC.BIQ.AFU.ARI.EFQ

Recuay
FL.1154
UF Aija
CN F.FL.ALO.ALO.ALO.ARI.AXC.AFU.AXC.AXC

recycling plants
USE **resource recovery facilities**

red
DL.34 (L)
CN D.DL.AFU.AFU.ALO

red alder
MT.1098 (L)
UF alder, red
Alnus oregona
Alnus rubra
CN M.MT.AFU.AFU.ALO.BIQ.DCU.AFU.AFU.AFU.ALO.BIQ

red antique porphyry
MT.621
UF antique porphyry, red
diorite, porphyritic
porphyrite
porphyritic diorite
porphyry, red antique
CN M.MT.AFU.AFU.AFU.DCU.AFU.AFU.AFU.ALO.AFU.ALO

red beech
MT.1111
UF beech, red
Nothofagus fusca
CN M.MT.AFU.AFU.ALO.BIQ.DCU.AFU.AFU.AFU.BCW.BOK

red-black burnished ware
USE **Khirbet Kerak ware**

red bole
MT.1674
UF Armenian bole
bole, Armenian
bole, red
clay, gilders red
gilders red clay
gold size, red burnish
red burnish gold size
red clay, gilders
size, red burnish gold
CN M.MT.AFU.AFU.ARI.AFU.AFU.ALO.ALO.BCW.AFU.ALO.AXC

red brass
MT.388
SN Brass having a reddish tint due to a high copper content. (W)
UF brass, red
CN M.MT.AFU.AFU.AFU.BZY.AFU.AFU.AFU.ALO.ARI.BIQ.AFU.ARI

red brown
USE **blackish red**
brownish orange
dark red
dark reddish orange
deep orange
grayish red
grayish yellowish pink
light brown
light grayish red
light reddish brown
moderate brown
moderate olive brown
moderate orange
moderate reddish brown
moderate reddish orange
moderate yellowish brown
pale yellowish pink
reddish gray
strong yellowish brown

red brown, deep
USE **grayish reddish brown**

red burnish gold size
USE **red bole**

red burnished ware
FL.3028
UF burnished ware, red

ware, red burnished
CN F.FL.ALO.AXC.ARI.BIQ.ALO.AXC.BIQ

red cedar
MT.1361 (L)
UF cedar, pencil
cedar, red
Juniperus virginiana
pencil cedar
CN M.MT.AFU.AFU.ALO.BIQ.DCU.AFU.AFU.ALO.BUE.ARI

red chalk
MT.49
SN Chalk composed of hematite diffused in clay and used for drawing since the Renaissance. Originally cut from deposits but later fabricated from the same material.
UF chalk, natural red
chalk, red
natural red chalk
red chalk, natural
sanguine
CN M.MT.AFU.AFU.AFU.ARI.ARI

red chalk, natural
USE **red chalk**

red clay, gilders
USE **red bole**

red earth
USE **moderate reddish brown**

Red-figure
FL.2645
CN F.FL.ALO.AXC.ALO.AFU.ALO.AXC.ARI.AXC

red fir
USE **Douglas fir**

red-gloss pottery
FL.2752
UF pottery, red-gloss
red-gloss ware
ware, red-gloss
CN F.FL.ALO.AXC.ALO.ALO.ALO.BUE.ALO.BCW

red-gloss ware
USE **red-gloss pottery**

red granite
MT.600
UF granite, red
CN M.MT.AFU.AFU.AFU.DCU.AFU.AFU.AFU.AFU.AFU.ARI.ALO.ARI

red gum
MT.1163
UF gum, red
CN M.MT.AFU.AFU.ALO.BIQ.DCU.AFU.AFU.AFU.DIO.AXC.AXC

red indigo
USE **orchil**

red iron oxide
USE **iron oxide red**

red juniper
USE **juniper**

red lead
MT.1701 (L)
UF lead tetroxide
lead, orange
lead, red
Mennige
mineral, orange
minium
orange lead
orange mineral
red, saturine
red, Saturn
saturine red
Saturn red
CN M.MT.AFU.AFU.ARI.AFU.AFU.ALO.ALO.BCW.ARI.BCW

red lead (color)
USE **deep reddish orange**
strong reddish orange
vivid reddish orange

red lead (iron oxide red)
USE **iron oxide red**

red-light districts
RG.267
ALT **red-light district**
CN V.RG.ALO.AFU.ALO.AFU.AFU

red lilac
USE **grayish purplish red**
moderate purplish red

red lithopone, cadmium
USE **cadmium red lithopone**

red locust
USE **black locust**

red lustrous ware
FL.2903
UF lustrous ware, red
ware, red lustrous
CN F.FL.ALO.AXC.ARI.ARI.ALO.ALO.AXC

red maple
MT.1223 (L)
UF Acer rubrum
maple, red
CN M.MT.AFU.AFU.ALO.BIQ.DCU.AFU.AFU.AFU.IFM.BIQ

red marble
MT.797
UF marble, red
CN M.MT.AFU.AFU.AFU.DCU.AFU.ARI.ARI.ARI.BCW

red marble, French
USE **Languedoc marble**
griotte marble

red oak
MT.1248 (L)
UF oak, red
Quercus borealis
Quercus rubia
CN M.MT.AFU.AFU.ALO.BIQ.DCU.AFU.AFU.AFU.IRA.DOI

red oak, southern
USE **southern red oak**

red ocher
MT.1675
UF ocher, red
CN M.MT.AFU.AFU.ARI.AFU.AFU.ALO.ALO.BCW.AFU.ALO.BCW

red ocher (color)
USE **moderate reddish brown**

Red Ocher (style)
FL.843
CN F.FL.ALO.ALO.ALO.AFU.ALO.ALO.ARI.AFU.CLM

red-on-black ware
FL.2905
UF ware, red-on-black
CN F.FL.ALO.AXC.ARI.ARI.ALO.ALO.BIQ

red-on-cream ware
FL.2876
UF ware, red-on-cream
CN F.FL.ALO.AXC.ARI.AFU.ALO.ARI.CLM

red-on-red ware
FL.3029
UF ware, red-on-red
CN F.FL.ALO.AXC.ARI.BIQ.ALO.AXC.BOK

red-on-white ware
FL.2906
UF Erimi ware
ware, Erimi
ware, red-on-white
CN F.FL.ALO.AXC.ARI.ARI.ALO.ALO.BOK

red orange
USE **strong reddish orange**
vivid red
vivid reddish orange
vivid yellowish pink

red orpiment
USE **realgar**

red oxide
USE **deep reddish brown**
iron oxide red
strong brown
strong reddish brown

red oxide, Spanish
USE **Spanish red oxide**

red-pattern burnished ware
FL.2943
UF burnished ware, red-pattern
ware, red-pattern burnished
CN F.FL.ALO.AXC.ARI.AXC.ALO.BIQ.CLM

red pigment

MT.1667
UF orange pigment
pigment, orange
pigment, red
CN M.MT.AFU.AFU.ARI.AFU.AFU.ALO.ALO.BCW

red pigment, artificial inorganic
USE **artificial inorganic red pigment**

red pigment, artificial organic
USE **synthetic organic red pigment**

red pigment, inorganic
USE **inorganic red pigment**

red pigment, organic
USE **organic red pigment**

red pigment, synthetic inorganic
USE **artificial inorganic red pigment**

red pigment, synthetic organic
USE **synthetic organic red pigment**

red pine
USE **ponderosa pine**

red pine (Norway pine)
USE **Norway pine**

red plum
USE **dark grayish purple**
dark purplish red
very dark purplish red

red-polished ware
FL.2842
UF ware, red-polished
CN F.FL.ALO.AXC.ALO.ARI.ALO.AFU.BCW

red polished ware
FL.2904
UF polished ware, red
ware, red polished
CN F.FL.ALO.AXC.ARI.ARI.ALO.ALO.BCW

red purple
USE **dark purplish red**
deep reddish purple

red purple, blackish
USE **dark purplish red**

red purple, grayish
USE **grayish purple**

red purple, pale
USE **pale purple**

red sandstone
USE **ferruginous sandstone**

red silver fir
USE **silver fir**

red slate
MT.867
UF slate, red
CN M.MT.AFU.AFU.AFU.DCU.AFU.ARI.BUE.AFU.ARI

red-slipped ware
FL.2877
UF ware, red-slipped
CN F.FL.ALO.AXC.ARI.AFU.ALO.ARI.CRG

red spruce
MT.1402 (L)
UF Canadian spruce
Picea rubens
Picea rubra
pine, spruce
spruce pine
spruce, Canadian
spruce, red
spruce, West Virginia
spruce, yellow
West Virginia spruce
yellow spruce
CN M.MT.AFU.AFU.ALO.BIQ.DCU.AFU.AFU.ALO.DOI.BIQ

red violet
USE **deep purple**
deep reddish purple
grayish purplish pink
grayish purplish red
light purplish pink
light reddish purple
moderate purple
moderate purplish pink
moderate reddish purple
strong purple
strong reddish purple
vivid purple

red violet, bright
USE **strong purple**
strong reddish purple
vivid purple
vivid reddish purple

red ware
USE **redware**

red ware (Persian pottery)
USE **early red ware**

red ware, black-topped
USE **black-topped red ware**

red ware, early
USE **early red ware**

red ware, white-slipped
USE **white-slipped red ware**

red wash ware
FL.2942
UF ware, red wash
wash ware, red
CN F.FL.ALO.AXC.ARI.AXC.ALO.BIQ.CFS

red-washed buff ware
FL.2944
UF buff ware, red-washed
ware, red-washed buff
CN F.FL.ALO.AXC.ARI.AXC.ALO.BIQ.CRG

red, acra
USE **quinacridone red**

red, acridone
USE **quinacridone red**

red, antimony
USE **antimony orange**

red, blackish
USE **blackish red**

red, blood
USE **moderate red**
strong red
vivid red

red, bluish
USE **deep purplish red**
moderate purplish red
strong purplish red
very deep purplish red

red, brick
USE **dark red**
grayish red
moderate red
strong reddish orange

red, bright
USE **strong red**
vivid red

red, bright yellowish
USE **vivid red**
vivid reddish orange

red, brown
USE **grayish red**
grayish reddish brown
light grayish red
vivid red

red, cadmium
USE **cadmium red**

red, cadmium (color)
USE **moderate red**
strong red
vivid red
vivid reddish orange

red, Chinese
USE **chrome red**

red, chrome
USE **chrome red**

red, dark
USE **dark red**

red, dark grayish
USE **dark grayish red**

red, dark Indian
USE **dark grayish red**
grayish red

red, dark purplish
USE **dark purplish red**

red, deep
USE **deep red**

red, deep purplish
USE **deep purplish red**

red, Derby
USE **chrome red**

red, dull
USE **dark red**
deep reddish brown
grayish red
moderate red
moderate reddish brown
strong reddish orange
very dark red

red, dull bluish
USE **dark purplish red**
moderate purplish red
very dark purplish red

red, dull yellowish
USE **grayish reddish orange**

red, earth
USE **moderate brown**

red, fuchsia
USE **deep purplish red**
moderate purplish red

red, garnet
USE **dark red**
deep red

red, geranium
USE **geranium red**

red, geranium (color)
USE **strong red**

red, grayish
USE **grayish red**

red, grayish purplish
USE **grayish purplish red**

red, gulf
USE **gulf red**

red, haematite
USE **dark grayish red**
dark red
grayish red
grayish reddish brown

red, Harrison's
USE **lithol red**

red, Indian
USE **Indian red**

red, Indian (color)
USE **dark reddish orange**
grayish red
strong reddish brown

red, Indian (iron oxide red)
USE **iron oxide red**

red, iron oxide
USE **iron oxide red**

red, iron oxide (color)
USE **strong brown**
strong reddish brown

red, lacquer
USE **deep reddish orange**

red, light
USE **deep yellowish pink**
grayish reddish orange
moderate orange
moderate red
moderate reddish orange

red, light grayish
USE **light grayish red**

red, light grayish purplish
USE **light grayish purplish red**

red, lithol
USE **lithol red**

red, madder
USE **moderate red**
moderate reddish orange
strong red
strong reddish orange

red, Mars
USE **dark reddish orange**
iron oxide red

red, metallic
USE **deep reddish brown**

red, moderate
USE **moderate red**

red, moderate purplish
USE **moderate purplish red**

red, orange
USE **moderate reddish orange**

red, orpiment
USE **moderate orange yellow**
strong orange yellow

red, pale
USE **light grayish red**
light reddish brown

red, para
USE **para red**

red, para (color)
USE **moderate red**
strong red

red, permanent
USE **moderate red**
strong red

red, Persian
USE **chrome red**

red, Pompeian
USE **Pompeian red**
Pozzuoli red

red, Pompeian (color)
USE **grayish red**
grayish reddish orange
moderate red

red, Pozzuoli
USE **Pozzuoli red**

red, purplish
USE **purplish red**

red, quinacridone
USE **quinacridone red**

red, quinacridone (color)
USE **deep reddish orange**
moderate red
strong red

red, rose
USE **dark red**
deep red
moderate purplish red
moderate red
vivid red

red, ruby
USE **deep red**

red, San Francisco
USE **San Francisco red**

red, saturine
USE **red lead**

red, Saturn
USE **red lead**

red, selenium
USE **cadmium red**

red, Spanish
USE **strong brown**
strong reddish brown

red, spectrum
USE **vivid red**

red, strong
USE **strong red**

red, strong purplish
USE **strong purplish red**

red, toluidine
USE **toluidine red**

red, Turkey
USE **madder**

red, Tuscan
USE **Tuscan red**

red, Venetian
USE **Venetian red**

red, Venetian (color)
USE **deep reddish brown**
moderate reddish brown
strong reddish brown

red, very dark
USE **very dark red**

red, very dark purplish
USE **very dark purplish red**

red, very deep
USE **very deep red**

red, very deep purplish
USE **very deep purplish red**

red, Victoria
USE **chrome red**

red, Vienna
USE **chrome red**

red, vivid
USE **vivid red**

red, vivid purplish
USE **vivid purplish red**

red, weak
USE **light reddish brown**

red, whelk
USE **Tyrian purple**

red, yellow
USE **brownish orange**
strong brown

red, yellowish
USE **dark reddish orange**
deep reddish orange
moderate reddish orange
strong reddish orange

redans
RT.1210
ALT **redan**
SN Small ravelins. (PDARC)
UF redents
CN V.RT.AFU.BUE.AFU.BZY.BZY.AFU

reddish black
DL.48
UF black, reddish
brown, ebony
centroid color 24
ebony brown
CN D.DL.AFU.AFU.ALO.BZY

reddish blue
USE **brilliant purplish blue**
dark purplish blue
deep purplish blue
light purplish blue
moderate purplish blue
strong purplish blue
very light purplish blue

reddish blue, bright
USE **vivid purplish blue**

reddish blue, dull
USE **blackish blue**
dark grayish blue
grayish blue
grayish purplish blue
pale blue
pale purplish blue
very pale blue
very pale purplish blue

reddish brown
DL.89
UF brown, reddish
CN D.DL.AFU.AFU.AXC.BZY.AFU

reddish brown dull
USE **blackish red**

reddish brown, dark
USE **dark reddish brown**

reddish brown, dark grayish
USE **dark grayish reddish brown**

reddish brown, deep
USE **deep reddish brown**

reddish brown, dull
USE **dark grayish red**
dark grayish reddish brown
dark red
dark reddish brown
grayish red
grayish reddish brown
light grayish reddish brown
light reddish brown
very dark red

reddish brown, grayish
USE **grayish reddish brown**

reddish brown, light
USE **light reddish brown**

reddish brown, light grayish
USE **light grayish reddish brown**

reddish brown, moderate
USE **moderate reddish brown**

reddish brown, pale
USE **light reddish brown**

reddish brown, strong
USE **strong reddish brown**

reddish gray
DL.46
UF brown, lilac
brown, red
centroid color 22
gray lilac
gray, lead
gray, reddish
lead gray
lilac brown
lilac, gray
red brown
CN D.DL.AFU.AFU.ALO.BUE

reddish gray, dark
USE **dark reddish gray**

reddish navy
USE **dark violet**

reddish orange
DL.68
UF orange, reddish
CN D.DL.AFU.AFU.ARI.BOK.AFU

reddish orange, bright
USE **vivid reddish orange**

reddish orange, dark
USE **dark reddish orange**

reddish orange, deep
USE **deep reddish orange**

reddish orange, dull
USE **grayish reddish orange**

reddish orange, grayish
USE **grayish reddish orange**

reddish orange, moderate
USE **moderate reddish orange**

reddish orange, strong
USE **strong reddish orange**

reddish orange, vivid
USE **vivid reddish orange**

reddish purple
DL.288
UF purple, reddish
CN D.DL.AFU.AFU.CFS.DCU.AFU

reddish purple, dark
USE **dark reddish purple**

reddish purple, deep
USE **deep reddish purple**

reddish purple, grayish
USE **grayish reddish purple**

reddish purple, light
USE **light reddish purple**

reddish purple, moderate
USE **moderate reddish purple**

reddish purple, reddish
USE **pale reddish purple**

reddish purple, strong
USE **strong reddish purple**

reddish purple, very dark
USE **very dark reddish purple**

reddish purple, vivid
USE **vivid reddish purple**

reddish violet
USE **dark reddish purple**
deep reddish purple
light reddish purple
moderate reddish purple
strong reddish purple
very dark reddish purple
very deep reddish purple

reddish violet, bright
USE **vivid reddish purple**

reddish violet, dull
USE **blackish purple**
dark grayish purple
grayish purple
grayish reddish purple
pale purple
pale reddish purple

reddish white
USE **pinkish white**
purplish white

reddish yellow

USE brilliant orange yellow
brilliant yellow
dark orange yellow
dark yellow
deep orange yellow
deep yellow
light orange
light orange yellow
light yellow
moderate orange
moderate orange yellow
moderate yellow
strong orange yellow
strong yellow

reddish yellow, bright
USE vivid orange yellow
vivid yellow

reddish yellow, dark
USE dark grayish yellow

reddish yellow, dull
USE grayish yellow
pale orange yellow
pale yellow

redents
USE redans

redevelopment, urban
USE urban renewal

redoubts
RK.454
ALT redoubt
SN Small, usually isolated, fortification works of any form, commonly square or polygonal in plan, used to defend a prominent point.
CN V.RK.AFU.ALO.ALO.BIQ.CFS

redstone
USE ferruginous sandstone

reducers, water
USE water reducers

reducing (photography)
USE reduction (photography)

reduction (photography)
KT.418
SN Reducing the density of a negative or print by dissolving some of the silver forming its image. (SWED)
UF reducing (photography)
CN K.KT.AFU.ALO.DUC.DIO.ARI.AXC.DCU

reduction, cost
USE cost control

reductions
VB.118
ALT reduction
SN Copies of works of art on a smaller scale. (THDAT)
CN V.VB.ALO.BZY.AFU.ARI

redware
MT.155 (R)
SN Earthenware, often unglazed, made of clays that range in color from tan to red or black that fire to a shade of red, usually wheel-thrown and fired at a relatively low temperature. (KNOPGP)
UF red ware
CN M.MT.AFU.AFU.AFU.AXC.ALO.ALO.AFU.ALO.AFU.BIQ

redwood
MT.1391 (L,R)
UF California redwood
redwood, California
sequoia
CN M.MT.AFU.AFU.ALO.BIQ.DCU.AFU.AFU.ALO.DCU

redwood, Baltic
USE Scotch pine

redwood, California
USE redwood

redwood, coast
USE Humboldt redwood

redwood, dawn
USE dawn redwood

redwood, Humboldt
USE Humboldt redwood

redwood, sierra
USE giant sequoia

Ree
USE Arikara

reed
MT.1031 (L)
SN Any of various tall grasses that grow especially in wetlands.
CN M.MT.AFU.AFU.ALO.BIQ.AXC.AXC

reed pens
TB.275
ALT reed pen
SN Pens made from the stalks of marsh reeds. (MAYER)
UF pens, reed
CN V.TB.AFU.ARI.CLM.AFU.ALO.DOI.BIQ

reed, bur
USE bur reed

reed, sea
USE sea reed

reeding
DG.116
SN Ornamentation composed of parallel convex moldings, particularly popular in the late 18th and early 19th centuries for furniture and silverwork.
CN D.DG.AFU.ARI.ALO.ARI.BCW

reefs
RD.225 (L)
ALT reef
SN Ranges of rock, coral, or sand with their surface at or just above the low tide mark. (DNE)
CN V.RD.ARI.AFU.AXC.AFU.ALO.AXC.BIQ

reel and bead moldings
USE bead and reel moldings

reeves, game
USE game wardens

refectories
RM.114 (A,B,R)
ALT refectory
SN Use for the dining halls of monasteries or other religious institutions. (W)
CN V.RM.AFU.DIO.ALO.BCW.BUE.ALO

refectory tables
TG.687
ALT refectory table
UF dining tables, long
great tables
hall tables
joined tables (refectory tables)
library tables (refectory tables)
long dining tables
long tables (refectory tables)
stretcher tables
tables, great
tables, hall
tables, joined (refectory tables)
tables, library (refectory tables)
tables, long dining
tables, long (refectory tables)
tables, refectory
tables, stretcher
CN V.TG.AFU.AFU.BIQ.BOK.AFU.CLM

reference librarians
HG.309
ALT reference librarian
UF librarians, reference
CN H.HG.AFU.AXC.BCW.ALO.BCW.ALO.AXC

reference services
HG.869 (L)
ALT reference service
SN Organizations or departments of organizations that provide direct answers to users' queries or refer them to sources of information that will satisfy the queries.
UF services, reference
CN H.HG.ALO.DIO.AFU.AXC

refineries
RK.653 (A)
ALT refinery
CN V.RK.AFU.ALO.ALO.CLM.ALO.ALO.AFU.AXC.CXA

refineries, oil
USE petroleum refineries

refineries, petroleum
USE petroleum refineries

refineries, sugar
USE **sugar refineries**

reflected ceiling plans
VD.52
ALT **reflected ceiling plan**
UF ceiling plans, reflected
plans, reflected ceiling
reflected plans
CN V.VD.AFU.AFU.BIQ.ALO.AXC.ALO.BCW

reflected color
BM.116
UF accidental color
color, accidental
color, reflected
CN B.BM.AFU.AFU.ARI.BOK.ALO.AFU.BUE

reflected light
BM.850
SN That portion of light that is deflected from a surface. (MAYER)
UF light, reflected
CN B.BM.CFS.AXC.ALO.AFU.ALO.AFU.ARI

reflected plans
USE **reflected ceiling plans**

reflecting dressing tables
USE **Rudd tables**

reflection holograms
VJ.36
ALT **reflection hologram**
UF holograms, reflection
CN V.VJ.AFU.AFU.ARI.ALO.AFU

reflections
BM.859 (L,R)
CN B.BM.CFS.AXC.ALO.AFU.ALO.ALO.BIQ

reflective glass
MT.284 (A,B)
SN Window glass coated on the outside with a transparent metallic coating that reflects light and radiant heat. (DAC)
UF glass, mirrored
glass, reflective
mirrored glass
CN M.MT.AFU.AFU.AFU.BIQ.AFU.AXC.CRG

reflective insulation
MT.2410
SN Foil-surfaced insulation whose insulating power is determined by the number of its reflective surfaces and which must be used in connection with an air space; also acts as a vapor barrier. (PUTNAM)
UF foil back insulation
insulation, foil back
insulation, reflective
CN M.MT.AFU.ARI.BZY.BCW.ARI.AFU.ALO.ALO

reflex cameras
TB.301 (L)
ALT **reflex camera**
SN Cameras with a viewing and focusing system that uses a mirror between the lens and focusing screen to give an upright image. (LANG)
UF cameras, reflex
CN V.TB.AFU.ARI.CLM.ARI.AFU.AFU.ALO.AXC

Reform Judaism
BM.672 (L)
ALT **Reform Jewish**
UF Liberal Judaism
CN B.BM.BZY.AFU.BOK.ARI

reform schools
USE **reformatories**

reform, land
USE **land reform**

Reformation
FL.3170 (L,R)
UF Protestant Reformation
Reformation, Protestant
CN F.FL.ALO.BCW.ALO.ARI.ALO

Reformation, Protestant
USE **Reformation**

reformatories
RK.730 (A,L,B)
ALT **reformatory**
SN Use for penal institutions primarily for youthful offenders, 12 to 19 years old, or first offenders of minor crimes, which provide educational and vocational training as means toward reforming behavior.
UF approved schools
borstals
halls, juvenile
homes, juvenile
homes, remand
institutions, juvenile
juvenile halls
juvenile homes
juvenile institutions
reform schools
remand homes
schools, approved
schools, reform
CN V.RK.AFU.ALO.ALO.CXA.AFU.BCW

Reformed French Protestant
USE **Huguenot**

reformers
HG.755 (L)
ALT **reformer**
CN H.HG.AFU.BCW.HZS.BUE

refraction
BM.860 (L)
SN The deflection from a straight path undergone by a light ray or energy wave when passing obliquely from one medium to another. (W)
UF dioptrics
CN B.BM.CFS.AXC.ALO.AFU.ALO.ALO.BOK

refractory brick
USE **fire brick**

refractory clay
USE **fireclay**

refractory materials
MT.2798 (L)
UF materials, refractory
CN M.MT.AFU.BCW.BZY.AFU

refrigerant systems
RT.1390
ALT **refrigerant system**
SN Systems in which a refrigerant is compressed, condensed, and expanded as a means of removing heat from a cold reservoir; the heat is rejected elsewhere at a higher temperature. (MEANS)
UF systems, refrigerant
CN V.RT.ALO.BCW.AFU.AFU.ALO.ARI

refrigeration
KT.730 (L,B)
ALT **refrigerated**
CN K.KT.AFU.ALO.GWW.ALO.ALO

refugee camps
RG.86 (B)
ALT **refugee camp**
SN Use for temporary, often spontaneously established, settlements of displaced peoples along borders of neighboring or nearby countries, generally having minimal shelter, supplies, and sanitary facilities and created without the granting of technical asylum.
UF asylum camps, first
camps, refugee
first asylum camps
havens, temporary
temporary havens
CN V.RG.AFU.AFU.BOK.BCW.BCW

refugees
HG.796 (L,B,R)
ALT **refugee**
SN Use for persons who have fled their native country or usual country of residence to escape danger or persecution. For persons who have withdrawn voluntarily from their native country, especially those who have renounced allegiance to it, use **expatriates.**
CN H.HG.AFU.BOK.CFS

refuges, bird
USE **bird sanctuaries**

refuges, wildlife
USE **wildlife refuges**

refurbishment
USE **renovation**

refuse chutes
RM.215 (B)
ALT **refuse chute**
UF chutes, garbage
chutes, refuse
chutes, rubbish
chutes, trash
garbage chutes
rubbish chutes
trash chutes
CN V.RM.AFU.DIO.ALO.DIO.ARI.AXC

refuse disposal
KG.127 (A,L,B)
UF disposal of refuse
disposal, refuse
disposal, solid waste
solid waste disposal
CN K.KG.AFU.AFU.BCW.ALO.CFS.AFU.AFU

Rega
USE **Lega**

Régence
FL.3216 (R)
UF Regency (French)
CN F.FL.ALO.BCW.ALO.ARI.BIQ.BIQ.ARI.ALO.ARI.AXC

Regency
FL.3316 (A,L,B,R)
CN F.FL.ALO.BCW.ALO.AXC.DIO.ALO.BCW.AFU

Regency (French)
USE **Régence**

Regency Revival
FL.3327 (R)
UF Revival, Regency
CN F.FL.ALO.BCW.ALO.AXC.DIO.ALO.BIQ.BCW

Regensburg porcelain
FL.3228 (R)
UF porcelain, Regensburg
CN F.FL.ALO.BCW.ALO.ARI.BIQ.BIQ.AXC.AFU.ARI

regents
HG.703 (L,R)
ALT **regent**
CN H.HG.AFU.AXC.CFS.CRG.CXA

Regina
FL.141
CN F.FL.ALO.AFU.ALO.ARI.BCW.AXC

regional atlases
VW.132
ALT **regional atlas**
UF atlases, regional
CN V.VW.AFU.AFU.AFU.FZU.AXC.AFU.AFU.AFU.AXC.AXC

regional development
USE **community development**

regional directories
VW.419
ALT **regional directory**
UF directories, regional
CN V.VW.AFU.AFU.ALO.EWY.AXC.AFU.BOK.BCW

regional maps
VW.229
ALT **regional map**
UF maps, regional
CN V.VW.AFU.AFU.AFU.FZU.AXC.AFU.ARI.AXC.DUC.BIQ

regional parks
RK.1460
ALT **regional park**
SN Generally smaller than national parks and providing a wide range of recreation facilities with less emphasis on the landscape value of the area.
UF parks, regional
CN V.RK.ALO.ALO.ARI.AFU.AXC

regional planning
KD.171 (A,L,B,R)
UF planning, regional
planning, town and country
town and country planning
CN K.KD.AFU.ALO.DUC.ARI

regional plans
VW.465
ALT **regional plan**
UF plans, regional
CN V.VW.AFU.AFU.ALO.FIM.ARI.ALO.ALO

regional plans (drawings)
USE **site plans**

regionalism (form of expression)
BM.181 (A,L,B)
ALT **regionalist (form of expression)**
SN Use for a general consciousness of and loyalty to a distinct subnational or supranational area usually characterized by a common culture, background, or interests.(W) For the specific movement in American painting in the 1930s and 1940s, use **Realist.**
CN B.BM.AFU.AFU.AXC.BUE

Regionalist
FL.1749 (R)
ALT **Regionalism**
SN Use for the movement within American Scene painting, concentrated in the rural midwestern United States in the 1930s and capturing the flavor of life there in a literal painting style.(PDAT) For the concept of a general consciousness of and loyalty to a distinct subnational or supranational area, use **regionalism (form of expression).**
CN F.FL.ALO.ALO.BCW.AFU.CFS.AFU.AFU

registering
KT.749
ALT **registered**
SN In multicolor printing, the precise aligning of the plates or stencils, usually by means of register marks so that each color successively printed will be aligned with the others. (MAYER)
CN K.KT.AFU.ALO.HCQ.ALO.BIQ.ARI

registering (information handling)
KG.105 (L,B)
SN Making a legal or official record or list of people or objects. Specifically, in museology, the process of creating a written record for an object in a collection in order to identify the object and to record information about it such as provenance, condition, or value.
UF listing
registration
CN K.KG.AFU.AFU.AXC.DOI

registers (HVAC components)
RT.1442
ALT **register (HVAC component)**
UF registers, supply
supply registers
CN V.RT.ALO.BCW.AFU.ALO.ARI.BZY

registers (lists)
VW.267 (L)
ALT **register (list)**
CN V.VW.AFU.AFU.AFU.FZU.BCW.AFU.BIQ

registers of electors
USE **voters' lists**

registers, accession
USE **accession registers**

registers, archival
USE **archival registers**

registers, baptismal
USE **baptismal registers**

registers, birth
USE **birth registers**

registers, bookkeeping
USE **bookkeeping registers**

registers, burial
USE **burial registers**

registers, church
USE **church registers**

registers, death
USE **death registers**

registers, deed
USE **deed registers**

registers, funeral
USE **funeral registers**

registers, guest
USE **guest registers**

registers, hotel

USE **hotel registers**

registers, land
USE **land registers**

registers, manufacturers'
USE **manufacturers' registers**

registers, marriage
USE **marriage registers**

registers, motel
USE **hotel registers**

registers, parish
USE **parish registers**

registers, social
USE **social registers**

registers, supply
USE **registers (HVAC components)**

registrars
HG.205 (L)
ALT **registrar**
SN Persons who create written records for the objects in a museum collection in order to identify the object and to record information about them such as provenance, condition, or value.
UF museum registrars
registrars, museum
CN H.HG.AFU.AXC.AXC.AXC.AXC

registrars (government and administration)
HG.689 (L)
ALT **registrar (government and administration)**
SN Persons who keep official records, especially the officials at educational institutions who maintain students' personal and academic records, issue grade reports, and mail out calendars and other official publications. (RHDEL2)
CN H.HG.AFU.AXC.CFS.CLM

registrars, museum
USE **registrars**

registration
USE **registering (information handling)**

registrations
VW.376
ALT **registration**
SN Documents attesting to acts of registering.
CN V.VW.AFU.AFU.ALO.DUC.ARI.AFU

registry marks
VW.724
ALT **registry mark**
UF marks, registry
CN V.VW.AFU.ALO.ALO.AFU.AXC.ALO.CLM

reglet inserts
TF.384
ALT **reglet insert**
UF inserts, reglet
CN V.TF.AFU.AFU.AFU.ALO.AFU.BZY.BOK

reglet moldings
RT.778
ALT **reglet molding**
SN Fillets or small flat-faced projections, as used in a fret molding or to cover a joint between two boards. (DAC)
UF moldings, reglet
CN V.RT.AFU.ALO.AFU.BOK.AFU.AFU.AXC.AXC.ARI

regulae
RT.779
ALT **regula**
SN In a Doric entablature, series of short bands beneath the taeniae, from which the guttae hang.
CN V.RT.AFU.ALO.AFU.BOK.AFU.AFU.AXC.AXC.AXC

regulating
KG.158 (L)
ALT **regulated**
SN Controlling according to rules, laws, or requirements. (RLG7)
CN K.KG.AFU.AFU.BIQ.CLM

regulation, rent
USE **rent control**

regulations
VW.999 (B)
ALT **regulation**
SN Use broadly for principles, rules, or laws designed to control or regulate behavior of individuals, corporations, or other entities.
CN V.VW.AFU.ARI.ALO.BCW.AFU.AFU.AFU.CLM

regulations, administrative
USE **administrative regulations**

regulations, building
USE **building codes**

rehabilitating
KG.136 (L,B)
ALT **rehabilitated**
SN Use for the function of restoring people to physical or mental health or good repute. Use also for the activity of returning to good condition deteriorated objects, structures, neighborhoods, or public facilities; may involve repair, renovation, conversion, expansion, remodeling, or reconstruction. For actions taken to prevent further changes or deterioration in things, use **preservation.** When deterioration has not occurred, use **renovation** for actions taken to improve the quality of structures.
CN K.KG.AFU.AFU.BCW.BOK

rehabilitation centers
RK.752 (A,L,B)
ALT **rehabilitation center**
UF centers, rehabilitation
CN V.RK.AFU.ALO.ALO.CXA.ALO.AFU.AXC.ARI

reigate stone
MT.715
UF stone, reigate
CN M.MT.AFU.AFU.AFU.DCU.AFU.ALO.AFU.ARI.AFU.ALO.ALO.AFU

Reims Style
FL.3133
UF Utrecht Psalter Style
CN F.FL.ALO.BCW.ALO.ALO.AFU.BOK.ARI.ARI.ALO

reincarnation
BM.687 (L,R)
UF rebirth
CN B.BM.BZY.ALO.AFU.BOK

reinforced concrete
MT.220 (A,L,B)
UF concrete, reinforced
ferro-concrete
CN M.MT.AFU.AFU.AFU.BCW.AFU.ARI.BOK

reinforced earth dams
USE **zoned earth dams**

reinforced monocoque construction
USE **monocoque construction**

reinforced plastic
MT.2113 (L)
UF fiber reinforced plastic
plastic, fiber reinforced
plastic, reinforced
reinforced plastic, fiber
CN M.MT.AFU.AFU.ARI.BUE.ALO.ARI.ARI

reinforced plastic, fiber
USE **reinforced plastic**

reinforced plastic, glass
USE **glass reinforced plastic**

reinforcers
USE **reinforcing materials**

reinforcing bars
MT.2385 (A,L)
SN Steel bars, usually with manufactured deformations, used in concrete and masonry construction to provide additional strength. (MEANS)
UF bars, reinforcing
reinforcing rods
rods, reinforcing
CN M.MT.AFU.ARI.BZY.ALO.AFU

reinforcing materials
MT.2648
UF materials, reinforcing
reinforcers
CN M.MT.AFU.ARI.HOE

reinforcing rods

USE **reinforcing bars**

reins
USE **springers**

relations, industrial
USE **industrial relations**

relations, international
USE **international relations**

relations, labor
USE **industrial relations**

relations, public
USE **public relations**

relative relief maps
USE **relief maps**

relay broadcast stations
USE **relay stations**

relay stations
RK.205 (A,L)
ALT **relay station**
SN Microwave communications stations set up to send and receive transmissions between other installations.
UF relay broadcast stations
relay transmitters
stations, relay
stations, relay broadcast
transmitters, relay
CN V.RK.AFU.ALO.ALO.ARI.AFU.ARI.ALO

relay transmitters
USE **relay stations**

release agents
USE **parting compounds**

releases
VW.381
ALT **release**
SN Documents giving permission for the use of an item requested.
CN V.VW.AFU.AFU.ALO.DUC.BIQ

releases (discharges)
USE **discharges**

releases, cable
USE **cable releases**

releases, press
USE **press releases**

releasing
KG.159
SN Discharging people from an institution, enterprise, or obligation. (RLG7)
CN K.KG.AFU.AFU.BIQ.CRG

relief
KT.537 (L,R)
SN Use to describe a surface that has been carved, molded, or stamped so that an image or design projects from or is sunk into a continuous surface.
CN K.KT.AFU.ALO.ELK.DIO.ALO.AXC

relief block printing
USE **block printing**

relief halftone
KT.438 (L)
SN A photomechanical process in which the image is broken up into a regular pattern of dots of varying sizes through the use of a screen; the plate is then etched, leaving the dots in relief.
UF halftone process
halftone, letterpress
halftone, relief
letterpress halftone
CN K.KT.AFU.ALO.DUC.DOI.BCW.AFU.AFU

relief halftones
VJ.21
ALT **relief halftone**
SN Photomechanical prints that are relief prints and that employ a halftone screen to break up the image into a regular pattern of dots so that gradations of tone may be reproduced.
UF halftone photomechanical prints
halftones
halftones, letterpress
halftones, relief
letterpress halftones
photomechanical prints, halftone
CN V.VJ.AFU.AFU.ALO.ARI.ALO

relief maps
VW.158 (L)
ALT **relief map**
SN Maps showing land or sea bottom relief in terms of height above or below a datum by any method, such as contours, hachures, shading, or tinting. (DOD)
UF hypsographic maps
hypsometric maps
maps, hypsographic
maps, hypsometric
maps, relative relief
maps, relief
relative relief maps
CN V.VW.AFU.AFU.AFU.FZU.AXC.AFU.ARI.AFU.CXA

relief printing
KT.468 (L)
SN Printing processes in which the nonprinting areas of the block or plate are carved, engraved, or etched away, leaving the original plane surface as the area to be printed. (MAYER)
UF printing, relief
printing, surface
surface printing
CN K.KT.AFU.ALO.DUC.DUC.ALO.BCW.ARI

relief process, wash-off
USE **Eastman Wash-off Relief (TM)**

relief services
USE **welfare services**

relief, Eastman wash-off
USE **Eastman Wash-off Relief (TM)**

relief, high
USE **high relief**

relieving arches
RT.275
ALT **relieving arch**
SN Arches which deflect the weight off of another arch, opening, or other structural member located beneath.
UF arches, discharging
arches, relieving
arches, rough
arches, safety
discharging arches
rough arches
safety arches
CN V.RT.AFU.AFU.AFU.BCW.AFU.AFU.ALO.ALO

religion
KD.74 (L,R)
SN Study of religious beliefs and traditions in human life and culture from the perspective of the humanistic disciplines. (PG)
CN K.KD.AFU.AFU.BUE.AFU

religion historians
USE **historians of religion**

religion, anthropology of
USE **anthropology of religion**

religion, comparative
USE **comparative religion**

religion, history of
USE **history of religion**

religion, philosophy of
USE **philosophy of religion**

religion, psychology of
USE **psychology of religion**

religion, sociology of
USE **sociology of religion**

religions
BM.609 (L)
CN B.BM.BZY.AFU

religious
HG.240
SN Members of religious orders or communities. (RHDEL2)
CN H.HG.AFU.AXC.AXC.BIQ.AFU.BUE

religious architecture
USE **religious buildings**

religious books
VW.536
ALT **religious book**
UF books, religious

CN V.VW.AFU.ALO.AFU.AFU.ALO.BUE

religious buildings
RK.1092 (A,L,B)
ALT **religious building**
UF architecture, ecclesiastical
architecture, liturgical
architecture, religious
buildings, religious
ecclesiastical architecture
facilities, religious
liturgical architecture
religious architecture
religious facilities
CN V.RK.AFU.ALO.ALO.FCS.BIQ

religious calendars
VW.90 (L)
ALT **religious calendar**
UF calendars, religious
CN V.VW.AFU.AFU.AFU.FZU.AFU.ARI

religious camps
RG.159 (A,L)
ALT **religious camp**
UF camps, religious
CN V.RG.AFU.AFU.DOI.AXC.ARI

religious communities
RG.188 (A,L)
ALT **religious community**
UF communities, religious
CN V.RG.AFU.AFU.DUC

religious drama
BM.281 (L,R)
UF drama, religious
CN B.BM.AFU.ARI.BIQ.BZY

religious ethics
KD.86 (L)
UF ethics, religious
CN K.KD.AFU.AFU.BUE.ALO.BIQ

religious facilities
USE **religious buildings**

religious museums
RK.411 (A)
ALT **religious museum**
UF museums of religious art
museums, religious
CN V.RK.AFU.ALO.ALO.BCW.AXC.ARI.BZY

religious symbolism
BM.16 (B,R)
SN Refers to the practice of representing tangible objects or personifications as signs of religious beliefs or ideals.
UF church symbolism
symbolism, church
symbolism, religious
CN B.BM.AFU.AFU.AFU.BZY.ARI

relining
USE **lining**

relocatable partitions
USE **demountable partitions**

relocating
KG.137 (L)
ALT **relocated**
SN Moving people or things from one residence or fairly permanent location to another, for the purpose of preserving or improving their safety or well-being.
CN K.KG.AFU.AFU.BCW.BUE

remailloteuse
USE **chauffeuses**

remand homes
USE **reformatories**

reminiscences
VW.446
ALT **reminiscence**
SN Narrations of past experiences. (AHD)
CN V.VW.AFU.AFU.ALO.FCS

remodeling
KT.629 (A,L,B)
ALT **remodeled**
SN Use for changes undertaken with the intention of altering the style or decorative appearance of rooms, spaces, or buildings or other structures, without regard necessarily to historically accurate forms or periods.
CN K.KT.AFU.ALO.FZU.ARI

remote sensing
KT.116 (A,L)
SN Use broadly for the capture and transmission of information by detecting devices located at a distance from the receiving device and for the detection of information beyond the reach of normal human capacity.
UF sensing, remote
CN K.KT.AFU.ALO.CXA.ALO

remote-station fire alarm systems
RT.1509
ALT **remote-station fire alarm system**
UF fire alarm systems, remote-station
systems, remote-staion fire alarm
CN V.RT.ALO.BIQ.AFU.AFU.AFU.AXC

removed sections
VD.77
ALT **removed section**
SN Use for sections that are set apart from, but adjacent to, a main view of the structure or object through which the section is taken.
UF sections, removed
CN V.VD.AFU.AFU.BIQ.ALO.BIQ.BUE

removers, paint
USE **paint removers**

Renaissance
FL.3166 (A,L,B,R)
CN F.FL.ALO.BCW.ALO.ARI.AFU

Renaissance perspective
USE **linear perspective**

Renaissance Plateresque
USE **Second Plateresque**

Renaissance Revival
FL.3273 (A,R)
UF American Renaissance
Neo-Renaissance
Renaissance, American
Revival, Renaissance
CN F.FL.ALO.BCW.ALO.AXC.CLM.BZY

Renaissance, American
USE **Renaissance Revival**

Renaissance, Byzantine
USE **Palaeologan**

Renaissance, Early
USE **Early Renaissance**

Renaissance, Harlem
USE **Harlem Renaissance**

Renaissance, High
USE **High Renaissance**

Renaissance, Late
USE **Late Renaissance**

Renaissance, Macedonian
USE **Macedonian Renaissance**

Renaissance, Mexican
USE **Mexican Muralist**

Renaissance, Negro
USE **Harlem Renaissance**

rendered projects
USE **renderings**

renderers
HG.99
ALT **renderer**
CN H.HG.AFU.AXC.AXC.AFU.AFU.ALO.AXC.BOK.AFU

rendering
KT.200
ALT **rendered**
SN Giving a technical drawing, as an elevation, a more or less complete indication of light and shadow, and sometimes of color.
CN K.KT.AFU.ALO.DUC.BZY.ALO.BZY

renderings
VD.135 (A,L)
ALT **rendering**
SN Use for architectural drawings, usually perspectives or elevations, showing shadows, textures, sometimes colors, often executed with watercolor washes, and showing some setting. Intended as visualizations of the full conception of the project.
UF architectural renderings
projects, rendered
projets rendus
rendered projects

rendus
CN V.VD.AFU.AXC.BUE

Rendile
FL.630 (L)
CN F.FL.ALO.AFU.AXC.AXC.ARI.DCU

rending axes
USE **froes**

rendus
USE **renderings**

renewal, urban
USE **urban renewal**

renovation
KT.630 (L,B)
ALT **renovated**
SN Use for the process of making changes to objects, especially buildings or other structures, with the intention of improving their physical condition. When such changes intend to return a building or structure to a state of historical correctness, use **restoration.** Distinguished from **rehabilitating** which refers to improving deteriorated structures.
UF refurbishment
CN K.KT.AFU.ALO.FZU.AXC

rent
BM.407 (A,L,B)
CN B.BM.ARI.EWY

rent and eviction control
USE **rent control**

rent control
BM.410 (A,L)
UF control, eviction
control, rent
control, rent and eviction
eviction control
regulation, rent
rent and eviction control
rent regulation
rent restriction
restriction, rent
CN B.BM.ARI.EWY.ARI

rent regulation
USE **rent control**

rent restriction
USE **rent control**

rent tables
TG.756 (N)
ALT **rent table**
SN Late 18th- and early 19th-century circular or octagonal pedestal tables which have a deep top with numerous drawers in the frieze; often the drawers are marked with days of the week or dates, as such tables were used by landlords for filing collected rents.
UF drum tables
tables, drum
tables, rent
CN V.TG.AFU.AFU.BIQ.BOK.ALO.ERE

rent, economic
USE **economic rent**

rent, ground
USE **ground rent**

rental housing
RG.79 (A,L)
UF housing, rental
leased housing
CN V.RG.AFU.AFU.BOK.AXC.AXC

repainting
USE **retouching**

repair shops
RK.611
ALT **repair shop**
UF shops, repair
CN V.RK.AFU.ALO.ALO.CLM.ALO.AFU.BCW

repairing
KT.631 (L)
ALT **repaired**
CN K.KT.AFU.ALO.FZU.BCW

repairmen
HG.51
ALT **repairman**
CN H.HG.AFU.AXC.ARI.CXA

repeater stations
RK.206 (A,L)
ALT **repeater station**
SN Microwave communications stations capable of boosting an incoming weak signal for retransmission on another frequency.
UF repeaters
stations, repeater
CN V.RK.AFU.ALO.ALO.ARI.AFU.ARI.ALO.AFU

repeaters
USE **repeater stations**

replicas
VB.121 (N,R)
ALT **replica**
SN Use for precise reproductions of valued objects, usually in the same dimensions as the original. For reproductions of an image alone, use **reproductions** or **facsimiles.** Use also when more than one similar object is produced by the same artist, craftsman, or studio, with little or no variation between them; if variation is apparent, use **versions.** Distinct from **forgeries** and **counterfeits,** which are produced with the intent to deceive.
CN V.VB.ALO.BZY.AFU.AXC.ALO

repointing
USE **pointing**

report cards
VW.1068 (L,N)
ALT **report card**
SN Statements of a student's academic record for a particular period, often including also an evaluation of the student's rate of progress. (GAHLM)
UF cards, report
CN V.VW.AFU.ARI.ALO.CRG.BCW

report writing
USE **technical writing**

reporters
HG.288 (L)
ALT **reporter**
CN H.HG.AFU.AXC.BCW.ALO.AFU.ARI.ARI

reporters, court
USE **law reporters**

reporters, law
USE **law reporters**

reporting
KG.42 (L)
SN Giving an account. (RLG7)
CN K.KG.AFU.AFU.ALO.BZY

reports
VW.447 (L)
ALT **report**
SN Documents containing presentations of facts or the record of some proceeding, investigation, or event. (ICA)
CN V.VW.AFU.AFU.ALO.FIM

reports, accident
USE **accident reports**

reports, annual
USE **annual reports**

reports, audit
USE **audits**

reports, conference
USE **proceedings**

reports, congressional committee
USE **congressional committee reports**

reports, corporation
USE **corporation reports**

reports, daily
USE **daily reports**

reports, damage
USE **damage reports**

reports, environmental impact
USE **environmental impact statements**

reports, interim
USE **progress reports**

reports, monthly
USE **monthly reports**

reports, official
USE **official reports**

reports, progress
USE **progress reports**

reports, quarterly
USE **quarterly reports**

reports, scientific
USE **technical reports**

reports, technical
USE **technical reports**

reports, test
USE **test reports**

repositories
RK.1211 (L)
ALT **repository**
SN Places where archives, manuscripts, books, or other documents are stored. (ALAG)
UF archive repositories
depositories
repositories, archive
CN V.RK.AFU.ALO.ALO.GFO.BCW

repositories, archive
USE **repositories**

repositories, gentleman's
USE **gentleman's repositories**

repoussé
KT.837 (L)
SN In metalwork, a technique for decorating a surface by hammering the reverse of the object, sometimes into a mold of wood that has been carved in intaglio, to create designs in relief. (MAYER)
UF repoussé work
CN K.KT.AFU.ALO.HOE.BCW.ALO .AXC.AXC

repoussé work
USE **repoussé**

repoussoir
BM.62
SN An element placed in the immediate foreground of a pictorial composition to direct the spectator's eye into the picture. (THDAT)
CN B.BM.AFU.AFU.ARI.AFU.BCW.ALO. BOK

representation
BM.196
SN A manner of expression by the artist in which the subject matter is presented so that the observer is reminded of actual visible forms. (AFTP)
CN B.BM.AFU.AFU.AXC.CLM.CFS

representation (governmental function)
USE **representing**

representation, continuous
USE **continuous representation**

representation, simultaneous
USE **simultaneous representation**

representational art
USE **figurative art**

Representatives (Members of Congress)
USE **Members of the House of Representatives**

representing
KG.185 (L)
SN Serving in a legislative body by authority delegated by persons subject to the laws enacted by that body, usually by election, to represent their wishes and interests. (WCOL)
UF representation (governmental function)
CN K.KG.AFU.ALO.ARI.BZY

reprints
VW.688 (L)
ALT **reprint**
SN Reproductions of printed matter. (WCOL)
CN V.VW.AFU.ALO.AFU.DZW.BIQ.CFS

reproductions
VB.119 (A,L,N,R)
ALT **reproduction**
SN Use with regard to art images, art objects, or antiques, reproduced without intent to deceive; implies more precise and faithful imitation than does the term **copies.** With regard to art images, includes photographic reproductions. Where the intent is to deceive, use **forgeries** or **counterfeits.** For documents, use **copies.**
CN V.VB.ALO.BZY.AFU.AXC

reproductions, photomechanical
USE **photomechanical prints**

reprographic art
USE **copy art**

Republican
FL.2712
CN F.FL.ALO.AXC.ALO.ALO.AFU.AXC .AFU

Republican, Late
USE **Late Republican**

Republican, Upper
USE **Upper Republican**

requisitions
VW.864
ALT **requisition**
SN Written demands that something be furnished; also demands or applications made, usually with authority, as a demand made by military authorities upon civilians for supplies. (GAHLM)
CN V.VW.AFU.ARI.AFU.BIQ.CXA.AXC. ARI.AFU

reredorters
RK.748
ALT **reredorter**
SN Latrines situated at the rear of Medieval convents or monasteries. (W)
UF latrinas
CN V.RK.AFU.ALO.ALO.CXA.ALO.AFU. ARI.AFU.AFU

reredoses
RT.1227 (A,L,R)
ALT **reredos**
SN Use for large structures above and behind Christian altars, usually containing figures and scenes; may form part of the inner side of an altar screen.
CN V.RT.AFU.BUE.ALO.ARI.ALO.AFU

research buildings
RK.1158 (A,L,B)
ALT **research building**
UF buildings, research
facilities, research
research facilities
CN V.RK.AFU.ALO.ALO.FIM.ALO

research centers
RK.1178 (A)
ALT **research center**
SN Use for places to conduct research that are generally part of larger organizations or corporate, industrial, or educational facilities. For independent places where research is conducted, use **research institutes.**
UF centers, research
CN V.RK.AFU.ALO.ALO.FIM.ALO.ARI

research facilities
USE **research buildings**

research institutes
RK.1179 (L,B)
ALT **research institute**
SN Use for separate, independent and generally self-sufficient places engaging in basic or applied research under contract or as nonprofit organizations. For places where research is conducted as part of a larger organization, use **research centers.**
UF institutes, research
CN V.RK.AFU.ALO.ALO.FIM.ALO.AXC

research laboratories
RK.1170 (B)
ALT **research laboratory**
SN Use for laboratories equipped for both basic and applied research, usually set up in support of a larger organization which may then test and implement the research results.
UF laboratories, research
CN V.RK.AFU.ALO.ALO.FIM.ALO.AFU. CLM

research libraries
RK.705 (L)

ALT **research library**
SN Libraries consisting of specialized documents, and providing facilities for undertaking exhaustive investigation. (LG)
UF libraries, research
CN V.RK.AFU.ALO.ALO.CRG.AXC.ALO .ARI.ALO

research methods
USE **methodology**

research parks, industrial
USE **industrial parks**

research stations
RK.1174 (B)
ALT **research station**
SN Use for relatively isolated places with facilities for personnel habitation on site and for conducting on-site observations of natural phenomena in specific fields. Distinct from **experiment stations** which are primarily for research and experimenting and generally are not physically isolated.
UF stations, research
CN V.RK.AFU.ALO.ALO.FIM.ALO.ALO .ALO

researchers
HG.733
ALT **researcher**
CN H.HG.AFU.BCW.FIM

researching
KG.26 (A,L,B)
CN K.KG.AFU.AFU.AFU.DIO

reservations, Indian
USE **Indian reservations**

Reserve Mogollon
FL.948
UF Mogollon, Reserve
CN F.FL.ALO.ALO.ALO.AFU.ALO.ARI. BIQ.BCW.BCW

reserves, forest
USE **forest reserves**

reserves, marine
USE **marine parks**

reserves, national
USE **national parks**

reserves, nature
USE **nature preserves**

reservoirs
RK.576 (A,L,N,B)
ALT **resevoir**
SN Use for places or receptacles where fluids are accumulated and retained until needed.
CN V.RK.AFU.ALO.ALO.CFS.ALO.BCW .BIQ

reservoirs, underground
USE **underground reservoirs**

resettlement
BM.1062 (A)
CN B.BM.CLM.AFU.BIQ

residence halls
USE **dormitories**

residences
USE **dwellings**

residences, artists'
USE **artists' houses**

residences, community based
USE **group homes**

residences, country
USE **country houses**

residences, interns'
USE **interns' residences**

residences, nurses'
USE **nurses' residences**

residences, official
USE **official residences**

residences, secondary
USE **second homes**

residential areas
USE **residential districts**

residential buildings
USE **dwellings**

residential developments, planned
USE **planned unit developments**

residential districts
RG.272 (B)
ALT **residential district**
UF areas, residential
residential areas
CN V.RG.ALO.AFU.ALO.BCW

residential facilities
USE **dwellings**

residential hotels
USE **apartment hotels**

residential housing
USE **dwellings**

residential mobility
BM.1053 (A,L)
UF mobility, residential
CN B.BM.CLM.AFU.ALO.ARI.ALO

residential schools
USE **boarding schools**

resin
MT.1466 (L)
SN Any of various solid or semisolid organic substances usually obtained from plant secretions, but sometimes from insects; soluble in organic solvents but not in water; commonly used in varnishes, printing inks, and sizes.
CN M.MT.AFU.AFU.ALO.BOK

resin-coated paper
MT.1948
UF paper, RC
paper, resin-coated
RC paper
CN M.MT.AFU.AFU.ARI.ALO.ALO.AXC. ARI.BOK.BCW

resin concrete
USE **polymer-impregnated concrete**

resin paint, acrylic
USE **acrylic paint**

resin-treated wood
USE **impregnated wood**

resin, acaroid
USE **acaroid resin**

resin, acetal
USE **acetal**

resin, acrylate
USE **acrylic**

resin, acrylic
USE **acrylic**

resin, alkyd
USE **alkyd resin**

resin, allyl
USE **allyl resin**

resin, amino
USE **amino resin**

resin, aminoaldehyde
USE **aminoaldehyde resin**

resin, epoxy
USE **epoxy**

resin, fluorocarbon
USE **fluoroplastic**

resin, fossil
USE **fossil resin**

resin, gum
USE **gum resin**

resin, juniper
USE **juniper resin**

resin, kauri
USE **kauri**

resin, phenol-formaldehyde
USE **phenolic**

resin, phenolic
USE **phenolic**

resin, phenylene-based
USE **phenylene-based resin**

resin, polyacrylic
USE **polyacrylate**

resin, polyamide
USE **nylon**

resin, polyformaldehyde

USE **acetal**

resin, propylene
USE **polypropylene**

resin, Rhoplex (TM)
USE **Rhoplex resin (TM)**

resin, styrene
USE **polystyrene**

resin, sulfone-based
USE **sulfone polymer**

resin, thermoplastic
USE **thermoplastic**

resin, thermosetting
USE **thermoset**

resin, urea
USE **urea-formaldehyde resin**

resin, urea-formaldehyde
USE **urea-formaldehyde resin**

resin, urethane
USE **polyurethane**

resin, vinyl
USE **vinyl**

resinate, copper
USE **copper resinate**

resins (plastics)
USE **plastics**

resins, artificial
USE **plastics**

resins, synthetic
USE **plastics**

resist
MT.2726
SN Any substance used to block out or mask temporarily a surface area in order to prevent or impede an action (as of a chemical) on the masked area. (MAYER)
UF acid resist
resist, acid
CN M.MT.AFU.ARI.IFM.BCW

resist-dyed cloth
MT.1884
UF cloth, resist-dyed
resist-dyed textiles
textiles, resist-dyed
CN M.MT.AFU.AFU.ARI.ALO.ALO.ALO.ARI.BCW

resist-dyed textiles
USE **resist-dyed cloth**

resist dyeing
KT.79
ALT **resist-dyed**
SN Dyeing cloth by repeatedly putting a resist on different parts of the pattern and placing the fabric in successive dye baths. (W)
UF dyeing, resist
printing, resist
resist printing
CN K.KT.AFU.ALO.BOK.ALO.ALO

resist printing
USE **resist dyeing**

resist, acid
USE **resist**

resistance brazing
KT.795
UF brazing, resistance
CN K.KT.AFU.ALO.HOE.BCW.ALO.AFU.AFU.AFU.BCW

resistance heating
USE **electric resistance heating**

resistance welding
KT.805 (L)
ALT **resistance-welded**
SN A form of electrical pressure welding in which the necessary heat is produced by a flow of current through the parts to be welded. Sufficient pressure to make the weld is applied simultaneously with the flow of current. (W)
UF electric resistance welding
welding, electric resistance
welding, resistance
CN K.KT.AFU.ALO.HOE.BCW.ALO.AFU.ALO.ALO.ALO

resistance, acid
USE **acid resistance**

resolution
USE **resolving**

resolutions
VW.782 (L)
ALT **resolution**
SN Formal expressions of the opinion formed by some superior authority on matters referred to its decision and forwarded to inferior authorities for their instruction and government. (BLACKS)
CN V.VW.AFU.ARI.AFU.ALO.CFS

resolving
KG.28 (L)
SN Settling disputes by informal process. (RLG7)
UF resolution
CN K.KG.AFU.AFU.AFU.DOI

resonance (seismic design)
BM.1026
CN B.BM.CFS.AXC.CLM.ALO.BIQ.AFU

resorcinol
MT.2325 (L)
SN A crystalline phenol, obtained naturally from various resins or artificially; used especially in making dyes, pharmaceuticals, and resins.
CN M.MT.AFU.ARI.ALO.ERE

resorts
RG.168 (A,L,B,R)
ALT **resort**
UF holiday resorts
CN V.RG.AFU.AFU.DOI.BZY

resorts, health
USE **health resorts**

resorts, seaside
USE **seaside resorts**

resorts, summer
USE **summer resorts**

resorts, winter
USE **winter resorts**

resource centers, funding
USE **funding agencies**

resource maps, mineral
USE **mineral resource maps**

resource recovery facilities
RK.655 (L)
ALT **resource recovery facility**
UF facilities, resource recovery
plants, recycling
recovery facilities, resource
recycling plants
waste recovery facilities
CN V.RK.AFU.ALO.ALO.CLM.ALO.ALO.AFU.AXC.DCU

resources development, water
USE **water resources development**

resources, energy
USE **energy resources**

resources, natural
USE **natural resources**

resources, power
USE **energy resources**

resources, visual
USE **visual resource collections**

respirators
TB.408 (L)
ALT **respirator**
SN Protective masks worn when working in an area with gas, fumes, smoke, or high dust density.
CN V.TB.AFU.ARI.DUC.ARI

responds
RT.661
ALT **respond**
SN Pilasters or half-colonettes, engaged to a wall, that carry one end of a vault rib.
CN V.RT.AFU.AFU.AFU.BIQ.BUE.ALO.AFU.BZY

rest areas
USE **roadside rest areas**

rest areas, roadside
USE **roadside rest areas**

rest beds

USE **daybeds**

rest homes
RK.753 (A,L,B,R)
ALT **rest home**
UF boarding homes
homes, boarding
homes, rest
homes, sheltered care
sheltered care homes
CN V.RK.AFU.ALO.ALO.CXA.ALO.AFU.AXC.AXC

rest homes, labor
USE **labor rest homes**

rest rooms
RM.71 (A)
ALT **rest room**
SN Use for public facilities containing toilets and lavatories, such as are found in office buildings, schools, transportation facilities, and other nonresidential locations.
UF lavatories, public
public lavatories
rooms, rest
CN V.RM.AFU.DIO.ALO.ALO.BIQ

restaurants
RK.111 (A,L,N,B,R)
ALT **restaurant**
CN V.RK.AFU.ALO.ALO.ALO.AFU.AXC

restaurants, communal
USE **soup kitchens**

restaurants, drive-in
USE **drive-in restaurants**

restaurants, fast food
USE **fast food restaurants**

restaurants, open-air
USE **outdoor cafés**

restaurants, quick-service
USE **fast food restaurants**

restaurants, self-service
USE **Automats (TM)**
cafeterias

Restauration
FL.3361
UF Charles X
CN F.FL.ALO.BCW.ALO.AXC.DIO.BCW.ALO.AXC

restoration
KT.633 (A,L,B,R)
ALT **restored**
SN Use for the process of making changes to an object or structure so that it will closely approximate its state at a specific time in its history. For changes not considering historical correctness, use **remodeling** or **renovation.** When changes are made to prevent further deterioration, use **preservation.**
UF restoring
CN K.KT.AFU.ALO.FZU.BIQ

Restoration (period)
FL.3196
UF Carolean
CN F.FL.ALO.BCW.ALO.ARI.BIQ.BIQ.AFU.AFU.ALO.ALO

restorers
HG.467 (L)
ALT **restorer**
CN H.HG.AFU.AXC.BUE.ALO.CLM

restoring
USE **restoration**

restrainers
MT.2326
SN Fluid that is used with a solvent when cleaning or stripping oil paintings to reduce the strength and slow down the activity of the solvent. (MAYER)
CN M.MT.AFU.ARI.ALO.EWY

restriction, rent
USE **rent control**

restrictions, height
USE **height restrictions**

restrictive covenants
BM.451 (B)
SN Agreements generally running with specific pieces of land, restricting the free use of that land with reference to particular purposes or occupancy by members of a particular group. (W)
UF covenants, restrictive
CN B.BM.BCW.BOK.AFU.AFU

resumes
VW.781 (L)
ALT **resume**
SN Brief records of one's personal history and experience submitted with a job application. (AHD)
UF curricula vitae
job resumes
vitas
CN V.VW.AFU.ARI.AFU.ALO.BZY.AXC

retables
RT.1228 (A,L,B,R)
ALT **retable**
SN Use for painted or sculpted panels attached at the back of a Christian altar's mensa.
CN V.RT.AFU.BUE.ALO.ARI.ALO.ALO

retail centers, strip
USE **shopping plazas**

retail inventories
USE **merchandise inventories**

retail stores
RK.179 (A,L,N)
ALT **retail store**
SN Use for places of business where goods are sold directly to the ultimate consumers.
UF stores, retail
CN V.RK.AFU.ALO.ALO.ALO.ARI.BIQ.ALO.BZY

retailers
HG.429
ALT **retailer**
CN H.HG.AFU.AXC.BOK.FCS.ALO.AFU

retailing districts
USE **shopping districts**

retaining walls
RT.587 (A,L,B)
ALT **retaining wall**
SN Includes walls, either freestanding or laterally braced, that hold back or support a bank of earth and walls constructed to resist lateral loads.
UF walls, retaining
CN V.RT.AFU.AFU.AFU.BIQ.BUE.AFU.ALO.AXC

retaining walls, crib
USE **cribbing**

retaining walls, gravity
USE **gravity walls**

retardants
MT.2327
CN M.MT.AFU.ARI.ALO.FCS

retardants, flame
USE **fireproofing agents**

retarded hemihydrate plaster
MT.2445
UF class B gypsum plaster
gypsum plaster, class B
hemihydrate plaster, retarded
plaster, class B gypsum
plaster, retarded hemihydrate
CN M.MT.AFU.ARI.CRG.AFU.AXC.AFU.AXC.AXC

retarded, mentally
USE **mentally handicapped**

retention basins, storm water
USE **storm water retention basins**

retention basins, water
USE **storm water retention basins**

retention schedules
USE **records schedules**

retention schedules, records
USE **records schedules**

reticular pattern
DG.131
SN Crossing or interlacing lines or series of lozenges, forming a net- or weblike pattern.
UF network pattern
pattern, network
pattern, reticular
CN D.DG.AFU.ARI.ALO.BIQ.BIQ

reticulated tracery

RT.1020
UF net tracery
tracery, net
tracery, reticulated
CN V.RT.AFU.ARI.ALO.BZY.AFU.AFU .ARI

retirement communities
RD.73 (A,L,B)
ALT **retirement community**
SN Use for self-contained residential communities for retired people which provide for most of the daily needs of the residents. For similar facilities offering more comprehensive services, use **life care communities.**
UF communities, retirement
retirement villages
villages, retirement
CN V.RD.AFU.BIQ.ARI

retirement homes
RK.347 (A)
ALT **retirement home**
UF homes, retirement
CN V.RK.AFU.ALO.ALO.AXC.ALO.BOK .BUE

retirement pensions
USE **pensions**

retirement villages
USE **retirement communities**

retouch varnish
MT.2475
SN A very thin solution of damar or other non-yellowing resin that the artist sprays or brushes over a dry, unfinished oil painting before the resumption of painting with fresh colors. (MAYER)
UF varnish, retouch
CN M.MT.AFU.ARI.CRG.AFU.BOK.AFU. ALO.ALO

retouching
KT.9 (L)
ALT **retouched**
SN Reworking small areas of a painting or photographic negative usually to cover damage or to mask unwanted features. (PDAT)
UF repainting
CN K.KT.AFU.ALO.ARI.AFU

retracted claw feet
TG.920
ALT **retracted claw foot**
UF claw feet, retracted
feet, retracted claw
CN V.TG.ALO.DZW.AFU.DCU.AFU.AFU .ALO

retreats
KM.140 (L)
SN Periods of withdrawal to a place of seclusion for the purpose of spiritual rest and restoration.
CN K.KM.AFU.DOI.ARI

retrieval services, information
USE **information retrieval services**

retrieval services, online
USE **information retrieval services**

retrieval, data
USE **information retrieval**

retrieval, information
USE **information retrieval**

retrieval, online
USE **online searching**

retrochoirs
RM.328
ALT **retrochoir**
UF backchoirs
CN V.RM.AFU.DIO.AXC.ALO.AFU.DUC

retrofitting
KT.634
ALT **retrofit**
SN Use for the process of furnishing a building or other object with new parts or equipment not available at the time of its manufacture.
CN K.KT.AFU.ALO.FZU.BOK

retrospective conversion
KG.86 (L)
SN Converting to machine-readable form data records from a manual or non-machine-readable file that are not converted in day-to-day processing. (ALAG)
UF conversion, retrospective
RECON
CN K.KG.AFU.AFU.AXC.BIQ.AFU.AFU

returns, census
USE **census records**

returns, election
USE **election returns**

returns, tax
USE **tax returns**

reuse, adaptive
USE **adaptive reuse**

revales
RT.756
ALT **revale**
SN Stone moldings, carved in place. (DAC)
CN V.RT.AFU.ALO.AFU.BOK.AFU.AFU. ALO.AFU

reveal joints
USE **recessed joints**

reveals
RT.1008
ALT **reveal**
SN Those portions of jambs of an opening or recess which are visible from the face of the wall back to the frame or other structure which may be placed between the jambs. (RS)
UF esconsons
revels
sconcheons
scuncheons
CN V.RT.AFU.ARI.ALO.BCW

revels
USE **reveals**

reversal film
MT.2242
UF film, reversal
CN M.MT.AFU.ALO.CXA.ALO.BUE

reversal paper
MT.1949
UF paper, reversal
CN M.MT.AFU.AFU.ARI.ALO.ALO.AXC .ARI.BOK.BIQ

reversal (solarization)
USE **solarization**

reverse
DC.21
SN Use with reference to the back, underside, or subordinate surface of a coin, medal, seal, or currency note. Use **verso** to refer to the reverse or subordinate side of a sheet of paper.
CN D.DC.AFU.ALO.ALO.BUE

reverse bevel locks
TF.215
ALT **reverse bevel lock**
UF bevel locks, reverse
locks, reverse bevel
CN V.TF.AFU.AFU.AFU.AFU.DIO.BIQ. AFU.DOI

reverse engraving on glass
USE **verre églomisé**

reverse ogee moldings
USE **cyma reversas**

reverse painting on glass
KT.767 (L,R)
SN Technique of applying paint to the back of a sheet of glass in reverse order, that is, with details and highlights first and background last. The finished picture is viewed from the front. (FOLKGL)
UF back painting
glass underpainting
mirror painting (reverse painting)
painting, back
painting, mirror (reverse painting)
underpainting, glass
CN K.KT.AFU.ALO.HOE.ALO.AXC.AFU

reverse perspective
USE **inverted perspective**

reverse serpentine
USE **oxbow**

reversible locks
TF.216
ALT **reversible lock**

SN Locks which can be adapted to fit a door of either hand. (MEANS)
UF locks, reversible
CN V.TF.AFU.AFU.AFU.AFU.DIO.BIQ .AFU.DUC

revetments
RT.662
ALT **revetment**
SN Any wall facings over less durable or attractive substances or constructions.
CN V.RT.AFU.AFU.AFU.BIQ.BUE.ALO. AFU.CFS

review, design
USE **design review**

reviewing
KG.29
SN Going over or examining critically or deliberately. (W)
CN K.KG.AFU.AFU.AFU.DUC

reviews
VW.307 (L)
ALT **review**
SN Reports or essays giving critical estimates of a work or performance. (AHD)
CN V.VW.AFU.AFU.ALO.BCW.ARI

reviews, book
USE **book reviews**

reviews, exhibition
USE **exhibition reviews**

reviews, film
USE **film reviews**

reviews, motion-picture
USE **film reviews**

reviews, movie
USE **film reviews**

reviews, moving-picture
USE **film reviews**

revisers
HG.734
ALT **reviser**
SN Use for those who revise, redraft, update, or otherwise make authorized changes to drawings, plans, models, manuscripts, printed texts, or any form of document, visual or verbal, originally created by others.
CN H.HG.AFU.BCW.FOG

revival
BM.303 (L,R)
SN Self-conscious use of earlier styles in new works of visual art, architecture, literature, or theatre, on a scale broader than quotations or pastiches, generally to the point of an artistic movement.
CN B.BM.AFU.AXC.DIO

Revival, Baroque
USE **Baroque Revival**

Revival, Byzantine
USE **Byzantine Revival**

Revival, Classic
USE **Classical Revival**

Revival, Classical
USE **Classical Revival**

Revival, Classical (North American)
USE **Federal**

Revival, Colonial
USE **Colonial Revival**

Revival, Egyptian
USE **Egyptian Revival**

Revival, Elizabethan
USE **Elizabethan Revival**

Revival, Georgian
USE **Georgian Revival**

Revival, Gothic
USE **Gothic Revival**

Revival, Greek
USE **Greek Revival**

Revival, Islamic
USE **Islamic Revival**

Revival, Jacobean
USE **Jacobean Revival**

Revival, Mayan
USE **Mayan Revival**

Revival, Mission
USE **Mission Style**

Revival, Moorish
USE **Islamic Revival**

Revival, Mudejar
USE **Mudejar Revival**

Revival, Neoclassical
USE **Classical Revival**

Revival, Norman
USE **Norman Revival**

Revival, Palaeologue
USE **Palaeologan**

Revival, Palladian
USE **Palladian**

Revival, Pueblo
USE **Pueblo Revival**

Revival, Pueblo-Spanish
USE **Pueblo Revival**

Revival, Queen Anne
USE **Queen Anne Style**

Revival, Regency
USE **Regency Revival**

Revival, Renaissance
USE **Renaissance Revival**

Revival, Rococo
USE **Rococo Revival**

Revival, Romanesque
USE **Romanesque Revival**

Revival, Saite
USE **Twenty-sixth Dynasty**

Revival, Spanish Colonial
USE **Spanish Colonial Revival**

Revival, Stuart
USE **Stuart Revival**

Revival, Tudor
USE **Tudor Revival**

Revival, Vernacular
USE **Old English**

Revival, Victorian
USE **Victorian Revival**

revivalists
USE **evangelists**

Revived Court Style, Kuba
USE **Kuba Revived Court Style**

Revived Kutani
USE **Saiko Kutani**

revolution
BM.1117 (R)
CN B.BM.CRG.BCW.CLM.AFU

revolved sections
VD.78
ALT **revolved section**
SN Use for orthographic drawings that show a section of a structure or object revolved 90 degrees and drawn on the main view.
UF rotated sections
sections, revolved
sections, rotated
CN V.VD.AFU.AFU.BIQ.ALO.BIQ.BZY

revolvers (swivel chairs)
USE **swivel chairs**

revolving bookcases
TG.406
ALT **revolving bookcase**
UF bookcases, circular
bookcases, revolving
bookcases, rotary
bookcases, tiered
circular bookcases
rotary bookcases
tiered bookcases
CN V.TG.AFU.AFU.AXC.ALO.ALO.BOK

revolving buildings
RK.1381 (A,B)
ALT **revolving building**
UF buildings, revolving
CN V.RK.AFU.ALO.AXC.BUE

revolving chairs
USE **swivel chairs**

revolving doors
RT.870 (B)
ALT **revolving door**
UF doors, revolving
CN V.RT.AFU.ARI.AFU.AFU.AFU.ALO.ARI.AFU.ARI.BCW.AFU

revolving stages
RM.369
ALT **revolving stage**
UF stages, revolving
turntables (revolving stages)
CN V.RM.AFU.DIO.AXC.AXC.ALO.BIQ.AFU.ARI

revolving stools
TG.273
ALT **revolving stool**
UF rotary stools
screw stools
stools, revolving
stools, rotary
stools, screw
stools, swivel
swivel stools
CN V.TG.AFU.AFU.ALO.AFU.ALO.AXC.ALO

reweaving
USE **weaving**

Rhages ware
USE **Rayy ware**

rhea
USE **ramie**

rhetoric
KD.88 (L,R)
SN Art of expressive speech or discourse; specifically the study of principles and rules of composition formulated by ancient critics and interpreted by classical scholars for application to discourse in the vernacular. (W)
CN K.KD.AFU.AFU.BZY

rhetoricians
HG.248 (R)
ALT **rhetorician**
CN H.HG.AFU.AXC.AXC.BOK

rhinestone
MT.241
CN M.MT.AFU.AFU.AFU.BIQ.AFU.AFU.ALO.AFU.AFU

rhizophora
USE **mangrove**

rhodamine pink
USE **strong purplish pink**

rhodamine purple
USE **vivid purplish red**

Rhodes ware
USE **Rhodian ware**

Rhodian
FL.2610
UF Camirian
Kameirian
Kamirian
CN F.FL.ALO.AXC.ALO.AFU.ALO.AXC.ALO.ARI.AXC

Rhodian pottery
USE **Rhodian ware**

Rhodian style Iznik pottery
USE **Rhodian ware**

Rhodian ware
FL.3523
UF Iznik pottery, Rhodian style
pottery, Rhodian
pottery, Rhodian style Iznik
Rhodes ware
Rhodian pottery
Rhodian style Iznik pottery
ware, Rhodes
ware, Rhodian
CN F.FL.ALO.BIQ.AFU.FOG.ALO.ALO.ARI

rhombuses
BM.779 (B)
ALT **rhomboid**
SN Equilateral parallelograms having, usually, obtuse angles. (WCOL)
CN B.BM.CFS.ARI.AXC.BCW.AFU.BIQ.ALO.AFU.ALO

Rhoplex resin (TM)
MT.2123
SN Acrylic resin emulsions of the Rhom & Haas Company, used for paints, textile finishes, and adhesives. (MH12)
UF resin, Rhoplex (TM)
CN M.MT.AFU.AFU.ARI.BUE.ALO.AXC.AFU.ALO.ALO

rhyolite
MT.605 (L)
UF liparite
CN M.MT.AFU.AFU.AFU.DCU.AFU.AFU.AFU.AFU.AFU.BCW

rhythm
BM.102 (L)
SN A continuance, flow, or sense of movement achieved by repetition of regular or patterned units. (AFTP)
UF continuity
CN B.BM.AFU.AFU.ARI.AXC

rib lath
MT.2414
SN Expanded-metal lath having V-shaped ribs to provide greater stiffness and to permit wider spacing of framing members. (DAC)
UF lath, rib
CN M.MT.AFU.ARI.BZY.BIQ.ALO

ribands
USE **ledger boards**

ribats
RG.135
ALT **ribat**
SN Use for multifunctional Islamic fortified outposts generally reserved for warriors of the Faith who are committed to defense of frontiers and to proselytizing.
CN V.RG.AFU.AFU.BZY.ALO.AXC

ribband-back chairs
USE **ribbon-back chairs**

ribbed arches
RT.257
ALT **ribbed arch**
SN Use for arches with the surface treated as a series of round-sectioned elements, akin to ribs in vaults, common in Gothic architecture.
UF arches, ribbed
CN V.RT.AFU.AFU.AFU.BCW.AFU.AFU.AFU.ELK.BIQ

ribbed domes
RT.395
ALT **ribbed dome**
SN Use for domes having ribs; also, domes, usually of wood or metal, with vertical members converging at the crown, intersected by horizontal members.
UF domes, ribbed
CN V.RT.AFU.AFU.AFU.BIQ.AFU.AFU.BIQ

ribbed floors, one-way
USE **one-way joist systems**

ribbed fluting
USE **cabled fluting**

ribbed vaults
RT.550 (A,B)
ALT **ribbed vault**
SN Vaults in which arched ribs are located along the groins to act as a framework or support for the infilling or vaulting cell. (IGA)
CN V.RT.AFU.AFU.AFU.BIQ.BOK.AFU.ARI.AFU.ALO

ribbon
MT.2264 (L,N)
CN M.MT.AFU.ALO.FIM

ribbon-back chairs
TG.149
ALT **ribbon-back chair**
SN Chairs with interwoven splats in the form of interlaced ribbons, such as those popularized by Chippendale and appearing in mid-18th century England and America.
UF chairs, ribbon-back
interlaced splat-back chairs
ribband-back chairs
CN V.TG.AFU.AFU.ALO.AFU.AFU.AFU.NIE.DIO

ribbon boards
USE **ledger boards**

ribbon development
BM.1080 (B)
SN Unplanned development of, usually commercial, buildings built side by side or adjoining, and stretching in continuous strings along both sides of a roadway.
UF development, ribbon
development, string
development, strip
string development
strip development
CN B.BM.CLM.ALO.ALO.ALO.AXC

ribbon saws
USE **band saws**

ribbon slate
MT.869
UF slate, ribbon
CN M.MT.AFU.AFU.AFU.DCU.AFU.ARI.BUE.AFU.AXC

ribbon strips
USE **ledger boards**

ribbonwork
MT.2779 (L)
CN M.MT.AFU.AXC.CLM

Ribe
FL.607 (L)
UF Waribe
CN F.FL.ALO.AFU.AXC.AXC.ALO.BOK.BIQ

ribs
RT.684 (R)
ALT **rib**
SN Projecting bands, usually of masonry, which support or decorate domes or vaults.
UF nervures
ribs, vault
vault ribs
CN V.RT.AFU.AFU.ALO.AFU.ARI

ribs, arch
USE **transverse ribs**

ribs, cross
USE **transverse ribs**

ribs, diagonal
USE **diagonal ribs**

ribs, flying
USE **flying ribs**

ribs, groin
USE **diagonal ribs**

ribs, intermediate
USE **tiercerons**

ribs, lierne
USE **liernes**

ribs, longitudinal ridge
USE **longitudinal ridge ribs**

ribs, ridge
USE **ridge ribs**

ribs, secondary
USE **tiercerons**

ribs, tertiary
USE **liernes**

ribs, transverse
USE **transverse ribs**

ribs, transverse ridge
USE **transverse ridge ribs**

ribs, vault
USE **ribs**

ribs, wall
USE **wall ribs**

rice oil
MT.2041 (L)
UF oil, rice
CN M.MT.AFU.AFU.ARI.ARI.AXC.ARI.CFS

rice paper
MT.1897
UF paper, rice
CN M.MT.AFU.AFU.ARI.ALO.ALO.AXC.AFU.ARI

rice straw
MT.1079
UF straw, rice
CN M.MT.AFU.AFU.ALO.BIQ.CRG.ALO

rich lime
USE **fat lime**

rich mortar
USE **fat mortar**

Richard, Igbo
USE **Igbo Richard**

Richardsonian Romanesque
FL.1738
UF Romanesque, Richardsonian
CN F.FL.ALO.ALO.BCW.AFU.BUE.BOK

riddles (founding tools)
TB.694
ALT **riddle (founding tool)**
SN Coarse sieves used for separating and grading granular material. (MEANS)
CN V.TB.AFU.BCW.BIQ.ALO.ARI

rides
USE **amusement rides**

rides, amusement
USE **amusement rides**

ridge beams
USE **ridgeboards**

ridge hangers, formed
USE **formed ridge hangers**

ridge ribs
RT.688
ALT **ridge rib**
SN The ribs along the longitudinal or transverse ridges of vaults. (PDARC)
UF ribs, ridge
CN V.RT.AFU.AFU.ALO.AFU.ARI.AXC

ridge ribs, longitudinal
USE **longitudinal ridge ribs**

ridge ribs, transverse
USE **transverse ridge ribs**

ridge rolls
USE **hip rolls**

ridge tile
MT.187
SN A tile which is curved in section, used to cover the ridge of a roof. (DAC)
UF crown tile
tile, crown
tile, ridge
CN M.MT.AFU.AFU.AFU.AXC.ALO.ALO.ALO.AFU.ALO.AXC.AFU.ARI.AXC

ridgeboards
RT.507
ALT **ridgeboard**
SN Longitudinal members at the apexes of roofs which support the upper ends of the rafters. (DAC)
UF beams, ridge
ridge beams
ridgepieces
ridgeplates
ridgepoles
roof trees
trees, roof
CN V.RT.AFU.AFU.AFU.BIQ.ARI.ALO.ALO.ALO.ARI

ridgepieces
USE **ridgeboards**

ridgeplates
USE **ridgeboards**

ridgepoles
USE **ridgeboards**

ridges
RT.470
ALT **ridge**
CN V.RT.AFU.AFU.BIQ.ARI.ALO.AFU.BOK

ridges (landform components)
RD.238 (L)
ALT **ridge (landform component)**
CN V.RD.ARI.AFU.AXC.ALO.BIQ

ridges, angle
USE **hip rafters**

ridges, beach
USE **beach ridges**

riding chairs
USE **chamber horses**

riding clubs
RK.1028 (L,B)
ALT **riding club**
UF clubs, equestrian

clubs, horseback riding
clubs, riding
equestrian clubs
horseback riding clubs
CN V.RK.AFU.ALO.ALO.EWY.AXC.AL O.AFU.ALO

riding halls
RK.1066 (A)
ALT **riding hall**
SN Indoor enclosures for horseback riding. (DOS)
UF halls, riding
houses, riding
riding houses
CN V.RK.AFU.ALO.ALO.EWY.AXC.BIQ .ALO.BCW

riding houses
USE **riding halls**

riding rings
RK.1499
ALT **riding ring**
UF rings (horse riding)
rings, riding
CN V.RK.ALO.ALO.BCW.BZY

riding schools
RK.816 (L,B)
ALT **riding school**
UF schools, riding
CN V.RK.AFU.ALO.ALO.CXA.ARI.ALO. CXA

riding trails
USE **bridle paths**

riffler files
TB.877 (N)
ALT **riffler file**
SN Curved files in a variety of shapes and cross sections; used for carving. (BLACKB)
UF files, riffler
files, woodcarver's
rifflers (files)
woodcarver's files
CN V.TB.AFU.BCW.CFS.ALO.AFU.CFS. AXC

riffler rasps
TB.982 (N)
ALT **riffler rasp**
SN Curved rasps in a variety of shapes and cross sections; used for carving.
UF rasps, riffler
rifflers (rasps)
CN V.TB.AFU.BCW.CFS.ALO.AFU.EFQ. ALO

rifflers (files)
USE **riffler files**

rifflers (rasps)
USE **riffler rasps**

rifle ranges
RG.149 (L,B)
ALT **rifle range**
UF ranges, rifle
CN V.RG.AFU.AFU.DIO.ARI.ALO

rigging plans
VD.32
ALT **rigging plan**
SN Drawings representing a side elevation of a ship and emphasizing the arrangement of the rigging.
UF plans, rigging
CN V.VD.AFU.AFU.BIQ.ALO.ALO.BIQ. ARI

right
DC.42
CN D.DC.AFU.ALO.ARI.DUC

right-angle bit tongs
USE **side tongs**

right-angle gauges
USE **try squares**

right of way
BM.476 (L)
SN A legal right of passage over another's ground. (W)
UF way, right of
CN B.BM.BCW.DIO

rights transfer, development
USE **development rights transfer**

rights, air
USE **air rights**

rights, airspace
USE **air rights**

rights, artists'
USE **artists' rights**

rights, civil
USE **civil rights**

rights, riparian
USE **riparian rights**

rights, water
USE **water rights**

rights, women's
USE **feminism**

rigid arches
RT.258
ALT **rigid arch**
SN Use for arches made of one piece of continuous deformed material, rather than of voussoirs.
UF arches, rigid
CN V.RT.AFU.AFU.AFU.BCW.AFU.AFU. AFU.ELK.BOK

rigid frames
RT.42
ALT **rigid frame**
SN Use for structural frames in which all columns and beams are rigidly connected, with no hinged joints.
UF frames, portal
frames, rigid
portal frames
CN V.RT.AFU.AFU.AFU.ALO.AXC.BCW

rigid insulation
MT.2411
UF board insulation
insulation, board
insulation, rigid
insulation, slab
slab insulation
CN M.MT.AFU.ARI.BZY.BCW.ARI.ALO

rigid joints
TF.663
ALT **rigid joint**
UF fixed joints
joints, fixed
joints, rigid
CN V.TF.ALO.ARI.ARI.BZY

rigid locks
USE **preassembled locks**

rigid pavements
RT.814
ALT **rigid pavement**
SN Pavements that provide high bending resistance and that distribute loads to the foundation over a relatively large area. (DAC)
UF pavements, rigid
CN V.RT.AFU.ALO.AFU.BZY.AFU.ALO

rigid structures
RT.11
ALT **rigid structure**
SN Use for structures that do not undergo appreciable changes in shape under the actions of loads.
UF structures, rigid
CN V.RT.AFU.AFU.AFU.AFU.ALO.ARI

rigidity
BM.956
CN B.BM.CFS.AXC.BZY.BOK.BZY

rigs, drilling
USE **drilling rigs**

rigs, offshore
USE **offshore rigs**

rigs, offshore drilling
USE **offshore rigs**

rigs, oil
USE **oil rigs**

rim locks
TF.217
ALT **rim lock**
SN Door locks applied to the surface of a door with its strike applied to the face of the jamb. (DITTRI)
UF box locks
locks, box
locks, rim
locks, surface
surface door locks
surface locks
CN V.TF.AFU.AFU.AFU.AFU.DIO.BIQ .AFU.DZW

rim locks, auxiliary

USE **auxiliary rim locks**

rimers
USE **taper augers**

Rimpa School
USE **Sotatsu-Korin School**

rinceaux
DG.148
ALT **rinceau**
SN Use for a pattern of scrolling stems and leaves, especially of acanthus and in classicizing decoration. For other leafy scrollwork, use **scrolling foliage.**
CN D.DG.AFU.ARI.ALO.CRG.ARI.AFU

Rinderi
FL.219
CN F.FL.ALO.AFU.AXC.AFU.AFU.ALO.ALO.CRG

rinding irons
USE **barking irons**

ring crosses
USE **Celtic crosses**

ring dating, hydration
USE **neutron activation analysis**

ring dogs
TB.1068 (N)
ALT **ring dog**
SN Pocket-sized cant hooks for rolling logs. (SLOANE)
UF dogs, ring
CN V.TB.AFU.BCW.CFS.ALO.ALO.BZY.AFU.AFU

ring-groove nails
USE **ring-shank nails**

ring handles
TF.82
ALT **ring handle**
UF handles, loop
handles, ring
loop handles
pulls, ring
ring pulls
CN V.TF.AFU.AFU.AFU.AFU.CFS.BCW.AFU.CRG

ring pulls
USE **ring handles**

ring roads
USE **beltways**

ring-shank nails
TF.399
ALT **ring-shank nail**
SN Nails with ring like grooves around the shank to improve their grip. (MEANS)
UF annular nails
annular ring nails
nails, ring-shank
ring-groove nails
ringlock nails
CN V.TF.AFU.AFU.AFU.ALO.AFU.CFS.AFU.CRG

ring-shaped
USE **annular**

ring ware, base
USE **base ring ware**

ringas
USE **Borneo rosewood**

ringed columns
USE **banded columns**

Ringerike Style
FL.3149
CN F.FL.ALO.BCW.ALO.ALO.AFU.BOK.ARI.BUE.ARI

ringlock nails
USE **ring-shank nails**

rings (horse riding)
USE **riding rings**

rings, door
USE **door rings**

rings, flush
USE **flush rings**

rings, riding
USE **riding rings**

rings, shaft
USE **shaft rings**

rings, tension
USE **tension rings**

rinks
USE **skating rinks**

rinks, hockey
USE **ice hockey rinks**

rinks, ice hockey
USE **ice hockey rinks**

rinks, ice-skating
USE **ice-skating rinks**

rinks, roller-skating
USE **roller-skating rinks**

rinks, skating
USE **skating rinks**

Rinman's green
USE **cobalt green**

rinsing
USE **washing**

Rio Bec
FL.1041
CN F.FL.ALO.ALO.ALO.ALO.AFU.ALO.ARI.ALO.AFU.ARI

riparian rights
BM.478 (L)
SN The right of one owning waterfront land to have access to and use of the shore and water. (W)
UF rights, riparian
CN B.BM.BCW.DOI.AFU

rippers
TB.45
ALT **ripper**
SN Tractor-drawn devices with protruding teeth; used to penetrate and disrupt the earth's surface up to 3 feet in depth.
CN V.TB.AFU.ARI.AFU.ARI.BIQ

ripping bars
USE **pinch bars**

ripping chisels
TB.864 (N)
ALT **ripping chisel**
SN Bent chisels used to clear out mortises or seams. (DAC)
UF chisels, ripping
CN V.TB.AFU.BCW.CFS.ALO.AFU.BUE.BIQ

ripple-burnished ware
FL.2843
UF ware, ripple-burnished
CN F.FL.ALO.AXC.ALO.ARI.ALO.AFU.BIQ

riprap
RK.563
SN Use for layers, facings, or protective embankments comprised of large irregular and randomly placed stones to prevent erosion, scour or sloughing; also the stone so used.
CN V.RK.AFU.ALO.ALO.CFS.ALO.ALO.BIQ

ripsaws
TB.1028 (N)
ALT **ripsaw**
SN Long, typically coarse-toothed hand saws, whose teeth are cut at a 60 degree angle, and have a chisel-like ripping action; used for cutting wood in the direction of the grain.
UF saws, rip
CN V.TB.AFU.BCW.CFS.ALO.AFU.EWY.BUE.BIQ

risen moldings
USE **bolection moldings**

risers
RT.1122 (B)
ALT **riser**
SN The vertical faces of steps.
CN V.RT.AFU.BIQ.AXC.ALO.BIQ.ALO.ALO

risers (piping)
RT.1472 (L)
ALT **riser (piping)**
CN V.RT.ALO.BCW.ALO.ARI.BZY.BCW

rising arches
USE **rampant arches**

rising butt hinges

USE **rising hinges**

rising hinges
TF.103
ALT **rising hinge**
SN Door hinges fabricated with a slope on the knuckle which causes the door to rise when opened. Rising hinges are used when there are obstructions along the door's bottom edge, such as carpeting. (MEANS)
UF butt hinges, rising
door hinges, gravity
gravity door hinges
hinges, gravity door
hinges, rising
hinges, rising butt
rising butt hinges
CN V.TF.AFU.AFU.AFU.AFU.CLM.AFU.ARI.AXC

rising stretchers
USE **saltire stretchers**

rising suns
DG.44
ALT **rising sun**
SN Motifs of a semicircle with projecting fanlike rays.
UF motifs, sunrise
sunrise motifs
suns, rising
CN D.DG.AFU.AFU.CXA.ARI

rising-top writing tables
TG.580
ALT **rising-top writing table**
UF tables, rising-top writing
writing tables, rising-top
CN V.TG.AFU.AFU.AXC.ALO.BZY.FUA.CFS

risk, environmental
USE **environmental impact**

rituals
KM.146 (L,R)
SN Procedures performed in a set, precise manner, often regularly repeated. (W)
CN K.KM.AFU.EFQ

river beds
RD.161
ALT **river bed**
UF beds, river
CN V.RD.ARI.AFU.AFU.ALO.AXC

river birch
MT.1121
UF Betula nigra
birch, black
birch, river
black birch
CN M.MT.AFU.AFU.ALO.BIQ.DCU.AFU.AFU.AFU.BIQ.BOK

river charts
VW.217
ALT **river chart**
UF charts, river
CN V.VW.AFU.AFU.AFU.FZU.AXC.AFU.ARI.AXC.DIO.ALO.ALO.ARI

river maple
USE **silver maple**

river marble
MT.691
UF marble, river
CN M.MT.AFU.AFU.AFU.DCU.AFU.ALO.AFU.ALO.ALO.ALO.ALO

river rapids
USE **rapids**

river towns
RD.69
ALT **river town**
UF towns, river
CN V.RD.AFU.BCW.BCW.ARI

riverbanks
RD.162 (B)
ALT **riverbank**
SN The land margins of rivers.
UF banks (riverbanks)
CN V.RD.ARI.AFU.AFU.ALO.BCW

riverfronts
RK.1595 (A,L,B)
ALT **riverfront**
CN V.RK.ALO.ARI.CLM.AFU.ALO

rivers
RD.138 (L,B,R)
ALT **river**
CN V.RD.ARI.AFU.AFU.AFU.AFU.ARI.AFU

rivers, lath
USE **froes**

Riverton
FL.823
CN F.FL.ALO.ALO.ALO.AFU.ALO.ALO.AFU.CFS

rivet punches
USE **starting punches**

rivet sets
TB.677
ALT **rivet set**
SN Tools used to shape the head of a rivet. (DAC)
UF punches, setting
sets, rivet
setting punches
CN V.TB.AFU.BCW.BIQ.AFU.ALO.CFS

riveters
HG.606
ALT **riveter**
CN H.HG.AFU.AXC.BZY.AFU.ELK

riveting
KT.53 (L)
ALT **riveted**
SN Forming a permanent connection between two or more pieces of material by passing a rivet through aligned holes. (STEIN)
CN K.KT.AFU.ALO.BCW.BCW.AXC

rivets
TF.465 (N)
ALT **rivet**
SN Small cylindrical pieces of soft metal, used to fasten two metal plates or a metal plate and a piece of wood together. (PUTNAM)
CN V.TF.AFU.AFU.AFU.ALO.AFU.DCU

rivulets
USE **brooks**

rivurets
USE **brooks**

roachstone
USE **travertine**

road bridges
RK.1292
ALT **road bridge**
UF bridges, road
CN V.RK.AFU.ALO.ALO.GLI.ALO.AFU.ALO.ARI.ALO

road engineering
USE **highway engineering**

road engineers
USE **transportation engineers**

road junctions
USE **intersections**

road maps
VW.220 (L)
ALT **road map**
UF highway maps
maps, highway
maps, road
CN V.VW.AFU.AFU.AFU.FZU.AXC.AFU.ARI.AXC.DIO.BCW

roadbeds
RM.506
ALT **roadbed**
SN The beds or foundations of railroads on which the ties, rails, and ballast rest; also the earth foundations of highways, streets, or roads. (W)
CN V.RM.ALO.ALO.ALO.ARI.ALO

roadhouses
RK.123 (B)
ALT **roadhouse**
CN V.RK.AFU.ALO.ALO.ALO.AFU.BCW

roads
RK.1513 (A,L,B,R)
ALT **road**
CN V.RK.ALO.ALO.BIQ.ARI

roads, access
USE **access roads**

roads, approach
USE **access roads**

roads, arterial
USE **arterial streets**
arterials

roads, bridle
USE **bridle paths**

roads, bypass
USE **bypasses**

roads, elevated
USE **elevated roads**

roads, express
USE **expressways**

roads, frontage
USE **service roads**

roads, highway access
USE **access roads**

roads, limited access
USE **limited access highways**

roads, local
USE **secondary roads**

roads, macadamized
USE **macadamized roads**

roads, main
USE **primary roads**

roads, military
USE **military roads**

roads, minor
USE **secondary roads**

roads, multi-level
USE **multi-level roads**

roads, one-way
USE **one-way streets**

roads, pedestrian
USE **pedestrian streets**

roads, post
USE **post roads**

roads, primary
USE **primary roads**

roads, private
USE **private roads**

roads, ring
USE **beltways**

roads, secondary
USE **secondary roads**

roads, service
USE **service roads**

roads, subsidiary
USE **secondary roads**

roads, sunken
USE **sunken roads**

roads, toll
USE **turnpikes**

roadside crosses
USE **wayside crosses**

roadside improvement
BM.1067 (A,L)
UF beautification, highway
highway beautification
improvement, roadside
planting, roadside
roadside planting
CN B.BM.CLM.ALO.AFU.ALO

roadside planting
USE **roadside improvement**

roadside rest areas
RM.490 (A,L)
ALT **roadside rest area**
SN Turn-outs along roadways used as public rest stops; often having shade trees or shelters, toilets, picnic tables, and trash cans. (DLA)
UF rest areas
rest areas, roadside
safety rests
CN V.RM.ALO.ALO.ALO.ALO.CLM

roadsides
RM.491 (A,L)
ALT **roadside**
SN Strips of land adjoining roads and adjacent to the shoulder, when both are present. (W)
CN V.RM.ALO.ALO.ALO.ALO.CRG

roadways
RM.492 (B)
ALT **roadway**
UF carriageways
CN V.RM.ALO.ALO.ALO.ALO.CXA

Robinia
USE **locust**

Robinia pseudoacacia
USE **black locust**

Robinson Crusoe playgrounds
USE **adventure playgrounds**

Robles
FL.1045
CN F.FL.ALO.ALO.ALO.ALO.AFU.ALO .ARI.ALO.ALO.ALO.AFU

Rocaille
FL.3186 (R)
CN F.FL.ALO.BCW.ALO.ARI.BIQ.BCW. ARI

rock
MT.892 (L,B,R)
CN M.MT.AFU.AFU.AFU.DCU.ALO.CFS

rock asphalt
MT.978 (L)
SN A sandstone or limestone naturally impregnated with asphalt. (MH)
UF asphalt, rock
bituminous rock
rock, bituminous
CN M.MT.AFU.AFU.ALO.ALO.AFU.AFU .ALO.AXC

rock churches
USE **cave churches**
rock-cut churches

rock crystal
USE **quartz crystal**

rock-cut architecture
RK.1367 (A,R)
SN Use for structures excavated into living rock; distinguished from **cave architecture,** which denotes the use of existing rock cavities.
UF architecture, rock-cut
CN V.RK.AFU.ALO.ARI.AXC.BOK

rock-cut churches
RK.1098 (A,L,B)
ALT **rock-cut church**
SN Use for churches whose spaces are cut into the living rock; distinguished from **cave churches,** which utilize natural cavities in the earth's surface.
UF churches, rock-cut
rock churches
CN V.RK.AFU.ALO.ALO.FCS.BIQ.ALO. AFU.ARI

rock-cut temples
RK.1129 (A)
ALT **rock-cut temple**
UF temples, rock-cut
CN V.RK.AFU.ALO.ALO.FCS.BIQ.BZY. AFU.ALO

rock-cut tombs
RK.492 (A,L)
ALT **rock-cut tomb**
UF rock-hewn tombs
rock-tombs
tombs, rock-cut
CN V.RK.AFU.ALO.ALO.BOK.BUE.AFU. BOK

rock dash
USE **pebble dash**

rock-drills
TB.588 (L)
ALT **rock-drill**
SN High-powered pnuematic or electrically driven devices or machines used for boring holes into rock. (MEANS)
UF drills, rock
CN V.TB.AFU.BCW.BCW.ALO.CLM .AXC

rock elm
MT.1148
UF elm, hickory
elm, rock
hickory elm
CN M.MT.AFU.AFU.ALO.BIQ.DCU.AFU .AFU.AFU.DCU.AXC

rock-faced brick
USE **ashlar brick**

rock-fill dams
RK.538 (L)
ALT **rock-fill dam**

SN Use for dams built mainly of rocks of various sizes with a waterproof case or covering.
UF dams, rock-fill
rockfill dams
CN V.RK.AFU.ALO.ALO.CFS.AFU.ARI.ARI.ALO

rock gardens
RK.1413 (A,L,B)
ALT **rock garden**
UF gardens, rock
rockeries
CN V.RK.ALO.AFU.AFU.AFU.BUE

rock-hewn tombs
USE **rock-cut tombs**

rock lath
USE **gypsum board**

rock maple
USE **sugar maple**

rock men
USE **quarriers**

rock shelters
RK.1184 (A,L)
ALT **rock shelter**
UF shelters, rock
CN V.RK.AFU.ALO.ALO.FOG.ARI

rock-tombs
USE **rock-cut tombs**

rock, acid igneous
USE **acid igneous rock**

rock, arenaceous
USE **sandstone**

rock, argillaceous
USE **argillaceous rock**

rock, basic
USE **basic igneous rock**

rock, basic igneous
USE **basic igneous rock**

rock, bituminous
USE **rock asphalt**

rock, calcareous
USE **carbonate rock**

rock, calico
USE **Potomac breccia**

rock, carbonate
USE **carbonate rock**

rock, coquina
USE **coquina rock**

rock, coral
USE **coral limestone**

rock, crushed
USE **crushed stone**

rock, extrusive
USE **volcanic rock**

rock, igneous
USE **igneous rock**

rock, intermediate igneous
USE **intermediate igneous rock**

rock, intrusive
USE **plutonic rock**

rock, metamorphic
USE **metamorphic rock**

rock, plutonic
USE **plutonic rock**

rock, pyroclastic
USE **pyroclastic rock**

rock, rudaceous
USE **rudaceous rock**

rock, sedimentary
USE **sedimentary rock**

rock, volcanic
USE **volcanic rock**

rocker stamping
KT.160
ALT **rocker stamped**
UF stamping, rocker
CN K.KT.AFU.ALO.DOI.DUC.ALO

rockeries
USE **rock gardens**

rockers (bends)
USE **bends**

rockers (chairs)
USE **rocking chairs**

rockers, Boston
USE **Boston rockers**

rockers, Lincoln
USE **Lincoln rockers**

rockers, mammy's
USE **cradle benches**

rockers, platform
USE **platform rockers**

rockfill dams
USE **rock-fill dams**

rocking benches
USE **cradle benches**

rocking chairs
TG.225 (L,N,R)
ALT **rocking chair**
UF chairs, rocking
rockers (chairs)
CN V.TG.AFU.AFU.ALO.AFU.AFU.AXC.ARI

rocking chairs, Boston
USE **Boston rockers**

rocking chairs, Grecian
USE **Lincoln rockers**

rocking chairs, Lincoln
USE **Lincoln rockers**

rocking chairs, platform
USE **platform rockers**

rocking chairs, swing
USE **platform rockers**

rocking chairs, Windsor
USE **Windsor rocking chairs**

rocking settees
USE **cradle benches**

Rockingham royal black marble
MT.778
UF black marble, Rockingham royal
marble, Rockingham royal black
CN M.MT.AFU.AFU.AFU.DCU.AFU.ARI.ARI.ARI.AFU.BIQ

Rococo
FL.3176 (A,L,B,R)
CN F.FL.ALO.BCW.ALO.ARI.BCW

Rococo Revival
FL.3274 (A,R)
UF French, Old
Neo-Rococo
Old French
Revival, Rococo
CN F.FL.ALO.BCW.ALO.AXC.CLM.CFS

rod anchors
TF.298
ALT **rod anchor**
UF anchors, rod
CN V.TF.AFU.AFU.AFU.ALO.AFU.AFU.CFS

rod-back Windsor chairs
USE **square-back Windsor chairs**

rodded joints
USE **concave joints**

rodeos
KM.44 (L,R)
CN K.KM.AFU.AXC.ARI

rods
MT.2265
CN M.MT.AFU.ALO.FOG

rods, lightning
USE **lightning rods**

rods, mixing
USE **stirring rods**

rods, prying
USE **flagging irons**

rods, radius
USE **radius tools**

rods, reinforcing
USE **reinforcing bars**

rods, stirring
USE **stirring rods**

rods, tension
USE **tie rods**

USE **tie rods**

rods, tie
USE **tie rods**

roestone
USE **oolitic limestone**

role, sex
USE **sex role**

roll-and-fillet moldings
RT.793
ALT **roll-and-fillet molding**
SN Moldings of nearly circular cross section with narrow bands or fillets on the face. (DAC)
UF moldings, roll-and-fillet
CN V.RT.AFU.ALO.AFU.BOK.AFU.AFU.AXC.BZY.AFU

roll billet moldings
RT.762
ALT **roll billet molding**
SN Common Norman moldings consisting of a series of billets which are cylindrical in cross section, usually staggered in alternate rows. (HAS)
UF billet moldings, roll
billet moldings, round
moldings, roll billet
moldings, round billet
round billet moldings
CN V.RT.AFU.ALO.AFU.BOK.AFU.AFU.ARI.ARI.AFU

roll cabinets, pianola
USE **pianola roll cabinets**

roll fill dams
USE **rolled-fill dams**

roll film
MT.2243
UF film, roll
CN M.MT.AFU.ALO.CXA.ALO.BZY

roll insulation
MT.2408
UF insulation, roll
CN M.MT.AFU.ARI.BZY.BCW.ARI.AFU.ALO

roll moldings
RT.792
ALT **roll molding**
SN Any convex, rounded molding which has a partly cylindrical form; commonly used to refer to Gothic or Romanesque rather than classical forms.
UF annular moldings
boltels
boultines
bowtells
edge rolls
moldings, annular
moldings, roll
moldings, round
rolls, edge
round moldings
CN V.RT.AFU.ALO.AFU.BOK.AFU.AFU.AXC.BZY

roll-over arms
USE **rolled arms**

roll-paper, stripping
USE **stripping film**

roll-top Windsor chairs
TG.110
ALT **roll-top Windsor chair**
SN Square-back Windsor chairs with a turned cross piece framed at the top of the back posts and accompanied by one or two horizontal cross slats at mid-back and sometimes with short spindles between the seat and lower slat. (EVANS)
UF chairs, roll-top Windsor
Windsor chairs, roll-top
CN V.TG.AFU.AFU.ALO.AFU.AFU.AFU.MLC.CFS.AXC

roll-up doors
RT.871 (B)
ALT **roll-up door**
SN Manual or automatic doors made up of small horizontal interlocking metal slats which are guided in a track.
UF doors, roll-up
doors, rolling
rolling doors
CN V.RT.AFU.ARI.AFU.AFU.AFU.ALO.ARI.AFU.ARI.BIQ

rolled arms
TG.814
ALT **rolled arm**
UF arms, roll-over
arms, rolled
roll-over arms
CN V.TG.ALO.ALO.AFU.AFU.AXC

rolled-fill dams
RK.536
ALT **rolled-fill dam**
UF dams, rolled-fill
roll fill dams
CN V.RK.AFU.ALO.ALO.CFS.AFU.ARI.ARI.AFU.AFU

rolled glass
MT.264
SN A flat glass of considerable thickness made by passing a roller over molten glass. (W)
UF cast plate glass
glass, cast plate
glass, rolled
CN M.MT.AFU.AFU.AFU.BIQ.AFU.ARI.CFS

rolled patterned glass
USE **figured glass**

roller catches
USE **roller latches**

roller coasters
RK.1006 (A,L,R)
ALT **roller coaster**
UF coasters, roller
CN V.RK.AFU.ALO.ALO.EWY.AFU.AFU.ARI

roller conveyors
TB.368
ALT **roller conveyor**
SN Conveyors consisting of fixed-location rollers over which materials are moved by gravity or propulsion. (W)
UF conveyors, roller
CN V.TB.AFU.ARI.DCU.AFU.AFU.ARI

roller joints
TF.600
ALT **roller joint**
SN Joints which allow rotations to occur freely except in the direction perpendicular to the support. (DS)
UF joints, roller
CN V.TF.ALO.AFU.FCS

roller latches
TF.178
ALT **roller latch**
UF catches, roller
latches, roller
roller catches
CN V.TF.AFU.AFU.AFU.AFU.DIO.BCW.AFU.BCW

roller painting
KT.250 (L)
ALT **roller painted**
UF painting, roller
CN K.KT.AFU.ALO.DUC.CXA.ALO.AXC.ALO

roller pin nails, shade
USE **shade roller pin nails**

roller rinks
USE **roller-skating rinks**

roller-skating rinks
RK.1053 (L,B)
ALT **roller-skating rink**
UF rinks, roller-skating
roller rinks
CN V.RK.AFU.ALO.ALO.EWY.AXC.BIQ.AFU.AXC.ALO

rollers (compacting equipment)
TB.28 (N)
ALT **roller (compacting equipment)**
SN Heavy, self-propelled or towed devices used to compact granular fill. (MEANS)
CN V.TB.AFU.ARI.AFU.ALO.ALO

rollers, barn-door
USE **barn-door rollers**

rollers, paint
USE **paint rollers**

rollers, tamping
USE **sheepsfoot rollers**

rollers, tandem

USE **tandem rollers**

rolling doors
USE **roll-up doors**

rolling mills
RK.647 (L,N,B)
ALT **rolling mill**
UF mills, rolling
mills, steel rolling
steel rolling mills
CN V.RK.AFU.ALO.ALO.CLM.ALO.ALO.AFU.AXC.BUE.AXC.AFU

rolling-up
KT.695
CN K.KT.AFU.ALO.GRC.BUE.ALO

rollock arches
USE **rowlock arches**

rolls
VW.270
ALT **roll**
SN Documents consisting of one or more membranes of parchment or sheets of paper in which the membranes or sheets are sewn together end to end and rolled. (ICA)
CN V.VW.AFU.AFU.AFU.FZU.BCW.AFU.BOK.AFU

rolls (rosters)
USE **rosters**

rolls, charter
USE **charter rolls**

rolls, court
USE **judicial records**

rolls, curb
USE **knuckle joints**

rolls, edge
USE **roll moldings**

rolls, electors'
USE **voters' lists**

rolls, hip
USE **hip rolls**

rolls, liberate
USE **liberate rolls**

rolls, membership
USE **membership lists**

rolls, microfilm
USE **microfilms**

rolls, muster
USE **muster rolls**

rolls, ridge
USE **hip rolls**

rolltop desks
TG.549 (N)
ALT **rolltop desk**
SN Use for desks that close by means of a flexible shutter of convex shape and composed of horizontal slats of wood. Distinguished from **tambour desks** which close by means of upright reeded or slatted shutters.
UF desks, rolltop
CN V.TG.AFU.AFU.AXC.ALO.BZY.DIO

rollwork
USE **strapwork**

Roman
FL.2711 (A,L,B,R)
CN F.FL.ALO.AXC.ALO.ALO.AFU.AXC

Roman arches
USE **semicircular arches**

Roman brick
MT.82
SN Brick whose nominal dimensions are 2 2/3 x 4 x 12 inches. (MEANS)
UF brick, Roman
CN M.MT.AFU.AFU.AFU.AXC.ALO.AFU.AFU.AFU.CRG

Roman Catholicism
USE **Catholicism**

Roman cement
USE **natural cement**
pozzolan cement

Roman Empire
USE **Imperial**

Roman ink
USE **atramentum**

Roman linen
MT.1854
UF linen, Roman
CN M.MT.AFU.AFU.ARI.ALO.ALO.ALO.AFU.AXC.AFU

Roman ocher
USE **golden ocher**

Roman pewter
MT.418
SN Ancient pewter containing 70% tin and 30% lead, with other elements such as iron present as impurities. (MH)
UF pewter, Roman
CN M.MT.AFU.AFU.AFU.BZY.AFU.AFU.AFU.ALO.BUE.ALO.BOK

Roman sepia
MT.2505
UF sepia, Roman
CN M.MT.AFU.ARI.CRG.ALO.ALO.BZY.AFU

Roman tile
MT.176 (R)
UF tile, Roman
CN M.MT.AFU.AFU.AFU.AXC.ALO.ALO.ALO.AFU.ALO.AXC.AFU.AFU.ARI

Roman white
USE **white lead**

Roman, Late
USE **Late Antique**

Romanellian
FL.2482
CN F.FL.ALO.AXC.AFU.AXC.BUE

Romanesque
FL.3092 (A,L,B,R)
CN F.FL.ALO.BCW.ALO.ALO.AFU.ALO

Romanesque Revival
FL.3275 (A,L,R)
UF Neo-Romanesque
Revival, Romanesque
CN F.FL.ALO.BCW.ALO.AXC.CLM.CLM

Romanesque, First
USE **First Romanesque**

Romanesque, Richardsonian
USE **Richardsonian Romanesque**

Romanian
FL.3055 (L)
CN F.FL.ALO.BCW.AFU.DIO

Romanist
FL.3180
ALT **Romanism**
UF Italianate (Romanist)
Italianizing
CN F.FL.ALO.BCW.ALO.ARI.BIQ.ARI

Romano-British
FL.2735
CN F.FL.ALO.AXC.ALO.ALO.ALO.BCW.ALO

Romantic
FL.3260 (R)
ALT **Romanticism**
UF Romantic movement
Romanticist
CN F.FL.ALO.BCW.ALO.AXC.BZY

Romantic movement
USE **Romantic**

romanticism (form of expression)
BM.182 (L)
ALT **romantic (form of expression)**
SN Use for the approach to visual art, literature, theater, and music that emphasizes the emotional, dramatic, or exotic.
CN B.BM.AFU.AFU.AXC.BZY

Romanticist
USE **Romantic**

rondavels
RK.239 (A,B)
ALT **rondavel**
SN Use for the native round huts of southern Africa, usually built of mud and thatch. (W)
CN V.RK.AFU.ALO.ALO.AXC.ALO.AFU.BOK.ARI

ronde bosse, en
USE **en ronde bosse**

rood lofts
RT.1247 (L)

ALT rood loft
UF holy lofts
lofts, holy
lofts, rood
CN V.RT.AFU.BUE.ALO.ARI.CRG

rood screens
RT.1252 (A,R)
ALT **rood screen**
SN Screens erected in churches between the nave and the choir or chancel supporting the rood (cross) in the center. (RS)
UF screens, rood
CN V.RT.AFU.BUE.ALO.ARI.CXA.ALO.ALO

rood spires
USE **crossing towers**

rood steeples
USE **crossing towers**

rood towers
USE **crossing towers**

roof dormers
USE **dormers**

roof galleries
USE **widow's walks**

roof gardens
RK.1430 (A,B)
ALT **roof garden**
UF gardens, roof
CN V.RK.ALO.AFU.AFU.ARI.ARI

roof guards
USE **snow guards**

roof lights
USE **skylights**

roof parking garages
RK.1227 (B)
ALT **roof parking garage**
UF garages, roof parking
parking garages, roof
CN V.RK.AFU.ALO.ALO.GFO.BUE.ALO.AFU.AFU

roof plates
RT.704
ALT **roof plate**
SN Wall plates which receive the lower ends of the rafters of a roof. (DAC)
UF plates, rafter
plates, roof
plates, top
rafter plates
top plates
CN V.RT.AFU.AFU.ALO.ALO.ARI.ALO.AFU

roof principals
USE **roof trusses**

roof purlins
USE **purlins**

roof systems, one-way floor and
USE **one-way structural systems**

roof systems, two-way floor and
USE **two-way structural systems**

roof ties
USE **tie beams**

roof tile
USE **roofing tile**

roof trees
USE **ridgeboards**

roof trusses
RT.381 (A,L,B)
ALT **roof truss**
UF principals, roof
roof principals
trusses, roof
CN V.RT.AFU.AFU.AFU.BCW.CLM.AFU.ALO.ALO

roof valleys
USE **valleys (roof components)**

roof, lean-to
USE **shed roofs**

roofed ingles
USE **inglenooks**

roofers
HG.607
ALT **roofer**
CN H.HG.AFU.AXC.BZY.AFU.ERE

roofing
MT.2393 (A,L)
SN Any material used as a roof covering (such as shingles, slate, sheet metal, or tile) to make it wind- and waterproof, and often to provide thermal insulation. (DAC)
CN M.MT.AFU.ARI.BZY.AXC.ALO

roofing granules
MT.903
SN Graded particles of crushed rock, slate, slag, porcelain, or tile used as surfacing in asphalt roofing and shingles. (MH)
UF granules, roofing
CN M.MT.AFU.AFU.AFU.DCU.ARI.AFU.ALO

roofing hammers
USE **clench hammers**

roofing nails
TF.444
ALT **roofing nail**
SN Special purpose short threaded nails each having a large head and usually galvanized or aluminum with a neoprene or plastic washer to aid in fastening roof coverings. (MEANS)
UF nails, roofing
CN V.TF.AFU.AFU.AFU.ALO.AFU.CFS.ALO.DIO

roofing nails, nonleaking
USE **lead-capped nails**

roofing sand
MT.2072
SN A fine white silica sand. (MH)
UF sand, roofing
CN M.MT.AFU.AFU.ARI.BOK.ALO.BOKn.AFU.ARI

roofing slate
MT.872 (A,B)
UF slate, roofing
CN M.MT.AFU.AFU.AFU.DCU.AFU.ARI.BUE.ALO.ALO

roofing tile
MT.172 (L,B)
SN A tile for roofing usually of burnt clay, concrete, or asbestos cement; available in many configurations and types such as plain tiles, single-lap tiles, and interlocking tiles. (DAC)
UF roof tile
tile, roof
tile, roofing
CN M.MT.AFU.AFU.AFU.AXC.ALO.ALO.ALO.AFU.ALO.AXC.AFU

roofing tile, pan-and-roll
USE **pan-and-roll roofing tile**

roofing, built-up
USE **built-up roofing**

roofing, composition
USE **built-up roofing**

roofs
RT.409 (A,L,B,R)
ALT **roof**
UF rooves
CN V.RT.AFU.AFU.AFU.BIQ.ARI.AFU

roofs, arched barrel
USE **barrel roofs**

roofs, barrel shell
USE **barrel roofs**

roofs, butterfly
USE **butterfly roofs**

roofs, butterfly-shell
USE **butterfly roofs**

roofs, clipped gable
USE **jerkinhead roofs**

roofs, collar
USE **collar beam roofs**

roofs, collar beam
USE **collar beam roofs**

roofs, compass
USE **compass roofs**

roofs, compass-headed
USE **compass roofs**

roofs, cottage
USE **single-framed roofs**

roofs, couple
USE **couple roofs**

roofs, cradle
USE **barrel roofs**
compass roofs

roofs, curb
USE **curb roofs**

roofs, double
USE **double-framed roofs**

roofs, double-framed
USE **double-framed roofs**

roofs, double-gable
USE **double-gable roofs**

roofs, double hip
USE **mansard roofs**

roofs, double pitch
USE **gable roofs**

roofs, dual-pitched
USE **curb roofs**

roofs, false thatched
USE **false thatched roofs**

roofs, flat
USE **flat roofs**

roofs, French
USE **French roofs**

roofs, gable
USE **gable roofs**

roofs, gable-on-hip
USE **gable-on-hip roofs**

roofs, gambrel
USE **gambrel roofs**

roofs, half-span
USE **shed roofs**

roofs, hammer-beam
USE **hammer-beam roofs**

roofs, hanging
USE **suspension roofs**

roofs, helm
USE **helm roofs**

roofs, hip
USE **hip roofs**

roofs, hipped gable
USE **jerkinhead roofs**

roofs, jerkinhead
USE **jerkinhead roofs**

roofs, king-post
USE **king-post roofs**

roofs, lamella
USE **lamella structures**

roofs, mansard
USE **mansard roofs**

roofs, northlight
USE **sawtooth roofs**

roofs, ogee
USE **ogee roofs**

roofs, open
USE **open-timbered roofs**

roofs, open-timbered
USE **open-timbered roofs**

roofs, parallel gable
USE **double-gable roofs**

roofs, pavilion
USE **pyramidal roofs**

roofs, pent (skirt roofs)
USE **skirt roofs**

roofs, penthouse (shed roofs)
USE **shed roofs**

roofs, penthouse (skirt roofs)
USE **skirt roofs**

roofs, pitched
USE **pitched roofs**

roofs, platform
USE **platform roofs**

roofs, principal rafter
USE **double-framed roofs**

roofs, pyramidal
USE **pyramidal roofs**

roofs, pyramidal hipped
USE **pyramidal roofs**

roofs, queen-post
USE **queen-post roofs**

roofs, rainbow
USE **rainbow roofs**

roofs, saddle
USE **saddleback roofs**

roofs, saddleback
USE **saddleback roofs**

roofs, sawtooth
USE **sawtooth roofs**

roofs, shed
USE **shed roofs**

roofs, shell
USE **shell structures**

roofs, shreadhead
USE **jerkinhead roofs**

roofs, single
USE **single-framed roofs**

roofs, single-framed
USE **single-framed roofs**

roofs, skirt
USE **skirt roofs**

roofs, suspended
USE **suspension roofs**

roofs, suspension
USE **suspension roofs**

roofs, terrace
USE **terrace roofs**

roofs, trough
USE **double-gable roofs**

roofs, trussed rafter
USE **barrel roofs**

roofs, whaleback
USE **rainbow roofs**

rooftops
RM.54
ALT **rooftop**
CN V.RM.AFU.DIO.AFU.BCW.BIQ

room-by-room inventories
VW.1019
ALT **room-by-room inventory**
UF inventories, room-by-room
CN V.VW.AFU.ARI.ALO.BCW.AFU.ALO.ALO.AFU.AFU.AFU.AFU.AFU

room dividers
RT.517
ALT **room divider**
SN Use for entities that serve to divide interior spaces, often incorporating bookshelves, cabinets, or drawers. For interior, sometimes permanent, walls that separate one portion of a building from another, use **partitions.**
UF dividers (interior walls)
dividers, room
dividers, space
space dividers
CN V.RT.AFU.AFU.AFU.BIQ.AXC

room-door locks
TF.242
ALT **room-door lock**
UF inside-door locks
locks, inside-door
locks, room-door
CN V.TF.AFU.AFU.AFU.AFU.DIO.BIQ.ALO.ALO.BZY

rooming houses
USE **lodging houses**

rooms
RM.279 (A,L,B,R)
ALT **room**
UF chambers (rooms)
CN V.RM.AFU.DIO.ARI.ALO.CXA

rooms, anechoic
USE **anechoic rooms**

rooms, archives
USE **archives rooms**

rooms, assembly
USE **assembly rooms**

rooms, baggage

USE **baggage rooms**

rooms, banking
USE **banking rooms**

rooms, banquet
USE **banquet halls**

rooms, billiard
USE **billiard rooms**

rooms, boiler
USE **boiler rooms**

rooms, breakfast
USE **breakfast rooms**

rooms, changing
USE **dressing rooms**

rooms, clean
rooms, clean
USE **clean rooms**

rooms, cold storage
USE **cold storage rooms**

rooms, committee
USE **conference rooms**

rooms, common
USE **common rooms**

rooms, computer
USE **computer rooms**

rooms, conference
USE **conference rooms**

rooms, control
USE **control rooms**

rooms, dining
USE **dining rooms**

rooms, drawing
USE **drawing rooms**

rooms, dressing
USE **dressing rooms**

rooms, emergency
USE **emergency rooms**

rooms, family
USE **family rooms**

rooms, feed
USE **feed rooms**

rooms, Florida
USE **solariums**

rooms, game
USE **game rooms**

rooms, gaming
USE **gaming rooms**

rooms, green
USE **green rooms**

rooms, gun
USE **gun rooms**

rooms, harness
USE **tack rooms**

rooms, hobby
USE **recreation rooms**

rooms, keeping
USE **keeping rooms**

rooms, laundry
USE **laundry rooms**

rooms, living
USE **living rooms**

rooms, locker
USE **locker rooms**

rooms, lumber
USE **storerooms**

rooms, meeting
USE **conference rooms**

rooms, morning
USE **morning rooms**

rooms, mud
USE **mud rooms**

rooms, music
USE **music rooms**

rooms, operating
USE **operating rooms**

rooms, period
USE **period rooms**

rooms, powder
USE **lavatories (rooms)**

rooms, presence
USE **presence chambers**

rooms, pump
USE **pump rooms**

rooms, reading
USE **reading rooms**

rooms, rec
USE **recreation rooms**

rooms, reception
USE **reception rooms**

rooms, recovery
USE **recovery rooms**

rooms, recreation
USE **recreation rooms**

rooms, rest
USE **rest rooms**

rooms, rumpus
USE **playrooms**
recreation rooms

rooms, sample
USE **sample rooms**

rooms, screening
USE **screening rooms**

rooms, sewing
USE **sewing rooms**

rooms, sitting
USE **sitting rooms**

rooms, smoking
USE **smoking rooms**

rooms, steam
USE **steam rooms**

rooms, strong
USE **vaults (strong rooms)**

rooms, sun
USE **solariums**

rooms, supper
USE **supper rooms**

rooms, tack
USE **tack rooms**

rooms, tea
USE **tea rooms**

rooms, throne
USE **throne rooms**

rooms, tool
USE **toolsheds**

rooms, utility
USE **utility rooms**

rooms, waiting
USE **waiting rooms**

rooms, wash
USE **lavatories (rooms)**

rooms, writing
USE **writing rooms**

root
MT.1064
CN M.MT.AFU.AFU.ALO.BIQ.BZY

root cellars
RM.189 (L,N)
ALT root cellar
SN Cellars, partially or wholly underground and usually covered with dirt, where root crops and other crops are stored. (RHDEL2)
UF cellars, root
CN V.RM.AFU.DIO.ALO.DCU.ARI.ALO

root madder
USE **madder**

roots (mathematics)
BM.816 (L)
SN Quantities that when taken as factors the number of times indicated produce other quantities. (W)
CN B.BM.CFS.ARI.BZY

rooves
USE **roofs**

rope
MT.1974 (L,N)
CN M.MT.AFU.AFU.ARI.ALO.ALO.BIQ.

ALO

rope-knot gardens
USE knot gardens

rope ladders
TB.483 (N)
ALT **rope ladder**
SN Ladders with sidepieces of rope and rungs of rope, wood, or metal. (W)
UF flipper-floppers
Jacob's ladders
ladders, Jacob's
ladders, rope
ladders, sea
sea ladders
CN V.TB.AFU.ARI.ERE.ALO.BCW

rope-makers
HG.571 (L)
ALT **rope-maker**
CN H.HG.AFU.AXC.BUE.AXC.DIO

rope moldings
USE **cable moldings**

rope works
USE **roperies**

rope, wire
USE **cable**

roperies
RK.656 (A,B)
ALT **ropery**
UF rope works
CN V.RK.AFU.ALO.ALO.CLM.ALO.ALO.AFU.AXC.DIO

ropework
MT.2780 (L)
CN M.MT.AFU.AXC.CRG

rose
USE **dark pink**
dark purplish pink
dark yellowish pink
deep purplish pink
deep yellowish pink
grayish purplish red
grayish red
grayish yellowish pink
light pink
light purplish pink
light yellowish pink
moderate pink
moderate purplish red
moderate red
moderate reddish orange
moderate yellowish pink
pale purple
pale yellowish pink
strong purplish red
strong red
strong yellowish pink
vivid pink
vivid purplish red
vivid yellowish pink

Rose + Croix
USE **Rosicrucian**

rose beige, light
USE **brownish pink**
grayish yellowish pink

rose brown
USE **dark grayish red**
deep purplish red
deep red
grayish red
grayish reddish brown
very deep purplish red
very deep red
vivid red

rose brown, dark
USE **dark grayish red**
dark reddish gray

rose brown, light
USE **dark grayish red**
grayish red

rose carmine
USE **moderate purplish red**
strong purplish red
vivid purplish red

rose carthame
USE **safflower (red pigment)**

rose chestnut, Indian
USE **gangaw**

rose clench nails
TF.414
ALT **rose clench nail**
UF clench nails, rose
nails, rose clench
CN V.TF.AFU.AFU.AFU.ALO.AFU.CFS.AFU.DCU.CLM.AFU

Rose et Croix
USE **Rosicrucian**

rose flat nails
TF.415
ALT **rose flat nail**
UF flat nails, rose
nails, rose flat
CN V.TF.AFU.AFU.AFU.ALO.AFU.CFS.AFU.DCU.CLM.ALO

rose gold
MT.395
UF gold, rose
CN M.MT.AFU.AFU.AFU.BZY.AFU.AFU.AFU.ALO.AXC.AFU.ARI

rose gray
USE **brownish gray**
grayish red

rose lake
USE **dark purplish red**
grayish purplish red
moderate pink

rose lilac
USE **dark purplish pink**
grayish purplish red
light reddish purple
moderate purplish red

rose madder
USE **strong purplish red**
vivid purplish red

rose madder (alizarin madder)
USE **alizarin madder**

rose marble
USE **pink marble**

rose mauve
USE **dark grayish purple**
dark purplish red
grayish purple

rose nails
TF.413
ALT **rose nail**
SN Wrought nails with cone-shaped heads. (MEANS)
UF nails, rose
CN V.TF.AFU.AFU.AFU.ALO.AFU.CFS.AFU.DCU.CLM

rose pink
USE **light purplish pink**
moderate purplish pink
vivid purplish red

rose pink, deep
USE **strong purplish pink**

rose plum
USE **dark purplish red**
grayish purplish red
grayish reddish purple

rose purple
USE **brilliant purple**
light purple
light reddish purple

rose purple, pale
USE **light purple**

rose quartz
MT.560
UF quartz, rose
CN M.MT.AFU.AFU.AFU.CFS.AFU.GRC.AFU.BIQ

rose red
USE **dark red**
deep red
moderate purplish red
moderate red
vivid red

rose sharp nails
TF.416
ALT **rose sharp nail**
UF nails, rose sharp
sharp nails, rose
CN V.TF.AFU.AFU.AFU.ALO.AFU.CFS.AFU.DCU.CLM.ARI

rose taupe
USE **dark gray**
dark reddish gray
grayish brown
grayish purple
grayish red

grayish reddish brown

rose taupe, dark
USE **brownish gray**
dark reddish gray

rose violet
USE **deep purplish red**
deep reddish purple
moderate purplish pink
moderate purplish red
moderate reddish purple

rose violet, bright
USE **deep purplish pink**

rose windows
RT.930 (A,L,B,R)
ALT **rose window**
SN Round Medieval windows, containing tracery disposed in a radial manner. (HAS)
UF Catherine-wheel windows
marigold windows
wheel windows
windows, Catherine-wheel
windows, marigold
windows, rose
windows, wheel
CN V.RT.AFU.ARI.AFU.AFU.BOK.AFU.AFU.DZW

rose, bright
USE **deep pink**
deep purplish pink
grayish purplish red
moderate purplish red
strong purplish red
strong red
vivid purplish red

rose, bright fuchsia
USE **moderate purplish red**

rose, carmine
USE **deep purplish pink**
grayish red
moderate purplish red
moderate red
strong purplish red
strong red
vivid red

rose, dark
USE **moderate purplish red**
moderate red

rose, deep
USE **deep pink**
moderate purplish red
moderate red

rose, dull
USE **light grayish red**
moderate purplish pink

rose, fuchsia
USE **moderate purplish red**
strong purplish red
vivid purplish red

rose, geranium
USE **moderate red**
strong red

rose, light
USE **moderate purplish pink**

rose, light orchid
USE **deep purplish pink**
moderate purplish pink

rose, lilac
USE **deep purplish pink**
light grayish red
light purplish pink
moderate purplish red
strong reddish purple

rose, magenta
USE **dark purplish red**
deep purplish red
moderate purplish red

rose, orchid
USE **deep purplish pink**

rose, salmon
USE **light yellowish pink**

rose, taupe
USE **dark reddish gray**

roseaker
USE **realgar**

rosemary oil
MT.1990
SN A pungent essential oil obtained from the flowering tops of rosemary and used chiefly in soaps, colognes, hair lotions, pharmaceutical preparations,(W) and as a retardant in oil paints. (MAYER)
UF oil of rosemary
oil, rosemary
CN M.MT.AFU.AFU.ARI.ARI.AFU.ARI.AFU.ARI

rosemary pine
USE **longleaf pine**
shortleaf pine

roses (backplates)
TF.261
ALT **rose (backplate)**
SN Small round backplates that serve as a mounting for a doorknob or lever door handle and intervene between it and the door. (DITTRI)
CN V.TF.AFU.AFU.AFU.AFU.DZW.AFU.AFU

roses, Tudor
USE **Tudor roses**

rosettes
DG.60 (R)
ALT **rosette**
SN Motifs of formalized roses, with petals radiating from the center; sometimes used for any small circular ornament radiating from the center. (IDO)
CN D.DG.AFU.AFU.DIO.BZY

rosewood
MT.1296 (L)
SN Any of various valuable cabinet woods from tropical trees of a dark red or purplish color streaked and variegated with black. (W)
UF melanorrhoea
CN M.MT.AFU.AFU.ALO.BIQ.DCU.AFU.AFU.AFU.LCM

rosewood, Borneo
USE **Borneo rosewood**

rosewood, Brazilian
USE **Brazilian rosewood**

rosewood, Ceylon
USE **Ceylon rosewood**

rosewood, East Indian
USE **East Indian rosewood**

rosewood, Honduran
USE **cocobolo**

rosewood, Indian
USE **East Indian rosewood**

Rosh Hashanah
KM.88 (L)
UF Jewish New Year
New Year, Jewish
CN K.KM.AFU.CFS.ARI.CLM

Rosicrucian
FL.3302
ALT **Rosicrucianism**
UF Rose + Croix
Rose et Croix
CN F.FL.ALO.BCW.ALO.AXC.DCU.CLM

rosin
MT.1506 (L)
SN A resin obtained from pine; used chiefly in making varnish, paper size, soap, and adhesives.
UF colophony
Greek pitch
pitch, Greek
CN M.MT.AFU.AFU.ALO.BOK.DOI

rosin ester
USE **ester gum**

rosin-sized paper
MT.1930
UF paper, rosin-sized
CN M.MT.AFU.AFU.ARI.ALO.ALO.AXC.ARI.ALO.ALO

Röslein
USE **fleurons**

Ross board (TM)
MT.1920
SN Trade name for a large and varied line of textured boards that are similar to coquille boards. (MAYER)
UF board, Ross (TM)
CN M.MT.AFU.AFU.ARI.ALO.ALO.AXC

.ALO.BIQ.AFU.BOK

Rossen
FL.2494
CN F.FL.ALO.AXC.AFU.BCW.BZY

rosso antico
USE **rouge antique marble**

rosso brecciato
MT.757
UF marmor Lydium
CN M.MT.AFU.AFU.AFU.DCU.AFU.ARI.ARI.ALO.AFU.CFS

rosso de levanto marble
MT.801
UF marble, rosso de levanto
CN M.MT.AFU.AFU.AFU.DCU.AFU.ARI.ARI.ARI.BCW.AXC

rosso di francia
MT.817
CN M.MT.AFU.AFU.AFU.DCU.AFU.ARI.ARI.ARI.BIQ.CXA

rosters
VW.269 (N)
ALT **roster**
SN Use generally for any list of names of persons enrolled or enlisted for a particular purpose, as a list of names of military personnel enrolled for active duty.
UF rolls (rosters)
CN V.VW.AFU.AFU.AFU.FZU.BCW.AFU.BOK

rostral columns
RK.897
ALT **rostral column**
SN Columns erected in honor of a naval triumph and ornamented with the rostra or prows of ships.
UF columnae rostratae
columns, rostral
CN V.RK.AFU.ALO.ALO.DOI.AFU.BCW.AFU

rotaries
USE **traffic circles**

rotary bookcases
USE **revolving bookcases**

rotary cylinder desks
USE **rotary desks**

rotary desks
TG.562
ALT **rotary desk**
UF cylinder desks, rotary
desks, rotary
desks, rotary cylinder
rotary cylinder desks
CN V.TG.AFU.AFU.AXC.ALO.BZY.FIM.AFU

rotary kilns
TB.93 (L)
ALT **rotary kiln**
SN Long cylindrical kilns lined with refractory, inclined at a slight angle, and rotated at slow speed. (MHDSTT)
UF kilns, rotary
CN V.TB.AFU.ARI.ALO.ARI.ALO.AFU.ARI

rotary stools
USE **revolving stools**

rotated indexes
VW.428 (L)
ALT **rotated index**
SN Indexes in which each significant element of a multiword index entry appears as a filing element.
UF indexes, permuted
indexes, rotated
permuted indexes
CN V.VW.AFU.AFU.ALO.EWY.BOK.AFU.ARI

rotated sections
USE **revolved sections**

rotation
BM.899 (L)
UF motion, rotational
rotational motion
CN B.BM.CFS.AXC.BIQ.AFU.AXC.BIQ

rotational molding
KT.150
SN Plastics forming process in which a granular, powdered, or liquid plastic is introduced into a mold which is closed and rotated horizontally and vertically. The plastic is forced against the walls of the mold. (DIETZ)
UF molding, rotational
CN K.KT.AFU.ALO.DOI.CRG.AXC

rotational motion
USE **rotation**

rotondas
USE **rotundas**

Rotse
USE **Lozi**

rottenstone
MT.692 (L)
SN A soft, friable, earthy stone of light gray to olive color, used as an abrasive for metal and wood finishing. (MH)
CN M.MT.AFU.AFU.AFU.DCU.AFU.ALO.AFU.ALO.ALO.ALO.ARI

rotundas
RM.280 (L,R)
ALT **rotunda**
SN Use for large round rooms.
UF rotondas
CN V.RM.AFU.DIO.ARI.ALO.DCU

rotundas (buildings)
RK.27 (A,L,R)
ALT **rotunda (building)**
CN V.RK.AFU.ALO.AFU.ALO.CFS

rouge
MT.2577
SN A hydrated iron oxide used for polishing metals and in break-in lubricants for aluminum bronze bearings. (MH)
UF polishing rouge
rouge, polishing
CN M.MT.AFU.ARI.CRG.AXC.ALO

rouge antique marble
MT.802
UF marble, rouge antique
rosso antico
CN M.MT.AFU.AFU.AFU.DCU.AFU.ARI.ARI.ARI.BCW.BCW

rouge de cadmium
USE **cadmium red**

rouge de chrome
USE **chrome red**

rouge flambé
USE **sang de boeuf**

rouge (Indian red)
USE **Indian red**

rouge végétal
USE **safflower (red pigment)**

rouge, green
USE **green rouge**

rouge, polishing
USE **rouge**

rough
DC.139 (L,B)
ALT **roughness**
CN D.DC.AFU.BCW.BCW

rough arches
USE **relieving arches**

rough-axed brick
USE **axed brick**

rough bucks
USE **door bucks**

rough-cut joints
TF.620
SN Mortar joints that are flush with the faces of the blocks. (MEANS)
UF flat joints
flush joints (mortar joints)
flush masonry joints
hick joints
joints, flat
joints, flush (mortar joints)
joints, hick
joints, plain cut
joints, rough-cut
masonry joints, flush
plain cut joints
CN V.TF.ALO.ARI.ALO.AFU.ARI.AFU

rough drafts
USE **first drafts**

rough files

TB.517
ALT **rough file**
SN Files having the coarsest cutting ridges. (W)
UF files, rough
CN V.TB.AFU.ARI.EWY.ALO.CFS.ALO

rough hardware
TF.286
SN Hardware that is used in the construction of buildings and other structures, such as screws, nuts, and bolts, and that is generally meant to be concealed.
UF hardware, rough
CN V.TF.AFU.AFU.AFU.ALO

rough lumber
MT.1429
SN Lumber that has not been dressed since it was sawed. (W)
UF lumber, rough
CN M.MT.AFU.AFU.ALO.BIQ.DCU.ALO .BOK.ALO.AFU.ALO

rough sills
RT.705
ALT **rough sill**
SN Horizontal members laid across the bottom of an unfinished opening to act as a base during construction of window frames. (MEANS)
UF sills, rough
CN V.RT.AFU.AFU.ALO.ALO.AXC

rough strings
USE **carriage pieces**

rough, Alma
USE **Alma rough**

roughcast
MT.2459
SN Plaster made of lime mixed with shells or pebbles and used for covering buildings usually by being thrown from a trowel forcibly against a wall. (W)
UF harling
slap-dash
CN M.MT.AFU.ARI.CRG.AFU.AXC.ARI. BCW

roughing planes
TB.968 (N)
ALT **roughing plane**
SN Planes with a single cutting iron, used for rough-shaping or preliminary planing; suited for rougher work than the jack plane. (SALAM)
UF cow planes
hunter planes
planes, cow
planes, hunter
planes, roughing
planes, scrub
planes, scud
planes, scurfing
scrub planes
scud planes
scurfing planes
CN V.TB.AFU.BCW.CFS.ALO.AFU.DUC. BIQ

round
DC.70
CN D.DC.AFU.ARI.DCU

Round Arch Style
USE **Rundbogenstil**

round arches
USE **semicircular arches**

round billet moldings
USE **roll billet moldings**

round-both-ways planes
USE **cooper's stoup planes**

round chairs (corner chairs)
USE **corner chairs**

round-edge equalling files
USE **joint files**

round files
TB.718 (N)
ALT **round file**
SN Round tapering files, 4 to 20 inches long, used for enlarging holes and shaping curves.
UF files, mousetail
files, rat tail
files, round
mousetail files
rat tail files
CN V.TB.AFU.BCW.BIQ.ARI.ALO.ARI. AXC

round-front
DC.109
CN D.DC.AFU.ARI.EWY.BZY

Round Head phase
FL.69
CN F.FL.ALO.AFU.AFU.ARI.ALO

round keys
TF.536
ALT **round key**
UF keys, round
CN V.TF.AFU.ALO.ARI.AFU.BZY

round-lip tongs
TB.762 (N)
UF tongs, round-lip
CN V.TB.AFU.BCW.BIQ.AXC.ALO.AXC .CRG

round moldings
USE **roll moldings**

round mortise-and-tenon joints
TF.679
ALT **round mortise-and-tenon joint**
UF joints, round mortise-and-tenon
CN V.TF.ALO.ARI.AXC.ALO.BCW.ALO

round planes
TB.960 (N)
ALT **round plane**
SN Planes with a convex blade for cutting hollow molding patterns; usually paired with hollow planes in sets. (MERCER)
UF planes, round
CN V.TB.AFU.BCW.CFS.ALO.AFU.DUC. AXC.AFU.BUE

round planes (guttering planes)
USE **guttering planes**

round saws
USE **crown saws**

round shaves
USE **scorpers**

round shaves, one-hand
USE **closed scorpers**

Round Style
FL.701
SN Style of African sculpture, characteristically naturalistic, gentle, and organic, featuring rounded shapes, and giving the impression of flesh over the bone structure. (LAANP)
CN F.FL.ALO.AFU.BCW.ALO

round-top Windsor chairs
USE **sack-back Windsor chairs**

round towers
RK.36 (A,L,B)
ALT **round tower**
SN Use for circular stone towers which taper toward the top, have a conical stone cap, four to five internal floors, and an entry door high above the ground; common in Ireland, associated with churches, and probably built between the 10th and 12th centuries.
UF towers, round
CN V.RK.AFU.ALO.AFU.ALO.DCU.ARI

roundabout chairs
USE **corner chairs**

roundabouts
USE **corner chairs**

roundabouts (traffic circles)
USE **traffic circles**

roundels
RT.632
ALT **roundel**
SN Use for circular panels, usually sculptured or otherwise decorated, set as decorative elements in an architectural context. For similarly shaped and decorated motifs in two-dimensional media, use **medallions (ornament areas).**
CN V.RT.AFU.AFU.AFU.BIQ.BUE.ALO. AFU.ARI.AXC

roundels (moldings)
USE **bead moldings**

roundels (windows)
USE **oculi**

rounder planes
TB.969 (N)
ALT **rounder plane**
SN Planes with a cutting blade set in a stock that has a round hole in it and is twisted down over a piece of work; used to make round stock such as broom handles and spokes. (MERCER)
UF planes, rounder
planes, witchet
witchet planes
CN V.TB.AFU.BCW.CFS.ALO.AFU.DUC.BOK

roundhouses
RK.1243 (L,N,R)
ALT **roundhouse**
SN Circular buildings for housing and repairing locomotives. (W)
UF circular engine houses
engine houses (railway buildings)
engine houses, circular
houses, circular engine
CN V.RK.AFU.ALO.ALO.GLI.AFU.ALO.AFU.ARI

rounding planes (forkstaffs)
USE **forkstaffs**

roundsils
USE **compass planes**

rout chairs
TG.82
ALT **rout chair**
SN Term used by Chippendale for small painted chairs with rush seats used at general entertainments. (GILBR2)
UF chairs, fly
chairs, rout
fly chairs
CN V.TG.AFU.AFU.ALO.AFU.AFU.AFU.JOC

route maps
USE **line-route maps**

routers
TB.985 (N)
ALT **router**
SN Electrically driven devices with various bits; used for cutting grooves and channels in wood. (MEANS)
CN V.TB.AFU.BCW.CFS.ALO.AFU.ERE

routes, truck
USE **truck routes**

roving
MT.1979
CN M.MT.AFU.AFU.ARI.ALO.ALO.BIQ.BIQ.AFU

row dwellings
USE **row houses**

row houses
RK.265 (A,L,B,R)
ALT **row house**
SN Use for urban dwellings attached in a series of three or more. For individual freestanding urban dwellings use **townhouses.**
UF dwellings, row
houses, row
row dwellings
row housing
townhouses (row houses)
CN V.RK.AFU.ALO.ALO.AXC.ALO.AFU.CRG.BIQ

row housing
USE **row houses**

rowlock arches
RT.249
ALT **rowlock arch**
SN Arches, usually of brick, in which the voussoirs are arranged in separate concentric rings.
UF arches, rollock
arches, rowlock
rollock arches
CN V.RT.AFU.AFU.AFU.BCW.AFU.AFU.AFU.ELK.AFU.AFU

royal blue
USE **artificial ultramarine blue**
dark blue
deep blue
deep purplish blue
moderate blue
moderate purplish blue
strong blue
strong purplish blue
vivid blue
vivid purplish blue

royal blue, deep
USE **dark blue**
deep blue
deep purplish blue
moderate purplish blue

royal chapels
RM.312 (L,B)
ALT **royal chapel**
SN Private chapels for a royal court. (ODCC)
UF chapels royal
chapels, court
chapels, palace
chapels, royal
court chapels
palace chapels
CN V.RM.AFU.DIO.AXC.ALO.AFU.AXC.BUE

royal green
USE **chrome green**

royal palaces
RK.341 (B)
ALT **royal palace**
UF palaces, royal
CN V.RK.AFU.ALO.ALO.AXC.ALO.BOK.BOK.ALO.AXC

royal scarlet
USE **iodine scarlet**

royal tombs
RK.497
ALT **royal tomb**
UF tombs, royal
CN V.RK.AFU.ALO.ALO.BOK.BUE.ALO.AFU

Rozwi
FL.137
UF Barozwi
CN F.FL.ALO.AFU.ALO.ARI.BCW

RRT
USE **rapid rail transit systems**

Ru ware
FL.1949
UF Ju Chou ware
Ju ware
ware, Ju
ware, Ju Chou
ware, Ru
CN F.FL.ALO.ARI.ALO.AFU.AFU.AXC.ARI.BIQ

Ruanda
FL.687 (L)
UF Rwanda
CN F.FL.ALO.AFU.AXC.AXC.BOK.DIO

rubbed joints
TF.601
ALT **rubbed joint**
SN For joining two narrow boards. Both boards are planed smooth, coated with glue, and rubbed together until all air pockets and excess glue are expelled from the joint. No clamping is necessary and the joint is extremely strong. (MEANS)
UF joints, rubbed
CN V.TF.ALO.AFU.FIM

rubber
MT.1500 (L)
UF natural rubber
rubber, natural
CN M.MT.AFU.AFU.ALO.BOK.CFS.ALO

rubber (brick)
USE **cutter**

rubber, artificial
USE **elastomers**

rubber, butyl
USE **butyl rubber**

rubber, chloroprene
USE **neoprene**

rubber, EPR
USE **ethylene-propylene elastomer**

rubber, ethylene-propylene
USE **ethylene-propylene elastomer**

rubber, foam
USE **foam rubber**

rubber, natural
USE **rubber**

rubber, NBR
USE **nitrile elastomer**

rubber, nitrile
USE **nitrile elastomer**

rubber, silicone
USE **silicone rubber**

rubber, sponge
USE **foam rubber**

rubber, styrene-butadiene
USE **styrene-butadiene rubber**

rubber, synthetic
USE **elastomers**

rubber, synthetic natural
USE **polyisoprene**

rubbing stones
USE **floatstones**

rubbing varnish
MT.2478
UF varnish, rubbing
CN M.MT.AFU.ARI.CRG.AFU.BOK.AFU.BCW

rubbing, brass
USE **brass rubbing**

rubbish chutes
USE **refuse chutes**

rubbish dumps
USE **dumps**

rubble
MT.893 (B)
SN Rough, broken stones or bricks. (PUTNAM)
CN M.MT.AFU.AFU.AFU.DCU.ALO.CLM

rubble arches
USE **rustic arches**

rubble concrete
MT.205 (B)
SN Form of concrete reinforced by broken stones or brick. (PUTNAM)
UF concrete, rubble
CN M.MT.AFU.AFU.AFU.BCW.AFU.AFU.BZY

Rubenism
BM.197
SN Artistic theory in France, current from the second half of the 17th century to the early 18th century, advocating the primacy of color over line. (PDAT)
UF Color, Party of
colorism
Party of Color
CN B.BM.AFU.AFU.AXC.CLM.CLM

Rubens' brown
USE **Van Dyke brown**

rubstones
USE **floatstones**

ruby
MT.500 (L,R)
SN A red variety of the mineral corundum that ranks with the best grades of precious stones as a gemstone; off-color rubies are used for watch and instrument bearings. (MH)
CN M.MT.AFU.AFU.AFU.CFS.AFU.BUE.ALO

ruby (color)
USE **dark red**
deep purplish red
deep red
moderate red

ruby red
USE **deep red**

rudaceous rock
MT.733
UF psephite
rock, rudaceous
CN M.MT.AFU.AFU.AFU.DCU.AFU.ALO.ALO.ARI

Rudd dressing chests
TG.494
ALT **Rudd dressing chest**
UF chests, Rudd dressing
dressing chests, Rudd
CN V.TG.AFU.AFU.AXC.ALO.BCW.CLM

Rudd dressing tables
USE **Rudd tables**

Rudd tables
TG.737
ALT **Rudd table**
SN Dressing tables with two drawers in the sides which swing out and provide mirrors on a quadrant so that a woman could see herself at any angle. (DEF)
UF dressing tables, reflecting
dressing tables, Rudd
reflecting dressing tables
Rudd dressing tables
tables, reflecting dressing
tables, Rudd
tables, Rudd dressing
CN V.TG.AFU.AFU.BIQ.BOK.ALO.CLM.AXC.ALO

rudenture
USE **cabling**

Rufijic
FL.611
CN F.FL.ALO.AFU.AXC.AXC.ALO.BUE.ARI

rugby fields
RK.1484 (B)
ALT **rugby field**
UF fields, rugby
grounds, rugby
rugby grounds
CN V.RK.ALO.ALO.BCW.AFU.BOK

rugby grounds
USE **rugby fields**

rugmaking
KT.530 (L)
CN K.KT.AFU.ALO.ELK.DCU

ruin marble
MT.693
UF marble, ruin
CN M.MT.AFU.AFU.AFU.DCU.AFU.ALO.AFU.ALO.ALO.ALO.AXC

ruined cities
RD.39 (A,L,B)
ALT **ruined city**
UF cities, ruined
ruined towns
ruined villages
towns, ruined
villages, ruined
CN V.RD.AFU.ARI.ARI

ruined towns
USE **ruined cities**

ruined villages
USE **ruined cities**

ruins
RK.1392 (A,L,R)
ALT **ruin**
SN Use generally for remains of buildings or groups of buildings that have been destroyed or are in a state of great disrepair or decay.
CN V.RK.AFU.ALO.BCW.ARI

ruins, artificial
USE **artificial ruins**

ruins, sham
USE **artificial ruins**

Rukana
USE **Ica**

Rukn-ad-Din Sulayman II
FL.3557
CN F.FL.ALO.BIQ.AFU.HIK.ARI.BCW

Rukuba
FL.220 (L)
CN F.FL.ALO.AFU.AXC.AFU.AFU.ALO.ALO.CXA

rule joints
TF.689
ALT **rule joint**
SN Joints formed by two boards with curved edges; favored for dropleaf tables because they minimize the gap between a table top and its leaf in the closed position. (NEF)
UF joints, rule
CN V.TF.ALO.ARI.AXC.ARI.BIQ

rulers (people)
HG.690 (L,R)
ALT **ruler (person)**
UF sovereigns
CN H.HG.AFU.AXC.CFS.CRG

rules
VW.783 (L)
ALT **rule**
SN Authoritative directions for conduct, especially those governing procedure in a legislative body or in a game, sport, or contest. (AHD)
CN V.VW.AFU.ARI.AFU.ALO.CLM

rules of order
USE **rules of procedure**

rules of procedure
VW.784 (L)
ALT **rule of procedure**
SN Rules made by a legislative body concerning the mode and manner of conducting its business and for the purpose of making an orderly and proper disposition of the matters before it. (BLACKS)
UF order, rules of
procedure, rules of
rules of order
CN V.VW.AFU.ARI.AFU.ALO.CLM.AFU

rules, featheredge
USE **featheredge rules**

rules, parallel
USE **parallel rules**

ruling pens
TB.276 (N)
ALT **ruling pen**
SN Basic drafting implements used to inscribe lines of uniform thickness; usually guided by a straight edge, curve, or template. (MAYER)
UF pens, ruling
CN V.TB.AFU.ARI.CLM.AFU.ALO.DOI.BOK

rum cherry
USE **black cherry**

Rum, Seljuk of
USE **Seljuk of Rum**

rumble seats (wagon seats)
USE **wagon seats**

rumble strips
RM.493
ALT **rumble strip**
SN Series of rough or slightly raised strips of pavement on a highway, intended to slow down the speed of vehicles. (RHDEL2)
UF strips, rumble
CN V.RM.ALO.ALO.ALO.ALO.DCU

rumi
USE **arabesques**

rummage sales
KM.155 (L)
SN Sales of miscellaneous articles, old or new, as items contributed to raise money for charity, of unclaimed goods at a wharf or warehouse, or of odds and ends of merchandise at a shop. (RHDEL2)
UF jumble sales
sales, jumble
sales, rummage
sales, white elephant
white elephant sales
CN K.KM.AFU.ELK.BCW

rumpus rooms
USE **playrooms**
recreation rooms

Rundbogenstil
FL.3385 (B,R)
UF Round Arch Style
CN F.FL.ALO.BCW.ALO.AXC.DIO.BIQ.AXC.AFU

runner feet
TG.910
ALT **runner foot**
UF bar feet
feet, bar
feet, runner
CN V.TG.ALO.DZW.AFU.BUE

runners
TG.889
ALT **runner**
SN Narrow strips applied to the bottom edge of a drawer to provide a good running surface on the framing.
CN V.TG.ALO.DCU.ALO.AFU

runners (bends)
USE **bends**

runners, draw
USE **lopers**

running bond
MT.2752
SN Pattern bond consisting of all stretchers and where the vertical joints of one course fall midway between the joints of the courses above and below.
UF bond, running
bond, stretcher
stretcher bond
CN M.MT.AFU.AXC.BIQ.AFU.AFU.AXC

running decoration
USE **running ornament**

running dog
USE **wave scrolls**

running ornament
DG.99
SN Use for ornament in the form of a continuous pattern that proceeds directionally, as in a band. For patterns that extend more broadly over a surface, use **allover patterns.**
UF band patterns (running ornament)
continuous linear pattern
decoration, running
linear pattern, continuous
ornament, progressive
ornament, running
pattern, continuous linear
patterns, band (running ornament)
patterns, running
progressive ornament
running decoration
running patterns
CN D.DG.AFU.ARI.AFU.ARI

running patterns
USE **running ornament**

running tracks
RK.1500 (A,B)
ALT **running track**
UF tracks, running
CN V.RK.ALO.ALO.BCW.CFS

runoff
BM.419 (L,B)
UF surface water drainage
CN B.BM.AXC.AFU.AFU.AFU

runs, bobsled
USE **bobsled runs**

runs, toboggan
USE **toboggan runs**

runways
RK.1507 (A,L,B)
ALT **runway**
UF airport runways
runways, airport
CN V.RK.ALO.ALO.BIQ.AFU.AXC

runways, airport
USE **runways**

rural community development
USE **rural development**

rural development
BM.1070 (A,L)
UF community development, rural
development, rural
economic development, rural
rural community development
rural economic development
CN B.BM.CLM.ALO.ALO.AFU.AFU

rural economic development
USE **rural development**

rural exodus
USE **rural-urban migration**

rural fringes
USE **urban fringes**

rural housing
RG.66 (L,B)
UF housing, rural
CN V.RG.AFU.AFU.BOK.ARI.AFU

rural land use
BM.1046 (A,L)
UF land use, rural
use, rural land
CN B.BM.CLM.AFU.AFU.ALO

rural planning
KD.172 (B)

UF country planning
planning, country
planning, rural
CN K.KD.AFU.ALO.DUC.AXC

rural sociology
KD.190 (L)
UF sociology, rural
CN K.KD.AFU.ALO.ELK.ALO

rural-urban fringes
USE **urban fringes**

rural-urban migration
BM.1054 (A,L)
UF exodus, rural
migration, rural-urban
rural exodus
CN B.BM.CLM.AFU.ALO.ARI.ARI

Rusafah pottery
USE **Rusapha ware**

Rusapha ware
FL.3568
UF pottery, Rusafah
Rusafah pottery
ware, Rusapha
CN F.FL.ALO.BIQ.AFU.HIK.BCW.BIQ

rush
MT.1036
CN M.MT.AFU.AFU.ALO.BIQ.AXC .BCW

rush irons
USE **flagging irons**

rushing levers
USE **flagging irons**

rushwork
MT.2781 (L)
CN M.MT.AFU.AXC.CXA

Russian
FL.3056 (L,B)
CN F.FL.ALO.BCW.AFU.DOI

Russian maple
USE **European birch**

rust-inhibiting paint
MT.2548
UF paint, rust-inhibiting
CN M.MT.AFU.ARI.CRG.ALO.BCW.ARI. BZY

rust inhibitors
MT.2317
UF inhibitors, rust
CN M.MT.AFU.ARI.ALO.DCU.ALO

rust joints
TF.664
ALT **rust joint**
SN Watertight pipe connections that use iron filings as a catalyst to induce rusting in iron pipe joints. (MEANS)
UF joints, rust
CN V.TF.ALO.ARI.ARI.CFS

rust removing agents
MT.2727
UF agents, rust removing
CN M.MT.AFU.ARI.IFM.BIQ

Rustam
USE **Rüstem**

Rüstem
FL.3582
UF Rustam
CN F.FL.ALO.BIQ.AFU.IFM.AFU.AXC

Rustic
FL.3285 (A,L,R)
CN F.FL.ALO.BCW.ALO.AXC.CXA.ARI

rustic arches
RT.259
ALT **rustic arch**
SN Use for arches built of large, rough, and irregular stones, abundantly mortared.
UF arches, rubble
arches, rustic
rubble arches
CN V.RT.AFU.AFU.AFU.BCW.AFU.AFU. AFU.ELK.BUE

rustic brick
MT.101
UF brick, rustic
CN M.MT.AFU.AFU.AFU.AXC.ALO.AFU .ALO.BIQ.ALO

rustic joints
TF.630
ALT **rustic joint**
SN Sunken joints between building stones. (PUTNAM)
UF joints, rustic
CN V.TF.ALO.ARI.ALO.AFU.AXC

rustic limestone
MT.697
UF limestone, rustic
CN M.MT.AFU.AFU.AFU.DCU.AFU.ALO .AFU.ALO.ALO.ARI.ALO

Rustic order
RT.55
SN Use for an architectural order employing rusticated columns.
UF order, Rustic
CN V.RT.AFU.AFU.AFU.ARI.ARI.BCW

rustic work
USE **rustication**

rusticated columns
USE **banded columns**

rustication
DG.117 (A,B,R)
ALT **rusticated**
SN Surface pattern originally for stone but frequently simulated in other materials, giving the effect of large blocks with deep, wide joints.
UF rustic work
CN D.DG.AFU.ARI.ALO.ARI.BIQ

rusting
KT.897 (A,B)
ALT **rusted**
SN The formation of a reddish, brittle coating on metal usually caused by its exposure to moist air. (WCOL)
CN K.KT.ALO.BCW.ALO.ALO

rustproofing
KT.597
ALT **rustproof**
CN K.KT.AFU.ALO.FOG.ARI

rutters
USE **portolanos**

ruttiers
USE **portolanos**

Rwanda
USE **Ruanda**

Ryokuyo
FL.2032
CN F.FL.ALO.ARI.ALO.ALO.ALO.ALO. ALO.DCU

S chairs
TG.83
ALT **S chair**
UF chairs, S
CN V.TG.AFU.AFU.ALO.AFU.AFU.AFU .JTW

S-scrolls
DG.67
ALT **S-scroll**
SN Ornamental scrolls that uncoil in one direction and then reverse to coil in the other.
CN D.DG.AFU.AFU.DOI.ARI

Sabaean
FL.2888
CN F.FL.ALO.AXC.ARI.ALO.AFU.AXC

Sabattier effect
KT.911
UF edge reversal
effect, Sabattier
CN K.KT.ALO.BOK.AFU

Sabbath schools
USE **Sunday schools**

saber saws
TB.1030 (N)
ALT **saber saw**
SN Keyhole-style saws with a short blade that is supported in a pistol-style grip; frequently having interchangeable blades for different purposes.
UF bayonet saws
saws, bayonet
saws, saber
CN V.TB.AFU.BCW.CFS.ALO.AFU.EWY. BUE.BOK

sabre legs
TG.950
ALT **sabre leg**
SN Legs, curved lika a cavalry sabre, square or round in section and

tapering gently toward the base. Derived from the Greek klismos and much used on late 18th-century and early 19th-century chairs and sofas. (DDA)
UF legs, sabre
legs, scimitar
legs, Waterloo
scimitar legs
Waterloo legs
CN V.TG.ALO.FIM.AFU.AFU.BIQ

Sac
USE **Sauk**

saccharoidal marble
USE **white marble**

sacella
RK.1146
ALT **sacellum**
SN Use for small ancient Roman shrines, usually built as enclosures open to the sky.
CN V.RK.AFU.ALO.ALO.FCS.BOK.BOK

Sachian
USE **Saka**

Sacian
USE **Saka**

sack-back Windsor chairs
TG.104
ALT **sack-back Windsor chair**
SN Windsor armchairs with a horizontal U-shaped arm rail and back of medium height consisting of spindles contained within a curved bow anchored in the arm rail. (EVANS)
UF chairs, hoop-back Windsor
chairs, loop-back Windsor
chairs, round-top Windsor
chairs, sack-back Windsor
hoop-back Windsor chairs
loop-back Windsor chairs
round-top Windsor chairs
Windsor chairs, hoop-back
Windsor chairs, loop-back
Windsor chairs, round-top
Windsor chairs, sack-back
CN V.TG.AFU.AFU.ALO.AFU.AFU.AFU.MLC.BUE

sacraria
RM.332
ALT **sacrarium**
SN May be used broadly for any consecrated place in ancient Roman or Christian architecture, but more specific terms are preferred, such as **chapels, shrines, sacristies,** or **sanctuaries.**
CN V.RM.AFU.DIO.AXC.ALO.ALO

sacristies
RM.329 (A,R)
ALT **sacristy**
SN Rooms in or attached to churches where the sacred utensils and vestments are kept. (W)
UF vestries
CN V.RM.AFU.DIO.AXC.ALO.AFU.DZW

saddle-back coping brick
MT.96
UF brick, saddle-back coping
CN M.MT.AFU.AFU.AFU.AXC.ALO.AFU.ALO.AXC.AFU

saddle boards
RT.488
ALT **saddle board**
SN Strips of wood or metal covering the ridges of a roof. (W)
UF boards, comb
boards, saddle
comb boards
CN V.RT.AFU.AFU.AFU.BIQ.ARI.ALO.AFU.BZY

saddle cheek chairs
USE **easy chairs**

saddle hangers, channel
USE **channel saddle hangers**

saddle hangers, plate
USE **plate saddle hangers**

saddle joints
USE **water joints**

saddle roofs
USE **saddleback roofs**

saddle scaffolds
TB.491
ALT **saddle scaffold**
SN Scaffolds erected so as to bridge the ridge of a roof; usually used during chimney repair. (MEANS)
UF scaffolds, saddle
CN V.TB.AFU.ARI.ERE.ARI.ARI

saddle seats
TG.973
ALT **saddle seat**
SN Chair seats shaped like the cup of a saddle with a slight center ridge at the front edge; most often used on Windsor chairs. (FAIRB)
UF seats, saddle
CN V.TG.ALO.GLI.AFU.ALO.AFU

saddle style hangers
TF.364
ALT **saddle style hanger**
UF hangers, saddle style
CN V.TF.AFU.AFU.AFU.ALO.AFU.BOK.ARI.ARI.ALO.AFU

saddleback roofs
RT.429
ALT **saddleback roof**
SN Use for gable roofs on towers.
UF roofs, saddle
roofs, saddleback
saddle roofs
CN V.RT.AFU.AFU.AFU.BIQ.ARI.AFU.AFU.AFU.BOK.AXC.ALO

saddlebag houses
RK.262
ALT **saddlebag house**
SN Use either for central-chimney double-pen houses or for one-and-a-half-story dogtrot houses. (TEXLOG)
UF houses, saddlebag
saddlebags (houses)
CN V.RK.AFU.ALO.ALO.AXC.ALO.AFU.CRG.ARI.ALO

saddlebags (houses)
USE **saddlebag houses**

saddlers
HG.572
ALT **saddler**
CN H.HG.AFU.AXC.BUE.AXC.DOI

saddles
USE **doorsills**

saddles, beam
USE **beam hangers**

sadness
USE **melancholy**

safari chairs
USE **director's chairs**

safari parks
RG.233
ALT **safari park**
SN Distinguished from **wild animal parks** by the lack of restrictions on animal movement and by the mingling of animals and the visiting public, who generally drive through the parks in their own vehicles.
UF game parks
parks, game
parks, safari
CN V.RG.AFU.AFU.ELK.ARI.AFU

Safavid
FL.3531 (A,L)
CN F.FL.ALO.BIQ.AFU.GRC

safelights
TB.336 (N)
ALT **safelight**
SN Darkroom lights of a color and intensity that will not noticeably affect light-sensitive photographic materials. (LANG)
CN V.TB.AFU.ARI.CLM.ARI.ALO.CFS

safes, food
USE **kitchen safes**

safes, kitchen
USE **kitchen safes**

safety
BM.207 (A,L,B)
CN B.BM.AFU.ALO.BOK

safety arches
USE **relieving arches**

safety base

USE **safety film**

safety-base film
USE **safety film**

safety belts
TB.411 (N)
ALT **safety belt**
UF belts, safety
harnesses, safety
safety harnesses
CN V.TB.AFU.ARI.DUC.AXC

safety curtains
USE **asbestos curtains**

safety engineers
HG.644 (L)
ALT **safety engineer**
UF engineers, safety
CN H.HG.AFU.AXC.BZY.BCW.CXA

safety film
MT.2244 (L)
SN Photographic film with a base of cellulose acetate, triacetate, or polyester that will not ignite spontaneously. (ICPEP)
UF base, safety
film, non-flam
film, safety
film, safety-base
non-flam film
safety base
safety-base film
CN M.MT.AFU.ALO.CXA.ALO.CFS

safety glass
MT.285 (L,B)
UF glass, laminated
glass, nonshattering
glass, safety
glass, shatterproof
laminated glass
nonshattering glass
shatterproof glass
CN M.MT.AFU.AFU.AFU.BIQ.AFU.AXC.CXA

safety harnesses
USE **safety belts**

safety nets
TB.412
ALT **safety net**
UF nets, safety
CN V.TB.AFU.ARI.DUC.BCW

safety rails
TF.273
ALT **safety rail**
UF rails, safety
CN V.TF.AFU.AFU.AFU.AFU.ELK

safety rails, toilet
USE **toilet safety rails**

safety rests
USE **roadside rest areas**

safety, electrical
USE **electrical safety**

safety, fire
USE **fire safety**

Saffarid
FL.3544 (L)
CN F.FL.ALO.BIQ.AFU.GWW

safflower (colorant)
MT.1530 (L)
SN Dye prepared from flower heads of the safflower and now used chiefly in the Orient for dyeing silk and cotton light red. (W)
CN M.MT.AFU.AFU.ARI.AFU.AFU.AFU.AFU.AFU.AXC.CLM

safflower oil
MT.2018
SN A pale, non-yellowing drying oil of good film-forming properties and excellent color retention. (MAYER)
UF oil, safflower
CN M.MT.AFU.AFU.ARI.ARI.AXC.AFU.BZY

safflower (red pigment)
MT.1694
SN An obsolete, fugitive, red lake made from safflower dye, a natural dyestuff made from the dried petals of the safflower plant. (MAYER)
UF carthame
rose carthame
rouge végétal
CN M.MT.AFU.AFU.ARI.AFU.AFU.ALO.ALO.BCW.ALO.BOK

saffron
MT.1531 (L)
SN A fugitive yellow natural dyestuff prepared from the dried flowers of Crocus sativus. (MAYER)
CN M.MT.AFU.AFU.ARI.AFU.AFU.AFU.AFU.AFU.AXC.CRG

Saftgrün
USE **sap green**

Sagittarius symbols
DG.82 (R)
ALT **Sagittarius symbol**
CN D.DG.AFU.AFU.ERE.BZY

Sahaptin
USE **Nez Percé**

Sai
USE **Sao Empire**
Saô

Saiko Kutani
FL.2028
UF Hachiroemon Kutani
Kutani, Hachiroemon
Kutani, Revived
Kutani, Saiko
Revived Kutani
Wakasugi ware
ware, Wakasugi
CN F.FL.ALO.ARI.ALO.ALO.ALO.ALO.ALO.CFS.ARI

sail lofts
RM.233
ALT **sail loft**
UF lofts, sail
CN V.RM.AFU.DIO.ALO.DOI.CFS

sail plans
VD.33
ALT **sail plan**
SN Drawings representing a side elevation of a ship's sails, masts, spars, and standing rigging. (ENK)
UF plans, sail
CN V.VD.AFU.AFU.BIQ.ALO.ALO.BIQ.AXC

sail vaults
USE **pendentive domes**

sailcloth
MT.1860
SN A strong, heavy canvas, used chiefly for sails, tents, and upholstery. (W)
CN M.MT.AFU.AFU.ARI.ALO.ALO.ALO.ALO.ARI.AFU

Sailendra
FL.2380
UF Shailéndra
CN F.FL.ALO.ARI.BCW.ARI.ALO.AXC.AFU.AFU.AFU

sailmakers
HG.573
ALT **sailmaker**
CN H.HG.AFU.AXC.BUE.AXC.DUC

Saint Andrew's crosses
DG.15
ALT **Saint Andrew's cross**
SN Crosses in the form of the letter X. (MAYER)
UF crosses, Saint Andrew's
cruces decussatae
saltires
CN D.DG.AFU.AFU.ARI.BZY

Saint Anne marble
MT.779
UF marble, Saint Anne
CN M.MT.AFU.AFU.AFU.DCU.AFU.ARI.ARI.ARI.AFU.BOK

Saint Anthony's crosses
USE **tau crosses**

Saint Clément pottery
FL.3369 (R)
UF pottery, Saint Clément
CN F.FL.ALO.BCW.ALO.AXC.DIO.BCW.AXC.ALO.AFU

Saint Lawrence Island Eskimo
FL.1202
UF Eskimo, Saint Lawrence Island
CN F.FL.ALO.ALO.ARI.AFU.AFU.AFU.AFU.AXC

saints
HG.797 (L,R)
ALT **saint**

CN H.HG.AFU.BOK.CLM

Saisunaga-Nanda
FL.2192
UF Pre-Maurya
CN F.FL.ALO.ARI.AXC.ALO.AFU.ARI .AFU

Saite Dynasty (Twenty-eighth Dynasty)
USE **Twenty-eighth Dynasty**

Saite Dynasty (Twenty-sixth Dynasty)
USE **Twenty-sixth Dynasty**

Saite period (Twenty-eighth Dynasty)
USE **Twenty-eighth Dynasty**

Saite Period (Twenty-sixth Dynasty)
USE **Twenty-sixth Dynasty**

Saite Revival
USE **Twenty-sixth Dynasty**

Saiva
USE **Sivaism**

Saivism
USE **Sivaism**

Saka
FL.2143 (L)
UF Chaka
Massagetae
Sachian
Sacian
CN F.FL.ALO.ARI.ARI.ALO.AFU.ARI

Sakalava
FL.560 (L)
CN F.FL.ALO.AFU.AXC.ARI.ARI.BIQ

Sakya School
FL.2184
UF Ngor School
Nor School
Sakyapa
CN F.FL.ALO.ARI.AXC.AFU.BOK.AFU. BOK

Sakyapa
USE **Sakya School**

Salaihid
USE **Sulayhid**

Salampasu
FL.447
UF Basalampasu
CN F.FL.ALO.AFU.AXC.ALO.ALO.AFU. AFU.CLM

salaries
BM.375 (L,B)
SN Use for fixed compensation paid regularly to employees for ongoing work or services, on the basis of periods longer than days. For such compensation paid on an hourly, daily, or piecework basis, use **wages**.
CN B.BM.ARI.AXC.ARI

sale catalogs
VW.110
ALT **sale catalog**
UF catalogs, sale
CN V.VW.AFU.AFU.AFU.FZU.ALO.ALO .ARI.AFU.ARI

sales letters
VW.27 (L)
ALT **sales letter**
UF letters, sales
CN V.VW.AFU.AFU.AFU.BIQ.AFU.ARI. BZY

sales personnel
HG.426 (L)
UF personnel, sales
salesclerks
salesmen
saleswomen
CN H.HG.AFU.AXC.BOK.FCS

sales records
VW.860 (R)
ALT **sales record**
SN Documents that serve as the evidence or record of cash and credit sales, including sales orders, tickets, slips, invoices, journals and summaries, and customers' ledgers. (GAHLM)
UF records, sales
CN V.VW.AFU.ARI.AFU.BIQ.CXA.AXC

sales, garage
USE **garage sales**

sales, jumble
USE **rummage sales**

sales, rummage
USE **rummage sales**

sales, tag
USE **garage sales**

sales, white elephant
USE **rummage sales**

sales, yard
USE **garage sales**

salesclerks
USE **sales personnel**

salesmen
USE **sales personnel**

saleswomen
USE **sales personnel**

Salic
USE **Salian**

Salinan
FL.1262 (L)
CN F.FL.ALO.ALO.ARI.AFU.ALO.DOI

Salinar
FL.1151
CN F.FL.ALO.ALO.ALO.ARI.AXC.AFU. AXC.AFU

saline water
USE **salt water**

Salish
FL.1356 (L)
CN F.FL.ALO.ALO.ARI.AFU.BIQ.FCS

Salish (Flathead)
USE **Flathead**

Salish, Coast
USE **Coast Salish**

Salix
USE **willow**

Salix alba
USE **white willow**

Salix iasiandra
USE **western black willow**

Salix melanostach
USE **Japanese willow**

Salix nigra
USE **black willow**

Saljuk
USE **Seljuk**

sally ports
RT.889
ALT **sally port**
SN Large gates or passages in a fortified place suitable for the use of troops making a sortie; also, similar passages especially through the corner story of buildings forming a quadrangle. (W)
UF ports, sally
CN V.RT.AFU.ARI.AFU.AFU.ARI.AFU .AFU

salmon
USE **light orange**
light yellowish pink
moderate yellowish pink
strong yellowish pink

salmon brick
USE **place brick**

salmon rose
USE **light yellowish pink**

salmon, light
USE **light yellowish pink**

Salomonicas
USE **spiral columns**

salons
RM.179 (L,R)
ALT **salon**
SN Use for spacious, usually formal and elegantly furnished rooms, used largely for entertaining.
CN V.RM.AFU.DIO.ALO.CXA.CRG

salons, beauty
USE **beauty shops**

salons, hairdressing
USE **beauty shops**

saloon tables

TG.782
ALT **saloon table**
SN Sturdy tables, sometimes fitted with coasters or pockets, generally having a shelf under the top to hold glasses and steins so the top could remain clear for card playing. (PC)
UF tables, saloon
CN V.TG.AFU.AFU.BIQ.BOK.ARI.ALO.AXC

saloons
RK.106 (A,L,N)
ALT **saloon**
SN Use for public refreshment places with more emphasis on drinking, normally alcoholic beverages, than on eating, and offering a stage show or other type of public entertainment in the main room, but providing no overnight accommodations; use **pubs** for similar facilities, but generally offering no staged entertainment; use **taverns** for establishments offering overnight accommodations as well as food and drink but no staged entertainment.
CN V.RK.AFU.ALO.ALO.ALO.AFU.AFU.ARI

Salor
FL.3591
UF Salur
CN F.FL.ALO.BIQ.AFU.IFM.ARI.AXC

salt flats
RD.216
ALT **salt flat**
UF flats, salt
CN V.RD.ARI.AFU.AXC.AFU.ALO.ARI.AFU.AFU

salt glaze
MT.2569 (R)
SN A clear, glasslike ceramic coating with a distinctive uneven surface produced by throwing common table salt into a hot kiln. (DARIS)
UF glaze, salt
CN M.MT.AFU.ARI.CRG.ARI.ARI.AFU.ARI.AXC

salt paper photoprints
USE **salted paper prints**

salt paper prints
USE **salted paper prints**

salt paper processes
USE **salted paper processes**

salt print process
USE **salted paper processes**

salt prints
USE **salted paper prints**

salt processes, iron
USE **iron processes**

salt water
MT.318 (L)
UF saline water
water, saline
water, salt
CN M.MT.AFU.AFU.AFU.BOK.BOK.AFU.ARI

salt, spirits of
USE **hydrochloric acid**

saltbox houses
RK.252 (A,R)
ALT **saltbox house**
SN Denotes houses with two stories in front and one in back and with an asymmetrical gable roof where the rear slope is longer than the front slope.
UF catslide houses
houses, catslide
houses, lean-to
houses, saltbox
lean-to houses
CN V.RK.AFU.ALO.ALO.AXC.ALO.AFU.CLM.BIQ

salted paper
MT.1950
UF paper, plain salted
paper, salted
plain salted paper
salted paper, plain
CN M.MT.AFU.AFU.ARI.ALO.ALO.AXC.ARI.BOK.BOK

salted paper photoprints
USE **salted paper prints**

salted paper prints
VJ.58
ALT **salted paper print**
SN Photographic prints whose light-sensitive salts are in the fibers of the paper rather than in a binder; the image is positive and is printed out rather than developed out. Use **calotypes** only for paper negatives made by Talbot's patented calotype process. Use **photogenic drawings** only for Talbot's printed-out paper negatives.
UF calotype photoprints
calotype positives
calotype prints
paper prints, salted
photoprints, calotype
photoprints, salted paper
positives, calotype
prints, calotype
prints, salt
prints, salt paper
prints, salted paper
salt paper photoprints
salt paper prints
salt prints
salted paper photoprints
CN V.VJ.AFU.AFU.ARI.ARI.AXC.CFS

salted paper processes
KT.361
SN Use for photographic processes in which the light-sensitive salt is formed in the fibers of the paper rather than in a binder. Sometimes designed to be developed out, as in the calotype process, and sometimes printed out, as when making salted paper prints.
UF plain salted paper processes
salt paper processes
salt print process
CN K.KT.AFU.ALO.DUC.DIO.ALO.DUC

salted paper, plain
USE **salted paper**

saltire stretchers
TG.1001
ALT **saltire stretcher**
UF arched stretchers
hooped stretchers
rising stretchers
stretchers, arched
stretchers, hooped
stretchers, rising
stretchers, saltire
CN V.TG.ALO.HIK.ALO.ALO.AXC.AFU

saltires
USE **Saint Andrew's crosses**

saltwater aquariums
USE **marine aquariums**

saltworks
RK.637 (R)
SN Factories where salt is made on a commercial scale. (W)
CN V.RK.AFU.ALO.ALO.CLM.ALO.ALO.AFU.AXC.BCW.BIQ

Salur
USE **Salor**

salvation
BM.688 (L,R)
CN B.BM.BZY.ALO.AFU.BUE

Samanid
FL.3545
CN F.FL.ALO.BIQ.AFU.HCQ

Samarkand School
FL.3575
CN F.FL.ALO.BIQ.AFU.HTY.AFU.ALO

Samarqand
USE **Afrasiab**

Samarra
FL.2954
CN F.FL.ALO.AXC.ARI.BCW.AFU.AFU.AFU.ARI

Samarra pottery
USE **Samarra ware**

Samarra ware
FL.3429
UF pottery, Samarra
Samarra pottery
ware, Samarra

CN F.FL.ALO.BIQ.AFU.AFU.AFU.ALO

Sambor Prei Kuk
FL.2324
CN F.FL.ALO.ARI.BCW.ALO.AFU.ALO.AXC

Samburu
FL.631 (L)
UF Loikpo
CN F.FL.ALO.AFU.AXC.AXC.ARI.DIO

Samian
FL.2694
CN F.FL.ALO.AXC.ALO.AFU.ALO.BCW.ALO.CRG

Samian ware
FL.2754
UF ware, Samian
CN F.FL.ALO.AXC.ALO.ALO.ALO.BUE.ALO.BIQ.AFU

sammel brick
MT.123
UF brick, sammel
CN M.MT.AFU.AFU.AFU.AXC.ALO.AFU.AXC.AFU.AFU.ALO.ARI

Samoan
FL.3699 (L)
CN F.FL.ALO.BOK.AXC.BUE

sample books
VW.554 (R)
ALT **sample book**
UF books, sample
books, specimen
specimen books
CN V.VW.AFU.ALO.AFU.AFU.ALO.BZY

sample rooms
RM.102
ALT **sample room**
SN Use for showrooms in hotels specially arranged for the display of merchandise by traveling salesmen.
UF rooms, sample
CN V.RM.AFU.DIO.ALO.AXC.ARI.ARI

samples
VB.110 (L)
ALT **sample**
UF specimens
CN V.VB.ALO.BUE.BOK

San
FL.553 (L)
UF Bushmen
CN F.FL.ALO.AFU.AXC.ARI.ALO.ARI

San Blas
FL.1550 (L)
CN F.FL.ALO.ALO.ARI.ALO.BOK.AFU.ALO

San Cristoval Island
FL.3668 (L)
CN F.FL.ALO.BOK.ALO.BOK.BIQ

San Francisco Mogollon
FL.949
UF Mogollon, San Francisco
CN F.FL.ALO.ALO.ALO.AFU.ALO.ARI.BIQ.BCW.BIQ

San Francisco red
FL.947
UF red, San Francisco
CN F.FL.ALO.ALO.ALO.AFU.ALO.ARI.BIQ.BCW.AXC.AFU.ALO

San Ildefonso
FL.1472
CN F.FL.ALO.ALO.ARI.AFU.CFS.CRG.AFU.BIQ

San José Mogote
FL.1052
CN F.FL.ALO.ALO.ALO.ALO.AFU.ALO.AXC.AFU.AFU

San Juan Plumbate
USE **San Juan (pottery style)**

San Juan (pottery style)
FL.1046
UF Plumbate, San Juan
San Juan Plumbate
CN F.FL.ALO.ALO.ALO.ALO.AFU.ALO.ARI.ALO.ALO.ALO.ALO

San Juan (Rio Grande Pueblo)
FL.1473
CN F.FL.ALO.ALO.ARI.AFU.CFS.CRG.AFU.BOK

San Pedro Cochise
FL.931
UF Cochise, San Pedro
CN F.FL.ALO.ALO.ALO.AFU.ALO.ARI.BIQ.ALO.ALO

SAN (styrene-acrylonitrile)
USE **styrene-acrylonitrile**

San-ts'ai
USE **Sancai**

Sanage
FL.2033
CN F.FL.ALO.ARI.ALO.ALO.ALO.ALO.ALO.DIO

sanatoriums
RK.755 (A,L,B)
ALT **sanatorium**
SN Use for health care facilities for the chronically ill.
UF sanitariums
CN V.RK.AFU.ALO.ALO.CXA.ALO.AFU.AXC.BCW

Sanaviron
FL.1625 (L)
CN F.FL.ALO.ALO.ARI.ARI.ALO.ALO.BZY

Sanborn maps
USE **fire insurance maps**

Sancai
FL.1950
UF San-ts'ai
three-color ware
ware, three-color
CN F.FL.ALO.ARI.ALO.AFU.AFU.AXC.ARI.BOK

sanctuaries
RM.333 (B,R)
ALT **sanctuary**
SN Includes the most sacred spaces of religious buildings and the parts of Christian churches containing the altar.
UF agiasteria
CN V.RM.AFU.DIO.AXC.ALO.ARI

sanctuaries (shrines)
USE **shrines**

sanctuaries, bird
USE **bird sanctuaries**

sanctuaries, fire
USE **fire temples**

sanctuaries, marine
USE **marine parks**

sanctuaries, wildlife
USE **wildlife refuges**

sand
MT.2068 (L,B)
CN M.MT.AFU.AFU.ARI.BOK.ALO.BOK

sand bars
RD.226 (L)
ALT **sand bar**
UF bars, sand
sandbanks
shoals
CN V.RD.ARI.AFU.AXC.AFU.ALO.AXC.BOK

sand-blast
USE **sandblasting**

sand casting
KT.135 (L)
ALT **sand cast**
SN The process of casting metal sculpture, especially hollow bronzes, in a mold made of foundry sand. (MAYER)
UF casting, sand
CN K.KT.AFU.ALO.DOI.ARI.AXC

sand concrete, foamed
USE **foamed sand concrete**

sand dunes
USE **dunes**

sand-faced brick
USE **sand-struck brick**

sand-lime brick
MT.43 (L,B)
UF brick, sand-lime
CN M.MT.AFU.AFU.AFU.ALO.ALO.ALO

sand-struck brick
MT.136

SN Brick formed in a mold that has been sprinkled with sand to facilitate removal. (MEANS)
UF brick, sand-faced
brick, sand-struck
sand-faced brick
CN M.MT.AFU.AFU.AFU.AXC.ALO.AFU .AXC.ALO.ALO.ALO.AFU

sand, building
USE **building sand**

sand, flooring
USE **flooring sand**

sand, foundry
USE **foundry sand**

sand, glass
USE **glass sand**

sand, green
USE **green earth**

sand, molding
USE **foundry sand**

sand, paving
USE **paving sand**

sand, roofing
USE **roofing sand**

sand, sandblast
USE **sandblast sand**

sand, silica
USE **silica sand**

sandalwood
MT.1395 (L)
SN A compact close-grained fragrant yellowish wood that is the heartwood of an Indo-Malayan parasitic tree. (W)
CN M.MT.AFU.AFU.ALO.BIQ.DCU.AFU .AFU.ALO.DIO

sandarac
MT.1508
SN Hard, brittle resin from the Callitris quadrivalis or alerce tree; widely employed for making protective and decorative coatings and artists' paint vehicles. (AHMT)
CN M.MT.AFU.AFU.ALO.BOK.DUC

sandarac (pigment)
USE **realgar**

sandarach
USE **moderate orange yellow**
strong orange yellow
vivid reddish orange

Sandawe
FL.591 (L)
CN F.FL.ALO.AFU.AXC.AXC.AFU.BZY

sandbanks
USE **sand bars**

sandblast sand
MT.2077
SN Sand employed in a blast of air for cleaning castings, removal of paint, cleaning of metal articles, and for giving a dull, rough finish to glass or metal goods. (MH)
UF sand, sandblast
CN M.MT.AFU.AFU.ARI.BOK.ALO.BOK .BCW

sandblasters
USE **sandblasting equipment**

sandblasting
KT.67 (L)
ALT **sandblasted**
SN Using sand, propelled by an air blast, on a metal, masonry, concrete, or other surface to remove dirt, rust, or paint, or to decorate it with a rough texture. (DAC)
UF sand-blast
CN K.KT.AFU.ALO.BIQ.AFU.AFU

sandblasting equipment
TB.497 (L)
SN Equipment used for cleaning or removing surfaces by a controlled stream of pressure-ejected material consisting of sand or manufactured grit. (STEIN)
UF equipment, sandblasting
sandblasters
CN V.TB.AFU.ARI.EWY.AFU.AFU

sanders
TB.520 (L,N)
ALT **sander**
SN Machines designed to smooth wood and remove saw or lathe marks and other imperfections; ranging in size from hand-held to large drums or belts capable of surfacing a full-size panel. (MEANS)
CN V.TB.AFU.ARI.EWY.ALO.CXA

Sanders blue
USE **ultramarine blue**

sanders, belt
USE **belt sanders**

sanders, contour
USE **contour sanders**

sanders, disk
USE **disk sanders**

sanders, drum
USE **sanding disks**

sanders, power
USE **power sanders**

sanders, spindle
USE **spindle sanders**

Sandia
FL.746
CN F.FL.ALO.ALO.ALO.AFU.AFU.ARI. ALO.AFU.ALO

sanding
KT.602
ALT **sanded**
SN Smoothing a surface with abrasive paper or cloth, either by hand or by machine. (DAC)
CN K.KT.AFU.ALO.FUA.AFU.AFU

sanding blocks
TB.526
ALT **sanding block**
SN Devices which hold a piece of sandpaper for sanding by hand. (DAC)
UF blocks, sanding
CN V.TB.AFU.ARI.EWY.ALO.DCU

sanding disks
TB.1130
ALT **sanding disk**
SN Disks or drums with an attached abrasive for power tool application in sanding. (W)
UF disks, sanding
drum sanders
sanders, drum
CN V.TB.ALO.DIO

sanding machines
TB.498 (L)
ALT **sanding machine**
SN Stationary machines having a moving belt, disk, or spindle with an abrasive surface, usually a sandpaper; used for smoothing surfaces. (MEANS)
UF machines, sanding
CN V.TB.AFU.ARI.EWY.AFU.ALO

sanding slips
USE **contour sanders**

sanding wheels
TB.1135 (N)
ALT **sanding wheel**
UF wheels, sanding
CN V.TB.ALO.DUC.ARI

sandpaper
TB.503 (N)
SN Tough paper coated with an abrasive material, such as silica, garnet, silicon carbide, or aluminum oxide; used for smoothing and polishing.
CN V.TB.AFU.ARI.EWY.ALO.AFU.ARI

sandstone
MT.701 (A,L,R)
SN A consolidated sand rock, consisting of sand grains united with a natural cementing material; the most common sand in sandstone is quartz, with considerable feldspar, lime, mica, and clayey matter. (MH)
UF arenaceous rock
psammites
rock, arenaceous
CN M.MT.AFU.AFU.AFU.DCU.AFU.ALO .AFU.ARI

sandstone, Amherst

USE **Amherst sandstone**

sandstone, Aquia
USE **Aquia Creek sandstone**

sandstone, Aquia Creek
USE **Aquia Creek sandstone**

sandstone, argillaceous
USE **argillaceous sandstone**

sandstone, calcareous
USE **calcareous sandstone**

sandstone, Dunn County
USE **Dunville sandstone**

sandstone, Dunville
USE **Dunville sandstone**

sandstone, feldspathic
USE **feldspathic sandstone**

sandstone, ferruginous
USE **ferruginous sandstone**

sandstone, graywether
USE **sarsen**

sandstone, micaceous
USE **micaceous sandstone**

sandstone, Portland
USE **Portland sandstone**

sandstone, Potsdam
USE **Potsdam sandstone**

sandstone, red
USE **ferruginous sandstone**

sandstone, Seneca
USE **Seneca sandstone**

sandstone, silica
USE **siliceous sandstone**

sandstone, siliceous
USE **siliceous sandstone**

sandstone, Stancliffe
USE **Stancliffe sandstone**

sandstorms
KM.122 (L)
CN K.KM.AFU.CXA.BIQ.BIQ

sandwich beams
USE **flitch beams**

sandwich construction
KT.34 (L)
SN Consists of two thin, dense, strong, and hard facing layers of plastic, metal, or wood bonded with adhesives to a core of lightweight material to form a panel. (BCMTC)
UF construction, sandwich
CN K.KT.AFU.ALO.BCW.ARI.AFU.BIQ.AFU

Sandwich Island
USE **Hawaiian**

sandwich materials
USE **composite materials**

sandy limestone
USE **siliceous limestone**

sang de boeuf
MT.2570
SN An opaque claret red to brownish red reduced copper glaze developed in China during the Kanxi period and used chiefly in porcelain ware. (W)
UF rouge flambé
CN M.MT.AFU.ARI.CRG.ARI.ARI.AFU.ARI.BCW

sanghas
RG.200
ALT **sangha**
SN Use for communities of Buddhist monks; may also be used for Jain religious communities.
CN V.RG.AFU.AFU.DUC.BOK

Sangkalok
USE **Sawankhalok**

Sango
FL.535 (L)
CN F.FL.ALO.AFU.AXC.ALO.ALO.BIQ.ALO.CFS

Sangoan
FL.54
CN F.FL.ALO.AFU.AFU.ALO.ALO.ALO

Sangu
FL.406
UF Shango
CN F.FL.ALO.AFU.AXC.ALO.AFU.ALO.BOK

sanguine
USE **red chalk**

sanitariums
USE **sanatoriums**

sanitary drainage
USE **sanitary drainage systems**

sanitary drainage systems
RT.1446
ALT **sanitary drainage system**
SN Use for building drainage systems that carry away waste matter from sinks and toilets.
UF drainage systems, sanitary
drainage, sanitary
sanitary drainage
sanitary systems
systems, sanitary
systems, sanitary drainage
CN V.RT.ALO.BCW.ALO.AFU.AFU

sanitary engineering
KD.220 (A,L)
UF engineering, sanitary
CN K.KD.AFU.ARI.BIQ.AXC.ALO.AFU

sanitary engineers
HG.633 (L)
ALT **sanitary engineer**
UF engineers, sanitary
CN H.HG.AFU.AXC.BZY.BCW.BCW.ALO

sanitary fittings
USE **plumbing fixtures**

sanitary landfills
RK.1472 (L)
ALT **sanitary landfill**
SN Use for refuse dumps over which layers of earth or ashes are heaped regularly to control pests and odors.
UF landfills, sanitary
CN V.RK.ALO.ALO.AXC.AFU.ALO.AFU

sanitary sewers
RK.545
ALT **sanitary sewer**
SN Use for sewers that carry liquid and solid wastes from, for example, dwellings, businesses, and factories, and that do not carry ground, surface, or storm waters.
UF sewers, sanitary
CN V.RK.AFU.ALO.ALO.CFS.ALO.AFU.ALO.AFU.ALO

sanitary systems
USE **sanitary drainage systems**

Sanjo Street School
FL.2102
CN F.FL.ALO.ARI.ALO.ALO.ALO.BCW.AXC

Sankore
FL.89
CN F.FL.ALO.AFU.ALO.AFU.BOK.ALO

Sanpoil
FL.1419 (L)
CN F.FL.ALO.ALO.ARI.AFU.BUE.DIO

Santa Ana
FL.1474
CN F.FL.ALO.ALO.ARI.AFU.CFS.CRG.AFU.BUE

Santa Clara
FL.1475
CN F.FL.ALO.ALO.ARI.AFU.CFS.CRG.AFU.BZY

Santa Cruz Island
FL.3669 (L)
CN F.FL.ALO.BOK.ALO.BOK.BOK

Santa Maria
FL.1089
CN F.FL.ALO.ALO.ALO.ALO.ALO.ALO.AFU.AXC

Santa Maria (pottery style)
FL.1189
UF Diaguita, Northern
Northern Diaguita
CN F.FL.ALO.ALO.ALO.ARI.BCW.ALO.AFU.AXC

Santa Rosa-Swift Creek

FL.896
CN F.FL.ALO.ALO.ALO.AFU.ALO.ALO.BOK.CFS

Santarém
FL.1129
CN F.FL.ALO.ALO.ALO.ARI.ARI.ALO.ALO

Santee Dakota
FL.1398 (L)
UF Dakota, Santee
Sisseton
CN F.FL.ALO.ALO.ARI.AFU.BOK.FCS.AFU.AFU

Santo Domingo
FL.1476
CN F.FL.ALO.ALO.ARI.AFU.CFS.CRG.AFU.CFS

santorin
MT.637
SN A lightweight, gray, volcanic tuff, used as pozzolana. (DAC)
CN M.MT.AFU.AFU.AFU.DCU.AFU.AFU.ALO.ALO.ALO.AXC.ALO

Saô
FL.372
UF Sai
So
CN F.FL.ALO.AFU.AXC.AFU.AXC.ALO.BIQ

Sao Empire
FL.119
UF Chad Civilization
Sai
So
CN F.FL.ALO.AFU.ALO.AFU.BZY

sap
MT.1059 (L)
CN M.MT.AFU.AFU.ALO.BIQ.BUE.BIQ

sap green
MT.1646
UF bladder green
green, bladder
green, iris
green, sap
iris green
Saftgrün
verd vessie
vert de Vessie
CN M.MT.AFU.AFU.ARI.AFU.AFU.ALO.ALO.AXC.ALO.ARI

sap houses
USE **sugar houses**

sap pine
USE **loblolly pine**

Sapahn
USE **Sapo**

Sapan
USE **Sapo**

Sapi-Portuguese
FL.174
UF Bulom
Sherbro (Sapi-Portuguese)
CN F.FL.ALO.AFU.ARI.AFU.ALO

Sapo
FL.315
UF Pahn
Sapahn
Sapan
CN F.FL.ALO.AFU.AXC.AFU.ARI.ARI.ARI.AFU

saponified oil
MT.1999
UF oil, saponified
CN M.MT.AFU.AFU.ARI.ARI.ARI.AXC

saponin
MT.1060 (L)
SN Powdered bark of the soapbark tree that has a foamy, soaplike character when mixed with water; used chiefly as a mild detergent in picture cleaning. (MAYER)
CN M.MT.AFU.AFU.ALO.BIQ.BUE.BOK

sappanwood
MT.1128
UF Caesalpinia sappan
CN M.MT.AFU.AFU.ALO.BIQ.DCU.AFU.AFU.AFU.BUE.AFU

sapphire
MT.501 (L,R)
CN M.MT.AFU.AFU.AFU.CFS.AFU.BUE.ARI

sapphire blue
USE **dark blue**
deep purplish blue
strong blue
strong purplish blue
vivid blue
vivid purplish blue

sapphire blue, deep
USE **dark blue**
deep blue
moderate purplish blue

Sarab ware
FL.3030
UF ware, Sarab
CN F.FL.ALO.AXC.ARI.BIQ.ALO.AXC.BUE

Saracenic
FL.3605 (L,B)
CN F.FL.ALO.BIQ.ARI

Saragash phase
FL.2136
CN F.FL.ALO.ARI.ARI.AFU.BIQ.BCW.ARI

Sarakole
USE **Soninke**

sarasins
USE **portcullises**

Sarawak
FL.2399
CN F.FL.ALO.ARI.BCW.BCW.ALO

Sarcee
USE **Sarsi**

sarcocolla
MT.1055
SN Gum from some species of Astragalus or Penaea, mentioned in ancient writings and also in English 18th- and early 19th-century painting recipes.
CN M.MT.AFU.AFU.ALO.BIQ.BUE.AXC.BOK

sarcophagi (cellerets)
USE **cellerets**

sardonyx
MT.549 (R)
SN An onyx marked by parallel layers of sard and of mineral of another color. (W)
CN M.MT.AFU.AFU.AFU.CFS.AFU.GRC.AFU.ARI.AFU.ALO.AFU

Sargonid
FL.2969
CN F.FL.ALO.AXC.ARI.BCW.AFU.AXC.ALO

Sari ware
FL.3548
UF ware, Sari
CN F.FL.ALO.BIQ.AFU.HCQ.AFU.ALO

Sarmatian
FL.1803 (L,R)
CN F.FL.ALO.ARI.AFU.AXC.DCU

Sarnath
FL.2202
CN F.FL.ALO.ARI.AXC.ALO.AFU.ARI.BIQ.AFU

Sarqaq
FL.794
CN F.FL.ALO.ALO.ALO.AFU.ALO.AFU.ALO.AFU.ARI

Sarrancolin marble
MT.758
SN A variegated French breccia marble, usually with gray, red, or yellow predominating, quarried near Sarrancolin in the Pyrenees. (MAYER)
UF marble, Sarrancolin
CN M.MT.AFU.AFU.AFU.DCU.AFU.ARI.ARI.ALO.AFU.CLM

Sarreguemines pottery
FL.3370 (R)
UF pottery, Sarreguemines
CN F.FL.ALO.BCW.ALO.AXC.DIO.BCW.AXC.ALO.ALO

sarsen
MT.894
SN A large, loose residual mass of stone

left after the erosion of a once continuous bed or layer; also, one of the large sandstone blocks scattered over the English chalk downs. (W)
UF druid stone
gray wether
graywether sandstone
heathstone
sandstone, graywether
stone, druid
wether, gray
CN M.MT.AFU.AFU.AFU.DCU.ALO.CRG

Sarsi
FL.1238 (L)
UF Sarcee
CN F.FL.ALO.ALO.ARI.AFU.AFU.ARI.DCU

Saryk
FL.3592
UF Saryq
CN F.FL.ALO.BIQ.AFU.IFM.ARI.BCW

Saryq
USE **Saryk**

sash-bars
USE **muntins**

sash chains
TF.29
ALT **sash chain**
SN Metal chains used in place of sash cords to connect a vertically hung sash with its counterweight. (MEANS)
UF chains, sash
CN V.TF.AFU.AFU.AFU.AFU.ALO.ALO

sash chisels
TB.865
ALT **sash chisel**
SN Chisels having a wide blade honed on both sides; used for deep cutting, such as the mortises in pulley stiles. (MEANS)
UF chisels, pocket
chisels, sash
pocket chisels
CN V.TB.AFU.BCW.CFS.ALO.AFU.BUE.BOK

sash clamps
TB.1053
ALT **sash clamp**
SN Somewhat lighter versions of joiner's clamps. (SALAM)
UF clamps, sash
CN V.TB.AFU.BCW.CFS.ALO.ALO.BCW.AXC.AFU

sash cords
TF.30
ALT **sash cord**
SN Ropes connecting a sash with its counterweight in a double-hung window. (MEANS)
UF cords, sash
CN V.TF.AFU.AFU.AFU.AFU.ALO.ARI

sash counterweights
USE **sash weights**

sash fasteners
USE **window locks**

sash fasts
USE **window locks**

sash fillister planes
TB.919
ALT **sash fillister plane**
SN Planes with projecting arms, used to cut grooves on the side farthest from the worker.
UF planes, sash fillister
CN V.TB.AFU.BCW.CFS.ALO.AFU.DUC.ALO.BCW.ALO

sash holders
USE **window locks**

sash lifts
TF.31
ALT **sash lift**
SN Devices attached to a sash rail by which the window may be raised or lowered; may be flush-mounted cups or surface-mounted bars or hooks.
UF lifts, sash
lifts, window
pulls, sash
pulls, window
sash pulls
window lifts
window pulls
CN V.TF.AFU.AFU.AFU.AFU.ALO.AXC

sash locks
USE **window locks**

sash pins
TF.32
ALT **sash pin**
SN Narrow rods inserted through holes drilled into both upper and lower sashes so that the lower sash may be held partly opened yet immobile. (DITTRI)
UF pins, sash
CN V.TF.AFU.AFU.AFU.AFU.ALO.BCW

sash plan corners
USE **ovolo corners**

sash planes
TB.926 (N)
ALT **sash plane**
SN Planes having special notched cutters, used for trimming the inside of a window frame or doorframe. (DAC)
UF planes, sash
CN V.TB.AFU.BCW.CFS.ALO.AFU.DUC.ALO.BZY

sash pulls
USE **sash lifts**

sash weights
TF.33
ALT **sash weight**
SN Weights, usually cast iron, used to balance vertically hung windows. (MEANS)
UF counterweights, sash
sash counterweights
weights, sash
CN V.TF.AFU.AFU.AFU.AFU.ALO.BIQ

sashes
RT.974 (N)
ALT **sash**
SN The frames in which window lights are set. (PUTNAM)
UF sashes, window
window sashes
CN V.RT.AFU.ARI.AFU.AFU.BOK.ALO.BCW

sashes, window
USE **sashes**

sassafras
MT.1306
CN M.MT.AFU.AFU.ALO.BIQ.DCU.AFU.AFU.AFU.LIG

Sassafras albidum
USE **American sassafras**

Sassafras officinale
USE **oleum sassafras**

sassafras, American
USE **American sassafras**

sassafras, oleum
USE **oleum sassafras**

Sassanian
FL.3017 (A,L,B,R)
CN F.FL.ALO.AXC.ARI.BIQ.AFU.BIQ

satellite cities
RD.62 (A,L)
ALT **satellite city**
SN Use for smaller cities on the outskirts of larger metropolitan areas that are independent of the larger city's jurisdiction but within its economic and social orbit. (LOC)
UF cities, satellite
communities, satellite
satellite communities
satellite towns (satellite cities)
towns, satellite (satellite cities)
CN V.RD.AFU.BCW.ALO

satellite cities (new towns)
USE **new towns**

satellite communities
USE **satellite cities**

satellite towns (new towns)
USE **new towns**

satellite towns (satellite cities)
USE **satellite cities**

satellite tracking stations
RK.207 (A,L)
ALT **satellite tracking station**

UF earth stations
ground stations
stations, earth
stations, ground
stations, satellite tracking
tracking stations, satellite
CN V.RK.AFU.ALO.ALO.ARI.AFU.ARI.ARI

satin
MT.1875 (L)
SN Cloth, usually of silk but also of wool and linen, that is shiny on one side and dull on the other, created by a special weave leaving numerous warp floats on the surface. (NYLAN)
CN M.MT.AFU.AFU.ARI.ALO.ALO.ALO.ALO.DIO

satinee
MT.1305
UF Ferolia guianensis
CN M.MT.AFU.AFU.ALO.BIQ.DCU.AFU.AFU.AFU.LCM.BCW

satinwood
MT.1309
SN Very hard yellowish brown wood of an East Indian tree (Cloroxylon swietenia) of the family Meliaceae; has a satiny luster and is used especially for fine woodwork and tools. (W)
CN M.MT.AFU.AFU.ALO.BIQ.DCU.AFU.AFU.AFU.LOA

satire
BM.11 (L,B,R)
CN B.BM.AFU.AFU.AFU.BOK

satirists
HG.190 (L)
ALT **satirist**
CN H.HG.AFU.AXC.AXC.ARI.AFU.AFU.CFS

Satsuma
FL.2035 (L)
CN F.FL.ALO.ARI.ALO.ALO.ALO.ALO.ALO.DOI

saturation
USE **intensity**

saturine red
USE **red lead**

Saturn red
USE **red lead**

Satvahana
USE **Andhra**

saucer adzes
USE **hollowing adzes**

saucer domes
RT.396
ALT **saucer dome**
SN Domes with a rise less than the radius. (DAC)
UF domes, saucer
domes, segmental
segmental domes
CN V.RT.AFU.AFU.AFU.BIQ.AFU.AFU.BOK

Sauk
FL.1331 (L)
UF Sac
CN F.FL.ALO.ALO.ARI.AFU.BCW.BZY

Saulteaux
FL.1223 (L)
UF Northern Ojibwa
Ojibwa, Northern
CN F.FL.ALO.ALO.ARI.AFU.AFU.ALO.BIQ

saunas
RM.80 (A,L,B,R)
ALT **sauna**
UF baths, Finnish
Finnish baths
CN V.RM.AFU.DIO.ALO.ALO.BUE

Saunders blue
USE **ultramarine blue**

Sauveterrian
FL.2483
CN F.FL.ALO.AXC.AFU.AXC.BZY

Sava
FL.3569
CN F.FL.ALO.BIQ.AFU.HIK.BCW.BOK

Savannah River
FL.828
CN F.FL.ALO.ALO.ALO.AFU.ALO.ALO.ALO.ARI

savannas
RD.249 (L)
ALT **savanna**
SN Treeless plains; used especially for land in the southeast United States; also tropical or subtropical grassland usually containing scattered trees or shrubs. (W)
CN V.RD.ARI.AFU.BCW.ALO.AFU.AFU.BCW

savin
USE **juniper**

savings banks
RK.132 (L)
ALT **savings bank**
UF banks, savings
CN V.RK.AFU.ALO.ALO.ALO.ALO.AFU.BCW

Savonarola chairs
TG.118
ALT **Savonarola chair**
SN Collector's term for Italian Renaissance chairs with numerous crosspieces linked up along the sides. Named for the 15th-century reforming monk, although it is questionable that such chairs were actually used by him.
UF chairs, Savonarola
chairs, Savonarola cross
cross chairs, Savonarola
Savonarola cross chairs
CN V.TG.AFU.AFU.ALO.AFU.AFU.AFU.MWQ.ALO

Savonarola cross chairs
USE **Savonarola chairs**

saw benches
USE **bench saws**

saw blades
TB.1117
ALT **saw blade**
UF blades, saw
CN V.TB.ALO.AXC.AFU

saw clamps
TB.1055 (N)
ALT **saw clamp**
SN Clamps used to hold saw blades during sharpening. (HUMMEL)
UF blocks, whetting
clamps, saw
whetting blocks
CN V.TB.AFU.BCW.CFS.ALO.ALO.BCW.BIQ

saw filing horses
USE **saw-sharpening horses**

saw-kerf binding
KT.517
SN Type of bookbinding in which slanted binding cuts are made in the back edge of a book; useful for old magazines or books too deteriorated to be sewn for rebinding. (CRBOOK)
UF binding, saw-kerf
CN K.KT.AFU.ALO.ELK.ARI.ALO

saw sets
TB.442 (N)
ALT **saw set**
SN Plier-like tools which set the teeth of a saw after they have been sharpened. They may be adjusted for use on different saws. (BLACKB)
CN V.TB.AFU.ARI.EFQ.ALO.BUE

saw-sharpening horses
TB.474 (N)
ALT **saw-sharpening horse**
SN Horses used to hold saw blades in place during sharpening.
UF horses, saw filing
horses, saw-sharpening
saw filing horses
CN V.TB.AFU.ARI.ERE.AFU.ALO

Sawankhalok
FL.2425
UF Sangkalok
Swankalok
CN F.FL.ALO.ARI.BCW.BOK.ALO.ALO

sawbuck tables
TG.698
ALT **sawbuck table**

SN A variant form of trestle table with an X-shaped trestle at either end.
UF braced tables
tables, braced
tables, sawbuck
CN V.TG.AFU.AFU.BIQ.BOK.AFU.DUC.AXC

sawbucks
USE **sawhorses**

sawdust
MT.1454 (L)
UF waste, wood
wood waste
CN M.MT.AFU.AFU.ALO.BIQ.DCU.ALO.CXA

sawed joints
TF.613
ALT **sawed joint**
UF joints, sawed
CN V.TF.ALO.ARI.AFU.ARI

sawhorses
TB.475 (L,N)
ALT **sawhorse**
SN Four-legged supports, usually used in pairs, made primarily to hold wood while being sawed. (DAC)
UF finishing horses
horses, finishing
horses, saw
sawbucks
CN V.TB.AFU.ARI.ERE.AFU.ARI

sawing
KT.88 (L)
ALT **sawed**
CN K.KT.AFU.ALO.BUE.ALO

sawing tackles
TB.476 (N)
ALT **sawing tackle**
SN X- or Y-shaped wood devices used to support logs during sawing.
UF tackles, sawing
CN V.TB.AFU.ARI.ERE.AFU.ARI.AFU

sawmills
RK.657 (A,L,B)
ALT **sawmill**
SN Factories in which logs are converted to lumber by running them through a series of saws. (MEANS)
CN V.RK.AFU.ALO.ALO.CLM.ALO.ALO.AFU.AXC.DOI

sawmills, gang
USE **gang sawmills**

sawmills, gate-type
USE **gate saws**

sawmills, muley
USE **muley sawmills**

sawmills, up-and-down
USE **up-and-down sawmills**

Sawos
FL.3652 (L)
UF Tshuosh
CN F.FL.ALO.BOK.ALO.BCW.ALO.BCW.AFU.BIQ

saws
TB.133 (L,N,B,R)
ALT **saw**
SN Cutting tools having thin, flat metal blades, bands, or stiff plates with cutting teeth along the edges. (DAC)
CN V.TB.AFU.ARI.AXC.ALO.CLM

saws, angle
USE **dovetail saws**

saws, back
USE **backsaws**

saws, band
USE **band saws**

saws, bayonet
USE **saber saws**

saws, bead
USE **bead saws**

saws, bench
USE **bench saws**

saws, betty
USE **felloe saws**

saws, blitz
USE **blitz-back saws**

saws, blitz-back
USE **blitz-back saws**

saws, board
USE **pit saws**

saws, bow
USE **bow saws**

saws, bracket
USE **fretsaws**

saws, buck
USE **bucksaws**

saws, buhl
USE **buhl saws**

saws, buzz
USE **circular saws**

saws, cabinet
USE **cabinet saws**

saws, carcass
USE **carcass saws**

saws, chain
USE **chain saws**

saws, chair web
USE **web saws**

saws, circular
USE **circular saws**

saws, compass
USE **compass saws**

saws, concrete
USE **concrete saws**

saws, coping
USE **coping saws**

saws, corner
USE **dovetail saws**

saws, crosscut
USE **crosscut saws**

saws, crown
USE **crown saws**

saws, cylinder
USE **crown saws**

saws, donkey
USE **felloe saws**

saws, dovetail
USE **dovetail saws**

saws, drunken
USE **drunken saws**

saws, electric-portable
USE **electric-portable saws**

saws, endless
USE **band saws**

saws, felloe
USE **felloe saws**

saws, frame
USE **frame saws**

saws, frame pit
USE **frame pit saws**

saws, gate
USE **gate saws**

saws, grooving
USE **stairbuilder's saws**

saws, grub
USE **grub saws**

saws, hand
USE **hand saws**

saws, hole
USE **crown saws**

saws, inlaying
USE **buhl saws**

saws, Jesus
USE **felloe saws**

saws, keyhole
USE **keyhole saws**

saws, lock
USE **locksaws**

saws, long
USE **crosscut saws**

saws, miter
USE **miter-box saws**
tenon saws

saws, miter-box
USE **miter-box saws**

saws, notching
USE **stairbuilder's saws**

saws, one-man crosscut
USE **one-man crosscut saws**

saws, open
USE **open saws**

saws, open pit
USE **open pit saws**

saws, pad
USE **keyhole saws**

saws, panel
USE **panel saws**

saws, pendulum
USE **pendulum saws**

saws, pit
USE **pit saws**

saws, plank
USE **pit saws**

saws, port
USE **compass saws**

saws, portable circular
USE **electric-portable saws**

saws, rabbet
USE **rabbet saws**

saws, radial-arm
USE **radial-arm saws**

saws, ribbon
USE **band saws**

saws, rip
USE **ripsaws**

saws, round
USE **crown saws**

saws, saber
USE **saber saws**

saws, scribing
USE **coping saws**

saws, scroll
USE **scroll saws**

saws, sheave
USE **crown saws**

saws, skill
USE **electric-portable saws**

saws, square hole
USE **square hole saws**

saws, stairbuilder's
USE **stairbuilder's saws**

saws, sweep
USE **bow saws**

saws, swing
USE **pendulum saws**

saws, table
USE **table saws**

saws, tenon
USE **tenon saws**

saws, thwart
USE **two-handed crosscut saws**

saws, trenching
USE **stairbuilder's saws**

saws, trepan
USE **crown saws**

saws, turning
USE **bow saws**

saws, two-handed crosscut
USE **two-handed crosscut saws**

saws, two-man crosscut
USE **two-handed crosscut saws**

saws, up-and-down
USE **felloe saws**

saws, veneer
USE **veneer saws**

saws, web
USE **web saws**

saws, wobble
USE **drunken saws**

saws, woodcutter's
USE **bucksaws**

sawtooth roofs
RT.437 (B)
ALT **sawtooth roof**
SN Roof systems that have a number of parallel roof surfaces of triangular section with a profile similar to the teeth in a saw; usually the steeper side is glazed. (DAC)
UF northlight roofs
roofs, northlight
roofs, sawtooth
CN V.RT.AFU.AFU.AFU.BIQ.ARI.AFU.AFU.AFU.BZY

sawyer's props
TB.477 (N)
ALT **sawyer's prop**
SN Supports consisting of two crossed wood clubs; used to support logs that are being sawed. (SLOANE)
UF props, sawyer's
CN V.TB.AFU.ARI.ERE.AFU.ARI.ALO

sawyers
HG.546
ALT **sawyer**
CN H.HG.AFU.AXC.BUE.ARI.DIO.ARI

saxes
USE **zaxes**

Saxon blue
USE **smalt**

Saxony green
USE **cobalt green**

Sayaco
USE **Amahuaca**

Sb
USE **antimony**

SBS
USE **sick building syndrome**

scabbard planes
USE **splint planes**

scabbing hammers
USE **scabbling hammers**

scabbling hammers
TB.607
ALT **scabbling hammer**
SN Hammers used for rough-dressing stone, with one end pointed for picking. (MEANS)
UF hammers, scabbling
scabbing hammers
CN V.TB.AFU.BCW.BCW.ALO.EFQ.BIQ

scaenae
RT.1271
ALT **scaena**
SN In ancient theaters, the structures facing the audience and forming the background before which performances were given. (RHDEL2)
UF skene
CN V.RT.AFU.BUE.ARI.BIQ.AFU

scaenae frontes
RT.1274
ALT **scaena frons**
SN Use for the facades of the stage buildings of Roman theaters.
CN V.RT.AFU.BUE.ARI.BIQ.ALO.ALO

scaffold nails
USE **double-headed nails**

scaffolders
HG.608
ALT **scaffolder**
CN H.HG.AFU.AXC.BZY.AFU.EWY

scaffolding, bracket
USE **bracket scaffolding**

scaffolding, bricklayer's
USE **bricklayer's scaffolding**

scaffolding, suspended
USE **suspended scaffolding**

scaffolds
TB.488 (A,L,B)
ALT **scaffold**
SN Temporary elevated platforms or structures for supporting workmen, materials, and tools.
UF staging
CN V.TB.AFU.ARI.ERE.ARI

scaffolds, hanging

USE **suspended scaffolding**

scaffolds, saddle
USE **saddle scaffolds**

scaffolds, trestle
USE **trestle scaffolds**

scagliola
MT.2460 (A,B)
SN Plaster of Paris or cement mixed with pigments, marble dust, and other inert fragments and sometimes glue. (MAYER)
UF marmorino
CN M.MT.AFU.ARI.CRG.AFU.AXC.ARI.BIQ

scalars
BM.817 (L)
CN B.BM.CFS.ARI.CFS

scale
BM.87 (R)
CN B.BM.AFU.AFU.ARI.AFU.ERE

scale drawings
VD.7
ALT **scale drawing**
UF drawings, scale
CN V.VD.AFU.AFU.BCW

scale ornament
USE **scale pattern**

scale pattern
DG.137
SN Pattern in which rows of curved or faceted elements successively overlap one another, resembling fish scales.
UF diaper pattern, petal
fish scale pattern
ornament, scale
pattern, fish scale
pattern, scale
petal diaper pattern
scale ornament
scaling
CN D.DG.AFU.ARI.ALO.BUE.AFU

scaleboard planes
USE **splint planes**

scales, fish
USE **fish scales**

scaling
USE **scale pattern**

scallop shell
MT.948
UF escallop shell
scollop shell
shell, scallop
CN M.MT.AFU.AFU.ALO.AFU.DUC.BCW

scallop work
USE **scalloping**

scalloped capitals
RT.131
ALT **scalloped capital**
SN Capitals in which the four sides are shaped into a series of curves resembling truncated cones.
UF capitals, scalloped
CN V.RT.AFU.AFU.AFU.AXC.BIQ.ALO.ARI.AFU.DIO

scalloping
DG.118
ALT **scalloped**
SN Ornament in the form of a series of small convex curves; often used as an edging.
UF scallop work
scallops
CN D.DG.AFU.ARI.ALO.ARI.BOK

scalloping punches
TB.676 (N)
ALT **scalloping punch**
UF punches, scalloping
CN V.TB.AFU.BCW.BIQ.AFU.ALO.BZY.BUE

scallops
USE **scalloping**

scampers
USE **scorpers**

Scandinavian
FL.3057 (L,B)
CN F.FL.ALO.BCW.AFU.DUC

scantling
MT.1448
SN Any square-edged piece of hardwood of nonstandard dimensions. (DAC)
CN M.MT.AFU.AFU.ALO.BIQ.DCU.ALO.BOK.ARI.BIQ.ALO

scapes
USE **apophyges**

Scapigliatura
FL.3406
CN F.FL.ALO.BCW.ALO.AXC.DIO.BOK.BCW.ARI

scarcements
RT.677
ALT **scarcement**
SN Setbacks in the face of a wall or in an earthen embankment; also, footings or ledges formed by the setting back of a wall. (HAS)
CN V.RT.AFU.AFU.AFU.BIQ.BUE.ALO.ALO.BUE

scarf joints
TF.690
ALT **scarf joint**
SN Joints made by beveling the ends of two pieces of lumber or plywood to be joined. The cut on each piece is angled so that the surfaces of the two pieces being joined are flush. (MEANS)
UF joints, scarf
joints, scarfed
joints, scarped
scarfed joints
scarped joints
CN V.TF.ALO.ARI.AXC.ARI.BOK

scarfed joints
USE **scarf joints**

Scarified-Guacamayo
FL.1088
CN F.FL.ALO.ALO.ALO.ALO.ALO.ALO.AFU.ARI

scarified ware
FL.1102
UF ware, scarified
CN F.FL.ALO.ALO.ALO.ALO.ALO.ALO.ALO.AXC.ARI

scarifiers
TB.628
ALT **scarifier**
SN Plastering tools with long wirelike teeth; used to scratch the surface of unset plaster providing a sufficient bond for the next coat.
CN V.TB.AFU.BCW.BCW.ALO.GRC.AXC

scarifiers (earthmoving equipment)
TB.46 (N)
ALT **scarifier (earthmoving equipment)**
SN Machines or attachments for a tractor or grader having a long tooth or series of teeth that can be lowered to tear up surface soil or pavement. (DAC)
CN V.TB.AFU.ARI.AFU.ARI.BOK

scarifying
KT.691
ALT **scarified**
SN A type of pottery decoration consisting of alternate groups of incised lines and patches, usually in red color. Characteristic of Pre-Hispanic Central America. (MUSER)
CN K.KT.AFU.ALO.GRC.BIQ.AFU

scarlet
USE **deep pink**
moderate red
strong red
strong reddish orange
vivid red
vivid reddish orange

scarlet lake
USE **moderate red**
strong red

scarlet madder
USE **strong yellowish pink**

scarlet madder (natural dye)
USE **madder**

scarlet oak
MT.1249

UF oak, scarlet
Quercus coccinea
CN M.MT.AFU.AFU.ALO.BIQ.DCU.AFU.AFU.AFU.IRA.DUC

scarlet red
USE **vivid red**

scarlet vermilion
MT.1686
SN The bluish, or least yellowish, variety of vermilion. (MAYER)
UF vermilion, scarlet
CN M.MT.AFU.AFU.ARI.AFU.AFU.ALO.ALO.BCW.AFU.AXC.BCW

scarlet vermilion (color)
USE **vivid reddish orange**

scarlet ware
FL.2996
UF ware, scarlet
CN F.FL.ALO.AXC.ARI.BCW.ALO.BCW.BOK

scarlet, brilliant
USE **iodine scarlet**

scarlet, iodine
USE **iodine scarlet**

scarlet, pure
USE **iodine scarlet**

scarlet, royal
USE **iodine scarlet**

scarped joints
USE **scarf joints**

scarps
USE **escarpments**

scarps (landform components)
USE **escarpments (landform components)**

scattered-site housing
RG.72 (A)
SN Public housing units, either new or rehabilitated, located on noncontiguous sites and intended to promote racial integration by placing relatively small housing units within the context of existing neighborhoods.
UF housing, scattered-site
CN V.RG.AFU.AFU.BOK.AXC.AFU.ALO.AFU.AFU

scaupers
USE **scorpers**

scene stills
USE **film stills**

Scene, American
USE **American Scene**

scenes, genre
USE **genre**

scenic lookouts
USE **overlooks**

scenic recreation areas
USE **recreation areas**

scenographers
USE **theater designers**

scenography
USE **theater design**

sceuophylacia
USE **diaconica**

Schadographs
USE **photograms**

schedules
VW.290 (N)
ALT **schedule**
SN Documents showing the order or sequence of planned events, such as lists of arrivals and departures of buses, trains, or airplanes.
UF timetables
CN V.VW.AFU.AFU.AFU.FZU.BOK

schedules (contract documents)
VW.805
ALT **schedule (contract document)**
SN Lists or tables of working drawings or descriptions of the components of a building.
CN V.VW.AFU.ARI.AFU.ARI.ARI

schedules, census
USE **census records**

schedules, comprehensive record
USE **records schedules**

schedules, disposition
USE **records schedules**

schedules, general
USE **general records schedules**

schedules, general records
USE **general records schedules**

schedules, progress
USE **progress schedules**

schedules, records retention
USE **records schedules**

schedules, retention
USE **records schedules**

schedules, tariff
USE **tariff schedules**

schedules, transfer
USE **records schedules**

scheduling
KG.160 (L)
SN Establishing appointed times for events or for the start and completion of projects or series of events.
CN K.KG.AFU.AFU.BIQ.CXA

Scheele's green
MT.1654
UF green, Scheele's
CN M.MT.AFU.AFU.ARI.AFU.AFU.ALO.ALO.AXC.ARI.BIQ.AFU

Scheele's green (color)
USE **moderate yellow green**
strong yellow green
strong yellowish green

schematic design drawings
USE **schematic drawings**

schematic drawings
VD.99
ALT **schematic drawing**
SN Use for diagrammatic drawings done early in the design process of an architectural project, usually drawn to scale and showing the entire project.
UF design drawings, schematic
drawings, schematic
schematic design drawings
CN V.VD.AFU.ALO.AXC.ARI

schemes, preliminary
USE **preliminary drawings**

schinopsis
USE **quebracho**

schist
MT.849
SN A rock, the constituent minerals of which have assumed a position in more or less closely parallel layers due to metamorphic action. (DAC)
CN M.MT.AFU.AFU.AFU.DCU.AFU.ARI.BIQ

schizzi
USE **preliminary sketches**

schlieren photography
KT.402 (L)
SN Use for quasi-photographic techniques to record different densities in a gas as a pattern of colored bands of light and dark; frequently used to record patterns of radiated heat; not all forms of this technique require a camera and lens.
UF photography, schlieren
CN K.KT.AFU.ALO.DUC.DIO.ARI.ARI.CFS.ARI

schneck oak
USE **southern red oak**

Schnitzer's green
USE **chromium oxide green**

Schnörkelstil
USE **Jugendstil**

scholars
HG.769 (L)
ALT **scholar**
SN Persons who have engaged in advanced study and acquired expertise in some special field along with accuracy and skill in investigation and powers of critical analysis in interpretation of such knowledge.

(W)
CN H.HG.AFU.BIQ.BUE

scholarships
BM.395 (L)
CN B.BM.ARI.CRG.ALO.ARI.AFU

scholasticism
BM.523 (L,R)
CN B.BM.BIQ.AXC.EFQ

school
BM.304
SN Group or succession of persons who in some area of thought or practice are disciples of the same master or are united by a general similarity of principles and methods; also the doctrine or practice followed by such a group of persons.(OCA) In art history, a group of artists working under the influence of a single master or possessing similarity because they practice the same local style. (THDAT)
CN B.BM.AFU.AXC.DOI

school camps
RG.161 (L,B)
ALT **school camp**
UF camps, school
CN V.RG.AFU.AFU.DOI.AXC.AXC

school clock and program systems
USE **clock and program systems**

school complexes
USE **educational complexes**

school districts
RG.259 (L)
ALT **school district**
SN Administrative areas having their own board and power of taxation and serving as the smallest units for administration of a public school system. (W)
UF districts, school
CN V.RG.ALO.AFU.AFU.BOK

school facilities
USE **schools**

school farms
RG.11 (L)
ALT **school farm**
SN Use for farms attached to education facilities either for the purpose of teaching agriculture or providing meats and produce to the parent institution.
UF farms, school
CN V.RG.AFU.AFU.AFU.AFU.ARI.AXC

school libraries
RK.701 (L,B)
ALT **school library**
SN Libraries established in schools for the use of teachers and students. (LG)
UF libraries, school
CN V.RK.AFU.ALO.ALO.CRG.AXC.ALO.ALO

school media centers
USE **learning resource centers**

School of Aphrodisias
USE **Aphrodisian**

School of Meditation
USE **Ch'an**

school records
VW.1063 (L)
ALT **school record**
UF records, school
CN V.VW.AFU.ARI.ALO.CRG

school yearbooks
VW.614 (L)
ALT **school yearbook**
UF yearbooks, school
CN V.VW.AFU.ALO.AFU.CXA.AFU.AFU.AFU.AFU

schoolhouses
USE **schools**

schoolrooms
USE **classrooms**

schools
RK.793 (A,L,N,B,R)
ALT **school**
UF academies (schools)
buildings, educational
educational buildings
facilities, school
facilities, teaching
school facilities
schoolhouses
teaching facilities
CN V.RK.AFU.ALO.ALO.CXA.ARI

schools of architecture
USE **architectural schools**

schools of art
USE **art schools**

schools of nursing
USE **nursing schools**

schools, aeronautical
USE **aeronautical schools**

schools, alternative
USE **free schools**

schools, approved
USE **reformatories**

schools, architectural
USE **architectural schools**

schools, art
USE **art schools**

schools, aviation
USE **aeronautical schools**

schools, boarding
USE **boarding schools**

schools, business
USE **business schools**

schools, church
USE **parochial schools**

schools, commercial
USE **business schools**

schools, consolidated
USE **consolidated schools**

schools, day
USE **day schools**

schools, denominational
USE **parochial schools**

schools, dental
USE **dental schools**

schools, diocesan
USE **parochial schools**

schools, divinity
USE **theological seminaries**

schools, elementary
USE **elementary schools**

schools, engineering
USE **engineering schools**

schools, finishing
USE **preparatory schools**

schools, free
USE **free schools**

schools, grade
USE **elementary schools**

schools, grammar
USE **elementary schools**

schools, Hebrew
USE **Hebrew schools**

schools, high
USE **high schools**

schools, hospital-training
USE **nursing schools**

schools, independent
USE **private schools**

schools, infant
USE **nursery schools**

schools, Jewish day
USE **yeshivas**

schools, Jewish religious
USE **Hebrew schools**

schools, junior high
USE **junior high schools**

schools, language
USE **language schools**

schools, law
USE **law schools**

schools, martial arts

USE **martial arts training centers**

schools, medical
USE **medical schools**

schools, middle
USE **middle schools**

schools, military
USE **military academies**

schools, music
USE **music schools**

schools, naval
USE **naval schools**

schools, nursery
USE **nursery schools**

schools, nursing
USE **nursing schools**

schools, parish
USE **parochial schools**

schools, parochial
USE **parochial schools**

schools, play
USE **play schools**

schools, polytechnical
USE **polytechnics**

schools, preparatory
USE **preparatory schools**

schools, primary
USE **elementary schools**

schools, private
USE **private schools**

schools, public
USE **public schools**

schools, reform
USE **reformatories**

schools, residential
USE **boarding schools**

schools, riding
USE **riding schools**

schools, Sabbath
USE **Sunday schools**

schools, secondary
USE **high schools**

schools, Sunday
USE **Sunday schools**

schools, technical
USE **vocational schools**

schools, trade
USE **vocational schools**

schools, vocational
USE **vocational schools**

schoolyards
RK.1497
ALT **schoolyard**
CN V.RK.ALO.ALO.BCW.BUE.ARI

schranks
TG.601 (N)
ALT **schrank**
SN Use with reference to an originally German type of wardrobe for the storage of clothes and linens; generally with two paneled doors and sometimes having one side with drawers and shelves and the other side an open space for hanging clothes.
UF kunstschranks
shonks
CN V.TG.AFU.AFU.AXC.ALO.CXA.ARI

Schwedler domes
RT.397
ALT **Schwedler dome**
SN Use for domes consisting of an irregular triangular mesh of hinged bars, as introduced by Schwedler in Berlin in 1863.
UF domes, Schwedler
CN V.RT.AFU.AFU.AFU.BIQ.AFU.AFU.BUE

Schweinfurt green
USE **emerald green**

Schweinfurter Grün
USE **emerald green**

scialbo
USE **intonaco**

science centers
USE **science museums**

science fiction
BM.269 (L,R)
UF fiction, science
CN B.BM.AFU.ARI.BIQ.ARI.AFU

science historians
USE **historians of science**

science museums
RK.412 (A,L,B)
ALT **science museum**
UF centers, science
museums, science
science centers
CN V.RK.AFU.ALO.ALO.BCW.AXC.ARI.CFS

science photography
USE **scientific photography**

science, ceramic
USE **ceramic science**

science, computer
USE **computer science**

science, domestic
USE **home economics**

science, information
USE **information science**

science, library
USE **library science**

science, marine
USE **oceanography**

science, optical
USE **optics**

science, political
USE **political science**

science, polymer
USE **polymer science**

science, soil
USE **soil science**

science, textile
USE **textile science**

sciences
KD.194 (L,B,R)
CN K.KD.AFU.ARI

sciences, atmospheric
USE **meteorology**

sciences, biological
USE **biological sciences**

sciences, earth
USE **earth sciences**

sciences, environmental
USE **environmental sciences**

sciences, geodetic
USE **geodesy**

sciences, health
USE **health sciences**

sciences, materials
USE **materials sciences**

sciences, occult
USE **occult sciences**

sciences, physical
USE **physical sciences**

sciences, social
USE **social sciences**

scientific illustration
KT.209 (L,R)
UF illustration, scientific
CN K.KT.AFU.ALO.DUC.CLM.BOK

scientific illustrations
VB.49 (L,R)
ALT **scientific illustration**
UF illustrations, scientific
CN V.VB.AFU.ALO.AXC.ALO.ARI

scientific illustrators
HG.147
ALT **scientific illustrator**
UF illustrators, scientific
CN H.HG.AFU.AXC.AXC.AFU.AFU.ALO.BCW.AFU.ALO.ALO.ARI

scientific instruments
TB.541 (L)

ALT **scientific instrument**
UF instruments, scientific
CN V.TB.AFU.AXC.ALO.AXC

scientific photographers
HG.121
ALT **scientific photographer**
SN Persons engaged in scientific photography.
UF photographers, scientific
CN H.HG.AFU.AXC.AXC.AFU.AFU.ALO.AXC.DOI.AXC

scientific photography
KT.306 (L)
SN The activity of producing photographs that document or illustrate scientific phenomena.
UF photography, science
photography, scientific
science photography
CN K.KT.AFU.ALO.DUC.DIO.AFU.DIO

scientific reports
USE **technical reports**

scientific societies
HG.901 (L)
ALT **scientific society**
UF societies, scientific
CN H.HG.ALO.DUC.BZY

scientists
HG.325 (L,R)
ALT **scientist**
CN H.HG.AFU.AXC.BIQ.AFU.AFU

scientists, conservation
USE **conservators**

scientists, information
USE **information scientists**

scientists, medical
USE **medical scientists**

scientists, political
USE **political scientists**

scillops
USE **taper augers**

scimatia
USE **cymatia**

scimitar legs
USE **sabre legs**

scissor beam trusses
USE **scissors trusses**

scissors
TB.137 (L,N)
SN Cutting tools consisting of two beveledged cutting blades with handles and being movable past one another on a pivot in the center by which they are held together. (W)
CN V.TB.AFU.ARI.AXC.ALO.CRG

scissors chairs
USE **X-chairs**

scissors trusses
RT.371
ALT **scissors truss**
SN Trusses used to support a pitched roof; the ties cross each other and are connected to the opposite rafters at an intermediate point along their length. (DAC)
UF scissor beam trusses
trusses, scissor beam
trusses, scissors
CN V.RT.AFU.AFU.AFU.BCW.CLM.AFU.AFU.AFU.CFS

scoinson arches
USE **back arches**

scollop shell
USE **scallop shell**

sconcheon arches
USE **back arches**

sconcheons
USE **reveals**

scones (masonry units)
USE **splits**

scooper planes
TB.970 (N)
ALT **scooper plane**
SN Small planes used to hollow out scoops and shovels. (SLOANE)
UF planes, scooper
planes, scoopmaker
scoopmaker planes
CN V.TB.AFU.BCW.CFS.ALO.AFU.DUC.BUE

scoopmaker planes
USE **scooper planes**

scorers
TB.361
ALT **scorer**
SN Instruments used for scoring a variety of materials.
CN V.TB.AFU.ARI.CXA.BCW

scores
VW.56
ALT **score**
SN Original and entire drafts or transcripts of musical compositions or arrangements, with the parts of all the different instruments or voices written on staffs one above another, so that they can be read at a glance. (GAHLM)
UF music scores
CN V.VW.AFU.AFU.AFU.DOI.AFU

scoria
MT.479
SN The refuse, dross, or slag left after melting or smelting metal. (RHDEL2)
CN M.MT.AFU.AFU.AFU.BZY.ALO.BOK

scoring
KT.168
ALT **scored**
SN The act or process of marking with lines, scratches, or notches. (W)
CN K.KT.AFU.ALO.DOI.ERE.AXC

scorpers
TB.1032 (N)
ALT **scorper**
SN Tools, usually with a curved blade, which are a cross between an adz and a drawknife; used to hollow curved surfaces.
UF inshaves
inside shaves
round shaves
scampers
scaupers
shaves, inside
shaves, round
CN V.TB.AFU.BCW.CFS.ALO.AFU.FCS

scorpers, closed
USE **closed scorpers**

scorpers, open
USE **open scorpers**

Scorpio symbols
DG.83
ALT **Scorpio symbol**
CN D.DG.AFU.AFU.ERE.CFS

Scotch fir
USE **Scotch pine**

Scotch pine
MT.1385 (L)
UF archangel fir
Baltic pine
Baltic redwood
Danzig fir
Danzig pine
deal, yellow
fir, archangel
fir, Danzig
fir, memel
fir, Scotch
fir, Scots
memel fir
northern pine
pine, Baltic
pine, Danzig
pine, northern
pine, Scotch
pine, Scots
pine, yellow (Scotch pine)
Pinus sylvestris
redwood, Baltic
Scotch fir
Scots fir
Scots pine
yellow deal
yellow pine (Scotch pine)
CN M.MT.AFU.AFU.ALO.BIQ.DCU.AFU.AFU.ALO.CXA.DIO

scotches
TB.618

SN Bricklayer's tools having a cutting edge on each side; used for cutting, trimming, and dressing brick or stone. (DAC)
UF scutches
skutches
CN V.TB.AFU.BCW.BCW.ALO.FOG.ALO

scotias
RT.791 (B)
ALT **scotia**
SN Deep concave moldings, especially one at the base of a column in classical architecture. (HAS)
UF gorges (scotias)
trochili
trochilus
CN V.RT.AFU.ALO.AFU.BOK.AFU.mAFU.AXC.BUE

Scots fir
USE **Scotch pine**

Scots pine
USE **Scotch pine**

Scottish
FL.3041 (L,B)
CN F.FL.ALO.BCW.AFU.AXC.ALO

Scottish Baronial
FL.3334
UF Baronial, Scottish
CN F.FL.ALO.BCW.ALO.AXC.DIO.ALO.BOK.ARI

Scottsbluff
FL.758 (L)
CN F.FL.ALO.ALO.ALO.AFU.AFU.ARI.ALO.ARI.ALO.BCW

SCR brick
MT.79
SN Brick wider and longer than most other brick; used chiefly for garden walls.
UF brick, SCR
CN M.MT.AFU.AFU.AFU.AXC.ALO.AFU.AFU.AFU.BZY.AFU

scrap metal
MT.470 (L)
UF metal, scrap
CN M.MT.AFU.AFU.AFU.BZY.AFU.ARI.ALO

scrap yards
USE **junkyards**

scrapbooks
VW.517 (L,N)
ALT **scrapbook**
SN Blank books, sometimes loose-leaf, in which printed items, pictures, manuscript items, and memorabilia may be mounted. (GAHLM)
CN V.VW.AFU.ALO.AFU.AFU.AFU.CXA

scraper planes
USE **cabinet scrapers**

scraperboard
USE **scratchboard**

scrapers
TB.527 (L,N)
ALT **scraper**
SN Any of various tools used for scraping, producing a clean or a smooth finished surface, cutting grooves, or shaping objects by scraping away superfluous material. (W)
CN V.TB.AFU.ARI.EWY.ALO.DIO

scrapers (earthmoving equipment)
TB.47 (L,N)
ALT **scraper (earthmoving equipment)**
SN Digging, hauling, and grading machinery having a cutting edge, a carrying bowl, a movable front wall or apron, and a dumping or ejecting mechanism. (MEANS)
CN V.TB.AFU.ARI.AFU.ARI.BUE

scrapers, block
USE **block scrapers**

scrapers, box
USE **box scrapers**

scrapers, cabinet
USE **cabinet scrapers**

scrapers, wall
USE **wall scrapers**

scraping
KT.622
ALT **scraped**
CN K.KT.AFU.ALO.FUA.DUC

scratch awls
USE **scribe awls**

scratch tools
TB.624
ALT **scratch tool**
SN A variety of hand tools used to scratch a plaster surface to increase bonding of the successive coat. (MEANS)
UF tools, scratch
CN V.TB.AFU.BCW.BCW.ALO.GRC

scratchboard
MT.1921
SN Cardboard coated with a smooth layer, usually of gesso, and then with drawing ink. An image is made by scraping away areas of ink and exposing the white layer. (MAYER)
UF scraperboard
CN M.MT.AFU.AFU.ARI.ALO.ALO.AXC.ALO.BIQ.AFU.BUE

screeds
TB.629 (N)
ALT **screed**
SN In cement masonry flatwork, the wood or metal straightedges used to strike off or level newly placed concrete. (PUTNAM)
UF strikeoffs
CN V.TB.AFU.BCW.BCW.ALO.GWW

screen desks
USE **lady's screen writing tables**

screen-door catches
USE **screen-door latches**

screen-door latches
TF.190
ALT **screen-door latch**
SN Light locking or latching devices for use on a screen door and operated by a knob, a lever handle, or a handle and push button. (MEANS)
UF catches, screen-door
latches, screen-door
screen-door catches
CN V.TF.AFU.AFU.AFU.AFU.DIO.BCW.ALO.BOK

screen doors
RT.859 (L,N)
ALT **screen door**
UF doors, screen
CN V.RT.AFU.ARI.AFU.AFU.AFU.ALO.ARI.AFU.AFU.BOK.BCW

screen facades
RT.598
ALT **screen facade**
SN Use generally for facades constructed to conceal the shape or size of the buildings to which they are attached, as by exceeding them in height or width; if the intention is to give a more imposing appearance, use **false fronts.**
UF facades, screen
CN V.RT.AFU.AFU.AFU.BIQ.BUE.AFU.ARI.ALO.AFU.AFU.ALO

screen plate process, Dufay's
USE **Dufaycolor**

screen plate processes
USE **screen processes**

screen processes
KT.314 (L)
SN Photographic processes that produce an additive color image using a screen of minute red, green, and blue filters to record the relative intensity of each hue on a panchromatic, black-and-white emulsion which is processed to form a transparency. When viewed through a similar filter, each filter contributes its hue with its intensity modulated by the silver image.
UF color screen processes
processes, screen
screen plate processes
screen processes, color
CN K.KT.AFU.ALO.DUC.DIO.ALO.AFU.ALO

screen processes, color
USE **screen processes**

screen tables
USE **lady's screen writing tables**

screen walls
USE **pierced walls**

screen writers
HG.191 (L)
ALT **screen writer**
UF writers, screen
CN H.HG.AFU.AXC.AXC.ARI.AFU.AFU.CLM

screen writing tables, lady's
USE **lady's screen writing tables**

screening rooms
RM.131 (A)
ALT **screening room**
UF rooms, screening
CN V.RM.AFU.DIO.ALO.BIQ.BIQ

screenplays
VW.74 (L)
ALT **screenplay**
SN Written forms of stories prepared for motion picture productions, including description of characters, details of scenes and settings, dialogue, and stage directions. (GAHLM)
UF film scripts
scripts, film
CN V.VW.AFU.AFU.AFU.ERE.ARI

screens
TG.3 (L,N,R)
ALT **screen**
CN V.TG.AFU.AFU.AFU

screens passages
RM.92
ALT **screens passage**
SN In Medieval halls, the spaces between the screens (which act as visual barriers) and the doors to the service rooms (buttery, kitchen, pantry). (HAS)
UF passages, screens
CN V.RM.AFU.DIO.ALO.ARI.AXC.AXC

screens, altar
USE **altar screens**

screens, banner
USE **pole screens**

screens, chancel
USE **chancel screens**

screens, cheval
USE **cheval fire screens**

screens, cheval fire
USE **cheval fire screens**

screens, choir
USE **choir screens**

screens, draught
USE **folding screens**

screens, extension fire
USE **extension fire screens**

screens, fire
USE **fire screens**

screens, folding
USE **folding screens**

screens, folding fire
USE **folding fire screens**

screens, horse fire
USE **cheval fire screens**

screens, lady' writing fire
USE **lady's writing fire screens**

screens, organ
USE **organ screens**

screens, pole
USE **pole screens**

screens, pole fire
USE **pole screens**

screens, rood
USE **rood screens**

screens, shoji
USE **shoji**

screens, sliding fire
USE **sliding fire screens**

screens, tripod fire
USE **pole screens**

screens, tripod pole
USE **pole screens**

screens, writing fire
USE **writing fire screens**

screw anchors
TF.299
ALT **screw anchor**
SN Metal, plastic, or fiber shells inserted into a hole in masonry, plaster, or concrete, which expand when the screw is driven in. (MEANS)
UF anchors, screw
CN V.TF.AFU.AFU.AFU.ALO.AFU.AFU.CLM

screw augers
USE **spiral augers**

screw boxes
TB.1038
ALT **screw box**
SN Wood or iron tools used to cut threads on wood screws or pegs.
UF boxes, screw
CN V.TB.AFU.BCW.CFS.ALO.AFU.FOG

screw clamps
TB.1056 (N)
ALT **screw clamp**
SN Any clamps set by means of a screw; especially those used in woodworking which have two parallel jaws for holding together work to be pressed.
UF clamps, hand
clamps, handscrew
clamps, screw
hand clamps
hand screws
handscrew clamps
screws, hand
CN V.TB.AFU.BCW.CFS.ALO.ALO.BCW.BOK

screw-cutting machines
TB.701 (L,N)
ALT **screw-cutting machine**
SN A form of turret lathe usually having a hollow spindle through which a bar can be fed to be machined into bolts, studs, and other screws. (W)
UF machines, screw
machines, screw-cutting
machines, thread-cutting
screw machines
thread-cutting machines
CN V.TB.AFU.BCW.BIQ.ARI.AFU.AFU.AFU.AFU

screw jacks
USE **jackscrews**

screw machines
USE **screw-cutting machines**

screw nails
USE **drivescrews**

screw plates
TB.733 (N)
ALT **screw plate**
SN Flat metal plates with one or more holes with a cutting edge for threading screws, pipes, or rods by hand. (W)
UF plates, screw
CN V.TB.AFU.BCW.BIQ.ARI.ALO.BUE.AXC

screw stairs
USE **spiral stairs**

screw starters
USE **gimlets**

screw stools
USE **revolving stools**

screw taps
USE **taps**

screwdrivers
TB.195 (L,N)
ALT **screwdriver**
SN Hand tools with a handle and a shank with a tip shaped to fit the recess in the head of a screw; used to drive or remove screws. (MEANS)
UF turnscrews
CN V.TB.AFU.ARI.BOK.ALO

screwdrivers, offset
USE **offset screwdrivers**

screwdrivers, Phillips head
USE **Phillips head screwdrivers**

screwdrivers, ratchet
USE **ratchet screwdrivers**

screwdrivers, spiral ratchet
USE **spiral ratchet screwdrivers**

screwing
KT.54
ALT **screwed**
CN K.KT.AFU.ALO.BCW.BCW.BCW

screwless knobs
TF.62
ALT **screwless knob**
SN Door knobs that are attached to the spindles using special wrenches, rather than the more common side screw. (MEANS)
UF knobs, screwless
CN V.TF.AFU.AFU.AFU.AFU.CFS.AXC.AFU.ALO

screws
TF.466 (L,N,B)
ALT **screw**
SN Cylindrical fasteners having a head with a slot or recess and helical or spiral threading, to be inserted by rotating, as with a screwdriver. (W)
CN V.TF.AFU.AFU.AFU.ALO.AFU.DIO

screws, adjusting
USE **adjusting screws**

screws, Allen
USE **Allen screws**

screws, cap
USE **cap screws**

screws, clamping
USE **clamping screws**

screws, coach
USE **lag bolts**

screws, cylinder
USE **cylinder screws**

screws, drive
USE **drivescrews**

screws, hand
USE **screw clamps**

screws, lag
USE **lag bolts**

screws, machine
USE **machine screws**

screws, Phillips head
USE **Phillips head screws**

screws, set
USE **setscrews**

screws, sheet metal
USE **sheet metal screws**

screws, shutter
USE **shutter screws**

screws, stop
USE **stop screws**

screws, stop bead
USE **stop bead screws**

screws, thumb
USE **thumbscrews**

screws, wood
USE **wood screws**

scribbles
USE **doodles**

scribe awls
TB.833 (N)
ALT **scribe awl**
SN Sharp pointed steel instruments used for laying out work, especially on hard wood. (PUTNAM)
UF awls, chisel-end marking
awls, marking
awls, scratch
awls, scribe
chisel-end marking awls
marking awls
marking awls, chisel-end
scratch awls
scribers (awls)
scribes (awls)
CN V.TB.AFU.BCW.CFS.ALO.AFU.ARI.ARI

scribed joints
USE **coped joints**

scribers
TB.362
ALT **scriber**
SN Pointed instruments used to mark lines in wood, metal, or brick. (MEANS)
CN V.TB.AFU.ARI.CXA.BIQ

scribers (awls)
USE **scribe awls**

scribes
HG.468 (L,R)
ALT **scribe**
SN Persons who inscribe or copy texts, especially those who transcribed, copied, and edited manuscripts in the days before mechanical printing.
CN H.HG.AFU.AXC.BUE.ALO.CRG

scribes (awls)
USE **scribe awls**

scribing saws
USE **coping saws**

scrinium
USE **arcae**

scriptoires
USE **desks**

scriptoria
RM.153 (R)
ALT **scriptorium**
SN Rooms used for the copying of manuscripts before the era of printing.
CN V.RM.AFU.DIO.ALO.CFS.BCW

scripts
VW.71 (N)
ALT **script**
SN Written texts of stage plays, screenplays, and radio or television broadcasts. (GAHLM)
CN V.VW.AFU.AFU.AFU.ERE

scripts, exhibit
USE **exhibit scripts**

scripts, film
USE **screenplays**

scripts, radio
USE **radio scripts**

scripts, television
USE **television scripts**

scritoires
USE **escritoires**

scroll feet
TG.911
ALT **scroll foot**
SN Feet in the form of a tight scroll; especially those found on mid-18th-century English chair legs. (DDA)
UF feet, French scroll
feet, French (scroll feet)
feet, knulled
feet, knurl
feet, knurl toe
feet, scroll
feet, scrolled toe
feet, tern
feet, whorl
French feet (scroll feet)
French scroll feet
knulled feet
knurl feet
knurl toe feet
knurled feet
scrolled feet
scrolled toe feet
tern feet
whorl feet
CN V.TG.ALO.DZW.AFU.BZY

scroll-over arms
USE **scrolled arms**

scroll patterns
USE **scrollwork**

scroll saws
TB.1014 (L,N)
ALT **scroll saw**
SN Hand saws set in a deep U-shaped frame with a thin blade, which is slightly wider than the blade of a fretsaw; especially suited to cutting curves.
UF saws, scroll
CN V.TB.AFU.BCW.CFS.ALO.AFU.EWY.BCW.BOK

scroll, linen
USE **linenfold**

scroll, Spanish
USE **Spanish feet**

scrolled arms
TG.815
ALT **scrolled arm**
SN Arms in which the support rises from the seat rail curving first toward the front and then toward the back, and leveling out for the armrest. Used in the Queen Anne and Early Georgian periods. (TOMLIN)
UF arms, scroll-over
arms, scrolled
arms, voluted
scroll-over arms
voluted arms
CN V.TG.ALO.ALO.AFU.AFU.BCW

scrolled backs
TG.829
ALT **scrolled back**
UF backs, scrolled
CN V.TG.ALO.AXC.AFU.ALO

scrolled feet
USE **scroll feet**

scrolled toe feet
USE **scroll feet**

scrolling foliage
DG.147
SN Running or allover patterns in which stems and leaves coil, spiral, and branch out into further curves and spirals.
UF foliage scrolls
scrolls, foliage
CN D.DG.AFU.ARI.ALO.CRG.ARI

scrolls
VW.624 (L)
ALT **scroll**
SN Written documents on rolls, as of parchment or papyrus.
CN V.VW.AFU.ALO.AFU.DCU

scrolls (motifs)
DG.64 (L,R)
ALT **scroll (motif)**
SN General term for motifs consisting of a spirally wound band. For simple motifs of coiled lines, use **spirals**; for scroll-shaped architectural elements use other terms, such as **consoles** and **volutes**; for a series of scrolls, in running or allover patterns, use **scrollwork.**
UF scrolls, spiral
scrowls
spiral scrolls
CN D.DG.AFU.AFU.DOI

scrolls, cloud
USE **cloud scrolls**

scrolls, evolute
USE **wave scrolls**

scrolls, foliage
USE **scrolling foliage**

scrolls, foliate
USE **leaf scrolls**

scrolls, inhabited
USE **inhabited scrolls**

scrolls, leaf
USE **leaf scrolls**

scrolls, peopled
USE **inhabited scrolls**

scrolls, spiral
USE **scrolls (motifs)**

scrolls, vine
USE **vine scrolls**

scrolls, Vitruvian
USE **Vitruvian scrolls**

scrolls, wave
USE **wave scrolls**

scrollwork
DG.144
SN Use for running or allover patterns based on scrolls, which usually branch and flow out from each other.
UF patterns, scroll
scroll patterns
CN D.DG.AFU.ARI.ALO.CRG

scrowls
USE **scrolls (motifs)**

scrub brushes
TB.352 (N)
ALT **scrub brush**
UF brushes, scrub
CN V.TB.AFU.ARI.CRG.ALO.ALO.ARI

scrub pine
MT.1386 (L)
UF Jersey pine
pine, Jersey
pine, scrub
pine, spruce
pine, yellow (scrub pine)
Pinus virginiana
spruce pine
yellow pine (scrub pine)
CN M.MT.AFU.AFU.ALO.BIQ.DCU.AFU.AFU.ALO.CXA.DOI

scrub planes
USE **roughing planes**

scruffing
USE **dragging**

scrutoires (bureau-bookcases)
USE **bureau-bookcases**

scrutoires (desks)
USE **desks**

scrutoirs
USE **desks**

scrutoirs (desks and bookcases)
USE **secretaries**

scud planes
USE **roughing planes**

scuffing
USE **dragging**

sculleries
RM.234 (B)
ALT **scullery**
SN Rooms off the kitchen for storing and washing dishes and food. (W)
CN V.RM.AFU.DIO.ALO.DOI.CLM

sculptors
HG.136 (A,L,B,R)
ALT **sculptor**
CN H.HG.AFU.AXC.AXC.AFU.AFU.ALO.AXC.DZW

sculptors, animal
USE **animal sculptors**

sculpture
KT.532 (A,L,B,R)
CN K.KT.AFU.ALO.ELK.DIO.AFU

sculpture gardens
RK.1424 (A,L,B,R)
ALT **sculpture garden**
SN Gardens designed to display sculpture, publicly or privately.
UF gardens, sculpture
CN V.RK.ALO.AFU.AFU.ALO.BUE

Sculpture Movement, New
USE **New Sculpture Movement**

sculpture techniques
KT.533 (L,R)
CN K.KT.AFU.ALO.ELK.DIO.ALO

sculpture, postal
USE **correspondence art**

scumbling
KT.234
ALT **scumbled**
SN Applying a thin, semiopaque or translucent coating of paint over a previously painted surface without entirely obscuring it. (GOTTS)
CN K.KT.AFU.ALO.DUC.CXA.ALO.AFU.CRG

scuncheons
USE **reveals**

Scuola Metafisica
USE **Metaphysical**

scupper nails
TF.400
ALT **scupper nail**
UF nails, scupper
CN V.TF.AFU.AFU.AFU.ALO.AFU.CFS.AFU.CXA

scurfing planes
USE **roughing planes**

scutcheons
USE **escutcheons (hardware)**

scutches
USE **scotches**

Scythian
FL.3021 (L,R)
CN F.FL.ALO.AXC.ARI.BIQ.ALO.ARI

sea charts
USE **marine charts**

sea chests
TG.468 (L,N)
ALT **sea chest**
UF chests, sea
chests, ship
ship chests
CN V.TG.AFU.AFU.AXC.ALO.AXC.DZW

sea ladders
USE **rope ladders**

sea level canals
USE **interoceanic canals**

sea painters
USE **marine painters**

sea-pieces
USE **seascapes**

sea ports
USE **ports**

sea reed
MT.1035
UF grass, marrum
marrum grass
reed, sea
CN M.MT.AFU.AFU.ALO.BIQ.AXC.AXC.AXC

sealants
USE **sealing compounds**

sealed double glazing
USE **double windows**

sealing
KT.671 (L)
ALT **sealed**
CN K.KT.AFU.ALO.GRC.AFU.BIQ

sealing compounds
MT.2649 (A,L,B)
UF compounds, sealing
jointing materials
materials, jointing
sealants
CN M.MT.AFU.ARI.HTY

sealmakers
HG.574 (L)
ALT **sealmaker**
CN H.HG.AFU.AXC.BUE.AXC.DZW

seals
VW.763 (L,B,R)
ALT **seal**
CN V.VW.AFU.ALO.ALO.ARI

seamen
HG.735
ALT **seaman**
SN Persons whose occupations are the handling, working, or navigating of ships at sea. (W)
CN H.HG.AFU.BCW.FUA

seamers
TB.678
ALT **seamer**
SN Hand tools used in making sheet metal joints or seams. (MEANS)
CN V.TB.AFU.BCW.BIQ.AFU.ALO.CLM

seamers, double
USE **double seamers**

seams, beaded dovetail
USE **beaded dovetail seams**

seams, bottom double
USE **bottom double seams**

seams, cap strip
USE **cap strip seams**

seams, corner double
USE **corner double seams**

seams, elbow
USE **elbow seams**

seams, flange dovetail
USE **flange dovetail seams**

seams, grooved
USE **grooved seams**

seams, insert bottom
USE **insert bottom seams**

seams, lap
USE **lap bottom seams**

seams, lap bottom
USE **lap bottom seams**

seams, Pittsburgh lock
USE **Pittsburgh lock seams**

seams, plain dovetail
USE **plain dovetail seams**

seams, single bottom
USE **single bottom seams**

seams, standing
USE **standing seams**

seamstresses
USE **sewers (textile workers)**

search services, data
USE **information retrieval services**

search services, online
USE **information retrieval services**

searching
KG.95 (L)
SN Systematically examining records in a file or collection for the purpose of locating specific data or records. (ALAG)
CN K.KG.AFU.AFU.AXC.CRG.ALO.AFU

searching, database
USE **online searching**

searching, online
USE **online searching**

searching, subject
USE **subject searching**

seas
RD.129 (L,B,R)
ALT **sea**
SN The shallower salt water areas of the earth lying on the margins of continents; loosely applied as a proper name to any specific bodies of water. For the main water areas of the earth, lying in basins, use **oceans.**
CN V.RD.ARI.AFU.AFU.AFU.AFU.AFU.ALO

seascapes
VB.77 (L,R)
ALT **seascape**
UF marine subjects
sea-pieces
waterscapes
CN V.VB.AFU.AXC.BIQ

seashell
USE **shell**

seashore resorts
USE **seaside resorts**

seashores
RD.231 (L,R)
ALT **seashore**
UF seasides
CN V.RD.ARI.AFU.AXC.AFU.ALO.AXC.BUE.AXC

seaside alder
MT.1099
UF alder, Formosan
alder, seaside
Alnus maritima
Formosan alder
CN M.MT.AFU.AFU.ALO.BIQ.DCU.AFU.AFU.AFU.ALO.BOK

seaside resorts
RG.171 (A,L,B)
ALT **seaside resort**
UF lidos
resorts, seaside
seashore resorts
CN V.RG.AFU.AFU.DOI.BZY.ALO

seaside towns
USE **coastal towns**

seasides
USE **seashores**

seasonal dwellings
RK.276

ALT **seasonal dwelling**
UF dwellings, seasonal
CN V.RK.AFU.ALO.ALO.AXC.ALO.ALO.ARI

seasons
BM.1036 (L,R)
CN B.BM.CFS.AXC.CRG.ARI

seat curbs
USE **fender stools**

seat frames
TG.978
ALT **seat frame**
UF frames, seat
CN V.TG.ALO.GLI.ALO.AFU

seat furniture
USE **seating furniture**

seat hangers, formed
USE **formed seat hangers**

seat ottomans
USE **ottomans**

seat rails
TG.979
ALT **seat rail**
SN Frames on which the seat is built.
UF lists (seat rails)
rails, seat
CN V.TG.ALO.GLI.ALO.ALO

seating furniture
TG.18 (L)
UF furniture, seat
furniture, seating
seat furniture
CN V.TG.AFU.AFU.ALO

seats
TG.970 (L)
ALT **seat**
SN The part of seating furniture on which one sits.
CN V.TG.ALO.GLI.AFU

seats, cabriole
USE **cabriole sofas**

seats, coil-spring
USE **coil-spring seats**

seats, compass
USE **compass seats**

seats, concave
USE **hollowed seats**

seats, country
USE **country houses**

seats, county
USE **county seats**

seats, deacon's
USE **deacon's benches**

seats, dipped
USE **hollowed seats**

seats, drop-in
USE **slip seats**

seats, dropped
USE **hollowed seats**

seats, garden
USE **garden seats**

seats, hall
USE **hall seats**

seats, hollowed
USE **hollowed seats**

seats, horseshoe
USE **compass seats**

seats, loose
USE **slip seats**

seats, love
USE **love seats**

seats, meeting house
USE **deacon's benches**

seats, monk's
USE **chair-tables**

seats, ottoman
USE **ottoman footstools**

seats, parish
USE **parish seats**

seats, reading
USE **daybeds**

seats, rumble (wagon seats)
USE **wagon seats**

seats, saddle
USE **saddle seats**

seats, slip
USE **slip seats**

seats, turf
USE **turf seats**

seats, wagon
USE **wagon seats**

seats, window
USE **window seats**

seawalls
RK.558 (A,L)
ALT **seawall**
SN Walls built as breakwaters specifically to protect land from erosion or other damage due to wave action.
CN V.RK.AFU.ALO.ALO.CFS.ALO.ALO.AFU.ARI

Sebennyte Dynasty
USE **Thirtieth Dynasty**

Sebilian
FL.2786
CN F.FL.ALO.AXC.ALO.ARI.AFU.ALO.ALO

secco
KT.235
SN Technique of painting a mural on dried lime plaster. (MAYER)
UF dry fresco
fresco à secco
fresco-secco
fresco, dry
secco-fresco
CN K.KT.AFU.ALO.DUC.CXA.ALO.AFU.CXA

secco-fresco
USE **secco**

Secession Movement
FL.3261 (A,R)
UF Sezession
CN F.FL.ALO.BCW.ALO.AXC.CFS

Secession style
USE **Sezessionstil**

Sechín
USE **Cerro Sechín**

Second Dynasty
FL.2794
UF 2nd Dynasty
Dynasty, Second
CN F.FL.ALO.AXC.ALO.ARI.AFU.AXC.ALO

Second Empire
FL.3363 (A,B,R)
UF Mansard Style
CN F.FL.ALO.BCW.ALO.AXC.DIO.BCW.ALO.BIQ

Second Golden Age (Byzantine)
USE **Middle Byzantine**

second homes
RK.281 (A,L)
ALT **second home**
UF homes, second
residences, secondary
secondary residences
CN V.RK.AFU.ALO.ALO.AXC.ALO.ALO.AXC

Second Intermediate period
FL.2806
UF Intermediate period, Second
CN F.FL.ALO.AXC.ALO.ARI.AFU.BOK

Second Persian Domination
USE **Thirty-first Dynasty**

Second Persian period
USE **Thirty-first Dynasty**

Second Plateresque
FL.3246
UF Plateresque, Renaissance
Plateresque, Second
Renaissance Plateresque
CN F.FL.ALO.BCW.ALO.ARI.BIQ.BIQ.BUE.ALO.ALO

Second Pointed
USE **Decorated Style**

Second Pompeian Style

USE **Second Style**

second printing
USE **double-printing**

Second Style
FL.2767
UF Architectural Style
Pompeian Style, Second
Second Pompeian Style
CN F.FL.ALO.AXC.ALO.ALO.ALO.
CFS.AFU.ALO

Secondaire
USE **Rayonnant**

secondary colors
BM.117
SN Colors which results from mixing two primary colors.
UF colors, secondary
CN B.BM.AFU.AFU.ARI.BOK.ALO.
AFU.BZY

secondary education
KD.125 (L,B)
SN Branch of education covering grades 7 or 8 through to the end of high school. (ERIC)
UF education, secondary
education, secondary school
secondary school education
CN K.KD.AFU.ALO.BOK.AFU.ARI

secondary residences
USE **second homes**

secondary ribs
USE **tiercerons**

secondary roads
RK.1556
ALT **secondary road**
UF local roads
minor roads
roads, local
roads, minor
roads, secondary
roads, subsidiary
subsidiary roads
CN V.RK.ALO.ALO.BIQ.ARI.ALO.BZY

secondary school education
USE **secondary education**

secondary schools
USE **high schools**

secondary supports
USE **mounts (artists' materials)**

secondary wood
MT.1412
UF wood, secondary
CN M.MT.AFU.AFU.ALO.BIQ.DCU.
AFU.ALO.AXC

secondhand stores
USE **thrift shops**

secret doors
RT.862
ALT **secret door**
UF doors, secret
pseudothyra
CN V.RT.AFU.ARI.AFU.AFU.AFU.ALO.
ARI.AFU.ALO.ALO

secret drawers
TG.883
ALT **secret drawer**
UF drawers, secret
CN V.TG.ALO.DCU.AFU.ALO.AXC

secret gardens
USE **giardini segreti**

secret gate latches
TF.191
ALT **secret gate latch**
SN Surface-mounted latches operated by a concealed button or other device, usually used on bank gates.
UF gate latches, secret
latches, secret gate
CN V.TF.AFU.AFU.AFU.AFU.DIO.
BCW.ALO.BUE

secret hinges
USE **invisible hinges**

secret ink
USE **invisible ink**

secret societies
HG.902 (L)
ALT **secret society**
UF societies, secret
CN H.HG.ALO.DUC.CFS

secrétaires à abattant
TG.535
ALT **secrétaire à abattant**
SN French desks with a vertical fall front enclosing drawers and pigeonholes; usually with a cupboard below, but sometimes raised up on tall legs. (PC)
UF drop-front secrétaires
secrétaires en armoire
secrétaires en tombeau
secrétaires, drop-front
CN V.TG.AFU.AFU.AXC.ALO.BZY.
BUE.AFU

secrétaires à capucin
USE **secrétaires à la Bourgogne**

secrétaires à cylindre
USE **bureaux à cylindre**

secrétaires à dessus brisé
USE **bureaux en pente**

secrétaires à la Bourgogne
TG.550
ALT **secrétaire à la Bourgogne**
SN Multipurpose commode like desks containing a set of drawers which could be mechanically raised from the back section of the piece. (PC)
UF bureaux à la Bourgogne
secrétaires à capucin
tables à la Bourgogne
CN V.TG.AFU.AFU.AXC.ALO.BZY.DOI

secrétaires à panse
USE **bureaux à cylindre**

secrétaires à pupitre
USE **bureaux en pente**

secrétaires à rouleau
USE **bureaux à cylindre**

secrétaires en armoire
USE **secrétaires à abattant**

secrétaires en pente
USE **bureaux en pente**

secrétaires en pente à écran
USE **écrans à secrétaire**

secrétaires en tombeau
USE **bureaux en pente**
secrétaires à abattant

secrétaires, drop-front
USE **secrétaires à abattant**

secretaries
TG.551 (N,R)
ALT **secretary**
SN Writing desks or cabinets with a fall-front desk drawer.(BEARD) Popular term for **desks and bookcases.**
UF escritoires (secretaries)
scrutoirs (desks and bookcases)
secretaries escritoir
CN V.TG.AFU.AFU.AXC.ALO.BZY.DUC

secretaries and bookcases, cylinder
USE **cylinder desks and bookcases**

secretaries (clerical workers)
HG.34 (L)
ALT **secretary (clerical worker)**
CN H.HG.AFU.AXC.ALO.BOK.AFU.AFU

secretaries escritoir
USE **secretaries**

secretaries, bookcase and
USE **secretary-bookcases**

secretaries, cabinet office
USE **Wooton cabinet office secretaries**

secretaries, gentleman's
USE **gentleman's secretaries**

secretaries, lady's
USE **lady's secretaries**

secretaries, Wooton cabinet office
USE **Wooton cabinet office secretaries**

secretaries, Wooton patent
USE **Wooton cabinet office secretaries**

secretary and bookcases
USE **secretary-bookcases**

secretary-bookcases
TG.407
ALT **secretary-bookcase**

UF bookcase and secretaries
bookcases, secretary and
secretaries, bookcase and
secretary and bookcases
CN V.TG.AFU.AFU.AXC.ALO.ALO.BUE

secretary bookcases
USE **desks and bookcases**

secretary-cabinets
USE **desks and bookcases**

secretary desks
USE **bureau-bookcases**
desks and bookcases

secretary drawers
TG.884
ALT **secretary drawer**
SN Fall-front drawers often incorporated in bookcases or as the upper drawer in chests of drawers to provide a level surface convenient for writing.
UF drawers, secretary
drawers, writing
writing drawers
CN V.TG.ALO.DCU.AFU.ALO.BCW

secretary's chairs
USE **typewriter chairs**

section drawings
USE **sections**

section modulus
BM.914
SN The moment of inertia of the area of the cross section of a structural member divided by the distance from the center of gravity to the farthest point of the section; a measure of the flexural strength of the beam. (DAC)
UF modulus, section
CN B.BM.CFS.AXC.BIQ.ARI.ARI

section plans
USE **sections**

section, golden
USE **golden section**

sectional bookcases
TG.408
ALT **sectional bookcase**
UF bookcases, sectional
CN V.TG.AFU.AFU.AXC.ALO.ALO.BZY

sectional elevations
VD.28
ALT **sectional elevation**
SN Use for orthographic drawings that show a structure as partly an exterior elevation and partly an interior elevation. If only a small portion of exterior is taken away, use **broken-out sections.** For smaller, symmetrical objects shown as half exterior and half interior, use **half sections.**
UF elevation-sections
elevations, sectional
CN V.VD.AFU.AFU.BIQ.ALO.ALO.BCW

sectional furniture
TG.804
SN Furniture made up of modular units capable of use separately or in various combinations. (W)
UF furniture, interchangeable
furniture, sectional
interchangeable furniture
CN V.TG.AFU.ARI.CFS.AFU

sectional ladders
TB.484
ALT **sectional ladder**
SN Non-self-supporting portable ladders, nonadjustable in length, consisting of two or more sections so constructed that the sections may be combined to function as a single ladder. (STEIN)
UF ladders, sectional
CN V.TB.AFU.ARI.ERE.ALO.BIQ

sectional perspectives
VD.83
ALT **sectional perspective**
SN Use for drawings in which a structure or object is cut away in orthographic section, and a perspective is projected back from this plane.
UF perspectival sections
perspectives, sectional
sections, perspectival
CN V.VD.AFU.AFU.BIQ.ARI.AXC

sections
VD.67
ALT **section**
SN Orthographic drawings of a building, object, or site as if cut through and exposed at one specific plane.
UF drawings, section
full sections
general sections
plans, section
section drawings
section plans
sections, full
sections, general
CN V.VD.AFU.AFU.BIQ.ALO.BIQ

sections, auxiliary
USE **auxiliary sections**

sections, axial
USE **longitudinal sections**

sections, broken-out
USE **broken-out sections**

sections, building
USE **longitudinal sections**

sections, channel
USE **channel beams**

sections, cross
USE **cross sections**

sections, full
USE **sections**

sections, general
USE **sections**

sections, half
USE **half sections**

sections, longitudinal
USE **longitudinal sections**

sections, oblique
USE **oblique sections**

sections, offset
USE **offset sections**

sections, partial
USE **partial sections**

sections, perspectival
USE **sectional perspectives**

sections, removed
USE **removed sections**

sections, revolved
USE **revolved sections**

sections, rotated
USE **revolved sections**

sections, strip
USE **partial sections**

sections, transverse
USE **cross sections**

security guards
HG.52
ALT **security guard**
SN Persons employed by an institution or organization to provide physical protection from break-ins, theft, or vandalism.
UF guards, security
officers, security
security officers
CN H.HG.AFU.AXC.ARI.DCU

security officers
USE **security guards**

security systems
RT.1522 (L)
ALT **security system**
UF systems, security
CN V.RT.ALO.BIQ.ALO

security, building
USE **burglary protection**

security, housing
USE **burglary protection**

sedan chairs
TG.84 (L,N,R)
ALT **sedan chair**
SN Portable chairs borne on two long poles; generally with elaborate upholstery and decoration.
UF chairs, sedan
chairs, stick (sedan chairs)

chaises à porteur
stick chairs (sedan chairs)
CN V.TG.AFU.AFU.ALO.AFU.AFU.AFU.JZQ

Seders
KM.40 (L)
CN K.KM.AFU.ARI.AXC.CLM

sedia Dantesca
USE **Dante chairs**

sedilia
RT.1256 (R)
ALT **sedile**
SN Use for series of seats, usually three and of stone, located to the south of the choir for the officiating clergy.
CN V.RT.AFU.BUE.ALO.ARI.DCU

sedimentary rock
MT.638 (L)
SN Rock, such as sandstone or limestone, formed from materials deposited as sediments. (DAC)
UF rock, sedimentary
CN M.MT.AFU.AFU.AFU.DCU.AFU.ALO

sedimentation basins
USE **settling basins**

sediments, aeolian
USE **aeolian landforms**

seed
MT.1066 (L)
CN M.MT.AFU.AFU.ALO.BIQ.CFS.AFU

seed oil, tobacco
USE **tobacco seed oil**

seedpods
USE **pods**

seepage pits
RT.1493
ALT **seepage pit**
SN Covered pits with open-jointed linings through which the septic tank effluent it receives may seep or leach into the surrounding porous soil. (STEIN)
UF pits, seepage
seepage wells
wells, seepage
CN V.RT.ALO.BCW.ALO.ARI.CLM

seepage wells
USE **seepage pits**

segment arches
USE **segmental arches**

segmental arches
RT.240
ALT **segmental arch**
SN Arches in the shape of a segment of a circle that is less than a semicircle.
UF arches, segment
arches, segmental
segment arches
CN V.RT.AFU.AFU.AFU.BCW.AFU.AFU.AFU.DCU

segmental arches, pointed
USE **pointed segmental arches**

segmental arches, two-centered
USE **pointed segmental arches**

segmental domes
USE **saucer domes**

segmental pediments
RT.675
ALT **segmental pediment**
SN Pediments with a top in the form of a segmental arch.
UF pediments, segmental
CN V.RT.AFU.AFU.AFU.BIQ.BUE.ALO.ALO.BIQ.ARI

seigneuries
RG.260
ALT **seigneury**
SN Use for the complete domain of a lord, especially a feudal lord.
CN V.RG.ALO.AFU.AFU.BUE

seillages
USE **water benches**

seismic design
BM.1025 (L)
UF design, earthquake-resistant
design, seismic
earthquake design
earthquake-resistant design
CN B.BM.CFS.AXC.CLM.ALO.BIQ

seismic joints
TF.607
ALT **seismic joint**
SN Joints used to separate extremely long buildings into a series of adjacent volumes to resist earthquake damage. (DS)
UF joints, seismic
CN V.TF.ALO.ALO.BCW

seismicity maps
VW.191
ALT **seismicity map**
SN Maps showing earthquake-related structural features of the earth.
UF maps, seismicity
CN V.VW.AFU.AFU.AFU.FZU.AXC.AFU.ARI.AXC.BCW.BIQ

seismological stations
RK.1177 (L)
ALT **seismological station**
UF earthquake stations
stations, earthquake
stations, seismological
CN V.RK.AFU.ALO.ALO.FIM.ALO.ALO.ALO.ARI

Sekani
FL.1239
CN F.FL.ALO.ALO.ARI.AFU.AFU.ARI.DIO

Seke
FL.193
CN F.FL.ALO.AFU.AXC.AFU.AFU.AFU.ALO.BUE

Sekki
USE **Yakishime**

Seldjuk
USE **Seljuk**

select bibliographies
USE **selective bibliographies**

select limestone
MT.698
SN A dense, fine-grain stone with only minor variations of grain and texture and no pore spaces larger than 1 mm. (WATSON)
UF limestone, select
CN M.MT.AFU.AFU.AFU.DCU.AFU.ALO.AFU.ALO.ALO.ARI.ARI

select lumber
MT.1442
SN In carpentry, boards with few defects and suitable for fine finished work. (PUTNAM)
UF lumber, select
CN M.MT.AFU.AFU.ALO.BIQ.DCU.ALO.BOK.ARI.AXC

selecting
KG.13
UF choosing
CN K.KG.AFU.AFU.AFU.BOK.AFU

selections
USE **excerpts**

selective bibliographies
VW.257
ALT **selective bibliography**
UF bibliographies, partial
bibliographies, select
bibliographies, selective
partial bibliographies
select bibliographies
CN V.VW.AFU.AFU.AFU.FZU.BCW.AFU.ALO.ARI

selenite
MT.523
SN A variety of gypsum occurring in transparent crystals or crystalline masses. (W)
CN M.MT.AFU.AFU.AFU.CFS.AFU.DUC.ARI

selenium
MT.576
SN A nonmetallic element obtained chiefly as a by-product in copper refining. (WCOL)
CN M.MT.AFU.AFU.AFU.CRG

selenium red
USE **cadmium red**

Seleucid
FL.3015 (A,L,B)
CN F.FL.ALO.AXC.ARI.BIQ.AFU.AXC

Self-destructive
USE **Auto-destructive**

self-expression
BM.36
CN B.BM.AFU.AFU.ALO.BIQ.AFU

self-help housing (A,L,B)
RG.76
SN Use for housing built or renovated by nonprofit groups or single families whose labor is counted as part of the homeowner's equity. (HUD)
UF housing, self-help
CN V.RG.AFU.AFU.BOK.AXC.AFU.BIQ

self-instructional materials
VW.360
ALT **self-instructional material**
UF materials, self-instructional
CN V.VW.AFU.AFU.ALO.CXA.BZY

self-latching bolts
TF.558
ALT **self-latching bolt**
UF bolts, self-latching
CN V.TF.AFU.ALO.AXC.AFU.BUE

self-portraits (L,R)
VB.76
ALT **self-portrait**
CN V.VB.AFU.AXC.BCW.ALO

self-service restaurants
USE **Automats (TM)**
cafeterias

self-service shops
USE **self-service stores**

self-service stores (L,B)
RK.180
ALT **self-service store**
UF self-service shops
shops, self-service
stores, self-service
CN V.RK.AFU.ALO.ALO.ALO.ARI.BIQ.ALO.CFS

Selim I
FL.3491
UF Selim the Grim
CN F.FL.ALO.BIQ.AFU.FOG.AFU.CFS

Selim II
FL.3493
UF Selim the Sot
CN F.FL.ALO.BIQ.AFU.FOG.AFU.CRG

Selim III
FL.3509
CN F.FL.ALO.BIQ.AFU.FOG.AFU.GFO

Selim the Grim
USE **Selim I**

Selim the Sot
USE **Selim II**

Seljuk (A,L,B,R)
FL.3549
UF Saljuk
Seldjuk
CN F.FL.ALO.BIQ.AFU.HIK

Seljuk of Anatolia
USE **Seljuk of Rum**

Seljuk of Kirman
FL.3551
CN F.FL.ALO.BIQ.AFU.HIK.ALO

Seljuk of Rum
FL.3552
UF Anatolian Seljuq
Rum, Seljuk of
Seljuk of Anatolia
Seljuq, Anatolian
CN F.FL.ALO.BIQ.AFU.HIK.ARI

Seljuk of Syria
FL.3561
CN F.FL.ALO.BIQ.AFU.HIK.AXC

Seljuk, Great
USE **Great Seljuk**

Seljuq, Anatolian
USE **Seljuk of Rum**

sellae
USE **stools**

sellae curulis
TG.272
ALT **sella curulis**
SN Ancient Roman folding stools used by senators and magistrates.
UF chairs, curule
chaises curules
curule chairs
CN V.TG.AFU.AFU.ALO.AFU.ALO.AXC.AFU.BIQ

selling (L)
KG.171
CN K.KG.AFU.ALO.AFU.BOK

selours
USE **testers**

Semainean period
USE **Early Dynastic (Egyptian)**

semainiers
TG.495
ALT **semainier**
SN Chests of drawers having seven drawers and intended to hold a week's supply of clothing; of a type originally made in 18th-century France. (PC)
CN V.TG.AFU.AFU.AXC.ALO.BCW.CRG

semanticists
HG.173
ALT **semanticist**
CN H.HG.AFU.AXC.AXC.ALO.AFU.ARI

semantics (L,R)
KD.46
SN Study of meanings in language and of changes in those meanings. (ERIC)
CN K.KD.AFU.AFU.AXC.AFU.ALO.BOK

semi-monocoque construction
USE **monocoque construction**

semiarches
RT.241
ALT **semiarch**
SN Arches having only one half of their sweep developed, as in a flying buttress. (DAC)
CN V.RT.AFU.AFU.AFU.BCW.AFU.AFU.AFU.DIO

semicircles
BM.787
ALT **semicircular**
CN B.BM.CFS.ARI.AXC.BCW.AFU.BOK

semicircular arches
RT.242
ALT **semicircular arch**
SN Round arches whose intrados is a full semicircle. (DAC)
UF arches, barrel
arches, circular
arches, compass-headed
arches, Roman
arches, round
arches, semicircular
barrel arches
circular arches
compass-headed arches
Roman arches
round arches
CN V.RT.AFU.AFU.AFU.BCW.AFU.AFU.AFU.DOI

semicolumns
USE **half columns**

semiconductors (L)
MT.2581
SN Materials which are capable of being partly conductors of electricity and partly insulators. (MH)
CN M.MT.AFU.ARI.CXA.AFU.AFU

semidetached houses
USE **double houses**

semidomes
RT.398
ALT **semidome**
SN Use for domes consisting of one quarter of a sphere, such as would surmount an arched niche.
UF cul-de-fours
domes, half
half domes
CN V.RT.AFU.AFU.AFU.BIQ.AFU.AFU.BZY

semidrying oil
MT.2025
SN A vegetable oil such as corn or soy bean oil, that can be made to dry or form a solid film by chemical treatment, but does not do so on simple exposure to air, as does a drying oil; not used in artists' oil paints. (MAYER)

UF oil, semidrying
CN M.MT.AFU.AFU.ARI.ARI.AXC.ALO

semiellipses
BM.788
ALT **semielliptical**
CN B.BM.CFS.ARI.AXC.BCW.AFU.BUE

semielliptical arches
USE **elliptical arches**

seminaries
USE **theological seminaries**

seminaries, Jewish theological
USE **rabbinical seminaries**

seminaries, rabbinical
USE **rabbinical seminaries**

seminaries, theological
USE **theological seminaries**

seminars
KM.50 (L,B)
CN K.KM.AFU.BCW.AXC

Seminole
FL.1439 (L)
CN F.FL.ALO.ALO.ARI.AFU.BZY.CFS

semiotics
KD.52 (L,B,R)
SN Theory and study of signs and symbols dealing especially with their function in languages, including syntax, semantics, and pragmatics. (ERIC)
CN K.KD.AFU.AFU.AXC.ALO.ARI

semiprecious stones
MT.574 (L,R)
UF stones, semiprecious
CN M.MT.AFU.AFU.AFU.CFS.ALO.AXC

semiskilled workers
HG.27
ALT **semiskilled worker**
SN Use for persons possessing skills in a limited range of activities that demand less training, experience, and independent judgement than is required of skilled workers. (ERIC)
UF workers, semiskilled
CN H.HG.AFU.AXC.ALO.ARI

sems
TF.472
CN V.TF.AFU.AFU.AFU.ALO.AFU.
DIO.AFU.AXC.AFU

Sena
FL.2211
UF Pala-Sena (Sena)
CN F.FL.ALO.ARI.AXC.ALO.AFU.
AXC.BCW

Senate records
VW.1037
ALT **Senate record**
UF records, Senate
CN V.VW.AFU.ARI.ALO.BCW.AFU.
ARI.ALO.AFU.ARI

Senators
HG.680 (L)
ALT **Senator**
CN H.HG.AFU.AXC.CFS.CFS.BCW.ARI

Seneca
FL.1297 (L)
CN F.FL.ALO.ALO.ARI.AFU.ARI.BCW.
BCW

Seneca sandstone
MT.721
UF sandstone, Seneca
CN M.MT.AFU.AFU.AFU.DCU.AFU.
ALO.AFU.ARI.AFU.ALO.AXC.ALO.
ALO

Senegal ebony
USE **African blackwood**

Sengele
FL.536
UF Basengele
CN F.FL.ALO.AFU.AXC.ALO.ALO.
BIQ.ALO.CLM

Sengoku
FL.1969
CN F.FL.ALO.ARI.ALO.ALO.AFU.
ALO.ARI.AFU

senior centers
RK.1191 (A,L,B)
ALT **senior center**
SN Use for drop-in centers for elderly, ambulatory adults that provide classes and unsupervised activities and programs, but no medical services.
UF centers, senior
CN V.RK.AFU.ALO.ALO.FUA.ALO.ALO

senior citizens
USE **aged**

sensation
BM.594 (L)
UF feeling
CN B.BM.BUE.CLM

senses
BM.724 (L,R)
UF five senses
CN B.BM.CFS.AFU.BCW

sensing, remote
USE **remote sensing**

sensitized paper
USE **photographic paper**

sensitometry
KT.510 (L)
SN Any process of measuring sensitivity. (W)
CN K.KT.AFU.ALO.EFQ.ARI

sensitometry, photographic
USE **photographic sensitometry**

sensors, flame
USE **flame detectors**

sensuality
BM.600 (L,R)
SN Purely animal or physical part of human nature; the senses and appetites of the physical body. (W)
CN B.BM.BUE.CRG

Sentani
USE **Lake Sentani**

sentencing
KG.206 (L)
SN Condemning to penalty or punishment. (W)
CN K.KG.AFU.ALO.BCW.BOK.BIQ

sentry boxes
RK.871
ALT **sentry box**
SN Huts or boxes to shelter a sentry at his post. (W)
UF boxes, sentry
CN V.RK.AFU.ALO.ALO.DIO.ALO.BCW

Senufo
FL.361 (L)
UF Siena
CN F.FL.ALO.AFU.AXC.AFU.AXC.
AFU.CRG

separable lenses
USE **convertible lenses**

separate
USE **detached**

separate contracts
VW.884
ALT **separate contract**
SN Contracts made between owners and builders other than general contractors for the construction of portions of a project. (STEIN)
UF contracts, separate
CN V.VW.AFU.ARI.AFU.BOK.BOK.
ALO.ALO.AFU.ARI

separating
KT.635 (L)
ALT **separated**
UF separation
CN K.KT.AFU.ALO.GFO

separation
USE **separating**

separation negatives
USE **color separation negatives**

separation negatives, color
USE **color separation negatives**

separation positives
USE **color separation positives**

separation, color
USE **color separation**

separations, grade
USE **grade separations**

sepia

MT.2504
UF cuttlefish ink
ink, cuttlefish
CN M.MT.AFU.ARI.CRG.ALO.ALO.BZY

sepia (color)
USE **dark grayish yellowish brown**
dark olive brown
light brownish gray
moderate olive brown

sepia brown
USE **dark grayish yellowish brown**
dark olive brown
dark yellowish brown

sepia intermediates
USE **sepia prints**

sepia platinotype
KT.360
SN Photographic process that is a variant of the platinum process in which citrate of mercury is introduced, giving sepia tones to the print.
UF platinotype, sepia
sepiatype (platinotype)
CN K.KT.AFU.ALO.DUC.DIO.ALO.DOI.AFU

sepia prints
VW.694
ALT **sepia print**
SN Use for brownline prints on translucent paper, usually used as intermediates from which more prints can be made and usually made by a diazo process; distinct from **brownprints,** which show a white image on brown background.
UF intermediates, sepia
prints, sepia
prints, sepia process
prints, Van Dyke (sepia prints)
sepia intermediates
sepia process prints
sepias
Van Dyke prints (sepia prints)
CN V.VW.AFU.ALO.AFU.DZW.BIQ.CRG.ARI.AFU

sepia process prints
USE **sepia prints**

sepia, Roman
USE **Roman sepia**

sepias
USE **sepia prints**

sepiatype (platinotype)
USE **sepia platinotype**

Sepik
FL.3645 (L)
UF Sepik River
CN F.FL.ALO.BOK.ALO.BCW.ALO.BCW

Sepik River
USE **Sepik**

Sepik, Lower
USE **Lower Sepik**

Sepik, Middle
USE **Middle Sepik**

sepiolite
USE **meerschaum**

septaria
MT.731
CN M.MT.AFU.AFU.AFU.DCU.AFU.ALO.ALO.AFU.AFU

septic tanks
RT.1494 (L,B)
ALT **septic tank**
SN Watertight reservoirs or tanks that receive sewage and by sedimentation and bacterial action effect a process of clarification and partial purification. (STEIN)
UF tanks, septic
CN V.RT.ALO.BCW.ALO.ARI.CRG

sepulchers
RT.1221
ALT **sepulcher**
SN Receptacles for relics in Christian altars. (HAS)
CN V.RT.AFU.BUE.ALO.ALO.ALO.AXC

sepulchers (tombs)
USE **tombs**

sepulchers, Easter
USE **Easter sepulchers**

sepulchral chapels
RM.313 (A,L,B)
ALT **sepulchral chapel**
SN Use for small chapels containing individual or family tombs. For rooms devoted to funeral services in funeral homes, use **funeral chapels.**
UF chapels, monumental
chapels, mortuary
chapels, sepulchral
monumental chapels
mortuary chapels
CN V.RM.AFU.DIO.AXC.ALO.AFU.AXC.BZY

sepulchral monuments
RK.476 (A,L,B,R)
ALT **sepulchral monument**
UF monuments, sepulchral
CN V.RK.AFU.ALO.ALO.BOK.BOK

sequential art
USE **serial art**

sequential photography
USE **chronophotography**

sequoia
USE **redwood**

Sequoia sempervirens
USE **Humboldt redwood**

sequoia, giant
USE **giant sequoia**

Sequoidendron giganteum
USE **giant sequoia**

seraya
USE **Borneo mahogany**

Serer
FL.342 (L)
CN F.FL.ALO.AFU.AXC.AFU.ARI.BIQ.BOK

Seri
FL.1483 (L)
CN F.FL.ALO.ALO.ARI.AFU.CFS.CXA

serial art
BM.252 (L,R)
SN Use for works of art created as a series, a popular genre since the late 19th century, especially in Minimal art of the 1960s.
UF art, sequential
art, serial
art, series
imagery, serial
sequential art
serial imagery
serialism
series art
CN B.BM.AFU.ARI.BCW.FCS

serial imagery
USE **serial art**

serial photography
USE **chronophotography**

serial publications
USE **serials**

serialism
USE **serial art**

serials
VW.611 (L,B,R)
ALT **serial**
SN Publications in any medium issued in successive parts bearing numerical or chronological designations and intended to be continued indefinitely. (AACR2)
UF publications, serial
serial publications
CN V.VW.AFU.ALO.AFU.CXA.AFU

series
VW.76 (L)
SN Includes publications which bear a collective title in addition to their individual titles and works similar in character that are issued in sequence.
CN V.VW.AFU.AFU.AFU.EWY

series (mathematics)
BM.818 (L)
UF progressions (mathematics)
CN B.BM.CFS.ARI.CLM

series art

USE serial art

series, arithmetic
USE **arithmetic progressions**

series, monographic
USE **monographic series**

serigraphers
HG.133 (L)
ALT **serigrapher**
CN H.HG.AFU.AXC.AXC.AFU.AFU.ALO.AXC.DUC.BCW

serigraphy
KT.467 (L,R)
SN Printmaking technique where ink or paint is brushed through a fine screen made of cloth and masks are used to produce the design. (THDAT)
UF printing, silk screen
silk screen printing
silkscreening
CN K.KT.AFU.ALO.DUC.DUC.ALO.BCW.ALO.AXC

serliana
USE **Palladian windows**

sermons
VW.473 (L,R)
ALT **sermon**
SN Religious discourses delivered as part of a church service. (AHD)
UF homilies
CN V.VW.AFU.AFU.ALO.FOG.ARI

serpent columns
RT.96
ALT **serpent column**
SN Use for columns depicting serpents, features of Toltec architecture.
UF columns, serpent
CN V.RT.AFU.AFU.AFU.AXC.BIQ.AFU.AFU.CRG

serpentina comune
MT.854
UF marmor ligusticum
CN M.MT.AFU.AFU.AFU.DCU.AFU.ARI.BOK.AXC

serpentine
DC.71
SN Winding, meandering, or sinuous in shape.(W) Used especially with reference to furniture pieces, the fronts of which are shaped in alternating concave and convex curves. For other features, such as arches or moldings, composed of flowing, wavelike curves, use **undulating**. For features consisting of or bounded by curved lines in general use **curvilinear**.
CN D.DC.AFU.ARI.DIO

serpentine (rock)
MT.850 (L)
CN M.MT.AFU.AFU.AFU.DCU.AFU.ARI.BOK

serpentine-front
DC.110
CN D.DC.AFU.ARI.EWY.CFS

serpentine, reverse
USE **oxbow**

Serrano
FL.1263 (L)
CN F.FL.ALO.ALO.ARI.AFU.ALO.DUC

serre papiers
TG.441
ALT **serre papier**
SN Pieces of furniture fitted with pigeonholes or compartments to hold paper; either resting on a specially made cabinet placed at one end of a bureau plat or on the top of the bureau plat itself. (PC)
CN V.TG.AFU.AFU.AXC.ALO.ARI.ALO.DIO

serres-bijoux
USE **jewel cabinets**

servants
HG.53 (L,R)
ALT **servant**
CN H.HG.AFU.AXC.ARI.DIO

servants' halls
RM.394
ALT **servants' hall**
SN Use for rooms where servants gather and dine.
UF halls, servants'
CN V.RM.AFU.DIO.BCW.BCW

servants, civil
USE **government employees**

servants, public
USE **government employees**

servers
TG.595 (N)
ALT **server**
UF serving tables
tables, serving
CN V.TG.AFU.AFU.AXC.ALO.CRG.BZY

servers (sideboard tables)
USE **sideboard tables**

service books
USE **choirbooks**

service cores
RM.217 (B)
ALT **service core**
SN Use for areas rising through the centers of buildings, devoted to such service functions as pipe chases, air ducts, elevators, fire stairs, and rest rooms.
UF cores (service cores)
CN V.RM.AFU.DIO.ALO.DIO.BCW

service elevators
RT.1315
ALT **service elevator**
UF elevators, service
CN V.RT.ALO.ALO.AFU.ARI.ALO.ALO.ARI

service pipes
RT.1473
ALT **service pipe**
SN Use for water supply pipes which lead from supply sources to the buildings.
UF pipes, service
CN V.RT.ALO.BCW.ALO.ARI.BZY.BIQ

service roads
RK.1557 (L,B)
ALT **service road**
UF frontage roads
roads, frontage
roads, service
CN V.RK.ALO.ALO.BIQ.ARI.ALO.CFS

service sinks
USE **slop sinks**

service station buildings
USE **service stations**

service stations
RK.1254 (A,L,B,R)
ALT **service station**
SN Use for establishments that primarily sell gasoline, lubricating oils, and other merchandise, such as tires and batteries, for motor vehicles and that often also perform minor repair work. (SIC)
UF automobile service stations
buildings, service station
filling stations
gasoline service stations
gasoline stations
petrol filling stations
petrol stations
service station buildings
stations, automobile service
stations, filling
stations, gasoline
stations, petrol
stations, service
CN V.RK.AFU.ALO.ALO.GLI.AFU.ARI.BOK

serviced land
USE **improved land**

services, A and I
USE **abstracting and indexing services**

services, abstracting and indexing
USE **abstracting and indexing services**

services, armed
USE **armed forces**

services, bibliographical
USE **bibliographic utilities**

services, data search
USE **information retrieval services**

services, emergency
USE **emergency services**

services, indexing and abstracting
USE **abstracting and indexing services**

services, information
USE **information services**

services, information retrieval
USE **information retrieval services**

services, information storage and retrieval
USE **information retrieval services**

services, municipal
USE **public services**

services, online reference
USE **online reference services**

services, online search
USE **information retrieval services**

services, public
USE **public services**

services, reference
USE **reference services**

services, relief
USE **welfare services**

services, social
USE **social services**

services, welfare
USE **welfare services**

serving boards
USE **sideboards**

serving tables
USE **servers**
sideboard tables

serviteurs-fidèle
TG.768
ALT **serviteur-fidèle**
SN French 18th-century term for small tiered tables, usually of tripod form, with movable arms to support candlesticks; generally used by women both for work and for reading. (PC)
CN V.TG.AFU.AFU.BIQ.BOK.ALO.GWW.AFU

serviteurs-muets
USE **dumbwaiters (stands)**

servitude
USE **easement**
slavery

Sesklo
FL.2533
CN F.FL.ALO.AXC.ALO.AFU.AFU.AFU.ALO

sessile oak
MT.1250 (L)
UF oak, sessile
Quercus sessiliflora
CN M.MT.AFU.AFU.ALO.BIQ.DCU.AFU.AFU.AFU.IRA.DZW

set hammers
TB.665 (N)
ALT **set hammer**
SN Hammer like tools having a grooved or hollowed-out face; used as a swage when riveting sheet metal. (PUTNAM)
UF hammers, set
CN V.TB.AFU.BCW.BIQ.AFU.ALO.BIQ.BCW

set squares
TB.447 (N)
ALT **set square**
SN Drafting instruments having straight edges that may be set at any desired angle with the edge of a drawing board. (W)
UF squares, set
CN V.TB.AFU.ARI.EFQ.ALO.BZY.AXC

set squares (triangles)
USE **triangles (tools)**

set tubs
USE **laundry trays**

setback buttresses
RT.80
ALT **setback buttress**
SN Use for buttresses set back slightly from the corners of buildings.
UF buttresses, setback
CN V.RT.AFU.AFU.AFU.AXC.AXC.BCW

setback (formal concept)
BM.88
SN Withdrawal of the face of a building to a line some distance to the rear of the building line or to the rear of the wall below to reduce the obstruction the upper stories offer to sunlight and air reaching the lower stories and street. (W)
CN B.BM.AFU.AFU.ARI.AFU.EWY

setback (zoning law)
BM.485
SN Distance from the curb or other established line within which no building may be erected. (STEIN)
CN B.BM.BCW.DUC.BIQ

Seto-guro
FL.2039
CN F.FL.ALO.ARI.ALO.ALO.ALO.ALO.ALO.DUC.ARI

Seto ware
FL.2036 (L)
UF pottery, Seto
ware, Seto
CN F.FL.ALO.ARI.ALO.ALO.ALO.ALO.ALO.DUC

Seto, Ki
USE **Ki Seto**

Seto, Ko
USE **Ko Seto**

Seto, Old
USE **Ko Seto**

Seto, Yellow
USE **Ki Seto**

sets
VB.99 (N)
ALT **set**
SN Use with reference to a group of things designed to be used or viewed together.
CN V.VB.ALO.BOK.BZY

sets, brick
USE **brick sets**

sets, nail
USE **nail sets**

sets, rivet
USE **rivet sets**

sets, stage
USE **stage sets**

setscrews
TF.473
ALT **setscrew**
UF screws, set
CN V.TF.AFU.AFU.AFU.ALO.AFU.DIO.AFU.BCW

Settchuyo
FL.2001
UF Eclectic Style
CN F.FL.ALO.ARI.ALO.ALO.ALO.AFU.BZY

settee beds
USE **settle beds**

settees
TG.300 (N,R)
ALT **settee**
SN Seats with a back and usually arms; large enough for two or more persons. (DDA)
UF têtes
CN V.TG.AFU.AFU.ALO.ALO.BUE

settees, chair-back
USE **chair-back settees**

settees, Darby and Joan
USE **chair-back settees**

settees, Knole
USE **Knole settees**

settees, rocking
USE **cradle benches**

settees, Windsor
USE **Windsor settees**

setters-out
HG.470
ALT **setter-out**
SN Carpenters or metalworkers who line out the details of the work. (W)
CN H.HG.AFU.AXC.BUE.ALO.CXA

setting punches

USE **rivet sets**

settle beds
TG.370
ALT **settle bed**
SN Settles convertible into beds.
UF banc lits
beds, settee
beds, settle
settee beds
CN V.TG.AFU.AFU.ARI.AFU.AFU.DZW

settle benches
USE **settles**

settle-tables
TG.286 (N)
ALT **settle-table**
UF settles, table
table-settles
CN V.TG.AFU.AFU.ALO.ALO.AFU.AFU.BIQ.ARI

settlement of land
USE **land settlement**

settlement of structures
BM.1027 (A,L)
UF structures, settlement of
CN B.BM.CFS.AXC.CLM.ALO.BOK

settlement, land
USE **land settlement**

settlements
RD.1 (A,L)
ALT **settlement**
SN Designates places or areas occupied, modified, or planned to be inhabited by communities of human populations and that contain enough societal functions to be relatively self-sufficient.
UF human settlements
CN V.RD.AFU

settlements, agricultural
USE **agricultural settlements**

settlements, collective
USE **collective settlements**

settlements, communal
USE **collective settlements**

settlements, mining
USE **mining towns**

settlements, moon
USE **lunar bases**

settlements, squatter
USE **squatter settlements**

settles
TG.283 (N,R)
ALT **settle**
SN Long seats of two basic types: a low-back bench with arms and a bench with a high, usually solid, back and with arms and wings. For settles with hinged seats use **box settles.**
UF benches, settle
settle benches
CN V.TG.AFU.AFU.ALO.ALO.AFU.AFU.BIQ

settles, box
USE **box settles**

settles, hooded
USE **hooded settles**

settles, storage
USE **box settles**

settles, table
USE **settle-tables**

settling basins
RK.579 (L)
ALT **settling basin**
UF basins, sedimentation
basins, settling
sedimentation basins
settling tanks
CN V.RK.AFU.ALO.ALO.CFS.ALO.BCW.BOK

settling tanks
USE **settling basins**

Seventeenth Dynasty
FL.2811
UF 17th Dynasty
Dynasty, Seventeenth
CN F.FL.ALO.AXC.ALO.ARI.AFU.BOK.BCW

Seventh Dynasty
FL.2797
UF 7th Dynasty
Dynasty, Seventh
CN F.FL.ALO.AXC.ALO.ARI.AFU.BCW.AFU

Severan
FL.2724 (R)
CN F.FL.ALO.AXC.ALO.ALO.AFU.AXC.ALO.BUE

Severe Style
FL.2695
CN F.FL.ALO.AXC.ALO.AFU.ALO.BCW.ALO.CXA

severies
USE **vault bays**

sewage disposal
KG.128 (L,B)
UF disposal, sewage
CN K.KG.AFU.AFU.BCW.ALO.CFS.AFU.ALO

sewage disposal plants
USE **sewage treatment plants**

sewage sumps
USE **sumps**

sewage treatment
USE **solid waste management**

sewage treatment plants
RK.587 (A,L,B)
ALT **sewage treatment plant**
UF plants, sewage treatment
sewage disposal plants
treatment plants, sewage
CN V.RK.AFU.ALO.ALO.CFS.ALO.BCW.CRG.ARI

sewer brick
USE **blue brick**

sewerage system, combined
USE **combined sewers**

sewers
RK.542 (A,L,B)
ALT **sewer**
CN V.RK.AFU.ALO.ALO.CFS.ALO.AFU.ALO

sewers (textile workers)
HG.530 (R)
ALT **sewer (textile worker)**
UF seamstresses
CN H.HG.AFU.AXC.BUE.ARI.CXA.BCW

sewers, branch
USE **branch sewers**

sewers, combined
USE **combined sewers**

sewers, intercepting
USE **intercepting sewers**

sewers, lateral
USE **lateral sewers**

sewers, main
USE **main sewers**

sewers, outfall
USE **outfall sewers**

sewers, sanitary
USE **sanitary sewers**

sewers, storm
USE **storm sewers**

sewers, trunk
USE **main sewers**

sewing
KT.567 (L,R)
ALT **sewn**
CN K.KT.AFU.ALO.ELK.DUC.ARI

sewing rooms
RM.235
ALT **sewing room**
UF rooms, sewing
CN V.RM.AFU.DIO.ALO.DOI.CRG

sewing tables
USE **work tables**

sewing, side
USE **side sewing**

sex
BM.731 (L,R)
CN B.BM.CFS.AFU.BIQ

sex discrimination
BM.1108 (L)
SN Use for discriminatory behavior directed against either sex.
UF discrimination, sex
sexism
CN B.BM.CRG.BCW.ARI.BCW

sex role
BM.1131 (L)
UF role, sex
CN B.BM.CRG.BUE.BCW

sexism
USE **sex discrimination**

sexpartite vaults
RT.527
ALT **sexpartite vault**
SN Vaults divided into six vaulting cells.
UF hexapartite vaults
six-part vaults
vaults, hexapartite
vaults, sexpartite
vaults, six-part
CN V.RT.AFU.AFU.AFU.BIQ.BOK.
AFU.AFU.AFU.AFU.ARI

sexuality
BM.601
CN B.BM.BUE.CXA

Sezession
USE **Secession Movement**

Sezessionstil
FL.3309 (B)
UF Secession style
CN F.FL.ALO.BCW.ALO.AXC.DIO.
AFU.AFU

sfumato
KT.288 (R)
SN In oil painting, the creation of soft, delicately blended effects by the fusion of one tone into another, particularly in glazes. (MAYER)
CN K.KT.AFU.ALO.DUC.DCU.BUE

sgabelles
TG.41
ALT **sgabelle**
SN Term used outside of Italy to describe 16th-century Italian wooden side chairs having a solid carved back and small, usually octagonal, seat supported on carved end boards in the front and back, instead of legs.
CN V.TG.AFU.AFU.ALO.AFU.AFU.
AFU.CFS.ALO

sgraffito
KT.478 (L,B,R)
SN The technique of scratching through one surface layer, such as on a wall or slip on a pot, so as to reveal another layer of contrasting color. (THDAT)
UF decoration, graffito
graffiato
graffito decoration
CN K.KT.AFU.ALO.DUC.DZW

sgraffito, dry
USE **dry sgraffito**

shackles, raft
USE **raft shackles**

shacks
RK.241 (A)
ALT **shack**
UF shanties
CN V.RK.AFU.ALO.ALO.AXC.ALO.
AFU.BZY

shacks, pole
USE **log cabins**

shade
BM.861 (L)
CN B.BM.CFS.AXC.ALO.AFU.ALO.
ALO.BUE

shade roller pin nails
TF.446
ALT **shade roller pin nail**
UF nails, shade roller pin
pin nails, shade roller
roller pin nails, shade
CN V.TF.AFU.AFU.AFU.ALO.AFU.CFS.
ALO.DOI

shaded-relief maps
VW.161
ALT **shaded-relief map**
SN Maps on which relief is made to appear three-dimensional by the use of graded shadow effect. (DOD)
UF maps, shaded-relief
CN V.VW.AFU.AFU.AFU.FZU.AXC.
AFU.ARI.AFU.CXA.ARI

shades, sun
USE **brise-soleils**

shading
KT.289
ALT **shaded**
SN The darkening of areas of a picture to indicate shadows.
CN K.KT.AFU.ALO.DUC.DCU.BZY

shadow joints
USE **recessed joints**

shadow pictures
USE **photograms**

shadowgraphs (photograms)
USE **photograms**

shadowgraphs (radiographs)
USE **radiographs**

shadows
BM.862 (A,L,B,R)
ALT **shadow**
CN B.BM.CFS.AXC.ALO.AFU.ALO.
ALO.BZY

shadows, cast
USE **cast shadows**

Shaft Grave period
FL.2551
CN F.FL.ALO.AXC.ALO.AFU.AFU.
ALO.ALO.ALO.AFU

shaft graves
RK.493 (A)
ALT **shaft grave**
UF graves, pit
graves, shaft
pit graves
pit tombs
shaft tombs
tombs, pit
tombs, shaft
CN V.RK.AFU.ALO.ALO.BOK.BUE.
AFU.BUE

shaft rings
RT.147
ALT **shaft ring**
UF cimbiae
rings, shaft
CN V.RT.AFU.AFU.AFU.AXC.BIQ.
ALO.AXC.ALO.AXC

shaft tombs
USE **shaft graves**

shafts (column components)
RT.142
ALT **shaft (column component)**
SN The portions of columns, colonettes, or pilasters between the base and the capital. (HAS)
CN V.RT.AFU.AFU.AFU.AXC.BIQ.
ALO.AXC.AFU

shafts (Medieval columns)
RT.97
ALT **shaft (Medieval column)**
SN Use for small columns in Medieval architecture that are usually attached to walls, piers, or the like.
CN V.RT.AFU.AFU.AFU.AXC.BIQ.
AFU.AFU.CXA

shafts (spaces)
RM.281
ALT **shaft (space)**
SN Well-like passages or enclosed vertical spaces in a building. (RHDEL2)
CN V.RM.AFU.DIO.ARI.ALO.DIO

shafts (tool components)
TB.1131
ALT **shaft (tool components)**
CN V.TB.ALO.DOI

shafts, air
USE **air shafts**

shafts, baluster
USE **baluster columns**

shafts, jamb
USE **jamb shafts**

shafts, mine
USE **mine shafts**

shafts, nook

USE nook shafts

shaftways
USE **hoistways**

shagbark hickory
MT.1179
UF Carya ovata
hickory, shagbark
hickory, shellbark
shellbark hickory
CN M.MT.AFU.AFU.ALO.BIQ.DCU.AFU.AFU.AFU.ELK.BOK

shagreen
USE **sharkskin**

Shah Alam
FL.2228
CN F.FL.ALO.ARI.AXC.ALO.AFU.BIQ.ALO.AFU.AFU

Shah Jahan
FL.2233
CN F.FL.ALO.ARI.AXC.ALO.AFU.BIQ.ALO.AFU.BIQ

Shah Period
USE **Gurkha**

Shahristan
FL.1824
CN F.FL.ALO.ARI.AFU.AXC.ELK.CLM.ARI

Shai
FL.310
CN F.FL.ALO.AFU.AXC.AFU.ARI.ALO.BOK

Shaibanid
USE **Uzbek**

Shailéndra
USE **Sailendra**

Shaivism
USE **Sivaism**

Shake
FL.421 (L)
UF Kota (Shake)
CN F.FL.ALO.AFU.AXC.ALO.AFU.AXC.BZY

Shaker
BM.649 (A,L,B)
CN B.BM.BZY.AFU.ALO.AXC.BOK

shakes
MT.1455 (L)
SN Shingles or clapboard formed by splitting a short log into tapered radial sections. (RHDEL2)
CN M.MT.AFU.AFU.ALO.BIQ.DCU.ALO.DCU

Shakhrinau
FL.1805
CN F.FL.ALO.ARI.AFU.AXC.DIO

shale
MT.645 (L,B)
CN M.MT.AFU.AFU.AFU.DCU.AFU.ALO.AFU.AFU.BCW

shale, blue
USE **bluestone**

shale, clay
USE **clay shale**

sham doors
USE **false doors**

sham ruins
USE **artificial ruins**

shamanism
BM.707 (L,R)
ALT **shamanistic**
CN B.BM.BZY.ALO.ARI.DCU

Shambala
FL.653 (L)
UF Washambala
CN F.FL.ALO.AFU.AXC.AXC.BCW.CRG

shammy
USE **chamois**

shamoy
USE **chamois**

Shang
FL.1854 (A,L)
CN F.FL.ALO.ARI.ALO.AFU.AFU.ALO.BCW

Shanga
FL.547
CN F.FL.ALO.AFU.AXC.ARI.AFU.BCW

Shanghai
FL.1935
CN F.FL.ALO.ARI.ALO.AFU.AFU.AXC.ALO.CFS

Shango
USE **Sangu**

Shankadi
FL.498
CN F.FL.ALO.AFU.AXC.ALO.ALO.BCW.BCW.ALO.AFU

shanks
TB.695
ALT **shank**
SN Handles by which a ladle of molten metal can be carried by one or more men. (W)
CN V.TB.AFU.BCW.BIQ.ALO.AXC

shanties
USE **shacks**

shantyboats
USE **houseboats**

shantytowns
RG.279 (A,L,B)
ALT **shantytown**
CN V.RG.ALO.AFU.ALO.BCW.ALO

shap granite
MT.599
UF granite, shap
CN M.MT.AFU.AFU.AFU.DCU.AFU.AFU.AFU.AFU.AFU.ARI.ALO.ALO.ALO

shape
BM.89 (A)
CN B.BM.AFU.AFU.ARI.AFU.FCS

shape factors
BM.1024
UF factors, shape
CN B.BM.CFS.AXC.CLM.ALO.BCW.ALO

shaped dormers
RT.482
ALT **shaped dormer**
SN Use for dormers having decoratively multicurved tops or sides.
UF dormers, shaped
CN V.RT.AFU.AFU.AFU.BIQ.ARI.ALO.AFU.BUE.AXC.BIQ

shaped gables
RT.640
ALT **shaped gable**
SN Gables each side of which is multicurved. (HAS)
UF gables, shaped
CN V.RT.AFU.AFU.AFU.BIQ.BUE.ALO.AFU.AXC.AFU.BIQ

shaped stretchers
TG.1002
ALT **shaped stretcher**
UF stretchers, shaped
CN V.TG.ALO.HIK.ALO.ALO.BCW

shaping
USE **forming**

shards
USE **sherds**

share certificates
USE **stock certificates**

sharkskin
MT.952
UF shagreen
CN M.MT.AFU.AFU.ALO.AFU.DZW.ALO.AFU

Sharp-focus Realist
USE **Photorealist**

sharp nails, rose
USE **rose sharp nails**

sharpeners, knife
USE **whetstones**

sharpeners, pencil
USE **pencil sharpeners**

sharpening stones
USE **whetstones**

Shasta
FL.1264 (L)
CN F.FL.ALO.ALO.ARI.AFU.ALO.DZW

shatterproof glass
USE **safety glass**

shavehooks
TB.528
ALT **shavehook**
SN Small tools with interchangeable heads used to scratch metal and wood surfaces.
CN V.TB.AFU.ARI.EWY.ALO.DIO.AFU

shaves, draft
USE **drawknives**

shaves, hollow
USE **hollowing drawknives**

shaves, inside
USE **scorpers**

shaves, one-hand round
USE **closed scorpers**

shaves, round
USE **scorpers**

shaving blocks
TB.1073 (N)
ALT **shaving block**
SN Blocks used in conjunction with the woodworker's body to hold a piece of wood in place during shaving.
UF blocks, shaving
CN V.TB.AFU.BCW.CFS.ALO.ALO.CRG

shaving chairs
USE **corner chairs**

shaving knives
USE **drawknives**

shaving stands
TG.651 (N)
ALT **shaving stand**
SN Various types of stands with adjustable mirrors used by men when dressing or shaving.
UF barbières
shaving tables
stands, shaving
tables, shaving
CN V.TG.AFU.AFU.BIQ.BCW.ALO.DUC

shaving tables
USE **shaving stands**

shavings
MT.2266
SN Thin layers or shreds of material that have been cut or sliced from another material or object.
CN M.MT.AFU.ALO.FUA

Shawnee
FL.1440 (L)
UF Piqua
CN F.FL.ALO.ALO.ARI.AFU.BZY.CLM

Shaybanid
USE **Uzbek**

sheaf-back chairs
TG.147
ALT **sheaf-back chair**
SN Modern term for chair backs, made in the mid-18th century, with a waisted, pierced splat, which resembles the shape of a wheatsheaf. (GLOAG)
UF chairs, sheaf-back
chairs, wheatsheaf-back
wheatsheaf-back chairs
CN V.TG.AFU.AFU.ALO.AFU.AFU.AFU.NIE.CXA.ARI

sheaf catalogs
USE **loose-leaf catalogs**

shear force, internal
USE **shear stress**

shear strength
BM.963
SN The maximum shear stress which a material or soil is capable of sustaining. (DAC)
UF strength, shear
CN B.BM.CFS.AXC.BZY.BOK.CLM.BCW

shear stress
BM.921 (L)
UF internal shear force
shear force, internal
stress, shear
CN B.BM.CFS.AXC.BIQ.ARI.BCW.BCW

shear walls
RT.590 (A)
ALT **shear wall**
SN Walls which in their own plane carry shear resulting from forces such as wind, blast, or earthquakes. (DAC)
UF walls, shear
CN V.RT.AFU.AFU.AFU.BIQ.BUE.AFU.ALO.BCW

shearing sheds
USE **woolsheds**

shears
TB.138 (L,N)
SN Cutting implements similar or identical to scissors, but typically larger. (W)
CN V.TB.AFU.ARI.AXC.ALO.CXA

shears, alligator
USE **lever shears**

shears, bench
USE **bench shears**

shears, circle
USE **circle shears**

shears, crocodile
USE **lever shears**

shears, lever
USE **lever shears**

shears, sheet
USE **sheet shears**

sheathing
MT.2415 (A)
SN The covering, usually wood boards, plywood, or wallboards, placed over the exterior studding or rafters of a building; provides a base for the application of wall or roof siding. (DAC)
CN M.MT.AFU.ARI.BZY.BOK

sheathing nails
TF.447
ALT **sheathing nail**
UF nails, sheathing
CN V.TF.AFU.AFU.AFU.ALO.AFU.CFS.ALO.DUC

sheathing paper
USE **building paper**

sheave saws
USE **crown saws**

shed dormers
RT.483
ALT **shed dormer**
SN Dormers whose eaves lines are parallel to the eaves lines of the main roof instead of being gabled; provide more attic space than gabled dormers. (DAC)
UF dormers, shed
CN V.RT.AFU.AFU.AFU.BIQ.ARI.ALO.AFU.BUE.AXC.BOK

shed roofs
RT.434 (B)
ALT **shed roof**
SN Pitched roofs with only one slope.
UF half-span roofs
lean-to roofs
pent roofs (shed roofs)
penthouse roofs (shed roofs)
roof, lean-to
roofs, half-span
roofs, penthouse (shed roofs)
roofs, shed
CN V.RT.AFU.AFU.AFU.BIQ.ARI.AFU.AFU.AFU.BOK.BUE

sheds
RK.1212 (A,N,B)
ALT **shed**
CN V.RK.AFU.ALO.ALO.GFO.BIQ

sheds, bicycle
USE **bicycle sheds**

sheds, carriage
USE **carriage houses**

sheds, cattle
USE **cow sheds**

sheds, chicken
USE **chicken houses**

sheds, cow
USE **cow sheds**

sheds, cycle
USE **bicycle sheds**

sheds, drying
USE **drying sheds**

sheds, hop
USE **hop barns**

sheds, locomotive
USE **train sheds**

sheds, lumber
USE **lumber sheds**

sheds, machinery
USE **machinery sheds**

sheds, shearing
USE **woolsheds**

sheds, tobacco
USE **tobacco barns**

sheds, train
USE **train sheds**

sheds, weaving
USE **weaving sheds**

sheep barns
RK.51
ALT **sheep barn**
UF barns, sheep
CN V.RK.AFU.ALO.ALO.AFU.AFU.AFU.ALO.ARI

sheep farms
RG.12 (L,B)
ALT **sheep farm**
UF farms, sheep
CN V.RG.AFU.AFU.AFU.AFU.ARI.BCW

sheepcotes
USE **sheepfolds**

sheepfolds
RK.93 (R)
ALT **sheepfold**
SN Pens or shelters for sheep. (W)
UF sheepcotes
sheephouses
CN V.RK.AFU.ALO.ALO.AFU.ALO.CRG

sheephouses
USE **sheepfolds**

sheepsfoot rollers
TB.29
ALT **sheepsfoot roller**
SN Self-propelled or towed drum like rollers with projecting studs that penetrate the surface of the ground; used to obtain deep compaction of fill material. (DAC)
UF rollers, tamping
tamping rollers
CN V.TB.AFU.ARI.AFU.ALO.ALO.AFU

sheer plans
VD.34
ALT **sheer plan**
SN Drawings that are broadside elevations of a ship, emphasizing the ship's lines. When appearing with a body plan and a half-breadth plan, use **lines drawings** for the set. For more detailed broadside elevations, use **outboard profiles.**
UF plans, sheer
CN V.VD.AFU.AFU.BIQ.ALO.ALO.BIQ.BCW

sheet
MT.2267 (B)
SN Use for any material in sheet form; especially used with reference to metal.
UF sheeting
CN M.MT.AFU.ALO.FZU

sheet film
USE **cut film**

sheet glass
MT.250 (B)
UF glass, heavy sheet
glass, sheet
glass, window
heavy sheet glass
sheet glass, heavy
window glass
CN M.MT.AFU.AFU.AFU.BIQ.AFU.ALO.AXC

sheet glass, heavy
USE **sheet glass**

sheet metal screws
TF.475 (N)
ALT **sheet metal screw**
SN Usually self-tapping screws, either round, flat, or pan-headed, threaded from tip to head, and used without a nut for fastening lapped sheet metal and some other materials. (MEANS)
UF screws, sheet metal
CN V.TF.AFU.AFU.AFU.ALO.AFU.DIO.AFU.BIQ

sheet metal workers
HG.518
ALT **sheet metal worker**
UF workers, sheet metal
CN H.HG.AFU.AXC.BUE.ARI.CFS.ARI.BZY

sheet metal worker's snips
USE **tin snips**

sheet music
VW.57 (N)
SN Music printed on unbound sheets of paper. (WCOL)
UF music, sheet
CN V.VW.AFU.AFU.AFU.DOI.ALO

sheet shears
TB.726 (N)
SN Large, foot operated machines that cut sheet metal square to a fence with a guillotine like action. (PC)
UF guillotines (shears)
shears, sheet
CN V.TB.AFU.BCW.BIQ.ARI.ALO.BIQ.BCW

sheeting
USE **sheet**

sheetrock
USE **gypsum board**

sheets, balance
USE **balance sheets**

sheets, contact
USE **contact sheets**

sheets, proof
USE **contact sheets**

sheets, tear
USE **tear sheets**

sheets, time
USE **time sheets**

Sheffield plate
MT.463 (L,R)
UF plate, Sheffield
CN M.MT.AFU.AFU.AFU.BZY.AFU.ALO.AXC.AFU.ALO.AFU

shelf brackets
TF.38 (N)
ALT **shelf bracket**
SN Structural members secured to a wall or upright, from which they also project to support a shelf. (MEANS)
UF brackets, shelf
shelf supports
supports, shelf
CN V.TF.AFU.AFU.AFU.AFU.ARI.ALO

shelf hardware
TF.510
UF hardware, shelf
CN V.TF.AFU.AFU.ALO.BUE

shelf lists
VW.271
ALT **shelf list**
SN Lists of the holdings in a library, records center, or archives, arranged in the order of the contents of each shelf. (ICA)
UF lists, shelf
CN V.VW.AFU.AFU.AFU.FZU.BCW.AFU.BUE

shelf supports
USE **shelf brackets**

shell
MT.943 (L,R)
UF seashell
CN M.MT.AFU.AFU.ALO.AFU.DUC

shell augers
TB.827 (N)
ALT **shell auger**
UF augers, pod
augers, shell
augers, snail
pod augers
snail augers
CN V.TB.AFU.BCW.CFS.ALO.AFU.ALO.BIQ

shell augers (nose augers)
USE **nose augers**

shell augers, taper
USE **taper augers**

shell bits
TB.1112 (N)
ALT **shell bit**
SN Gouge-shaped bits for boring holes in wood.
UF bits, shell
CN V.TB.ALO.ARI.DCU

shell cabinets
TG.426
ALT **shell cabinet**
UF cabinets, shell
CN V.TG.AFU.AFU.AXC.ALO.ARI.ALO.AXC.ARI

shell chairs
USE **diamond chairs**

shell construction
USE **shell structures**

shell marble
MT.764
SN A dark, gray brown marble, closely packed with fossil shells, which when polished gives a brilliant gleam. (MAYER)
UF fire marble
marble, fire
marble, shell
CN M.MT.AFU.AFU.AFU.DCU.AFU.ARI.ARI.ALO.BOK

shell middens
USE **middens**

shell mounds
USE **middens**

shell roofs
USE **shell structures**

shell structures
RT.518 (A,L,B,R)
ALT **shell structure**
SN Use for curved enclosing structures, almost always of concrete and very thin in relation to their span, and depending for structural stability on actions that may be computed by the membrane theory.
UF construction, shell
roofs, shell
shell construction
shell roofs
shells (structures)
structural shells
structures, shell
structures, thin shell
thin shell structures
CN V.RT.AFU.AFU.AFU.BIQ.BCW

shell, oyster
USE **oyster shell**

shell, scallop
USE **scallop shell**

shell, tortoise
USE **tortoise shell**

shellac
MT.2431 (L)
SN An alcohol-soluble resin, the most highly refined form of lac; also the varnish made by dissolving it in alcohol. (MAYER)
UF shellac varnish
varnish, shellac
CN M.MT.AFU.ARI.CRG.AFU.ARI.ALO

shellac varnish
USE **shellac**

shellac, orange
USE **orange shellac**

shellac, white
USE **white shellac**

shellbark hickory
USE **shagbark hickory**

shellbark hickory, big
USE **big shellbark hickory**

shells (structures)
USE **shell structures**

shells, band
USE **band shells**

shells, orchestra
USE **band shells**

shellstone
USE **coquina rock**

Shelly limestone
MT.657
UF limestone, Shelly
CN M.MT.AFU.AFU.AFU.DCU.AFU.ALO.AFU.ALO.ALO.AFU.AFU.AFU.BCW

shelter
USE **housing**

shelterbelts
USE **windbreaks**

sheltered care homes
USE **rest homes**

sheltered workshops
RK.791 (L,B)
ALT **sheltered workshop**
SN Places providing job training and vocational rehabilitation for the disadvantaged, whether due to physical handicap or lack of experience or education.
UF workshops for the handicapped
workshops, sheltered
CN V.RK.AFU.ALO.ALO.CXA.ALO.ALO.BOK

shelters
RK.1181 (A,B)
ALT **shelter**
SN Use generally for structures providing some degree of protection, refuge, or defense; if possible, use a more specific term.
CN V.RK.AFU.ALO.ALO.FOG

shelters, air raid
USE **air raid shelters**

shelters, animal
USE **animal shelters**

shelters, animal (farm structures)
USE **animal housing**

shelters, atomic bomb
USE **nuclear bomb shelters**

shelters, bicycle
USE **bicycle sheds**

shelters, bomb
USE **air raid shelters**

shelters, bus
USE **bus shelters**

shelters, fallout
USE **nuclear bomb shelters**

shelters, nuclear bomb
USE **nuclear bomb shelters**

shelters, radiation
USE **nuclear bomb shelters**

shelters, rock
USE **rock shelters**

shelves
TG.982
ALT **shelf**
CN V.TG.ALO.GRC

shelves, book
USE **bookshelves**

shelves, china
USE **china shelves**

shelves, corner
USE **corner shelves**

shelves, hanging (cupboards)
USE **hanging cupboards**

shelves, sliding
USE **sliding shelves**

shelves, standing (bookshelves)
USE **bookshelves**

Sheng-wen
FL.1842
CN F.FL.ALO.ARI.ALO.AFU.AFU.AFU.ARI.AFU

shepherds
HG.363 (L,R)
ALT **shepherd**
CN H.HG.AFU.AXC.BIQ.ALO.AXC.AFU.ALO.AFU

sherardizing

KT.824
ALT **sherardized**
SN Coating steel with a thin corrosion-resistant cladding of zinc. (DAC)
CN K.KT.AFU.ALO.HOE.BCW.ALO.ALO.AXC

Sheraton
FL.3339 (R)
CN F.FL.ALO.BCW.ALO.AXC.DIO.ALO.BUE.ARI

Sherbro
FL.332
UF Bulom
CN F.FL.ALO.AFU.AXC.AFU.ARI.BCW.CLM

Sherbro (Afro-Portuguese)
USE **Afro-Portuguese**

Sherbro (Sapi-Portuguese)
USE **Sapi-Portuguese**

sherds
VB.96 (N)
ALT **sherd**
SN Limited to fragments of pottery or glass.
UF shards
CN V.VB.ALO.BOK.BIQ.AFU

sheriffs
HG.686 (L)
ALT **sheriff**
CN H.HG.AFU.AXC.CFS.CFS.CLM

Shetinasha
USE **Chitimacha**

sheverets
USE **cheverets**

Shi'a
BM.665 (L)
ALT **Shi'ite**
UF Shi'ism
Shi'ite Islam
Shia
CN B.BM.BZY.AFU.BCW.AFU

Shi'ism
USE **Shi'a**

Shi'ite Islam
USE **Shi'a**

Shia
USE **Shi'a**

Shibe
FL.2132
CN F.FL.ALO.ARI.ARI.AFU.BIQ.AXC

Shichi-jo
USE **Shichijo Street School**

Shichijo Street School
FL.2103
UF Shichi-jo
CN F.FL.ALO.ARI.ALO.ALO.ALO.BCW.BCW

shield-back chairs
TG.150
ALT **shield-back chair**
SN Chair designs made fashionable in the 1780s by George Hepplewhite. The rail and stile form the shape of a shield. (BEARD)
UF chairs, shield-back
chairs, urn back
chairs, vase back
urn back chairs
vase back chairs
CN V.TG.AFU.AFU.ALO.AFU.AFU.AFU.NIE.DOI

shielded metal arc welding
KT.803 (L)
SN Arc welding in which a flux-coated metal electrode is consumed to form a pool of filler metal and a gas shield around the weld area. (STEIN)
UF arc welding, shielded metal
metal arc welding, shielded
welding, shielded metal arc
CN K.KT.AFU.ALO.HOE.BCW.ALO.AFU.ALO.ALO.AFU.ALO

shields (heraldry)
USE **escutcheons (coats of arms)**

Shields of David
USE **Stars of David**

shields, David's
USE **Stars of David**

shields, erasing
USE **erasing shields**

Shien
USE **Tien**

shift joints
USE **break joints**

shift, color
USE **color shift**

Shigaraki
FL.2040 (L)
CN F.FL.ALO.ARI.ALO.ALO.ALO.ALO.ALO.DZW

Shijo
FL.2065
CN F.FL.ALO.ARI.ALO.ALO.ALO.ARI.DUC

Shiki
FL.2041
CN F.FL.ALO.ARI.ALO.ALO.ALO.ALO.ALO.EFQ

Shilluk
FL.632 (L)
CN F.FL.ALO.AFU.AXC.AXC.ARI.DOI

Shimmei
FL.2002
CN F.FL.ALO.ARI.ALO.ALO.ALO.AFU.CFS

Shin
BM.623 (L)
UF Pure Land sect (Japan)
CN B.BM.BZY.AFU.AFU.BIQ.ALO

Shinden
FL.2003 (A)
CN F.FL.ALO.ARI.ALO.ALO.ALO.AFU.CLM

shingle nails
TF.448
ALT **shingle nail**
SN Nails of galvanized steel, aluminum alloy, or coated steel, often having a threaded shank. (MEANS)
UF nails, shingle
nails, siding
siding nails
CN V.TF.AFU.AFU.AFU.ALO.AFU.CFS.ALO.DZW

shingle punches
TB.977 (N)
ALT **shingle punch**
SN Hinged tools with a stable bed for punching holes in shingles. (MERCER)
UF punches, shingle
CN V.TB.AFU.BCW.CFS.ALO.AFU.DZW.AXC

shingle spruce
USE **white spruce**

Shingle Style
FL.1739 (A,L,B,R)
CN F.FL.ALO.ALO.BCW.AFU.BUE.BUE

shingle tile
MT.177
SN A flat clay tile used for roofing. (DAC)
UF tile, shingle
CN M.MT.AFU.AFU.AFU.AXC.ALO.ALO.ALO.AFU.ALO.AXC.AFU.AFU.AXC

shingles
MT.2396 (A,L,N,B)
ALT **shingle**
SN Units of wood, asphaltic material, slate, tile, concrete, asbestos cement, or other material cut to stock dimensions; used chiefly for roofing. (DAC)
CN M.MT.AFU.ARI.BZY.AXC.ARI

shingling
KT.587
ALT **shingled**
CN K.KT.AFU.ALO.ERE.BOK

shingling hatchets
TB.894 (N)
ALT **shingling hatchet**
SN Hatchets with flared blades and nail-driving polls; used to split and nail wood roof shingles.
UF hatchets, shingling
CN V.TB.AFU.BCW.CFS.ALO.AFU.

DCU.AXC

Shingon
BM.624 (L)
UF True Word sect (Japan)
CN B.BM.BZY.AFU.AFU.BIQ.ARI

Shino
FL.2042 (L)
CN F.FL.ALO.ARI.ALO.ALO.ALO.
ALO.ALO.ELK

Shinto
BM.675 (A,L)
UF Shintoism
CN B.BM.BZY.AFU.CFS

Shintoism
USE **Shinto**

shiny
DC.140
SN Having a reflective surface finish less bright than glossy and giving less of an impression of depth in the finish than a lustrous surface.
CN D.DC.AFU.BCW.BIQ

ship auger bits
TB.1099
ALT **ship auger bit**
SN Large, long, auger bits with a very open twist that may or may not terminate in a screw end. (BLACKB)
UF auger bits, ship
augers, ship (bits)
bits, ship auger
ship augers (bits)
CN V.TB.ALO.ARI.AFU.AFU

ship augers (bits)
USE **ship auger bits**

ship axes
USE **shipwright's axes**

ship building yards
USE **shipyards**

ship carpenter's adzes
USE **shipwright's adzes**

ship carpenter's axes
USE **shipwright's axes**

ship-carpenter's mallets
USE **caulking mallets**

ship chests
USE **sea chests**

ship locks
TF.252
ALT **ship lock**
SN Locks made of bronze for use on ships, usually of heavy construction. (STEIN)
UF locks, ship
CN V.TF.AFU.AFU.AFU.AFU.DIO.BIQ.
ALO.AXC

ship pitch
USE **navy pitch**

ship plans
USE **ships plans**

ship terminals
USE **marine terminals**

ship's maul hammers
USE **top maul hammers**

Shipaya
FL.1595
CN F.FL.ALO.ALO.ARI.ARI.AFU.GFO

shipbuilder's axes
USE **shipwright's axes**

shipbuilders
HG.609
ALT **shipbuilder**
SN Persons employed in the construction of ships. (OED)
UF shipwrights
CN H.HG.AFU.AXC.BZY.AFU.FCS

shipbuilding works
USE **shipyards**

Shipibo
FL.1596 (L)
UF Sipibo
CN F.FL.ALO.ALO.ARI.ARI.AFU.GLI

shiplap joints
USE **covered joints**

shiplap siding
MT.2400
UF siding, shiplap
CN M.MT.AFU.ARI.BZY.AXC.AXC.ARI

shipmasters
HG.736
ALT **shipmaster**
SN Masters or commanders of nonmilitary ships.
CN H.HG.AFU.BCW.FUA.AFU

shipment records
USE **shipping records**

shippers
HG.54
ALT **shipper**
CN H.HG.AFU.AXC.ARI.DOI

shippers' guides
VW.503 (L)
ALT **shippers' guide**
UF guides, shippers'
CN V.VW.AFU.ALO.AFU.AFU.AFU.
BZY.AFU.ALO

shipping
KT.759 (L)
ALT **shipped**
CN K.KT.AFU.ALO.HIK.ARI

shipping records
VW.933
ALT **shipping record**
SN Records of goods or cargo shipped.
UF records, shipment
records, shipping
shipment records
CN V.VW.AFU.ARI.AFU.CFS

shippo
USE **cloisonné**

ships drawings
USE **ships plans**

ships lines
USE **lines drawings**

ships plans
VD.156 (L)
ALT **ship plan**
SN Use as a general designation for drawings that specify the structure or arrangement of a ship, whether plan views, elevations, or sections. May be construction drawings, to be used for constructing a ship, or measured drawings made after an existing ship.
UF drawings, ships
plans, ships
ship plans
ships drawings
CN V.VD.AFU.BIQ.BOK

ships' logs
VW.52 (N)
ALT **ship's log**
SN Daily records of the progress of a ship at sea, with notes on the weather and important incidents of the voyage. (GAHLM)
UF logs, ships'
CN V.VW.AFU.AFU.AFU.DCU.AXC

ships' manifests
VW.936
ALT **ships' manifest**
SN Lists or invoices of cargo on a ship, usually containing marks or indication of contents or commodity, consignee, and other pertinent information for use at terminals or customhouses. (GAHLM)
UF manifests, ships'
CN V.VW.AFU.ARI.AFU.CFS.ALO.AFU

ships' papers
VW.1073 (L)
ALT **ships' paper**
SN Papers which must be carried by a vessel on a voyage, in order to furnish evidence of its national character, nature and destination of cargo, and of compliance with navigation laws. (BLACKS)
UF papers, ships'
CN V.VW.AFU.ARI.ALO.CXA

ships' passenger lists
VW.283 (L)
ALT **ship's passenger list**
SN Lists of persons traveling on a ship.
UF lists, ships' passenger
passenger lists, ships'

CN V.VW.AFU.AFU.AFU.FZU.BCW.
ALO.BIQ.AFU

shipways
USE **slipways**

shipwright's adzes
TB.818 (N)
ALT **shipwright's adz**
SN Very broad, flat adzes having a spur or punch on the back of the head which can be used as a nail set. (BLACKB)
UF adzes, ship carpenter's
adzes, shipwright's
ship carpenter's adzes
CN V.TB.AFU.BCW.CFS.ALO.AFU.
AFU.BUE

shipwright's axes
TB.845 (N)
ALT **shipwright's ax**
UF axes, boatbuilder's
axes, carpenter's
axes, ship
axes, ship carpenter's
axes, shipbuilder's
axes, shipwright's
boatbuilder's axes
carpenter's axes
ship axes
ship carpenter's axes
shipbuilder's axes
wheelwright's axes
CN V.TB.AFU.BCW.CFS.ALO.AFU.
AXC.BZY

shipwrights
USE **shipbuilders**

shipyards
RG.228 (L,B,R)
ALT **shipyard**
SN Places or enclosures where boats or ships are built or repaired. (W)
UF boatyards
ship building yards
shipbuilding works
works, shipbuilding
CN V.RG.AFU.AFU.EFQ.ARI.BCW

shipyards, naval
USE **naval shipyards**

Shira
FL.407 (L)
UF Ashira
Eshira
Sira
CN F.FL.ALO.AFU.AXC.ALO.AFU.
ALO.BUE

shires
HG.809
ALT **shire**
CN H.HG.ALO.ALO.BUE

Shivaism
USE **Sivaism**

shoals
USE **sand bars**

Shobwa
FL.440
CN F.FL.ALO.AFU.AXC.ALO.ALO.
AFU.AFU.AXC.BIQ

shoe racks
TF.271
ALT **shoe rack**
UF racks, shoe
CN V.TF.AFU.AFU.AFU.AFU.EFQ.ALO

shoe shops
USE **shoe stores**

shoe stores
RK.154 (A,B)
ALT **shoe store**
UF shoe shops
shops, shoe
stores, shoe
CN V.RK.AFU.ALO.ALO.ALO.ARI.
BIQ.AFU.AXC.AFU

shoe tongs
TB.763 (N)
SN Tongs with cupped jaws for gripping horseshoes. (SMITH)
UF tongs, shoe
CN V.TB.AFU.BCW.BIQ.AXC.ALO.
AXC.CXA

shoemakers
HG.575 (L)
ALT **shoemaker**
UF cobblers
CN H.HG.AFU.AXC.BUE.AXC.EFQ

shoes (furniture components)
TG.834
ALT **shoe (furniture component)**
SN Disk-shaped turned or shaped terminations on furniture legs used especially during the 17th and 18th centuries. (W)
CN V.TG.ALO.AXC.ALO.AXC

Shoin
FL.2004 (L)
CN F.FL.ALO.ARI.ALO.ALO.ALO.
AFU.CRG

shoji
RT.818
SN Paper screens serving as wall partitions or sliding doors. (W)
UF screens, shoji
shoji screens
CN V.RT.AFU.ALO.AFU.CFS

shoji screens
USE **shoji**

Shona
FL.548 (L)
CN F.FL.ALO.AFU.AXC.ARI.AFU.BIQ

shonks
USE **schranks**

shooting galleries
RK.1044 (N,B)
ALT **shooting gallery**
SN Indoor ranges or covered structures equipped with targets for practice or competition with firearms. (W)
UF galleries, shooting
CN V.RK.AFU.ALO.ALO.EWY.AXC.BCW

shooting galleries (theaters)
USE **nickelodeons**

shooting preserves
USE **preserves**

shooting ranges
RG.147 (L,B)
ALT **shooting range**
UF ranges, shooting
CN V.RG.AFU.AFU.DIO.ARI

shoots, miter
USE **miter boards**

shop chairs
USE **tall chairs**

shop drawings
VD.118
ALT **shop drawing**
UF drawings, shop
drawings, subcontractors'
subcontractors' drawings
CN V.VD.AFU.ALO.DCU.AXC

shop fronts
USE **storefronts**

shop lumber
USE **factory lumber**

shopkeepers
HG.430
ALT **shopkeeper**
CN H.HG.AFU.AXC.BOK.FCS.ALO.
AFU.AFU

shopping arcades
RG.43 (A,L,B,R)
ALT **shopping arcade**
SN Use for covered passageways lined with shops or booths; usually found in urban settings and linking two or more thoroughfares.
UF arcades (shopping arcades)
arcades, shopping
galleries (shopping arcades)
passages (shopping arcades)
CN V.RG.AFU.AFU.AXC.ALO.AFU

shopping centers
RG.42 (A,L,B,R)
ALT **shopping center**
SN Concentrations of stores, markets, and service establishments, along with parking facilities, often in a suburban location. (DAC)
UF centers, shopping
CN V.RG.AFU.AFU.AXC.ALO

shopping centers, underground
USE **underground shopping centers**

shopping districts
RG.268
ALT **shopping district**
UF districts, retailing
districts, shopping
precincts, shopping
retailing districts
shopping precincts
CN V.RG.ALO.AFU.ALO.AFU.ALO

shopping malls
RG.44 (A,L,B)
ALT **shopping mall**
UF malls (shopping centers)
malls, shopping
CN V.RG.AFU.AFU.AXC.ALO.ALO

shopping plazas
RG.45
ALT **shopping plaza**
UF corporate plazas
plazas, corporate
plazas, shopping
retail centers, strip
strip retail centers
CN V.RG.AFU.AFU.AXC.ALO.ARI

shopping precincts
USE **shopping districts**

shops
USE **workshops**

shops (stores)
USE **stores**

shops (work spaces)
USE **workshops (work spaces)**

shops, antique
USE **antique stores**

shops, autobody
USE **body shops**

shops, baker's
USE **bakeries**

shops, beauty
USE **beauty shops**

shops, betting
USE **betting parlors**

shops, blacksmith
USE **smithies**

shops, body
USE **body shops**

shops, chemist's
USE **drugstores**

shops, coffee
USE **coffee shops**

shops, florist
USE **florist shops**

shops, flower
USE **florist shops**

shops, forge
USE **smithies**

shops, grocery
USE **grocery stores**

shops, jewelry
USE **jewelry stores**

shops, machine
USE **machine shops**

shops, paint
USE **paint shops**

shops, pawnbroker's
USE **pawnshops**

shops, pet
USE **pet shops**

shops, repair
USE **repair shops**

shops, self-service
USE **self-service stores**

shops, shoe
USE **shoe stores**

shops, tea
USE **tea rooms**
tea stores

shops, thrift
USE **thrift shops**

shops, variety
USE **variety stores**

Shorchuk
FL.1820
UF Sorcuq
CN F.FL.ALO.ARI.AFU.AXC.ELK.CFS

shorea
USE **lauan**

shorelines
USE **coastlines**

shorers
HG.611
ALT **shorer**
CN H.HG.AFU.AXC.BZY.AFU.FIM

shores
RD.227 (L)
ALT **shore**
SN Use either generally for strips of land bordering large bodies of water or specifically for the areas of land between the lowest low-water spring tide and the highest point of storm waves; for the line forming the boundary between land and sea, use **coastlines.**
UF coasts
CN V.RD.ARI.AFU.AXC.AFU.ALO.AXC.BUE

shores (structural elements)
RT.202
ALT **shore (structural element)**
SN Use for pieces of lumber used as temporary supports, as when in an oblique position to hold a wall under pressure or as a component of formwork.
UF props
CN V.RT.AFU.AFU.AFU.AXC.DIO

shoring
KT.651 (L,B)
ALT **shored**
UF jacking up
propping
CN K.KT.AFU.ALO.GLI.AFU.BCW

shoro
RK.34
SN Use for towerlike structures holding bells in Buddhist monasteries. (PAINE3)
UF shuro
CN V.RK.AFU.ALO.AFU.ALO.DCU.AFU.ALO

short-jointer planes
TB.938 (N)
ALT **short-jointer plane**
SN Two-man, two-handled planes used to make the edges of boards smooth and square in the joining of long staves. (MERCER)
UF planes, pull
planes, short-jointer
pull planes
CN V.TB.AFU.BCW.CFS.ALO.AFU.DUC.ARI.AFU.ARI.ARI

short term loads
USE **impact loads**

shortleaf pine
MT.1387 (L)
UF North Carolina pine
pine, North Carolina
pine, pitch
pine, rosemary
pine, shortleaf
pine, spruce
pine, yellow (shortleaf pine)
Pinus echinata
Pinus mitis
pitch pine
rosemary pine
spruce pine
yellow pine (shortleaf pine)
CN M.MT.AFU.AFU.ALO.BIQ.DCU.AFU.AFU.ALO.CXA.DUC

Shoshone
FL.1316 (L)
UF Snake
CN F.FL.ALO.ALO.ARI.AFU.AXC.BZY

Shoshone, Western
USE **Western Shoshone**

Shoshone, Wind River
USE **Wind River Shoshone**

shot
MT.2255 (L)
CN M.MT.AFU.ALO.DOI.ARI.AFU.AFU

shot-firers
USE **blasters**

shot holes
USE **loopholes**

shot towers
RK.644
ALT **shot tower**
SN High towers, usually round, in which shot is made by dropping molten lead from an upper story into a cistern of water. (HAS)
UF towers, shot
CN V.RK.AFU.ALO.ALO.CLM.ALO.ALO.AFU.AXC.BUE.ALO

shotblasting
KT.68 (L)
SN Use for a type of abrasive cleaning where hardened, cast metal shot is used as the abrasive, as distinguished from **sandblasting,** where sand is used.
CN K.KT.AFU.ALO.BIQ.AFU.ALO

shotcrete
USE **gunite**

shotgun houses
RK.269 (A)
ALT **shotgun house**
SN Houses in which all the rooms are in direct line with one another usually front to back,(W) common in the 19th century in southern United States cities; also, narrow gable-front dwellings one room wide. (FGAH)
UF houses, shotgun
CN V.RK.AFU.ALO.ALO.AXC.ALO.AFU.CRG.BOK

shoulder planes
TB.927 (N)
ALT **shoulder plane**
SN Planes with the stock the same width as the blade, often with one side of the blade sharpened to cut at the same time as the bottom; often used for cleaning up around tenons. (PC)
UF planes, shoulder
CN V.TB.AFU.BCW.CFS.ALO.AFU.DUC.ALO.CFS

shouldered arches
RT.243
ALT **shouldered arch**
SN Spanning members consisting of straight lintels carried on corbels projecting into the opening and usually cut into hollow curves under the projecting ends. (W)
UF arches, shouldered
CN V.RT.AFU.AFU.AFU.BCW.AFU.AFU.AFU.DUC

shouldered dovetail joints
TF.674
ALT **shouldered dovetail joint**
UF dovetail joints, shouldered
joints, shouldered dovetail
CN V.TF.ALO.ARI.AXC.ALO.ALO.ALO

shoulders (furniture components)
TG.835
ALT **shoulder (furniture component)**
CN V.TG.ALO.AXC.ALO.BCW

shoulders (roads)
RM.494
ALT **shoulder (road)**
SN Either of the two edges or borders along a road, especially that portion on which vehicles can be parked in emergencies. (RHDEL2)
UF highway shoulders
shoulders, highway
CN V.RM.ALO.ALO.ALO.ALO.DIO

shoulders, gable
USE **gable shoulders**

shoulders, highway
USE **shoulders (roads)**

shoved joints
TF.623
ALT **shoved joint**
SN Vertical joints in brickwork made by laying the brick in a bed of mortar and shoving the brick toward the last brick laid. (MEANS)
UF joints, shoved
CN V.TF.ALO.ARI.ALO.AFU.ARI.ARI

shovel dozers
TB.35
ALT **shovel dozer**
SN Tractors equipped with a front-mounted bucket that can be used for pushing, digging, and truck loading. (STEIN)
UF dozers, shovel
CN V.TB.AFU.ARI.AFU.ARI.AFU.ALO

shovels
TB.381 (L,N,R)
ALT **shovel**
SN Tools consisting of a broad blade or scoop attached to a long handle; used for taking up, removing, or throwing loose matter, such as earth, snow, or coal. (RHDEL2)
CN V.TB.AFU.ARI.DCU.ALO.ALO

shovels, drag
USE **backhoes**

shovels, power
USE **power shovels**

shovels, pull
USE **backhoes**

shovels, steam
USE **steam shovels**

show-card colors
USE **poster color**

show cards
USE **business cards**

show houses
USE **decorators' show houses**

show rafters
RT.489
ALT **show rafter**
SN Use for rafters, often ornamental, visible beneath a cornice.
UF rafters, show
CN V.RT.AFU.AFU.AFU.BIQ.ARI.ALO.AFU.CFS

show-windows
RT.954 (A,L,R)
ALT **show-window**
SN Any windows used or designed for the display of goods or advertising material, whether fully or partly enclosed or entirely open at the rear; may have a platform raised above street level. (DAC)
UF display windows
windows, display
CN V.RT.AFU.ARI.AFU.AFU.BOK.AFU.ALO.ALO

Showa
FL.1990 (A)
CN F.FL.ALO.ARI.ALO.ALO.AFU.BIQ.ARI

showcases
TG.585 (N,R)
ALT **showcase**
SN Glazed boxes, cases, or cabinets for displaying and protecting wares in a store. (W)
UF cases, display
display cases
vitrines (showcases)
CN V.TG.AFU.AFU.AXC.ALO.CLM.AFU

shower-baths
USE **showers**

shower stalls
RM.81 (N)
ALT **shower stall**
UF stalls, shower
CN V.RM.AFU.DIO.ALO.ALO.BZY

showers
RT.1483 (L,N,B)
ALT **shower**
UF shower-baths
CN V.RT.ALO.BCW.ALO.ARI.CFS.BCW

showmen
USE **performing artists**

showrooms
RM.99 (A,L,B)
ALT **showroom**
SN Use for rooms devoted to the display of merchandise for sale.
CN V.RM.AFU.DIO.ALO.AXC.ARI

showrooms, automobile
USE **automobile showrooms**

showrooms, furniture

USE **furniture showrooms**

shows (exhibitions)
USE **exhibitions**

shows, garden
USE **garden shows**

shows, trade
USE **trade shows**

shreadhead roofs
USE **jerkinhead roofs**

shrines
RK.1139 (A,L,N,B,R)
ALT **shrine**
UF holy places
places, holy
sanctuaries (shrines)
CN V.RK.AFU.ALO.ALO.FCS.BOK

shrines, Torah
USE **arks**

shrinkage
KT.915
ALT **shrunk**
CN K.KT.ALO.BUE.ARI

Shrivijaya
USE **Srivijaya**

shriving-seats
USE **confessionals**

shrubs
RD.272 (L,B)
ALT **shrub**
CN V.RD.ARI.AFU.BCW.ALO.ALO.
ALO.ALO

Shu-fu
USE **Shufu**

Shuara
USE **Jivaro**

shuffleboard courts
RK.1017
ALT **shuffleboard court**
UF courts, shuffleboard
shuffleboards
CN V.RK.AFU.ALO.ALO.EWY.ALO.BUE

shuffleboards
USE **shuffleboard courts**

Shufu
FL.1951
UF Shu-fu
CN F.FL.ALO.ARI.ALO.AFU.AFU.AXC.
ARI.BUE

shumard oak
MT.1251
UF oak, shumard
Quercus shumardii
CN M.MT.AFU.AFU.ALO.BIQ.DCU.
AFU.AFU.AFU.IRA.EFQ

Shun-chih
USE **Shunzhi**

Shunga
USE **Sunga**

Shunzhi
FL.1910
UF Shun-chih
CN F.FL.ALO.ARI.ALO.AFU.AFU.
ALO.DOI.AFU

shuro
USE **shoro**

Shuswap
FL.1420 (L)
CN F.FL.ALO.ALO.ARI.AFU.BUE.DOI

shut-off valves
TF.284
ALT **shut-off valve**
UF valves, shut-off
CN V.TF.AFU.AFU.AFU.AFU.EWY.BIQ

shutter bars
TF.34
ALT **shutter bar**
SN Hinged bars used to fasten a pair of shutters together in the closed position. (MEANS)
UF bars, shutter
CN V.TF.AFU.AFU.AFU.AFU.ALO.BOK

shutter dogs
TF.35
ALT **shutter dog**
SN Ornamental gravitating catches used to hold opened shutters back against the exterior surface surrounding a window. (DITTRI)
UF dogs, shutter
holdbacks, shutter
shutter holdbacks
shutter turns
turns, shutter
CN V.TF.AFU.AFU.AFU.AFU.ALO.BUE

shutter doors
USE **louver doors**

shutter hardware
USE **window hardware**

shutter hinges
TF.138
ALT **shutter hinge**
SN Hinges designed to swing shutters. (BROWNL)
UF hinges, shutter
CN V.TF.AFU.AFU.AFU.AFU.CLM.
ALO.BCW

shutter holdbacks
USE **shutter dogs**

shutter knobs
TF.67
ALT **shutter knob**
UF knobs, shutter
CN V.TF.AFU.AFU.AFU.AFU.CFS.AXC.
ALO.ARI

shutter screws
TF.484
ALT **shutter screw**
UF screws, shutter
CN V.TF.AFU.AFU.AFU.ALO.AFU.
DIO.ALO.AFU

shutter turns
USE **shutter dogs**

shutters
RT.1009 (A,N,B,R)
ALT **shutter**
SN Movable screens, covers, or similar contrivances to close an opening, especially a window. (RS)
UF blinds (shutters)
CN V.RT.AFU.ARI.ALO.BIQ

shutters, boxing
USE **folding shutters**

shutters, folding
USE **folding shutters**

shutting posts
RT.900
ALT **shutting post**
SN Posts at the side of a gate against which it shuts. (HAS)
UF posts, shutting
CN V.RT.AFU.ARI.AFU.AFU.ARI.ALO.
AFU.ALO.ARI

shutting stiles
USE **lock stiles**

Sî Tép
USE **Sri Deb**

Sia
USE **Zia**

Sialk pottery
FL.3031
UF pottery, Sialk
CN F.FL.ALO.AXC.ARI.BIQ.ALO.
AXC.BZY

Siamese
USE **Thai**

Siberian
FL.2119 (L,B)
CN F.FL.ALO.ARI.ARI

Siberian larch
MT.1365 (L)
UF larch, Siberian
Larix russica
Larix sibirica
CN M.MT.AFU.AFU.ALO.BIQ.DCU.
AFU.AFU.ALO.BZY.ARI

siccatives
USE **driers**

Siches
FL.1135
CN F.FL.ALO.ALO.ALO.ARI.AXC.
AFU.AFU.ARI

Sicilian
FL.2640
CN F.FL.ALO.AXC.ALO.AFU.ALO.

AXC.ALO.BIQ.BUE

Sicilian brown
USE **raw umber**

sick building syndrome
BM.719 (A,L)
SN Use for illnesses and ailments that seem to be induced in occupants of a building by conditions inside the building.
UF SBS
syndrome, sick building
CN B.BM.CFS.AFU.AFU.ALO

side
DC.22
SN Related to or situated at or towards the side of something.
UF flank
CN D.DC.AFU.ALO.ALO.BZY

side altars
RT.1216
ALT **side altar**
SN In churches, altars subordinate to the high altar, often placed in a bay of the nave. (RS)
UF altars, side
CN V.RT.AFU.BUE.ALO.ALO.AFU.ALO

side chairs
TG.85 (N)
ALT **side chair**
SN Term generally applied to a wide range of chairs without arms to distinguish them from armchairs. (DOWNS)
UF chairs, occasional
chairs, side
chairs, single
occasional chairs
single chairs
CN V.TG.AFU.AFU.ALO.AFU.AFU.
AFU.KFK

side chairs, cantilevered
USE **Cesca chairs**

side-cut brick
MT.142
UF brick, side-cut
CN M.MT.AFU.AFU.AFU.AXC.ALO.
AFU.AXC.ALO.AXC.AFU.ALO

side cutters
TB.788
ALT **side cutter**
SN Clippers used for cutting off the ends of cane. (HAND)
UF cutters, side
CN V.TB.AFU.BCW.BUE.AXC

side elevations
RM.10
ALT **side elevation**
UF elevations, end
elevations, flank
elevations, side
end elevations
flank elevations
CN V.RM.AFU.BCW.AXC

side-facing gables
USE **side gables**

side gables
RT.641
ALT **side gable**
UF gables, side
gables, side-facing
side-facing gables
CN V.RT.AFU.AFU.AFU.BIQ.BUE.
ALO.AFU.AXC.AFU.BOK

side hooks
USE **bench hooks**

side hung windows
USE **casement windows**

side knives
USE **froes**

side lights
RT.962
ALT **side light**
SN Framed areas of fixed glass alongside a door or window opening. (DAC)
UF flanking windows
lights, margin
lights, side
margin lights
windows, flanking
winglights
CN V.RT.AFU.ARI.AFU.AFU.BOK.
AFU.ARI.BCW

side locking joints
USE **interlocking joints**

side nails
TF.427
ALT **side nail**
UF nails, side
CN V.TF.AFU.AFU.AFU.ALO.AFU.CFS.
AFU.DIO.BUE

side notes
USE **marginalia**

side sewing
KT.518
ALT **side sewn**
SN Bookbinding process where unfolded single sheets of paper are bound together, the sheets are then glued together, a cloth hinge is applied, and the pages are sewn. (CRBOOK)
UF flat stitching
sewing, side
side stitching
stab-stitching
stitching, flat
stitching, side
stitching, stab
CN K.KT.AFU.ALO.ELK.ARI.ARI

side shows
KM.63 (L)
CN K.KM.AFU.BOK.AXC.BIQ

side stitching
USE **side sewing**

side tables
TG.774 (N)
ALT **side table**
SN Tables designed to stand against the wall, generally with one side undecorated. (DDA)
UF tables, side
CN V.TG.AFU.AFU.BIQ.BOK.ARI.
AFU.ALO

side tables (sideboard tables)
USE **sideboard tables**

side tongs
TB.764 (N)
UF bit tongs, right-angle
right-angle bit tongs
tongs, right-angle bit
tongs, side
CN V.TB.AFU.BCW.BIQ.AXC.ALO.
AXC.DCU

sideboard tables
TG.757 (N)
ALT **sideboard table**
SN Side tables, some of which may have tops attached to the wall, which are used in a dining room. For low, wide chests of drawers or case pieces on legs also used in dining rooms, use **sideboards.**
UF buffets (sideboard tables)
servers (sideboard tables)
serving tables
side tables (sideboard tables)
tables, serving
tables, side (sideboard tables)
tables, sideboard
CN V.TG.AFU.AFU.BIQ.BOK.ALO.EWY

sideboards
TG.586 (N,R)
ALT **sideboard**
SN Generally low, wide chests of drawers or case pieces on legs with cupboard space; placed along the wall of a dining room and used for storage and serving.(FAIRB) For side tables used along the walls of dining rooms, use **sideboard tables.**
UF boards, serving
dressers (sideboards)
serving boards
CN V.TG.AFU.AFU.AXC.ALO.CRG

sideboards, celleret
USE **celleret sideboards**

sideboards, pedestal
USE **pedestal end sideboards**

sideboards, pedestal end
USE **pedestal end sideboards**

sideboards, slab
USE **slab sideboards**

siderite

MT.516 (L)
SN An iron carbonate, containing theoretically 48.2% iron. (MH)
UF carbonate ore
iron ore, spathic
ironstone
ore, carbonate
ore, spathic iron
spathic iron ore
CN M.MT.AFU.AFU.AFU.CFS. AFU.
CXA.BIQ

siderographers
HG.463
ALT **siderographer**
SN Persons who engrave steel, especially to reproduce original engravings on metal plates used to print bank notes, bonds, and other securities.
CN H.HG.AFU.AXC.BUE.ALO.CFS.BZY

siderography
KT.679 (L,R)
SN The art of engraving steel.
UF steel engraving
CN K.KT.AFU.ALO.GRC.ARI.ALO

sidetracks
USE **sidings**

sidewalk elevators
RT.1313
ALT **sidewalk elevator**
UF elevators, sidewalk
CN V.RT.ALO.ALO.AFU.ARI.ALO.
ALO.AFU.ALO

sidewalks
RM.495 (A,L,B,R)
ALT **sidewalk**
UF banquettes (sidewalks)
pavements (sidewalks)
CN V.RM.ALO.ALO.ALO.ALO.DOI

sidewalks, moving
USE **moving walkways**

siding
MT.2397 (A,L,B)
SN Exterior wall covering on houses or other structures.
UF cladding (siding)
weatherboarding
CN M.MT.AFU.ARI.BZY.AXC.AXC

siding nails
USE **shingle nails**

siding tracks
USE **sidings**

siding, barn
USE **barnboard**

siding, bevel
USE **clapboard siding**

siding, clapboard
USE **clapboard siding**

siding, shiplap
USE **shiplap siding**

siding, weatherboard
USE **clapboard siding**

sidings
RM.507 (L)
ALT **siding**
SN Short railroad tracks connected by switches or points at one or more places with the main track and used especially to enable trains to pass each other. (W)
UF railroad sidings
sidetracks
siding tracks
tracks, siding
CN V.RM.ALO.ALO.ALO.ARI.ARI

Siebold's beech
MT.1112
UF beech, Siebold's
Fagus crenata
CN M.MT.AFU.AFU.ALO.BIQ.DCU.
AFU.AFU.AFU.BCW.BUE

sieges à la reine
USE **chaises à la reine**

sièges à langer
USE **chauffeuses**

sièges courants
TG.208
ALT **siège courant**
SN French 18th-century chairs that stood in the center of a room and could be moved. Distinct from **sièges meublants** which were largely decorative and were positioned against the wall. (PC)
CN V.TG.AFU.AFU.ALO.AFU.AFU.
ARI.ARI.AFU

sièges de nourrice
USE **chauffeuses**

sièges meublants
TG.209
ALT **siège meublant**
SN French 18th-century chairs that were positioned against the wall. Their use was governed by strict protocol and sièges meublants were usually not sat on, but rather meant to be a part of the architectural decoration of a room. Distinct from **sièges courants** which stood in the center of a room and could be moved. (PC)
CN V.TG.AFU.AFU.ALO.AFU.AFU.
ARI.ARI.ALO

Siena
USE **Senufo**

siena
USE **strong reddish brown**

Siena marble
MT.845
UF giallo di Siena
marble, Siena
CN M.MT.AFU.AFU.AFU.DCU.AFU.
ARI.ARI.ARI.BUE.ALO

Sienaerde
USE **raw sienna**

sienna
MT.1628
CN M.MT.AFU.AFU.ARI.AFU.AFU.
ALO.ALO.ARI.ARI.AXC

sienna brown
USE **moderate brown**

sienna, burnt
USE **burnt sienna**

sienna, burnt (color)
USE **dark reddish orange**
strong reddish brown

sienna, raw
USE **raw sienna**

sienna, raw (color)
USE **brownish orange**
dark orange yellow
light brown
strong yellowish brown

Sierra Leone copal
MT.1484
UF copal, Sierra Leone
CN M.MT.AFU.AFU.ALO.BOK.ARI.AXC

sierra redwood
USE **giant sequoia**

sight
BM.726 (L,R)
UF eyesight
vision
CN B.BM.CFS.AFU.BCW.ALO

sight lines
BM.165 (B)
SN Lines that define an unimpeded field of vision,(RHDEL2) as within rooms or open spaces or along city streets.
UF lines, sight
CN B.BM.AFU.AFU.ARI.BOK.DCU

sigillata ware, Western
USE **Western sigillata ware**

sigmas
USE **cyrtostyles**

sign and symbol handbooks
VW.403 (L)
ALT **sign and symbol handbook**
UF handbooks, sign and symbol
CN V.VW.AFU.AFU.ALO.EWY.ARI.
ALO.BIQ

signal boxes
USE **signal towers**

signal gantries
RM.508 (L,B)
ALT **signal gantry**
SN Structures supporting a number of railroad signals for several tracks.

(W)
UF gantries (railroads)
gantries, signal
CN V.RM.ALO.ALO.ALO.ARI.AXC

signal systems
USE **communication systems**

signal towers
RK.1312
ALT **signal tower**
UF boxes, signal
signal boxes
towers, signal
CN V.RK.AFU.ALO.ALO.GLI.ARI.
ALO.AFU

signals, traffic
USE **traffic signals**

signatures
VW.45 (A,L,B,R)
ALT **signature**
SN Persons' names written in their own hand.
UF autographs (signatures)
CN V.VW.AFU.AFU.AFU.CRG.AXC

signers
HG.737
ALT **signer**
CN H.HG.AFU.BCW.FZU

significant form
BM.493
SN Certain combinations of lines, colors, and spatial elements that excite pure aesthetic emotion; term coined by art critic Clive Bell. (MGHDIC)
UF form, significant
CN B.BM.BIQ.AFU.BIQ

signs (symbols)
USE **symbols**

signs, zodiac
USE **zodiac symbols**

sikharas
RM.421
ALT **sikhara**
SN In the temple architecture of India, towers or spires, usually tapering in a convex curve.
CN V.RM.AFU.DZW.ARI

Sikhism
BM.676 (L)
ALT **Sikh**
CN B.BM.BZY.AFU.CLM

Sikkimese
FL.2172
CN F.FL.ALO.ARI.AXC.AFU.BCW

sil
USE **yellow ocher**

silane
MT.2177
SN Any of several silica hydrides. (W)
CN M.MT.AFU.AFU.ARI.BUE.ALO.
AXC.ALO.BUE.AFU

silencers, door
USE **door silencers**

silhouettes
VB.6 (L,R)
ALT **silhouette**
SN Use for portraits cut from dark paper and, by extension, for dark images showing no interior detail set against light backgrounds.
CN V.VB.AFU.AFU.AXC

silica
MT.541 (R)
CN M.MT.AFU.AFU.AFU.CFS.AFU.GRC

silica (white pigment)
MT.1755
UF quartz (pigment)
CN M.MT.AFU.AFU.ARI.AFU.AFU.
ALO.ALO.BOK.ALO.CXA

silica glass
USE **fused silica glass**

silica glass, fused
USE **fused silica glass**

silica sand
MT.2075 (L)
UF sand, silica
CN M.MT.AFU.AFU.ARI.BOK.ALO.
BOK.ARI.AFU

silica sandstone
USE **siliceous sandstone**

silicate brick, calcium
USE **calcium silicate brick**

silicate glass, lead
USE **lead glass**

silicate paint
MT.2529
SN A paint, the vehicle of which consists chiefly of water glass; used especially for painting on mortar. (W)
UF paint, silicate
CN M.MT.AFU.ARI.CRG.ALO.BCW.
AFU.BCW

silicate, potash
USE **muscovite (mica)**

silicate, sodium
USE **water glass**

siliceous limestone
MT.687
UF arenaceous limestone
cherty limestone
limestone, arenaceous
limestone, cherty
limestone, sandy
limestone, siliceous
sandy limestone
CN M.MT.AFU.AFU.AFU.DCU.AFU.
ALO.AFU.ALO.ALO.AFU.ALO.BCW

siliceous sandstone
MT.723
UF orthoquartzite
sandstone, silica
sandstone, siliceous
silica sandstone
CN M.MT.AFU.AFU.AFU.DCU.AFU.
ALO.AFU.ARI.AFU.ALO.BIQ

silicon
MT.577 (L)
CN M.MT.AFU.AFU.AFU.CXA

silicon bronze
MT.390
SN Applied to two classes of copper-silicon alloys, one of which is nearly pure copper, fluxed with silicon, and the other includes many copper-base alloys, some of which may be brasses of aluminum bronzes. (MH)
UF bronze, silicon
CN M.MT.AFU.AFU.AFU.BZY.AFU.
AFU.AFU.ALO.ARI.BOK

silicone
MT.2176 (L,B)
UF silicone, thermoset
thermoset silicone
CN M.MT.AFU.AFU.ARI.BUE.ALO.
AXC.ALO.BUE

silicone elastomer
MT.2093
UF elastomer, silicone
CN M.MT.AFU.AFU.ARI.BUE.AFU.
AFU.CLM

silicone epoxy
MT.2170
UF epoxy, silicone
CN M.MT.AFU.AFU.ARI.BUE.ALO.
AXC.ALO.BCW.ARI

silicone rubber
MT.2091 (L)
SN Rubber made from silicone elastomers and characterized by its retention of flexibility, resilience, and tensile strength over a wide temperature range and its resistance to weathering and many chemicals. (W)
UF rubber, silicone
CN M.MT.AFU.AFU.ARI.BUE.AFU.
AFU.BZY.AFU

silicone, thermoset
USE **silicone**

silk
MT.1818 (L,R)
CN M.MT.AFU.AFU.ARI.ALO.AFU.
AFU.AFU.ARI

silk cotton
USE **kapok**

silk screen printing
USE **serigraphy**

silk, Chinese
USE **Chinese silk**

silk, glass
USE **glass wool**

silkscreening
USE **serigraphy**

sill anchors
TF.325
ALT **sill anchor**
SN Anchor bolts used to fasten a sill to its foundation. (MEANS)
UF anchors, plate
anchors, sill
plate anchors
CN V.TF.AFU.AFU.AFU.ALO.AFU.ALO.ALO.BCW

sill courses
RT.626
ALT **sill course**
SN In stone masonry, stringcourses set at window sill level; commonly differentiated from the wall by their greater projection, their finish, or their thickness. (HAS)
UF courses, sill
CN V.RT.AFU.AFU.AFU.BIQ.BUE.ALO.AFU.ALO.CFS.AXC

sill plates
RT.702 (A)
ALT **sill plate**
SN Horizontal timbers at the bottom of the frame of a wood structure, that rest on the foundation. (DAC)
UF beams, ground
bottom plates
ground beams
ground plates
groundsills
mudsills
plates, bottom
plates, ground
plates, sill
sills (sill plates)
solepieces
soleplates
CN V.RT.AFU.AFU.ALO.ALO.ARI.AFU

Silla
USE **Unified Silla Kingdom**

Silla Kingdom, Unified
USE **Unified Silla Kingdom**

Silla Kingdom, United
USE **Unified Silla Kingdom**

Silla, Great
USE **Unified Silla Kingdom**

Silla, Old
USE **Old Silla**

sillónes de cadera
TG.119
ALT **sillón de cadera**
SN Medieval Spanish type of X-chairs, often with inlaid decoration. (DDA)
CN V.TG.AFU.AFU.ALO.AFU.AFU.AFU.MWQ.ARI

sillónes de frailero
USE **fraileros**

sillónes fraileros
USE **fraileros**

sills
RT.1013 (A,N,B)
ALT **sill**
SN Members forming the lower sides of openings.
UF cills
CN V.RT.AFU.ARI.ALO.BOK

sills (sill plates)
USE **sill plates**

sills (window frame components)
USE **window sills**

sills, lug
USE **lug sills**

sills, rough
USE **rough sills**

sills, slip
USE **slip sills**

sills, window
USE **window sills**

silos
RK.99 (A,L,N,B)
ALT **silo**
SN Use for tall, usually cylindrical, structures in which animal feed is stored and which are normally sealed to exclude air and promote fermentation of green fodder (silage) without spoilage.
UF grain silos
silos, grain
CN V.RK.AFU.ALO.ALO.AFU.ARI.ARI

silos, grain
USE **silos**

silos, guided missile
USE **guided missile silos**

silos, missile
USE **guided missile silos**

siltstone
MT.706 (L)
CN M.MT.AFU.AFU.AFU.DCU.AFU.ALO.AFU.ARI.AFU.AFU.ARI

siltstone (clay stone)
USE **clay stone**

silver
MT.444 (L,R)
CN M.MT.AFU.AFU.AFU.BZY.AFU.AFU.ARI.DCU.AFU

silver (color)
USE **medium gray**

silver albumen prints
USE **albumen prints**

silver albumen process
USE **albumen process**

silver alloys
MT.404 (L)
UF alloys, silver
CN M.MT.AFU.AFU.AFU.BZY.AFU.AFU.AFU.ALO.BOK

silver birch
MT.1122 (L)
UF Betula pendula
birch, common
birch, silver
birch, white
common birch
white birch
CN M.MT.AFU.AFU.ALO.BIQ.DCU.AFU.AFU.AFU.BIQ.BUE

silver bromide
MT.309
UF bromide (silver bromide)
bromide, silver
CN M.MT.AFU.AFU.AFU.BOK.AXC.AFU.AFU

silver chloride
MT.310
UF chloride, silver
CN M.MT.AFU.AFU.AFU.BOK.AXC.AFU.ALO

silver-dye bleach process
KT.371
SN A subtractive color photographic process in which dyes present in the emulsion are bleached, leaving only those dyes that correspond to the image color.
UF bleach-out process
bleach process, dye
dye bleach process
dye bleaching process
dye destruction process
silver-dye process
CN K.KT.AFU.ALO.DUC.DIO.ALO.DZW.ALO

silver-dye process
USE **silver-dye bleach process**

silver fir
MT.1353 (L)
UF Abies amabilis
cascadis fir
fir, cascadis
fir, red silver
fir, silver
red silver fir
silver fir, red
CN M.MT.AFU.AFU.ALO.BIQ.DCU.AFU.AFU.ALO.BIQ.ARI

silver fir, red
USE **silver fir**

silver gelatin dry plate
USE **gelatin dry plate process**

silver gelatin negatives
USE **gelatin silver negatives**

silver gelatin photonegatives
USE **gelatin silver negatives**

silver gelatin photoprints
USE **gelatin silver prints**

silver gelatin phototransparencies
USE **gelatin silver transparencies**

silver gelatin prints
USE **gelatin silver prints**

silver gelatin process
USE **gelatin silver process**

silver gelatin transparencies
USE **gelatin silver transparencies**

silver gray
USE **light brownish gray**
light olive brown
medium gray

silver halide
MT.308 (L)
UF halide, silver
CN M.MT.AFU.AFU.AFU.BOK.AXC.AFU

silver iodide
MT.311
UF iodide, silver
CN M.MT.AFU.AFU.AFU.BOK.AXC.AFU.ARI

silver maple
MT.1224
UF Acer saccharinum
maple, river
maple, silver
maple, soft
maple, white
river maple
soft maple
white maple
CN M.MT.AFU.AFU.ALO.BIQ.DCU.AFU.AFU.AFU.IFM.BOK

silver marks
VW.737 (R)
ALT **silver mark**
UF marks, silver
CN V.VW.AFU.ALO.ALO.AFU.AXC.ARI.CLM

silver mines
RG.103 (L)
ALT **silver mine**
UF mines, silver
CN V.RG.AFU.AFU.BUE.AFU.ALO.BIQ

silver mirroring
KT.903
SN A symptom of oxidative-reductive deterioration in photographs. (REILLY)
UF mirroring, silver
silvering-out
CN K.KT.ALO.BCW.BUE

silver negatives, gelatin
USE **gelatin silver negatives**

silver nitrate
MT.446 (L)
UF nitrate, silver
CN M.MT.AFU.AFU.AFU.BZY.AFU.AFU.ARI.DCU.ALO.AFU

silver orthophosphate
USE **silver phosphate**

silver phosphate
MT.447 (L)
UF orthophosphate, silver
phosphate, silver
silver orthophosphate
CN M.MT.AFU.AFU.AFU.BZY.AFU.AFU.ARI.DCU.ALO.ALO

silver pink
USE **grayish pink**

silver plate
MT.462 (L)
UF plate, silver
CN M.MT.AFU.AFU.AFU.BZY.AFU.ALO.AXC.AFU.ALO

silver points
TB.257
ALT **silver point**
SN Pointed rods of silver used in conjunction with specially treated paper to produce delicate drawings. (MAYER)
CN V.TB.AFU.ARI.CLM.AFU.ALO.CLM.ARI

silver prints, albumen
USE **albumen prints**

silver prints, gelatin
USE **gelatin silver prints**

silver salt processes
USE **photographic processes**

silver spruce
USE **sitka spruce**

silver stain
MT.2466 (B)
SN Solution of silver salts used to alter the color of local areas of stained glass. (MAYER)
UF stain, silver
CN M.MT.AFU.ARI.CRG.AFU.BIQ.ALO

silver transparencies, gelatin
USE **gelatin silver transparencies**

silver wattle
MT.1204
UF Acacia dealbata
wattle, silver
CN M.MT.AFU.AFU.ALO.BIQ.DCU.AFU.AFU.AFU.HCQ.BCW

silver, German
USE **German silver**

silver, sterling
USE **sterling silver**

silvered glass
MT.265 (R)
SN Thin glass blown with double walls and sealed after silvering of the enclosed surfaces; used to produce ornamental wares. (W)
UF glass, mercury
glass, silvered
mercury glass
CN M.MT.AFU.AFU.AFU.BIQ.AFU.ARI.CLM

silvering
KT.717 (L)
ALT **silvered**
SN The act or process of covering with silver. (W)
CN K.KT.AFU.ALO.GRC.CRG.ARI

silvering-out
USE **silver mirroring**

silversmithing
KT.785 (L,R)
CN K.KT.AFU.ALO.HOE.BCW.AFU.BOK

silversmiths
HG.500 (L,R)
ALT **silversmith**
CN H.HG.AFU.AXC.BUE.ARI.CFS.AFU.BOK

silversmiths' marks
VW.756
ALT **silversmith's mark**
UF marks, silversmiths'
CN V.VW.AFU.ALO.ALO.AFU.AXC.AXC.DIO

simas
USE **cymas**

Simirinche
USE **Piro**

simple beams
RT.317
ALT **simple beam**
SN Structural beams which have their ends free and rest only on supports at each end. (DAC)
UF beams, simple
CN V.RT.AFU.AFU.AFU.BCW.ALO.ARI.ALO

simple joints
TF.680
ALT **simple joint**
UF joints, simple
CN V.TF.ALO.ARI.AXC.ARI

simple solution varnish
MT.2485
SN A varnish made by dissolving a resin directly in a volatile solvent. (MAYER)
UF cold cut varnish
varnish, cold cut
varnish, simple solution
CN M.MT.AFU.ARI.CRG.AFU.BOK.ALO.ALO

Simple Style
FL.2649
CN F.FL.ALO.AXC.ALO.AFU.ALO.AXC.ARI.AXC.AXC

simple trusses
USE **trussed rafters**

simple vaults
RT.536
ALT **simple vault**
SN Vaults that have a smooth intrados without ribs or cross arches. (W)
UF vaults, simple
CN V.RT.AFU.AFU.AFU.BIQ.BOK.AFU.ALO

simplicity
BM.103 (A,L)
SN Absence of intricacy or excessive ornament in form, structure, or appearance.
CN B.BM.AFU.AFU.ARI.BCW

simulation methods
BM.1158 (L)
UF methods, simulation
CN B.BM.DIO.ARI.ALO

simultaneism
BM.183 (R)
ALT **simultaneity**
SN Concept in early 20th-century visual art, theater, and literature regarding the expression of multiple awareness of things happening in different places at the same time or extended in time, challenging the traditional idea of unity of time, action, and place. (OCTCA)
CN B.BM.AFU.AFU.AXC.CFS

simultaneity (simultaneous representation)
USE **simultaneous representation**

simultaneous contrast
BM.128
SN The phenomenon through which the same color can reveal different hues, depending only on the colors surrounding it. (BLCT)
UF contrast, simultaneous
CN B.BM.AFU.AFU.ARI.BOK.ALO.ALO.AFU.ARI

simultaneous representation
BM.166
SN Representation of an object, person, or structure in such a way that its most essential features are all seen in one view without regard to perspective or a single point of view. (PDAT)
UF representation, simultaneous
simultaneity (simultaneous representation)
CN B.BM.AFU.AFU.ARI.BOK.DIO

Sinabo
FL.1597
CN F.FL.ALO.ALO.ARI.ARI.AFU.GRC

Sinagua
FL.954 (L)
CN F.FL.ALO.ALO.ALO.AFU.ALO.ARI.BIQ.BIQ.ARI

Singalese
USE **Sri Lankan**

Singapore damar
MT.1488
UF damar, Singapore
CN M.MT.AFU.AFU.ALO.BOK.AXC.AFU.AFU

singers
HG.79 (L,R)
ALT **singer**
UF vocalists
CN H.HG.AFU.AXC.AXC.AFU.AFU.AFU.BIQ.BIQ.BOK

Singhalese
USE **Sri Lankan**

Singhasari
FL.2383
CN F.FL.ALO.ARI.BCW.ARI.ALO.AXC.ALO.AFU.AFU

single beds
USE **twin beds**

single bottom seams
TF.661
ALT **single bottom seam**
UF bottom seams, single
seams, single bottom
CN V.TF.ALO.ARI.ARI.BUE.CRG

single bow Windsor chairs
USE **single rod-back Windsor chairs**

single-center arches
USE **one-centered arches**

single chairs
USE **side chairs**

single-cleat ladders
TB.485
ALT **single-cleat ladder**
SN Ladders which consist of a pair of side rails, usually parallel, connected together with cleats that are joined to the side rails at regular intervals. (DAC)
UF ladders, single-cleat
CN V.TB.AFU.ARI.ERE.ALO.BOK

single company towns
USE **company towns**

single contracts
VW.885
ALT **single contract**
SN Contracts for construction where all work is contracted under the responsibility of a single or prime general contractor. (STEIN)
UF contracts, single
CN V.VW.AFU.ARI.AFU.BOK.BOK.ALO.ALO.AFU.AXC

single counting-house desks
USE **counting-house desks**

single dwelling units
USE **single-family dwellings**

single-family dwellings
RK.348 (L)
ALT **single-family dwelling**
UF dwellings, single-family
houses, one-family
houses, single-family
one-family houses
single dwelling units
single-family houses
units, single dwelling
CN V.RK.AFU.ALO.ALO.AXC.ALO.BOK.BZY

single-family houses
USE **single-family dwellings**

single-framed roofs
RT.446
ALT **single-framed roof**
SN Use for roofs in which the common rafters do not transfer their loads to secondary support members, such as rafters or purlins.
UF cottage roofs
roofs, cottage
roofs, single
roofs, single-framed
single roofs
CN V.RT.AFU.AFU.AFU.BIQ.ARI.AFU.ALO.ALO.AFU

single-hung windows
RT.946
ALT **single-hung window**
SN Movable windows having a single sash. (DAC)
UF windows, single-hung
CN V.RT.AFU.ARI.AFU.AFU.BOK.AFU.AFU.EWY.ARI.ARI

single lens reflex cameras
TB.302 (L,N)
ALT **single lens reflex camera**
SN Cameras which allow the user to see the exact image formed by the picture-taking lens, by means of a hinged mirror between the lens and film. (LANG)
UF cameras, single lens reflex
SLRs
CN V.TB.AFU.ARI.CLM.ARI.AFU.AFU.ALO.AXC.AFU

single-pen houses
RK.270 (A)
ALT **single-pen house**
SN Use for log dwellings consisting of only a single room, or pen.
UF houses, single-pen
single-pens
CN V.RK.AFU.ALO.ALO.AXC.ALO.AFU.CRG.BUE

single-pens

USE **single-pen houses**

single rod-back Windsor chairs
TG.111
ALT **single rod-back Windsor chair**
SN Square-back Windsor chairs with a single turned rod across the top usually capping the back posts. (EVANS)
UF chairs, single bow Windsor
chairs, single rod-back Windsor
single bow Windsor chairs
Windsor chairs, single bow
Windsor chairs, single rod-back
CN V.TG.AFU.AFU.ALO.AFU.AFU.AFU.MLC.CFS.BCW

single roofs
USE **single-framed roofs**

single span bridges
RK.1283
ALT **single span bridge**
UF bridges, single span
CN V.RK.AFU.ALO.ALO.GLI.ALO.AFU.AFU.BIQ

single-story
DC.97 (L,B)
UF 1-story
one-story
CN D.DC.AFU.ARI.ERE.BOK.AFU

single strength window glass
MT.253
UF glass, single strength window
window glass, single strength
CN M.MT.AFU.AFU.AFU.BIQ.AFU.ALO.AXC.ALO

single-view drawings
USE **pictorial drawings**

single-weight paper
MT.1951
UF paper, single-weight
CN M.MT.AFU.AFU.ARI.ALO.ALO.AXC.ARI.BOK.BUE

Sinhalese
USE **Sri Lankan**

Sinkiuse
FL.1421 (L)
UF Columbia
Sinkiuse-Columbia
CN F.FL.ALO.ALO.ARI.AFU.BUE.DUC

Sinkiuse-Columbia
USE **Sinkiuse**

sinks
RT.1484 (N)
ALT **sink**
CN V.RT.ALO.BCW.ALO.ARI.CFS.BIQ

sinks, dental
USE **dental sinks**

sinks, dry
USE **dry sinks**

sinks, service
USE **slop sinks**

sinks, slop
USE **slop sinks**

sinks, wash
USE **wash sinks**

sinopia
MT.1676
CN M.MT.AFU.AFU.ARI.AFU.AFU.ALO.ALO.BCW.AFU.ALO.BIQ

sinopie
VD.104 (R)
ALT **sinopia**
CN V.VD.AFU.ALO.BOK.AFU.AFU

Sinú
FL.1110
CN F.FL.ALO.ALO.ALO.ARI.AFU.ALO

Sioux
FL.1396 (L)
CN F.FL.ALO.ALO.ARI.AFU.BOK.FCS

Sipibo
USE **Shipibo**

Sira
USE **Shira**

Sirmur
FL.2300
CN F.FL.ALO.ARI.AXC.ALO.AFU.BZY.BIQ.ARI

Sirohi
FL.2296
CN F.FL.ALO.ARI.AXC.ALO.AFU.BZY.BCW.BCW.CLM

sisal
MT.1837 (L,B)
UF fiber, sisal
hemp, sisal
sisal fiber
sisal hemp
CN M.MT.AFU.AFU.ARI.ALO.AFU.AFU.ALO.DCU

sisal fiber
USE **sisal**

sisal hemp
USE **sisal**

sisal, Mexican
USE **henequen**

sisal, Yucatan
USE **henequen**

Sisala
FL.364 (L)
UF Isala
Sissala
CN F.FL.ALO.AFU.AXC.AFU.AXC.AFU.CXA

Sissala
USE **Sisala**

Sisseton
USE **Santee Dakota**

sister's cylinder bookcases
USE **cylinder desks and bookcases**

site analysis
KT.16 (B)
SN Includes the complete examination, investigation, and testing of surface and subsurface soil and conditions at a site. (MEANS)
UF analysis, site
site investigation
CN K.KT.AFU.ALO.AXC.AXC

site investigation
USE **site analysis**

site layouts
USE **site plans**

site plans
VD.39
ALT **site plan**
UF drawings, layout
layout drawings
layouts, site
local plans
location plans
plans, local
plans, location
plans, plot
plans, regional (drawings)
plans, site
plans, vicinity
plot plans
regional plans (drawings)
site layouts
vicinity plans
CN V.VD.AFU.AFU.BIQ.ALO.AXC.AFU.ALO

site surveys
USE **topographic surveys**

sites
RG.203 (L)
ALT **site**
CN V.RG.AFU.AFU.DZW

sites, archaeological
USE **archaeological sites**

sites, building
USE **building sites**

sites, camp
USE **camp sites**

sites, caravan
USE **trailer camps**

sites, construction
USE **building sites**

sites, endangered
USE **endangered places**

sites, factory
USE **industrial sites**

sites, historic
USE **historic sites**

sites, imperiled
USE **endangered places**

sites, industrial
USE **industrial sites**

sites, launch
USE **launch complexes**

sites, nuclear test
USE **nuclear test sites**

sites, pilgrimage
USE **pilgrimage centers**

sites, test
USE **test sites**

Sitka
FL.1359
CN F.FL.ALO.ALO.ARI.AFU.BIQ.FIM

sitka spruce
MT.1403 (L)
UF Picea sitchensis
silver spruce
spruce, silver
spruce, sitka
spruce, Western
Western spruce
CN M.MT.AFU.AFU.ALO.BIQ.DCU.
AFU.AFU.ALO.DOI.BOK

Sittanavasal
FL.2301
CN F.FL.ALO.ARI.AXC.ALO.AFU.BZY.
BIQ.AXC

sitting rooms
RM.180 (A,L)
ALT **sitting room**
SN Use for rooms for sitting and relaxation, often located adjacent to bedrooms and generally more private than living rooms or parlors.
UF rooms, sitting
CN V.RM.AFU.DIO.ALO.CXA.CXA

Siuslaw
FL.1360 (L)
CN F.FL.ALO.ALO.ARI.AFU.BIQ.FOG

Sivaism
BM.662 (L)
ALT **Sivaite**
UF Saiva
Saivism
Shaivism
Shivaism
CN B.BM.BZY.AFU.AXC.ALO

six-back chairs
USE **slat-back chairs**

six-board chests
USE **board chests**

Six Dynasties
FL.1867 (L)
CN F.FL.ALO.ARI.ALO.AFU.AFU.
ALO.BUE

Six Nations
USE **Iroquois**

six-part vaults
USE **sexpartite vaults**

Sixteenth Dynasty
FL.2810
UF 16th Dynasty
Dynasty, Sixteenth
CN F.FL.ALO.AXC.ALO.ARI.AFU.
BOK.AXC

sixteenth plate
DC.131
SN A photographic plate size, about 1 3/8 by 1 5/8 inches.
CN D.DC.AFU.AXC.BIQ.BIQ

Sixth Dynasty
FL.2791
UF 6th Dynasty
Dynasty, Sixth
CN F.FL.ALO.AXC.ALO.ARI.AFU.ARI.
AXC

sixth-form colleges
USE **high schools**

sixth plate
DC.132
SN A photograhic plate size, usually 2 3/4 by 3 1/4 inches.
UF medium plate
CN D.DC.AFU.AXC.BIQ.BOK

size
BM.801 (L,B)
UF dimensions
CN B.BM.CFS.ARI.AXC.BUE

size (materials)
MT.2728
UF sizing (materials)
CN M.MT.AFU.ARI.IFM.BOK

size, animal
USE **animal size**

size, gold
USE **gold size**

size, red burnish gold
USE **red bole**

size, viscose
USE **viscose size**

sizing
KT.721 (L)
ALT **sized**
SN Application of a penetrating liquid to fill pores, to isolate coatings, or to make surfaces suitable to receive coatings. (AHMT)
CN K.KT.AFU.ALO.GRC.DCU

sizing (materials)
USE **size (materials)**

Skagit
FL.1361 (L)
CN F.FL.ALO.ALO.ARI.AFU.BIQ.FUA

skateboarding parks
RG.182 (A,L,B)
ALT **skateboarding park**
UF parks, skateboarding
skateparks
CN V.RG.AFU.AFU.DOI.CFS.ARI

skateparks
USE **skateboarding parks**

skating rinks
RK.1050 (A,L,B,R)
ALT **skating rink**
UF rinks
rinks, skating
CN V.RK.AFU.ALO.ALO.EWY.AXC.
BIQ.AFU.AXC

skeet ranges
RG.150
ALT **skeet range**
UF ranges, skeet
CN V.RG.AFU.AFU.DIO.ARI.ARI

skeleton keys
TF.538
ALT **skeleton key**
SN Keys with large parts of the bit filed away to enable it to open low quality locks as master keys. (W)
UF keys, skeleton
CN V.TF.AFU.ALO.ARI.AFU.CFS

skene
USE **scaenae**

skenographiae
USE **perspective drawings**

skeps
USE **beehives**

sketch maps
VW.177
ALT **sketch map**
SN Rough, freehand maps of the principal features of a locale, as one drawn from memory. (RHDEL2)
UF maps, sketch
CN V.VW.AFU.AFU.AFU.FZU.AXC.
AFU.ARI.ARI.AXC

sketchbooks
VW.518 (A,R)
ALT **sketchbook**
SN Pads of paper used for sketching. (AHD)
UF sketchpads
CN V.VW.AFU.ALO.AFU.AFU.AFU.DCU

sketchbooks, artists'
USE **artists' sketchbooks**

sketches
VB.7 (L,N)
ALT **sketch**
SN Use for rough or summary art works; less finished than studies. Though sketches are often in the drawing medium, the term **drawings** in general implies more finished works than

does sketches.
UF macchie
CN V.VB.AFU.AFU.BCW

sketches, biographical
USE **biographies**

sketches, composition
USE **composition sketches**

sketches, conceptual
USE **conceptual drawings**

sketches, detail
USE **detail studies**

sketches, developed
USE **design development drawings**

sketches, developmental
USE **preliminary sketches**

sketches, initial
USE **preliminary sketches**

sketches, literary
USE **essays**

sketches, outline
USE **preliminary sketches**

sketches, preliminary
USE **preliminary sketches**

sketches, preliminary (underdrawings)
USE **underdrawings**

sketches, thumbnail
USE **thumbnail sketches**

sketches, travel
USE **travel sketches**

sketching
KT.480 (L,B)
ALT **sketched**
CN K.KT.AFU.ALO.DUC.EFQ

sketchpads
USE **sketchbooks**

skew arches
USE **oblique arches**

skew blocks
USE **kneelers (gable components)**

skew bridges
RK.1284
ALT **skew bridge**
SN Bridges built obliquely from bank to bank. (W)
UF bridges, skew
CN V.RK.AFU.ALO.ALO.GLI.ALO.AFU.AFU.BOK

skew butts
USE **kneelers (gable components)**

skew chisels
TB.866 (N)
ALT **skew chisel**
SN Chisels with a sharp cutting edge cut at an oblique angle and having beveled sides. (MEANS)
UF chisels, skew
CN V.TB.AFU.BCW.CFS.ALO.AFU.BUE.BUE

skew planes
TB.925 (N)
ALT **skew plane**
SN Planes in which the mouth and edge of the iron are obliquely across the face. (DAC)
UF planes, skew
CN V.TB.AFU.BCW.CFS.ALO.AFU.DUC.ALO.BUE.ARI

skews
USE **kneelers (gable components)**

ski jumps
RK.1079 (B)
ALT **ski jump**
UF jumps, ski
CN V.RK.AFU.ALO.ALO.EWY.BIQ.ARI

ski-lift stations
RK.1067 (B)
ALT **ski-lift station**
UF chair-lift stations
stations, chair-lift
stations, ski-lift
CN V.RK.AFU.ALO.ALO.EWY.AXC.BIQ.ALO.BIQ

ski lifts
RK.1080 (A,L)
ALT **ski lift**
UF chair lifts (ski lifts)
lifts, chair (ski lifts)
lifts, ski
CN V.RK.AFU.ALO.ALO.EWY.BIQ.AXC

ski lodges
RK.962 (A,B)
ALT **ski lodge**
UF lodges, ski
CN V.RK.AFU.ALO.ALO.ELK.BOK.ARI

ski slopes, artificial
USE **artificial ski slopes**

ski trails
RG.186
ALT **ski trail**
UF trails, ski
CN V.RG.AFU.AFU.DOI.CLM.ARI

skiagrams
USE **radiographs**

skiagraphs
USE **radiographs**

skid rows
RG.277 (L)
ALT **skid row**
CN V.RG.ALO.AFU.ALO.BCW.AFU.AXC

skill saws
USE **electric-portable saws**

skilled workers
HG.28
ALT **skilled worker**
SN Use for persons qualified in a particular occupation, trade, or craft requiring a high degree of skill, usually in a wide range of related activities performed with a minimum of direction or supervision. (ERIC)
UF workers, skilled
CN H.HG.AFU.AXC.ALO.AXC

skimmers (founding tools)
TB.696 (N)
ALT **skimmer (founding tool)**
SN Tools for removing impurities from the surface of molten metal. (HAND)
CN V.TB.AFU.BCW.BIQ.ALO.BCW

skin
MT.949 (L)
CN M.MT.AFU.AFU.ALO.AFU.DZW

skinning
KT.623
ALT **skinned**
SN Use for the process of removing the outer layer of something, such as the removal of original paint when restoring a painting.
CN K.KT.AFU.ALO.FUA.DZW

skins, stressed
USE **stressed skin structures**

skirt roofs
RT.435
ALT **skirt roof**
SN Small, usually false portions of roofing between the stories of a building. (W)
UF pent roofs (skirt roofs)
penthouse roofs (skirt roofs)
roofs, pent (skirt roofs)
roofs, penthouse (skirt roofs)
roofs, skirt
CN V.RT.AFU.AFU.AFU.BIQ.ARI.AFU.AFU.AFU.BOK.BZY

skirting boards
USE **baseboards**

skirtings
USE **baseboards**

skirts (furniture components)
USE **aprons (furniture components)**

skittle alleys
RK.1059 (B)
ALT **skittle alley**
UF alleys, skittle
CN V.RK.AFU.ALO.ALO.EWY.AXC.BIQ.ALO.AFU.AFU

Skopasian
FL.2696
CN F.FL.ALO.AXC.ALO.AFU.ALO.BCW.ALO.DCU

skotch fasteners
TF.485
ALT **skotch fastener**

SN Devices used for making or strengthening any type of wood joint. The curved prongs draw both sides of a joint firmly together. (PUTNAM)
UF fasteners, skotch
CN V.TF.AFU.AFU.AFU.ALO.AFU.DOI

skull crackers
USE **wrecking balls**

skunk spruce
USE **white spruce**

skutches
USE **scotches**

skybridges
RK.1288
ALT **skybridge**
SN Bridgelike structures for pedestrians built to link one building with another across an alley or street; for the network of interconnecting walkways incorporating skybridges, use **skywalks.** (RHDEL2)
UF bridges, flying
bridges, skywalk
flying bridges
skywalk bridges
CN V.RK.AFU.ALO.ALO.GLI.ALO.AFU.ALO.AFU.AFU

skylights
RT.999 (A,L,N,B)
ALT **skylight**
SN Openings in a roof, glazed or filled with other transparent or translucent material, either in a horizontal plane or substantially tilted, serving to admit light to a space below.
UF lights, roof
roof lights
CN V.RT.AFU.ARI.AFU.ARI.ARI.AXC

skylines
RD.292 (A,B)
ALT **skyline**
SN Outlines, especially of a series of buildings, as seen against the sky.
CN V.RD.ARI.ALO.ALO.ALO

skyscrapers
RK.13 (A,L,B,R)
ALT **skyscraper**
SN Use for exceptionally tall buildings of skeletal frame construction.
UF blocks, tower
buildings, high
buildings, tall
high buildings
tall buildings
tower blocks
CN V.RK.AFU.ALO.AFU.AFU.AFU.ARI.ALO

skywalk bridges
USE **skybridges**

skywalks
RK.1578 (A,B)
ALT **skywalk**
SN Denotes generally enclosed and climate controlled pedestrian walkways or networks of them consisting of bridgelike structures over streets, second-story corridors within buildings and various activity hubs connecting retail and service establishments, usually in a downtown area;(TQ) for the individual bridgelike structures over streets, use **skybridges.**
UF elevated walkways
skyways
walkways, elevated
CN V.RK.ALO.ALO.BUE.BIQ

skyways
USE **expressways**
skywalks
throughways

skywriting
KT.487 (L)
CN K.KT.AFU.ALO.DUC.EWY.ARI

slab blocks
RK.28
ALT **slab block**
UF blocks, slab
buildings, slab
slab buildings
slabs (buildings)
CN V.RK.AFU.ALO.AFU.ALO.CLM

slab buildings
USE **slab blocks**

slab-forming
USE **slab method**

slab foundations
RT.169
ALT **slab foundation**
SN Use for foundations consisting only of a floor slab, thickened to support walls and columns, but not supported by other foundation structures.
UF foundations, slab
CN V.RT.AFU.AFU.AFU.AXC.BUE.ARI.AFU.ARI

slab frames
USE **slab tables**

slab insulation
USE **rigid insulation**

slab method
KT.874
SN A technique of forming pottery by hand, in which a mass of wet clay is flattened to a slab with a rolling pin. The slab may be beat into various shapes, joined to other slaps with slip, or paddled over a wood form. (MAYER)
UF slab-forming
CN K.KT.AFU.ALO.HOE.BOK.BCW

slab sideboards
TG.596
ALT **slab sideboard**
SN Sideboards generally fitted for the display of plates and therefore without cabinets or storage compartments. (BLACK)
UF sideboards, slab
CN V.TG.AFU.AFU.AXC.ALO.CRG.CFS

slab tables
TG.688
ALT **slab table**
SN Period term for 18th-century tables with marble tops. Use **mixing tables** for marble-topped tables with a superstructure containing drawers for decanters and a tambour roll top which descends to cover the marble slab when the table is not in use.
UF drinking tables (slab tables)
frames, slab
marble tables (slab tables)
marble-topped tables
mixing tables (slab tables)
pier tables (slab tables)
slab frames
tables, drinking (slab tables)
tables, marble (slab tables)
tables, marble-topped
tables, mixing (slab tables)
tables, pier (slab tables)
tables, slab
CN V.TG.AFU.AFU.BIQ.BOK.AFU.CRG

slabs
RT.25 (A,L,B)
ALT **slab**
SN Use for flat, thick plates, usually of concrete, functioning as structural elements and capable of sustaining loads, often serving as floors and roofs; also, use collectively, for the structural systems based on such elements.
UF concrete slabs
slabs, concrete
CN V.RT.AFU.AFU.AFU.ALO.ARI.ALO.AFU

slabs (buildings)
USE **slab blocks**

slabs, altar
USE **mensas**

slabs, concrete
USE **slabs**

slabs, flat
USE **flat slab systems**

slabs, ink
USE **inkstones**

slabs, solid
USE **one-way solid slab systems**

slabs, two-direction spanning
USE **two-way structural systems**

slabs, two-way waffle
USE **waffle slabs**

slabs, waffle
USE **waffle slabs**

slag
MT.2046 (L,B)
CN M.MT.AFU.AFU.ARI.AXC.AXC

slag cement
MT.33 (L)
UF cement, slag
CN M.MT.AFU.AFU.AFU.ALO.AFU.AFU.CXA

slag cement, portland
USE **portland slag cement**

slag concrete
MT.206
SN Relatively lightweight concrete made with blast-furnace slag as the coarse aggregate. (DAC)
UF concrete, slag
CN M.MT.AFU.AFU.AFU.BCW.AFU.AFU.CFS

slag concrete, foamed
USE **foamed slag concrete**

slag heaps
RK.1474 (B)
ALT **slag heap**
UF heaps, slag
CN V.RK.ALO.ALO.AXC.ALO

slag plaster
MT.2448
SN Plaster having crushed blast-furnace slag as the aggregate. (DAC)
UF plaster, slag
CN M.MT.AFU.ARI.CRG.AFU.AXC.AFU.BOK

slaked lime
USE **hydrated lime**

slaked plaster of Paris
MT.2444
SN Produced by soaking plaster of Paris overnight so that it loses its setting power; used to make gesso in the Middle Ages. (MAYER)
UF plaster of Paris, slaked
CN M.MT.AFU.ARI.CRG.AFU.AXC.AFU.AXC.ARI.ALO

slant elevators
RT.1309
ALT **slant elevator**
UF elevators, inclined
elevators, slant
inclined elevators
CN V.RT.ALO.ALO.AFU.ARI.ALO.AFU.ARI

slant-front desks
TG.536 (N)
ALT **slant-front desk**
UF desks, slant-front
CN V.TG.AFU.AFU.AXC.ALO.BZY.BUE.ALO

slap-dash
USE **roughcast**

slash pine
USE **Cuban pine**

slat
MT.2268
CN M.MT.AFU.ALO.GFO

slat-back chairs
TG.152
ALT **slat-back chair**
SN Chairs with horizontal slats across the back.
UF chairs, ladder-back
chairs, six-back
chairs, slat-back
ladder-back chairs
six-back chairs
CN V.TG.AFU.AFU.ALO.AFU.AFU.AFU.NIE.DUC

slat-back Windsor chairs
TG.112
ALT **slat-back Windsor chair**
SN Square-back Windsor chairs with a slat across the upper back framed between the back posts. (EVANS)
UF chairs, slat-back Windsor
Windsor chairs, slat-back
CN V.TG.AFU.AFU.ALO.AFU.AFU.AFU.MLC.CFS.BIQ

slat-bending clamps
TB.1057
ALT **slat-bending clamp**
SN Clamps used in chair making to force slats to retain a curved shape. (HUMMEL)
UF clamps, slat-bending
CN V.TB.AFU.BCW.CFS.ALO.ALO.BCW.BUE

slat conveyors
TB.369
ALT **slat conveyor**
SN Conveyors consisting of one or more endless chains to which horizontal spaced slats are attached to form a moving support for the objects being conveyed. (W)
UF conveyors, slat
CN V.TB.AFU.ARI.DCU.AFU.AFU.AXC

slat doors
USE **louver doors**

slat houses
USE **lathhouses**

slate
MT.861 (A,L,B,R)
UF slatestone
CN M.MT.AFU.AFU.AFU.DCU.AFU.ARI.BUE

slate (color)
USE **blackish blue**
bluish gray
dark bluish gray
dark gray
dark grayish blue
dark grayish green
dark greenish gray
dark purplish blue
dark purplish gray
grayish purplish blue
greenish gray
pale green
purplish gray

slate black
USE **black**

slate black, bluish
USE **dark blue**

slate black, greenish
USE **dark gray**
dark greenish gray

slate blue
USE **dark bluish gray**
grayish blue
grayish purplish blue
moderate bluish green

slate blue, deep
USE **grayish blue**

slate gray
USE **dark gray**
medium gray

slate green
USE **dark grayish green**
dark greenish gray
grayish green
greenish gray
light grayish olive
light olive gray
moderate green
moderate olive green
strong olive green

slate green, dark
USE **blackish green**
dark grayish green
dark green
very dark green

slate green, deep
USE **dark greenish gray**

slate olive
USE **dark greenish gray**

slate olive, deep
USE **dark greenish gray**

slate orchid
USE **grayish purple**

slate purple
USE **dark grayish purple**
dark reddish purple
grayish purple
grayish reddish purple

slate violet
USE **dark grayish purple**
dark purplish gray
grayish purple

slate violet, dark
USE **dark purplish gray**
grayish purple

slate violet, deep
USE **grayish purple**

slate, black
USE **black slate**

slate, blackboard
USE **blackboard slate**

slate, blackish
USE **dark gray**

slate, blue
USE **blue slate**

slate, dark green blue
USE **dark blue**
dark grayish blue

slate, dark violet
USE **grayish blue**

slate, gray
USE **gray slate**

slate, green
USE **green slate**

slate, green blue
USE **grayish blue**

slate, purple
USE **purple slate**

slate, red
USE **red slate**

slate, ribbon
USE **ribbon slate**

slate, roofing
USE **roofing slate**

slate, structural
USE **structural slate**

slate, wrestler
USE **wrestler slate**

slatestone
USE **slate**

slating
KT.588
SN The installation of slate shingles, as on a roof or wall. (DAC)
CN K.KT.AFU.ALO.ERE.BUE

slating hammers
USE **zaxes**

slating nails, cut
USE **cut slating nails**

slats
TG.836
ALT **slat**
SN Flat narrow bands of wood, often set in a horizontal series across the back of chairs and other seating furniture.
UF cross rails
rails, cross
CN V.TG.ALO.AXC.ALO.BIQ

slats (louvers)
USE **louvers**

slats, bed
USE **bed slats**

slaughterhouses
RK.636 (A,L,B,R)
ALT **slaughterhouse**
UF abattoirs
meatworks
CN V.RK.AFU.ALO.ALO.CLM.ALO.
ALO.AFU.AXC.BCW.BCW.ALO

Slave
FL.1240 (L)
UF Etchaottine
CN F.FL.ALO.ALO.ARI.AFU.AFU.ARI.
DOI

slave cabins
USE **slave quarters**

slave dwellings
USE **slave quarters**

slave houses
USE **slave quarters**

slave keeping
USE **slavery**

slave quarters
RK.349 (A)
ALT **slave quarter**
UF cabins, slave
dwellings, slave
houses, slave
quarters, slave
slave cabins
slave dwellings
slave houses
CN V.RK.AFU.ALO.ALO.AXC.ALO.
BOK.CFS

slavery
BM.1115 (A,L,R)
UF servitude
slave keeping
CN B.BM.CRG.BCW.CFS

Slavic
FL.3116 (A,L,R)
UF Slavonic
CN F.FL.ALO.BCW.ALO.ALO.AFU.
BOK.ALO.AXC

Slavonic
USE **Slavic**

sledgehammers
TB.465 (N)
ALT **sledgehammer**
SN Large heavy hammers that are usually wielded with both hands and used especially for driving stakes and breaking stone. (W)
UF hammers, striking
striking hammers
CN V.TB.AFU.ARI.ELK.AFU.AXC

sleeper walls
RT.591 (B)
ALT **sleeper wall**
SN Dwarf walls that carry a joist supporting a floor, usually perforated to permit the passage of air for ventilation.
UF walls, sleeper
CN V.RT.AFU.AFU.AFU.BIQ.BUE.
AFU.ALO.BIQ

sleepers, sofa
USE **sofa beds**

sleeping chairs
TG.196
ALT **sleeping chair**
SN Upholstered armchairs with a winged back which by means of a ratchet can be adjusted to any desired angle; first made in the Restoration period. (DDA)
UF chairs, sleeping
CN V.TG.AFU.AFU.ALO.AFU.AFU.
ALO.ERE

sleeping porches
RM.249 (A)
ALT **sleeping porch**
SN Porches or rooms having open sides or many windows arranged to permit sleeping in the open air. (W)
UF porches, sleeping
CN V.RM.AFU.DIO.ARI.AFU.BIQ.AFU

Sleepy Hollow chairs
TG.86
ALT **Sleepy Hollow chair**
SN Upholstered armchairs, often with a button-tufted back, having a single piece forming a high sloping back and a concave seat; of a type made in America in the mid-19th to early 20th centuries.
UF chairs, Sleepy Hollow
CN V.TG.AFU.AFU.ALO.AFU.AFU.
AFU.KLE

sleet
BM.752
CN B.BM.CFS.ALO.AXC.ALO.BIQ.ARI

sleigh beds
TG.371 (N)
ALT **sleigh bed**
SN Use for beds with two ends of equal height intended to stand lengthwise along the wall.
UF beds, boat
beds, French (sleigh beds)
beds, gondola
beds, gondola-shaped
beds, Grecian
beds, sleigh
boat beds
French beds (sleigh beds)
gondola beds
gondola-shaped beds
Grecian beds

CN V.TG.AFU.AFU.ARI.AFU.AFU.EFQ

Sliammon
USE **Comox**

slices (slicks)
USE **slicks**

slickers, derby
USE **darbies**

slicks
TB.860 (N)
ALT **slick**
SN Giant paring chisels which are pushed by the hands and shoulder rather than struck. (BLACKB)
UF slices (slicks)
CN V.TB.AFU.BCW.CFS.ALO.AFU.BUE.ALO.BCW.AFU

sliders
USE **slides (furniture components)**

slides
VJ.85 (L,N,R)
ALT **slide**
SN Positive transparencies in mounts suitable for projection, usually 35mm film in a mount of 2 by 2 inches.
CN V.VJ.AFU.AFU.BCW.AXC

slides (furniture components)
TG.984
ALT **slide (furniture component)**
SN Horizontal panels that slide out of the body of a piece to increase the surface area temporarily.
UF sliders
CN V.TG.ALO.GWW

slides, black-and-white
USE **black-and-white slides**

slides, candle
USE **candle slides**

slides, color
USE **color slides**

slides, lantern
USE **lantern slides**

slides, magic lantern
USE **lantern slides**

slides, water
USE **water slides**

sliding bevels
USE **bevel squares**

sliding-door keys
TF.539
ALT **sliding-door key**
SN Keys adapted for use with a mortise lock and a cup escutcheon on sliding doors; its length is usually adjustable. (STEIN)
UF keys, sliding-door
CN V.TF.AFU.ALO.ARI.AFU.CLM

sliding-door latches
USE **sliding-door locks**

sliding-door locks
TF.243
ALT **sliding-door lock**
UF latches, sliding-door
locks, sliding-door
sliding-door latches
CN V.TF.AFU.AFU.AFU.AFU.DIO.BIQ.ALO.ALO.CFS

sliding-door pulls
TF.90
ALT **sliding-door pull**
UF pulls, sliding-door
CN V.TF.AFU.AFU.AFU.AFU.CFS.BCW.ALO.ARI.ALO

sliding doors
RT.872 (L,B)
ALT **sliding door**
SN Doors that slide sideways.
UF doors, sliding
CN V.RT.AFU.ARI.AFU.AFU.AFU.ALO.ARI.AFU.ARI.BOK

sliding fire screens
TG.10
ALT **sliding fire screen**
SN Period term for 18th-century fire screens supported upon a stand, which may be extended by means of sliding panels.
UF fire screens, sliding
screens, sliding fire
CN V.TG.AFU.AFU.AFU.AFU.BCW

sliding joints
USE **housed joints**

sliding shelves
TG.983
ALT **sliding shelf**
UF shelves, sliding
CN V.TG.ALO.GRC.AFU

sliding tongs
TB.765 (N)
SN Tongs primarily used by clock- and watchmakers to hold pins, arbors, or other small objects while they are being filed. (HUMMEL)
UF buckle tongs
clamping-pliers
tongs, buckle
tongs, sliding
CN V.TB.AFU.BCW.BIQ.AXC.ALO.AXC.DIO

sliding windows
RT.951
ALT **sliding window**
UF windows, sliding
CN V.RT.AFU.ARI.AFU.AFU.BOK.AFU.AFU.EWY.BIQ

sling chairs
TG.87
ALT **sling chair**
SN Any of several varieties of chairs having a seat and back formed from a single sheet of canvas, leather, or the like, and hanging loosely on a frame. (RHDEL2)
UF chairs, sling
CN V.TG.AFU.AFU.ALO.AFU.AFU.AFU.KQY

slingers
HG.590
ALT **slinger**
SN Workers who attach slings to articles for hoisting. (W)
CN H.HG.AFU.AXC.BZY.AFU.BUE.AFU

slings
TB.1128 (L)
ALT **sling**
SN Hoist components usually consisting of looped lines used to hold securely something to be hoisted, lowered, carried, or suspended. (W)
CN V.TB.ALO.CXA.AFU

slip
MT.59 (L)
SN A clay which, in its natural state, contains sufficient flux to be used for glazing. (MAYER)
UF clay, slip
slip clay
CN M.MT.AFU.AFU.AFU.AXC.AFU.AFU.BOK

slip casting
KT.875 (L)
ALT **slip cast**
SN The process of forming clayware by pouring slip into plaster molds. (W)
UF casting, slip
CN K.KT.AFU.ALO.HOE.BOK.BIQ

slip clay
USE **slip**

slip clay, Albany
USE **Albany slip clay**

slip glaze
MT.2571
UF glaze, slip
CN M.MT.AFU.ARI.CRG.ARI.ARI.AFU.ARI.BIQ

slip joints
TF.631
ALT **slip joint**
UF joints, slip
CN V.TF.ALO.ARI.ALO.AFU.BCW

slip seats
TG.976
ALT **slip seat**
SN Upholstered or carved seats that have their own frame and fit loosely into the frame of the chair.
UF drop-in seats
loose seats
seats, drop-in
seats, loose
seats, slip
CN V.TG.ALO.GLI.AFU.ARI.ALO

slip sills
RT.982
ALT **slip sill**
SN Use for window sills that consist of a stone slab just as long as the window is wide and fitting into the walls between the jamb; distinguished from **lug sills** which are longer than the width of the window opening and are let in to the wall on each side.
UF sills, slip
CN V.RT.AFU.ARI.AFU.AFU.BOK.ALO.BOK.ALO.ALO.ALO

slip trailing
KT.873
SN The application of slip to a piece of pottery with a syringelike device so as to create slightly raised linear decoration. (MAYER)
UF pastillage
trailing
trailing, slip
CN K.KT.AFU.ALO.HOE.BOK.AXC.BCW

slip ware, white
USE **white slip ware**

slip, brick
USE **brick slip**

slipper chairs
TG.89 (N)
ALT **slipper chair**
SN High-backed, low-seated chairs without arms and often upholstered; intended for bedroom use.
UF chairs, slipper
CN V.TG.AFU.AFU.ALO.AFU.AFU.AFU.KWS

slippery elm
MT.1149
UF elm, slippery
Ulmus fulva
Ulmus rubra
CN M.MT.AFU.AFU.ALO.BIQ.DCU.AFU.AFU.AFU.DCU.BCW

slips
RK.1599
ALT **slip**
SN Use for unoccupied, open water spaces set between adjacent piers or perpendicular to landing places, especially those spaces which can accommodate only one vessel at a time; when such spaces are alongside land places, use **berths.** Use **docks** for open water spaces when occupied by vessels made fast to landing places.
CN V.RK.ALO.ARI.CLM.ALO.ARI

slips, building
USE **slipways**

slips, draw
USE **lopers**

slips, gouge
USE **gouge slips**

slips, sanding
USE **contour sanders**

slipways
RK.680
ALT **slipway**
SN The structures inclined toward the water on which a ship may be built or lowered into the water; may also be used for the guides which support the ship's hull.
UF berths, building
building berths
building slips
shipways
slips, building
CN V.RK.AFU.ALO.ALO.CLM.BCW.AFU

slit deal planes
USE **tongue-and-groove planes**

slits, vision
USE **loopholes**

slitting planes
USE **splint planes**

slop brick
USE **water-struck brick**

slop sinks
RT.1487
ALT **slop sink**
SN Deep sinks, usually set low, especially used for emptying pails of dirty water. (DAC)
UF service sinks
sinks, service
sinks, slop
CN V.RT.ALO.BCW.ALO.ARI.CFS.BIQ.ARI

slope
BM.811 (A,B)
CN B.BM.CFS.ARI.AXC.BZY

slope beds
USE **field beds**

slopes
RD.239 (L)
ALT **slope**
CN V.RD.ARI.AFU.AXC.ALO.BOK

slot anchors
TF.300
ALT **slot anchor**
UF anchors, furring
anchors, slot
furring anchors
CN V.TF.AFU.AFU.AFU.ALO.AFU.AFU.CRG

slots, letter
USE **letter-box plates**

slots, mail
USE **letter-box plates**

sloughs
USE **swamps**

slow-curing asphalt
MT.986
UF asphalt, slow-curing
CN M.MT.AFU.AFU.ALO.ALO.AFU.AXC.ALO

sloyd knives
TB.909
ALT **sloyd knife**
SN Woodworker's knives having fixed, single blades, used in woodcarving, slicing, and trimming. (DAC)
UF knives, sloyd
CN V.TB.AFU.BCW.CFS.ALO.AFU.DOI.BCW

SLRs
USE **single lens reflex cameras**

slues
USE **swamps**

sluice gates
RT.896 (A,L,N)
ALT **sluice gate**
UF floodgates
gates, sluice
CN V.RT.AFU.ARI.AFU.AFU.ARI.ALO.AFU.AFU.AXC

sluices
RK.517 (L,N)
ALT **sluice**
SN Artificial passages for water, fitted with a valve or gate for stopping or regulating the flow. (W)
CN V.RK.AFU.ALO.ALO.CFS.AFU.AFU.ARI

sluing arches
USE **splayed arches**

slum clearance
BM.1074 (A,L,B)
UF clearance, slum
CN B.BM.CLM.ALO.ALO.AFU.ALO.ARI

slums
RG.278 (A,L,B)
ALT **slum**
CN V.RG.ALO.AFU.ALO.BCW.AFU.BCW

slurry-trenches
USE **diaphragm walls**

slurry-walls
USE **diaphragm walls**

small
DC.124 (A,B)
CN D.DC.AFU.AXC.BCW

small-leafed lime
MT.1314
UF lime, small-leafed
Tilia cordata

CN M.MT.AFU.AFU.ALO.BIQ.DCU.
AFU.AFU.AFU.LZO.ARI

Small Vehicle
USE **Hinayana**

small writing desks, lady's
USE **lady's writing tables**

smallholdings
RD.287
ALT **smallholding**
SN Pieces of land rented or sold to a farmer or other laborer by county or local authorities for purposes of cultivation, often as a supplement to primary income.
CN V.RD.ARI.ALO.AFU.AFU.AXC.AFU

smalt
MT.1603
UF azure blue
bleu d'émail
blue, azure
blue, dumont
blue, Hungary
blue, Saxon
dumont blue
Hungary blue
Saxon blue
Smalte
CN M.MT.AFU.AFU.ARI.AFU.AFU.ALO.
ALO.ALO.ARI.BUE

smalt (color)
USE **deep blue**

smalt blue
USE **moderate blue**
vivid purplish blue

smalt, green
USE **cobalt green**

Smalte
USE **smalt**

Sman gsar
USE **New Menri School**

smart buildings
USE **intelligent buildings**

smashers, atom
USE **particle accelerators**

smell
BM.728 (L,R)
CN B.BM.CFS.AFU.BCW.ARI

smeltermen
HG.507
ALT **smelterman**
UF smelters (metalworkers)
CN H.HG.AFU.AXC.BUE.ARI.CFS.ALO.
BCW

smelters
RK.645 (B)
ALT **smelter**
UF mills, smelting
plants, smelting
smelting mills
smelting plants
smelting works
works, smelting
CN V.RK.AFU.ALO.ALO.CLM.ALO.
ALO.AFU.AXC.BUE.ARI

smelters (metalworkers)
USE **smeltermen**

smelting
KT.852 (L)
SN To melt or fuse ore, often with an accompanying chemical change, usually to separate the metal. (W)
CN K.KT.AFU.ALO.HOE.BCW.ALO.
BIQ.BOK

smelting mills
USE **smelters**

smelting plants
USE **smelters**

smelting works
USE **smelters**

Smillie's bath
MT.2723
SN Solution of hydrochloric acid and potassium chlorate used as a mordant in aquatint. (MAYER)
UF bath, Smillie's
CN M.MT.AFU.ARI.IFM.ARI.ALO.AFU

smith's braces
TB.849
ALT **smith's brace**
SN Various iron braces used in conjunction with a drill when exceptional drilling pressure is needed.
UF braces, smith's
CN V.TB.AFU.BCW.CFS.ALO.AFU.BIQ.
ALO

smith's drills
USE **drill clamps**

Smithfield
FL.63 (L)
CN F.FL.ALO.AFU.AFU.ALO.BCW.AFU

smithies
RK.1326 (A,L,B,R)
ALT **smithy**
UF blacksmith shops
forge shops
forges (smithies)
shops, blacksmith
shops, forge
CN V.RK.AFU.ALO.ALO.GRC.AFU

smithing, brass
USE **brass-smithing**

smiths
USE **metalworkers**

smock mills
RK.668
ALT **smock mill**
SN Use for windmills having a timber cap revolving on top of a polygonal lower structure clad in siding.
UF mills, smock
smock windmills
windmills, smock
CN V.RK.AFU.ALO.ALO.CLM.ALO.
ALO.ALO.ALO.AFU

smock windmills
USE **smock mills**

smog
BM.432 (L,B)
CN B.BM.AXC.BCW.AFU.AFU.ALO

smoke
MT.2048 (R)
CN M.MT.AFU.AFU.ARI.BCW

smoke abatement
KG.124 (L,B)
UF abatement, smoke
CN K.KG.AFU.AFU.BCW.ALO.BZY.ALO

smoke detectors
RT.1515 (A,L,B)
ALT **smoke detector**
UF detectors, smoke
CN V.RT.ALO.BIQ.AFU.AFU.ALO.ARI

smoke-pipes
USE **flues**

smoke towers
USE **smokestacks**

smokehouses
RK.638 (B)
ALT **smokehouse**
CN V.RK.AFU.ALO.ALO.CLM.ALO.
ALO.AFU.AXC.BCW.BOK

smoker's cabinets
USE **smoking stands**

smoker's stands
USE **smokers**

smokers
TG.652 (N)
ALT **smoker**
SN Ashtrays mounted on a low pedestal stand generally used along side of a sofa. Distinct from **smoking stands** which are small stands or cabinets with zinc-lined compartments used to store smoking supplies.
UF ashtray stands
cigarette tables
smoker's stands
smoking stands (ashtrays)
stands, ashtray
stands, smoker's
stands, smoking (ashtrays)
tables, cigarette
CN V.TG.AFU.AFU.BIQ.BCW.ALO.DZW

smokestacks
RT.1134 (A,L,N)
ALT **smokestack**
SN Use for large chimneys through which smoke and gases of combus-

tion are discharged.
UF smoke towers
towers, smoke
CN V.RT.AFU.BOK.AFU.AFU.ALO

smoking chairs
TG.197
ALT **smoking chair**
SN Chairs with compartments for smoking equipment.
UF chairs, smoking
chairs, strapple
strapple chairs
CN V.TG.AFU.AFU.ALO.AFU.AFU.ALO.EWY

smoking rooms
RM.181
ALT **smoking room**
SN Rooms set apart for smoking, as in hotels or clubhouses. (RHDEL2)
UF rooms, smoking
CN V.RM.AFU.DIO.ALO.CXA.DCU

smoking stands
TG.653
ALT **smoking stand**
SN Small stands or cabinets with zinc-lined compartments used to store smoking supplies. Distinct from **smokers'** which are ashtrays mounted on a low pedestal stand.
UF cabinets, smoker's
smoker's cabinets
stands, smoking
CN V.TG.AFU.AFU.BIQ.BCW.ALO.EFQ

smoking stands (ashtrays)
USE **smokers**

smooth
DC.141
ALT **smoothness**
CN D.DC.AFU.BCW.BOK

smoothing planes
TB.939 (N)
ALT **smoothing plane**
SN Short planes, often coffin-shaped; the last plane used on a wood surface to give it the utmost degree of smoothness.
UF coffin planes
planes, coffin
planes, smoothing
CN V.TB.AFU.BCW.CFS.ALO.AFU.DUC.ARI.AFU.AXC

smoothing planes, compass
USE **compass planes**

SMSAs
USE **Standard Metropolitan Statistical Areas**

snack bars
RK.108 (A,B)
ALT **snack bar**
SN Eating facilities where quick, light meals, refreshments, or snacks are served, usually at a counter . (DAC)
UF bars, snack
CN V.RK.AFU.ALO.ALO.ALO.AFU.AFU.AXC

snack tables
TG.758
ALT **snack table**
UF tables, snack
tables, TV
TV tables
CN V.TG.AFU.AFU.BIQ.BOK.ALO.FCS

snail augers
USE **shell augers**

Snake
USE **Shoshone**

snake curves
USE **flexible curves**

snake feet
TG.930
ALT **snake foot**
SN S-curved legs with thin ankles which broaden to a shaped foot not unlike the head of a snake; used on tripod tables from the early 18th century. (PAIN)
UF feet, snake
CN V.TG.ALO.DZW.AFU.DCU.BOK

snakeskin
MT.959
CN M.MT.AFU.AFU.ALO.AFU.DZW.AXC.BCW

snap header
USE **brickbat**

snap tables
USE **tilt-top tables**

snap-tie hangers
TF.345
ALT **snap-tie hanger**
UF hangers, snap-tie
CN V.TF.AFU.AFU.AFU.ALO.AFU.BOK.ALO.ALO.ARI

snapshots
VJ.100 (L)
ALT **snapshot**
SN Photographs made with simple cameras without artistic pretensions or commercial considerations; beginning especially in 1888 with the appearance of the first roll film box camera.(COE) Snapshots thus are most often recognizable in that they are photographs that were processed not by the photographer but by a commercial concern.
CN V.VJ.AFU.ARI.AFU.BIQ

snarling irons
TB.680 (N)
ALT **snarling iron**
SN Tools with a long beak, used in making raised work on metal surfaces by repercussion. (W)
UF irons, snarling
CN V.TB.AFU.BCW.BIQ.AFU.ALO.CRG

snedding axes
USE **lopping axes**

snipe-bill hinges
USE **cotter pin hinges**

snipe hinges
USE **cotter pin hinges**

snipping
KT.89
ALT **snipped**
CN K.KT.AFU.ALO.BUE.ARI

snips
USE **tin snips**

snips, sheet metal worker's
USE **tin snips**

snips, tin
USE **tin snips**

Snoqualmi
USE **Snuqualmi**

snow
BM.753 (L,R)
CN B.BM.CFS.ALO.AXC.ALO.BIQ.AXC

snow boards
USE **snow guards**

snow crystals
USE **snowflakes**

snow fences
RM.440 (L)
ALT **snow fence**
SN Fences of laths wired together, set perpendicular to the direction of prevailing winds to catch drifting snow. (DAC)
UF fences, snow
CN V.RM.ALO.AFU.BCW.BIQ

snow guards
RT.490
ALT **snow guard**
SN Devices used to prevent snow from sliding off a roof.
UF boards, snow
guards, roof
guards, snow
rails, snow
roof guards
snow boards
snow rails
CN V.RT.AFU.AFU.AFU.BIQ.ARI.ALO.AFU.CLM

snow loads
BM.1018 (L,B)
CN B.BM.CFS.AXC.CLM.ALO.ARI.CRG

snow rails
USE **snow guards**

snowflake white
USE **white lead**

snowflakes
DG.45
ALT **snowflake**
SN Use for decorative motifs based on the hexagonal crystal formation of snowflakes.
UF crystals, snow
snow crystals
CN D.DG.AFU.AFU.CXA.AXC

snowstorms
KM.123
CN K.KM.AFU.CXA.BIQ.BOK

Snuqualmi
FL.1362
UF Snoqualmi
CN F.FL.ALO.ALO.ARI.AFU.BIQ.FZU

So
USE **Sao Empire**
Saô

soak-stain technique
KT.236
SN A method of painting which produces soft stains or blots of color through the use of heavily diluted paint on unsized canvas. (THDAT)
CN K.KT.AFU.ALO.DUC.CXA.ALO.AFU.DCU

soap
MT.2049 (L,R)
CN M.MT.AFU.AFU.ARI.BIQ

soap (brick)
MT.83
CN M.MT.AFU.AFU.AFU.AXC.ALO.AFU.AFU.AFU.CXA

soap dispensers
TF.145
ALT **soap dispenser**
UF dispensers, soap
CN V.TF.AFU.AFU.AFU.AFU.CRG.ALO

soap valves
TF.285
ALT **soap valve**
UF valves, soap
CN V.TF.AFU.AFU.AFU.AFU.EWY.BOK

soap, soft
USE **soft soap**

soap, tincture of green
USE **soft soap**

soapstone
MT.875 (L,R)
SN Massive, soft rock that contains a high proportion of talc; used in building for laboratory sinks, bench tops, and electrical panels,(DAC) and by artists for carving.
CN M.MT.AFU.AFU.AFU.DCU.AFU.ARI.BZY

soapstone (white pigment)
USE **talc (white pigment)**

Sobo
USE **Urhobo**

soccer fields
RK.1485 (L,B)
ALT **soccer field**
UF fields, soccer
football pitches
pitches, football
pitches, soccer
soccer pitches
CN V.RK.ALO.ALO.BCW.AFU.BUE

soccer pitches
USE **soccer fields**

social anthropologists
HG.254
ALT **social anthropologist**
SN Anthropologists who study human cultures, especially with respect to social structure, language, law, politics, religion, magic, art, and technology.
UF anthropologists, cultural
anthropologists, social
cultural anthropologists
CN H.HG.AFU.AXC.BCW.AFU.AFU.ARI

social anthropology
KD.99 (L)
UF anthropology, cultural
anthropology, social
cultural anthropology
CN K.KD.AFU.ALO.AFU.BOK

social centers
USE **community centers**

social classes
HG.883 (L,R)
ALT **social class**
SN Levels in human populations distinguished by degree of wealth or privilege, modes of labor, way of life, or other social, economic, or cultural factors. (TSIT)
UF class differences
classes, social
social stratification
stratification, social
CN H.HG.ALO.DOI.ALO

social conflict
BM.1116 (L)
UF conflict, social
CN B.BM.CRG.BCW.CLM

social customs
USE **customs**

Social Darwinism
BM.1092 (L)
SN Theory in sociology that sociocultural advance is the product of intergroup conflict and competition and that therefore the socially elect classes (those possessing wealth and power) possess biological superiority in the struggle for existence. (W)
UF Darwinism, Social
CN B.BM.CRG.AXC

social deviancy
USE **deviant behavior**

social ethics
BM.499 (L)
UF ethics, social
CN B.BM.BIQ.ALO.ALO

social history
KD.145 (L)
SN History that concentrates on the sociocultural aspects of the life, customs, trends, and institutions of a people. (ERIC)
UF history, social
CN K.KD.AFU.ALO.CLM.AFU.BCW

social institutions
HG.861 (L)
ALT **social institution**
UF institutions, social
CN H.HG.ALO.CXA.ARI

social issues
BM.1093 (L)
UF issues, social
problems, social
social problems
CN B.BM.CRG.BCW

social mobility
BM.1124 (L)
SN Use for changes in the social status of individuals or groups.
UF mobility, social
CN B.BM.CRG.BIQ

social problems
USE **social issues**

social psychology
KD.183 (L)
SN Study of how people are affected by others and by their social environment. (PG)
UF psychology, social
CN K.KD.AFU.ALO.EFQ.AFU.ARI

social realism
BM.179 (L,R)
ALT **social realist**
SN Use for works depicting realistic situations with tones of social protest, common especially in the 1930s and 1940s. For the representational art in Communist countries sanctioned by the government, use **Socialist Realist.**
UF realism, social
CN B.BM.AFU.AFU.AXC.BOK.AFU

social registers
VW.412 (L)
ALT **social register**
SN Directories listing persons of social prominence in a community. (AHD)
UF bluebooks

directories, elite
elite directories
registers, social
CN V.VW.AFU.AFU.ALO.EWY.AXC.AFU.BCW

social sciences
KD.89 (L,R)
SN Sciences dealing with the institutions and functioning of human society and with the interpersonal relationships of individuals as members of society. (W)
UF sciences, social
CN K.KD.AFU.ALO

social services
HG.875
ALT **social service**
SN Use for organized assistance provided by public or private agencies and organizations to individual community members. For essential on-going services provided by the government relating directly to the protection and maintenance of the lives and property of community members as a whole, use **public services.**
UF services, social
CN H.HG.ALO.DIO.BCW

social status
BM.1125 (L)
UF class status
socioeconomic status
status, class
status, social
status, socioeconomic
CN B.BM.CRG.BOK

social stratification
USE **social classes**

social structure
BM.1126 (L)
UF structure, social
CN B.BM.CRG.BUE

social tables
USE **drinking stands**

social welfare
USE **welfare services**

social workers
HG.322 (L)
ALT **social worker**
SN Persons engaged in social work or professionally trained specialists in social work. (W)
UF workers, social
CN H.HG.AFU.AXC.BCW.ALO.BOK

socialism
BM.564 (L,R)
CN B.BM.BOK.BZY.CFS

Socialism, National
USE **National Socialism**

Socialist Realist
FL.3418 (L,R)
ALT **Socialist Realism**
SN Use for the representational style sanctioned by the government in Communist countries. For works depicting realistic situations with a tone of social protest, use **social realism.**
UF Realist, Socialist
CN F.FL.ALO.BCW.ALO.AXC.DIO.BZY.ALO.BCW

societies
HG.892 (L,B)
ALT **society**
CN H.HG.ALO.DUC

societies' buildings
RK.1201 (A,B)
ALT **societies' building**
UF association buildings
buildings, association
buildings, foundation
buildings, organizations'
buildings, societies'
buildings, society and association
foundation buildings
organizations' buildings
society and association buildings
CN V.RK.AFU.ALO.ALO.FZU

societies, archaeological
USE **archaeological societies**

societies, architectural
USE **architectural societies**

societies, botanical
USE **garden clubs**
horticultural societies

societies, charitable
USE **charitable societies**

societies, educational
USE **educational societies**

societies, garden
USE **garden clubs**

societies, historical
USE **historical societies**

societies, horticultural
USE **horticultural societies**

societies, scientific
USE **scientific societies**

societies, secret
USE **secret societies**

societies, standards
USE **standards organizations**

societies, technical
USE **technical societies**

societies, tribal
USE **tribes**

society and association buildings
USE **societies' buildings**

Society Island
FL.3700 (L)
CN F.FL.ALO.BOK.AXC.BZY

socioeconomic status
USE **social status**

sociolinguistics
KD.38 (L)
CN K.KD.AFU.AFU.AXC.AFU.AFU.BCW

sociologists
HG.278 (L)
ALT **sociologist**
CN H.HG.AFU.AXC.BCW.AFU.CFS

sociology
KD.188 (L,B,R)
SN Science of society, social institutions, and social relationships; specifically the systematic study of the development, structure, and function of human groups conceived as processes of interaction or as organized patterns of collective behavior. (W)
CN K.KD.AFU.ALO.ELK

sociology of knowledge
KD.191 (L)
UF knowledge, sociology of
CN K.KD.AFU.ALO.ELK.ARI

sociology of religion
KD.79 (L)
UF religion, sociology of
CN K.KD.AFU.AFU.BUE.AFU.BCW

sociology, Frankfurt school of
USE **critical theory**

sociology, historical
USE **historical sociology**

sociology, rural
USE **rural sociology**

sociology, urban
USE **urban sociology**

socket chisels
TB.867 (N)
ALT **socket chisel**
SN Chisels that have a tapering hollow tang to recieve a handle. (W)
UF chisels, socket
CN V.TB.AFU.BCW.CFS.ALO.AFU.BUE.BZY

socket wrenches
TB.779 (N)
ALT **socket wrench**
SN Box wrenches with a recessed socket that fits over a nut; used for tightening or removing nuts. (MEANS)
UF sockets (wrenches)
wrenches, socket
CN V.TB.AFU.BCW.BIQ.AXC.ALO.BIQ.BUE

sockets (power outlets)
USE **power outlets**

sockets (wrenches)
USE **socket wrenches**

sockets, foot
USE **foot sockets**

sockets, wall
USE **power outlets**

socles
RT.67 (A)
ALT **socle**
SN Plain blocks or plinths forming the low pedestals of statues, columns, or the like; also plain faces, or plinths, at the lower part of a wall or pedestal. (PARKER)
UF zocles
CN V.RT.AFU.AFU.AFU.AXC.ARI.AFU.AFU

sod
MT.2060
UF turf
CN M.MT.AFU.AFU.ARI.BOK.AFU.BCW

soda chairs
USE **ice-cream parlor chairs**

soda fountain chairs
USE **ice-cream parlor chairs**

soda glass, lime
USE **soda lime glass**

soda lime glass
MT.245
SN A lime glass in which soda is used. (W)
UF glass, lime
glass, lime soda
glass, soda lime
lime glass
lime glass, soda
lime soda glass
soda glass, lime
CN M.MT.AFU.AFU.AFU.BIQ.AFU.AFU.BCW

soda pulp
MT.1057
UF pulp, soda
CN M.MT.AFU.AFU.ALO.BIQ.BUE.BCW.AFU

soda, caustic
USE **sodium hydroxide**

sodalities
USE **confraternities**

sodium hydroxide
MT.305 (L)
UF caustic soda
hydroxide, sodium
soda, caustic
CN M.MT.AFU.AFU.AFU.BOK.ALO.ALO

sodium silicate
USE **water glass**

sofa beds
TG.316 (N)
ALT **sofa bed**
SN Sofas that can be converted into beds.
UF beds, convertible
beds, sofa
canapés en lit
canapés-lits
convertible beds
convertible sofas
lits-canapés
sleepers, sofa
sofa sleepers
sofas, convertible
CN V.TG.AFU.AFU.ALO.ALO.BZY.BOK

sofa sleepers
USE **sofa beds**

sofa tables
TG.777 (N)
ALT **sofa table**
SN Similar to pembroke tables but with flaps at the ends. In the late Regency period the end-flaps disappeared and the term was used a synonym for occasional tables. (BEARD)
UF davenport tables
tables, davenport
tables, sofa
CN V.TG.AFU.AFU.BIQ.BOK.ARI.AFU.ARI

sofa writing tables
TG.581
ALT **sofa writing table**
UF tables, sofa writing
writing tables, sofa
CN V.TG.AFU.AFU.AXC.ALO.BZY.FUA.CLM

sofas
TG.307 (N,R)
ALT **sofa**
SN Long, upholstered seating forms with a back and two ends; primarily used for sitting rather than reclining. Distinct from **couches** which have a back support and one end and are primarily used for reclining rather than sitting.
UF couches (sofas)
sophas
CN V.TG.AFU.AFU.ALO.ALO.BZY

sofas, bar-back
USE **chair-back settees**

sofas, cabriole
USE **cabriole sofas**

sofas, convertible
USE **sofa beds**

sofas, Grecian
USE **Grecian couches**

sofas, recamier
USE **Grecian couches**

sofas, turkey
USE **ottomans**

soffit vents
RT.991
ALT **soffit vent**
UF vents, soffit
CN V.RT.AFU.ARI.AFU.ALO.BCW.AFU

soffits
RT.819
ALT **soffit**
SN The underside of a part or member of a building (as of an overhang, ceiling, staircase, cornice, or entablature). (W)
UF pieces, plancier
plancier pieces
planciers
CN V.RT.AFU.ALO.AFU.CLM

soft blue violet
USE **brilliant violet**

soft brick
MT.120
SN Weak, non-weather-resistant brick fired at low temperature ranges or remote from the fire in the kiln; suitable for use as backing brick.
UF brick, soft
brick, soft-burned
brick, underburned
brick, unfired
soft-burned brick
underburned brick
unfired brick
CN M.MT.AFU.AFU.AFU.AXC.ALO.AFU.AXC.AFU.AFU.ALO

soft-burned brick
USE **soft brick**

soft coal
USE **bituminous coal**

soft-ground etching
KT.460
ALT **soft-ground etched**
SN Use for the intaglio process in which a ground of a soft substance, such as vaseline or tallow, is applied thinly to a plate allowing the rendering of textures. (MAYER)
UF etching, soft-ground
vernis mou
CN K.KT.AFU.ALO.DUC.DUC.ALO.BCW.AFU.AXC.ARI

soft maple
USE **silver maple**

soft-mud brick
MT.135
SN Brick produced by a process of forming wet clay in molds. (PCMC)
UF brick, soft-mud
CN M.MT.AFU.AFU.AFU.AXC.ALO.AFU.AXC.ALO.ALO.ALO

soft paste porcelain

MT.147 (R)
UF porcelain, soft paste
CN M.MT.AFU.AFU.AFU.AXC.ALO.ALO.AFU.AFU.ALO

soft soap
MT.2050
UF green soap, tincture of
soap, soft
soap, tincture of green
tincture of green soap
CN M.MT.AFU.AFU.ARI.BIQ.AFU

Soft Style
USE **International Gothic**

soft ware
FL.3032
UF ware, soft
CN F.FL.ALO.AXC.ARI.BIQ.ALO.AXC.CFS

soft water
MT.319
UF water, soft
CN M.MT.AFU.AFU.AFU.BOK.BOK.AFU.AXC

soft yellow
USE **light yellow**

softball fields
RK.1486
ALT **softball field**
UF fields, softball
CN V.RK.ALO.ALO.BCW.AFU.BZY

softeners, water
USE **water softeners**

software
VW.653 (A,L)
SN Sets of computer programs, procedures, and associated documentation concerned with the operation of data processing systems. (ICA)
UF computer programs
programs, computer
CN V.VW.AFU.ALO.AFU.DZW.ALO.BUE

softwood
MT.1331 (L,B)
UF gymnosperm
CN M.MT.AFU.AFU.ALO.BIQ.DCU.AFU.AFU.ALO

Soga (African)
FL.688
UF Basoga
CN F.FL.ALO.AFU.AXC.AXC.BOK.DOI

Soga (Japanese painting style)
FL.2066
CN F.FL.ALO.ARI.ALO.ALO.ALO.ARI.DZW

Sogdian
FL.1821 (L)
UF K'ana-chu
Kankju
CN F.FL.ALO.ARI.AFU.AXC.ELK.CLM

sohnhofen stone
USE **solnhofen stone**

soil
MT.2051 (L,B)
SN Includes unconsolidated material on the earth's surface formed by the weathering of rock and that portion of the earth's surface that can support plant life.
CN M.MT.AFU.AFU.ARI.BOK

soil cement
MT.34 (L,B)
SN Portland cement mixed with the existing soil to serve as a paving or surfacing material. (DLA)
UF cement, soil
CN M.MT.AFU.AFU.AFU.ALO.AFU.AFU.DCU

soil drainage
USE **land drainage**

soil maps
VW.192 (L)
ALT **soil map**
SN Charts or maps indicating various existing soils in an area and often indicating particular soil use. (DLA)
UF maps, soil
maps, soil survey
soil survey maps
CN V.VW.AFU.AFU.AFU.FZU.AXC.AFU.ARI.AXC.BCW.BOK

soil mechanics
BM.733 (L)
SN The application of the principles of mechanics and hydraulics to engineering problems dealing with soil as an engineering material. (DAC)
UF mechanics, soil
CN B.BM.CFS.ALO.AFU

soil percolation
BM.420 (L)
UF percolation, soil
soil water percolation
CN B.BM.AXC.AFU.ALO

soil permeability
BM.979 (L)
UF permeability, soil
CN B.BM.CFS.AXC.BZY.BZY.ALO.AFU

soil pollution
BM.433 (L)
UF pollution, soil
CN B.BM.AXC.BCW.AFU.ALO

soil profiles
VD.66 (L)
ALT **soil profile**
SN Vertical sections of soil showing the nature and sequence of the various layers, as developed by deposition, weathering, or both. (DAC)
UF profiles, soil
CN V.VD.AFU.AFU.BIQ.ALO.BCW.AFU

soil science
KD.279 (L,B)
UF science, soil
CN K.KD.AFU.ARI.CLM.ARI.CLM

soil stacks
RT.1475
ALT **soil stack**
SN Stacks that convey the discharge of one or more sanitary units. (STEIN)
UF stacks, soil
CN V.RT.ALO.BCW.ALO.ARI.BZY.BOK.AFU

soil structure
BM.734 (L)
SN Arrangement and state of aggregation of soil particles in a soil mass. (DAC)
UF structure, soil
CN B.BM.CFS.ALO.AFU.AFU

soil survey maps
USE **soil maps**

soil water percolation
USE **soil percolation**

soil, borrow
USE **borrow soil**

Solanki
FL.2213 (L)
CN F.FL.ALO.ARI.AXC.ALO.AFU.AXC.BOK

solar-assisted heat pumps
RT.1426
ALT **solar-assisted heat pump**
UF heat pumps, solar-assisted
pumps, solar-assisted heat
CN V.RT.ALO.BCW.AFU.ALO.AFU.BIQ.AFU

solar buildings
RK.1382 (A,L,R)
ALT **solar building**
UF buildings, solar
buildings, sun-heated
sun-heated buildings
CN V.RK.AFU.ALO.AXC.BZY

solar charts
VW.241 (B)
ALT **solar chart**
UF charts, solar
CN V.VW.AFU.AFU.AFU.FZU.AXC.ALO.BIQ

solar collectors
TB.394 (A,L)
ALT **solar collector**
SN Any devices intended to collect solar radiation and convert it into energy. (MEANS)
UF collectors, solar
CN V.TB.AFU.ARI.DOI.BIQ

solar greenhouses
RK.67 (A,L)
ALT **solar greenhouse**

UF greenhouses, solar
greenhouses, solar-heated
greenhouses, sun-heated
solar-heated greenhouses
sun-heated greenhouses
CN V.RK.AFU.ALO.ALO.AFU.AFU.BOK.AFU.AXC

solar-heated greenhouses
USE solar greenhouses

solar heating
RT.1396 (A,L,B)
UF heating, solar
CN V.RT.ALO.BCW.AFU.AFU.ARI.AXC

solar heating, active
USE **active solar heating**

solar heating, passive
USE **passive solar heating**

solar houses
RK.318 (A,L,B)
ALT **solar house**
UF houses, solar
CN V.RK.AFU.ALO.ALO.AXC.ALO.BCW.BIQ

solar orientation
BM.80 (A)
SN The placing of buildings in relation to the sun. (DAC)
UF orientation, solar
CN B.BM.AFU.AFU.ARI.AFU.DUC.AFU

solar power
BM.877 (L,B,R)
UF ambient energy
energy, ambient
power, solar
CN B.BM.CFS.AXC.ALO.ALO.ARI.AXC

solar power plants
RG.113 (L)
ALT **solar power plant**
UF plants, solar power
power plants, solar
CN V.RG.AFU.AFU.BUE.ARI.ARI

solar radiation
BM.865 (L)
UF radiation, solar
CN B.BM.CFS.AXC.ALO.AFU.ARI.AFU

solar water heaters
RT.1500 (L)
ALT **solar water heater**
UF heaters, solar water
water heaters, solar
CN V.RT.ALO.BCW.ALO.ARI.DIO.AFU

solariums
RM.284 (A,B)
ALT **solarium**
SN Use generally for rooms or loggias designed to receive maximum sunlight.
UF Florida rooms
rooms, Florida
rooms, sun
sun rooms
CN V.RM.AFU.DIO.ARI.ALO.DOI

solarization
KT.419
ALT **solarized**
UF edge reversal
reversal (solarization)
CN K.KT.AFU.ALO.DUC.DIO.ARI.AXC.DIO

solars
RM.285
ALT **solar**
SN Certain upper floor rooms in Medieval houses that are smaller than halls and reserved for private family use.
UF solers
sollars
sollers
CN V.RM.AFU.DIO.ARI.ALO.DUC

solder
MT.420 (L)
CN M.MT.AFU.AFU.AFU.BZY.AFU.AFU.AFU.ALO.BUE.ARI

solder, fine
USE **fine solder**

solder, gold
USE **chrysocolla**

solder, hard
USE **hard solder**

solder, medium
USE **medium solder**

soldering
KT.789 (L)
ALT **soldered**
SN The joining of two metal surfaces by means of a metallic alloy, usually of lead and tin. (MAYER)
CN K.KT.AFU.ALO.HOE.BCW.ALO.AFU.AFU

soldering coppers
USE **soldering irons**

soldering guns
TB.747
ALT **soldering gun**
SN Tools with a pistol grip and a small electrically heated bit that reaches operating temperatures rapidly; used to solder electrical components. (MEANS)
UF guns, soldering
CN V.TB.AFU.BCW.BIQ.AXC.ALO.ALO

soldering irons
TB.748 (N)
ALT **soldering iron**
SN Tools for joining metals with solder, having a wedge-shaped metal bit, usually of copper, which is heated. (DAC)
UF coppers, soldering
irons, soldering
soldering coppers
CN V.TB.AFU.BCW.BIQ.AXC.ALO.ARI

soldier arches
RT.260
ALT **soldier arch**
SN Use for flat arches in brick, with the bricks set with their long sides vertical.
UF arches, soldier
CN V.RT.AFU.AFU.AFU.BCW.AFU.AFU.AFU.ELK.BZY

soldiers' monuments
RK.908 (L)
ALT **soldiers' monument**
UF monuments, soldiers'
CN V.RK.AFU.ALO.ALO.DOI.ALO.AXC

solepieces
USE **sill plates**

soleplates
USE **sill plates**

solers
USE **solars**

solicitors
HG.321 (L)
ALT **solicitor**
CN H.HG.AFU.AXC.BCW.ALO.BIQ.AXC.AXC

solid
DC.144
SN Having an interior filled with matter. (W)
CN D.DC.AFU.BIQ.ALO

solid brick
MT.90
SN A brick which meets the specifications for a solid masonry unit. (DAC)
UF brick, solid
CN M.MT.AFU.AFU.AFU.AXC.ALO.AFU.AFU.ALO.AXC

solid-core doors
RT.856
ALT **solid-core door**
SN Doors having cores of solid wood or mineral composition. (DAC)
UF doors, solid
doors, solid-core
solid doors
CN V.RT.AFU.ARI.AFU.AFU.AFU.ALO.ARI.AFU.AFU.BOK.ALO.ALO

solid doors
USE **solid-core doors**

solid moldings
USE **struck moldings**

solid newel stairs
RT.1079
ALT **solid newel stair**
SN Stairs whose tapered treads wind around, and engage in, a central newel. (HAS)

UF stairs, solid newel
vices
vises (stairs)
vyses
CN V.RT.AFU.BIQ.AXC.AFU.AFU.BIQ.AXC

solid slabs
USE **one-way solid slab systems**

solid vaults
RT.555
ALT **solid vault**
SN Use for vaults without ribs.
UF vaults, solid
CN V.RT.AFU.AFU.AFU.BIQ.BOK.AFU.ARI.AFU.ARI

solid waste disposal
USE **refuse disposal**

solid waste management
KG.125 (A,L)
UF management, solid waste
sewage treatment
waste management, solid
CN K.KG.AFU.AFU.BCW.ALO.CFS

solids
MT.2290 (L)
CN M.MT.AFU.ALO.JCO.AXC

solids (geometric)
BM.789
SN Geometric figures having three dimensions.
CN B.BM.CFS.ARI.AXC.BCW.ALO

solio paper
MT.1952
UF paper, solio
CN M.MT.AFU.AFU.ARI.ALO.ALO.AXC.ARI.BOK.BZY

soliums
USE **thrones**

sollars
USE **solars**

sollers
USE **solars**

solnhofen stone
MT.686
SN A blue gray Bavarian limestone. (MAYER)
UF lithograph stone
lithographic stone
sohnhofen stone
stone, lithograph
stone, lithographic
stone, solnhofen
CN M.MT.AFU.AFU.AFU.DCU.AFU.ALO.AFU.ALO.ALO.AFU.ALO.AXC.ALO

Solomon Island
FL.3662 (L,B)
UF British Solomon Island
Solomon Island, British
CN F.FL.ALO.BOK.ALO.BOK

Solomon Island, British
USE **Solomon Island**

Solomonic columns
USE **spiral columns**

Solomonic order
USE **spiral columns**

Solongo
USE **Sorongo**

solubility
BM.941 (L)
CN B.BM.CFS.AXC.BZY.ARI.ALO

soluble dyes, oil
USE **oil soluble dyes**

soluble dyes, water
USE **water soluble dyes**

soluble glass
USE **water glass**

solutions, anti-freeze
USE **antifreeze**

Solutrian
FL.2472 (L)
CN F.FL.ALO.AXC.AFU.ARI.ALO.BIQ

solvent, petroleum
USE **mineral spirits**

solvents
MT.2659 (L)
SN Any material, usually liquid, having the power of dissolving another material. (MH12)
UF solvents, volatile
volatile solvents
CN M.MT.AFU.ARI.HZS

solvents, aromatic
USE **aromatic hydrocarbons**

solvents, coal tar
USE **coal tar solvents**

solvents, volatile
USE **solvents**

Somali
FL.633 (L,B)
CN F.FL.ALO.AFU.AXC.AXC.ARI.DUC

somatology
USE **physical anthropology**

somnoes
TG.750
ALT **somnoe**
UF zommos
CN V.TG.AFU.AFU.BIQ.BOK.ALO.DIO.AFU

Sondergotik
FL.3145
CN F.FL.ALO.BCW.ALO.ALO.AFU.BOK.ARI.BOK.AFU.ALO

Song
FL.1893 (L)
UF Sung
CN F.FL.ALO.ARI.ALO.AFU.AFU.ALO.CXA

song books
VW.555 (L,R)
ALT **song book**
SN Books containing brief musical compositions written or adapted for singing.
UF books, song
CN V.VW.AFU.ALO.AFU.AFU.ALO.CFS

Song, Northern
USE **Northern Song**

Song, Southern
USE **Southern Song**

Songa Mnara
FL.165
CN F.FL.ALO.AFU.ALO.AXC.BCW

Songhai
FL.120 (L)
CN F.FL.ALO.AFU.ALO.AFU.CFS

Songo
FL.459 (L)
CN F.FL.ALO.AFU.AXC.ALO.ALO.ALO.BUE

Songomeno
USE **Nkutshu**

songs
VW.58 (L)
ALT **song**
SN Musical compositions, generally short, containing words.
CN V.VW.AFU.AFU.AFU.DOI.ARI

songwriters
USE **lyricists**

Songye
FL.500 (L)
UF Basonge
CN F.FL.ALO.AFU.AXC.ALO.ALO.BCW.BOK

sonic engineering
USE **acoustical engineering**

sonic engineers
USE **acoustical engineers**

Soninke
FL.378 (L)
UF Sarakole
CN F.FL.ALO.AFU.AXC.AFU.AXC.ARI.ALO

sons
HG.11 (L)
ALT **son**
CN H.HG.AFU.ALO.AFU.ALO

Sonyo
FL.484 (L)
CN F.FL.ALO.AFU.AXC.ALO.ALO.AXC.AXC.BCW

soot
MT.2047 (L)
CN M.MT.AFU.AFU.ARI.AXC.BCW

soot brown
USE **bister**

soot doors
RT.1148
ALT **soot door**
UF doors, soot
CN V.RT.AFU.BOK.AFU.ALO.CRG

sophas
USE **sofas**

Sorcuq
USE **Shorchuk**

sorel cement
USE **oxychloric cement**

Sorongo
FL.485
UF Solongo
CN F.FL.ALO.AFU.AXC.ALO.ALO.AXC.AXC.BIQ

sorority houses
RK.225 (B)
ALT **sorority house**
UF houses, sorority
CN V.RK.AFU.ALO.ALO.AXC.AFU.BUE

sorrow
USE **grief**

Sotatsu-Korin School
FL.2067 (L)
UF Korin School
Rimpa School
CN F.FL.ALO.ARI.ALO.ALO.ALO.ARI.EFQ

Sotho
FL.572 (L)
UF Basuto
Suto
CN F.FL.ALO.AFU.AXC.ARI.BCW.ARI

sotto in su
BM.167
SN Representation of architecture and figures, usually on a ceiling, shown from below in extreme foreshortening.
UF di sotto in su
frog perspective
perspective, frog
CN B.BM.AFU.AFU.ARI.BOK.DOI

sound
BM.994 (L,B,R)
CN B.BM.CFS.AXC.CFS.AFU

sound absorption
BM.997 (L,B)
UF absorption, sound
CN B.BM.CFS.AXC.CFS.ALO.ALO

sound engineering
USE **acoustical engineering**

sound engineers
USE **acoustical engineers**

sound insulation
USE **acoustical insulation**
soundproofing

sound recordings
VW.631 (L)
ALT **sound recording**
SN Discs, tapes, filaments, or other media on which sound has been recorded. (ICA)
UF audio recordings
recordings, audio
recordings, sound
CN V.VW.AFU.ALO.AFU.DZW.AFU.AFU

sound reverberation
USE **echo**

sound stages
RM.238
ALT **sound stage**
SN Rooms or studios made acoustically suitable (as by soundproofing) for producing sound motion pictures. (W)
UF stages, sound
CN V.RM.AFU.DIO.ALO.DOI.CXA.ALO

sound studios
RM.236 (A,L,B)
ALT **sound studio**
UF studios, sound
CN V.RM.AFU.DIO.ALO.DOI.CXA

sound tapes
USE **audio tapes**

sound transmission
BM.998 (L,B)
UF transmission, sound
CN B.BM.CFS.AXC.CFS.ALO.ARI

sounding boards
RT.1246 (N,B)
ALT **sounding board**
UF abat-voix
boards, sounding
CN V.RT.AFU.BUE.ALO.ARI.CLM.ALO.AFU

soundproofing
KT.598 (A,L,B)
ALT **soundproof**
UF insulation, sound
sound insulation
CN K.KT.AFU.ALO.FOG.AXC

soup kitchens
RK.792 (B)
ALT **soup kitchen**
UF communal restaurants
kitchens, soup
restaurants, communal
CN V.RK.AFU.ALO.ALO.CXA.ALO.ALO.BUE

sour cherry
MT.1290 (L)
UF cherry, sour
Prunus cerasus
CN M.MT.AFU.AFU.ALO.BIQ.DCU.AFU.AFU.AFU.KLE.ARI.ALO.AFU

sour gum
USE **tupelo**

sour tupelo
USE **ogeche tupelo**

sources, energy
USE **energy resources**

souterrains
RM.93 (A,L,B,R)
ALT **souterrain**
SN Use for underground passages or chambers.
UF underground vaults
vaults, underground
CN V.RM.AFU.DIO.ALO.ARI.AXC.BCW

south
DC.50
CN D.DC.AFU.ALO.AXC.BCW

South American
FL.716 (L,B)
UF American, South
CN F.FL.ALO.ALO.AFU.AXC

South American mahogany
MT.1212
UF baywood
Cuban mahogany
Honduras mahogany
mahogany, Cuban
mahogany, Honduras
mahogany, South American
mahogany, Spanish
Spanish mahogany
Swietenia macrophylla
Swietenia mahogani
CN M.MT.AFU.AFU.ALO.BIQ.DCU.AFU.AFU.AFU.HTY.ARI.AFU

South Asian
FL.2151 (L)
UF Asian, South
Indian Subcontinent
CN F.FL.ALO.ARI.AXC

South Indian
FL.2297
UF Indian, South
CN F.FL.ALO.ARI.AXC.ALO.AFU.BZY.BIQ

South Italian
FL.2631
UF Italian, South
Italiote
CN F.FL.ALO.AXC.ALO.AFU.ALO.AXC.ALO.BIQ

South Seas
USE **Pacific**

southeast
DC.51
CN D.DC.AFU.ALO.AXC.BIQ

Southeast Asian
FL.2307 (L)
UF Asian, Southeast
Greater Indian
CN F.FL.ALO.ARI.BCW

Southern and Northern Dynasties
USE **Northern and Southern Dynasties**

Southern Buddhism
USE **Theravada**

Southern Ch'i
USE **Southern Qi**

Southern Cheyenne
FL.1378
UF Cheyenne, Southern
CN F.FL.ALO.ALO.ARI.AFU.BOK.BIQ.ALO

Southern Dynasties
FL.1875
UF Dynasties, Southern
CN F.FL.ALO.ARI.ALO.AFU.AFU.ALO.BUE.AFU.ALO

Southern Paiute
FL.1319
UF Paiute, Southern
CN F.FL.ALO.ALO.ARI.AFU.AXC.CFS

southern pine
USE **longleaf pine**

Southern Qi
FL.1876 (L)
UF Ch'i, Southern
Qi
Qi, Southern
Southern Ch'i
CN F.FL.ALO.ARI.ALO.AFU.AFU.ALO.BUE.AFU.ALO.AFU

southern red oak
MT.1252
UF oak, schneck
oak, southern red
oak, Texas
Quercus falcata
red oak, southern
schneck oak
Texas oak
CN M.MT.AFU.AFU.ALO.BIQ.DCU.AFU.AFU.AFU.IRA.ELK

Southern School
FL.1936
CN F.FL.ALO.ARI.ALO.AFU.AFU.AXC.ALO.CLM

Southern School (Nanga)
USE **Nanga**

Southern Song
FL.1895
UF Song, Southern
Southern Sung
Sung, Southern
CN F.FL.ALO.ARI.ALO.AFU.AFU.ALO.CXA.ALO

Southern Sung
USE **Southern Song**

southern white cedar
USE **white cypress**

southern yellow pine
MT.1388 (L)
UF Georgia pine
hard pine
hill pine
pine, Georgia
pine, hard
pine, hill
pine, southern yellow
yellow pine, southern
CN M.MT.AFU.AFU.ALO.BIQ.DCU.AFU.AFU.ALO.CXA.DZW

southwest
DC.52
CN D.DC.AFU.ALO.AXC.BOK

souvenir albums
VW.492
ALT **souvenir album**
UF albums, souvenir
CN V.VW.AFU.ALO.AFU.AFU.AFU.ALO.BIQ

souvenirs
VB.111 (L,R)
ALT **souvenir**
UF keepsakes
CN V.VB.ALO.BUE.BUE

sovereigns
USE **rulers (people)**

soya glue
USE **soybean glue**

soyabean oil
USE **soybean oil**

soybean glue
MT.2355 (L)
SN Vegetable protein glue made from extracted soya bean meal; has greater adhesive power and water resistance than most other vegetable glues; marketed dry and used chiefly for interior plywood. (DAC)
UF glue, soya
glue, soybean
soya glue
CN M.MT.AFU.ARI.ARI.AFU.ALO.ALO.ALO.AXC

soybean oil
MT.2019 (L)
SN A pale yellow drying oil obtained from soya beans; used in paints and varnishes, sometimes mixed with linseed oil. (DAC)
UF oil, soyabean
oil, soybean
soyabean oil
CN M.MT.AFU.AFU.ARI.ARI.AXC.AFU.CFS

spa buildings
USE **spas**

space
BM.90 (A,L)
CN B.BM.AFU.AFU.ARI.AFU.FIM

space bases
USE **extraterrestrial bases**

space colonies
RD.63 (L)
ALT **space colony**
SN Use only for large communities established in space or on natural extraterrestrial bodies. For smaller manned installations established on natural extraterrestrial bodies for specific functions use **extraterrestrial bases.** Use **space stations** for manned artificial satellites placed in a fixed orbit and serving as a base for specific functions (e.g., scientific observations or the refueling of spaceships).
UF colonies, space
CN V.RD.AFU.BCW.ARI

space dividers
USE **room dividers**

space frame structures
USE **space frames**

space frames
RT.375 (A,B)
ALT **space frame**
SN Use for trusses in which the members are arranged three-dimensionally rather than in only one plane.
UF frames, grid space
frames, space
grid space frames
space frame structures
space frames, grid
space trusses
structures, space frame
three-dimensional trusses
trusses, space
trusses, three-dimensional
CN V.RT.AFU.AFU.AFU.BCW.CLM.AFU.AFU.ALO

space frames, grid
USE **space frames**

space laboratories
USE **space stations**

space perception
BM.590 (A,L)
UF perception, sound
CN B.BM.BUE.BOK.ALO

space photography
KT.397 (L)
SN Use for the taking of photographs from beyond the earth's atmosphere. For photography of celestial bodies or astronomical phenomena, use **astronomical photography.** For pho-

tography of the earth from aircraft, use **aerial photography.**
UF photography, space
CN K.KT.AFU.ALO.DUC.DIO.ARI.ARI.BZY.BCW

space planning
KT.105 (B)
UF planning, space
spatial planning
CN K.KT.AFU.ALO.CFS.BZY.AFU

space platforms
USE **space stations**

space stations
RK.1362 (A,L,N,R)
ALT **space station**
SN Use for manned artificial satellites designed to revolve in a fixed orbit and to serve as a base for specific functions (e.g., scientific observations or the refueling of spaceships). For manned installations established on natural extraterrestrial bodies for specific functions, use **extraterrestrial bases.** For larger communities established in space or on natural extraterrestrial bodies, use **space colonies.**
UF laboratories, manned orbital
laboratories, space
manned orbital laboratories
orbital laboratories, manned
platforms, space
space laboratories
space platforms
stations, space
CN V.RK.AFU.ALO.ARI.AXC.AXC.ALO

space trusses
USE **space frames**

space utilization
BM.210 (L,B)
UF utilization, space
CN B.BM.AFU.ALO.BUE

space, defensible
USE **defensible space**

space, negative
USE **negative space**

space, personal
USE **personal space**

space, pictorial
USE **pictorial space**

spaces, crawl
USE **crawl spaces**

spaces, open
USE **open spaces**

Spackle (TM)
MT.2612
SN A paste used to fill holes and cracks in plaster, wallboard, wood, or other surfaces. (MEANS)
UF cement, joint
joint cement
spackling compound
CN M.MT.AFU.ARI.DZW.BCW

spackling
KT.125
ALT **spackled**
SN The rectifying of a defect in a plaster wall or mural painting by digging out the defective spot and filling it in with a plastic gesso, plaster of Paris, Keene's cement or other similar material. (AHMT)
CN K.KT.AFU.ALO.DCU.AXC

spackling compound
USE **Spackle (TM)**

spade feet
USE **therm feet**

spade gouges
USE **bent gouges**

spade pulls
TF.84
ALT **spade pull**
SN Hand-forged pulls with mounting plates shaped like spade blades. (DITTRI)
UF pulls, spade
CN V.TF.AFU.AFU.AFU.AFU.CFS.BCW.AFU.CXA

spalliera
USE **wainscoting**

spalling
KT.925 (A)
SN Breaking or chipping of masonry or pavement at joints, cracks, or edges, usually resulting in fragments with feather edges. (STEIN)
CN K.KT.ALO.BZY.BIQ

span
BM.1028
SN The distance between the supports of a transverse structural member or between the abutments of an arch. (W)
CN B.BM.CFS.AXC.CLM.ALO.BUE

span-rails
USE **stretchers**

spandrel glass
MT.272
SN Clear glass with colored ceramic enamel fired on one side, used for spandrels and similar applications. (STEIN)
UF glass, spandrel
spandrelite
CN M.MT.AFU.AFU.AFU.BIQ.AFU.AXC.AFU.ARI

spandrel steps
RT.1116
ALT **spandrel step**
SN Solid steps, as those worked from one piece of stone, having more or less the section of a right-angled triangle, the hypoteneuse forming part of the sloping soffit of the flight. (RS)
UF steps, spandrel
CN V.RT.AFU.BIQ.AXC.ALO.BIQ.AFU.AXC

spandrelite
USE **spandrel glass**

spandrels
RT.678 (A,B)
ALT **spandrel**
SN The triangular spaces enclosed by the haunches of an arch, the horizontal drawn from the level of the apex, and the verticals drawn from the springings. (PDARC)
CN V.RT.AFU.AFU.AFU.BIQ.BUE.ALO.ALO.BZY

spandrels (vaulting cells)
USE **vaulting cells**

Spanish
FL.3062 (L,B)
CN F.FL.ALO.BCW.AFU.DZW

Spanish back chairs
USE **square-back chairs**

Spanish black
USE **vine black**

Spanish brown
USE **strong reddish brown**

Spanish cedar
MT.1340
UF cedar, Central American
cedar, cigar-box
cedar, Spanish
Cedrela odorata
Central American cedar
cigar-box cedar
CN M.MT.AFU.AFU.ALO.BIQ.DCU.AFU.AFU.ALO.ALO.BOK

Spanish chestnut
USE **European chestnut**

Spanish Colonial
FL.3247 (A)
UF Colonial, Spanish
CN F.FL.ALO.BCW.ALO.ARI.BIQ.BIQ.BUE.ARI

Spanish Colonial Revival
FL.1724 (A)
UF Colonial Revival, Spanish
Revival, Spanish Colonial
CN F.FL.ALO.ALO.BCW.AFU.ARI.AFU

Spanish feet
TG.913
ALT **Spanish foot**
SN Popular in the late 17th century, feet in which the scroll turns under, towards the back. (TOMLIN)
UF feet, paintbrush
feet, Portuguese

feet, Spanish
feet, tassel
paintbrush feet
pe de pincels
Portuguese feet
scroll, Spanish
Spanish scroll
tassel feet
CN V.TG.ALO.DZW.AFU.CLM

Spanish licorice
MT.1622
UF licorice, Spanish
CN M.MT.AFU.AFU.ARI.AFU.AFU.ALO.ALO.ARI.ALO.BIQ

Spanish mahogany
USE **South American mahogany**

Spanish red
USE **strong brown**
strong reddish brown

Spanish red oxide
MT.1677
UF oxide, Spanish red
red oxide, Spanish
CN M.MT.AFU.AFU.ARI.AFU.AFU.ALO.ALO.BCW.AFU.ALO.BOK

Spanish scroll
USE **Spanish feet**

Spanish tile
MT.178 (B)
SN Clay roofing tile, approximately semicylindrical in shape; laid in cornices with the units having their convex sides alternately up and down. (DAC)
UF mission tile
tile, mission
tile, Spanish
CN M.MT.AFU.AFU.AFU.AXC.ALO.ALO.ALO.AFU.ALO.AXC.AFU.AFU.BCW

spanners
USE **wrenches**

spanning slabs, one-direction
USE **one-way structural systems**

spar axes
USE **mast axes**

spar varnish
MT.2480
SN A varnish made with durable oils and resins, used on exterior wood surfaces because of its superior weather-resistant qualities. Suitable for use on the spars of ships. (DAC)
UF varnish, spar
CN M.MT.AFU.ARI.CRG.AFU.BOK.AFU.BIQ

spar, heavy
USE **blanc fixe**

spark guards
USE **fire screens**

spars
USE **common rafters**

sparver beds
TG.328
ALT **sparver bed**
SN Medieval beds with a conical bowl- or tent-shaped canopy suspended over the head half of the bed. (THORN1)
UF beds, sparver
beds, sperver
sparver bedsteads
sperver beds
CN V.TG.AFU.AFU.ARI.AFU.AFU.ARI.ARI

sparver bedsteads
USE **sparver beds**

spas
RG.170 (A,L,B,R)
ALT **spa**
UF baths, mineral
buildings, spa
kursaals
mineral baths
spa buildings
CN V.RG.AFU.AFU.DOI.BZY.AFU.AFU

spathic iron ore
USE **siderite**

spatial articulation
USE **articulation**

spatial behavior
BM.585 (L)
UF behavior, proxemic
behavior, spatial
proxemic behavior
CN B.BM.BUE.AXC.ALO

spatial planning
USE **space planning**

Spatialist
FL.3751 (R)
ALT **Spatialism**
UF Movimento spaziale
Spazialismo
CN F.FL.ALO.BUE.ARI.HTY

spattering
KT.696
ALT **spattered**
SN Applying paint or ink so as to cover a surface with irregular, sparse patterns of fine specks.(MAYER) Use **splashing** when the paint or ink more randomly covers wide areas.
CN K.KT.AFU.ALO.GRC.BUE.ARI

Spazialismo
USE **Spatialist**

speakers
USE **lecturers**

spec houses
USE **speculative houses**

special librarians
HG.310 (L)
ALT **special librarian**
UF librarians, special
CN H.HG.AFU.AXC.BCW.ALO.BCW.ALO.BCW

special libraries
RK.703 (L,B)
ALT **special library**
SN Privately owned libraries that form a unit of a business firm or other organization and usually serve only the staff or members of their organization. (W)
UF libraries, special
CN V.RK.AFU.ALO.ALO.CRG.AXC.ALO.ARI

special-purpose maps
USE **thematic maps**

specialists
HG.771
ALT **specialist**
CN H.HG.AFU.BIQ.BZY

specialists, film production
USE **filmmakers**

specialists, population
USE **demographers**

specialty stores
RK.181 (L)
ALT **specialty store**
UF stores, specialty
CN V.RK.AFU.ALO.ALO.ALO.ARI.BIQ.ALO.CLM

specific gravity
BM.943 (L)
UF gravity, specific
CN B.BM.CFS.AXC.BZY.AXC.AFU

specific heat
BM.989 (L)
SN The number of calories required to raise 1 gram of a material 1 degree Celsius in temperature. (MH)
UF heat, specific
CN B.BM.CFS.AXC.BZY.CFS.BOK

specification writing
KG.108 (A,L)
SN Use for the activity of documenting in writing the requirements of a project.
UF writing, specification
CN K.KG.AFU.AFU.AXC.DZW.AFU

specifications
VW.793 (A,L,B)
ALT **specification**
SN Detailed and exact statements of particulars, especially statements prescribing materials, dimensions, and workmanship for something to be built, installed, or manufactured. (AHD)
CN V.VW.AFU.ARI.AFU.ARI.AFU.ARI

specifications, base bid
USE **base bid specifications**

specifications, closed
USE **closed specifications**

specifications, commercial
USE **commercial specifications**

specifications, master
USE **master specifications**

specifications, or-equal
USE **or-equal specifications**

specifications, outline
USE **outline specifications**

specifications, performance
USE **performance specifications**

specifications, preliminary
USE **preliminary specifications**

specifications, product
USE **product specifications**

specifications, proprietary
USE **proprietary specifications**

specimen books
USE **sample books**

specimens
USE **samples**

spectroscopy, x-ray
USE **x-ray spectroscopy**

spectrum
BM.140
SN Systematic arrangement of visible energy rays by wavelength, seen as a band of rainbow colors when sunlight is passed through a prism.
CN B.BM.AFU.AFU.ARI.BOK.ALO.ALO.BIQ

spectrum red
USE **vivid red**

speculating
KG.172 (L,B)
SN Engaging in business transactions in the anticipation of profit from changes in the economic situation.
CN K.KG.AFU.ALO.AFU.BUE

speculative houses
RK.321 (B)
ALT **speculative house**
SN Use for homes built without a particular client and in hopes, but with no assurances, of sales.
UF houses, speculative
spec houses
CN V.RK.AFU.ALO.ALO.AXC.ALO.BIQ.AFU

Spedos type
FL.2680
CN F.FL.ALO.AXC.ALO.AFU.ALO.BCW.AFU.AXC

speech
BM.605 (L,R)
CN B.BM.BUE.DCU

speech handicapped
USE **mutes**

speeches
VW.470 (L,N)
ALT **speech**
SN Documents containing the text of any public address or talk.
UF addresses
CN V.VW.AFU.AFU.ALO.FOG

speed
BM.901 (L)
UF velocity
CN B.BM.CFS.AXC.BIQ.AFU.AXC.BOK

speedways
USE **automobile racetracks**
expressways
throughways

spelk planes
USE **splint planes**

speoses
RK.1130
ALT **speos**
SN Use especially with reference to ancient Egyptian temples, shrines, or tombs cut into the living rock.
CN V.RK.AFU.ALO.ALO.FCS.BIQ.BZY.AFU.ALO.AFU

spermaceti
MT.2196 (L)
SN Wax from the head cavity of the sperm whale or of the dolphin; formerly used for candles, but now used chiefly as a fine wax for ointments. (MH12)
CN M.MT.AFU.AFU.ARI.BZY.AFU.ARI

sperone
MT.636
UF lapis gabinus
CN M.MT.AFU.AFU.AFU.DCU.AFU.AFU.ALO.ALO.ALO.AXC.AFU.AFU

sperver beds
USE **sparver beds**

sphaeristeria
RK.1068
ALT **sphaeristerium**
SN Use for ancient Roman structures adapted to ball playing.
CN V.RK.AFU.ALO.ALO.EWY.AXC.BIQ.ALO.BOK

spheres
BM.797 (L,R)
ALT **spherical**
CN B.BM.CFS.ARI.AXC.BCW.ALO.BCW

spice cabinets
TG.442 (N)
ALT **spice cabinet**
SN Cabinets with the interior divided into nests of small drawers for holding spices.
UF cabinets, spice
CN V.TG.AFU.AFU.AXC.ALO.ARI.ALO.DOI

spice chests
TG.469 (N,R)
ALT **spice chest**
SN Miniature chests holding innumerable small drawers; made to stand on a table or chest of drawers. (DOWNS)
UF chests, spice
CN V.TG.AFU.AFU.AXC.ALO.AXC.EFQ

spice cupboards
TG.520
ALT **spice cupboard**
SN Small cupboards, usually hanging, to hold spices; often miniatures of 18th-century floor cabinets. (ARON)
UF cupboards, spice
CN V.TG.AFU.AFU.AXC.ALO.BUE.DCU

spider-leg tables
TG.699
ALT **spider-leg table**
SN Tables with very slender supports, sometimes of gate-leg design. (GILBR2)
UF spider tables
tables, spider-leg
CN V.TG.AFU.AFU.BIQ.BOK.AFU.DUC.BCW

spider tables
USE **spider-leg tables**

spigot-and-socket joints
USE **bell-and-spigot joints**

spike lavender, oil of
USE **spike oil**

spike oil
MT.1989
UF oil of spike lavender
oil, spike
spike lavender, oil of
CN M.MT.AFU.AFU.ARI.ARI.AFU.ARI.AFU.ALO.AFU

spikes
TF.486 (L,N)
ALT **spike**
SN Very heavy nails, usually square in cross section, and 3 to 12 inches long. (MEANS)
CN V.TF.AFU.AFU.AFU.ALO.AFU.DUC

spikes, barge
USE **boat spikes**

spikes, boat
USE **boat spikes**

spikes, gutter
USE **gutter spikes**

spikes, Hertfordshire
USE **needle spires**

spillways
RM.463 (N)
ALT **spillway**
SN Passages, as a paved apron or channel, for surplus water over or around a dam or similar obstruction. (W)
UF wasteways
wasteweirs (spillways)
CN V.RM.ALO.ALO.AFU.ARI

spindle-back chairs
TG.155
ALT **spindle-back chair**
UF chairs, spindle-back
chairs, stick-back
stick-back chairs
CN V.TG.AFU.AFU.ALO.AFU.AFU.AFU.NIE.DZW

spindle beds
USE **spool beds**

spindle sanders
TB.525
ALT **spindle sander**
SN Sanding machines in which the sandpaper is carried on a small-diameter vertical drum located on the work table of the machine. (DAC)
UF sanders, spindle
CN V.TB.AFU.ARI.EWY.ALO.CXA.BCW

spindles
TG.986
ALT **spindle**
SN One of a series of slender turned rods set in vertical rows to fill open areas such as chair backs.
CN V.TG.ALO.HCQ

spindles, arrow
USE **arrow spindles**

spindles, split
USE **split spindles**

Spindlework
USE **Gingerbread**

spinet desks
TG.554
ALT **spinet desk**
UF desks, spinet
CN V.TG.AFU.AFU.AXC.ALO.BZY.DZW

spinners
HG.531
ALT **spinner**
CN H.HG.AFU.AXC.BUE.ARI.CXA.BIQ

spinning
KT.570 (L,R)
ALT **spun**
SN The process of making fibers or filaments into yarn or thread. (W)
CN K.KT.AFU.ALO.ELK.DUC.AXC

spinning (metal)
USE **metal-spinning**

spinning, hand
USE **hand spinning**

spirae
USE **toruses**

spiral augers
TB.828 (N)
ALT **spiral auger**
SN Augers which terminate in a screw worm.
UF augers, screw
augers, spiral
augers, twist
screw augers
twist augers
CN V.TB.AFU.BCW.CFS.ALO.AFU.ALO.BOK

spiral bits
TB.1113 (N)
ALT **spiral bit**
SN Boring bits that resemble twist drills in having two deep vertical grooves, but having a steeper cutting angle.
UF augers, twist (bits)
bits, spiral
bits, twist
twist augers (bits)
twist bits
CN V.TB.ALO.ARI.DIO

spiral columns
RT.99 (B,R)
ALT **spiral column**
SN Columns so shaped as to present a twisted or spiral form. (HAS)
UF columns, Solomonic
columns, spiral
columns, twisted
columns, wreathed
order, Solomonic
Salomonicas
Solomonic columns
Solomonic order
twisted columns
wreathed columns
CN V.RT.AFU.AFU.AFU.AXC.BIQ.AFU.AFU.DCU

spiral ratchet screwdrivers
TB.199
ALT **spiral ratchet screwdriver**
SN Screwdrivers having a blade that rotates with respect to the handle, as the handle is pushed inward toward the blade; permits a screw to be driven easily and with speed. (DAC)
UF ratchet screwdrivers, spiral
screwdrivers, spiral ratchet
CN V.TB.AFU.ARI.BOK.ALO.AXC

spiral scrolls
USE **scrolls (motifs)**

spiral stairs
RT.1075
ALT **spiral stair**
SN Staircases that are circular in plan, consisting entirely of winders or wedge-shaped steps. (PUTNAM)
UF caracoles
circular stairs
coakels
cockle stairs
cokels
corkscrew stairs
helical stairs
screw stairs
stairs, circular
stairs, cockle
stairs, corkscrew
stairs, helical
stairs, screw
stairs, spiral
stairs, turnpike
stairs, winding
turnpike stairs
winding stairs
CN V.RT.AFU.BIQ.AXC.AFU.AFU.BIQ

spiral stairs, double
USE **double spiral stairs**

spiral vaults
RT.541
ALT **spiral vault**
SN Annular vaults with a spiral axis used for supporting the steps of a spiral stair. (RS)
UF vaults, spiral
CN V.RT.AFU.AFU.AFU.BIQ.BOK.AFU.ALO.AFU.ARI.AFU

spirals
BM.798 (A,L,B,R)
ALT **spiral**
SN When in reference to ornament, use for simple coiled lines, and prefer **scrolls** or **scrollwork** for more complex forms.
CN B.BM.CFS.ARI.AXC.BCW.ARI

spirals, divergent
USE **trumpet spirals**

spirals, evolute
USE **wave scrolls**

spirals, trumpet
USE **trumpet spirals**

spire lights
RT.963
ALT **spire light**
SN Windows in a spire, frequently found in Early English and occasionally in Perpendicular Style architecture.
UF lights, spire
CN V.RT.AFU.ARI.AFU.AFU.BOK.AFU.ARI.BIQ

spirelets
RM.408 (B)
ALT **spirelet**
SN Small spires as those found on pinnacles or turrets. (HAS)
CN V.RM.AFU.DOI.ALO.AFU.BCW

spires
RM.403 (A,L,N,B,R)

ALT **spire**
SN Use for tall structures that are at least roughly pyramidal, polygonal, or conical and that rise from towers or roofs.
CN V.RM.AFU.DOI.ALO.AFU

spires, broach
USE **broach spires**

spires, needle
USE **needle spires**

spires, rood
USE **crossing towers**

spirit
USE **alcohol**

spirit duplicating
KT.183 (L)
SN Printing process utilizing master sheets that release color through type identations when a colorless chemical fluid is applied. (W)
UF copying processes, fluid
duplicating, fluid
duplicating, spirit
fluid copying processes
fluid duplicating
CN K.KT.AFU.ALO.DUC.BOK.ALO

spirit of hartshorn
USE **ammonia water**

spirit of the age
USE **Zeitgeist**

spirit of the nation
USE **Volksgeist**

spirit photographs
VJ.130 (L)
ALT **spirit photograph**
SN Photographs that purport to be visual records of ectoplasmic or other manifestations of persons in a state of existence equivalent to or beyond death. (ICPEP)
UF ghost photographs
photographs, ghost
photographs, spirit
CN V.VJ.AFU.AXC.BCW

spirit photography
KT.307 (L)
SN The techniques or the activity of making spirit photographs.
UF photography, spirit
CN K.KT.AFU.ALO.DUC.DIO.AFU.DOI

spirit stain
MT.2467
SN A penetrating, alcohol-soluble dye used to stain wood, producing deep color and little fiber swelling. (DAC)
UF stain, spirit
CN M.MT.AFU.ARI.CRG.AFU.BIQ.ARI

spirit varnish
MT.2486
UF varnish, spirit
CN M.MT.AFU.ARI.CRG.AFU.BOK.ALO.ARI

spiritism
USE **spiritualism**

spirits of salt
USE **hydrochloric acid**

spirits of turpentine
USE **gum turpentine**

spirits, Cologne
USE **ethyl alcohol**

spirits, Columbian
USE **methyl alcohol**

spirits, gum
USE **gum turpentine**

spirits, mineral
USE **mineral spirits**

spirits, petroleum
USE **mineral spirits**

spirits, Texaco
USE **mineral spirits**

spirits, white
USE **mineral spirits**

spiritualism
BM.524 (L,R)
SN Use with reference to endeavors to communicate with the souls of the dead or other spirits.
UF spiritism
CN B.BM.BIQ.AXC.ELK

spitals
USE **hospitals**

splads
USE **splats**

splashboards
TG.825
ALT **splashboard**
SN Shaped extensions of backboards. (KETCH)
CN V.TG.ALO.ARI.AFU

splashing
KT.697
SN Applying a liquid, such as ink or paint, in a scattered, usually random pattern. For the similar technique resulting in a surface covered with fine specks, use **spattering.**
CN K.KT.AFU.ALO.GRC.BUE.AXC

splat-back Windsor chairs
TG.105
ALT **splat-back Windsor chair**
SN Term generally applied to any Windsor chair, of square or round back, having a central vertical back splat. (EVANS)
UF chairs, splat-back Windsor
Windsor chairs, splat-back
CN V.TG.AFU.AFU.ALO.AFU.AFU.AFU.MLC.BZY

splats
TG.837
ALT **splat**
SN Central, vertical members on a chair back, generally shaped or pierced. (DDA)
UF back splats
splads
splats, back
CN V.TG.ALO.AXC.ALO.BOK

splats, back
USE **splats**

splay brick
MT.84
SN A brick, one side of which is beveled. (DAC)
UF brick, cant
brick, splay
cant brick
CN M.MT.AFU.AFU.AFU.AXC.ALO.AFU.AFU.AFU.DCU

splay-leg tables
USE **cricket tables**

splayed
DC.72
SN Having the parts or members spread apart, extended outwards, or lying wide and flat.
CN D.DC.AFU.ARI.DOI

splayed arches
RT.272
ALT **splayed arch**
SN Use for arches with intradoses having a greater radius at one face of the arch than at the other.
UF arches, sluing
arches, splayed
sluing arches
CN V.RT.AFU.AFU.AFU.BCW.AFU.AFU.AFU.FCS.ALO

splayed-leg stools
USE **cricket stools**

splicers
USE **film splicers**

splicers, film
USE **film splicers**

splices, halved
USE **half-lap joints**

splicing
KT.62 (L)
ALT **spliced**
CN K.KT.AFU.ALO.BCW.CLM

spline chisels
TB.789
ALT **spline chisel**
SN Chisels used for removing old cane strips from furniture. (HAND)
UF chisels, spline
CN V.TB.AFU.BCW.BUE.BCW

spline joints
TF.691
ALT **spline joint**
SN Joints in which a thin strip of wood (spline), acts as an independent tongue that fits simultaneously into corresponding grooves cut in two butted or mitered boards. (NEF)
UF joints, spline
joints, spline miter
miter joints, spline
spline miter joints
CN V.TF.ALO.ARI.AXC.ARI.BUE

spline miter joints
USE **spline joints**

splint planes
TB.971 (N)
ALT **splint plane**
SN Planes used to produce a shaving of wood for such purposes as basketry. (SALAM)
UF chip planes
pill box planes
planes, chip
planes, pill box
planes, scabbard
planes, scaleboard
planes, slitting
planes, spelk
planes, splint
scabbard planes
scaleboard planes
slitting planes
spelk planes
CN V.TB.AFU.BCW.CFS.ALO.AFU.DUC.BZY

split axes
USE **froes**

split bamboo
MT.1028
UF bamboo, split
CN M.MT.AFU.AFU.ALO.BIQ.AXC.AFU.AFU

split dead bolts
TF.555
ALT **split dead bolt**
UF bolts, split dead
dead bolts, split
CN V.TF.AFU.ALO.AXC.AFU.BCW.AFU

split-level houses
RK.253 (B)
ALT **split-level house**
UF houses, split-level
CN V.RK.AFU.ALO.ALO.AXC.ALO.AFU.CLM.BOK

split-quills
USE **gouge bits**

split spindles
TG.988
ALT **split spindle**
UF spindles, split
CN V.TG.ALO.HCQ.ALO

splits
MT.2763
UF scones (masonry units)
CN M.MT.AFU.AXC.BIQ.ALO.ARI

splitting chisels
TB.581 (N)
ALT **splitting chisel**
SN Tools used to break up rock. (HAND)
UF chisels, splitting
CN V.TB.AFU.BCW.BCW.ALO.BZY.BCW

splitting wedges
TB.1042
ALT **splitting wedge**
UF cleaving wedges
wedges, cleaving
wedges, splitting
wedges, wood-splitting
wood-splitting wedges
CN V.TB.AFU.BCW.CFS.ALO.AFU.FZU.AFU

spoil areas
USE **spoil banks**

spoil banks
RK.1475 (L)
ALT **spoil bank**
SN Areas created by the deposited spoil or overburdened material prior to backfilling; also, that part of a mine where the coal and other minerals that are not marketable are left. (HUNTED)
UF areas, spoil
banks, spoil
coal tips
heaps, spoil
spoil areas
spoil heaps
tips, coal
CN V.RK.ALO.ALO.AXC.ARI

spoil heaps
USE **spoil banks**

spoils (architecture)
USE **spolia**

Spokan
FL.1422 (L)
CN F.FL.ALO.ALO.ARI.AFU.BUE.DZW

spoke dogs
TB.1063 (N)
ALT **spoke dog**
SN Sticks used by wheelwrights to force the outer ends of spokes into the rim. (RHDEL2)
UF dogs, spoke
CN V.TB.AFU.BCW.CFS.ALO.ALO.BIQ.ALO

spoke lathes
TB.797 (N)
ALT **spoke lathe**
SN Lathes in a variety of forms; used for turning irregular forms. (KNIGHT)
UF lathes, spoke
CN V.TB.AFU.BCW.CFS.AFU.AFU.AXC

spokeshaves
TB.1039 (N)
ALT **spokeshave**
SN Carpenter's tools used for shaping curved edges, consisting of a blade set between two handles and used as a drawknife or planing tool. (MEANS)
CN V.TB.AFU.BCW.CFS.ALO.AFU.FUA

spokeshaves, chamfer
USE **chamfer spokeshaves**

spolia
VB.112
SN Architectural materials reused; usually pieces built into a new fabric. A term used especially for ancient and Medieval instances of the practice.
UF spoils (architecture)
CN V.VB.ALO.BUE.BZY

spolvero
KT.744
SN In fresco, transferring a pricked drawing onto the final plaster layer by dusting it with a cloth sack filled with charcoal powder, leaving an outline of the design on the fresh intonaco. (FFF)
CN K.KT.AFU.ALO.HCQ.ALO.AXC.AFU

sponge
MT.962 (L)
CN M.MT.AFU.AFU.ALO.AFU.EFQ

sponge rubber
USE **foam rubber**

spontaneous architecture
USE **vernacular architecture**

spool beds
TG.373
ALT **spool bed**
UF beds, Jenny Lind
beds, spindle
beds, spool
Jenny Lind beds
spindle beds
CN V.TG.AFU.AFU.ARI.AFU.AFU.ELK

spoon-back chairs
TG.156
ALT **spoon-back chair**
SN The name sometimes given to early 18th-century chairs in which the back has a gentle double curve designed to fit the back of the sitter. Also a mid-19th century chair with a rounded, waisted back and short legs. (TOMLIN)
UF chairs, spoon-back
spoon-backs
CN V.TG.AFU.AFU.ALO.AFU.AFU.AFU.NIE.EFQ

spoon-backs
USE **spoon-back chairs**

spoon bits
TB.1114 (N)
ALT **spoon bit**
SN Bits shaped like a half cylinder; used with a brace for drilling dowel holes. (MEANS)
UF bits, chair
bits, dowel
bits, pin
bits, quill
bits, spoon
chair bits
dowel bits
pin bits
quill bits
CN V.TB.ALO.ARI.DOI

spoon gouges
USE **bent gouges**

spoons, mud
USE **mud spoons**

spoons, quarryman's mud
USE **mud spoons**

sporting goods stores
RK.165 (A,L)
ALT **sporting goods store**
UF stores, sporting goods
CN V.RK.AFU.ALO.ALO.ALO.ARI.BIQ.AFU.DIO

sporting houses
USE **brothels**

sports
BM.335 (L,B,R)
CN B.BM.ALO.ALO.BOK

sports arenas
USE **arenas**

sports buildings
RK.1045 (A,B)
ALT **sport building**
UF athletics buildings
buildings, athletics
buildings, sports
facilities, sports
halls, sports
pavilions, sports
sports facilities
sports halls
sports pavilions
CN V.RK.AFU.ALO.ALO.EWY.AXC.BIQ

sports centers
USE **sports complexes**

sports clubs
USE **athletic clubs**

sports complexes
RG.174 (A,L,B,R)
ALT **sports complex**
UF athletic facilities
centers, sports
complexes, sports
facilities, athletic
facilities, sports
sports centers
sports facilities
CN V.RG.AFU.AFU.DOI.CFS

sports facilities
USE **sports buildings**
sports complexes

sports grounds
USE **athletic fields**

sports halls
USE **sports buildings**

sports museums
RK.423 (L)
ALT **sports museum**
UF museums, sports
CN V.RK.AFU.ALO.ALO.BCW.AXC.ARI.CLM

sports pavilions
USE **sports buildings**

spot boards
USE **hawks**

spotlighting
RT.1362
CN V.RT.ALO.AXC.AFU.BZY

spouses
HG.15 (L)
ALT **spouse**
CN H.HG.AFU.ALO.ARI

spout adzes
USE **guttering adzes**

spout planes
USE **guttering planes**

sprawl, urban
USE **urban sprawl**

spray painting
KT.237 (L)
ALT **spray painted**
UF paint spraying
painting, spray
CN K.KT.AFU.ALO.DUC.CXA.ALO.AFU.DIO

sprayed concrete
USE **gunite**

spraying, flock
USE **flocking**

spread foundations
RT.166
ALT **spread foundation**
SN Use for foundations that sustain loads by distributing them over a large planar surface.
UF foundations, spread
CN V.RT.AFU.AFU.AFU.AXC.BUE.ARI.AFU

spreaders
TB.51
ALT **spreader**
SN Devices or machines for metering granular material such as gravel or crushed stone, from a feed hopper and distributing it over a given area.
CN V.TB.AFU.ARI.AFU.AXC

spreaders, concrete
USE **concrete spreaders**

sprezzatura
BM.44
SN Use for the effect conveyed by some works of art of skillful execution done without apparent effort.
CN B.BM.AFU.AFU.ALO.CRG

sprig bits
USE **bradawls**

spring
BM.1038 (L,R)
UF springtime
CN B.BM.CFS.AXC.CRG.ARI.ALO

Spring and Autumn Annals
FL.1863 (L)
UF Ch'un-ch'iu
Chunqiu
CN F.FL.ALO.ARI.ALO.AFU.AFU.ALO.BIQ.AFU.AFU

spring bolts, window
USE **window spring bolts**

spring chairs, centripetal
USE **centripetal spring chairs**

spring clamps
TB.1058
ALT **spring clamp**
SN Any clamps which exert pressure by a spring; used to hold parts together during gluing or as a temporary electric connection. (MEANS)
UF clamps, spring
CN V.TB.AFU.BCW.CFS.ALO.ALO.BCW.BZY

spring hinges
TF.126
ALT **spring hinge**
SN Hinges containing one or more springs to move a door into a closed position. They may be either single- or double-acting. (BROWNL)
UF hinges, spring
CN V.TF.AFU.AFU.AFU.AFU.CLM.AFU.FOG

spring hinges, double-acting
USE **double-acting spring hinges**

spring hinges, jamb
USE **jamb spring hinges**

spring latches
TF.179
ALT **spring latch**
SN Plain latches, generally used on interior doors and having no locking mechanisms. (STEIN)
UF latches, spring
CN V.TF.AFU.AFU.AFU.AFU.DIO.BCW.

AFU.BIQ

spring needles
TB.533
ALT **spring needle**
SN Fine steel needles that have a butt at one end and a long flexible hook at the other that curves back to the shank of the needle. (W)
UF needles, spring
CN V.TB.AFU.ARI.FCS.ALO.AFU

spring tongs
USE **tweezers**

springers
RT.697
ALT **springer**
SN The lower voussoirs, or bottom stones of an arch, which rest immediately on an impost. (HAS)
UF lines, springing
reins
springing lines
CN V.RT.AFU.AFU.ALO.AFU.AXC.ALO

springers, gable
USE **kneelers (gable components)**

springhouses
RK.74 (N)
ALT **springhouse**
SN Buildings enclosing a natural spring; sufficiently cool for use as a storehouse of milk and other dairy products. (DAC)
CN V.RK.AFU.ALO.ALO.AFU.AFU.CLM

springing lines
USE **springers**

springs
RD.151 (L)
ALT **spring**
SN Water issuing naturally from the rock or soil upon the land or into a body of surface water. (STEIN)
CN V.RD.ARI.AFU.AFU.AFU.ALO.AXC

springs, bed
USE **bedsprings**

springs, box
USE **box springs**

springtime
USE **spring**

sprinklers, fire
USE **fire sprinklers**

sprocket pieces
USE **sprockets**

sprockets
RT.516
ALT **sprocket**
SN In roofing, strips of wood fixed to the upper side of rafters at the eaves, that raise the edge of the eaves and form a break in the roof line. (DAC)
UF cocking pieces
pieces, cocking
pieces, sprocket
sprocket pieces
CN V.RT.AFU.AFU.AFU.BIQ.ARI.ALO.ALO.AXC

spruce
MT.1396 (L)
UF Picea
CN M.MT.AFU.AFU.ALO.BIQ.DCU.AFU.AFU.ALO.DOI

spruce fir
USE **common spruce**

spruce fir (Norway spruce)
USE **Norway spruce**

spruce ocher
MT.1791
UF ocher, spruce
CN M.MT.AFU.AFU.ARI.AFU.AFU.ALO.ALO.BUE.ARI.CFS.AXC

spruce pine
USE **Cuban pine**
black spruce
blue spruce
eastern hemlock
pond pine
red spruce
scrub pine
shortleaf pine
white spruce

spruce, black
USE **black spruce**

spruce, blue
USE **blue spruce**

spruce, bog
USE **bog spruce**

spruce, Canadian
USE **red spruce**
white spruce

spruce, Colorado
USE **blue spruce**

spruce, Colorado blue
USE **blue spruce**

spruce, common
USE **common spruce**

spruce, Douglas
USE **Douglas fir**

spruce, Engelmann
USE **Engelmann spruce**

spruce, European
USE **common spruce**

spruce, hemlock
USE **eastern hemlock**

spruce, Norway
USE **Norway spruce**

spruce, red
USE **red spruce**

spruce, shingle
USE **white spruce**

spruce, silver
USE **sitka spruce**

spruce, sitka
USE **sitka spruce**

spruce, skunk
USE **white spruce**

spruce, West Himalayan
USE **West Himalayan spruce**

spruce, West Virginia
USE **red spruce**

spruce, Western
USE **sitka spruce**

spruce, white
USE **white spruce**

spruce, white (Norway spruce)
USE **Norway spruce**

spruce, yellow
USE **red spruce**

sprue cutters
TB.712 (N)
ALT **sprue cutter**
SN Cutters used for clipping off the excess sprues of molded metal after the mold has been removed. (HAND)
UF cutters, sprue
CN V.TB.AFU.BCW.BIQ.ARI.ALO.ALO.BCW

sprung floors
RT.746
ALT **sprung floor**
UF floors, sprung
CN V.RT.AFU.ALO.AFU.BIQ.AFU.AXC

spud wrenches
TB.772
ALT **spud wrench**
SN Tools with a long tapering steel handle with an open-end wrench at one end; used primarily in plumbing to tighten large square nuts and to align holes.
UF wrenches, spud
CN V.TB.AFU.BCW.BIQ.AXC.ALO.BIQ.AFU.ALO

spuds
USE **barking irons**

spur braces
USE **spurs**

spur dikes
USE **wing dams**

spurs
RT.208
ALT **spur**
SN Use for diagonal braces connecting posts and tie beams or rafters.
UF braces, spur

spur braces
CN V.RT.AFU.AFU.AFU.AXC.DOI.AFU.AFU.ARI

spurs (erosion protection works)
USE **wing dams**

spurs (griffes)
USE **griffes**

squabs
TG.981
ALT **squab**
SN Common term for removable stuffed seat cushions in the 17th and 18th centuries; term also seems to have been applied to large padded seats. (DEF)
CN V.TG.ALO.GLI.ALO.ARI

square-back chairs
TG.157
ALT **square-back chair**
UF chairs, Spanish back
chairs, square-back
Spanish back chairs
CN V.TG.AFU.AFU.ALO.AFU.AFU.AFU.NIE.ELK

square-back Windsor chairs
TG.106
ALT **square-back Windsor chair**
SN Term introduced in the 19th century for any Windsor chair, with or without arms, of a square or nearly square back. (EVANS)
UF birdcage Windsor chairs
chairs, birdcage Windsor
chairs, chicken-coop Windsor
chairs, rod-back Windsor
chairs, square-back Windsor
chairs, Windsor rod-back
chicken-coop Windsor chairs
rod-back Windsor chairs
Windsor chairs, birdcage
Windsor chairs, chicken-coop
Windsor chairs, rod-back
Windsor chairs, square-back
Windsor rod-back chairs
CN V.TG.AFU.AFU.ALO.AFU.AFU.AFU.MLC.CFS

square bay windows
RT.914
ALT **square bay window**
UF bay windows, square
windows, square bay
CN V.RT.AFU.ARI.AFU.AFU.BOK.AFU.AFU.ALO.AXC

square bolts
TF.559
ALT **square bolt**
UF bolts, square
CN V.TF.AFU.ALO.AXC.AFU.BZY

square easy chairs
TG.65
ALT **square easy chair**
SN Term used to differentiate between easy chairs with straight backs as opposed to those with circular backs. (MONTGO)
UF chairs, square easy
chairs, straight-back easy
easy chairs, square
easy chairs, straight-back
straight-back easy chairs
CN V.TG.AFU.AFU.ALO.AFU.AFU.AFU.FZU.BCW

square hole saws
TB.1022
ALT **square hole saw**
SN Type of compass saw with teeth at the heel edge that are set out at 90 degrees to the blade; used to cut corners. (DISSTO)
UF saws, square hole
CN V.TB.AFU.BCW.CFS.ALO.AFU.EWY.BUE.ALO.ARI

square legs (Marlborough legs)
USE **Marlborough legs**

squares
RK.1444 (A,L,B,R)
ALT **square**
SN Use for open public spaces in cities or towns, usually rectilinear, surrounded by buildings, and located at the junction of two or more thoroughfares.
UF city squares
public squares
squares, city
squares, public
CN V.RK.ALO.AFU.ARI

squares (carpenter's squares)
USE **carpenter's squares**

squares (geometric figures)
BM.778 (L,R)
ALT **square (geometric figure)**
CN B.BM.CFS.ARI.AXC.BCW.AFU.BIQ.ALO.AFU.AFU.AFU

squares (tools)
TB.443 (L,N)
ALT **square (tool)**
SN Tools consisting of two perpendicular arms, usually made of wood, metal, plastic, or a combination of these materials, fixed together so as to form a right angle; used for marking right angles or testing the squareness of sides, edges, or surfaces.
CN V.TB.AFU.ARI.EFQ.ALO.BZY

squares, bevel
USE **bevel squares**

squares, carpenter's
USE **carpenter's squares**

squares, city
USE **squares**

squares, framing
USE **carpenter's squares**

squares, market
USE **marketplaces**

squares, miter
USE **miter squares**

squares, public
USE **squares**

squares, set
USE **set squares**

squares, set (triangles)
USE **triangles (tools)**

squares, steel
USE **carpenter's squares**

squares, tee
USE **T-squares**

squares, try
USE **try squares**

squaring
KT.157
ALT **squared**
SN To form with right angles and straight edges. (W)
CN K.KT.AFU.ALO.DOI.DOI

squaring off
USE **squaring (transferring technique)**

squaring (transferring technique)
KT.751
SN A method for transferring a drawing to another surface on a different scale, especially to a larger surface that is to be painted, such as a canvas or a wall. (MAYER)
UF squaring off
CN K.KT.AFU.ALO.HCQ.ALO.BOK

squash courts
RK.1018 (A,B)
ALT **squash court**
UF courts, squash
squash racquet courts
CN V.RK.AFU.ALO.ALO.EWY.ALO.BZY

squash racquet courts
USE **squash courts**

squatter settlements
RD.75 (A,L)
ALT **squatter settlement**
UF settlements, squatter
CN V.RD.AFU.BIQ.AXC

squatters
HG.738 (A,L,B)
ALT **squatter**
SN Persons who settle on land without a right or title. (W)
CN H.HG.AFU.BCW.GFO

squeezed joints
TF.693
ALT **squeezed joint**
SN Joints formed by coating surfaces of

two pieces with cement and squeezing them together. (MEANS)
UF joints, squeezed
CN V.TF.ALO.ARI.AXC.ARI.BZY

squeezers, brad
USE **brad pushers**

squinch arches
USE **squinches**

squinches
RT.282 (A)
ALT **squinch**
SN Arches across the interior corners of a square or polygonal structure forming a transition to a circular or polygonal superstructure.
UF arches, squinch
arches, trumpet
squinch arches
trumpet arches
CN V.RT.AFU.AFU.AFU.BCW.AFU.AFU.ARI.BCW

squint brick
MT.85
SN A building stone or brick of special shape to be used at an oblique corner. (DAC)
UF brick, squint
CN M.MT.AFU.AFU.AFU.AFU.AXC.ALO.AFU.AFU.AFU.DIO

squint windows
USE **squints**

squints
RT.964
ALT **squint**
SN Small openings, often obliquely cut, in the wall of a church, generally so placed as to afford a view of the high altar from the transept or aisles. (DAC)
UF eucharistic windows
squint windows
windows, eucharistic
windows, squint
CN V.RT.AFU.ARI.AFU.AFU.BOK.AFU.ARI.BOK

squirrel cages (furniture components)
USE **birdcages (furniture components)**

Sri Deb
FL.2414
UF Crideb
Sî Tép
CN F.FL.ALO.ARI.BCW.BOK.AFU.BZY

Sri Lankan
FL.2304 (L,B)
UF Ceylonese
Singalese
Singhalese
Sinhalese
CN F.FL.ALO.ARI.AXC.ARI

Sriksetra
USE **Pyu**

Srindrajayavarman
FL.2351
CN F.FL.ALO.ARI.BCW.ALO.ARI.AFU.EFQ

Srindravarman
FL.2350
CN F.FL.ALO.ARI.BCW.ALO.ARI.AFU.DZW

Srivijaya
FL.2379 (L)
UF Shrivijaya
CN F.FL.ALO.ARI.BCW.ARI.ALO.AXC.AFU.AFU

Srivijaya (Thai)
FL.2418 (L)
CN F.FL.ALO.ARI.BCW.BOK.AFU.CXA

stab-stitching
USE **side sewing**

stability analysis
USE **structural stability**

stability of structures
USE **structural stability**

stability, structural
USE **structural stability**

stabilization
USE **stabilizing**

stabilizers
MT.2328 (L)
SN Includes materials, such as waxes, aqueous solutions, or certain inert pigments, added to artists' colors in order to keep pigment in suspension and the oil from separating; (AHMT) also, any materials that improve the behavior of another material.
UF agents, stabilizing
stabilizing agents
CN M.MT.AFU.ARI.ALO.FIM

stabilizers, heat
USE **heat stabilizers**

stabilizers, ultraviolet
USE **ultraviolet stabilizers**

stabilizers, UV
USE **ultraviolet stabilizers**

stabilizing
KT.642 (L)
ALT **stabilized**
UF stabilization
CN K.KT.AFU.ALO.GLI

stabilizing (strengthening)
USE **strengthening**

stabilizing agents
USE **stabilizers**

stables
RK.94 (A,L,N,B,R)
ALT **stable**
CN V.RK.AFU.ALO.ALO.AFU.ALO.CXA

stables (carriage houses)
USE **carriage houses**

stacco
KT.737
SN The process of detaching a fresco painting from the wall by removing the pigment layer and a layer of intonaco. Cloth is glued to the painted surface and, when dry, the cloth, painting, and plaster are stripped from the wall. (FFF)
CN K.KT.AFU.ALO.HCQ.AFU.AFU

stack bond
MT.2753
SN Purely pattern bond with no overlapping of units, so that all vertical joints are aligned.
UF block bond
bond, block
bond, stack
CN M.MT.AFU.AXC.BIQ.AFU.AFU.BCW

stack tables
USE **nesting tables**

stackable chairs
USE **stacking chairs**

stacking chairs
TG.230
ALT **stacking chair**
UF chairs, stackable
chairs, stacking
stackable chairs
CN V.TG.AFU.AFU.ALO.AFU.AFU.AXC.AXC

stacking stools
TG.274
ALT **stacking stool**
UF stools, stacking
CN V.TG.AFU.AFU.ALO.AFU.ALO.AXC.ARI

stacking tables
USE **nesting tables**

stacks (piping)
RT.1474
ALT **stack (piping)**
SN Vertical mains of a system of soil, waste, or vent piping extending through one or more stories. (STEIN)
CN V.RT.ALO.BCW.ALO.ARI.BZY.BOK

stacks, chimney
USE **chimney stacks**

stacks, soil
USE **soil stacks**

stacks, vent
USE **vent stacks**

stacks, waste
USE **waste stacks**

stackwood construction

USE **stovewood construction**

stadiums
RK.1054 (A,L,N,B,R)
ALT **stadium**
SN Large usually unroofed buildings with tiers of seats for spectators built in various shapes and enclosing a field used for sports events. (W)
UF coliseums
CN V.RK.AFU.ALO.ALO.EWY.AXC.BIQ.AFU.BCW

stadiums, baseball
USE **baseball stadiums**

stadiums, football
USE **football stadiums**

staff
MT.2269
CN M.MT.AFU.ALO.GLI

staff manuals
USE **employees' manuals**

Staffordshire blue brick
USE **blue brick**

staffs, bed
USE **bed slats**

stage equipment
USE **stage machinery**

stage floors
RT.1275
ALT **stage floor**
SN The surface of a stage, commonly made of wood, on which the players perform. (TL)
UF boards (stage floors)
floors, stage
CN V.RT.AFU.BUE.ARI.BOK

stage houses
RM.364
ALT **stage house**
SN Parts of theaters holding the stage and the space above it. (IDTL)
UF houses, stage
CN V.RM.AFU.DIO.AXC.AXC.ALO.BCW

stage lighting
RT.1379 (A,L,B)
UF lighting, stage
CN V.RT.ALO.AXC.AXC.ARI

stage lofts
USE **fly lofts**

stage machinery
RM.373 (L)
SN Use for all machinery and equipment effecting movement on the stage, including groove systems, devices for flying figures, etc.
UF equipment, stage
machinery, stage
machinery, theatrical
stage equipment
theatrical machinery
CN V.RM.AFU.DIO.AXC.AXC.ALO.BIQ.ALO.ALO

stage sets
RT.1277 (A,L,B,R)
ALT **stage set**
UF sets, stage
CN V.RT.AFU.BUE.ARI.BUE.AFU

stages
RM.366
ALT **stage**
SN In theaters or auditoriums, the areas visible to the audience and commonly framed by a proscenium arch and in which the performance occurs.
CN V.RM.AFU.DIO.AXC.AXC.ALO.BIQ.AFU

stages (stories)
USE **stories**

stages, apron
USE **forestages**

stages, inner
USE **chambers**

stages, landing
USE **landings (marine structures)**

stages, revolving
USE **revolving stages**

stages, sound
USE **sound stages**

stages, thrust
USE **thrust stages**

stages, upper
USE **upper stages**

staggered joints
USE **break joints**

staging
USE **scaffolds**

staging, bracket
USE **bracket scaffolding**

stain
MT.2464 (L,B,R)
SN A varnish containing enough pigment or dye to alter the appearance or tone of wood, or to equalize the color in wood. (MH)
CN M.MT.AFU.ARI.CRG.AFU.BIQ

stain, oil
USE **oil stain**

stain, silver
USE **silver stain**

stain, spirit
USE **spirit stain**

stain, varnish
USE **varnish stain**

stain, water
USE **water stain**

stained glass
MT.266 (A,L,N,B,R)
UF glass, stained
CN M.MT.AFU.AFU.AFU.BIQ.AFU.ARI.CRG

staining
KT.83 (L,R)
ALT **stained**
CN K.KT.AFU.ALO.BOK.AXC

stainless steel
MT.351 (A,B,R)
SN A large and widely used family of iron-chromium alloys, known for their corrosion resistance, and nonrusting quality. (MH)
UF steel, stainless
CN M.MT.AFU.AFU.AFU.BZY.AFU.AFU.AFU.AFU.ALO.AFU.ALO.AFU.ALO

stainless steel, austenitic
USE **austenitic stainless steel**

stainless steel, hardenable
USE **martensitic stainless steel**

stainless steel, martensitic
USE **martensitic stainless steel**

stair carpet holders
TF.276
ALT **stair carpet holder**
UF carpet holders, stair
holders, stair carpet
CN V.TF.AFU.AFU.AFU.AFU.ERE

stair dormers
RT.484
ALT **stair dormer**
SN Dormers built sufficiently wide to accommodate the upper part of a staircase leading to an upper half-floor or attic. (HAS)
UF dormers, stair
CN V.RT.AFU.AFU.AFU.BIQ.ARI.ALO.AFU.BUE.AXC.BUE

stair-ends
USE **strings**

stair landings
USE **landings**

stair nosing planes
USE **nosing planes**

stair planes
USE **capping planes**

stair towers
RM.422
ALT **stair tower**
SN Use for clearly articulated, often towerlike, building appendages containing only stairs.
UF towers, stair
CN V.RM.AFU.DZW.AXC

stair treads
USE **treads**

stairbuilder's planes
USE **capping planes**
handrail planes

stairbuilder's saws
TB.993 (N)
ALT **stairbuilder's saw**
SN Short lengths of saw blade with shaped wood grips fitted along the upper edge, and sometimes made adjustable for depth of cut; used to cut the sides of grooves across or at an angle with the grain. (SALAM)
UF grooving saws
notching saws
saws, grooving
saws, notching
saws, stairbuilder's
saws, trenching
trenching saws
CN V.TB.AFU.BCW.CFS.ALO.AFU.EWY.AFU.BIQ

staircases
USE **stairs**

staircases, moving
USE **escalators**

stairs
RT.1068 (A,L,N,B,R)
ALT **stair**
SN A series of steps or flights of steps connected by landings for passing from one level to another. (W)
UF staircases
stairways
CN V.RT.AFU.BIQ.AXC.AFU

stairs, angle
USE **quarter-turn stairs**

stairs, cantilevered
USE **flying stairs**

stairs, circular
USE **spiral stairs**

stairs, cockle
USE **spiral stairs**

stairs, corkscrew
USE **spiral stairs**

stairs, disappearing
USE **disappearing stairs**

stairs, dogleg
USE **dogleg stairs**

stairs, double return
USE **double return stairs**

stairs, double spiral
USE **double spiral stairs**

stairs, fire
USE **fire stairs**

stairs, flying
USE **flying stairs**

stairs, full-turn
USE **one-turn stairs**

stairs, geometrical
USE **geometrical stairs**

stairs, half-space
USE **halfpace stairs**

stairs, half-turn
USE **half-turn stairs**

stairs, halfpace
USE **halfpace stairs**

stairs, helical
USE **spiral stairs**

stairs, hollow newel
USE **hollow newel stairs**

stairs, newel
USE **newel stairs**

stairs, one-turn
USE **one-turn stairs**

stairs, open newel
USE **open newel stairs**

stairs, open well
USE **open well stairs**

stairs, quarter-turn
USE **quarter-turn stairs**

stairs, quarterpace
USE **quarterpace stairs**

stairs, screw
USE **spiral stairs**

stairs, solid newel
USE **solid newel stairs**

stairs, spiral
USE **spiral stairs**

stairs, straight
USE **straight stairs**

stairs, straight-run
USE **straight stairs**

stairs, three-quarter turn
USE **three-quarter turn stairs**

stairs, turnpike
USE **spiral stairs**

stairs, water
USE **water stairs**

stairs, winding
USE **spiral stairs**

stairs, wreathed
USE **geometrical stairs**

stairways
USE **stairs**

stairways, disappearing
USE **disappearing stairs**

stairways, electric
USE **escalators**

stairwells
RM.94
ALT **stairwell**
SN Use for spaces, extending through one or more floors, that contain staircases.
CN V.RM.AFU.DIO.ALO.ARI.BCW

stairwells, pressurized
USE **pressurized stairwells**

stake anvils
USE **stakes**

stakes
TB.681 (N)
ALT **stake**
SN Small anvils used for the working of thin sheet metal, so called because they are supported by a sharp vertical prop which is inserted into a hole in the workbench. (DAC)
UF anvils, stake
stake anvils
CN V.TB.AFU.BCW.BIQ.AFU.ALO.CXA

stakes, beakhorn
USE **beakhorn stakes**

stakes, blowhorn
USE **blowhorn stakes**

stakes, creasing
USE **creasing stakes**

stakes, double-creasing
USE **double-creasing stakes**

stakes, hatchet
USE **hatchet stakes**

stakes, hollow-mandrel
USE **hollow-mandrel stakes**

stakes, needle case
USE **needle case stakes**

stakes, planishing
USE **planishing stakes**

stalactite work
USE **muqarnas**

stalk
MT.1073
CN M.MT.AFU.AFU.ALO.BIQ.CLM

stalk, leaf
USE **leafstalk**

stalls (carrels)
USE **carrels**

stalls (choir stalls)
USE **choir stalls**

stalls (church fixtures)
RT.1257 (B)
ALT **stall (church fixture)**
SN Fixed seats for clergy and choristers, enclosed at back and sides. (RS)
CN V.RT.AFU.BUE.ALO.ARI.DIO

stalls (stable spaces)

RM.344
ALT **stall (stable space)**
SN Divisions of stables or barns, each accommodating one animal. (W)
CN V.RM.AFU.DIO.AXC.ARI.ARI

stalls, box
USE **box stalls**

stalls, choir
USE **choir stalls**

stalls, shower
USE **shower stalls**

stambas
USE **lats**

stamp albums
VW.493 (L)
ALT **stamp album**
UF albums, stamp
CN V.VW.AFU.ALO.AFU.AFU.AFU.ALO.BOK

stamp-decorated ware
USE **stamped ware**

stamped ware
FL.147
UF stamp-decorated ware
ware, stamp-decorated
ware, stamped
CN F.FL.ALO.AFU.ALO.ARI.BOK.ARI

stamping
KT.158
ALT **stamped**
SN Impressing, marking, or forming materials or objects or their surfaces, such as shaping metal in a die or embossing soft clay. (W)
CN K.KT.AFU.ALO.DOI.DUC

stamping, check
USE **check stamping**

stamping, die
USE **die stamping**

stamping, rocker
USE **rocker stamping**

stamps (tools)
TB.450 (N)
ALT **stamp (tool)**
SN Instruments for stamping, such as dies or tools for impressing or marking a design or pattern on metal, paper, or other soft or absorbent material. (W)
UF dies (stamps)
CN V.TB.AFU.ARI.EFQ.ALO.CFS

stamps, back
USE **back stamps**

stamps, brick
USE **brick stamps**

stamps, poster
USE **poster stamps**

Stancliffe sandstone
MT.728
UF sandstone, Stancliffe
CN M.MT.AFU.AFU.AFU.DCU.AFU.ALO.AFU.ARI.AFU.ALO.BIQ.BCW

stand oil
MT.2000
SN Heavy viscous material resulting from the polymerization of an oil, such as linseed oil; used chiefly in painting and glazing mediums; unlike raw oil, tends not to yellow with age. (AHMT)
UF oil, polymerized
oil, stand
polymerized oil
CN M.MT.AFU.AFU.ARI.ARI.ARI.BCW

standard coil hangers
TF.346
ALT **standard coil hanger**
UF hangers, standard coil
CN V.TF.AFU.AFU.AFU.ALO.AFU.BOK.ALO.ALO.AXC

standard detail drawings
VD.151
ALT **standard detail drawing**
SN Use for detail drawings made by an architectural office for reuse on more than one project.
UF detail drawings, standard
drawings, standard detail
CN V.VD.AFU.BIQ.ARI.AFU

standard deviation
BM.830 (L)
UF deviation, standard
CN B.BM.CFS.ARI.CRG.ALO.BIQ

standard lenses
TB.321
ALT **standard lens**
SN Lenses whose focal lengths are approximately equal to the film format with which they are used. (LANG)
UF lenses, normal
lenses, prime
lenses, standard
normal lenses
prime lenses
CN V.TB.AFU.ARI.CLM.ARI.AFU.ALO.BOK.BCW

standard limestone
MT.699
SN A less dense stone with more variation of grain and more and larger pore spaces than pure limestone. (WATSON)
UF limestone, standard
CN M.MT.AFU.AFU.AFU.DCU.AFU.ALO.AFU.ALO.ALO.ARI.AXC

Standard Metropolitan Statistical Areas
RG.263
ALT **Standard Metropolitan Statistical Area**
SN Areas, used mainly for census and federal funding allocation, having a dominant central city with a combined minimum population of 50,000 and with a surrounding urbanized coummunity that is economically and socially integrated with the central city. (DOP)
UF Areas, Standard Metropolitan Statistical
Metropolitan Statistical Areas, Standard
SMSAs
Statistical Areas, Standard Metropolitan
CN V.RG.ALO.AFU.AFU.BZY.ALO

standard painted ware
FL.3033
UF painted ware, standard
ware, standard painted
CN F.FL.ALO.AXC.ARI.BIQ.ALO.AXC.CLM

standard portland cement
MT.18
UF cement, portland normal
cement, standard portland
cement, type I portland
normal portland cement
portland cement, normal
portland cement, standard
portland cement, type I
type I portland cement
CN M.MT.AFU.AFU.AFU.ALO.AFU.AFU.ARI.AFU.BOK

standard ware
USE **Hassuna standard ware**

standard ware, Hassuna
USE **Hassuna standard ware**

standardization
BM.1142 (L,B)
CN B.BM.CXA.ALO.AXC

standards
BM.1159 (L,B)
CN B.BM.DIO.AXC

standards organizations
HG.827 (B)
ALT **standards organization**
UF organizations, standards
societies, standards
standards societies
CN H.HG.ALO.BCW.BUE

standards societies
USE **standards organizations**

standards (trussing coffers)
USE **trussing coffers**

standards, professional
USE **professional standards**

standby power systems
USE **emergency power supply**

standing desks

TG.555
ALT **standing desk**
SN Slant-top desks having a high writing surface, designed to be used while standing.
UF desks, standing
CN V.TG.AFU.AFU.AXC.ALO.BZY.EFQ

standing seams
TF.662
ALT **standing seam**
SN Seams, in sheet metal and roofing, made by turning up two adjacent edges and folding the upstanding parts over on themselves. (MEANS)
UF seams, standing
CN V.TF.ALO.ARI.ARI.BUE.CXA

standing shelves (bookshelves)
USE **bookshelves**

standing stones
RK.892 (A,L,N,B)
ALT **standing stone**
UF menhirs
peristeles
stones, standing
CN V.RK.AFU.ALO.ALO.DOI.AFU.ARI.ARI

standpipes
RK.580 (L)
ALT **standpipe**
SN Use for tanks or vertical pipes connected to watersupply systems and used to insure uniform pressure or to store water for emergency use.
CN V.RK.AFU.ALO.ALO.CFS.ALO.BCW.BUE

stands
TG.616 (L)
ALT **stand**
CN V.TG.AFU.AFU.BIQ.BCW

stands (grandstands)
USE **grandstands**

stands, ashtray
USE **smokers**

stands, basin
USE **basin stands**

stands, bidet
USE **bidets (box stools)**

stands, book
USE **bookstands**

stands, bouquet
USE **plant stands**

stands, bowl
USE **basin stands**

stands, cabinet
USE **cabinet stands**

stands, cabinets and
USE **cabinets on stands**

stands, cabinets on
USE **cabinets on stands**

stands, cake
USE **muffin stands**

stands, card
USE **card stands**

stands, casket
USE **cabinet stands**

stands, corner
USE **corner shelves**

stands, corner basin
USE **corner basin stands**

stands, corner enclosed basin
USE **corner enclosed basin stands**

stands, dictionary
USE **bookstands**

stands, dressing
USE **dressing stands**

stands, drinking
USE **drinking stands**

stands, enclosed basin
USE **enclosed basin stands**

stands, flower
USE **plant stands**

stands, fruit
USE **produce stands**

stands, gentleman's dressing
USE **gentleman's dressing stands**

stands, globe
USE **globe stands**

stands, hall
USE **hall stands**

stands, hat
USE **hat stands**

stands, hat and cloak
USE **hat stands**

stands, hat and coat
USE **hat stands**

stands, inclosed basin
USE **enclosed basin stands**

stands, kettle
USE **kettle stands**

stands, Koran
USE **Koran stands**

stands, lady's dressing
USE **lady's dressing stands**

stands, map
USE **map stands**

stands, muffin
USE **muffin stands**

stands, music
USE **music stands**

stands, palm
USE **plant stands**

stands, plant
USE **plant stands**

stands, pole and
USE **pole screens**

stands, portfolio
USE **portfolio stands**

stands, produce
USE **produce stands**

stands, reading
USE **music stands**
reading desks

stands, shaving
USE **shaving stands**

stands, smoker's
USE **smokers**

stands, smoking
USE **smoking stands**

stands, smoking (ashtrays)
USE **smokers**

stands, taxi
USE **taxi stands**

stands, tea kettle
USE **kettle stands**
tea tables

stands, telephone
USE **telephone tables**

stands, tiered
USE **tiered stands**

stands, tined kettle
USE **kettle stands**

stands, toilet
USE **basin stands**

stands, towel
USE **towel racks**

stands, tray
USE **tray stands**

stands, umbrella
USE **umbrella stands**

stands, urn
USE **kettle stands**

stands, vegetable
USE **produce stands**

stands, washhand
USE **washstands**

stands, washing
USE **washstands**

stands, Windsor
USE **Windsor stands**

stanhopes
VJ.120

ALT **stanhope**
SN Miniature photographs, mounted under a magnifying glass, that might be inserted in jewelry or used for other decorative purposes. (HCOP)
CN V.VJ.AFU.ARI.ALO.BZY.AFU

stannaries
USE **tin mines**

stannate, lead
USE **lead stannate**

staple extractors
USE **staple pullers**

staple guns
TB.200
ALT **staple gun**
SN Spring-driven guns used to drive staples. (MEANS)
UF guns, staple
staplers (staple guns)
CN V.TB.AFU.ARI.BOK.ARI

staple nails
TF.417
ALT **staple nail**
UF nails, staple
CN V.TF.AFU.AFU.AFU.ALO.AFU.CFS.AFU.DCU.CRG

staple pullers
TB.423 (N)
ALT **staple puller**
UF extractors, staple
pullers, staple
staple extractors
CN V.TB.AFU.ARI.DZW.BIQ

staplers
TB.201 (L,N)
ALT **stapler**
SN Small usually hand-held devices for inserting wire staples that bind two or more materials together. (W)
CN V.TB.AFU.ARI.BOK.AXC

staplers (staple guns)
USE **staple guns**

staples
TF.489 (L)
ALT **staple**
SN Double-pointed, U-shaped pieces of metal used to attach wire mesh, insulation batts, building paper, usually driven with a staple gun. (MEANS)
CN V.TF.AFU.AFU.AFU.ALO.AFU.DZW

stapling
KT.55
ALT **stapled**
CN K.KT.AFU.ALO.BCW.BCW.BIQ

star charts
USE **astronomical charts**

star coral
MT.918
SN Any of numerous stony corals belonging to Orbicella and related genera in which the polyp cavities are round or polygonal and contain conspicuous radiating septa. (W)
UF coral, star
CN M.MT.AFU.AFU.ALO.AFU.BIQ.AFU

star drills
USE **plugging chisels**

star expansion bolts
TF.312
ALT **star expansion bolt**
SN Fasteners used in concrete, consisting of two semicircular shields that are forced apart, to bear on the walls of a hole, as a bolt is driven into the shields. (MEANS)
UF bolts, star expansion
expansion bolts, star
CN V.TF.AFU.AFU.AFU.ALO.AFU.ALO.AFU.AXC.AFU

star-forts
RK.451
ALT **star-fort**
SN Redoubts formed by a number of re-entering and salient angles, the sides of which flank each other. (UMD)
CN V.RK.AFU.ALO.ALO.BIQ.BOK.AXC

star maps
USE **astronomical charts**

star-ribbed vaults
USE **stellar vaults**

star-shaped
USE **stellate**

star vaults
USE **stellar vaults**

Starcevo
FL.2495
CN F.FL.ALO.AXC.AFU.BCW.CFS

starch
MT.1061 (L)
CN M.MT.AFU.AFU.ALO.BIQ.BUE.BUE

starch gum
USE **dextrine**

starch-resist cloth
MT.1886
UF cloth, starch-resist
CN M.MT.AFU.AFU.ARI.ALO.ALO.ALO.ARI.BCW.ALO

starch, arrowroot
USE **arrowroot**

stars
DG.46
ALT **star**
SN Use for the conventionalized figures derived from astronomical stars, having radiating points of any number.
CN D.DG.AFU.AFU.CXA.BCW

Stars of David
DG.47 (L)
ALT **Star of David**
SN Six-pointed stars composed of two equilateral triangles, one superimposed upside down on the other. (HAS)
UF David's shields
Magen Davids
Mogen Davids
Shields of David
shields, David's
CN D.DG.AFU.AFU.CXA.BCW.AFU

starters, screw
USE **gimlets**

starting punches
TB.978 (N)
ALT **starting punch**
SN Plain steel rods, about 8 to 10 inches long, usually tapered toward one end; used for driving bolts out of holes. (SALAM)
UF punches, rivet
punches, starting
rivet punches
CN V.TB.AFU.BCW.CFS.ALO.AFU.DZW.BCW

starved joints
TF.694
ALT **starved joint**
SN Poorly bonded glue joints resulting from the use of too little glue. (MEANS)
UF joints, starved
CN V.TF.ALO.ARI.AXC.ARI.CFS

state and environment
USE **environmental policy**

state arts agencies
USE **art commissions**

state atlases
VW.131
ALT **state atlas**
UF atlases, state
CN V.VW.AFU.AFU.AFU.FZU.AXC.AFU.AFU.AFU.AXC.ARI

state beds
TG.374
ALT **state bed**
SN Grand, lavishly upholstered beds intended for princes and noblemen. (BEARD)
UF beds, state
CN V.TG.AFU.AFU.ARI.AFU.AFU.ERE

state capitols
USE **capitols**

state chairs
TG.166
ALT **state chair**
SN High-back chairs with elaborate ornamentation, made especially for display. (BLACK)
UF chairs, state
CN V.TG.AFU.AFU.ALO.AFU.AFU.ALO.

ARI.ALO

state colleges
RK.845 (L)
ALT **state college**
UF colleges, state
CN V.RK.AFU.ALO.ALO.CXA.ARI.AXC.BIQ.AFU.ARI

state directories
VW.418
ALT **state directory**
UF directories, state
CN V.VW.AFU.AFU.ALO.EWY.AXC.AFU.BOK.AXC

state domain
USE **public domain**

state government
BM.547 (L)
UF government, state
CN B.BM.BOK.BOK.ALO.ARI

state government records
VW.1047 (L)
ALT **state government record**
SN Records made or received by an agency of a state government and maintained in the conduct of state government business.
UF government records, state
records, state government
CN V.VW.AFU.ARI.ALO.BCW.ALO.ALO

state guidebooks
VW.507
ALT **state guidebook**
UF guidebooks, state
CN V.VW.AFU.ALO.AFU.AFU.AFU.BZY.ALO.ALO

state libraries
RK.698 (L)
ALT **state library**
SN Libraries maintained by state funds, whose broad function is to preserve state records and publications for the use of state officials and citizens. (ERIC)
UF libraries, state
CN V.RK.AFU.ALO.ALO.CRG.AXC.AFU.AXC

state maps
VW.230
ALT **state map**
UF maps, state
CN V.VW.AFU.AFU.AFU.FZU.AXC.AFU.ARI.AXC.DUC.BOK

state parks
RK.1466 (A,L)
ALT **state park**
UF parks, state
CN V.RK.ALO.ALO.ARI.ALO.ARI

state penitentiaries
USE **state prisons**

state prisons
RK.729
ALT **state prison**
UF penitentiaries, state
prisons, state
state penitentiaries
CN V.RK.AFU.ALO.ALO.CXA.AFU.AXC.ALO.ARI

state universities
RK.848 (L)
ALT **state university**
UF universities, state
CN V.RK.AFU.ALO.ALO.CXA.ARI.AXC.BIQ.ARI.AFU

statehouses
USE **capitols**

stately homes
USE **mansions**

statements, back
USE **bank statements**

statements, environmental impact
USE **environmental impact statements**

statements, financial
USE **financial statements**

statements, profit and loss
USE **profit and loss statements**

states
HG.810
ALT **state**
CN H.HG.ALO.ALO.BZY

states (nations)
USE **nations**

states, ideal
USE **utopias**

statesmen
HG.704 (L,R)
ALT **statesman**
CN H.HG.AFU.AXC.CFS.CXA

static loads
USE **dead loads**

statically determinate structures
RT.12
ALT **statically determinate structure**
SN Use for structures having no more than three unknown reactions, so that the reactions can be found through simple application of the basic equations of statics.
UF determinate structures
structures, determinate
structures, statically determinate
CN V.RT.AFU.AFU.AFU.AFU.ALO.AXC

statically indeterminate structures
RT.13
ALT **statically indeterminate structure**
SN Use for structures having connections or supports that provide more than the minimum needed for stability.
UF indeterminate structures
structures, indeterminate
structures, statically indeterminate
CN V.RT.AFU.AFU.AFU.AFU.ALO.BCW

statics
BM.903 (L)
SN The relations among forces that produce equilibrium among material bodies. (W)
CN B.BM.CFS.AXC.BIQ.ALO

statics, graphic
USE **graphic statics**

station point
BM.157
SN Includes the implied location in a perspective system where the viewer would be standing and the fixed actual observation point for viewing a perspectival picture.
UF point, station
CN B.BM.AFU.AFU.ARI.BOK.CFS.BCW

stations
RK.1263 (A,L,N,B)
ALT **station**
SN Use for intermediate stopping places along transportation routes; for the end points of such routes, use **terminals.**
UF depots
CN V.RK.AFU.ALO.ALO.GLI.AFU.AXC

stations, ambulance
USE **ambulance stations**

stations, automobile service
USE **service stations**

stations, broadcasting
USE **broadcasting stations**

stations, bus
USE **bus stations**

stations, chair-lift
USE **ski-lift stations**

stations, coastguard
USE **coastguard stations**

stations, earth
USE **satellite tracking stations**

stations, earthquake
USE **seismological stations**

stations, electrical supply
USE **electrical supply stations**

stations, experiment
USE **experiment stations**

stations, filling
USE **service stations**

stations, fire
USE **fire stations**

stations, gasoline
USE **service stations**

stations, generating

USE **power plants**

stations, ground
USE **satellite tracking stations**

stations, ice
USE **ice stations**

stations, lift
USE **pumping stations**

stations, manual
USE **manual stations**

stations, manual fire alarm
USE **manual stations**

stations, meteorological
USE **meteorological stations**

stations, nurses'
USE **nurses' stations**

stations, petrol
USE **service stations**

stations, police
USE **police stations**

stations, power
USE **power plants**

stations, public comfort
USE **comfort stations**

stations, pumping
USE **pumping stations**

stations, radio
USE **radio stations**

stations, railroad
USE **railroad stations**

stations, relay
USE **relay stations**

stations, relay broadcast
USE **relay stations**

stations, repeater
USE **repeater stations**

stations, research
USE **research stations**

stations, satellite tracking
USE **satellite tracking stations**

stations, seismological
USE **seismological stations**

stations, service
USE **service stations**

stations, ski-lift
USE **ski-lift stations**

stations, space
USE **space stations**

stations, subway
USE **subway stations**

stations, telegraph
USE **telegraph stations**

stations, telephone
USE **telephone exchanges**

stations, television
USE **television stations**

stations, transformer
USE **electric substations**

stations, union
USE **union stations**

stations, water pumping
USE **pumping stations**

stations, weather
USE **meteorological stations**

stations, weigh
USE **weigh stations**

statistical areas
RG.261
ALT **statistical area**
UF areas, statistical
CN V.RG.ALO.AFU.AFU.BZY

Statistical Areas, Standard Metropolitan
USE **Standard Metropolitan Statistical Areas**

statistical atlases
VW.127
ALT **statistical atlas**
UF atlases, statistical
CN V.VW.AFU.AFU.AFU.FZU.AXC.AFU.AFU.AFU.ARI

statisticians
HG.347 (L)
ALT **statistician**
CN H.HG.AFU.AXC.BIQ.AFU.AFU.CLM.AFU

statistics
BM.823 (L,B,R)
CN B.BM.CFS.ARI.CRG.AFU

stats
VW.689 (B)
ALT **stat**
SN Use for reproductions, usually of documents, made with the Photostat (TM) machine or similar machines.
UF Photostats (TM)
CN V.VW.AFU.ALO.AFU.DZW.BIQ.CLM

statuary bronze
MT.380
SN Bronze with a smooth, reddish surface used for statues, plaques, hardware, and other objects. (MH12)
UF bronze, statuary
CN M.MT.AFU.AFU.AFU.BZY.AFU.AFU.AFU.ALO.ARI.BCW.ALO.BCW

statuary limestone
MT.700
SN A very fine, uniform-grained buff limestone used for sculpture and fine carvings. (WATSON)
UF limestone, statuary
CN M.MT.AFU.AFU.AFU.DCU.AFU.ALO.AFU.ALO.ALO.ARI.BCW

statuary marble
MT.770
SN Marble of the purest white and of finely crystalline form used in architecture and sculpture. (W)
UF marble, statuary
CN M.MT.AFU.AFU.AFU.DCU.AFU.ARI.ARI.ALO.BUE

statuary marble, Colorado yule
USE **Colorado yule statuary marble**

statuary marble, Vermont white
USE **Vermont white statuary marble**

statuary porcelain
USE **Parian ware**

status, class
USE **social status**

status, social
USE **social status**

status, socioeconomic
USE **social status**

statutes
VW.1027 (L,B,R)
ALT **statute**
SN Acts of a legislature declaring, commanding, or prohibiting something, expressed according to the forms necessary to constitute law. For regulations having the force of law issued by a government agency in order to interpret or implement the provisions of a statute, use **administrative regulations.**
UF instruments, statutory
statutory instruments
CN V.VW.AFU.ARI.ALO.BCW.AFU.ARI.AFU.ARI

statutory instruments
USE **statutes**

stave
MT.2270 (L)
SN One of a number of narrow boards used to build up a curved surface. (DAC)
CN M.MT.AFU.ALO.GRC

stave churches
RK.1099 (A,L,B,R)
ALT **stave church**
SN Wood churches with walls of vertical planks, used from at least the 9th century, especially in Scandinavia.
UF churches, mast
churches, stave
mast churches
CN V.RK.AFU.ALO.ALO.FCS.BIQ.ALO.AFU.AXC

stave wrenches
USE **flagging irons**

stayed bridges
USE **cable-stayed bridges**

stayed cable structures
USE **cable-stayed structures**

stayed girder bridges
USE **cable-stayed bridges**

stays
RT.203
ALT **stay**
SN Use for elements, long in relation to their width and usually set on a diagonal, that serve to stiffen or stabilize a member or a structure.
CN V.RT.AFU.AFU.AFU.AXC.DOI

stays (stretchers)
USE **stretchers**

stays, barn-door
USE **barn-door stays**

stays, casement
USE **casement stays**

steam
MT.326 (L)
CN M.MT.AFU.AFU.AFU.BOK.BOK.ARI.ALO.AFU

steam baths
RK.1072 (L,B)
ALT **steam bath**
UF baths, steam
baths, thermal
baths, vapor
thermal baths
vapor baths
CN V.RK.AFU.ALO.ALO.EWY.BCW.ALO

steam boilers
RT.1413 (L,N)
ALT **steam boiler**
UF boilers, steam
CN V.RT.ALO.BCW.AFU.ALO.AFU.ALO.ALO

steam-electric plants
USE **steam power plants**

steam electric power plants, coal-fired
USE **coal-fired power plants**

steam engines
TB.389 (L,N)
ALT **steam engine**
SN Engines driven or worked by steam. (W)
UF engines, steam
CN V.TB.AFU.ARI.DOI.ALO.ALO

steam heating
RT.1399 (L)
UF heating, steam
CN V.RT.ALO.BCW.AFU.AFU.ARI.BCW

steam power plants
RG.115 (L)
ALT **steam power plant**
UF plants, steam-electric
plants, steam power
power plants, steam
steam-electric plants
CN V.RG.AFU.AFU.BUE.ARI.AXC

steam rooms
RM.82
ALT **steam room**
UF rooms, steam
CN V.RM.AFU.DIO.ALO.ALO.CFS

steam shovels
TB.50 (L)
ALT **steam shovel**
SN Power shovels operated by steam from an integral boiler. (MEANS)
UF shovels, steam
CN V.TB.AFU.ARI.AFU.ARI.BZY.AFU.AFU

steam turbines
TB.400 (L,N)
ALT **steam turbine**
SN Turbines that are driven by the pressure of steam which is discharged at high velocity against the turbine vanes. (W)
UF turbines, steam
CN V.TB.AFU.ARI.DOI.BUE.AXC

steamer chairs
USE **deck chairs**

steamrollers
TB.30 (N)
ALT **steamroller**
SN Steam driven road rollers. (W)
CN V.TB.AFU.ARI.AFU.ALO.ALO.ALO

steamship terminals
USE **marine terminals**

steatite
MT.877 (L)
CN M.MT.AFU.AFU.AFU.DCU.AFU.ARI.BZY.ALO

steatite (white pigment)
USE **talc (white pigment)**

steel
MT.342 (A,L,B,R)
CN M.MT.AFU.AFU.AFU.BZY.AFU.AFU.AFU.AFU.ALO

steel (color)
USE **dark gray**

steel alloys
MT.348 (L,B)
UF alloy steels
alloys, steel
steels, alloy
CN M.MT.AFU.AFU.AFU.BZY.AFU.AFU.AFU.AFU.ALO.AFU.ALO

steel-aluminum alloys
MT.356 (L)
UF alloys, steel-aluminum
CN M.MT.AFU.AFU.AFU.BZY.AFU.AFU.AFU.AFU.ALO.AFU.ALO.AXC

steel blue
USE **Prussian blue**
grayish blue

steel blue, dark
USE **grayish blue**

steel bronze
USE **phosphor bronze**

steel engraving
USE **siderography**

steel foundries
USE **steel mills**

steel gray
USE **dark gray**

steel mills
RK.646 (A,L,N,B)
ALT **steel mill**
UF foundries
mills, steel
steel foundries
steelworks
CN V.RK.AFU.ALO.ALO.CLM.ALO.ALO.AFU.AXC.BUE.AXC

steel rolling mills
USE **rolling mills**

steel squares
USE **carpenter's squares**

steel-to-steel beam hangers
TF.356
ALT **steel-to-steel beam hanger**
UF beam hangers, steel-to-steel
hangers, steel-to-steel beam
CN V.TF.AFU.AFU.AFU.ALO.AFU.BOK.ARI.ALO.AFU

steel wool
MT.480
SN A matted mass of long, fine steel fibers; especially used for cleaning and polishing surfaces. (DAC)
UF wool, steel
CN M.MT.AFU.AFU.AFU.BZY.ALO.BUE

steel, alloy constructional
USE **high-strength low-alloy steel**

steel, austenitic stainless
USE **austenitic stainless steel**

steel, carbon
USE **carbon steel**

steel, chrome
USE **chrome steel**

steel, chrome-vanadium
USE **chrome-vanadium steel**

steel, hardenable stainless
USE **martensitic stainless steel**

steel, high-carbon
USE **high-carbon steel**

steel, high-strength low-alloy
USE **high-strength low-alloy steel**

steel, HSLA
USE **high-strength low-alloy steel**

steel, low-alloy
USE **high-strength low-alloy steel**

steel, low-carbon
USE **low-carbon steel**

steel, machine
USE **low-carbon steel**

steel, machinery
USE **low-carbon steel**

steel, martensitic stainless
USE **martensitic stainless steel**

steel, medium-carbon
USE **medium-carbon steel**

steel, mild
USE **low-carbon steel**

steel, nickel
USE **nickel steel**

steel, ordinary
USE **carbon steel**

steel, plain carbon
USE **carbon steel**

steel, stainless
USE **stainless steel**

steel, straight carbon
USE **carbon steel**

steel, structural
USE **structural steel**

steel, titanium
USE **titanium steel**

steels, alloy
USE **steel alloys**

steelwork
MT.2772 (L)
CN M.MT.AFU.AXC.BOK.BOK

steelworks
USE **steel mills**

steeplejacks
HG.612 (L)
ALT **steeplejack**
CN H.HG.AFU.AXC.BZY.AFU.FOG

steeples
RM.400 (A,L,B,R)
ALT **steeple**
SN Use for towers terminated by spires or approximations of spires; refers to the entire construction of tower, spire, and lantern, if present.
CN V.RM.AFU.DOI.AFU

steeples, crown
USE **crown steeples**

steeples, rood
USE **crossing towers**

steinkisten
USE **megalithic chamber tombs**

stelae
RK.903 (A,L,B)
ALT **stele**
SN Upright stone slabs, plain or decorated, used as commemorative markers.
CN V.RK.AFU.ALO.ALO.DOI.AFU.BOK

stellar vaults
RT.554
ALT **stellar vault**
SN Vaults whose rib patterns suggest a star. (HAS)
UF star-ribbed vaults
star vaults
vaults, star
vaults, star-ribbed
vaults, stellar
CN V.RT.AFU.AFU.AFU.BIQ.BOK.AFU.ARI.AFU.ALO.AXC

stellate
DC.117
UF star-shaped
CN D.DC.AFU.ARI.FCS.BCW

stencil duplicating
KT.184
SN A method of producing multiple copies of documents from a specially prepared wax master. A particular kind of ink is forced through the cuts in the stencil and transferred to the paper. (LG)
UF duplicating, stencil
CN K.KT.AFU.ALO.DUC.BOK.ARI

stencilers
HG.113
ALT **stenciler**
CN H.HG.AFU.AXC.AXC.AFU.AFU.ALO.AXC.CXA.ALO.ARI

stenciling
KT.752 (A,L,R)
ALT **stenciled**
SN Method of creating multiple copies of a design by cutting it out of a thin yet durable sheet, such as thin brass or plastic, and dabbing, pouncing, spraying, or rubbing a color substance through the openings. (MAYER)
CN K.KT.AFU.ALO.HCQ.ALO.BUE

stencils (images)
VB.14 (A,L)
ALT **stencil (image)**
SN Images produced by using sheets of celluloid, cardboard, or other material in which desired lettering or designs have been cut out so that ink or paint applied to the sheets will reproduce the designs on the surface beneath. (AHD)
CN V.VB.AFU.AFU.BIQ

stenographer's chairs
USE **typewriter chairs**

stenographer's stools
USE **typewriter chairs**

stenographers
HG.35 (L)
ALT **stenographer**
CN H.HG.AFU.AXC.ALO.BOK.AFU.ALO

step-and-hook devices
USE **stepped frets**

step chairs
TG.198 (N)
ALT **step chair**
SN Chairs convertible into a stepladder. (W)
UF chairs, step
chairs, step-ladder
step-ladder chairs
CN V.TG.AFU.AFU.ALO.AFU.AFU.ALO.FCS

step gables
USE **crow-stepped gables**

step-ladder chairs
USE **step chairs**

step nosing planes
USE **nosing planes**

step ornament
USE **step pattern**

step pattern
DG.132
SN A pattern in which a series of small right angles produces a steplike edge, usually proceeding a few steps up and then down again.
UF ornament, step
pattern, step
pattern, stepped
step ornament
stepped pattern
CN D.DG.AFU.ARI.ALO.BIQ.BOK

step stools
TG.259 (L,N)
ALT **step stool**
SN Stools with one or two steps that often fold away beneath the seat. (W)
UF stools, step
CN V.TG.AFU.AFU.ALO.AFU.ALO.ALO.AXC

stepladders
TB.486 (N)
ALT **stepladder**
SN Portable sets of flat broad steps or treads, with a frame hinged to the back for steadying. (W)
CN V.TB.AFU.ARI.ERE.ALO.BUE

stepped arches
RT.261
ALT **stepped arch**
SN Use for arches in which some or all

of the voussoirs have their edges cut horizontally and vertically, so as to continue or parallel the jambs of the wall.
UF arches, stepped
CN V.RT.AFU.AFU.AFU.BCW.AFU.AFU.AFU.ELK.CFS

stepped flashing
RT.738
SN Metal flashing used at the intersection of a wall and a sloping roof; the upper edge steps up to follow the general inclination of the roof. (DAC)
UF flashing, stepped
CN V.RT.AFU.ALO.AFU.BCW.ARI

stepped frets
DG.142
ALT **stepped fret**
SN Decorative motif comprised of diagonally rising steps and ending in an angular curved hook.
UF devices, step-and-hook
frets, stepped
hooks, steps and
step-and-hook devices
steps and hooks
xicalcoliuhqui
CN D.DG.AFU.ARI.ALO.CFS.AFU

stepped pattern
USE **step pattern**

stepped wells
USE **baolis**

steps
RT.1111 (L,B)
ALT **step**
SN Stair units that consist of one tread and one riser, or any similar element providing a horizontal surface on which to support the foot of a person descending or ascending. (DAC)
CN V.RT.AFU.BIQ.AXC.ALO.BIQ.AFU

steps and hooks
USE **stepped frets**

steps, balanced
USE **balanced steps**

steps, bed
USE **bed steps**

steps, bullnose
USE **bullnose steps**

steps, commode
USE **commode steps**

steps, corbel
USE **crowsteps**

steps, dancing
USE **balanced steps**

steps, hanging
USE **hanging steps**

steps, library
USE **library steps**

steps, radial
USE **winders (steps)**

steps, spandrel
USE **spandrel steps**

steps, tapered
USE **winders (steps)**

steps, turret
USE **turret steps**

steps, wheel
USE **winders (steps)**

stereo cameras
USE **stereoscopic cameras**

stereo cards
USE **stereographs**

stereo pairs
USE **stereoscopic photographs**

stereo views
USE **stereoscopic photographs**

stereobates
RM.15
ALT **stereobate**
SN Use for substructures supporting the columns of Greek temples.
CN V.RM.AFU.BOK.ALO

stereograms
USE **stereographs**
stereoscopic photographs

stereographs
VJ.104 (N)
ALT **stereograph**
SN Use for stereoscopic photographs that are prints mounted on cards. Sometimes used as a synonym of stereoscopic photographs.
UF card stereographs
stereo cards
stereograms
CN V.VJ.AFU.ARI.AFU.BOK.ARI

stereographs, parallax
USE **parallax stereographs**

stereographs, tissue
USE **tissue stereographs**

stereophotogrammetry
USE **photogrammetry**

stereophotographs
USE **stereoscopic photographs**

stereophotography
USE **stereoscopic photography**

stereos (photographs)
USE **stereoscopic photographs**

stereoscopes
TB.340 (L,N)
ALT **stereoscope**
SN Viewers in which pairs of stereoscopic images combine when viewed into a single image with apparent depth. (LANG)
CN V.TB.AFU.ARI.CLM.ARI.ARI.AFU

stereoscopic cameras
TB.304 (L,N)
ALT **stereoscopic camera**
SN Cameras designed to take simultaneous images of the same subject from viewpoints separated by the same distance as that between the eyes. (LANG)
UF cameras, stereo
cameras, stereoscopic
stereo cameras
CN V.TB.AFU.ARI.CLM.ARI.AFU.AFU.ALO.BCW

stereoscopic photographs
VJ.101 (N)
ALT **stereoscopic photograph**
SN Use for pairs of photographs taken with two lenses such that, when viewed with special devices, the two images appear to form a single, three-dimensional image. May be daguerreotypes, negatives, or other forms. For those mounted on cards, the most common type, use **stereographs.**
UF photographs, stereoscopic
stereo pairs
stereo views
stereograms
stereophotographs
stereos (photographs)
sterescopic views
views, stereo
CN V.VJ.AFU.ARI.AFU.BOK

stereoscopic photography
KT.390 (L,R)
SN Use for techniques to produce the appearance of three-dimensionality in photographs by using two images made at slightly different positions, mounting them side-by-side, and viewing the pair through a stereoscope or other device.
UF photography, stereoscopic
stereophotography
CN K.KT.AFU.ALO.DUC.DIO.ARI.ARI.BOK

stereotomy
KT.161 (L,R)
SN Process of cutting solid materials, such as stone, into certain shapes or figures. (RHDEL2)
CN K.KT.AFU.ALO.DOI.DZW

stereotypers
HG.464
ALT **stereotyper**
CN H.HG.AFU.AXC.BUE.ALO.CFS.CFS

sterescopic views
USE **stereoscopic photographs**

sterling silver
MT.405
UF silver, sterling
CN M.MT.AFU.AFU.AFU.BZY.AFU.AFU.AFU.ALO.BOK.AFU

stibium
USE **antimony**

Stichbandkeramik
FL.2504
UF Banded ware, Incised
Incised Banded ware
Stroked ware
ware, Incised Banded
ware, Stroked
CN F.FL.ALO.AXC.AFU.BCW.DCU.AFU.ALO

stick
MT.2271 (L,R)
CN M.MT.AFU.ALO.GWW

stick-back chairs
USE **spindle-back chairs**

stick chairs (sedan chairs)
USE **sedan chairs**

Stick Style
FL.1740 (A,L,R)
CN F.FL.ALO.ALO.BCW.AFU.BUE.BZY

sticks, bed
USE **bed slats**

sticks, chalk
USE **chalk sticks**

sticks, charcoal
USE **charcoal sticks**

sticks, gig
USE **radius tools**

stiff-mud brick
MT.139
SN Brick made of clay mixed with only enough water to produce plasticity, and extruded through a die.
UF brick, stiff-mud
CN M.MT.AFU.AFU.AFU.AXC.ALO.AFU.AXC.ALO.AXC

stiffness
BM.957
SN The material property which is measured by the rate at which the stress in a material increases with strain. (MH)
CN B.BM.CFS.AXC.BZY.BOK.CFS

stigmatization
BM.689 (L,R)
SN The appearance of wounds on the hands, feet, and side corresponding to those received by Christ upon crucifixion, which have appeared, inexplicably, on some people who intensely contemplate the Passion of Christ. (NCE)
CN B.BM.BZY.ALO.AFU.BZY

Stijl, De
USE **De Stijl**

stil de grain brun
USE **Dutch pink**

stil de grain vert
USE **Dutch pink**

Stile Boito
FL.3399
CN F.FL.ALO.BCW.ALO.AXC.DIO.BOK.ARI.AFU

Stile Floreale
USE **Stile Liberty**

Stile Liberty
FL.3397 (A,L,B,R)
UF Liberty Style
Neo-Liberty
Stile Floreale
CN F.FL.ALO.BCW.ALO.AXC.DIO.BOK.ALO

Stile Umberto
FL.3400
UF Cinquecentismo
Neo-cinquecento
CN F.FL.ALO.BCW.ALO.AXC.DIO.BOK.ARI.ALO

stiles
RT.825
ALT **stile**
SN Vertical members in woodwork or furniture, such as in a door, a sash, or a chest of drawers, into which secondary members are fitted.
CN V.RT.AFU.ALO.ALO.AXC

stiles (stairs)
RT.1096 (N)
ALT **stile (stair)**
SN Sets of steps, or frameworks of bars and steps, for crossing over a fence or wall. (DAC)
CN V.RT.AFU.BIQ.AXC.AFU.ALO.BCW

stiles, butt
USE **hinge stiles**

stiles, hanging
USE **hinge stiles**

stiles, hinge
USE **hinge stiles**

stiles, lock
USE **lock stiles**

stiles, locking
USE **lock stiles**

stiles, shutting
USE **lock stiles**

still lifes
VB.78 (L,R)
ALT **still life**
CN V.VB.AFU.AXC.BOK

still photographers
HG.123
ALT **still photographer**
UF photographers, still
CN H.HG.AFU.AXC.AXC.AFU.AFU.ALO.AXC.DOI.BCW

Stillbay
FL.56
CN F.FL.ALO.AFU.AFU.ALO.ARI.AFU

stilling basins
RM.464 (L)
ALT **stilling basin**
SN Depressions in a channel or reservoir deep enough to reduce the turbulence or velocity of the flow. (W)
UF basins, stilling
CN V.RM.ALO.ALO.AFU.AXC

stillrooms
RM.203
ALT **stillroom**
CN V.RM.AFU.DIO.ALO.DCU.CRG

stills
USE **distilleries**

stills (photographs)
USE **film stills**

stills, film
USE **film stills**

stilt houses
RK.254 (B)
ALT **stilt house**
UF houses, stilt
CN V.RK.AFU.ALO.ALO.AXC.ALO.AFU.CLM.BUE

stilted arches
RT.244
ALT **stilted arch**
SN Arches whose curves begin above the impost. (HAS)
UF arches, stilted
CN V.RT.AFU.AFU.AFU.BCW.AFU.AFU.AFU.DZW

stilted vaults
RT.533
ALT **stilted vault**
SN Compound vaults in which intersecting barrel vaults are of differing widths, the ridges of the same height but the springing lines of different height, producing a groin line of double curvature. (RS)
UF vaults, stilted
CN V.RT.AFU.AFU.AFU.BIQ.BOK.AFU.AFU.AFU.ALO.ALO.ALO

stilts
RT.201 (A)
ALT **stilt**
SN Use for posts that raise a structure above ground or water level.
CN V.RT.AFU.AFU.AFU.AXC.DCU.ALO.ALO

stipple engravers

HG.128 (L)
ALT **stipple engraver**
UF engravers, stipple
CN H.HG.AFU.AXC.AXC.AFU.AFU.ALO.AXC.DUC.AFU.ALO

stipple engraving
KT.455 (L)
SN Use for the printmaking technique used much in the late 18th and early 19th centuries for the reproduction of drawings in which the design was laid into the plate with dotted lines.
UF engraving, stipple
CN K.KT.AFU.ALO.DUC.DUC.ALO.BCW.AFU.ARI.AXC

stippling
KT.698 (L)
ALT **stippled**
SN Use for the process or effect of applying paint, ink, or other medium in small dots.
CN K.KT.AFU.ALO.GRC.BUE.BCW

stirring rods
TB.337 (N)
ALT **stirring rod**
SN Glass or plastic rods often having a thick disc at one end for crushing tablets or crystals; used to stir solutions while dissolving chemicals. (FOCAL)
UF mixing rods
rods, mixing
rods, stirring
CN V.TB.AFU.ARI.CLM.ARI.ALO.CLM

stitching
KT.569
ALT **stitched**
SN Fastening together materials by an in-and-out movement of thread or wire. (W)
CN K.KT.AFU.ALO.ELK.DUC.ARI.ALO

stitching, flat
USE **side sewing**

stitching, side
USE **side sewing**

stitching, stab
USE **side sewing**

stoas
RK.1199 (A,L)
ALT **stoa**
CN V.RK.AFU.ALO.ALO.FUA.BUE

stock brick
MT.132
UF brick, stock
CN M.MT.AFU.AFU.AFU.AXC.ALO.AFU.AXC.ALO.AFU.ARI

stock certificates
VW.835 (L,N)
ALT **stock certificate**
SN Certificates of a corporation or joint stock company that a named person is owner of the designated number of shares of stock. (BLACKS)
UF certificates of stock
certificates, share
certificates, stock
share certificates
stock, certificates of
CN V.VW.AFU.ARI.AFU.BIQ.CFS.BOK

stock exchanges
RK.135 (A,L,B,R)
ALT **stock exchange**
UF exchanges, stock
CN V.RK.AFU.ALO.ALO.ALO.ALO.ALO.ALO

stock howels
USE **howell planes**

stock inventories
USE **merchandise inventories**

stock knives
USE **block knives**

stock, certificates of
USE **stock certificates**

stock, dimension
USE **dimension lumber**

stockades
RK.455
ALT **stockade**
CN V.RK.AFU.ALO.ALO.BIQ.CLM

stockades, elephant
USE **elephant houses**

stockbrokers
HG.408 (L)
ALT **stockbroker**
CN H.HG.AFU.AXC.BOK.BZY.AFU.AFU

stocks
USE **braces (woodworking tools)**

stocks, bit
USE **braces (woodworking tools)**

stocks, breast
USE **braces (woodworking tools)**

stockyards
RK.1567 (A,L)
ALT **stockyard**
SN Enclosed spaces with pens, stables, and sheds, where beef cattle are confined for fattening prior to market; usually associated with a railroad line.
CN V.RK.ALO.ALO.BOK

stoicism
BM.525 (R)
CN B.BM.BIQ.AXC.ERE

stomps
USE **stumps**

stone
MT.578 (A,B,R)
CN M.MT.AFU.AFU.AFU.DCU

Stone Age
FL.7 (L,R)
UF Age, Stone
CN F.FL.AFU.BCW.AFU

Stone Age, Middle
USE **Mesolithic**

Stone Age, New
USE **Neolithic**

Stone Age, Old
USE **Paleolithic**

stone anchors
TF.303
ALT **stone anchor**
UF anchors, stone
CN V.TF.AFU.AFU.AFU.ALO.AFU.AFU.CRG.ARI

stone brick
USE **hard-burned brick**

stone circles
USE **cromlechs**

stone-cutters' marks
USE **masons' marks**

stone dust
MT.895
SN Pulverized stone used to fill the spaces between irregular stones and produce a stable surface. (DAC)
UF dust, stone
pulverized stone
stone, pulverized
CN M.MT.AFU.AFU.AFU.DCU.ALO.CXA

stone green
USE **green earth**

stone hands
USE **makeup arrangers**

stone ocher
USE **Oxford ocher**

stone pine, Japanese
USE **Japanese stone pine**

stone quarries
USE **quarries**

stone tables
USE **megalithic chamber tombs**

stone yellow
USE **Oxford ocher**

stone, Alberene
USE **Alberene stone**

stone, Armenian
USE **azurite**

stone, artificial
USE **artificial stone**

stone, Barnack
USE **Barnack stone**

stone, Bath

USE **Bath stone**

stone, Bedford
USE **Bedford stone**

stone, beer
USE **beer stone**

stone, Bologna
USE **blanc fixe**

stone, broken
USE **crushed stone**

stone, building
USE **building stone**

stone, Caen
USE **Caen stone**

stone, cement
USE **hydraulic limestone**

stone, China
USE **petuntze**

stone, Claudian
USE **Porta Santa marble**

stone, clay
USE **clay stone**

stone, clipsham
USE **clipsham stone**

stone, coade
USE **coade stone**

stone, concretionary
USE **concretionary stone**

stone, coral
USE **coral limestone**

stone, crushed
USE **crushed stone**

stone, cut
USE **dimension stone**

stone, dimension
USE **dimension stone**

stone, dressed
USE **dressed stone**

stone, druid
USE **sarsen**

stone, gingerbread
USE **carstone**

stone, kane
USE **Caen stone**

stone, Ketton
USE **Ketton stone**

stone, lithograph
USE **solnhofen stone**

stone, lithographic
USE **solnhofen stone**

stone, Lydian
USE **touchstone**

stone, Minnesota
USE **Minnesota stone**

stone, monumental
USE **monumental stone**

stone, pagoda
USE **pagoda stone**

stone, paving
USE **paving stone**

stone, Portland
USE **Portland stone**

stone, pulverized
USE **stone dust**

stone, purbeck
USE **purbeck marble**

stone, reigate
USE **reigate stone**

stone, solnhofen
USE **solnhofen stone**

stone, vein
USE **ultramarine blue**

stone, Weldon
USE **Weldon stone**

stone, Wyoming Valley
USE **Wyoming Valley stone**

stonecutter's chisels
USE **tooth chisels**

stonecutters
HG.613 (R)
ALT **stonecutter**
CN H.HG.AFU.AXC.BZY.AFU.FUA

stonecutting
KT.90 (A,L,B,R)
SN Use generally for the process of cutting or dressing stone.
CN K.KT.AFU.ALO.BUE.AXC

stonemasons
HG.601 (A,L,B,R)
ALT **stonemason**
CN H.HG.AFU.AXC.BZY.AFU.DIO.AXC

stones, altar
USE **mensas**

stones, barge
USE **barge stones**

stones, boundary
USE **boundary stones**

stones, carborundum
USE **carborundum stones**

stones, heel
USE **heel stones**

stones, lich
USE **lich stones**

stones, oil
USE **oil stones**

stones, parpend
USE **perpends**

stones, precious
USE **precious stones**

stones, rubbing
USE **floatstones**

stones, semiprecious
USE **semiprecious stones**

stones, sharpening
USE **whetstones**

stones, standing
USE **standing stones**

stones, table
USE **megalithic chamber tombs**

stones, through
USE **perpends**

stoneware
MT.157 (L,R)
CN M.MT.AFU.AFU.AFU.AXC.ALO.ALO.AFU.ALO.ARI

stoneware, Nassau
USE **Westerwald stoneware**

stoneware, Punch'ong
USE **Punch'ong ware**

stoneware, Westerwald
USE **Westerwald stoneware**

stonework
MT.2755 (A,L,B)
SN Masonry construction in stone. (DAC)
CN M.MT.AFU.AXC.BIQ.AFU.ARI

Stoney
USE **Assiniboin**

stools
TG.232 (L,N,B,R)
ALT **stool**
SN Most common type of seat furniture until the 19th century. Distinct from **benches** in that they seat only one person; usually distinguished from **chairs** in that they have no back, however, tall seating pieces at a bar or counter are called stools though they sometimes have backs. Generally made in two types; one supported on four straight legs and the other with legs arranged crosswise.
UF sellae
CN V.TG.AFU.AFU.ALO.AFU.ALO

stools, bar
USE **barstools**

stools, box
USE **box stools**

stools, buffet
USE **buffet stools**

stools, close

USE **close stools**

stools, coffin
USE **joint stools**

stools, counter
USE **counter stools**

stools, creepie
USE **cutty stools**

stools, cricket
USE **cricket stools**

stools, cricket (buffet stools)
USE **buffet stools**

stools, cross-legged
USE **folding stools**

stools, cutty
USE **cutty stools**

stools, dressing
USE **dressing stools**

stools, fender
USE **fender stools**

stools, fishing
USE **fishing stools**

stools, folding
USE **folding stools**

stools, French (window seats)
USE **window seats**

stools, gout
USE **gout stools**

stools, hearth
USE **fender stools**

stools, joint
USE **joint stools**

stools, joyned
USE **joint stools**

stools, library
USE **library steps**

stools, low
USE **joint stools**

stools, lunch
USE **counter stools**

stools, lunch counter
USE **counter stools**

stools, milking
USE **milking stools**

stools, music
USE **music stools**

stools, necessary
USE **close stools**

stools, piano
USE **music stools**

stools, prayer
USE **prayer stools**

stools, revolving
USE **revolving stools**

stools, rotary
USE **revolving stools**

stools, screw
USE **revolving stools**

stools, stacking
USE **stacking stools**

stools, stenographer
USE **typewriter chairs**

stools, step
USE **step stools**

stools, swivel
USE **revolving stools**

stools, Thebes
USE **Thebes stools**

stools, three-legged
USE **three-legged stools**

stools, vanity
USE **dressing stools**

stools, window
USE **window seats**

stools, Windsor
USE **Windsor stools**

stoops
RM.55
ALT **stoop**
SN Porches, platforms, entrance stairways, or small verandas at house doors. (W)
CN V.RM.AFU.DIO.AFU.BCW.BOK

stoops, box
USE **box stoops**

stop bead screws
TF.477
ALT **stop bead screw**
UF bead screws, stop
screws, stop bead
CN V.TF.AFU.AFU.AFU.ALO.AFU.DIO.AFU.BOK.AFU

stop keys
TF.540
ALT **stop key**
UF keys, stop
CN V.TF.AFU.ALO.ARI.AFU.CRG

stop lights
USE **traffic signals**

stop moldings
RT.757
ALT **stop molding**
SN Struck moldings which are terminated short of the end of the member into which they are cut. (DAC)
UF moldings, stop
CN V.RT.AFU.ALO.AFU.BOK.AFU.AFU.ALO.ALO

stop screws
TF.476
ALT **stop screw**
UF screws, stop
CN V.TF.AFU.AFU.AFU.ALO.AFU.DIO.AFU.BOK

stopping knives (putty knives)
USE **putty knives**

stops, bench
USE **bench stops**

stops, bench (bench dogs)
USE **bench dogs**

stops, truck
USE **truck stops**

stopways
USE **overruns**

storage
BM.211 (B)
CN B.BM.AFU.ALO.BZY

storage and retrieval services, information
USE **information retrieval services**

storage devices
TB.173 (L)
ALT **storage device**
SN Computer devices that can receive data and retain it for subsequent retrieval. (DOC)
UF computer storage devices
devices, computer storage
devices, storage
storage devices, computer
CN V.TB.AFU.ARI.BCW.AXC.BCW

storage devices, computer
USE **storage devices**

storage facilities
RK.1206
ALT **storage facility**
UF facilities, storage
CN V.RK.AFU.ALO.ALO.GFO

storage racks
USE **racks**

storage settles
USE **box settles**

storage systems, ice
USE **ice storage systems**

storage systems, water
USE **water storage systems**

storage tanks
RK.1220 (L,N)
ALT **storage tank**
UF tanks, storage
CN V.RK.AFU.ALO.ALO.GFO.BOK

storage tanks, liquid gas
USE **gasoline tanks**

storage tanks, oil
USE **oil storage tanks**

storage tanks, water
USE **water storage tanks**

storage, information
USE **information storage**

storax
MT.1509
SN Grayish brown, fragrant balsam obtained from the bark of an Asiatic tree. (W)
CN M.MT.AFU.AFU.ALO.BOK.DZW

store buildings
USE **stores**

store-door handles
TF.92
ALT **store-door handle**
SN Heavy grips or pulls mounted on sectional or elongated plates and provided with a thumbpiece to operate the latch trip of a store-door lock. (BROWNL)
UF handles, store-door
CN V.TF.AFU.AFU.AFU.AFU.CFS.BIQ

store-door locks
TF.244
ALT **store-door lock**
UF locks, store-door
CN V.TF.AFU.AFU.AFU.AFU.DIO.BIQ .ALO.ALO.CLM

store-door locks, combined
USE **combined store-door locks**

storefronts
RT.599 (A,L,B,R)
ALT **storefront**
SN Sides of stores or store buildings facing a street and usually containing window display spaces. (RHDEL2)
UF fronts, shop
shop fronts
CN V.RT.AFU.AFU.AFU.BIQ.BUE.AFU. ARI.ALO.AFU.AFU.ARI

storehouses
USE **warehouses**

storerooms
RM.204 (B)
ALT **storeroom**
UF lumber rooms
rooms, lumber
CN V.RM.AFU.DIO.ALO.DCU.CXA

stores
RK.148 (A,L,N,B,R)
ALT **store**
UF buildings, store
shops (stores)
store buildings
CN V.RK.AFU.ALO.ALO.ALO.ARI.BIQ

stores, antique
USE **antique stores**

stores, chain
USE **chain stores**

stores, clothing
USE **clothing stores**

stores, company
USE **company stores**

stores, confectionery
USE **confectioneries**

stores, convenience
USE **convenience stores**

stores, cooperative
USE **cooperative stores**

stores, country
USE **general stores**

stores, department
USE **department stores**

stores, dime
USE **variety stores**

stores, discount
USE **discount houses**

stores, five-and-ten-cent
USE **variety stores**

stores, furniture
USE **furniture stores**

stores, general
USE **general stores**

stores, grocery
USE **grocery stores**

stores, hardware
USE **hardware stores**

stores, industrial
USE **company stores**

stores, jewelry
USE **jewelry stores**

stores, ordnance
USE **ordnance depots**

stores, outlet
USE **outlet stores**

stores, pet
USE **pet shops**

stores, retail
USE **retail stores**

stores, secondhand
USE **thrift shops**

stores, self-service
USE **self-service stores**

stores, shoe
USE **shoe stores**

stores, specialty
USE **specialty stores**

stores, sporting goods
USE **sporting goods stores**

stores, tea
USE **tea stores**

stores, ten-cent
USE **variety stores**

stores, toy
USE **toy stores**

stores, variety
USE **variety stores**

storicismo
USE **historicism**

stories
RM.409 (N)
ALT **story**
SN Use for the habitable spaces between two floors of a building or between a floor and the roof, and for the horizontal divisions of the exteriors of buildings which tend to correspond to this division of the interior spaces.
UF floors (stories)
stages (stories)
CN V.RM.AFU.DUC

storm caves
USE **storm cellars**

storm cellars
RM.145
ALT **storm cellar**
SN Use for wholly or partially underground refuges from tornadoes or other violent storms.
UF caves, storm
cellars, cyclone
cellars, storm
cellars, tornado
cyclone cellars
storm caves
tornado cellars
CN V.RM.AFU.DIO.ALO.BZY.ALO

storm doors
RT.863 (L)
ALT **storm door**
UF doors, storm
doors, weather
weather doors
CN V.RT.AFU.ARI.AFU.AFU.AFU.ALO .ARI.AFU.ALO.ARI

storm drainage systems
USE **storm water systems**

storm drains
RT.1458 (L)
ALT **storm drain**
SN Drains used for conveying rainwater, subsurface water, condensate, cooling water, or other similar discharges, but not sewage or industrial waste, to point of disposal. (DAC)
UF drains, storm
CN V.RT.ALO.BCW.ALO.ARI.AXC.ARI

storm sewers
RK.546 (L)

ALT **storm sewer**
UF sewers, storm
CN V.RK.AFU.ALO.ALO.CFS.ALO.AFU.ALO.AFU.ARI

storm water retention basins
RK.581 (L)
ALT **storm water retention basin**
UF basins, storm water retention
basins, water retention
retention basins, storm water
retention basins, water
water retention basins
CN V.RK.AFU.ALO.ALO.CFS.ALO.BCW.BZY

storm water systems
RT.1450
ALT **storm water system**
UF drainage systems, storm
storm drainage systems
systems, storm drainage
systems, storm water
water systems, storm
CN V.RT.ALO.BCW.ALO.ALO

storm windows
RT.956 (L)
ALT **storm window**
UF windows, storm
CN V.RT.AFU.ARI.AFU.AFU.BOK.AFU.ALO.ARI

stormproof building
USE **stormproof construction**

stormproof construction
KT.47 (L)
UF building, stormproof
construction, stormproof
stormproof building
CN K.KT.AFU.ALO.BCW.ARI.ALO.BCW

storms
KM.113 (L,B,R)
SN Violent disturbances of the atmosphere attended by wind and usually by rain, snow, sleet, and hail. (W)
CN K.KM.AFU.CXA.BIQ

storms, ice
USE **ice storms**

stoups
RM.57 (R)
ALT **stoup**
SN Basins at the entrance of a church used to contain holy water. (W)
UF holy water stoups
CN V.RM.AFU.DIO.AFU.BCW.BOK.ALO

stove bolts
TF.326
ALT **stove bolt**
SN Common bolts each having a round or flat head and a slot for a screwdriver. (MEANS)
UF bolts, stove
CN V.TF.AFU.AFU.AFU.ALO.AFU.ALO.ALO.BIQ

stoves
TB.102 (A,L,N,B,R)
ALT **stove**
SN Portable or fixed apparatuses that furnish heat for warmth or cooking, commonly using coal, oil, gas, wood, or electricity as a source of power. (RHDEL2)
CN V.TB.AFU.ARI.ALO.ARI.AXC

stoves (greenhouses)
USE **greenhouses**

stoves, palm
USE **palm houses**

stovewood construction
KT.37 (A,L)
SN Building technique using short firewood-sized logs set in piles perpendicular to the length of walls and held in place by mortar or wooden frames. (WB&S)
UF construction, log-end
construction, stackwood
construction, stovewood
log-end construction
stackwood construction
CN K.KT.AFU.ALO.BCW.ARI.AFU.BOK.AFU

stowing adzes
USE **trussing adzes**

Straight
FL.3303
SN Use with regard to a photography style of the early 20th century.
CN F.FL.ALO.BCW.ALO.AXC.DCU.CRG

straight arches
USE **flat arches**

straight-back easy chairs
USE **square easy chairs**

straight banding
DG.110
SN Decorative inlaid border of contrasting woods cut along the length of the grain, generally used on the edges and rims of furniture. (DDA)
UF banding, straight
CN D.DG.AFU.ARI.ALO.ARI.AFU.ARI

straight block planes
USE **strike blocks**

straight carbon steel
USE **carbon steel**

straight flights
USE **straight stairs**

straight-front
DC.111
CN D.DC.AFU.ARI.EWY.CLM

straight-front desks
USE **fall-front desks**

straight legs
USE **Marlborough legs**

straight-lip tongs
USE **flat tongs**

straight-peen hammers
TB.462 (N)
ALT **straight-peen hammer**
SN Hammers having a blunt chisel-shaped peen whose edge is parallel to the handle. (DAC)
UF hammers, straight-peen
CN V.TB.AFU.ARI.ELK.AFU.ALO.ARI

straight-run stairs
USE **straight stairs**

straight stairs
RT.1080
ALT **straight stair**
SN Stairs which rise in one direction only, without turns. (RS)
UF flights, straight
stairs, straight
stairs, straight-run
straight flights
straight-run stairs
CN V.RT.AFU.BIQ.AXC.AFU.AFU.BOK

straight tracks
USE **leys**

straightedges
TB.451
ALT **straightedge**
SN Any flat heavy bar used for ruling and cutting mats, paper, leather, glass, and other materials in a straight line. (MAYER)
CN V.TB.AFU.ARI.EFQ.ALO.CLM

strainers, web
USE **web strainers**

straining arches
RT.276
ALT **straining arch**
SN Use for arches serving to resist thrust, as in flying buttresses.
UF arches, straining
CN V.RT.AFU.AFU.AFU.BCW.AFU.AFU.ALO.ARI

straining beams
RT.508
ALT **straining beam**
SN In a truss, horizontal struts above the tie beam or above a line joining the feet of the rafters, commonly between the joists at mid-span. (DAC)
UF beams, straining
pieces, strutting
strutting pieces
CN V.RT.AFU.AFU.AFU.BIQ.ARI.ALO.ALO.ALO.AXC

strains
BM.915 (L,R)
SN Ratios of change in size or shape of elements subjected to stress to the

original size or shape of those elements. (DS)
CN B.BM.CFS.AXC.BIQ.ARI.AXC

strap
MT.2272
CN M.MT.AFU.ALO.HCQ

strap anchors
TF.304
ALT **strap anchor**
UF anchors, strap
CN V.TF.AFU.AFU.AFU.ALO.AFU.AFU.CXA

strap footings
USE **continuous footings**

strap hinges
TF.130
ALT **strap hinge**
SN Surface-mounted hinges with one leaf or both leaves elongated to accommodate additional fasteners. (MEANS)
UF flap hinges
hinges, flap
hinges, strap
CN V.TF.AFU.AFU.AFU.AFU.CLM.AFU.FUA.AFU

strap ornament
USE **strapwork**

straphangers
TF.339
ALT **straphanger**
CN V.TF.AFU.AFU.AFU.ALO.AFU.BOK.AFU.ALO

strapped walls
USE **battened walls**

strapple chairs
USE **smoking chairs**

strappo
KT.738
SN The process by which a fresco is detached when the plaster on which it is painted has greatly deteriorated; the color layer is removed by a strong glue without removing excessive amounts of plaster. (FFF)
CN K.KT.AFU.ALO.HCQ.AFU.ALO

straps (hardware)
TF.490 (N)
ALT **strap (hardware)**
SN Metal plates fastened across the intersection of two or more timbers. (MEANS)
CN V.TF.AFU.AFU.AFU.ALO.AFU.EFQ

straps, hinge
USE **hinge straps**

strapwork
DG.152 (L,R)
SN Ornament consisting of twisted and intertwined bands (based on leather strips or ribbons); popular in Northern Europe during the 16th and 17th centuries and in 19th-century revivals. (LDDO)
UF ornament, strap
rollwork
strap ornament
CN D.DG.AFU.ARI.ALO.CXA

Strasbourg faïence
FL.3223
UF faïence and porcelain, Strasbourg
faïence, Strasbourg
porcelain, Strasbourg
pottery, Strasbourg
Strasbourg porcelain
Strasbourg pottery
CN F.FL.ALO.BCW.ALO.ARI.BIQ.BIQ.ARI.ALO.AXC.AXC

Strasbourg porcelain
USE **Strasbourg faïence**

Strasbourg pottery
USE **Strasbourg faïence**

Strasbourg turpentine
MT.1476
SN An oleoresin or balsam obtained from Central European fir trees, used by artists as an ingredient of vehicles and mastics and other varnishes. (MAYER)
UF turpentine, Strasbourg
CN M.MT.AFU.AFU.ALO.BOK.AFU.BIQ

strass
USE **paste (glass)**

stratification, social
USE **social classes**

stratigraphers
HG.344
ALT **stratigrapher**
CN H.HG.AFU.AXC.BIQ.AFU.AFU.BZY.AXC

straw
MT.1077 (L,R)
CN M.MT.AFU.AFU.ALO.BIQ.CRG

straw work
MT.2782 (L,R)
UF work, straw
CN M.MT.AFU.AXC.DCU

straw, barley
USE **barley straw**

straw, rice
USE **rice straw**

straw, wheat
USE **wheat straw**

Strawberry Hill Gothic
USE **Gothic Revival**

strawboard
MT.1891
SN Pasteboard made of straw, certain grasses, and other low-cellulose paper materials. (MH)
CN M.MT.AFU.AFU.ARI.ALO.ALO.ARI.ALO

streamlining
KT.162 (L,B)
ALT **streamlined**
CN K.KT.AFU.ALO.DOI.EFQ

streams
RD.139 (L,R)
ALT **stream**
UF watercourses
CN V.RD.ARI.AFU.AFU.AFU.AFU.ARI.ALO

street art
BM.253 (L,R)
SN Use for outdoor mural paintings decorating buildings in public thoroughfares in the 20th century, sometimes intended to draw attention to urban problems such as drugs, discrimination against minorities, or police brutality.
UF art, street
street works
works, street
CN B.BM.AFU.ARI.BCW.FIM

street directories
VW.415 (L)
ALT **street directory**
UF directories, street
CN V.VW.AFU.AFU.ALO.EWY.AXC.AFU.BOK.AFU

street elevations
RM.11
ALT **street elevation**
UF elevations, street
CN V.RM.AFU.BCW.BCW

street furniture
RM.496 (A,B,R)
SN Benches, signs, light fixtures, and receptacles provided as part of the design of a road. (DAC)
UF furniture, street
CN V.RM.ALO.ALO.ALO.ALO.DUC

street-level views
USE **eye-level views**

street lighting
RD.118 (A,L,B)
UF lighting, street
CN V.RD.ALO.AXC.ALO

street maps
VW.221 (L)
ALT **street map**
SN Maps depicting public ways or highways in a city or town. (AHD)
UF maps, street
plans, street
street plans
CN V.VW.AFU.AFU.AFU.FZU.AXC.AFU.ARI.AXC.DIO.BCW.AFU

street plans

USE **street maps**

street-railroads
RD.103 (A,L)
ALT **street-railroad**
SN Designates light rail train systems operating along streets in urban areas; replaced horse-drawn rail vehicles during the 19th century prior to the popularity of self-propelled streetcar systems.
UF railways, street
street railways
CN V.RD.ALO.ARI.AFU.AFU.ALO.AFU.ARI

street railways
USE **street-railroads**

street works
USE **street art**

streetcar lines
USE **streetcar systems**

streetcar systems
RD.104 (A,L)
ALT **streetcar system**
SN Use for rail transit systems consisting of single cars or short multiunit trains operated manually with electric power, on exclusive right of way along streets, for an intermediate number of passengers.
UF streetcar lines
systems, streetcar
tramlines
tramways
trolleycar lines
CN V.RD.ALO.ARI.AFU.AFU.ALO.AFU.AXC

streetlamps
USE **streetlights**

streetlights
RM.500 (N)
ALT **streetlight**
SN Use for lights providing illumination to roads and highways as well as streets.
UF streetlamps
CN V.RM.ALO.ALO.ALO.ALO.DUC.AXC

streets
RK.1526 (A,L,B,R)
ALT **street**
CN V.RK.ALO.ALO.BIQ.ARI.AFU.ALO

streets, arterial
USE **arterial streets**

streets, dead-end
USE **dead-end streets**

streets, foot
USE **pedestrian streets**

streets, main
USE **main streets**

streets, one way
USE **one way streets**

streets, pedestrian
USE **pedestrian streets**

streets, private
USE **private roads**

streets, through
USE **through streets**

streets, walking
USE **pedestrian streets**

Strefizm
USE **Zonist**

strength of materials
BM.909 (A,L,B)
UF materials, strength of
CN B.BM.CFS.AXC.BIQ.ARI

strength, bursting
USE **bursting strength**

strength, fatigue
USE **fatigue strength**

strength, impact
USE **impact strength**

strength, shear
USE **shear strength**

strength, ultimate
USE **ultimate strength**

strength, yield
USE **yield strength**

strengthening
KT.643
ALT **strengthened**
UF stabilizing (strengthening)
CN K.KT.AFU.ALO.GLI.AFU

stress
BM.916 (L,R)
SN Resultant condition of applied force; condition existant in a body when its internal structure or surfaces resist a force that produces or tends to produce deformation in the body. (STEIN)
CN B.BM.CFS.AXC.BIQ.ARI.BCW

stress analysis
USE **structural analysis**

stress, axial
USE **axial stress**

stress, bearing
USE **bearing stress**

stress, bending
USE **bending stress**

stress, combined
USE **combined stress**

stress, crowding
USE **overcrowding**

stress, shear
USE **shear stress**

stress, temperature
USE **thermal stress**

stress, thermal
USE **thermal stress**

stress, torsional
USE **torsional stress**

stress, twisting
USE **torsional stress**

stress, yield
USE **yield strength**

stressed-skin construction
KT.35 (B)
SN Construction in which a thin material on the exterior surface of a building is utilized to carry loads. (DAC)
UF construction, stressed-skin
CN K.KT.AFU.ALO.BCW.ARI.AFU.BIQ.ALO

stressed-skin structures
RT.519 (A)
ALT **stressed-skin structure**
SN Use for structures in which both a thin outer surface and the framework carry loads. (COWAN)
UF skins, stressed
stressed skins
structures, stressed-skin
CN V.RT.AFU.AFU.AFU.BIQ.BIQ

stressed skins
USE **stressed-skin structures**

stressing, post
USE **post tensioning**

stretch yarn
MT.1980 (L)
SN Synthetic yarns that will stretch under tension and contract when released; usually made from thermoplastic filaments used especially for hosiery. (W)
UF yarn, stretch
CN M.MT.AFU.AFU.ARI.ALO.ALO.BIQ.BIQ.ALO

stretcher bond
USE **running bond**

stretcher tables
USE **refectory tables**

stretcher tables, tavern
USE **tavern tables**

stretchers
TG.996
ALT **stretcher**
SN Horizontal members connecting and supporting the legs of furniture. (BEARD)
UF barrs
entretoises

span-rails
stays (stretchers)
underbracing
CN V.TG.ALO.HIK.ALO.ALO

stretchers (masonry units)
MT.2764
SN Masonry units laid horizontally and with their lengths parallel with the face of the wall. (DAC)
CN M.MT.AFU.AXC.BIQ.ALO.AXC

stretchers, arched
USE **saltire stretchers**

stretchers, block and spindle
USE **block and spindle stretchers**

stretchers, block and turned
USE **block and spindle stretchers**

stretchers, box
USE **box stretchers**

stretchers, crescent
USE **crescent stretchers**

stretchers, cross
USE **cross stretchers**

stretchers, cruciform
USE **cross stretchers**

stretchers, diagonal
USE **cross stretchers**

stretchers, diagonal cross shaped
USE **cross stretchers**

stretchers, hooped
USE **saltire stretchers**

stretchers, rising
USE **saltire stretchers**

stretchers, saltire
USE **saltire stretchers**

stretchers, shaped
USE **shaped stretchers**

stretching
KT.163
ALT **stretched**
CN K.KT.AFU.ALO.DOI.ELK

Stridenist
USE **Estridentismo**

strigil ornament
USE **strigillation**

strigil pattern
USE **strigillation**

strigillation
DG.114
ALT **strigillated**
SN A curving fluted pattern; common on Roman sarcophagi and in Neoclassical ornament. (LDDO)
UF ornament, strigil
pattern, strigil
strigil ornament
strigil pattern
CN D.DG.AFU.ARI.ALO.ARI.ARI.ALO

strike blocks
TB.940
ALT **strike block**
SN Planes shorter than a jointer plane, about 11 or 12 inches long, with its blade set at less of a pitch than a normal jointer; used for fitting a short joint.
UF block planes, straight
blocks, strike
planes, straight block
straight block planes
CN V.TB.AFU.BCW.CFS.ALO.AFU.DUC.ARI.AFU.BCW

strike plates
USE **strikes**

strikeoffs
USE **screeds**

strikes
TF.515
ALT **strike**
SN Fastenings on a door frame into which a bolt is projected to secure a door. (DITTRI)
UF keepers
strike plates
CN V.TF.AFU.ALO.AFU.ALO

strikes (events)
KM.160 (L)
SN Temporary stoppages of work by workers designed to enforce compliance with demands made on employers or government. (W)
CN K.KM.AFU.EWY.ALO

strikes, box
USE **box strikes**

strikes, dustproof
USE **dustproof strikes**

strikes, mortise
USE **mortise strikes**

strikes, surface
USE **surface strikes**

strikes, universal
USE **universal strikes**

striking
KG.161 (L)
SN Engaging in a temporary stoppage of work in order to bring about compliance with demands. (W)
CN K.KG.AFU.AFU.BIQ.DCU

striking blocks
TB.657
ALT **striking block**
UF blocks, striking
CN V.TB.AFU.BCW.BIQ.AFU.ALO.ARI.BCW

striking hammers
USE **sledgehammers**

string
MT.1975 (L,N)
CN M.MT.AFU.AFU.ARI.ALO.ALO.BIQ.ARI

string development
USE **ribbon development**

stringboards
USE **face strings**

stringcourses
RT.622 (B)
ALT **stringcourse**
SN Horizontal bands of masonry, generally narrower than other courses, extending across the face of a wall and in some instances continuing across piers or engaged columns; may be flush or projecting and may be flat surfaced, molded, or otherwise shaped. (HAS)
UF belt courses
cordons
courses, belt
CN V.RT.AFU.AFU.AFU.BIQ.BUE.ALO.AFU.ALO.CFS

stringers
USE **strings**

stringers, wall
USE **wall strings**

strings
RT.1124 (B)
ALT **string**
SN In a stair, inclined boards which support the ends of the steps. (HAS)
UF carriages (stair components)
horses (stair components)
stair-ends
stringers
CN V.RT.AFU.BIQ.AXC.ALO.BOK

strings, cut
USE **open strings**

strings, face
USE **face strings**

strings, finish
USE **face strings**

strings, open
USE **open strings**

strings, outer
USE **face strings**

strings, rough
USE **carriage pieces**

strings, wall
USE **wall strings**

strip
MT.2273
CN M.MT.AFU.ALO.HIK

strip development

USE **ribbon development**

strip films
USE **filmstrips**

strip footings
USE **continuous footings**

strip-lining
KT.646
SN Use for the painting conservation technique where a deteriorated canvas is strengthened by affixing a strip of canvas to its outside edge. (RUHEMA)
CN K.KT.AFU.ALO.GLI.AFU.ALO.AFU

strip maps
VW.156
ALT **strip map**
UF maps, strip
CN V.VW.AFU.AFU.AFU.FZU.AXC.AFU.ARI.AFU.CLM.AXC

strip mining
KT.618 (L)
CN K.KT.AFU.ALO.FUA.CXA.AFU

strip retail centers
USE **shopping plazas**

strip seams, cap
USE **cap strip seams**

strip sections
USE **partial sections**

strip windows
RT.931
ALT **strip window**
SN Several windows set directly adjacent, without intervening wall space, so as to form a horizontal band of fenestration; found in buildings of Modernist style.
UF windows, strip
CN V.RT.AFU.ARI.AFU.AFU.BOK.AFU.AFU.EFQ

strip, bark
USE **bark strip**

striped pattern
USE **stripes**

stripes
DG.133
UF pattern, striped
striped pattern
CN D.DG.AFU.ARI.ALO.BIQ.BUE

stripped joints
TF.628
ALT **stripped joint**
SN In brickwork, raked joints used with bricks of rough texture. (DAC)
UF joints, stripped
CN V.TF.ALO.ARI.ALO.AFU.ARI.AXC.ARI.AFU

stripping
KT.624
ALT **stripped**
SN The process of removing an outer layer of material.
CN K.KT.AFU.ALO.FUA.EFQ

stripping emulsion
USE **stripping film**

stripping film
MT.1953
UF emulsion, stripping
film, stripping
paper, stripping
roll-paper, stripping
stripping emulsion
stripping paper
stripping roll-paper
CN M.MT.AFU.AFU.ARI.ALO.ALO.AXC.ARI.BOK.CFS

stripping paper
USE **stripping film**

stripping roll-paper
USE **stripping film**

strips, cartoon
USE **comics**

strips, comic
USE **comics**

strips, commercial
USE **commercial strips**

strips, cover
USE **cover moldings**

strips, furring
USE **furring strips**

strips, girt
USE **ledger boards**

strips, landing
USE **airstrips**

strips, microfilm
USE **microfilm strips**

strips, pilaster
USE **pilaster strips**

strips, ribbon
USE **ledger boards**

strips, rumble
USE **rumble strips**

strips, weather
USE **weather strips**

stroboscopic photography
KT.382
SN Photography of moving objects by repeated flashes or a pulsating light source. (RILA)
UF photography, stroboscopic
CN K.KT.AFU.ALO.DUC.DIO.ARI.ARI.AFU.AFU

Stroked ware
USE **Stichbandkeramik**

strong blue
DL.215
UF artificial ultramarine
blue, bright
blue, bright copen
blue, cerulean (color)
blue, copen
blue, dull
blue, genuine ultramarine
blue, Paris
blue, Prussian (color)
blue, royal
blue, sapphire
blue, strong
bright blue
bright copen blue
bright ultramarine
centroid color 178
cerulean blue (color)
copen blue
copen blue, bright
dull blue
French ultramarine
genuine ultramarine blue
Paris blue
Prussian blue (color)
royal blue
sapphire blue
ultramarine
ultramarine blue, genuine
ultramarine, artificial
ultramarine, bright
ultramarine, French
CN D.DL.AFU.AFU.BZY.ARI

strong bluish green
DL.198
UF blue green
blue green, dark
blue, bright
blue, bright turquoise
blue, vivid turquoise
bluish green, strong
bright blue
bright emerald green
bright green
bright jade green
bright turquoise
bright turquoise blue
bright turquoise green
centroid color 160
dark blue green
emerald green (color)
emerald green, bright
emerald green, vivid
green, bright
green, bright emerald
green, bright jade
green, bright turquoise
green, emerald (color)
green, jade
green, strong bluish
green, turquoise
green, vivid emerald
green, vivid turquoise
jade green
jade green, bright
turquoise blue, bright

turquoise blue, vivid
turquoise (color)
turquoise green
turquoise green, bright
turquoise green, vivid
turquoise, bright
turquoise, vivid
vivid emerald green
vivid turquoise
vivid turquoise blue
vivid turquoise green
CN D.DL.AFU.AFU.BUE.DCU.ALO.ARI

strong brown
DL.77
UF brown, gold
brown, light copper
brown, orange
brown, strong
brown, yellow
centroid color 55
copper brown, light
gold brown
iron oxide red (color)
light copper brown
orange brown
red oxide
red, iron oxide (color)
red, Spanish
red, yellow
Spanish red
terra cotta (color)
yellow brown
yellow red
CN D.DL.AFU.AFU.AXC.AFU

strong green
DL.166
UF blue green
blue green, bright
blue green, dark
bright blue green
bright emerald green
bright green
bright jade green
bright kelly green
centroid color 141
chrome green (color)
chrysocolla green
dark blue green
emerald green (color)
emerald green, bright
green, bright
green, bright emerald
green, bright jade
green, bright kelly
green, chrome (color)
green, chrysocolla
green, emerald (color)
green, kelly
green, Ming
green, strong
green, viridian
jade green, bright
kelly green
kelly green, bright
Ming green
transparent chromium oxide
viridian (color)
viridian green
CN D.DL.AFU.AFU.BUE.ARI

strong greenish blue
DL.235
UF blue, bright
blue, bright cerulean
blue, bright peacock
blue, bright turquoise
blue, brilliant peacock
blue, cerulean (color)
blue, cobalt (color)
blue, kingfisher
blue, light cerulean
blue, peacock
blue, strong greenish
blue, turquoise
blue, vivid cerulean
blue, vivid peacock
blue, vivid turquoise
bright blue
bright cerulean blue
bright peacock blue
bright turquoise blue
brilliant peacock blue
centroid color 169
cerulean blue (color)
cerulean blue, bright
cerulean blue, light
cerulean blue, vivid
cobalt blue (color)
cobalt ultramarine
greenish blue, strong
kingfisher blue
light cerulean blue
peacock blue
peacock blue, bright
peacock blue, brilliant
peacock blue, vivid
turquoise blue
turquoise blue, bright
turquoise blue, vivid
ultramarine, cobalt
vivid cerulean blue
vivid peacock blue
vivid turquoise blue
CN D.DL.AFU.AFU.BZY.DCU.AFU.ARI

strong greenish yellow
DL.137
UF bright chartreuse yellow
centroid color 99
chartreuse
chartreuse yellow
chartreuse yellow, bright
chartreuse yellow, light
greenish yellow, strong
light chartreuse yellow
lime yellow
strontium yellow (color)
yellow, bright chartreuse
yellow, chartreuse
yellow, light chartreuse
yellow, lime
yellow, strong greenish
yellow, strontium (color)
CN D.DL.AFU.AFU.BCW.CRG.ALO.ARI

strong oil
MT.2002
UF oil, strong
CN M.MT.AFU.AFU.ARI.ARI.ARI.BCW.ALO

strong olive green
DL.206
UF bluish olive
centroid color 123
green, slate
green, strong olive
olive green, strong
olive, bluish
slate green
CN D.DL.AFU.AFU.BUE.DCU.ARI.AFU

strong orange
DL.63
UF bright orange
brown orange
cadmium orange (color)
cadmium yellow (color)
centroid color 50
Mars yellow (color)
orange, bright
orange, cadmium (color)
orange, orpiment
orange, strong
orange, yellow
orpiment orange
yellow orange
yellow, cadmium (color)
yellow, Mars (color)
CN D.DL.AFU.AFU.ARI.ARI

strong orange yellow
DL.128 (L)
UF bright yellow
brown orange
cadmium yellow (color)
centroid color 68
chrome yellow (color)
chrome, deep
deep chrome
gold yellow
golden yellow
ocher, yellow (color)
orange yellow, strong
orange, brown
orange, yellowish
orpiment red
realgar (color)
red, orpiment
reddish yellow
sandarach
yellow ocher (color)
yellow, bright
yellow, cadmium (color)
yellow, gold
yellow, golden
yellow, reddish
yellow, strong orange
yellowish orange
CN D.DL.AFU.AFU.BCW.CRG.AFU.ARI

strong pink
DL.5
UF alizarine pink

centroid color 2
pink, alizarine
pink, strong
CN D.DL.AFU.AFU.AFU.ALO

strong purple
DL.269
UF bright red violet
bright violet
centroid color 218
cobalt violet (color)
litho purple
magenta (color)
manganese violet (color)
mauve (color)
mineral violet
permanent violet
purple, litho
purple, strong
red violet
red violet, bright
violet, bright
violet, cobalt (color)
violet, maganese (color)
violet, mineral
violet, permanent
CN D.DL.AFU.AFU.CFS.ARI

strong purplish blue
DL.245
UF artificial ultramarine
blue violet, dull
blue violet, grayish
blue, French
blue, permanent
blue, reddish
blue, royal
blue, sapphire
blue, strong purplish
blue, violet
bluish violet, light
bright ultramarine
centroid color 196
della robbia
dull blue violet
French blue
French ultramarine
grayish blue violet
light bluish violet
light violet blue
permanent blue
purplish blue, strong
reddish blue
royal blue
sapphire blue
ultramarine
ultramarine, artificial
ultramarine, bright
ultramarine, French
ultramarine, violet
violet blue
violet blue, light
violet ultramarine
violet, light bluish
CN D.DL.AFU.AFU.BZY.DCU.ALO.ARI

strong purplish pink
DL.17
UF bluish pink
centroid color 247
deep rose pink
pink, bluish
pink, deep rose
pink, rhodamine
pink, strong purplish
purplish pink, strong
rhodamine pink
rose pink, deep
CN D.DL.AFU.AFU.AFU.CLM.AFU.ALO

strong purplish red
DL.52
UF bluish red
bright rose
carmine (color)
carmine lake
carmine rose
carmine, rose
centroid color 255
cerise pink
fuchsia
fuchsia rose
lake, carmine
lake, madder
madder lake
madder pink
madder, rose
magenta (color)
pink, cerise
pink, madder
purplish red, strong
red, bluish
red, strong purplish
rose
rose carmine
rose madder
rose, bright
rose, carmine
rose, fuchsia
CN D.DL.AFU.AFU.ALO.CFS.AFU.ALO

strong red
DL.36
UF blood red
bright red
bright rose
cadmium carmine
cadmium red (color)
cadmium vermilion
carmine (color)
carmine lake
carmine rose
carmine, cadmium
centroid color 12
English vermilion (color)
fuchsia
geranium red (color)
geranium rose
lake (color)
lake, carmine
lake, madder
lake, scarlet
madder (color)
madder lake
madder red
para red (color)
permanent red
quinacridone red (color)
red, blood
red, bright
red, cadmium (color)
red, geranium (color)
red, madder
red, para (color)
red, permanent
red, quinacridone (color)
red, strong
rose
rose, bright
rose, carmine
rose, geranium
scarlet
scarlet lake
vermilion, cadmium
vermilion, English (color)
CN D.DL.AFU.AFU.ALO.ALO

strong reddish brown
DL.90
UF brown, orange
brown, Spanish
brown, strong reddish
burnt sienna (color)
centroid color 40
Indian red (color)
iron oxide red (color)
orange brown
red oxide
red, Indian (color)
red, iron oxide (color)
red, Spanish
red, Venetian (color)
reddish brown, strong
siena
sienna, burnt (color)
Spanish brown
Spanish red
terra cotta (color)
Venetian red (color)
CN D.DL.AFU.AFU.AXC.BZY.AFU.AFU

strong reddish orange
DL.70
UF brick red
centroid color 35
dull red
light vermilion
madder (color)
madder red
orange vermilion (color)
orange, red
orange, strong reddish
red lead (color)
red orange
red, brick
red, dull
red, madder
red, yellowish
reddish orange, strong
scarlet
vermilion (color)
vermilion, light
vermilion, orange (color)
yellowish red
CN D.DL.AFU.AFU.ARI.BOK.AFU.ALO

strong reddish purple
DL.290
UF bright fuchsia purple
bright red violet
centroid color 237
dark fuchsia
dull dark purple
dull magenta purple
fuchsia purple
fuchsia purple, bright
fuchsia purple, light
fuchsia, dark
light fuchsia purple
lilac rose
magenta (color)
magenta purple, dull
orchid
orchid, purple
purple orchid
purple, bright fuchsia
purple, dull dark
purple, dull magenta
purple, fuchsia
purple, light fuchsia
purple, strong reddish
red violet
red violet, bright
reddish purple, strong
reddish violet
rose, lilac
violet, red
violet, reddish
CN D.DL.AFU.AFU.CFS.DCU.AFU.ALO

strong rooms
USE **vaults (strong rooms)**

strong violet
DL.257
UF blue violet, dull
blue violet, grayish
bluish violet
bluish violet, deep dull
bluish violet, dull
centroid color 207
deep dull bluish violet
dull blue violet
dull bluish violet
grayish blue violet
ultramarine, violet
violet ultramarine
violet, bluish
violet, deep dull bluish
violet, dull bluish
violet, strong
CN D.DL.AFU.AFU.BZY.DCU.ARI.ARI

strong yellow
DL.114
UF aureolin (color)
bronze gold
buff, orange
centroid color 84
chrome yellow, light
gamboge (color)
gold, bronze
gold, light
light chrome yellow
light gold
light orange yellow
ocher (color)
orange buff
orange yellow, light
orpiment (color)
pastel yellow
reddish yellow
Turner's yellow (color)
yellow, light chrome
yellow, pastel
yellow, reddish
yellow, strong
yellow, Turner's (color)
yellow, zinc (color)
zinc yellow (color)
CN D.DL.AFU.AFU.BCW.ARI

strong yellow green
DL.157
UF bright chartreuse
bright lime green
centroid color 117
chartreuse
chartreuse, bright
green, bright lime
green, light lime
green, lime
green, Scheele's (color)
green, strong yellow
light lime green
lime green
lime green, bright
lime green, light
Scheele's green (color)
yellow green, strong
CN D.DL.AFU.AFU.BOK.ARI

strong yellowish brown
DL.99
UF bistre
brown, red
brown, strong yellowish
brown, yellow
centroid color 74
gold ocher, transparent (color)
ocher (color)
ocher, transparent gold (color)
raw sienna (color)
red brown
sienna, raw (color)
topaz (color)
transparent gold ocher (color)
yellow brown
yellowish brown, strong
CN D.DL.AFU.AFU.AXC.BZY.ALO.AFU

strong yellowish green
DL.187
UF bright green
bright kelly green
centroid color 131
emerald (color)
emerald green (color)
green, bright
green, bright kelly
green, emerald (color)
green, kelly
green, Paris
green, Scheele's (color)
green, strong yellowish
kelly green
kelly green, bright
Paris green
Scheele's green (color)
yellowish green, strong
CN D.DL.AFU.AFU.BUE.DCU.AFU.ARI

strong yellowish pink
DL.26
UF bright peach
centroid color 26
madder, scarlet
peach (color)
peach, bright
pink, strong yellowish
rose
salmon
scarlet madder
vermilion (color)
yellowish pink, strong
CN D.DL.AFU.AFU.AFU.CLM.ALO.ALO

strongholds
USE **fortresses**

strontian yellow
USE **strontium yellow**

strontium chromate
USE **strontium yellow**

strontium chrome
USE **strontium yellow**

strontium yellow
MT.1793
UF chrome, strontium
jaune de strontium
strontian yellow
strontium chromate
strontium chrome
Strontiumgelb
ultramarine yellow
ultramarine, yellow
yellow ultramarine
yellow, strontian
yellow, strontium
yellow, ultramarine
CN M.MT.AFU.AFU.ARI.AFU.AFU.ALO.ALO.BUE.ARI.CLM

strontium yellow (color)
USE **brilliant greenish yellow**
strong greenish yellow

Strontiumgelb
USE **strontium yellow**

strops
TB.728 (N)
ALT **strop**
SN Bands usually of leather backed with liner canvas, for sharpening blades. (W)
CN V.TB.AFU.BCW.BIQ.ARI.ALO.BOK

struck joints
TF.621
ALT **struck joint**
SN Masonry joints in which excess mor-

tar is removed by a stroke of a trowel. (MEANS)
UF joints, struck
CN V.TF.ALO.ARI.ALO.AFU.ARI.AFU.AFU

struck moldings
RT.755
ALT **struck molding**
SN Moldings cut into, rather than added to or applied to, a member. (HAS)
UF moldings, solid
moldings, struck
solid moldings
CN V.RT.AFU.ALO.AFU.BOK.AFU.AFU.ALO

structural aluminum
MT.430 (L)
UF aluminum, structural
CN M.MT.AFU.AFU.AFU.BZY.AFU.AFU.ARI.AFU.AFU

structural analysis
BM.1000
UF analysis, stress
analysis, structural
stress analysis
CN B.BM.CFS.AXC.CLM.AFU

structural anthropology
KD.100 (L)
UF anthropology, structural
CN K.KD.AFU.ALO.AFU.BUE

structural clay tile
MT.168
SN A hollow clay tile composed of burnt clay, shale, fireclay, or mixtures thereof. (DAC)
UF clay tile, structural
hollow tile
tile, hollow
tile, structural clay
CN M.MT.AFU.AFU.AFU.AXC.ALO.ALO.ALO.AFU.ALO.ARI

structural colors
BM.118 (L)
UF colors, structural
CN B.BM.AFU.AFU.ARI.BOK.ALO.AFU.CFS

structural drawings
VD.159
ALT **structural drawing**
UF drawings, structural
CN V.VD.AFU.BIQ.BUE

structural dynamics
USE **dynamics**

structural engineering
KD.222 (L)
SN Branch of civil engineering dealing primarily with the design and construction of structures such as bridges, buildings, and dams. (W)
UF engineering, structural
CN K.KD.AFU.ARI.BIQ.AXC.AXC

structural engineers
HG.634 (B)
ALT **structural engineer**
UF engineers, structural
CN H.HG.AFU.AXC.BZY.BCW.BCW.ARI

structural failures
BM.1029 (A,L,B)
UF failures, structural
CN B.BM.CFS.AXC.CLM.ALO.BZY

structural foam
MT.2105
UF foam, structural
CN M.MT.AFU.AFU.ARI.BUE.ALO.ALO.ALO.AFU

structural frames
RT.37 (A,L)
ALT **structural frame**
SN All the members of buildings or structures required to transmit loads to the ground. (DAC)
UF frames (structural frames)
frames, structural
CN V.RT.AFU.AFU.AFU.ALO.AXC

structural geology
KD.270 (L)
SN Use for the study of individual geological structures such as anticlines, thrust vaults, and lineations.(BADGLE) For the study of larger-scale units of the earth's crust, use **tectonics (geology).**
UF geology, structural
CN K.KD.AFU.ARI.CLM.ARI.ARI.ALO

structural glass, Carrara
USE **Carrara structural glass**

structural iron
MT.360 (L)
UF iron, structural
CN M.MT.AFU.AFU.AFU.BZY.AFU.AFU.AFU.AFU.ARI

structural loads
USE **loads**

structural lumber
MT.1443
SN Lumber that is five inches or more in both thickness and width. (PUTNAM)
UF lumber, structural
structural timber
timber, structural
CN M.MT.AFU.AFU.ALO.BIQ.DCU.ALO.BOK.ARI.BCW

structural shells
USE **shell structures**

structural slate
MT.874
UF slate, structural
CN M.MT.AFU.AFU.AFU.DCU.AFU.ARI.BUE.ALO.ARI

structural stability
BM.1032 (A,L,B)
UF analysis, stability
stability analysis
stability of structures
stability, structural
structures, stability of
CN B.BM.CFS.AXC.CLM.ALO.CFS

structural steel
MT.359 (A,L)
SN Steel, rolled in a variety of shapes, such as beams, bars, or sheets, and used as load-bearing structural members. (DAC)
UF steel, structural
CN M.MT.AFU.AFU.AFU.BZY.AFU.AFU.AFU.AFU.ALO.ALO.AFU

structural surveys
VW.366
ALT **structural survey**
UF surveys, structural
CN V.VW.AFU.AFU.ALO.DCU.AFU.ALO

structural systems, one-way
USE **one-way structural systems**

structural systems, two-way
USE **two-way structural systems**

structural timber
USE **structural lumber**

structuralism
BM.292 (L,R)
ALT **structuralist**
SN Theory or method applicable in many fields in which interrelations of constituent elements (as of a work of literature, an activity, or an approach) are regarded as more significant than the elements in isolation; sometimes applied to all human activity and its products, such that even thought itself is seen as constructed and not natural.
CN B.BM.AFU.AXC.AXC.ARI

structure, social
USE **social structure**

structure, soil
USE **soil structure**

structures
RK.3 (A,L)
ALT **structure**
SN Use for constructions of any kind artificially fabricated of parts joined together in some definite manner and which may or may not provide enclosure or shelter.
CN V.RK.AFU.AFU.AFU

structures (structural elements)
RT.4 (A)
ALT **structure (structural element)**
SN The general classes of load-distributing devices, based on structural principles, used in built works.
CN V.RT.AFU.AFU.AFU.AFU

structures, air-inflated
USE **air-inflated structures**

structures, air-supported
USE **air-supported structures**

structures, balloon
USE **pneumatic structures**

structures, cable
USE **cable structures**

structures, cable net
USE **cable net structures**

structures, cable-stayed
USE **cable-stayed structures**

structures, determinate
USE **statically determinate structures**

structures, double-cable
USE **double-cable structures**

structures, expandable
USE **air-supported structures**

structures, extraterrestrial
USE **extraterrestrial structures**

structures, flexible
USE **nonrigid structures**

structures, folded
USE **folded plate structures**

structures, folded plate
USE **folded plate structures**

structures, garden
USE **garden structures**

structures, hydraulic
USE **hydraulic structures**

structures, indeterminate
USE **statically indeterminate structures**

structures, inflatable
USE **air-inflated structures**

structures, lamella
USE **lamella structures**

structures, large span
USE **large span structures**

structures, long span
USE **large span structures**

structures, marine
USE **marine structures**

structures, membrane
USE **membrane structures**

structures, net
USE **cable net structures**

structures, nonrigid
USE **nonrigid structures**

structures, offshore
USE **offshore structures**

structures, plate
USE **plate structures**

structures, pneumatic
USE **pneumatic structures**

structures, post-and-beam
USE **post-and-beam structures**

structures, rigid
USE **rigid structures**

structures, settlement of
USE **settlement of structures**

structures, shell
USE **shell structures**

structures, space frame
USE **space frames**

structures, stability of
USE **structural stability**

structures, statically determinate
USE **statically determinate structures**

structures, statically indeterminate
USE **statically indeterminate structures**

structures, stayed cable
USE **cable-stayed structures**

structures, stressed-skin
USE **stressed-skin structures**

structures, subaquatic
USE **submarine structures**

structures, submarine
USE **submarine structures**

structures, suspended
USE **suspension structures**

structures, suspension
USE **suspension structures**

structures, temporary
USE **temporary structures**

structures, tensegrity
USE **tensegrity structures**

structures, tensile
USE **tensile structures**

structures, tension
USE **tensile structures**

structures, tent
USE **tent structures**

structures, thin shell
USE **shell structures**

structures, trabeated
USE **post-and-beam structures**

structures, tube
USE **tube structures**

structures, tube-in-tube
USE **tube structures**

structures, underground
USE **underground structures**

structures, underwater
USE **submarine structures**

Structurist
USE **Constructionist**

strutbeams
USE **collar beams**

struts
USE **braces**

strutting pieces
USE **straining beams**

strutting, herringbone
USE **cross bridging**

Stselax
FL.916
CN F.FL.ALO.ALO.ALO.AFU.ALO.ARI.ARI.BCW

Stuart
FL.3194 (L,B,R)
CN F.FL.ALO.BCW.ALO.ARI.BIQ.BIQ.AFU.AFU.ALO

Stuart Revival
FL.3328 (R)
UF Revival, Stuart
CN F.FL.ALO.BCW.ALO.AXC.DIO.ALO.BIQ.BIQ

stubs, check
USE **check stubs**

stucco
MT.2461 (A,L,B,R)
CN M.MT.AFU.ARI.CRG.AFU.AXC.ARI.BOK

stucco-lustro technique
KT.228
SN A fresco method using equal parts of white slaked pit lime and marble grit. The surface is ironed with a hot iron to produce a gloss. (WEHLTE)
CN K.KT.AFU.ALO.DUC.CXA.ALO.AFU.BIQ.ALO

stuccoing
KT.722
ALT **stuccoed**
CN K.KT.AFU.ALO.GRC.DIO

stud drivers
TB.21
ALT **stud driver**
SN Devices for driving a hardened steel fastener into concrete or other hard material, consisting of a hand-held driver that positions the fastener. A blow on the head of the driver forces the fastener into the material. (MEANS)
UF drivers, stud
CN V.TB.AFU.ARI.AFU.AFU.AXC

stud guns
TB.22
ALT **stud gun**

SN Stud drivers in which the impact is provided by the firing of a blank cartridge. (DAC)
UF explosive actuated guns
guns, explosive actuated
guns, plug-driving
guns, stud
plug-driving guns
CN V.TB.AFU.ARI.AFU.AFU.AXC.AFU

stud welding
KT.804 (L)
SN Type of arc welding process in which elements are joined by heating between a metal stud and the other work part until their surfaces are joined. (STEIN)
UF welding, stud
CN K.KT.AFU.ALO.HOE.BCW.ALO.AFU.ALO.ALO.AFU.ARI

studbooks
VW.557 (L)
ALT **studbook**
SN Official records, in book form, of the pedigree of purebred animals. (W)
CN V.VW.AFU.ALO.AFU.AFU.ALO.CLM

student aid
BM.394 (L)
UF aid, student
financial aid, student
student financial aid
CN B.BM.ARI.CRG.ALO.ARI

student centers
USE **student unions**

student chairs
TG.194
ALT **student chair**
SN Term used in the late 19th century for a type of upholstered armchair intended to be used as reading chairs in dormitories.
UF chairs, student
CN V.TG.AFU.AFU.ALO.AFU.AFU.ALO.EFQ.AFU

student commons
USE **student unions**

student drawings
VD.142
ALT **student drawing**
UF drawings, student
drawings, thesis
thesis drawings
CN V.VD.AFU.BCW.ALO

student financial aid
USE **student aid**

student housing
RG.87 (A,L,B)
UF college housing
housing, college
housing, student
CN V.RG.AFU.AFU.BOK.BCW.BIQ

student mobility
BM.1055 (L)
SN Geographic mobility of students from one region or school district to another. (ERIC)
UF mobility, student
CN B.BM.CLM.AFU.ALO.ARI.AXC

student projects
BM.42 (A)
UF projects, student
CN B.BM.AFU.AFU.ALO.CLM.AFU

student unions
RK.1200 (A,L,B)
ALT **student union**
UF centers, college community
centers, student
college community centers
college unions
commons, student
community centers, college
student centers
student commons
unions, college
unions, student
CN V.RK.AFU.ALO.ALO.FUA.BZY

students
HG.772 (L)
ALT **student**
UF pupils
CN H.HG.AFU.BIQ.CFS

studies
VB.58
ALT **study**
SN Use for works in any medium of the visual arts that explore a subject or are preliminary to a separate, more finalized work; more finished than sketches.
UF études
CN V.VB.AFU.ALO.BOK

studies (rooms)
RM.154
ALT **study (room)**
CN V.RM.AFU.DIO.ALO.CFS.BIQ

studies, anatomical
USE **anatomical studies**

studies, Biblical
USE **Biblical studies**

studies, composition
USE **composition studies**

studies, detail
USE **detail studies**

studies, drapery
USE **drapery studies**

studies, feasibility
USE **feasibility studies**

studies, figure
USE **figure studies**

studies, legal
USE **law**

studies, liberal
USE **liberal arts**

studies, museum
USE **museology**

studies, population
USE **demography**

studies, preliminary
USE **preparatory studies**

studies, preparatory
USE **preparatory studies**

studies, urban
USE **urban studies**

studio apartments
RM.270 (A)
ALT **studio apartment**
UF apartments, bachelor
apartments, efficiency
apartments, studio
bachelor apartments
efficiency apartments
CN V.RM.AFU.DIO.ARI.ALO.BIQ.AFU.AXC

studio portraiture
USE **commercial portraiture**

Studio-Stil
USE **Jugendstil**

studiolos
RM.103 (L,R)
ALT **studiolo**
SN Small chambers or studies in private homes housing collections of art works or biological or geological specimens, popular during the Italian Renaissance.
CN V.RM.AFU.DIO.ALO.AXC.AXC

studios
HG.904 (A,L,B,R)
ALT **studio**
SN Use for groups consisting of a master artist or an architect and his or her assistants or pupils, especially in the 19th and 20th centuries; earlier, use **workshops.**
UF ateliers
bottegas
CN H.HG.ALO.DZW

studios (work spaces)
RM.239 (A,L,B,R)
ALT **studio (work space)**
SN Use for spaces set aside for an artist to work, whether a painter, photographer, or other artist.
UF ateliers (work spaces)
CN V.RM.AFU.DIO.ALO.DOI.DCU

studios, broadcasting
USE **broadcasting studios**

studios, motion-picture
USE **motion-picture studios**

studios, radio
USE **radio studios**

studios, recording
USE **recording studios**

studios, sound
USE **sound studios**

studios, television
USE **television studios**

studios, TV
USE **television studios**

studs
RT.706
ALT **stud**
SN Series of vertical structural members which act as the supporting elements in a wall or partition. (DAC)
CN V.RT.AFU.AFU.ALO.ALO.BCW

studs (fasteners)
TF.491
ALT **stud (fastener)**
SN Bosses, rivets, or nails with a large head for ornament or protection.
CN V.TF.AFU.AFU.AFU.ALO.AFU.ELK

studs, upholstery
USE **upholstery studs**

study guides, examination
USE **examination study guides**

stuff, coarse
USE **coarse stuff**

stuff, dimension
USE **dimension lumber**

stuff, fine
USE **fine stuff**

stump beds
TG.376
ALT **stump bed**
SN Term used by Chippendale for low beds without any superstructure, generally used by servants. (GILBR2)
UF beds, stump
CN V.TG.AFU.AFU.ARI.AFU.AFU.EWY

stump legs
TG.951
ALT **stump leg**
SN Furniture legs in which the foot is formed by a continuation of the surfaces of a square leg in an outward flare.
UF legs, stump
CN V.TG.ALO.FIM.AFU.AFU.BOK

stumping
KT.251
ALT **stumped**
SN A drawing technique, using a cigar-shaped implement called a stump, to blend or smudge charcoal, soft pencil, pastel, chalk, or crayon. (MAYER)
CN K.KT.AFU.ALO.DUC.CXA.ALO.AXC
.ARI

stumps
TB.282 (N)
ALT **stump**
SN Cigar-shaped implements often pointed at both ends, consisting of tightly rolled leather, paper, or felt; used in drawing to blend or smudge charcoal, soft pencil, pastel, chalk, or crayon. (MAYER)
UF stomps
CN V.TB.AFU.ARI.CLM.AFU.ALO.ELK

stumps, arm
USE **arm supports**

stupas
RK.1148 (A,L)
ALT **stupa**
SN Use for Buddhist relic mounds of earth, brick, or stone, dominated by a hemispherical or bulbous dome set on a square or circular base and topped by a small pavilionlike structure and a spire.
UF chedi
pai t'a
thats
thupas
topes
CN V.RK.AFU.ALO.ALO.FCS.BUE

style
BM.305 (A,L,R)
SN Configuration of artistic elements that together constitute a manner of expression peculiar to a certain epoch, people, or individual. (MGHDIC)
CN B.BM.AFU.AXC.DUC

Style 1200
USE **Early Gothic**

Style Guimard
USE **Art Nouveau**

style manuals
VW.352 (L)
ALT **style manual**
UF manuals, style
style sheets
CN V.VW.AFU.AFU.ALO.CXA.BIQ.AXC

Style Moderne
USE **Art Deco**

style sheets
USE **style manuals**

style, court
USE **court style**

style, palace
USE **court style**

stylebooks
VW.532 (L)
ALT **stylebook**
CN V.VW.AFU.ALO.AFU.AFU.ALO.BCW
.BCW

stylebooks, architectural
USE **domestic stylebooks**

stylebooks, domestic
USE **domestic stylebooks**

stylists
HG.532
ALT **stylist**
CN H.HG.AFU.AXC.BUE.ARI.CXA.BOK

stylization
BM.12
SN Representation of natural appearances, sounds, and motions, such as shapes, speech, and gestures, more in accordance with artistic ideals or conventions than with observation of individual examples of these forms.
CN B.BM.AFU.AFU.AFU.BUE

stylobates
RM.16 (A,R)
ALT **stylobate**
SN Use for the course of pavement on which columns rest in Greek temples. For similar features in other building types, including Roman or Etruscan temples, use **podiums.**
CN V.RM.AFU.BOK.ARI

stylographs
TB.270 (N)
ALT **stylograph**
SN Fountain pens that have a fine writing point fitted with a needle which by the pressure of the point on a surface is pushed back to release the flow of ink. (W)
UF needle-point pens
pens, needle-point
Rapidographs (TM)
CN V.TB.AFU.ARI.CLM.AFU.ALO.DOI.
ALO.AFU

styluses
TB.284 (N)
ALT **stylus**
SN Any small pencil-shaped instruments with a hard point, usually metal; used for incising lines on a soft surface or for transferring drawings. (MAYER)
CN V.TB.AFU.ARI.CLM.AFU.ALO.ERE

styluses, light
USE **light pens**

styrene
MT.2701
SN A fragrant, liquid, unsaturated hydrocarbon used chiefly in making synthetic rubber, resins, and plastics and in improving drying oils. (W)
CN M.MT.AFU.ARI.HZS.AFU.BUE

styrene-acrylonitrile
MT.2150
UF SAN (styrene-acrylonitrile)
CN M.MT.AFU.AFU.ARI.BUE.ALO.AXC.

AFU.DUC

styrene-butadiene copolymer
USE **styrene-butadiene rubber**

styrene-butadiene elastomer
USE **styrene-butadiene rubber**

styrene-butadiene rubber
MT.2095 (L)
UF bunas
copolymer, sytrene-butadiene
elastomer, sytrene-butadiene
GR-S
rubber, styrene-butadiene
styrene-butadiene copolymer
styrene-butadiene elastomer
CN M.MT.AFU.AFU.ARI.BUE.AFU.AFU.CRG

styrene resin
USE **polystyrene**

Styrofoam (TM)
MT.2149
SN Polystyrene expanded into a multicellular mass that has one-sixth the weight of cork and will withstand temperatures above 170 degrees F. (MH)
CN M.MT.AFU.AFU.ARI.BUE.ALO.AXC.AFU.DOI.AFU

SU
USE **sulfone polymer**

Su-Song
FL.1937
CN F.FL.ALO.ARI.ALO.AFU.AFU.AXC.ALO.CRG

Sub-Apennine
FL.2704
CN F.FL.ALO.AXC.ALO.ALO.AFU.AFU.BCW

sub-bucks
USE **door bucks**

Sub-geometric
FL.2568
CN F.FL.ALO.AXC.ALO.AFU.AFU.ARI.ALO.AXC

Sub-Imperial Mughal
FL.2239
CN F.FL.ALO.ARI.AXC.ALO.AFU.BIQ.ALO.ALO.ARI

sub-layer
USE **subbing layer**

Sub-Mycenaean
FL.2554
CN F.FL.ALO.AXC.ALO.AFU.AFU.ALO.ALO.ARI.ALO

subaquatic structures
USE **submarine structures**

subarches
RT.283
ALT **subarch**
SN Minor arches beneath and enclosed by outer arches. (HAS)
CN V.RT.AFU.AFU.AFU.BCW.AFU.AFU.ARI.BIQ

subassemblies
USE **subassembly drawings**

subassembly drawings
VD.114
ALT **subassembly drawing**
UF detail assemblies
drawings, subassembly
drawings, subcomponent
subassemblies
subcomponent drawings
CN V.VD.AFU.ALO.DCU.AFU.ALO

subbasements
RM.415
ALT **subbasement**
SN Use to designate stories beneath basements.
CN V.RM.AFU.DUC.BIQ

subbidders
HG.402
ALT **subbidder**
CN H.HG.AFU.AXC.BOK.BCW.AFU

subbing layer
MT.2363
SN The layer of a photograph placed directly on the glass or film or paper base prior to addition of the binder. (SAPSP)
UF coating, substratum
layer, subbing
sub-layer
substratum coating
CN M.MT.AFU.ARI.ARI.ARI.ALO

subcomponent drawings
USE **subassembly drawings**

subcontracting
KG.194 (L)
CN K.KG.AFU.ALO.BCW.AFU.ALO

subcontractor bonds
VW.909
ALT **subcontractor bond**
UF bonds, subcontractor
CN V.VW.AFU.ARI.AFU.BOK.BOK.AXC.BCW.AFU

subcontractors
HG.619 (B)
ALT **subcontractor**
CN H.HG.AFU.AXC.BZY.ALO.ARI

subcontractors' drawings
USE **shop drawings**

subcontracts
VW.886
ALT **subcontract**
SN Contracts subordinate to another contract, made or intended to be made between the contracting parties, on one part, or some of them, and a third party (subcontractor). (BLACKS)
CN V.VW.AFU.ARI.AFU.BOK.BOK.ALO.ALO.AFU.BCW

subdivision of land
USE **land subdivision**

subdivision, land
USE **land subdivision**

subdivision, real estate
USE **land subdivision**

subdivisions
RG.238
ALT **subdivision**
SN Areas of land divided into blocks or lots, provided with streets or roads and open spaces, and then offered for sale or lease.
CN V.RG.AFU.ALO.ARI

subfloors
RT.749
ALT **subfloor**
SN Use for layers of boards or plywood sheets laid directly on joists and surmounted by the finish flooring, sometimes with a layer of underlayment in between.
CN V.RT.AFU.ALO.AFU.BIQ.ALO.AFU

subject analysis
KG.106 (L)
SN Examining the content of documents, either textual or pictorial, in order to determine what they are about or of.
UF analysis, content
analysis, subject
content analysis
CN K.KG.AFU.AFU.AXC.DUC

subject authority files
VW.591
ALT **subject authority file**
UF authority files, subject
files, subject authority
CN V.VW.AFU.ALO.AFU.BIQ.ALO.AFU.ALO

subject bibliographies
VW.258
ALT **subject bibliography**
UF bibliographies, subject
CN V.VW.AFU.AFU.AFU.FZU.BCW.AFU.ALO.AXC

subject cataloging
KG.74 (L)
SN Allocating subject headings to records for items in a library or other collection. (LG)
CN K.KG.AFU.AFU.AXC.AXC.AXC.ALO

subject catalogs
VW.99 (L)
ALT **subject catalog**
UF catalogs, subject
CN V.VW.AFU.AFU.AFU.FZU.ALO.AFU.

AXC.ALO

subject indexes
VW.441
ALT **subject index**
UF indexes, subject
CN V.VW.AFU.AFU.ALO.EWY.BOK.ARI .ALO

subject searching
KG.97
UF searching, subject
CN K.KG.AFU.AFU.AXC.CRG.ALO.AFU. ALO

Sublime, the
BM.494 (L,R)
SN Use for the conception or expression of awe-inspiring grandeur in a work of art.
UF the Sublime
CN B.BM.BIQ.AFU.BOK

submarine archaeology
USE **underwater archaeology**

submarine bases
RG.130 (B)
ALT **submarine base**
UF bases, submarine
CN V.RG.AFU.AFU.BZY.AFU.AXC.ALO

submarine photography
USE **underwater photography**

submarine structures
RK.1366 (B)
UF structures, subaquatic
structures, submarine
structures, underwater
subaquatic structures
underwater structures
CN V.RK.AFU.ALO.ARI.AXC.BIQ.ALO

submaster keys
TF.541
ALT **submaster key**
SN Keys capable of controlling a subordinate group of master-keyed locks, each having a different key of its own, but all in turn controlled by the main master key. (STEIN)
UF keys, submaster
CN V.TF.AFU.ALO.ARI.AFU.CXA

subminiature cameras
TB.294 (L)
ALT **subminiature camera**
SN Cameras using a film format smaller than 35mm. (LANG)
UF cameras, subminiature
CN V.TB.AFU.ARI.CLM.ARI.AFU.AFU .AFU.AXC.AFU

Subminoan
FL.2558
CN F.FL.ALO.AXC.ALO.AFU.AFU.ALO. ARI.ARI

submittals
VW.919
ALT **submittal**
CN V.VW.AFU.ARI.AFU.BOK.BOK.CRG

subpoenas
VW.1011 (L)
ALT **subpoena**
SN Commands to appear at a certain time and place to give testimony upon a certain matter. (BLACKS)
CN V.VW.AFU.ARI.ALO.BCW.AFU.ALO. AFU.ALO

subrails
RT.1129
ALT **subrail**
SN On a staircase, members which are fixed to the upper edge of a closed string to receive the balusters. (DAC)
CN V.RT.AFU.BIQ.AXC.ALO.BUE

subscribers, lists of
USE **subscription lists**

subscription lists
VW.265
ALT **subscription list**
SN Lists or records of subscriptions and subscribers. (GAHLM)
UF lists of subscribers
lists, subscription
subscribers, lists of
CN V.VW.AFU.AFU.AFU.FZU.BCW.AFU. AXC.AFU

subsequent locks
TF.224
ALT **subsequent lock**
SN Time locks constructed to lock by the action of a clock at a predetermined time subsequent to and irrespective of the time of the closing of the door. (STEIN)
UF locks, subsequent
CN V.TF.AFU.AFU.AFU.AFU.DIO.BIQ .AFU.ERE.ALO

subsidences (earth movements)
KM.108 (A,L,B)
UF land subsidences
subsidences, land
CN K.KM.AFU.CXA.ALO.BCW

subsidences, land
USE **subsidences (earth movements)**

subsidiary roads
USE **secondary roads**

subsidies
BM.391 (A,L)
SN Grants or gifts of money or other property made by way of financial aid. (W)
CN B.BM.ARI.CRG.ALO

subsidization
USE **subsidizing**

subsidizing
KG.48
ALT **subsidized**
SN Providing direct material aid, most often monetary, to persons, groups, or enterprises, usually for the purpose of supporting or promoting the recipient.
UF subsidization
CN K.KG.AFU.AFU.ARI.ALO.AFU.AFU

substances
USE **materials**

substances, hazardous
USE **hazardous substances**

substances, toxic
USE **hazardous substances**

substations
USE **electric substations**

substations, electric
USE **electric substations**

substratum coating
USE **subbing layer**

substructures
RT.6 (B)
ALT **substructure**
SN The foundation or understructure of a building; supports the superstructure. (DAC)
CN V.RT.AFU.AFU.AFU.AFU.AFU.AFU

subtractive color mixture
USE **subtractive mixture**

subtractive color processes
KT.365
SN Photographic processes using cyan, magenta, and yellow dyes or inks to produce a full-color image. Each dye permits two of the primary colors to pass, while blocking the third; a combination of two dyes (on separate filters) will allow only a single primary to pass.
UF subtractive processes (photography)
CN K.KT.AFU.ALO.DUC.DIO.ALO.DZW

subtractive mixture
BM.127
SN Mixture of color pigments, so called because reflected light is reduced as pigment colors are combined. (PREBLE)
UF color mixture, subtractive
mixture, subtractive
subtractive color mixture
CN B.BM.AFU.AFU.ARI.BOK.ALO.ALO. AFU.ALO.ALO

subtractive processes (photography)
USE **subtractive color processes**

subtreasury locks
TF.220
ALT **subtreasury lock**
SN Locks for use on metal doors of the small chests or boxes within a fireproof safe. (STEIN)
UF locks, subtreasury

CN V.TF.AFU.AFU.AFU.AFU.DIO.BIQ .AFU.EFQ

suburban growth
BM.1083 (A,B)
UF growth, suburban
CN B.BM.CLM.ALO.AXC.AFU

suburban homes
USE **suburban houses**

suburban houses
RK.299 (L)
ALT **suburban house**
UF homes, suburban
houses, suburban
suburban homes
CN V.RK.AFU.ALO.ALO.AXC.ALO.AXC .AFU.ALO

suburban landscapes
RD.293
ALT **suburban landscape**
SN Town and country areas with heterogeneous patchy mixture of residential areas, commercial centers, cropland, managed vegetation, and natural areas. (LNDECO)
UF landscapes, suburban
suburbscapes
CN V.RD.ARI.ALO.ALO.ARI

suburban rail
USE **commuter railroads**

suburbs
RD.64 (A,L,B,R)
ALT **suburb**
SN Compactly developed or developing, usually residential, areas on the outskirts of a central city; distinguished from central cities by their more homogeneous socio-economic and physical character, although rarely is there an identifiable boundary between suburbs and central cities.
UF faubourgs
CN V.RD.AFU.BCW.AXC

suburbs, garden
USE **garden suburbs**

suburbscapes
USE **suburban landscapes**

subventions
BM.390 (L)
CN B.BM.ARI.CRG.AFU.AFU

subway lines
USE **subways**

subway stations
RK.1246 (A,L)
ALT **subway station**
UF stations, subway
CN V.RK.AFU.ALO.ALO.GLI.AFU.ALO. ALO

subways
RD.108 (A,L,B,R)
ALT **subway**
UF metros
railroads, underground
railways, underground
subway lines
U-bahns
underground railroads
underground railway systems
underground railways
undergrounds
CN V.RD.ALO.ARI.AFU.AFU.ALO.AXC. AFU

succinite
MT.1495
UF amber, Prussian
Prussian amber
CN M.MT.AFU.AFU.ALO.BOK.BOK .AFU.AFU

Succos
USE **Sukkot**

sudatione
RM.77
ALT **sudatio**
SN Rooms in the Roman bath or gymnasium between the laconicum, sudatorium, or stove, and the caldarium or warm bath where athletes retired to remove sweat from their bodies. (RS)
CN V.RM.AFU.DIO.ALO.ALO.BOK. BCW

sudatoria
RM.78
ALT **sudatorium**
SN Hot air baths for inducing sweating; also such rooms in Roman baths.
UF laconica
CN V.RM.AFU.DIO.ALO.ALO.BOK.BIQ

Sue ware
FL.2043
UF Sueki
Sue(ki)
ware, Sue
CN F.FL.ALO.ARI.ALO.ALO.ALO.ALO. ALO.ERE

Sueki
USE **Sue ware**

Sue(ki)
USE **Sue ware**

suffering
BM.598 (L,R)
CN B.BM.BUE.CLM.AXC

suffragettes
HG.758 (L)
ALT **suffragette**
CN H.HG.AFU.BCW.HZS.BUE.ALO.AFU

suffragists
HG.757
ALT **suffragist**
CN H.HG.AFU.BCW.HZS.BUE.ALO

Sufism
BM.666 (L)
ALT **Sufi**
CN B.BM.BZY.AFU.BCW.ALO

sugar barns
USE **sugar houses**

sugar cane bagasse
USE **bagasse**

sugar chests
TG.470
ALT **sugar chest**
SN Specialized furniture form most popular in the American South; generally having a hinged lid on top covering a large divided storage chamber for brown and white sugar. (FAIRB)
UF chests, sugar
CN V.TG.AFU.AFU.AXC.ALO.AXC.ELK

sugar factories
USE **sugar refineries**

sugar houses
RK.75 (A)
ALT **sugar house**
UF barns, sugar
houses, sap
houses, sugar
sap houses
sugar barns
CN V.RK.AFU.ALO.ALO.AFU.AFU.CRG

sugar-lift aquatint
USE **lift-ground**

sugar maple
MT.1225 (L)
UF Acer saccharum
hard maple
maple, hard
maple, rock
maple, sugar
rock maple
CN M.MT.AFU.AFU.ALO.BIQ.DCU.AFU .AFU.AFU.IFM.BUE

sugar pine
MT.1389 (L)
UF pine, sugar
Pinus lambertiana
CN M.MT.AFU.AFU.ALO.BIQ.DCU.AFU .AFU.ALO.CXA.EFQ

sugar refineries
RK.639 (L,B)
ALT **sugar refinery**
UF factories, sugar
refineries, sugar
sugar factories
CN V.RK.AFU.ALO.ALO.CLM.ALO.ALO .AFU.AXC.BCW.BUE

Sui
FL.1884 (L)
CN F.FL.ALO.ARI.ALO.AFU.AFU.ALO. BZY

Suibokuga
FL.2069
CN F.FL.ALO.ARI.ALO.ALO.ALO.ARI

.ERE

suicides
KM.139 (L,R)
CN K.KM.AFU.DOI.ALO.ARI

Suiko
USE Asuka

suing
USE litigating

suitcase beds
TG.377
ALT suitcase bed
UF beds, suitcase
CN V.TG.AFU.AFU.ARI.AFU.AFU.FCS

suites
RM.271
ALT suite
SN Successions of connected rooms, generally on one floor, that are occupied as one unit. (RS)
CN V.RM.AFU.DIO.ARI.ALO.BIQ.ALO

suites (furniture)
TG.605
ALT suite (furniture)
CN V.TG.AFU.AFU.BCW

Suk
USE Pokot

Sukhodaya
USE Sukhothai

Sukhothai
FL.2415 (L)
UF Sukhodaya
CN F.FL.ALO.ARI.BCW.BOK.AFU.CFS

Sukiya
FL.2005 (L)
CN F.FL.ALO.ARI.ALO.ALO.ALO.AFU.CXA

sukkahs
RK.1152 (A)
ALT sukkah
SN Temporary structures roofed with branches and adorned with fruits or vegetables, built near a house or synagogue, and used as dining or living areas during the Jewish festival of Sukkot.
UF sukkot (structures)
CN V.RK.AFU.ALO.ALO.FCS.BZY

Sukkot
KM.89 (L,R)
UF Feast of Tabernacles
Succos
Tabernacles, Feast of
CN K.KM.AFU.CFS.ARI.CRG

sukkot (structures)
USE sukkahs

Suku
FL.470 (L)
UF Basuku
CN F.FL.ALO.AFU.AXC.ALO.ALO.ARI.CFS

Sukuma
FL.654 (L)
CN F.FL.ALO.AFU.AXC.AXC.BCW.CXA

Sulaiman I
USE Süleyman I

Sulawesi
FL.2387 (L)
UF Celebes
CN F.FL.ALO.ARI.BCW.ARI.ALO.BCW

Sulayhid
FL.3570
UF Salaihid
CN F.FL.ALO.BIQ.AFU.HOE

Sulayman b. Qutalmish
FL.3553
CN F.FL.ALO.BIQ.AFU.HIK.ARI.AFU

Süleyman I
FL.3487
UF Sulaiman I
Süleyman the Lawgiver
Süleyman the Magnificent
CN F.FL.ALO.BIQ.AFU.FOG.AFU.BIQ

Süleyman II
FL.3492
CN F.FL.ALO.BIQ.AFU.FOG.AFU.CLM

Süleyman the Lawgiver
USE Süleyman I

Süleyman the Magnificent
USE Süleyman I

sulfate-resistant cement
MT.19
SN A portland cement which is low in tricalcium aluminate; has a reduced susceptibility to attack by dissolved sulfates in water or soil. (DAC)
UF cement, sulfate-resistant
cement, sulfate-resisting
cement, type V portland
portland cement, type V
type V portland cement
CN M.MT.AFU.AFU.AFU.ALO.AFU.AFU.ARI.AFU.BUE

sulfate-resistant concrete
MT.230
UF concrete, sulfate-resistant
CN M.MT.AFU.AFU.AFU.BCW.AFU.AXC.BUE

sulfate, barium
USE blanc fixe

sulfide
MT.1006 (L)
SN Organic compound characterized by a sulfur atom attached to two carbon atoms. (WCOL)
UF sulphide
CN M.MT.AFU.AFU.ALO.AXC.BUE

sulfiding
KT.904
ALT sulfided
SN A deteriorative process affecting silver photographic images, in which the silver reacts with sulphur from the air or from within the print itself to form silver sulfide, causing the print to yellow and fade. (REILLY)
CN K.KT.ALO.BCW.BZY

sulfoaluminate cement
USE expanding cement

sulfone-based resin
USE sulfone polymer

sulfone polymer
MT.2151
UF polymer, sulfone
polysulfone
resin, sulfone-based
SU
sulfone-based resin
CN M.MT.AFU.AFU.ARI.BUE.ALO.AXC.AFU.DZW

sulfur
MT.561 (L,B)
UF brimstone
CN M.MT.AFU.AFU.AFU.CFS.AFU.GWW

sulfur cement
MT.35 (L)
UF cement, sulfur
cement, sulphur
cement, supersulphate
lute (cement)
sulphur cement
supersulphate cement
CN M.MT.AFU.AFU.AFU.ALO.AFU.AFU.DIO

sulfur dioxide
MT.313 (L)
SN A colorless gas used chiefly as a refrigerant, as a preservative, in bleachings, and for making other chemicals. (MH)
UF dioxide, sulfur
CN M.MT.AFU.AFU.AFU.BOK.BIQ

sulfuric acid
MT.302 (L)
UF acid, sulfuric
CN M.MT.AFU.AFU.AFU.BOK.AFU.BOK

Sulka
FL.3623
CN F.FL.ALO.BOK.ALO.ARI.ALO

Sullan
FL.2715
CN F.FL.ALO.AXC.ALO.ALO.AFU.AXC.AFU.ARI

sulphate, calcium
USE gypsum

sulphide
USE sulfide

sulphur cement
USE **sulfur cement**

sulphur (color)
USE **light greenish yellow**

Sulphur Spring Cochise
FL.932
UF Cochise, Sulphur Spring
CN F.FL.ALO.ALO.ALO.AFU.ALO.ARI.BIQ.ALO.ARI

sulphur yellow
USE **brilliant greenish yellow**
light greenish yellow
pale greenish yellow
vivid greenish yellow
vivid yellow

Sultanabad pottery
USE **Sultanabad ware**

Sultanabad ware
FL.3459
UF pottery, Sultanabad
Sultanabad pottery
ware, Sultanabad
CN F.FL.ALO.BIQ.AFU.DIO.ALO.ARI

Sultanate
FL.2302 (A)
CN F.FL.ALO.ARI.AXC.ALO.AFU.BZY.BOK

Sultanate of Delhi
USE **Delhi Sultanate**

sultanes
USE **ottomans**

sultanes (lits de repos)
USE **daybeds**

Sumatran
FL.2388 (L)
UF Suvarnadvipa
CN F.FL.ALO.ARI.BCW.ARI.ALO.BIQ

Sumba
FL.2390
CN F.FL.ALO.ARI.BCW.ARI.ALO.BOK

Sumbawa
FL.2391 (L)
CN F.FL.ALO.ARI.BCW.ARI.ALO.BUE

Sumbwa
FL.655
CN F.FL.ALO.AFU.AXC.AXC.BCW.DCU

Sumerian
FL.2964 (L)
CN F.FL.ALO.AXC.ARI.BCW.AFU.ALO.AXC

Sumero-Akkadian
FL.2986
CN F.FL.ALO.AXC.ARI.BCW.ALO.ARI

sumi
USE **Japanese ink**

sumi painting
USE **sumie**

sumie
KT.260 (L)
SN Painting carried out entirely in black ink, with no additional color but often giving the impression of color through manipulation of tone. (THDAT)
UF painting, sumi
sumi painting
CN K.KT.AFU.ALO.DUC.CXA.ALO.BCW.ARI

Sumiyoshi (architecture style)
FL.2006
CN F.FL.ALO.ARI.ALO.ALO.ALO.AFU.DCU

Sumiyoshi (painting style)
FL.2070
CN F.FL.ALO.ARI.ALO.ALO.ALO.ARI.EWY

summaries
VW.78
ALT **summary**
CN V.VW.AFU.AFU.AFU.FCS

summations
BM.821
CN B.BM.CFS.ARI.CLM.ARI

summer
BM.1039 (L,R)
UF summertime
CN B.BM.CFS.AXC.CRG.ARI.ARI

summer beds
TG.361
ALT **summer bed**
SN Term used by Sheraton for a fanciful design which incorporates two twin beds sharing a common tester and having a passageway between the beds to allow easy access for servants.
UF beds, summer
CN V.TG.AFU.AFU.ARI.AFU.AFU.BZY.ALO.BCW

summer camps
RG.162 (A,L)
ALT **summer camp**
UF camps, summer
CN V.RG.AFU.AFU.DOI.AXC.BCW

summer cottages
USE **summer houses**

summer homes
USE **summer houses**

summer houses
RK.277 (A,L,B)
ALT **summer house**
SN Homes in the country used as summer residences. (DAC)
UF cottages, summer
homes, summer
houses, summer
summer cottages
summer homes
CN V.RK.AFU.ALO.ALO.AXC.ALO.ALO.ARI.AFU

summer palaces
RK.344 (A)
ALT **summer palace**
UF palaces, summer
CN V.RK.AFU.ALO.ALO.AXC.ALO.BOK.BOK.ALO.BCW

summer resorts
RG.172 (A,L)
ALT **summer resort**
UF resorts, summer
CN V.RG.AFU.AFU.DOI.BZY.ARI

summerbeams
RT.314
ALT **summerbeam**
SN Horizontal beams supporting the ends of floor joists or resting on posts and supporting the wall above. (DAC)
UF summers
CN V.RT.AFU.AFU.AFU.BCW.ALO.ALO.BOK

summers
USE **summerbeams**

summertime
USE **summer**

summonses
VW.1012 (L)
ALT **summons**
SN Instruments delivered by a sheriff or other appropriate party, notifying a person that a court action has been commenced against the person and that the person is required to appear in court on the day named to answer the complaint. (BLACKS)
CN V.VW.AFU.ARI.ALO.BCW.AFU.ALO.AFU.ARI

Sumo
FL.1560 (L)
CN F.FL.ALO.ALO.ARI.ALO.BOK.CLM

sump pits
USE **sumps**

sumps
RT.1495
ALT **sump**
SN Tanks or pits, located below the normal grade of the gravity system, and that receive the discharge from drains or other wastes; must be emptied by mechanical means. (STEIN)
UF pits, sump
sewage sumps
sump pits
sumps, sewage
CN V.RT.ALO.BCW.ALO.ARI.CXA

sumps, sewage
USE **sumps**

sun-baked brick
USE **sun-dried brick**

sun breakers
USE **brise-soleils**

sun decks
RM.52 (A,L)
ALT **sun deck**
SN Decks or flat roofs intended for sunbathing. (MEANS)
UF decks, sun
CN V.RM.AFU.DIO.AFU.BCW.AXC.ALO

sun-dried brick
MT.124
UF brick, sun-baked
brick, sun-dried
brick, sun-dried mud
brick, unburnt
brick, unfired
mud brick, sun-dried
sun-baked brick
sun-dried mud brick
unburnt brick
unfired brick
CN M.MT.AFU.AFU.AFU.AXC.ALO.AFU.AXC.AFU.ALO

sun-dried mud brick
USE **sun-dried brick**

sun-heated buildings
USE **solar buildings**

sun-heated greenhouses
USE **solar greenhouses**

sun louvers
USE **brise-soleils**

sun-planes
TB.948 (N)
ALT **sun-plane**
SN Planes with a semicircular shape when viewed from above; used to smooth and level the ends of the staves of barrels after the barrels have been assembled. (MERCER)
UF cooper's levellers
levellers, cooper's
planes, sun
CN V.TB.AFU.BCW.CFS.ALO.AFU.DUC.ARI.BUE

sun rooms
USE **solariums**

sun shades
USE **brise-soleils**

sun snakes, double
USE **swastikas**

sun-thickened oil
MT.2004
UF oil, sun-thickened
CN M.MT.AFU.AFU.ARI.ARI.ARI.BIQ

sun yellow
USE **nickel-titanium yellow**

sunburst lights
USE **fanlights**

sunbursts
DG.48
ALT **sunburst**
CN D.DG.AFU.AFU.CXA.BIQ

Sunday schools
RK.817 (L)
ALT **Sunday school**
UF Sabbath schools
schools, Sabbath
schools, Sunday
CN V.RK.AFU.ALO.ALO.CXA.ARI.ALO.DCU

Sundi
FL.486
CN F.FL.ALO.AFU.AXC.ALO.ALO.AXC.AXC.BOK

sunflower oil
MT.2020 (L)
SN A pale yellow drying oil with a pleasant odor and taste obtained from the large seeds of the common sunflower plant. (MH)
UF oil, sunflower
CN M.MT.AFU.AFU.ARI.ARI.AXC.AFU.CLM

sunflower yellow
USE **orpiment**

Sung
USE **Song**

Sung, Northern
USE **Northern Song**

Sung, Southern
USE **Southern Song**

Sunga
FL.2195
UF Shunga
CN F.FL.ALO.ARI.AXC.ALO.AFU.ARI.ARI

sunk fences
USE **ha-has**

sunk fillets
RT.780
ALT **sunk fillet**
SN Fillet moldings that are produced by cutting a groove in a plane surface.
UF fillets, sunk
CN V.RT.AFU.ALO.AFU.BOK.AFU.AFU.AXC.AXC.BCW

sunken fences
USE **ha-has**

sunken-floor huts
USE **sunken huts**

sunken huts
RK.29 (A)
ALT **sunken hut**
SN Denotes semi-underground buildings forming self-contained structures without a built floor, common to England and northern Europe throughout the first millennium AD and used variously for such functions as houses, storehouses, and workshops; use **pit dwellings** for prehistoric houses whose floors are generally deeply set below ground level.
UF Grubenhäuser
huts, sunken
sunken-floor huts
CN V.RK.AFU.ALO.AFU.ALO.CRG

sunken roads
RK.1562
ALT **sunken road**
UF roads, sunken
CN V.RK.ALO.ALO.BIQ.ARI.ARI.ARI

sunlight
BM.849 (L,B)
SN Use with reference to the direct light of the sun; for the light of day in general, use **daylight.**
UF sunshine
CN B.BM.CFS.AXC.ALO.AFU.ALO.AFU.ALO.AFU

Sunni
BM.667 (L)
UF Sunni Islam
CN B.BM.BZY.AFU.BCW.ARI

Sunni Islam
USE **Sunni**

sunrise motifs
USE **rising suns**

suns, rising
USE **rising suns**

sunshine
USE **sunlight**

Supai
USE **Havasupai**

super-security prisons
USE **maximum-security prisons**

superba
USE **composite white**

superba white
USE **composite white**

superblocks
RK.1582
ALT **superblock**
SN Designates very large, usually residential, city blocks often formed by consolidating several smaller blocks and often barred to through traffic and crossed by pedestrian walks.
CN V.RK.ALO.ARI.ALO.AFU

supercapitals
USE **impost blocks**

supercilia
RT.781
ALT **supercilium**
SN The flat bands above the uppermost moldings or cymas of cornices, or the small bands above and below the scotia of an Attic base. (RS)
CN V.RT.AFU.ALO.AFU.BOK.AFU.AFU.AXC.AXC.BIQ

supercoat
MT.2574
UF antiabrasion layer
coat, top
layer, antiabrasion
layer, nonabrasion
nonabrasion layer
overcoat
supercoating
top coat
CN M.MT.AFU.ARI.CRG.ARI.BCW

supercoating
USE **supercoat**

superconductors
MT.2582 (L)
SN Materials that have a complete lack of measurable electrical resistance at very low temperatures. (MH)
CN M.MT.AFU.ARI.CXA.AFU.ALO

superhighways
USE **throughways**

superintendents
HG.655
ALT **superintendent**
CN H.HG.AFU.AXC.CFS.AFU.AFU.ARI

Supermannerist
FL.3752 (R)
ALT **Supermannerism**
UF Mega-decoration
CN F.FL.ALO.BUE.ARI.HZS

supermarkets
RK.143 (A,L,B)
ALT **supermarket**
SN Large, self-service, retail markets which sell food, household goods, and household merchandise. (DAC)
UF hypermarkets
CN V.RK.AFU.ALO.ALO.ALO.ARI.AXC.ARI

supernatural
BM.502 (L,R)
CN B.BM.BIQ.ARI.ALO

superoxol
MT.2381
SN Bleach and oxidizing agent used especially in conservation of art work. (MAYER)
CN M.MT.AFU.ARI.BUE.AFU

Superrealist
USE **Photorealist**

superstructures
RT.7
ALT **superstructure**
SN Structures built on something else; also, that part of a structure which receives the live load directly. (DAC)
CN V.RT.AFU.AFU.AFU.AFU.AFU.ALO

supersulphate cement
USE **sulfur cement**

supervising
KG.155 (L)
SN Overseeing activity in an organization. (RLG7)
CN K.KG.AFU.AFU.BIQ.BUE.BIQ

supervising architects
HG.89
ALT **supervising architect**
SN Architects who guide, review, or approve the work of other architects or supervisory personnel. (STEIN)
UF architects, supervising
CN H.HG.AFU.AXC.AXC.AFU.AFU.ALO.ALO.BIQ

supervisors
HG.658 (L)
ALT **supervisor**
CN H.HG.AFU.AXC.CFS.AFU.ALO.AFU

supper canterburies
USE **canterburies (stands)**

supper rooms
RM.120
ALT **supper room**
SN Rooms found in large houses and hotels intended for meals that are part of late evening entertainments.
UF rooms, supper
CN V.RM.AFU.DIO.ALO.BCW.CXA

supper trays (canterburies)
USE **canterburies (stands)**

supplementary lighting
RT.1363
UF lighting, supplementary
CN V.RT.ALO.AXC.AFU.CFS

supplements
VW.474
ALT **supplement**
SN Sections added to books or documents to give further information or to correct errors. Includes separate sections devoted to special subjects inserted into newspapers or periodicals. (AHD)
CN V.VW.AFU.AFU.ALO.FUA

suppliers
HG.433
ALT **supplier**
CN H.HG.AFU.AXC.BOK.FIM

supply registers
USE **registers (HVAC components)**

supply stations, electrical
USE **electrical supply stations**

supply systems, water
USE **water supply systems**

supply, electric power
USE **power supply**

supply, power
USE **power supply**

supporting
KT.652
ALT **supported**
CN K.KT.AFU.ALO.GLI.AFU.BIQ

supports (artists' materials)
MT.2366 (R)
ALT **support (artist's material)**
SN Material on the surface of which an image resides, as in paintings, drawings, prints, or photographs. For secondary materials on which supports are mounted, use **mounts (artists' materials).**
UF bases (artists' materials)
primary supports
supports, primary
surfaces (artists' materials)
CN M.MT.AFU.ARI.BCW.AFU

supports (furniture components)
TG.989
ALT **support (furniture component)**
CN V.TG.ALO.HIK

supports, arm
USE **arm supports**

supports, birdcage
USE **birdcages (furniture components)**

supports, dolphin
USE **dolphin supports**

supports, drawer
USE **drawer supports**

supports, melon bulb
USE **melon bulb supports**

supports, primary
USE **supports (artists' materials)**

supports, secondary
USE **mounts (artists' materials)**

supports, shelf
USE **shelf brackets**

Suprematist
FL.3419 (R)
ALT **Suprematism**
CN F.FL.ALO.BCW.ALO.AXC.DIO.BZY.ALO.BIQ

suqs
USE **bazaars**

surbased arches
RT.246
ALT **surbased arch**
SN Use for semicircular arches in which the rise is less than half the span.
UF arches, surbased

CN V.RT.AFU.AFU.AFU.BCW.AFU.AFU.
AFU.EFQ

surbased vaults
RT.560
ALT **surbased vault**
SN Vaults formed by the portion of any curve where the height is less than half the span. (NICH)
UF testudines
vaults, surbased
CN V.RT.AFU.AFU.AFU.BIQ.BOK.AFU.
ARI.ALO.AFU

surbases
USE **caps (pedestal components)**

sure cards
USE **cartes-de-visite**

surety bonds
VW.910 (L)
ALT **surety bond**
SN Legal instruments under which one party guarantees to pay a second party for the debt, default, or failure to perform of a third party.
UF bonds, surety
CN V.VW.AFU.ARI.AFU.BOK.BOK.AXC.
BIQ

surface-active agents
MT.2732 (L)
SN Substances useful for their cleaning, wetting, dispersing, or similar powers. (W)
UF agents, surface-active
surfactants
CN M.MT.AFU.ARI.IFM.BUE

surface arcades
USE **blind arcades**

surface-coatings
USE **coatings**

surface color
USE **local color**

surface door locks
USE **rim locks**

surface hardening
KT.842 (L)
ALT **surface hardened**
SN Hardening the surface of a metal by case-hardening or other method, such as by induction or flame. (W)
UF hardening, surface
CN K.KT.AFU.ALO.HOE.BCW.ALO.
BCW.AXC

surface hinges
TF.129
ALT **surface hinge**
SN Hinges, often ornamental, mounted on a face of a door rather than the edge. (MEANS)
UF hinges, surface
CN V.TF.AFU.AFU.AFU.AFU.CLM.AFU.
FUA

surface locks
USE **rim locks**

surface printing
USE **relief printing**

surface properties
BM.976
UF properties, surface
CN B.BM.CFS.AXC.BZY.BZY

surface strikes
TF.519
ALT **surface strike**
SN Strikes projecting slightly beyond the face of a door jamb. (DITTRI)
UF strikes, surface
CN V.TF.AFU.ALO.AFU.ALO.AXC

surface water drainage
USE **runoff**

surfaced lumber
USE **dressed lumber**

surfaces (artists' materials)
USE **supports (artists' materials)**

surfactants
USE **surface-active agents**

surgeons
HG.388 (L)
ALT **surgeon**
CN H.HG.AFU.AXC.BIQ.ALO.BCW.
BOK.AFU

surgeries, doctors'
USE **medical offices**

surgery
KG.189 (L)
SN Performing manual or operative procedures to treat diseases, injuries, or deformities. (RHDEL2)
UF operating (surgery)
CN K.KG.AFU.ALO.AXC.AFU

surgical clinics
RK.745 (L)
ALT **surgical clinic**
UF clinics, surgical
CN V.RK.AFU.ALO.ALO.CXA.ALO.AFU.
ALO.BCW

surmounted arches
RT.245
ALT **surmounted arch**
SN Use for semicircular stilted arches.
UF arches, surmounted
CN V.RT.AFU.AFU.AFU.BCW.AFU.AFU.
AFU.DZW.AFU

surmounted vaults
RT.543
ALT **surmounted vault**
SN Vaults formed by the portion of any curve where the height is greater than half the span. (NICH)
UF vaults, surmounted
CN V.RT.AFU.AFU.AFU.BIQ.BOK.AFU.
ALO.AFU.BCW

Surrealist
FL.3304 (A,L,B,R)
ALT **Surrealism**
CN F.FL.ALO.BCW.ALO.AXC.DCU.CXA

surrounds
RT.1014
ALT **surround**
SN The visible bordering elements around a door, window, or other opening.
CN V.RT.AFU.ARI.ALO.BUE

survey drawings
USE **measured drawings**

survey maps
USE **topographic surveys**

survey plans
USE **topographic surveys**

surveying
KT.117 (A,L,R)
ALT **surveyed**
CN K.KT.AFU.ALO.CXA.ARI

surveying, archaeological
USE **archaeological surveying**

surveying, land
USE **topographical surveying**

surveying, photographic
USE **photographic surveying**

surveying, topographical
USE **topographical surveying**

surveyors
HG.648 (A,L,B)
ALT **surveyor**
CN H.HG.AFU.AXC.BZY.BUE

surveyors, quantity
USE **quantity surveyors**

surveys (inventories)
USE **inventories**

surveys (land)
USE **land surveys**

surveys (questionnaires)
USE **questionnaires**

surveys, architectural
USE **architectural surveys**

surveys, building
USE **building surveys**

surveys, cadastral
USE **cadastral maps**

surveys, historic structure
USE **architectural surveys**

surveys, insurance
USE **insurance surveys**

surveys, land
USE **land surveys**

surveys, plot

USE **topographic surveys**

surveys, quantity
USE **quantity surveys**

surveys, records
USE **records surveys**

surveys, site
USE **topographic surveys**

surveys, structural
USE **structural surveys**

surveys, topographic
USE **topographic surveys**

Suryavarman I
FL.2334
CN F.FL.ALO.ARI.BCW.ALO.ARI.AFU.ALO

Suryavarman II
FL.2343
CN F.FL.ALO.ARI.BCW.ALO.ARI.AFU.CLM

suspended
DC.43
SN Connected to a support located above.
CN D.DC.AFU.ALO.ARI.DZW

suspended ceilings
RT.732 (A,B)
ALT **suspended ceiling**
SN Nonstructural ceilings suspended below the overhead structural slab or from the structural elements of a building, and not bearing on the walls. (DAC)
UF ceilings, drop
ceilings, false
ceilings, suspended
drop ceilings
false ceilings
CN V.RT.AFU.ALO.AFU.ALO.CLM

suspended floors
RT.747 (A,B)
ALT **suspended floor**
SN Floors which span the entire distance between end supports without additional support in the middle. (DAC)
UF floors, suspended
CN V.RT.AFU.ALO.AFU.BIQ.AFU.BCW

suspended roofs
USE **suspension roofs**

suspended scaffolding
TB.492
SN Scaffolding supported by cables or metal straps. (PUTNAM)
UF hanging scaffolds
scaffolding, suspended
scaffolds, hanging
CN V.TB.AFU.ARI.ERE.ARI.AXC

suspended structures
USE **suspension structures**

suspending agents
MT.2331
UF agents, suspending
CN M.MT.AFU.ARI.ALO.FOG

suspension bridges
RK.1301 (A,L)
ALT **suspension bridge**
UF bridges, suspension
CN V.RK.AFU.ALO.ALO.GLI.ALO.AFU.ARI.BOK

suspension roofs
RT.443 (A,L,B)
ALT **suspension roof**
SN Roofs in which the loads are carried by cables. (DAC)
UF hanging roofs
roofs, hanging
roofs, suspended
roofs, suspension
suspended roofs
CN V.RT.AFU.AFU.AFU.BIQ.ARI.AFU.ALO.AFU

suspension structures
RT.20 (B)
ALT **suspension structure**
UF structures, suspended
structures, suspension
suspended structures
CN V.RT.AFU.AFU.AFU.ALO.AFU.AXC

Susquehanna
FL.1305 (L)
CN F.FL.ALO.ALO.ARI.AFU.ARI.CRG

Sussex marble
MT.769
UF marble, Sussex
CN M.MT.AFU.AFU.AFU.DCU.AFU.ARI.ARI.ALO.BOK.BCW

Sutaio
FL.1379
CN F.FL.ALO.ALO.ARI.AFU.BOK.BIQ.ARI

Sutherland tables
TG.678
ALT **Sutherland table**
SN Swing-leg, dropleaf tables with a very narrow central portion; of a type made in England from the early 19th century. (DDA)
UF tables, Sutherland
CN V.TG.AFU.AFU.BIQ.BOK.AFU.AXC.BIQ

Suto
USE **Sotho**

Suvarnadvipa
USE **Sumatran**

Suwannee
FL.742
CN F.FL.ALO.ALO.ALO.AFU.AFU.ARI.AFU.BIQ

Suzdalian
USE **Vladimir-Suzdalian**

Suzuki School
FL.2095
CN F.FL.ALO.ARI.ALO.ALO.ALO.AXC.BZY.CLM

Svat Valley
USE **Swat Valley**

swages
TB.690 (N)
ALT **swage**
SN Tools used for various purposes but especially to set the teeth of saws, and in sheet metal work, hand tools used to shape material to the desired form. (PUTNAM)
CN V.TB.AFU.BCW.BIQ.AFU.ALO.DCU

swaging
KT.853 (L)
ALT **swaged**
SN Finishing the cross section of a metal item to size or shape. (ALMEID)
CN K.KT.AFU.ALO.HOE.BCW.ALO.BIQ.BUE

Swahili
FL.608 (A,L)
CN F.FL.ALO.AFU.AXC.AXC.ALO.BUE

swales
RD.213
ALT **swale**
SN Use either for long, narrow land depressions, especially on shores and largely parallel to coastlines, or for narrow, valleylike features formed where two slopes intersect.
CN V.RD.ARI.AFU.AXC.AFU.ALO.ALO.ARI

swamp gum
USE **tupelo**

swamp oak
USE **pin oak**

swamp pine
USE **Cuban pine**
loblolly pine

swamp tupelo
MT.1161
UF gum, water
Nyssa biflora
tupelo, swamp
water gum
CN M.MT.AFU.AFU.ALO.BIQ.DCU.AFU.AFU.AFU.DIO.AXC.ARI.ARI

swamp white oak
MT.1253
UF oak, swamp white
Quercus bicolor
white oak, swamp
CN M.MT.AFU.AFU.ALO.BIQ.DCU.AFU.AFU.AFU.IRA.ERE

swamps

RD.174 (L)
ALT **swamp**
UF sloughs
slues
CN V.RD.ARI.AFU.ARI.BIQ

swan arms
TG.816
ALT **swan arm**
UF arms, swan
arms, swan-neck
swan-neck arms
CN V.TG.ALO.ALO.AFU.AFU.BIQ

swan chairs
TG.90
ALT **swan chair**
UF chairs, swan
chairs, swan easy
easy chairs, swan
swan easy chairs
CN V.TG.AFU.AFU.ALO.AFU.AFU.AFU.LCM

swan easy chairs
USE **swan chairs**

swan-neck arms
USE **swan arms**

Swankalok
USE **Sawankhalok**

swastikas
DG.69 (L,B,R)
ALT **swastika**
SN Figures in which two lines or bands cross each other and form four arms of equal length that are bent at right angles.
UF double sun snakes
fylfots
hammers, Thor's
sun snakes, double
Thor's hammers
CN D.DG.AFU.AFU.DUC.AFU

swastikas, three-armed
USE **triskelions**

Swat
FL.2173
CN F.FL.ALO.ARI.AXC.AFU.BIQ

Swat Valley
FL.2174
UF Svat Valley
Uddiyana
CN F.FL.ALO.ARI.AXC.AFU.BIQ.AFU

Swatow ware
FL.1952
UF ware, Swatow
CN F.FL.ALO.ARI.ALO.AFU.AFU.AXC.ARI.BZY

sways
USE **braces (woodworking tools)**

Swazi
FL.564 (L)
CN F.FL.ALO.AFU.AXC.ARI.AXC.ARI

sweat lodges
USE **sweathouses**

sweathouses
RK.1073 (R)
ALT **sweathouse**
UF lodges, sweat
sweat lodges
CN V.RK.AFU.ALO.ALO.EWY.BCW.ALO.AFU

Swedish
FL.3061 (L,B)
CN F.FL.ALO.BCW.AFU.DUC.AXC

sweep braces
USE **medial braces**

sweep saws
USE **bow saws**

sweeps
USE **braces (woodworking tools)**

sweet birch
MT.1123
UF Betula lenta
birch, black
birch, cherry
birch, mahogany
birch, sweet
black birch
cherry birch
mahogany birch
CN M.MT.AFU.AFU.ALO.BIQ.DCU.AFU.AFU.AFU.BIQ.BZY

sweet buckeye
USE **yellow buckeye**

sweet cherry
MT.1291 (L)
UF cherry, sweet
cherry, wild
gean
mazzard
Prunus avium
wild cherry
CN M.MT.AFU.AFU.ALO.BIQ.DCU.AFU.AFU.AFU.KLE.ARI.ALO.ALO

sweet chestnut
USE **European chestnut**

sweet chestnut, American
USE **American chestnut**

sweet gum
MT.1164 (L)
UF gum, sweet
Liquidambar styraciflua
CN M.MT.AFU.AFU.ALO.BIQ.DCU.AFU.AFU.AFU.DIO.AXC.BCW

swell'd front
USE **blockfront**

swelled chamfers
USE **wave moldings**

swelled friezes
USE **pulvinated friezes**

swept dormers
USE **eyebrow dormers**

swept-leg chairs
USE **Trafalgar chairs**

Swietenia
MT.1211
CN M.MT.AFU.AFU.ALO.BIQ.DCU.AFU.AFU.AFU.HTY.ARI

Swietenia macrophylla
USE **South American mahogany**

Swietenia mahagoni
USE **West Indies mahogany**

Swietenia mahogani
USE **South American mahogany**

swimming baths
USE **swimming pools**

swimming pools
RK.1075 (A,L,N,B,R)
ALT **swimming pool**
UF baths, swimming
natatoriums
pools, swimming
swimming baths
CN V.RK.AFU.ALO.ALO.EWY.BCW.ARI

swing bridges
RK.1281
ALT **swing bridge**
SN Drawbridges that open and close to river craft by rotating around a central pier. (W)
UF bridges, swing
swivel bridges
CN V.RK.AFU.ALO.ALO.GLI.ALO.AFU.AFU.AXC.AXC

swing cribs
USE **swinging cribs**

swing doors
USE **swinging doors**

swing legs
TG.956
ALT **swing leg**
SN Use for a hinged leg, without a stretcher, which swings out to support the drop leaf of a table, such as found on card tables. For similar legs with a stretcher, use **gate legs**.
UF fly legs
legs, fly
legs, swing
CN V.TG.ALO.FIM.AFU.ALO.ALO

swing rocking chairs
USE **platform rockers**

swing saws
USE **pendulum saws**

swinging cradles
TG.333
ALT **swinging cradle**
UF cradles, swinging

CN V.TG.AFU.AFU.ARI.AFU.AFU.AXC.ALO.ALO

swinging crib beds
USE **swinging cribs**

swinging cribs
TG.336
ALT **swinging crib**
UF beds, swinging crib
cribs, swinging
swing cribs
swinging crib beds
CN V.TG.AFU.AFU.ARI.AFU.AFU.AXC.ARI.ALO

swinging doors
RT.874
ALT **swinging door**
SN Doors equipped with hardware which enable them to swing 90 degrees in either direction from the plane of their frame. (DAC)
UF doors, double-acting
doors, swing
doors, swinging
double-acting doors
swing doors
CN V.RT.AFU.ARI.AFU.AFU.AFU.ALO.ARI.AFU.ARI.BUE

swinging latch bolts
TF.560
ALT **swinging latch bolt**
SN Latch bolts hinged to a lock or door and operated by swinging rather than sliding. (MEANS)
UF bolts, hinged latch
bolts, swinging latch
hinged latch bolts
latch bolts, hinged
latch bolts, swinging
CN V.TF.AFU.ALO.AXC.AFU.CFS

swinging posts
USE **hanging posts**

Swiss
FL.3063 (L,B)
CN F.FL.ALO.BCW.AFU.EFQ

switch gear, electric
USE **switchboards**

switch plates
TF.268
ALT **switch plate**
UF plates, switch
CN V.TF.AFU.AFU.AFU.AFU.DZW.ARI.AFU

switchboards
RT.1350 (L,N,B)
ALT **switchboard**
SN Use for large panels, frames, or other assemblies on which are mounted switches, fuses, instruments, and protective devices; for smaller panels containing switches and fuses or circuit breakers, use **panelboards.**
UF electric switch gear
switch gear, electric
CN V.RT.ALO.ARI.ALO.DCU

switches
USE **electric switches**

switches, electric
USE **electric switches**

switching yards
USE **marshalling yards**

swivel bridges
USE **swing bridges**

swivel chairs
TG.231 (N)
ALT **swivel chair**
SN Chairs with a revolving seat on a fixed frame.
UF chairs, revolving
chairs, swivel
revolvers (swivel chairs)
revolving chairs
CN V.TG.AFU.AFU.ALO.AFU.AFU.AXC.BCW

swivel stools
USE **revolving stools**

Sword Style
FL.2526
CN F.FL.ALO.AXC.AFU.BOK.ALO.ALO.ARI

swordsmiths
HG.519 (L)
ALT **swordsmith**
CN H.HG.AFU.AXC.BUE.ARI.CFS.ARI.CFS

swordsmiths' marks
VW.757 (L,R)
ALT **swordsmith's mark**
UF marks, swordsmiths'
CN V.VW.AFU.ALO.ALO.AFU.AXC.AXC.DOI

SX-70 (TM) process
USE **internal dye diffusion transfer process**

sycamore
MT.1268 (L)
UF American plane
American sycamore
buttonball
buttonwood
plane, American
Platanus occidentalis
sycamore, American
CN M.MT.AFU.AFU.ALO.BIQ.DCU.AFU.AFU.AFU.JZQ.ALO

sycamore, American
USE **sycamore**

syenite
MT.616 (L)
CN M.MT.AFU.AFU.AFU.DCU.AFU.AFU.AFU.AFU.ARI.ARI

syllabi
VW.1069 (L)
ALT **syllabus**
SN Outlines or brief statements of the main points of a lecture or course of study. (AHD)
CN V.VW.AFU.ARI.ALO.CRG.BIQ

symbolic color
BM.17 (L)
SN Color associated with a certain personage in Christian art; also any use of color in a symbolic sense. (MGHDIC)
UF color, symbolic
symbolism of colors
CN B.BM.AFU.AFU.AFU.BZY.AXC

symbolic numbers
USE **number symbolism**

symbolism
BM.13 (L,B,R)
CN B.BM.AFU.AFU.AFU.BZY

Symbolism (art movement)
USE **Symbolist**

symbolism of colors
USE **symbolic color**

symbolism of numbers
USE **number symbolism**

symbolism, church
USE **religious symbolism**

symbolism, number
USE **number symbolism**

symbolism, religious
USE **religious symbolism**

Symbolist
FL.3305 (L,R)
ALT **Symbolist movement**
UF Symbolism (art movement)
CN F.FL.ALO.BCW.ALO.AXC.DCU.DCU

symbols
VB.65 (L,B,R)
ALT **symbol**
SN Use for visible signs (which can include figures, such as personifications, or objects) that stand for something else, often something abstract or invisible.
UF signs (symbols)
CN V.VB.AFU.ALO.BUE

symbols, zodiac
USE **zodiac symbols**

symmetrical balance
USE **bilateral symmetry**

symmetry
BM.93 (A,L,B,R)
ALT **symmetrical**
CN B.BM.AFU.AFU.ARI.AFU.FOG

symmetry, approximate
USE **approximate symmetry**

symmetry, axial
USE **axial symmetry**

symmetry, bilateral
USE **bilateral symmetry**

symmetry, dynamic
USE **approximate symmetry**

symmetry, radial
USE **radial symmetry**

sympathetic ink
USE **invisible ink**

symphony halls
USE **concert halls**

symposia
KM.98 (L,B,R)
UF colloquiums
CN K.KM.AFU.CRG.AFU.AFU

synagogues
RK.1125 (A,L,N,B,R)
ALT **synagogue**
UF Jewish temples
tabernacles (synagogues)
temples, Jewish
CN V.RK.AFU.ALO.ALO.FCS.BIQ.BUE

synasol
USE **denatured alcohol**

Synchromist
FL.1754 (L,R)
ALT **Synchromism**
CN F.FL.ALO.ALO.BCW.AFU.CFS.BIQ

syncretism
BM.526 (L,R)
SN Reconciliation or union of conflicting (as religious) beliefs or an effort intending such. (W)
CN B.BM.BIQ.AXC.EWY

syndrome, sick building
USE **sick building syndrome**

synecdoche
BM.24 (R)
CN B.BM.AFU.AFU.AFU.CFS.BIQ

synesthesia
BM.599 (L,R)
CN B.BM.BUE.CLM.BCW

syngraphai
VW.887
ALT **syngraph**
SN Written contracts signed by both or all parties. (OED)
CN V.VW.AFU.ARI.AFU.BOK.BOK.ALO.ALO.AFU.BIQ

Synnadicum marble
USE **pavonazzetto**

synodal halls
USE **chapter houses**

synonyms, dictionaries of
USE **dictionaries of synonyms**

synopses
VW.82
ALT **synopsis**
SN Brief statements or outlines of a subject. (AHD)
CN V.VW.AFU.AFU.AFU.FCS.AXC

syntactics
USE **syntax**

syntax
KD.47 (L,R)
UF grammar
syntactics
CN K.KD.AFU.AFU.AXC.AFU.ALO.BUE

synthetic binders
MT.2371
UF binders, synthetic
CN M.MT.AFU.ARI.BIQ.ARI

Synthetic Cubist
FL.3294
ALT **Synthetic Cubism**
UF Collage Cubist
Cubist, Collage
Cubist, Synthetic
CN F.FL.ALO.BCW.ALO.AXC.DCU.ARI.ALO

synthetic detergents
USE **detergents**

synthetic dye
MT.1537
UF dye, synthetic
CN M.MT.AFU.AFU.ARI.AFU.AFU.AFU.AFU.ALO

synthetic fiber
MT.1838 (L)
UF fiber, synthetic
CN M.MT.AFU.AFU.ARI.ALO.AFU.ALO

synthetic inorganic black pigment
USE **artificial inorganic black pigment**

synthetic inorganic blue pigment
USE **artificial inorganic blue pigment**

synthetic inorganic brown pigment
USE **artificial inorganic brown pigment**

synthetic inorganic green pigment
USE **artificial inorganic green pigment**

synthetic inorganic red pigment
USE **artificial inorganic red pigment**

synthetic inorganic violet pigment
USE **artificial inorganic violet pigment**

synthetic inorganic yellow pigment
USE **artificial inorganic yellow pigment**

synthetic madder
USE **alizarin madder**

synthetic natural rubber
USE **polyisoprene**

synthetic organic black pigment
MT.1578
UF artificial organic black pigment
black pigment, artificial organic
black pigment, synthetic organic
organic black pigment, artificial
organic black pigment, synthetic
pigment, artificial organic black
pigment, synthetic organic black
CN M.MT.AFU.AFU.ARI.AFU.AFU.ALO.ALO.AFU.ARI

synthetic organic blue pigment
MT.1605
UF artificial organic blue pigment
blue pigment, artificial organic
blue pigment, synthetic organic
organic blue pigment, artificial
organic blue pigment, synthetic
pigment, artificial organic blue
pigment, synthetic organic blue
CN M.MT.AFU.AFU.ARI.AFU.AFU.ALO.ALO.ALO.AXC

synthetic organic green pigment
MT.1660
UF artificial organic green pigment
green pigment, artificial organic
green pigment, synthetic organic
organic green pigment, artificial
organic green pigment, synthetic
pigment, artificial organic green
pigment, synthetic organic green
CN M.MT.AFU.AFU.ARI.AFU.AFU.ALO.ALO.AXC.AXC

synthetic organic pigment
MT.1562 (L)
UF artificial organic pigment
coal-tar color
coal-tar dye
color, coal-tar
dye, coal-tar
organic pigment, artificial
organic pigment, synthetic
pigment, artificial organic
pigment, synthetic organic
CN M.MT.AFU.AFU.ARI.AFU.AFU.ALO.AFU.ALO.ALO

synthetic organic red pigment
MT.1702
UF artificial organic red pigment
organic red pigment, artificial
organic red pigment, synthetic
pigment, artificial organic red
pigment, synthetic organic red
red pigment, artificial organic
red pigment, synthetic organic
CN M.MT.AFU.AFU.ARI.AFU.AFU.ALO.ALO.BCW.AXC

synthetic organic violet pigment
MT.1722
UF artificial organic violet pigment
organic violet pigment, artificial
organic violet pigment, synthetic
pigment, artificial organic violet
pigment, synthetic organic violet

violet pigment, artificial organic
violet pigment, synthetic organic
CN M.MT.AFU.AFU.ARI.AFU.AFU.ALO.ALO.BIQ.AXC

synthetic organic yellow pigment
MT.1797
UF artificial organic yellow pigment
organic yellow pigment, artificial
organic yellow pigment, synthetic
pigment, artificial organic yellow
pigment, synthetic organic yellow
yellow pigment, artificial organic
yellow pigment, synthetic organic
CN M.MT.AFU.AFU.ARI.AFU.AFU.ALO.ALO.BUE.AXC

synthetic resins
USE **plastics**

synthetic rubber
USE **elastomers**

synthetic wax
MT.2203
UF wax, synthetic
CN M.MT.AFU.AFU.ARI.BZY.ARI

Synthetist
FL.3379 (R)
ALT **Synthetism**
SN Use when referring to the work of Gauguin and the Pont-Aven School.
CN F.FL.ALO.BCW.ALO.AXC.DIO.BCW.BCW.BUE

Syrian
FL.2931 (L,B)
CN F.FL.ALO.AXC.ARI.AXC.ALO.BCW

Syrian gray-black ware
FL.2945
UF burnished ware, gray (Syrian)
gray burnished ware (Syrian)
gray-black ware, Syrian
ware, gray burnished (Syrian)
ware, Syrian gray-black
CN F.FL.ALO.AXC.ARI.AXC.ALO.BIQ.CXA

Syro-Hittite
FL.2864
CN F.FL.ALO.AXC.ARI.AFU.ALO.ALO

Syro-Phoenician
FL.2930
CN F.FL.ALO.AXC.ARI.AXC.ALO.AXC.AFU

Syros phase
FL.2541
CN F.FL.ALO.AXC.ALO.AFU.AFU.ALO.AFU.AFU.AXC

syrup
MT.2274 (L)
CN M.MT.AFU.ALO.HOE

systematic bibliographies
USE **systematic enumerative bibliographies**

systematic catalogs
USE **classified catalogs**

systematic enumerative bibliographies
VW.261
ALT **systematic enumerative bibliography**
UF bibliographies, enumerative
bibliographies, systematic
bibliographies, systematic enumerative
enumerative bibiographies, systematic
enumerative bibliographies
systematic bibliographies
CN V.VW.AFU.AFU.AFU.FZU.BCW.AFU.ALO.BCW

Systemic
FL.3753 (R)
SN Use with reference to abstract paintings of the 1960s and 1970s that repeat or vary a motif from work to work or within a work.
CN F.FL.ALO.BUE.ARI.IFM

systems
BM.1161 (L,B,R)
SN Use broadly to designate complex assemblies of entities and activities, arranged according to some scheme or plan, and intended to perform specific functions.
CN B.BM.DIO.BCW

systems analysis
KT.18 (L)
UF analysis, systems
CN K.KT.AFU.ALO.AXC.BCW

systems analysts
HG.358
ALT **systems analyst**
UF analysts, systems
CN H.HG.AFU.AXC.BIQ.ALO.ARI

Systems art
FL.3754 (R)
SN Use for art influenced by systems analysis, dealing, for example, with systems of natural phenomena, social signs, or the art world itself.
UF art, Systems
CN F.FL.ALO.BUE.ARI.ILG

systems engineering
KD.233 (L)
SN Branch of engineering involving the design of relatively large-scale, complex systems. (PG)
UF engineering, systems
CN K.KD.AFU.ARI.BIQ.CRG

systems, air conditioning
USE **air conditioning**

systems, air distribution
USE **air distribution systems**

systems, auxiliary fire alarm
USE **auxiliary fire alarm systems**

systems, building
USE **building systems**

systems, bus
USE **bus transit systems**

systems, bus transit
USE **bus transit systems**

systems, chilled water
USE **chilled water systems**

systems, clock and program
USE **clock and program systems**

systems, communication
USE **communication systems**

systems, communication (infrastructural systems)
USE **telecommunication systems**

systems, conveying
USE **conveying systems**

systems, cooling
USE **air cooling**

systems, downfeed
USE **downfeed systems**

systems, drainage
USE **drainage systems**

systems, electric wiring
USE **electric wiring**

systems, electrical
USE **electrical systems**

systems, fire alarm
USE **fire alarm systems**

systems, fire detection
USE **fire detectors**

systems, fire extinguishing
USE **fire extinguishing systems**

systems, fire protection
USE **fire protection systems**

systems, fireplace
USE **fireplaces**

systems, flat plate
USE **flat plate systems**

systems, flat slab
USE **flat slab systems**

systems, flat slab and beam
USE **two-way beam and slab systems**

systems, flat slab and drop panel
USE **flat slab systems**

systems, forced-air heating
USE **forced air heating**

systems, generative (copy art)
USE **copy art**

systems, gravity warm air
USE **gravity heating**

systems, grounded
USE **grounded systems**

systems, heating
USE **heating systems**

systems, ice storage
USE **ice storage systems**

systems, incremental air conditioning
USE **incremental air conditioning**

systems, intercom
USE **intercom systems**

systems, intercommunication
USE **intercom systems**

systems, intermission alarm
USE **intermission alarm systems**

systems, irrigation
USE **irrigation systems**

systems, local fire alarm
USE **local fire alarm systems**

systems, mechanical
USE **mechanical systems**

systems, monorail
USE **monorails**

systems, motor bus
USE **bus transit systems**

systems, one-way beam and slab
USE **one-way beam and slab systems**

systems, one-way flat plate
USE **one-way solid slab systems**

systems, one-way joist
USE **one-way joist systems**

systems, one-way pan joist
USE **one-way joist systems**

systems, one-way solid slab
USE **one-way solid slab systems**

systems, one-way structural
USE **one-way structural systems**

systems, passive solar heating
USE **passive solar heating**

systems, plumbing
USE **plumbing systems**

systems, police communication
USE **police communication systems**

systems, proprietary fire alarm
USE **proprietary fire alarm systems**

systems, public address
USE **public address systems**

systems, rail transit
USE **rail transit systems**

systems, rapid rail transit
USE **rapid rail transit systems**

systems, refrigerant
USE **refrigerant systems**

systems, remote-staion fire alarm
USE **remote-station fire alarm systems**

systems, sanitary
USE **sanitary drainage systems**

systems, sanitary drainage
USE **sanitary drainage systems**

systems, school clock and program
USE **clock and program systems**

systems, security
USE **security systems**

systems, signal
USE **communication systems**

systems, storm drainage
USE **storm water systems**

systems, storm water
USE **storm water systems**

systems, streetcar
USE **streetcar systems**

systems, telecommunication
USE **telecommunication systems**

systems, telephone
USE **telephone systems**

systems, television antenna
USE **television antenna systems**

systems, transit
USE **transit systems**

systems, transportation
USE **transit systems**

systems, trolleybus
USE **trolleybus systems**

systems, two-way
USE **two-way structural systems**

systems, two-way beam and slab
USE **two-way beam and slab systems**

systems, two-way flat plate
USE **flat plate systems**

systems, two-way structural
USE **two-way structural systems**

systems, unit air conditioning
USE **unit air conditioning**

systems, upfeed
USE **upfeed systems**

systems, urban rail
USE **urban rail systems**

systems, urban transit
USE **urban transit systems**

systems, ventilation
USE **ventilation**

systems, wall
USE **wall systems**

systems, warm air heating
USE **warm air heating**

systems, water
USE **plumbing systems**

systems, water storage
USE **water storage systems**

systems, water supply
USE water supply systems

systems, wiring
USE **electric wiring**

Szeletian
FL.2463
CN F.FL.ALO.AXC.AFU.ARI.AFU.ARI

T and G joints
USE **tongue-and-groove joints**

T-beams
RT.713
ALT **T-beam**
CN V.RT.AFU.AFU.ALO.ARI.BCW

T bevels
USE **bevel squares**

T hinges
TF.131
ALT **T hinge**
SN T-shaped, surface-mounted hinges. The cross arm of the T is fixed to a doorframe or post while the length of the T supports a door or gate. (MEANS)
UF hinges, T
CN V.TF.AFU.AFU.AFU.AFU.CLM.AFU.FUA.ALO

T-squares
TB.448 (L,N)
ALT **T-square**
SN Squares in the shape of a T, used in technical and architectural drawing. The short arm slides along the edge of a drawing board keeping the long arm in a parallel state. (MEANS)
UF squares, tee
tee squares
CN V.TB.AFU.ARI.EFQ.ALO.BZY.BCW

t'ai miao
RK.1147
SN Use for Chinese great ancestral shrines, usually associated with palace buildings.
CN V.RK.AFU.ALO.ALO.FCS.BOK.BUE

T'ang
USE **Tang**

T'ien-ch'i
USE **Tianqi**

T'ien-T'ai
BM.620 (L)
CN B.BM.BZY.AFU.AFU.BCW.AXC

T'ung-chih
USE **Tongzhi**

Tabagayab
USE **Tazaba-Gyab**

tabby
MT.36 (L)
SN A mixture of lime and water with shells, gravel, or stones which, when dry, is as hard as rock; used as a building material. (DAC)
CN M.MT.AFU.AFU.AFU.ALO.AFU.AFU DOI

tabernacles (aediculae)
USE **aediculae**

tabernacles (altar components)
RT.1222 (L,N)
ALT **tabernacle (altar component)**
SN Ornamental receptacles, attached to Christian altars, for vessels containing the sacred host. (NCE)
CN V.RT.AFU.BUE.ALO.ALO.ALO.BCW

tabernacles (churches)
USE **churches**

tabernacles (synagogues)
USE **synagogues**

Tabernacles, Feast of
USE **Sukkot**

tabernae
RK.183
ALT **taberna**
SN Roman one-room, rectangular chambers opening directly off the street and used primarily as shops or booths.
CN V.RK.AFU.ALO.ALO.ALO.ARI.BIQ.ALO.CRG

table beds
TG.347
ALT **table bed**
SN Dual-purpose side tables having a hinged top and a front containing a folding bed. (GILBR2)
UF beds, table
bedsteads, table
table bedsteads
CN V.TG.AFU.AFU.ARI.AFU.AFU.BIQ.AFU.BOK

table bedsteads
USE **table beds**

table boards
USE **tables**

table-bureau
USE **tables à écrire**

table-chairs
USE **chair-tables**

table chairs, child's
USE **highchairs**

table desks
USE **portable desks**

table planes
USE **table round planes**

table round planes
TB.928
ALT **table round plane**
SN Molding planes in matched pairs used for making rule joints on the flaps of folding tables or desks. (SALAM)
UF planes, table
planes, table round
table planes
CN V.TB.AFU.BCW.CFS.ALO.AFU.DUC.ALO.CLM

table saws
TB.1003
ALT **table saw**
SN Circular saws that are set below the surface of a table having a slot through which the saw blade protrudes.(DAC) The blade can be raised or lowered to control the depth of cut, and it can usually be tilted to provide a cut of a particular angle.
UF saws, table
CN V.TB.AFU.BCW.CFS.ALO.AFU.EWY.AXC.BCW

table-settles
USE **settle-tables**

table stones
USE **megalithic chamber tombs**

tables
TG.665 (L,N,R)
ALT **table**
SN Articles of furniture consisting of a flat, slab like top supported on one or more legs or supports. (RHDEL2)
UF boards (tables)
boards, table
mensae
table boards
trapeza
CN V.TG.AFU.AFU.BIQ.BOK

tables à abattant
USE **dropleaf tables**

tables à écrire
TG.582
ALT **table à écrire**
SN Writing tables often with a leather-covered slide and sometimes with an adjustable hinged panel for reading. Distinguished from **bureaux plats** by their much smaller size. (PC)
UF table-bureau
tables-écritoire
tables en écritoire
CN V.TG.AFU.AFU.AXC.ALO.BZY.FUA.CRG

tables à fleurs
USE **jardinières**

tables à gradin
USE **bonheurs-du-jour**

tables à jouer
USE **gaming tables**

tables à la Bourgogne
USE **secrétaires à la Bourgogne**

tables à la tronchin
TG.689
ALT **table à la tronchin**
SN Tables with adjustable tops which could be raised by means of a ratchet so that they could be used as standing desks. (GRANDJ)
CN V.TG.AFU.AFU.BIQ.BOK.AFU.CXA

tables à ouvrage
USE **work tables**

tables ambulantes
TG.684
ALT **table ambulante**
SN 18th-century French term for any small, easily portable table. (DDA)
UF ambulantes
petites tables (tables ambulantes)
tables correntilles
CN V.TG.AFU.AFU.BIQ.BOK.AFU.BZY.AFU

tables and desks, combined dressing
USE **bureau tables**

tables chiffonnières
USE **tables en chiffonnière**

tables correntilles
USE **tables ambulantes**

tables d'en cas
USE **night tables**

tables de brelan
TG.717
ALT **table de brelan**
SN Circular card tables with a depression in the center for the cards and for a candlestick. (VERLET)
CN V.TG.AFU.AFU.BIQ.BOK.ALO.AXC.AXC

tables de chevet
USE **night tables**

tables de jeu
USE **gaming tables**

tables de nuit
USE **night tables**

tables de salon
TG.685
ALT **table de salon**
SN Small movable tables sometimes with a porcelain or marble top. (PC)
CN V.TG.AFU.AFU.BIQ.BOK.AFU.BZY.AFU.AFU

tables de toilette
USE **toilettes**

tables de tric-trac
TG.745
ALT **table de tric-trac**

SN French gaming tables incorporating a tric-trac (backgammon board), the latter most often housed in a well and covered by a removable top, veneered on one side with a chess board and on the other with a baize or leather covered surface for the playing of cards. (PC)
UF tric-tracs (gaming tables)
CN V.TG.AFU.AFU.BIQ.BOK.ALO.CRG.ARI

tables (documents)
VW.249 (L,B)
ALT **table (document)**
SN Condensed, orderly arrangements of data, especially those in which the data are arranged in columns and rows. (AHD)
CN V.VW.AFU.AFU.AFU.FZU.AXC.BCW

tables-écritoire
USE **tables à écrire**

tables en cas
USE **night tables**

tables en chiffonnière
TG.769
ALT **table en chiffonnière**
SN Small ladies' work tables in its classic form with galleries around its top and the shelf joining its legs to provide shallow receptacles into which one could plance chiffons (scraps of ribbon and cloth) and other needlework materials; either square or circular in form and generally having three drawers, the uppermost sometimes fitted with writing equipment. (PC)
UF chiffonnières (table)
tables chiffonnières
CN V.TG.AFU.AFU.BIQ.BOK.ALO.GWW.ALO

tables en crachoir
TG.705
ALT **table en crachoir**
SN Term for French tables with a deep rim or gallery around the top. (DDA)
CN V.TG.AFU.AFU.BIQ.BOK.AFU.DZW.ARI

tables en écritoire
USE **tables à écrire**

tables en guéridon
USE **guéridons**

tables en vide-poche
USE **vide-poches**

tables (panels)
USE **panels**

tables servantes
USE **dumbwaiters (stands)**

tables volantes
TG.690
ALT **table volante**
SN Elaborate mechanical tables that could sink or rise through the floor to be replenished with food. (WATSON)
CN V.TG.AFU.AFU.BIQ.BOK.AFU.DCU

tables, architect's
USE **drawing tables**

tables, artist's
USE **drawing tables**

tables, backgammon
USE **backgammon tables**

tables, bag
USE **work tables**

tables, bagatelle
USE **bagatelle tables**

tables, banquet
USE **dining tables**

tables, basset
USE **basset tables**

tables, Beau-Brommel dressing
USE **Beau-Brummel dressing tables**

tables, bed
USE **bed tables**

tables, bedside
USE **night tables**

tables, bench
USE **bench tables**

tables, billiard
USE **billiard tables**

tables, braced
USE **sawbuck tables**

tables, bracket
USE **console tables**

tables, breakfast
USE **breakfast tables**

tables, bureau
USE **bureau tables**

tables, bureau dressing
USE **bureau tables**

tables, butterfly
USE **butterfly tables**

tables, cabinet
USE **cabinet stands**

tables, café
USE **ice-cream tables**

tables, calling card
USE **card stands**

tables, capstan
USE **capstan tables**

tables, capstan expanding
USE **capstan tables**

tables, card
USE **card tables**

tables, Carlton
USE **Carlton House tables**

tables, Carlton House
USE **Carlton House tables**

tables, center
USE center tables

tables, chamber
USE **chamber tables**

tables, checker
USE **chess tables**

tables, chess
USE **chess tables**

tables, china
USE **china tables**

tables, cigarette
USE **smokers**

tables, clap
USE **console tables**

tables, cocktail
USE **cocktail tables**

tables, coffee
USE **coffee tables**

tables, combined writing and dressing
USE **bureau tables**

tables, commode
USE **commode dressing tables**

tables, communion
USE **communion tables**

tables, console
USE **console tables**

tables, conversion
USE **conversion tables**

tables, corbel
USE **corbel tables**

tables, corner
USE **handkerchief tables**

tables, counter
USE **counters**

tables, credence
USE **credences**

tables, cricket
USE **cricket tables**

tables, davenport
USE **sofa tables**

tables, déjeuner
USE **déjeuner tables**

tables, dining
USE **dining tables**

tables, dining-room

tables, occasional
USE **occasional tables**

tables, ombre
USE **ombre tables**

tables, oyster
USE **oyster tables**

tables, parlor
USE **parlor tables**

tables, pastry
USE **pastry tables**

tables, pedestal
USE **pedestal tables**

tables, pedestal base
USE **pedestal tables**

tables, Pembroke
USE **Pembroke tables**

tables, phone
USE **telephone tables**

tables, picnic
USE **picnic tables**

tables, piecrust
USE **piecrust tables**

tables, pier
USE **pier tables**

tables, pier-console
USE **pier tables**

tables, pier (slab tables)
USE **slab tables**

tables, pillar and claw
USE **pillar and claw tables**

tables, pillar and claw dining
USE **pillar and claw dining tables**

tables, pillar and claw Pembroke
USE **pillar and claw Pembroke tables**

tables, pillar pedestal
USE **pedestal tables**

tables, pool
USE **pool tables**

tables, pouch
USE **work tables**

tables, quartetto
USE **quartetto tables**

tables, radio
USE **radio tables**

tables, refectory
USE **refectory tables**

tables, reflecting dressing
USE **Rudd tables**

tables, rent
USE **rent tables**

tables, rising-top writing
USE **rising-top writing tables**

tables, Rudd
USE **Rudd tables**

tables, Rudd dressing
USE **Rudd tables**

tables, saloon
USE **saloon tables**

tables, sawbuck
USE **sawbuck tables**

tables, screen
USE **lady's screen writing tables**

tables, serving
USE **servers**
sideboard tables

tables, sewing
USE **work tables**

tables, shaving
USE **shaving stands**

tables, side
USE **side tables**

tables, side (sideboard tables)
USE **sideboard tables**

tables, sideboard
USE **sideboard tables**

tables, slab
USE **slab tables**

tables, snack
USE **snack tables**

tables, snap
USE **tilt-top tables**

tables, social
USE **drinking stands**

tables, sofa
USE **sofa tables**

tables, sofa writing
USE **sofa writing tables**

tables, spider-leg
USE **spider-leg tables**

tables, splay-leg
USE **cricket tables**

tables, stack
USE **nesting tables**

tables, stone
USE **megalithic chamber tombs**

tables, stretcher
USE **refectory tables**

tables, Sutherland
USE **Sutherland tables**

tables, tailor's
USE **tailor's tables**

tables, tambour writing
USE **tambour writing tables**

tables, tavern
USE **tavern tables**

tables, tavern stretcher
USE **tavern tables**

tables, tea
USE **tea tables**

tables, telephone
USE **telephone tables**

tables, telescope
USE **telescope tables**

tables, telescope dining
USE **telescope tables**

tables, three-part dining
USE **three-part dining tables**

tables, tier
USE **tiered stands**

tables, tilt-top
USE **tilt-top tables**

tables, tip
USE **tilt-top tables**

tables, tip-top
USE **tilt-top tables**

tables, tip-up
USE **tilt-top tables**

tables, toddy
USE **drinking stands**

tables, toilet
USE **dressing tables**

tables, trestle
USE **trestle tables**

tables, triangular dropleaf
USE **handkerchief tables**

tables, tripod
USE **tripod tables**

tables, tripod-base
USE **tripod tables**

tables, tripod card
USE **tripod card tables**

tables, turn up
USE **tilt-top tables**

tables, TV
USE **snack tables**

tables, upright-top
USE **tilt-top tables**

tables, urn
USE **kettle stands**

tables, water
USE **water tables**

tables, Windsor
USE **Windsor tables**

tables, wine
USE **drinking stands**

tables, work
USE **work tables**

tables, writing
USE **writing tables**

tablet-arm chairs
TG.199 (N)
ALT **tablet-arm chair**
SN Armchairs with one flat arm wide enough to use as a writing surface.
UF arms, tablet
chairs, tablet
chairs, tablet-arm
tablet arms
tablet chairs
CN V.TG.AFU.AFU.ALO.AFU.AFU.ALO.FIM

tablet arms
USE **tablet-arm chairs**
writing arms

tablet chairs
USE **tablet-arm chairs**

tablet top chairs
USE **Trafalgar chairs**

tablet-top Windsor chairs
TG.113
ALT **tablet-top Windsor chair**
SN Square-back Windsor chairs with a cross panel capping and usually extending beyond the top of the back posts. Such chairs can have backs consisting of long spindles, cross slats, one or more cross slats with short spindles, or a vertical back splat. (EVANS)
UF chairs, tablet-top Windsor
Windsor chairs, tablet-top
CN V.TG.AFU.AFU.ALO.AFU.AFU.AFU.MLC.CFS.BOK

tablets
VW.625 (L,B,R)
ALT **tablet**
CN V.VW.AFU.ALO.AFU.DIO

tablets, digitizing
USE **graphics tablets**

tablets, graphics
USE **graphics tablets**

tablina
RM.286
ALT **tablinum**
SN Use for rooms located at the far end of the atria in ancient Roman houses.
CN V.RM.AFU.DIO.ARI.ALO.DZW

tabourets
TG.250 (N)
ALT **tabouret**
SN French term for stools, originally of drum shape; in the 18th century it applied to any stool with fixed upright legs, as distinct from **pliants,** which had folding crossed legs. 18th-century tabourets were rectangular, not drum-shaped, with upholstered seats. For similar seats supported on six or more legs use **banquettes.** (DDA)
CN V.TG.AFU.AFU.ALO.AFU.ALO.AFU.CFS

tabourets de pied
USE **footstools**

tabourets en chancelière
TG.251
ALT **tabouret en chanceli ère**
SN 18th-century tabourets, often lavishly carved and sometimes surrounded by a back on three sides so that they resembled the end of a miniature duchesse brisée. (WATSON)
CN
V.TG.AFU.AFU.ALO.AFU.ALO.AFU.CFS.AFU

tabourets en X
USE **X-chairs**

Tabrez marble
MT.677
UF marble, Tabrez
CN M.MT.AFU.AFU.AFU.DCU.AFU.ALO.AFU.ALO.ALO.AFU.AFU.BCW.ALO

Tabriz School (Il-Khanid)
FL.3455
CN F.FL.ALO.BIQ.AFU.DIO.AFU.AFU.ALO

Tabriz School (Safavid)
FL.3536
CN F.FL.ALO.BIQ.AFU.GRC.AFU.AXC

tabularia
RK.687
ALT **tabularium**
SN Use for ancient Roman archive buildings. (JBW-P)
CN V.RK.AFU.ALO.ALO.CRG.AFU.ALO

Tabwa
FL.502
CN F.FL.ALO.AFU.AXC.ALO.ALO.BCW.BUE

tacamahac
USE **balsam poplar**

Tachiste
FL.3718 (R)
ALT **Tachisme**
SN Use for French painting similar to American Action Painting, including that of the late 1940s sometimes called Abstraction Lyrique. Use **Lyrical Abstraction** for the continuation of Abstract Expressionism into the 1960s and 1970s (e.g., Guston, Frankenthaler).
UF Abstraction Lyrique
CN F.FL.ALO.BUE.ARI.ARI.AFU

tachylite
MT.631
SN Volcanic glass from Oahu, Hawaii, used for making ornamental articles. (MH)
UF basalt glass
glass, basalt
Hawaiian obsidian
obsidian, Hawaiian
CN M.MT.AFU.AFU.AFU.DCU.AFU.AFU.ALO.ALO.ALO.AFU.ARI

tack claws
USE **tack pulls**

tack hammers
TB.1082 (N)
ALT **tack hammer**
SN Lightweight hammers that have usually one magnetized face and are used for holding and driving tacks. (W)
UF hammers, tack
CN V.TB.AFU.BCW.CFS.ALO.ARI.AFU.AXC

tack lifters
USE **tack pulls**

tack pulls
TB.424 (N)
ALT **tack pull**
SN Small hand tools with a handle and a slightly bent bifurcated end for removing tacks or nails. (W)
UF cat's paws
claws, nail
claws, tack
lifters, tack
nail claws
pulls, tack
tack claws
tack lifters
tack wrenches
wrenches, tack
CN V.TB.AFU.ARI.DZW.BOK

tack rooms
RM.346
ALT **tack room**
SN Rooms in or attached to a horse barn or stable for the storage and maintenance of riding tack and often of stud records or for the display of prizes or other honors of the stable. (W)
UF harness rooms
rooms, harness
rooms, tack
CN V.RM.AFU.DIO.AXC.ARI.AXC

tack wrenches
USE **tack pulls**

tacking irons
TB.338 (N)
ALT **tacking iron**
SN Electric, straight-handled irons used

for dry mounting photographs by holding paper, dry-mounting tissue, and cardboard in place until they are put in a dry-mounting press, where they are thoroughly bound. (MAYER)
UF irons, tacking
CN V.TB.AFU.ARI.CLM.ARI.ALO.CRG

tackles
USE **block and tackle**

tackles, sawing
USE **sawing tackles**

tacks
TF.493 (L,N)
ALT **tack**
CN V.TF.AFU.AFU.AFU.ALO.AFU.ERE

tacks, carpet
USE **carpet tacks**

tacks, double pointed
USE **double pointed tacks**

tactical maps
VW.166
ALT **tactical map**
SN Large-scale maps used for tactical and administrative purposes. (DOD)
UF maps, tactical
CN V.VW.AFU.AFU.AFU.FZU.AXC.AFU.ARI.ALO.ALO

tactile perception
USE **touch**

tactile values
BM.169
SN Surface characteristics perceptible by touch.
UF values, tactile
CN B.BM.AFU.AFU.ARI.BOK.DUC.AFU

Tactilist
FL.3407
ALT **Tactilism**
UF Tattilismo
CN F.FL.ALO.BCW.ALO.AXC.DIO.BOK.BCW.AXC

Tada
FL.117
CN F.FL.ALO.AFU.ALO.AFU.BUE.CRG.ALO

taeniae
RT.782
ALT **taenia**
SN Narrow raised bands, particularly the topmost members of the Doric architrave. (DAC)
CN V.RT.AFU.ALO.AFU.BOK.AFU.AFU.AXC.AXC.BOK

tag sales
USE **garage sales**

Tagar
FL.2133
CN F.FL.ALO.ARI.ARI.AFU.BIQ.BCW

Tahitian
FL.3701 (L)
CN F.FL.ALO.BOK.AXC.BZY.AFU

Tahltan
FL.1241
UF Nahane, Western
Western Nahane
CN F.FL.ALO.ALO.ARI.AFU.AFU.ARI.DUC

Tahuantinsuyo
USE **Inca horizon**

Tai
USE **Thai**

taigas
RD.252 (L)
ALT **taiga**
SN Forests, usually coniferous, adjacent to arctic tundras. (ALLABY)
UF boreal forests
forests, boreal
CN V.RD.ARI.AFU.BCW.ALO.AFU.ARI

tailor's tables
TG.759
ALT **tailor's table**
UF tables, tailor's
CN V.TG.AFU.AFU.BIQ.BOK.ALO.FIM

tailors
HG.533 (L)
ALT **tailor**
CN H.HG.AFU.AXC.BUE.ARI.CXA.BUE

tailpieces
USE **lookouts (roof components)**

tails, devil's
USE **jumpers**

Taino
FL.1106 (L)
CN F.FL.ALO.ALO.ALO.ALO.ARI.ARI

Tairona
FL.1669 (L)
CN F.FL.ALO.ALO.ARI.ARI.BCW.DUC

Taisha
USE **Izumo Taisha**

Taisho
FL.1989
CN F.FL.ALO.ARI.ALO.ALO.AFU.BIQ.ALO

Taita
USE **Teita**

Tajin
FL.1005
UF El Tajin
CN F.FL.ALO.ALO.ALO.ALO.AFU.ALO.ALO.AFU.AFU

Takatori pottery
USE **Takatori ware**

Takatori ware
FL.2044 (L)
UF pottery, Takatori
Takatori pottery
ware, Takatori
CN F.FL.ALO.ARI.ALO.ALO.ALO.ALO.ALO.EWY

Takli
FL.788
CN F.FL.ALO.ALO.ALO.AFU.ALO.AFU.AFU.ARI.ALO

Takulli
USE **Carrier**

Takuma
FL.2068
CN F.FL.ALO.ARI.ALO.ALO.ALO.ARI.ELK

Talaing
FL.2314
CN F.FL.ALO.ARI.BCW.AFU.BCW

Talbot-Klic process
USE **photogravure**

Talbotype
USE **calotype**

Talbotypes
USE **calotypes**

talc
MT.562 (L)
CN M.MT.AFU.AFU.AFU.CFS.AFU.HCQ

talc (white pigment)
MT.1756 (L)
UF soapstone (white pigment)
steatite (white pigment)
CN M.MT.AFU.AFU.ARI.AFU.AFU.ALO.ALO.BOK.ALO.DCU

Talensi
USE **Tallensi**

tales, folk
USE **folk tales**

Tali-Barzu
FL.1806
CN F.FL.ALO.ARI.AFU.AXC.DOI

tall buildings
USE **skyscrapers**

tall chairs
TG.91
ALT **tall chair**
SN Chairs with tall legs and a high seat, such as those used at counters.
UF chairs, counting-house
chairs, high (tall chairs)
chairs, shop
chairs, tall
counting-house chairs
high chairs (tall chairs)
shop chairs
CN V.TG.AFU.AFU.ALO.AFU.AFU.AFU.LIG

tall chests of drawers
USE **chiffoniers**

tall-post beds
USE **high-post beds**

tallboys
TG.493
ALT **tallboy**
SN Tall case pieces generally having seven or more drawers divided by a cornice into two sections with the lower section supported on raised legs. For the equivalent American pieces, use **high chests of drawers.**
CN V.TG.AFU.AFU.AXC.ALO.BCW.CFS.AFU

tallboys (chimney pots)
RT.1143
ALT **tallboy (chimney pot)**
SN Chimney pots of long and slender form, intended to improve the draft. (HAS)
CN V.RT.AFU.BOK.AFU.ALO.BOK.AFU

Tallensi
FL.365 (L)
UF Talensi
CN F.FL.ALO.AFU.AXC.AFU.AXC.AFU.DCU

talon and ball feet
USE **claw-and-ball feet**

talon moldings
USE **cymas**

talons
TG.935
ALT **talon**
UF claws
CN V.TG.ALO.DZW.ALO.AXC

talus walls
USE **battered walls**

tamarack, western
USE **western larch**

Tamba
FL.2045 (L)
CN F.FL.ALO.ARI.ALO.ALO.ALO.ALO.ALO.FCS

Tamberma
FL.387 (L)
CN F.FL.ALO.AFU.AXC.AFU.AXC.ARI.ARI.BIQ

tambour desks
TG.557 (N)
ALT **tambour desk**
SN Use for American desks with upright reeded or slatted shutters that cover up the nest of drawers and pigeonholes. Distinct from English **tambour writing tables**, which are a modification of the cylinder desk with tambour shutters instead of a curved solid cylinder. Distinct from **rolltop desks** which close by means of a flexible shutter of convex shape composed of horizontal slats of wood.
UF desks, tambour
CN V.TG.AFU.AFU.AXC.ALO.BZY.ELK

tambour writing tables
TG.558
ALT **tambour writing table**
SN Use for English desks which are a modification of the cylinder desk, having tambour shutters instead of a curved cylinder. Distinct from the American **tambour desk,** which has upright reeded or slatted shutters that cover up the rest of the drawers and pigeonholes. (MONTGO)
UF tables, tambour writing
writing tables, tambour
CN V.TG.AFU.AFU.AXC.ALO.BZY.ERE

tamped earth
USE **rammed earth**

tampers
TB.26 (N)
ALT **tamper**
SN Compaction devices for consolidating a granular material such as soil, backfill, or unformed concrete; usually powered by a motor. (DAC)
CN V.TB.AFU.ARI.AFU.ALO.AFU.AFU

tamping
USE **compaction**

tamping rollers
USE **sheepsfoot rollers**

tan
USE **light yellowish brown**
moderate yellowish brown

tan, light
USE **light yellowish brown**

tan, light mustard
USE **light olive**

tan, mustard
USE **light olive brown**
moderate olive

Tanaina
FL.1242 (L)
UF Knaiakhotana
CN F.FL.ALO.ALO.ARI.AFU.AFU.ARI.DZW

Tanana
FL.1243 (L)
UF Nabesnatana
Nebesna
Tenankutchin
Upper Tanana
CN F.FL.ALO.ALO.ARI.AFU.AFU.ARI.EFQ

tandem rollers
TB.31
ALT **tandem roller**
SN Units of two rollers of equal diameter placed one behind the other on the same track. (MEANS)
UF rollers, tandem
CN V.TB.AFU.ARI.AFU.ALO.ALO.ARI

Tang
FL.1885 (A,L)
UF T'ang
CN F.FL.ALO.ARI.ALO.AFU.AFU.ALO.CFS

Tang, Later
USE **Later Tang**

tangile
USE **lauan**

Tanite Dynasty
USE **Twenty-first Dynasty**

tank farms
RG.121
ALT **tank farm**
SN Designates areas where a large number of high capacity storage tanks are located, usually used for crude oil or other petroleum products.
UF farms, tank
CN V.RG.AFU.AFU.BUE.AXC

tanks, developing
USE **developing tanks**

tanks, gasoline
USE **gasoline tanks**

tanks, liquid gas storage
USE **gasoline tanks**

tanks, oil storage
USE **oil storage tanks**

tanks, petrol
USE **gasoline tanks**

tanks, septic
USE **septic tanks**

tanks, storage
USE **storage tanks**

tanks, water
USE **water tanks**

tanks, water storage
USE **water storage tanks**

tanneries
RK.658 (A,B,R)
ALT **tannery**
UF factories, leather
leather factories
CN V.RK.AFU.ALO.ALO.CLM.ALO.ALO.AFU.AXC.DUC

tanners
HG.489 (L)
ALT **tanner**
CN H.HG.AFU.AXC.BUE.ARI.BZY.AXC

tanning
KT.774 (L)
ALT **tanned**
CN K.KT.AFU.ALO.HOE.AXC.AFU.ALO

Tantric Buddhism

USE **Vajrayana**

tantrism
BM.708 (A,L)
ALT **tantric**
CN B.BM.BZY.ALO.ARI.DIO

Tantrism (Buddhist)
USE **Vajrayana**

Tao-kuang
USE **Daoguang**

Taoism
BM.677 (L,R)
ALT **Taoist**
CN B.BM.BZY.AFU.CRG

Taos
FL.1477 (L)
CN F.FL.ALO.ALO.ARI.AFU.CFS.CRG.AFU.CLM

tap augers
USE **taper augers**

tap dance
KD.8 (L)
SN Dance in which the rhythm or rhythmic variation is audibly tapped out with the toes or heels by dancers wearing shoes with special hard soles or with metal taps. (RHDEL2)
UF dance, tap
CN K.KD.AFU.AFU.AFU.AFU.AFU.AFU.ALO

tap wrenches
TB.780 (N)
ALT **tap wrench**
SN Wrenches used to turn taps. (W)
UF wrenches, tap
CN V.TB.AFU.BCW.BIQ.AXC.ALO.BIQ.BZY

tapa
USE **bark cloth**

tape
MT.2275
CN M.MT.AFU.ALO.HTY

tape recordings
USE **audio tapes**

tape, adhesive
USE **adhesive tape**

tape, friction
USE **friction tape**

tape, masking
USE **masking tape**

taper augers
TB.829 (N)
ALT **taper auger**
SN Augers made in the form of a tapered, conical half-funnel, with one or both of the exposed edges side-sharpened to cut laterally. (SALAM)
UF augers, pump
augers, tap
augers, taper
augers, taper shell
pump augers
reamers (taper augers)
rimers
scillops
shell augers, taper
tap augers
taper shell augers
CN V.TB.AFU.BCW.CFS.ALO.AFU.ALO.BUE

taper shell augers
USE **taper augers**

taper taps
TB.736 (N)
ALT **taper tap**
SN Cone-shaped or slightly tapered taps.
UF taps, taper
CN V.TB.AFU.BCW.BIQ.ARI.ALO.BUE.BCW.ALO

tapered steps
USE **winders (steps)**

tapes, audio
USE **audio tapes**

tapes, magnetic
USE **magnetic tapes**

tapes, paper
USE **paper tapes**

tapes, sound
USE **audio tapes**

tapes, video
USE **videotapes**

tapestry
KT.556 (L,R)
CN K.KT.AFU.ALO.ELK.DUC.AFU.BOK.AXC

tapestry marks
VW.738 (R)
ALT **tapestry mark**
UF marks, tapestry
CN V.VW.AFU.ALO.ALO.AFU.AXC.ARI.CRG

tapia
MT.2059
UF tobi
CN M.MT.AFU.AFU.ARI.BOK.AFU.AXC.ALO

tapioca
USE **cassava**

tapioca plant
USE **cassava**

tapissiers
HG.541
ALT **tapissier**
SN Dealers in or makers of tapestries. (W)
CN H.HG.AFU.AXC.BUE.ARI.CXA.CFS.BCW

tapping out
KT.699
SN A procedure used to transfer small amounts of mixed printing ink to paper so as to examine the accuracy of the color. (TBL)
CN K.KT.AFU.ALO.GRC.BUE.BIQ

taps
TB.734 (L,N)
ALT **tap**
SN Tools for forming internal screw threads. (W)
UF screw taps
taps, screw
CN V.TB.AFU.BCW.BIQ.ARI.ALO.BUE.BCW

taps, bib
USE **faucets**

taps, plug
USE **plug taps**

taps, screw
USE **taps**

taps, taper
USE **taper taps**

taps, water
USE **faucets**

taquillónes
TG.471
ALT **taquillón**
SN Paneled chests often used as cabinet stands. (PAYNE)
CN V.TG.AFU.AFU.AXC.ALO.AXC.ERE

tar
MT.987 (L)
SN A black solid mass obtained in the destructive distillation of coal, peat, wood, petroleum, or other organic material. (MH)
CN M.MT.AFU.AFU.ALO.ALO.ALO

tar paper
MT.1929
SN Heavy paper coated or impregnated with tar for use especially in building. (W)
UF bituminised paper
paper, bituminised
paper, tar
CN M.MT.AFU.AFU.ARI.ALO.ALO.AXC.ARI.ALO.AFU.AFU

tar, coal
USE **coal tar**

tar, pine
USE **pine tar**

tar, wood
USE **wood tar**

Tarahumara
FL.1492 (L,R)

CN F.FL.ALO.ALO.ARI.ALO.AFU.AXC

Tarascan
FL.1497 (L)
CN F.FL.ALO.ALO.ARI.ALO.ALO.AFU

Tarawa Atoll
USE **Cook Island**

Tardenoisian
FL.2484 (L)
CN F.FL.ALO.AXC.AFU.AXC.CFS

target ranges
USE **ranges**

tariff
BM.411 (L)
CN B.BM.ARI.FCS

tariff schedules
VW.285 (L)
ALT **tariff shcedule**
SN Series or lists of rates of duties imposed by a government on imported or exported goods. (AHD)
UF schedules, tariff
CN V.VW.AFU.AFU.AFU.FZU.BCW.ALO.BOK.AFU

tarns
RD.133
ALT **tarn**
SN Designates small mountain lakes, often with no apparent inlet, usually formed in a blocked bowl-shaped depression eroded by ice.
CN V.RD.ARI.AFU.AFU.AFU.AFU.ALO.AFU.ALO

Tarquinian
FL.2710
CN F.FL.ALO.AXC.ALO.ALO.AFU.ARI.ARI

tarras
USE **trass**

tarrases
RM.382
ALT **tarrase**
SN Use for the upper stage acting areas, in front of the chamber, of Elizabethan theaters.
UF terraces (theaters)
CN V.RM.AFU.DIO.AXC.AXC.ALO.BUE.ALO.ALO

Tarrietia javanica
USE **lumbayo**

tarsia
USE **intarsia**

Tartar
FL.3606 (L,R)
UF Tatar
CN F.FL.ALO.BIQ.AXC

Taruga
FL.111
CN F.FL.ALO.AFU.ALO.AFU.BUE.BZY.AFU

tas-de-charges
RT.568
ALT **tas-de-charge**
SN The courses of vault ribs at the point where the ribs begin to spring and separate from the wall bonding; the point of the vault's maximum outward thrust.
CN V.RT.AFU.AFU.AFU.BIQ.BOK.ALO.BIQ.AFU

Tashtyk
FL.2138
CN F.FL.ALO.ARI.ARI.AFU.BOK

Tasian
USE **Badarian**

tasio
MT.836
UF greco livido
marble, Thasian
marmor thasium
Thasian marble
CN M.MT.AFU.AFU.AFU.DCU.AFU.ARI.ARI.ARI.BOK.DOI

task forces
HG.853
ALT **task force**
SN Committees, usually of experts or specialists, formed for analyzing, investigating, or solving a specific problem. (RHDEL2)
UF forces, task
working groups
CN H.HG.ALO.BZY.AFU

task lighting
RT.1368
UF lighting, task
CN V.RT.ALO.AXC.ALO.AXC

Tasmanian
FL.3617 (L)
CN F.FL.ALO.BOK.AFU.ALO.ARI

Tasmanian blackwood
USE **Australian locust**

tassel feet
USE **Spanish feet**

taste (aesthetics)
BM.495 (B,R)
CN B.BM.BIQ.AFU.BUE

taste (senses)
BM.729 (L,R)
SN Sense by which the flavor or savor of things is perceived when they are brought into contact with the tongue. (RHDEL2)
CN B.BM.CFS.AFU.BCW.AXC

Tatar
USE **Tartar**

Tattilismo
USE **Tactilist**

tatting
KT.550 (L)
ALT **tatted**
SN Making by hand a delicate lace, by looping and knotting with a single cotton thread and a small shuttle, making varied designs of rings and semicircles. (W)
CN K.KT.AFU.ALO.ELK.DUC.AFU.BIQ.AFU

tattoo artists
HG.138 (L)
ALT **tattoo artist**
UF artists, tattoo
CN H.HG.AFU.AXC.AXC.AFU.AFU.ALO.AXC.EFQ

tattooing
KT.481 (L,R)
ALT **tattooed**
SN The procedure of marking or coloring the skin by pricking in coloring matter so as to form indelible marks as figures or by production of scars. (W)
CN K.KT.AFU.ALO.DUC.ELK

tattoos
VB.68
ALT **tattoo**
CN V.VB.AFU.ARI.ALO

tau crosses
DG.16
ALT **tau cross**
SN T-shaped crosses. (IDO)
UF crosses, St. Anthony's
crosses, tau
cruces commissae
Saint Anthony's crosses
CN D.DG.AFU.AFU.ARI.CFS

taupe
USE **brownish gray**

taupe brown
USE **brownish gray**
dark grayish purple
grayish brown
grayish red
grayish reddish brown

taupe gray
USE **dark purplish gray**
purplish gray

taupe rose
USE **dark reddish gray**

taupe, dark mauve
USE **dark grayish red**
dark purplish gray

taupe, dark orchid
USE **dark grayish purple**
dark purplish gray

taupe, dark rose
USE **brownish gray**
dark reddish gray

taupe, mauve
USE **dark grayish purple**
dark purplish gray
dark reddish gray
grayish purplish red

taupe, orchid
USE **dark grayish purple**
grayish purple

taupe, rose
USE **dark gray**
dark reddish gray
grayish brown
grayish purple
grayish red
grayish reddish brown

Taurus symbols
DG.84 (R)
ALT **Taurus symbol**
CN D.DG.AFU.AFU.ERE.CLM

tavern stretcher tables
USE **tavern tables**

tavern tables
TG.691
ALT **tavern table**
SN Small, low tables with box stretchers and, generally, turned legs and overhanging tops; designed for a variety of domestic uses, not necessarily exclusively for taverns.
UF stretcher tables, tavern
tables, tavern
tables, tavern stretcher
tavern stretcher tables
CN V.TG.AFU.AFU.BIQ.BOK.AFU.DIO

taverns
RK.124 (A,L,N,B,R)
ALT **tavern**
SN Primarily 17th- to early 19th-century English and American places of eating, drinking, and public accommodations, which often became local centers of social gatherings; distinguished from **inns** which emphasize their overnight accommodations and also provide food and drinking facilities; for establishments that emphasize drinking, especially liquors, use **pubs** or **saloons.**
UF bars (taverns)
CN V.RK.AFU.ALO.ALO.ALO.AFU.BIQ

Tawakoni
FL.1402 (L)
CN F.FL.ALO.ALO.ARI.AFU.BOK.FIM.AFU

Tawana
USE **Tswana**

tax bills
VW.938
ALT **tax bill**
UF bills, tax
CN V.VW.AFU.ARI.AFU.CLM.AFU

tax brick
MT.76
UF brick, tax
CN M.MT.AFU.AFU.AFU.AXC.ALO.AFU.AFU.AFU.BOK.AFU

tax collectors
HG.667 (R)
ALT **tax collector**
UF collectors, tax
CN H.HG.AFU.AXC.CFS.BIQ.ALO

tax forms
USE **tax returns**

tax incentives
BM.396 (A,L)
SN Special exemptions or provisions for businesses such as accelerated depreciation allowances, credits, and deductions, intended to encourage socially or economically desirable activities. (LCSH)
UF incentives, tax
CN B.BM.ARI.CRG.ARI

tax maps
USE **cadastral maps**

tax records
VW.937
ALT **tax record**
UF records, tax
CN V.VW.AFU.ARI.AFU.CLM

tax returns
VW.939 (L)
ALT **tax return**
UF forms, tax
returns, tax
tax forms
CN V.VW.AFU.ARI.AFU.CLM.ALO

tax warrant books
USE **warrant books**

taxation
USE **taxing**

taxes
BM.566 (L)
CN B.BM.BOK.CLM

taxi stands
RM.502
ALT **taxi stand**
SN Places where taxis may park awaiting hire. (W)
UF cabstands
stands, taxi
CN V.RM.ALO.ALO.ALO.ALO.DZW

taxi tracks
USE **taxiways**

taxidermy
KT.540 (L)
SN Preparing lifelike representations of animals by stuffing the skin or molding it around a model of the specimen. (W)
CN K.KT.AFU.ALO.ELK.DOI

taxing
KG.186 (L,B)
UF taxation
CN K.KG.AFU.ALO.ARI.CFS

taxiways
RK.1509
ALT **taxiway**
SN A usually paved strip for taxiing at an airport. (W)
UF taxi tracks
tracks, taxi
CN V.RK.ALO.ALO.BIQ.AFU.BCW

Taxus
USE **yew**

Tayacian
FL.2454
CN F.FL.ALO.AXC.AFU.AFU.BCW

Tazaba-Gyab
FL.1784
UF Tabagayab
Tazabagyab
CN F.FL.ALO.ARI.AFU.ARI.BCW

Tazabagyab
USE **Tazaba-Gyab**

Tazumal
FL.1082
CN F.FL.ALO.ALO.ALO.ALO.ALO.AFU.BCW

tchahar taqs
USE **chahar taqs**

Tchambuli
USE **Chambri**

Tchefuncte
FL.863 (L)
CN F.FL.ALO.ALO.ALO.AFU.ALO.ALO.ARI.ARI.BZY

Tchien
USE **Tien**

Tchula
FL.850 (L)
CN F.FL.ALO.ALO.ALO.AFU.ALO.ALO.ARI.ALO.BIQ

tea boards
USE **tea tables**

tea caddies
TG.473
ALT **tea caddy**
SN Smaller versions of tea chests, usually fitted with one or more wood or tin (sometimes silver) canisters in which tea was stored under lock and key. (MONTGO)
UF caddies, tea
CN V.TG.AFU.AFU.AXC.ALO.AXC.EWY.AFU

tea caddies (tea tables)
USE **tea tables**

tea carts
USE **tea wagons**

tea chest, book
USE **tea chests**

tea chests
TG.472 (L)
ALT **tea chest**
SN Square wooden cases usually fixed with sheet lead or tin and used for exporting tea. (W)
UF book tea chests
chests, book tea
chests, tea
tea chest, book
CN V.TG.AFU.AFU.AXC.ALO.AXC.EWY

tea gardens
RK.1425 (A)
ALT **tea garden**
SN Traditionally, formal settings for the Japanese tea ceremony;(OCG) by extension, today, outdoor public places serving teas and other light refreshments (W).
UF gardens, tea
tea-house gardens
CN V.RK.ALO.AFU.AFU.ALO.BZY

tea-house gardens
USE **tea gardens**

tea-huts
USE **teahouses**

tea kettle stands
USE **kettle stands**
tea tables

tea poys
USE **tea tables**

tea rooms
RK.122 (A,L,B)
ALT **tea room**
SN Establishments where tea and other nonalchoholic refreshments and light meals are served.
UF rooms, tea
shops, tea
tea shops
CN V.RK.AFU.ALO.ALO.ALO.AFU.AXC.CFS

tea shops
USE **tea rooms**
tea stores

tea stores
RK.166
ALT **tea store**
UF shops, tea
stores, tea
tea shops
CN V.RK.AFU.ALO.ALO.ALO.ARI.BIQ.AFU.DOI

tea tables
TG.760 (N)
ALT **tea table**
UF boards, tea
caddies, tea (tea tables)
kettle stands, tea
poys, tea
stands, tea kettle
tables, tea
tea boards
tea caddies (tea tables)
tea kettle stands
tea poys
CN V.TG.AFU.AFU.BIQ.BOK.ALO.FOG

tea trolleys
USE **tea wagons**

tea wagons
TG.762 (N)
ALT **tea wagon**
SN Small tables on wheels used in serving tea and light refreshments. (W)
UF carts, tea
tea carts
tea trolleys
trolleys, tea
wagons, tea
CN V.TG.AFU.AFU.BIQ.BOK.ALO.FUA

teacher training colleges
USE **teachers colleges**

teachers
HG.299 (L)
ALT **teacher**
UF faculty
instructors
CN H.HG.AFU.AXC.BCW.ALO.ARI.ARI

teachers colleges
RK.818 (L,B)
ALT **teachers college**
UF colleges, teachers
normal schools
schools, normal
teacher training colleges
CN V.RK.AFU.ALO.ALO.CXA.ARI.ALO.DIO

teachers, private
USE **tutors**

teaching
KG.175 (L,R)
UF educating
instruction
training
CN K.KG.AFU.ALO.ALO.ALO

teaching facilities
USE **schools**

teaching hospitals
RK.772 (A,L,B)
ALT **teaching hospital**
SN Hospitals where formal medical training takes place, usually affiliated with nursing or medical schools.
UF hospitals, teaching
CN V.RK.AFU.ALO.ALO.CXA.ALO.AFU.BCW.ALO.BUE

teaching, case
USE **case method**

teahouses
RK.1340 (A,L,B)
ALT **teahouse**
SN Designates small buildings for the Japanese tea ceremony.
UF chashitsu
tea-huts
CN V.RK.AFU.ALO.ARI.AFU.BUE

teak
MT.1310 (L)
UF Indian oak
oak, Indian
Tectona grandis
CN M.MT.AFU.AFU.ALO.BIQ.DCU.AFU.AFU.AFU.LTU

teak, gray
USE **white beech**

teal
USE **dark bluish green**
moderate bluish green
moderate greenish blue

teal blue
USE **dark grayish blue**
dark greenish blue
moderate greenish blue

teal blue, bright
USE **dark greenish blue**
moderate greenish blue

teal blue, dark
USE **dark grayish blue**
dark greenish blue

teal blue, deep
USE **dark bluish green**
dark greenish blue
moderate greenish blue

teal blue, medium
USE **moderate greenish blue**

teal gray
USE **dark bluish gray**
dark gray

teal green
USE **dark bluish green**
moderate bluish green

teal green, dark
USE **dark bluish green**

teal green, deep
USE **dark bluish green**

teal, dark
USE **dark bluish green**
dark grayish blue
grayish blue
very dark bluish green

teal, deep
USE **dark bluish green**

teal, medium
USE **moderate greenish blue**

tear sheets
VW.626
ALT **tear sheet**
SN Sheets torn from a publication, usually to send as proof of insertion to an advertiser whose advertisement appears on it. (W)
UF sheets, tear
CN V.VW.AFU.ALO.AFU.DOI

teastors
USE **testers**

technical colleges
USE **polytechnics**

technical dictionaries
VW.404 (L)
ALT **technical dictionary**
UF dictionaries, technical
CN V.VW.AFU.AFU.ALO.EWY.ARI.ALO.BOK

technical drawings
VD.109 (L,N,R)
ALT **technical drawing**
SN Use for the broad class of drawings that are intended for constructional, mechanical, or mapping purposes and that follow precise conventions of scale and projection.
UF drawings, engineering
drawings, technical
engineering drawings
CN V.VD.AFU.ALO.CRG

technical illustration
KT.215 (L,R)
UF illustration, technical
CN K.KT.AFU.ALO.DUC.CLM.BUE

technical illustrations
VB.55 (L,R)
ALT **technical illustration**
UF illustrations, technical
CN V.VB.AFU.ALO.AXC.ALO.AXC

technical manuals
VW.353 (L)
ALT **technical manual**
UF manuals, technical
CN V.VW.AFU.AFU.ALO.CXA.BIQ.BCW

technical pens
TB.277
ALT **technical pen**
SN Fountain pens with a tubular, needle like point whose ink supply is controlled by a check valve and released only when pressure is placed on the point; used for drawing precise, even lines. (ADAG)
UF pens, technical
CN V.TB.AFU.ARI.CLM.AFU.ALO.DOI.BUE

technical reports
VW.467 (L)
ALT **technical report**
UF reports, scientific
reports, technical
scientific reports
CN V.VW.AFU.AFU.ALO.FIM.BCW

technical schools
USE **vocational schools**

technical societies
HG.903 (L)
ALT **technical society**
UF societies, technical
CN H.HG.ALO.DUC.CLM

technical writing
KG.107 (L)
UF report writing
writing, report
writing, technical
CN K.KG.AFU.AFU.AXC.DZW

technicians
HG.29 (L)
ALT **technician**
SN Practical specialists in the technical details of a subject or occupation. (W)
CN H.HG.AFU.AXC.ALO.AXC.AFU

technicians, conservation
USE **conservators**

technique
BM.307 (R)
SN The manner in which an artist or craftsman uses the technical elements of a medium to achieve a desired aesthetic effect.
CN B.BM.AFU.AXC.DZW

techniques
KT.4 (L,R)
ALT **technique**
SN Use for the manner or method by which an activity is performed. Use **processes** when referring generally to the activities or procedures followed to produce some end.
UF methods
CN K.KT.AFU.AFU.ALO

technological museums
USE **technology museums**

technology
BM.1133 (L,B,R)
UF applied science
CN B.BM.CXA.AFU

technology museums
RK.401 (L)
ALT **technology museum**
UF museums, technology
technological museums
CN V.RK.AFU.ALO.ALO.BCW.AXC.ARI.AXC.BUE

technology, alternative
USE **appropriate technology**

technology, appropriate
USE **appropriate technology**

technology, information
USE **information technology**

technology, intermediate
USE **appropriate technology**

Tectona grandis
USE **teak**

tectonics
BM.318
SN In recent architectural theory, the consideration of loads and stresses in architectural designs.
CN B.BM.AFU.AXC.ELK.AFU.ALO

tectonics (geology)
KD.271 (L)
SN Use for the study of the form, pattern, and evolution of large-scale units of the earth's crust, such as basins, disturbed belts, forelands, and continental shelves.(BADGLE) For the study of smaller, individual geological structures, use **structural geology.**
CN K.KD.AFU.ARI.CLM.ARI.ARI.ARI

tee bevels
USE **bevel squares**

tee squares
USE **T-squares**

teenagers
HG.7 (L)
ALT **teenager**
UF adolescents
CN H.HG.AFU.AFU.ARI.ALO

teepees
USE **tipis**

Tehuelche
FL.1698 (L)
UF Tzoneca
Tzoneka
CN F.FL.ALO.ALO.ARI.ARI.BOK.CLM

Teita
FL.656 (L)
UF Taita
CN F.FL.ALO.AFU.AXC.AXC.BCW.DIO

Teke
FL.471 (L)
UF Bateke
CN F.FL.ALO.AFU.AXC.ALO.ALO.ARI.CLM

Tekke
FL.3593
CN F.FL.ALO.BIQ.AFU.IFM.ARI.BIQ

tekkes
RG.201
ALT **tekke**
SN Use only for dervish monasteries; for rest houses for Islamic pilgrims, use **hospices.**
CN V.RG.AFU.AFU.DUC.BUE

telamones

USE **atlantes**

telecommunication
USE **telecommunications**

telecommunication networks
USE **telecommunication systems**

telecommunication systems
RD.88 (A,L,R)
ALT **telecommunication system**
UF communication systems (infrastructural systems)
networks, telecommunication
systems, communication (infrastructural systems)
systems, telecommunication
telecommunication networks
CN V.RD.ALO.ALO

telecommunications
KD.115 (L)
UF telecommunication
CN K.KD.AFU.ALO.ARI.BCW

telegrams
VW.29 (L,N)
ALT **telegram**
SN Messages sent by telegraph. (GAHLM)
UF cablegrams
CN V.VW.AFU.AFU.AFU.BIQ.AFU.BCW

telegraph offices
RK.208 (B)
ALT **telegraph office**
UF offices, telegraph
CN V.RK.AFU.ALO.ALO.ARI.AFU.ARI.AXC

telegraph stations
RK.209 (L,B,R)
ALT **telegraph station**
UF stations, telegraph
CN V.RK.AFU.ALO.ALO.ARI.AFU.ARI.BCW

telephone area code maps
VW.206 (L)
ALT **telephone area code map**
UF area code maps, telephone
maps, telephone area code
CN V.VW.AFU.AFU.AFU.FZU.AXC.AFU.ARI.AXC.CXA

telephone books
USE **telephone directories**

telephone booths
RK.215 (A,N,B,R)
ALT **telephone booth**
UF booths, phone
booths, telephone
boxes, call
call boxes
phone booths
CN V.RK.AFU.ALO.ALO.ARI.ARI

telephone directories
VW.413 (L,N)
ALT **telephone directory**
SN Directories of the names of telephone subscribers with corresponding addresses and telephone numbers. (AHD)
UF books, phone
books, telephone
directories, telephone
phone books
telephone books
CN V.VW.AFU.AFU.ALO.EWY.AXC.AFU.BIQ

telephone exchanges
RK.210 (L,B)
ALT **telephone exchange**
UF exchanges, telephone
stations, telephone
telephone stations
CN V.RK.AFU.ALO.ALO.ARI.AFU.ARI.BIQ

telephone networks
USE **telephone systems**

telephone poles
USE **utility poles**

telephone stands
USE **telephone tables**

telephone stations
USE **telephone exchanges**

telephone systems
RD.90 (L)
ALT **telephone system**
UF networks, telephone
systems, telephone
telephone networks
telephony
CN V.RD.ALO.ALO.ALO

telephone tables
TG.763
ALT **telephone table**
UF phone tables
stands, telephone
tables, phone
tables, telephone
telephone stands
CN V.TG.AFU.AFU.BIQ.BOK.ALO.FZU

telephony
USE **telephone systems**

telephoto lenses
TB.320 (L)
ALT **telephoto lens**
SN Long focal length lenses which enlarge distant subjects within their narrow angle of view. (LANG)
UF lenses, telephoto
CN V.TB.AFU.ARI.CLM.ARI.AFU.ALO.BOK.AXC.AFU

telephotography
KT.391 (L)
SN Photography of distant objects using either a telephoto lens or a telescope.
UF telescopic photography
CN K.KT.AFU.ALO.DUC.DIO.ARI.ARI.BUE

teleprinters
USE **page printers**

telescope dining tables
USE **telescope tables**

telescope tables
TG.725
ALT **telescope table**
SN Extension dining tables invented during the Victorian period, which received their name from the slide action by which their length is varied. (BLACK)
UF dining tables, telescope
tables, telescope
tables, telescope dining
telescope dining tables
CN V.TG.AFU.AFU.BIQ.BOK.ALO.BZY.AFU.AFU

telescopic photography
USE **telephotography**

television antenna systems
RT.1289
ALT **television antenna system**
UF antenna systems, television
systems, television antenna
CN V.RT.ALO.AFU.AFU.BIQ

television broadcasting
KD.112 (L)
UF broadcasting, television
CN K.KD.AFU.ALO.ARI.ALO.ALO

television cameras
TB.296 (L,N)
ALT **television camera**
UF cameras, television
CN V.TB.AFU.ARI.CLM.ARI.AFU.AFU.AFU.BIQ

television personalities
HG.80 (L)
ALT **television personality**
UF personalities, television
CN H.HG.AFU.AXC.AXC.AFU.AFU.AFU.BOK

television scripts
VW.75 (L)
ALT **television script**
SN Written texts of television productions or broadcasts.
UF scripts, television
CN V.VW.AFU.AFU.AFU.ERE.AXC

television stations
RK.204 (A,L)
ALT **television station**
UF stations, television
CN V.RK.AFU.ALO.ALO.ARI.AFU.ARI.AFU.ALO

television studios
RM.225 (A,B)
ALT **television studio**

SN Use for the series of rooms specifically designed for the origination of live or taped television programs;(MHDSTT) for the larger facilities, including offices and equipment, from where the transmissions are sent and received, use **television stations.**
UF studios, television
studios, TV
TV studios
CN V.RM.AFU.DIO.ALO.DOI.ARI.ALO

television towers
RK.213 (B)
ALT **television tower**
UF towers, television
towers, transmitter
transmitter towers
CN V.RK.AFU.ALO.ALO.ARI.ALO.ALO

Tellem
FL.90
CN F.FL.ALO.AFU.ALO.AFU.BOK.ARI

tells
RD.41 (A)
ALT **tell**
SN Use for artificial mounds consisting of the accumulation of debris from successive settlement levels; common in regions where mud brick is used.
CN V.RD.AFU.ARI.ARI.AFU.AFU

Tem
FL.388 (L)
UF Kotokoli
Temba
CN F.FL.ALO.AFU.AXC.AFU.AXC.ARI.ARI.BOK

Temba
USE **Tem**

Tembé
FL.1598 (L)
UF Guajajara
Tenetehara
CN F.FL.ALO.ALO.ARI.ARI.AFU.GWW

Tembu
FL.565 (L)
CN F.FL.ALO.AFU.AXC.ARI.AXC.AXC

temene
RG.258
ALT **temenos**
UF hiera
CN V.RG.ALO.AFU.AFU.BIQ.BCW

Temne
FL.333 (L)
UF Timne
CN F.FL.ALO.AFU.AXC.AFU.ARI.BCW.CRG

tempera
MT.2518
SN Mixtures of pigments and any number of water-soluble vehicles, especially egg, glue, or casein, that leave a matte surface when dry. (A-Z)
CN M.MT.AFU.ARI.CRG.ALO.BCW.AFU.ALO.ARI

tempera, casein
USE **casein paint**

tempera, egg
USE **egg tempera**

tempera, gum
USE **gum tempera**

tempera, oil
USE **oil tempera**

tempera, polymer
USE **polymer paint**

temperate climate
BM.743
SN Climate characterized by variable, moderate temperatures, intermediate between polar and tropical types. (EBMIC)
CN B.BM.CFS.ALO.AXC.ALO.AFU.ARI

temperature
BM.842 (L,B)
CN B.BM.CFS.AXC.ALO.AFU.AFU.ALO.AXC

temperature detectors
RT.1513
ALT **temperature detector**
UF detectors, temperature
CN V.RT.ALO.BIQ.AFU.AFU.ALO.AFU.ALO

temperature stress
USE **thermal stress**

tempering
KT.733 (L)
ALT **tempered**
SN The process of heating metal, glass, or other material to a temperature below the transformation stage and then cooling it at a controlled rate to change its hardness, strength, or toughness. (HORNB)
CN K.KT.AFU.ALO.GWW.ARI.ALO

templates
TB.453 (A,N)
ALT **template**
SN Guiding tools used for duplicating shapes.
CN V.TB.AFU.ARI.EFQ.ALO.CRG

templates, dovetail
USE **dovetail templates**

Temple Mound I
FL.767
CN F.FL.ALO.ALO.ALO.AFU.AFU.AXC.ALO.ALO.AFU

Temple Mound II
FL.768
CN F.FL.ALO.ALO.ALO.AFU.AFU.AXC.ALO.ALO.ALO

Temple Mound period
FL.766 (L)
UF Mississippian culture
CN F.FL.ALO.ALO.ALO.AFU.AFU.AXC.ALO.ALO

temple towers
USE **ziggurats**

temples
RK.1126 (A,L,N,B,R)
ALT **temple**
UF fanes
CN V.RK.AFU.ALO.ALO.FCS.BIQ.BZY

temples, cave
USE **cave temples**

temples, fire
USE **fire temples**

temples, hypaethral
USE **hypaethral temples**

temples, Jewish
USE **synagogues**

temples, masonic
USE **masonic buildings**

temples, mortuary
USE **mortuary temples**

temples, rock-cut
USE **rock-cut temples**

temporary architecture
USE **temporary buildings**

temporary buildings
RK.1384 (A,L,B,R)
ALT **temporary building**
UF architecture, temporary
buildings, temporary
temporary architecture
CN V.RK.AFU.ALO.AXC.CFS.AFU

temporary havens
USE **refugee camps**

temporary housing
RG.61 (A,B)
UF housing, temporary
CN V.RG.AFU.AFU.BOK.ALO.AFU

temporary structures
RK.1383 (L,R)
ALT **temporary structure**
SN Nonpermanent structures erected for festive or sporting events or to provide access to or protection or support of facilities under construction.
UF structures, temporary
CN V.RK.AFU.ALO.AXC.CFS

Tempyo
USE **Late Nara**

ten-cent stores
USE **variety stores**

Tena
USE **Ingalik**

Tenankutchin
USE **Tanana**

tenants
HG.739 (A,L)
ALT **tenant**
CN H.HG.AFU.BCW.GLI

Tenayuca
USE **Aztec II**

Tendai
BM.625 (L)
CN B.BM.BZY.AFU.AFU.BIQ.AXC

tendering
USE **bidding**

tenders
USE **bids**

tenement houses
RK.365 (A,L,B,R)
ALT **tenement house**
SN Use only for buildings containing rental apartments that are in large cities, occupied by poorer people, generally built to minimum standards of sanitation, safety, and comfort, and often in run-down condition.
UF houses, tenement
tenements
CN V.RK.AFU.ALO.ALO.AXC.AXC.ALO.ARI

tenements
USE **tenement houses**

tenements, dumbbell
USE **dumbbell tenements**

Tenetehara
USE **Tembé**

Tenino
FL.1423
CN F.FL.ALO.ALO.ARI.AFU.BUE.EFQ

Tenjiku-yo
USE **Daibutsuyo**

Tenjiku yo
USE **Daibutsuyo**

Tenjikuyo
USE **Daibutsuyo**

Tennessee marble
MT.837
UF marble, Tennessee
CN M.MT.AFU.AFU.AFU.DCU.AFU.ARI.ARI.ARI.BOK.DUC

Tennessee pink marble
MT.796
UF marble, Tennessee pink
pink marble, Tennessee
CN M.MT.AFU.AFU.AFU.DCU.AFU.ARI.ARI.ARI.AXC.AFU

tennis clubs
RK.1029 (A,L,B)
ALT **tennis club**
UF clubs, tennis
CN V.RK.AFU.ALO.ALO.EWY.AXC.ALO.AFU.ARI

tennis courts
RK.1019 (A,L,B,R)
ALT **tennis court**
UF courts, lawn tennis
courts, tennis
lawn tennis courts
CN V.RK.AFU.ALO.ALO.EWY.ALO.CFS

tennis courts, indoor
USE **indoor tennis courts**

Tenochtitlán
USE **Aztec III**

tenon-cutting bits
TB.1115 (N)
ALT **tenon-cutting bit**
SN Bits with sharpened edges or saw teeth at the opening, used to cut round wood plugs or dowels.
UF annular bits
bits, annular
bits, cock plug
bits, deck dowelling
bits, pivot
bits, plug
bits, plug center
bits, tenon-cutting
center bits, plug
cock plug bits
deck dowelling bits
pivot bits
plug bits
plug center bits
CN V.TB.ALO.ARI.DUC

tenon saws
TB.994 (N)
ALT **tenon saw**
SN Medium-sized backsaws whose blade is stiffened on the back by a metal strip, and a handle which is usually closed like a hand saw.
UF miter saws
saws, miter
saws, tenon
CN V.TB.AFU.BCW.CFS.ALO.AFU.EWY.AFU.BOK

tensegrities
USE **tensegrity structures**

tensegrity structures
RT.376
ALT **tensegrity structure**
SN Stable, three-dimensional structures consisting of members under tension that are contiguous and members under compression that are not. (OEDSUP)
UF structures, tensegrity
tensegrities
CN V.RT.AFU.AFU.AFU.BCW.CLM.AFU.AFU.ALO.AFU

tensile strength
BM.964
CN B.BM.CFS.AXC.BZY.BOK.CLM.BIQ

tensile structures
RT.14 (A,L,B)
ALT **tensile structure**
UF structures, tensile
structures, tension
tension structures
CN V.RT.AFU.AFU.AFU.AFU.ALO.BIQ

tension rings
RT.402
ALT **tension ring**
SN Use for rings or chains that encircle domes in order to contain their outward thrusts.
UF rings, tension
CN V.RT.AFU.AFU.AFU.BIQ.AFU.ALO.ALO

tension rods
USE **tie rods**

tension structures
USE **tensile structures**

tensioning, post
USE **post tensioning**

tent beds
USE **field beds**

tent bedsteads
USE **field beds**

tent ceilings
USE **camp ceilings**

tent structures
RT.407 (A)
ALT **tent structure**
UF structures, tent
tents (structures)
CN V.RT.AFU.AFU.AFU.BIQ.ALO.ALO

tent trailers
USE **camping trailers**

Tenth Dynasty
FL.2800
UF 10th Dynasty
Dynasty, Tenth
CN F.FL.ALO.AXC.ALO.ARI.AFU.BCW.AXC

tents
RK.356 (A,L,N,B,R)
ALT **tent**
CN V.RK.AFU.ALO.ALO.AXC.ARI.BIQ

tents (structures)
USE **tent structures**

Teocalco
USE **Aztec IV**

Teotihuacán
FL.1001
CN F.FL.ALO.ALO.ALO.ALO.AFU.ALO.

AFU.ALO.ARI

Teotihuacan I
USE **Tzacualli**

Teotihuacan II
USE **Miccaotli**

Teotihuacan III
USE **Tlamimilolpa**

Teotihuacan IIIa
USE **Xolalpan**

Teotihuacan IV
USE **Metepec**

Tepalcingo
FL.1714
CN F.FL.ALO.ALO.AXC.ALO.AFU.ARI.AXC

Tepecano
FL.1493 (L)
CN F.FL.ALO.ALO.ARI.ALO.AFU.BCW

tepees
USE **tipis**

Tepehuan
FL.1494 (L)
CN F.FL.ALO.ALO.ARI.ALO.AFU.BIQ

tepes
RD.43
ALT **tepe**
SN Tells (artificial mounds resulting from layers of human habitation) in Persia.
CN V.RD.AFU.ARI.ARI.AFU.AFU.ALO

Tepeu
FL.1015
CN F.FL.ALO.ALO.ALO.ALO.AFU.ALO.ARI.AFU.AFU.BIQ

tepidaria
RM.79
ALT **tepidarium**
SN In ancient Roman baths, spaces containing water of intermediate temperatures between the caldarrium and the frigidarium. (RS)
CN V.RM.AFU.DIO.ALO.ALO.BOK.BOK

Tepqui
FL.1612
CN F.FL.ALO.ALO.ARI.ARI.ALO.AFU.BZY

Tequislatec
FL.1522
UF Chontal de Oaxaca
CN F.FL.ALO.ALO.ARI.ALO.AXC.CXA

terebinth
USE **turpentine**

terminal buildings (airports)
USE **airport terminals**

terminal care facilities
RK.756 (L)
ALT **terminal care facility**
UF facilities, terminal care
hospices (terminal care)
CN V.RK.AFU.ALO.ALO.CXA.ALO.AFU.AXC.BIQ

Terminalia superba
USE **limba**

terminally ill
HG.798 (L)
UF ill, terminally
CN H.HG.AFU.BOK.CRG

terminals
RK.1264 (L,N,B)
ALT **terminal**
UF centers, transport
terminals, transportation
transport centers
transportation terminals
CN V.RK.AFU.ALO.ALO.GLI.AFU.BCW

terminals (computers)
USE **computer terminals**

terminals, air
USE **airport terminals**

terminals, airport
USE **airport terminals**

terminals, bus
USE **bus terminals**

terminals, computer
USE **computer terminals**

terminals, freight
USE **freight terminals**

terminals, marine
USE **marine terminals**

terminals, motor bus
USE **bus terminals**

terminals, motor-truck
USE **truck terminals**

terminals, passenger
USE **passenger terminals**

terminals, railroad
USE **railroad terminals**

terminals, ship
USE **marine terminals**

terminals, steamship
USE **marine terminals**

terminals, transportation
USE **terminals**

terminals, truck
USE **truck terminals**

terminological control
USE **authority control**

terminology
BM.1162 (A,L,B,R)
SN Technical or special terms or expressions used in a particular field. (W)
CN B.BM.DIO.BIQ

tern feet
USE **scroll feet**

terneplate
MT.467
SN Sheet steel coated with an alloy of 80% lead and 20% tin; widely used for roofing and construction work.
CN M.MT.AFU.AFU.AFU.BZY.AFU.ALO.AXC.ALO.ARI

terpenes
MT.2702 (L)
CN M.MT.AFU.ARI.HZS.AFU.BZY

terra alba
USE **gypsum**

terra cotta (color)
USE **brownish orange**
dark reddish orange
deep orange
grayish reddish orange
light reddish brown
moderate reddish brown
strong brown
strong reddish brown

terra di Siena
USE **raw sienna**

terra orellana
USE **annatto**

terra sienna
USE **brownish orange**

Terra sigillata
FL.2753
CN F.FL.ALO.AXC.ALO.ALO.ALO.BUE.ALO.BIQ

terrace houses
RK.268 (A,L,B,R)
ALT **terrace house**
SN Designates lines of dwellings situated on a sloping, terraced, or similar site.
UF dwelling terraces
houses, terrace
terraces (houses)
terraces (row houses)
terraces, dwelling
CN V.RK.AFU.ALO.ALO.AXC.ALO.AFU.CRG.BIQ.ARI

terrace roofs
RT.416
ALT **terrace roof**
SN Use for flat roofs having masonry paving and therefore being usable as living space.
UF roofs, terrace
CN V.RT.AFU.AFU.AFU.BIQ.ARI.AFU.AFU.AFU.ARI.AFU

terrace walls
RM.446

ALT **terrace wall**
UF walls, terrace
CN V.RM.ALO.AFU.BOK.ARI

terraces
RM.455 (A,L,B,R)
ALT **terrace**
SN Use for level paved or planted areas, usually elevated above surrounding terrain and adjacent to buildings or parts of garden complexes.
CN V.RM.ALO.AFU.CFS.BIQ

terraces (houses)
USE **terrace houses**

terraces (row houses)
USE **terrace houses**

terraces (theaters)
USE **tarrases**

terraces, dwelling
USE **terrace houses**

terracotta
MT.193 (A,L,B,R)
SN A baked or fired clay, usually brownish red, widely used since ancient times for pottery, small sculptures, and roof tiles. (MAYER)
CN M.MT.AFU.AFU.AFU.AXC.ALO.AXC

terrain analysis
KT.19
SN The process of studying and interpreting the land surface and subsurface conditions of a geographical area using, for example, aerial photography or computer models.
UF analysis, terrain
CN K.KT.AFU.ALO.AXC.BIQ

Terramare
FL.2705 (L)
CN F.FL.ALO.AXC.ALO.ALO.AFU.AFU.BIQ

terrazzo
MT.897 (A,L,B)
SN Marble aggregate concrete that is cast in place or precast and ground smooth; used especially as a decorative surfacing on floors and walls. (DAC)
CN M.MT.AFU.AFU.AFU.DCU.ALO.DCU

terre d'ombre
USE **umber**

terre d'ombre brûlée
USE **burnt umber**

terre d'ombre naturelle
USE **raw umber**

terre de Cassel
USE **Van Dyke brown**

terre de Sienne brûlée
USE **burnt sienna**

terre verte
USE **grayish green**
green earth

terre verte brûlée
USE **transparent brown**

terre verte, dark
USE **grayish green**

terre verte, light
USE **moderate bluish green**

terrepleins
RT.1194
ALT **terreplein**
SN Use for the top platform or horizontal surface behind the parapet of a rampart.
CN V.RT.AFU.BUE.AFU.BCW.ALO.BCW

terrestrial globes
VW.137 (L,R)
ALT **terrestrial globe**
UF globes, terrestrial
CN V.VW.AFU.AFU.AFU.FZU.AXC.AFU.ALO.ALO

territorial records
VW.1051
ALT **territorial record**
UF records, territorial
CN V.VW.AFU.ARI.ALO.BCW.ALO.BCW

territoriality
BM.606 (L)
SN The interpersonal behavior regulator, which covers the defining of a space, and the creation of visible and invisible boundaries to that space.
UF human territoriality
CN B.BM.BUE.DIO

territories
HG.811 (L)
ALT **territory**
SN Regions or districts under the jurisdiction of a potential authority, not admitted as a state or province but having its own local government and legislature.
CN H.HG.ALO.ALO.CFS

terrorism
BM.1118 (L,R)
UF political violence
violence, political
CN B.BM.CRG.BCW.CLM.ALO

Tertiaire
USE **Flamboyant**

tertiary ribs
USE **liernes**

terylene
USE **Dacron (TM)**

Tes phase
FL.2137
CN F.FL.ALO.ARI.ARI.AFU.BIQ.BCW.AXC

Teshik-Kala
USE **Teshik-Tash**

Teshik-Tash
FL.1766
UF Teshik-Kala
CN F.FL.ALO.ARI.AFU.AFU.ARI

Teso
FL.689 (L)
UF Bakedi
Bateso
Iteso
CN F.FL.ALO.AFU.AXC.AXC.BOK.DUC

tesserae
MT.2276 (L)
SN Small, squarish pieces of colored marble, glass, or tile used in making mosaics. (DAC)
CN M.MT.AFU.ALO.HZS

test reports
VW.469
ALT **test report**
SN Reports on the results of tests or examinations.
UF reports, test
CN V.VW.AFU.AFU.ALO.FIM.BCW.ALO

test sites
RG.214
ALT **test site**
SN Locations where, usually very destructive, weapons are exploded distant from an observation point; also, where scientific field explorations or investigations are conducted, as in archaeology or geology. For complexes where weapons are tested under close scrutiny, use **proving grounds.**
UF sites, test
CN V.RG.AFU.AFU.DZW.BIQ

test sites, atomic
USE **nuclear test sites**

test sites, nuclear
USE **nuclear test sites**

testamentary, letters
USE **letters testamentary**

tester beds
TG.356 (N)
ALT **tester bed**
SN Beds with a rooflike component supported above the bed by the posts. For beds with testers that only cover the head half of the bed, use **half-tester beds.** Use **canopy beds** when the rooflike component is suspended from the ceiling as opposed to being supported on posts.
UF beds, canopy (tester beds)
beds, four-posted
beds, plantation
beds, tester

canopy beds (tester beds)
four-posted beds
four-posters
plantation beds
CN V.TG.AFU.AFU.ARI.AFU.AFU.BZY.ALO

testers
TG.858
ALT **tester**
SN Rooflike components supported above the bed by posts and covering the whole area of the bed. Use **flying testers** for rooflike components generally cantilevered from the headboard and extending over the whole area of the bed. Use **half-testers** for similar forms which only extend over the head half of the bed. Use **canopies** for rooflike components suspended over the head of the bed by means of a cord or chain attached to the ceiling.
UF canopies (testers)
celters
celures
selours
teastors
testours
CN V.TG.ALO.BIQ.CRG

testers, drop
USE **drop testers**

testers, flying
USE **flying testers**

testers, half-headed
USE **half-testers**

testimonials
VW.323 (L)
ALT **testimonial**
SN Documents containing affirmation of another's character; also, tributes for a person's service or achievements. (AHD)
CN V.VW.AFU.AFU.ALO.BOK.BIQ

testimonies
VW.475 (L)
ALT **testimony**
SN Solemn declarations, usually made orally by a witness under oath in response to interrogation by a lawyer or authorized public official, reduced to writing. (GAHLM)
CN V.VW.AFU.AFU.ALO.FZU

testing
KG.31 (A,L,B)
SN Examining and measuring critically the qualities or abilities of something or someone, often with reference to established standards.
CN K.KG.AFU.AFU.AFU.DZW

testours
USE **testers**

tests
USE **examinations**

testudines
USE **surbased vaults**

Tesuque
FL.1478
CN F.FL.ALO.ALO.ARI.AFU.CFS.CRG.AFU.CRG

tête-à-têtes
USE **confidantes**

Tetela
FL.503 (L)
UF Batetela
CN F.FL.ALO.AFU.AXC.ALO.ALO.BCW.BZY

têtes
USE **settees**

têtes (confidantes)
USE **confidantes**

tethering posts
USE **hitching posts**

Teton
FL.1399 (L)
UF Lakota
CN F.FL.ALO.ALO.ARI.AFU.BOK.FCS.ALO

tetraconchs
RK.17 (R)
ALT **tetraconch**
CN V.RK.AFU.ALO.AFU.ALO.AFU.AFU

tetrahedrons
BM.796 (N)
ALT **tetrahedron**
CN B.BM.CFS.ARI.AXC.BCW.ALO.AXC.ARI

tetrapylons
RK.505
ALT **tetrapylon**
UF quadrifrontes
CN V.RK.AFU.ALO.ALO.BUE.BOK

Tetrarchic
FL.2726
CN F.FL.ALO.AXC.ALO.ALO.AFU.AXC.ARI.AFU

tetraskeles
USE **tetraskelions**

tetraskelions
DG.68
ALT **tetraskelion**
SN Figures in which four arms radiate out from a center and curve or bend in the same direction. (IDO)
UF tetraskeles
CN D.DG.AFU.AFU.DUC

tetrastyle
DC.95
CN D.DC.AFU.ARI.ERE.BIQ.CRG

tetrole copolymer
USE **furan**

tetroles
USE **furan**

tevahs
USE **bemas**

Texaco spirits
USE **mineral spirits**

Texas marble
MT.838
UF marble, Texas
CN M.MT.AFU.AFU.AFU.DCU.AFU.ARI.ARI.ARI.BOK.DZW

Texas oak
USE **southern red oak**

textbooks
VW.520 (L)
ALT **textbook**
SN Books used as standard works for the formal study of a particular subject. (AHD)
CN V.VW.AFU.ALO.AFU.AFU.AFU.DIO

textbooks, programmed
USE **programmed textbooks**

textile crafts
USE **textile working**

textile engineering
USE **textile science**

textile fabrics
USE **textiles**

textile factories
USE **textile mills**

textile mill buildings
USE **textile mills**

textile mills
RK.659 (A,L,B,R)
ALT **textile mill**
UF buildings, textile mill
factories, textile
mills, textile
textile factories
textile mill buildings
CN V.RK.AFU.ALO.ALO.CLM.ALO.ALO.AFU.AXC.DZW

textile museums
RK.389 (L)
ALT **textile museum**
UF museums, textile
CN V.RK.AFU.ALO.ALO.BCW.AXC.ARI.AFU.BIQ

textile science
KD.249
SN Field concerned with the performance properties of fibers, the molecular structure relating to these properties, and the interaction of fibers in structures; also the physics and engineering requirements for the production, control, and evalua-

tion of fibers, yarns, and fabrics. (PG)
UF engineering, textile
science, textile
textile engineering
CN K.KD.AFU.ARI.BZY.AXC

textile workers
HG.525 (L)
ALT **textile worker**
UF workers, textile
CN H.HG.AFU.AXC.BUE.ARI.CXA

textile working
KT.541 (L,R)
UF textile crafts
CN K.KT.AFU.ALO.ELK.DUC

textiles
MT.1876 (A,L,B,R)
SN Use specifically for cloth composed of fibers that are woven.
UF fabric
fabrics, textile
textile fabrics
CN M.MT.AFU.AFU.ARI.ALO.ALO.ALO.ALO.DOI

textiles, resist-dyed
USE **resist-dyed cloth**

texts, exhibition
USE **exhibit scripts**

texture
BM.168 (L,B,R)
SN Visual and tactile surface characteristics. (W)
CN B.BM.AFU.AFU.ARI.BOK.DUC

texture floats
TB.597
ALT **texture float**
SN Plastering tools such as carpet or cork floats; used for texturing plaster. (PUTNAM)
UF floats, texture
CN V.TB.AFU.BCW.BCW.ALO.DIO.BCW

Tezoyuca
FL.984
CN F.FL.ALO.ALO.ALO.ALO.AFU.ALO.AFU.AFU.BCW

Thabas-zi-ka-Mambo
FL.142
CN F.FL.ALO.AFU.ALO.ARI.BCW.BCW

thackstone
MT.904
CN M.MT.AFU.AFU.AFU.DCU.ARI.AFU.ARI

Thai
FL.2401 (L,B)
UF Siamese
Tai
CN F.FL.ALO.ARI.BCW.BOK

Thai, Northern
USE **Northern Thai**

Thakuri
FL.2161
CN F.FL.ALO.ARI.AXC.AFU.AXC.AFU.AXC

Thalo blue
USE **phthalocyanine blue**

Thalo blue (color)
USE **dark greenish blue**
very dark greenish blue

Thanksgiving
KM.76 (L)
CN K.KM.AFU.CFS.ALO.ARI

Thap-mam
USE **Binh Dinh**

Thasian marble
USE **tasio**

thatched roofs, false
USE **false thatched roofs**

thatching
KT.589 (B)
ALT **thatched**
SN The technique of arranging plant material, especially straw, in a thick mat with the individual parts parallel and sloping so as to shed water, used as roofing for houses. (W)
CN K.KT.AFU.ALO.ERE.BZY

Thatôn
FL.2311
CN F.FL.ALO.ARI.BCW.AFU.ALO.AFU

thats
USE **stupas**

thawing
KT.734 (L)
ALT **thawed**
CN K.KT.AFU.ALO.GWW.AXC

the Antique
USE **Antique, the**

the Beautiful
USE **beauty**

the Ideal
USE **Ideal, the**

The Levant
USE **Levantine**

the Picturesque
USE **Picturesque, the**

the Sublime
USE **Sublime, the**

theater
KD.12 (L,R)
SN Use for the professionally oriented study of theater, involving training, practice, and study in the processes of doing theater. For the academically oriented study of theater, use **drama.**
UF arts, theater
theater arts
CN K.KD.AFU.AFU.AFU.AFU.AFU.BCW

theater arts
USE **theater**

theater auditoriums
RM.357
ALT **theater auditorium**
SN Use for the seating areas of theaters.
UF auditoriums (theater spaces)
auditoriums, theater
CN V.RM.AFU.DIO.AXC.AXC.AFU.BZY

theater boxes
USE **boxes (audience spaces)**

theater design
KT.106 (L,R)
SN Design of all visual aspects of a stage production, including scenery, properties, lighting, costume, and make-up.
UF design, theater
scenography
CN K.KT.AFU.ALO.CFS.CFS

theater designers
HG.161
ALT **theater designer**
UF designers, theater
scenographers
CN H.HG.AFU.AXC.AXC.AFU.AFU.ALO.BCW.CFS

theater museums
RK.426 (L)
ALT **theater museum**
UF museums, theater
CN V.RK.AFU.ALO.ALO.BCW.AXC.ARI.CRG

theater programs
VW.70 (L,N)
ALT **theater program**
SN Printed or written lists of the acts, scenes, selections, or other features composing a theater performance, including the names of the performers. (GAHLM)
UF programs, theater
CN V.VW.AFU.AFU.AFU.ELK.ALO

theaters
RK.931 (A,L,N,B,R)
ALT **theater**
UF playhouses (theaters)
CN V.RK.AFU.ALO.ALO.EFQ.ARI.BCW

theaters-in-the-round
USE **arena theaters**

theaters, arena
USE **arena theaters**

theaters, drive-in
USE **drive-in theaters**

theaters, film
USE **movie theaters**

theaters, lecture
USE lecture halls

theaters, miniature
USE miniature theaters

theaters, movie
USE movie theaters

theaters, open-air
USE open-air theaters

theaters, operating
USE operating rooms

theaters, outdoor
USE open-air theaters

theaters, puppet
USE puppet theaters

theaters, variety
USE variety theaters

theatrical costumers
USE costume designers

theatrical machinery
USE stage machinery

Theban
FL.2813
CN F.FL.ALO.AXC.ALO.ARI.AFU.BOK.BOK

Thebes stools
TG.252
ALT Thebes stool
UF stools, Thebes
CN V.TG.AFU.AFU.ALO.AFU.ALO.AFU.CLM

theft
BM.1098 (L,R)
CN B.BM.CRG.BCW.ALO.ALO

thematic maps
VW.167
ALT thematic map
SN Maps designed primarily to meet specific requirements. (DOD)
UF maps, special-purpose
maps, thematic
special-purpose maps
CN V.VW.AFU.AFU.AFU.FZU.AXC.AFU.ARI.ALO.ARI

theme parks
RG.153 (A,L,B,R)
ALT theme park
UF parks, theme
CN V.RG.AFU.AFU.DOI.AFU.AFU

Thénard's blue
USE cobalt blue

theocracy
BM.542 (L)
CN B.BM.BOK.BOK.AFU.AXC

Theodosian
FL.3070 (L)
CN F.FL.ALO.BCW.ALO.AFU.ALO.AFU.AFU

theologians
HG.243 (L)
ALT theologian
CN H.HG.AFU.AXC.AXC.BIQ.AFU.BZY

theological seminaries
RK.822 (A,L,B,R)
ALT theological seminary
UF divinity schools
schools, divinity
seminaries
seminaries, theological
CN V.RK.AFU.ALO.ALO.CXA.ARI.ALO.DOI.ARI

theology
KD.87 (L,R)
SN Study of religious doctrines and practices as understood within a particular religious tradition, usually from the viewpoint of committed religious believers. (PG)
CN K.KD.AFU.AFU.BUE.ALO.BOK

theophany
BM.690 (L,R)
CN B.BM.BZY.ALO.AFU.CFS

theoretical designs
USE theoretical drawings

theoretical drawings
VD.110
ALT theoretical drawing
SN Use for drawings intended as experiments rather than designs to be executed and that are not so speculative as fantastic and visionary art or architecture.
UF designs, theoretical
drawings, theoretical
theoretical designs
CN V.VD.AFU.ALO.CXA

theoretical linguistics
KD.39
UF linguistics, theoretical
CN K.KD.AFU.AFU.AXC.AFU.ALO

theorists
HG.740
ALT theorist
CN H.HG.AFU.BCW.GRC

theory
BM.1163 (A,L,B,R)
SN Body of generalizations and principles developed in association with practice in a field of activity and forming its content as an intellectual discipline. (W)
CN B.BM.DIO.BOK

theory of function
USE functionalism

theory of knowledge
USE epistemology

theory of literature
USE literary theory

theory of value
USE axiology

theory, architectural
USE architectural theory

theory, art
USE art theory

theory, critical
USE critical theory

theory, literary
USE literary theory

theosophy
BM.709 (L,R)
CN B.BM.BZY.ALO.ARI.DOI

Theran
FL.2612
CN F.FL.ALO.AXC.ALO.AFU.ALO.AXC.ALO.ARI.BCW

therapists
HG.277 (L)
ALT therapist
SN Persons trained in applying occupational or physical measures in the treatment or rehabilitation of patients. (W)
CN H.HG.AFU.AXC.BCW.AFU.BZY.AFU

therapists, physical
USE physical therapists

therapy, art
USE art therapy

therapy, creative arts
USE art therapy

Theravada
BM.612 (L)
UF Buddhism, Pali
Buddhism, Southern
Buddhism, Theravada
Pali Buddhism
Southern Buddhism
Theravada Buddhism
CN B.BM.BZY.AFU.AFU.AFU.AFU

Theravada Buddhism
USE Theravada

therm feet
TG.914
ALT therm foot
SN Furniture feet in the form of a tapered square block, much used in the second half of the 18th century. (TOMLIN)
UF arrow feet
connelly feet
feet, arrow
feet, connelly
feet, haines
feet, plinth
feet, spade
feet, therm

feet, turned spade
haines feet
plinth feet
spade feet
thermed feet
thimble toes
toes, thimble
turned spade feet
CN V.TG.ALO.DZW.AFU.CRG

therm legs
TG.952
ALT **therm leg**
SN Tapered furniture legs that are square in section. (W)
UF legs, therm
CN V.TG.ALO.FIM.AFU.AFU.BUE

therm windows
USE **Diocletian windows**

thermae
RK.782 (A,B)
SN Use for monumental ancient Roman bath buildings. For public or private ancient Roman baths or bath buildings of ordinary size use **balnea.**
CN V.RK.AFU.ALO.ALO.CXA.ALO.AFU.BZY.ALO

thermal baths
USE **steam baths**

thermal breaks
TF.608
ALT **thermal break**
SN Elements of low conductivity placed between two conductive materials to limit heat flow; for use in metal windows of curtain walls that are to be used in cold climates. (MEANS)
UF breaks, thermal
CN V.TF.ALO.ALO.BIQ

thermal bridges
KT.927 (A)
SN Use for conditions that result across some construction details under certain climatic situations causing heat loss and unwanted heat flow in rooms and spaces.
UF bridges, cold
bridges, heat
bridges, thermal
cold bridges
heat bridges
CN K.KT.ALO.CFS

thermal conductivity
BM.990
UF conductivity, thermal
CN B.BM.CFS.AXC.BZY.CFS.BUE

thermal copying
USE **thermography**

thermal cutting
KT.830
UF cutting, thermal
CN K.KT.AFU.ALO.HOE.BCW.ALO.ARI.BCW

thermal efficiency
BM.844 (B)
UF efficiency, thermal
CN B.BM.CFS.AXC.ALO.AFU.AFU.ALO.BCW

thermal energy conversion plants, ocean
USE **ocean thermal energy conversion plants**

thermal expansion
USE **expansion**

thermal insulating materials
USE **thermal insulation**

thermal insulation
MT.2405 (L,B)
SN A material providing high resistance to heat flow; usually made of mineral wool, cork, asbestos, foam glass, foamed plastic, or diatomaceous earth, fabricated in the form of batts, blankets, blocks, boards, granular fill and loose fill. (DAC)
UF heat insulation
insulating materials, thermal
insulation, heat
insulation, thermal
materials, thermal insulating
thermal insulating materials
CN M.MT.AFU.ARI.BZY.BCW.ARI

thermal pollution
BM.441 (L)
UF heat pollution
pollution, heat
pollution, thermal
CN B.BM.AXC.BCW.ALO.BCW

thermal process
USE **thermography**

thermal properties
BM.982 (A,L)
UF properties, thermal
CN B.BM.CFS.AXC.BZY.CFS

thermal stress
BM.922 (A,L)
UF stress, temperature
stress, thermal
temperature stress
CN B.BM.CFS.AXC.BIQ.ARI.BCW.BIQ

thermed feet
USE **therm feet**

thermic copying
USE **thermography**

thermodynamics
BM.902 (L,R)
CN B.BM.CFS.AXC.BIQ.AFU.BCW

thermography
KT.482 (L,R)
SN Use for copying or printing processes which involve the use of heat, including document copying processes that use heat-sensitive paper and the raised-printing process in which matter printed by letterpress is dusted with powder and heated to make the lettering rise, thus giving an engraved appearance, as on business cards and stationery.
UF copying, heat
copying, thermal
copying, thermic
embossing, imitation
heat copying
imitation embossing
printing, raised-letter
raised-letter printing
thermal copying
thermal process
thermic copying
CN K.KT.AFU.ALO.DUC.ERE

thermoluminescence
BM.858 (L,R)
CN B.BM.CFS.AXC.ALO.AFU.ALO.ALO.BCW.AFU

thermoluminescence dating
KT.507 (A,L)
SN Method of dating objects by heating them to 400 to 500 degrees Celsius and measuring the release of stored energy in the form of light. (HOL-HZR)
UF dating, thermoluminescence
CN K.KT.AFU.ALO.EFQ.AFU.BOK

thermopane
USE **insulating glass**

thermoplastic
MT.2116 (L)
SN Plastics that become soft when heated and hard when cooled, no matter how often these processes are repeated, because of little or no cross-bonding between molecules. (MH12)
UF polymer, thermoplastic
resin, thermoplastic
thermoplastic polymer
thermoplastic resin
CN M.MT.AFU.AFU.ARI.BUE.ALO.AXC.AFU

thermoplastic polyester
MT.2180
UF polyester, thermoplastic
CN M.MT.AFU.AFU.ARI.BUE.ALO.AXC.ARI.AFU.AFU

thermoplastic polyimide
MT.2184
UF PI-tp
polyimide, thermoplastic
CN M.MT.AFU.AFU.ARI.BUE.ALO.AXC.ARI.ALO.AFU

thermoplastic polymer
USE **thermoplastic**

thermoplastic resin
USE **thermoplastic**

thermoset
MT.2158 (L)
SN Plastics with strong intermolecular bonding that become rigid by chemical reaction and that are not remeltable. (MH12)
UF plastic, thermosetting
resin, thermosetting
thermosetting plastic
thermosetting resin
CN M.MT.AFU.AFU.ARI.BUE.ALO .AXC.ALO

thermoset polyester
MT.2182
UF PES-ts
polyester, thermoset
CN M.MT.AFU.AFU.ARI.BUE.ALO AXC.ARI.AFU.ALO

thermoset polyimide
MT.2185
UF PI-ts
polyimide, thermoset
CN M.MT.AFU.AFU.ARI.BUE.ALO .AXC.ARI.ALO.ALO

thermoset silicone
USE **silicone**

thermosetting plastic
USE **thermoset**

thermosetting powders
USE **powder coatings**

thermosetting resin
USE **thermoset**

thesauri
VW.443 (L,R)
ALT **thesaurus**
SN Controlled vocabularies of semantically related terms usually covering one field of knowledge. (ICA)
CN V.VW.AFU.AFU.ALO.EWY.BUE

thesauri, monolingual
USE **monolingual thesauri**

thesauri, multilingual
USE **multilingual thesauri**

thesaurus construction
KG.100
UF construction, thesaurus
CN K.KG.AFU.AFU.AXC.CRG.BCW

theses
VW.1070 (L,B,R)
ALT **thesis**
SN Discourses advancing an original point of view as a result of research, especially as a requirement for an academic degree. (AHD)
CN V.VW.AFU.ARI.ALO.CRG.BOK

theses, masters
USE **masters theses**

thesis drawings
USE **student drawings**

thickeners
MT.2332
CN M.MT.AFU.ARI.ALO.FUA

thickness
BM.808
CN B.BM.CFS.ARI.AXC.BUE.BOK

thieves
HG.715 (L)
ALT **thief**
CN H.HG.AFU.BCW.BOK.ARI

thimble toes
USE **therm feet**

thin masonry vaults
USE **timbrel vaults**

thin oil
MT.2003
UF oil, thin
CN M.MT.AFU.AFU.ARI.ARI.ARI .BCW.ARI

Thin Orange
FL.1048
UF Orange, Thin
CN F.FL.ALO.ALO.ALO.ALO.AFU .ALO.ARI.ALO.ALO.ARI

thin shell structures
USE **shell structures**

Thinite
FL.2795
CN F.FL.ALO.AXC.ALO.ARI.AFU .AXC.ARI

thinners
MT.2712
SN Any volatile liquid used for thinning or diluting paints and varnishes. (MAYER)
UF diluents
paint thinners
thinners, paint
CN M.MT.AFU.ARI.HZS.ALO.ALO

thinners, paint
USE **thinners**

thinning files
USE **joint files**

thioindigo violet
MT.1725
UF violet, thioindigo
CN M.MT.AFU.AFU.ARI.AFU.AFU .ALO.ALO.BIQ.AXC.ARI

thiokol
USE **polysulfide elastomer**

Third Dynasty
FL.2788
UF 3rd Dynasty
Dynasty, Third
CN F.FL.ALO.AXC.ALO.ARI.AFU.ARI .AFU

Third Dynasty of Ur
FL.2971
UF Ur III
CN F.FL.ALO.AXC.ARI.BCW.AFU .BCW.AFU

Third Golden Age (Byzantine)
USE **Palaeologan**

Third Intermediate period
FL.2820
CN F.FL.ALO.AXC.ALO.ARI.AFU.BZY

Third Pointed
USE **Perpendicular Style**

Third Pompeian Style
USE **Third Style**

Third Style
FL.2768
UF Capricious Style
Ornate Style (Third Style)
Pompeian Style, Third
Third Pompeian Style
CN F.FL.ALO.AXC.ALO.ALO.ALO.CFS. AFU.ARI

Thirteenth Dynasty
FL.2807
UF 13th Dynasty
Dynasty, Thirteenth
CN F.FL.ALO.AXC.ALO.ARI.AFU.BOK. AFU

Thirtieth Dynasty
FL.2831
UF 30th Dynasty
Dynasty, Thirtieth
Sebennyte Dynasty
CN F.FL.ALO.AXC.ALO.ARI.AFU.CFS. BCW

Thirty-first Dynasty
FL.2832
UF Dynasty, Thirty-first
Second Persian Domination
Second Persian period
CN F.FL.ALO.AXC.ALO.ARI.AFU.CFS .BIQ

thirty-five millimeter cameras
USE **35mm cameras**

Thlingchadine
USE **Dogrib**

tholoi
RK.30 (A)
ALT **tholos**

SN Use to designate circular buildings of classical date, with or without a peristyle.
CN V.RK.AFU.ALO.AFU.ALO.CXA

tholos tombs
RK.494
ALT **tholos tomb**
SN Use for circular masonry tombs, primarily of Mycenaean Greece, constructed with a corbeled dome, entered via a long walled passageway, and covered by a mound.
UF beehive tombs
tombs, beehive
tombs, tholos
CN V.RK.AFU.ALO.ALO.BOK.BUE.AFU BZY

Thompson
FL.1424 (L)
UF Ntlakyapamuk
CN F.FL.ALO.ALO.ARI.AFU.BUE.ELK

Thon buri
USE **Thonburi**

Thonburi
FL.2416
UF Thon buri
CN F.FL.ALO.ARI.BCW.BOK.AFU.CLM

thong drills
USE **bow drills**

Thonga
FL.549 (L)
UF Bathonga
Tsonga
CN F.FL.ALO.AFU.AXC.ARI.AFU.BOK

Thor's hammers
USE **swastikas**

thorn
MT.1081 (L)
CN M.MT.AFU.AFU.ALO.BIQ.CXA

thorn ware
FL.2757
UF ware, thorn
CN F.FL.ALO.AXC.ALO.ALO.ALO.BUE .ALO.BOK

thoroughfares
USE **highways**

Thought painting
USE **Gedankenmalerei**

thread
MT.1976 (L,N,R)
CN M.MT.AFU.AFU.ARI.ALO.ALO.BIQ. AXC

thread cabinets
TG.443
ALT **thread cabinet**
UF cabinets, thread
CN V.TG.AFU.AFU.AXC.ALO.ARI.ALO. DUC

thread-cutting machines
USE **screw-cutting machines**

thread escutcheons
TF.266
ALT **thread escutcheon**
UF escutcheons, thread
CN V.TF.AFU.AFU.AFU.AFU.DZW.ALO. AXC

three-armed swastikas
USE **triskelions**

three-bay barns
USE **English barns**

three-centered arches
RT.268
ALT **three-centered arch**
SN Arches struck from three centers.
UF arches, three-centered
CN V.RT.AFU.AFU.AFU.BCW.AFU.AFU. AFU.EWY.ARI

Three Circle Mogollon
FL.950
UF Mogollon, Three Circle
CN F.FL.ALO.ALO.ALO.AFU.ALO.ARI. BIQ.BCW.BOK

three-color carbro process
KT.358
SN A subtractive color photographic process to make permanent color pigment prints. Three separate carbro transfer sheets are made, each corresponding to one of the subtractive primaries (cyan, magenta, and yellow); the sheets are transferred in register to a single support to form the image.
UF carbro tri-color
carbro trichrome
trichrome carbro process
tricolor carbro
Vivex
CN K.KT.AFU.ALO.DUC.DIO.ALO.DIO. ALO.AFU

three-color photography
USE **three-color processes**

three-color processes
KT.374 (L)
SN Photographic process producing full-color images using only three colors; may be additive or subtractive color processes.
UF photography, three-color
three-color photography
tri-color processes
trichromatic processes
trichrome processes
CN K.KT.AFU.ALO.DUC.DIO.ALO.EFQ

three-color ware
USE **Sancai**

three-deckers
RK.243 (A)
ALT **three-decker**
UF houses, triple-decker
triple-decker houses
triple-deckers
CN V.RK.AFU.ALO.ALO.AXC.ALO.AFU. CFS.AFU

three-deckers (pulpits)
RT.1244
ALT **three-decker (pulpit)**
SN Church pulpits with a clerk's desk at the bottom, reader's desk above, and pulpit on top.
CN V.RT.AFU.BUE.ALO.ARI.CLM.AFU. ALO

three-dimensional
DC.73
CN D.DC.AFU.ARI.DUC

three-dimensional trusses
USE **space frames**

three-hinged arches
RT.264
ALT **three-hinged arch**
SN Use for wood or metal arches that are hinged at the two springing points and at the crown.
UF arches, three-hinged
arches, three-pinned
three pinned arches
CN V.RT.AFU.AFU.AFU.BCW.AFU.AFU. AFU.ERE.ALO

Three Kingdoms (Chinese)
FL.1880 (L)
CN F.FL.ALO.ARI.ALO.AFU.AFU.ALO. BUE.ALO

Three Kingdoms (Korean)
FL.2109
CN F.FL.ALO.ARI.ALO.ARI.AFU.ALO

three-legged stools
TG.253
ALT **three-legged stool**
UF stools, three-legged
CN V.TG.AFU.AFU.ALO.AFU.ALO.AFU. CRG

three-part dining tables
TG.728
ALT **three-part dining table**
UF dining tables, three-part
tables, three-part dining
CN V.TG.AFU.AFU.BIQ.BOK.ALO.BZY. AXC

three-part vaults
USE **tripartite vaults**

three pinned arches
USE **three-hinged arches**

three-point locks
TF.221
ALT **three-point lock**
SN Assemblies that latch a pair of doors or the active leaf of a door at three points. (MEANS)
UF locks, three-point

CN V.TF.AFU.AFU.AFU.AFU.DIO.BIQ.
AFU.ELK

three-point perspective
KT.276
UF perspective, three-point
CN K.KT.AFU.ALO.DUC.DCU.BIQ.AXC.
ARI

three-point perspectives
VD.87
ALT **three-point perspective**
UF oblique perspectives
perspectives, oblique
perspectives, three-point
CN V.VD.AFU.AFU.BIQ.ARI.BCW.ARI

three-quarter closer
USE **king closer**

three-quarter size beds
TG.383
ALT **three-quarter size bed**
UF beds, three-quarter size
CN V.TG.AFU.AFU.ARI.AFU.ALO.ARI

three-quarter turn stairs
RT.1089
ALT **three-quarter turn stair**
SN Stairs which turn 270 degrees as they progress from bottom to top.
UF stairs, three-quarter turn
CN V.RT.AFU.BIQ.AXC.AFU.AFU.BZY.
ARI

three-quarter views
VB.28
ALT **three-quarter view**
UF views, three-quarter
CN V.VB.AFU.AFU.BOK.ALO.BUE.AFU

three-seated chairs
USE **indiscrets**

three-story
DC.99
UF 3-story
CN D.DC.AFU.ARI.ERE.BOK.ARI

three-tone drawings
VD.136
ALT **three-tone drawing**
UF chiaroscuro drawings
drawings, chiaroscuro
drawings, three-tone
CN V.VD.AFU.AXC.BZY

threnys
USE **footstools**

threshold combs
RT.1326
ALT **threshold comb**
UF combs, threshold
CN V.RT.ALO.ALO.ALO.ALO.AFU

threshold plates
RT.1327
ALT **threshold plate**
UF plates, threshold
CN V.RT.ALO.ALO.ALO.ALO.ALO

thresholds
RT.842
ALT **threshold**
SN Strips fastened to the floor beneath a door, usually required to cover the joint when two types of floor material meet; may provide weather protection on external doors. (HAS)
CN V.RT.AFU.ARI.AFU.AFU.AFU.ALO.
ALO.ALO.BCW

thrift shops
RK.184 (L)
ALT **thrift shop**
SN Retail stores that sell secondhand goods at reduced prices. (RHDEL2)
UF secondhand stores
shops, thrift
stores, secondhand
CN V.RK.AFU.ALO.ALO.ALO.ARI.BIQ.
ALO.CXA

throat moldings
USE **cavetto moldings**

throats, chimney
USE **chimney throats**

throats, fireplace
USE **chimney throats**

throne rooms
RM.159
ALT **throne room**
SN Chief rooms of state containing the throne. (RS)
UF rooms, throne
CN V.RM.AFU.DIO.ALO.CLM.ARI

thrones
TG.167 (A,L,R)
ALT **throne**
UF chairs, coronation
coronation chairs
soliums
CN V.TG.AFU.AFU.ALO.AFU.AFU.ALO.
ARI.ARI

thronoi
TG.168
ALT **thronos**
CN V.TG.AFU.AFU.ALO.AFU.AFU.ALO.
ARI.ARI.AFU

through stones
USE **perpends**

through streets
RK.1546
ALT **through street**
SN Streets along which traffic has the right of way over vehicles entering or crossing at intersections. (RHDEL2)
UF streets, through
CN V.RK.ALO.ALO.BIQ.ARI.AFU.ALO.
ARI.ARI

through trusses
RT.379
ALT **through truss**
SN Bridge trusses supporting loads on their lower chords.
UF deck trusses
trusses, deck
trusses, through
CN V.RT.AFU.AFU.AFU.BCW.CLM.AFU.
ALO.AFU.AFU

throughways
RK.1521 (L,B)
ALT **throughway**
SN Use for divided, multilane highways with full grade separation and total control of access; can be freeways or turnpikes.
UF motorways
skyways
speedways
superhighways
CN V.RK.ALO.ALO.BIQ.ARI.AFU.AFU
.ARI.AFU.ALO

throw bolts, double
USE **double throw bolts**

throwers
USE **froes**

throwing (pottery technique)
KT.876
ALT **thrown**
SN The process of making a ceramic object on a potter's wheel. (THDAT)
CN K.KT.AFU.ALO.HOE.BOK.BOK

thru-screw knobs
TF.63
ALT **thru-screw knob**
SN Knobs with a hole through which to receive a mounting screw. (DITTRI)
UF knobs, thru-screw
CN V.TF.AFU.AFU.AFU.AFU.CFS.AXC
.AFU.ARI

thrust keys
USE **push keys**

thrust stages
RM.370
ALT **thrust stage**
SN Open stages that project into the audience.
UF stages, thrust
CN V.RM.AFU.DIO.AXC.AXC.ALO.BIQ.
AFU.AXC

thuja accidentalis
USE **American arbor vitae**

Thule
FL.795 (L)
CN F.FL.ALO.ALO.ALO.AFU.ALO.AFU.
ALO.AFU.AXC

Thule, Western
USE **Western Thule**

thumb bolts
TF.170
ALT **thumb bolt**
SN Door bolts operated by a rotating

thumbpiece or a small knob. (STEIN)
UF bolts, thumb
CN V.TF.AFU.AFU.AFU.AFU.DIO.ARI.BOK

thumb latches
TF.180
ALT **thumb latch**
UF latches, thumb
CN V.TF.AFU.AFU.AFU.AFU.DIO.BCW.AFU.BOK

thumb moldings
USE **gadrooning**

thumb planes
TB.972
ALT **thumb plane**
SN Any of a variety of small narrow planes 1 to 5 inches in length.
UF planes, thumb
CN V.TB.AFU.BCW.CFS.ALO.AFU.DUC.CFS

thumb turns
TF.569
ALT **thumb turn**
UF turns, thumb
CN V.TF.AFU.ALO.AXC.BZY

thumbnail sketches
VD.137
ALT **thumbnail sketch**
UF sketches, thumbnail
CN V.VD.AFU.AXC.CFS

thumbscrews
TF.478 (N)
ALT **thumbscrew**
SN Screws each having a head that is either curled or flattened so it can be turned with a thumb and fingers. (MEANS)
UF screws, thumb
CN V.TF.AFU.AFU.AFU.ALO.AFU.DIO.AFU.BUE

thumbtacks
TF.496
ALT **thumbtack**
CN V.TF.AFU.AFU.AFU.ALO.AFU.ERE.ARI

thunderstorms
KM.124 (L,R)
CN K.KM.AFU.CXA.BIQ.BUE

thupas
USE **stupas**

Thuringian ware
FL.3389 (L,R)
UF ware, Thuringian
CN F.FL.ALO.BCW.ALO.AXC.DIO.BIQ.BCW.ARI

thus, gum
USE **gum thus**

thuya occidentalis
USE **American arbor vitae**

thwart saws
USE **two-handed crosscut saws**

thymeles
RK.1087
ALT **thymele**
SN Use for altars standing in the center of a Greek theater orchestra.
CN V.RK.AFU.ALO.ALO.FCS.AFU.AXC

Tiahuanaco
FL.1161 (L)
CN F.FL.ALO.ALO.ALO.ARI.AXC.AFU.BCW.ARI

Tiahuanaco, Costal
USE **Pacheco**

Tianqi
FL.1907
UF T'ien-ch'i
CN F.FL.ALO.ARI.ALO.AFU.AFU.ALO.DIO.CFS

Tibetan
FL.2175 (L,B)
CN F.FL.ALO.ARI.AXC.AFU.BOK

tickets
VW.627 (N)
ALT **ticket**
SN Includes documents, usually slips of paper or cardboard, serving as evidence that the holder has paid a fare or admission or is entitled to some service.
CN V.VW.AFU.ALO.AFU.DUC

tickets, admission
USE **admission tickets**

tickets, bottle
USE **wine labels**

tickets, election
USE **ballots**

tickets, library
USE **library cards**

tickets, readers'
USE **library cards**

tickets, time
USE **time sheets**

tickets, traffic
USE **traffic tickets**

Ticomán
FL.983
UF Cuicuilco
CN F.FL.ALO.ALO.ALO.ALO.AFU.ALO.AFU.AFU.AXC

tidal electric plants
USE **tidal power plants**

tidal energy electric generating plants
USE **tidal power plants**

tidal energy plants
USE **tidal power plants**

tidal power plants
RG.112 (L)
ALT **tidal power plant**
UF electric generating plants, tidal energy
electric plants, tidal
plants, tidal power
power plants, tidal
power stations, wave
tidal electric plants
tidal energy electric generating plants
tidal energy plants
wave power stations
CN V.RG.AFU.AFU.BUE.ARI.ALO.ALO

tidal waves
KM.126 (L,R)
UF tsunamis
waves, tidal
CN K.KM.AFU.CXA.BOK

tide mills
RK.666 (B)
ALT **tide mill**
SN Mills operated by the tidal currents. (W)
UF mills, tide
CN V.RK.AFU.ALO.ALO.CLM.ALO.ALO.ALO.AFU.AFU

tides
BM.735 (L)
CN B.BM.CFS.ALO.ALO

tie and dye cloth
MT.1887
UF cloth, tie and dye
CN M.MT.AFU.AFU.ARI.ALO.ALO.ALO.ARI.BCW.ARI

tie bars
USE **tie rods**

tie beams
RT.509
ALT **tie beam**
SN Use for the members that form the base of the roof truss and prevent the rafters from spreading.
UF beams, tie
main ties
pieces, tie
roof ties
tie pieces
ties, main
ties, roof
CN V.RT.AFU.AFU.AFU.BIQ.ARI.ALO.ALO.ALO.BCW

tie bolts
USE **tie rods**

tie-dyeing
KT.81 (L)
ALT **tie-dyed**
CN K.KT.AFU.ALO.BOK.ALO.ARI

tie hangers
TF.347
ALT **tie hanger**

UF hangers, tie
CN V.TF.AFU.AFU.AFU.ALO.AFU.BOK.ALO.ALO.BCW

tie pieces
USE **tie beams**

tie racks
TF.272
ALT **tie rack**
UF racks, tie
CN V.TF.AFU.AFU.AFU.AFU.EFQ.ARI

tie rods
MT.2387 (L)
SN Rods used as a connecting member or brace, especially to counteract the spreading action of vaults or roofs.
UF bolts, tie
rods, tension
rods, tie
tension rods
tie bars
tie bolts
CN M.MT.AFU.ARI.BZY.ALO.ALO

Tien
FL.316
UF Shien
Tchien
CN F.FL.ALO.AFU.AXC.AFU.ARI.ARI.ARI.ALO

tier tables
USE **tiered stands**

tiercerons
RT.691
ALT **tierceron**
SN Secondary ribs springing from a main springer and leading to the ridge rib. (STOK)
UF intermediate ribs
ribs, intermediate
ribs, secondary
secondary ribs
CN V.RT.AFU.AFU.ALO.AFU.ARI.BCW

tiered bookcases
USE **revolving bookcases**

tiered stands
TG.620
ALT **tiered stand**
UF stands, tiered
tables, tier
tier tables
CN V.TG.AFU.AFU.BIQ.BCW.AFU.ARI

tiers (wythes)
USE **wythes**

ties (hardware)
TF.497 (B)
ALT **tie (hardware)**
SN Tensile units adapted to holding concrete forms secure against the lateral pressure of unhardened concrete, with or without provision for removal of metal to a specified distance from the finished concrete surfaces. (MEANS)
CN V.TF.AFU.AFU.AFU.ALO.AFU.EWY

ties, anchor
USE **anchor ties**

ties, angle
USE **angle braces**

ties, collar
USE **collar beams**

ties, dragon
USE **dragon ties**

ties, main
USE **tie beams**

ties, roof
USE **tie beams**

tiger maple
MT.1226
UF maple, tiger
CN M.MT.AFU.AFU.ALO.BIQ.DCU.AFU.AFU.AFU.IFM.BZY

Tiger ware
FL.3188
UF ware, Tiger
CN F.FL.ALO.BCW.ALO.ARI.BIQ.BCW.AXC.AFU

tight pin hinges
USE **fast-pin hinges**

Tigong
FL.221
CN F.FL.ALO.AFU.AXC.AFU.AFU.ALO.ALO.DCU

Tikar
FL.194 (L)
CN F.FL.ALO.AFU.AXC.AFU.AFU.AFU.ARI

Tikopia
FL.3670 (L)
CN F.FL.ALO.BOK.ALO.BOK.BUE

tile
MT.2277 (A,L,B,R)
SN Thin piece of resilient material used especially for covering floors and walls; any material in the form of a tile.
CN M.MT.AFU.ALO.IFM

tile block printing
KT.473 (L)
UF block printing, tile
printing, tile block
CN K.KT.AFU.ALO.DUC.DUC.ALO.BCW.ARI.ALO.ARI

tile flooring
MT.2392 (L)
UF flooring, tile
CN M.MT.AFU.ARI.BZY.AXC.AFU.ALO

tile laying
KT.590 (L,B)
ALT **tiled**
UF laying, tile
tiling
CN K.KT.AFU.ALO.ERE.CFS

tile, acoustical
USE **acoustical tile**

tile, arris
USE **arris tile**

tile, bonnet hip
USE **bonnet hip tile**

tile, book
USE **book tile**

tile, ceramic
USE **ceramic tile**

tile, cone
USE **bonnet hip tile**

tile, cone hip
USE **bonnet hip tile**

tile, cover
USE **cover tile**

tile, covering
USE **cover tile**

tile, crease
USE **crest tile**

tile, cress
USE **crest tile**

tile, crest
USE **crest tile**

tile, crown
USE **ridge tile**

tile, drainage
USE **draintile**

tile, facing
USE **wall tile**

tile, faience
USE **faience tile**

tile, field
USE **draintile**

tile, fireproofing
USE **fireproofing tile**

tile, French
USE **French tile**

tile, geometrical
USE **mathematical tile**

tile, hip
USE **hip tile**

tile, hollow
USE **structural clay tile**

tile, mathematical
USE **mathematical tile**

tile, mission
USE **Spanish tile**

tile, pan-and-roll roofing
USE **pan-and-roll roofing tile**

tile, partition
USE **partition tile**

tile, paving
USE **paving tile**

tile, quarry
USE **quarry tile**

tile, ridge
USE **ridge tile**

tile, Roman
USE **Roman tile**

tile, roof
USE **roofing tile**

tile, roofing
USE **roofing tile**

tile, shingle
USE **shingle tile**

tile, Spanish
USE **Spanish tile**

tile, structural clay
USE **structural clay tile**

tile, valley
USE **valley tile**

tile, wall
USE **wall tile**

tile, weather
USE **weather tile**

Tilia
USE **linden**

Tilia americana
USE **linden**

Tilia cordata
USE **small-leafed lime**

Tilia europea
USE **common lime**

Tilia vulgaris
USE **common lime**

tiling
USE **tile laying**

tiling plaster
USE **gypsum cement**

till locks
USE **drawer locks**

Tillamook
FL.1363 (L)
CN F.FL.ALO.ALO.ARI.AFU.BIQ.GFO

tills
TG.885
ALT **till**
SN Drawers or boxes fitted in a larger piece of furniture; frequently found in Medieval chests and sometimes in 16th- and 17th-century cupboards. (DEF)
CN V.TG.ALO.DCU.AFU.ALO.BIQ

tilt hammers
USE **helve hammers**

tilt-top tables
TG.706
ALT **tilt-top table**
SN Tripod tables, usually with circular tops, which are hinged to tilt to a vertical position. (FAIRB)
UF snap tables
tables, snap
tables, tilt-top
tables, tip
tables, tip-top
tables, tip-up
tables, turn up
tables, upright-top
tip tables
tip-top tables
tip-up tables
turn up tables
upright-top tables
CN V.TG.AFU.AFU.BIQ.BOK.AFU.DZW.AXC

tilting chests
TG.474
ALT **tilting chest**
UF chests, tilting
CN V.TG.AFU.AFU.AXC.ALO.AXC.FCS

tilting dozers
TB.36
ALT **tilting dozer**
SN Bulldozers whose blades can be pivoted on a horizontal center pin to cut down on either side. (STEIN)
UF dozers, tilting
CN V.TB.AFU.ARI.AFU.ARI.AFU.ARI

tilting fillets
USE **eaves boards**

timber
MT.1445 (A,L,B)
CN M.MT.AFU.AFU.ALO.BIQ.DCU.ALO.BOK.ARI.BCW.ALO

timber yards
USE **lumberyards**

timber, clean
USE **clear lumber**

timber, structural
USE **structural lumber**

timbers, cased-in
USE **cased beams**

Timbira
FL.1683 (L)
CN F.FL.ALO.ALO.ARI.ARI.BIQ.CLM

timbrel vaults
RT.557
ALT **timbrel vault**
SN Use for vaults of separate masonry units, but very thin, and deriving their rigidity from curvature rather than massiveness.
UF masonry vaults, thin
thin masonry vaults
vaults, thin masonry
vaults, timbrel
CN V.RT.AFU.AFU.AFU.BIQ.BOK.AFU.ARI.AFU.AXC

Timbú
FL.1699
CN F.FL.ALO.ALO.ARI.ARI.BOK.CRG

Timbuktu
FL.91
CN F.FL.ALO.AFU.ALO.AFU.BOK.AXC

timchent
MT.2449
SN A hard, quick-drying plaster processed from river silt used in Saharan building for making building blocks, as mortar, and for rendering. (OLIVER)
CN M.MT.AFU.ARI.CRG.AFU.AXC.AFU.BUE

time
BM.1033 (L,R)
CN B.BM.CFS.AXC.CRG

time books
VW.852
ALT **time book**
SN Books in which hours spent on a job by workers are recorded. (GAHLM)
UF books, time
CN V.VW.AFU.ARI.AFU.BIQ.CXA.AFU.BZY.ARI

time cards
VW.853
ALT **time card**
SN Cards, either maintained by each employee or stamped by a time clock, recording the arrival and departure of an employee each day. (AHD)
UF cards, time
time-clock cards
CN V.VW.AFU.ARI.AFU.BIQ.CXA.AFU.BZY.AXC

time-clock cards
USE **time cards**

time-lapse photography
KT.383 (L)
SN Technique of taking a series of photographs at set intervals to record changes that take place slowly with time, such as the growth of a plant. Usually played back as a motion picture.
UF photography, time-lapse
CN K.KT.AFU.ALO.DUC.DIO.ARI.ARI.AFU.ALO

time locks

TF.222
ALT **time lock**
UF chronometer locks
locks, chronometer
locks, time
CN V.TF.AFU.AFU.AFU.AFU.DIO.BIQ.AFU.ERE

time sheets
VW.854
ALT **time sheet**
SN Sheets for recording the times of arrival and departure of workers and for recording the amount of time spent upon each job; also sheets for totalling the hours worked by each worker during a pay period. (GAHLM)
UF sheets, time
tickets, time
time tickets
CN V.VW.AFU.ARI.AFU.BIQ.CXA.AFU.BZY.BCW

time tickets
USE **time sheets**

time zone maps
VW.207
ALT **time zone map**
SN Small-scale charts of the world designed to show the legal time on land. (DOD)
UF maps, time zone
zone maps, time
CN V.VW.AFU.AFU.AFU.FZU.AXC.AFU.ARI.AXC.DCU

timetables
USE **schedules**

Timne
USE **Temne**

timonox
USE **antimony white**

Timor
FL.2392 (L)
CN F.FL.ALO.ARI.BCW.ARI.ALO.BZY

Timote
FL.1633
CN F.FL.ALO.ALO.ARI.ARI.ARI.BIQ

Timucua
FL.1441 (L,R)
UF Utina
CN F.FL.ALO.ALO.ARI.AFU.BZY.CRG

Timurid
FL.3571 (A,L)
CN F.FL.ALO.BIQ.AFU.HTY

tin
MT.448 (L,R)
CN M.MT.AFU.AFU.AFU.BZY.AFU.AFU.ARI.DIO

tin alloys
MT.406 (L)
UF alloys, tin
CN M.MT.AFU.AFU.AFU.BZY.AFU.AFU.AFU.ALO.BUE

tin brass
USE **naval brass**

tin mines
RG.104 (L,B)
ALT **tin mine**
UF mines, tin
stannaries
CN V.RG.AFU.AFU.BUE.AFU.ALO.BOK

tin snips
TB.727 (N)
SN Sharp cutters used for snipping pieces of sheet metal. (HAND)
UF sheet metal worker's snips
snips
snips, sheet metal worker's
snips, tin
CN V.TB.AFU.BCW.BIQ.ARI.ALO.BIQ.BIQ

tin white
MT.1734
SN Stannic oxide, used to produce an opaque white in ceramics. (MAYER)
UF ceruse of tin
tin, ceruse of
white, tin
CN M.MT.AFU.AFU.ARI.AFU.AFU.ALO.ALO.BOK.AFU.BOK

tin, ceruse of
USE **tin white**

tincture of green soap
USE **soft soap**

tined kettle stands
USE **kettle stands**

Ting ware
USE **Ding ware**

Ting yao
USE **Ding ware**

tinkers
HG.520 (L)
ALT **tinker**
CN H.HG.AFU.AXC.BUE.ARI.CFS.ARI.CLM

tinners
USE **tinsmiths**

tinsmithing
KT.786 (L,R)
CN K.KT.AFU.ALO.HOE.BCW.AFU.BUE

tinsmiths
HG.501 (L)
ALT **tinsmith**
UF tinners
CN H.HG.AFU.AXC.BUE.ARI.CFS.AFU.BUE

tint
BM.134
SN Color obtained by mixing a basic hue with white in order to lighten it. (A-Z)
CN B.BM.AFU.AFU.ARI.BOK.ALO.ALO.ALO.BCW

tinting
KT.84 (L)
ALT **tinted**
CN K.KT.AFU.ALO.BOK.BCW

tinting, hand
USE **hand coloring**

tintype
KT.323 (L)
SN A variant of the wet collodion process producing a direct positive image on a thin sheet of lacquered metal (usually iron, never tin).
UF ferrotype
melainotype
CN K.KT.AFU.ALO.DUC.DIO.ALO.BCW.ARI

tintypes
VJ.34 (L,N,R)
ALT **tintype**
SN Photographs produced by the wet collodion process directly on lacquered metal, usually iron.
UF ferrotypes
melainotypes
CN V.VJ.AFU.AFU.ARI.AFU.BCW

tintypes, gem
USE **gem photographs**

tinware
MT.478 (L,R)
CN M.MT.AFU.AFU.AFU.BZY.ALO.BIQ.AFU

tip tables
USE **tilt-top tables**

tip-top tables
USE **tilt-top tables**

tip-up tables
USE **tilt-top tables**

tipis
RK.357 (L,N,R)
ALT **tipi**
SN Use for conical tent dwellings of poles gathered together at the top, spread into a circle on the ground, and covered with skins or canvas; common to Native American tribes of the Great Plains.
UF teepees
tepees
CN V.RK.AFU.ALO.ALO.AXC.ARI.BIQ.AFU

tipping
USE **tipping in**

tipping in
KT.63
ALT **tipped in**

SN Use for the process of inserting a single leaf, errata slip, or illustration into a book with a narrow edge of paste that binds it to the following page. (LG)
UF tipping
CN K.KT.AFU.ALO.BCW.CRG

tips, coal
USE **spoil banks**

tiring houses
RM.375
ALT **tiring house**
SN Portions of the theater backstage used as a place for dressing and storage, for a green room, and sometimes for an inner stage. (TL)
UF attiring houses
houses, attiring
houses, tiring
houses, tyreing
tyreing houses
CN V.RM.AFU.DIO.AXC.AXC.ALO.BOK.AFU

tirio
MT.839
UF greco turchiniccio
marmor tyrium
CN M.MT.AFU.AFU.AFU.DCU.AFU.ARI.ARI.ARI.BOK.EFQ

tissue paper
MT.1923 (L)
UF paper, tissue
CN M.MT.AFU.AFU.ARI.ALO.ALO.AXC.ALO.BOK

tissue stereographs
VJ.105
ALT **tissue stereograph**
SN Stereoscopic photographs on tissue paper mounted between sheets of glass or in a cardboard frame. (SAPSP)
UF French tissues
stereographs, tissue
tissues, French
CN V.VJ.AFU.ARI.AFU.BOK.AXC

tissue, dry-mounting
USE **mounting tissue**

tissue, mounting
USE **mounting tissue**

tissues, French
USE **tissue stereographs**

titanates
MT.2333 (L)
CN M.MT.AFU.ARI.ALO.FZU

titanium
MT.449 (L)
CN M.MT.AFU.AFU.AFU.BZY.AFU.AFU.ARI.DOI

titanium barium white
MT.1736
UF white, titanium barium
CN M.MT.AFU.AFU.ARI.AFU.AFU.ALO.ALO.BOK.AFU.BUE.AFU

titanium calcium white
MT.1737
UF white, titanium calcium
CN M.MT.AFU.AFU.ARI.AFU.AFU.ALO.ALO.BOK.AFU.BUE.ALO

titanium dioxide
USE **titanium white**

titanium steel
MT.357 (L)
UF steel, titanium
CN M.MT.AFU.AFU.AFU.BZY.AFU.AFU.AFU.AFU.ALO.AFU.ALO.BCW

titanium white
MT.1735 (L)
UF blanc titane
titanium dioxide
titanox
Titanweiss
white, titanium
CN M.MT.AFU.AFU.ARI.AFU.AFU.ALO.ALO.BOK.AFU.BUE

titanox
USE **titanium white**

Titanweiss
USE **titanium white**

tithe barns
RK.52 (B)
ALT **tithe barn**
SN Barns built for storing agricultural produce, taxes, or other contributions paid in support of religious establishments or parishes; common in England.
UF barns, tithe
CN V.RK.AFU.ALO.ALO.AFU.AFU.AFU.ALO.AXC

tithing
KG.215 (L)
SN Paying or exacting as payment a tenth part of income, crops, or other material resources.
CN K.KG.AFU.ALO.BIQ.AXC

title
BM.474
CN B.BM.BCW.CXA.ALO.ALO.ALO

title deeds
USE **deeds**

title indexes
VW.442
ALT **title index**
UF indexes, title
CN V.VW.AFU.AFU.ALO.EWY.BOK.ARI.ARI

tituli
USE **domus ecclesiae**

Tiv
FL.222 (L)
UF Munshi
CN F.FL.ALO.AFU.AXC.AFU.AFU.ALO.ALO.DIO

tlachtlis
USE **ball courts**

Tlahuica
FL.1504 (L)
CN F.FL.ALO.ALO.ARI.ALO.ARI.BCW.AFU

Tlalpan
FL.977
CN F.FL.ALO.ALO.ALO.ALO.AFU.ALO.AFU.AFU.AFU

Tlamimilolpa
FL.989
UF Teotihuacan III
CN F.FL.ALO.ALO.ALO.ALO.AFU.ALO.AFU.AFU.CFS

Tlapanec
FL.1523 (L)
CN F.FL.ALO.ALO.ARI.ALO.AXC.DCU

Tlatelolco
USE **Aztec IV**

Tlatilco
FL.978 (L)
CN F.FL.ALO.ALO.ALO.ALO.AFU.ALO.AFU.AFU.ALO

Tlaxcalan
FL.1505 (L)
CN F.FL.ALO.ALO.ARI.ALO.ARI.BCW.ALO

Tlingit
FL.1364 (L)
UF Kolosh
CN F.FL.ALO.ALO.ARI.AFU.BIQ.GLI

TLRs
USE **twin-lens cameras**

TNT
MT.2588
UF tolite
trinitrotoluene
trinitrotoluol
trotyl
CN M.MT.AFU.ARI.DIO.ARI

toad tunnels
RK.1307
ALT **toad tunnel**
SN Tunnels built to give toads, moving to breeding ponds in mating season, safe passage beneath roads.
UF tunnels, toad
CN V.RK.AFU.ALO.ALO.GLI.ALO.ALO.ARI

toad's-eye views
USE **worm's-eye views**

Toba (Chaco)
FL.1650 (L)

CN F.FL.ALO.ALO.ARI.ARI.AXC.DIO

tobacco
MT.1040 (L,R)
CN M.MT.AFU.AFU.ALO.BIQ.BIQ.ALO

tobacco barns
RK.100 (N)
ALT **tobacco barn**
UF barns, tobacco
sheds, tobacco
tobacco sheds
CN V.RK.AFU.ALO.ALO.AFU.AXC

tobacco cloth
MT.1851
SN A loose-weave cotton fabric, used especially to shade growing tobacco plants. (W)
UF cloth, tobacco
CN M.MT.AFU.AFU.ARI.ALO.ALO.ALO.AFU.ALO.AXC

tobacco seed oil
MT.2021
UF oil, tobacco seed
seed oil, tobacco
TSO
CN M.MT.AFU.AFU.ARI.ARI.AXC.AFU.CRG

tobacco sheds
USE **tobacco barns**

tobi
USE **tapia**

Tobikhar
USE **Gabrieliño**

toboggan runs
RK.1081 (B)
ALT **toboggan run**
UF runs, toboggan
CN V.RK.AFU.ALO.ALO.EWY.BIQ.BCW

tocineras
TG.764
ALT **tocinera**
SN Small kitchen tables dedicated to pork-salting and sausage-making. (BYNE)
CN V.TG.AFU.AFU.BIQ.BOK.ALO.GFO

toddy tables
USE **drinking stands**

toes, thimble
USE **therm feet**

Tofinu
FL.308 (L)
CN F.FL.ALO.AFU.AXC.AFU.ARI.ALO.BCW.AFU

Togbo
FL.537
CN F.FL.ALO.AFU.AXC.ALO.ALO.BIQ.ALO.CRG

toggle bolts
TF.319
ALT **toggle bolt**
SN Bolt and nut assemblies used to fasten objects to a hollow wall or a wall accessible from only one side. The nut has pivoted wings that close against a spring when the nut end of the assembly is pushed through a hole and open on the other side. (MEANS)
UF bolts, toggle
CN V.TF.AFU.AFU.AFU.ALO.AFU.ALO.AFU.CLM

Tohil
FL.1025
CN F.FL.ALO.ALO.ALO.ALO.AFU.ALO.ARI.AFU.ALO.BZY

Tohil Plumbate
FL.1047
CN F.FL.ALO.ALO.ALO.ALO.AFU.ALO.ARI.ALO.ALO.ALO.ARI

toilet compartments
RM.83 (B)
ALT **toilet compartment**
UF compartments, toilet
partitions, toilet
toilet partitions
CN V.RM.AFU.DIO.ALO.ALO.CLM

toilet paper holders
TF.146
ALT **toilet paper holder**
UF holders, paper
holders, toilet paper
paper holders
paper holders, toilet
CN V.TF.AFU.AFU.AFU.AFU.CRG.ARI

toilet partitions
USE **toilet compartments**

toilet safety rails
TF.275
ALT **toilet safety rail**
UF rails, toilet safety
safety rails, toilet
CN V.TF.AFU.AFU.AFU.AFU.ELK.ALO

toilet stands
USE **basin stands**

toilet table beds
TG.348
ALT **toilet table bed**
UF toilet table bedsteads
CN V.TG.AFU.AFU.ARI.AFU.AFU.BIQ.AFU.BOK.AFU

toilet table bedsteads
USE **toilet table beds**

toilet tables
USE **dressing tables**

toilet tank levers
TF.257
ALT **toilet tank lever**
UF levers, toilet tank
CN V.TF.AFU.AFU.AFU.AFU.DOI.AFU

toilets
RT.1489 (L,B)
ALT **toilet**
SN Plumbing fixtures consisting typically of a water-flushed bowl with a toilet seat. (W)
UF water closets
WCs
CN V.RT.ALO.BCW.ALO.ARI.CFS.BOK

toilets, public
USE **comfort stations**

toilets, waterless
USE **waterless toilets**

toilettes
TG.738
ALT **toilette**
SN French term applied to a variety of dressing tables.
UF poudreuses
tables de toilette
CN V.TG.AFU.AFU.BIQ.BOK.ALO.CLM.AXC.ARI

toilettes en papillon
TG.740
ALT **toilette en papillon**
SN Heart-shaped dressing tables with drawers springing out at each side somewhat like butterfly wings. (WATSON)
CN V.TG.AFU.AFU.BIQ.BOK.ALO.CLM.AXC.ARI.ALO

Tojolabal
FL.1540 (L)
UF Canabal
CN F.FL.ALO.ALO.ARI.ALO.BIQ.AFU.BZY

Tokoname
FL.2046
CN F.FL.ALO.ARI.ALO.ALO.ALO.ALO.ALO.FIM

Tokugawa
USE **Edo (Japanese period)**

Tokugawa, Early
USE **Early Edo**

Tokugawa, Late
USE **Late Edo**

Tolai
FL.3624 (L)
CN F.FL.ALO.BOK.ALO.ARI.ARI

tolerances
BM.1144 (L,B)
UF engineering tolerances
fits (engineering)
CN B.BM.CXA.ALO.AXC.ALO

Tolima
FL.1111
CN F.FL.ALO.ALO.ALO.ARI.AFU.ARI

tolite
USE **TNT**

toll bridges
RK.1293 (L)
ALT **toll bridge**
UF bridges, toll
CN V.RK.AFU.ALO.ALO.GLI.ALO.AFU.ALO.ARI.ALO.AFU

toll plazas
RK.1256 (A,L)
ALT **toll plaza**
UF plazas, toll
CN V.RK.AFU.ALO.ALO.GLI.AFU.ARI.BUE.AFU

toll roads
USE **turnpikes**

tollbooths
RK.1257 (A)
ALT **tollbooth**
CN V.RK.AFU.ALO.ALO.GLI.AFU.ARI.BUE.ALO

tollgates
RK.1258 (N)
ALT **tollgate**
CN V.RK.AFU.ALO.ALO.GLI.AFU.ARI.BUE.ARI

tollhouses
RK.1259 (L,N,B)
ALT **tollhouse**
CN V.RK.AFU.ALO.ALO.GLI.AFU.ARI.BUE.AXC

tollways
USE **turnpikes**

Tolowa
FL.1365 (L)
CN F.FL.ALO.ALO.ARI.AFU.BIQ.GRC

Toltec
FL.1002 (L,B)
CN F.FL.ALO.ALO.ALO.ALO.AFU.ALO.AFU.ALO.AXC

Tolú
FL.1670
CN F.FL.ALO.ALO.ARI.ARI.BCW.DZW

tolu balsam
MT.1477
UF balsam, tolu
CN M.MT.AFU.AFU.ALO.BOK.AFU.BOK

toluene
MT.2673 (L)
UF benzene, methyl
methyl benzene
CN M.MT.AFU.ARI.HZS.AFU.BIQ.ALO.ALO

toluidine red
MT.1709
UF red, toluidine
CN M.MT.AFU.AFU.ARI.AFU.AFU.ALO.ALO.BCW.AXC.BOK

Tom Thumb courses
USE **miniature golf courses**

Toma
USE **Loma**

tomahawks (twivels)
USE **twivels**

tomb towers
USE **chullpas**
gumbads

Tomba
USE **Ntomba**

tombs
RK.480 (A,L,B,R)
ALT **tomb**
SN Elaborations constructed over or around burial sites; for simple interments in the earth, use **graves**.
UF sepulchers (tombs)
CN V.RK.AFU.ALO.ALO.BOK.BUE

tombs, altar
USE **altar tombs**

tombs, beehive
USE **tholos tombs**

tombs, chamber
USE **chamber tombs**

tombs, cist
USE **cist graves**

tombs, high
USE **altar tombs**

tombs, megalithic chamber
USE **megalithic chamber tombs**

tombs, pit
USE **shaft graves**

tombs, rock-cut
USE **rock-cut tombs**

tombs, royal
USE **royal tombs**

tombs, shaft
USE **shaft graves**

tombs, tholos
USE **tholos tombs**

tombstone lights
RT.932
ALT **tombstone light**
SN Small windows with lights in the shape of an arched tombstone; usually in the transom above a doorway. (HAS)
UF lights, tombstone
CN V.RT.AFU.ARI.AFU.AFU.BOK.AFU.AFU.ELK

tombstones
RK.479 (A,L,N,B,R)
ALT **tombstone**
UF gravestones
headstones
CN V.RK.AFU.ALO.ALO.BOK.BOK.ARI

Tonalist
FL.1755 (L,R)
ALT **Tonalism**
CN F.FL.ALO.ALO.BCW.AFU.CFS.BOK

tone
BM.135
SN Use for the variation of color produced by changes in intensity or value.
CN B.BM.AFU.AFU.ARI.BOK.ALO.ALO.ALO.BIQ

tone drawings
VD.138
ALT **tone drawing**
SN Use for drawings in which surfaces and planes are indicated by contrast between different tones or values, rather than by lines.
UF drawings, tone
drawings, value
value drawings
CN V.VD.AFU.AXC.CLM

tone, mass
USE **mass color**

toner, para
USE **para red**

Tonga
FL.580 (L)
UF Batonga
CN F.FL.ALO.AFU.AXC.ARI.BOK.ALO

Tongan
FL.3702 (L)
UF Friendly Island
CN F.FL.ALO.BOK.AXC.CFS

tongs
TB.222 (L)
SN Any of numerous devices used for taking hold of objects, consisting commonly of two metal pieces that are joined at one end or near one end by a pivot or spring, forming the two jaws which are used for gripping.
CN V.TB.AFU.ARI.CFS.BCW

tongs, anvil
USE **pickup tongs**

tongs, bolt
USE **bolt tongs**

tongs, box
USE **box tongs**

tongs, box hammer
USE **box hammer tongs**

tongs, buckle
USE **sliding tongs**

tongs, chain
USE **chain tongs**

tongs, clip
USE **clip tongs**

tongs, crook-bit

USE **crook-bit tongs**

tongs, draw
USE **clip tongs**

tongs, eye
USE **hammer tongs**

tongs, flat
USE **flat tongs**

tongs, hammer
USE **hammer tongs**

tongs, hollow-bit
USE **hollow-bit tongs**

tongs, hoop
USE **hoop tongs**

tongs, nail
USE **nail tongs**

tongs, pickup
USE **pickup tongs**

tongs, pincer
USE **pincer tongs**

tongs, right-angle bit
USE **side tongs**

tongs, round-lip
USE **round-lip tongs**

tongs, shoe
USE **shoe tongs**

tongs, side
USE **side tongs**

tongs, sliding
USE **sliding tongs**

tongs, spring
USE **tweezers**

tongs, straight-lip
USE **flat tongs**

tongs, V-lip
USE **hollow-bit tongs**

tongue-and-groove joints
TF.695
ALT **tongue-and-groove joint**
SN Joints made by fitting a projecting rib on one piece into a groove in another. If the pieces are metal, the joint may also be welded. For plastic or wood pieces, the joint may be glued. (MEANS)
UF joints, T and G
joints, tongue-and-groove
T and G joints
CN V.TF.ALO.ARI.AXC.ARI.CLM

tongue-and-groove planes
TB.930
ALT **tongue-and-groove plane**
SN Planes with two blades which are used to cut a tongue. One of the blades may be covered so that the remaining blade cuts a groove into which the tongue will fit. (BLACKB)
UF matching planes
planes, matching
planes, slit deal
planes, tongue-and-groove
slit deal planes
CN V.TB.AFU.BCW.CFS.ALO.AFU.DUC.ALO.CXA

tongue-and-lip joints
TF.696
ALT **tongue-and-lip joint**
SN Tongue-and-groove joints in which the tongue is wedge-shaped and the groove is tapered to receive it. (MEANS)
UF joints, tongue-and-lip
CN V.TF.ALO.ARI.AXC.ARI.CLM.AFU

tongue planes
TB.929 (N)
ALT **tongue plane**
SN Planes with a notch in the center; used to cut a center ridge, or tongue.
UF planes, tongue
CN V.TB.AFU.BCW.CFS.ALO.AFU.DUC.ALO.CRG

Tongzhi
FL.1917 (L)
UF T'ung-chih
CN F.FL.ALO.ARI.ALO.AFU.AFU.ALO.DOI.BUE

toning
KT.261
ALT **toned**
SN In oil painting, altering the pervading color by an overall glaze or scumble. (MAYER)
CN K.KT.AFU.ALO.DUC.CXA.ALO.BCW.AXC

toning (photography)
KT.420 (L)
ALT **toned (photography)**
SN In photographic processing, converting some or all of the silver in a black-and-white image using inorganic salts or mordant dyes, and usually altering the overall tone of the image.
CN K.KT.AFU.ALO.DUC.DIO.ARI.AXC.DOI

toning, dye
USE **dye toning**

toning, metallic
USE **metallic toning**

Tonkawa
FL.1442 (L)
CN F.FL.ALO.ALO.ARI.AFU.BZY.CXA

Tonkin
FL.2446
CN F.FL.ALO.ARI.BCW.BUE.ALO.AXC

Tonocoté
FL.1626 (L)
CN F.FL.ALO.ALO.ARI.ARI.ALO.ALO.CFS

Too-an-hooch Indians
USE **Twana**

tool rooms
USE **toolsheds**

tooled joints
TF.624
ALT **tooled joint**
SN Masonry joints in which the mortar has been shaped or worked before it sets. (MEANS)
UF joints, tooled
CN V.TF.ALO.ARI.ALO.AFU.ARI.AXC

toolhouses
USE **toolsheds**

tooling
KT.723
ALT **tooled**
CN K.KT.AFU.ALO.GRC.DOI

toolmakers
HG.576
ALT **toolmaker**
CN H.HG.AFU.AXC.BUE.AXC.ELK

tools
TB.5 (L,R)
ALT **tool**
SN Use for objects, especially those hand-held, for performing or facilitating mechanical operations.
UF implements
CN V.TB.AFU.AFU.ALO

tools, caulking
USE **caulking irons**

tools, claw
USE **tooth chisels**

tools, drawing
USE **drawing instruments**

tools, fantail
USE **fishtail tools**

tools, fireplace
USE **firesets**

tools, fishtail
USE **fishtail tools**

tools, hand
USE **hand tools**

tools, machine
USE **machine tools**

tools, parting
USE **parting tools**

tools, pitching
USE **pitching chisels**

tools, pneumatic
USE **pneumatic tools**

tools, power

USE power tools

tools, radius
USE **radius tools**

tools, scratch
USE **scratch tools**

tools, veining
USE **veiners**

tools, woodworking
USE **woodworking tools**

toolsheds
RK.1218 (L)
ALT **toolshed**
UF rooms, tool
tool rooms
toolhouses
CN V.RK.AFU.ALO.ALO.GFO.BIQ.BCW.AFU

toon
MT.1341
UF cedar, Chinese
Cedrela sinensis
Cedrela toona
Chinese cedar
Chinese toon
toon, Chinese
CN M.MT.AFU.AFU.ALO.BIQ.DCU.AFU.AFU.ALO.ALO.BUE

toon, Chinese
USE **toon**

tooth
MT.963 (L)
CN M.MT.AFU.AFU.ALO.AFU.ELK

tooth chisels
TB.582 (N)
ALT **tooth chisel**
SN Chisels especially designed for cutting stone. (PUTNAM)
UF chisels, stonecutter's
chisels, tooth
claw tools
stonecutter's chisels
tools, claw
CN V.TB.AFU.BCW.BCW.ALO.BZY.BIQ

toothbrush holders
TF.147 (N)
ALT **toothbrush holder**
UF holders, toothbrush
CN V.TF.AFU.AFU.AFU.AFU.CRG.AXC

toothing planes
TB.949 (N)
ALT **toothing plane**
SN Planes with a serrated blade mounted nearly vertical; used to roughen a surface prior to application of a veneer. (MEANS)
UF planes, toothing
CN V.TB.AFU.BCW.CFS.ALO.AFU.DUC.ARI.BZY

top
DC.23
CN D.DC.AFU.ALO.ALO.CFS

top coat
USE **supercoat**

top hangers, flush
USE **flush top hangers**

top hung windows
USE **awning windows**

top maul hammers
TB.1083 (N)
ALT **top maul hammer**
SN Round-faced hammers with chamfered necks and a heavy tapering peen; used by shipwrights to drive large nails and spikes. (SALAM)
UF hammers, ship's mauls
hammers, top maul
mauls, pin
pin mauls
ship's maul hammers
CN V.TB.AFU.BCW.CFS.ALO.ARI.AFU.BCW

top plates
USE **roof plates**

top-rails (crest rails)
USE **crest rails**

Topanga
FL.904
CN F.FL.ALO.ALO.ALO.AFU.ALO.ARI.AFU.BCW

topaz
MT.565 (L)
CN M.MT.AFU.AFU.AFU.CFS.AFU.HIK

topaz (color)
USE **dark orange yellow**
light yellowish brown
strong yellowish brown

topes
USE **stupas**

topiary
RM.456 (A,L,R)
SN Use for trees or shrubs pruned and trained into various geometric, zoomorphic, or fantastic shapes.
UF topiary work
CN V.RM.ALO.AFU.CFS.BOK

topiary work
USE **topiary**

topographic maps
VW.162 (L)
ALT **topographic map**
SN Maps that chart the features of a relatively small area, usually portraying its relief features or surface configuration through the use of contour lines.
UF maps, topographic
CN V.VW.AFU.AFU.AFU.FZU.AXC.AFU.ARI.AFU.CXA.AXC

topographic surveys
VW.931 (L)
ALT **topographic survey**
SN Surveys of the surface configuration of an area, including natural and man-made features.
UF maps, survey
plans, survey
plot surveys
site surveys
survey maps
survey plans
surveys, plot
surveys, site
surveys, topographic
CN V.VW.AFU.ARI.AFU.BZY.BCW.AFU

topographical illustrations
USE **topographical views**

topographical surveying
KT.120 (L,B)
SN Recording the configuration of a surface, including its relief and the locations of its natural and man-made features, usually indicated by means of contour lines. (DAC)
UF land surveying
surveying, land
surveying, topographical
CN K.KT.AFU.ALO.CXA.ARI.ARI

topographical views
VB.79 (R)
ALT **topographical view**
SN Use for pictorial or photographic representations that faithfully (though not necessarily with total accuracy) depict actual locations. May be **landscapes** or **city views**, though those terms imply invention whereas **topographical views** implies recording of appearances. For faithful drawings of individual buildings, use **measured drawings**, **record drawings**, or **as-built drawings**.
UF illustrations, topographical
topographical illustrations
views, topographical
CN V.VB.AFU.AXC.BUE

topography
BM.736 (A,L,R)
SN The configuration of a surface indicating its relief and the position of its natural and man-made features. (W)
CN B.BM.CFS.ALO.ARI

toponymy
KD.50 (L,R)
SN Etymological study of the place-names of a region or language. (W)
CN K.KD.AFU.AFU.AXC.ALO.AFU.AFU

Toposa
USE **Topotha**

Topotha
FL.634 (L)

UF Toposa
CN F.FL.ALO.AFU.AXC.AXC.ARI.DZW

topping axes
USE **lopping axes**

topping joints
TF.614
ALT **topping joint**
SN In concrete finishing, a space or break of about 1/8 inch made at regular intervals, particularly over expansion joints, to allow for contraction and expansion in the topping layer of sidewalks, driveways, and similar structures. (PUTNAM)
UF joints, topping
CN V.TF.ALO.ARI.AFU.AXC

toppings out
KM.16 (B)
SN Ceremonies that celebrate the structure of a building under construction reaching its highest point.
CN K.KM.AFU.ARI.ALO.AFU

Toprak-Kala
FL.1807
CN F.FL.ALO.ARI.AFU.AXC.DUC

tops, bonnet
USE **bonnet tops**

tops, closed bonnet
USE **bonnet tops**

tops, dished
USE **china tables**

tops, hooded
USE **bonnet tops**

tops, monitor
USE **monitors (roof appendages)**

Torah shrines
USE **arks**

toranas
RK.506
ALT **torana**
CN V.RK.AFU.ALO.ALO.BUE.BUE

torch brazing
KT.796
SN Brazing in which the flame of a gas torch is used to heat the metals and brazing materials. (HORNB)
UF brazing, torch
CN K.KT.AFU.ALO.HOE.BCW.ALO.AFU.AFU.AFU.BIQ

torchères
TG.654 (N)
ALT **torchère**
SN Use for very tall stands, generally carved and gilt, intended to hold candelabra. (PC)
UF guéridons porte-luminaire
guéridons-torchère
CN V.TG.AFU.AFU.BIQ.BCW.ALO.ELK

torches
TB.103 (L,N)
ALT **torch**
SN Any of various portable devices for emitting an unusually hot flame. (W)
CN V.TB.AFU.ARI.ALO.ARI.BCW

torches, acetylene
USE **acetylene torches**

torches, kerosene
USE **kerosene torches**

torches, oxyacetylene
USE **oxyacetylene torches**

torches, oxyhydrogen
USE **oxyhydrogen torches**

torchis
MT.127
CN M.MT.AFU.AFU.AFU.AXC.ALO.AFU.AXC.AFU.ALO.AFU.ALO

Tori
FL.2104
CN F.FL.ALO.ARI.ALO.ALO.ALO.BCW.BIQ

tori (moldings)
USE **toruses**

torii
RK.507 (A,L)
SN Use for gateways to Shinto shrines, generally composed of two columns and two horizontal spanning members often with slight upward curvature at their ends.
CN V.RK.AFU.ALO.ALO.BUE.BZY

Torii School
FL.2082 (L)
CN F.FL.ALO.ARI.ALO.ALO.ALO.AXC.BOK

tornado cellars
USE **storm cellars**

tornadoes
KM.117 (L,R)
SN Violent, destructive whirling winds, accompanied by funnel-shaped clouds, that progress in a narrow path over the land. (W)
UF twisters (tornadoes)
CN K.KM.AFU.CXA.BIQ.ALO.ALO

Torobo
USE **Dorobo**

torque
BM.900 (L)
CN B.BM.CFS.AXC.BIQ.AFU.AXC.BIQ.AFU

Torres Strait
FL.3658 (L)
CN F.FL.ALO.BOK.ALO.BCW.ALO.BIQ

torsional stress
BM.923
UF stress, torsional
stress, twisting
twisting stress
CN B.BM.CFS.AXC.BIQ.ARI.BCW.BOK

tortillons
TB.283
ALT **tortillon**
SN Small stumps of tightly rolled gray or white paper, usually pointed at one end only; used to blend charcoal and pastel. (MAYER)
CN V.TB.AFU.ARI.CLM.AFU.ALO.ELK.AFU

tortoise shell
MT.966 (L,R)
UF shell, tortoise
CN M.MT.AFU.AFU.ALO.AFU.ERE

toruses
RT.787
ALT **torus**
SN Bold projecting moldings, convex in shape, generally forming the lowest member of a base over the plinth. (DAC)
UF spirae
tori (moldings)
CN V.RT.AFU.ALO.AFU.BOK.AFU.AFU.AXC.BCW.ARI

Tosa School
FL.2071 (L)
CN F.FL.ALO.ARI.ALO.ALO.ALO.ARI.FCS

tot lots
RK.1498
ALT **tot lot**
SN Designates special play areas set aside for children, particularly preschool age children.
UF lots, tot
playlots
CN V.RK.ALO.ALO.BCW.BUE.AXC

totalitarianism
BM.556 (L,R)
CN B.BM.BOK.BZY.ARI.AFU

totemism
BM.711 (L,R)
CN B.BM.BZY.ALO.ARI.DUC

Totonac
FL.1508 (L)
CN F.FL.ALO.ALO.ARI.ALO.ARI.BUE

Touareg
USE **Tuareg**

touch
BM.730 (L,R)
UF feeling
perception, tactile
tactile perception
CN B.BM.CFS.AFU.BCW.BCW

touchstone
MT.557
SN A cherty flint used for testing gold

and silver by the streak left on the stone by the metal.
UF Lydian stone
stone, Lydian
CN M.MT.AFU.AFU.AFU.CFS.AFU.GRC.AFU.AXC.ARI

toupie feet
TG.908
ALT **toupie foot**
SN Furniture feet in the shape of spinning tops. (WATS)
UF feet, toupie
CN V.TG.ALO.DZW.AFU.BIQ.AFU.AFU

tourelles
USE **turrets**

touring chairs
TG.200 (N)
ALT **touring chair**
SN Late 19th- and early 20th-century chairs used on boardwalks for tourists; not to be confused with **invalid's chairs.** (PC)
UF chairs, touring
CN V.TG.AFU.AFU.ALO.AFU.AFU.ALO.FOG

tourism
BM.398 (A,L,B)
SN Use broadly for that industry providing facilities and services to people traveling for recreation. (W)
UF tourist trade
trade, tourist
CN B.BM.ARI.CXA.AFU

tourist cabins
RK.280
ALT **tourist cabin**
SN One of a number of small, individually housed units in a motel. (DAC)
UF cabins, tourist
CN V.RK.AFU.ALO.ALO.AXC.ALO.ALO.ARI.ALO.AFU

tourist courts
USE **motor courts**

tourist information centers
USE **information centers**

tourist maps
VW.168 (L)
ALT **tourist map**
UF maps, tourist
CN V.VW.AFU.AFU.AFU.FZU.AXC.AFU.ARI.ALO.AXC

tourist towns
RD.58 (A,B)
ALT **tourist town**
UF tourist villages
towns, tourist
villages, tourist
CN V.RD.AFU.AXC.BZY

tourist trade
USE **tourism**

tourist villages
USE **tourist towns**

tourmaline
MT.566 (L)
UF turmaline
CN M.MT.AFU.AFU.AFU.CFS.AFU.HOE

Tournai porcelain
FL.3239 (L)
UF porcelain, Tournai
CN F.FL.ALO.BCW.ALO.ARI.BIQ.BIQ.BIQ.ALO.ALO

tournaments
KM.45 (L,R)
CN K.KM.AFU.AXC.AXC

tours
KM.94 (A,B)
CN K.KM.AFU.CLM.ARI

tours, grand
USE **grand tours**

towel bars
TF.148
ALT **towel bar**
SN Bars which are mounted to a wall, counter, or other surface on which towels and washcloths are hung.
UF bars, towel
holders, towel
towel holders
CN V.TF.AFU.AFU.AFU.AFU.CRG.BCW

towel dispensers, hand
USE **hand towel dispensers**

towel holders
USE **towel bars**

towel horses
USE **towel racks**

towel racks
TG.615 (N)
ALT **towel rack**
SN Racks for holding towels with two or more horizontal members, either freestanding or hung on the wall.
UF airers, linen
horses, towel
linen airers
racks, towel
rails, towel
stands, towel
towel horses
towel rails
towel stands
CN V.TG.AFU.AFU.BIQ.AXC.AXC

towel rails
USE **towel racks**

towel stands
USE **towel racks**

tower blocks
USE **skyscrapers**

tower bolts
TF.551
ALT **tower bolt**
SN Modified form of barrel bolts, in which the locking bar is shortened. (STEIN)
UF bolts, tower
CN V.TF.AFU.ALO.AXC.AFU.ALO.AFU

tower buildings
RK.14 (B)
ALT **tower building**
SN Use for modern high-rise buildings whose main mass rises, with the tall slender proportions of a tower, from a larger low base.
UF buildings, tower
CN V.RK.AFU.ALO.AFU.AFU.AFU.ARI.ARI

tower cranes
TB.68 (L)
ALT **tower crane**
SN Type of crane consisting of a fixed vertical mast which is topped by a rotating boom, equipped with a winch for hoisting and lowering loads and placing them at any location within the diameter of the boom. (DAC)
UF cranes, tower
CN V.TB.AFU.ARI.AFU.BCW.AXC.BOK

tower-tombs
RK.495
ALT **tower-tomb**
SN Used to designate ancient Roman funerary structures of several stories usually rising from a stepped square or rectangular base and topped by a pyramidal, domical, or flat roof.
CN V.RK.AFU.ALO.ALO.BOK.BUE.AFU.CFS

towers
RK.31 (A,L,N,B,R)
ALT **tower**
CN V.RK.AFU.ALO.AFU.ALO.DCU

towers (building divisions)
RM.417 (A,L,N,B,R)
ALT **tower (building division)**
SN Use for parts of buildings with walls rising considerably above the rest, usually with vertical proportions, and to some extent architecturally distinct.
CN V.RM.AFU.DZW

towers of silence
RK.467 (L)
ALT **tower of silence**
SN Circular stone platforms on which Parsees of India leave their dead to be devoured by vultures. (RHDEL2)

UF dokhmas
CN V.RK.AFU.ALO.ALO.BOK.ARI.AFU.BCW

towers, bell
USE **bell towers**

towers, central
USE **crossing towers**

towers, church
USE **church towers**

towers, clock
USE **clock towers**

towers, control
USE **control towers**

towers, cooling
USE **cooling towers**

towers, crossing
USE **crossing towers**

towers, fire
USE **fire towers**

towers, fire (building divisions)
USE **fire towers (building divisions)**

towers, gate
USE **gate towers**

towers, lantern
USE **crossing towers**

towers, launch
USE **launch towers**

towers, lookout
USE **watchtowers**

towers, maiden
USE **keeps**

towers, martello
USE **martello towers**

towers, observation
USE **watchtowers**

towers, office
USE **office towers**

towers, peel
USE **bastel houses**

towers, radio
USE **radio towers**

towers, rood
USE **crossing towers**

towers, round
USE **round towers**

towers, shot
USE **shot towers**

towers, signal
USE **signal towers**

towers, smoke
USE **smokestacks**

towers, stair
USE **stair towers**

towers, television
USE **television towers**

towers, temple
USE **ziggurats**

towers, tomb
USE **chullpas**
gumbads

towers, transmission
USE **transmission towers**

towers, transmitter
USE **radio towers**
television towers

towers, wall
USE **wall towers**

towers, water
USE **water towers**

town and country planning
USE **regional planning**

town halls
RK.999 (A,L,N,B,R)
ALT **town hall**
UF halls, town
halls, village
village halls
CN V.RK.AFU.ALO.ALO.ERE.ALO.AFU.BIQ

town houses
RK.301 (A,L,B)
ALT **town house**
SN Use only for individual freestanding urban homes. For attatched urban homes each having its own private entrance, use **row houses.**
UF houses, town
houses, urban
urban houses
CN V.RK.AFU.ALO.ALO.AXC.ALO.AXC.AFU.ARI

Town lattice trusses
RT.372
ALT **Town lattice truss**
SN Lattice trusses usually made of wood, patented by Ithul Town in 1820.
UF lattice trusses
lattice trusses, Town
trusses, lattice
trusses, Town lattice
CN V.RT.AFU.AFU.AFU.BCW.CLM.AFU.AFU.AFU.CLM

town meetings
KM.100 (L)
UF meetings, town
CN K.KM.AFU.CRG.ARI

town planners
USE **city planners**

town planning
USE **city planning**

town plans
USE **city plans**

townhouses (row houses)
USE **row houses**

towns
RD.9 (A,L,B,R)
ALT **town**
SN Distinctions among villages, towns, and cities are relative and vary according to their individual regional contexts. Towns generally are units of compact settlement larger than villages and less important and internally complex than cities in the region.
CN V.RD.AFU.AFU.ALO.ARI

towns, cantonment
USE **cantonments**

towns, cathedral
USE **cathedral cities**

towns, coastal
USE **coastal towns**

towns, college
USE **college towns**

towns, company
USE **company towns**

towns, factory
USE **industrial towns**

towns, fortified
USE **fortified towns**

towns, ghost
USE **ghost towns**

towns, hill
USE **hill towns**

towns, ideal
USE **ideal cities**

towns, industrial
USE **industrial towns**

towns, market
USE **market towns**

towns, military
USE **military towns**

towns, mill
USE **mill towns**

towns, mining
USE **mining towns**

towns, new
USE **new towns**

towns, old
USE **old towns**

towns, pilgrimage
USE **pilgrimage centers**

towns, river
USE **river towns**

towns, ruined
USE **ruined cities**

towns, satellite (new towns)
USE **new towns**

towns, satellite (satellite cities)
USE **satellite cities**

towns, seaside
USE **coastal towns**

towns, tourist
USE **tourist towns**

towns, university
USE **university towns**

townscapes
RD.294 (A,B)
ALT **townscape**
SN Use to designate the built forms of towns, cities, or other built-up areas, in combination, as perceived visually and aesthetically. For representations of towns or cities, as in drawings or photographs, use **city views.**
UF cityscapes
CN V.RD.ARI.ALO.ALO.AXC

townscapes (views)
USE **city views**

township maps
VW.225
ALT **township map**
UF maps, township
CN V.VW.AFU.AFU.AFU.FZU.AXC.AFU.ARI.AXC.DUC.ALO

townships
RG.247 (L,B)
ALT **township**
CN V.RG.ALO.AFU.AFU.ALO.AXC

toxic substances
USE **hazardous substances**

toy making
KT.572 (L)
CN K.KT.AFU.ALO.ELK.DZW

toy stores
RK.167 (A,B)
ALT **toy store**
UF stores, toy
toyshops
CN V.RK.AFU.ALO.ALO.ALO.ARI.BIQ.AFU.DUC

Toyok
FL.1826
CN F.FL.ALO.ARI.AFU.AXC.ELK.CRG

toyshops
USE **toy stores**

Tra-kieu
FL.2442
CN F.FL.ALO.ARI.BCW.BUE.ALO.ALO.AFU.ARI

trabeated structures
USE **post-and-beam structures**

trace element analysis
KT.12
SN Analyzing an artifact to find out what trace elements are present, and in what proportion, especially to determine the source of the raw materials from which the artifact was made.
UF analysis, trace element
CN K.KT.AFU.ALO.AXC.AFU.AFU

tracers, curve
USE **flexible curves**

tracery
RT.1016 (L,B,R)
SN Ornamental openwork of masonry, originally found in the upper parts of Gothic windows; also, similar motifs and forms in various materials applied decoratively, as on walls, furniture, and other objects.
CN V.RT.AFU.ARI.ALO.BZY.AFU

tracery, bar
USE **bar tracery**

tracery, blank
USE **blind tracery**

tracery, blind
USE **blind tracery**

tracery, curvilinear
USE **flowing tracery**

tracery, drop
USE **drop tracery**

tracery, flowing
USE **flowing tracery**

tracery, net
USE **reticulated tracery**

tracery, panel
USE **perpendicular tracery**

tracery, perpendicular
USE **perpendicular tracery**

tracery, plate
USE **plate tracery**

tracery, rectilinear
USE **perpendicular tracery**

tracery, reticulated
USE **reticulated tracery**

tracery, undulating
USE **flowing tracery**

tracery, wheel
USE **wheel tracery**

tracery, wye
USE **Y-tracery**

traces (area plans)
VD.44
ALT **trace (area plan)**
CN V.VD.AFU.AFU.BIQ.ALO.AXC.AFU.ARI

trachelia
USE **necking**

tracing
KT.755
ALT **traced**
SN Copying from an original by drawing over it onto a thin piece of paper. (MAYER)
CN K.KT.AFU.ALO.HCQ.ALO.BZY

tracing cloth
MT.1877 (L)
SN Made from thin, fine cotton or linen cloth, glazed on one or both sides; used for making tracings in ink. (MH)
UF cloth, tracing
CN M.MT.AFU.AFU.ARI.ALO.ALO.ALO.ALO.DUC

tracing paper
MT.1937
SN Any translucent paper which, when laid over an existing image, permits the image to be seen and traced.
UF paper, tracing
CN M.MT.AFU.AFU.ARI.ALO.ALO.AXC.ARI.AXC.AXC

tracing paper, albanene
USE **tracing vellum**

tracing vellum
MT.1938
UF albanene tracing paper
paper, albanene tracing
tracing paper, albanene
vellum, tracing
CN M.MT.AFU.AFU.ARI.ALO.ALO.AXC.ARI.AXC.AXC.AFU

tracing wheels (pouncing)
USE **perforating wheels**

tracings
VD.139
ALT **tracing**
CN V.VD.AFU.AXC.CRG

track-type tractors
USE **crawler tractors**

tracking stations, satellite
USE **satellite tracking stations**

tracklaying tractors
USE **crawler tractors**

tracks (racetracks)
USE **racetracks**

tracks, bicycle
USE **cycling paths**
velodromes

tracks, cycling
USE **cycling paths**

tracks, dog
USE **dog tracks**

tracks, indoor
USE **indoor tracks**

tracks, running
USE **running tracks**

tracks, siding
USE **sidings**

tracks, taxi
USE **taxiways**

tract houses
RK.322 (A,B,R)
ALT **tract house**
SN Use for groups of similarly designed houses located in subdivisions; used to distinguish from those houses that are custom designed and built.
UF houses, tract
CN V.RK.AFU.ALO.ALO.AXC.ALO.BIQ.ALO

traction elevators
RT.1321
ALT **traction elevator**
SN Use for elevators in which the motion of the car is obtained by means of friction between the traction sheave and the hoisting cable, as is usually the case in 20th-century installations.
UF elevators, traction
CN V.RT.ALO.ALO.AFU.ARI.ALO.ARI.AXC

tractors, crawler
USE **crawler tractors**

tractors, track-type
USE **crawler tractors**

tractors, tracklaying
USE **crawler tractors**

tracts (land areas)
RD.306
ALT **tract (land area)**
CN V.RD.ARI.ALO.ARI.AXC

tracts (pamphlets)
VW.607 (L)
ALT **tract (pamphlet)**
SN Pamphlets containing short propagandist discourses, especially on religious, political, or social subjects. (LG)
CN V.VW.AFU.ALO.AFU.CFS.AFU

tracts, census
USE **census tracts**

trade
BM.412 (L,R)
SN Use for the activity of buying, selling, or bartering commodities.(W) For the broad field of commercial or mercantile activity involving the exchange of commodities, services, or financial resources, use **business.**
CN B.BM.ARI.FIM

trade associations
HG.828
ALT **trade association**
UF associations, trade
CN H.HG.ALO.BCW.BZY

trade bibliographies
VW.262
ALT **trade bibliography**
SN Bibliographies issued for, and usually by, booksellers and publishers to facilitate the sale of books.
UF bibliographies, trade
CN V.VW.AFU.AFU.AFU.FZU.BCW.AFU.ALO.BIQ

trade cards
USE **business cards**

trade catalogs
USE **commercial catalogs**

trade directories
USE **commercial directories**

trade fairs
USE **trade shows**

trade-in housing
RG.80 (L)
UF housing, trade-in
CN V.RG.AFU.AFU.BOK.AXC.BCW

trade marts
RK.187 (A)
ALT **trade mart**
SN Designates buildings or building complexes providing wholesalers with a single location having display spaces for product vendors of various trades, such as apparel, furnishings, or business equipment.
UF marts, merchandise
marts, trade
merchandise marts
CN V.RK.AFU.ALO.ALO.ALO.ARI.BOK

trade porcelain, China
USE **Chinese export porcelain**

trade schools
USE **vocational schools**

trade shows
KM.156 (L,B)
UF fairs, trade
shows, trade
trade fairs
CN K.KM.AFU.ELK.BIQ

trade unions
HG.829 (A,L,B,R)
ALT **trade union**
UF industrial unions
labor unions
unions
unions, industrial
unions, labor
unions, trade
CN H.HG.ALO.BCW.CFS

trade, art
USE **art trade**

trade, boards of
USE **boards of trade**

trade, tourist
USE **tourism**

trademarks
VW.725 (L,R)
ALT **trademark**
SN The names, symbols, figures, letters, words, or other marks adopted and used by a manufacturer or merchant in order to designate his goods and to distinguish them from any others; usually registered with a governmental agency to assure its use exclusively by the owner of the mark. (RHDEL2)
UF marks, merchant
merchant marks
CN V.VW.AFU.ALO.ALO.AFU.AXC.ALO.CRG

traders
USE **merchants**

trades
USE **industries**

tradesmen's cards
USE **business cards**

trading posts
RK.185 (L)
ALT **trading post**
UF posts, trading
CN V.RK.AFU.ALO.ALO.ALO.ARI.BIQ.ALO.DCU

traditionalism
BM.367 (L)
CN B.BM.ALO.ALO.CLM.FOG

Trafalgar chairs
TG.92
ALT **Trafalgar chair**
SN Use for various types of 19th-century chairs with nautical motifs and often a tablet top and a backrail incorporating cable molding. Made after the Battle of Trafalgar in 1805.
UF Bouneparte chairs
chairs, Bouneparte
chairs, Nelson's
chairs, swept-leg
chairs, tablet top
chairs, Trafalgar
chairs, Waterloo
chairs, Wellington
Nelson's chairs
swept-leg chairs
tablet top chairs
Waterloo chairs

Wellington chairs
CN V.TG.AFU.AFU.ALO.AFU.AFU.AFU.LOA

traffic
BM.1152 (A,L,B,R)
CN B.BM.DCU.ALO.ALO

traffic circles
RM.481 (A)
ALT **traffic circle**
SN Circular arrangements constructed at the intersection of two or more roads in order to facilitate the passage from one road to another. (RHDEL2)
UF circles (road junctions)
circles, traffic
circles, turning
rotaries
roundabouts (traffic circles)
turning circles
CN V.RM.ALO.ALO.ALO.ALO.BOK.ALO

traffic control towers (airports)
USE **control towers**

traffic engineering
KD.223 (L)
SN Branch of civil engineering concerned with the design and construction of streets and roads that will best facilitate traffic movement. (RHDEL2)
UF engineering, traffic
CN K.KD.AFU.ARI.BIQ.AXC.BCW

traffic engineers
HG.635 (L)
ALT **traffic engineer**
UF engineers, traffic
CN H.HG.AFU.AXC.BZY.BCW.BCW.AXC

traffic islands
RM.503 (A)
ALT **traffic island**
SN Paved or planted islands in roadways designed to guide the flow of traffic. (W)
UF islands, traffic
CN V.RM.ALO.ALO.ALO.ALO.EFQ

traffic lights
USE **traffic signals**

traffic loads
BM.1019
UF loads, traffic
CN B.BM.CFS.AXC.CLM.ALO.ARI.CXA

traffic noise
BM.424 (L,B)
UF noise, traffic
CN B.BM.AXC.ALO.AFU.ALO

traffic signals
RM.501 (L,N)
ALT **traffic signal**
SN Usually electrically operated signals (as a system of colored lights) for warning and controlling traffic. (W)
UF lights, stop
lights, traffic
signals, traffic
stop lights
traffic lights
CN V.RM.ALO.ALO.ALO.ALO.DUC.BCW

traffic tickets
VW.920
ALT **traffic ticket**
UF tickets, traffic
CN V.VW.AFU.ARI.AFU.BOK.BOK.CXA

tragacanth, gum
USE **gum tragacanth**

tragedy
BM.284 (L,R)
CN B.BM.AFU.ARI.BIQ.CFS

trailer camps
RG.163 (A,L)
ALT **trailer camp**
SN Distinguished from **mobile home parks** by being only for the temporary parking of travel trailers, camping trailers, motorized homes, or the like for recreational purposes.
UF camps, trailer
caravan sites
courts, trailer
parks, trailer
sites, caravan
trailer courts
trailer parks
trailer parks, travel
travel trailer parks
CN V.RG.AFU.AFU.DOI.AXC.BIQ

trailer courts
USE **trailer camps**

trailer parks
USE **trailer camps**

trailer parks, travel
USE **trailer camps**

trailers, camper
USE **travel trailers**

trailers, camping
USE **camping trailers**

trailers, tent
USE **camping trailers**

trailers, travel
USE **travel trailers**

trailing
USE **slip trailing**

trailing, slip
USE **slip trailing**

trails
RG.183 (A,L,B)
ALT **trail**
CN V.RG.AFU.AFU.DOI.CLM

trails, archaeological
USE **heritage trails**

trails, bridle
USE **bridle paths**

trails, heritage
USE **heritage trails**

trails, nature
USE **nature trails**

trails, riding
USE **bridle paths**

trails, ski
USE **ski trails**

train sheds
RM.146 (B)
ALT **train shed**
SN The parts of railroad stations that cover the tracks. (W)
UF locomotive sheds
sheds, locomotive
sheds, train
CN V.RM.AFU.DIO.ALO.BZY.ARI

trainees
HG.773
ALT **trainee**
CN H.HG.AFU.BIQ.CLM

training
USE **teaching**

training camps, military
USE **military training camps**

training centers, martial arts
USE **martial arts training centers**

training manuals
VW.356 (L)
ALT **training manual**
UF manuals, training
CN V.VW.AFU.AFU.ALO.CXA.BIQ.BIQ

training, architectural
USE **architectural education**

Trajanic
FL.2721 (R)
CN F.FL.ALO.AXC.ALO.ALO.AFU.AXC.ALO.BCW

tram depots
RK.1245 (A,B)
ALT **tram depot**
UF depots, tram
CN V.RK.AFU.ALO.ALO.GLI.AFU.ALO.AFU.AXC

tramlines
USE **streetcar systems**

tramways
USE **streetcar systems**

Trân
FL.2431
CN F.FL.ALO.ARI.BCW.BUE.AFU.AXC

Trans-avantgarde
FL.3755 (R)
UF Transavanguardia
CN F.FL.ALO.BUE.ARI.IRA

transactions
USE **proceedings**

Transavanguardia
USE **Trans-avantgarde**

transcendentalism
BM.527 (L,R)
CN B.BM.BIQ.AXC.FCS

transcripts
VW.83 (N)
ALT **transcript**
SN Use both for copies transcribed from an original text or document and also for written records of words originally spoken, such as of court proceedings, broadcasts, or oral histories.
CN V.VW.AFU.AFU.AFU.FIM

transepts
RM.331 (A,B,R)
ALT **transept**
SN Transverse parts of cruciform churches. (W)
CN V.RM.AFU.DIO.AXC.ALO.AFU.EFQ

transfer lithography
KT.464
SN Lithography in which the drawing is made on paper and then transferred to the stone for printing. (MAYER)
UF lithography, transfer
CN K.KT.AFU.ALO.DUC.DUC.ALO.BCW.ALO.AFU.ALO

transfer molding
KT.151
SN Plastics molding technique in which a measured charge of thermosetting molding powder is preheated in a pot and forced by a plunger through a short channel or runners into a heated cavity or cavities where it hardens. (DIETZ)
UF molding, transfer
CN K.KT.AFU.ALO.DOI.CRG.BCW

transfer of development rights
USE **development rights transfer**

transfer paper
MT.1956
UF paper, transfer
CN M.MT.AFU.AFU.ARI.ALO.ALO.AXC.ARI.BZY

transfer printing
KT.750 (L,R)
ALT **transfer printed**
SN Process of decorating enamel, ceramics, and glass by printing a design from an engraved plate onto paper, then, while the ink is still wet, pressing the design onto the surface to be decorated.
UF printing, transfer
CN K.KT.AFU.ALO.HCQ.ALO.BIQ.AXC

transfer prints, dye
USE **dye transfer prints**

transfer prints, dye diffusion
USE **dye diffusion transfer prints**

transfer process, dye
USE **dye transfer process**

transfer schedules
USE **records schedules**

transferring
KT.736
ALT **transferred**
SN Use for the transporting of images from one surface to another, such as the separating of a paint film from its mount and moving it to a new support, and for processes of precisely copying or reforming an image on another surface, as in pouncing.
CN K.KT.AFU.ALO.HCQ.AFU

transfers, collodion
USE **collodion transfers**

transformer stations
USE **electric substations**

transformers
RT.1351 (L,N)
ALT **transformer**
UF electric transformers
transformers, electric
CN V.RT.ALO.ARI.ALO.DIO

transformers, electric
USE **transformers**

transit systems
RD.91 (A,L)
ALT **transit system**
UF systems, transit
systems, transportation
transportation systems
CN V.RD.ALO.ARI

transit systems, bus
USE **bus transit systems**

transit systems, rail
USE **rail transit systems**

transit systems, rapid rail
USE **rapid rail transit systems**

transit systems, urban
USE **urban transit systems**

transit systems, urban rail
USE **urban rail systems**

transit, automated guideway
USE **people-movers**
personal rapid transit

transit, bus
USE **bus transit systems**

transit, city
USE **local transit**

transit, community
USE **local transit**

transit, fixed-guideway
USE **rail transit systems**

transit, light guideway
USE **personal rapid transit**

transit, light rail
USE **light rail transit**

transit, local
USE **local transit**

transit, mass
USE **public transit**

transit, municipal
USE **local transit**

transit, personal rail
USE **personal rapid transit**

transit, personal rapid
USE **personal rapid transit**

transit, public
USE **public transit**

transit, rail
USE **rail transit systems**

transit, rapid
USE **rapid rail transit systems**

transit, urban
USE **urban transit systems**

transition zones
RG.288
ALT **transition zone**
SN Designates areas undergoing an orderly conversion from one predominant use to another, as from residential to higher density residential plus commercial. (LOC)
UF zones, transition
CN V.RG.ALO.AFU.ALO.BIQ.ARI

Transitional
FL.2328
UF Formative Angkor
CN F.FL.ALO.ARI.BCW.ALO.ALO

Transitional blue-and-white ware
USE **Kraak porcelain**

Transitional period Plateau
FL.778
UF Plateau, Transitional period
CN F.FL.ALO.ALO.ALO.AFU.AFU.BCW.ARI.ALO

Transitional Style
USE **Early Gothic**

Transitional ware
USE **Kraak porcelain**

Transitional, Choga Mami
USE **Choga Mami Transitional**

translating
KG.109 (L)
SN The activity of comprehending, analyzing, and expressing written or spoken material in a different language from the original. (PG)
CN K.KG.AFU.AFU.AXC.EFQ

translations
VW.84 (L)
ALT **translation**
SN Translated versions of a text. (AHD)
CN V.VW.AFU.AFU.AFU.FOG

translators
HG.293 (L)
ALT **translator**
CN H.HG.AFU.AXC.BCW.ALO.AFU.BCW

transliterations
VW.478 (L)
ALT **transliteration**
CN V.VW.AFU.AFU.ALO.GFO

translucency
BM.974 (B)
ALT **translucent**
SN The ability of a substance to transmit light without allowing clear visibility. (MAYER)
CN B.BM.CFS.AXC.BZY.BUE.BCW

transmission holograms
VJ.37
ALT **transmission hologram**
UF holograms, transmission
CN V.VJ.AFU.AFU.ARI.ALO.ALO

transmission lines
USE **power lines**

transmission towers
RK.214
ALT **transmission tower**
SN Use only for tall concrete, metal, or timber structures of various plans designed to carry power lines; for tall metal structures used to hold radio or television antennas, use **radio towers** or **television towers.**
UF towers, transmission
CN V.RK.AFU.ALO.ALO.ARI.ALO.ARI

transmission, heat
USE **heat transmission**

transmission, sound
USE **sound transmission**

transmitted light
BM.851
UF light, transmitted
CN B.BM.CFS.AXC.ALO.AFU.ALO.AFU.AXC

transmitter towers
USE **radio towers**
television towers

transmitters, relay
USE **relay stations**

transom bars
USE **transoms**

transom catches
TF.50
ALT **transom catch**
SN Locks used on transoms, having the latch bolt operated by a ring-shaped part that is moved by using a pole with a hook on its end. (MEANS)
UF catches, transom
CN V.TF.AFU.AFU.AFU.AFU.BCW.BZY

transom lights
USE **transom windows**

transom windows
RT.965
ALT **transom window**
SN The openings above transoms when fitted as windows. (RS)
UF lights, transom
transom lights
windows, transom
CN V.RT.AFU.ARI.AFU.AFU.BOK.AFU.ARI.BUE

transoms
RT.1030
ALT **transom**
SN Horizontal members across a window or door opening near the top.
UF bars, transom
transom bars
CN V.RT.AFU.ARI.ALO.CFS

Transoxiana
USE **Central Asian**

transparencies
VJ.59 (L,N,R)
ALT **transparency**
SN Use for positive photographs (i.e, reproducing appearances without tonal reversal), designed for viewing by transmitted light. Can also refer to transparent nonphotographic images that are designed for projection viewing or as intermediates for reproduction.
UF diapositives
phototransparencies
positive transparencies
transparencies, positive
CN V.VJ.AFU.AFU.ARI.AXC

transparencies, black-and-white
USE **black-and-white transparencies**

transparencies, color
USE **color transparencies**

transparencies, color separation
USE **color separation positives**

transparencies, gelatin silver
USE **gelatin silver transparencies**

transparencies, lantern slide
USE **lantern slides**

transparencies, positive
USE **transparencies**

transparencies, positive color
USE **color transparencies**

transparency
BM.975
ALT **transparent**
SN Quality or state of transmitting light without appreciable scattering so that bodies lying beyond are entirely visible. (OCA)
CN B.BM.CFS.AXC.BZY.BUE.BIQ

transparent brown
MT.1613
UF brown, transparent
brown, Verona
brown, Veronese
burnt green earth
burnt terre verte
gebrannte grüne Erde
green earth, burnt
terre verte brûlée
Verona brown
Veronese brown
CN M.MT.AFU.AFU.ARI.AFU.AFU.ALO.ALO.ARI.AFU.AFU

transparent chromium oxide
USE **moderate green**
strong green

transparent chromium oxide green
USE **viridian**

transparent gold ocher
MT.1788
UF gold ocher, transparent
ocher, transparent gold
CN M.MT.AFU.AFU.ARI.AFU.AFU.ALO.ALO.BUE.ARI.CFS.AFU.AFU

transparent gold ocher (color)
USE **brownish orange**
strong yellowish brown

transparent white pigment
MT.1742
UF extender white pigment
inert white pigment
pigment, extender white
pigment, inert white
pigment, transparent white
white pigment, extender
white pigment, inert
white pigment, transparent
CN M.MT.AFU.AFU.ARI.AFU.AFU.ALO.ALO.BOK.ALO

transparent yellow
USE **pale yellow**

transport centers
USE **terminals**

transport, air
USE **air transport**

transport, water
USE **water transport**

transportable buildings
USE **portable buildings**

transportation
BM.1146 (L,B,R)
CN B.BM.DCU.AFU

transportation buildings
RK.1232 (A,L,N)
ALT **transportation building**
UF buildings, transportation
facilities, transportation
transportation facilities
CN V.RK.AFU.ALO.ALO.GLI.AFU

transportation engineering
KD.224 (L)
UF engineering, transportation
CN K.KD.AFU.ARI.BIQ.AXC.BIQ

transportation engineers
HG.636
ALT **transportation engineer**
UF engineers, road
engineers, transportation
road engineers
CN H.HG.AFU.AXC.BZY.BCW.BCW.BCW

transportation facilities
USE **transportation buildings**

transportation maps
VW.208
ALT **transportation map**
UF maps, transportation
CN V.VW.AFU.AFU.AFU.FZU.AXC.AFU.ARI.AXC.DIO

transportation museums
RK.402 (A,L,B)
ALT **transportation museum**
UF museums, transportation
CN V.RK.AFU.ALO.ALO.BCW.AXC.ARI.AXC.BZY

transportation noise
BM.425 (L)
UF noise, transportation
CN B.BM.AXC.ALO.AFU.ARI

transportation planning
KD.173 (A,L,B)
UF planning, transportation
CN K.KD.AFU.ALO.DUC.BCW

transportation systems
USE **transit systems**

transportation systems, urban
USE **urban transit systems**

transportation terminals
USE **terminals**

transportation, cable
USE **cable railroads**

transportation, city
USE **urban transportation**

transportation, demand responsive
USE **paratransit**

transportation, metropolitan
USE **urban transportation**

transportation, municipal
USE **urban transportation**

transportation, urban
USE **urban transportation**

transporting
KT.756 (L)
ALT **transported**
UF moving
CN K.KT.AFU.ALO.HIK

transubstantiation
BM.691 (L,R)
SN Miraculous change by which according to Roman Catholic and Orthodox Eastern dogma the eucharistic elements at their consecration become the body and blood of Christ while keeping only the appearances of bread and wine. (W)
UF presence, real
real presence
CN B.BM.BZY.ALO.AFU.CLM

transverse
DC.12
SN Lying, situated, or placed across; crossing from side to side. (W)
UF crossing
crosswise
CN D.DC.AFU.ALO.AFU.BIQ

transverse arches
RT.284
ALT **transverse arch**
SN Use for arches which separate the bays of vaults; for arches across a nave or hall that support walls rather than vaults, use **diaphragm arches.**
UF arches, transverse
CN V.RT.AFU.AFU.AFU.BCW.AFU.AFU.ARI.BOK

transverse barrel vaults
USE **barrel vaults**

transverse ribs
RT.692
ALT **transverse rib**
SN Ribs which span at right angles to the longitudinal axis of the space being spanned, dividing it into bays or compartments. (DAC)
UF arch ribs
arcs doubleaux
cross ribs
ribs, arch
ribs, cross
ribs, transverse
CN V.RT.AFU.AFU.ALO.AFU.ARI.BIQ

transverse ridge ribs
RT.690
ALT **transverse ridge rib**
SN Ridge ribs running at right angles to the longitudinal axis of the space spanned by the vault.
UF ribs, transverse ridge
ridge ribs, transverse
CN V.RT.AFU.AFU.ALO.AFU.ARI.AXC.ALO

transverse sections
USE **cross sections**

trap doors
RT.851
ALT **trap door**
SN Doors fitted to an opening in a horizontal or nearly horizontal surface, as a floor or roof, through which a person ascends head first and descends feet first. (RS)
UF doors, trap
CN V.RT.AFU.ARI.AFU.AFU.AFU.ALO.ARI.AFU.AFU.BIQ

trapeza
USE **tables**

trapeziums
BM.786
ALT **trapezial**
CN B.BM.CFS.ARI.AXC.BCW.AFU.BIQ.BUE

trapezoids
BM.780 (L)
ALT **trapezoidal**
SN Quadrilateral figures having one pair of parallel and one pair of nonparallel sides. (RHDEL2)
CN B.BM.CFS.ARI.AXC.BCW.AFU.BIQ.ALO.ALO

trappers
HG.379 (L)
ALT **trapper**
CN H.HG.AFU.AXC.BIQ.ALO.AXC.BZY

traprock
USE **diabase**

traps (plumbing systems)
RT.1496 (L)
ALT **trap (plumbing system)**
SN Fittings or devices so designed and constructed as to provide, when properly vented, a liquid seal that will prevent the back passage of air without materially affecting the flow of sewage or waste water. (STEIN)
CN V.RT.ALO.BCW.ALO.ARI.DCU

traps (theater elements)
RT.1280
ALT **trap (theater element)**
SN Openings for the passage of actors or objects, commonly in the stage floor. (TL)
CN V.RT.AFU.BUE.ARI.BZY

traps, fixture
USE **fixture traps**

traps, house
USE **house traps**

trash chutes
USE **refuse chutes**

trass
MT.632
SN Volcanic material found in the Rhine district of Germany that is similar to pozzolan cement. (MH)
UF tarras
CN M.MT.AFU.AFU.AFU.DCU.AFU.AFU.ALO.ALO.ALO.ALO

travailleuses
USE **work tables**

travel
BM.336 (L)
CN B.BM.ALO.ALO.BUE

travel agencies
RK.196 (A,L,B)
ALT **travel agency**
UF agencies, travel
travel bureaus
CN V.RK.AFU.ALO.ALO.ALO.AXC.BUE

travel agents
HG.411 (A,L)
ALT **travel agent**
UF agents, travel
CN H.HG.AFU.AXC.BOK.BZY.AXC

travel bureaus
USE **travel agencies**

travel guidebooks
VW.504 (L)
ALT **travel guidebook**
UF guidebooks, travel
guides, holiday
holiday guides
CN V.VW.AFU.ALO.AFU.AFU.AFU.BZY.AFU.ARI

travel photography
KT.308 (L)
UF photography, travel
CN K.KT.AFU.ALO.DUC.DIO.AFU.DUC

travel sketches
VB.13
ALT **travel sketch**
UF sketches, travel
CN V.VB.AFU.AFU.BCW.BCW

travel trailer parks
USE **trailer camps**

travel trailers
RK.359 (L,N)
ALT **travel trailer**
SN Designates portable vehicles, not exceeding 8 feet wide and 32 feet long, designed as temporary dwellings for travel or recreational purposes.
UF camper trailers
campers
trailers, camper
trailers, travel
CN V.RK.AFU.ALO.ALO.AXC.ARI.BOK

traveler's letters of credit
USE **letters of credit**

travelers
HG.741 (L,R)
ALT **traveler**
UF voyagers
CN H.HG.AFU.BCW.GWW

travelers' checks
VW.831 (L)
ALT **traveler's check**
SN Internationally redeemable drafts purchasable from a bank, express company, or travel agency, in various denominations, valid only with the holder's own endorsement against his/her original signature. (AHD)
UF checks, travelers'
CN V.VW.AFU.ARI.AFU.BIQ.CFS.ARI.ALO

traveling bidets
TG.237
ALT **traveling bidet**
SN Bidets made to rise out a chest.(FHSJ) Use **portable bidets** for those with legs made to screw off and tops made to lock.
UF bidets, traveling
CN V.TG.AFU.AFU.ALO.AFU.ALO.AFU.AFU.AFU.ALO

traveling chests
USE **trussing coffers**

traveling coffers
USE **trussing coffers**

traveling cranes
TB.69 (L)
ALT **traveling crane**
SN Tower cranes which are mounted on crawlers, rubber tires, or rails. (DAC)
UF cranes, traveling
CN V.TB.AFU.ARI.AFU.BCW.AXC.BOK.AFU

traveling desks
TG.559
ALT **traveling desk**
UF desks, traveling
CN V.TG.AFU.AFU.AXC.ALO.BZY.EWY

traveling exhibitions
KM.69 (L,B)
UF exhibitions, traveling
CN K.KM.AFU.BUE.AXC

travelogs
VW.479
ALT **travelogs**
CN V.VW.AFU.AFU.ALO.GLI

travertine
MT.675 (L)
UF calc sinter
calcareous tufa
lapis tiburtinus
limestone, tufaceous
roachstone
tufa, calcareous
tufaceous limestone
CN M.MT.AFU.AFU.AFU.DCU.AFU.ALO.AFU.ALO.ALO.AFU.AFU.BCW

tray ceilings
USE **camp ceilings**

tray stands
TG.655
ALT **tray stand**
UF stands, tray
CN V.TG.AFU.AFU.BIQ.BCW.ALO.ERE

trays, laundry
USE **laundry trays**

trays, supper (canterburies)
USE **canterburies (stands)**

TRB
USE **Funnel Beaker**

TRBK
USE **Funnel Beaker**

treadmills
TB.395 (L,N)
ALT **treadmill**
SN Apparatus for producing rotary motion by the weight of men or animals treading on a succession of moving steps or a belt that forms a kind of continuous path, as around the periphery of a pair of horizontal cylinders. (RHDEL2)
CN V.TB.AFU.ARI.DOI.BOK

treads
RT.1123 (N,B)
ALT **tread**
SN The horizontal parts of steps. (DAC)
UF stair treads
treads, stair
CN V.RT.AFU.BIQ.AXC.ALO.BIQ.ALO.ARI

treads, stair
USE **treads**

treasure, national
USE **cultural property**

treasuries
RM.205 (A)
ALT **treasury**
SN Includes both freestanding buildings and rooms or spaces that serve as storage places for valuable objects.
CN V.RM.AFU.DIO.ALO.DCU.DCU

treaties
VW.900 (L)
ALT **treaty**
SN Agreements or contracts made between two or more states, formally signed by duly authorized representatives, and usually ratified by the

lawmaking authority of the states, as treaties of peace or alliance, or commercial treaties. (GAHLM)
CN V.VW.AFU.ARI.AFU.BOK.BOK.ALO.AXC.AFU

treating
KG.190 (L)
SN Providing patients with medical care.
CN K.KG.AFU.ALO.AXC.ALO

treatises
VW.85 (A,R)
ALT **treatise**
SN Formal and systematic written expositions of the principles of a subject, generally longer and more detailed than essays.
CN V.VW.AFU.AFU.AFU.FUA

treatment plants, sewage
USE **sewage treatment plants**

treatment plants, water
USE **water treatment plants**

tree dwellings
USE **tree houses**

tree farms
RG.13 (L)
ALT **tree farm**
UF farms, tree
CN V.RG.AFU.AFU.AFU.AFU.ARI.BIQ

tree houses
RK.311 (A,L,B,R)
ALT **tree house**
UF houses, tree
tree dwellings
tree-top houses
CN V.RK.AFU.ALO.ALO.AXC.ALO.AXC.ALO.BIQ

tree ring dating
USE **dendrochronology**

tree-top houses
USE **tree houses**

tree, bean
USE **catalpa**

tree, camphor
USE **camphorwood**

tree, gum arabic
USE **Acacia**

tree, Indian bean
USE **catalpa**

treenails
TF.500 (N)
ALT **treenail**
SN Long pins of hardwood used for fastening planks or timbers in some post-and-beam construction. (DAC)
UF trenails
trunnels
CN V.TF.AFU.AFU.AFU.ALO.AFU.FCS

treenware
MT.1456 (L,R)
UF woodenware
CN M.MT.AFU.AFU.ALO.BIQ.DCU.ALO.DIO

trees
RD.273 (L,B,R)
ALT **tree**
CN V.RD.ARI.AFU.BCW.ALO.ALO.ALO.ARI

trees, canopy
USE **canopy trees**

trees, deciduous
USE **deciduous trees**

trees, door
USE **door jambs**

trees, family
USE **genealogical tables**

trees, hall
USE **hall stands**

trees, roof
USE **ridgeboards**

trees, understory
USE **understory trees**

trefoils
DG.31
ALT **trefoil**
SN Figures of three equal arcs or lobes, separated by cusps.
CN D.DG.AFU.AFU.BIQ.BUE

trellis-back chairs
USE **lattice-back chairs**

trellis windows
USE **lattice windows**

trellis-work
USE **trellises**

trellises
RK.1331 (A,L,N,B)
ALT **trellis**
SN Arbors or frameworks for the support of vines. (HAS)
UF garden lattices
lattices, garden
trellis-work
CN V.RK.AFU.ALO.ARI.AFU.AFU.ALO

Trempealeau
FL.824
UF Hopewell, Trempealeau
Trempealeau Hopewell
CN F.FL.ALO.ALO.ALO.AFU.ALO.ALO.AFU.CLM

Trempealeau Hopewell
USE **Trempealeau**

trenails
USE **treenails**

trench excavators
USE **trenching machines**

trench jacks
TB.374
ALT **trench jack**
SN Screw or hydraulic-type jacks used as a cross bracing in a trench shoring system. (STEIN)
UF jacks, trench
CN V.TB.AFU.ARI.DCU.AFU.ALO.ARI

trenchers (machines)
USE **trenching machines**

trenches
RK.1354 (B)
ALT **trench**
CN V.RK.AFU.ALO.ARI.AXC.ARI.AFU.ARI

trenches, leaching
USE **leaching fields**

trenching machines
TB.42 (L,N)
ALT **trenching machine**
SN Self-propelled machines with a side-mounted shovel or chain of buckets; used to excavate trenches. (MEANS)
UF ditchers
ditching machines
excavators, trench
machines, ditching
machines, trenching
trench excavators
trenchers (machines)
CN V.TB.AFU.ARI.AFU.ARI.ARI.AXC

trenching planes
USE **dado planes**

trenching saws
USE **stairbuilder's saws**

trepan saws
USE **crown saws**

trespoli
TG.765
ALT **trespolos**
SN Italian type of small, spindly three-legged tables, especially popular in 18th-century Venice. (DDA)
CN V.TG.AFU.AFU.BIQ.BOK.ALO.GLI

tressels
USE **trestle scaffolds**

trestle ladders
TB.487
ALT **trestle ladder**
SN Self-supporting portable ladders, nonadjustable in length, consisting of two sections hinged at the top to form equal angles with the base. (STEIN)
UF ladders, trestle
CN V.TB.AFU.ARI.ERE.ALO.BZY

trestle scaffolds
TB.493 (N,B)
ALT **trestle scaffold**
SN Braced framework, usually consist-

ing of a horizontal beam supported at each end by a pair of spreading legs which serve as braces. (PUTNAM)
UF scaffolds, trestle
tressels
CN V.TB.AFU.ARI.ERE.ARI.BCW

trestle tables
TG.700
ALT **trestle table**
SN Use for tables with a removable board top resting on two or three trestle supports connected by a longitudinal bar instead of legs. For tables with X-shaped trestle supports use **sawbuck tables.**
UF tables, trestle
CN V.TG.AFU.AFU.BIQ.BOK.AFU.DUC.BIQ

trestles
TG.841
ALT **trestle**
SN Table supports of Medieval origin, consisting of two or more inverted T or Y shapes braced by a stretcher or brackets. (CTSB)
CN V.TG.ALO.BCW.AFU

trestles (bridges)
RK.1285 (L,N)
ALT **trestle (bridge)**
SN A braced framework of timbers, piles, or steelwork usually of considerable height for carrying a road or railroad over a depression. (W)
CN V.RK.AFU.ALO.ALO.GLI.ALO.AFU.AFU.BUE

trestles (equipment)
USE **horses**

trestles, A
USE **A trestles**

trestles, A-shaped
USE **A trestles**

tri-color processes
USE **three-color processes**

triacetate (cellulose triacetate)
USE **cellulose triacetate**

triacetate, cellulose
USE **cellulose triacetate**

trial calendars
USE **dockets**

trials
KM.157 (L)
CN K.KM.AFU.ERE

triangles
BM.774 (L,B)
ALT **triangular**
CN B.BM.CFS.ARI.AXC.BCW.AFU.BIQ.AFU

triangles (tools)
TB.455 (L,N)
ALT **triangle (tool)**
SN Implements of flat plastic, wood, or other material, made in a great number of triangular shapes and sizes; used as guides for drawing lines at various angles. (MAYER)
UF set squares (triangles)
squares, set (triangles)
CN V.TB.AFU.ARI.EFQ.ALO.CXA

triangular arches
USE **miter arches**

triangular dropleaf tables
USE **handkerchief tables**

tribal societies
USE **tribes**

tribes
HG.882 (L,R)
ALT **tribe**
SN Social groups, the members of which are held to be descended from a common ancestor, composed of numerous families, clans, or villages. They commonly occupy a specific geographic territory, possess cultural, religious, and linguistic homogeneity, and are united politically under one head or chief. (W)
UF societies, tribal
tribal societies
CN H.HG.ALO.DOI.AFU.ARI

Tribhuvanadityavarman
FL.2346
CN F.FL.ALO.ARI.BCW.ALO.ARI.AFU.DCU

tribunes
RM.38
ALT **tribune**
SN Stories in basilican churches that are above the nave arcade and contain a substantial gallery passage; distinct from **triforiums,** which always are at the level just below the side roof and do not have large passages.
CN V.RM.AFU.DIO.AFU.AXC.BCW

tribunes (apses)
USE **apses**

tric-tracs (gaming tables)
USE **tables de tric-trac**

trichromatic processes
USE **three-color processes**

trichrome carbro process
USE **three-color carbro process**

trichrome processes
USE **three-color processes**

Trichterbecher
USE **Funnel Beaker**

Trichterrandbecher
USE **Funnel Beaker**

triclinia
RM.116
ALT **triclinium**
SN Dining rooms in Roman houses; were usually furnished with a low table and surrounded on three sides by couches. (RS)
CN V.RM.AFU.DIO.ALO.BCW.BZY.AFU

triclinia (couches)
TG.391
ALT **triclinium (couch)**
SN Ancient Roman couches, used for dining and therefore generally lacking head and foot boards. (RICHTE)
CN V.TG.AFU.AFU.ARI.ALO.AXC.AFU

tricloroethane
MT.2708 (L)
CN M.MT.AFU.ARI.HZS.AFU.CFS

tricolor carbro
USE **three-color carbro process**

triconchs
RK.18 (R)
ALT **triconch**
CN V.RK.AFU.ALO.AFU.ALO.AFU.ALO

tricoteuses
TG.770
ALT **tricoteuse**
SN Ladies' work tables with tray tops and sometimes shelves; from 'tricoter', to knit, but used for a variety of needlework forms. A 19th-century term used mainly for 18th-century pieces. (PC)
CN V.TG.AFU.AFU.BIQ.BOK.ALO.GWW.ARI

tridarn cupboards
USE **tridarns**

tridarns
TG.519
ALT **tridarn**
SN Welsh cupboards in three stages, the lower two stages closed by doors and the upper stage opened for display.
UF cabinets, Welsh
cupboards, tridarn
cupboards, Welsh
tridarn cupboards
Welsh cabinets
Welsh cupboards
CN V.TG.AFU.AFU.AXC.ALO.BUE.CXA.AXC

trifid feet
TG.915
ALT **trifid foot**
SN Furniture feet having the form of three connected lobes.
UF drake feet
duck feet
Dutch feet
feet, drake
feet, duck
feet, Dutch

feet, trifid
feet, triphid
feet, web
triphid feet
web feet
CN V.TG.ALO.DZW.AFU.CXA

triforia
USE **triforiums**

triforiums
RM.416 (A)
ALT **triforium**
SN Stories in basilican church interiors that correspond to the level between the vaulting and the aisle roof, or the vaulting of the tribune and the tribune roof; may or may not contain a small passage. Distinct from **tribunes,** which always have substantial passages.
UF triforia
CN V.RM.AFU.DUC.BOK

trigger bolts
USE **auxiliary dead latches**

triglyphs
RT.353 (B)
ALT **triglyph**
SN The characteristic ornaments of the Doric frieze, consisting of a slightly raised block of three vertical bands separated by V-shaped grooves. (HAS)
CN V.RT.AFU.AFU.AFU.BCW.BZY.ALO.ARI.ALO.ARI

trigonometry
KD.257 (L)
SN Branch of mathematics dealing with the relations holding among the sides and angles of triangles and among closely related magnitudes, especially with methods of deducing from given parts other required parts. (W)
CN K.KD.AFU.ARI.CFS.BOK

trilithons
RK.893
ALT **trilithon**
SN Use for megalithic prehistoric structures comprised of two monolithic upright stones topped by a monolithic lintel. For smaller structures formed by two or more large standing stones capped by monolithic horizontal slabs, use **megalithic chamber tombs.**
UF triliths
CN V.RK.AFU.ALO.ALO.DOI.AFU.ARI.AXC

triliths
USE **trilithons**

trim, campaign
USE **campaign trim**

trimetric drawings
VD.19
ALT **trimetric drawing**
SN Use for axonometric drawings in which the three spatial axes are unequally inclined to the plane of projection (drawing surface), and the ratio of foreshortening is different for all three.
UF anisometric projections
drawings, trimetric
projections, anisometric
projections, trimetric
trimetric projections
CN V.VD.AFU.AFU.BIQ.AFU.AXC

trimetric projection
KT.285
SN Axonometric projection in which the three spatial axes are unequally inclined to the plane of projection (drawing surface), and the ratio of foreshortening is different for all three axes.
UF projection, trimetric
CN K.KT.AFU.ALO.DUC.DCU.BOK.ALO.AFU.AXC

trimetric projections
USE **trimetric drawings**

trimmers (frame components)
RT.707
ALT **trimmer (frame component)**
SN Pieces of timber inserted in a roof, floor, or wooden partition to support a header, which in turn supports the ends of the joists, rafters, or studs. Also, small horizontal beams, as in a floor, into which the ends of one or more joists are framed. (DAC)
UF joists, trimming
trimming joists
CN V.RT.AFU.AFU.ALO.ALO.BIQ

trimmers, window
USE **window dressers**

trimming
KT.91
ALT **trimmed**
CN K.KT.AFU.ALO.BUE.BCW

trimming joists
USE **trimmers (frame components)**

trinitrotoluene
USE **TNT**

trinitrotoluol
USE **TNT**

trinity columns
RK.898
ALT **trinity column**
SN Religious memorials, triangular in plan. (W)
UF columns, trinity
CN V.RK.AFU.ALO.ALO.DOI.AFU.BCW.ALO

trip-hammers
TB.466 (N)
ALT **trip-hammer**
SN Massive power hammers having a helve that is tripped and allowed to fall by cam or lever action. (W)
CN V.TB.AFU.ARI.ELK.AFU.BCW

tripacks
MT.2237
SN Color photographic film formed of three separate emulsions bound in register. For film with an integral, three-layer emulsion, use **integral tripacks.**
CN M.MT.AFU.ALO.CXA.ALO.ARI.AXC

tripacks, integral
USE **integral tripacks**

tripartite vaults
RT.525
ALT **tripartite vault**
SN Vaults divided into three vaulting cells.
UF three-part vaults
vaults, three-part
vaults, tripartite
CN V.RT.AFU.AFU.AFU.BIQ.BOK.AFU.AFU.AFU.AFU.AFU

triphid feet
USE **trifid feet**

triple-decker houses
USE **three-deckers**

triple-deckers
USE **three-deckers**

triple-hung windows
RT.947
ALT **triple-hung window**
SN Windows having three vertically sliding sashes.
UF windows, triple-hung
CN V.RT.AFU.ARI.AFU.AFU.BOK.AFU.AFU.EWY.ARI.AXC

tripod-base tables
USE **tripod tables**

tripod card tables
TG.718
ALT **tripod card table**
UF card tables, tripod
tables, tripod card
CN V.TG.AFU.AFU.BIQ.BOK.ALO.AXC.BCW

tripod fire screens
USE **pole screens**

tripod pole screens
USE **pole screens**

tripod stands
USE **tripods (stands)**

tripod tables
TG.701
ALT **tripod table**
SN Tables with a pedestal base support-

ed by three legs. (FAIRB)
UF tables, tripod
tables, tripod-base
tripod-base tables
CN V.TG.AFU.AFU.BIQ.BOK.AFU.DUC.BOK

tripods
TB.324 (L,N)
ALT **tripod**
SN Three-legged supports for stabilizing the camera while permitting it to be tilted, turned, raised, or lowered. (SWED)
CN V.TB.AFU.ARI.CLM.ARI.AFU.ALO.BUE

tripods (stands)
TG.625
ALT **tripod (stand)**
UF tripod stands
CN V.TG.AFU.AFU.BIQ.BCW.AFU.BCW.ALO

Tripolye
FL.2496
UF Cucuteni-Tripolye
Tripolye-Cucuteni
CN F.FL.ALO.AXC.AFU.BCW.CLM

Tripolye-Cucuteni
USE **Tripolye**

trips
USE **journeys**

Trique
FL.1524 (L)
CN F.FL.ALO.ALO.ARI.ALO.AXC.DIO

triquetras
DG.32
ALT **triquetra**
SN Triangle-shaped figures formed of three interlaced arcs or loops. (W)
CN D.DG.AFU.AFU.BIQ.BZY

triskeles
USE **triskelions**

triskelions
DG.70 (L)
ALT **triskelion**
SN Figures composed of three curved or bent branches radiating from a center. (W)
UF swastikas, three-armed
three-armed swastikas
triskeles
CN D.DG.AFU.AFU.DZW

triumphal arches
RK.895 (A,L,B,R)
ALT **triumphal arch**
UF arches, triumphal
CN V.RK.AFU.ALO.ALO.DOI.AFU.AXC.AFU

triumphal arches (church components)
USE **chancel arches**

trivium
KD.297
SN Group of studies in the Middle Ages forming the elementary division of the seven liberal arts and consisting of grammar, rhetoric, and logic. (W)
CN K.KD.AFU.BCW.ALO.AFU

Trobriand Island
FL.3641 (L)
CN F.FL.ALO.BOK.ALO.BCW.ALO.ARI.ARI

trochili
USE **cavetto moldings**
scotias

trochilus
USE **scotias**

trois couleurs
USE **à trois crayons**

trois crayons
USE **à trois crayons**

trolleybus systems
RD.96 (B)
ALT **trolleybus system**
SN Use for free-wheeled transit systems consisting of buslike vehicles, whose power comes from overhead cables to which the trolleybuses are attached, and of routes that intermingle with general street traffic.
UF systems, trolleybus
CN V.RD.ALO.ARI.AFU.AFU.AFU.AFU.AFU

trolleycar lines
USE **streetcar systems**

trolleys, tea
USE **tea wagons**

trompe-l'oeil
BM.147 (A,L,B,R)
SN French term meaning deception of the eye, applied to images so realistic that they may fool the viewer into thinking that the objects or scenes represented are real rather than images. (MAYER)
CN B.BM.AFU.AFU.ARI.BOK.BUE.AFU

trompe-l'oeil architecture
USE **fictive architecture**

trompes
RT.214
ALT **trompe**
SN Use for segments of vaults used externally as the supports of projecting features.
CN V.RT.AFU.AFU.AFU.AXC.DUC

tropaea
USE **trophies**

trophies
RK.909 (L,R)
ALT **trophy**
SN Use for triumphal monuments erected, as permanent reminders of military victories, in the land of the vanquished.
UF tropaea
CN V.RK.AFU.ALO.ALO.DOI.ALO.BCW

tropical climate
BM.744 (A,L,B)
SN Climate characterized by high temperatures and heavy precipitation, either throughout the year or alternating with dry seasons.
UF climate, tropical
CN B.BM.CFS.ALO.AXC.ALO.AFU.AXC

tropical forests
USE **jungles**

tropical rain forests
USE **rain forests**

trotyl
USE **TNT**

Troubadour
FL.3355
UF Cathedral Style
CN F.FL.ALO.BCW.ALO.AXC.DIO.BCW.AFU

trough roofs
USE **double-gable roofs**

troughs, eave
USE **gutters (storm water systems)**

troughs, mixing
USE **mixing troughs**

trowels
TB.630 (N)
ALT **trowel**
SN Flat hand tools having a broad steel blade; used to apply, spread, and shape plaster or mortar or to smooth the surface of unformed concrete. (DAC)
UF plasterer's trowels
trowels, plasterer's
CN V.TB.AFU.BCW.BCW.ALO.HCQ

trowels, angle
USE **margin trowels**

trowels, brick
USE **brick trowels**

trowels, buttering
USE **buttering trowels**

trowels, corner
USE **corner trowels**

trowels, inside corner
USE **inside corner trowels**

trowels, margin
USE **margin trowels**

trowels, mechanical
USE **mechanical trowels**

trowels, outside corner

USE **outside corner trowels**

trowels, plasterer's
USE **trowels**

trowels, pointing
USE **pointing trowels**

trowels, power
USE **mechanical trowels**

Troyville
FL.864
CN F.FL.ALO.ALO.ALO.AFU.ALO.ALO.ARI.ARI.CFS

truck cranes
TB.70 (L)
ALT **truck crane**
SN Materials-handling machines consisting of a crane which is mounted on a truck-type vehicle to provide mobility and maneuverability. (DAC)
UF cranes, truck
cranes, truck-mounted
truck-mounted cranes
CN V.TB.AFU.ARI.AFU.BCW.AXC.BUE

truck-mounted cranes
USE **truck cranes**

truck routes
RK.1558 (L)
ALT **truck route**
UF routes, truck
CN V.RK.ALO.ALO.BIQ.ARI.ALO.CLM

truck stops
RK.1260 (L)
ALT **truck stop**
UF stops, truck
CN V.RK.AFU.ALO.ALO.GLI.AFU.ARI.BZY

truck terminals
RK.1261 (L)
ALT **truck terminal**
UF motor-truck terminals
terminals, motor-truck
terminals, truck
CN V.RK.AFU.ALO.ALO.GLI.AFU.ARI.CFS

truckle beds
USE **trundle beds**

true laurel
USE **laurel**

True Word sect (China)
USE **Chen-Yen**

True Word sect (Japan)
USE **Shingon**

trueing planes
USE **trying planes**

Truk
FL.3680 (L)
CN F.FL.ALO.BOK.ARI.ALO.ALO

trulli
RK.248 (L,R)
ALT **trullo**
SN Designates traditional houses of some towns of South Italy, circular in plan and constructed with distinctive conical roofs of corbeled, dry-walled masonry.
CN V.RK.AFU.ALO.ALO.AXC.ALO.AFU.CLM.ALO.ALO

trumeaux
RT.885
ALT **trumeau**
SN The central supports of Medieval doorways. (HAS)
CN V.RT.AFU.ARI.AFU.AFU.AFU.ALO.BCW

trumpet arches
USE **squinches**

trumpet legs
TG.953
ALT **trumpet leg**
SN Turned legs that resemble a trumpet standing on end; characteristic of William and Mary period furniture. (CTSB)
UF legs, trumpet
CN V.TG.ALO.FIM.AFU.AFU.BZY

trumpet motifs
USE **trumpet spirals**

trumpet motifs, Celtic
USE **trumpet spirals**

trumpet pattern
USE **trumpet spirals**

trumpet spirals
DG.71
SN Use for the diverging spiral motif within a circle common in Celtic and Insular art.
UF blind trumpets
Celtic trumpet motifs
divergent spirals
motifs, trumpet
pattern, trumpet
spirals, divergent
spirals, trumpet
trumpet motifs
trumpet motifs, Celtic
trumpet pattern
trumpets, blind
CN D.DG.AFU.AFU.EFQ

trumpets, blind
USE **trumpet spirals**

trundle beds
TG.351 (N)
ALT **trundle bed**
SN Low bedsteads mounted on wheels so that they can be trundled under a standing bed when not in use. (TOMLIN)
UF beds, truckle
beds, trundle
beds, trunk
truckle beds
trunk beds
wheelbeds
CN V.TG.AFU.AFU.ARI.AFU.AFU.BIQ.ALO.ALO

trunk beds
USE **trundle beds**

trunk nails
TF.449
ALT **trunk nail**
UF nails, trunk
CN V.TF.AFU.AFU.AFU.ALO.AFU.CFS.ALO.EFQ

trunk sewers
USE **main sewers**

trunnels
USE **treenails**

truss bridges
RK.1302 (A,L)
ALT **truss bridge**
UF bridges, truss
CN V.RK.AFU.ALO.ALO.GLI.ALO.AFU.ARI.BUE

truss clips
TF.332
ALT **truss clip**
SN Clip connectors used in assembling trusses or in joining timber end to end. (PUTNAM)
UF clips, truss
CN V.TF.AFU.AFU.AFU.ALO.AFU.ARI.BCW

trussed joists
USE **open web joists**

trussed rafter roofs
RT.454
ALT **trussed rafter roof**
UF roofs, trussed rafter
CN V.RT.AFU.AFU.AFU.BIQ.ARI.AFU.ALO.ARI.BIQ

trussed rafter roofs (collar beam roofs)
USE **collar beam roofs**

trussed rafters
RT.383
ALT **trussed rafter**
SN Assemblies of structural members in a roof forming a rigid framework of triangular shapes.
UF rafters, trussed
simple trusses
trusses, simple
CN V.RT.AFU.AFU.AFU.BCW.CLM.AFU.ALO.ALO.ALO

trusses
RT.356 (A,L,B,R)
ALT **truss**
SN Assemblages of members (as beams, bars, or rods) typically arranged in a triangle or combinations of triangles to form a rigid framework (as for

supporting a load over a wide area) that cannot be deformed by the application of exterior force without deformation of one or more of its members. (W)
CN V.RT.AFU.AFU.AFU.BCW.CLM.AFU

trusses, Belfast
USE **bowstring trusses**

trusses, Belgian
USE **Fink trusses**

trusses, bowstring
USE **bowstring trusses**

trusses, bridge
USE **bridge trusses**

trusses, Burr arch
USE **Burr arch trusses**

trusses, camelback
USE **crescent trusses**

trusses, crescent
USE **crescent trusses**

trusses, curved
USE **crescent trusses**

trusses, deck
USE **through trusses**

trusses, fan
USE **fan Fink trusses**

trusses, fan Fink
USE **fan Fink trusses**

trusses, Fink
USE **Fink trusses**

trusses, French
USE **Fink trusses**

trusses, hammer-beam
USE **hammer-beam trusses**

trusses, Howe
USE **Howe trusses**

trusses, jack
USE **jack trusses**

trusses, king-post
USE **king-post trusses**

trusses, lattice
USE **Town lattice trusses**

trusses, Linville
USE **Whipple trusses**

trusses, Parker
USE **Parker trusses**

trusses, planar
USE **planar trusses**

trusses, pony
USE **pony trusses**

trusses, Pratt
USE **Pratt trusses**

trusses, queen
USE **queen-post trusses**

trusses, queen-post
USE **queen-post trusses**

trusses, roof
USE **roof trusses**

trusses, scissor beam
USE **scissors trusses**

trusses, scissors
USE **scissors trusses**

trusses, simple
USE **trussed rafters**

trusses, space
USE **space frames**

trusses, three-dimensional
USE **space frames**

trusses, through
USE **through trusses**

trusses, Town lattice
USE **Town lattice trusses**

trusses, Vierendeel
USE **Vierendeel trusses**

trusses, Warren
USE **Warren trusses**

trusses, Whipple
USE **Whipple trusses**

trussing adzes
TB.819 (N)
ALT **trussing adz**
SN Adzes with dull blades; used to strike barrel hoops into place. (SALAM)
UF adzes, stowing
adzes, trussing
stowing adzes
CN V.TB.AFU.BCW.CFS.ALO.AFU.AFU.BZY

trussing coffers
TG.459
ALT **trussing coffer**
SN Wood boxes, often covered in leather and tooled in gilt or bound with iron, which were used as traveling trunks to store papers, valuables, and clothes; of a type made in the late Medieval period.
UF coffers, traveling
coffers, trussing
standards (trussing coffers)
traveling chests
traveling coffers
CN V.TG.AFU.AFU.AXC.ALO.AXC.CLM.ARI

trust receipts
VW.837 (L)
ALT **trust receipt**
SN Documents in which are expressed security transactions. (BLACKS)
UF receipts, trust
CN V.VW.AFU.ARI.AFU.BIQ.CRG

trustees
HG.742
ALT **trustee**
CN H.HG.AFU.BCW.HCQ

trustees, boards of
USE **boards of trustees**

trusts
USE **foundations (organizations)**

truth
BM.529 (L,R)
CN B.BM.BIQ.BCW

try squares
TB.449 (N)
ALT **try square**
SN Squares usually consisting of a thin blade made of wood or metal which is attached at a right angle to the end of a thicker stock which may be placed against the edge of a drawing board or the like; predominately used to draw or mark something at right angles.
UF gauges, right-angle
right-angle gauges
squares, try
CN V.TB.AFU.ARI.EFQ.ALO.BZY.BIQ

trying planes
TB.941 (N)
ALT **trying plane**
SN Long planes, 22 to 24 inches long, used for smoothing boards. (MERCER)
UF planes, trueing
planes, trying
trueing planes
CN V.TB.AFU.BCW.CFS.ALO.AFU.DUC.ARI.AFU.BIQ

tsars
USE **czars**

Tsattine
USE **Beaver**

Tsaya
FL.472
CN F.FL.ALO.AFU.AXC.ALO.ALO.ARI.CLM.AFU

Tsetsaut
FL.1244
CN F.FL.ALO.ALO.ARI.AFU.AFU.ARI.ELK

Tshitolian
FL.66
CN F.FL.ALO.AFU.AFU.ALO.BCW.AXC

Tshogo
USE **Tsogo**

Tshuosh
USE **Sawos**

Tsilkotin
USE **Chilcotin**

Tsimshian
FL.1366 (L)
CN F.FL.ALO.ALO.ARI.AFU.BIQ.GWW

TSO
USE **tobacco seed oil**

Tsoede
FL.115
CN F.FL.ALO.AFU.ALO.AFU.BUE.CRG

Tsogo
FL.423 (L)
UF Ashogo
Mitsogo
Tshogo
CN F.FL.ALO.AFU.AXC.ALO.AFU.BCW

Tsonga
USE **Thonga**

Tsuga
USE **hemlock**

Tsuga canadensis
USE **eastern hemlock**

Tsuga heterophylla
USE **western hemlock**

Tsuga mertensiana
USE **mountain hemlock**

tsunamis
USE **tidal waves**

Tswana
FL.573 (L)
UF Batwana
Tawana
CN F.FL.ALO.AFU.AXC.ARI.BCW.AXC

Tuareg
FL.698 (L)
UF Touareg
CN F.FL.ALO.AFU.AXC.BCW.AXC.ALO

tub-back easy chairs
USE **circular easy chairs**

tub chairs
USE **barrel chairs**
circular easy chairs

Tübatulabal
FL.1265 (L)
CN F.FL.ALO.ALO.ARI.AFU.ALO.EFQ

tube-in-tube structures
USE **tube structures**

tube mills
RK.648 (N)
ALT **tube mill**
UF mills, tube
CN V.RK.AFU.ALO.ALO.CLM.ALO.
ALO.AFU.AXC.BUE.AXC.AFU.AFU

tube structures
RT.44
ALT **tube structure**
SN Use for rigid frame structures with closely spaced exterior columns rigidly connected to spandrel beams, the exterior framework carrying all lateral loads, as in the Sears Tower, Chicago.
UF structures, tube
structures, tube-in-tube
tube-in-tube structures
CN V.RT.AFU.AFU.AFU.ALO.AXC.BCW.
ALO

tube wells
USE **driven wells**

tubes, pneumatic
USE **pneumatic tubes**

tubing
MT.2282 (L)
SN Any material in the form of a tube. (DAC)
CN M.MT.AFU.ALO.ILG

tubs
USE **bathtubs**

tubs, laundry
USE **laundry trays**

tubs, set
USE **laundry trays**

Tubuai Island
USE **Austral Island**

tubular locks
TF.219
ALT **tubular lock**
SN Locks having a case that requires a bored, round hole rather than a rectangular mortise. The face plate and the lock case are fastened together as a unit. (BROWNL)
UF locks, tubular
CN V.TF.AFU.AFU.AFU.AFU.DIO.BIQ.
AFU.DZW.ALO

Tucano
FL.1599 (L)
UF Tukano
CN F.FL.ALO.ALO.ARI.ARI.AFU.HCQ

Tuchokwe
USE **Chokwe**

tuck and pat pointing
USE **pointing**

tuck joint pointing
USE **pointing**

tuck pointing
USE **pointing**

Tudor
FL.3192 (A,L,B,R)
CN F.FL.ALO.BCW.ALO.ARI.BIQ.BIQ.
AFU.AFU.AFU

Tudor arches
RT.238
ALT **Tudor arch**
SN Use for four-centered pointed arches.
UF arches, four-centered Tudor
arches, Tudor
four-centered pointed arches
four-centered Tudor arches
pointed arches, four-centered
CN V.RT.AFU.AFU.AFU.BCW.AFU.AFU.
AFU.CRG.BUE

Tudor flowers
DG.61
ALT **Tudor flower**
SN Ornamental motifs like an upright formalized ivy leaf, common in English Late Gothic and Tudor architecture, especially for brattishing. (PDARC)
UF flowers, Tudor
CN D.DG.AFU.AFU.DIO.CFS

Tudor Revival
FL.3329 (A,R)
UF Neo-Tudor
Revival, Tudor
CN F.FL.ALO.BCW.ALO.AXC.DIO.ALO.
BIQ.BOK

Tudor roses
DG.62
ALT **Tudor rose**
SN Conventionalized figures of roses in which one rose is superimposed over another, originally symbolizing the union of the houses of Lancaster and York in 1485.
UF roses, Tudor
CN D.DG.AFU.AFU.DIO.CLM

tufa
MT.633
SN Porous rock formed as a deposit from springs or streams, often calcareous. (W)
UF tufa, volcanic
volcanic tufa
CN M.MT.AFU.AFU.AFU.DCU.AFU.AFU.
ALO.ALO.ALO.ARI

tufa, calcareous
USE **travertine**

tufa, volcanic
USE **tufa**

tufaceous limestone
USE **travertine**

tuff
MT.634 (L)
SN Rock composed of the finer kinds of volcanic detritus. (MH)
CN M.MT.AFU.AFU.AFU.DCU.AFU.AFU.
ALO.ALO.ALO.AXC

Tughluq
FL.2240 (A,L)
CN F.FL.ALO.ARI.AXC.ALO.AFU.BIQ.
ARI

Tukano
USE **Tucano**

Tukete
USE **Kete**

Tula-Mazapán
USE **Aztec I**

Tulare
FL.1266
CN F.FL.ALO.ALO.ARI.AFU.ALO.ELK

tulipwood
MT.1315 (L)
UF canary whitewood
Liriodendron tulipifera
poplar, Virginia
poplar, yellow
Virginia poplar
whitewood
whitewood, canary
yellow poplar
CN M.MT.AFU.AFU.ALO.BIQ.DCU.
AFU.AFU.AFU.MFI

Tulunda
USE **Lunda**

Tulunid
FL.3576 (L)
CN F.FL.ALO.BIQ.AFU.HZS

Tumba
USE **Ntomba**

Tumbez
FL.1613
CN F.FL.ALO.ALO.ARI.ARI.ALO.AFU.
CFS

tumbler holders
TF.149
ALT **tumbler holder**
UF glass holders
holders, glass
holders, tumbler
CN V.TF.AFU.AFU.AFU.AFU.CRG.BIQ

tumbler locks, lever
USE **lever tumbler locks**

tumblers (lock components)
TF.570
ALT **tumbler (lock component)**
SN The mechanism in a lock holding the bolt until operated by a key. (MEANS)
CN V.TF.AFU.ALO.AXC.CFS

tumbling
USE **barreling**

tumbling courses
RT.627
ALT **tumbling course**
SN Sloping courses of brickwork which intersect horizontal courses. (HAS)
UF courses, tumbling
CN V.RT.AFU.AFU.AFU.BIQ.BUE.ALO.
AFU.ALO.CLM

tumeric
MT.1767
CN M.MT.AFU.AFU.ARI.AFU.AFU.ALO.
ALO.BUE.ALO.BIQ

Tumshuk
FL.1827
CN F.FL.ALO.ARI.AFU.AXC.ELK.CXA

tumuli
USE **burial mounds**

Tumulus period
FL.2511 (L)
CN F.FL.ALO.AXC.AFU.BIQ.AFU.ARI

Tumulus period (Kofun)
USE **Kofun**

Tun-huang
FL.1828
UF Dunhuang
CN F.FL.ALO.ARI.AFU.AXC.ELK.DCU

tundras
RD.253 (L)
ALT **tundra**
CN V.RD.ARI.AFU.BCW.ALO.AFU.AXC

tung oil
MT.2022 (L)
SN A semidrying oil used in hardwearing varnishes and enamels. (MAYER)
UF China wood oil
oil, China wood
oil, tung
wood oil, China
CN M.MT.AFU.AFU.ARI.ARI.AXC.AFU.
CXA

tung oil, Japanese
USE **Japanese tung oil**

tungsten
MT.450 (L)
SN Naturally occurring heavy white metal with a specific gravity of 19.6; has the highest melting point of all the metals; used chiefly in making alloy steel and magnets and in electronic applications. (MH)
CN M.MT.AFU.AFU.AFU.BZY.AFU.AFU.
ARI.DUC

tungsten blue
MT.1604
UF blue de tungstène
blue, tungsten
Wolframblau
CN M.MT.AFU.AFU.ARI.AFU.AFU.ALO.
ALO.ALO.ARI.BZY

Tunica
FL.1443 (L)
CN F.FL.ALO.ALO.ARI.AFU.BZY.DCU

tunnel kilns
TB.94 (A,L)
ALT **tunnel kiln**
UF cartunnel kilns
continuous kilns
kilns, cartunnel
kilns, continuous
kilns, tunnel
CN V.TB.AFU.ARI.ALO.ARI.ALO.AFU.
AXC

tunnel vaults
USE **barrel vaults**

tunneling
KT.613 (A,L)
CN K.KT.AFU.ALO.FUA.CFS.ALO

tunnels
RK.1304 (A,L,B,R)
ALT **tunnel**
CN V.RK.AFU.ALO.ALO.GLI.ALO.ALO

tunnels, highway
USE **highway tunnels**

tunnels, railroad
USE **railroad tunnels**

tunnels, toad
USE **toad tunnels**

tunnels, water
USE **water tunnels**

tuns, chimney
USE **chimney stacks**

Tup-Khona
FL.1808
CN F.FL.ALO.ARI.AFU.AXC.DZW

tupelo
MT.1162
UF cotton gum
gum, cotton
gum, sour
gum, swamp
gum, tupelo
Nyssa aquatica
sour gum
swamp gum
tupelo gum
CN M.MT.AFU.AFU.ALO.BIQ.DCU.
AFU.AFU.AFU.DIO.AXC.ARI.AXC

tupelo gum
USE **tupelo**

tupelo, black
USE **black gum**

tupelo, ogeche
USE **ogeche tupelo**

tupelo, sour
USE **ogeche tupelo**

tupelo, swamp
USE **swamp tupelo**

Tupí
FL.1684 (L)
CN F.FL.ALO.ALO.ARI.ARI.BIQ.CRG

Tupinamba
FL.1685 (L)
CN F.FL.ALO.ALO.ARI.ARI.BIQ.CXA

Tupinikin
FL.1686
CN F.FL.ALO.ALO.ARI.ARI.BIQ.DCU

Tura
FL.322 (L)
CN F.FL.ALO.AFU.AXC.AFU.ARI.BCW.AFU.AFU

turbines
TB.396 (L,N)
ALT **turbine**
SN Any of various machines which convert the kinetic energy of a moving fluid to mechanical energy; often used for driving an electric generator. (MEANS)
CN V.TB.AFU.ARI.DOI.BUE

turbines, gas
USE **gas turbines**

turbines, hydraulic
USE **hydraulic turbines**

turbines, impulse
USE **impulse turbines**

turbines, steam
USE **steam turbines**

Turcoman
USE **Turkman**

turf
USE **sod**

turf mazes
RK.1407
ALT **turf maze**
SN Use for labyrinthine garden features created by cutting shallow pathways into deep lawns; common during the Renaissance.
UF mazes, turf
CN V.RK.ALO.AFU.AFU.AFU.ARI.ARI.ALO.ALO

turf seats
RM.457
ALT **turf seat**
SN Use for raised seats or benches covered with turf, common in Medieval gardens.
UF seats, turf
turfed seats
CN V.RM.ALO.AFU.CFS.BUE

Turfan
FL.1829
CN F.FL.ALO.ARI.AFU.AXC.ELK.DIO

turfed seats
USE **turf seats**

Turkana
FL.635 (L)
CN F.FL.ALO.AFU.AXC.AXC.ARI.EFQ

turkey oak, European
USE **European turkey oak**

Turkey red
USE **madder**

turkey sofas
USE **ottomans**

Turkey umber
USE **umber**

turkey work chairs (Cromwellian chairs)
USE **Cromwellian chairs**

Turkish baths
RK.1074 (L,B)
ALT **Turkish bath**
UF baths, Turkish
hammams
CN V.RK.AFU.ALO.ALO.EWY.BCW.ALO.ALO

Turkish chairs
TG.93
ALT **Turkish chair**
UF chairs, Turkish
chairs, Turkish frame
frame chairs, Turkish
Turkish frame chairs
CN V.TG.AFU.AFU.ALO.AFU.AFU.AFU.LTU

Turkish domes
USE **onion domes**

Turkish frame chairs
USE **Turkish chairs**

Turkman
FL.3577 (L,B)
UF Turcoman
CN F.FL.ALO.BIQ.AFU.IFM

Turks, Ottoman
USE **Ottoman**

turmaline
USE **tourmaline**

turmeric
MT.1532 (L)
SN A yellow to reddish brown dyestuff obtained from the East Indian perennial herb, turmeric.
UF curcuma
CN M.MT.AFU.AFU.ARI.AFU.AFU.AFU.AFU.AFU.AXC.CXA

turn-up beds
USE **folding beds**
press beds

turn up tables
USE **tilt-top tables**

Turnbull's blue
USE **Prussian blue**

turned legs, baluster
USE **baluster legs**

turned spade feet
USE **therm feet**

turned three-square great chairs
USE **great chairs**

Turner's yellow
MT.1794
UF Cassel yellow
Kassler yellow
mineral yellow
Montpellier yellow
patent yellow
Verona yellow
yellow, Cassel
yellow, Kassler
yellow, mineral
yellow, Montpellier
yellow, patent
yellow, Turner's
yellow, Verona
CN M.MT.AFU.AFU.ARI.AFU.AFU.ALO.ALO.BUE.ARI.CRG

Turner's yellow (color)
USE **brilliant yellow**
light yellow
moderate yellow
strong yellow

turners
HG.547
ALT **turner**
CN H.HG.AFU.AXC.BUE.ARI.DIO.AXC

turning
KT.169 (L,R)
ALT **turned**
SN The shaping of objects by means of cutting tools while the material from which the objects are made rotates rapidly on a lathe. (DAC)
CN K.KT.AFU.ALO.DOI.ERE.BCW

turning bars
USE **chimney bars**

turning chisels
TB.868 (N)
ALT **turning chisel**
SN Tools with a rounded bevel on both sides, and a cuting edge which is square or skewed; used for paring and smoothing wood turned on a lathe.
UF chisels, turning
CN V.TB.AFU.BCW.CFS.ALO.AFU.BUE.CFS

turning circles
USE **traffic circles**

turning gouges
TB.889 (N)
ALT **turning gouge**
SN Tools used in turning to remove irregularities in the wood quickly and to smooth hollows. Commonly used by wheelwrights to turn wheel hubs.
UF gouges, turning
CN V.TB.AFU.BCW.CFS.ALO.AFU.CXA.BUE

turning saws
USE **bow saws**

turnip feet
TG.898
ALT **turnip foot**
SN Ball feet with small collars at their

bases. (CTSB)
UF feet, turnip
CN V.TG.ALO.DZW.AFU.AFU.AFU

turnkey contracts
VW.888
ALT **turnkey contract**
SN Those contracts in which a builder agrees to complete the work of building and installation to the point of readiness for occupancy. (BLACKS)
UF contracts, turnkey
CN V.VW.AFU.ARI.AFU.BOK.BOK.ALO.ALO.AFU.BOK

turnpike stairs
USE **spiral stairs**

turnpikes
RK.1524 (L)
ALT **turnpike**
SN Use for either high-speed multilane highways or 18th- and 19th-century thoroughfares along which tolls are collected from users; can be expressways or throughways.
UF roads, toll
toll roads
tollways
CN V.RK.ALO.ALO.BIQ.ARI.AFU.AFU.ARI.ALO.ALO

turns, cupboard
USE **cupboard turns**

turns, shutter
USE **shutter dogs**

turns, thumb
USE **thumb turns**

turnscrews
USE **screwdrivers**

turnsole
MT.1533
CN M.MT.AFU.AFU.ARI.AFU.AFU.AFU.AFU.AFU.AXC.DCU

turnstiles
RT.1046 (N)
ALT **turnstile**
SN Barriers which rotate on an axis and are usually so arranged as to allow the passage of a person through an opening only in one direction, one person at a time. (DAC)
CN V.RT.AFU.AXC.ALO.BCW

turntables (rail transportation structures)
RK.1313 (B)
ALT **turntable (rail transportation structure)**
UF railway turntables
CN V.RK.AFU.ALO.ALO.GLI.ARI.ALO.ALO

turntables (revolving stages)
USE **revolving stages**

turpentine
MT.2705 (L)
SN The traditional solvent or thinner for a drying oil (such as linseed oil) distilled from resin exuded by certain trees, such as the European larch, white fir, and the American longleaf pine. (TATEMT)
UF chian turpentine
oil of turpentine
terebinth
turpentine, chian
turpentine, oil of
CN M.MT.AFU.ARI.HZS.AFU.BZY.ARI

turpentine, Burgundy
USE **Burgundy turpentine**

turpentine, chian
USE **turpentine**

turpentine, gum
USE **gum turpentine**

turpentine, Jura
USE **Jura turpentine**

turpentine, oil of
USE **turpentine**

turpentine, spirits of
USE **gum turpentine**

turpentine, Strasbourg
USE **Strasbourg turpentine**

turpentine, Venice
USE **Venice turpentine**

turpentine, wood
USE **wood turpentine**

turquoise
MT.567 (L)
CN M.MT.AFU.AFU.AFU.CFS.AFU.HTY

turquoise (color)
USE **brilliant bluish green**
light bluish green
light greenish blue
moderate bluish green
moderate greenish blue
strong bluish green

turquoise blue
USE **light bluish green**
light greenish blue
moderate greenish blue
strong greenish blue

turquoise blue, bright
USE **brilliant greenish blue**
strong bluish green
strong greenish blue

turquoise blue, light
USE **very light greenish blue**

turquoise blue, medium
USE **moderate greenish blue**

turquoise blue, vivid
USE **moderate greenish blue**
strong bluish green
strong greenish blue

turquoise green
USE **brilliant bluish green**
light bluish green
light greenish blue
moderate bluish green
strong bluish green
vivid bluish green

turquoise green, bright
USE **brilliant bluish green**
light bluish green
moderate bluish green
strong bluish green

turquoise green, deep
USE **deep bluish green**

turquoise green, light
USE **very light bluish green**

turquoise green, pale
USE **very light bluish green**

turquoise green, pastel
USE **light bluish green**
very light bluish green

turquoise green, vivid
USE **strong bluish green**

turquoise, blue
USE **brilliant greenish blue**
light greenish blue

turquoise, bright
USE **brilliant bluish green**
strong bluish green

turquoise, light
USE **light bluish green**
light greenish blue
very light greenish blue

turquoise, vivid
USE **strong bluish green**

turquoises
USE **ottomans**

turret lathes
TB.700 (N)
ALT **turret lathe**
SN Lathes having a turret for holding various different cutting tools. (W)
UF lathes, turret
CN V.TB.AFU.BCW.BIQ.ARI.AFU.AFU.AFU

turret steps
RT.1119 (B)
SN Stone steps, triangular in section, forming spiral or solid newel stairs; they are tapered and have shaped ends which, laid upon each other, constitute the central column or solid newel. (HAS)
UF steps, turret
CN V.RT.AFU.BIQ.AXC.ALO.BIQ.AFU.BCW.ALO

turrets
RM.423 (L,N,B)

ALT **turret**
SN Use for small towers, especially when corbelled out from a corner.
UF tourelles
CN V.RM.AFU.DZW.BCW

turrets (theaters)
RM.377
ALT **turret (theater)**
SN Use for upper parts of tiring houses in Elizabethan theaters, possibly used as music galleries and for sound effects.
CN V.RM.AFU.DIO.AXC.AXC.ALO.BOK.ALO.AFU

turrets, watch
USE **bartizans**

Turu
FL.592 (L)
UF Nyaturu
Waniaturu
CN F.FL.ALO.AFU.AXC.AXC.AFU.CFS

Tusayan
USE **Hopi**

Tuscan
FL.2741 (B)
CN F.FL.ALO.AXC.ALO.ALO.ALO.BOK.ALO

Tuscan order
RT.56 (A,B,R)
UF order, Tuscan
CN V.RT.AFU.AFU.AFU.ARI.ARI.BIQ

Tuscan red
MT.1678
UF red, Tuscan
CN M.MT.AFU.AFU.ARI.AFU.AFU.ALO.ALO.BCW.AFU.ALO.BUE

Tuscan Villa Style
USE **Italian Villa Style**

Tuscarora
FL.1444 (L)
CN F.FL.ALO.ALO.ARI.AFU.BZY.DIO

Tuscarora (Iroquois)
FL.1298 (L)
CN F.FL.ALO.ALO.ARI.AFU.ARI.BCW.BIQ

tusche
MT.2506
SN The greasy liquid used with pen or brush in lithography. (GASCO)
CN M.MT.AFU.ARI.CRG.ALO.ALO.CFS

tusk
MT.964 (L)
CN M.MT.AFU.AFU.ALO.AFU.ELK.AFU

Tutania
USE **Tutanic metal**

Tutanic metal
MT.419
SN German utensil alloy, contains 88% to 92% tin, up to 3% copper, and 6% to 7.5% lead. (MH)
UF metal, Tutanic
Tutania
CN M.MT.AFU.AFU.AFU.BZY.AFU.AFU.AFU.ALO.BUE.ALO.BUE

Tutchone
FL.1245
CN F.FL.ALO.ALO.ARI.AFU.AFU.ARI.ERE

Tutelo
FL.1445 (L)
CN F.FL.ALO.ALO.ARI.AFU.BZY.DOI

tutenag
USE **bidri**

tutors
HG.301 (L)
ALT **tutor**
UF instructors, private
private instructors
private teachers
teachers, private
CN H.HG.AFU.AXC.BCW.ALO.ARI.ARI.ALO

Tuva
FL.2144 (L)
CN F.FL.ALO.ARI.ARI.ALO.AFU.AXC

Tuvalu
FL.3685 (L)
CN F.FL.ALO.BOK.ARI.BIQ

TV studios
USE **television studios**

TV tables
USE **snack tables**

Twa
FL.540
UF Batwa
CN F.FL.ALO.AFU.AXC.ALO.ALO.BIQ.ARI.AFU

Twana
FL.1367 (L)
UF Too-an-hooch Indians
CN F.FL.ALO.ALO.ARI.AFU.BIQ.HCQ

tweed
MT.1821 (L)
SN A woolen material with a rough, homespun surface effect. (EOT)
CN M.MT.AFU.AFU.ARI.ALO.AFU.AFU.AFU.AXC.AFU

tweezers
TB.223 (N)
SN Any of various small pincer-shaped tools used for plucking, holding, or manipulating. (W)
UF spring tongs
tongs, spring
CN V.TB.AFU.ARI.CFS.BIQ

Twelfth Dynasty
FL.2805
UF 12th Dynasty
Dynasty, Twelfth
CN F.FL.ALO.AXC.ALO.ARI.AFU.BIQ.ALO

Twentieth Dynasty
FL.2818
UF 20th Dynasty
Dynasty, Twentieth
CN F.FL.ALO.AXC.ALO.ARI.AFU.BUE.AXC

Twenty-eighth Dynasty
FL.2829
UF 28th Dynasty
Dynasty, Twenty-eighth
Saite Dynasty (Twenty-eighth Dynasty)
Saite period (Twenty-eighth Dynasty)
CN F.FL.ALO.AXC.ALO.ARI.AFU.CFS.ARI

Twenty-fifth Dynasty
FL.2825
UF 25th Dynasty
Dynasty, Twenty-fifth
Kushite Dynasty
Nubian Dynasty
CN F.FL.ALO.AXC.ALO.ARI.AFU.BZY.BCW

Twenty-first Dynasty
FL.2821
UF 21st Dynasty
Dynasty, Twenty-first
Tanite Dynasty
CN F.FL.ALO.AXC.ALO.ARI.AFU.BZY.AFU

twenty-four carat gold
USE **gold**

Twenty-fourth Dynasty
FL.2824
UF 24th Dynasty
Dynasty, Twenty-fourth
CN F.FL.ALO.AXC.ALO.ARI.AFU.BZY.AXC

Twenty-ninth Dynasty
FL.2830
UF 29th Dynasty
Dynasty, Twenty-ninth
Mendesian Dynasty
CN F.FL.ALO.AXC.ALO.ARI.AFU.CFS.AXC

Twenty-second Dynasty
FL.2822
UF 22nd Dynasty
Dynasty, Twenty-second
Libyan Dynasty
CN F.FL.ALO.AXC.ALO.ARI.AFU.BZY.ALO

Twenty-seventh Dynasty
FL.2828
UF 27th Dynasty
Dynasty, Twenty-seventh
First Persian period
Persian period

CN F.FL.ALO.AXC.ALO.ARI.AFU.CFS.
ALO

Twenty-sixth Dynasty
FL.2827
UF 26th Dynasty
Dynasty, Twenty-sixth
Revival, Saite
Saite Dynasty (Twenty-sixth Dynasty)
Saite Period (Twenty-sixth Dynasty)
Saite Revival
CN F.FL.ALO.AXC.ALO.ARI.AFU.CFS.
AFU

Twenty-third Dynasty
FL.2823
UF 23rd Dynasty
Dynasty, Twenty-third
Libyan Dynasty
CN F.FL.ALO.AXC.ALO.ARI.AFU.BZY.
ARI

twibills
USE **twivels**

Twightwees
USE **Miami**

twin beds
TG.380
ALT **twin bed**
SN Beds for one person, especially a matching pair in a bedroom.
UF beds, single
beds, twin
single beds
CN V.TG.AFU.AFU.ARI.AFU.ALO.AFU

twin cathedrals
USE **double churches**

twin churches
USE **double churches**

twin-lens cameras
TB.303 (L)
ALT **twin-lens camera**
SN Cameras having two lenses of the same focal length. One is used for viewing and focusing, the other for exposing the film. The lenses are mounted above each other. (LANG)
UF cameras, twin-lens
TLRs
CN V.TB.AFU.ARI.CLM.ARI.AFU.AFU.
ALO.AXC.ALO

twine
MT.1977 (L,N)
CN M.MT.AFU.AFU.ARI.ALO.ALO.BIQ.
BCW

twist augers
USE **spiral augers**

twist augers (bits)
USE **spiral bits**

twist bits
USE **spiral bits**

twist drills
TB.187 (L)
ALT **twist drill**
SN Drills with one or more spiral cutting grooves; used to drill holes in metal, wood, and plastic. (MEANS)
UF drills, twist
CN V.TB.AFU.ARI.BIQ.ALO.AFU.AFU.
BOK

twisted columns
USE **spiral columns**

twisters (tornadoes)
USE **tornadoes**

twisting stress
USE **torsional stress**

twivels
TB.844 (N)
ALT **twivel**
SN Small two-headed axes used for cutting mortises; one end is chisel-shaped and the other is a triangular knife.
UF axes, cross
cross axes
daders
knives, mortising
mortising knives
tomahawks (twivels)
twibills
two-bills
CN V.TB.AFU.BCW.CFS.ALO.AFU.AXC.
BUE.AFU

two-bills
USE **twivels**

two-centered arches
RT.267
ALT **two-centered arch**
SN Arches struck from two centers, resulting in a pointed arch. (HAS)
UF arches, two-centered
CN V.RT.AFU.AFU.AFU.BCW.AFU.AFU.
AFU.EWY.ALO

two-centered segmental arches
USE **pointed segmental arches**

two-color processes
KT.375
SN Photographic processes using two colors, usually red and green or orange and near-cyan, to synthesize the full color spectrum; may be additive or subtractive.
UF dichromatic processes
duochromatic processes
CN K.KT.AFU.ALO.DUC.DIO.ALO.ELK

two-dimensional
DC.74
CN D.DC.AFU.ARI.DZW

two-direction spanning slabs
USE **two-way structural systems**

two-family houses
USE **double houses**
duplex houses

two-handed crosscut saws
TB.1025 (N)
ALT **two-handed crosscut saw**
SN Large two-handled saws up to 7 feet in length, designed for use by two people and having a variety of tooth patterns.
UF saws, thwart
saws, two-handed crosscut
saws, two-man crosscut
thwart saws
two-man crosscut saws
CN V.TB.AFU.BCW.CFS.ALO.AFU.EWY.
BUE.ARI.ALO

two-hinged arches
RT.263
ALT **two-hinged arch**
SN Use for wood or metal arches hinged at the two springing points.
UF arches, two-hinged
CN V.RT.AFU.AFU.AFU.BCW.AFU.AFU.
AFU.ERE.AFU

two-man crosscut saws
USE **two-handed crosscut saws**

two-point latches
TF.187
ALT **two-point latch**
UF latches, two-point
CN V.TF.AFU.AFU.AFU.AFU.DIO.BCW.
ALO.AXC.AFU

two-point perspective
KT.275
UF perspective, two-point
CN K.KT.AFU.ALO.DUC.DCU.BIQ.AXC.
ALO

two-point perspectives
VD.88
ALT **two-point perspective**
UF angular perspectives
perspectives, angular
perspectives, two-point
CN V.VD.AFU.AFU.BIQ.ARI.BCW.AXC

two-story
DC.98 (A)
CN D.DC.AFU.ARI.ERE.BOK.ALO

two-way beam and slab systems
RT.33
ALT **two-way beam and slab system**
SN Use for structural systems based on concrete slabs in which loads are transferred in two directions, with a network of beams providing additional strength.
UF beam and slab systems, two-way
beam systems, flat slab and
flat slab and beam systems
systems, flat slab and beam
systems, two-way beam and slab
CN V.RT.AFU.AFU.AFU.ALO.ARI.ALO.
AFU.ALO.ARI

two-way construction

USE **two-way structural systems**

two-way flat plate systems
USE **flat plate systems**

two-way flat slab construction
USE **flat slab systems**

two-way flat slab systems
USE **flat slab systems**

two-way floor and roof systems
USE **two-way structural systems**

two-way structural systems
RT.30
ALT **two-way structural system**
SN Use for structural systems based on concrete slabs in which loads are transferred in two directions.
UF construction, two-way
floor and roof systems, two-way
roof systems, two-way floor and
slabs, two-direction spanning
structural systems, two-way
systems, two-way
systems, two-way structural
two-direction spanning slabs
two-way construction
two-way floor and roof systems
two-way systems
CN V.RT.AFU.AFU.AFU.ALO.ARI.ALO.AFU.ALO

two-way systems
USE **two-way structural systems**

two-way waffle slabs
USE **waffle slabs**

tying
KT.64
ALT **tied**
CN K.KT.AFU.ALO.BCW.CXA

tympana
RT.679 (A,L,R)
ALT **tympanum**
SN The triangular or segmental spaces enclosed by a pediment or an arch. (HAS)
CN V.RT.AFU.AFU.AFU.BIQ.BUE.ALO.ALO.CFS

type I portland cement
USE **standard portland cement**

type II portland cement
USE **modified portland cement**

type III cement
USE **high-early-strength cement**

type III portland cement
USE **high-early-strength cement**

type IV cement
USE **low-heat cement**

type ornaments
USE **printers' ornaments**

type V portland cement
USE **sulfate-resistant cement**

typescripts
VW.660
ALT **typescript**
SN Typed documents. (ICA)
CN V.VW.AFU.ALO.AFU.DZW.ARI.AFU.BCW

typesetters
HG.465
ALT **typesetter**
CN H.HG.AFU.AXC.BUE.ALO.CFS.CLM

typewriter chairs
TG.201 (N)
ALT **typewriter chair**
SN Revolving chairs, usually with a spring back, made for office use.
UF chairs, secretary's
chairs, stenographer's
chairs, typewriter
secretary's chairs
stenographer's chairs
stenographer's stools
stools, stenographer
CN V.TG.AFU.AFU.ALO.AFU.AFU.ALO.FUA

typhoons
KM.118 (L,B)
CN K.KM.AFU.CXA.BIQ.ALO.ARI

typical floor plans
VD.48
ALT **typical floor plan**
SN Plan of one story of a building that has numerous stories in that form.
UF floor plans, typical
plans, typical floor
CN V.VD.AFU.AFU.BIQ.ALO.AXC.ALO.AFU.ALO

typographers
HG.466
ALT **typographer**
CN H.HG.AFU.AXC.BUE.ALO.CFS.CRG

typographical devices
USE **printers' marks**

typology
BM.1164 (A,L,R)
SN Generally, the comparative study and analysis of the characteristics of things, including their grouping into classes on the basis of common characteristics. Specifically, the analysis of the origin and meaning of Biblical types, especially in comparing the Old and New Testaments.
CN B.BM.DIO.BUE

tyranny
USE **despotism**

tyreing houses
USE **tiring houses**

Tyrian purple
MT.1518
UF Grecian purple
purple, Grecian
purple, Tyrian
red, whelk
whelk red
CN M.MT.AFU.AFU.ARI.AFU.AFU.AFU.AFU.AFU.ARI

Tyrian purple (color)
USE **vivid purplish red**

Tyrolean green
MT.1640
UF green, Tyrolean
CN M.MT.AFU.AFU.ARI.AFU.AFU.ALO.ALO.AXC.AFU.ALO.ARI

Tzacualli
FL.987
UF Teotihuacan I
CN F.FL.ALO.ALO.ALO.ALO.AFU.ALO.AFU.AFU.BUE

Tzakol
FL.1014
CN F.FL.ALO.ALO.ALO.ALO.AFU.ALO.ARI.AFU.AFU.BCW

Tzeltal
FL.1541 (L)
CN F.FL.ALO.ALO.ARI.ALO.BIQ.AFU.CFS

Tzoneca
USE **Tehuelche**

Tzoneka
USE **Tehuelche**

Tzotzil
FL.1542 (L)
UF Zatzil
CN F.FL.ALO.ALO.ARI.ALO.BIQ.AFU.CLM

Tzutujil
FL.1545 (L)
UF Zutujil
CN F.FL.ALO.ALO.ARI.ALO.BIQ.AFU.CRG

U-bahns
USE **subways**

U-Thong
USE **Tong**

Tong
FL.2421
UF U-Thong
Uthong
CN F.FL.ALO.ARI.BCW.BOK.AFU.DOI

U.S.
USE **American**

Ubaid
FL.2959
CN F.FL.ALO.AXC.ARI.BCW.AFU.AFU.ALO.ARI

Ubaid 1
USE **Eridu**

Ubaid 2
USE **Hajji Muhammed**

Udaipur
USE **Mewar**

Udayadityavarman I
FL.2339
CN F.FL.ALO.ARI.BCW.ALO.ARI.AFU.BOK

Uddiyana
USE **Swat Valley**

Udi
FL.264 (L)
CN F.FL.ALO.AFU.AXC.AFU.ALO.ARI.AXC.AXC

ugliness
BM.496 (L,R)
SN That which evokes an awareness or feeling of deep revulsion or painfully disturbs a previously accepted aesthetic ideal. Can be considered as culturally defined or as an individual reaction. (LIA)
CN B.BM.BIQ.AFU.BZY

Ugrian
USE **Uighur**

Uighur
FL.1809 (L)
UF Ugrian
Uigur
Uygur
Yue-che
Yueh-Chi
CN F.FL.ALO.ARI.AFU.AXC.EFQ

Uigur
USE **Uighur**

Uki-e
FL.2083
CN F.FL.ALO.ARI.ALO.ALO.ALO.AXC.BUE

Ukiyo-e
FL.2084 (L,R)
UF Floating-world
CN F.FL.ALO.ARI.ALO.ALO.ALO.AXC.BZY

Ulmus americana
USE **American elm**

Ulmus fulva
USE **slippery elm**

Ulmus glabra
USE **wych elm**

Ulmus parrifolia
USE **Chinese elm**

Ulmus procera
USE **English elm**

Ulmus rubra
USE **slippery elm**

ultimate-load design
USE **plastic design**

ultimate strength
BM.965
SN The stress, calculated on the maximum value of the force and the original area of cross section, which causes fracture of the material. (MH)
UF strength, ultimate
CN B.BM.CFS.AXC.BZY.BOK.CLM.BOK

ultimate-strength analysis
USE **plastic design**

ultra-microfiche
USE **ultrafiche**

ultra white
USE **composite white**

Ultrabaroque
FL.1715
CN F.FL.ALO.ALO.AXC.ALO.AFU.ARI.BCW

ultrafiche
VW.670
SN Microfiche with a reduction ratio greater than 90 times. (ICA)
UF ultra-microfiche
CN V.VW.AFU.ALO.AFU.DZW.AXC.ALO.ALO

ultraism
USE **radicalism**

Ultraist
FL.3422
ALT **Ultraism**
CN F.FL.ALO.BCW.ALO.AXC.DIO.CFS.AFU

Ultramarinblau
USE **artificial ultramarine blue**

Ultramarinblau natürlich
USE **ultramarine blue**

ultramarine
USE **brilliant blue**
brilliant purplish blue
deep blue
grayish purplish blue
light blue
light purplish blue
light violet
moderate blue
moderate purplish blue
pale blue
pale purplish blue
strong blue
strong purplish blue
very light purplish blue
very pale purplish blue
vivid blue
vivid purplish blue

ultramarine ash
USE **ultramarine blue**

ultramarine ash, blue
USE **moderate blue**

ultramarine ash, gray
USE **light greenish gray**

ultramarine blue
MT.1586 (L)
UF ash, ultramarine
azure
azurro ultramarino
bleu d'azur
blue, lazuline
blue, Sanders
blue, Saunders
blue, ultramarine
genuine ultramarine
gray, mineral
lapis lazuli (ultramarine blue)
lazuline blue
mineral gray
outremer naturel
Sanders blue
Saunders blue
stone, vein
Ultramarinblau natürlich
ultramarine ash
ultramarine, genuine
vein stone
CN M.MT.AFU.AFU.ARI.AFU.AFU.ALO.ALO.ALO.AFU.BCW

ultramarine blue (color)
USE **vivid blue**
vivid purplish blue

ultramarine blue, artificial
USE **artificial ultramarine blue**

ultramarine blue, genuine
USE **strong blue**
vivid blue

ultramarine green
MT.1656
UF green, ultramarine
CN M.MT.AFU.AFU.ARI.AFU.AFU.ALO.ALO.AXC.ARI.BUE

ultramarine violet
MT.1714
UF outremer violet
Ultramarinviolett
violet ultramarine
violet, outremer
CN M.MT.AFU.AFU.ARI.AFU.AFU.ALO.ALO.BIQ.AFU.ARI

ultramarine yellow
USE **strontium yellow**

ultramarine, artificial
USE **strong blue**
strong purplish blue

ultramarine, bright
USE **strong blue**
strong purplish blue
vivid blue
vivid purplish blue

ultramarine, cobalt

USE **strong greenish blue**

ultramarine, deep
USE **moderate blue**
vivid blue
vivid purplish blue

ultramarine, French
USE **artificial ultramarine blue**
strong blue
strong purplish blue

ultramarine, genuine
USE **ultramarine blue**

ultramarine, Vienna
USE **cobalt blue**

ultramarine, violet
USE **strong purplish blue**
strong violet

ultramarine, yellow
USE **barium yellow**
strontium yellow

Ultramarinviolett
USE **ultramarine violet**

ultrasonic metal-cutting
KT.831 (L)
UF metal-cutting, ultrasonic
CN K.KT.AFU.ALO.HOE.BCW.ALO.ARI.BIQ

ultrasonic welding
KT.814 (L)
SN A solid-state welding process in which the metals are joined by the local application of high-frequency sound waves as the work parts are held together under pressure. (DAC)
UF welding, ultrasonic
CN K.KT.AFU.ALO.HOE.BCW.ALO.AFU.ALO.BIQ.ALO

ultraviolet photography
KT.403 (L)
UF photography, ultraviolet
UV photography
CN K.KT.AFU.ALO.DUC.DIO.ARI.ARI.CFS.AXC

ultraviolet radiation
BM.866 (L,B,R)
UF radiation, ultraviolet
Radiation, UV
UV radiation
CN B.BM.CFS.AXC.ALO.AFU.ARI.ALO

ultraviolet stabilizers
MT.2330
UF stabilizers, ultraviolet
stabilizers, UV
UV stabilizers
CN M.MT.AFU.ARI.ALO.FIM.ALO

Ulúa
FL.1083
CN F.FL.ALO.ALO.ALO.ALO.ALO.AFU.BIQ

Uluzzian
FL.2473
CN F.FL.ALO.AXC.AFU.ARI.ALO.BOK

Umatilla
FL.1425 (L)
CN F.FL.ALO.ALO.ARI.AFU.BUE.ERE

Umaua
USE **Carijona**

Umayyad
FL.3595 (L)
UF Omayyad
CN F.FL.ALO.BIQ.AFU.ILG

umber
MT.1631
UF brown, Cappagh
Cappagh brown
Cyprus umber
terre d'ombre
Turkey umber
umber, Cyprus
umber, Turkey
umbra
CN M.MT.AFU.AFU.ARI.AFU.AFU.ALO.ALO.ARI.ARI.BCW

umber brown
USE **grayish brown**

umber, burnt
USE **burnt umber**

umber, burnt (color)
USE **grayish reddish brown**
moderate brown

umber, Cyprus
USE **umber**

umber, raw
USE **raw umber**

umber, raw (color)
USE **dark yellowish brown**
moderate brown
moderate yellowish brown

umber, Turkey
USE **umber**

umbra
USE **umber**

Umbra gebrannt
USE **burnt umber**

Umbra natur
USE **raw umber**

umbrella domes
RT.399
ALT **umbrella dome**
SN Melonlike ribbed domes (either exterior or interior) found especially in Islamic architecture. (HAS)
UF conch domes
domes, conch
domes, melon
domes, parachute
domes, pumpkin
domes, umbrella
melon domes
parachute domes
pumpkin domes
CN V.RT.AFU.AFU.AFU.BIQ.AFU.AFU.CFS

umbrella nails
TF.418
ALT **umbrella nail**
UF nails, umbrella
CN V.TF.AFU.AFU.AFU.ALO.AFU.CFS.AFU.DCU.CXA

umbrella stands
TG.656 (N)
ALT **umbrella stand**
UF stands, umbrella
CN V.TG.AFU.AFU.BIQ.BCW.ALO.EWY

Umbundu
USE **Mbundu**

Umiro
USE **Lango**

Umm an-Nar
FL.2889
CN F.FL.ALO.AXC.ARI.ALO.AFU.BCW

Unanimist
FL.3306 (L)
ALT **Unanimism**
CN F.FL.ALO.BCW.ALO.AXC.DCU.DIO

unbleached beeswax
MT.2193
UF beeswax, unbleached
cera flava
CN M.MT.AFU.AFU.ARI.BZY.AFU.AFU.AFU.ALO

unbroken
DC.75
UF continuous
CN D.DC.AFU.ARI.EFQ

unbuilt designs
USE **unbuilt projects**

unbuilt projects
BM.43
SN Use for planned works of architecture that were never physically produced. For works other than architecture, use **unexecuted designs**.
UF designs, unbuilt
projects, unbuilt
unbuilt designs
CN B.BM.AFU.AFU.ALO.CLM.ALO

unburnt brick
USE **sun-dried brick**

uncalcined gypsum
MT.524
SN An effective, economical retarder in cement, used to control the setting of Portland cements and concrete. (HORNB)
UF gypsum, uncalcined
CN M.MT.AFU.AFU.AFU.CFS.AFU.DUC.

AXC

uncentered barrel vaults
USE **pitched-brick vaults**

unconscious
BM.607 (R)
SN The greater part of the psychic apparatus accumulated through life experience that is not ordinarily integrated or available to consciousness, considered by many psychologists to be a powerful motive force in overt behavior. (W)
CN B.BM.BUE.DOI

unction, extreme
USE **extreme unction**

underbracing
USE **stretchers**

underburned brick
USE **soft brick**

undercoat
USE **primer**

undercoverings
USE **underlayment**

underdrawings
VD.103 (R)
ALT **underdrawing**
SN Drawings preliminary to other works of art that are actually incorporated into those works. (MAYER)
UF drawings, preliminary (underdrawings)
preliminary drawings (underdrawings)
preliminary sketches (underdrawings)
sketches, preliminary (underdrawings)
CN V.VD.AFU.ALO.BOK.AFU

underengraving, glass
USE **verre églomisé**

underengraving, glass foil
USE **verre églomisé**

underglaze
USE **underglazing**

underglazing
KT.871
ALT **underglazed**
SN In ceramics, the application of color to the surface of a clay body before application of a transparent glaze. (MAYER)
UF underglaze
CN K.KT.AFU.ALO.HOE.BOK.AXC.ARI.AXC

underground buildings
RK.1370 (A,L,B)
ALT **underground building**
UF buildings, underground
CN V.RK.AFU.ALO.ARI.AXC.BUE.ALO

underground markets
USE **underground shopping centers**

underground railroads
USE **subways**

underground railway systems
USE **subways**

underground railways
USE **subways**

underground reservoirs
RK.578 (A,L)
ALT **underground reservoir**
UF reservoirs, underground
CN V.RK.AFU.ALO.ALO.CFS.ALO.BCW.BIQ.ALO

underground shopping centers
RG.46 (A,L)
ALT **underground shopping center**
UF markets, underground
shopping centers, underground
underground markets
CN V.RG.AFU.AFU.AXC.ALO.AXC

underground structures
RK.1368 (A,L,R)
ALT **underground structure**
UF structures, underground
CN V.RK.AFU.ALO.ARI.AXC.BUE

underground vaults
USE **souterrains**

undergrounds
USE **subways**

underlayment
RT.750
SN Plywood, hardboard, or other material placed on a subfloor to provide a smooth, even surface for applying the finish.
UF undercoverings
CN V.RT.AFU.ALO.AFU.BIQ.ALO.ALO

underpainting
KT.245 (R)
ALT **underpainted**
SN Application of a layer of paint that is intended to be seen through a subsequent paint layer. (QUICK)
CN K.KT.AFU.ALO.DUC.CXA.ALO.ARI.ALO

underpainting, glass
USE **reverse painting on glass**

underpasses
RM.475 (A,L,B)
ALT **underpass**
SN Grade separations where clearance to traffic on the upper level is obtained by depressing partially or completely the grade of the lower level. (W)
CN V.RM.ALO.ALO.ALO.ALO.AXC.ALO

underpitch vaults
RT.535
ALT **underpitch vault**
SN Constructions formed by the penetration of two vaults of unequal size, springing from the same level. (DAC)
UF vaults, underpitch
vaults, Welsh
Welsh vaults
CN V.RT.AFU.AFU.AFU.BIQ.BOK.AFU.AFU.AFU.ALO.ALO.ARI

understory trees
RD.279
ALT **understory tree**
UF trees, understory
CN V.RD.ARI.AFU.BCW.ALO.ALO.ALO.ARI.ALO.ALO

undertakers
HG.434 (L)
ALT **undertaker**
SN Persons who prepare the dead for burial and arrange and manage funerals. (RHDEL2)
UF morticians
CN H.HG.AFU.AXC.BOK.FOG

undertone
BM.119
SN Use for a color seen through, and modifying other colors.
CN B.BM.AFU.AFU.ARI.BOK.ALO.AFU.CLM

underwater archaeology
KD.107 (A,L)
SN Branch of archaeology that deals with the recovery of ancient objects found beneath the sea, as shipwrecks or remains from submerged human settlements, and with the techniques of underwater exploration, excavation, and retrieval. (RHDEL2)
UF archaeology, marine
archaeology, submarine
archaeology, underwater
marine archaeology
submarine archaeology
CN K.KD.AFU.ALO.ALO.BIQ

underwater buildings
RK.1371 (A,B)
ALT **underwater building**
UF buildings, underwater
CN V.RK.AFU.ALO.ARI.AXC.BZY

underwater photography
KT.398 (L)
UF photography, submarine
photography, underwater
submarine photography
CN K.KT.AFU.ALO.DUC.DIO.ARI.ARI.BZY.BIQ

underwater structures
USE **submarine structures**

underwriting

USE **insuring**

undulate bands
DG.100
ALT **undulate band**
SN Running ornament in which the main element curves back and forth from one side of the band to the other.
UF bands, undulate
CN D.DG.AFU.ARI.AFU.ARI.AFU

undulating
DC.76
SN Having a wavelike outline of flowing compound curves; used, for example, with reference to architectural features such as arches, moldings, and tracery. For furniture pieces, the fronts of which have alternating concave and convex surfaces, use **serpentine.** For features consisting of or bounded by curved lines in general, use **curvilinear.**
CN D.DC.AFU.ARI.ELK

undulating moldings
USE **wave moldings**

undulating tracery
USE **flowing tracery**

unemployment
BM.384 (L,B)
SN The state of being without a paying job. (RHDEL2)
CN B.BM.ARI.BZY.AFU

Unetician
FL.2512
CN F.FL.ALO.AXC.AFU.BIQ.AFU.AXC

unexecuted designs
BM.33 (A,R)
SN Use for planned works of art or architecture that were never physically produced. For architecture more specifically, use **unbuilt projects.**
UF designs, unexecuted
projects, unrealized
unrealized projects
CN B.BM.AFU.AFU.ALO.AXC.AFU

unfilled plastic
MT.2106
UF plastic, unfilled
CN M.MT.AFU.AFU.ARI.BUE.ALO.ALO.ARI

unfired brick
USE **soft brick**
sun-dried brick

Ungava
FL.1213
UF Inuit, Québec
Québec Inuit
CN F.FL.ALO.ALO.ARI.AFU.AFU.AFU.ALO.AFU.BOK

Unified Silla Kingdom
FL.2113
UF Great Silla
Silla
Silla Kingdom, Unified
Silla Kingdom, United
Silla, Great
United Silla Kingdom
CN F.FL.ALO.ARI.ALO.ARI.AFU.ARI

uniform loads
BM.1020 (B)
UF loads, uniform
CN B.BM.CFS.AXC.CLM.ALO.ARI.DCU

unimproved land
USE **raw land**

unincorporated areas
RD.45
ALT **unincorporated area**
UF areas, unincorporated
CN V.RD.AFU.ARI.AXC

union catalogs
VW.102 (L)
ALT **union catalog**
SN Catalogs combining in alphabetical sequence the contents of a number of catalogs or the contents of more than one library or other collection. (AHD)
UF catalogs, union
CN V.VW.AFU.AFU.AFU.FZU.ALO.AFU.BOK

union labels
VW.761 (L)
ALT **union label**
SN Identifying marks attached to goods indicating they have been produced by union labor. (W)
UF labels, union
CN V.VW.AFU.ALO.ALO.ALO.ALO

union lists
VW.272 (L)
ALT **union list**
UF lists, union
CN V.VW.AFU.AFU.AFU.FZU.BCW.AFU.BZY

union locks
USE **preassembled locks**

union stations
RK.1242
ALT **union station**
UF stations, union
CN V.RK.AFU.ALO.ALO.GLI.AFU.ALO.AFU.ALO.AFU.AFU

unions
USE **trade unions**

unions, college
USE **student unions**

unions, credit
USE **credit unions**

unions, industrial
USE **trade unions**

unions, labor
USE **trade unions**

unions, student
USE **student unions**

unions, trade
USE **trade unions**

unique image photographs
USE **direct positives**

Unist
FL.3420 (R)
ALT **Unism**
CN F.FL.ALO.BCW.ALO.AXC.DIO.BZY.ALO.BOK

unit air conditioning
RT.1386
UF air conditioning, unit
systems, unit air conditioning
unit air conditioning systems
unit systems
CN V.RT.ALO.BCW.AFU.AFU.AFU.ARI

unit air conditioning systems
USE **unit air conditioning**

unit construction
USE **modular construction**

unit developments, planned
USE **planned unit developments**

unit furniture
TG.803 (L)
SN Describes furniture made in related units, so that pieces such as wardrobes, chests, cupboards, bookcases, or writing desks, made in standard sizes, may be conveniently added to and rearranged.
UF furniture, unit
CN V.TG.AFU.ARI.CFS

unit locks
USE **preassembled locks**

unit systems
USE **unit air conditioning**

United Silla Kingdom
USE **Unified Silla Kingdom**

units, baseboard
USE **baseboard units**

units, emergency
USE **emergency medical centers**

units, flash
USE **flash attachments**

units, heat-distributing
USE **heat-distributing units**

units, masonry
USE **masonry units**

units, single dwelling
USE **single-family dwellings**

unity
BM.104 (L,B)
SN Appearance or condition of oneness or wholeness.
CN B.BM.AFU.AFU.ARI.BIQ

universal clamps
TB.1059
ALT **universal clamp**
SN Clamps consisting of two double-cranked arms with swivel shoes connected by a system of levers actuated by a central threaded rod which also carries a round shoe; usually used for corner-clamping large mitered frames. (SALAM)
UF clamps, combination
clamps, hexagon
clamps, universal
combination clamps
hexagon clamps
CN V.TB.AFU.BCW.CFS.ALO.ALO.BCW.CFS

universal dynamism
USE **dynamism**

universal strikes
TF.520
ALT **universal strike**
UF strikes, universal
CN V.TF.AFU.ALO.AFU.ALO.BCW

universities
RK.847 (A,L,B,R)
ALT **university**
CN V.RK.AFU.ALO.ALO.CXA.ARI.AXC.BIQ.ARI

universities, municipal
USE **urban universities**

universities, state
USE **state universities**

universities, urban
USE **urban universities**

university cities
USE **university towns**

university towns
RD.59 (L)
ALT **university town**
UF cities, university
towns, university
university cities
CN V.RD.AFU.AXC.CFS

Unkei
FL.2105
CN F.FL.ALO.ARI.ALO.ALO.ALO.BCW.BOK

Unkoku School
FL.2072
CN F.FL.ALO.ARI.ALO.ALO.ALO.ARI.FIM

unofficial art
USE **dissident art**

unrealized projects
USE **unexecuted designs**

unskilled labor
HG.30 (L)
SN Manual workers whose tasks require little or no training or experience. (ERIC)
UF labor, unskilled
unskilled workers
workers, unskilled
CN H.HG.AFU.AXC.ALO.BCW

unskilled workers
USE **unskilled labor**

unslaked lime
USE **quicklime**

unsymmetrical loads
USE **eccentric loads**

up-and-down sawmills
TB.806 (N)
ALT **up-and-down sawmill**
SN Machines which utilize a frame to support a vertical saw blade that moves up and down. (DISSTO)
UF sawmills, up-and-down
CN V.TB.AFU.BCW.CFS.AFU.BCW.AXC

up-and-down saws
USE **felloe saws**

upfeed systems
RT.1449
ALT **upfeed system**
UF systems, upfeed
upfeed water distribution
water distribution, upfeed
CN V.RT.ALO.BCW.ALO.AFU.ALO.ALO

upfeed water distribution
USE **upfeed systems**

upholstered joined backstools
USE **farthingale chairs**

upholsterers
HG.563
ALT **upholsterer**
CN H.HG.AFU.AXC.BUE.AXC.BUE.AXC

upholstering
USE **upholstery**

upholstery
KT.724
ALT **upholstered**
SN Covering with padding and fabric. (W)
UF upholstering
CN K.KT.AFU.ALO.GRC.DUC

upholstery studs
TF.492
ALT **upholstery stud**
UF studs, upholstery
CN V.TF.AFU.AFU.AFU.ALO.AFU.ELK.AFU

upper
DC.44
CN D.DC.AFU.ALO.ARI.EFQ

upper classes
HG.887 (L,R)
ALT **upper class**
UF classes, upper
CN H.HG.ALO.DOI.ALO.ARI

Upper Lithic
USE **Paleo-Indian**

Upper Paleolithic
FL.11
UF Paleolithic, Upper
CN F.FL.AFU.BCW.AFU.AFU.ARI

Upper Perigordian
FL.2471
UF Perigordian, Upper
CN F.FL.ALO.AXC.AFU.ARI.ALO.BCW.ALO

Upper Republican
FL.923
UF Republican, Upper
CN F.FL.ALO.ALO.ALO.AFU.ALO.ARI.AXC.BIQ

Upper Sepik
FL.3657
CN F.FL.ALO.BOK.ALO.BCW.ALO.BCW.ALO.AXC

upper stages
RM.379
ALT **upper stage**
SN Use for the upper level stages in Elizabethan and contemporary European theaters, including the chamber and tarrase in Elizabethan theaters, although the extent of its existence is controversial.
UF stages, upper
CN V.RM.AFU.DIO.AXC.AXC.ALO.BUE.AFU

Upper Tanana
USE **Tanana**

upright locks
TF.225
ALT **upright lock**
SN Locks whose major dimension is vertical. (STEIN)
UF locks, upright
CN V.TF.AFU.AFU.AFU.AFU.DIO.BIQ.AFU.EWY

upright-top tables
USE **tilt-top tables**

uprights
USE **back rails**

upset forging
KT.847 (L)
UF forging, upset
jumping up
CN K.KT.AFU.ALO.HOE.BCW.ALO.BIQ.ALO.AFU

Ur III
USE **Third Dynasty of Ur**

Urabá
FL.1671
UF Uruba
CN F.FL.ALO.ALO.ARI.ARI.BCW.EFQ

uranium
MT.451 (L,R)
CN M.MT.AFU.AFU.AFU.BZY.AFU.AFU.ARI.DZW

uranium yellow
MT.1795
UF yellow, uranium
CN M.MT.AFU.AFU.ARI.AFU.AFU.ALO.ALO.BUE.ARI.CXA

Urartian
FL.2859
CN F.FL.ALO.AXC.ARI.AFU.AFU.AXC

urban areas
RG.296 (L)
ALT **urban area**
SN Areas within city limits or closely linked to them by common use of public utilities or services. (DAC)
UF areas, urban
CN V.RG.ALO.ALO.BOK

urban atlases
USE **city atlases**

urban beautification
BM.1066 (L,R)
UF beautification, urban
city beautification
CN B.BM.CLM.ALO.AFU.AFU.AFU

urban blight
BM.1084
UF blight
CN B.BM.CLM.ALO.AXC.ALO

urban centers
USE **central cities**

urban communities
USE **cities**

urban decay
BM.1123
UF decay, urban
CN B.BM.CRG.BCW.CRG

urban design
USE **city planning**

urban development
BM.1071 (A,L,R)
UF development, urban
development, urban economic
urban economic development
CN B.BM.CLM.ALO.ALO.AFU.ALO

urban economic development
USE **urban development**

urban forestry
KD.236 (A,L)
UF city forestry
forestry, city
forestry, urban
CN K.KD.AFU.ARI.BOK.AFU.AFU

urban forests
RD.301
ALT **urban forest**
UF forests, urban
CN V.RD.ARI.ALO.ALO.BIQ.ALO.ALO

urban fringes
RG.297 (A)
ALT **urban fringe**
SN Use for settlement areas lying at the periphery of cities or suburbs where urban land uses meet rural land uses.
UF fringes, urban
rural fringes
rural-urban fringes
CN V.RG.ALO.ALO.BUE

urban geography
KD.137 (L)
UF geography, urban
CN K.KD.AFU.ALO.BZY.AXC

urban historians
HG.267 (A)
ALT **urban historian**
UF historians, urban
CN H.HG.AFU.AXC.BCW.AFU.BOK.AFU.ALO

urban history
KD.146 (L,B)
UF cities, history of
history of cities
history, urban
CN K.KD.AFU.ALO.CLM.AFU.BIQ

urban houses
USE **town houses**

urban infrastructure
USE **infrastructure**

urban land use
BM.1047 (L,R)
UF land use, urban
use, urban land
CN B.BM.CLM.AFU.AFU.ARI

urban landscapes
RD.295
ALT **urban landscape**
SN Landscapes with densely built-up districts and settlement areas and with distinctive skylines. (LNDECO)
UF landscapes, urban
CN V.RD.ARI.ALO.ALO.BCW

urban mass transit rail systems
USE **urban rail systems**

urban noise
USE **city noise**

urban parks
RK.1461 (A)
ALT **urban park**
SN Small parks serving central business districts, highly urban areas (including new towns), or commercial districts. (RPD)
UF city parks
city-wide parks
metropolitan parks
parks, city
parks, metropolitan
parks, urban
CN V.RK.ALO.ALO.ARI.AFU.BCW

urban planners
USE **city planners**

urban planning
USE **city planning**

urban rail
USE **urban rail systems**

urban rail systems
RD.114
ALT **urban rail system**
SN Includes rail transit systems serving primarily urban areas.
UF mass transit rail systems, urban
metropolitan railways
rail systems, urban
railways, metropolitan
systems, urban rail
transit systems, urban rail
urban mass transit rail systems
urban rail
urban rail transit systems
CN V.RD.ALO.ARI.AFU.ALO.AXC.AFU

urban rail transit systems
USE **urban rail systems**

urban rapid transit systems
USE **urban transit systems**

urban rapid transportation systems
USE **urban transit systems**

urban redevelopment
USE **urban renewal**

urban renewal
BM.1075 (L,B,R)
UF redevelopment, urban
renewal, urban
urban redevelopment
CN B.BM.CLM.ALO.ALO.AFU.ALO.AXC

urban-rural migration
BM.1056 (L)
SN Population shift from an urban to a rural environment. (LCSH)
UF migration, urban-rural
CN B.BM.CLM.AFU.ALO.ARI.BCW

urban sociology
KD.192 (L)
UF sociology, urban
CN K.KD.AFU.ALO.ELK.AXC

urban sprawl
BM.1085
UF sprawl, urban
CN B.BM.CLM.ALO.AXC.ARI

urban studies
KD.193 (L)
UF studies, urban
CN K.KD.AFU.ALO.ERE

urban transit
USE **urban transit systems**

urban transit systems
RD.113 (A,L)
ALT **urban transit system**
SN May include rail transit or free-wheeled systems.
UF rapid transit systems, urban
systems, urban transit
transit systems, urban
transit, urban
transportation systems, urban
urban rapid transit systems
urban rapid transportation systems
urban transit
urban transportation systems
CN V.RD.ALO.ARI.AFU.ALO.AXC

urban transportation
BM.1148 (A,L)
SN Use for general transportation in urban areas, whether by transit systems or private means.
UF city transportation
metropolitan transportation
municipal transportation
transportation, city
transportation, metropolitan
transportation, municipal
transportation, urban
CN B.BM.DCU.AFU.ALO

urban transportation systems
USE **urban transit systems**

urban universities
RK.849 (L)
ALT **urban university**
UF municipal universities
universities, municipal
universities, urban
CN V.RK.AFU.ALO.ALO.CXA.ARI.AXC.BIQ.ARI.ALO

urban views
USE **city views**

urbanists
USE **city planners**

urbanization
BM.1082 (A,L,R)
CN B.BM.CLM.ALO.AXC

urea-aminoplastic
USE **urea-formaldehyde resin**

urea formaldehyde
USE **urea-formaldehyde resin**

urea-formaldehyde resin
MT.2164 (L)
UF formaldehyde, urea
resin, urea
resin, urea-formaldehyde
urea-aminoplastic
urea formaldehyde
urea resin
CN M.MT.AFU.AFU.ARI.BUE.ALO.AXC.ALO.ARI.ALO

urea resin
USE **urea-formaldehyde resin**

urethane elastomer
MT.2096
UF elastomer, urethane
CN M.MT.AFU.AFU.ARI.BUE.AFU.AFU.CXA

urethane resin
USE **polyurethane**

Urfirnis ware
FL.2663
UF ware, Urfirnis
CN F.FL.ALO.AXC.ALO.AFU.ALO.AXC.AXC.BZY

Urhobo
FL.255 (L)
UF Sobo
CN F.FL.ALO.AFU.AXC.AFU.ALO.ALO.BUE

urinals
RT.1491 (L,N,B)
ALT **urinal**
SN Plumbing fixtures for receiving and draining away urine. (PBCD)
CN V.RT.ALO.BCW.ALO.ARI.CFS.BUE

urn back chairs
USE **shield-back chairs**

urn stands
USE **kettle stands**

urn tables
USE **kettle stands**

Urnes Style
FL.3150 (R)
CN F.FL.ALO.BCW.ALO.ALO.AFU.BOK.ARI.BUE.AXC

Urnfield
FL.2513
CN F.FL.ALO.AXC.AFU.BIQ.AFU.BCW

Uru
FL.1614 (L)
UF Huno
Puquina
CN F.FL.ALO.ALO.ARI.ARI.ALO.AFU.CLM

Uruba
USE Urabá

Uruguayan
FL.724 (L,B)
CN F.FL.ALO.ALO.AFU.AXC.BUE

Uruk
FL.2962
UF Protoliterate A-B
Warka
CN F.FL.ALO.AXC.ARI.BCW.AFU.ALO.ALO

use
BM.212 (L)
UF utilization
CN B.BM.AFU.ALO.CFS

use, dedication to public
USE **dedication to public use**

use, land
USE **land use**

use, mixed
USE **mixed use**

use, rural land
USE **rural land use**

use, urban land
USE **urban land use**

used car lots
RK.1512
ALT **used car lot**
UF car lots, used
lots, used car
CN V.RK.ALO.ALO.BIQ.ALO.ALO

user groups
HG.830
ALT **user group**
SN Members of a particular library's target groups and others who actually use the collection or services of the library.(ALAG) Also, formal or informal groups of people who use a particular database or retrieval product. (GROSCH)
UF groups, user
CN H.HG.ALO.BCW.CLM

users
HG.743
ALT **user**
SN Use generally for people who use any product or service of the information industry, such as software, thesauri, or indexes, including those who themselves use such resources to provide information services to others. For clients or patrons of a library, information center, or information retrieval service, prefer the more specific term **end users.**
CN H.HG.AFU.BCW.HIK

users, end
USE **end users**

Uspantec
FL.1546 (L)
CN F.FL.ALO.ALO.ARI.ALO.BIQ.AFU.CXA

ustrina
RK.463
ALT **ustrinum**
SN Designates ancient Roman places for burning corpses.
CN V.RK.AFU.ALO.ALO.BOK.ARI.AFU.

AFU.ALO

Usulután
FL.1049
CN F.FL.ALO.ALO.ALO.ALO.AFU.ALO.ARI.ALO.ALO.AXC

ut pictura poesis
BM.324 (R)
SN Use with reference to the various interpretations of this phrase from Horace's Ars Poetica in relation to pictorial arts.
CN B.BM.AFU.AXC.ELK.BOK

Utagawa School
FL.2096 (L)
CN F.FL.ALO.ARI.ALO.ALO.ALO.AXC.BZY.CRG

Ute
FL.1320 (L)
CN F.FL.ALO.ALO.ARI.AFU.AXC.CLM

utensils, fireplace
USE **firesets**

Uthman I
USE **Osman I**

Uthman III
USE **Osman III**

Uthong
USE **Tong**

utilitarianism
BM.528 (L,R)
SN Doctrine that usefulness is the highest good and that the determining characteristic of right conduct should be the usefulness of its consequence.
CN B.BM.BIQ.AXC.FIM

utilities
RD.116 (L,R)
ALT **utility**
SN Use for the basic service systems required for developed areas; for the government-regulated enterprises providing such services, use **public utilities.**
CN V.RD.ALO.AXC

utilities, bibliographic
USE **bibliographic utilities**

utilities, electric
USE **electric utilities**

utilities, municipal
USE **public utilities**

utilities, public
USE **public utilities**

utility cabinets
TG.444
ALT **utility cabinet**
UF cabinets, utility
CN V.TG.AFU.AFU.AXC.ALO.ARI.ALO.DZW

utility furniture
TG.805 (B)
SN Furniture of simple design which makes the most economical use of materials and labor; generally austere, well-proportioned, and unornamented.
UF furniture, utility
CN V.TG.AFU.ARI.CLM

utility hooks
TF.157
ALT **utility hook**
UF hooks, utility
CN V.TF.AFU.AFU.AFU.AFU.CXA.BOK

utility knives
TB.130 (N)
ALT **utility knife**
SN Cutting knives with a single-edge razor blade held between the two sides of the knife. (PUTNAM)
UF board knives
craft knives
knives, board
knives, craft
knives, utility
CN V.TB.AFU.ARI.AXC.ALO.BUE.ARI

utility plans
VD.53
ALT **utility plan**
UF plans, utility
CN V.VD.AFU.AFU.BIQ.ALO.AXC.ALO.BIQ

utility poles
RM.512 (L,N)
ALT **utility pole**
UF poles, telephone
poles, utility
telephone poles
CN V.RM.ALO.ALO.ARI.ARI

utility rooms
RM.218 (A)
ALT **utility room**
SN Rooms designed or used to house heating, laundry, or general maintenance equipment. (W)
UF rooms, utility
CN V.RM.AFU.DIO.ALO.DIO.BIQ

utilization
USE **use**

utilization, space
USE **space utilization**

Utina
USE **Timucua**

utopias
BM.567 (A,L,B,R)
SN Places of ideal perfection, especially with regard to laws, government, and social conditions.
UF ideal states
states, ideal
CN B.BM.BOK.CRG

Utpala
FL.2160
CN F.FL.ALO.ARI.AXC.AFU.AXC.AFU.ARI

Utrecht Psalter Style
USE **Reims Style**

UV photography
USE **ultraviolet photography**

UV radiation
USE **ultraviolet radiation**

UV stabilizers
USE **ultraviolet stabilizers**

Uwharrie
FL.829
CN F.FL.ALO.ALO.ALO.AFU.ALO.ALO.ALO.AXC

Uygur
USE **Uighur**

Uzbek
FL.3598 (L)
UF Ozbeg
Shaibanid
Shaybanid
CN F.FL.ALO.BIQ.AFU.IRA

V-gouges
USE **parting tools**

V-joints
TF.697
ALT **V-joint**
SN Joints at the edges of wood boards, formed so that a corresponding indented and projecting V meet.
CN V.TF.ALO.ARI.AXC.ARI.CRG

V-joints (mortar joints)
USE **V-shaped joints**

V-lip tongs
USE **hollow-bit tongs**

V-shaped joints
TF.629
ALT **V-shaped joint**
UF joints, V-shaped
V-joints (mortar joints)
V-tooled joints
CN V.TF.ALO.ARI.ALO.AFU.ARI.AXC.AXC

V-tooled joints
USE **V-shaped joints**

V.I.P. lounges
RM.176 (A)
ALT **V.I.P. lounge**
SN Lounges reserved for privileged and important individuals.
UF lounges, V.I.P.
CN V.RM.AFU.DIO.ALO.CXA.BZY.AFU

VA hospitals
USE **veterans' hospitals**

vacant land
USE **raw land**

vacant lots
RK.1589 (L)
ALT **vacant lot**
UF lots, vacant
CN V.RK.ALO.ARI.BUE.AFU

vacation homes
USE **vacation houses**

vacation houses
RK.279 (A,L,B)
ALT **vacation house**
UF holiday houses
homes, vacation
houses, holiday
houses, vacation
houses, weekend
vacation homes
weekend houses
CN V.RK.AFU.ALO.ALO.AXC.ALO.
ALO.ARI.ALO

vaccination centers
RK.739 (A,L)
ALT **vaccination center**
UF centers, immunization
centers, vaccination
immunization centers
CN V.RK.AFU.ALO.ALO.CXA.ALO.AFU.
AFU.AXC

vacuum brazing
KT.797 (L)
UF brazing, vacuum
CN K.KT.AFU.ALO.HOE.BCW.ALO.
AFU.AFU.AFU.BOK

vacuum forming
KT.152
SN Forming process in which heated plastic sheet is drawn against the mold surface by evacuating the air between it and the mold. (STEIN)
UF forming, vacuum
CN K.KT.AFU.ALO.DOI.CRG.BIQ

vacuum heating
RT.1400
UF heating, vacuum
CN V.RT.ALO.BCW.AFU.AFU.ARI.BCW.
AFU

Vai
FL.334 (L)
UF Vei
CN F.FL.ALO.AFU.AXC.AFU.ARI.BCW.
CXA

Vaisali (Nepalese)
FL.2171
UF Vasali
CN F.FL.ALO.ARI.AXC.AFU.AXC.ALO.
BCW

Vaishnavism
USE **Vaisnavism**

Vaisnavism
BM.663 (L)
ALT **Vaisnava**
UF Vaishnavism
CN B.BM.BZY.AFU.AXC.ARI

vaisseliers
USE **cupboards**

Vajrayana
BM.615 (L)
UF Buddhism, Vajrayana
Diamond Vehicle
Mantrayana
Tantric Buddhism
Tantrism (Buddhist)
Vajrayana Buddhism
CN B.BM.BZY.AFU.AFU.AXC

Vajrayana Buddhism
USE **Vajrayana**

valance lighting
RT.1378
UF lighting, valance
CN V.RT.ALO.AXC.AXC.ALO.ARI

Valdivia
FL.1113
CN F.FL.ALO.ALO.ALO.ARI.ALO.AFU

Valenciennes lace
MT.1872 (R)
SN Flat bobbin lace worked in one piece with the same thread forming both the ground and design. (EOT)
UF lace, Valenciennes
CN M.MT.AFU.AFU.ARI.ALO.ALO.
ALO.ALO.CXA.AFU.AFU

valentine's day cards
USE **valentines**

valentines
VW.571 (L,R)
ALT **valentine**
SN Greeting cards sent to a sweetheart on Saint Valentine's Day. (AHD)
UF valentine's day cards
CN V.VW.AFU.ALO.AFU.ARI.BOK.BCW

vales
USE **valleys**

valla
RT.1184
ALT **vallum**
SN Ramparts, especially palisaded ramparts, with which the Romans enclosed their camps. (HAS)
CN V.RT.AFU.BUE.AFU.BCW.AFU.AXC.
AFU

valley gutters
RT.1463
ALT **valley gutter**
UF gutters, valley
CN V.RT.ALO.BCW.ALO.ARI.BCW.AXC

valley jacks
RT.501
ALT **valley jack**
UF jacks, valley
CN V.RT.AFU.AFU.AFU.BIQ.ARI.ALO.
ALO.AFU.ARI.AFU

valley oak
USE **California white oak**

valley rafters
RT.503
ALT **valley rafter**
SN Use for rafters directly along the valley, at the intersection of two sloping planes.
UF rafters, valley
CN V.RT.AFU.AFU.AFU.BIQ.ARI.ALO.
ALO.AFU.BCW

valley tile
MT.188
SN A special roof tile, shaped and laid to form a valley. (DAC)
UF tile, valley
CN M.MT.AFU.AFU.AFU.AXC.ALO.
ALO.ALO.AFU.ALO.AXC.AFU.ARI.
BCW

Valley Yokuts
USE **Yokuts**

valleys
RD.210 (L)
ALT **valley**
SN Land depressions having a more flattish landscape, with less precipitous slopes, than canyons or gorges.
UF vales
CN V.RD.ARI.AFU.AXC.AFU.ALO.ALO.
AFU

valleys (roof components)
RT.491
ALT **valley (roof component)**
SN Internal angles in a roof formed by the meeting of two slopes.
UF roof valleys
CN V.RT.AFU.AFU.AFU.BIQ.ARI.ALO.
AFU.CRG

valonia oak
MT.1254 (L)
UF oak, valonia
CN M.MT.AFU.AFU.ALO.BIQ.DCU.
AFU.AFU.AFU.IRA.EWY

valuation
USE **appraising**

valuation, land
USE **land valuation**

Valuchazi
USE **Luchazi**

value
BM.414
UF economic value
value, economic
CN B.BM.ARI.FOG

value analysis
USE **cost benefit analysis**

value (color)

BM.136
SN Use for the degree of lightness or darkness of a color, white having the lightest value and black the darkest. When referring generally to the relative degree of lightness or darkness of a surface, use **brightness.**
UF brightness (color)
CN B.BM.AFU.AFU.ARI.BOK.ALO.ALO.ALO.BOK

value drawings
USE **tone drawings**

value engineering
USE **cost benefit analysis**

value theory
USE **axiology**

value, economic
USE **value**

value, philosophy of
USE **axiology**

value, theory of
USE **axiology**

values, tactile
USE **tactile values**

valves
TF.277 (L)
ALT **valve**
CN V.TF.AFU.AFU.AFU.AFU.EWY

valves, ball
USE **ball valves**

valves, float
USE **float valves**

valves, flush
USE **flush valves**

valves, foot pedal
USE **foot pedal valves**

valves, mixing pressure
USE **mixing pressure valves**

valves, shut-off
USE **shut-off valves**

valves, soap
USE **soap valves**

Van Dyke brown
MT.1623
SN Bituminous lignite or brown coal, containing manganese, obtained by open-cast mining, thus a natural organic pigment of vegetable origin. (MAYER)
UF bituminous earth
brown, Rubens'
brown, Van Dyke
Cassel earth
Cologne earth
earth of cullen
earth, bituminous
earth, Cassel
earth, Cologne
Kasslerbraun
Rubens' brown
terre de Cassel
CN M.MT.AFU.AFU.ARI.AFU.AFU.ALO.ALO.ARI.ALO.BOK

Van Dyke brown (color)
USE **grayish brown**
moderate brown

Van Dyke brown photoprints
USE **brownprints**

Van Dyke photoprints
USE **brownprints**

Van Dyke prints (brownprints)
USE **brownprints**

Van Dyke prints (sepia prints)
USE **sepia prints**

Van Eyck green
USE **verdigris**

Van Niekirk Ruins
FL.143
CN F.FL.ALO.AFU.ALO.ARI.BIQ

vanadium
MT.452 (L)
CN M.MT.AFU.AFU.AFU.BZY.AFU.AFU.ARI.EFQ

Vandal
FL.3114 (L,R)
CN F.FL.ALO.BCW.ALO.ALO.AFU.BOK.ALO.ALO.BOK

vandalism
BM.1100 (L,B,R)
UF destruction of property
property, destruction of
CN B.BM.CRG.BCW.ALO.ARI

vanishing area
BM.158
SN In a perspective system, an area where orthogonals converge in a general vicinity rather than a single point. (ARTBUL)
UF area, vanishing
CN B.BM.AFU.AFU.ARI.BOK.CFS.BIQ

vanishing axis
BM.159
SN Use for the axis toward which parallel lines converge in an axial perspective system.
UF axis, vanishing
CN B.BM.AFU.AFU.ARI.BOK.CFS.BOK

vanishing point
BM.160
UF point, vanishing
CN B.BM.AFU.AFU.ARI.BOK.CFS.BUE

vanities
USE **dressing tables**

vanity stools
USE **dressing stools**

Vanuatu
FL.3671 (L)
UF New Hebrides
CN F.FL.ALO.BOK.ALO.BUE

vapor barrier paint
USE **dampproofing paint**

vapor barriers
MT.2417
SN A moisture-impervious layer or coating, such as special paint or a membrane on roofing felt or on building paper, which prevents the passage of moisture or vapor into a material or structure. (DAC)
UF barriers, vapor
CN M.MT.AFU.ARI.BZY.BUE

vapor baths
USE **steam baths**

vapor pressure
BM.934 (L)
UF pressure, vapor
CN B.BM.CFS.AXC.BUE.AXC

vapor, water
USE **water vapor**

vaporization casting
USE **lost-wax process**

Varakhsha
FL.1825
CN F.FL.ALO.ARI.AFU.AXC.ELK.CLM.AXC

vargueños
TG.540
ALT **vargeuño**
SN 19th-century term for Spanish full-front writing cabinets, taking the form of a rectangular chest supported on a decorative trestle stand, called a pie de puente. The interior is often elaborately decorated and generally contains tiers of drawers which may be supplemented with pigeonholes and a small cupboard.
UF bargueños
escritorios
CN V.TG.AFU.AFU.AXC.ALO.BZY.BUE.ARI

variable hangers
TF.365
ALT **variable hanger**
UF hangers, variable
CN V.TF.AFU.AFU.AFU.ALO.AFU.BOK.ARI.ARI.ALO.ALO

variants
USE **versions**

variation orders
USE **change orders**

variegated limestone
MT.694
UF limestone, variegated
CN M.MT.AFU.AFU.AFU.DCU.AFU.

ALO.AFU.ALO.ALO.ALO.BCW

variegated marble
MT.803
UF marble, variegated
marble, veined
veined marble
CN M.MT.AFU.AFU.AFU.DCU.AFU.ARI.ARI.ARI.BIQ

variety shops
USE **variety stores**

variety stores
RK.186 (L)
ALT **variety store**
UF dime stores
five-and-dimes
five-and-ten-cent stores
five-and-tens
shops, variety
stores, dime
stores, five-and-ten-cent
stores, ten-cent
stores, variety
ten-cent stores
variety shops
CN V.RK.AFU.ALO.ALO.ALO.ARI.BIQ.ALO.DIO

variety theaters
RK.943 (L,B)
ALT **variety theater**
UF theaters, variety
CN V.RK.AFU.ALO.ALO.EFQ.ARI.BCW.ALO.AXC

varifocal lenses
USE **zoom lenses**

varnish
MT.2470 (L,B,R)
SN A solution of a resin in drying oil, which when spread out in a thin film, dries and hardens by evaporation of the volatile solvent, or by the oxidation of the oil, or both. Leaves a smooth, glossy coating on the surface. (MH12)
UF vernice liquida
CN M.MT.AFU.ARI.CRG.AFU.BOK

varnish stain
MT.2468
SN A varnish which is colored with a transparent material, leaving a colored coating on the surface; has less penetrating power than a true stain. (DAC)
UF stain, varnish
CN M.MT.AFU.ARI.CRG.AFU.BIQ.AXC

varnish, burnt-oil
USE **litho varnish**

varnish, coach
USE **coach varnish**

varnish, coachbuilder's
USE **coach varnish**

varnish, cold cut
USE **simple solution varnish**

varnish, finishing
USE **finishing varnish**

varnish, flat
USE **flat varnish**

varnish, floor
USE **finishing varnish**

varnish, gold
USE **gold varnish**

varnish, intermediate
USE **intermediate varnish**

varnish, isolating
USE **isolating varnish**

varnish, litho
USE **litho varnish**

varnish, matte
USE **flat varnish**

varnish, mixing
USE **mixing varnish**

varnish, oil
USE **oil varnish**

varnish, picture
USE **picture varnish**

varnish, retouch
USE **retouch varnish**

varnish, rubbing
USE **rubbing varnish**

varnish, shellac
USE **shellac**

varnish, simple solution
USE **simple solution varnish**

varnish, spar
USE **spar varnish**

varnish, spirit
USE **spirit varnish**

varnish, yellow
USE **yellow varnish**

varnishes, copal
USE **copal varnishes**

varnishing
KT.673 (L)
ALT **varnished**
SN The application to a surface of a resin in a volatile solvent, which dries to a hard, glossy, and usually transparent film. (MAYER)
CN K.KT.AFU.ALO.GRC.AFU.BOK

varnolene
USE **mineral spirits**

Vasali
USE **Vaisali (Nepalese)**

Vasara
USE **Vesara**

vase back chairs
USE **shield-back chairs**

Vaseline (TM)
USE **petroleum jelly**

Vasiliki ware
FL.2674
UF ware, Vasiliki
CN F.FL.ALO.AXC.ALO.AFU.ALO.AXC.BCW.CFS

Vat Kukut
USE **Wat Kukut**

vats
USE **wats**

vault bays
RT.564
ALT **vault bay**
SN Areas of vaulting limited by two transverse ribs. (HAS)
UF bays (vault components)
bays, vault
severies
CN V.RT.AFU.AFU.AFU.BIQ.BOK.ALO.ARI

vault cells
USE **vaulting cells**

vault ribs
USE **ribs**

vaulting capitals
RT.565
ALT **vaulting capital**
SN Use for the capitals of piers or colonnettes that appear to support vaults or ribs of vaults.
UF capitals, vaulting
CN V.RT.AFU.AFU.AFU.BIQ.BOK.ALO.AXC

vaulting cells
RT.566
ALT **vaulting cell**
SN Use for those compartments between the groins or ribs of a vault.
UF cells (vault components)
cells, vault
cells, vaulting
compartments, vaulting
spandrels (vaulting cells)
vault cells
vaulting compartments
webs
CN V.RT.AFU.AFU.AFU.BIQ.BOK.ALO.BCW

vaulting compartments
USE **vaulting cells**

vaulting courses
RT.567
ALT **vaulting course**
SN Horizontal courses made up of the abutments or springers of a vault;

generally made of stones set in projection or corbeled out, with horizontal beds. (RS)
UF courses, vaulting
CN V.RT.AFU.AFU.AFU.BIQ.BOK.ALO.BIQ

vaults
RT.521 (A,L,B,R)
ALT vault
SN Arched structures, usually of masonry and usually forming a ceiling or roof.
CN V.RT.AFU.AFU.AFU.BIQ.BOK.AFU

vaults (strong rooms)
RM.147 (L)
ALT **vault (strong room)**
SN Rooms for the safekeeping of valuables, commonly built of steel. (W)
UF rooms, strong
strong rooms
CN V.RM.AFU.DIO.ALO.BZY.AXC

vaults (tomb spaces)
RM.387 (A,L,B)
ALT **vault (tomb space)**
SN Use for spaces or containers for a casket in a burial site.
CN V.RM.AFU.DIO.AXC.BCW.ARI

vaults, annular
USE **annular vaults**

vaults, barrel
USE **barrel vaults**

vaults, canted
USE **pitched-brick vaults**

vaults, Catalan
USE **pitched-brick vaults**

vaults, cloister
USE **cloister vaults**

vaults, cloistered
USE **cloister vaults**

vaults, compound
USE **compound vaults**

vaults, conical
USE **expanding vaults**

vaults, conoidal
USE **conoidal vaults**

vaults, convex conoidal
USE **convex conoidal vaults**

vaults, corbel
USE **corbel vaults**

vaults, coved
USE **cloister vaults**

vaults, cradle
USE **barrel vaults**

vaults, cross
USE **groined vaults**

vaults, domical
USE **domical vaults**

vaults, eight-part
USE **octopartite vaults**

vaults, expanding
USE **expanding vaults**

vaults, fan
USE **fan vaults**

vaults, four-part
USE **quadripartite vaults**

vaults, groined
USE **groined vaults**

vaults, Guastavino
USE **Guastavino vaults**

vaults, half barrel
USE **half barrel vaults**

vaults, handkerchief
USE **pendentive domes**

vaults, hexapartite
USE **sexpartite vaults**

vaults, inclined barrel
USE **inclined barrel vaults**

vaults, lierne
USE **lierne vaults**

vaults, net
USE **net vaults**

vaults, octopartite
USE **octopartite vaults**

vaults, pitched-brick
USE **pitched-brick vaults**

vaults, ploughshare
USE **plowshare vaults**

vaults, plowshare
USE **plowshare vaults**

vaults, quadripartite
USE **quadripartite vaults**

vaults, rampant
USE **rampant barrel vaults**

vaults, rampant barrel
USE **rampant barrel vaults**

vaults, rear
USE **back arches**

vaults, sail
USE **pendentive domes**

vaults, sexpartite
USE **sexpartite vaults**

vaults, simple
USE **simple vaults**

vaults, six-part
USE **sexpartite vaults**

vaults, solid
USE **solid vaults**

vaults, spiral
USE **spiral vaults**

vaults, star
USE **stellar vaults**

vaults, star-ribbed
USE **stellar vaults**

vaults, stellar
USE **stellar vaults**

vaults, stilted
USE **stilted vaults**

vaults, surbased
USE **surbased vaults**

vaults, surmounted
USE **surmounted vaults**

vaults, thin masonry
USE **timbrel vaults**

vaults, three-part
USE **tripartite vaults**

vaults, timbrel
USE **timbrel vaults**

vaults, transverse barrel
USE **barrel vaults**

vaults, tripartite
USE **tripartite vaults**

vaults, tunnel
USE **barrel vaults**

vaults, uncentered barrel
USE **pitched-brick vaults**

vaults, underground
USE **souterrains**

vaults, underpitch
USE **underpitch vaults**

vaults, wagonhead
USE **barrel vaults**

vaults, Welsh
USE **underpitch vaults**

vaults, wine
USE **wine cellars**

vawcers
USE **voussoirs**

VDTs
USE **monitors**

VDUs
USE **monitors**

vectors
BM.831
CN B.BM.CFS.ARI.CXA

Vedic
FL.2190 (L)
UF Aryan
CN F.FL.ALO.ARI.AXC.ALO.AFU.ALO

vedute

VB.80 (A,R)
ALT **veduta**
SN Use for topographical views, especially 18th-century Italian paintings or prints, usually of cities.
CN V.VB.AFU.AXC.BUE.AFU

vedute ideate
VB.81
ALT **veduta ideata**
SN Scenes realistically conceived but whose elements are completely imaginary. Distinct from **capricci**, in which accurately rendered buildings are grouped in an arbitrary, imaginary arrangement. Use especially with reference to 18th-century Italian paintings and prints.
CN V.VB.AFU.AXC.BZY

vegetable adhesive
USE **vegetable glue**

vegetable black
USE **carbon black**
charcoal black

vegetable dye
MT.1519
UF dye, vegetable
CN M.MT.AFU.AFU.ARI.AFU.AFU.AFU.AFU.AFU.AXC

vegetable gardens
RK.1434 (L,N)
ALT **vegetable garden**
UF gardens, vegetable
CN V.RK.ALO.AFU.AFU.AXC.ARI

vegetable glue
MT.2351
UF adhesive, vegetable
glue, vegetable
vegetable adhesive
CN M.MT.AFU.ARI.ARI.AFU.ALO.ALO.ALO

vegetable oil
MT.1985 (L)
UF oil, vegetable
CN M.MT.AFU.AFU.ARI.ARI.AFU.ARI

vegetable pigment
USE **plant pigment**

vegetable stands
USE **produce stands**

vegetable violet
MT.1716
UF violet, vegetable
CN M.MT.AFU.AFU.ARI.AFU.AFU.ALO.ALO.BIQ.ALO.AFU

vegetable wax
MT.2204
UF wax, vegetable
CN M.MT.AFU.AFU.ARI.BZY.AXC

vegetation
RD.241 (L,B)
CN V.RD.ARI.AFU.BCW.AFU

vegetation fortifications
USE **plant fortifications**

Vehicle, Great
USE **Mahayana**

Vehicle, Lesser
USE **Hinayana**

Vehicle, Small
USE **Hinayana**

vehicles
MT.2372
SN Any liquid or substance in which pigment is dispersed, the whole forming a pigmented coating, such as paint or ink.
UF mediums (vehicles)
CN M.MT.AFU.ARI.BIQ.AXC

vehicles, recreational
USE **motor homes**

Vei
USE **Vai**

veilleuses
TG.318
ALT **veilleuse**
SN Type of French sofa with an undulating back; often made in matching pairs and placed on either side of the fireplace.
CN V.TG.AFU.AFU.ALO.ALO.BZY.BUE

vein stone
USE **ultramarine blue**

veined marble
USE **variegated marble**

veiners
TB.869
ALT **veiner**
SN Small, narrow V-shaped gouges used in woodworking. (W)
UF tools, veining
veining tools
CN V.TB.AFU.BCW.CFS.ALO.AFU.BUE.CLM

veining tools
USE **veiners**

velaria
RT.444 (A)
ALT **velarium**
UF velum (roofs)
CN V.RT.AFU.AFU.AFU.BIQ.ARI.AFU.ALO.AFU.AFU

Veldesche
USE **Jugendstil**

vellum
MT.961 (L)
CN M.MT.AFU.AFU.ALO.AFU.DZW.BCW.AFU

vellum, tracing
USE **tracing vellum**

velocity
USE **speed**

velodromes
RG.181 (B)
ALT **velodrome**
UF bicycle tracks
cycle racing tracks
cycle tracks
racing tracks, cycle
tracks, bicycle
CN V.RG.AFU.AFU.DOI.CFS.ALO.AXC

velum
MT.939
SN Material of woven animal hair that serves as a tent or covering. (OLIVER)
CN M.MT.AFU.AFU.ALO.AFU.CXA.ALO.AFU

velum (roofs)
USE **velaria**

velvet
MT.1878 (L,R)
SN A clothing and upholstery fabric in a wide range of constructions and weights made of silk, rayon, cotton, nylon, or wool and characterized by a short, soft, dense pile produced by weaving into a single cloth an extra warp which is looped over wires and later cut. (W)
CN M.MT.AFU.AFU.ARI.ALO.ALO.ALO.ALO.DZW

velvet, kasai
USE **cut-pile cloth**

Venda
FL.574 (L)
CN F.FL.ALO.AFU.AXC.ARI.BCW.BCW

vendors
HG.435 (L,R)
ALT **vendor**
SN Use for persons or agencies who offer goods for sale, especially those who create, market, and sell computers, software, automated systems, databases, and services.
CN H.HG.AFU.AXC.BOK.FUA

vendors, database
USE **online vendors**

vendors, information
USE **online vendors**

vendors, online
USE **online vendors**

veneer
MT.2283 (A,L,B)
CN M.MT.AFU.ALO.IRA

veneer hammers
TB.1084 (N)
ALT **veneer hammer**
SN Hammers used not for striking but for applying pressure to veneer after

it has been glued into position. (HAND)
UF hammers, veneer
CN V.TB.AFU.BCW.CFS.ALO.ARI.AFU.BIQ

veneer pins
TF.464
ALT **veneer pin**
UF pins, veneer
CN V.TF.AFU.AFU.AFU.ALO.AFU.CXA.BOK

veneer punches
TB.979 (N)
ALT **veneer punch**
SN Irregularly-shaped punches used when replacing damaged veneer.
UF punches, veneer
CN V.TB.AFU.BCW.CFS.ALO.AFU.DZW.BIQ

veneer saws
TB.1031 (N)
ALT **veneer saw**
SN Commonly defined as large frame saws whose saw web is set in the middle of a wood frame; used for cutting veneer from wood. The term also refers to a kind of backsaw with a slightly curved blade and a heavy wood back that serves as a handle. It is also a particular kind of circular saw. (SALAM)
UF saws, veneer
CN V.TB.AFU.BCW.CFS.ALO.AFU.EWY.BZY

veneer, burl
USE **burl veneer**

veneered walls
RT.580
ALT **veneered wall**
SN Walls with a masonry face that is attached, but not bonded, to the body of the wall and does not exert a common reaction under load. (PUTNAM)
UF walls, veneered
CN V.RT.AFU.AFU.AFU.BIQ.BUE.AFU.AFU.BZY

veneerers
HG.542
ALT **veneerer**
CN H.HG.AFU.AXC.BUE.ARI.DCU

veneering
KT.725 (L)
ALT **veneered**
CN K.KT.AFU.ALO.GRC.DZW

Venetian blue
USE **Egyptian blue**

Venetian glass
MT.267 (L)
UF glass, Venetian
CN M.MT.AFU.AFU.AFU.BIQ.AFU.ARI.CXA

Venetian red
MT.1679
UF red, Venetian
CN M.MT.AFU.AFU.ARI.AFU.AFU.ALO.ALO.BCW.AFU.ALO.BZY

Venetian red (color)
USE **deep reddish brown**
moderate reddish brown
strong reddish brown

Venetian windows
USE **Palladian windows**

Venezuelan
FL.725 (L,B)
CN F.FL.ALO.ALO.AFU.AXC.BZY

Venice turpentine
MT.1478
UF turpentine, Venice
CN M.MT.AFU.AFU.ALO.BOK.AFU.BUE

Venn diagrams
VW.244 (L)
ALT **Venn diagram**
SN Pictorial representations using circles and squares so positioned as to represent an operation in set theory. (AHD)
UF diagrams, Venn
Venn's diagrams
CN V.VW.AFU.AFU.AFU.FZU.AXC.ARI.ALO

Venn's diagrams
USE **Venn diagrams**

vent stacks
RT.1476
ALT **vent stack**
SN Vertical vent pipes installed primarily for the purpose of providing circulation of air to or from any part of the building drainage system. (STEIN)
UF stacks, vent
vents (plumbing components)
CN V.RT.ALO.BCW.ALO.ARI.BZY.BOK.ALO

ventilago
MT.1534
CN M.MT.AFU.AFU.ARI.AFU.AFU.AFU.AFU.AFU.AXC.DIO

ventilating brick
USE **air brick**

ventilating cowls
USE **cowls**

ventilation
RT.1404 (A,L,B,R)
UF systems, ventilation
ventilation systems
CN V.RT.ALO.BCW.AFU.AFU.AXC

ventilation systems
USE **ventilation**

ventilation, exhaust
USE **exhaust ventilation**

ventilation, mechanical
USE **mechanical ventilation**

ventilation, natural
USE **natural ventilation**

ventilation, passive
USE **natural ventilation**

ventilators
RT.1443 (N,B)
ALT **ventilator**
CN V.RT.ALO.BCW.AFU.ALO.ARI.CFS

vents
RT.990
ALT **vent**
SN Openings, as in a wall, serving as outlets for air, smoke, or fumes. (RHDEL2)
CN V.RT.AFU.ARI.AFU.ALO.BCW

vents (plumbing components)
USE **vent stacks**

vents, soffit
USE **soffit vents**

ventures, joint
USE **joint ventures**

Veracruz, Classic
USE **Classic Veracruz**

Veraguas
FL.1094
UF Classic Veraguas
Veraguas, Classic
CN F.FL.ALO.ALO.ALO.ALO.ALO.ALO.AFU.BZY

Veraguas, Classic
USE **Veraguas**

Veramin ware
FL.3460
UF ware, Veramin
CN F.FL.ALO.BIQ.AFU.DIO.ALO.AXC

verandas
USE **porches**

verd antico
USE **verd antique**

verd antique
MT.794
SN A green mottled or veined serpentine marble or calcareous serpentine. (WCOL)
UF antique green (marble)
lapis atracius
verd antico
verde antico
verde antique
CN M.MT.AFU.AFU.AFU.DCU.AFU.ARI.ARI.ARI.ARI.ARI

verd vessie
USE **sap green**

verde antico
USE **verd antique**

verde antique
USE **verd antique**

verde chrome
USE **chrome green**

verde di genoa
MT.855
CN M.MT.AFU.AFU.AFU.DCU.AFU.ARI.BOK.BCW

verde di levanto
MT.856
CN M.MT.AFU.AFU.AFU.DCU.AFU.ARI.BOK.BIQ

verde di pegli
MT.857
CN M.MT.AFU.AFU.AFU.DCU.AFU.ARI.BOK.BOK

verde di ponsevera
MT.858
CN M.MT.AFU.AFU.AFU.DCU.AFU.ARI.BOK.BUE

verde di prato
MT.859
CN M.MT.AFU.AFU.AFU.DCU.AFU.ARI.BOK.BZY

verde di ranocchia
MT.860
UF lapis ophites
ophicalcite
ophiolite
ophite
CN M.MT.AFU.AFU.AFU.DCU.AFU.ARI.BOK.CFS

verderame
USE **verdigris**

verdeterra
USE **green earth**

verdetta
USE **green earth**

verdigris
MT.1657 (R)
UF copper basic acetate
green, Montpellier
green, Van Eyck
Grünspan
Montpellier green
Van Eyck green
verderame
vert-de-gris
viride aeris
CN M.MT.AFU.AFU.ARI.AFU.AFU.ALO.ALO.AXC.ARI.BZY

verdigris (color)
USE **light green**
moderate yellowish green

verdigris green
USE **light green**

verditer
USE **blue verditer**

verditer green
USE **moderate yellowish green**

verditer, blue
USE **blue verditer**

verditer, blue (color)
USE **moderate blue**

vergeboards
USE **bargeboards**

verges
RT.493
ALT verge
SN Use for those portions of a roof that project beyond the gable, in effect the raking equivalent of eaves; use **eaves** for portions projecting beyond the walls, at the lower horizontal edges of roofs.
CN V.RT.AFU.AFU.AFU.BIQ.ARI.ALO.AFU.CXA.AFU

verism
BM.180 (L)
SN Extreme form of realism that repudiates idealization, nobility, and heroism in visual art, literature, and theater, aiming to reproduce exact descriptions or appearances of even repugnant subjects.
CN B.BM.AFU.AFU.AXC.BOK.ALO

Verismo
FL.3408
SN Use with reference to certain Italian sculpture of the mid-19th century.
CN F.FL.ALO.BCW.ALO.AXC.DIO.BOK.BCW.BCW

vermeil
MT.461 (R)
CN M.MT.AFU.AFU.AFU.BZY.AFU.ALO.AXC.AFU.AFU.AFU

vermiculation
DG.119
ALT **vermiculated**
SN A pattern of short, irregular wriggling channels imitating worm tracks, used as a surface decoration on stone. (LDDO)
CN D.DG.AFU.ARI.ALO.ARI.BUE

vermiculite
MT.537 (L)
CN M.MT.AFU.AFU.AFU.CFS.AFU.FUA.ARI

vermilion
MT.1681
SN Pigment composed of mercury sulfide, including the natural mineral and the artificially made compound.
UF cinnabar (vermilion)
natural vermilion
Zinnober
CN M.MT.AFU.AFU.ARI.AFU.AFU.ALO.ALO.BCW.AFU.AXC

vermilion (color)
USE **dark pink**
dark reddish orange
dark yellowish pink
deep reddish orange
deep yellowish pink
grayish red
light grayish red
moderate red
moderate reddish orange
strong reddish orange
strong yellowish pink
vivid red
vivid reddish orange

vermilion, American
USE **chrome red**

vermilion, antimony
USE **antimony vermilion**

vermilion, artificial
USE **grayish purplish red**

vermilion, cadmium
USE **moderate red**
strong red

vermilion, Chinese
USE **Chinese vermilion**

vermilion, Chinese (color)
USE **vivid red**

vermilion, dull
USE **moderate reddish orange**

vermilion, Dutch
USE **vivid reddish orange**

vermilion, English
USE **English vermilion**

vermilion, English (color)
USE **strong red**

vermilion, French
USE **vivid reddish orange**

vermilion, light
USE **strong reddish orange**
vivid reddish orange

vermilion, orange
USE **orange vermilion**

vermilion, orange (color)
USE **deep orange**
moderate reddish orange
strong reddish orange

vermilion, scarlet
USE **scarlet vermilion**

vermilion, scarlet (color)
USE **vivid reddish orange**

Vermont white statuary marble
MT.840
UF marble, Vermont white statuary
statuary marble, Vermont white

white statuary marble, Vermont
CN M.MT.AFU.AFU.AFU.DCU.AFU.ARI.ARI.ARI.BOK.ELK

vernacular architecture
BM.227 (A,L,B,R)
SN Use for indigenous architecture which is the product of craftsmen using traditional plans and construction methods and local building materials. (LCSH)
UF anonymous architecture
architecture, anonymous
architecture, folk
architecture, indigenous
architecture, non-pedigreed
architecture, spontaneous
architecture, vernacular
folk architecture
indigenous architecture
nonpedigreed architecture
spontaneous architecture
CN B.BM.AFU.ARI.AXC.BCW

Vernacular Revival
USE **Old English**

vernice liquida
USE **varnish**

vernis mou
USE **soft-ground etching**

Verona brown
USE **transparent brown**

Verona green
MT.1641
UF green, Verona
CN M.MT.AFU.AFU.ARI.AFU.AFU.ALO.ALO.AXC.AFU.ALO.AXC

Verona yellow
USE **Turner's yellow**

Veronese brown
USE **transparent brown**

Veronese green
USE **emerald green**

verre églomisé
KT.768 (R)
SN Use for the technique of decorating glass in which a painted, drawn, or gilded image is executed on the underside of the glass and backed with metal foil, usually gold or silver.
UF back painting
églomisé
engraving on glass, reverse
foil underengraving, glass
glass foil underengraving
glass underengraving
mirror painting (verre églomisé)
painting, back
painting, mirror (verre églomisé)
reverse engraving on glass
underengraving, glass
underengraving, glass foil
CN K.KT.AFU.ALO.HOE.ALO.AXC.ALO

versions
VB.122 (R)
ALT **version**
SN Use when a valued object is made by the same artist, craftsman, or studio that created an original on which it is closely based, and when the resulting work shows some variation from the original. If little or no variation is apparent, use **replicas**.
UF variants
CN V.VB.ALO.BZY.AFU.BCW

verso
DC.24
SN Use with reference to the reverse or subordinate side of a sheet of paper. Use **reverse** to refer to the back, underside, or subordinate surface of a coin, medal, seal, or currency note.
CN D.DC.AFU.ALO.ALO.CLM

vert anglais
USE **emerald green**

vert antique
MT.2491
CN M.MT.AFU.ARI.CRG.AFU.BUE

vert de chrome
USE **chrome green**

vert de cinabre
USE **chrome green**

vert de cobalt
USE **cobalt green**

vert-de-gris
USE **verdigris**

vert de Vessie
USE **sap green**

vert de zinc
USE **zinc chrome green**

vert émeraude
USE **emerald green**
viridian

vert Paul Véronèse
USE **emerald green**

vertebrate bands
DG.101
ALT **vertebrate band**
SN Running ornament in which forms are attached to a central feature that runs down the center of the band.
CN D.DG.AFU.ARI.AFU.ARI.ALO

vertical duplexes
USE **duplex houses**

vertical files
VW.587 (L)
ALT **vertical file**
SN Collections of documents such as pamphlets, sheets of paper, and mounted photographs that have been collected and arranged for ready reference, as in a library. (AHD)
UF files, pamphlet
files, vertical
pamphlet files
CN V.VW.AFU.ALO.AFU.BIQ.AFU.ARI

vertical lift bridges
USE **lift bridges**

verticality
BM.98
ALT **vertical**
SN Use for parallel relationships to a vertical axis in designs for graphic works, objects, and structures.
CN B.BM.AFU.AFU.ARI.AFU.FUA

very dark bluish green
DL.204
UF bluish green, very dark
centroid color 166
dark teal
green, hemlock
green, very dark bluish
hemlock green
teal, dark
CN D.DL.AFU.AFU.BUE.DCU.ALO.BOK.AFU

very dark brown
USE **dark brown**
dark yellowish brown

very dark gray
USE **brownish gray**
dark gray

very dark grayish brown
USE **dark grayish yellowish brown**
moderate olive brown

very dark green
DL.172
UF blue green, dark
centroid color 147
dark blue green
dark slate green
green, dark slate
green, hemlock
green, very dark
hemlock green
slate green, dark
CN D.DL.AFU.AFU.BUE.BOK.AFU

very dark greenish blue
DL.241
UF blue, Thalo (color)
blue, very dark greenish
centroid color 175
greenish blue, very dark
Thalo blue (color)
CN D.DL.AFU.AFU.BZY.DCU.AFU.BOK.AFU

very dark purple
DL.276
UF centroid color 225
plum purple
purple, plum

purple, very dark
CN D.DL.AFU.AFU.CFS.BOK.AFU

very dark purplish red
DL.57
UF black violet
bluish red, dull
brown, dark violet
centroid color 260
dark violet brown
dull bluish red
plum (color)
plum, red
purplish red, very dark
red plum
red, dull bluish
red, very dark purplish
violet brown, dark
violet, black
CN D.DL.AFU.AFU.ALO.CFS.AFU.BCW.AFU

very dark red
DL.41
UF brown, dull reddish
centroid color 17
dull red
dull reddish brown
garnet (color)
maroon
red, dull
red, very dark
reddish brown, dull
CN D.DL.AFU.AFU.ALO.BCW.AFU

very dark reddish purple
DL.296
UF centroid color 243
deep plum
plum (color)
plum, deep
purple, very dark reddish
reddish purple, very dark
reddish violet
violet, reddish
CN D.DL.AFU.AFU.CFS.DCU.AFU.BIQ.AFU

very dark yellowish green
DL.194
UF centroid color 138
chrome green (color)
dark hunter green
green, chrome (color)
green, dark hunter
green, hunter
green, hunter's
green, very dark yellowish
hunter green
hunter green, dark
hunter's green
yellowish green, very dark
CN D.DL.AFU.AFU.BUE.DCU.AFU.BOK.AFU

very deep purple
DL.271
UF centroid color 220
purple, very deep
CN D.DL.AFU.AFU.CFS.AXC.AFU

very deep purplish red
DL.54
UF bluish red
brown, rose
centroid color 257
purplish red, very deep
red, bluish
red, very deep purplish
rose brown
CN D.DL.AFU.AFU.ALO.CFS.AFU.ARI.AFU

very deep red
DL.38
UF brown carmine
brown, rose
carmine, brown
centroid color 14
maroon
red, very deep
rose brown
CN D.DL.AFU.AFU.ALO.ARI.AFU

very deep reddish purple
DL.292
UF centroid color 239
purple, very deep reddish
reddish violet
violet, reddish
CN D.DL.AFU.AFU.CFS.DCU.AFU.ARI.AFU

very deep yellowish green
DL.189
UF centroid color 133
green, very deep yellowish
yellowish green, very deep
CN D.DL.AFU.AFU.BUE.DCU.AFU.AXC.AFU

very light blue
DL.218
UF baby blue
blue, baby
blue, pale cerulean
blue, very light
centroid color 180
cerulean blue, pale
pale cerulean blue
CN D.DL.AFU.AFU.BZY.BCW.AFU

very light bluish green
DL.201
UF aqua green, bright
aqua green, light
aqua green, pale
bluish green, very light
bright aqua green
centroid color 162
emerald green, light
green, bright aqua
green, light aqua
green, light emerald
green, light turquoise
green, pale aqua
green, pale emerald
green, pale turquoise
green, pastel turquoise
green, very light bluish
light aqua green
light emerald green
light turquoise green
pale aqua green
pale emerald green
pale turquoise green
pastel turquoise green
turquoise green, light
turquoise green, pale
turquoise green, pastel
CN D.DL.AFU.AFU.BUE.DCU.ALO.BCW.AFU

very light gray
USE **light gray**

very light green
DL.169
UF blue green
centroid color 143
emerald green, pale
green, light mint
green, pale emerald
green, pale mint
green, very light
light mint green
mint green, light
mint green, pale
pale emerald green
pale mint green
CN D.DL.AFU.AFU.BUE.BCW.AFU

very light greenish blue
DL.238
UF aqua blue
aqua blue, light
aqua, bright
aqua, light
baby blue
blue, aqua
blue, baby
blue, light aqua
blue, light turquoise
blue, very light greenish
bright aqua
centroid color 171
greenish blue, very light
light aqua
light aqua blue
light turquoise
light turquoise blue
turquoise blue, light
turquoise, light
CN D.DL.AFU.AFU.BZY.DCU.AFU.BCW.AFU

very light purple
DL.273
UF centroid color 221
light lilac
lilac
lilac, light
purple, very light
CN D.DL.AFU.AFU.CFS.BCW.AFU

very light purplish blue
DL.248
UF blue, reddish

blue, very light purplish
centroid color 198
purplish blue, very light
reddish blue
ultramarine
CN D.DL.AFU.AFU.BZY.DCU.ALO.BCW.AFU

very light violet
DL.260
UF bluish violet
centroid color 209
lavender
lilac
violet, bluish
violet, very light
CN D.DL.AFU.AFU.BZY.DCU.ARI.BCW.AFU

very light yellowish green
DL.191
UF centroid color 134
emerald green (color)
green, emerald (color)
green, very light yellowish
yellowish green, very light
CN D.DL.AFU.AFU.BUE.DCU.AFU.BCW.AFU

very pale blue
DL.222
UF aqua blue, pale
aqua, pale
baby blue
blue, baby
blue, dull greenish
blue, dull reddish
blue, pale aqua
blue, pale grayish
blue, pastel
blue, very pale
centroid color 184
dull greenish blue
dull reddish blue
gray, pearl
grayish blue, pale
greenish blue, dull
pale aqua
pale aqua blue
pale grayish blue
pastel blue
pearl gray
reddish blue, dull
CN D.DL.AFU.AFU.BZY.BUE.AFU

very pale brown
USE **brownish pink**
light grayish yellowish brown
light yellowish brown
pale orange yellow

very pale green
DL.174
UF aqua green, pale
aqua, pale
blue green, pale
bluish green, dull
celadon (color)
centroid color 148
dull bluish green
dull green
green, dull
green, dull bluish
green, pale aqua
green, pale jade
green, pale mint
green, pastel
green, very pale
jade green, pale
mint green, pale
pale aqua
pale aqua green
pale blue green
pale jade green
pale mint green
pastel green
CN D.DL.AFU.AFU.BUE.BUE.AFU

very pale purple
DL.278
UF blue, pale periwinkle
bluish lavender, pale
bluish violet, dull
centroid color 226
dull bluish violet
dull violet
gray lilac
lavender, pale
lavender, pale bluish
lavender, pastel
lilac
lilac, gray
lilac, pale
lilac, pastel
pale bluish lavender
pale lavender
pale lilac
pale periwinkle blue
pastel lavender
pastel lilac
periwinkle blue, pale
purple, very pale
violet, dull
violet, dull bluish
CN D.DL.AFU.AFU.CFS.BUE.AFU

very pale purplish blue
DL.252
UF blue violet, pale grayish
blue, dull reddish
blue, pale periwinkle
blue, very pale purplish
centroid color 202
dull reddish blue
gray, lavender
grayish blue violet, pale
grayish blue, pale
lavender gray
pale grayish blue
pale grayish blue violet
pale periwinkle blue
periwinkle blue, pale
purplish blue, very pale
reddish blue, dull
ultramarine
CN D.DL.AFU.AFU.BZY.DCU.ALO.BUE.AFU

very pale violet
DL.264
UF blue, light periwinkle
bluish lavender, pale bluish
bluish violet, dull
centroid color 213
dull bluish violet
gray, lavender
lavender
lavender gray
lavender, pale bluish
light periwinkle blue
pale bluish lavender
periwinkle blue, light
violet, dull bluish
violet, very pale
CN D.DL.AFU.AFU.BZY.DCU.ARI.BUE.AFU

Vesara
FL.2249
UF Vasara
CN F.FL.ALO.ARI.AXC.ALO.AFU.BUE.ARI

vesper chairs
USE **prie-dieus**

vest-pocket parks
RK.1462
ALT **vest-pocket park**
SN Very small city parks, directly adjacent to and usually between buildings in a densely built area.
UF mini-parks
parkettes
parks, pocket
parks, vest-pocket
pocket parks
CN V.RK.ALO.ALO.ARI.AFU.BIQ

vestiaries
USE **wardrobes (rooms)**

vestibule-door locks
TF.245
ALT **vestibule-door lock**
UF locks, vestibule-door
CN V.TF.AFU.AFU.AFU.AFU.DIO.BIQ.ALO.ALO.CRG

vestibule latches
TF.192
ALT **vestibule latch**
UF latches, vestibule
CN V.TF.AFU.AFU.AFU.AFU.DIO.BCW.ALO.BZY

vestibules
RM.138 (A,L,B,R)
ALT **vestibule**
SN Use for spaces between the outer and inner doors to buildings, or for sheltered spaces, recessed in the mass of the building, just outside the outer doors. For spaces just inside the outer door but not separated from the building interior by any barrier such as a door, use **entrance halls.**

CN V.RM.AFU.DIO.ALO.BOK.BIQ

Vestorian blue
USE **Egyptian blue**

vestries
USE **sacristies**

vestry records
USE **church registers**
churchwardens' accounts

veterans' hospitals
RK.773 (L,B)
ALT **veterans' hospital**
UF hopsitals, veterans'
hospitals, VA
VA hospitals
CN V.RK.AFU.ALO.ALO.CXA.ALO.AFU.
BCW.ALO.BZY

veterinary colleges
RK.823 (A,L,B)
ALT **veterinary college**
UF colleges, veterinary
CN V.RK.AFU.ALO.ALO.CXA.ARI.ALO.
DUC

veterinary hospitals
RK.774 (A,L,B)
ALT **veterinary hospital**
UF animal hospitals
hospitals, animal
hospitals, veterinary
CN V.RK.AFU.ALO.ALO.CXA.ALO.
AFU.BCW.ALO.CFS

veterinary laboratories
RK.1171 (A,L,B)
ALT **veterinary laboratory**
UF laboratories, veterinary
CN V.RK.AFU.ALO.ALO.FIM.ALO.AFU.
CRG

veusurae
USE **voussoirs**

Vezzi porcelain
FL.3234 (R)
UF porcelain, Vezzi
CN F.FL.ALO.BCW.ALO.ARI.BIQ.BIQ.
BCW.ALO.ALO

viaducts
RK.1290 (A,L,B,R)
ALT **viaduct**
SN Bridges, usually resting on a series of arches, carrying roadways or railways over low-lying areas.
CN V.RK.AFU.ALO.ALO.GLI.ALO.AFU.
ALO.ARI

viaducts, railroad
USE **railroad bridges**

vibrating conveyors
TB.370 (L)
ALT **vibrating conveyor**
UF conveyors, vibrating
CN V.TB.AFU.ARI.DCU.AFU.AFU.BCW

vibration
BM.991 (A,L,B)
CN B.BM.CFS.AXC.BZY.CLM

Vibrationist
FL.3423
ALT **Vibrationism**
CN F.FL.ALO.BCW.ALO.AXC.DIO.CFS.
ALO

vicarages
RK.331 (A,L,B,R)
ALT **vicarage**
CN V.RK.AFU.ALO.ALO.AXC.ALO.
BOK.ARI.BCW

vice presidents
HG.656 (L)
ALT **vice president**
CN H.HG.AFU.AXC.CFS.AFU.AFU.AXC

viceroys
HG.687 (L)
ALT **viceroy**
SN Governing officials of countries, provinces, or territories who rule in the name of their sovereign. (WCOL)
CN H.HG.AFU.AXC.CFS.CFS.CRG

vices
USE **solid newel stairs**

vici
RG.283
ALT **vicus**
SN May be used generally for ancient Roman urban residential neighborhoods and for Roman or Medieval merchants' quarters or small villages, usually located outside the walls of nearby military settlements.
CN V.RG.ALO.AFU.ALO.BCW.ARI

vicinity plans
USE **site plans**

victoria card photographs
USE **victoria prints**

victoria card photoprints
USE **victoria prints**

Victoria green
USE **chrome green**

victoria prints
VJ.82
ALT **victoria print**
SN Use for card photographs on mounts measuring about 3 1/2 by 5 inches.
UF card photographs, victoria
prints, victoria
victoria card photographs
victoria card photoprints
CN V.VJ.AFU.AFU.BCW.AFU.BOK

Victoria red
USE **chrome red**

Victorian
FL.3317 (A,L,B,R)
CN F.FL.ALO.BCW.ALO.AXC.DIO.ALO.
BCW.ALO

Victorian Gothic
USE **Gothic Revival**

Victorian Revival
FL.3330 (R)
UF Revival, Victorian
CN F.FL.ALO.BCW.ALO.AXC.DIO.ALO.
BIQ.BUE

Victorian, Early
USE **Early Victorian**

Victorian, High
USE **High Victorian**

Victorian, Late
USE **Late Victorian**

victory gardens
RK.1435
ALT **victory garden**
SN Used to designate vegetable gardens cultivated to increase food production during the Second World War, especially in England and America.
UF gardens, victory
CN V.RK.ALO.AFU.AFU.AXC.ARI.AFU

vide-poches
TG.766
ALT **vide-poche**
SN Small bedroom tables, often of trestle form, with deeply rimmed tops and sometimes one or more shelves designed to hold the contents of a man's pockets when he undresses. First made in France in the 1720s and popular there and in England in the late 18th century. (PC)
UF tables en vide-poche
vuide-poches
CN V.TG.AFU.AFU.BIQ.BOK.ALO.GRC

video
KD.13
CN K.KD.AFU.AFU.AFU.AFU.AFU.BIQ

video arcades
RK.1035 (A)
ALT **video arcade**
UF arcades, video
video game arcades
CN V.RK.AFU.ALO.ALO.EWY.AXC.ARI.
AFU.ALO

video art
BM.264 (L,R)
SN An art form involving the creative exploitation of video technology to produce videotapes for viewing on a television screen or computer monitor. (RHDEL2)
UF art, video
CN B.BM.AFU.ARI.BCW.FOG.CFS

video cartridges
USE **videocassettes**

video cassettes
USE **videocassettes**

video discs

USE **videodiscs**

video disks
USE **videodiscs**

video game arcades
USE **video arcades**

video recordings
VW.638 (L)
ALT **video recording**
UF recordings, video
recordings, video tape
video tape recordings
videos
CN V.VW.AFU.ALO.AFU.DZW.AFU.ALO

video tape cartridges
USE **videocassettes**

video tape cassettes
USE **videocassettes**

video tape recordings
USE **video recordings**
videotapes

video tapes
USE **videotapes**

videocassettes
VW.642
ALT **video cassette**
SN Recordings on videotape contained in cassettes. (AHD)
UF cartridges, video
cartridges, video tape
cassettes, video tape
video cartridges
video cassettes
video tape cartridges
video tape cassettes
CN V.VW.AFU.ALO.AFU.DZW.AFU.ALO.ARI.AFU

videodisc recordings
USE **videodiscs**

videodiscs
VW.640 (L,R)
ALT **videodisc**
SN Flat circular media upon the surfaces of which images can be recorded and stored. (ICA)
UF discs, video
disks, video
recordings, videodisc
video discs
video disks
videodisc recordings
videodisks
CN V.VW.AFU.ALO.AFU.DZW.AFU.ALO.ALO

videodisks
USE **videodiscs**

videos
USE **video recordings**

videotapes
VW.641 (L,B)
ALT **videotape**
SN Magnetic tapes on which visual images are electronically recorded, with or without sound. (ICA)
UF tapes, video
video tape recordings
video tapes
CN V.VW.AFU.ALO.AFU.DZW.AFU.ALO.ARI

vieilles villes
USE **old towns**

Vienna blue
USE **cobalt blue**

Vienna green
USE **emerald green**

Vienna lake
USE **carmine**

Vienna red
USE **chrome red**

Vienna ultramarine
USE **cobalt blue**

Vientiane
FL.2396
CN F.FL.ALO.ARI.BCW.AXC.ARI

Vierendeel girders
USE **Vierendeel trusses**

Vierendeel trusses
RT.373
ALT **Vierendeel truss**
SN Open web trusses with vertical members but without diagonals and with rigid joints. (W)
UF girders, Vierendeel
trusses, Vierendeel
Vierendeel girders
CN V.RT.AFU.AFU.AFU.BCW.CLM.AFU.AFU.AFU.CRG

Vietnamese
FL.2426
UF Dai Co Viet
Dai Viet
CN F.FL.ALO.ARI.BCW.BUE

view albums
VW.489
ALT **view album**
SN Commercially published photographic albums popular from around 1885 on, containing pictures usually of one place or event. (HCOP)
UF albums, view
CN V.VW.AFU.ALO.AFU.AFU.AFU.ALO.ARI.AFU

view cameras
TB.305 (L,N)
ALT **view camera**
SN Large-format cameras which have a ground-glass screen at the image plane for viewing and focusing. (LANG)
UF cameras, field
cameras, flatbed
cameras, view
field cameras
flatbed cameras
CN V.TB.AFU.ARI.CLM.ARI.AFU.AFU.ALO.BIQ

viewpoint
BM.170
SN Point from which a viewer looks at an object or visual field. (A-Z)
CN B.BM.AFU.AFU.ARI.BOK.DZW

views
VB.15 (A,L)
ALT **view**
SN Use for depictions, including photographs, of places or things, especially to distinguish them from other information such as diagrams, working drawings, or verbal descriptions.
UF prospects (views)
CN V.VB.AFU.AFU.BOK

views, aerial
USE **aerial views**

views, aerial (perspective drawings)
USE **bird's-eye perspectives**

views, angle
USE **oblique views**

views, auxiliary
USE **auxiliary views**

views, balloon
USE **bird's-eye views**

views, bird's-eye
USE **bird's-eye views**

views, bird's-eye (perspective drawings)
USE **bird's-eye perspectives**

views, city
USE **city views**

views, close-up
USE **close-up views**

views, diagonal
USE **oblique views**

views, distant
USE **distant views**

views, expanded
USE **exploded drawings**

views, exploded
USE **exploded drawings**

views, exterior
USE **exterior views**

views, eye-level
USE **eye-level views**

views, full
USE **general views**

views, general
USE **general views**

views, ichnographic
USE **plan views**

views, interior
USE **interior views**

views, oblique
USE **oblique views**

views, overall
USE **general views**

views, partial
USE **partial views**

views, perspective
USE **perspective drawings**

views, pictorial
USE **pictorial drawings**

views, plan
USE **plan views**

views, profile (figures)
USE **profiles (figures)**

views, stereo
USE **stereoscopic photographs**

views, street-level
USE **eye-level views**

views, three-quarter
USE **three-quarter views**

views, toad's-eye
USE **worm's-eye views**

views, topographical
USE **topographical views**

views, urban
USE **city views**

views, whole
USE **general views**

views, worm's-eye
USE **worm's-eye views**

vignette daguerreotypes
USE **cameotypes**

vignettes
VB.32 (L,R)
ALT **vignette**
SN Engravings, drawings, photographs, or the like that are shaded off gradually at the edges. (RHDEL2)
CN V.VB.AFU.AFU.BUE

vignettes de fonts
USE **fleurons**

vignettes (scrollwork)
USE **vine scrolls**

viharas
RG.202
ALT **vihara**
SN Use primarily for Indian Buddhist monasteries; may also be used for Sinhalese Buddhist temples.
CN V.RG.AFU.AFU.DUC.BZY

Vijayanagar
FL.2223 (L)
CN F.FL.ALO.ARI.AXC.ALO.AFU.BCW.ALO

Viking
FL.3151 (A,L,R)
CN F.FL.ALO.BCW.ALO.ALO.AFU.BOK.ARI.BUE.BCW

Vili
FL.487 (L)
UF Bavili
CN F.FL.ALO.AFU.AXC.ALO.ALO.AXC.BCW

Villa Style, Italian
USE **Italian Villa Style**

Villa Style, Tuscan
USE **Italian Villa Style**

villae rusticae
RK.293
ALT **villa rustica**
SN Designates Roman villas serving agricultural purposes.
CN V.RK.AFU.ALO.ALO.AXC.ALO.AXC.AFU.AFU.AFU.ARI.AFU

villae suburbanae
RK.294
ALT **villa suburbana**
SN Designates often palatial buildings of the Italian Renaissance located just outside of town, suitable for spending the day but usually without bedrooms.
CN V.RK.AFU.ALO.ALO.AXC.ALO.AXC.AFU.AFU.AFU.ARI.ALO

villae urbanae
RK.295
ALT **villa urbana**
SN Designates Roman country houses located near the city and serving recreational, not agricultural purposes.
CN V.RK.AFU.ALO.ALO.AXC.ALO.AXC.AFU.AFU.AFU.ARI.ARI

village community centers
USE **community centers**

village greens
USE **greens**

village halls
USE **town halls**

village industries
USE **cottage industries**

village maps
VW.224 (L)
ALT **village map**
UF maps, village
CN V.VW.AFU.AFU.AFU.FZU.AXC.AFU.ARI.AXC.DUC.AFU

village museums
USE **museum villages**

Village, Old
USE **Old Village**

villages
RD.7 (A,L,B,R)
ALT **village**
SN Distinctions among villages, towns, and cities are relative and vary according to their individual regional contexts. Villages generally designate units of compact settlement, varying in size but usually larger than hamlets and smaller than towns and distinguished from the surrounding rural territory.
CN V.RD.AFU.AFU.ALO.ALO

villages, agricultural
USE **agricultural settlements**

villages, children's
USE **children's villages**

villages, company
USE **company towns**

villages, deserted
USE **deserted villages**

villages, factory
USE **factory villages**

villages, farming
USE **agricultural settlements**

villages, fishing
USE **fishing villages**

villages, lost
USE **lost cities**

villages, market
USE **market towns**

villages, model
USE **new towns**

villages, museum
USE **museum villages**

villages, olympic
USE **olympic villages**

villages, retirement
USE **retirement communities**

villages, ruined
USE **ruined cities**

villages, tourist
USE **tourist towns**

Villanovan
FL.2706
CN F.FL.ALO.AXC.ALO.ALO.AFU.ALO

villas
RK.292 (A,L,B,R)
ALT **villa**

SN Used since the Roman period to designate country houses, generally of some pretension, and often including their outbuildings and gardens.
CN V.RK.AFU.ALO.ALO.AXC.ALO.AXC.AFU.AFU.AFU.ARI

vimanas
RM.334
ALT **vimana**
SN Use for sanctuaries of later Indian temples; may also be used for earlier Indian temples as a whole, including sanctuary and attached porches.
CN V.RM.AFU.DIO.AXC.ALO.ARI.AFU

Viñaque
FL.1180
UF Wilkawaín
CN F.FL.ALO.ALO.ALO.ARI.AXC.ALO.ALO.BIQ

Vinca
FL.2497 (L)
CN F.FL.ALO.AXC.AFU.BCW.CRG

Vinca-Plocnik
FL.2498
CN F.FL.ALO.AXC.AFU.BCW.CRG.AFU

Vinca-Tordos
FL.2499
CN F.FL.ALO.AXC.AFU.BCW.CRG.ALO

vine black
MT.1573
UF black, blue
black, cork
black, drop
black, German
black, Spanish
black, vine
black, yeast
blue black
cork black
drop black
German black
noir de vigne
Rebenschwarz
Spanish black
yeast black
CN M.MT.AFU.AFU.ARI.AFU.AFU.ALO.ALO.AFU.AFU.AFU.ALO.ARI

vine charcoal
USE **charcoal sticks**

vine scrolls
DG.149
ALT **vine scroll**
SN Scrolling foliage consisting of grapevines with bunches of grapes.
UF scrolls, vine
vignettes (scrollwork)
CN D.DG.AFU.ARI.ALO.CRG.ARI.ALO

vinegar
MT.295 (L)
CN M.MT.AFU.AFU.AFU.BOK.AFU.AFU.AFU

vines
RD.271 (L)
ALT **vine**
UF climbing plants
vitaceae
CN V.RD.ARI.AFU.BCW.ALO.ALO.ALO.AFU.BOK

vineyards
RG.14 (L,R)
ALT **vineyard**
CN V.RG.AFU.AFU.AFU.AFU.ARI.BOK

vintage prints
VJ.40
ALT **vintage print**
SN Photographic prints made by the original photographer or soon after the picture was taken, as opposed to prints made much later or by someone else from the same negative,(HCOP) i.e., prints of the same historical vintage as the original photograph.
UF prints, vintage
CN V.VJ.AFU.AFU.ARI.ARI.ALO

vintners
HG.366 (L)
ALT **vintner**
SN Persons who make or sell wine. (RHDEL2)
CN H.HG.AFU.AXC.BIQ.ALO.AXC.AFU.ARI.ALO

vinyl
MT.2152 (L)
UF copolymer, vinyl
polymer, vinyl
resin, vinyl
vinyl copolymer
vinyl polymer
vinyl resin
CN M.MT.AFU.AFU.ARI.BUE.ALO.AXC.AFU.EFQ

vinyl copolymer
USE **vinyl**

vinyl polymer
USE **vinyl**

vinyl resin
USE **vinyl**

Vinza
FL.593
CN F.FL.ALO.AFU.AXC.AXC.AFU.CLM

violence, political
USE **terrorism**

violet
DL.254
CN D.DL.AFU.AFU.BZY.DCU.ARI

violet black
USE **dark grayish red**
dark purplish gray

violet black, dull
USE **black**

dark bluish gray
dark gray
dark grayish blue
dark grayish purple
dark purplish gray

violet blue
USE **strong purplish blue**

violet blue, dark dull
USE **grayish purplish blue**
grayish violet

violet blue, grayish
USE **light violet**

violet blue, light
USE **strong purplish blue**

violet blue, light grayish
USE **brilliant purplish blue**

violet blue, pale grayish
USE **light purplish blue**

violet brown
USE **dark purplish red**
grayish purple
grayish red

violet brown, dark
USE **blackish purple**
dark grayish purple
dark purplish red
very dark purplish red

violet carmine
MT.1717
UF carmine, violet
CN M.MT.AFU.AFU.ARI.AFU.AFU.ALO.ALO.BIQ.ALO.ALO

violet carmine (color)
USE **dark purplish red**
dark reddish purple

violet de cobalt
USE **cobalt violet**

violet gray
USE **purplish gray**

violet gray, blackish
USE **dark gray**
dark purplish gray

violet gray, dark
USE **dark gray**

violet gray, deep
USE **dark gray**
dark purplish gray
medium gray
purplish gray

violet gray, light
USE **medium gray**
purplish gray

violet gray, pale
USE **medium gray**
purplish gray

violet madder lake

USE **alizarin violet**

violet manganèse
USE **manganese violet**

violet pigment
MT.1710
UF pigments, violet
CN M.MT.AFU.AFU.ARI.AFU.AFU.ALO.ALO.BIQ

violet pigment, artificial inorganic
USE **artificial inorganic violet pigment**

violet pigment, artificial organic
USE **synthetic organic violet pigment**

violet pigment, inorganic
USE **inorganic violet pigment**

violet pigment, organic
USE **organic violet pigment**

violet pigment, synthetic inorganic
USE **artificial inorganic violet pigment**

violet pigment, synthetic organic
USE **synthetic organic violet pigment**

violet purple
USE **deep reddish purple**
vivid purple

violet slate
USE **grayish blue**

violet slate, dark
USE **grayish blue**

violet ultramarine
USE **strong purplish blue**
strong violet
ultramarine violet

violet wood
MT.1316
UF wood, violet
CN M.MT.AFU.AFU.ALO.BIQ.DCU.AFU.AFU.AFU.MLC

violet, alizarin
USE **alizarin violet**

violet, amethyst
USE **vivid purple**

violet, aniline
USE **light violet**
mauve

violet, anthracene
USE **moderate violet**

violet, black
USE **blackish purple**
dark grayish purple
dark purplish red
very dark purplish red

violet, blackish
USE **dark violet**
grayish violet
moderate violet

violet, blue
USE **light purplish blue**

violet, bluish
USE **brilliant violet**
dark violet
deep violet
light violet
moderate violet
strong violet
very light violet
vivid purplish blue
vivid violet

violet, bright
USE **moderate purple**
moderate violet
strong purple
vivid purple

violet, bright bluish
USE **vivid violet**

violet, bright reddish
USE **vivid reddish purple**

violet, bright rose
USE **deep purplish pink**

violet, brilliant
USE **brilliant violet**

violet, brown
USE **dark purplish red**
grayish purplish red

violet, Burgundy
USE **manganese violet**

violet, cobalt
USE **cobalt violet**

violet, cobalt (color)
USE **moderate purple**
strong purple

violet, dark
USE **dark violet**

violet, dark anthracene
USE **dark grayish purple**
dark purple

violet, dark bluish
USE **dark violet**
grayish purple
grayish violet

violet, dark dull bluish
USE **dark purple**
grayish violet
moderate violet

violet, dark madder
USE **dark grayish purple**

violet, dark naphthalene
USE **dark grayish purple**

violet, dark nigrosin
USE **dark purple**

violet, deep
USE **deep violet**

violet, deep dull bluish
USE **grayish purplish blue**
moderate violet
pale purplish blue
pale violet
strong violet

violet, dull
USE **blackish purple**
dark grayish purple
dark purplish red
grayish purple
grayish purplish red
grayish reddish purple
light grayish purplish red
pale purple
very pale purple

violet, dull bluish
USE **blackish purple**
brilliant violet
dark grayish purple
grayish violet
light violet
pale purple
pale violet
strong violet
very pale purple
very pale violet

violet, dull reddish
USE **blackish purple**
dark grayish purple
grayish purple
grayish reddish purple
pale purple
pale reddish purple

violet, gray
USE **purplish gray**

violet, grayish
USE **grayish violet**

violet, light
USE **light violet**

violet, light bluish
USE **brilliant purplish blue**
brilliant violet
strong purplish blue

violet, light dull bluish
USE **light violet**

violet, maganese (color)
USE **strong purple**

violet, manganese
USE **manganese violet**

violet, Mars
USE **Mars violet**

violet, Mars (color)
USE **dark grayish purple**
deep reddish brown

violet, methyl
USE **vivid violet**

violet, mineral

USE manganese violet
strong purple

violet, moderate
USE moderate violet

violet, naphthalene
USE dark reddish purple

violet, nigrosin
USE dark purple

violet, Nürnburg
USE manganese violet

violet, outremer
USE ultramarine violet

violet, pale
USE pale violet

violet, pale bluish
USE brilliant purplish blue

violet, Perkin's
USE mauve

violet, permanent
USE manganese violet
strong purple

violet, plum
USE dark purplish red

violet, quinacridone
USE quinacridone violet

violet, red
USE deep reddish purple
grayish purplish pink
grayish purplish red
light purplish pink
light reddish purple
moderate purple
moderate purplish pink
moderate reddish purple
strong reddish purple

violet, reddish
USE dark reddish purple
deep reddish purple
light reddish purple
moderate reddish purple
strong reddish purple
very dark reddish purple
very deep reddish purple

violet, rose
USE deep purplish red
deep reddish purple
moderate purplish pink
moderate purplish red
moderate reddish purple

violet, slate
USE grayish purple

violet, strong
USE strong violet

violet, thioindigo
USE thioindigo violet

violet, vegetable
USE vegetable violet

violet, very light
USE very light violet

violet, very pale
USE very pale violet

violet, vivid
USE vivid violet

violin makers
HG.567 (L)
ALT violin maker
CN H.HG.AFU.AXC.BUE.AXC.CLM.AFU

violin wood
USE common spruce

Virginia greenstone
MT.879
UF greenstone, Virginia
CN M.MT.AFU.AFU.AFU.DCU.AFU.
ARI.BZY.ARI

Virginia pine
USE loblolly pine

Virginia poplar
USE tulipwood

Virgo symbols
DG.85 (R)
ALT Virgo symbol
CN D.DG.AFU.AFU.ERE.CRG

viride aeris
USE verdigris

viridian
MT.1658
UF Casali's green
chromium oxide green, transparent
Chromoxidhydratgrün
green, Casali's
green, Guignet's
green, Mittler's
green, Pannetier's
green, transparent chromium oxide
Guignet's green
Mittler's green
oxide green, transparent chromium
Pannetier's green
transparent chromium oxide green
vert émeraude
CN M.MT.AFU.AFU.ARI.AFU.AFU.ALO.
ALO.AXC.ARI.CFS

viridian (color)
USE moderate green
strong green

viridian green
USE brilliant green
strong green

viridian green, dark
USE moderate green

vis-à-vis
USE confidantes

visas
VW.944 (L)
ALT visa
SN Official endorsements made on passports by proper officials denoting a passport has been examined and the bearer is permitted to proceed. (BLACKS)
CN V.VW.AFU.ARI.AFU.CRG.ARI

viscose size
MT.2731
UF size, viscose
CN M.MT.AFU.ARI.IFM.BOK.ARI

viscous filters
USE viscous impingement filters

viscous impingement filters
RT.1437
ALT viscous impingement filter
UF filters, viscous impingement
viscous filters
CN V.RT.ALO.BCW.AFU.ALO.ARI.AXC.
ALO

vises
TB.224 (N)
ALT vise
SN Gripping tools with adjustable jaws controlled by a lever or screw; used to clamp an object firmly in place while work is being done on it. (MEANS)
CN V.TB.AFU.ARI.CFS.BOK

vises (stairs)
USE solid newel stairs

vises, bench
USE bench vises

vises, box
USE box vises

vises, chain-pipe
USE chain-pipe vises

vises, chair
USE chair vises

vises, hand
USE hand vises

vises, leg
USE leg vises

vises, wire
USE wire vises

Visigothic
FL.3111 (L,R)
CN F.FL.ALO.BCW.ALO.ALO.AFU.
BOK.ALO.ALO.AXC.ALO

vision
USE sight

vision slits
USE loopholes

visionaries
HG.759 (R)
ALT visionary

CN H.HG.AFU.BCW.HZS.BZY

visionary architecture
BM.224 (A,B,R)
SN Use for architecture designs which are idealistic or futuristic.
UF architecture, futuristic
architecture, visionary
futuristic architecture
CN B.BM.AFU.ARI.AXC.ALO.AFU

visionary art
USE **fantastic art**

visiting cards
VW.580 (L,N,R)
ALT **visiting card**
SN Small cards bearing the name, and sometimes the address of a person or married couple for presentation, as when formally calling or visiting. (GAHLM)
UF calling cards
cards, calling
cards, visiting
cartes de visite (visiting cards)
CN V.VW.AFU.ALO.AFU.ARI.DCU

visitors
HG.745
ALT **visitor**
CN H.HG.AFU.BCW.HOE

visitors' books
VW.279
ALT **visitors' book**
UF books, visitors'
CN V.VW.AFU.AFU.AFU.FZU.BCW.ALO.ARI.ALO

visitors' centers
RK.690 (A,B)
ALT **visitor center**
SN Use for structures providing specific information about specific localities, buildings, or exhibitions through the display of printed or other material, or the sale or free distribution of literature.
UF centers, visitors'
CN V.RK.AFU.ALO.ALO.CRG.ARI.AFU

visual aids
USE **visual materials**

visual arts
KD.14 (L)
UF arts, visual
CN K.KD.AFU.AFU.AFU.AFU.ALO

visual collections
USE **visual resource collections**

visual materials
VW.695
ALT **visual material**
SN Items that convey information through images rather than text. Use a more specific term if possible.
UF aids, visual
materials, nonprint
materials, visual
media, visual
nonprint materials
visual aids
visual media
CN V.VW.AFU.ALO.AFU.DZW.BOK

visual materials (collections)
USE **visual resource collections**

visual media
USE **visual materials**

visual resource collections
HG.851
ALT **visual resource collection**
UF collections, visual
collections, visual resource
materials, visual (collections)
resources, visual
visual collections
visual materials (collections)
visual resources
CN H.HG.ALO.BUE.AXC

visual resources
USE **visual resource collections**

vitaceae
USE **vines**

vital records
VW.945
ALT **vital record**
SN Records of organizations which are vital to the continuity of a business in case of emergency or after a disaster. (ICA)
UF records, vital
CN V.VW.AFU.ARI.AFU.CXA

vital records (vital statistics records)
USE **vital statistics records**

vital statistics records
VW.946 (L)
ALT **vital statistics record**
SN Public records kept by a state, city, or other governmental subdivision, under a statutory provision, of births, deaths, marriages, diseases, divorces, and other life events. (BLACKS)
UF records, vital statistics
vital records (vital statistics records)
CN V.VW.AFU.ARI.AFU.DCU

vitas
USE **resumes**

vitreous enamel
USE **porcelain enamel**

vitrification
KT.928 (A)
ALT **vitrified**
CN K.KT.ALO.CLM

vitrified header
USE **glazed header**

vitrines
TG.428 (N)
ALT **vitrine**
SN Small cabinets with glass doors and generally glass shelves for the display of miniatures or art objects; developed in France and adopted elsewhere. Also took the form of tables with glass tops. (PC)
CN V.TG.AFU.AFU.AXC.ALO.ARI.ALO.AXC.AXC

vitrines (showcases)
USE **showcases**

Vitrolite (TM)
MT.273
SN Used for thick homogeneous opaque structural glass used especially for ornamental finish on surfaces exposed to the weather. (W)
CN M.MT.AFU.AFU.AFU.BIQ.AFU.AXC.AFU.AXC

Vitruvian scrolls
DG.151
ALT **Vitruvian scroll**
SN Use for wave scrolls when occurring in the context of classicizing styles.
UF scrolls, Vitruvian
Vitruvian waves
waves, Vitruvian
CN D.DG.AFU.ARI.ALO.CRG.AXC.AFU

Vitruvian waves
USE **Vitruvian scrolls**

vivariums
RK.1180 (L)
ALT **vivarium**
SN Use for structures built to raise or observe plants or land animals.
CN V.RK.AFU.ALO.ALO.FIM.ALO.BCW

Vivex
USE **three-color carbro process**

vivianite
USE **blue ocher**

vivid blue
DL.213
UF blue, bright
blue, cerulean (color)
blue, cobalt (color)
blue, genuine ultramarine
blue, methyl
blue, royal
blue, sapphire
blue, ultramarine (color)
blue, vivid
bright blue
bright ultramarine
centroid color 176
cerulean blue (color)
cobalt blue (color)
deep ultramarine
genuine ultramarine blue
methyl blue
royal blue
sapphire blue

ultramarine
ultramarine blue (color)
ultramarine blue, genuine
ultramarine, bright
ultramarine, deep
CN D.DL.AFU.AFU.BZY.AFU

vivid bluish green
DL.196
UF blue green
bluish green, bright
bluish green, vivid
bright bluish green
centroid color 158
green, bright bluish
green, turquoise
green, vivid bluish
turquoise green
CN D.DL.AFU.AFU.BUE.DCU.ALO.AFU

vivid cerulean blue
USE **strong greenish blue**

vivid chartreuse
USE **vivid yellow green**

vivid emerald green
USE **strong bluish green**

vivid green
DL.164
UF blue green, bright
bright blue green
bright green
centroid color 139
emerald (color)
green, bright
green, vivid
CN D.DL.AFU.AFU.BUE.AFU

vivid greenish blue
DL.233
UF blue, bright greenish
blue, cerulean (color)
blue, vivid greenish
bright greenish blue
centroid color 167
cerulean blue (color)
greenish blue, bright
greenish blue, vivid
CN D.DL.AFU.AFU.BZY.DCU.AFU.AFU

vivid greenish yellow
DL.135
UF bright chartreuse yellow
bright greenish yellow
bright lemon yellow
centroid color 97
chartreuse yellow, bright
greenish yellow, bright
greenish yellow, vivid
lemon yellow
sulphur yellow
yellow, bright chartreuse
yellow, bright greenish
yellow, lemon
yellow, sulphur
yellow, vivid greenish
CN D.DL.AFU.AFU.BCW.CRG.ALO.AFU

vivid orange
DL.61
UF bright orange
cadmium orange (color)
centroid color 48
chrome orange
orange, bright
orange, cadmium (color)
orange, chrome
orange, orpiment
orange, vivid
orpiment orange
CN D.DL.AFU.AFU.ARI.AFU

vivid orange yellow
DL.126
UF bright reddish yellow
bright yellowish orange
centroid color 66
chrome yellow (color)
orange yellow, vivid
orange, bright yellowish
reddish yellow, bright
yellow, bright reddish
yellow, chrome (color)
yellow, vivid orange
yellowish orange, bright
CN D.DL.AFU.AFU.BCW.CRG.AFU.AFU

vivid peacock blue
USE **strong greenish blue**

vivid pink
DL.4
UF carmine (color)
centroid color 1
pink, vivid
rose
CN D.DL.AFU.AFU.AFU.AFU

vivid purple
DL.267
UF amethyst violet
bright red violet
bright violet
centroid color 216
purple, vivid
red violet
red violet, bright
violet purple
violet, amethyst
violet, bright
CN D.DL.AFU.AFU.CFS.AFU

vivid purplish blue
DL.243
UF blue violet
blue violet, deep
blue violet, light
blue, bright reddish
blue, French
blue, phenyl
blue, royal
blue, sapphire
blue, smalt
blue, ultramarine (color)
blue, vivid purplish
bluish violet
bright reddish blue
bright ultramarine
centroid color 194
deep blue violet
deep ultramarine
French blue
light blue violet
phenyl blue
purplish blue, vivid
reddish blue, bright
royal blue
sapphire blue
smalt blue
ultramarine
ultramarine blue (color)
ultramarine, bright
ultramarine, deep
violet, bluish
CN D.DL.AFU.AFU.BZY.DCU.ALO.AFU

vivid purplish red
DL.51
UF bright bluish red
bright rose
carmine (color)
carmine, rose
centroid color 254
cerise
crimson
deep magenta
fuchsia
fuchsia purple
fuchsia rose
madder, rose
magenta (color)
magenta, deep
pink, rose
purple, fuchsia
purple, rhodamine
purple, Tyrian (color)
purplish red, vivid
red, vivid purplish
rhodamine purple
rose
rose carmine
rose madder
rose pink
rose, bright
rose, fuchsia
Tyrian purple (color)
CN D.DL.AFU.AFU.ALO.CFS.AFU.AFU

vivid red
DL.35
UF blood red
bright red
bright yellowish red
brown red
brown, rose
cadmium red (color)
carmine (color)
carmine lake
carmine rose
carmine, dark
centroid color 11
Chinese vermilion (color)
cochineal (color)
crimson
crimson madder

dark carmine
geranium lake
kermes (color)
lake (color)
lake, carmine
lake, geranium
madder, crimson
red orange
red, blood
red, bright
red, bright yellowish
red, brown
red, cadmium (color)
red, rose
red, spectrum
red, vivid
rose brown
rose red
rose, carmine
scarlet
scarlet red
spectrum red
vermilion (color)
vermilion, Chinese (color)
yellowish red, bright
CN D.DL.AFU.AFU.ALO.AFU

vivid reddish orange
DL.69
UF bright reddish orange
bright yellowish red
cadmium red (color)
centroid color 34
chrome orange
Dutch vermilion
French vermilion
light vermilion
minium (color)
orange lead
orange, bright reddish
orange, chrome
orange, red
orange, vivid reddish
red lead (color)
red orange
red, bright yellowish
red, cadmium (color)
reddish orange, bright
reddish orange, vivid
sandarach
scarlet
scarlet vermilion (color)
vermilion (color)
vermilion, Dutch
vermilion, French
vermilion, light
vermilion, scarlet (color)
yellowish red, bright
CN D.DL.AFU.AFU.ARI.BOK.AFU.AFU

vivid reddish purple
DL.289
UF bright red violet
bright reddish violet
centroid color 236
fuchsia
orchid purple
plum (color)
purple, orchid
purple, vivid reddish
red violet, bright
reddish purple, vivid
reddish violet, bright
violet, bright reddish
CN D.DL.AFU.AFU.CFS.DCU.AFU.AFU

vivid turquoise
USE **strong bluish green**

vivid turquoise blue
USE **moderate greenish blue**
strong bluish green
strong greenish blue

vivid turquoise green
USE **strong bluish green**

vivid violet
DL.255
UF blue violet
blue violet, deep
bluish violet
bluish violet, bright
bright bluish violet
bright violet
centroid color 205
deep blue violet
magenta (color)
methyl violet
violet, bluish
violet, bright bluish
violet, methyl
violet, vivid
CN D.DL.AFU.AFU.BZY.DCU.ARI.AFU

vivid yellow
DL.112
UF aureolin (color)
bright gold
bright reddish yellow
bright yellow
cadmium, light
canary yellow
centroid color 82
chrome yellow (color)
gold (color)
gold, bright
golden yellow
lemon yellow
light cadmium
reddish yellow, bright
sulphur yellow
yellow, bright
yellow, bright reddish
yellow, canary
yellow, chrome (color)
yellow, golden
yellow, lemon
yellow, sulphur
yellow, vivid
CN D.DL.AFU.AFU.BCW.AFU

vivid yellow green
DL.155
UF bright chartreuse
bright green yellow
bright lime green
bright yellowish green
centroid color 115
chartreuse green
chartreuse, bright
chartreuse, vivid
green yellow, bright
green, bright lime
green, bright yellowish
green, chartreuse
green, vivid yellow
lime green, bright
vivid chartreuse
yellow green, vivid
yellowish green, bright
CN D.DL.AFU.AFU.BOK.AFU

vivid yellowish green
DL.185
UF bright green
bright kelly green
bright yellowish green
centroid color 129
emerald (color)
green, bright
green, bright kelly
green, bright yellowish
green, Paris
green, vivid yellowish
kelly green, bright
Paris green
yellowish green, bright
yellowish green, vivid
CN D.DL.AFU.AFU.BUE.DCU.AFU.AFU

vivid yellowish pink
DL.25
UF centroid color 25
orange, red
pink, vivid yellowish
red orange
rose
yellowish pink, vivid
CN D.DL.AFU.AFU.AFU.CLM.ALO.AFU

Vladimir-Suzdalian
FL.3085
UF Suzdalian
CN F.FL.ALO.BCW.ALO.AFU.ALO.
BCW.ARI.ALO

vocabulary control
USE **authority control**

vocalists
USE **singers**

vocational education facilities
USE **vocational schools**

vocational guidance
KG.37 (L)
UF career guidance
guidance, vocational
occupational guidance
CN K.KG.AFU.AFU.ALO.AXC.AFU

vocational schools
RK.824 (A,L,B)
ALT **vocational school**
UF facilities, vocational education
schools, technical

schools, trade
schools, vocational
technical schools
trade schools
vocational education facilities
CN V.RK.AFU.ALO.ALO.CXA.ARI.ALO.DZW

void
USE **negative space**

volatile solvents
USE **solvents**

volcanic glass
USE **obsidian**

volcanic glass (white pigment)
USE **pumice (white pigment)**

volcanic rock
MT.624 (L)
UF extrusive rock
rock, extrusive
rock, volcanic
CN M.MT.AFU.AFU.AFU.DCU.AFU.AFU.ALO.ALO

volcanic tufa
USE **tufa**

volcanoes
RD.181 (L,R)
ALT **volcano**
CN V.RD.ARI.AFU.AXC.AFU.AFU.AFU.ARI

Volksgeist
BM.337
UF spirit of the nation
CN B.BM.ALO.ALO.BZY

volleyball courts
RK.1021
ALT **volleyball court**
UF courts, volleyball
CN V.RK.AFU.ALO.ALO.EWY.ALO.CLM

volsurae
USE **voussoirs**

volume
BM.809 (L,B)
CN B.BM.CFS.ARI.AXC.BUE.BUE

volume color
BM.120
SN A partly or wholly transparent color perceived as filling a space in three dimensions. (W)
UF bulky color
color, bulky
color, volume
CN B.BM.AFU.AFU.ARI.BOK.ALO.AFU.CRG

volume, negative
USE **negative space**

volumes, hollow
USE **negative space**

volumes, memorial
USE **Festschriften**

voluntary associations
HG.831 (L)
ALT **voluntary association**
UF associations, voluntary
CN H.HG.ALO.BCW.CRG

volunteers
HG.31 (L)
ALT **volunteer**
CN H.HG.AFU.AXC.ALO.BIQ

voluted arms
USE **scrolled arms**

volutes
RT.140 (A,B,R)
ALT **volute**
SN Term first applied to the spiral forms in Ionic and Composite capitals; sometimes used also for other three-dimensional scrolling elements in architecture and the decorative arts.
CN V.RT.AFU.AFU.AFU.AXC.BIQ.ALO.ARI.ALO.BUE

vomitories
RM.358
ALT **vomitory**
SN Entrances piercing the banks of seats of theaters or amphitheaters. (W)
CN V.RM.AFU.DIO.AXC.AXC.AFU.CFS

voodoo
KD.304 (L,R)
CN K.KD.AFU.BIQ.ARI.AFU

Vorticist
FL.3346 (L,R)
ALT **Vorticism**
CN F.FL.ALO.BCW.ALO.AXC.DIO.ALO.BZY.ARI

voters' lists
VW.287
ALT **voters' list**
UF electors' rolls
electors, registers of
lists, voters'
registers of electors
rolls, electors'
CN V.VW.AFU.AFU.AFU.FZU.BCW.ALO.BZY

voting districts
USE **election districts**

voting papers
USE **ballots**

voting precincts
USE **election districts**

vouchers
VW.866
ALT **voucher**
SN Documents serving as evidence or proof, specifically, a receipt or statement attesting to the expenditure or receipt of money, usually accompanied by bills or other evidence of indebtedness or expenditure. (ICA)
CN V.VW.AFU.ARI.AFU.BIQ.CXA.AXC.BCW

Vounous stage
FL.2894
CN F.FL.ALO.AXC.ARI.ARI.AFU.AFU.ALO

voussoir brick
USE **compass brick**

voussoirs
RT.694
ALT **voussoir**
SN Masonry units that form an arch or vault. (HAS)
UF arch blocks
blocks, arch
vawcers
veusurae
volsurae
CN V.RT.AFU.AFU.ALO.AFU.AXC

voyagers
USE **travelers**

voyeurism
BM.584 (R)
CN B.BM.BUE.AXC.AFU.AFU

voyeuses
TG.202
ALT **voyeuse**
SN 18th-century French term for rather low-seated chairs with a padded top to the back on which an occupant may rest the elbows when sitting astride the seat. First made in France about 1740 and later in England. (DDA)
UF chairs, conversation
chairs, gossiping
chaises caquetoires
chaises en voyeuse
conversation chairs
conversation-seats
gossiping chairs
CN V.TG.AFU.AFU.ALO.AFU.AFU.ALO.FZU

voyeuses à genoux
TG.203
ALT **voyeuse à genoux**
SN A special type of voyeuse designed for women to kneel on, as it was inelegant for them to sit astride. (DDA)
UF voyeuses en prie-dieu
voyeuses pour femme
voyeuses pour se mettre à genoux
CN V.TG.AFU.AFU.ALO.AFU.AFU.ALO.FZU.AFU

voyeuses en prie-dieu
USE **voyeuses à genoux**

voyeuses pour femme
USE **voyeuses à genoux**

voyeuses pour se mettre à genoux
USE **voyeuses à genoux**

vuide-poches
USE **vide-poches**

vulne windows
USE **lowside windows**

vyses
USE **solid newel stairs**

W-beams
USE **wide-flange beams**

W-trusses
USE **Fink trusses**

Wabanaki
USE **Abnaki**

Wabembe
USE **Bembe (Northeastern Zaire)**

Wabena
USE **Bena**

Wachaga
USE **Chagga**

Waco
FL.1403 (L)
CN F.FL.ALO.ALO.ARI.AFU.BOK.FIM.ALO

Wadi Rabah pottery
FL.2946
UF pottery, Wadi Rabah
CN F.FL.ALO.AXC.ARI.AXC.ALO.BIQ.DCU

Wadumbo
USE **Dumbo**

waffle flat plate construction
USE **waffle slabs**

waffle slabs
RT.34
ALT **waffle slab**
SN Two-way slab systems, with the slab reinforced by ribs running in both directions, creating a waffle pattern.
UF constructions, waffle flat plate
flat plate construction, waffle
slabs, two-way waffle
slabs, waffle
two-way waffle slabs
waffle flat plate construction
waffle slabs, two-way
CN V.RT.AFU.AFU.AFU.ALO.ARI.ALO.AFU.ALO.AXC

waffle slabs, two-way
USE **waffle slabs**

wages
BM.376 (L,B)
SN Use for compensation, usually in money, paid to employees for services rendered according to contract or other agreement, on an hourly, daily, or piecework basis. For such compensation paid on the basis of longer time periods, use **salaries**.
UF pay
CN B.BM.ARI.AXC.AXC

wagon benches
USE **wagon seats**

wagon roofs
USE **barrel roofs**

wagon seats
TG.319
ALT **wagon seat**
SN Plain, unupholstered settees, usually with slat backs, for use either indoors or in a wagon. (RHDEL2)
UF benches, wagon
rumble seats (wagon seats)
seats, rumble (wagon seats)
seats, wagon
wagon benches
CN V.TG.AFU.AFU.ALO.ALO.CFS

wagon vaults
USE **barrel vaults**

wagonhead vaults
USE **barrel vaults**

wagons, gypsy
USE **caravans**

wagons, tea
USE **tea wagons**

Wahehe
USE **Hehe**

Wahpekute
USE **Dakota**

wainscot chairs
TG.159
ALT **wainscot chair**
SN 16th- and 17th-century joined chairs having a solid paneled back and a plank seat; generally made of oak and often carved.
UF chairs, panel-back
chairs, wainscot
panel-back chairs
panelled-back chairs
CN V.TG.AFU.AFU.ALO.AFU.AFU.AFU.NIE.ERE

wainscoting
RT.655 (R)
SN Decorative or protective facings applied to the lower portion of an interior partition or wall, such as wood paneling. (DAC)
UF lambruscatura
spalliera
wainscots
CN V.RT.AFU.AFU.AFU.BIQ.BUE.ALO.AFU.BCW.BOK

wainscots
USE **wainscoting**

waists, chimney
USE **chimney throats**

waiters, wine
USE **wine coolers**

waiting rooms
RM.182 (A,B)
ALT **waiting room**
UF rooms, waiting
CN V.RM.AFU.DIO.ALO.CXA.DIO

Waiwai
FL.1600 (L)
UF Ouayeoue
Woyamana
CN F.FL.ALO.ALO.ARI.ARI.AFU.HIK

Waja
FL.205
CN F.FL.ALO.AFU.AXC.AFU.AFU.ALO.AFU.ARI

Wakasugi ware
USE **Saiko Kutani**

Wakerewe
USE **Kerewe**

wakes
KM.26
CN K.KM.AFU.ARI.ARI.BZY

Walapai
FL.1484 (L)
UF Hualapai
CN F.FL.ALO.ALO.ARI.AFU.CFS.DCU

Waldalgesheim Style
FL.2527
CN F.FL.ALO.AXC.AFU.BOK.ALO.ALO.AXC

walk-ups
RK.1387
ALT **walk-up**
SN Designates multistory apartment or commercial buildings lacking elevators.
CN V.RK.AFU.ALO.AXC.CLM

walking streets
USE **pedestrian streets**

walks
USE **walkways**

walks, captain's
USE **widow's walks**

walks, garden
USE **garden walks**

walks, moving
USE **moving walkways**

walks, widow's
USE **widow's walks**

walkways
RK.1568 (A,B)
ALT **walkway**
UF pedestrian ways
walks

ways, pedestrian
CN V.RK.ALO.ALO.BUE

walkways, covered
USE **covered walkways**

walkways, elevated
USE **skywalks**

walkways, moving
USE **moving walkways**

walkways, pedestrian
USE **footbridges**

wall anchors
USE **beam anchors**

wall arcades
USE **blind arcades**

wall-beds
USE **box beds**

wall board
USE **wallboard**

wall chases
USE **chases**

wall cranes
TB.71
ALT **wall crane**
SN Cranes with a horizontal arm supported from a wall or columns of a building. The arm may also support a trolley. (MEANS)
UF cranes, wall
CN V.TB.AFU.ARI.AFU.BCW.AXC.BZY

wall cupboards
USE **hanging cupboards**

wall desks
TG.560
ALT **wall desk**
UF desks, wall
CN V.TG.AFU.AFU.AXC.ALO.BZY.FCS

wall piers
RT.191
ALT **wall pier**
SN Use for piers, such as would include several columns or pilasters, that are thickenings of or projections from a wall.
UF piers, wall
CN V.RT.AFU.AFU.AFU.AXC.CRG.AFU.ALO.ARI

wall plates
RT.703
ALT **wall plate**
SN Horizontal members placed along the tops of walls or a series of studs to support joists or rafters.
UF plates, raising
plates, wall
raising plates
CN V.RT.AFU.AFU.ALO.ALO.ARI.ALO

wall plates (finish hardware)
TF.267
ALT **wall plate (finish hardware)**
SN Use for plates attached to walls to hide something unsightly.
UF plates, wall (finish hardware)
CN V.TF.AFU.AFU.AFU.AFU.DZW.ARI

wall ribs
RT.693
ALT **wall rib**
SN Ribs, usually decorative, located where a vault abuts a wall.
UF arcs formerets
formerets
ribs, wall
CN V.RT.AFU.AFU.ALO.AFU.ARI.BOK

wall scrapers
TB.529 (N)
ALT **wall scraper**
SN Scrapers with a wide flat blade; used primarily for cleaning walls of wallpaper. (BLACKB)
UF scrapers, wall
CN V.TB.AFU.ARI.EWY.ALO.DIO.ALO

wall sockets
USE **power outlets**

wall stringers
USE **wall strings**

wall strings
RT.1127
ALT **wall string**
SN Stair strings set against a wall. (DAC)
UF stringers, wall
strings, wall
wall stringers
CN V.RT.AFU.BIQ.AXC.ALO.BOK.ALO

wall systems
RT.586 (A)
ALT **wall system**
SN Curtain walls assembled from highly similar components, each combining two or more of the traditionally separate elements of windows, external finish wall, internal finish wall, and insulation.
UF systems, wall
CN V.RT.AFU.AFU.AFU.BIQ.BUE.AFU.ALO.ARI.AFU.AFU

wall tile
MT.2281 (B)
SN A glazed tile used as a facing on a wall. (DAC)
UF facing tile
tile, facing
tile, wall
CN M.MT.AFU.ALO.IFM.AXC

wall towers
RM.424
ALT **wall tower**
UF towers, wall
CN V.RM.AFU.DZW.BIQ

wallboard
MT.2214 (L,B)
UF dry wall
drywall
wall board
CN M.MT.AFU.ALO.ARI.AFU.AFU

wallboard nails
USE **gypsum board nails**

wallboard, gypsum
USE **gypsum board**

walled gardens
RK.1414 (A)
ALT **walled garden**
UF enclosed gardens
gardens, enclosed
gardens, walled
CN V.RK.ALO.AFU.AFU.AFU.BZY

wallpaper
MT.2401 (A,L,N,B,R)
SN Paper, or paperlike material, usually decorated in colors, which is pasted or otherwise affixed to walls or ceilings of rooms. (DAC)
CN M.MT.AFU.ARI.BZY.AXC.BCW

wallpaper brushes
TB.507 (N)
ALT **wallpaper brush**
UF brushes, paperhanging
brushes, wallpaper
paperhanging brushes
CN V.TB.AFU.ARI.EWY.ALO.ALO.ALO

walls
RT.570 (A,L,B,R)
ALT **wall**
SN Vertical architectural members used to define and divide spaces. (W)
CN V.RT.AFU.AFU.AFU.BIQ.BUE.AFU

walls, battened
USE **battened walls**

walls, battered
USE **battered walls**

walls, bearing
USE **loadbearing walls**

walls, blank
USE **blank walls**

walls, blind
USE **blank walls**

walls, boundary
USE **boundary walls**

walls, canted
USE **canted walls**

walls, cavity
USE **cavity walls**

walls, city
USE **city walls**

walls, crib retaining
USE **cribbing**

walls, curtain
USE **curtain walls**

walls, curtain (fortifications elements)
USE **curtain walls (fortification elements)**

walls, dead
USE **blank walls**

walls, defensive
USE **defensive walls**

walls, diaphragm
USE **diaphragm walls**

walls, dry
USE **dry laid walls**

walls, dry laid
USE **dry laid walls**

walls, dry stone
USE **dry laid walls**

walls, enclosure
USE **curtain walls**

walls, exterior
USE **exterior walls**

walls, external
USE **exterior walls**

walls, faced
USE **faced walls**

walls, fire
USE **fire walls**

walls, fire resistive
USE **fire walls**

walls, flood
USE **levees**

walls, foundation
USE **foundation walls**

walls, gable
USE **gable ends**

walls, gravity
USE **gravity walls**

walls, hollow
USE **cavity walls**

walls, hollow masonry
USE **cavity walls**

walls, interior
USE **interior walls**

walls, internal
USE **interior walls**

walls, loadbearing
USE **loadbearing walls**

walls, mass retaining
USE **gravity walls**

walls, mortarless
USE **dry laid walls**

walls, nonbearing
USE **nonbearing walls**

walls, parapet
USE **parapets**

walls, party
USE **party walls**

walls, perforated
USE **pierced walls**

walls, periphery
USE **exterior walls**

walls, pierced
USE **pierced walls**

walls, prayer
USE **qibla walls**

walls, proscenium
USE **proscenium walls**

walls, qibla
USE **qibla walls**

walls, retaining
USE **retaining walls**

walls, screen
USE **pierced walls**

walls, shear
USE **shear walls**

walls, sleeper
USE **sleeper walls**

walls, strapped
USE **battened walls**

walls, talus
USE **battered walls**

walls, terrace
USE **terrace walls**

walls, veneered
USE **veneered walls**

walls, window
USE **curtain walls**

walnut
MT.1317 (L)
UF Juglans regia
CN M.MT.AFU.AFU.ALO.BIQ.DCU.
AFU.AFU.AFU.MQW

walnut oil
MT.2024
SN A yellowish drying oil used especially for artist's paints. (MH)
UF oil, walnut
CN M.MT.AFU.AFU.ARI.ARI.AXC.AFU.
DCU

walnut, American
USE **black walnut**

walnut, American black
USE **black walnut**

walnut, black
USE **black walnut**

walnut, burled
USE **burled walnut**

walnut, common Persian
USE **English walnut**

walnut, East India
USE **East India walnut**

walnut, English
USE **English walnut**

walnut, European
USE **English walnut**

walnut, white
USE **butternut**

Wamakua
USE **Makua**

Wamawia
USE **Mawia**

Wan-li
USE **Wanli**

Wandala
USE **Mandara**

Wandorobo
USE **Dorobo**

Waniaturu
USE **Turu**

Wanika
USE **Mijikenda**

Wanli
FL.1906
UF Wan-li
CN F.FL.ALO.ARI.ALO.AFU.AFU.ALO.
DIO.BZY

want lists
VW.273 (L)
ALT **want list**
SN Use for lists of items lacking or needed, such as a list of books issued by a librarian or a list of objects wanted for a museum collection.
UF lists, want
CN V.VW.AFU.AFU.AFU.FZU.BCW.AFU.
CFS

Wapangwa
USE **Pangwa**

Wapogoro
USE **Pogoro**

Wappinger
FL.1306 (L)
CN F.FL.ALO.ALO.ARI.AFU.ARI.CXA

waqwaq
USE **arabesques**

war
BM.1119 (L,R)
CN B.BM.CRG.BCW.CLM.ARI

war cemeteries
RG.36 (L)
ALT **war cemetery**
UF cemeteries, military

cemeteries, war
military cemeteries
CN V.RG.AFU.AFU.ALO.ALO.BIQ

war memorials
RK.853 (A,L,B,R)
ALT **war memorial**
UF memorials, war
CN V.RK.AFU.ALO.ALO.DCU.AFU

war museums
USE **military museums**

war photographers
HG.124 (L)
ALT **war photographer**
UF photographers, war
CN H.HG.AFU.AXC.AXC.AFU.AFU.ALO.AXC.DOI.BIQ

war photography
KT.309 (L,R)
SN Use with regard to photography in war for the purposes of historical documentation. For military applications of photography, such as for mapping or training, use **military photography**. (LCSH)
UF photography, war
CN K.KT.AFU.ALO.DUC.DIO.AFU.DZW

war, civil
USE **civil war**

war, nuclear
USE **nuclear war**

ward files
USE **flat files**

warded keys
TF.542
ALT **warded key**
UF keys, warded
CN V.TF.AFU.ALO.ARI.AFU.DCU

warded locks
TF.226
ALT **warded lock**
SN Locks having for obstacles, projections cast in the keyhole opening or on the inside of the case. (STEIN)
UF locks, warded
CN V.TF.AFU.AFU.AFU.AFU.DIO.BIQ.AFU.FCS

wardens, game
USE **game wardens**

wardrobe hooks
TF.158
ALT **wardrobe hook**
SN Hooks with a single prong, for use on the side walls of closets and wardrobes. (BROWNL)
UF hooks, wardrobe
CN V.TF.AFU.AFU.AFU.AFU.CXA.BUE

wardrobes
TG.597 (N,B,R)
ALT **wardrobe**
SN Use for large upright pieces of furniture, especially those fitted with hooks, pegs, or rods, used for hanging clothes; generally having two large doors and may have a drawer or drawers below. Distinct from **clothes presses** in which clothes are stored on shelves.
UF chifforobes (wardrobes)
clothes cupboards
cupboards, clothes
garderobes (wardrobes)
CN V.TG.AFU.AFU.AXC.ALO.CXA

wardrobes (rooms)
RM.207 (B,R)
ALT **wardrobe (room)**
SN Use for rooms devoted to the storage, and sometimes the care, of clothes.
UF garderobes
vestiaries
CN V.RM.AFU.DIO.ALO.DCU.DIO

wardrobes, low
USE **low clothes presses**

wardrobes, wing
USE **wing clothes presses**

wards
USE **election districts**
precincts

wards, hospital
USE **hospital wards**

wards, maternity
USE **maternity wards**

ware, Agkhand
USE **Agkhand ware**

ware, Amol
USE **Amol ware**

ware, Amuq B
USE **Amuq B ware**

ware, Archaic
USE **Archaic ware**

ware, Archaic painted
USE **Archaic ware**
Hassuna Archaic ware

ware, Argive Miyan
USE **Argive Minyan ware**

ware, Arretine
USE **Arretine ware**

ware, Atchana
USE **Atchana ware**

ware, Ayios Onouphrios
USE **Ayios Onouphrios ware**

ware, Banded
USE **Bandkeramik**

ware, base ring
USE **base ring ware**

ware, basket
USE **basket ware**

ware, Billa
USE **Atchana ware**

ware, black-burnished
USE **black-burnished ware**

ware, black burnished (Helladic pottery)
USE **black burnished ware (Helladic pottery)**

ware, black lustrous
USE **black lustrous ware**

ware, black-mouthed
USE **black-mouthed ware**

ware, black-on-buff
USE **black-on-buff ware**

ware, black-on-red
USE **black-on-red ware**

ware, black-slip-and-combed
USE **black-slip-and-combed ware**

ware, black-topped red
USE **black-topped red ware**

ware, Böttger
USE **Böttger ware**

ware, brittle
USE **brittle ware**

ware, brittle-painted
USE **brittle-painted ware**

ware, brown-on-cream
USE **brown-on-cream ware**

ware, brown-slipped
USE **brown-slipped ware**

ware, Bucchereo
USE **Bucchero ware**

ware, buff
USE **buff ware**

ware, Calene
USE **Calene ware**

ware, Cappadocian
USE **Cappadocian ware**

ware, Çatal West
USE **Çatal West ware**

ware, ceramic
USE **ceramics**

ware, Ch'ing-pai
USE **Qingbai ware**

ware, channeled
USE **channeled ware**

ware, Chun
USE **Jun ware**

ware, Compagnie des Indes
USE **Compagnie des Indes ware**

ware, Corded

USE **Corded ware**

ware, crusted
USE **crusted ware**

ware, Cycladic white
USE **Cycladic white ware**

ware, Damascus
USE **Damascus ware**

ware, Daphne
USE **Daphne ware**

ware, dark-burnished
USE **dark-burnished ware**

ware, dark-faced burnished
USE **dark-faced burnished ware**

ware, dark-faced incised
USE **dark-faced incised ware**

ware, dark-on-light painted
USE **dark-on-light painted ware**

ware, dimple based
USE **dimple based ware**

ware, Ding
USE **Ding ware**

ware, early red
USE **early red ware**

ware, eggshell
USE **eggshell ware**

ware, Ephyraean
USE **Ephyraean ware**

ware, Erimi
USE **red-on-white ware**

ware, Faliscan
USE **Faliscan ware**

ware, Forum
USE **Forum ware**

ware, Fostat
USE **Fostat ware**

ware, Fustat
USE **Fostat ware**

ware, Gabri
USE **Gabri ware**

ware, Garrus
USE **Garrus ware**

ware, Gombroon
USE **Gombroon ware**

ware, gray
USE **gray ware**

ware, gray burnished
USE **gray burnished ware**

ware, gray burnished (Syrian)
USE **Syrian gray-black ware**

ware, Gray Minyan
USE **Gray Minyan ware**

ware, gritty buff
USE **gritty buff ware**

ware, Gurgan
USE **Gurgan ware**

ware, Habaner
USE **Habaner ware**

ware, Hanau
USE **Hanau pottery**

ware, Hassuna Archaic
USE **Hassuna Archaic ware**

ware, Hassuna standard
USE **Hassuna standard ware**

ware, Hsing
USE **Xing ware**

ware, Humber
USE **Humber ware**

ware, Hurrian
USE **Atchana ware**

ware, Incised Banded
USE **Stichbandkeramik**

ware, intermediate
USE **intermediate ware**

ware, Ismailabad
USE **Ismailabad ware**

ware, Iznik
USE **Iznik ware**

ware, Jesuit
USE **Jesuit ware**

ware, Ju
USE **Ru ware**

ware, Ju Chou
USE **Ru ware**

ware, Jun
USE **Jun ware**

ware, Kamares
USE **Kamares ware**

ware, Kashan
USE **Kashan ware**

ware, Kerman
USE **Kirman ware**

ware, Khabur
USE **Khabur ware**

ware, Khirbet Kerak
USE **Khirbet Kerak ware**

ware, Kirman
USE **Kirman ware**

ware, knobbed
USE **knobbed ware**

ware, Kubachi
USE **Kubachi ware**

ware, Kubatcha
USE **Kubachi ware**

ware, Kütahya
USE **Kütahya ware**

ware, Lakabi
USE **Lakabi ware**

ware, Laqabi
USE **Lakabi ware**

ware, latten
USE **pewter**

ware, light-on-dark
USE **light-on-dark ware**

ware, Linear
USE **Linienbandkeramik**

ware, lost color
USE **lost color ware**

ware, Luna
USE **Luna ware**

ware, Lung-ch'uan
USE **Longshan**

ware, Mashhad
USE **Meshhed ware**

ware, matt-painted
USE **matt-painted ware**

ware, Megarian
USE **Megarian**

ware, Meshhed
USE **Meshhed ware**

ware, metallic (Anatolian pottery)
USE **metallic ware (Anatolian pottery)**

ware, metallic (Levantine pottery)
USE **metallic ware (Levantine pottery)**

ware, mica-dusted
USE **micaceous ware**

ware, micaceous
USE **micaceous ware**

ware, Minai
USE **Minai ware**

ware, Minyan
USE **Minyan ware**

ware, multiple-brush painted
USE **multiple-brush painted ware**

ware, Nassau
USE **Westerwald stoneware**

ware, Nishapur
USE **Nishapur ware**

ware, orange-burnished
USE **orange-burnished ware**

ware, Palissy
USE **Palissy ware**

ware, Parian
USE **Parian ware**

ware, pattern-burnished
USE **pattern-burnished ware**

ware, Pergamene
USE **Pergamene ware**

ware, Pirgos
USE **Pyrgos ware**

ware, Punch'ong
USE **Punch'ong ware**

ware, Pyrgos
USE **Pyrgos ware**

ware, Qingbai
USE **Qingbai ware**

ware, Rakka
USE **Raqqa ware**

ware, raku
USE **raku**

ware, Raqqa
USE **Raqqa ware**

ware, Rayy
USE **Rayy ware**

ware, red-black burnished
USE **Khirbet Kerak ware**

ware, red burnished
USE **red burnished ware**

ware, red-gloss
USE **red-gloss pottery**

ware, red lustrous
USE **red lustrous ware**

ware, red-on-black
USE **red-on-black ware**

ware, red-on-cream
USE **red-on-cream ware**

ware, red-on-red
USE **red-on-red ware**

ware, red-on-white
USE **red-on-white ware**

ware, red-pattern burnished
USE **red-pattern burnished ware**

ware, red (Persian pottery)
USE **early red ware**

ware, red-polished
USF **red-polished ware**

ware, red polished
USE **red polished ware**

ware, red-slipped
USE **red-slipped ware**

ware, red wash
USE **red wash ware**

ware, red-washed buff
USE **red-washed buff ware**

ware, Rhages
USE **Rayy ware**

ware, Rhodes
USE **Rhodian ware**

ware, Rhodian
USE **Rhodian ware**

ware, ripple-burnished
USE ripple-burnished ware

ware, Ru
USE **Ru ware**

ware, Rusapha
USE **Rusapha ware**

ware, Samarra
USE **Samarra ware**

ware, Samian
USE **Samian ware**

ware, Sarab
USE **Sarab ware**

ware, Sari
USE **Sari ware**

ware, scarified
USE **scarified ware**

ware, scarlet
USE **scarlet ware**

ware, Seto
USE **Seto ware**

ware, soft
USE **soft ware**

ware, stamp-decorated
USE **stamped ware**

ware, stamped
USE **stamped ware**

ware, standard painted
USE **Hassuna standard ware**
standard painted ware

ware, Stroked
USE **Stichbandkeramik**

ware, Sue
USE **Sue ware**

ware, Sultanabad
USE **Sultanabad ware**

ware, Swatow
USE **Swatow ware**

ware, Syrian gray-black
USE **Syrian gray-black ware**

ware, Takatori
USE **Takatori ware**

ware, thorn
USE **thorn ware**

ware, three-color
USE **Sancai**

ware, Thuringian
USE **Thuringian ware**

ware, Tiger
USE **Tiger ware**

ware, Ting
USE **Ding ware**

ware, Transitional
USE **Kraak porcelain**

ware, Transitional blue-and-white
USE **Kraak porcelain**

ware, Urfirnis
USE **Urfirnis ware**

ware, Vasiliki
USE **Vasiliki ware**

ware, Veramin
USE **Veramin ware**

ware, Wakasugi
USE **Saiko Kutani**

ware, West Slope
USE **West Slope ware**

ware, Western sigillata
USE **Western sigillata ware**

ware, Westerwald
USE **Westerwald stoneware**

ware, white
USE **white ware**

ware, white cross-lined
USE **white cross-lined pottery**

ware, white-on-red
USE **white-on-red pottery**

ware, white painted
USE **white painted ware**

ware, white slip
USE **white slip ware**

ware, white-slipped red
USE **white-slipped red ware**

ware, Xing
USE **Xing ware**

ware, Yellow Minyan
USE **Yellow Minyan ware**

ware, yellow-slipped
USE **yellow-slipped ware**

ware, Yezd
USE **Yezd ware**

Warega
USE **Lega**

warehouse lists
USE **merchandise inventories**

warehouses
RK.1228 (A,L,N,B,R)
ALT **warehouse**
UF storehouses
CN V.RK.AFU.ALO.ALO.GFO.BZY

warehouses, bonded
USE **bonded warehouses**

warfare, guerilla
USE **guerilla warfare**

Wari
USE **Huari**

Waribe
USE **Ribe**

Warka
USE **Uruk**

warm air furnaces
RT.1416
ALT **warm air furnace**
UF furnaces, warm air
warm air heating furnaces
CN V.RT.ALO.BCW.AFU.ALO.AFU.
AXC.AFU

warm air heating
RT.1401 (L)
UF heating systems, warm air
heating, hot air
heating, warm air
hot air heating
systems, warm air heating
warm air heating systems
CN V.RT.ALO.BCW.AFU.AFU.ARI.BIQ

warm air heating furnaces
USE **warm air furnaces**

warm air heating systems
USE **warm air heating**

warm air systems, gravity
USE **gravity heating**

warm colors
BM.121
SN Colors commonly associated with fire, such as reds, oranges, and yellows, which suggest warmth and which appear to advance. (A-Z)
UF colors, warm
CN B.BM.AFU.AFU.ARI.BOK.ALO.AFU.
CXA

warm gray
USE **grayish yellow**

warmers, plate (furniture)
USE **plate warmers (furniture)**

warping
KT.929
ALT **warped**
SN Bending or twisting out of shape, such as that caused by drying, dampness, or heat. (W)
CN K.KT.ALO.CRG

warrant books
VW.940
ALT **warrant book**
SN Books which record the collection of unpaid taxes and the seizure and sale of property due to unpaid taxes. (BLACKS)
UF books, tax warrant
books, warrant
tax warrant books
CN V.VW.AFU.ARI.AFU.CLM.ARI

warranties
VW.898 (L)
ALT **warranty**
SN Guarantees with reference to goods offered for sale which assure that a breach may be answered by a claim for damages. (OCLD)
CN V.VW.AFU.ARI.AFU.BOK.BOK.ALO.
ARI.AFU

warrants
VW.382 (L)
ALT **warrant**
SN Documents giving authority to do something; especially used in civil and criminal law for the arrest of persons or for their production in court as witnesses.
CN V.VW.AFU.AFU.ALO.DUC.BOK

Warrau
FL.1634 (L)
CN F.FL.ALO.ALO.ARI.ARI.ARI.BOK

Warren girders
USE **Warren trusses**

Warren trusses
RT.374
ALT **Warren truss**
SN Trusses with parallel chords between which the braces and ties are set at the same angle so as to form a series of isoceles triangles. (RS)
UF girders, Warren
trusses, Warren
Warren girders
CN V.RT.AFU.AFU.AFU.BCW.CLM.AFU.
AFU.AFU.CXA

warrens, rabbit
USE **rabbit hutches**

Warri
USE **Itsekiri**

Warring Kingdoms
USE **Warring States**

Warring States
FL.1864 (L)
UF Chan-Kuo
Warring Kingdoms
Zhanquo
CN F.FL.ALO.ARI.ALO.AFU.AFU.ALO.
BIQ.AFU.ALO

Warrington-pattern hammers
TB.1085
ALT **Warrington-pattern hammer**
SN Hammers having a round face with a chamfered neck and a cross peen which tapers to a rounded tip; used as a general-purpose hammer. (SALAM)
UF hammers, Lancashire pattern riveting
hammers, Warrington-pattern
Lancashire pattern riveting hammers
CN V.TB.AFU.BCW.CFS.ALO.ARI.AFU.
BOK

Wasaramo
USE **Zaramo**

wash
MT.2550
SN Broad, thin film of highly diluted pigment. (A-Z)
CN M.MT.AFU.ARI.CRG.ALO.BOK

wash houses
USE **laundries**

wash-off relief process
USE **Eastman Wash-off Relief (TM)**

wash rooms
USE **lavatories (rooms)**

wash sinks
RT.1488
ALT **wash sink**
SN Use for large, deep sinks used for washing the arms and upper body and more commonly encountered in factories and hospitals than in houses; for smaller sinks for washing the hands and face, use **lavatories (sinks).**
UF sinks, wash
wash-up sinks
CN V.RT.ALO.BCW.ALO.ARI.CFS.BIQ.
AXC

wash-up sinks
USE **wash sinks**

wash ware, red
USE **red wash ware**

Washambala
USE **Shambala**

washers
USE **washing machines**

washers (fasteners)
TF.501 (N)
ALT **washer (fastener)**
CN V.TF.AFU.AFU.AFU.ALO.AFU.FIM

washers, air
USE **air washers**

washers, film
USE **film washers**

washfountains
RT.1492 (R)
ALT **washfountain**
SN Large usually circular wash basins, as in industrial plants, in which a spray of water activated by a foot pedal allows several workers to wash simultaneously. (RHDEL2)

CN V.RT.ALO.BCW.ALO.ARI.CFS.BZY

washhand stands
USE **washstands**

washhouses
RK.1344 (R)
ALT **washhouse**
CN V.RK.AFU.ALO.ARI.ARI.ALO

washi
MT.1966
CN M.MT.AFU.AFU.ARI.ALO.ALO.AXC.AXC.AFU.AXC

washing
KT.74
ALT **washed**
SN Cleansing with water or other liquid. (RHDEL2)
UF rinsing
CN K.KT.AFU.ALO.BIQ.BOK

washing machines
TB.345 (L,N)
ALT **washing machine**
SN Usually power-driven machines used for washing clothes and linens. (W)
UF machines, washing
washers
CN V.TB.AFU.ARI.CRG.AFU.ALO

washing stands
USE **washstands**

Washkuk
FL.3613 (L)
CN F.FL.ALO.BOK.AFU.AFU.ARI

Washo
FL.1321 (L)
CN F.FL.ALO.ALO.ARI.AFU.AXC.CRG

washroom accessories
USE **bathroom hardware**

washstands
TG.657 (N)
ALT **washstand**
SN Furniture combining features of a table and cupboard and used to hold articles (as a pitcher, basin, and towel) for washing the hands and face. (W)
UF commodes (washstands)
stands, washhand
stands, washing
washhand stands
washing stands
CN V.TG.AFU.AFU.BIQ.BCW.ALO.FCS

Wassily chairs
TG.94
ALT **Wassily chair**
UF Breuer chairs
chairs, Breuer
chairs, Wassily
CN V.TG.AFU.AFU.ALO.AFU.AFU.AFU.LZO

waste disposal
KG.126 (A,L,B)
UF disposal, waste
CN K.KG.AFU.AFU.BCW.ALO.CFS.AFU

waste lands
USE **wasteland**

waste management, solid
USE **solid waste management**

waste recovery facilities
USE **resource recovery facilities**

waste stacks
RT.1477
ALT **waste stack**
SN Stacks that are not soil stacks. (STEIN)
UF stacks, waste
CN V.RT.ALO.BCW.ALO.ARI.BZY.BOK.ARI

waste, wood
USE **sawdust**

wasteland
RD.307 (A,L)
UF waste lands
CN V.RD.ARI.ALO.ARI.BCW

wasteways
USE **spillways**

wasteweirs
RK.533
ALT **wasteweir**
CN V.RK.AFU.ALO.ALO.CFS.AFU.ARI.ALO.BOK.AFU

wasteweirs (spillways)
USE **spillways**

Wat Kukut
FL.2417
UF Vat Kukut
CN F.FL.ALO.ARI.BCW.BOK.AFU.CRG

watch making
KT.574 (L)
CN K.KT.AFU.ALO.ELK.EFQ

watch turrets
USE **bartizans**

watchmaker's files
USE **clockmaker's files**

watchmakers
HG.577 (L,R)
ALT **watchmaker**
CN H.HG.AFU.AXC.BUE.AXC.ERE

watchmen
HG.55 (L)
ALT **watchman**
CN H.HG.AFU.AXC.ARI.DUC

watchtowers
RK.37 (A,B)
ALT **watchtower**
UF lookout towers
observation towers
towers, lookout
towers, observation
CN V.RK.AFU.ALO.AFU.ALO.DCU.AXC

water
MT.314 (A,L,B,R)
CN M.MT.AFU.AFU.AFU.BOK.BOK

water bars
RT.1031
ALT **water bar**
SN Strips fixed to the sill of an external door or window to resist the penetration of water. (DAC)
UF bars, water
weatherbars
CN V.RT.AFU.ARI.ALO.CLM

water beds
TG.378 (L,N)
ALT **water bed**
SN Beds having a liquid-filled rubber or plastic mattress in a rigid, often heated, waterproof frame and providing a surface that conforms to the sleeper's body in any position. (RHDEL2)
UF beds, water
CN V.TG.AFU.AFU.ARI.AFU.AFU.FIM

water benches
TG.521 (N)
ALT **water bench**
SN Cupboards having a lower portion closed with doors for milk pails, an open shelf for water pails, and an upper section with shallow drawers; of a type made by the Pennsylvania Dutch.
UF benches, bucket
benches, milk
benches, water
bucket benches
milk benches
seillages
CN V.TG.AFU.AFU.AXC.ALO.BUE.DIO

water closets
USE **toilets**

water-conserving gardens
USE **xeriscapes**

water distribution, upfeed
USE **upfeed systems**

water districts
RG.264 (L)
ALT **water district**
UF districts, water
CN V.RG.ALO.AFU.AFU.CFS

water flow control works
USE **erosion protection works**

water gardens
RK.1415 (A,L,B)
ALT **water garden**
SN Gardens incorporating fountains and pools in which aquatic and other water-loving plants are grown. (DAC)
UF gardens, water
CN V.RK.ALO.AFU.AFU.AFU.CFS

water gates
RK.508 (L,B,R)
ALT **water gate**
UF gates, water
CN V.RK.AFU.ALO.ALO.BUE.CFS

water gilding
KT.716
SN Technique of adhering precious-metal leaf to a gesso or bole ground that is moistened with water before each leaf is laid. (MAYER)
UF gilding, water
CN K.KT.AFU.ALO.GRC.CRG.ALO.AXC

water glass
MT.2339 (L)
SN A water-soluble salt noted for powerful detergent and emulsifying properties, and for its suspending power. (MH)
UF glass, soluble
glass, water
silicate, sodium
sodium silicate
soluble glass
CN M.MT.AFU.ARI.ARI.AFU.AFU.AFU

water gum
USE **swamp tupelo**

water heaters
RT.1499 (L,N)
ALT **water heater**
UF heaters, water
CN V.RT.ALO.BCW.ALO.ARI.DIO

water heaters, solar
USE **solar water heaters**

water joints
TF.632
ALT **water joint**
SN Masonry joints protected from rain and snow by sloping the surface of the stone away from the wall, so it will shed water easily. (PUTNAM)
UF joints, saddle
joints, water
saddle joints
CN V.TF.ALO.ARI.ALO.AFU.BIQ

water leaf
DG.63
SN Various leaflike forms, usually unribbed and unserrated, used as decorative motifs, especially common in late 12th-century capitals.
UF hart's-tongue
leaf, lily
leaf, water
lily leaf
CN D.DG.AFU.AFU.DIO.CRG

water-lime
USE **natural cement**

water mains
RM.513 (L)
ALT **water main**
UF mains, water
CN V.RM.ALO.ALO.ARI.AXC

water mills
RK.665 (A,L,B,R)
ALT **water mill**
UF mills, water
CN V.RK.AFU.ALO.ALO.CLM.ALO.ALO.ALO.AFU

water paint, latex
USE **latex paint**

water-pattern
USE **guilloche**

water pollution
BM.434 (L)
UF pollution, water
CN B.BM.AXC.BCW.AFU.ARI

water-power
USE **hydroelectric power**

water-power electric plants
USE **hydroelectric power plants**

water pressure
BM.935
UF pressure, water
CN B.BM.CFS.AXC.BUE.BCW

water pumping stations
USE **pumping stations**

water purification plants
USE **water treatment plants**

water putty
MT.2658
UF putty, water
CN M.MT.AFU.ARI.HTY.ALO.AXC

water quality management
KG.129 (A,L)
UF management, water quality
quality management, water
CN K.KG.AFU.AFU.BCW.ALO.CLM

water reducers
MT.2334
UF admixtures, water-reducing
agents, water-reducing
reducers, water
water-reducing admixtures
water-reducing agents
CN M.MT.AFU.ARI.ALO.GFO

water-reducing admixtures
USE **water reducers**

water-reducing agents
USE **water reducers**

water-resistant materials
USE **waterproof materials**

water resources development
KG.134 (A,L)
UF development, water resources
resources development, water
CN K.KG.AFU.AFU.BCW.BCW.AFU

water retention basins
USE **storm water retention basins**

water rights
BM.477 (L)
UF rights, water
CN B.BM.BCW.DOI

water slides
RK.1007 (A)
ALT **water slide**
UF slides, water
CN V.RK.AFU.ALO.ALO.EWY.AFU.ALO

water softeners
MT.2335
SN Chemical compounds used for converting soluble scale-forming solids in water into insoluble forms. (MH)
UF softeners, water
CN M.MT.AFU.ARI.ALO.GLI

water soluble dyes
MT.1546
UF dyes, water soluble
soluble dyes, water
CN M.MT.AFU.AFU.ARI.AFU.AFU.AFU.ALO.ALO

water stain
MT.2469
UF stain, water
CN M.MT.AFU.ARI.CRG.AFU.BIQ.BCW

water stairs
RT.1097
ALT **water stair**
SN Stairs or steps communicating between any water level, as of a river, lake, or harbor, and the land, for convenience of embarkation or debarkation. (RS)
UF stairs, water
CN V.RT.AFU.BIQ.AXC.AFU.ALO.BIQ

water storage cisterns
USE **cisterns**

water storage systems
RD.121 (L)
ALT **water storage system**
UF storage systems, water
systems, water storage
water storage works
CN V.RD.ALO.AXC.ARI.ALO

water storage tanks
RT.1501
ALT **water storage tank**
UF storage tanks, water
tanks, water storage
CN V.RT.ALO.BCW.ALO.ARI.DOI

water storage works
USE **water storage systems**

water-struck brick
MT.137
UF brick, slop
brick, water-struck
slop brick
CN M.MT.AFU.AFU.AFU.AXC.ALO.

AFU.AXC.ALO.ALO.ALO.ALO

water-supply engineers
HG.632 (L)
ALT **water-supply engineer**
UF engineers, water-supply
CN H.HG.AFU.AXC.BZY.BCW.BCW.AFU.AFU

water supply systems
RD.119 (L,B)
ALT water supply system
SN Use for systems that supply water to and between buildings and other structures or to or from locations within communities or agricultural landscapes; use **plumbing systems** for water distribution systems within buildings.
UF supply systems, water
systems, water supply
CN V.RD.ALO.AXC.ARI

water systems
USE **plumbing systems**

water systems, chilled
USE **chilled water systems**

water systems, storm
USE **storm water systems**

water tables
RT.664
ALT **water table**
SN Stringcourses or other projecting members so devised as to guide water away from the face of the wall. (RS)
UF offsets
tables, water
CN V.RT.AFU.AFU.AFU.BIQ.BUE.ALO.AFU.CLM

water tanks
RK.582 (L,B)
ALT **water tank**
UF tanks, water
CN V.RK.AFU.ALO.ALO.CFS.ALO.BCW.CFS

water taps
USE **faucets**

water towers
RK.583 (A,L,N,B,R)
ALT **water tower**
UF towers, water
CN V.RK.AFU.ALO.ALO.CFS.ALO.BCW.CLM

water transport
BM.1149
UF transport, water
CN B.BM.DCU.AFU.ARI

water treatment plants
RK.588 (A,L)
ALT **water treatment plant**
UF plants, water treatment
treatment plants, water
water purification plants
CN V.RK.AFU.ALO.ALO.CFS.ALO.BCW.CRG.AXC

water tunnels
RK.1308 (A,L)
ALT **water tunnel**
SN Tunnels used to transport water in water supply systems. (MHDSTT)
UF tunnels, water
CN V.RK.AFU.ALO.ALO.GLI.ALO.ALO.AXC

water vapor
MT.325
UF vapor, water
CN M.MT.AFU.AFU.AFU.BOK.BOK.ARI.ALO

water wells
RK.593 (B)
ALT **water well**
UF wells, water
CN V.RK.AFU.ALO.ALO.CFS.ALO.BCW.CXA.AFU.ARI

water, ammonia
USE **ammonia water**

water, bodies of
USE **bodies of water**

water, distilled
USE **distilled water**

water, drinking
USE **drinking water**

water, fresh
USE **fresh water**

water, hard
USE **hard water**

water, potable
USE **drinking water**

water, saline
USE **salt water**

water, salt
USE **salt water**

water, soft
USE **soft water**

watercolor
MT.2523
SN A paint produced by mixing pigments with an aqueous vehicle; usually applied with a brush. (MCFAD)
CN M.MT.AFU.ARI.CRG.ALO.BCW.AFU.ALO.AXC

watercolor drawings
USE **watercolors**

watercolor painters
USE **watercolorists**

watercolor paintings
USE **watercolors**

watercolor paper
MT.1939
SN Paper used as both ground and support for watercolor. (MAYER)
UF paper, watercolor
CN M.MT.AFU.AFU.ARI.ALO.ALO.AXC.ARI.AXC.BCW

watercolor, black
USE **Japanese ink**

watercolor, opaque
USE **gouache**

watercolorists
HG.114 (L)
ALT **watercolorist**
UF painters, watercolor
watercolor painters
CN H.HG.AFU.AXC.AXC.AFU.AFU.ALO.AXC.CXA.ALO.AXC

watercolors
VD.161 (A,R)
ALT **watercolor**
UF watercolor drawings
watercolor paintings
CN V.VD.ARI

watercourses
USE **streams**

waterfalls
RD.163 (L,R)
ALT **waterfall**
SN Use for man-made waterfalls only if highly naturalistic in form and context; otherwise prefer **cascades** or **fountains.**
UF falls
CN V.RD.ARI.AFU.AFU.ALO.BIQ

waterfalls (man-made)
USE **cascades**

waterflow control works
USE **flood protection works**

waterfronts
RK.1593 (A,L,B)
ALT **waterfront**
CN V.RK.ALO.ARI.CLM.AFU

watering places
USE **health resorts**

waterless toilets
RT.1490
ALT **waterless toilet**
UF toilets, waterless
CN V.RT.ALO.BCW.ALO.ARI.CFS.BOK.AFU

Waterloo chairs
USE **Trafalgar chairs**

Waterloo legs
USE **sabre legs**

watermain maps
VW.205 (L)
ALT **watermain map**
UF maps, watermain

CN V.VW.AFU.AFU.AFU.FZU.AXC.AFU.
ARI.AXC.CRG.ARI

watermarks
VW.710 (L,R)
ALT **watermark**
SN Devices incorporated into paper as it is made and appearing as translucent areas; often used to give the name of the manufacturer and the date of the paper's manufacture.
UF filigrains
marks in paper
CN V.VW.AFU.ALO.ALO.AFU.AXC.AFU.
ALO

watermarks, impressed
USE **impressed watermarks**

waterproof cement
USE **natural cement**

waterproof materials
MT.2735
UF impervious material
material, impervious
materials, water-resistant
materials, waterproof
water-resistant materials
CN M.MT.AFU.ARI.ILG

waterproofing
KT.599 (A,L,B)
ALT **waterproof**
UF dampproofing
moisture-proofing
CN K.KT.AFU.ALO.FOG.BCW

waterproofing materials
MT.2736 (B)
SN Coatings or other materials, often of a bituminous type, that are impervious to water. (STEIN)
UF material, waterproofing
CN M.MT.AFU.ARI.IRA

waterscapes
USE **seascapes**

watershed maps
VW.188 (L)
ALT **watershed map**
UF maps, watershed
CN V.VW.AFU.AFU.AFU.FZU.AXC.AFU.
ARI.AXC.BCW.ARI.AFU

waterwheels
TB.401 (A,L,N,B)
ALT **waterwheel**
SN Wheels made to rotate by the direct action of water. (W)
CN V.TB.AFU.ARI.DOI.BZY

waterworks
RK.584 (A,L,B,R)
CN V.RK.AFU.ALO.ALO.CFS.ALO.BCW.
CRG

wats
RK.1131
ALT **wat**
SN Siamese Buddhist temples; may also be used for Siamese Buddhist monasteries.
UF vats
CN V.RK.AFU.ALO.ALO.FCS.BIQ.BZY.
AFU.ARI

wattle
MT.2418 (L)
SN A framework of interwoven rods, poles, or branches; used with daub as a building material. (DAC)
CN M.MT.AFU.ARI.BZY.BZY

wattle and daub
KT.41
SN Construction consisting of upright posts or stakes interwoven with twigs or tree branches and plastered with a mixture of clay and straw. (RHDEL2)
UF daub, wattle and
CN K.KT.AFU.ALO.BCW.ARI.AFU.CLM

wattle, silver
USE **silver wattle**

wave moldings
RT.768
ALT **wave molding**
SN Moldings decorated with a series of stylized representations of breaking waves. (HAS)
UF chamfers, swelled
moldings, undulating
moldings, wave
swelled chamfers
undulating moldings
CN V.RT.AFU.ALO.AFU.BOK.AFU.AFU.
ARI.BZY

wave pattern
DG.153
SN Use for decorative motifs consisting of wavy lines or other series of generally wavelike forms. For the specific running pattern of successive, connected spirals, use **wave scrolls**.
UF pattern, wave
wavy lines
CN D.DG.AFU.ARI.ALO.DCU

wave power stations
USE **tidal power plants**

wave scrolls
DG.150
ALT **wave scroll**
SN A running ornament consisting of a series of simple scrolls, each spiralling out from the center of the preceding one.
UF evolute scrolls
evolute spirals
running dog
scrolls, evolute
scrolls, wave
spirals, evolute
CN D.DG.AFU.ARI.ALO.CRG.AXC

waves, tidal
USE **tidal waves**

waves, Vitruvian
USE **Vitruvian scrolls**

wavs
USE **baolis**

wavy lines
USE **wave pattern**

wax
MT.2187 (L,R)
SN A variety of substances of animal and vegetable origin, which are fatty acids in combination with higher alcohols instead of with glycerin as in fats and oils. (MH)
CN M.MT.AFU.AFU.ARI.BZY

wax casting
USE **lost-wax process**

wax cloth
USE **wax resist cloth**

wax crayons
TB.245
ALT **wax crayon**
UF crayons, wax
CN V.TB.AFU.ARI.CLM.AFU.ALO.AXC.
AXC

wax museums
RK.427 (L,R)
ALT **wax museum**
UF cabinets, wax work
museums, wax
wax work cabinets
waxworks
CN V.RK.AFU.ALO.ALO.BCW.AXC.
ARI.CXA

wax painting
USE **encaustic painting**

wax print
USE **wax resist cloth**

wax-printed cloth
USE **wax resist cloth**

wax printing
USE **cerography**

wax process
USE **waxed-paper process**

wax resist cloth
MT.1888
UF cloth, wax
cloth, wax-printed
cloth, wax resist
print, wax
wax cloth
wax print
wax-printed cloth
CN M.MT.AFU.AFU.ARI.ALO.ALO.
ALO.ARI.BIQ

wax work cabinets
USE **wax museums**

wax, animal
USE **animal wax**

wax, candelilla
USE **candelilla wax**

wax, carnauba
USE **carnauba wax**

wax, Chinese insect
USE **Chinese insect wax**

wax, galician earth
USE **ozokerite**

wax, insect
USE **insect wax**

wax, Japan
USE **Japan wax**

wax, microcrystalline
USE **microcrystalline wax**

wax, mineral
USE **mineral wax**

wax, montan
USE **montan wax**

wax, paraffin
USE **paraffin**

wax, punic
USE **punic wax**

wax, synthetic
USE **synthetic wax**

wax, vegetable
USE **vegetable wax**

wax, white (beeswax)
USE **bleached beeswax**

wax, wool
USE **lanolin**

waxed-paper process
KT.364
SN Use for a number of closely related variants of the salted paper process in which the paper was made translucent by waxing before sensitizing. Do not use if a paper negative has been waxed after processing.
UF wax process
CN K.KT.AFU.ALO.DUC.DIO.ALO.DUC.ARI

waxworks
USE **wax museums**

way, right of
USE **right of way**

Wayang
FL.2386
CN F.FL.ALO.ARI.BCW.ARI.ALO.AXC.ARI

Wayo
FL.2007
CN F.FL.ALO.ARI.ALO.ALO.ALO.AFU.DIO

ways, bridle
USE **bridle paths**

ways, covered
USE **covered walkways**

ways, covered (fortification elements)
USE **covered ways (fortification elements)**

ways, pedestrian
USE **walkways**

ways, processional
USE **processional ways**

wayside crosses
RK.885 (R)
ALT **wayside cross**
SN Crosses erected by the side of the road in Roman Catholic countries as stations for prayer or as commemorations to local events. (RS)
UF crosses, roadside
crosses, wayside
roadside crosses
CN V.RK.AFU.ALO.ALO.DOI.AFU.ALO.ALO.ARI

WCs
USE **toilets**

weak red
USE **light reddish brown**

wealth
BM.415 (L,R)
SN All property or resources that have monetary or exchangeable value or economic utility. (WCOL)
CN B.BM.ARI.FUA

weapons ranges
USE **firing ranges**

weather
BM.738 (L,B,R)
CN B.BM.CFS.ALO.AXC.AFU

weather diaries
VW.53
ALT **weather diary**
UF diaries, weather
CN V.VW.AFU.AFU.AFU.DCU.BCW

weather doors
USE **storm doors**

weather maps
VW.222 (L)
ALT **weather map**
UF maps, weather
CN V.VW.AFU.AFU.AFU.FZU.AXC.AFU.ARI.AXC.DOI

weather stations
USE **meteorological stations**

weather strips
RT.1032 (A)
ALT **weather strip**
SN Pieces of metal, wood, or other material used to cover joints around doors and windows to prevent drafts and to keep out rain and snow. (PUTNAM)
UF strips, weather
weatherstripping
CN V.RT.AFU.ARI.ALO.CRG

weather-struck joints
TF.633
ALT **weather-struck joint**
SN Horizontal masonry joints sloped from a point inside the face of the wall to the face of the wall so the joint will shed water. (MEANS)
UF joints, weather-struck
joints, weathered
weathered joints
CN V.TF.ALO.ARI.ALO.AFU.BOK

weather tile
MT.171
SN Any of a series of tiles covering a wall and overlapped like shingles. (W)
UF tile, weather
CN M.MT.AFU.AFU.AFU.AXC.ALO.ALO.ALO.AFU.ALO.AXC

weatherbars
USE **water bars**

weatherboard siding
USE **clapboard siding**

weatherboarding
USE **siding**

weathered joints
USE **weather-struck joints**

weathering
KT.905 (L,B)
ALT **weathered**
CN K.KT.ALO.BCW.CFS

weatherstripping
USE **weather strips**

weathertightness
BM.981
ALT **weathertight**
SN Use for the condition of being secure against wind and rain.
CN B.BM.CFS.AXC.BZY.BZY.AXC

weave sheds
USE **weaving sheds**

weavers
HG.534 (L,R)
ALT **weaver**
CN H.HG.AFU.AXC.BUE.ARI.CXA.BZY

weaving
KT.551 (L,B,R)
ALT **woven**
UF reweaving
CN K.KT.AFU.ALO.ELK.DUC.AFU.BOK

weaving sheds
RK.683

ALT **weaving shed**
UF sheds, weaving
weave sheds
CN V.RK.AFU.ALO.ALO.CLM.BIQ.ALO

weaving, hand
USE **hand weaving**

weaving, loom
USE **loom weaving**

web clamps
TB.1060
ALT **web clamp**
SN Devices consisting of a fabric tape with a fastener that is secured with a wrench or screwdriver; used to hold carpentry work while gluing. (MEANS)
UF clamps, web
CN V.TB.AFU.BCW.CFS.ALO.ALO.BCW.CLM

web feet
USE **trifid feet**

web members
RT.386
ALT **web member**
SN In a truss, members which join the top and bottom chords. (DAC)
UF members, web
CN V.RT.AFU.AFU.AFU.BCW.CLM.ALO.ALO

web saws
TB.1006
ALT **web saw**
SN Framed bow saws with a light blade and handles at both ends. (DISSTO)
UF chair web saws
saws, chair web
saws, web
web saws, chair
CN V.TB.AFU.BCW.CFS.ALO.AFU.EWY.BCW.AFU.AFU

web saws, chair
USE **web saws**

web strainers
TB.534
ALT **web strainer**
SN Small wood tools used to give tension to the webbing which forms the foundation in most types of upholstery. (SALAM)
UF strainers, web
CN V.TB.AFU.ARI.FCS.ARI

webs
USE **vaulting cells**

wedding chests
USE **dower chests**

wedding invitations
VW.370
ALT **wedding invitation**
UF invitations, wedding
CN V.VW.AFU.AFU.ALO.DIO.AFU

wedding photography
KT.310 (L)
UF photography, wedding
CN K.KT.AFU.ALO.DUC.DIO.AFU.EFQ

weddings
KM.27 (L,R)
CN K.KM.AFU.ARI.ARI.CFS

wedge bittles
USE **beetles (mallets)**

wedge inserts
TF.385
ALT **wedge insert**
UF inserts, wedge
CN V.TF.AFU.AFU.AFU.ALO.AFU.BZY.BUE

wedges
TB.1041 (L,N)
ALT **wedge**
SN Pieces of wood or metal tapering to a thin edge; used to adjust elevation or tighten formwork. (MEANS)
UF gluts
CN V.TB.AFU.BCW.CFS.ALO.AFU.FZU

wedges, cleaving
USE **splitting wedges**

wedges, splitting
USE **splitting wedges**

wedges, wood-splitting
USE **splitting wedges**

Wee
FL.314 (L)
UF Gere
Guere
Kra
Kran
Ngere
Ouobe
Wobe
Wobi
CN F.FL.ALO.AFU.AXC.AFU.ARI.ARI.ARI

weed killers
USE **herbicides**

Weeden Island
FL.897 (L)
CN F.FL.ALO.ALO.ALO.AFU.ALO.ALO.BOK.CLM

weekend houses
USE **vacation houses**

weeping crosses
USE **preaching crosses**

Wei, Eastern
USE **Eastern Wei**

Wei, Northern
USE **Northern Wei**

Wei, Western
USE **Western Wei**

Weicher Stil
USE **International Gothic**

weigh-houses
USE **weigh stations**

weigh stations
RK.1262 (A,L,B)
ALT **weigh station**
UF stations, weigh
weigh-houses
CN V.RK.AFU.ALO.ALO.GLI.AFU.ARI.CLM

weight
BM.992 (L)
SN The force with which a body is attracted toward the earth or a celestial body by gravity. (W)
CN B.BM.CFS.AXC.BZY.CRG

weights, sash
USE **sash weights**

weirs
RK.532 (A,L)
ALT **weir**
SN Designates dams across waterways regulating water level or diverting or measuring water flow.
CN V.RK.AFU.ALO.ALO.CFS.AFU.ARI.ALO.BOK

weld
MT.1535
SN A bright yellow natural dyestuff. (MAYER)
UF arzica
gaude yellow
yellow, gaude
CN M.MT.AFU.AFU.ARI.AFU.AFU.AFU.AFU.AFU.AXC.DOI

welders
HG.508 (L)
ALT **welder**
CN H.HG.AFU.AXC.BUE.ARI.CFS.ALO.BIQ

welders, arc
USE **arc welding machines**

welders, electric
USE **arc welding machines**

welding
KT.798 (L,B)
ALT **welded**
SN To unite metal parts by melting the surfaces of the parts to be joined, either with or without adding molten material. (QUICK)
CN K.KT.AFU.ALO.HOE.BCW.ALO.AFU.ALO

welding, arc
USE **arc welding**

welding, braze
USE **braze welding**

welding, cold

USE **cold welding**

welding, electric
USE **electric welding**

welding, electric arc
USE **arc welding**

welding, electric resistance
USE **resistance welding**

welding, electron beam
USE **electron beam welding**

welding, fire
USE **forge welding**

welding, forge
USE **forge welding**

welding, friction
USE **friction welding**

welding, fusion
USE **fusion welding**

welding, gas
USE **gas welding**

welding, laser
USE **laser welding**

welding, pressure
USE **pressure welding**

welding, projection
USE **projection welding**

welding, resistance
USE **resistance welding**

welding, shielded metal arc
USE **shielded metal arc welding**

welding, stud
USE **stud welding**

welding, ultrasonic
USE **ultrasonic welding**

Weldon stone
MT.672
UF stone, Weldon
CN M.MT.AFU.AFU.AFU.DCU.AFU.ALO.AFU.ALO.ALO.AFU.AFU.ALO.BZY

welfare buildings
RK.783 (A,L,B)
ALT **welfare building**
UF buildings, welfare
centers, welfare
charitable institutions
facilities, welfare
institutions, charitable
welfare centers
welfare facilities
CN V.RK.AFU.ALO.ALO.CXA.ALO.ALO

welfare centers
USE **welfare buildings**

welfare facilities
USE **welfare buildings**

welfare services
HG.877 (L,B)
ALT **welfare service**
SN Organized public material assistance provided to financially needy individuals or families. (ERIC)
UF public welfare
relief services
services, relief
services, welfare
social welfare
welfare, public
welfare, social
CN H.HG.ALO.DIO.BCW.ALO

welfare, public
USE **welfare services**

welfare, social
USE **welfare services**

well-burned brick
USE **hard-burned brick**

well houses
RK.1345
ALT **well house**
UF houses, well
CN V.RK.AFU.ALO.ARI.ARI.ARI

Wellington chairs
USE **Trafalgar chairs**

wells
RK.589 (A,L,R)
ALT **well**
CN V.RK.AFU.ALO.ALO.CFS.ALO.BCW.CXA

wells, artesian
USE **artesian wells**

wells, driven
USE **driven wells**

wells, dug
USE **dug wells**

wells, escalator
USE **escalator wells**

wells, gas
USE **gas wells**

wells, holy
USE **holy wells**

wells, oil
USE **oil wells**

wells, seepage
USE **seepage pits**

wells, stepped
USE **baolis**

wells, tube
USE **driven wells**

wells, water
USE **water wells**

wellways
USE **escalator wells**

Welsh
FL.3042 (L,B)
CN F.FL.ALO.BCW.AFU.AXC.ARI

Welsh cabinets
USE **tridarns**

Welsh cupboards
USE **tridarns**

Welsh vaults
USE **underpitch vaults**

Wen-jen
USE Wen ren

Wen ren
FL.1938
UF Literati
Wen-jen
CN F.FL.ALO.ARI.ALO.AFU.AFU.AXC.ALO.CXA

Wenatchi
FL.1426 (L)
CN F.FL.ALO.ALO.ARI.AFU.BUE.EWY

Wessex
FL.2514
CN F.FL.ALO.AXC.AFU.BIQ.AFU.BIQ

west
DC.53
CN D.DC.AFU.ALO.AXC.BUE

West Himalayan spruce
MT.1405
UF Picea morinda
Picea smithiana
spruce, West Himalayan
CN M.MT.AFU.AFU.ALO.BIQ.DCU.AFU.AFU.ALO.DOI.BUE

West Indian boxwood
USE **Maracaibo boxwood**

West Indian ebony
USE **granadilla**

West Indies mahogany
MT.1214
UF mahogany, West Indies
Swietenia mahagoni
CN M.MT.AFU.AFU.ALO.BIQ.DCU.AFU.AFU.AFU.HTY.ARI.ALO

West Slope ware
FL.2623
UF ware, West Slope
CN F.FL.ALO.AXC.ALO.AFU.ALO.AXC.ALO.AXC.BOK

West Virginia spruce
USE **red spruce**

Western Apache
FL.1454
UF Apache, Western
CN F.FL.ALO.ALO.ARI.AFU.CFS.AFU.BIQ

Western Archaic
FL.732

UF Archaic, Western
CN F.FL.ALO.ALO.ALO.AFU.AFU.ALO.ALO

Western Arctic Inuit
FL.1214
UF Arctic Inuit, Western
Inuit, Mackenzie
Inuit, Western Arctic
Inuvialuit
Mackenzie Inuit
CN F.FL.ALO.ALO.ARI.AFU.AFU.AFU.ALO.AFU.BUE

western balsam poplar
USE **black cottonwood**

western black willow
MT.1329
UF black willow, western
Pacific willow
Salix iasiandra
willow, Pacific
willow, western black
willow, yellow
yellow willow
CN M.MT.AFU.AFU.ALO.BIQ.DCU.AFU.AFU.AFU.MWQ.ARI

Western Chin
USE **Western Jin**

Western Chou
USE **Western Zhou**

western frames
USE **platform frames**

western hackmatack
USE **western larch**

Western Han
FL.1850
UF Early Han
Former Han
CN F.FL.ALO.ARI.ALO.AFU.AFU.ALO.AFU.ALO

western hemlock
MT.1357 (L)
UF Alaskan pine
fir, gray
fir, Prince Albert
gray fir
hemlock, Pacific
hemlock, western
Pacific hemlock
pine, Alaskan
Prince Albert fir
Tsuga heterophylla
CN M.MT.AFU.AFU.ALO.BIQ.DCU.AFU.AFU.ALO.BOK.ARI

Western Indian
FL.2303
UF Gujarati
Indian, Western
CN F.FL.ALO.ARI.AXC.ALO.AFU.BZY.BUE

Western Jin
FL.1883
UF Chin, Western
Jin, Western
Western Chin
CN F.FL.ALO.ARI.ALO.AFU.AFU.ALO.BUE.ARI.ALO

western larch
MT.1366
UF fir, larch
hackmatack, western
larch fir
larch, Montana
larch, mountain
larch, western
Larix occidentalis
Montana larch
mountain larch
tamarack, western
western hackmatack
western tamarack
CN M.MT.AFU.AFU.ALO.BIQ.DCU.AFU.AFU.ALO.BZY.AXC

Western Nahane
USE **Tahltan**

Western Shoshone
FL.1317
UF Shoshone, Western
CN F.FL.ALO.ALO.ARI.AFU.AXC.BZY.AFU

Western sigillata ware
FL.2755
UF sigillata ware, Western
ware, Western sigillata
CN F.FL.ALO.AXC.ALO.ALO.ALO.BUE.ALO.BIQ.ALO

Western spruce
USE **sitka spruce**

Western-style
USE **Yoga**

western tamarack
USE **western larch**

Western Thule
FL.802
UF Thule, Western
CN F.FL.ALO.ALO.ALO.AFU.ALO.AFU.ALO.ALO.AFU.BCW

Western Wei
FL.1872
UF Wei, Western
CN F.FL.ALO.ARI.ALO.AFU.AFU.ALO.BUE.AFU.AFU.AFU.ALO

western white oak
MT.1255
UF oak, Oregon
oak, Oregon white
oak, western white
Oregon oak
Oregon white oak
Quercus garryana
white oak, Oregon
white oak, western
CN M.MT.AFU.AFU.ALO.BIQ.DCU.AFU.AFU.AFU.IRA.FCS

western yellow pine
USE **ponderosa pine**

Western Zhou
FL.1865
UF Chou, Western
Western Chou
Zhou, Western
CN F.FL.ALO.ARI.ALO.AFU.AFU.ALO.BIQ.ALO

Westerwald stoneware
FL.3229 (R)
UF Nassau stoneware
pottery, Westerwald
stoneware, Nassau
stoneware, Westerwald
ware, Nassau
ware, Westerwald
CN F.FL.ALO.BCW.ALO.ARI.BIQ.BIQ.AXC.AFU.AXC

Westport chairs
TG.95
ALT **Westport chair**
SN Angular lawn chairs, similar in form to the Adirondack chair, but constructed of boards rather than slats and heavier and more amply proportioned. Older than the classic Adirondack chair, it was patented by Harry C. Brunnell and manufactured between 1904 and 1930. (GIL-BOR)
UF chairs, Westport
CN V.TG.AFU.AFU.ALO.AFU.AFU.AFU.MFI

westworks
RM.425 (A,R)
ALT **westwork**
SN Use for the western ends of certain Carolingian and Ottonian churches, having an entrance hall, upper level chapel, and towers.
CN V.RM.AFU.EFQ

wet collodion glass negatives
USE **wet collodion negatives**

wet collodion negatives
VJ.15
ALT **wet collodion negative**
SN Use for negatives produced by the wet collodion process.
UF collodion negatives, wet
collodion wet plate photonegatives
glass negatives, wet collodion
negatives, wet collodion
negatives, wet plate
wet collodion glass negatives
wet plate negatives
wet plate photonegatives
CN V.VJ.AFU.AFU.AFU.BCW.AXC

wet collodion process
KT.324 (L)

SN Photographic process that uses a collodion binder which must be coated on the support, exposed, and developed before the collodion has become dry. A silver halide is the light-sensitive agent, and the process may be used to produce positives or negatives.
UF collodion wet process
wet plate process
CN K.KT.AFU.ALO.DUC.DIO.ALO.BCW.AXC

wet docks
RK.1324
ALT **wet dock**
SN Large watertight enclosures in which the water is maintained at the level of high tide so that vessels remain constantly afloat in them. (OED)
UF docks, wet
CN V.RK.AFU.ALO.ALO.GLI.ARI.ARI.BOK

wet plate negatives
USE **wet collodion negatives**

wet plate photographers
USE **photolithographers**

wet plate photonegatives
USE **wet collodion negatives**

wet plate process
USE **wet collodion process**

wether, gray
USE **sarsen**

wetlands
RD.167 (A,L)
ALT **wetland**
CN V.RD.ARI.AFU.ARI

wetting agents
MT.2734 (L)
SN Liquids or chemicals added to solutions to reduce the surface tension and give greater ease of mixing and stability,(MH12) such as liquid added to watercolor so that the paint will flow freely and take evenly on the paper. (MAYER)
UF agents, wetting
CN M.MT.AFU.ARI.IFM.BUE.ALO

Weymouth pine
USE **northern white pine**

WFs
USE **wide-flange beams**

whaleback roofs
USE **rainbow roofs**

wharves
RK.1321 (A,L,B,R)
ALT **wharf**
SN Use, in post-Second World War contexts, for structures built generally parallel to the shoreline so that vessels may moor alongside to receive or discharge cargo or passengers; prior to the mid-20th century, may refer broadly to any such landing places. For similar loading and unloading places built to extend from the shoreline out over water, use **piers (marine landings)**; if such places are artificial solid banks or shoreline extensions built parallel to the shoreline, use **quays.**
CN V.RK.AFU.ALO.ALO.GLI.ARI.ARI.AXC.ARI

whatnots
USE **étagères**

wheat straw
MT.1080
SN A source of pulp for paper, principally corrugated paper boards for insulation. (HORNB)
UF straw, wheat
CN M.MT.AFU.AFU.ALO.BIQ.CRG.ARI

wheatsheaf-back chairs
USE **sheaf-back chairs**

wheel-back chairs
TG.160
ALT **wheel-back chair**
SN Late 18th-century English chairs having round or oval backs with radiating spindles or bars resembling the spokes of a wheel. (ARON)
UF chairs, wheel-back
CN V.TG.AFU.AFU.ALO.AFU.AFU.AFU.NIE.EWY

wheel crosses
DG.17
ALT **wheel cross**
SN Circles enclosing four-spoke crosses, an ancient sign from which Celtic crosses may derive.
UF crosses, wheel
CN D.DG.AFU.AFU.ARI.CLM

wheel crosses (Celtic crosses)
USE **Celtic crosses**

wheel-engraving
KT.680
ALT **wheel-engraved**
SN The process of cutting or engraving glass pieces using a wheel or grindstone. (OCDA)
CN K.KT.AFU.ALO.GRC.ARI.ARI

wheel-head crosses
USE **Celtic crosses**

wheel lathes
TB.798
ALT **wheel lathe**
SN Lathes designed especially for turning locomotive and railroad car wheels. (W)
UF lathes, wheel
CN V.TB.AFU.BCW.CFS.AFU.AFU.BCW

wheel-mounted cranes
TB.72
ALT **wheel-mounted crane**
SN Cranes that consist of a rotating superstructure with power plant, operating machinery, and boom mounted on a mobile base or platform. Their function is to hoist and swing loads at various radii. (STEIN)
UF cranes, wheel-mounted
CN V.TB.AFU.ARI.AFU.BCW.AXC.CFS

wheel steps
USE **winders (steps)**

wheel tracery
RT.1021
SN Tracery radiating from a center, as the spokes of a wheel. (HAS)
UF tracery, wheel
CN V.RT.AFU.ARI.ALO.BZY.AFU.AFU.AXC

wheel windows
USE **rose windows**

wheelbeds
USE **trundle beds**

wheelchair ramps
RT.1066
ALT **wheelchair ramp**
UF ramps, wheelchair
CN V.RT.AFU.BIQ.ARI.AFU

wheelchairs
TG.184 (L,N,R)
ALT **wheelchair**
SN Chairs mounted on wheels that may either be pushed or propelled by the occupant by means of hand rims attached to the two large side wheels. (W)
CN V.TG.AFU.AFU.ALO.AFU.AFU.ALO.CLM.ARI

wheelhouses
RK.1244
ALT **wheelhouse**
CN V.RK.AFU.ALO.ALO.GLI.AFU.ALO.AFU.ARI.AFU

wheels
TB.1132 (L,N,R)
ALT **wheel**
SN Circular frameworks of wood, metal, or other hard material often with cogs or teeth on the rim used to transmit or modify force and motion in machinery or a mechanical contrivance. (W)
CN V.TB.ALO.DUC

wheels, abrasive
USE **grinding wheels**

wheels, color
USE **color wheels**

wheels, dotting
USE **dotting wheels**

wheels, ferris

USE **ferris wheels**

wheels, gin
USE **gins**

wheels, grinding
USE **grinding wheels**

wheels, perforating
USE **perforating wheels**

wheels, pounce
USE **perforating wheels**

wheels, sanding
USE **sanding wheels**

wheels, tracing (pouncing)
USE **perforating wheels**

wheelwright's adzes
TB.820 (N)
ALT **wheelwright's adz**
SN Curved adzes with a strong blade; used for hollowing the insides of wheel rims or the curved parts of coach frames. May also be used for hammering.
UF adzes, wheelwright's
CN V.TB.AFU.BCW.CFS.ALO.AFU.AFU.CFS

wheelwright's axes
USE **shipwright's axes**

wheelwrights
HG.578 (L)
ALT **wheelwright**
CN H.HG.AFU.AXC.BUE.AXC.EWY

whelk red
USE **Tyrian purple**

whetstones
TB.737 (N)
ALT **whetstone**
SN Hard stones used for sharpening edged tools. (MAYER)
UF hones
knife sharpeners
sharpeners, knife
sharpening stones
stones, sharpening
CN V.TB.AFU.BCW.BIQ.ARI.ALO.BZY

whetting blocks
USE **saw clamps**

whimbles
USE **braces (woodworking tools)**

whiplash curves
DG.72
ALT **whiplash curve**
SN Long and sinuous S-curves, sometimes resembling plant tendrils, common in Art Nouveau designs. (THDAT)
UF curves, whiplash
CN D.DG.AFU.AFU.ELK

Whipple trusses
RT.369
ALT **Whipple truss**
SN Use for double-intersection Pratt trusses having diagonal tension members and vertical compression members.
UF Linville trusses
trusses, Linville
trusses, Whipple
CN V.RT.AFU.AFU.AFU.BCW.CLM.AFU.AFU.AFU.BUE.ALO

whisk brooms
TB.348 (N)
ALT **whisk broom**
SN Small brooms with a short handles; used especially as a clothes brush or for light cleaning. (W)
UF brooms, whisk
CN V.TB.AFU.ARI.CRG.ALO.AFU.AFU

whiskers
MT.937
CN M.MT.AFU.AFU.ALO.AFU.CXA.AFU.ALO.ALO

white
DL.300 (L)
UF centroid color 263
drab gray, pale
oyster white (color)
pale drab gray
white, oyster (color)
CN D.DL.AFU.ALO.AFU

white ash
MT.1102 (L)
UF American ash
American white ash
ash, American
ash, American white
ash, Canadian
ash, white
Canadian ash
Fraxinus americana
white ash, American
CN M.MT.AFU.AFU.ALO.BIQ.DCU.AFU.AFU.AFU.ARI.ALO

white ash, American
USE **white ash**

white beech
MT.1113
UF beech, white
Binburra
cullonen
Gmelina leichhardti
gray teak
teak, gray
CN M.MT.AFU.AFU.ALO.BIQ.DCU.AFU.AFU.AFU.BCW.BZY

white beeswax, bleached
USE **bleached beeswax**

white birch
USE **silver birch**

white blue
USE **light bluish gray**

white bole
USE **kaolinite**

white cedar
USE **Port Orford cedar**

white cedar, Atlantic
USE **white cypress**

white cedar, southern
USE **white cypress**

white Cherokee marble
MT.841
UF marble, white Cherokee
CN M.MT.AFU.AFU.AFU.DCU.AFU.ARI.ARI.ARI.BOK.ERE

white collar workers
HG.32 (L)
ALT **white collar worker**
SN Workers whose duties consist primarily of nonmanual work which usually permits the wearing of street clothes, such as clerical, administrative, sales, professional, or technical work.
UF nonmanual workers
workers, nonmanual
workers, white collar
CN H.HG.AFU.AXC.ALO.BOK

white cross-lined pottery
FL.2845
UF cross-lined pottery, white
pottery, white cross-lined
ware, white cross-lined
CN F.FL.ALO.AXC.ALO.ARI.ALO.AFU.BOK.AFU

white cypress
MT.1346
UF Atlantic white cedar
cedar, Atlantic white
cedar, southern white
Chamaecyparis thyoides
cypress, white
southern white cedar
white cedar, Atlantic
white cedar, southern
CN M.MT.AFU.AFU.ALO.BIQ.DCU.AFU.AFU.ALO.AXC.ARI

white deal
USE **common spruce**

white elephant sales
USE **rummage sales**

white elm
USE **American elm**

white elm, American
USE **American elm**

white fir
USE **common spruce**

white fir (Norway spruce)
USE **Norway spruce**

white gold

MT.396
UF gold, white
CN M.MT.AFU.AFU.AFU.BZY.AFU.AFU.AFU.ALO.AXC.AFU.AXC

White-ground
FL.2650
CN F.FL.ALO.AXC.ALO.AFU.ALO.AXC.ARI.BCW

white hickory
USE **mockernut hickory**

white iron
MT.341
UF iron, white
CN M.MT.AFU.AFU.AFU.BZY.AFU.AFU.AFU.AFU.AFU.AXC

white lampblack
USE **zinc white**

white lead
MT.1738 (L)
UF blanc d'argent
blanc de plomb
Bleiweiss
ceruse
Cremnitz white
flake white
Kremnitz white
Krems white
Kremserweiss
lead, white
London white
Nottingham white
Roman white
snowflake white
white, Cremnitz
white, flake
white, Kremnitz
white, Krems
white, London
white, Nottingham
white, Roman
white, snowflake
CN M.MT.AFU.AFU.ARI.AFU.AFU.ALO.ALO.BOK.AFU.BZY

white lead, Dutch process
USE **Dutch process white lead**

white line prints
USE **blueprints**

white line process
KT.476
SN A type of wood engraving in which the design is carved into the surface, not raised from it. The effect is a white design on a black field. (QUICK)
CN K.KT.AFU.ALO.DUC.DUC.ALO.BCW.ARI.AXC

white-lined pottery
FL.2844
UF pottery, white-lined
CN F.FL.ALO.AXC.ALO.ARI.ALO.AFU.BOK

white mahogany
MT.1215 (L)
UF Khaya anthotheca
mahogany, white
primavera
CN M.MT.AFU.AFU.ALO.BIQ.DCU.AFU.AFU.AFU.HTY.AXC

white maple
USE **silver maple**

white marble
MT.818
UF marble, saccharoidal
marble, white
saccharoidal marble
CN M.MT.AFU.AFU.AFU.DCU.AFU.ARI.ARI.ARI.BOK

white metal
MT.424
SN Usually refers to the lead-antimony-tin alloys employed for machine bearings, packings, and linings, to the low-melting-point alloys used for toys, ornaments, and fusible metals, and to the metals used for printing type. (MH)
UF alloys, lead-antimony-tin
lead-antimony-tin alloys
metal, white
CN M.MT.AFU.AFU.AFU.BZY.AFU.AFU.AFU.ALO.BUE.AXC

white metal, Dutch
USE **Dutch white metal**

white metal, Hanover
USE **Hanover white metal**

white oak
MT.1256 (L)
UF oak, white
Quercus alba
CN M.MT.AFU.AFU.ALO.BIQ.DCU.AFU.AFU.AFU.IRA.FIM

white oak, California
USE **California white oak**

white oak, Oregon
USE **western white oak**

white oak, swamp
USE **swamp white oak**

white oak, western
USE **western white oak**

white-on-red
FL.1181
CN F.FL.ALO.ALO.ALO.ARI.AXC.ALO.ALO.BOK

white-on-red pottery
FL.2878
UF pottery, white-on-red
ware, white-on-red
white-on-red ware
CN F.FL.ALO.AXC.ARI.AFU.ALO.ARI.CXA

white-on-red ware
USE **white-on-red pottery**

white painted ware
FL.2907
UF painted ware, white
ware, white painted
CN F.FL.ALO.AXC.ARI.ARI.ALO.ALO.BUE

white pigment
MT.1726
UF pigment, white
CN M.MT.AFU.AFU.ARI.AFU.AFU.ALO.ALO.BOK

white pigment, extender
USE **transparent white pigment**

white pigment, inert
USE **transparent white pigment**

white pigment, opaque
USE **opaque white pigment**

white pigment, transparent
USE **transparent white pigment**

white pine
USE **common spruce**

white pine, Japanese
USE **Japanese white pine**

white pine, northern
USE **northern white pine**

white pine, Oregon
USE **ponderosa pine**

white poplar
MT.1279 (L)
UF poplar, white
Populus alba
CN M.MT.AFU.AFU.ALO.BIQ.DCU.AFU.AFU.AFU.KFK.ALO.BIQ

white shellac
MT.2433
SN Made by bleaching orange shellac with alkalies. (MH)
UF shellac, white
CN M.MT.AFU.ARI.CRG.AFU.ARI.ALO.ALO

white slip ware
FL.2908
UF slip ware, white
ware, white slip
CN F.FL.ALO.AXC.ARI.ARI.ALO.ALO.BZY

white-slipped red ware
FL.2879
UF red ware, white-slipped
ware, white-slipped red
CN F.FL.ALO.AXC.ARI.AFU.ALO.ARI.DCU

white spirits
USE **mineral spirits**

white spruce

MT.1406 (L)
UF Canadian spruce
Picea alba
pine, spruce
shingle spruce
skunk spruce
spruce pine
spruce, Canadian
spruce, shingle
spruce, skunk
spruce, white
CN M.MT.AFU.AFU.ALO.BIQ.DCU.AFU.AFU.ALO.DOI.BZY

white spruce (Norway spruce)
USE **Norway spruce**

white statuary marble, Vermont
USE **Vermont white statuary marble**

white walnut
USE **butternut**

white ware
FL.2947
UF ware, white
CN F.FL.ALO.AXC.ARI.AXC.ALO.BIQ.DIO

white ware, Cycladic
USE **Cycladic white ware**

white wax (beeswax)
USE **bleached beeswax**

white willow
MT.1330 (L)
UF Salix alba
willow, white
CN M.MT.AFU.AFU.ALO.BIQ.DCU.AFU.AFU.AFU.MWQ.AXC

white, aluminum hydrate
USE **aluminum hydrate white**

white, aluminum stearate
USE **aluminum stearate white**

white, anhydrite
USE **anhydrite white**

white, antimony
USE **antimony white**

white, baryta
USE **blanc fixe**

white, Becton
USE **lithopone**

white, bismuth
USE **bismuth white**

white, bluish
USE **bluish white**

white, bone
USE **bone white**

white, Bougival
USE **bismuth white**

white, brownish
USE **yellowish white**

white, Caledonian
USE **Caledonian white**

white, Charlton
USE **lithopone**

white, Chinese
USE **zinc white**

white, composite
USE **composite white**

white, constant
USE **blanc fixe**

white, Cremnitz
USE **white lead**

white, flake
USE **white lead**

white, greenish
USE **greenish white**

white, Griffith's patent zinc
USE **lithopone**

white, ivory
USE **pale yellow**

white, Jersey lily
USE **lithopone**

white, Kremnitz
USE **white lead**

white, Krems
USE **white lead**

white, lime
USE **chalk**

white, London
USE **white lead**

white, mineral
USE **gypsum**

white, mixed
USE **composite white**

white, Nottingham
USE **white lead**

white, Orr's zinc
USE **lithopone**

white, oyster
USE **oyster white**

white, oyster (color)
USE **light gray**
white

white, oyster shell
USE **oyster white**

white, pearl
USE **bismuth white**
light gray

white, permenent
USE **blanc fixe**

white, pinkish
USE **pinkish white**

white, process
USE **blanc fixe**

white, purplish
USE **purplish white**

white, reddish
USE **pinkish white**
purplish white

white, Roman
USE **white lead**

white, snowflake
USE **white lead**

white, superba
USE **composite white**

white, tin
USE **tin white**

white, titanium
USE **titanium white**

white, titanium barium
USE **titanium barium white**

white, titanium calcium
USE **titanium calcium white**

white, ultra
USE **composite white**

white, yellowish
USE **yellowish white**

white, zinc
USE **zinc white**

whiteprints
VW.690 (L)
ALT **whiteprint**
SN Copies made by light-sensitive processes, often the diazo process, usually of line drawings, in which black or colored lines appear on a white background. (AHD)
CN V.VW.AFU.ALO.AFU.DZW.BIQ.CRG

whitewash
MT.2516 (A,B)
SN One of the oldest paints, used for both exterior and interior surfaces. The principal ingredients are water and lime paste. (STEIN)
UF limewash
CN M.MT.AFU.ARI.CRG.ALO.BCW.AFU.ALO.AFU.ARI

whitewashing
KT.674 (B)
ALT **whitewashed**
UF limewashing
CN K.KT.AFU.ALO.GRC.AFU.BUE

whitewood
USE **tulipwood**

whitewood, canary
USE **tulipwood**

whiting
MT.2719 (L)

SN Chalk or precipitated calcium carbonate that has been ground and washed for use in paints, inks, and putty. (MH12)
CN M.MT.AFU.ARI.IFM.ALO.ALO

whittles, cooper's
USE **hoop-notching knives**

whittling
KT.170 (L)
ALT **whittled**
SN Forming or paring something, especially wood, by cutting off bits with a knife.
CN K.KT.AFU.ALO.DOI.ERE.BIQ

whole plate
DC.133
SN A photographic plate size, standard for daguerreotypes, 8 1/2 by 6 1/2 inches.
CN D.DC.AFU.AXC.BIQ.BUE

whole views
USE **general views**

wholesalers
HG.431
ALT **wholesaler**
UF jobbers
CN H.HG.AFU.AXC.BOK.FCS.ALO.ALO

whorehouses
USE **brothels**

whorl feet
USE **scroll feet**

Wichita
FL.1401 (L)
CN F.FL.ALO.ALO.ARI.AFU.BOK.FIM

wicker
MT.2285 (L,R)
SN Woven reed, rattan, twigs, or other material, especially used to construct furniture.
CN M.MT.AFU.ALO.IWU

wickerwork
MT.2783
CN M.MT.AFU.AXC.DIO

Wicklow granite
MT.596
UF granite, Wicklow
CN M.MT.AFU.AFU.AFU.DCU.AFU.AFU.AFU.AFU.AFU.ARI.ALO.AFU.ARI

wide-angle lenses
TB.322
ALT **wide-angle lens**
SN Lenses with a focal length considerably shorter than the diagonal of the format it fills. The lenses give a wide angle of view, and considerable depth of field. (LANG)
UF anamorphic lenses
lenses, anamorphic
lenses, wide-angle
CN V.TB.AFU.ARI.CLM.ARI.AFU.ALO.BOK.BIQ

wide-flange beams
RT.714
ALT **wide-flange beam**
UF beams, wide-flange
W-beams
WFs
CN V.RT.AFU.AFU.ALO.ARI.BIQ

widow's walks
RT.487
ALT **widow's walk**
SN Use for railed, unroofed platforms surmounting the roofs of American houses offering a view, especially of the sea; for rooftop outlooks that are enclosed, use **belvederes**; for rooftop structures that are usually ornamental, use **cupolas**.
UF captain's walks
galleries, roof
roof galleries
walks, captain's
walks, widow's
CN V.RT.AFU.AFU.AFU.BIQ.ARI.ALO.AFU.BUE.BOK

width
BM.810
CN B.BM.CFS.ARI.AXC.BUE.BZY

Wiener Aktionismus
FL.3756
CN F.FL.ALO.BUE.ARI.IWU

wigmakers
HG.579 (L)
ALT **wigmaker**
UF perukiers
CN H.HG.AFU.AXC.BUE.AXC.FCS

wigwams
RK.319 (L,N)
ALT **wigwam**
SN Houses of the Native Americans of the region of the Great Lakes and eastward having typically an arched top and consisting of a framework of poles overlaid with bark, rush mats, or hides. (W)
CN V.RK.AFU.ALO.ALO.AXC.ALO.BCW.BOK

wild animal parks
RG.234
ALT **wild animal park**
SN Distinguished from **safari parks** by the complete and planned separation of the visiting public from the animals, who are allowed to roam freely within bounded natural habitats.
UF animal parks
parks, animal
parks, wild animal
wildlife parks, zoological
zoological wildlife parks
CN V.RG.AFU.AFU.ELK.ARI.ALO

wild apple
USE **applewood**

wild cherry
USE **sweet cherry**

Wild Goat Style
FL.2604
CN F.FL.ALO.AXC.ALO.AFU.ALO.AXC.ALO.ALO.ARI

wilderness
RD.296
SN Designates wild and uncultivated regions left untouched in a natural state with no human control or interference (DNE); distinct from **nature preserves** in which plant and animal communities are protected and controlled; distinct from **wilderness areas** which are lands where natural growth is protected by legislation and recreation and industrial use are restricted.
CN V.RD.ARI.ALO.ALO.BIQ

wilderness areas
RK.1452 (L)
ALT **wilderness area**
SN Use for areas of land whose natural growth is protected by legislation and where recreation and industrial use are restricted;(RHDEL2) for wild and uncultivated regions left untouched in a natural state with no human control or interference, use **wilderness.**
UF areas, wilderness
CN V.RK.ALO.ALO.ALO.AFU

wildlife habitats
USE **wildlife refuges**

wildlife parks, zoological
USE **wild animal parks**

wildlife preserves
USE **wildlife refuges**

wildlife refuges
RK.1453 (L)
ALT **wildlife refuge**
UF habitats, wildlife
preserves, wildlife
refuges, wildlife
sanctuaries, wildlife
wildlife habitats
wildlife preserves
wildlife sanctuaries
CN V.RK.ALO.ALO.ALO.ALO

wildlife sanctuaries
USE **wildlife refuges**

Wilkawaín
USE **Viñaque**

will to form
USE **Kunstwollen**

William and Mary
FL.3197 (R)
CN F.FL.ALO.BCW.ALO.ARI.BIQ.BIQ.AFU.AFU.ALO.ARI

willow
MT.1326 (L)
UF Salix
CN M.MT.AFU.AFU.ALO.BIQ.DCU.AFU.AFU.AFU.MWQ

willow knives
TB.786 (N)
ALT willow knife
SN Knives with a long curved blade, used in rushworking.
UF knives, willow
CN V.TB.AFU.BCW.BUE.ALO.ALO

willow, black
USE **black willow**

willow, Japanese
USE **Japanese willow**

willow, Pacific
USE **western black willow**

willow, western black
USE **western black willow**

willow, white
USE **white willow**

willow, yellow
USE **western black willow**

wills
VW.921 (L,R)
ALT will
SN Legal instruments in which a person declares the disposition of his/her property, to take effect after his/her death, and which is revocable during the lifetime of that person. (BLACKS)
CN V.VW.AFU.ARI.AFU.BOK.BOK.DCU

Wilton
FL.64 (L)
CN F.FL.ALO.AFU.AFU.ALO.BCW.ALO

wimble bits
USE **nose bits**

wimbles, breast
USE **braces (woodworking tools)**

winches
TB.82 (L,N)
ALT winch
SN Stationary hoisting machines having a rotating drum around which a cable, rope, or chain is wrapped. (MEANS)
UF machines, winding
winding machines
CN V.TB.AFU.ARI.AFU.BCW.BCW.ALO.AXC

wind
BM.754 (L,B,R)
CN B.BM.CFS.ALO.AXC.ALO.BOK

wind beams
USE **collar beams**

wind braces
RT.209
ALT wind brace
SN Braces, such as struts, which strengthen a structure or framework against the wind. (DAC)
UF braces, wind
CN V.RT.AFU.AFU.AFU.AXC.DOI.AFU.AFU.AXC

wind-electric power plants
USE **wind power plants**

wind farms
USE **wind power plants**

wind loads
BM.1015 (A,L)
UF loads, wind
CN B.BM.CFS.AXC.CLM.ALO.ARI.BZY.ALO

wind plants
USE **wind power plants**

wind power
BM.878 (A,L)
UF power, wind
CN B.BM.CFS.AXC.ALO.ALO.ARI.BCW

wind power plants
RG.120
ALT wind power plant
UF farms, wind
plants, wind power
power plants, wind
wind-electric power plants
wind farms
wind plants
CN V.RG.AFU.AFU.BUE.ARI.BCW

Wind River Shoshone
FL.1318
UF Shoshone, Wind River
CN F.FL.ALO.ALO.ARI.AFU.AXC.BZY.ALO

windbreaks
RM.458 (L,B)
ALT windbreak
UF shelterbelts
CN V.RM.ALO.AFU.CLM

winders (steps)
RT.1117
SN Steps, more or less wedge-shaped, whose tread is wider at one end than the other. (DAC)
UF radial steps
steps, radial
steps, tapered
steps, wheel
tapered steps
wheel steps
CN V.RT.AFU.BIQ.AXC.ALO.BIQ.AFU.BCW

winders, dancing
USE **balanced steps**

winding engines
USE **windlasses**

winding machines
USE **winches**

winding stairs
USE **spiral stairs**

windlasses
TB.83 (L,N)
ALT windlass
SN Devices used to lift heavy objects, usually consisting of a horizontal drum turned by a lever or crank. A cable runs from the object over a pulley to the drum where lengths of cable are wound or unwound to move the object. (MEANS)
UF engines, winding
winding engines
CN V.TB.AFU.ARI.AFU.BCW.BCW.ALO.BCW

Windmill Hill
FL.2500
CN F.FL.ALO.AXC.AFU.BCW.CXA

windmills
RK.667 (A,L,N,B,R)
ALT windmill
CN V.RK.AFU.ALO.ALO.CLM.ALO.ALO.ALO.ALO

windmills, smock
USE **smock mills**

window benches
USE **window seats**

window boards
USE **window sills**

window boxes
RT.975 (B)
ALT window box
SN Boxes, usually elongated, containing soil and used for growing ornamental plants, placed on a windowsill or at the level of a sill.
UF boxes, flower
boxes, window
flower boxes
CN V.RT.AFU.ARI.AFU.AFU.BOK.ALO.BIQ

window chair
USE **window chairs**

window chairs
TG.216
SN Low-back chairs with wide seats; intended to be used in the embrasure of a window.
UF chairs, window
window chair
CN V.TG.AFU.AFU.ALO.AFU.AFU.ARI.AXC.BIQ

window dressers

HG.152
ALT **window dresser**
UF dressers, window
trimmers, window
window trimmers
CN H.HG.AFU.AXC.AXC.AFU.AFU.ALO.BCW.ARI.AFU

window fittings
USE **window hardware**

window frames
RT.977 (N)
ALT **window frame**
SN Frames, boxed for sliding sashes, or solid and rebated for casements, which are set in walls to receive and hold windows. (RS)
UF frames, window
linings, window
window linings
CN V.RT.AFU.ARI.AFU.AFU.BOK.ALO.BOK.AFU

window furniture
USE **window hardware**

window glass
USE **sheet glass**

window glass, double strength
USE **double strength window glass**

window glass, single strength
USE **single strength window glass**

window guards
RT.1044 (L)
ALT **window guard**
SN Metal protective grilles, often of elaborate, decorative character. (DAC)
UF guards, window
railings, window
window railings
CN V.RT.AFU.AXC.ALO.ARI.AFU

window hardware
TF.511 (R)
SN All the devices, fittings, or assemblies necessary to operate a window, such as catches, sash cords, fasteners, hinges, handles, locks, pulls, pulleys, and sash weights. (MEANS)
UF fittings, window
furniture, window
hardware, shutter
hardware, window
shutter hardware
window fittings
window furniture
CN V.TF.AFU.AFU.ALO.BZY

window heads
RT.979
ALT **window head**
SN The upper horizontal cross members or decorative elements of window frames. (HAS)
UF heads, window
CN V.RT.AFU.ARI.AFU.AFU.BOK.ALO.BOK.ALO.AFU

window lifts
USE **sash lifts**

window linings
USE **window frames**

window locks
TF.253 (N)
ALT **window lock**
SN Any fastening devices which hold two window sashes together to prevent their opening or rattling. Sash fasts are usually attached to the meeting rails of a double-hung window. (MEANS)
UF fasteners, sash
fasts, sash
holders, sash
locks, sash
locks, window
sash fasteners
sash fasts
sash holders
sash locks
CN V.TF.AFU.AFU.AFU.AFU.DIO.BIQ.ALO.BCW

window panes
USE **lights**

window pulls
USE **sash lifts**

window railings
USE **window guards**

window sashes
USE **sashes**

window seats
TG.292 (N,B)
ALT **window seat**
SN Use for freestanding or built-in benches intended for use in the embrasure of a window.
UF benches, window
French stools (window seats)
seats, window
stools, French (window seats)
stools, window
window benches
window stools
CN V.TG.AFU.AFU.ALO.ALO.AFU.ALO.BCW

window sills
RT.980 (N,B)
ALT **window sill**
SN The horizontal bottom member of a window frame.
UF boards, window
sills (window frame components)
sills, window
window boards
CN V.RT.AFU.ARI.AFU.AFU.BOK.ALO.BOK.ALO.ALO

window spring bolts
TF.255
ALT **window spring bolt**
SN Spring bolts for holding a sliding sash in any desired position, open or shut; used with unbalanced sashes. (BROWNL)
UF bolts, window spring
spring bolts, window
CN V.TF.AFU.AFU.AFU.AFU.DIO.BOK

window stools
USE **window seats**

window trimmers
USE **window dressers**

window walls
USE **curtain walls**

windowless buildings
RK.1388 (B)
ALT **windowless building**
UF buildings, windowless
CN V.RK.AFU.ALO.AXC.CRG

windowlights
USE **lights**

windows
RT.906 (A,L,B,R)
ALT **window**
SN An opening in the wall of a building, serving to admit light, usually to permit vision, and often to admit air.
UF lights (windows)
CN V.RT.AFU.ARI.AFU.AFU.BOK.AFU

windows, awning
USE **awning windows**

windows, basement
USE **basement windows**

windows, bay
USE **bay windows**

windows, blank
USE **false windows**

windows, blind
USE **false windows**

windows, bow
USE **bow windows**

windows, box-head
USE **jib-headed windows**

windows, bull's-eye
USE **oculi**

windows, cabinet
USE **cabinet windows**

windows, camber
USE **camber windows**

windows, casement
USE **casement windows**

windows, Catherine-wheel
USE **rose windows**

windows, Chicago
USE **Chicago windows**

windows, classroom
USE **classroom windows**

windows, combination
USE **combination windows**

windows, compass
USE **bow windows**

windows, coupled
USE **coupled windows**

windows, curved
USE **bow windows**

windows, Diocletian
USE **Diocletian windows**

windows, display
USE **show-windows**

windows, door
USE **French doors**

windows, double
USE **double windows**

windows, double frame
USE **double windows**

windows, double-hung
USE **double-hung windows**

windows, eucharistic
USE **squints**

windows, false
USE **false windows**

windows, fan
USE **fanlights**

windows, fixed
USE **fixed windows**

windows, flanking
USE **side lights**

windows, floor to ceiling
USE **floor to ceiling windows**

windows, French
USE **French doors**

windows, frieze
USE **frieze band windows**

windows, frieze band
USE **frieze band windows**

windows, gemel
USE **coupled windows**

windows, heat insulation
USE **double windows**

windows, hinged
USE **hinged windows**

windows, hopper
USE **hopper windows**

windows, jalousie
USE **jalousie windows**

windows, jib-headed
USE **jib-headed windows**

windows, Judas
USE **peepholes**

windows, jut
USE **bay windows**

windows, lancet
USE **lancet windows**

windows, lantern
USE **lantern lights**

windows, lattice
USE **lattice windows**

windows, loop
USE **loop windows**

windows, louver
USE **louver windows**

windows, lowside
USE **lowside windows**

windows, marigold
USE **rose windows**

windows, offertory
USE **lowside windows**

windows, oriel
USE **oriel windows**

windows, paired
USE **coupled windows**

windows, Palladian
USE **Palladian windows**

windows, picture
USE **picture windows**

windows, pivoting
USE **pivoting windows**

windows, projected
USE **projected windows**

windows, projecting
USE **projected windows**

windows, psychiatric
USE **psychiatric windows**

windows, rose
USE **rose windows**

windows, side hung
USE **casement windows**

windows, single-hung
USE **single-hung windows**

windows, sliding
USE **sliding windows**

windows, square bay
USE **square bay windows**

windows, squint
USE **squints**

windows, storm
USE **storm windows**

windows, strip
USE **strip windows**

windows, therm
USE **Diocletian windows**

windows, top hung
USE **awning windows**

windows, transom
USE **transom windows**

windows, trellis
USE **lattice windows**

windows, triple-hung
USE **triple-hung windows**

windows, Venetian
USE **Palladian windows**

windows, vulne
USE **lowside windows**

windows, wheel
USE **rose windows**

Windsor armchairs, continuous-bow
USE **continuous-bow Windsor armchairs**

Windsor blue, pale
USE **light blue**

Windsor chairs
TG.96 (L)
ALT **Windsor chair**
SN Chairs having a seat that is a shaped and contoured plank drilled with sockets on the upper and lower surfaces to anchor the back and undercarriage and having the rear legs and a back that are separate rather than continuous members. The elements of the back are vertical, horizontal, or curved, and spindles may or may not be present. (EVANS)
UF chairs, Windsor
CN V.TG.AFU.AFU.ALO.AFU.AFU.AFU.MLC

Windsor chairs, balloon-back
USE **balloon-back Windsor chairs**

Windsor chairs, birdcage
USE **square-back Windsor chairs**

Windsor chairs, bow-back
USE **bow-back Windsor chairs**

Windsor chairs, chicken-coop
USE **square-back Windsor chairs**

Windsor chairs, comb-back
USE **high-back Windsor chairs**

Windsor chairs, continuous arm
USE **continuous-bow Windsor armchairs**

Windsor chairs, dining
USE **bow-back Windsor chairs**

Windsor chairs, double bow-back
USE **double rod-back Windsor chairs**

Windsor chairs, double rod-back
USE **double rod-back Windsor chairs**

Windsor chairs, fan-back
USE **fan-back Windsor chairs**

Windsor chairs, firehouse
USE **low-back Windsor chairs**

Windsor chairs, gunstock
USE **gunstock Windsor chairs**

Windsor chairs, high-back
USE **high-back Windsor chairs**

Windsor chairs, hoop-back
USE **sack-back Windsor chairs**

Windsor chairs, lath-back
USE **lath-back Windsor chairs**

Windsor chairs, loop-back
USE **sack-back Windsor chairs**

Windsor chairs, low-back
USE **low-back Windsor chairs**

Windsor chairs, oval-back
USE **bow-back Windsor chairs**

Windsor chairs, pillow back
USE **high-back Windsor chairs**

Windsor chairs, rod-back
USE **square-back Windsor chairs**

Windsor chairs, roll-top
USE **roll-top Windsor chairs**

Windsor chairs, round-top
USE **sack-back Windsor chairs**

Windsor chairs, sack-back
USE **sack-back Windsor chairs**

Windsor chairs, single bow
USE **single rod-back Windsor chairs**

Windsor chairs, single rod-back
USE **single rod-back Windsor chairs**

Windsor chairs, slat-back
USE **slat-back Windsor chairs**

Windsor chairs, splat-back
USE **splat-back Windsor chairs**

Windsor chairs, square-back
USE **square-back Windsor chairs**

Windsor chairs, tablet-top
USE **tablet-top Windsor chairs**

Windsor chairs, writing-arm
USE **writing-arm Windsor chairs**

Windsor continuous-arm armchairs
USE **continuous-bow Windsor armchairs**

Windsor low-back armchairs
USE **low-back Windsor chairs**

Windsor rocking chairs
TG.229
ALT **Windsor rocking chair**
SN Any Windsor chair with the legs supported on bends for rocking. (EVANS)
UF chairs, Windsor rocking
rocking chairs, Windsor
CN V.TG.AFU.AFU.ALO.AFU.AFU.AXC.ARI.AXC

Windsor rod-back chairs
USE **square-back Windsor chairs**

Windsor settees
TG.306
ALT **Windsor settee**
UF settees, Windsor
CN V.TG.AFU.AFU.ALO.ALO.BUE.BIQ

Windsor stands
TG.622
ALT **Windsor stand**
SN Stands usually having three legs braced with stretchers which socket directly into a small, usually round, top. (EVANS)
UF stands, Windsor
CN V.TG.AFU.AFU.BIQ.BCW.AFU.AXC

Windsor stools
TG.254
ALT **Windsor stool**
SN Stools of varied height consisting of a horizontal plank of varied shape supported on three or four turned or shaved legs, frequently braced by stretchers, which socket directly into the plank. (EVANS)
UF stools, Windsor
CN V.TG.AFU.AFU.ALO.AFU.ALO.AFU.CXA

Windsor tables
TG.692
ALT **Windsor table**
SN Tables with a top, usually round, supported on legs which socket directly into the top; such tables have three legs braced by stretchers. (EVANS)
UF tables, Windsor
CN V.TG.AFU.AFU.BIQ.BOK.AFU.DOI

Windsor writing chairs
USE **writing-arm Windsor chairs**

windstorms
KM.125 (L)
CN K.KM.AFU.CXA.BIQ.BZY

wine cellarets
USE **wine coolers**

wine cellarettes
USE **cellerets**

wine cellars
RM.190 (A,B)
ALT **wine cellar**
SN Use for rooms in which wine is stored, whether below ground level or not.
UF cellars, wine
houses, pitcher
pitcher houses
vaults, wine
wine vaults
CN V.RM.AFU.DIO.ALO.DCU.ARI.ARI

wine chests
USE **cellerets**

wine cisterns
USE **wine coolers**

wine coolers
TG.602 (R)
ALT **wine cooler**
SN Use for metal-lined tubs or stands for cooling bottles of wine. For small chests or cabinets designed to store wine or liquor use **cellarettes.**
UF cellarets, wine
cisterns (wine coolers)
cisterns, wine
coolers (wine coolers)
coolers, wine
waiters, wine
wine cellarets
wine cisterns
wine waiters
CN V.TG.AFU.AFU.AXC.ALO.DCU

wine factories
USE **wineries**

wine labels
VW.762 (L,R)
ALT **wine label**
UF bottle tickets
decanter labels
labels, decanter
labels, wine
tickets, bottle
CN V.VW.AFU.ALO.ALO.ALO.ARI

wine lists
VW.288
ALT **wine list**
UF lists, wine
CN V.VW.AFU.AFU.AFU.FZU.BCW.ALO.CFS

wine tables
USE **drinking stands**

wine vaults
USE **wine cellars**

wine waiters
USE **wine coolers**

wineries
RK.625 (A,L,B,R)
ALT **winery**
UF factories, wine
wine factories
CN V.RK.AFU.ALO.ALO.CLM.ALO.ALO.AFU.AXC.AFU.AXC

wing-back chairs
USE **easy chairs**

wing chairs
USE **easy chairs**

wing clothes presses
TG.516
ALT **wing clothes press**
UF clothes presses, wing
presses, wing clothes
wardrobes, wing
wing wardrobes
CN V.TG.AFU.AFU.AXC.ALO.BUE.CXA.AFU.ALO

wing dams
RK.564
ALT **wing dam**
SN Use for impermeable, rigid barriers built out from a bank of a river or stream diverting the current to prevent or encourage scour. For similar structures located at the seashore use **groins (erosion protection works)**; when such structures are built to control shoaling use **jetties.**
UF dams, wing
dikes, spur
spur dikes
spurs (erosion protection works)
CN V.RK.AFU.ALO.ALO.CFS.ALO.ALO.BOK

wing keys
TF.543
ALT **wing key**
UF keys, wing
CN V.TF.AFU.ALO.ARI.AFU.DIO

wing nuts
TF.454
ALT **wing nut**
SN Nuts provided with winglike projections to facilitate turning by fingers and thumb. (MEANS)
UF nuts, wing
CN V.TF.AFU.AFU.AFU.ALO.AFU.CLM.AXC

wing wardrobes
USE **wing clothes presses**

winged claw feet
TG.921
ALT **winged claw foot**
UF claw feet, winged
feet, winged claw
CN V.TG.ALO.DZW.AFU.DCU.AFU.AFU.ARI

winglights
USE **side lights**

wings (building divisions)
RM.426
ALT **wing (building division)**
SN Subsidiary parts of buildings extending out from the main portion. (HAS)
UF extensions (building divisions)
CN V.RM.AFU.ELK

wings (furniture components)
TG.838
ALT **wing (furniture component)**
SN The two forward extensions to the sides of the back on an easy chair.
UF checks (furniture backs)
lugs
CN V.TG.ALO.AXC.ALO.BUE

wings (theaters)
RM.383
ALT **wing (theater)**
SN The areas offstage and to the side of the acting area. (IDTL)
CN V.RM.AFU.DIO.AXC.AXC.ALO.BZY

wings, chimney
USE **chimney wings**

Winnebago
FL.1332 (L)
CN F.FL.ALO.ALO.ARI.AFU.BCW.CFS

Winooski marble
MT.842
UF marble, Winooski
CN M.MT.AFU.AFU.AFU.DCU.AFU.ARI.ARI.ARI.BOK.EWY

winter
BM.1040 (L,R)
UF wintertime
CN B.BM.CFS.AXC.CRG.ARI.AXC

winter gardens
RK.68 (A,B)
ALT **winter garden**
SN Use primarily for large greenhouses with plants and facilities for public entertainment, popular in the 19th century; may also be used for areas planted for winter display.
UF gardens, winter
CN V.RK.AFU.ALO.ALO.AFU.AFU.BOK.AFU.BCW

winter resorts
RG.173 (A,L)
ALT **winter resort**
UF resorts, winter
winter sports resorts
CN V.RG.AFU.AFU.DOI.BZY.AXC

winter sports resorts
USE **winter resorts**

wintertime
USE **winter**

Winthrop desks
USE **Governor Winthrop desks**

Wintun
FL.1267 (L)
CN F.FL.ALO.ALO.ARI.AFU.ALO.ERE

wire
MT.481 (L)
SN A filament or slender rod of drawn metal. (DAC)
CN M.MT.AFU.AFU.AFU.BZY.ALO.BZY

wire anchors, dovetail
USE **dovetail wire anchors**

wire brads, flat-head
USE **flat-head wire brads**

wire brushes
TB.353 (N)
ALT **wire brush**
UF brushes, wire
CN V.TB.AFU.ARI.CRG.ALO.ALO.AXC

wire-cut brick
MT.140
SN Brick cut to size by a wire before firing. (DLA)
UF brick, wire-cut
CN M.MT.AFU.AFU.AFU.AXC.ALO.AFU.AXC.ALO.AXC.AFU

wire cutters
TB.713 (N)
ALT **wire cutter**
UF cutters, wire
CN V.TB.AFU.BCW.BIQ.ARI.ALO.ALO.BIQ

wire hangers, metal-to-wood
USE **metal-to-wood wire hangers**

wire hangers, nicked hanging
USE **nicked hanging wire hangers**

wire photographs
VJ.124 (L)
ALT **wire photograph**
SN Photographs converted to electrical signals, transmitted over wires, and then reformed into images.
UF news wire photos
photographs, wire
CN V.VJ.AFU.ARI.ALO.CXA

wire plates
USE **drawplates**

wire recordings
VW.637
ALT **wire recording**
SN Recordings of sound on a spool of wire rather than on magnetic tape. (AHD)
UF recordings, wire
CN V.VW.AFU.ALO.AFU.DZW.AFU.AFU.AXC

wire rope
USE **cable**

wire vises
TB.227
ALT **wire vise**
SN Clamps used to hold wire while it is filed and hammered into a rivet head.
UF vises, wire
CN V.TB.AFU.ARI.CFS.BOK.ARI

wire, barbed
USE **barbed wire**

wire, chicken
USE **chicken wire**

wire, piano
USE **piano wire**

wired glass
MT.287 (B)
UF glass, wired
CN M.MT.AFU.AFU.AFU.BIQ.AFU.AXC.CXA.ALO

wirework
MT.2773
CN M.MT.AFU.AXC.BOK.BUE

wiring systems
USE **electric wiring**

wiring, electric
USE **electric wiring**

Wishosk
USE **Wiyot**

Wishram
FL.1427 (L)
CN F.FL.ALO.ALO.ARI.AFU.BUE.FCS

witchet planes
USE **rounder planes**

withes
USE **wythes**

wives
HG.17 (L)
ALT **wife**
CN H.HG.AFU.ALO.ARI.ALO

Wiyot
FL.1268 (L)
UF Humboldt Bay Indians
Indians, Humboldt Bay
Wishosk
CN F.FL.ALO.ALO.ARI.AFU.ALO.EWY

woad
MT.1536 (L)
SN Blue dye similar to indigo obtained from the leaves of the woad plant, a herbaceous biennial, and used as a pigment in the Middle Ages. (GETTEN)
CN M.MT.AFU.AFU.ARI.AFU.AFU.AFU.AFU.AFU.AXC.DUC

wobble saws
USE **drunken saws**

Wobe
USE **Wee**

Wobi
USE **Wee**

Wodaabe
FL.394 (L)
CN F.FL.ALO.AFU.AXC.AFU.AXC.AXC.ALO.ARI

Wolframblau
USE **tungsten blue**

Wolof
FL.347 (L)
UF Jolof
CN F.FL.ALO.AFU.AXC.AFU.ARI.BIQ.BZY

womb chairs
TG.115
ALT **womb chair**
UF chairs, womb
CN V.TG.AFU.AFU.ALO.AFU.AFU.AFU.MQW

women
HG.20 (L,R)
ALT **woman**
CN H.HG.AFU.ARI.ALO

women's liberation movement
USE **feminism**

women's movement
USE **feminism**

women's rights
USE **feminism**

Wongo
FL.448
UF Bawongo
CN F.FL.ALO.AFU.AXC.ALO.ALO.AFU.AFU.CRG

wood
MT.1083 (A,L,B,R)
UF wooden
CN M.MT.AFU.AFU.ALO.BIQ.DCU.AFU

wood alcohol
USE **methyl alcohol**

wood-block printing
KT.474
SN Distinguished from wood engraving in that the lines and fine details of the design are left standing rather than cut into the wood. Wood-block printing produces prints composed of strong, wide lines against a light background, whereas wood engraving produces finer white lines on a dark background.
UF printing, wood-block
printing, woodcut
woodcut printing
woodcut process
CN K.KT.AFU.ALO.DUC.DUC.ALO.BCW.ARI.ALO.AXC

wood-carvers
HG.548 (A,L)
ALT **wood-carver**
CN H.HG.AFU.AXC.BUE.ARI.DIO.BCW

wood charcoal
MT.1046
UF charcoal, wood
CN M.MT.AFU.AFU.ALO.BIQ.BUE.ARI.AFU

wood-cut engravers
USE **wood engravers**

wood engravers
HG.134 (L,R)
ALT **wood engraver**
UF artists, woodblock
block cutters
block engravers
cutters, block
engravers, block
engravers, wood
engravers, wood-cut
finishers, wood-type
wood-cut engravers
wood-type finishers
woodblock artists
CN H.HG.AFU.AXC.AXC.AFU.AFU.ALO.AXC.DUC.BIQ

wood engraving
KT.477 (L,R)
SN Distinguished from wood block-printing in that an end-grain wood-block is always used, which allows lines to be cut freely and in any direction, and that the lines are cut with burins and other engraving tools. Wood engraving produces prints composed of white lines on a dark background, whereas wood-block printing results in wider dark lines on a light background.
UF engraving, wood
xylography
CN K.KT.AFU.ALO.DUC.DUC.ALO.BCW.ARI.BCW

wood frame construction
USE **frame construction**

wood oil, China
USE **tung oil**

wood preservatives
MT.2642 (A,L)
SN Chemicals, such as creosote or sodium fluoride, used to prevent or retard the decay of wood, especially by repelling fungi and insects. (DAC)
UF preservatives, wood
CN M.MT.AFU.ARI.HCQ.ALO.AFU

wood products
MT.1413 (L)
UF products, wood
CN M.MT.AFU.AFU.ALO.BIQ.DCU.ALO

wood-pulp
MT.1058 (L)
CN M.MT.AFU.AFU.ALO.BIQ.BUE.BCW.ALO

wood-pulp board
USE **pulpboard**

wood pulp paper
MT.1898
UF groundwood paper
paper, groundwood
paper, wood pulp
CN M.MT.AFU.AFU.ARI.ALO.ALO.AXC.AFU.AXC

wood screws
TF.479
ALT **wood screw**
SN Helically threaded fasteners that cut

their way into wood when turned under axial pressure. (MEANS)
UF screws, wood
CN V.TF.AFU.AFU.AFU.ALO.AFU.DIO.AFU.BZY

wood-splitting wedges
USE **splitting wedges**

wood tar
MT.989 (L)
SN Tar obtained by the destructive distillation of wood; used as a preservative. (W)
UF tar, wood
CN M.MT.AFU.AFU.ALO.ALO.ALO.ALO

wood-to-masonry hangers
TF.363
ALT **wood-to-masonry hanger**
UF hangers, wood-to-masonry
CN V.TF.AFU.AFU.AFU.ALO.AFU.BOK.ARI.ARI.ALO

wood-to-steel joist hangers
TF.366
ALT **wood-to-steel joist hanger**
UF hangers, wood-to-steel joist
joist hangers, wood-to-steel
CN V.TF.AFU.AFU.AFU.ALO.AFU.BOK.ARI.ARI.ARI

wood-to-wood hangers
TF.369
ALT **wood-to-wood hanger**
UF hangers, wood-to-wood
CN V.TF.AFU.AFU.AFU.ALO.AFU.BOK.ARI.ARI.AXC

wood turpentine
MT.2707
SN Turpentine obtained from waste wood, chips, or sawdust by steam extraction or destructive distillation. (MH12)
UF turpentine, wood
CN M.MT.AFU.ARI.HZS.AFU.BZY.ARI.ALO

wood-type finishers
USE **wood engravers**

wood waste
USE **sawdust**

wood, balsa
USE **balsa wood**

wood, campeachy
USE **logwood**

wood, cocus
USE **granadilla**

wood, compregnated
USE **impregnated wood**

wood, comressed
USE **compressed wood**

wood, densified
USE **compressed wood**

wood, dry
USE **air-dried lumber**

wood, Hungarian yellow
USE **young fustic**

wood, impregnated
USE **impregnated wood**

wood, jacaranda
USE **Brazilian rosewood**

wood, London plane
USE **London plane wood**

wood, Maltese
USE **mahoe**

wood, plane
USE **plane wood**

wood, plastic
USE **plastic wood**

wood, plastic-impregnated
USE **impregnated wood**

wood, pressed
USE **compressed wood**

wood, pressure-treated
USE **pressure-treated wood**

wood, primary
USE **primary wood**

wood, resin-treated
USE **impregnated wood**

wood, secondary
USE **secondary wood**

wood, violet
USE **violet wood**

wood, violin
USE **common spruce**

wood, zebra
USE **marblewood**

woodblock artists
USE **wood engravers**

woodburning
USE **pyrography**

Woodburytype
KT.427 (L)
SN A photomechanical process that produces continuous tone images in slight relief. A gelatin relief is prepared by a bichromate process and then used to make an intaglio plate. This plate is used as a mold and is filled with pigmented gelatin; the gelatin layer is then pressed onto a paper support. Widely used for fine book illustration from about 1875 to 1900.
CN K.KT.AFU.ALO.DUC.DOI.ALO

Woodburytypes
VJ.26
ALT **Woodburytype**
SN Photomechanical prints produced by the process called Woodburytype.
CN V.VJ.AFU.AFU.ALO.BOK

woodcarver's files
USE **riffler files**

woodcarvers (printmakers)
USE **woodcutters**

woodcarving
KT.880 (L,B,R)
SN Use for the art of fashioning or ornamenting objects of wood by cutting with a sharp implement. (WCOL)
CN K.KT.AFU.ALO.HOE.BUE.AFU.ALO

woodchips
MT.1465 (L)
CN M.MT.AFU.AFU.ALO.BIQ.DCU.ALO.DUC

woodcut printing
USE **wood-block printing**

woodcut process
USE **wood-block printing**

woodcutter's saws
USE **bucksaws**

woodcutters
HG.135
ALT **woodcutter**
SN People who make woodcut blocks or the prints from them.
UF woodcarvers (printmakers)
CN H.HG.AFU.AXC.AXC.AFU.AFU.ALO.AXC.DUC.BOK

wooden
USE **wood**

woodenware
USE **treenware**

Woodland Tradition
FL.761
CN F.FL.ALO.ALO.ALO.AFU.AFU.AXC.AFU.AFU

woodlands
RD.254
ALT **woodland**
SN Distinct vegetation landscapes dominated by trees, often used for grazing or hunting but not for timber or cultivation; for tracts of land with trees often acting as barriers or boundaries but otherwise minimally utilized, use **woods**; for timber-producing land or unmanaged wilderness of dense growth, use **forests.**
CN V.RD.ARI.AFU.BCW.ALO.AFU.BCW

woods
RD.255 (B)
ALT **wood**
SN Tracts of land with trees, often act-

ing as boundaries or barriers, but otherwise minimally utilized; smaller and less wild than forests. For landscapes dominated by trees and having various uses, prefer **woodlands.**
CN V.RD.ARI.AFU.BCW.ALO.AFU.BIQ

woodsheds
RK.1219 (N)
ALT **woodshed**
CN V.RK.AFU.ALO.ALO.GFO.BIQ.BIQ

woodwork
MT.2784 (A,L,B,R)
SN Interior fittings of wood, such as moldings and staircases; also work done in or with wooden objects or parts made of wood. (PUTNAM)
CN M.MT.AFU.AXC.DOI

woodworkers
HG.543 (A,L,R)
ALT **woodworker**
CN H.HG.AFU.AXC.BUE.ARI.DIO

woodworking
KT.878 (L,R)
SN Use broadly for the activity of fashioning in wood. For the art of making fine furniture and intricate woodwork, use **cabinetmaking.** Use **carpentry** for constructing buildings and other structures with wood, including the installation of floors, windows, and other trim work.
CN K.KT.AFU.ALO.HOE.BUE.AFU

woodworking machinery
TB.792 (L)
UF machinery, woodworking
CN V.TB.AFU.BCW.CFS.AFU

woodworking tools
TB.807 (L)
ALT **woodworking tool**
UF tools, woodworking
CN V.TB.AFU.BCW.CFS.ALO

woody plants
RD.263 (L)
ALT **woody plant**
UF plants, woody
CN V.RD.ARI.AFU.BCW.ALO.ALO.ALO

wool
MT.1820 (L,R)
SN Refers especially to the fine, soft, curly hair or fleece of the sheep, but also refers to wool of the alpaca, vicuna, certain goats, and a few other animals. (MH)
CN M.MT.AFU.AFU.ARI.ALO.AFU.AFU.AFU.AXC

wool-fat
USE **lanolin**

wool wax
USE **lanolin**

wool, glass
USE **glass wool**

wool, lead
USE **lead wool**

wool, steel
USE **steel wool**

woolen mills
RK.663
ALT **woolen mill**
UF mills, woolen
CN V.RK.AFU.ALO.ALO.CLM.ALO.ALO.AFU.AXC.DZW.AXC

woolsheds
RK.76 (L)
ALT **woolshed**
UF shearing sheds
sheds, shearing
CN V.RK.AFU.ALO.ALO.AFU.AFU.CXA

woonerven
RG.284
ALT **woonerf**
SN Use for protected residential areas in which most vehicular traffic has its destination within the designated area, curb distinctions between street and sidewalk have been eliminated, and streets are shared by pedestrians and vehicles; originated in Holland.
CN V.RG.ALO.AFU.ALO.BCW.AXC

Wooton cabinet office secretaries
TG.563
ALT **Wooton cabinet office secretary**
UF cabinet office secretaries
office secretaries, Wooton cabinet
office secretaries, cabinet
secretaries, cabinet office
secretaries, Wooton cabinet office
secretaries, Wooton patent
Wooton patent secretaries
CN V.TG.AFU.AFU.AXC.ALO.BZY.FIM.ALO

Wooton desks
TG.561
ALT **Wooton desk**
SN Term used loosely to describe Wooton cabinet office secretaries and rotary desks, each invented by William S. Wooton.
UF desks, Wooton
CN V.TG.AFU.AFU.AXC.ALO.BZY.FIM

Wooton patent secretaries
USE **Wooton cabinet office secretaries**

work camps
USE **prison camps**

work tables
TG.767 (N)
ALT **work table**
SN Tables for holding working materials and implements; especially small tables with drawers and often with a suspended cloth bag for holding needlework.
UF bag tables
Martha Washington tables
pouch tables
sewing tables
tables à ouvrage
tables, bag
tables, Martha Washington
tables, pouch
tables, sewing
tables, work
travailleuses
CN V.TG.AFU.AFU.BIQ.BOK.ALO.GWW

work, authority
USE **authority control**

work, straw
USE **straw work**

workbenches
TB.494 (L,N)
ALT **workbench**
SN Strong heavy waist-high tables on which the work of mechanics, machinists, and carpenters is performed. (W)
UF benches, carpenter's
carpenter's benches
CN V.TB.AFU.ARI.ERE.AXC

workbooks
VW.362
ALT **workbook**
SN Booklets containing problems and exercises in which a student may directly write or calculate. (AHD)
CN V.VW.AFU.AFU.ALO.CXA.CFS

worked lumber
MT.1426
SN Lumber that in addition to being dressed has been matched, shiplapped, or patterned. (PUTNAM)
UF lumber, worked
CN M.MT.AFU.AFU.ALO.BIQ.DCU.ALO.BOK.ALO.AFU.AFU.AFU

worker's housing
USE **industrial housing**

workers
HG.23 (L,R)
ALT **worker**
CN H.HG.AFU.AXC.ALO

workers, blue collar
USE **blue collar workers**

workers, clerical
USE **clerical workers**

workers, construction
USE **construction workers**

workers, furniture
USE **furniture workers**

workers, manual
USE **blue collar workers**

workers, migrant
USE **migrant workers**

workers, nonmanual
USE **white collar workers**

workers, office
USE **clerical workers**

workers, semiskilled
USE **semiskilled workers**

workers, sheet metal
USE **sheet metal workers**

workers, skilled
USE **skilled workers**

workers, social
USE **social workers**

workers, textile
USE **textile workers**

workers, unskilled
USE **unskilled labor**

workers, white collar
USE **white collar workers**

workhouses
RK.732 (L)
ALT **workhouse**
SN Use for places of confinement and correction, established since the 16th century, using hard labor and strict discipline as reformative measures for lesser offenders and vagrants. For welfare buildings providing charitable care and work for the poor, use **almshouses.**
UF bettering houses
bridewell houses
bridewells
houses of correction
houses, bettering
houses, bridewell
CN V.RK.AFU.ALO.ALO.CXA.AFU.BIQ

workhouses (almshouses)
USE **almshouses**

working class
HG.890 (L)
UF class, laboring
class, working
laboring class
CN H.HG.ALO.DOI.ALO.AXC

working drawings
VD.111 (N,B)
ALT **working drawing**
SN Use for final drawings from which a structure, object, or work of art is made. For drawings done in developing a work, use **sketches, studies, preliminary drawings, preparatory drawings,** or **design drawings.**
UF drawings, production
drawings, working
production drawings
CN V.VD.AFU.ALO.DCU

working groups
USE **task forces**

working-men's gardens
USE **community gardens**

workmanship
USE **craftsmanship**

works (art)
USE **works of art**

works (factories)
USE **factories**

works of art
VB.88
ALT **work of art**
SN Use for works of the fine or decorative arts when their aesthetic nature is emphasized, as opposed to their qualities as discrete objects. A work of art may exist as one part of a larger object, e.g., a mural painting or a painting on a piece of furniture. When emphasis is on the works as objects, as in conservation or inventorying, use **art objects.**
UF art, works of
artworks
works (art)
CN V.VB.ALO.BIQ

works, agricultural
USE **agricultural buildings**

works, collected
USE **collected works**

works, erosion protection
USE **erosion protection works**

works, flood protection
USE **flood protection works**

works, genre
USE **genre**

works, glass
USE **glass factories**

works, hydraulic construction
USE **hydraulic structures**

works, land reclamation
USE **land reclamation works**

works, public
USE **public works**

works, railway
USE **railway buildings**

works, reclamation
USE **land reclamation works**

works, shipbuilding
USE **shipyards**

works, smelting
USE **smelters**

works, street
USE **street art**

works, water flow control
USE **erosion protection works**

works, waterflow control
USE **flood protection works**

worksheets
VW.120
ALT **worksheet**
SN Documents used in making preliminary plans, auxiliary computations, notes, or comments as a guide in doing some piece of work. (W)
CN V.VW.AFU.AFU.AFU.FZU.ARI.AXC

workshops
HG.905 (A,L,B,R)
ALT **workshop**
SN Use for groups of artists or craftsmen collaborating to produce works, often under a master's name. In the 19th and 20th centuries (when a master artist takes on pupils rather than apprentices), use **studios.**
UF ateliers
bottegas
shops
CN H.HG.ALO.EFQ

workshops (seminars)
KM.51 (L)
CN K.KM.AFU.BCW.AXC.AFU

workshops (work spaces)
RM.240 (A,L,B,R)
ALT **workshop (work space)**
SN Use for rooms set aside for specific work to be done, especially machine work.
UF ateliers (work spaces)
shops (work spaces)
CN V.RM.AFU.DIO.ALO.DOI.DIO

workshops for the handicapped
USE **sheltered workshops**

workshops, sheltered
USE **sheltered workshops**

workyards
USE **adventure playgrounds**

world atlases
VW.134
ALT **world atlas**
UF atlases, world
CN V.VW.AFU.AFU.AFU.FZU.AXC.AFU.AFU.AFU.AXC.BIQ

world maps
VW.232 (L,B)
ALT **world map**
UF maps, world
CN V.VW.AFU.AFU.AFU.FZU.AXC.AFU.ARI.AXC.DUC.BZY

World of Art
USE **Mir Iskusstva**

world's fairs
KM.66 (A,L,B)
UF fairs, world's

CN K.KM.AFU.BUE.AFU.AFU

worm's-eye perspectives
VD.89
ALT **worm's-eye perspective**
SN Use for perspective drawings having a viewpoint well below normal eye level. For images with low viewpoints where perspective is not employed or not emphasized, use **worm's-eye views.**
UF frog perspectives
perspectives, frog
perspectives, worm's-eye
CN V.VD.AFU.AFU.BIQ.ARI.BCW.BCW

worm's-eye views
VB.31
ALT **worm's-eye view**
SN Use for views having a viewpoint well below normal eye level; if these are architectural drawings in precise perspective, use **worm's-eye perspectives.**
UF toad's-eye views
views, toad's-eye
views, worm's-eye
CN V.VB.AFU.AFU.BOK.ALO.CLM

worship
BM.712 (L)
CN B.BM.BZY.ALO.AXC

Wothly's process
USE **Wothlytype**

Wothlytype
KT.376
SN Process of making photographic prints using a printing-out paper that has light-sensitive salts of uranium and silver in a collodion binder.
UF Wothly's process
CN K.KT.AFU.ALO.DUC.DIO.ALO.ERE

wove paper
MT.1970
SN Has a woven or even appearance in transmitting light. First made about 1755, most modern papers are wove. (TATEMT)
UF paper, wove
CN M.MT.AFU.AFU.ARI.ALO.ALO.AXC.AXC.BCW

Woyamana
USE **Waiwai**

Woyo
FL.489
UF Bawoyo
CN F.FL.ALO.AFU.AXC.ALO.ALO.AXC.BIQ.AFU

wrack, grass
USE **eelgrass**

wrapping materials
MT.2737 (L,R)
UF materials, wrapping
CN M.MT.AFU.ARI.IWU

wrapping paper
MT.1957 (N)
UF paper, wrapping
CN M.MT.AFU.AFU.ARI.ALO.ALO.AXC.ARI.CFS

wrath
USE **anger**

wreathed columns
USE **spiral columns**

wreathed stairs
USE geometrical stairs

wreaths (stair components)
RT.1128
ALT **wreath (stair component)**
SN Curved portions of strings or handrails which follow turns in a geometrical stair, usually a quarter circle, and therefore corresponding to a portion of the surface of a vertical cylinder. (DAC)
CN V.RT.AFU.BIQ.AXC.ALO.BOK.ARI

wreckers
HG.615
ALT **wrecker**
SN Persons whose business is the demolition and removal of buildings or other structures, often including the salvaging of material.
UF demolishers
CN H.HG.AFU.AXC.BZY.AFU.FZU

wrecking
USE **demolition**

wrecking balls
TB.23 (N)
ALT **wrecking ball**
SN Rounded, heavy, metal or concrete demolition devices swung on a cable from the boom of a crane to break through concrete or masonry constructions. (MEANS)
UF ball breakers
balls, breaker
balls, headache
balls, wrecking
breaker balls
breakers, ball
crackers, skull
headache balls
skull crackers
CN V.TB.AFU.ARI.AFU.AFU.BCW

wrecking bars
USE **pinch bars**

wrenches
TB.202 (L,N)
ALT **wrench**
SN Hand tools consisting of a handle and a jaw at one end; used to turn or hold a bolt, nut, pipe, or fitting. The jaw may be shaped for a specific-sized object or may be adjustable. (MEANS)
UF spanners
CN V.TB.AFU.ARI.BOK.BCW

wrenches, adjustable
USE **adjustable wrenches**

wrenches, Allen
USE **Allen wrenches**

wrenches, Allen head
USE **Allen wrenches**

wrenches, bed
USE **bed wrenches**

wrenches, chain pipe
USE **chain tongs**

wrenches, crescent
USE **adjustable wrenches**

wrenches, impact
USE **impact wrenches**

wrenches, monkey
USE **monkey wrenches**

wrenches, open-end
USE **open-end wrenches**

wrenches, pipe
USE **pipe wrenches**

wrenches, socket
USE **socket wrenches**

wrenches, spud
USE **spud wrenches**

wrenches, stave
USE **flagging irons**

wrenches, tack
USE **tack pulls**

wrenches, tap
USE **tap wrenches**

wrestler slate
MT.873
UF slate, wrestler
CN M.MT.AFU.AFU.AFU.DCU.AFU.ARI.BUE.ALO.ALO.AFU

wrinkling
KT.926
ALT **wrinkled**
SN The formation of small ridges or furrows on a formerly smooth surface.
UF crinkling
CN K.KT.ALO.BZY.BOK

writers
USE **authors**

writers, editorial
USE **editorial writers**

writers, lyric
USE **lyricists**

writers, screen
USE **screen writers**

writers, song
USE **lyricists**

writing
KT.483 (L,B,R)
CN K.KT.AFU.ALO.DUC.EWY

writing and dressing tables, combined
USE **bureau tables**

writing-arm Windsor chairs
TG.114
ALT **writing-arm Windsor chair**
SN Any Windsor chair having one shaped, flat leaf, in lieu of a standard arm, used as a writing surface. (EVANS)
UF chairs, writing-arm Windsor
Windsor chairs, writing-arm
Windsor writing chairs
writing chairs, Windsor
CN V.TG.AFU.AFU.ALO.AFU.AFU.AFU.MLC.CLM

writing arms
TG.818
ALT **writing arm**
SN Broad, flat arms on chairs intended to serve as a writing surface.
UF arms, tablet
arms, writing
boards, writing
tablet arms
writing boards
CN V.TG.ALO.ALO.AFU.ALO.AFU

writing boards
USE **writing arms**

writing chairs (corner chairs)
USE **corner chairs**

writing chairs, Windsor
USE **writing-arm Windsor chairs**

writing desks
TG.564 (R)
ALT **writing desk**
SN Box like nests of drawers enclosed in the front by a flap that drops down to form a writing surface. (THORN2)
UF desks, writing
CN V.TG.AFU.AFU.AXC.ALO.BZY.FOG

writing desks (portable desks)
USE **portable desks**

writing desks, lady's small
USE **lady's writing tables**

writing desks, portable
USE **portable desks**

writing drawers
USE **secretary drawers**

writing fire screens
TG.12
ALT **writing fire screen**
UF fire screens, writing
screens, writing fire
CN V.TG.AFU.AFU.AFU.AFU.BIQ

writing fire screens, gentleman's
USE **gentleman's writing fire screens**

writing fire screens, lady's
USE **lady's writing fire screens**

writing instruments
TB.233 (L,N)
ALT **writing instrument**
UF instruments, writing
CN V.TB.AFU.ARI.CLM.AFU.AFU.ARI

writing paper
MT.1959 (N)
SN Paper intended for writing upon with ink; usually finished with a smooth surface and sized. (W)
UF paper, writing
CN M.MT.AFU.AFU.ARI.ALO.ALO.AXC.ARI.CLM

writing rooms
RM.155
ALT **writing room**
SN Use for rooms set aside for writing, as in a residence, hotel, or club.
UF rooms, writing
CN V.RM.AFU.DIO.ALO.CFS.BOK

writing table and dressing stands, combination
USE **lady's cabinet dressing tables**

writing tables
TG.566 (N)
ALT **writing table**
SN Use for flat-top desks on long legs, generally taking the form of a table with one long drawer in the apron. Use **writing desks** for similar forms having a superstructure with pigeonholes for writing materials.
UF bureaux (writing tables)
tables, writing
CN V.TG.AFU.AFU.AXC.ALO.BZY.FUA

writing tables, cylinder fall
USE **cylinder fall desks**

writing tables, gentleman's
USE **gentleman's writing tables**

writing tables, kidney library
USE **kidney tables**

writing tables, kneehole
USE **kneehole desks**

writing tables, lady's
USE **lady's writing tables**

writing tables, lady's cylinder
USE **lady's writing tables**

writing tables, lady's screen
USE **lady's screen writing tables**

writing tables, library
USE **library tables**

writing tables, rising-top
USE **rising-top writing tables**

writing tables, sofa
USE **sofa writing tables**

writing tables, tambour
USE **tambour writing tables**

writing, report
USE **technical writing**

writing, specification
USE **specification writing**

writing, technical
USE **technical writing**

writs
VW.1013 (L)
ALT **writ**
SN Orders in writing, issued under seal (in the name of the sovereign or a court or judicial officer) from the proper authority, commanding the person to whom it is directed to perform or refrain from performing an act specified therein. (GAHLM)
CN V.VW.AFU.ARI.ALO.BCW.AFU.ALO.AFU.AXC

wrong irons
USE **barking irons**

wrought iron
MT.361 (A,L,B,R)
SN A commercially pure iron of fibrous nature made by melting white cast iron, passing an oxidizing flame over it, and rolling it into a mass; valued for its corrosion resistance and ductility. (MH12)
UF iron, wrought
CN M.MT.AFU.AFU.AFU.BZY.AFU.AFU.AFU.AFU.AXC

wrought iron (color)
USE **dark gray**

Wu
FL.1939 (L)
CN F.FL.ALO.ARI.ALO.AFU.AFU.AXC.ALO.DCU

Wu-ts'ai
USE **Wucai**

Wucai
FL.1953
UF five-color porcelain
porcelain, five-color
Wu-ts'ai
CN F.FL.ALO.ARI.ALO.AFU.AFU.AXC.ARI.CFS

Wum
FL.200
UF Aghem
CN F.FL.ALO.AFU.AXC.AFU.AFU.AFU.ARI.BIQ

Wumu
FL.422
UF Bawumbu
CN F.FL.ALO.AFU.AXC.ALO.AFU.AXC.CFS

Wurkun
FL.232
CN F.FL.ALO.AFU.AXC.AFU.AFU.ALO.ARI.BUE

Wuvulu Island
FL.3686
UF Matty Island
CN F.FL.ALO.BOK.ARI.BOK

Wyandot
USE **Huron**

wych elm
MT.1150
UF elm, wych
Ulmus glabra
CN M.MT.AFU.AFU.ALO.BIQ.DCU.AFU.AFU.AFU.DCU.BIQ

wye tracery
USE **Y-tracery**

Wyoming Valley stone
MT.712
UF stone, Wyoming Valley
CN M.MT.AFU.AFU.AFU.DCU.AFU.ALO.AFU.ARI.AFU.ALO.AFU.AFU.ARI

wythes
RT.665
SN Continuous vertical sections of masonry, one unit in thickness. (ACME)
UF tiers (wythes)
withes
CN V.RT.AFU.AFU.AFU.BIQ.BUE.ALO.AFU.CRG

X-chairs
TG.116
ALT **X-chair**
SN Chairs with X-shaped frames; often designed to fold.
UF chairs, hip-joint
chairs, scissors
chairs, X-shaped
hip-joint chairs
scissors chairs
tabourets en X
X-frames
X-shaped chairs
X-stools
CN V.TG.AFU.AFU.ALO.AFU.AFU.AFU.MWQ

X-frames
USE **X-chairs**

x-ray absorbing glass
USE **x-ray protective glass**

x-ray photographs
USE **radiographs**

x-ray photography
USE **radiography**

x-ray protective glass
MT.288
UF glass, x-ray absorbing
glass, x-ray protective
glass, x-ray rejecting
glass, x-ray resistant
protective glass, x-ray
x-ray absorbing glass
x-ray rejecting glass
x-ray resistant glass
CN M.MT.AFU.AFU.AFU.BIQ.AFU.AXC.DCU

x-ray rejecting glass
USE **x-ray protective glass**

x-ray resistant glass
USE **x-ray protective glass**

x-ray spectroscopy
KT.20 (L)
UF spectroscopy, x-ray
CN K.KT.AFU.ALO.AXC.BOK

x-rays
BM.867 (L,B,R)
CN B.BM.CFS.AXC.ALO.AFU.ARI.ARI

x-rays (radiographs)
USE **radiographs**

X-shaped chairs
USE **X-chairs**

X-shaped legs
USE **curule legs**

X-stools
USE **X-chairs**

X-stools, folding
USE **folding stools**

X-stretchers
USE **cross stretchers**

xanthine orange
USE **deep orange**

xanthorrhoea
USE **acaroid resin**

Xe
FL.1010
CN F.FL.ALO.ALO.ALO.ALO.AFU.ALO.ARI.AFU.AFU.AFU

xenodochia
RK.949
ALT **xenodochium**
SN Use for establishments providing for the care and accommodation of pilgrims and strangers, especially in Classical through Medieval contexts.
CN V.RK.AFU.ALO.ALO.ELK.ARI.ALO

xeriscape gardens
USE **xeriscapes**

xeriscapes
RK.1426
ALT **xeriscape**
SN Use for gardens or landscapes designed for low water maintenance by plant selection, planting techniques, and irrigation systems tolerant of low water input.
UF drought-resistant gardens
drought-tolerant gardens
gardens, drought-resistant
gardens, drought-tolerant
gardens, low-water input
gardens, water-conserving
gardens, xeriscape
low-water input gardens
water-conserving gardens
xeriscape gardens
CN V.RK.ALO.AFU.AFU.ALO.CFS

xerographic art
USE **copy art**

xerographic copies
VW.687
ALT **xerographic copy**
UF copies, xerographic
CN V.VW.AFU.ALO.AFU.DZW.BIQ.BZY.AFU.AFU

xerographic process
USE **xerography**

xerography
KT.182 (L,R)
SN A dry, nonchemical photographic process in which an electrostatic image remains after exposure and is developed by the deposition of a fine powder. (NEBL62)
UF xerographic process
xeroxing
CN K.KT.AFU.ALO.DUC.BOK.AFU.AFU.AFU

Xerox art
USE **copy art**

xeroxing
USE **xerography**

Xhosa
FL.566 (L)
UF Xosa
CN F.FL.ALO.AFU.AXC.ARI.AXC.BCW

Xia
FL.1852
UF Chou
Hsia
CN F.FL.ALO.ARI.ALO.AFU.AFU.ALO.ARI

Xianfeng
FL.1916 (L)
UF Hsien-feng
CN F.FL.ALO.ARI.ALO.AFU.AFU.ALO.DOI.BOK

Xiaotun
FL.1859
UF Hsiao-t'un
CN F.FL.ALO.ARI.ALO.AFU.AFU.ALO.BCW.ALO.ALO

xicalcoliuhqui
USE **stepped frets**

Xing ware
FL.1954

UF Hsing ware
ware, Hsing
ware, Xing
CN F.FL.ALO.ARI.ALO.AFU.AFU.AXC.ARI.CLM

Xingú
FL.1601
CN F.FL.ALO.ALO.ARI.ARI.AFU.HOE

Xolalpan
FL.990
UF Teotihuacan IIIa
CN F.FL.ALO.ALO.ALO.ALO.AFU.ALO.AFU.AFU.CLM

Xometla
USE **Coyotlatelco**

Xosa
USE **Xhosa**

Xuande
FL.1900
UF Hsuan-te
CN F.FL.ALO.ARI.ALO.AFU.AFU.ALO.DIO.ARI

Xuantong
FL.1919 (L)
UF Hsuan-t'ung
CN F.FL.ALO.ARI.ALO.AFU.AFU.ALO.DOI.CFS

xylene
MT.2674 (L)
CN M.MT.AFU.ARI.HZS.AFU.BIQ.ALO.ARI

xylography
USE **wood engraving**

Y chairs
TG.120
ALT **Y chair**
UF chairs, Y
CN V.TG.AFU.AFU.ALO.AFU.AFU.AFU.NCK

Y-tracery
RT.1022
UF tracery, wye
wye tracery
CN V.RT.AFU.ARI.ALO.BZY.AFU.AFU.BCW

Ya` Furid
FL.3601
CN F.FL.ALO.BIQ.AFU.IWU

Ya`qub
FL.3585
CN F.FL.ALO.BIQ.AFU.IFM.AFU.BOK

yacca gum
USE **acaroid resin**

yacht basins
USE **marinas**

yacht clubs
RG.187 (A,L,B)
ALT **yacht club**
UF clubs, yacht
CN V.RG.AFU.AFU.DOI.CRG

Yachting Style
USE **Art Nouveau**

yachtsmen
HG.746
ALT **yachtsman**
SN Persons who own or sail a yacht or are enthusiasts of yachting. (RHDEL2)
CN H.HG.AFU.BCW.HTY

Yadava
FL.2219 (L)
CN F.FL.ALO.ARI.AXC.ALO.AFU.AXC.CXA

Yadkin
FL.830
CN F.FL.ALO.ALO.ALO.AFU.ALO.ALO.ALO.BCW

Yaelima
FL.449
CN F.FL.ALO.AFU.AXC.ALO.ALO.AFU.AFU.CXA

Yahano
USE **Diegueño**

Yahgan
FL.1700 (L)
UF Yamana
CN F.FL.ALO.ALO.ARI.ARI.BOK.CXA

Yahi
USE **Yana**

Yaka
FL.473 (L)
UF Bayaka
CN F.FL.ALO.AFU.AXC.ALO.ALO.ARI.CRG

Yakima
FL.1428 (L)
CN F.FL.ALO.ALO.ARI.AFU.BUE.FIM

Yakishime
FL.2047
UF Sekki
CN F.FL.ALO.ARI.ALO.ALO.ALO.ALO.ALO.FOG

Yakuba
USE **Dan**

yalis
RK.278 (A)
ALT **yali**
SN Use for Turkish summer mansions, especially when located at waterside.
CN V.RK.AFU.ALO.ALO.AXC.ALO.ALO.ARI.AFU.AFU

Yamachawan
FL.2034
CN F.FL.ALO.ARI.ALO.ALO.ALO.ALO.ALO.DIO.AFU

Yamana
USE **Yahgan**

Yamato-e
FL.2073 (L)
CN F.FL.ALO.ARI.ALO.ALO.ALO.ARI.FOG

Yana
FL.1269 (L)
UF Yahi
CN F.FL.ALO.ALO.ARI.AFU.ALO.FCS

Yangere
FL.538
CN F.FL.ALO.AFU.AXC.ALO.ALO.BIQ.ALO.CXA

Yangshao
FL.1843
UF Painted Pottery
CN F.FL.ALO.ARI.ALO.AFU.AFU.AFU.ARI.ALO

Yankee barns
USE **English barns**

Yankton
FL.1400 (L)
CN F.FL.ALO.ALO.ARI.AFU.BOK.FCS.ARI

Yans
USE **Yanzi**

Yanzi
FL.474 (L)
UF Bayanzi
Yans
CN F.FL.ALO.AFU.AXC.ALO.ALO.ARI.CXA

Yao
FL.671 (L)
CN F.FL.ALO.AFU.AXC.AXC.BIQ.DCU

Yap
FL.3681 (L)
CN F.FL.ALO.BOK.ARI.ALO.ARI

Yaqui
FL.1495 (L)
CN F.FL.ALO.ALO.ARI.ALO.AFU.BOK

yard lumber
MT.1446
SN Lumber up to 5 inches thick intended for general building construction. (DAC)
UF lumber, yard
CN M.MT.AFU.AFU.ALO.BIQ.DCU.ALO.BOK.ARI.BIQ

yard sales
USE **garage sales**

yards
RK.1600 (A)
ALT **yard**
CN V.RK.ALO.ARI.CRG

yards, hump
USE **marshalling yards**

yards, marshalling
USE **marshalling yards**

yards, railroad
USE **railroad yards**

yards, scrap
USE **junkyards**

yards, switching
USE **marshalling yards**

yards, timber
USE **lumberyards**

Yarkhoto
FL.1830
CN F.FL.ALO.ARI.AFU.AXC.ELK.DOI

Yarmukian
FL.2918
UF Jericho Pottery Neolithic A
CN F.FL.ALO.AXC.ARI.AXC.AFU.ALO.ALO

yarn
MT.1978 (L,N)
SN Bundle of fibers twisted or laid together to form continuous strands. (MH12)
CN M.MT.AFU.AFU.ARI.ALO.ALO.BIQ.BIQ

yarn, stretch
USE **stretch yarn**

Yasovarman I
FL.2335
CN F.FL.ALO.ARI.BCW.ALO.ARI.AFU.ARI

Yasovarman II
FL.2345
CN F.FL.ALO.ARI.BCW.ALO.ARI.AFU.CXA

Yatsumune
USE **Gongen**

Yaure
FL.289
CN F.FL.ALO.AFU.AXC.AFU.ARI.AFU.AFU.AXC.AFU

Yavapai
FL.1485 (L)
UF Apache, Mohave
Mohave Apache
CN F.FL.ALO.ALO.ARI.AFU.CFS.DIO

yaya
USE **lancewood**

Yayoi
FL.1971 (L)
CN F.FL.ALO.ARI.ALO.ALO.AFU.ARI.AFU

yearbooks
VW.613 (L,N)
ALT yearbook
SN Books published annually as a report or summary of the statistics or facts of a calendar year and intended as reference books. (GAHLM)
CN V.VW.AFU.ALO.AFU.CXA.AFU.AFU.AFU

yearbooks, school
USE **school yearbooks**

yeast black
USE **vine black**

Yebu
USE **Ijebu**

Yecuana
USE **Makiritaré**

Yela
FL.517
UF Boyela
CN F.FL.ALO.AFU.AXC.ALO.ALO.BIQ.AFU.AFU.CLM

yellow
DL.111 (L)
CN D.DL.AFU.AFU.BCW

yellow beige
USE **light yellowish brown**
moderate yellowish brown

yellow berry
USE **buckthorn berry**

yellow birch
MT.1124 (L)
UF Betula alleghaniensis
Betula lutea
birch, yellow
CN M.MT.AFU.AFU.ALO.BIQ.DCU.AFU.AFU.AFU.BIQ.CFS

yellow brass
USE **cartridge brass**

yellow brown
USE **brownish orange**
brownish pink
dark orange yellow
dark reddish orange
light brown
light olive
light reddish brown
moderate orange
strong brown
strong yellowish brown

yellow buckeye
MT.1091
UF Aesculus flava
Aesculus octandra
buckeye, sweet
buckeye, yellow
sweet buckeye
CN M.MT.AFU.AFU.ALO.BIQ.DCU.AFU.AFU.AFU.AFU.AFU.AXC

yellow buff
USE **grayish yellow**
light yellowish brown
moderate orange yellow
pale orange yellow
pale yellow

yellow carmine
MT.1768
UF carmine, yellow
CN M.MT.AFU.AFU.ARI.AFU.AFU.ALO.ALO.BUE.ALO.BOK

yellow cedar
USE **yellow cypress**

yellow cypress
MT.1347 (L)
UF cedar, yellow
Chamaecyparis nootkatensis
cypress, yellow
Cypressus nootkatensis
yellow cedar
CN M.MT.AFU.AFU.ALO.BIQ.DCU.AFU.AFU.ALO.AXC.AXC

yellow deal
USE **Scotch pine**

yellow earth
USE **moderate orange yellow**
yellow ocher

yellow fir
USE **Douglas fir**

yellow green
DL.154
UF green, yellow
CN D.DL.AFU.AFU.BOK

yellow green, brilliant
USE **brilliant yellow green**

yellow green, dark dull
USE **grayish olive green**
moderate olive green

yellow green, deep
USE **deep yellow green**

yellow green, deep dull
USE **dark yellowish green**
moderate olive green
moderate yellow green

yellow green, grayish
USE **grayish yellow green**

yellow green, light
USE **light yellow green**

yellow green, moderate
USE **moderate yellow green**

yellow green, pale
USE **pale yellow green**

yellow green, strong
USE **strong yellow green**

yellow green, vivid
USE **vivid yellow green**

yellow lake
MT.1800
UF lake, yellow
CN M.MT.AFU.AFU.ARI.AFU.AFU.ALO.ALO.BUE.AXC.ARI

yellow lead monoxide
USE **litharge**

yellow lithopone, cadmium
USE **cadmium yellow lithopone**

yellow marble
MT.843
UF marble, yellow
CN M.MT.AFU.AFU.AFU.DCU.AFU.ARI.ARI.ARI.BUE

yellow marble, Lisbon
USE **Lisbon yellow marble**

Yellow Minyan ware
FL.2661
UF Minyan ware, Yellow
ware, Yellow Minyan
CN F.FL.ALO.AXC.ALO.AFU.ALO.AXC.AXC.BOK.ARI

yellow ocher
MT.1792
UF chamois (yellow ocher)
earth, yellow
gelb Ocker
Italian ocher
minette
ocher, Italian
ocher, yellow
ocre jaune
sil
yellow earth
CN M.MT.AFU.AFU.ARI.AFU.AFU.ALO.ALO.BUE.ARI.CFS.BCW

yellow ocher (color)
USE **dark orange yellow**
moderate orange yellow
strong orange yellow

yellow orange
USE **moderate orange**
strong orange

yellow orange, pale
USE **light yellowish pink**

yellow oxide of iron
USE **Mars yellow**

yellow pigment
MT.1757
UF pigment, yellow
CN M.MT.AFU.AFU.ARI.AFU.AFU.ALO.ALO.BUE

yellow pigment, artificial inorganic
USE **artificial inorganic yellow pigment**

yellow pigment, artificial organic
USE **synthetic organic yellow pigment**

yellow pigment, inorganic
USE **inorganic yellow pigment**

yellow pigment, organic
USE **organic yellow pigment**

yellow pigment, synthetic inorganic
USE **artificial inorganic yellow pigment**

yellow pigment, synthetic organic
USE **synthetic organic yellow pigment**

yellow pine
MT.1390 (L)
CN M.MT.AFU.AFU.ALO.BIQ.DCU.AFU.AFU.ALO.CXA.ELK

yellow pine (loblolly pine)
USE **loblolly pine**

yellow pine (ponderosa pine)
USE **ponderosa pine**

yellow pine (Scotch pine)
USE **Scotch pine**

yellow pine (scrub pine)
USE **scrub pine**

yellow pine (shortleaf pine)
USE **shortleaf pine**

yellow pine, southern
USE **southern yellow pine**

yellow pine, western
USE **ponderosa pine**

yellow poplar
USE **tulipwood**

yellow red
USE **brownish orange**
strong brown

Yellow Seto
USE **Ki Seto**

yellow-slipped ware
FL.2597
UF ware, yellow-slipped
CN F.FL.ALO.AXC.ALO.AFU.ALO.AXC.AFU.BCW

yellow spruce
USE **red spruce**

yellow ultramarine
USE **barium yellow**
strontium yellow

yellow varnish
MT.2484
SN Damar resin dissolved in linseed oil and heated. (MAYER)
UF varnish, yellow
CN M.MT.AFU.ARI.CRG.AFU.BOK.ALO.AFU.ALO

yellow willow
USE **western black willow**

yellow wood, Hungarian
USE **young fustic**

yellow, alizarin
USE **alizarin yellow**

yellow, amber
USE **brilliant yellow**
light yellow

yellow, aniline
USE **deep yellow**

yellow, antimony
USE **Naples yellow**
moderate orange yellow

yellow, arsenic
USE **orpiment**

yellow, Aurora
USE **cadmium yellow**

yellow, barium
USE **barium yellow**

yellow, barium (color)
USE **brilliant yellow**
light greenish yellow
moderate greenish yellow

yellow, baryta
USE **barium yellow**

yellow, bright
USE **brilliant orange yellow**
light orange yellow
moderate orange yellow
strong orange yellow
vivid yellow

yellow, bright chartreuse
USE **strong greenish yellow**
vivid greenish yellow

yellow, bright greenish
USE **vivid greenish yellow**

yellow, bright reddish
USE **vivid orange yellow**
vivid yellow

yellow, brilliant
USE **Naples yellow**
brilliant yellow

yellow, brilliant orange
USE **brilliant orange yellow**

yellow, brownish
USE **dark orange yellow**

yellow, cadmium
USE **cadmium yellow**

yellow, cadmium (color)
USE **moderate orange**
moderate orange yellow
strong orange
strong orange yellow

yellow, canary
USE **brilliant yellow**
light yellow
vivid yellow

yellow, Cassel
USE **Turner's yellow**

yellow, chartreuse
USE **brilliant greenish yellow**
light greenish yellow
moderate greenish yellow
strong greenish yellow

yellow, Chinese
USE orpiment

yellow, chrome
USE chrome yellow

yellow, chrome (color)
USE vivid orange yellow
vivid yellow

yellow, citron
USE light greenish yellow
moderate greenish yellow
zinc yellow

yellow, cobalt
USE cobalt yellow

yellow, cobalt (color)
USE brilliant yellow

yellow, dark
USE dark yellow

yellow, dark grayish
USE dark grayish yellow

yellow, dark greenish
USE dark greenish yellow

yellow, dark orange
USE dark orange yellow

yellow, deep
USE deep yellow

yellow, deep cadmium
USE deep cadmium yellow

yellow, deep chrome
USE moderate orange yellow

yellow, deep greenish
USE deep greenish yellow

yellow, deep orange
USE deep orange yellow

yellow, dull
USE grayish yellow
light orange yellow

yellow, dull greenish
USE light olive
pale greenish yellow

yellow, dull reddish
USE dark grayish yellow
grayish yellow
pale orange yellow
pale yellow

yellow, earth
USE light yellowish brown

yellow, ferrite
USE Mars yellow

yellow, Flemish
USE massicot

yellow, gaude
USE weld

yellow, gold
USE moderate orange yellow
strong orange yellow

yellow, golden
USE dark orange yellow
moderate orange yellow
strong orange yellow
vivid yellow

yellow, grayish
USE grayish yellow

yellow, grayish greenish
USE grayish greenish yellow

yellow, greenish
USE greenish yellow

yellow, Hansa
USE Hansa yellow

yellow, Indian
USE Indian yellow

yellow, Indian (color)
USE brilliant orange yellow
light orange yellow
moderate orange yellow

yellow, iron
USE Mars yellow

yellow, ivory
USE pale yellow

yellow, Kassler
USE Turner's yellow

yellow, king's
USE orpiment

yellow, lead-tin
USE lead stannate

yellow, Leipzig
USE chrome yellow

yellow, lemon
USE barium yellow
brilliant greenish yellow
brilliant yellow
deep greenish yellow
deep yellow
light yellow
vivid greenish yellow
vivid yellow

yellow, lemon cadmium
USE lemon cadmium yellow

yellow, light
USE light yellow

yellow, light chartreuse
USE brilliant greenish yellow
light greenish yellow
moderate greenish yellow
strong greenish yellow

yellow, light chrome
USE strong yellow

yellow, light citron
USE light greenish yellow

yellow, light greenish
USE light greenish yellow

yellow, light lemon
USE brilliant greenish yellow
light greenish yellow

yellow, light orange
USE light orange yellow

yellow, lime
USE brilliant yellow green
strong greenish yellow

Yellow, Mapico
USE Mars yellow

yellow, Mars
USE Mars yellow

yellow, Mars (color)
USE dark orange yellow
deep orange yellow
moderate orange
strong orange

yellow, massicot
USE light yellow
pale yellow

yellow, middle cadmium
USE middle cadmium yellow

yellow, mineral
USE Turner's yellow

yellow, moderate
USE moderate yellow

yellow, moderate greenish
USE moderate greenish yellow

yellow, moderate orange
USE moderate orange yellow

yellow, monolite
USE Hansa yellow

yellow, Montpellier
USE Turner's yellow

yellow, Naples
USE Naples yellow

yellow, Naples (color)
USE brilliant yellow
grayish yellow
light yellow
moderate yellow
pale yellow

yellow, nickel-titanium
USE nickel-titanium yellow

yellow, olive
USE dark greenish yellow
dark yellow
deep greenish yellow
light olive
moderate olive
pale yellow

yellow, orange
USE orange yellow

yellow, orange cadmium
USE **cadmium orange**

yellow, orient
USE **deep cadmium yellow**

yellow, pale
USE **pale yellow**

yellow, pale cadmium
USE **pale cadmium yellow**

yellow, pale greenish
USE **pale greenish yellow**

yellow, pale lemon
USE **light greenish yellow**

yellow, pale orange
USE **pale orange yellow**

yellow, Paris
USE **chrome yellow**

yellow, pastel
USE **light greenish yellow**
light yellow
moderate greenish yellow
moderate yellow
pale greenish yellow
strong yellow

yellow, patent
USE **Turner's yellow**

yellow, permanent
USE **barium yellow**
moderate orange yellow

yellow, primrose
USE **zinc yellow**

yellow, reddish
USE **brilliant orange yellow**
brilliant yellow
dark orange yellow
dark yellow
deep orange yellow
deep yellow
light orange
light orange yellow
light yellow
moderate orange
moderate orange yellow
moderate yellow
strong orange yellow
strong yellow

yellow, soft
USE **light yellow**

yellow, stone
USE **Oxford ocher**

yellow, strong
USE **strong yellow**

yellow, strong greenish
USE **strong greenish yellow**

yellow, strong orange
USE **strong orange yellow**

yellow, strontian
USE **strontium yellow**

yellow, strontium
USE **strontium yellow**

yellow, strontium (color)
USE **brilliant greenish yellow**
strong greenish yellow

yellow, sulfur
USE **light greenish yellow**

yellow, sulphur
USE **brilliant greenish yellow**
pale greenish yellow
vivid greenish yellow
vivid yellow

yellow, sun
USE **nickel-titanium yellow**

yellow, sunflower
USE **orpiment**

yellow, transparent
USE **pale yellow**

yellow, Turner's
USE **Turner's yellow**

yellow, Turner's (color)
USE **brilliant yellow**
light yellow
moderate yellow
strong yellow

yellow, ultramarine
USE **strontium yellow**

yellow, uranium
USE **uranium yellow**

yellow, Verona
USE **Turner's yellow**

yellow, vivid
USE **vivid yellow**

yellow, vivid greenish
USE **vivid greenish yellow**

yellow, vivid orange
USE **vivid orange yellow**

yellow, zinc
USE **zinc yellow**

yellow, zinc (color)
USE **strong yellow**

yellowberries lake
USE **Persian berries lake**

yellowish brown
DL.98
UF brown, yellowish
CN D.DL.AFU.AFU.AXC.BZY.ALO

yellowish brown, dark
USE **dark yellowish brown**

yellowish brown, dark grayish
USE **dark grayish yellowish brown**

yellowish brown, deep
USE **deep yellowish brown**

yellowish brown, dull
USE **dark grayish yellowish brown**
dark yellowish brown
grayish yellowish brown
light grayish yellowish brown
light yellowish brown
moderate yellowish brown

yellowish brown, grayish
USE **grayish yellowish brown**

yellowish brown, light
USE **light yellowish brown**

yellowish brown, light grayish
USE **light grayish yellowish brown**

yellowish brown, moderate
USE **moderate yellowish brown**

yellowish brown, pale
USE **light grayish yellowish brown**

yellowish brown, strong
USE **strong yellowish brown**

yellowish gray
DL.123
UF alabaster (color)
beige gray
bisque
buff
centroid color 93
drab gray
gray, beige
gray, yellowish
olive gray, pale
pale olive gray
putty (color)
CN D.DL.AFU.AFU.BCW.CLM

yellowish green
DL.184
UF green, yellowish
CN D.DL.AFU.AFU.BUE.DCU.AFU

yellowish green, bright
USE **vivid yellow green**
vivid yellowish green

yellowish green, brilliant
USE **brilliant yellowish green**

yellowish green, dark
USE **dark yellowish green**

yellowish green, deep
USE **deep yellowish green**

yellowish green, dull
USE **grayish yellow green**
pale yellow green

yellowish green, light
USE **light yellowish green**

yellowish green, moderate
USE **moderate yellowish green**

yellowish green, pale
USE **pale green**

yellowish green, strong
USE **strong yellowish green**

yellowish green, very dark
USE **very dark yellowish green**

yellowish green, very deep
USE **very deep yellowish green**

yellowish green, very light
USE **very light yellowish green**

yellowish green, vivid
USE **vivid yellowish green**

yellowish olive
USE **moderate olive**

yellowish olive, light
USE **dark greenish yellow**

yellowish orange
USE **brilliant orange yellow**
dark orange yellow
deep orange yellow
light orange yellow
moderate orange yellow
strong orange yellow

yellowish orange, bright
USE **vivid orange yellow**

yellowish orange, dark
USE **dark orange yellow**

yellowish orange, pale
USE **pale orange yellow**

yellowish pink
DL.24
UF pink, yellowish
CN D.DL.AFU.AFU.AFU.CLM.ALO

yellowish pink, dark
USE **dark yellowish pink**

yellowish pink, deep
USE **deep yellowish pink**

yellowish pink, grayish
USE **grayish yellowish pink**

yellowish pink, light
USE **light yellowish pink**

yellowish pink, moderate
USE **moderate yellowish pink**

yellowish pink, pale
USE **pale yellowish pink**

yellowish pink, strong
USE **strong yellowish pink**

yellowish pink, vivid
USE **vivid yellowish pink**

yellowish red
USE **dark reddish orange**
deep reddish orange
moderate reddish orange
strong reddish orange

yellowish red, bright
USE **vivid red**
vivid reddish orange

yellowish red, dull
USE **grayish reddish orange**

yellowish white
DL.122
UF brownish white
buff
centroid color 92
cream
eggshell
ivory (color)
white, brownish
white, yellowish
CN D.DL.AFU.AFU.BCW.CFS

Yellowknife
USE **Chipewyan**

Yelwa
FL.118
UF Kainji Dam Area
CN F.FL.ALO.AFU.ALO.AFU.BUE.CXA

yeshivas
RK.829 (A,L)
SN Use for Hebrew-English day schools providing both secular and religious instruction, usually operated under Orthodox Jewish auspices.
UF Jewish day schools
schools, Jewish day
CN V.RK.AFU.ALO.ALO.CXA.ARI.ARI.AFU.ARI

yew
MT.1407 (L)
UF Taxus
CN M.MT.AFU.AFU.ALO.BIQ.DCU.AFU.AFU.ALO.DUC

Yezd ware
FL.3543
UF ware, Yezd
CN F.FL.ALO.BIQ.AFU.GRC.ALO.BCW

Yi
FL.2114 (L)
UF Li (Yi)
CN F.FL.ALO.ARI.ALO.ARI.AFU.AXC

yield point
USE **yield strength**

yield strength
BM.966
UF point, yield
strength, yield
stress, yield
yield point
yield stress
CN B.BM.CFS.AXC.BZY.BOK.CLM.BUE

yield stress
USE **yield strength**

Yinxu
USE **Anyang (Shang style)**

Yofuaha
USE **Chorotí**

Yoga
FL.2074
UF Western-style
CN F.FL.ALO.ARI.ALO.ALO.ALO.ARI.FUA

yokes
TG.839
ALT yoke
UF yolks
CN V.TG.ALO.AXC.ALO.BZY

Yokohama-e
FL.2097
CN F.FL.ALO.ARI.ALO.ALO.ALO.AXC.BZY.CXA

Yokuts
FL.1270 (L)
UF Foothill Yokuts
Mariposan
Valley Yokuts
Yokuts, Foothill
Yokuts, Valley
CN F.FL.ALO.ALO.ARI.AFU.ALO.FIM

Yokuts, Foothill
USE **Yokuts**

Yokuts, Valley
USE **Yokuts**

yolk, egg
USE **egg yolk**

yolks
USE **yokes**

Yom ha-Kippurim
USE **Yom Kippur**

Yom Kippur
KM.90 (L)
UF Atonement, Day of
Day of Atonement
Yom ha-Kippurim
CN K.KM.AFU.CFS.ARI.CXA

Yombe
FL.488 (L)
UF Bayombe
Mayombe
CN F.FL.ALO.AFU.AXC.ALO.ALO.AXC.BIQ

Yomud
FL.3594 (L)
CN F.FL.ALO.BIQ.AFU.IFM.ARI.BOK

Yongle
FL.1899
UF Yung-lo
CN F.FL.ALO.ARI.ALO.AFU.AFU.ALO.DIO.ALO

Yongzheng
FL.1912 (L)
UF Yung-cheng
CN F.FL.ALO.ARI.ALO.AFU.AFU.ALO.DOI.ARI

York chairs

USE fiddle-back chairs

Yoruba
FL.269 (L)
CN F.FL.ALO.AFU.AXC.AFU.ALO.BCW

young fustic
MT.1764
UF fustet
fustic, young
Hungarian yellow wood
wood, Hungarian yellow
yellow wood, Hungarian
CN M.MT.AFU.AFU.ARI.AFU.AFU.ALO.ALO.BUE.ALO.ARI.AFU

Young's modulus
USE modulus of elasticity

youth
HG.5 (L)
CN H.HG.AFU.AFU.ARI

youth centers
RK.1192 (A,L,B)
ALT youth center
UF centers, youth
clubs, youth
youth clubs
CN V.RK.AFU.ALO.ALO.FUA.ALO.ARI

youth clubs
USE youth centers

youth hostels
RK.951 (A,L,B)
ALT youth hostel
UF children's hostels
hostels, children's
hostels, youth
CN V.RK.AFU.ALO.ALO.ELK.AXC.AFU

Yüan
FL.1896 (A)
CN F.FL.ALO.ARI.ALO.AFU.AFU.ALO.DCU

yuca
USE cassava

Yucatan sisal
USE henequen

Yucatec
FL.1529
CN F.FL.ALO.ALO.ARI.ALO.BCW.ARI

Yuchi
FL.1446 (L)
CN F.FL.ALO.ALO.ARI.AFU.BZY.DUC

Yue-che
USE Uighur

Yueh-Chi
USE Uighur

Yugoslav
FL.3064 (L,B)
CN F.FL.ALO.BCW.AFU.ELK

Yuit
FL.1203 (L)
CN F.FL.ALO.ALO.ARI.AFU.AFU.AFU.AFU.BCW

Yuki
FL.1271 (L)
UF Yukian
CN F.FL.ALO.ALO.ARI.AFU.ALO.FOG

Yukian
USE Yuki

Yuman
FL.1486 (L)
CN F.FL.ALO.ALO.ARI.AFU.CFS.DOI

Yuman, California
USE California Yuman

Yuman, Peninsula
USE Peninsula Yuman

Yunca
FL.1615 (L)
CN F.FL.ALO.ALO.ARI.ARI.ALO.AFU.CRG

Yung-cheng
USE Yongzheng

Yung-lo
USE Yongle

Yupik
FL.1204 (L)
CN F.FL.ALO.ALO.ARI.AFU.AFU.AFU.AFU.BIQ

Yurok
FL.1272
CN F.FL.ALO.ALO.ARI.AFU.ALO.FUA

yurts
RK.358 (A,L)
ALT yurt
SN Use for circular tentlike structures consisting of skins or felt stretched over a collapsible lattice framework. (W)
UF jurts
CN V.RK.AFU.ALO.ALO.AXC.ARI.BIQ.ALO

Z anchors
TF.305
ALT Z anchor
UF anchors, Z
CN V.TF.AFU.AFU.AFU.ALO.AFU.AFU.DCU

Zacatenco
FL.979
CN F.FL.ALO.ALO.ALO.ALO.AFU.ALO.AFU.AFU.ARI

zaccab
MT.2078
SN Fine white clay mixed with lime; used chiefly as building and plastering material, and for sculpture. (MAYER)
CN M.MT.AFU.AFU.ARI.BOK.ALO.BUE

Zaman-Baba
FL.1785
CN F.FL.ALO.ARI.AFU.ARI.BIQ

Zamuco
FL.1651 (L)
CN F.FL.ALO.ALO.ARI.ARI.AXC.DOI

Zand
FL.3602
UF Zanj (Zand)
CN F.FL.ALO.BIQ.AFU.JCO

Zande
FL.524 (L)
UF Azande
CN F.FL.ALO.AFU.AXC.ALO.ALO.BIQ.AFU.ALO.BCW

Zanj
FL.166 (L)
CN F.FL.ALO.AFU.ALO.AXC.BIQ

Zanj (Zand)
USE Zand

Zanzibar copal
MT.1485
UF copal, Zanzibar
CN M.MT.AFU.AFU.ALO.BOK.ARI.BCW

zapatero
USE Maracaibo boxwood

Zapotec
FL.1063 (B)
CN F.FL.ALO.ALO.ALO.ALO.AFU.ALO.AXC.ALO.ARI

Zaramo
FL.612 (L)
UF Wasaramo
CN F.FL.ALO.AFU.AXC.AXC.ALO.BUE.AXC

Zaraut-Say
FL.1767
CN F.FL.ALO.ARI.AFU.AFU.AXC

Zarzian
FL.3001
CN F.FL.ALO.AXC.ARI.BIQ.AFU.AFU.ALO

Zatzil
USE Tzotzil

Zawi Chemi Shanidar
FL.3002 (L)
CN F.FL.ALO.AXC.ARI.BIQ.AFU.AFU.ARI

zaxes
TB.569 (N)
ALT zax
SN Slate cutter's hammers which have a point at the back of the head; used for making nail holes in slate. (DAC)
UF hammers, slating
saxes
slating hammers
CN V.TB.AFU.BCW.BCW.ALO.AXC.ALO

zinc chromate
zinc chrome
Zinkgelb
CN M.MT.AFU.AFU.ARI.AFU.AFU.ALO.ALO.BUE.ARI.DCU

zinc yellow (color)
USE **strong yellow**

zincography
KT.446 (L)
SN Process of preparing a printing surface on a zinc plate; may be prepared for lithographic printing or etched for relief printing.
UF lithozincography
CN K.KT.AFU.ALO.DUC.DUC.ALO.AXC

Zinkgelb
USE **zinc yellow**

Zinkgrün
USE **zinc chrome green**

Zinkweiss
USE **zinc white**

Zinnober
USE **vermilion**

zinnober green
USE **chrome green**

Zinnobergrün
USE **chrome green**

zionists
HG.760 (L)
ALT **zionist**
CN H.HG.AFU.BCW.HZS.CFS

zip code maps
VW.201
ALT **zip code map**
UF code maps, zip
maps, zip code
CN V.VW.AFU.AFU.AFU.FZU.AXC.AFU.ARI.AXC.CLM.AFU

zircon
MT.568 (L)
CN M.MT.AFU.AFU.AFU.CFS.AFU.HZS

zirconium oxide
MT.1741 (L)
SN A white powder produced by treating zircon and used as a pigment. (MAYER)
UF baddeleyite
CN M.MT.AFU.AFU.ARI.AFU.AFU.ALO.ALO.BOK.AFU.CLM

Zirid
FL.3603
UF Zayrid
CN F.FL.ALO.BIQ.AFU.JII

zocles
USE **socles**

zodiac signs
USE **zodiac symbols**

zodiac symbols
DG.73 (L,B,R)
ALT **zodiac symbol**
SN Use for those images of animals and objects that symbolize the twelve signs of the zodiac.
UF signs, zodiac
symbols, zodiac
zodiac signs
CN D.DG.AFU.AFU.ERE

zommos
USE **somnoes**

zone maps, time
USE **time zone maps**

zoned earth dams
RK.537
ALT **zoned earth dam**
SN Dams in which the fill, usually earth, rocks, or clay, is zoned by systematic distribution of materials according to their strength and permeability characteristics, generally built over an impervious core. (STEIN)
UF dams, reinforced earth
dams, zoned earth
earth dams, reinforced
earth dams, zoned
reinforced earth dams
CN V.RK.AFU.ALO.ALO.CFS.AFU.ARI.ARI.AFU.ALO

Zoned Hachure horizon
FL.1123
CN F.FL.ALO.ALO.ALO.ARI.ARI.AFU.AFU

zones
RG.285
ALT **zone**
SN Areas set off by a governing body for specific use, such as residential, commercial, or industrial. (STEIN)
CN V.RG.ALO.AFU.ALO.BIQ

zones, buffer
USE **buffer zones**

zones, commercial
USE **business districts**

zones, demilitarized
USE **demilitarized zones**

zones, transition
USE **transition zones**

zoning
KG.187 (A,L,B)
ALT **zoned**
SN Regulating land use for stated purposes. (RLG7)
CN K.KG.AFU.ALO.ARI.CLM

zoning boards
HG.840 (L)
ALT **zoning board**
UF boards of zoning adjustment
boards, zoning
CN H.HG.ALO.BIQ.BUE

zoning law
KD.167 (A,L,B)
UF law, zoning
CN K.KD.AFU.ALO.DOI.BOK

zoning maps
VW.169 (L)
ALT **zoning map**
SN Maps delineating the boundaries of districts which, along with the zoning text, comprise the zoning ordinances. (LOFZ)
UF maps, zoning
CN V.VW.AFU.AFU.AFU.FZU.AXC.AFU.ARI.ALO.BCW

zoning ordinances
VW.1031
ALT **zoning ordinance**
SN Ordinances that establish the permitted uses of the land in a particular district or zone and dictate such things as lot sizes and building placements.
UF ordinances, zoning
CN V.VW.AFU.ARI.ALO.BCW.AFU.ARI.AFU.ARI.ALO.AFU

Zonist
FL.3410
ALT **Zonism**
UF Strefizm
CN F.FL.ALO.BCW.ALO.AXC.DIO.BUE.AFU

Zonolite concrete (TM)
MT.209
SN A form of concrete which acts as an insulator. (PUTNAM)
UF concrete, Zonolite (TM)
CN M.MT.AFU.AFU.AFU.BCW.AFU.ALO.AFU.AFU

zoological gardens
USE **zoos**

zoological illustration
KT.213 (L,R)
UF illustration, zoological
CN K.KT.AFU.ALO.DUC.CLM.BOK.AFU.ARI

zoological illustrations
VB.53 (L,R)
ALT **zoological illustration**
UF illustrations, zoological
CN V.VB.AFU.ALO.AXC.ALO.ARI.AFU.ARI

zoological museums
RK.422 (A,L)
ALT **zoological museum**
UF museums, zoological
CN V.RK.AFU.ALO.ALO.BCW.AXC.ARI.CFS.BOK

zoological wildlife parks
USE **wild animal parks**

zoologists
HG.332 (L)
ALT **zoologist**
CN H.HG.AFU.AXC.BIQ.AFU.AFU.ALO.AXC

zoology
KD.209 (L,R)
CN K.KD.AFU.ARI.ARI.BZY

zoom lenses
TB.323 (L)
ALT zoom lens
SN Lenses which are constructed to allow continuously variable focal lengths within a specific range. The effective aperture and foucs settings remain unchanged throughout such adjustments. (LANG)
UF lenses, varifocal
lenses, zoom
varifocal lenses
CN V.TB.AFU.ARI.CLM.ARI.AFU.ALO.BOK.BOK

zoomorphic
DC.118
CN D.DC.AFU.ARI.FCS.BIQ

zoophori
DG.90
ALT **zoophorus**
SN Ornamental bands decorated with human figures or animals.
CN D.DG.AFU.ALO.ARI.AFU

zoophoric columns
RK.899
ALT **zoophoric column**
SN Columns supporting a figure or figures of one or more people or animals. (HAS)
UF columns, zoophoric
CN V.RK.AFU.ALO.ALO.DOI.AFU.BCW.ARI

zoos
RG.229 (A,L,B,R)
ALT **zoo**
UF zoological gardens
CN V.RG.AFU.AFU.ELK

zoos, children's
USE **children's zoos**

zoos, jungle
USE **open-air zoos**

zoos, open-air
USE **open-air zoos**

zoos, outdoor
USE **open-air zoos**

Zopfstil
FL.3383 (R)
CN F.FL.ALO.BCW.ALO.AXC.DIO.BIQ.ARI

Zoque
FL.1525 (L)
CN F.FL.ALO.ALO.ARI.ALO.AXC.DOI

Zoroastrianism
BM.678 (L,R)
ALT **Zoroastrian**
CN B.BM.BZY.AFU.CXA

Zulu
FL.567 (L)
CN F.FL.ALO.AFU.AXC.ARI.AXC.BIQ

Zumper
FL.223
UF Jompre
CN F.FL.ALO.AFU.AXC.AFU.AFU.ALO.ALO.DOI

Zuñi
FL.1482 (L,R)
CN F.FL.ALO.ALO.ARI.AFU.CFS.CRG ALO.ALO

Zutujil
USE **Tzutujil**